CASES AND MATERIALS ON
TRADEMARK LAW
Second Edition

■ ■ ■

Glynn Lunney
Professor of Law
Texas A&M University School of Law

AMERICAN CASEBOOK SERIES®

WEST
ACADEMIC
PUBLISHING

© 2010 Thomson Reuters
© 2016 LEG, Inc. d/b/a West Academic
    444 Cedar Street, Suite 700
    St. Paul, MN 55101
    1-877-888-1330

Printed in the United States of America

ISBN: 978-0-314-29000-7

For my sons

SUMMARY OF CONTENTS

TABLE OF CONTENTS

TABLE OF CASES

The principal cases are in bold type.

CASES AND MATERIALS ON
TRADEMARK LAW
Second Edition

CHAPTER 1

INTRODUCTION

■ ■ ■

A. COMPETITION: FAIR AND UNFAIR

In approaching the issue of competition, we can start from one of two general positions. First, we can adopt as our general rule the principle that copying or imitation, and the resulting competition that they generate, is fair, legal and permissible, and then define exceptional circumstances where that general rule does not apply. Or second, we can adopt as our general rule the principle that any copying or imitation is unfair and illegal, and then define exceptional circumstances where copying and imitation are permissible. As you read the following cases, see if you can determine which approach the Court adopts.

INTERNATIONAL NEWS SERVICE V. THE ASSOCIATED PRESS
248 U.S. 215 (1918)

PITNEY, J.

The parties are competitors in the gathering and distribution of news and its publication for profit in newspapers throughout the United States. The Associated Press, which was complainant in the District Court, is a cooperative organization, incorporated under the Membership Corporations Law of the State of New York, its members being individuals who are either proprietors or representatives of about 950 daily newspapers published in all parts of the United States. That a corporation may be organized under that act for the purpose of gathering news for the use and benefit of its members and for publication in newspapers owned or represented by them, is recognized by an amendment enacted in 1901 (Laws N.Y. 1901, c. 436). Complainant gathers in all parts of the world, by means of various instrumentalities of its own, by exchange with its members, and by other appropriate means, news and intelligence of current and recent events of interest to newspaper readers and distributes it daily to its members for publication in their newspapers. The cost of the service, amounting approximately to $3,500,000 per annum, is assessed upon the members and becomes a part of their costs of operation, to be recouped, presumably with profit, through the publication of their several newspapers. Under complainant's by-laws each member agrees upon assuming membership that news

1

received through complainant's service is received exclusively for publication in a particular newspaper, language, and place specified in the certificate of membership, that no other use of it shall be permitted, and that no member shall furnish or permit anyone in his employ or connected with his newspaper to furnish any of complainant's news in advance of publication to any person not a member. And each member is required to gather the local news of his district and supply it to the Associated Press and to no one else.

Defendant is a corporation organized under the laws of the State of New Jersey, whose business is the gathering and selling of news to its customers and clients, consisting of newspapers published throughout the United States, under contracts by which they pay certain amounts at stated times for defendant's service. It has wide-spread news-gathering agencies; the cost of its operations amounts, it is said, to more than $2,000,000 per annum; and it serves about 400 newspapers located in the various cities of the United States and abroad, a few of which are represented, also, in the membership of the Associated Press.

The parties are in the keenest competition between themselves in the distribution of news throughout the United States; and so, as a rule, are the newspapers that they serve, in their several districts.

Complainant in its bill, defendant in its answer, have set forth in almost identical terms the rather obvious circumstances and conditions under which their business is conducted. The value of the service, and of the news furnished, depends upon the promptness of transmission, as well as upon the accuracy and impartiality of the news; it being essential that the news be transmitted to members or subscribers as early or earlier than similar information can be furnished to competing newspapers by other news services, and that the news furnished by each agency shall not be furnished to newspapers which do not contribute to the expense of gathering it. And further, to quote from the answer: "Prompt knowledge and publication of world-wide news is essential to the conduct of a modern newspaper, and by reason of the enormous expense incident to the gathering and distribution of such news, the only practical way in which a proprietor of a newspaper can obtain the same is, either through cooperation with a considerable number of other newspaper proprietors in the work of collecting and distributing such news, and the equitable division with them of the expenses thereof, or by the purchase of such news from some existing agency engaged in that business."

The bill was filed to restrain the pirating of complainant's news by defendant in three ways: First, by bribing employees of newspapers published by complainant's members to furnish Associated Press news to defendant before publication, for transmission by telegraph and telephone to defendant's clients for publication by them; Second, by inducing Associated Press members to violate its by-laws and permit defendant to obtain news before publication; and Third, by copying news from bulletin boards and from early editions of complainant's newspapers and selling this, either bodily or after rewriting it, to defendant's customers.

The District Court, upon consideration of the bill and answer, with voluminous affidavits on both sides, granted a preliminary injunction under the first and second heads; but refused at that stage to restrain the systematic practice admittedly pursued by defendant, of taking news bodily from the bulletin boards and early editions of complainant's newspapers and selling it as its own. The court expressed itself as satisfied that this practice amounted to unfair trade, but as the legal question was one of first impression it considered that the allowance of an injunction should await the outcome of an appeal. 240 Fed. Rep. 983, 996. Both parties having appealed, the Circuit Court of Appeals sustained the injunction order so far as it went, and upon complainant's appeal modified it and remanded the cause with directions to issue an injunction also against any bodily taking of the words or substance of complainant's news until its commercial value as news had passed away. 245 Fed. Rep. 244, 253. The present writ of certiorari was then allowed. 245 U.S. 644.

The only matter that has been argued before us is whether defendant may lawfully be restrained from appropriating news taken from bulletins issued by complainant or any of its members, or from newspapers published by them, for the purpose of selling it to defendant's clients. Complainant asserts that defendant's admitted course of conduct in this regard both violates complainant's property right in the news and constitutes unfair competition in business. And notwithstanding the case has proceeded only to the stage of a preliminary injunction, we have deemed it proper to consider the underlying questions, since they go to the very merits of the action and are presented upon facts that are not in dispute. As presented in argument, these questions are: 1. Whether there is any property in news; 2. Whether, if there be property in news collected for the purpose of being published, it survives the instant of its publication in the first newspaper to which it is communicated by the news-gatherer; and 3. Whether defendant's admitted course of conduct in appropriating for commercial use matter taken from bulletins or early editions of Associated Press publications constitutes unfair competition in trade.

The federal jurisdiction was invoked because of diversity of citizenship, not upon the ground that the suit arose under the copyright or other laws of the United States. Complainant's news matter is not copyrighted. It is said that it could not, in practice, be copyrighted, because of the large number of dispatches that are sent daily; and, according to complainant's contention, news is not within the operation of the copyright act. Defendant, while apparently conceding this, nevertheless invokes the analogies of the law of literary property and copyright, insisting as its principal contention that, assuming complainant has a right of property in its news, it can be maintained (unless the copyright act be complied with) only by being kept secret and confidential, and that upon the publication with complainant's consent of uncopyrighted news by any of complainant's members in a newspaper or upon a bulletin board, the right of property is lost, and the subsequent use of the news by the public or by defendant for any purpose whatever becomes lawful.

. . . In considering the general question of property in news matter, it is necessary to recognize its dual character, distinguishing between the substance of the information and the particular form or collocation of words in which the writer has communicated it.

No doubt news articles often possess a literary quality, and are the subject of literary property at the common law; nor do we question that such an article, as a literary production, is the subject of copyright by the terms of the act as it now stands. . . .

But the news element—the information respecting current events contained in the literary production—is not the creation of the writer, but is a report of matters that ordinarily are *publici juris*; it is the history of the day. It is not to be supposed that the framers of the Constitution, when they empowered Congress "to promote the progress of science and useful arts, by securing for limited times to authors and inventors the exclusive right to their respective writings and discoveries" (Const., Art I, § 8, par. 8), intended to confer upon one who might happen to be the first to report a historic event the exclusive right for any period to spread the knowledge of it.

We need spend no time, however, upon the general question of property in news matter at common law, or the application of the copyright act, since it seems to us the case must turn upon the question of unfair competition in business. And, in our opinion, this does not depend upon any general right of property analogous to the common-law right of the proprietor of an unpublished work to prevent its publication without his consent; nor is it foreclosed by showing that the benefits of the copyright act have been waived. We are dealing here not with restrictions upon publication but with the very facilities and processes of publication. The peculiar value of news is in the spreading of it while it is fresh; and it is evident that a valuable property interest in the news, as news, cannot be maintained by keeping it secret. Besides, except for matters improperly disclosed, or published in breach of trust or confidence, or in violation of law, none of which is involved in this branch of the case, the news of current events may be regarded as common property. What we are concerned with is the business of making it known to the world, in which both parties to the present suit are engaged. That business consists in maintaining a prompt, sure, steady, and reliable service designed to place the daily events of the world at the breakfast table of the millions at a price that, while of trifling moment to each reader, is sufficient in the aggregate to afford compensation for the cost of gathering and distributing it, with the added profit so necessary as an incentive to effective action in the commercial world. The service thus performed for newspaper readers is not only innocent but extremely useful in itself, and indubitably constitutes a legitimate business. The parties are competitors in this field; and, on fundamental principles, applicable here as elsewhere, when the rights or privileges of the one are liable to conflict with those of the other, each party is under a duty so to conduct its own business as not unnecessarily or unfairly to injure that of the other. *Hitchman Coal & Coke Co.* v. *Mitchell*, 245 U.S. 229, 254.

Obviously, the question of what is unfair competition in business must be determined with particular reference to the character and circumstances of the business. The question here is not so much the rights of either party as against the public but their rights as between themselves. See *Morison* v. *Moat*, 9 Hare, 241, 258. And although we may and do assume that neither party has any remaining property interest as against the public in uncopyrighted news matter after the moment of its first publication, it by no means follows that there is no remaining property interest in it as between themselves. For, to both of them alike, news matter, however little susceptible of ownership or dominion in the absolute sense, is stock in trade, to be gathered at the cost of enterprise, organization, skill, labor, and money, and to be distributed and sold to those who will pay money for it, as for any other merchandise. Regarding the news, therefore, as but the material out of which both parties are seeking to make profits at the same time and in the same field, we hardly can fail to recognize that for this purpose, and as between them, it must be regarded as *quasi* property, irrespective of the rights of either as against the public.

In order to sustain the jurisdiction of equity over the controversy, we need not affirm any general and absolute property in the news as such. The rule that a court of equity concerns itself only in the protection of property rights treats any civil right of a pecuniary nature as a property right (*In re Sawyer*, 124 U.S. 200, 210; *In re Debs*, 158 U.S. 564, 593); and the right to acquire property by honest labor or the conduct of a lawful business is as much entitled to protection as the right to guard property already acquired. *Truax* v. *Raich*, 239 U.S. 33, 37–38; *Brennan* v. *United Hatters*, 73 N.J.L. 729, 742; *Barr* v. *Essex Trades Council*, 53 N.J. Eq. 101. It is this right that furnishes the basis of the jurisdiction in the ordinary case of unfair competition. . . .

Not only do the acquisition and transmission of news require elaborate organization and a large expenditure of money, skill, and effort; not only has it an exchange value to the gatherer, dependent chiefly upon its novelty and freshness, the regularity of the service, its reputed reliability and thoroughness, and its adaptability to the public needs; but also, as is evident, the news has an exchange value to one who can misappropriate it.

The peculiar features of the case arise from the fact that, while novelty and freshness form so important an element in the success of the business, the very processes of distribution and publication necessarily occupy a good deal of time. Complainant's service, as well as defendant's, is a daily service to daily newspapers; most of the foreign news reaches this country at the Atlantic seaboard, principally at the City of New York, and because of this, and of time differentials due to the earth's rotation, the distribution of news matter throughout the country is principally from east to west; and, since in speed the telegraph and telephone easily outstrip the rotation of the earth, it is a simple matter for defendant to take complainant's news from bulletins or early editions of complainant's members in the eastern cities and at the mere cost of telegraphic transmission cause it to be published in western papers issued at least as early as those served by complainant. Besides this, and irrespective of time differentials, irregularities in telegraphic transmission on different lines, and the normal consumption of time in printing and distributing the newspaper, result in permitting pirated news to be placed in the hands of defendant's readers sometimes simultaneously with the service of competing Associated Press papers, occasionally even earlier.

Defendant insists that when, with the sanction and approval of complainant, and as the result of the use of its news for the very purpose for which it is distributed, a portion of complainant's members communicate it to the general public by posting it upon bulletin boards so that all may read, or by issuing it to newspapers and distributing it indiscriminately, complainant no longer has the right to control the use to be made of it; that when it thus reaches the light of day it becomes the common possession of all to whom it is accessible; and that any purchaser of a newspaper has the right to communicate the intelligence which it contains to anybody and for any purpose, even for the purpose of selling it for profit to newspapers published for profit in competition with complainant's members.

The fault in the reasoning lies in applying as a test the right of the complainant as against the public, instead of considering the rights of complainant and defendant, competitors in business, as between themselves. The right of the purchaser of a single newspaper to spread knowledge of its contents gratuitously, for any legitimate purpose not unreasonably interfering with complainant's right to make merchandise of it, may be admitted; but to transmit that news for commercial use, in competition with complainant—which is what defendant has done and seeks to justify—is a very different matter. In doing this defendant, by its very act, admits that it is taking material that has been acquired by complainant as the result of organization and the expenditure of labor, skill, and money, and which is salable by complainant for money, and that defendant in appropriating it and selling it as its own is endeavoring to reap where it has not sown, and by disposing of it to newspapers that are competitors of complainant's members is appropriating to itself the harvest of those who have sown. Stripped of all disguises, the process amounts to an unauthorized interference with the normal operation of complainant's legitimate business precisely at the point where the profit is to be reaped, in order to divert a material portion of the profit from those who have earned it to those who have not; with special advantage to defendant in the competition because of the fact that it is not burdened with any part of the expense of gathering the news. The transaction speaks for itself, and a court of equity ought not to hesitate long in characterizing it as unfair competition in business.

The underlying principle is much the same as that which lies at the base of the equitable theory of consideration in the law of trusts—that he who has fairly paid the price should have the beneficial use of the property. Pom. Eq. Jur., § 981. It is no answer to say that complainant spends its money for that which is too fugitive or evanescent to be the subject of property. That might, and for the purposes of the discussion we are assuming that it would, furnish an answer in a common-law controversy. But in a court of equity, where the question is one of unfair competition, if that which complainant has acquired fairly at substantial cost may be sold fairly at substantial profit, a competitor who is misappropriating it for the purpose of disposing of it to his own profit and to the disadvantage of complainant cannot be heard to say that it is too fugitive or evanescent to be regarded as property. It has all the attributes of property necessary for determining that a misappropriation of it by a competitor is unfair competition because contrary to good conscience.

The contention that the news is abandoned to the public for all purposes when published in the first newspaper is untenable. Abandonment is a question of intent, and the entire organization of the Associated Press negatives such a purpose. The cost of the service would be prohibitive if the reward were to be so limited. No single newspaper, no small group of newspapers, could sustain the expenditure. Indeed, it is one of the most obvious results of defendant's theory that, by permitting indiscriminate publication by anybody and everybody for purposes of profit in competition with the news-gatherer, it would render publication profitless, or so little profitable as in effect to cut off the service by rendering the cost prohibitive in comparison with the return. The practical needs and requirements of the business are reflected in complainant's by-laws which have been referred to. Their effect is that publication by each member must be deemed not by any means an abandonment of the news to the world for any and all purposes, but a publication for limited purposes; for the benefit of the readers of the bulletin or the newspaper as such; not for the purpose of making merchandise of it as news, with the result of depriving complainant's other members of their reasonable opportunity to obtain just returns for their expenditures.

It is to be observed that the view we adopt does not result in giving to complainant the right to monopolize either the gathering or the distribution of the news, or, without complying with the copyright act, to prevent the reproduction of its news articles; but only postpones participation by complainant's competitor in the processes of distribution and reproduction of news that it has not gathered, and only to the extent necessary to prevent that competitor from reaping the fruits of complainant's efforts and expenditure, to the partial exclusion of complainant, and in violation of the principle that underlies the maxim *sic utere tuo*, etc.

It is said that the elements of unfair competition are lacking because there is no attempt by defendant to palm off its goods as those of the complainant, characteristic of the most familiar, if not the most typical, cases of unfair competition. *Howe Scale Co.* v. *Wyckoff, Seamans & Benedict*, 198 U.S. 118, 140. But we cannot concede that the right to equitable relief is confined to that class of cases. In the present case the fraud upon complainant's rights is more direct and obvious. Regarding news matter as the mere material from which these two competing parties are endeavoring to make money, and treating it, therefore, as *quasi* property for the purposes of their business because they are both selling it as such, defendant's conduct differs from the ordinary case of unfair competition in trade principally in this that, instead of selling its own goods as those of complainant, it substitutes misappropriation in the place of misrepresentation, and sells complainant's goods as its own.

Besides the misappropriation, there are elements of imitation, of false pretense, in defendant's practices. The device of rewriting complainant's news articles, frequently resorted to, carries its own comment. The habitual failure to give credit to complainant for that which is taken is significant. Indeed, the entire system of appropriating complainant's news and transmitting it as a commercial product to defendant's clients and patrons amounts to a false representation to them and to their newspaper readers that the news transmitted is the result of defendant's own investigation in the field. But these elements, although accentuating the wrong, are not the essence of it. It is something more than the advantage of celebrity of which complainant is being deprived.

The doctrine of unclean hands is invoked as a bar to relief; it being insisted that defendant's practices against which complainant seeks an injunction are not different from the practice attributed to complainant, of utilizing defendant's news published by its subscribers. At this point it becomes necessary to consider a distinction that is drawn by complainant, and, as we understand it, was recognized by defendant also in the submission of proofs in the District Court, between two kinds of use that may be made by one news agency of news taken from the bulletins and newspapers of the other. The first is the bodily appropriation of a statement of fact or a news article, with or without rewriting, but without independent investigation or other expense. This form of pirating was found by both courts to have been pursued by defendant systematically with respect to complainant's news, and against it the Circuit Court of Appeals granted an injunction. This practice complainant denies having pursued, and the denial was sustained by the finding of the District Court. It is not contended by defendant that the finding can be set aside, upon the proofs as they now stand. The other use is to take the news of a rival agency as a "tip" to be investigated, and if verified by independent investigation the news thus gathered is sold. This practice complainant admits that it has pursued and still is willing that defendant shall employ.

Both courts held that complainant could not be debarred on the ground of unclean hands upon the score of pirating defendant's news, because not shown to be guilty of sanctioning this practice.

As to securing "tips" from a competing news agency, the District Court (240 Fed. Rep. 991, 995), while not sanctioning the practice, found that both parties had adopted it in accordance with common business usage, in the belief that their conduct was technically lawful, and hence did not find in it any sufficient ground for attributing unclean hands to complainant. The Circuit Court of Appeals (245 Fed. Rep. 247) found that the tip habit, though discouraged by complainant, was "incurably journalistic," and that there was "no difficulty in discriminating between the utilization of 'tips' and the bodily appropriation of another's labor in accumulating and stating information."

We are inclined to think a distinction may be drawn between the utilization of tips and the bodily appropriation of news matter, either in its original form or after rewriting and without independent investigation and verification; whatever may appear at the final hearing, the proofs as they now stand recognize such a distinction; both parties avowedly recognize the practice of taking tips, and neither party alleges it to be unlawful or to amount to unfair competition in business. . . .

In the case before us, in the present state of the pleadings and proofs, we need go no further than to hold, as we do, that the admitted pursuit by complainant of the practice of taking news items published by defendant's subscribers as tips to be investigated, and, if verified, the result of the investigation to be sold—the practice having been followed by defendant also, and by news agencies generally—is not shown to be such as to constitute an unconscientious or inequitable attitude towards its adversary so as to fix upon complainant the taint of unclean hands, and debar it on this ground from the relief to which it is otherwise entitled.

There is some criticism of the injunction that was directed by the District Court upon the going down of the mandate from the Circuit Court of Appeals. In brief, it restrains any taking or gainfully using of the complainant's news, either bodily or in substance, from bulletins issued by the complainant or any of its members, or from editions of their newspapers, *"until its commercial value as news to the complainant and all of its members has passed away."* The part complained of is the clause we have italicized; but if this be indefinite, it is no more so than the criticism. Perhaps it would be better that the terms of the injunction be made specific, and so framed as to confine the restraint to an extent consistent with the reasonable protection of complainant's newspapers, each in its own area and for a specified time after its publication, against the competitive use of pirated news by defendant's customers. But the case presents practical difficulties; and we have not the materials, either in the way of a definite suggestion of amendment, or in the way of proofs, upon which to frame a specific injunction; hence, while not expressing approval of the form adopted by the District Court, we decline to modify it at this preliminary stage of the case, and will leave that court to deal with the matter upon appropriate application made to it for the purpose.

The decree of the Circuit Court of Appeals will be *Affirmed*.

MR. JUSTICE CLARKE took no part in the consideration or decision of this case.

MR. JUSTICE HOLMES (concurring):

When an uncopyrighted combination of words is published there is no general right to forbid other people repeating them—in other words there is no property in the combination or in the thoughts or facts that the words express. Property, a creation of law, does not arise from value, although exchangeable—a matter of fact. Many exchangeable values may be destroyed intentionally without compensation. Property depends upon exclusion by law from interference, and a person is not excluded from using any combination of words merely because someone has used it before, even if it took labor and genius to make it. If a given person is to be prohibited from making the use of words that his neighbors are free to make some other ground must be found. One such ground is vaguely expressed in the phrase unfair trade. This means that the words are repeated by a competitor in business in such a way as to convey a misrepresentation that materially injures the person who first used them, by appropriating credit of some kind which the first user has earned. The ordinary case is a representation by device, appearance, or other indirection that the defendant's goods come from the plaintiff. But the only reason why it is actionable to make such a representation is that it tends to give the defendant an advantage in his competition with the plaintiff and that it is thought undesirable that an advantage should be gained in that way. Apart from that the defendant may use such unpatented devices and uncopyrighted combinations of words as he likes. The ordinary case, I say, is palming off the defendant's product as the plaintiff's, but the same evil may follow from the opposite falsehood— from saying, whether in words or by implication, that the plaintiff's product is the defendant's, and that, it seems to me, is what has happened here.

Fresh news is got only by enterprise and expense. To produce such news as it is produced by the defendant represents by implication that it has been acquired by the defendant's enterprise and at its expense. When it comes from one of the great news-collecting agencies like the Associated Press, the source generally is indicated, plainly importing that credit; and that such a representation is implied may be inferred with some confidence from the unwillingness of the defendant to give the credit and tell the truth. If the plaintiff produces the news at the same time that the defendant does, the defendant's presentation impliedly denies to the plaintiff the credit of collecting the facts and assumes that credit to the defendant. If the plaintiff is later in western cities it naturally will be supposed to have obtained its information from the defendant. The falsehood is a little more subtle, the injury a little more indirect, than in ordinary cases of unfair trade, but I think that the principle that condemns the one condemns the other. It is a question of how strong an infusion of fraud is necessary to turn a flavor into a poison. The dose seems to me strong enough here to need a remedy from the law. But as, in my view, the only ground of complaint that can be recognized without legislation is the implied misstatement, it can be corrected by stating the truth; and a suitable acknowledgment of the source is all that the plaintiff can require. I think that within the limits recognized by the decision of the Court the defendant should be enjoined from publishing news obtained from the Associated Press for hours after publication by the plaintiff unless it gives express credit to the Associated Press; the number of hours and the form of acknowledgment to be settled by the District Court.

MR. JUSTICE MCKENNA concurs in this opinion.

MR. JUSTICE BRANDEIS dissenting.

. . . The sole question for our consideration is this: Was the International News Service properly enjoined from using, or causing to be used gainfully, news of which it acquired knowledge by lawful means (namely, by reading publicly posted bulletins or papers purchased by it in the open market) merely because the news had been originally gathered by the Associated Press and continued to be of value to some of its members, or because it did not reveal the source from which it was acquired?

. . . It is . . . suggested, that the fact that defendant does not refer to the Associated Press as the source of the news may furnish a basis for the relief. But the defendant and its subscribers, unlike members of the Associated Press, were under no contractual obligation to disclose the source of the news; and there is no rule of law requiring acknowledgment to be made where uncopyrighted matter is reproduced. The International News Service is said to mislead its subscribers into believing that the news transmitted was originally gathered by it and that they in turn mislead their readers. There is, in fact, no representation by either of any kind. Sources of information are sometimes given because required by contract; sometimes because naming the source gives authority to an otherwise incredible statement; and sometimes the source is named because the agency does not wish to take the responsibility itself of giving currency to the news. But no representation can properly be implied from omission to mention the source of information except that the International News Service is transmitting news which it believes to be credible. . . .

The great development of agencies now furnishing country-wide distribution of news, the vastness of our territory, and improvements in the means of transmitting intelligence, have made it possible for a news agency or newspapers to obtain, without paying compensation, the fruit of another's efforts and to use news so obtained gainfully in competition with the original collector. The injustice of such action is obvious. But to give relief against it would involve more than the application of existing rules of law to new facts. It would require the making of a new rule in analogy to existing ones. The unwritten law possesses capacity for growth; and has often satisfied new demands for justice by invoking analogies or by expanding a rule or principle. This process has been in the main wisely applied and should not be discontinued. Where the problem is relatively simple, as it is apt to be when private interests only are involved, it generally proves adequate. But with the increasing complexity of society, the public interest tends to become omnipresent; and the problems presented by new demands for justice cease to be simple. Then the creation or recognition by courts of a new private right may work serious injury to the general public, unless the boundaries of the right are definitely established and wisely guarded. In order to reconcile the new private right with the public interest, it may be necessary to prescribe limitations and rules for its enjoyment; and also to provide administrative machinery for enforcing the rules. It is largely for this reason that, in the effort to meet the many new demands for justice incident to a rapidly changing civilization, resort to legislation has latterly been had with increasing frequency.

. . . Courts are ill-equipped to make the investigations which should precede a determination of the limitations which should be set upon any property right in news or of the circumstances under which news gathered by a private agency should be deemed affected with a public interest. Courts would be powerless to prescribe the detailed regulations essential to full enjoyment of the rights conferred or to introduce the machinery required for enforcement of such regulations. Considerations such as these should lead us to decline to establish a new rule of law in the effort to redress a newly-disclosed wrong, although the propriety of some remedy appears to be clear.

NOTES FOR DISCUSSION

1. *Competition and Copying.* Both historically, and today, the general rule in the United States is that copying and imitation are legal absent some specific common law or statutory exception. Did the *INS* Court follow that approach? Over time, starting from a given rule with a narrow set of exceptions, the exceptions can grow until they reach the point where it's better to think of the exceptions as swallowing and thereby becoming the general rule. Does the *INS* holding reach that point?

While there are a variety of reasons why copying or imitation might not be legal in a specific case, the *INS* Court identifies two different reasons why INS's copying of AP's news should be considered "unfair," rather than "fair," competition. What are they?

The first justification, captured by the term "misappropriation," is the threat that INS's actions pose to the incentives for AP to engage in news gathering. Here, the concern is that INS's copying will enable INS to offer the same product at a substantially lower price than AP. Given this lower price, so many consumers—newspapers, in this case—will switch to INS that AP will no longer have sufficient incentive to engage in news gathering at all, or so the Court asserts. To prevent this, the Court recognizes a new cause of action for misappropriation to prevent INS from bodily appropriating AP's stories.

This incentives-based—or property-based—justification for a prohibition on copying is usually associated with copyright and patent. The Court's recognition of a new cause of action based upon this rationale raises several issues. First, is the Court correct in its reasoning that absent protection, INS's actions will drive AP out of business? Second, even if the Court is correct, are there other costs to recognizing the cause of action that should be considered? Third, even if recognizing such a cause of action is desirable (based upon the answer to these first two questions), is the Court the right institution to recognize the new cause of action or should it wait for the legislature to act?

The second justification, mentioned in passing by the majority and emphasized by Justice Holmes in his concurrence, is captured by the phrase "palming off." This is the traditional basis for trademark and unfair competition law. Here, the wrong lies in tricking or deceiving consumers into buying goods or services from Company A believing that they come from Company B. In that context, the paradigm case of unfair competition occurs when Company A sells its own goods or services as if they were Company B's. What would such a traditional case of passing off look like in the context of *INS v. AP*?

Both the majority and Justice Holmes, in his concurrence, suggest that this deception-based justification for finding certain types of competition unfair may apply to INS's actions. Instead of passing off INS's news as if it were from AP, however, Justice Holmes suggests that INS is passing off AP's news as if it were from INS. Because it reverses the parties' roles, we refer to this type of passing off as "reverse" passing off. It's easy to see the consumer harm from traditional or forward passing off. Consumers believe they are buying a product that they know and trust from Company B, and they actually receive a potentially inferior product from Company A. What is the harm to consumers from reverse passing off?

Is the Court serious in its invocation of that rationale, or is it simply trying to minimize the appearance of judicial activism inherent in its recognition of an altogether new cause of action for misappropriation? If the passing off aspect were the real basis for the Court's decision, what should be the scope of relief provided in the injunction?

2. *Property-Based Misappropriation, Part I: Will INS's Copying Drive AP Out of Business?* Is the Court persuasive in its prediction of the likely result of continued copying by INS? The Court's decision rests on the notion that newspapers receiving their news from AP would switch to INS, because INS's copying allowed it to offer the same news at a lower price than AP, and that this would eventually drive AP out of business. The result would be that no news-gathering activities would take place at all.

While this is a nice story, is it supported by the facts? For the copying competitor story to apply, two things must happen. First, the copying must substantially reduce INS's costs so that it can offer the news at a noticeably lower price. That provides AP's subscribers a reason to switch. Yet, it does not appear that INS's copying has enabled it to offer the news at a lower price. As the Court explained at the outset of its opinion, 950 papers were members of AP and shared AP's $3.5 million annual operating budget. Thus, AP membership cost approximately $3,700 annually. In contrast, only 400 papers belonged to INS and shared its $2 million annual budget. Thus, INS membership cost $5,000 annually. If INS was not less expensive than AP, even with its copying, why would newspapers switch?

Second, even if the copying enabled INS to offer the news at a lower price, there is still a question whether customers would switch to the INS product. Consider if you ran a newspaper, what sort of price difference would be sufficient to persuade you to switch from a news *gathering* organization to a news *copying* organization? Would you have concerns that some of the news might get lost or become inaccurate as a result of INS's rewriting? Would you have concerns that you might not get the stories in as timely a fashion?

As a factual matter, at the time of its suit against INS, AP had a reputation for accuracy and timeliness that INS lacked. This reputation may have been an important selling point for readers of AP newspapers. If that were indeed the case, AP newspapers would have an incentive to continue their relationships with AP even if its costs were higher. For a detailed discussion of some of the market forces at work behind INS v. AP, *see* Douglas G. Baird, *The Story of INS v. AP: Property, Natural Monopoly, and the Uneasy Legacy of a Concocted Controversy*, in INTELLECTUAL PROPERTY STORIES 9 (Jane C. Ginsburg & Rochelle C. Dreyfuss, eds., 2006).

3.   *Reasoning and Labels*. In its opinion, the Court talks about "reaping where another has sown" and "quasi property." Are these reasons for the outcome, or are they rhetorical flourishes meant to capture the Court's conclusions? If "reaping where another has sown" is necessarily unfair, why does the Court legitimize the practice of using each other's stories so long as each new service verifies the story independently—a practice the Court refers to as obtaining "tips"?

4.   *Property-Based Misappropriation, Part II: Other Costs*. Even if the facts matched the Court's story and it was plausible that INS's actions presented some real threat to AP's continued existence, that alone does not justify recognizing a cause of action. In such a case, the costs of not recognizing the cause of action are plain, but we still must consider the costs of recognizing the cause of action. For example, after the Court enjoins INS from copying AP's news, where could INS get the news?

Presumably, the general answer is that INS could go out and gather the news for itself. However, England had evicted INS's news gathering center from its country because INS had reported stories during World War I without first obtaining the approval of British censors. So what options did INS have? If INS could not copy obtain this information from AP, where could INS newspapers go for their news about the progress of the War? Could an INS newspaper subscribe to AP for the news?

Because of the organizational arrangement of AP, subscriber newspapers had "franchise rights" which allowed them to prevent competitor newspapers from becoming members of the organization. After the Court's injunction against INS, AP newspapers became the only newspapers with access to recent news and developments concerning the war then taking place in Europe. This resulted in AP newspapers obtaining virtual monopolies in the cities and regions where they circulated. *See* Baird, *supra*.

Assuming the Court's decision was correct about the potential harm to AP from INS's copying, how should we balance that harm against the resulting monopolization obtained by AP newspapers? Could the Court have denied injunctive relief and only granted damages, thereby creating a near equivalent of a compulsory license? Or does the Court's emphasis on "equity" as a justification for recognizing the cause of action foreclose such a result? Alternatively, is it practical to believe that INS could go to its competitor and negotiate a license to copy AP's news?

5.   *Historical Context: The General Common Law*. What law is the Court applying? Is it the law of a particular state? Is it some uncodified

federal common law? Before the Supreme Court's decision in *Erie R.R. Co. v. Tompkins*, 304 U.S. 64 (1938), federal courts were not bound to apply a particular state's law in deciding cases based on diversity jurisdiction. Rather, federal courts sitting in diversity could decide cases according to a "general common law" consisting of general principles and common law doctrines without regard to the common law as given by the highest court in any particular state. The cause of action for misappropriation created in *INS v. AP* was part of this "general common law."

There were numerous problems with such a general common law. Most importantly, if a legislature disagreed with the Court's decision in *INS*, which legislative body could overturn it? Congress? State legislatures? Which state legislature?

This and other problems led the Court in *Erie RR* to abrogate the general common law. After the *Erie RR* decision, *INS* itself was no longer binding law on any court, federal or state. Congress did not include a misappropriation cause of action in the Trademark Act of 1946, more commonly known as the Lanham Act, after its principal sponsor, Fritz Lanham, D-Texas. While there have been efforts in recent years to create a federal cause of action for misappropriation, particularly with respect to digital databases, at this time, misappropriation remains solely an issue of state law. After *Erie RR*, it became a matter of choice for state courts, or state legislatures, either to adopt *INS*-style misappropriation as the substantive law of their jurisdiction or to reject it. To date, over a dozen states have adopted the doctrine by judicial decision; New York courts having decided the greatest number of misappropriation cases. *See* Edmund J. Sease, *Misappropriation Is 75 Years Old: Should We Bury It or Revive It?*, 70 N. DAK. L. REV. 781, 801–02 (1994).

6.   *Historical Context: The Lochner Era.* Decided in 1918, the *INS* decision falls in the middle of an era of Supreme Court jurisprudence known as the *Lochner* era, named after the Court's decision in *Lochner v. New York*, 198 U.S. 45 (1905). During this era, lasting from the mid-1890s through the mid-1930s, the Court systematically struck down nearly two hundred federal and state laws on substantive due process grounds. At least two of the hallmarks of the *Lochner* era—a lack of deference to legislatures and a strong preference for private property and laissez-faire markets—are on display in *INS v. AP*.

During the *Lochner* era, two Justices systematically dissented from those decisions in which the Court used substantive due process to strike down federal and state statutes—Justices Holmes and Brandeis. When the Court rejected the *Lochner* approach in the mid-1930s, through a series of decisions beginning with *Nebbia v. New York*, 291 U.S. 502 (1934), the *Lochner*-era dissents of these two Justices became the foundation of what has become the Court's present approach to constitutional jurisprudence. Should we follow a similar jurisprudential approach to *INS*?

Even during the *Lochner* era, lower courts had begun to question whether the judicially-created doctrine of misappropriation could coexist with statutory patents and copyrights. Finding no easy way to reconcile the potential tensions, courts of appeal began to limit *INS* to its facts. For example, in *Cheney Bros. v. Doris Silk Corp.*, 35 F.2d 279 (2d Cir. 1929), a fabric designer asserted that the copying of its popular fabric designs constituted misappropriation. As in *INS*, the designer had made a substantial investment in creating new designs, and defendant's copying enabled the defendant to offer the same designs at a lower price. Nevertheless, the Second Circuit, in an opinion by Judge Hand, rejected the claim.

In doing so, the court began with the general proposition that absent some specific statutory or common law protection, "[o]thers may imitate at their pleasure." *Cheney Bros.*, 35 F.2d at 280. While the court recognized that the rationale of the *INS* decision might encompass the copying of silk designs, Judge Hand refused to extend *INS* beyond its facts. As Judge Hand explained:

> Although [the *INS* case] concerned another subject-matter— pirated news dispatches—we agree that, if it meant to lay down a general doctrine, it would cover this case; at least, the language of the majority opinion goes so far. We do not believe that it did. While it is of course true that law ordinarily speaks in general terms, there are cases where the occasion is at once the justification for, and the limit of, what is decided. This appears to us such an instance; we think that no more was covered than situations substantially similar to those then at bar. The difficulties of understanding it otherwise are insuperable. We are to suppose that the court meant to create a sort of common-law patent or copyright for reasons of justice. Either would flagrantly conflict with the scheme which Congress has for more than a century devised to cover the subject-matter.

Is there any sensible way to limit the reach of the misappropriation doctrine? Or does the doctrine almost necessarily "flagrantly conflict" with the statutory patent and copyright schemes?

7. *The Modern Misappropriation Doctrine.* Relying on the reasoning of Justice Brandeis's dissent and the treatment of *INS* in cases such as *Cheney Bros.*, the Restatement (Third) of Unfair Competition pronounced the death of the doctrine of misappropriation in 1995. See Restatement (Third) of Unfair Competition § 38, cmt. b (ALI 1995).

The Restatement position notwithstanding, misappropriation retains some life even today. For example, in *Board of Trade v. Dow Jones & Co.*, 98 Ill.2d 109, 74 Ill.Dec. 582, 456 N.E.2d 84 (1983), the Illinois Supreme Court found an actionable misappropriation when the Board of Trade proposed offering a futures contract based upon the Dow Jones Industrial Average. The court reasoned that Dow Jones invested time and money in identifying the specific stocks to include in its Industrial Average, so that the Average provided a meaningful indication of the stock market's performance as a whole. Because of this investment, the court ruled that the Board of Trade could not offer a futures contract based upon the index without Dow Jones's permission.

The Second Circuit recognized a misappropriation cause of action under New York state law, but reached a different result in *National Basketball Ass'n v. Motorola, Inc.,* 105 F.3d 841 (2d Cir. 1997). In that case, the NBA sued to enjoin Motorola from sending scores and other statistics about NBA basketball games to users of a mobile pager service. The court refused to enjoin the practice, reasoning that Motorola's pager service did not compete with the NBA's primary business of producing basketball games and licensing broadcast rights because the pager was not a replacement for viewing the games, either televised or live. Furthermore, because Motorola went to considerable expense to acquire and broadcast the statistical information regarding the basketball games over its network, it was not "free riding" on information that NBA expended time and effort to produce.

Similarly, in *United States Golf Ass'n v. St. Andrews Systems, Data-Max, Inc.,* 749 F.2d 1028 (3d Cir. 1984), the plaintiff's golf handicapping formula was used by defendant's own handicapping service. The court refused to enjoin the defendant from using the handicap because the defendant's use of the formula did not destroy the plaintiff's incentive to create it.

Does misappropriation serve a useful role in allowing courts of equity to protect intellectual property rights that are not covered by federal or state protections but perhaps should be? If so, how liberally should courts apply the doctrine? For an argument that the doctrine should be abolished, *see* Richard A. Posner, *Misappropriation: A Dirge*, 40 HOUS. L. REV. 621 (2003).

DASTAR CORP. V. TWENTIETH CENTURY FOX FILM CORP.
539 U.S. 23 (2003)

SCALIA, J.

In this case, we are asked to decide whether § 43(a) of the Lanham Act, 15 U.S.C. § 1125(a), prevents the unaccredited copying of a work, and if so, whether a court may double a profit award under § 1117(a), in order to deter future infringing conduct.

I

In 1948, three and a half years after the German surrender at Reims, General Dwight D. Eisenhower completed Crusade in Europe, his written account of the allied campaign in Europe during World War II. Doubleday published the book, registered it with the Copyright Office in 1948, and granted exclusive television rights to an affiliate of respondent Twentieth Century Fox Film Corporation (Fox). Fox, in turn, arranged for Time, Inc., to produce a television series, also called Crusade in Europe, based on the book, and Time assigned its copyright in the series to Fox. The television series, consisting of 26 episodes, was first broadcast in 1949. It combined a soundtrack based on a narration of the book with film footage from the United States Army, Navy, and Coast Guard, the British Ministry of Information and War Office, the National Film Board of Canada, and unidentified "Newsreel Pool Cameramen." In 1975, Doubleday renewed the copyright on the book as the " 'proprietor of copyright in a work made for hire.' " App. to Pet for Cert. 9a. Fox, however, did not renew the copyright on the Crusade television series, which expired in 1977, leaving the television series in the public domain.

In 1988, Fox reacquired the television rights in General Eisenhower's book, including the exclusive right to distribute the Crusade television series on video and to sub-license others to do so. Respondents SFM Entertainment and New Line Home Video, Inc., in turn, acquired from Fox the exclusive rights to distribute Crusade on video. SFM obtained the negatives of the original television series, restored them, and repackaged the series on videotape; New Line distributed the videotapes.

Enter petitioner Dastar. In 1995, Dastar decided to expand its product line from music compact discs to videos. Anticipating renewed interest in World War II on the 50th anniversary of the war's end, Dastar released a video set entitled World War II Campaigns in Europe. To make Campaigns, Dastar purchased eight beta cam tapes of the *original* version of the Crusade television series, which is in the public domain, copied them, and then edited the series. Dastar's Campaigns series is slightly more than half as long as the original Crusade television series. Dastar substituted a new opening sequence, credit page, and final closing for those of the Crusade television series; inserted new chapter-title sequences and narrated chapter introductions; moved the "recap" in the Crusade television series to the beginning and retitled it as a "preview"; and removed references to and images of the book. Dastar created new packaging for its Campaigns series and (as already noted) a new title.

Dastar manufactured and sold the Campaigns video set as its own product. The advertising states: "Produced and Distributed by: *Entertainment Distributing*" (which is owned by Dastar), and makes no reference to the Crusade television series. Similarly, the screen credits state "DASTAR CORP presents" and "an ENTERTAINMENT DISTRIBUTING Production," and list as executive producer, producer, and associate producer, employees of Dastar. Supp App. 2–3, 30. The Campaigns videos themselves also make no reference to the Crusade television series, New Line's Crusade videotapes, or the book. Dastar sells its Campaigns videos to Sam's Club, Costco, Best Buy, and other retailers and mail-order companies for $25 per set, substantially less than New Line's video set.

In 1998, respondents Fox, SFM, and New Line brought this action alleging that Dastar's sale of its Campaigns video set infringes Doubleday's copyright in General Eisenhower's book and, thus, their exclusive television rights in the book. Respondents later amended their complaint to add claims that Dastar's sale of Campaigns "without proper credit" to the Crusade television series constitutes "reverse passing off" in violation of § 43(a) of the Lanham Act, 15 U.S.C. § 1125(a), and in violation of state unfair-competition law. App. to Pet. for Cert. 31a. On cross-motions for summary judgment, the District Court found for respondents on all three counts, *id.*, at 54a–55a, treating its resolution of the Lanham Act claim as controlling on the state-law unfair-competition claim because "the ultimate test under both is whether the public is likely to be deceived or confused," *id.*, at 54a. The court awarded Dastar's profits to respondents and doubled them pursuant to § 35 of the Lanham Act, 15 U.S.C. § 1117(a), to deter future infringing conduct by petitioner.

The Court of Appeals for the Ninth Circuit affirmed the judgment for respondents on the Lanham Act claim, but reversed as to the copyright claim and remanded. 34 Fed. Appx. 312, 316 (2002). (It said nothing with regard to the state-law claim.) With respect to the Lanham Act claim, the Court of Appeals reasoned that "Dastar copied substantially the entire *Crusade in Europe* series created by Twentieth Century Fox, labeled the resulting product with a different name and marketed it without attribution to Fox [,and] therefore committed a 'bodily appropriation' of Fox's series." *Id.*, at 314. It concluded that "Dastar's 'bodily appropriation' of Fox's original [television] series is sufficient to establish the reverse passing off." *Ibid.* The court also affirmed the District Court's award under the Lanham Act of twice Dastar's profits. We granted certiorari *Dastar Corp. v. Twentieth Century Fox Film Corp.*, 537 U.S. 1099 (2003).

II

The Lanham Act was intended to make "actionable the deceptive and misleading use of marks," and "to protect persons engaged in . . . commerce against unfair competition." 15 U.S.C. § 1127. While much of the Lanham Act addresses the registration, use, and infringement of trademarks and related marks, § 43(a), 15 U.S.C. § 1125(a) is one of the few provisions that goes beyond trademark protection. As originally enacted, § 43(a) created a federal remedy against a person who used in commerce either "a false designation of origin, or any false description or representation" in connection with "any goods or services." 60 Stat. 441. As the Second Circuit accurately observed with regard to the original enactment, however—and as remains true after the 1988 revision— § 43(a) "does not have boundless application as a remedy for unfair trade practices," *Alfred Dunhill, Ltd.* v. *Interstate Cigar Co.*, 499 F.2d 232, 237 (1974). "Because of its inherently limited wording, § 43(a) can never be a federal 'codification' of the overall law of 'unfair competition,'" 4 J.

McCarthy Trademarks and Unfair Competition § 27:7, p 27–14 (4th ed. 2002) (McCarthy), but can apply only to certain unfair trade practices prohibited by its text.

Although a case can be made that a proper reading of § 43(a), as originally enacted, would treat the word "origin" as referring only "to the geographic location in which the goods originated," *Two Pesos, Inc.* v. *Taco Cabana, Inc.*, 505 U.S. 763, 777 (1992) (Stevens, J., concurring in judgment), the Courts of Appeals considering the issue, beginning with the Sixth Circuit, unanimously concluded that it "does not merely refer to geographical origin, but also to origin of source or manufacture," *Federal-Mogul-Bower Bearings, Inc.* v. *Azoff*, 313 F.2d 405, 408 (1963), thereby creating a federal cause of action for traditional trademark infringement of unregistered marks. See 4 McCarthy § 27:14; *Two Pesos, supra,* at 768. Moreover, every Circuit to consider the issue found § 43(a) broad enough to encompass reverse passing off. The Trademark Law Revision Act of 1988 made clear that § 43(a) covers origin of production as well as geographic origin. Its language is amply inclusive, moreover, of reverse passing off—if indeed it does not implicitly adopt the unanimous court-of-appeals jurisprudence on that subject.

Thus, as it comes to us, the gravamen of respondents' claim is that, in marketing and selling Campaigns as its own product without acknowledging its nearly wholesale reliance on the Crusade television series, Dastar has made a "false designation of origin, false or misleading description of fact, or false or misleading representation of fact, which . . . is likely to cause confusion . . . as to the origin . . . of his or her goods." See, *e.g.,* Brief for Respondents 8, 11. That claim would undoubtedly be sustained if Dastar had bought some of New Line's Crusade videotapes and merely repackaged them as its own. Dastar's alleged wrongdoing, however, is vastly different: it took a creative work in the public domain— the Crusade television series—copied it, made modifications (arguably minor), and produced its very own series of videotapes. If "origin" refers only to the manufacturer or producer of the physical "goods" that are made available to the public (in this case the videotapes), Dastar was the origin. If, however, "origin" includes the creator of the underlying work that Dastar copied, then someone else (perhaps Fox) was the origin of Dastar's product. At bottom, we must decide what § 43(a)(1)(A) of the Lanham Act means by the "origin" of "goods."

III

The dictionary definition of "origin" is "the fact or process of coming into being from a source," and "that from which anything primarily proceeds; source." Webster's New International Dictionary 1720–1721 (2d ed. 1949). And the dictionary definition of "goods" (as relevant here) is "[w]ares; merchandise." *Id.,* at 1079. We think the most natural understanding of the "origin" of "goods"—the source of wares—is the producer of the tangible product sold in the marketplace, in this case the physical Campaigns videotape sold by Dastar. The concept might be stretched (as it was under the original version of § 43(a)) to include not only the actual producer, but also the trademark owner who commissioned or assumed responsibility for ("stood behind") production of the physical product. But as used in the Lanham Act, the phrase "origin of goods" is in our view incapable of connoting the person or entity that originated the ideas or communications that "goods" embody or contain. Such an extension would not only stretch the text, but it would be out of accord with the history and purpose of the Lanham Act and inconsistent with precedent.

Section 43(a) of the Lanham Act prohibits actions like trademark infringement that deceive consumers and impair a producer's goodwill. It forbids, for example, the Coca-Cola Company's passing off its product as Pepsi-Cola or reverse passing off Pepsi-Cola as its product. But the brand-loyal consumer who prefers the drink that the Coca-Cola Company or PepsiCo sells, while he believes that that company produced (or at least stands behind the production of) that product, surely does not necessarily believe that that company was the "origin" of the drink in the sense that it was the very first to devise the formula. The consumer who buys a branded product does not automatically assume that the brand-name company is the same entity that came up with the idea for the product, or designed the product—and typically does not care whether it is. The words of the Lanham Act should not be stretched to cover matters that are typically of no consequence to purchasers.

It could be argued, perhaps, that the reality of purchaser concern is different for what might be called a communicative product—one that is valued not primarily for its physical qualities, such as a hammer, but for the intellectual content that it conveys, such as a book or, as here, a video. The purchaser of a novel is interested not merely, if at all, in the identity of the producer of the physical tome (the publisher), but also, and indeed primarily, in the identity of the creator of the story it conveys (the author). And the author, of course, has at least as much interest in avoiding passing-off (or reverse passing-off) of his creation as does the publisher. For such a communicative product (the argument goes) "origin of goods" in § 43(a) must be deemed to include not merely the producer of the physical item (the publishing house Farrar, Straus and Giroux, or the video producer Dastar) but also the creator of the content that the physical item conveys (the author Tom Wolfe, or—assertedly—respondents).

The problem with this argument according special treatment to communicative products is that it causes the Lanham Act to conflict with the law of copyright, which addresses that subject specifically. The right to copy, and to copy without attribution, once a copyright has expired, like "the right to make [an article whose patent has expired]—including the right to make it in precisely the shape it carried when patented—passes to the public." *Sears, Roebuck & Co.* v. *Stiffel Co.*, 376 U.S. 225, 230 (1964); see also *Kellogg Co.* v. *National Biscuit Co.*, 305 U.S. 111, 121–122 (1938). "In general, unless an intellectual property right such as a patent or copyright protects an item, it will be subject to copying." *TrafFix Devices, Inc.* v. *Marketing Displays, Inc.*, 532 U.S. 23, 29 (2001). The rights of a patentee or copyright holder are part of a "carefully crafted bargain," *Bonito Boats, Inc.* v. *Thunder Craft Boats, Inc.*, 489 U.S. 141, 150–151 (1989), under which, once the patent or copyright monopoly has expired, the public may use the invention or work at will and without attribution. Thus, in construing the Lanham Act, we have been "careful to caution against misuse or over-extension" of trademark and related protections into areas traditionally occupied by patent or copyright. *TrafFix*, 532 U.S., at 29. "The Lanham Act," we have said, "does not exist to reward manufacturers for their innovation in creating a particular device; that is the purpose of the patent law and its period of exclusivity." *Id.*, at 34. Federal trademark law "has no necessary relation to invention or discovery," *Trade-Mark Cases,* 100 U.S. 82, 94 (1879), but rather, by preventing competitors from copying "a source-identifying mark," "reduces the customer's costs of shopping and making purchasing decisions," and "helps assure a producer that it (and not an imitating competitor) will reap the financial, reputation-related rewards associated with a desirable product," *Qualitex Co.* v. *Jacobson Products Co.*, 514 U.S. 159, 163–164 (1995) (internal quotation marks and citation omitted). Assuming for the sake of argument that Dastar's representation of itself as the "Producer" of its videos amounted to a representation that it originated the creative work conveyed by the videos, allowing a cause of action under § 43(a) for that representation would create a species of mutant copyright law that limits the public's "federal right to 'copy and to use,' " expired copyrights, *Bonito Boats, supra*, at 165.

When Congress has wished to create such an addition to the law of copyright, it has done so with much more specificity than the Lanham Act's ambiguous use of "origin." The Visual Artists Rights Act of 1990, § 603(a), 104 Stat. 5128, provides that the author of an artistic work "shall have the right . . . to claim authorship of that work." 17 U.S.C. § 106A(a)(1)(A) [17 USCS § 106A(a)(1)(A)]. That express right of attribution is carefully limited and focused: It attaches only to specified "works of visual art," § 101, is personal to the artist, §§ 106A(b) and (e), and endures only for "the life of the author," at § 106A(d)(1). Recognizing in § 43(a) a cause of action for misrepresentation of authorship of noncopyrighted works (visual or otherwise) would render these limitations superfluous. A statutory interpretation that renders another statute superfluous is of course to be avoided. *E.g., Mackey* v. *Lanier Collection Agency & Service, Inc.*, 486 U.S. 825, 837, and n.11 (1988).

Reading "origin" in § 43(a) to require attribution of uncopyrighted materials would pose serious practical problems. Without a copyrighted work as the basepoint, the word "origin" has no discernable limits. A video of the MGM film Carmen Jones, after its copyright has expired, would presumably require attribution not just to MGM, but to Oscar Hammerstein II (who wrote the musical on which the film was based), to Georges Bizet (who wrote the opera on which the musical was based), and to Prosper Merimee (who wrote the novel on which the opera was based). In many cases, figuring out who is in the line of "origin" would be no simple task. Indeed, in the present case it is far from clear that respondents have that status. Neither SFM nor New Line had anything to do with the production of the Crusade television series—they merely were licensed to distribute the video version. While Fox might have a claim to being in the line of origin, its involvement with the creation of the television series was limited at best. Time, Inc., was the principal if not the exclusive creator, albeit under arrangement with Fox. And of course it was neither Fox nor Time, Inc., that shot the film used in the Crusade television series. Rather, that footage came from the United States Army, Navy, and Coast Guard, the British Ministry of Information and War Office, the National Film Board of Canada, and unidentified "Newsreel Pool Cameramen." If anyone has a claim to being the *original* creator of the material used in both the Crusade television series and the Campaigns videotapes, it would be those groups, rather than Fox. We do not think the Lanham Act requires this search for the source of the Nile and all its tributaries.

Another practical difficulty of adopting a special definition of "origin" for communicative products is that it places the manufacturers of those products in a difficult position. On the one hand, they would face Lanham Act liability for *failing* to credit the creator of a work on which their lawful copies are based; and on the other hand they could face Lanham Act liability for *crediting* the creator if that should be regarded as implying the creator's "sponsorship or approval" of the copy, 15 U.S.C. § 1125(a)(1)(A). In this case, for example, if Dastar had simply "copied [the television series] as Crusade in Europe and sold it as Crusade in Europe," without changing the title or packaging (including the original credits to Fox), it is hard to have confidence in respondents' assurance that they "would not be here on a Lanham Act cause of action," Tr. of Oral Arg. 35.

Finally, reading § 43(a) of the Lanham Act as creating a cause of action for, in effect, plagiarism—the use of otherwise unprotected works and inventions without attribution—would be hard to reconcile with our previous decisions. For example, in *Wal-Mart Stores, Inc.* v. *Samara Brothers, Inc.*, 529 U.S. 205 (2000), we considered whether product-design trade dress can ever be inherently distinctive. Wal-Mart produced "knockoffs" of children's clothes designed and manufactured by Samara

Brothers, containing only "minor modifications" of the original designs. *Id.*, at 208. We concluded that the designs could not be protected under § 43(a) without a showing that they had acquired "secondary meaning," *id.*, at 214, so that they " 'identify the source of the product rather than the product itself,' " *id.*, at 211 (quoting *Inwood Laboratories, Inc.* v. *Ives Laboratories, Inc.*, 456 U.S. 844, 851, n. 11 (1982)). This carefully considered limitation would be entirely pointless if the "original" producer could turn around and pursue a reverse-passing-off claim under exactly the same provision of the Lanham Act. Samara would merely have had to argue that it was the "origin" of the designs that Wal-Mart was selling as its own line. It was not, because "origin of goods" in the Lanham Act referred to the producer of the clothes, and not the producer of the (potentially) copyrightable or patentable designs that the clothes embodied.

Similarly under respondents' theory, the "origin of goods" provision of § 43(a) would have supported the suit that we rejected in *Bonito Boats*, 489 U.S. 141, where the defendants had used molds to duplicate the plaintiff's unpatented boat hulls (apparently without crediting the plaintiff). And it would have supported the suit we rejected in *TrafFix*, 532 U.S. 23: The plaintiff, whose patents on flexible road signs had expired, and who could not prevail on a trade-dress claim under § 43(a) because the features of the signs were functional, would have had a reverse-passing-off claim for unattributed copying of his design.

In sum, reading the phrase "origin of goods" in the Lanham Act in accordance with the Act's common-law foundations (which were *not* designed to protect originality or creativity), and in light of the copyright and patent laws (which *were*), we conclude that the phrase refers to the producer of the tangible goods that are offered for sale, and not to the author of any idea, concept, or communication embodied in those goods. *Cf.* 17 U.S.C. § 202 (distinguishing between a copyrighted work and "any material object in which the work is embodied"). To hold otherwise would be akin to finding that § 43(a) created a species of perpetual patent and copyright, which Congress may not do. *See Eldred* v. *Ashcroft*, 537 U.S. 186, 208 (2003).

The creative talent of the sort that lay behind the Campaigns videos is not left without protection. The original film footage used in the Crusade television series could have been copyrighted, *see* 17 U.S.C. § 102(a)(6), as was copyrighted (as a compilation) the Crusade television series, even though it included material from the public domain, *see* § 103(a). Had Fox renewed the copyright in the Crusade television series, it would have had an easy claim of copyright infringement. And respondents' contention that Campaigns infringes Doubleday's copyright in General Eisenhower's book is still a live question on remand. If, moreover, the producer of a video that substantially copied the Crusade series were, in advertising or promotion, to give purchasers the impression that the video was quite different from that series, then one or more of the respondents might have a cause of action—not for reverse passing off under the "confusion . . . as to the origin" provision of § 43(a)(1)(A), but for misrepresentation under the "misrepresents the nature, characteristics [or] qualities" provision of § 43(a)(1)(B). For merely saying it is the producer of the video, however, no Lanham Act liability attaches to Dastar. . . .

Because we conclude that Dastar was the "origin" of the products it sold as its own, respondents cannot prevail on their Lanham Act claim. We thus have no occasion to consider whether the Lanham Act permitted an award of double petitioner's profits. The judgment of the Court of Appeals for the Ninth Circuit is reversed, and the case is remanded for further proceedings consistent with this opinion.

It is so ordered.

JUSTICE BREYER took no part in the consideration or decision of this case.

NOTES FOR DISCUSSION

1. *The History of False Attribution Claims under the Common Law.* False or misleading attribution claims in Anglo-American jurisprudence have a long pedigree. As Judge Frank once pointed out: "[Lord] Byron obtained an injunction [in 1816] from an English court restraining the publication of a book purporting to contain his poems only, but which included some not of his authorship." *Granz v. Harris*, 198 F.2d 585, 589 (2d Cir. 1952) (Frank, J., concurring) (citing *Byron v. Johnston*, 2 Mer. 28, 35 Eng. Rep. 851 (1816)). By the early twentieth century, American courts had recognized three separate types of false or misleading attributions that would give rise to a claim for unfair competition. First, courts recognized a cause of action for attributing work to an author that was not in fact the author's work. *See, e.g., Prouty v. National Broadcasting Co., Inc.*, 26 F.Supp. 265 (D. Mass. 1939); *Packard v. Fox Film Corp.*, 207 App. Div. 311, 313, 202 N.Y.S. 164 (Sup. Ct. N.Y. 1923) (releasing film not based upon plaintiff's story "The Iron Rider" under that title constituted actionable unfair competition). Second, courts recognized a cause of action for failing to credit an author for her work. *See, e.g., Packard*, 207 App. Div. at 313–14. Third, courts recognized a cause of action for distortion, where a defendant held out "the artist as author of a version which substantially departs from the original." *Granz*, 198 F.2d at 589 (Frank, J., concurring).

At the same time, however, courts consistently rejected any extension of the unfair competition rubric that would create a substitute for, or an effectively perpetual, copyright. For example, in the *Mark Twain Case*, Samuel Clemens argued that his *nom de plume* had acquired secondary meaning and become a trademark. *Clemens v. Belford, Clark & Co.*, 14 F. 728 (C.C.N.D. Ill. 1883). As a consequence, he argued, no one could use his pen name "Mark Twain" without his permission, even on Mr. Clemens's own uncopyrighted writings. Recognizing Mr. Clemens's arguments as an attempt to circumvent the requirements and limitations on statutory copyright, the court rejected Mr. Clemens's unfair competition claims. *Id.* at 732.

However, while the court rejected Mr. Clemens's claims with respect to the use of his pen name on his own writings, it also recognized that had the attribution been false—had Mr. Clemens not in fact been the author of the work(s) at issue—the attribution would have been actionable. As the court explained:

> [A]n author of acquired reputation, and, perhaps, a person who has not obtained any standing before the public as a writer, may restrain another from the publication of literary matter purporting to have been written by him, but which, in fact, was never so written. In other words, no person has the right to hold another out to the world as the author of literary matter which he never wrote; and the same rule would undoubtedly apply in favor of a person known to the public under a nom de plume, because no one has the right, either expressly or by implication, falsely or untruly to charge another with the composition or authorship of a literary production which he did not write. Any other rule would permit writers of inferior merit to put their compositions before the public under the names of writers of high standing and authority, thereby perpetrating a fraud not only on the writer whose name is used, but also on the public.

Id. at 731.

2. *Misattribution Claims under Section 43(a).* In the mid-1970s, lawyers began bringing attribution claims under Section 43(a) of the Trademark Act of 1946. Congress originally intended section 43(a) to create a narrowly tailored cause of action for false representations with respect to geographic origin—the place where the product was made. Beginning with the decision in *L'Aiglon Apparel, Inc. v. Lana Lobell, Inc.*, 214 F.2d 649 (3d Cir. 1954), however, courts began to take the provision as a roving commission to root out whatever competition they perceived as unfair. In the attribution context, the claims generally arose within the film and literary contexts, and were based on the theory that the improper attribution of credit to an author or actor constituted a "false designation of origin" in violation of section 43(a).

One such case was *Gilliam v. American Broadcasting Inc.*, 538 F.2d 14 (2d Cir. 1976). In that case, members of the British comedy group Monty Python had licensed their *Flying Circus* television program to the BBC with the express condition that it not be materially altered without consultation of the creators. The BBC then licensed the program to ABC, which aired a truncated version of the series in the United States. Although the Second Circuit enjoined the program on the grounds that the alterations violated the terms of the copyright license, the Second Circuit also suggested that ABC's alteration of the show "impaired the integrity" to such an extent that associating the altered work with Monty Python constituted an actionable "false designation of origin" under section 43(a).

Several years later, the Ninth Circuit decided *Smith v. Montoro*, 648 F.2d 602 (9th Cir. 1981), in which an actor brought a misattribution claim against a film producer for removing the actor's name from the film credits, and replacing it with a made-up name. The court sustained the actor's misattribution claim under Section 43(a), relying on the importance of protecting the good will and reputation of an actor's name as a rationale for its decision.

Note the different rationales underlying the courts' decisions. Some courts have interpreted the Lanham Act to protect consumers against confusion as to the source of a particular work or product, whereas others have recognized a producer's economic interest in being properly identified as the "source" of a particular artistic work or product. Which of these interests better comports with the actual purposes of the statute? Are both of these interests just different sides of the same coin? Some courts applying the consumer protection rationale have imposed a standing requirement that a plaintiff bringing an attribution claim under 43(a) must assert some sort of economic injury in order for the claim to succeed. *See, e.g., Waldman Pub. Corp. v. Landoll, Inc.*, 43 F.3d 775 (2d Cir. 1994).

3.   *A Split Develops.* Although both the Second and Ninth Circuits recognized misattribution claims under section 43(a), they adopted differing standards for liability. The Second Circuit adopted a standard based on the "substantial similarity" standard in copyright law. *See King v. Innovation Books*, 976 F.2d 824 (2d Cir. 1992). Under this standard, so long as a defendant's work was "substantially similar" to the plaintiff's, a defendant was liable under 43(a) if he/she failed to attribute the work to the plaintiff. In adopting this standard, the Second Circuit concluded that such "substantial similarity" would suffice to cause consumer confusion as to the origin of particular works.

The Ninth Circuit, on the other hand, required a "bodily appropriation" before failing to credit the plaintiff would constitute an actionable misattribution under section 43(a). *See Shaw v. Lindheim*, 919 F.2d 1353 (9th Cir. 1990). This approach is based on the conclusion that "substantial similarity" alone is not enough to cause consumer confusion as to the source of a product or work. Rather, such a product or work must be "bodily appropriated" before the defendant's failure to attribute the work to the plaintiff would create actionable confusion. *See Cleary v. News Corp.*, 30 F.3d 1255 (9th Cir. 1994).

This split provided a nominal justification for the Court's decision to grant certiorari in *Dastar*, but as a practical matter, Dastar's failure to credit Time Life Films represented an actionable misattribution under either Circuit's approach.

4.   *The Search for the Nile.* In rejecting all misattribution claims under section 43(a), the Court emphasizes the difficulties that incorporating such a doctrine into 43(a) would present. Yet, although misattribution claims have been recognized for nearly two hundred years, the Court fails to cite any specific cases as examples of its parade of horribles. Why is that?

Presumably, part of the reason is the nature of the remedy available in these cases. If the wrong is improper attribution, then the remedy should be proper attribution. Given the limited nature of the remedy available, relatively few misattribution claims were filed, and usually they were filed only where the value of proper attribution, or the harm from a false or misleading attribution, was substantial.

What was 20th Century Fox's goal in this case? Was it to require Dastar to label its videotapes with an indication that the series is "based on 'Crusades in Europe'"? Or was it to stop Dastar from offering the same videotape at a lower price? If Fox's goals were the latter illegitimate goal, rather than the former legitimate goal, should that be a basis for denying the right altogether? Or should courts simply limit the remedy available to proper attribution?

5.   *What Was the Doctrinal Holding of the Court?* Does the language of the Trademark Act require that the words "designation of origin" be read to exclude the author of a creative work? Does it prohibit consumers from attaching authorship connotations to trademarks?

We begin, as a doctrinal matter, with the language of the Trademark Act itself. For reasons that will be discussed in connection with the *Sugar Busters* case in Chapter 6, Time could not register the title of Eisenhower's book as a trademark. Could Time Life Films have registered the title of the series when the series first aired on television? Would you register the title as a trademark or service mark? Section 45 of the Trademark Act defines a service mark as:

> any word, name, symbol, or device, or any combination thereof used by a person . . . to identify and distinguish the services of one person . . . from the service of others and to indicate the source of the services. . . . Titles, character names, and other distinctive features of radio or television programs may be registered as service marks notwithstanding that they, or the programs, may advertise the goods of the sponsor.

15 U.S.C. § 1127 (2015).

For a television series, what is the tangible product to which the Court refers? Does the definition of a service mark recognize authorship as the sort of information that a mark can convey? What sort of information does a title of a television show or the name of a character in a radio program convey? Who made the tangible product?

In *Gensler & Associates v. Strabala*, 764 F.3d 735 (7th Cir. 2014), the Seventh Circuit refused to extend *Dastar's* holding to service marks. Mr.

Strabala was an architect who had worked at the Gensler firm. When he left and started his own firm, he claimed that he had designed five projects for which the Gensler firm was the architect of record. Gensler sued, alleging a violation of section 43(a). The district court followed *Dastar* and dismissed the claim. The Seventh Circuit reversed. Preparing the architectural designs was a service, not a good, and as a result, *Dastar* did not control. *Id.* at 736.

What sort of information do consumers rely on marks associated with books and other communicative works to tell them? Does the mark "New York Times" on a newspaper or the mark "Newsweek" on a magazine tell a consumer solely about the quality of the paper and ink used in printing the paper? Or does it tell the consumer something about the quality and editorial slant likely to be found in the newspaper or magazine? If consumers in fact use marks as a source of information about the quality and nature of the authorship they will likely find in a given work, why shouldn't trademark law protect those consumer understandings?

6.   *Forward versus Reverse Confusion.* Like *INS*, this case concerns reverse passing off, or reverse confusion, rather than traditional passing off. How, if at all, does Dastar's failure to credit Time Life Films harm or potentially harm consumers? What would forward confusion look like in this type of case, and how, if at all, would it harm consumers? Are the harms equally serious? Should the Court have held that reverse confusion is not actionable? Or is the doctrinal interpretation of "origins" a better approach?

Will the Court or lower courts stick to the doctrinal "origins" holding in a case involving more traditional forward confusion? For example, how would the following case come out under *Dastar's* holding: JS wants to publish his first novel, but is afraid that it will not sell as well as he hopes. Therefore, while he correctly identifies the publisher of his novel (i.e. the company who prints the physical copies), he states that "John Grisham" is the author of the novel. Is this misattribution actionable under section 43(a) after *Dastar*?

As we shall see, section 43(a) contains two prohibitions. Section 43(a)(1)(A) prohibits false representations "likely to cause confusion . . . as to the origin, sponsorship, or approval of his or her goods, services, or commercial activities." 15 U.S.C. § 1125(a)(1)(A) (2015). Section 43(a)(1)(B) prohibits false representations "which in commercial advertising . . . misrepresents the nature, characteristics, qualities, or geographic origin of his or her or another's goods, services, or commercial activities." 15 U.S.C. § 1125(a)(1)(B) (2015). *Dastar* dealt with section 43(a)(1)(A). Can a plaintiff avoid *Dastar's* reach by alleging a violation of section 43(a)(1)(B)? *See Sybersound Records, Inc. v. UAV Corp.*, 517 F.3d 1137, 1144 (9th Cir. 2008) (holding that whether the public performance or reproduction of a musical work is properly licensed is not a "characteristic" of the good and so cannot support a false advertising claim, but suggesting that inaccurate representations of "the original song and artist" may be actionable).

7.   *Perpetual Copyright.* If the sole remedy awarded 20th Century Fox had been proper labeling, "Based on 'Crusades in Europe,'" how would the

case have come out? Would such a remedy be equivalent to perpetual copyright? Would it negate the risk of pretextual claims?

8. *The Aftermath of* Dastar.

(i) As the Court mentioned, the trial court in *Dastar* found that Dastar had also infringed the copyright in Eisenhower's underlying book on which the television series was based. The copyright issue was not before the Court, however, because the Ninth Circuit had remanded it to the district court to determine whether Fox had properly renewed the copyright in Eisenhower's book. On remand, the district court held, and in a subsequent appeal, the Ninth Circuit affirmed, that the copyright in Eisenhower's book had been properly renewed. *Twentieth Century Fox Film Corp. v. Entertainment Distributing*, 429 F.3d 869 (9th Cir. 2005), *cert. denied sub nom. Dastar Corp. v. Random House*, 548 U.S. 919 (2006). As a result, despite the Court's decision in *Dastar*, Dastar is legally unable to distribute its videotape series. Because the videotape series is based on Eisenhower's book, making or distributing copies of the Dastar videotape would infringe the copyright in Eisenhower's book. Moreover, because the courts found Eisenhower's book to be created as a work-made-for-hire under copyright law, the copyright in the book belongs to Fox. Thus, to make or distribute copies of its videotapes, Dastar must either obtain Fox's consent or wait for the copyright in the book to expire. Given that Eisenhower's book was originally published in 1948, the copyright in the book will expire in 2042, at least under the presently applicable copyright term. 17 U.S.C. § 304(b) (2015).

(ii) In justifying its decision, the Court wrote: "The right to copy, and to copy without attribution, once a copyright has expired, like 'the right to make [an article whose patent has expired]—including the right to make it in precisely the shape it carried when patented—passes to the public.'" Does that language effectively limit the Court's holding to works with expired copyrights? Or does the "origin means producer of the tangible good" holding control even with respect to misattribution claims for works still protected by copyright? *See, e.g., Zyla v. Wadsworth*, 360 F.3d 243 (1st Cir. 2004) (holding that *Dastar* bars a section 43(a) for the failure to credit a co-author even where underlying work is still within its copyright term).

(iii) Does the *Dastar* holding apply to state unfair competition claims alleging misattribution? Because state unfair competition law is usually a common law doctrine, not tied to the particular "origins" statutory language found in section 43(a), an argument can be made that *Dastar* does not limit the availability of a state unfair competition remedy for misattribution. However, on remand in *Dastar* itself, the district court held that because the relief available under state unfair competition law and section 43(a) are "substantially congruent," the Court's decision effectively barred the availability of state law relief as well. *Twentieth Century Fox Film Corp. v. Dastar Corp.*, 68 U.S.P.Q.2d (BNA) 1536 (C.D. Cal. 2003). According to the district court, "the Supreme Court's construction of 'origin' impliedly rejected any consumer confusion regarding [Dastar's] product." Holding such confusion to be an essential element of the state unfair competition cause of action, the district court rejected Fox's state unfair competition claims. Do you agree with the district court that the Court's "construction of 'origin' impliedly rejected any consumer confusion"? In its *Dastar* opinion, did the Court agree that the reach of section 43(a) and state unfair competition law are "substantially congruent"?

9.   *Understanding the Role of Trademarks.*

Consider the following colloquy between Justice Souter and Ms. Cendali, the attorney for Fox, during the *Dastar* oral argument:

Ms. Cendali: But the purposes of the Lanham Act, as this Court has made clear numerous occasions, most—very recently in *Qualitex*, is to let consumers be able to know when they're getting a product, if they want to get—if they like it, they want to get other things from that product—from that supplier, they can.

Question: Dastar knows who to plagiarize.

(Laughter.)

Question: When—when I see the Dastar name, I'm getting good stuff.

(Laughter.)

Ms. Cendali: Well—well, Your Honor, you just don't know whether the next person they plagiarize is going to be as good as Twentieth Century Fox—

Question: That's why I'm relying—yes, but I'm relying on them.

(Laughter.)

Question: They—they knew who to copy the first time. It seems to me that is just as much a—a guarantee that they'll know who to copy the next time, as if they had made it themselves.

Ms. Cendali: Well, the other problem with it, beyond the fact that they are deprived, because you have no idea whether the next time they copy will be as good as the first time, you're also depriving the consumer of the ability to end up buying two of the same product, a very real possibility that they would recognize.

Question: That's right, and they—and they can go to—and they can go to Dastar and raise the devil. They said, you didn't tell us that you copied that other thing. We'll never buy Dastar again. But they know exactly who to blame.

Ms. Cendali: They don't know who to blame because if someone buys Campaigns and Crusade, they will not know who cheated them. They will not be able to tell. The products are lodged with the Court. The Court can look at them. If you bought them both, if I bought my dad one for Christmas and another one for him for his birthday, he's not going to be happy to find he has 2 hours of the same—two copies of the same 7-hour videotape. And in page 205 of the record, it's clear that there are 7 hours of content in that.

Question: But the same point. Why can't he sue or you sue Dastar?

Ms. Cendali: You wouldn't know who to sue. And maybe he also would think—

Question: You sue the person you bought it from.

Ms. Cendali: But it could have been Fox. He wouldn't have known who was the one telling the truth. Moreover, he also wouldn't know—maybe he would think, you know what?

Question: Well, he can sue—he can sue them both and find out.

(Laughter.)

Ms. Cendali: I don't know if that's—that's the—the best way the law should deal with it. Going back to Justice Scalia's question, though, about origin, there's nothing in the Lanham Act to suggest that Congress wanted to limit the word origin to just the manufacture of a product.

Who has the better of the argument? Is there anything more that Ms. Cendali could have said to persuade Justice Souter to her point of view? Consider the following analysis derived from Glynn S. Lunney, Jr., *Distinguishing* Dastar: *Consumer Protection, Moral Rights, and Section 43(a)*, in CONSUMER PROTECTION IN THE AGE OF THE "INFORMATION ECONOMY" (2006).

Justice Souter's suggestion that the Dastar brand can become synonymous with good copying is attractive and quite plausible in the right circumstances. Walmart might be an example of a company that has built precisely such a reputation. But there are three problems with relying on it to justify the *Dastar* outcome. First, even if one accepts the reasoning implicit in Justice Souter's line of questioning, his analysis would lead not to the *Dastar* Court's rule—that section 43(a) does not protect authorial identifications—but to a distinction between traditional and reverse passing off. It might justify Dastar's actions, but it would not similarly justify allowing someone to identify John Grisham as the author of a novel that Grisham did not write.

Second, to the extent that we want to leave Dastar room to develop a reputation as an effective copier, requiring Dastar to state that its videotape series is "based on" the earlier Time Life television series would not frustrate Dastar's efforts in that regard. To the contrary, such an acknowledgement would make it easier for consumers to understand precisely what role Dastar is playing in producing its videotapes. Consumers would then have the information necessary to choose between the Dastar and the authorized versions, given the expected differences in quality and price. They would also have a more accurate information set available to make decisions with respect to future purchases of Dastar videotape series. If they knew that Dastar had copied from Time in this instance, for example, consumers could consider whether given the source material Dastar copies next time, the expectation of quality formed based upon Dastar's copying of the Time series should carry over. That consumers care about the derivation of the Dastar videotapes, while they don't care about the derivation of Walmart's imitations of physical goods, is a crucial distinction. Moreover, the risk that consumers will buy both the two World War II videotapes believing them to be different does not arise for physical goods, such as clothing, where the design is immediately evident from a pre-purchase visual examination.

Third, and most important, Justice Souter's suggested consumer lawsuit misses the point of trademarks and branding. As Benjamin Klein and Keith Leffler have shown, branding serves as a guarantee of quality in circumstances where the costs of a formal warranty enforced through a legal mechanism are prohibitive. *See* Benjamin Klein & Keith B. Leffler, *The Role of Market Forces in Assuring Contractual Performance*, 89 J. POL. ECON. 615 (1981). When products are differentiated through branding, if a consumer is dissatisfied with something she purchases, she does not need to sue and incur the considerable transaction costs a formal warranty mechanism would entail. She can simply take her business elsewhere next time. This threat—to take her business elsewhere—becomes both: (i) an incentive to invest in the quality of the goods or services provided today; and (ii) an implicit penalty for failing to do so. But for this system to work, a consumer must know who to blame; hence, trademark law's prohibition on the use of confusingly similar marks generally. Moreover, because the system is designed as an alternative to a formal, legally enforced warranty of product quality, requiring a consumer to sue to determine which of two trademarks should receive the blame defeats the very purpose of the trademark system. If a lawsuit to ensure product quality is necessary in any event, then the trademark system has failed as an alternative form of quality control.

Given the consumer interest at stake, particularly in misattribution cases involving traditional passing off, the question is how to protect that interest without unduly threatening consumers' equally strong interest in copying and the competition it engenders. Although the *Dastar* Court's parade of horribles exaggerated the potential cost of recognizing a right against misattribution, there is some truth in the concern that a rule requiring proper labeling can become a prohibition on copying itself. In theory, at least, there should not be much profit in the republication of public domain works. So long as the legality of the copying at issue is clear (and perhaps it never is), we should expect near-perfect competition among copiers, and as a result, none of the copiers should earn much in the way of economic rents. Given the relatively small expected profit from republication, even a relatively small risk of litigation and its attendant costs can eliminate the profit opportunity and successfully deter entry.

If we recognize a right against misattribution for communicative works, individuals whose works are no longer (or never were) protected by copyright will want to use that right to nitpick the labeling of copies in order to render any attempt at copying the underlying work unprofitable. As a result, the wide gulf between a requirement of proper labeling and a prohibition on copying, in theory, may prove far narrower in practice.

Is there some way to structure a cause of action for false or misleading attribution so that it protects consumers from material deception without becoming a "mutant species of copyright"? Alternatively, if we humor Justice Souter, what cause of action could a disappointed consumer bring against either Dastar or Fox upon buying both videotapes and finding the same seven hours of materials being offered under different titles?

B. THE CONSTITUTIONAL BASIS OF FEDERAL TRADEMARK PROTECTION

The Constitution, in article I, section 8, clause 8, specifically authorizes Congress to enact legislation to grant "authors and inventors, the exclusive right to their respective writings and discoveries." Pursuant to that authority, Congress enacted the first copyright and patent statutes in 1790. However, there is no similarly specific authorization for Congress to enact trademark legislation. Instead, trademark law was left entirely to the states until Congress enacted the first federal trademark statute in 1870. Soon thereafter, the question arose whether Congress had the constitutional authority to enact a trademark statute.

THE TRADE-MARK CASES
100 U.S. 82 (1879)

MILLER, J.

The three cases whose titles stand at the head of this opinion are criminal prosecutions for violations of what is known as the trade-mark legislation of Congress. The first two are indictments in the southern district of New York, and the last is an information in the southern district of Ohio. In all of them the judges of the circuit courts in which they are pending have certified to a difference of opinion on what is substantially the same question; namely, are the acts of Congress on the subject of trade-marks founded on any rightful authority in the Constitution of the United States?

The entire legislation of Congress in regard to trade-marks is of very recent origin. It is first seen in sects. 77 to 84, inclusive, of the act of July 8, 1870, entitled "An Act to revise, consolidate, and amend the statutes relating to patents and copyrights." 16 Stat. 198. The part of this act relating to trade-marks is embodied in chap. 2, tit. 60, sects. 4937 to 4947, of the Revised Statutes.

It is sufficient at present to say that they provide for the registration in the Patent Office of any device in the nature of a trade-mark to which any person has by usage established an exclusive right, or which the person so registering intends to appropriate by that act to his exclusive use; and they make the wrongful use of a trade-mark, so registered, by any other person, without the owner's permission, a cause of action in a civil suit for damages. Six years later we have the act of Aug. 14, 1876 (19 Stat. 141), punishing by fine and imprisonment the fraudulent use, sale, and counterfeiting of Trademarks registered in pursuance of the statutes of the United States, on which the informations and indictments are founded in the cases before us.

The right to adopt and use a symbol or a device to distinguish the goods or property made or sold by the person whose mark it is, to the exclusion of use by all other persons, has been long recognized by the common law and the chancery courts of England and of this country, and by the statutes of some of the States. It is a property right for the violation of which damages may be recovered in an action at law, and the continued violation of it will be enjoined by a court of equity, with compensation for past infringement. This exclusive right was not created by the act of Congress, and does not now depend upon it for its enforcement. The whole system of trade-mark property and the civil remedies for its protection existed long anterior to that act, and have remained in full force since its passage.

These propositions are so well understood as to require neither the citation of authorities nor an elaborate argument to prove them.

As the property in trade-marks and the right to their exclusive use rest on the laws of the States, and, like the great body of the rights of person and of property, depend on them for security and protection, the power of Congress to legislate on the subject, to establish the conditions on which these rights shall be enjoyed and exercised, the period of their duration, and the legal remedies for their enforcement, if such power exist at all, must be found in the Constitution of the United States, which is the source of all the powers that Congress can lawfully exercise.

In the argument of these cases this seems to be conceded, and the advocates for the validity of the acts of Congress on this subject point to two clauses of the Constitution, in one or in both of which, as they assert, sufficient warrant may be found for this legislation.

The first of these is the eighth clause of sect. 8 of the first article. That section, manifestly intended to be an enumeration of the powers expressly granted to Congress, and closing with the declaration of a rule for the ascertainment of such powers as are necessary by way of implication to carry into efficient operation those expressly given, authorizes Congress, by the clause referred to, "to promote the progress of science and useful arts, by securing for limited times, to authors and inventors, the exclusive right to their respective writings and discoveries."

As the first and only attempt by Congress to regulate the Right of trade-marks is to be found in the act of July 8, 1870, to which we have referred, entitled "An Act to revise, consolidate, and amend the statutes relating to Patents and Copyrights," terms which have long since become technical, as referring, the one to inventions and the other to the writings of authors, it is a reasonable inference that this part of the statute also was, in the opinion of Congress, an exercise of the power found in that clause of the Constitution. It may also be safely assumed that until a critical examination of the subject in the courts became necessary, it was mainly if not wholly to this clause that the advocates of the law looked for its support.

Any attempt, however, to identify the essential characteristics of a trade-mark with inventions and discoveries in the arts and sciences, or with the writings of authors, will show that the effort is surrounded with insurmountable difficulties.

The ordinary trade-mark has no necessary relation to invention or discovery. The trade-mark recognized by the common law is generally the growth of a considerable period of use, rather than a sudden invention. It is often the result of accident rather than design, and when under the act of Congress it is sought to establish it by registration, neither originality, invention, discovery, science, nor art is in any way essential to the right conferred by that act. If we should endeavor to classify it under the head of writings of authors, the objections are equally strong. In this, as in regard to inventions, originality is required. And while the word writings may be liberally construed, as it has been, to include original designs for engravings, prints, & c., it is only such as are original, and are founded in the creative powers of the mind. The writings which are to be protected are the fruits of intellectual labor, embodied in the form of books, prints, engravings and the like. The trade-mark may be, and generally is, the adoption of something already in existence as the distinctive symbol of the party using it. At common law the exclusive right to it grows out of its use, and not its mere adoption. By the act of Congress this exclusive right attaches upon registration. But in neither case does it depend upon novelty, invention, discovery, or any work of the brain. It requires no fancy or imagination, no genius, no laborious thought. It is simply founded on priority of appropriation. We look in vain in the statute for any other qualification or condition. If the symbol, however plain, simple, old, or well-known, has been first appropriated by the claimant as his distinctive trade-mark, he may by registration secure the right to its exclusive use. While such legislation may be a judicious aid to the common law on the subject of trade-marks, and may be within the competency of legislatures whose general powers embrace that class of subjects, we are unable to see any such power in the constitutional provision concerning authors and inventors, and their writings and discoveries.

The other clause of the Constitution supposed to confer the requisite authority on Congress is the third of the same section, which, read in connection with the granting clause, is as follows: "The Congress shall have power to regulate commerce with foreign nations, and among the several States, and with the Indian tribes."

The argument is that the use of a trade-mark—that which alone gives it any value—is to identify a particular class or quality of goods as the manufacture, produce, or property of the person who puts them in the general market for sale; that the sale of the article so distinguished is commerce; that the trade-mark is, therefore, a useful and valuable aid or instrument of commerce, and its regulation by virtue of the clause belongs to Congress, and that the act in question is a lawful exercise of this power.

Every species of property which is the subject of commerce, or which is used or even essential in commerce, is not brought by this clause within the control of Congress. . . .

The question, therefore, whether the trade-mark bears such a relation to commerce in general terms as to bring it within congressional control, when used or applied to the classes of commerce which fall within that control, is one which, in the present case, we propose to leave undecided. We adopt this course because when this court is called on in the course of the administration of the law to consider whether an act of Congress, or of any other department of the government, is within the constitutional authority of that department, a due respect for a co-ordinate branch of the government requires that we shall decide that it has transcended its powers only when that is so plain that we cannot avoid the duty.

In such cases it is manifestly the dictate of wisdom and judicial propriety to decide no more than is necessary to the case in hand. That such has been the uniform course of this court in regard to statutes passed by Congress will readily appear to anyone who will consider the vast amount of argument presented to us assailing them as unconstitutional, and he will count, as he may do on his fingers, the instances in which this court has declared an act of Congress void for want of constitutional power.

Governed by this view of our duty, we proceed to remark that a glance at the commerce clause of the Constitution discloses at once what has been often the subject to comment in this court and out of it, that the power of regulation there conferred on Congress is limited to commerce with foreign nations, commerce among the States, and commerce with the Indian tribes. While bearing in mind the liberal construction, that commerce with foreign nations means commerce between citizens of the United States and citizens and subjects of foreign nations, and commerce among the States means commerce between the individual citizens of different States, there still remains a very large amount of commerce, perhaps the largest, which, being trade or traffic between citizens of the same State, is beyond the control of Congress.

When, therefore, Congress undertakes to enact a law, which can only be valid as a regulation of commerce, it is reasonable to expect to find on the face of the law, or from its essential nature, that it is a regulation of commerce with foreign nations, or among the several States, or with the Indian tribes. If not so limited, it is in excess of the power of Congress. If its main purpose be to establish a regulation applicable to all trade, to commerce at all points, especially if it be apparent that it is designed to govern the commerce wholly between citizens of the same State, it is obviously the exercise of a power not confided to Congress.

We find no recognition of this principle in the chapter on trade-marks in the Revised Statutes. We would naturally look for this in the description of the class for persons who are entitled to register a trade-mark, or in reference to the goods to which it should be applied. If, for instance, the statute described persons engaged in a commerce between the different States, and related to the use of trade-marks in such commerce, it would be evident that Congress believed it was acting under the clause of the Constitution which authorizes it to regulate commerce among the States. So if, when the trade-mark has been registered, Congress had protected its use on goods sold by a citizen of one State to another, or by a citizen of a foreign State to a citizen of the United States, it would be seen that Congress was at least intending to exercise the power of regulation conferred by that clause of the Constitution. But no such idea is found or suggested in this statute. Its language is: "Any person or firm domiciled in the United States, and any corporation created by the United States, or of any State or Territory thereof," or any person residing in a foreign country which by treaty or convention affords similar privileges to our citizens, may by registration obtain protection for his trademark. Here is no requirement that such person shall be engaged in the kind of commerce which Congress is authorized to regulate. It is a general declaration that anybody in the United States, and anybody in any other country which permits us to do the like, may, by registering a trade-mark, have it fully protected. So, while the person registering is required to furnish "a statement of the class of merchandise, and the particular description of the goods comprised in such class, by which the trade-mark has been or is intended to be appropriated," there is no hint that the goods are to be transported from one State to another, or between the United States and foreign countries. Sect. 4939 is intended to impose some restriction upon the Commissioner of Patents in the matter of registration, but no limitation is suggested in regard to persons or property engaged in the different classes of commerce mentioned in the Constitution. The remedies provided by the act when the right of the owner of the registered trade-mark is infringed, are not confined to the case of a trade-mark used in foreign or inter-state commerce.

It is therefore manifest that no such distinction is found in the act, but that its broad purpose was to establish a universal system of trade-mark registration, for the benefit of all who had already used a trade-mark, or who wished to adopt one in the future, without regard to the character of the trade to which it was to be applied or the residence of the owner, with the solitary exception that those who resided in foreign countries which extended no such privileges to us were excluded from them here.

It has been suggested that if Congress has power to regulate trade-marks used in commerce with foreign nations and among the several States, these statutes shall be held valid in that class of cases, if no further. To this there are two objections: First, the indictments in these cases do not show that the trade-marks which are wrongfully used were trade-marks used in that kind of commerce. Secondly, while it may be true that when one part of a statute is valid and constitutional, and another part is unconstitutional and void, the court may enforce the valid part where they are distinctly separable so that each can stand alone, it is not within the judicial province to give to the words used by Congress a narrower meaning than they are manifestly intended to bear in order that crimes may be punished which are not described in language that brings them within the constitutional power of that body.... If we should, in the case before us, undertake to make by judicial construction a law which Congress did not make, it is quite probable we should do what, if the matter were now before that body, it would be unwilling to do; namely, make a trade-mark law which is only partial in its operation, and which would complicate the rights which parties would hold, in some instances under the act of Congress, and in others under State law.

In what we have here said we wish to be understood as leaving untouched the whole question of the treaty-making power over trade-marks, and of the duty of Congress to pass any laws necessary to carry treaties into effect.

While we have, in our references in this opinion to the trade-mark legislation of Congress, had mainly in view the act of 1870, and the civil remedy which that act provides, it was because the criminal offences described in the act of 1876 are, by their express terms, solely referable to frauds, counterfeits, and unlawful use of trade-marks which were registered under the provisions of the former act. If that act is unconstitutional, so that the registration under it confers no lawful right, then the criminal enactment intended to protect that right falls with it.

The questions in each of these cases being an inquiry whether these statutes can be upheld in whole or in part as valid and constitutional, must be answered in the negative; and it will be

So certified to the proper circuit courts.

NOTES FOR DISCUSSION

1. *The Trademark Acts of 1881 and 1905: Invoking the Commerce Clause.* Following *The Trademark Cases*, Congress acted quickly to address the Court's concerns by clarifying that Congress was acting under its Commerce Clause authority, rather than its authority under article I, section 8, clause 8 (the so-called "Patent and Copyright Clause"). The Commerce Clause, which is found in Article I, section 8, clause 3, provides:

> Congress shall have power . . . to regulate Commerce with foreign Nations, and among the several States, and with the Indian tribes. . . .

U.S. Const., art. I, sec. 8, cl. 3.

Just two years after *The Trademark Cases*, in the Trademark Act of 1881, Congress provided for registration of trademarks that were either "used in commerce with foreign nations, or with the Indian tribes, provided such owner shall be domiciled in the United States, or located in any foreign country or tribes, which by treaty, convention, or law, affords similar [registration] privileges to citizens of the United States." Act of Mar. 3, 1881, 46 Cong., 3d Sess., 21 Stat. 502, 502.

Establishing the basic framework that remains even today, the 1881 Act provided that registration would constitute "prima facie evidence of ownership." *Id.*, § 7, at 503. It further prohibited the infringement of a registered trademark. *Id.* at 503–04.

In 1905, Congress re-enacted the Trademark Act. Rather than limiting protection to those trademarks used in commerce with foreign nations or Indian tribes, however, Congress expanded protection in the Trademark Act of 1905 to trade-marks used in commerce "among the several States." Trademark Act of 1905, Pub. L. No. 84, 58th Cong., 3d Sess., 33 Stat. 724, 724.

2. *The Trademark Act of 1946.* Congress's reliance on its Commerce Clause authority to enact trademark legislation has continued in the Trademark Act currently in force, the Trademark Act of 1946. Also known as the Lanham Act, the Trademark Act of 1946 presently allows the registration of trademarks which are used in commerce. It further specifically defines commerce to mean "all commerce which may lawfully be regulated by Congress." 15 U.S.C. § 1127. It also includes the "in commerce" limitation in

defining what conduct constitutes infringement. 15 U.S.C. §§ 1051(a)(1) ("The owner of a trademark used in commerce may request registration. . . ."), 1114(1)(a) ("Any person who shall, without the consent of the registrant— used in commerce any reproduction, counterfeit, copy, or colorable imitation . . . shall be liable in a civil action.").

3.   *The Scope of Congress's Commerce Clause Authority.* Both the Trademark Acts of 1905 and 1946 limited their jurisdictional reach to trademarks used in interstate commerce, and thus nominally had the same jurisdictional scope. In fact, however, their reach differed dramatically because the Supreme Court radically broadened the scope of Congress's Commerce Clause power between 1905 and 1946.

So what counts as "Commerce . . . among the several States"? If a product is made in one state and then shipped and sold to a consumer in another state, such a sale would likely have qualified as interstate commerce in both 1905 and 1946. But what if the product is made in one state and sold to a citizen and resident of the same state? Or what if the product is not even sold? What if a farmer grows her own crop and her family consumes it? In 1905, purely intrastate conduct of this sort likely fell outside the scope of Congress's Commerce Clause authority to regulate. However, during the Great Depression, the federal government enacted a wide array of regulatory programs in an attempt to improve the economic situation. To allow Congress greater leeway to address the perceived demands imposed by the crisis, the Court embraced a broader vision of Congress's Commerce Clause authority. *See NLRB v. Jones & Laughlin Steel Corp.*, 301 U.S. 1 (1937) (upholding the National Labor Relations Act against a challenge that it was beyond Congress's authority under the Commerce Clause and marking the start of the Court's recognition of a broader reach to the Congress's Commerce Clause authority).

Indeed, as a result of one such Great Depression measure—the Agricultural Adjustment Act, the Court expressly addressed whether Congress's Commerce Clause authority extended to the case of a farmer growing and consuming his own food. In *Wickard v. Filburn*, the Court held that it did. 317 U.S. 111, 128–29 (1942). As the Court explained:

But if we assume that [the wheat] is never marketed, it supplies a need of the man who grew it which would otherwise be reflected by purchases in the open market. Home-grown wheat in this sense competes with wheat in commerce.

Id. at 129.

What sort of use of a trademark is thus sufficient to invoke the federal act? May a hairdresser in a small, rural town, well off the beaten path, in Louisiana who has long used the name "Hair We Are" for her salon where she serves an entirely local clientele, drawn entirely from Louisiana, seek federal registration of her mark? May a national chain that claims it used that mark first for its hair salons sue the Louisiana hairdresser under the federal act?

Or is the Louisiana hairdresser outside the scope of Congress's Commerce Clause power?

Even after the Court expanded Commerce Clause jurisdiction in the 1930s and 1940s, some courts continued to cling to the view that a realm of purely intrastate commerce beyond Congress's reach persisted. For example, in *Fairway Foods, Inc. v. Fairway Markets, Inc.*, the Ninth Circuit addressed whether the Trademark Act could reach the activities of a retail grocery that purchased and sold all of its food and other products within the county of Los Angeles. 227 F.2d 193 (9th Cir. 1955). The court said no. "[T]he activities of retail grocers purchasing and selling their wares exclusively intrastate are not a permissible field for Congressional regulation under the Commerce power." *Id.* at 198.

Today, however, the notion of such a purely intrastate commercial realm is almost entirely gone.

C. PERSPECTIVES ON TRADEMARK POLICY

When it enacted the Trademark Act, Congress identified two purposes the Act was intended to serve:

> One is to protect the public so it may be confident that, in purchasing a product bearing a particular trade-mark which it favorably knows, it will get the product which it asks for and wants to get. Secondly, where the owner of a trade-mark has spent energy, time, and money in presenting to the public the product, he is protected in his investment from its misappropriation by pirates and cheats.

S. Rep. No. 79–1333 (1946), *reprinted in* 1946 U.S.C.C.A.N. 1274, 1274.

Are these two different purposes or a single purpose from two different perspectives? Consider the classic case of trademark infringement. In the classic case, Company B brands its products with a trademark identical to that of established Company A so that consumers looking for Company A's products buy Company B's product by mistake instead. In this instance, barring Company B's use of such a confusingly similar trademark protects both consumers and Company A. Here, the two purposes Congress identified are in fact the same purpose from two different perspectives.

The interests of consumers and the trademark owner do not always coincide so nicely, however. Consider the following cases:

> 1) A company wants to market its perfume as a duplicate of Chanel No. 5 at a fraction of the price. Chanel objects. Who should win? *See Smith v. Chanel, Inc.*, 402 F.2d 562 (9th Cir. 1968).
>
> 2) A company wants to manufacture and sell t-shirts bearing the blue and white color scheme of, and bearing the words Dallas

Cowboys. The Dallas Cowboys object. Who should win? *See Boston Prof'l Hockey v. Dallas Cap & Emblem Mfg., Inc.,* 510 F.2d 1004 (5th Cir. 1975).

We will consider these two cases in detail in later chapters, but for now, would you say that the interests of consumers and the trademark owner coincide or conflict in these two cases? In both of these cases, allowing the use would likely prove beneficial for consumers. Allowing the use would promote competition, providing consumers with a second source for the same, or near identical, products. The second source would also likely offer its version of the product at a lower price, which would in turn put pressure on the original source to lower its price too. Moreover, as long as the products could still be distinguished in some other way, consumers would have a choice between purchasing the trademark owner's original at a somewhat higher price or purchasing the copy at a somewhat lower price. For these reasons, consumers would likely prefer that the court allow the use.

The trademark owner, on the other hand, would almost certainly object to both of these proposed uses. While in truth the trademark owner would object primarily because competition would lower its profits, the trademark owner would likely phrase its objection in different terms. The trademark owner might phrase its objection using the language of *INS v. AP*, and argue that the defendants were "reaping where it had not sown," or it might argue that the competitor was improperly seeking to free ride on the goodwill the trademark owner had created. In either case, the gist of the trademark owner's argument is that having created the value of the trademark, the owner is entitled to control its use.

This conflict arises for two reasons. First, a single trademark can play different informational roles. Chanel No. 5 on a perfume bottle, or Dallas Cowboys on a t-shirt, can tell consumers who made (or licensed) the product. It can also tell us what the perfume is likely to smell like, or enable one consumer to tell others which team he or she supports. When a mark in fact serves different informational roles, which should the law choose to recognize and protect? Second, whether we allow or prohibit another's use of a trademark also has important implications for competition. Competition brings lower prices, higher quality, and greater variety. For those reasons, consumers favor competition. For precisely the same reasons, trademark owners would prefer to avoid it as much as possible.

When the interests of consumers and the trademark owner do not coincide, whose interests should we prefer? Over the years, the courts have gone different ways on this issue. Indeed, if you have looked ahead, you already know that the Ninth Circuit allowed the use in the Chanel No. 5 case, while the Fifth Circuit prohibited the use in a case with facts analogous to the Dallas Cowboys example. Generalizations are therefore difficult. Nonetheless, in an article, somewhat provocatively entitled *Trademark Monopolies*, I have suggested that the general trend of trademark law over the course of the twentieth century has been a gradual shift from a consumer-centric perspective, which I denominated "deception-based" trademark, towards a trademark owner-centric perspective, which I denominated "property-based" trademark. 48 EMORY L.J. 367 (1999).

Thus, courts in the first half of the twentieth century tended to tie trademark protection fairly closely to traditional passing off. In *Prestonettes v. Coty*, for example, decided in 1924, Justice Holmes wrote: "A trademark only gives the right to prohibit the use of it so far as to protect the owner's good will against the sale of another's product as his." 264 U.S. 359, 368 (1924). Over time, however, this deception-based focus faded and courts began to embrace a more expansive and protective, property-based vision of trademarks.

Thus, in 1942, Justice Frankfurter offered perhaps the broadest statement of the reasons for trademark protection in *Mishawaka Rubber & Woolen Mfg. Co. v. S.S. Kresge Co.*:

> The protection of trade-marks is the law's recognition of the psychological function of symbols. If it is true that we live by symbols, it is no less true that we purchase goods by them. A trade-mark is a merchandising short-cut which induces a purchaser to select what he wants, or what he has been led to believe he wants. The owner of a mark exploits this human propensity by making every effort to impregnate the atmosphere of the market with the drawing power of a congenial symbol. Whatever the means employed, the aim is the same—to convey through the mark, in the minds of potential customers, the desirability of the commodity upon which it appears. Once this is attained, the trade-mark owner has something of value. If another poaches upon the commercial magnetism of the symbol he has created, the owner can obtain legal redress.

316 U.S. 203, 205 (1942).

If we focus on consumers, and adopt a deception-based justification for trademarks, then the sole purpose of trademark law is to enable consumers to find precisely what they are looking for when they are shopping. If you were looking for the real thing at the grocery store, and were faced with a shelf lined with identical white cans with the identical word "Cola" on them how would you find the taste that you've been looking for? Would you have to open each can and taste each product until you found the right one? From this perspective, we protect things as trademarks to make it easier for consumers to match their desires to a particular product in the marketplace. Economists refer to this as minimizing consumer "search costs," *see*, *e.g.*, William M. Landes &

Richard A. Posner, *Trademark Law: An Economic Perspective,* 30 J.L. & ECON. 265, 268–69 (1987), but a sophisticated knowledge of economics is not necessary to understand the practical advantages that trademarks offer consumers.

With consumers as our central focus, defining the boundaries of trademark protection becomes a balance between two competing concerns. On the one hand, we want to minimize the risks of consumer confusion and minimize consumer search costs. But confusion is not all that consumers are concerned with. If it were, we could simply prohibit "competition altogether. If there were only one source for sodas, one source for breakfast cereal, and one source for clothing, then consumers would invariably purchase such goods from the corresponding producer. In such a world, confusion over the source of goods would simply not arise." Lunney, *Trademark Monopolies,* 38 Emory L.J., at 433. Although consumers do not want to be confused, they are also intensely interested in the lower prices and increased variety that competition can bring. Some consumers may, and apparently do, prefer the taste of Pepsi over Coke. In crafting our trademark law, we must therefore ensure that in attempting to minimize confusion, we also leave ample room for competition.

If, on the other hand, we adopt the property-based approach to trademarks, the focus shifts from consumers to the trademark owner. Trademarks are property, so the argument goes, and so we should protect them in the ways we protect property ordinarily. Taken to its logical extent, this line of arguments seems to suggest that we should grant the trademark owner that "full and despotic dominion" that Blackstone famously, or perhaps infamously, attributed to landowners under English law. Under this view, a trademark has value no longer simply as a means for "conveying otherwise indiscernible information about a product, but as a valuable product in itself." *Id.* at 371.

While playing on some of the themes found in traditional deception-based trademark law, this shift from viewing a trademark as a source of information about a product, to viewing the trademark as the product, has sharply changed the emphasis and context in which trademark's traditional themes have played out. Under this property-based view of trademark law, confusion becomes not just a question of probable confusion as to source, but possible confusion over any connection between the plaintiff and the allegedly infringing use. Similarly, the need for incentives that trademark law addresses becomes not just a question of minimizing consumer deception to ensure a market that generates accurate pricing signals, but a matter of rewarding and thereby encouraging investment in the marks themselves. And, trademarks become property not merely in the formal, legal sense of a right assigned to an entity reasonably well-placed to protect and vindicate the mark's information function, but in the more ordinary, more substantive, and ultimately more absolute sense of a thing belonging fully and completely to its owner.

Id. at 371–72.

For its underlying justification, this property-based approach relies largely on analogies to the incentives-based approaches found in patent and copyright. However, as both *Dastar* and *The Trademark Cases* suggest there are important structural differences between these legal regimes. Patent and copyright laws' common incentives-based purpose is reflected in three defining characteristics found in both regimes. First, to receive a patent or copyright, an individual must create something that is, in some sense, new, whether a novel and nonobvious invention for patent, or an original work of authorship for copyright. Second, as a general rule, we initially assign ownership of the patent or copyright to the creative individual, whether inventor for patent or author for copyright. Third, the Constitution limits both patents and copyrights to "limited times." Both regimes provide the inventor or author a period of exclusivity in which to recover their invention or authorship costs, presently set at twenty years for patent and life-plus-seventy years for copyright. Having provided a sufficient incentive, the rights expire, and the right to practice the invention or to copy the work passes to the public.

In sharp contrast, the structure of trademark reflects none of these characteristics. First, to receive trademark protection, it is not necessary that you create something new. Although some trademarks are coined terms, such as Exxon or Kodak, many are simply existing words or combinations of words, such as Ford or International Business Machines. As a general rule, trademark protection arises not from creating something new, but from using a word or symbol in a manner that leads consumers to associate that word or symbol with the products or services of a particular company or individual. Second, trademark rights are awarded not to the individual who conceived or created a particular mark or slogan, but to the entity that actually uses the mark to sell its goods or services. Third, trademark rights are not tied to some specific statutory time period. As a general rule, trademarks remain protected as long as the mark retains its brand significance or distinctiveness.

As an alternative to the incentives-based justification, the property-based vision of trademarks also seems to derive in part from our instinctive dislike of "the copyist's opportunism." *Smith v. Chanel, Inc.,* 402 F.2d 562, 568 (9th Cir. 1968). This notion, whether phrased as "reaping where you have not sown" or "free-riding on another's goodwill," continues to play an important role in pushing for broader trademark protection. Courts know that competition is desirable, but they do not like copying. The resulting battle between intellect and emotion leads to sharply disparate outcome in trademark cases with seemingly similar facts, as some courts rule with their minds and others with their hearts. As the late Professor Ralph Brown so eloquently expressed it:

> . . . the imperfect stabilization of functionality (and related issues) probably stemmed not from judicial obtuseness, but from . . . the persistent urge [to use trademark and unfair competition law] to create some general protection against copiers. That urge has never achieved dominant expression in the cases. But it runs along like the Manichean heresy, forever pitting the forces of light and the alleged forces of darkness.

Ralph S. Brown, *Product Simulation: A Right or a Wrong?*, 64 COLUM. L. REV. 1216, 1227 (1964).

As you read through the casebook, watch for instances when courts embrace a deception-based approach to trademarks and when they embrace a property-based approach.

NOTES FOR DISCUSSION

1. *Markets Without Trademarks.* As you consider the role of trademarks, can you think of any markets in which there are no trademarks? Can you think of any products that you have purchased over the last few weeks that were not branded? In those markets, how did you find what you were looking for? If the products were sufficiently inexpensive that a formal breach of warranty claim would be impractical if you were dissatisfied with the quality of the products, what assurance of quality did you have? If you were dissatisfied with the quality of the product you purchased, what would you do?

2. *Deception-Based versus Property-Based.* How would you classify *Dastar*? How would you classify *INS*?

3. *The Limits of Trademark Protection.* Identifying the limits of deception-based trademark protection is a relatively straightforward exercise of determining whether consumers, as a whole, would be better or worse off by extending trademark protection in a particular case, recognizing that the resolution of any given case will likely become a rule governing similar cases going forward. What are the limits of property-based trademark protection? Should any use of a trademark without its owner's consent constitute trademark infringement?

4. *Rights and Value.* If someone creates value, should we award them a legal right protecting it? This question is interesting for its own sake and also raises a chicken-and-egg situation about which comes first. Do we protect value by creating rights? Or do rights create value? In this regard, Felix Cohen has remarked: "The vicious circle inherent in this reasoning is plain. It purports to base legal protection upon economic value, when, as a

matter of actual fact, the economic value of a sales device depends upon the extent to which it will be legally protected." *Transcendental Nonsense and the Functional Approach,* 35 COLUM. L. REV. 809, 815 (1935).

CHAPTER 2

PREREQUISITES FOR TRADEMARK PROTECTION: USE

■ ■ ■

In the United States, the first prerequisite for trademark protection is use. Under the common law, use marked the point in time where trademark protection could begin. When Congress enacted the Trademark Act of 1946, it required that a trademark be in "use in commerce" in order to be registered. For domestic trademark owners, that remains the law today. As we shall see in Chapter 6, use also plays a central role, as part of the abandonment doctrine, in defining where trademark protection ends.

Despite its central role in trademark law, Congress did not define use when it adopted the Trademark Act of 1946. Instead, Congress relied on the common law's understanding of the term to which we now turn.

A. THE TRADITIONAL USE REQUIREMENT

BLUE BELL, INC. v. FARAH MFG. CO.
508 F.2d 1260 (5th Cir. 1975)

GEWIN, J.

In the spring and summer of 1973 two prominent manufacturers of men's clothing created identical trademarks for goods substantially identical in appearance. Though the record offers no indication of bad faith in the design and adoption of the labels, both Farah Manufacturing Company (Farah) and Blue Bell, Inc. (Blue Bell) devised the mark "Time Out" for new lines of men's slacks and shirts. Both parties market their goods on a national scale, so they agree that joint utilization of the same trademark would confuse the buying public. Thus, the only question presented for our review is which party established prior use of the mark in trade. A response to that seemingly innocuous inquiry, however, requires us to define the chameleonic term "use" as it has developed in trademark law.

After a full development of the facts in the district court both parties moved for summary judgment. The motion of Farah was granted and that of Blue Bell denied. It is not claimed that summary judgment procedure was inappropriate; the controversy presented relates to the application of the proper legal principles to undisputed facts. A permanent injunction was granted in favor of Farah but no damages were awarded, and Blue Bell was allowed to fill all orders for garments bearing the Time Out label received by it as of the close of business on December 5, 1973. For the reasons hereinafter stated we affirm.

Farah conceived of the Time Out mark on May 16, after screening several possible titles for its new stretch menswear. Two days later the firm adopted an hourglass logo and authorized an extensive advertising campaign bearing the new insignia. Farah presented its fall line of clothing, including Time Out slacks, to sales personnel on June 5. In the meantime, patent counsel had given clearance for use of the mark after scrutiny of current federal registrations then on file. One of Farah's top executives demonstrated samples of the Time Out garments to large customers in Washington, D.C. and New York, though labels were not attached to the slacks at that time. Tags containing the new design were completed June 27. With favorable evaluations of marketing potential from all sides, Farah sent one pair of slacks bearing the Time Out mark to each of its twelve regional sales managers on July 3. Sales personnel paid for the pants, and the garments became their property in case of loss.

Following the July 3 shipment, regional managers showed the goods to customers the following week. Farah received several orders and production began. Further shipments of sample garments were mailed to the rest of the sales force on July 11 and 14. Merchandising efforts were fully operative by the end of the month. The first shipments to customers, however, occurred in September.

Blue Bell, on the other hand, was concerned with creating an entire new division of men's clothing, as an avenue to reaching the "upstairs" market. Though initially to be housed at the Hicks-Ponder plant in El Paso, the new division would eventually enjoy separate headquarters. On June 18 Blue Bell management arrived at the name Time Out to identify both its new division and its new line of men's sportswear. Like Farah, it received clearance for use of the mark from counsel. Like Farah, it inaugurated an advertising campaign. Unlike Farah, however, Blue Bell did not ship a dozen marked articles of the new line to its sales personnel. Instead, Blue Bell authorized the manufacture of several hundred labels bearing the words Time Out and its logo shaped like a referee's hands forming a T. When the labels were completed on June 29, the head of the embryonic division flew them to El Paso. He instructed shipping personnel to affix the new Time Out labels to slacks that already bore the "Mr. Hicks" trademark. The new tags, of varying sizes and colors, were randomly attached to the left hip pocket button of slacks and the left hip pocket of jeans. Thus, although no change occurred in the design or manufacture of the pants, on July 5 several hundred pair left El Paso with two tags.

Blue Bell made intermittent shipments of the doubly-labeled slacks thereafter, though the out-of-state customers who received the goods had ordered clothing of the Mr. Hicks variety. Production of the new Time Out merchandise began in the latter part of August, and Blue Bell held a sales meeting to present its fall designs from September 4–6. Sales personnel solicited numerous orders, though shipments of the garments were not scheduled until October.

By the end of October Farah had received orders for 204,403 items of Time Out sportswear, representing a retail sales value of over $2,750,000. Blue Bell had received orders for 154,200 garments valued at over $900,000. Both parties had commenced extensive advertising campaigns for their respective Time Out sportswear.

Soon after discovering the similarity of their marks, Blue Bell sued Farah for common law trademark infringement and unfair competition, seeking to enjoin use of the Time Out trademark on men's clothing. Farah counter-claimed for similar injunctive relief. The district court found that Farah's July 3 shipment and sale constituted a valid use in trade, while Blue Bell's July 5 shipment was a mere "token" use insufficient at law to create trademark rights. While we affirm the result reached by the trial court as to Farah's priority of use, the legal grounds upon which we base our decision are somewhat different from those undergirding the district court's judgment.

Federal jurisdiction is predicated upon diversity of citizenship, since neither party has registered the mark pursuant to the Lanham Act. Given the operative facts surrounding manufacture and shipment from El Paso, the parties agree the Texas law of trademarks controls. In 1967 the state legislature enacted a Trademark Statute. Section 16.02 of the Act explains that a mark is "used" when it is affixed to the goods and "the goods are sold, displayed for sale, or otherwise publicly distributed." Thus the question whether Blue Bell or Farah established priority of trademark use depends upon interpretation of the cited provision. Unfortunately, there are no Texas cases construing § 16.02. This court must therefore determine what principles the highest state court would utilize in deciding such a question. In view of the statute's stated purpose to preserve common law rights, we conclude the Texas Supreme Court would apply the statutory provision in light of general principles of trademark law.

A trademark is a symbol (word, name, device or combination thereof) adopted and used by a merchant to identify his goods and distinguish them from articles produced by others. Ownership of a mark requires a combination of both appropriation and use in trade. Thus, neither conception of the mark, nor advertising alone establishes trademark rights at common law. Rather, ownership of a trademark accrues when goods bearing the mark are placed on the market.

The exclusive right to a trademark belongs to one who first uses it in connection with specified goods. Such use need not have gained wide public recognition, and even a single use in trade may sustain trademark rights if followed by continuous commercial utilization.

The initial question presented for review is whether Farah's sale and shipment of slacks to twelve regional managers constitutes a valid first use of the Time Out mark. Blue Bell claims the July 3 sale was merely an internal transaction insufficiently public to secure trademark ownership. After consideration of pertinent authorities, we agree.

Secret, undisclosed internal shipments are generally inadequate to support the denomination "use." Trademark claims based upon shipments from a producer's plant to its sales office, and vice versa, have often been disallowed. Though none of the cited cases dealt with *sales* to intra-corporate personnel, we perceive that fact to be a distinction without a difference. The sales were not made to customers, but served as an accounting device to charge the salesmen with their cost in case of loss. The fact that some sales managers actively solicited accounts bolsters the good faith of Farah's intended use, but does not meet our essential objection: that the "sales" were not made to the public.

The primary, perhaps singular purpose of a trademark is to provide a means for the consumer to separate or distinguish one manufacturer's goods from those of another. Personnel within a corporation can identify an item by style number or other unique code. A trademark aids the public in selecting particular goods. As stated by the First Circuit:

> But to hold that a sale or sales are the *sine qua non* of a use sufficient to amount to an appropriation would be to read an unwarranted limitation into the statute, for so construed registration would have to be denied to any manufacturer who adopted a mark to distinguish or identify his product, and perhaps applied it thereon for years, if he should in practice lease his goods rather than sell them, as many manufacturers of machinery do. It seems to us that although evidence of sales is highly persuasive, the question of use adequate to establish appropriation remains one to be decided on the facts of each case, and that evidence showing, first, adoption, and, second, *use in a way sufficiently public to identify or distinguish the marked goods in an appropriate segment of the public mind as those of the adopter of the mark*, is competent to establish ownership. . . .

New England Duplicating Co. v. Mendes, 190 F.2d 415, 418 (1st Cir. 1951) (Emphasis added). Similarly, the Trademark Trial and Appeal Board has reasoned:

To acquire trademark rights there has to be an "open" use, that is to say, a use has to be made to the relevant class of purchasers or prospective purchasers since a trademark is intended to identify goods and distinguish those goods from those manufactured or sold by others. There was no such "open" use rather the use can be said to be an "internal" use, which cannot give rise to trademark rights.

Sterling Drug, Inc. v. Knoll A. G. Chemische Fabriken, [159 U.S.P.Q. 628, 631 (T.T.A.B. 1968)].

Farah nonetheless contends that a recent decision of the Board so undermines all prior cases relating to internal use that they should be ignored. In *Standard Pressed Steel Co. v. Midwest Chrome Process Co.*, 183 U.S.P.Q. 758 (TTAB 1974) the agency held that internal shipment of marked goods from a producer's manufacturing plant to its sales office constitutes a valid "use in commerce" for registration purposes.

An axiom of trademark law has been that the right to register a mark is conditioned upon its actual use in trade. Theoretically, then, common law use in trade should precede the use in commerce upon which Lanham Act registration is predicated. Arguably, since only a trademark owner can apply for registration, any activity adequate to create registrable rights must perforce also create trademark rights. A close examination of the Board's decision, however, dispels so mechanical a view. The tribunal took meticulous care to point out that its conclusion related solely to registration use rather than ownership use.

It has been recognized and especially so in the last few years that, in view of the expenditures involved in introducing a new product on the market generally and the attendant risk involved therein prior to the screening process involved in resorting to the federal registration system and in the absence of an "intent to use" statute, a token sale or a single shipment in commerce *may be sufficient to support an application to register a trademark* in the Patent Office notwithstanding that the evidence may not show what disposition was made of the product so shipped. That is, the fact that a sale or a shipment of goods bearing a trademark was *designed primarily to lay a foundation for the filing of an application for registration* does not, per se, invalidate any such application or subsequent registration issued thereon. . . .

Inasmuch as it is our belief that a most liberal policy should be followed in a situation of this kind [*in which dispute as to priority of use and ownership of a mark is not involved*], applicant's initial shipment of fasteners, although an intra-company transaction in that it was to a company sales representative, was a bona fide shipment. . . .

Standard Pressed Steel Co. v. Midwest Chrome Process Co., [183 U.S.P.Q. 758, 764–65 (T.T.A.B. 1974)] (Emphasis added).

Priority of use and ownership of the Time Out mark are the only issues before this court. The language fashioned by the Board clearly indicates a desire to leave the common law of trademark ownership intact. The decision may demonstrate a reversal of the presumption that ownership rights precede registration rights, but it does not affect our analysis of common law use in trade. Farah had undertaken substantial preliminary steps toward marketing the Time Out garments, but it did not establish ownership of the mark by means of the July 3 shipment to its sales managers. The gist of trademark rights is actual use in trade. Though technically a "sale", the July 3 shipment was not "publicly distributed" within the purview of the Texas statute.

Blue Bell's July 5 shipment similarly failed to satisfy the prerequisites of a bona fide use in trade. Elementary tenets of trademark law require that labels or designs be affixed to the merchandise actually intended to bear the mark in commercial transactions. Furthermore, courts have recognized that the usefulness of a mark derives not only from its capacity to identify a certain manufacturer, but also from its ability to differentiate between different classes of goods produced by a single manufacturer. Here customers had ordered slacks of the Mr. Hicks species, and Mr. Hicks was the fanciful mark distinguishing these slacks from all others. Blue Bell intended to use the Time Out mark on an entirely new line of men's sportswear, unique in style and cut, though none of the garments had yet been produced.

While goods may be identified by more than one trademark, the use of each mark must be bona fide. Mere adoption of a mark without bona fide use, in an attempt to reserve it for the future, will not create trademark rights. In the instant case Blue Bell's attachment of a secondary label to an older line of goods manifests a bad faith attempt to reserve a mark. We cannot countenance such activities as a valid use in trade. Blue Bell therefore did not acquire trademark rights by virtue of its July 5 shipment.

We thus hold that neither Farah's July 3 shipment nor Blue Bell's July 5 shipment sufficed to create rights in the Time Out mark. Based on a desire to secure ownership of the mark and superiority over a competitor, both claims of alleged use were chronologically premature. Essentially, they took a time out to litigate their differences too early in the game. The question thus becomes whether we should continue to stop the clock for a remand or make a final call from the appellate bench. While a remand to the district court for further factual development would not be improper in these circumstances, we believe the interests of judicial economy and the parties' desire to terminate the litigation demand that we decide, if possible, which manufacturer first used the mark in trade.

Careful examination of the record discloses that Farah shipped its first order of Time Out clothing to customers in September of 1973. Blue Bell, approximately one month behind its competitor at other relevant stages of development, did not mail its Time Out garments until at least October. Though sales to customers are not the *sine qua non* of trademark use, they are determinative in the instant case. These sales constituted the first point at which the public had a chance to associate Time Out with a particular line of sportswear. Therefore, Farah established priority of trademark use; it is entitled to a decree permanently enjoining Blue Bell from utilization of the Time Out trademark on men's garments.

The judgment of the trial court is affirmed.

ZAZU DESIGNS V. L'OREAL, S.A.
979 F.2d 499 (7th Cir. 1992)

EASTERBROOK, CIRCUIT JUDGE

In 1985 Cosmair, Inc., concluded that young women craved pink and blue hair. To meet the anticipated demand, Cosmair developed a line of "hair cosmetics"—hair coloring that is easily washed out. These inexpensive products, under the name ZAZU, were sold in the cosmetic sections of mass merchandise stores. Apparently the teenagers of the late 1980s had better taste than Cosmair's marketing staff thought. The product flopped, but its name gave rise to this trademark suit. Cosmair is the United States licensee of L'Oreal, S.A., a French firm specializing in perfumes, beauty aids, and related products. Cosmair placed L'Oreal's marks on the bottles and ads. For reasons the parties have not explained, L'Oreal rather than Cosmair is the defendant even though the events that led to the litigation were orchestrated in New York rather than Paris. L'Oreal does not protest, so for simplicity we refer to Cosmair and L'Oreal collectively as "L'Oreal."

L'Oreal hired Wordmark, a consulting firm, to help it find a name for the new line of hair cosmetics. After checking the United States Trademark Register for conflicts, Wordmark suggested 250 names. L'Oreal narrowed this field to three, including ZAZU, and investigated their availability. This investigation turned up one federal registration of ZAZU as a mark for clothing and two state service mark registrations including that word. One of these is Zazu Hair Designs; the other was defunct.

Zazu Hair Designs is a hair salon in Hinsdale, Illinois, a suburb of Chicago. We call it "ZHD" to avoid confusion with the ZAZU mark. (ZHD employs an acute accent and L'Oreal did not; no one makes anything of the difference.) The salon is a partnership between Raymond R. Koubek and Salvatore J. Segretto, hairstylists who joined forces in 1979. ZHD registered ZAZU with Illinois in 1980 as a trade name for its salon. L'Oreal called the salon to find out if ZHD was selling its own products. The employee who answered reported that the salon was not but added, "we're working on it". L'Oreal called again; this time it was told that ZHD had no products available under the name ZAZU.

L'Oreal took the sole federal registration, held by Riviera Slacks, Inc., as a serious obstacle. Some apparel makers have migrated to cosmetics, and if Riviera were about to follow Ralph Lauren (which makes perfumes in addition to shirts and skirts) it might have a legitimate complaint against a competing use of the mark. *Sands, Taylor & Wood Co. v. Quaker Oats Co.,* 978 F.2d 947 (7th Cir. 1992). Riviera charged L'Oreal $125,000 for a covenant not to sue if L'Oreal used the ZAZU mark on cosmetics. In April 1986, covenant in hand and satisfied that ZHD's state trade name did not prevent the introduction of a national product, L'Oreal made a small interstate shipment of hair cosmetics under the ZAZU name. It used this shipment as the basis of an application for federal registration, filed on June 12, 1986. By August L'Oreal had advertised and sold its products nationally.

Unknown to L'Oreal, Koubek and Segretto had for some time aspired to emulate Vidal Sassoon by marketing shampoos and conditioners under their salon's trade name. In 1985 Koubek began meeting with chemists to develop ZHD's products. Early efforts were unsuccessful; no one offered a product that satisfied ZHD. Eventually ZHD received acceptable samples from Gift Cosmetics, some of which Segretto sold to customers of the salon in plain bottles to which he taped the salon's business card. Between November 1985 and February 1986 ZHD made a few other sales. Koubek shipped two bottles to a friend in Texas, who paid $13. He also made two shipments to a hair stylist friend in Florida—40 bottles of shampoo for $78.58. These were designed to interest the Floridian in the future marketing of the product line. These bottles could not have been sold to the public, because they lacked labels listing the ingredients and weight. See 21 U.S.C. § 362(b); 15 U.S.C. §§ 1452, 1453(a); 21 C.F.R. §§ 701.3, 701.13(a). After L'Oreal's national marketing was under way, its representatives thrice visited ZHD and found that the salon still had no products for sale under the ZAZU name. Which is not to say that ZHD was supine. Late in 1985 ZHD had ordered 25,000 bottles silkscreened with the name ZAZU. Later it ordered stick-on labels listing the ingredients of its products. In September 1986 ZHD began to sell small quantities of shampoo in bottles filled (and labeled) by hand in the salon. After the turn of the year ZHD directed the supplier of the shampoo and conditioner to fill some bottles; the record does not reveal how many.

After a bench trial the district court held that ZHD's sales gave it an exclusive right to use the ZAZU name nationally for hair products. 9

U.S.P.Q.2d 1972 (N.D. Ill. 1988). The court enjoined L'Oreal from using the mark (a gesture, since the product had bombed and L'Oreal disclaimed any interest in using ZAZU again). It also awarded ZHD $100,000 in damages on account of lost profits and $1 million more to pay for corrective advertising to restore luster to the ZAZU mark. . . . [L'Oreal appealed.]

I

Federal law permits the registration of trademarks and the enforcement of registered marks. Through § 43(a) of the Lanham Act, 15 U.S.C. § 1125(a), a provision addressed to deceit, it also indirectly allows the enforcement of unregistered marks. But until 1988 federal law did not specify how one acquired the rights that could be registered or enforced without registration. That subject fell into the domain of state law, plus federal common law elaborating on the word "use" in § 43(a). *Two Pesos, Inc. v. Taco Cabana, Inc.,* 505 U.S. 763, 768 (1992); *id.* at 785–86 (Thomas, J., concurring). See also 15 U.S.C. § 1127 (" 'trademark' includes any word . . . used by a person"). At common law, "use" meant sales to the public of a product with the mark attached. *Trade-Mark Cases,* 100 U.S. 82, 94–95 (1879).

"Use" is neither a glitch in the Lanham Act nor a historical relic. By insisting that firms use marks to obtain rights in them, the law prevents entrepreneurs from reserving brand names in order to make their rivals' marketing more costly. Public sales let others know that they should not invest resources to develop a mark similar to one already used in the trade. Only active use allows consumers to associate a mark with particular goods and notifies other firms that the mark is so associated.

Under the common law, one must win the race to the marketplace to establish the exclusive right to a mark. Registration modifies this system slightly, allowing slight sales plus notice in the register to substitute for substantial sales without notice. 15 U.S.C. § 1051(a). (The legislation in 1988 modifies the use requirement further, but we disregard this.) ZHD's sales of its product are insufficient use to establish priority over L'Oreal. A few bottles sold over the counter in Hinsdale, and a few more mailed to friends in Texas and Florida, neither link the ZAZU mark with ZHD's product in the minds of consumers nor put other producers on notice. As a practical matter ZHD had no product, period, until months after L'Oreal had embarked on its doomed campaign.

In finding that ZHD's few sales secured rights against the world, the district court relied on cases such as *Department of Justice v. Calspan Corp.,* 578 F.2d 295 (C.C.P.A. 1978), which hold that a single sale, combined with proof of intent to go on selling, permit the vendor to register the mark. But use sufficient to register a mark that soon is widely distributed is not necessarily enough to acquire rights in the absence of registration. The Lanham Act allows only trademarks "used in commerce" to be registered. 15 U.S.C. § 1051(a). Courts have read "used" in a way that allows firms to seek protection for a mark before investing substantial sums in promotion. See *Fort Howard Paper Co. v. Kimberly-Clark Corp.*, 55 C.C.P.A. 947, 390 F.2d 1015 (C.C.P.A. 1968). Liberality in registering marks is not problematic, because the registration gives notice to latecomers, which token use alone does not. Firms need only search the register before embarking on development. Had ZHD registered ZAZU, the parties could have negotiated before L'Oreal committed large sums to marketing.

ZHD applied for registration of ZAZU after L'Oreal not only had applied to register the mark but also had put its product on the market nationwide. Efforts to register came too late. At oral argument ZHD suggested that L'Oreal's knowledge of ZHD's plan to enter the hair care market using ZAZU establishes ZHD's superior right to the name. Such an argument is unavailing. Intent to use a mark, like a naked registration, establishes no rights at all. . . . ZHD made first use of ZAZU in connection with hair services in Illinois, but this does not translate to a protectable right to market hair *products* nationally. The district court construed L'Oreal's knowledge of ZHD's use of ZAZU for salon services as knowledge "of [ZHD's] superior rights in the mark." 9 U.S.P.Q.2d at 1978. ZHD did not, however, have superior rights in the mark as applied to hair products, because it neither marketed such nor registered the mark before L'Oreal's use. Because the mark was not registered for use in conjunction with hair products, any knowledge L'Oreal may have had of ZHD's plans is irrelevant.

Imagine the consequences of ZHD's approach. Businesses that knew of an intended use would not be entitled to the mark even if they made the first significant use of it. Businesses with their heads in the sand, however, could stand on the actual date they introduced their products, and so would have priority over firms that intended to use a mark but had not done so. Ignorance would be rewarded—and knowledgeable firms might back off even though the rivals' "plans" or "intent" were unlikely to come to fruition. Yet investigations of the sort L'Oreal undertook prevent costly duplication in the development of trademarks and protect consumers from the confusion resulting from two products being sold under the same mark. L'Oreal should not be worse off because it made inquiries and found that, although no one had yet used the mark for hair products, ZHD intended to do so. Nor should a potential user have to bide its time until it learns whether other firms are serious about marketing a product. The use requirement rewards those who act quickly in getting new products in the hands of consumers. Had L'Oreal discovered that ZHD had a product on the market under the ZAZU mark or that ZHD had registered ZAZU for hair products, L'Oreal could have chosen another mark before committing extensive marketing resources. Knowledge that

ZHD planned to use the ZAZU mark in the future does not present an obstacle to L'Oreal's adopting it today.

Occasionally courts suggest that "bad faith" adoption of a mark defeats a claim to priority. See *California Cedar Products Co. v. Pine Mountain Corp.,* 724 F.2d 827, 830 (9th Cir. 1984); *Stern Electronics, Inc. v. Kaufman,* 669 F.2d 852, 857 (2d Cir. 1982); *Blue Bell v. Farah,* 508 F.2d at 1267. Although ZHD equates L'Oreal's knowledge of its impending use with "bad faith," the cases use the term differently. In each instance the court applied the label "bad faith" to transactions designed merely to reserve a mark, not to link the name to a product ready to be sold to the public. In *California Cedar Products,* for example, two firms sprinted to acquire the abandoned DURAFLAME mark. One shipped some of its goods in the abandoning company's wrapper with a new name pasted over it. Two days later the other commenced bona fide sales under the DURAFLAME mark. The court disregarded the first shipment, calling it "both premature and in bad faith", and held that the first firm to make bona fide sales to customers was the prior user. "Bad faith" was no more than an epithet stapled to the basic conclusion: that reserving a mark is forbidden, so that the first producer to make genuine sales gets the rights. If these cases find a parallel in our dispute, ZHD occupies the place of the firm trying to reserve a mark for "intended" exploitation. ZHD doled out a few samples in bottles lacking labeling necessary for sale to the public. Such transactions are the sort of pre-marketing maneuvers that these cases hold insufficient to establish rights in a trademark.

The district court erred in equating a use sufficient to support registration with a use sufficient to generate nationwide rights in the absence of registration. Although whether ZHD's use is sufficient to grant it rights in the ZAZU mark is a question of fact on which appellate review is deferential, *California Cedar Products,* 724 F.2d at 830; cf. *Scandia Down Corp. v. Euroquilt, Inc.,* 772 F.2d 1423, 1428–29 (7th Cir. 1985), the extent to which ZHD used the mark is not disputed. ZHD's sales of hair care products were insufficient as a matter of law to establish national trademark rights at the time L'Oreal put its electric hair colors on the market. . . .

REVERSED AND REMANDED

CUDAHY, CIRCUIT JUDGE, dissenting.

On the important issue of good faith, L'Oreal's conduct here merits a very hard look. In the case of Riviera, a *men's* clothing retailer, L'Oreal was careful to pay $125,000 for an agreement not to sue. Yet men's clothing and hair cosmetics marketed to women hardly seem related at all. On the other hand, a women's hair salon developing a line of hair care products is a purveyor of goods and services that seem closely related to hair cosmetics. Therefore, L'Oreal's knowledge of ZHD's use defeats any claim L'Oreal may have to priority.

One of the keys here seems to be the use of ZAZU as a service mark connected with the provision of salon services by ZHD. A service mark can be infringed by its use on a closely related product. . . . A service and a product are related if buyers are likely to assume a common source or sponsorship. The salon services and hair products at issue in this case, which are nearly as kindred as a service and product can be, offer the paradigmatic illustration of things that are closely related. Thus the majority's disregard for ZHD's substantial use of ZAZU in connection with salon services is unfounded.

As the majority correctly notes, the standard for granting federal registration is somewhat less exacting than that for establishing common law trademark rights. *See La Societe Anonyme des Parfums le Galion v. Jean Patou, Inc.,* 495 F.2d 1265 (2d Cir. 1974). But that distinction is so slight as to be inconsequential here. While any bona fide transaction that is more than a "mere sham" will, when combined with intent to continue use, suffice to support federal registration, any use greater than de minimis will still warrant trademark protection in the absence of registration. *See SweeTarts v. Sunline, Inc.,* 380 F.2d 923, 929 (8th Cir. 1967) (market penetration "need not be large" but must be "significant enough to pose the real likelihood of confusion"). Thus, bona fide test marketing or small experimental sales—indeed, any use that is not nominal or token—can satisfy the test.

In this case, ZHD's use of the ZAZU mark, both in its highly successful salon service business, which drew some out-of-state clients, and in its local and interstate product sales to customers and to a potential marketer, surely is more than de minimis. The extensive evidence of ZHD's intent to step up hair product sales—such as its order for 25,000 ZAZU-emblazoned bottles and its inquiry about advertising rates in a national magazine—bolsters this assessment. Even if ZHD did fail to demonstrate more than a de minimis market penetration nationally, at the very least it successfully established exclusive rights within its primary area of operation. The salon's substantial advertising, increasing revenue and staff and preliminary product sales indicate sufficient market penetration to afford trademark protection in that region.

L'Oreal concedes that ZHD has exclusive rights to use ZAZU for salon services in the Hinsdale area. Those exclusive rights also preclude L'Oreal from using the mark on hair products in the local area because of the likelihood of confusion between those products and ZHD's salon services, even apart from any confusion between the two parties' *products.* Given the deferential standard of review on the factual question of use, therefore, I think it clear that ZHD has achieved market penetration and exclusive rights to the ZAZU mark at the very least in the Chicago area.

ZHD's contention that its rights in the ZAZU mark extend beyond the local area is enhanced by evidence that L'Oreal did not, as we have noted, act in good faith. The majority's consideration of the good faith issue minimizes the important role good faith plays in trademark disputes, particularly disputes involving unregistered marks. Bad faith can defeat claims to priority. *See, e.g., A.J. Canfield Co. v. Honickman,* 808 F.2d 291 (3d Cir. 1986) (stating the doctrine that a senior user "has enforceable rights against any junior user who adopted the mark with knowledge of its senior use"). Contrary to the majority's narrow characterization of bad faith as a concept employed solely to deter attempts to reserve marks prior to genuine sales, courts have examined junior users' good faith in a variety of contexts. In fact, this court has held that a good faith junior user is simply one that begins using a mark without knowledge that another party already is using it. *The Money Store v. Harriscorp Finance, Inc.,* 689 F.2d 666, 674 (7th Cir. 1982). And while such knowledge may not automatically negate good faith, only the most unusual situations encompass both knowledge and good faith.

In sum, I believe ZHD's sale of ZAZU services and products constituted sufficient use to establish exclusive trademark rights in the Chicago area, if not nationally. In any event, L'Oreal's pursuit of its line of hair cosmetics in spite of its knowledge of ZHD's use defeats L'Oreal's position. Therefore, I respectfully dissent.

NOTES FOR DISCUSSION

1.   *The Purpose of the Use Requirement.* According to the *Blue Bell* court, what is the purpose of the use requirement? Does the *Zazu* court agree or does it articulate a different purpose or purposes for the use requirement?

Generally, when we identify the purpose of a given legal requirement, we then apply the requirement to a given set of facts by asking whether the purpose was satisfied. If the purpose of the use requirement is to lead consumers to draw a connection between a product, a manufacturer, and a mark, why was Blue Bell's dual labeling of the Mr. Hicks' clothing insufficient to establish use? Doesn't it create an association between Blue Bell, clothing, and the mark Time Out? Even if the Mr. Hicks' line is a different style than the clothing line Blue Bell eventually intended to market under the Time Out label, doesn't the Mr. Hicks' line tell consumers something about the likely quality and characteristics of the eventual Time Out line? When we deal with the question of infringement in Chapter 7, we'll see that a defendant's unauthorized use of a similar mark on a similar product constitutes infringement if it creates a likelihood of consumer confusion either as to source, that the plaintiff made the defendant's products, or association, that the plaintiff and defendant are affiliated or related companies. Why isn't a use that creates an association between one of

Blue Bell's lines and the mark sufficient, given that all of Blue Bell's lines have a single, common source—Blue Bell?

Alternatively, if the purpose of the use requirement is to alert competitors that a mark is already taken, so that they may choose a different mark, why wasn't Zazu Design's use of Zazu for hair care products sufficient? Did Zazu Design use the mark sufficiently to bring it to L'Oreal's attention? Wasn't the purpose of the use requirement, as Judge Easterbrook articulates it, therefore satisfied?

2.   *Good Faith, Bad Faith.* Both courts talk about the good or bad faith of the users. Do they interpret "bad faith" in the same manner, or do they give different meanings to the phrase? What role does the party's good or bad faith play in each decision?

We will see good faith and bad faith again, in Chapter 3, dealing with remote geographic use, in Chapter 7, in connection with the infringement analysis, and in Chapter 10, in connection with trademark infringement on the Internet. Unfortunately, just as in *Blue Bell* and *Zazu Designs*, we will find that bad faith means different things in each of these contexts and sometimes different things to different courts even within a given context. Moreover, courts are not always careful to keep the different meanings good faith may have in these different contexts separate, and will improperly cite cases addressing the meaning of good faith from one context as authority for its definition in another context. For an example of such a mistake, see *GTE Corp. v. Williams*, 904 F.2d 536, 541–42 (10th Cir. 1990) (Logan, J.) (relying on definition of good faith in the infringement context to define good faith in the remote junior user context). These sorts of doctrinal difficulties are unfortunately common in trademark law. As Judge Sneed once exclaimed: "Trademark infringement is a peculiarly complex area of the law. Its hallmarks are doctrinal confusion, conflicting results, and judicial prolixity." *HMH Pub. Co. v. Brincat*, 504 F.2d 713, 716 (9th Cir. 1974).

3.   *Use and Priority: Tacking.* In both *Blue Bell* and *Zazu*, the parties picked one mark and stuck with it, but sometimes a party changes the nature or appearance of its trademark over time. When a party changes its mark, what is its priority date: (i) the date it began using the original version of the mark; or (ii) the date it began using the revised or new version of the mark? We resolve this issue in trademark law using a doctrine known as tacking. When the original and revised marks are "legal equivalents," in that they create the same continuing commercial impression, then the trademark owner may "tack" the use of the original onto the use of the revised mark. In such a case, the mark owner may claim the date of first use of the original version of the mark as its priority date. If the two marks are not legal equivalents, because they do not create the same continuing commercial impression, then the trademark owner may not tack. In such a case, the mark owner may claim priority based solely upon the date of first use of the revised version of the mark. Whether two versions of a mark are legal equivalents is a question of fact for the jury. *See Hana Financial, Inc. v. Hana Bank*, 135 S.Ct. 907 (2015).

4. *Use and Priority: The Case of Descriptive Marks.* Although we shall study the issue in more detail in Chapter 4, the second prerequisite for trademark protection is distinctiveness. Both Time Out for men's sportswear and Zazu for hair care products qualify as inherently distinctive marks. As a result, first use determines priority. However, for descriptive marks, marks that describe the associated products or services, priority is determined not by which party is the first to use the mark, but by which party, through advertising, marketing, and sales, successfully creates a secondary meaning or acquires distinctiveness first.

5. *Hair Care and Hair Care Products.* Judge Cudahy in dissent argues that Zazu Designs had satisfied the use requirement for use with respect to the services of the hair salon. As Judge Cudahy argues, and as we shall see in Chapter 7, under trademark's likelihood of confusion infringement standard, L'Oreal's use of the same mark on hair care products constitutes trademark infringement if the plaintiff's service and the defendant's product are sufficiently related that consumers are likely to believe that L'Oreal's Zazu hair coloring products come from Zazu Designs. How does the majority respond to Judge Cudahy on this issue?

6. *Solving the Problem of Competing Priority.* How should we solve the problem of competing priority, well-illustrated by the facts of *Blue Bell*? Two producers both in good faith and without knowledge of the other's intentions adopt the same mark for the same products. Both begin to gear up marketing campaigns and spend considerable resources before they roll out their products. If they had known of the other's intentions, one of the producers could readily have switched to another mark, and likely would have, if it had known of the other's intentions before investing too much in the first mark. The difficulty with the common law approach is that the two parties may not become aware of each other's intentions until shortly before actual use begins, as in *Blue Bell*. At that point, if the parties have already invested considerable resources in the mark, a use-based priority rule actually encourages each party to expend even more resources trying to get to the market first.

From a social perspective, this is problematic for two reasons. First, it is wasteful. Both entities spend money promoting their respective goods under the mark, but in the end, only one can continue to use it. The resources spent by the other entity on the mark are simply wasted. Second, this approach can also lead to consumer confusion. In racing for actual use, both entities are likely to make some actual use of the mark before a court can step in and resolve the priority dispute. Even when this overlap is short, as in *Blue Bell*, the months of overlap, where both entities are offering similar products with the same mark, may create lingering, residual consumer confusion that could last for years.

The easiest way to address these difficulties would be to tie ownership to registration, rather than use, and simply allow parties to register whatever trademarks they wish as a way of reserving those marks for future use. This is the solution that much of the world has adopted. In most countries, trademark rights are tied to registration and not to use. The United States has long rejected such an approach, however, on the grounds that there is a limited supply of inherently strong marks—marks that will be attractive to consumers instantly and without large marketing expenditures—and if we allow registration without use, everyone will race to register all the good marks. Do you think that concern is persuasive? Should we simply allow registration without use?

For many years under the Trademark Act of 1946, courts used the so-called "token use" doctrine to create something like a registration-based system for creating trademark rights. Although the Trademark Act of 1946 has always required "use in commerce" in order to register a domestic mark, under the token use doctrine, even a token interstate shipment of goods bearing the claimed trademark, such as the shipments Koubek made to his friends in Texas and Florida in *Zazu Designs*, would suffice. This interpretation of use facilitated early registration of the mark, yet because it entailed some non-trivial expenses, tended to discourage registration unless the party was working towards a more general, bona fide, commercial use.

The token use doctrine did not facilitate early registration for all industries, however. How would an airplane manufacturer or a restaurant make a token use? As a result, in the Trademark Law Revision Act of 1988, Congress expressly rejected the token use doctrine. It amended the definition of "use in commerce" in section 45 of the Trademark Act to mean "the bona fide use of a mark in the ordinary course of trade, and not made merely to reserve a right in a mark." 15 U.S.C. § 1127. Congress did, however, recognize the problems that might arise in competing priority cases such as *Blue Bell*. Rather than rely on token use to facilitate early registration, Congress created a new mechanism, known as the "intent to use" or "ITU" application. As an alternative to the traditional use application, the ITU provisions allow a person to file an application to register a trademark federally if the person has "a bona fide intention, under circumstances showing the good faith of such person, to use a trademark in commerce." Pub. L. No. 667, 100th Cong., 2d Sess., § 103, 102 Stat. 3935, 3935–36, *codified at* 15 U.S.C. § 1051(b)(1) (2015). We shall study the intent-to-use process in more detail shortly.

7.   *Priority and Consumer Confusion: Of Equities and Calendars.* How would you resolve the following case: For years, General Mills had used the mark Kimberly for high-quality women's clothes. In March and April 1979, rumors began circulating within the fashion trade that General Mills intended to cease use of the Kimberly mark. Upon hearing these rumors, two of General Mills' competitors, Don Sophisticates and Sweater Bee, both tried to purchase the mark from General Mills. However, rather than sell the mark, General Mills decided it would abandon the mark instead, and formally did so on May 7, 1979.

In response, a "free-for-all" ensued. Don Sophisticates began shipments of its own apparel bearing the Kimberly mark beginning, according to the district court, on May 9, 1979. In the meantime, Sweater Bee was not idle and began making its own shipments of Kimberly branded goods on May 10th. Yet a third company, Bayard Shirt joined the fray, shipping its Kimberly branded goods on May 11th.

Under the rules of priority we have studied, who should own the Kimberly mark following General Mills' abandonment? If we award ownership to any one of these three companies, will some consumers be confused and assume that General Mills is still the source of Kimberly goods? How can we address that risk?

In *Manhattan Industries, Inc. v. Sweater Bee Banff, Ltd.*, 627 F.2d 628 (2d Cir. 1980), the court held that all three began use sufficiently close in time that all three companies held a legal right to use the Kimberly mark. To avoid confusion, the court required each to create Kimberly labels sufficiently distinct so that consumers could readily distinguish them, one from another, and could also distinguish each of their Kimberly labels from General Mills'. To justify this resolution, the court insisted "that the concept of priority in the law of trademarks is applied 'not in its calendar sense' but on the basis of 'the equities involved.'" (*quoting Chandon Champagne Corp. v. San Marino Wine Corp.*, 335 F.2d 531, 534 (2d Cir. 1964)). What do you think of the court's solution?

8.   *Ownership, Use, and Advertising Agencies.* Jerry Bryant has come to you for legal advice. He prepares advertising campaigns, with both advertisements and associated slogans, such as "One Call, That's All," for plaintiffs personal injury attorneys. He has clients around the country and shoots the same sets of commercials, using the same slogans, for each of them, which then air for his clients in their respective geographic markets. For his fee, he charges his clients a percentage of the money that they spend on placing the advertisements. One of his clients, Glen Lerner of Las Vegas, Nevada, no longer wants to work with Mr. Bryant, but wants to keep using the slogan. Mr. Bryant contends *inter alia* that because he came up with the slogan and prepared the advertisements for his clients that he should own the slogan as a service mark. Based upon these facts, will trademark law provide Mr. Bryant a basis for stopping his former client from continuing to use the slogan? If Mr. Bryant prepares and runs advertisements for another personal injury attorney in Las Vegas featuring One Call, That's All, will Mr. Bryant be liable to Mr. Lerner for trademark infringement? *See Invision Production & Media Servs. v. Lerner*, 2009 WL 766502 (9th Cir. 2009) (affirming award of attorneys' fees to Lerner as an exceptional case under Trademark Act, finding that advertising agency had no reasonable basis for claiming ownership of "One Call, That's All" mark and had willfully infringed Lerner's rights in mark by preparing and running advertisements for another attorney using mark in Las Vegas); *see also Arvelo v. American Int'l Insurance Co.*, 875 F.Supp. 95, 100–01 (D.P.R.) (holding that client who actually used the slogan, and not the advertising agency who created it, owned the trademark rights in the slogan), *aff'd without op.*, 66 F.3d 306 (1st Cir. 1995), *cert. denied*, 516 U.S. 1117 (1996); *Invisible, Inc. v. National Broadcasting Co.*, 212 U.S.P.Q. (BNA) 576, 577–78 (C.D. Cal. 1980) (same);

Gordon Bennett & Associates, Inc. v. Volkswagen of America, Inc., 186 U.S.P.Q. (BNA) 271, 272–73 (N.D. Cal. 1975) (same).

What other legal theories might be available to Mr. Bryant? As a general rule, copyright does not protect short phrases or slogans. 37 C.F.R. § 202.1 (2015) (stating that copyright protection is not available for "words and short phrases, such as names, titles, and slogans"); *see also Alberto-Culver Co. v. Andrea Dumon, Inc.*, 466 F.2d 705, 710 (7th Cir. 1972) (holding that the phrase "most personal sort of deodorant" which appeared on the back of a deodorant spray can was not subject to copyright protection). Mr. Bryant might also try to license Mr. Lerner's use of the mark, and claim under trademark law that Mr. Lerner's use therefore "inures" to Mr. Bryant's benefit. 15 U.S.C. § 1055. However, for the use of a licensee to inure to the licensor's benefit and thus count as use by the licensor, Mr. Bryant must control the quality of legal services Mr. Lerner offers under the One Call service mark. 15 U.S.C. §§ 1055 (allowing use of a licensee to inure to the benefit of the licensor if the two are related companies), 1127 (defining companies as related where the licensor controls the quality of the goods or services the licensee offers in connection with the mark). This quality-control requirement is an aspect of the naked license doctrine that we shall examine in more detail in Chapter 6. (Incidentally, the desire to avoid this quality-control requirement is also the reason that L'Oreal and Riviera Slacks phrased their agreement as a "covenant not to sue," rather than as a permission or license to use.) Assume for now that Mr. Bryant cannot satisfy the quality control requirement. Are there any other legal theories Mr. Bryant could assert? Is there any way to draft his agreement with his attorney clients going forward to ensure that he controls the use of the slogans in this type of situation?

B. ANALOGOUS USE

The *Blue Bell* court expressly stated that "neither conception of the mark, nor advertising alone establishes trademark rights at common law." Although historically true, in the years following *Blue Bell*, this rule came into question. In many industries, extensive advertising campaigns often precede actual sales of the associated goods or services by months, if not years. In some cases, the money spent on these advertising campaigns constitutes a significant fraction of the associated goods' costs. If one person has spent significant sums advertising a mark in connection with products or services that are not yet available but soon will be, may another swoop in and claim ownership of the mark by actually using the mark first? Consider the following case.

MARYLAND STADIUM AUTHORITY V. BECKER

806 F.Supp. 1236 (D. Md. 1992)

MOTZ, DISTRICT JUDGE

The Maryland Stadium Authority ("MSA") has brought this action against Roy G. Becker, asserting claims under Section 43(a) of the Lanham Act, 15 U.S.C. § 1125(a), and for unfair competition under Maryland common law. MSA, the owner of the baseball park in which the Baltimore Orioles play, alleges that Becker has wrongfully used the mark "Camden Yards" in connection with the sale of tee shirts and several other items of clothing. Discovery has been completed, and the parties have filed cross-motions for summary judgment.

I.

MSA is a public corporation created in 1986 by the Maryland General Assembly to plan, build and operate a sports complex, including a baseball park and, possibly, a football stadium (in the event that Baltimore is again awarded a franchise by the National Football League). Md. Fin. Inst. Code Ann., § 13–702 (1992 Supp.). In 1987 the General Assembly approved MSA's recommendation that the sports complex be constructed at Camden Yards, an area which for over a century had been a center of operations for the Baltimore & Ohio Railroad in downtown Baltimore.

In 1989 demolition of old buildings at the site commenced, and in early 1991 the superstructure of the new park began to rise from the ground. The park was scheduled to be completed for the start of the 1992 season, and throughout the summer of 1991, as public excitement grew, there was extensive public debate as to what it should be called. The two names most prominently mentioned were "Camden Yards" and "Oriole Park." In October 1991 the debate ended in compromise with the announcement that the name "Oriole Park at Camden Yards" had been chosen.

Construction proceeded apace during the long winter months, and on a cold but glorious afternoon in early April, 1992, the park was first opened for an exhibition game between the Baltimore Orioles and the New York Mets (a team last seen, unhappily, in Baltimore in the 1969 World Series). The following day the Orioles official season began with a game against the Cleveland Indians (who, even more unhappily, had beaten the Orioles 19 out of 21 times in 1954 when Memorial Stadium, the Birds' former park, had been opened).

In the meantime, in July 1991, Becker had begun selling tee shirts outside Memorial Stadium. These tee shirts bore the lettering "Camden Yards means baseball," "Baltimore, Maryland," and "1992," and displayed a design including an oriole, crossed baseball bats and a baseball diamond. Becker continued his street vendoring until the last day of the

1991 baseball season. He also sold his shirts by direct mail, through sports bars and stores, and by advertising in a local publication known as the "Penny Saver."

On August 22, 1991, MSA wrote to Becker demanding that he cease use of the name Camden Yards. Becker did not respond to the letter, and MSA filed this suit on September 23, 1991.

II.

Section 43(a) of the 1947 [*sic*—1946] Lanham Act creates a federal claim for unfair competition by prohibiting the use in interstate commerce of any "false designation of origin, or any false description or representation, including words or other symbols tending falsely to describe or represent the same. . . ." 15 U.S.C. § 1125(a) (1988). This provision protects against trademark, service mark, trade dress and trade name infringement even though the mark or name in question has not been federally registered.

The two basic elements necessary to establish infringement of an unregistered mark are "(1) the adoption and use of a mark and [the] entitlement to enforce it, and (2) the adoption and use by a junior user of a mark that is likely to cause confusion that goods or services emanate from the senior owner." *Quality Inns Int'l, Inc. v. McDonald's Corp.*, 695 F. Supp. 198, 209 (D. Md. 1988). Thus, "the gist of a claim for trademark infringement . . . is a sanction against one who trades by confusion on the goodwill or reputation of another, whether by intention or not." *Perini*, 915 F.2d at 124.

"Word marks" are classified into four categories: generic, descriptive, suggestive, and arbitrary or fanciful. *Perini*, 915 F.2d at 124. Geographic locations are considered descriptive word marks. See American *Waltham Watch Co. v. United States Watch Co.*, 173 Mass. 85, 53 N.E. 141 (1899) (Holmes, J.). To obtain trademark rights in a descriptive word mark and satisfy the first element of infringement, MSA must prove that: (a) it adopted and used the mark, and (b) the mark acquired secondary meaning. *Perini*, 915 F.2d at 125.

III.

As a threshold matter, Becker argues that MSA's use of the name Camden Yards as the name of the sports complex was insufficient to create trademark rights prior to July 1991 because MCA had not sold goods or services with the Camden Yards mark by that time. The argument is without merit. Although the sale or shipment of goods in commerce is necessary as part of a valid trademark application, *see In re Cedar Point, Inc.*, 220 U.S.P.Q. 533, 535–36 (TTAB 1983), the sale of goods or services using an unregistered mark is not necessary to establish use of the mark. *See New England Duplicating Co. v. Mendes*, 190 F.2d 415, 418 (1st Cir. 1951). Advertising and promotion is sufficient to obtain rights in a mark as long as they occur "within a commercially reasonable time prior to the actual rendition of service . . . ," *Kinark Corp. v. Camelot, Inc.*, 548 F. Supp. 429, 442 (D.N.J. 1982), and as long as the totality of acts "create[s] association of the goods or services and the mark with the user thereof." New *West Corp. v. NYM Co. of California, Inc.*, 595 F.2d 1194, 1200 (9th Cir. 1979) (citing *Hotel Corp. of America v. Inn America, Inc.*, 153 U.S.P.Q. (BNA) 574, 576 (1967)); *see also Selfway, Inc. v. Travelers Petroleum, Inc.*, 579 F.2d 75, 79 (C.C.P.A. 1978). Therefore, the questions which must be resolved are (1) whether MSA had adopted and used the Camden Yards mark prior to July, 1991, (2) whether the mark had obtained secondary meaning and (3) whether Becker's use of the mark creates a likelihood of confusion. As will be seen, the latter two questions merge.

A.   Adoption and Use of the Mark

The name Camden Yards first became associated with the proposed sports complex in 1987 when the Maryland General Assembly approved MSA's recommendation that the complex be constructed at the location of B&O's former railroad yard in Baltimore City. The General Assembly specifically defined the site as "85 acres in Baltimore City in the area bounded by Camden Street on the north, Russell Street on the west, Osten Street on the south, and Howard Street and Interstate 395 on the east." Md. Fin. Inst. Code Ann. § 13–709(f) (1992 Supp.).

MSA, itself, has referred to the project as the Camden Yards sports complex for many years. In November 1988 it formulated a "Camden Yards Sports Complex Development Plan" for "a major professional sports complex accommodating both a baseball park and a football stadium in the area of Camden Yards." This plan was disseminated to both the public and the press. Beginning in July 1989, MSA published a bi-monthly baseball newsletter that contained such phrases as "ball park at Camden Yards," "Camden Yards site," and "Camden Yards industrial area." The newsletter (as well as other brochures and pamphlets making reference to Camden Yards) was distributed to the press, to 2,500 readers and to members of the public who made inquiries about the new sports complex. Beginning in September 1989, MSA distributed to the press and sold to the public photographic renditions of the sports complex and baseball park, entitling them "Camden Yards Sports Complex" or "Camden Yards Ball Park." It also published drawings entitled "Camden Yards stadium properties" depicting the area where the sports complex was to be built. Likewise, its 1990 annual report, distributed to the Governor's office, members of the Maryland General Assembly, the news media and the Pratt Library, specifically referred to the Camden Yards sports complex.

MSA held a number of promotional events at Camden Yards which included media briefings and photo opportunities. At the "Wrecking Ball" and "Grand Slam" in June and November 1989, over 4,000 members of the public watched the demolition of various buildings which had been standing in the Camden Yards area. In February 1990, Pete Harnisch, Elrod Hendricks and Randy Milligan came to pitch, catch and hit the first balls thrown over the actual location of home plate at the new stadium. In April 1990, MSA began conducting regular tours of the Camden Yards sports complex. The name Camden Yards was used in publicizing all of these events.

MSA also generated public interest in the historical qualities of Camden Yards. In January 1990, it sponsored an "Archeological Open House" during which 1,000 people toured the location of the saloon once managed by George Herman Ruth, Sr., father of Babe Ruth. On March 27 and 28, 1990, it sponsored "Student Press Days" in which 200 middle and high school students studied the archeology of the area. It prepared a pamphlet detailing Camden Yards' archeological significance and distributed it to the Governor's Office, to the General Assembly, at locations visited by a mobile publicity van, to the Babe Ruth Museum and to members of the public who asked about the complex. MSA even designed a continuing education course, given at the University of Maryland, Baltimore County, entitled "The Camden Yards Ballpark—Baltimore's New Stadium," which covered various aspects of the sports complex, including the area's history and archeology.

Baltimore's 1991 baseball season was a remarkable one. While the team's performance on the field was rather dismal, attendance figures soared. Nostalgic and sentimental by nature, Oriole fans flocked to old Memorial Stadium to see a baseball game there just one more time. On the final day of the season, poignant closing ceremonies were held during which waves of Orioles from different eras streamed onto the field to say goodbye to the old ballpark on 33rd Street. But just as those ceremonies dramatically culminated in digging up home plate, transporting it by limousine and placing it at its new downtown home, so too throughout Memorial Stadium's last baseball season talk about the new ballpark had constantly been in the air. It represented the hope of the future and was on the mind and in the heart of every true Oriole fan. What would it be called? Oriole Park or Camden Yards? Controversy raged, from bar room to living room, from State House to penthouse. When it appeared that perhaps an impasse had been reached, such bland alternatives as "Harbor Stadium" crept into discussion. But one thing was certain: by the summer of 1991, whatever the official name of the ballpark might end up to be, Camden Yards had, as Becker's own tee shirts proclaimed, come to "mean baseball."

In short, at the time that Becker started his business, MSA's promotional efforts had already borne fruit. For any reasonable person to have made any association other than baseball with the Camden Yards name would have been as unlikely as Boog Powell hitting an inside-the-park home run, Paul Blair playing too deep, Brooks Robinson dropping a pop-up, Frank Robinson not running out a ground ball, Jim Palmer giving up a grand slam home run, Don Stanhouse pitching an easy 1–2–3 inning, or Cal Ripken, Jr., missing a game because of a cold. It is of such stuff that summary judgment is made. *Anderson v. Liberty Lobby, Inc.*, 477 U.S. 242 (1986); *Celotex Corp. v. Catrett*, 477 U.S. 317 (1986).

B. Secondary Meaning

In addition to proving its use of the Camden Yards mark, MSA also must establish that the mark has a secondary meaning. "Secondary meaning is the consuming public's understanding that the mark, when used in context, refers, not to what the descriptive word ordinarily describes, but to the particular business that the mark is meant to identify. For example, the descriptive phrase 'quick stop' used to describe convenience stores would only acquire secondary meaning if a substantial portion of the consuming public were to associate the term with a particular business." *Perini*, 915 F.2d at 125. Plaintiff has the burden to show secondary meaning (1) in the defendant's trade area, and (2) prior to the time the defendant entered the market. *Id.* at 125–26.

As I have already noted in discussing the adoption and use question, the factual record establishes beyond dispute that by July 1991 MSA's promotional efforts and the media coverage given to the new baseball park had conferred a secondary meaning upon the name Camden Yards. *See generally Perini*, 915 F.2d at 125. But if any doubt were to exist on the issue, it is dispelled by the fact that Becker intentionally copied the Camden Yards mark. Everything surrounding his use of the mark was baseball related. His tee shirts made reference to baseball in Baltimore and had baseball bats, a baseball diamond and an oriole on them. He sold the shirts outside of Memorial Stadium to baseball fans. He conducted his business under the name "Camden Yards Stadium." Under Fourth Circuit law this evidence of intentional direct copying "establishes a prima facie case of secondary meaning sufficient to shift the burden or persuasion to the defendant on that issue." *See Osem Food Indus. Ltd. v. Sherwood Foods, Inc.*, 917 F.2d 161, 163 (4th Cir. 1990) (*quoting M. Kramer Mfg. Co. v. Andrews*, 783 F.2d 421, 448 (4th Cir. 1986)). Becker has presented absolutely no evidence which would meet this burden.

C. Likelihood of Confusion

The only remaining issue is whether Becker's use of the Camden Yards mark is likely to cause confusion that such goods were in fact produced by MSA. *See Perini*, 915 F.2d at 127. In order for likelihood of confusion to exist, it is not necessary that the public know that MSA is the owner of the mark. All that needs to be shown is that the public knew that the clothing in issue likely would have come from a single source. See *M. Kramer Mfg. Co.*, 783 F.2d at 449. Further, "the test is not only the danger that defendant's use of the [trademarks] will confuse plaintiff's customers, but the likelihood of danger that such use will confuse the public in general, including plaintiff's customers, defendant's customers and other members of the public." *AMP Inc. v. Foy*, 540 F.2d 1181, 1183 (4th Cir. 1976).

Intentional copying of a mark raises a presumption of likelihood of confusion just as it raises a presumption of secondary meaning. *See Osem Food Indus. Ltd.*, 917 F.2d at 165; *Boston Athletic Ass'n v. Sullivan*, 867 F.2d 22, 9 U.S.P.Q. 2d (BNA) 1690, 1699 (1st Cir. 1989). Again, Becker has presented absolutely no evidence to overcome this presumption. And again, the presumption aside, the undisputed evidence establishes that the baseball related designs which Becker placed upon his tee shirts entitles MSA to summary judgment on the likelihood of confusion issue.

For the reasons stated in the opinion entered herein, this 12th day of November 1992, . . . Defendant is permanently enjoined from using the name "Camden Yards" on any tee-shirts, hats, sweat shirts or other items of clothing which he manufacturers, distributes or sells or in connection with advertising or promoting the distribution or sale of such products. . . .

NOTES FOR DISCUSSION

1.   *The Role of Analogous Use.* But for the analogous use doctrine, how would the case have come out? Would MSA have been able to enjoin Becker's use? If not, would Becker have established rights in Camden Yards as a trademark for his merchandise? Would those rights enable him to enjoin MSA from selling Camden Yards merchandise?

2.   *Consistency with the Statute.* Section 1127 of the Trademark Act, in relevant part, provides:

> For purposes of this Chapter, a mark shall be deemed to be in use in commerce—(1) on goods when—(A) it is placed in any manner on the goods . . . , and (B) the goods are sold or transported in commerce, and (2) on services when it is used or displayed in the sale or advertising of services and the services are rendered in commerce. . . .

15 U.S.C. § 1127 (definition of "use in commerce").

What use did MSA make of Camden Yards that satisfied this definition? Can you identify the goods that MSA sold or the services that MSA rendered before Becker's use began? Did MSA use Camden Yards as a mark after Becker's use began? Is that essential to establish MSA's trademark rights in Camden Yards? In other words, is the analogous use doctrine simply a timing rule? So long as actual use began at some point, for example, by offering tickets to a baseball game, MSA may backdate its priority in the mark to the date when advertising for the tickets began. Or is the analogous use doctrine an independent basis for trademark rights? In other words, under the analogous use doctrine, may MSA claim trademark rights in Camden Yards based simply upon promotional efforts even if it never offers any good or service in connection with the mark?

C. FEDERAL REGISTRATION AND THE INTENT TO USE ALTERNATIVE

Since the Trademark Act of 1905, Congress has authorized the federal registration of trademarks that are used in commerce. As we have seen, tying registration to use left open the possibility of competing firms adopting confusingly similar marks for similar goods, entirely unaware of the other's intentions. To avoid this, courts developed the token use doctrine. Under this doctrine, a person could make a token interstate shipment, obtain federal registration before undertaking an expensive marketing campaign, and thereby warn others of the person's intent to claim the mark.

While this approach worked reasonably well, it created a confusing dichotomy between the meanings "use" had for purposes of registration and for purposes of priority. To eliminate this dichotomy and to formalize a process that would facilitate early claiming of trademarks, Congress made two significant amendments to the Trademark Act in the Trademark Law Revision Act of 1988. First, it expressly defined "use in commerce" as "the bona fide use of a mark in the ordinary course of trade, and not made merely to reserve a right in a mark." 15 U.S.C. § 1127 (definition of "use in commerce"). This definition effectively abolished the token use doctrine, given that almost by definition, a "token" use is neither "bona fide" nor "in the ordinary course of trade," and is "made merely to reserve a right in a mark." Second, it added the ITU application process to the Trademark Act. 15 U.S.C. § 1051(b), (c), (d).

As a result, today, a person may apply for federal registration either if the person is using the mark in commerce, under section 1051(a) (known as a "use" application), or if the person "has a bona fide intention . . . to use a trademark in commerce" (known as an "ITU" application). Under the statute, when a person files either a use application or an ITU application, the Patent and Trademark Office will process them similarly. For either type of application, the Patent and Trademark Office will examine the claimed mark to determine whether it qualifies for registration. 15 U.S.C. § 1062. Usually, this examination focuses on whether the matter sought to be registered runs afoul of any of the prohibitions set forth in section 2 of the Act. 15 U.S.C. § 1052. If the examiner concludes that the mark is eligible for registration, then the application will be published in the Official Gazette of the Patent and Trademark Office. After the mark is published, any person who believes that "he would be damaged by the registration of the mark" has thirty days in which to file an opposition to the registration. 15 U.S.C. § 1063.

At this point, the similar treatment of use and ITU applications ends. For a use application, if the PTO approves the application and a successful opposition is not filed, the mark "shall be registered" and "a certificate of registration shall be issued." 15 U.S.C. § 1063(b)(1). In contrast, for an ITU application, the applicant receives only a "notice of allowance." 15 U.S.C. § 1063(b)(2). What's the difference between these two?

Under the statute, a certificate of registration "shall be prima facie evidence of the validity of the registered mark, and of the registration of the mark, of the registrant's ownership of the mark, and of the registrant's exclusive right to use the registered mark in commerce on or in connection with the goods or services specified in the certificate." 15 U.S.C. § 1057(b). Registration also provides "constructive notice of the registrant's claim of ownership thereof," as of the mark's registration date. 15 U.S.C. § 1072. Further, "[c]ontingent on the registration of a mark on the principal register, . . . the filing of the application shall constitute constructive use of the mark, conferring a right of priority, nationwide in effective, on or in connection with the goods or services specified in the registration." 15 U.S.C. § 1057(c).

In contrast, a notice of allowance provides none of these rights. In fact, a notice of allowance provides effectively no substantive rights at all. It merely gives the applicant a window of time in which to begin use of the mark, while holding the applicant's place in line. In order to obtain substantive rights from an ITU application, an applicant must somehow use her ITU application to obtain a certificate of registration. In enacting the ITU provisions, Congress provided two such paths.

First, if the ITU applicant begins using the mark in commerce while the PTO is examining her application, the applicant may amend her application to allege use. 15 U.S.C. § 1051(c). Amending her application will convert the application from an ITU application into a use application, so that at the end of the day, if her application is successful, the applicant receives a certificate of registration directly. Second, if the applicant does not amend her application during the examination process and therefore receives a notice of allowance after publication, she may convert her notice of allowance into a certificate of registration by filing a verified statement that she is using the mark in commerce on the specified goods or services. 15 U.S.C. § 1051(d). An applicant has an initial six-month window in which to begin use and file a statement of use once her notice of allowance is issued. 15 U.S.C. § 1051(d)(1). An applicant may further request up to five six-month extensions of time in which to file her statement of use. 15 U.S.C. § 1051(d)(2). If an applicant obtains all five extensions, she will have a total of three years from the date on which the notice of allowance issued to begin use and file a statement of use. Once a statement of use is filed and accepted by the

PTO, then "the mark shall be registered" and "a certificate of registration shall be issued." 15 U.S.C. § 1051(d)(1).

Thus, although a person may file an application for registration based upon a bona fide intent to use, in order to register her mark and obtain her certificate of registration, she must actually begin use of the mark in commerce. How then do the ITU provisions help solve priority disputes such as those we saw in *Blue Bell*? First, simply as a practical matter, ITU applications are made available through the PTO's online databases almost as soon as they are filed. This makes it easier for companies to identify potential trademark conflicts before they arise, and to switch to some unclaimed mark before any significant expense has been incurred. Second, while a notice of allowance itself provides no substantive rights, if an applicant successfully uses the ITU procedure to obtain a certificate of registration, either by amending the application to allege use or by timely filing a statement of use, then section 1057(c) gives that applicant constructive use of, and hence priority in, her mark from the date that she filed her ITU application.

To see how this is supposed to work, consider how the dispute between Blue Bell and Farah over Time Out would likely have worked out had it arisen in 2003, instead of 1973. If Farah conceives of the mark in May, how can it use the ITU provisions to assert a claim for Time Out? If it files an ITU application for Time Out for use in connection with men's sportswear at the end of May, what advice would you give Blue Bell, as its attorney, when it decided on using the same mark in June and soon thereafter found Farah's ITU application in the PTO's database? On the other hand, if Farah did not file an ITU application, but Blue Bell did in late June, and Farah found it in the PTO's database in July, what advice would you give Farah?

In this second hypothetical, would you advise Farah to hurry its line to the market first and then, based upon Farah's actual use, seek to enjoin Blue Bell from using the mark? After all, if Farah can begin use quickly enough and can use that actual use to enjoin Blue Bell's use under the common law priority rules, then Blue Bell will never begin use. If Blue Bell is unable to begin use, then it will not be able to file a statement of use, and thus will not be able to obtain the certificate of registration necessary to backdate Blue Bell's priority under 1057(c). Or will it? Consider the following case.

WARNERVISION ENTERTAINMENT, INC. V.
EMPIRE OF CAROLINA, INC.

101 F.3d 259 (2d Cir. 1996)

VAN GRAAFEILAND, CIRCUIT JUDGE

Empire of Carolina, Inc., Empire Industries, Inc. and Empire Manufacturing, Inc. (hereafter "Empire") and Thomas Lowe Ventures, Inc. d/b/a Playing Mantis (hereafter "TLV") appeal from orders of the United States District Court for the Southern District of New York (Baer, J.) preliminarily enjoining appellants from violating WarnerVision Entertainment Inc.'s trademark "Real Wheels," and denying Empire's cross-motion for injunctive relief. *See* 915 F. Supp. 639 and 919 F. Supp. 717. The appeal was argued on an emergency basis on May 31, 1996, and on June 12, 1996, we issued an order vacating the preliminary injunction with an opinion to follow. This is the opinion.

Appellants contend that the grant of preliminary relief in WarnerVision's favor should be reversed on any of several grounds. We limit our holding to one—the district court's misapplication of 15 U.S.C. § 1057(c), part of the intent-to-use ("ITU") provisions of the Lanham Act, to the facts of the instant case. This error constitutes an abuse of discretion. *See Reuters Ltd. v. United Press Int'l, Inc.*, 903 F.2d 904, 907 (2d Cir. 1990).

Prior to 1988, an applicant for trademark registration had to have used the mark in commerce before making the application. Following the enactment of the ITU provisions in that year, a person could seek registration of a mark not already in commercial use by alleging a bona fide intent to use it. *See* 15 U.S.C. § 1051(b). Registration may be granted only if, absent a grant of extension, the applicant files a statement of commercial use within six months of the date on which the Commissioner's notice of allowance pursuant to 15 U.S.C. § 1063(b) is issued. *See* 15 U.S.C. § 1051(d); *see also Eastman Kodak Co. v. Bell & Howell Document Management Prods. Co.*, 994 F.2d 1569, 1570 (Fed. Cir. 1993). The ITU applicant is entitled to an extension of another six months, and may receive further extensions from the Commissioner for an additional twenty-four months. 15 U.S.C. § 1051(d)(2). If, but only if, the mark completes the registration process and is registered, the ITU applicant is granted a constructive use date retroactive to the ITU filing date. 15 U.S.C. § 1057(c). This retroactive dating of constructive use permits a more orderly development of the mark without the risk that priority will be lost. The issue we now address is whether the creator of a mark who files an ITU application pursuant to 15 U.S.C. § 1051(b) can be preliminarily enjoined from engaging in the commercial use required for full registration by 15 U.S.C. § 1051(d) on motion of the holder of a similar mark who commenced commercial use of its mark subsequent to the creator's ITU application but prior to the ITU applicant's commercial use. A brief statement of the pertinent facts follows.

On September 9, 1994, TLV sent the Patent and Trademark Office ("PTO") an ITU application for the mark "Real Wheels," stating an intent-to-use the mark in commerce on or in connection with "the following goods/services: wheels affiliated with 1/64th and 1/43rd scale toy vehicles." The application was filed on September 23, 1994. Around the same time, two other companies, apparently acting in innocence and good faith, decided that the "Real Wheels" mark would fit the products they were preparing to market. One of them, Buddy L, a North Carolina manufacturer that had been marketing toy replicas of vehicles for many years, selected the name for its 1995 line of vehicle replicas. The other, WarnerVision Entertainment Inc., found the name suitable for certain of its home videos which featured motorized vehicles. The videos and vehicles were shrink-wrapped together in a single package. Both companies ordered trademark searches for conflicts in the name, but, because TLV's application had not yet reached the PTO database, no conflict was found.

Both companies then filed for registration of their mark. However, because WarnerVision's application was filed on January 3, 1995, three days before Buddy L's, it was approved, and Buddy L's was rejected. Buddy L nonetheless continued with its marketing efforts and entered into negotiations with TLV for a possible license based on TLV's ITU application.

Unfortunately, Buddy L encountered financial problems, and on March 3, 1995, it filed for relief under Chapter 11 of the Bankruptcy Law as a debtor in possession. Thereafter, in an auction sale approved by the Bankruptcy Court, Buddy L sold substantially all of its assets to Empire. On October 20, 1995, Empire purchased from TLV all of TLV's title and interest in and to the Real Wheels product line, trademarks and good will associated therewith, including the September 23, 1994 ITU application. At the same time, Empire licensed TLV to use the Real Wheels mark for toy automobiles. On November 13, 1995, WarnerVision brought the instant action.

In granting the preliminary injunction at issue, the district court quoted the Supreme Court's admonition in *Connecticut Nat'l Bank v. Germain*, 503 U.S. 249, 253–54 (1992), to the effect that when the words of a statute are unambiguous, judicial inquiry as to its meaning is complete. 919 F. Supp. at 719. We do not quarrel with this statement as a general proposition; however, we question its application in the instant case. Section 1057(c) of Title 15, the statute at issue, provides that, "contingent on the registration of a mark . . . the filing of the application to register such mark shall constitute constructive use of the mark, conferring a right of priority, nationwide in effect. . . ." Empire is not claiming constructive use based on registration. Registration will not take place until after the section 1051(d) statement of use is filed and further examination is had of the application for registration. See *Eastman Kodak*, 994 F.2d at 1570. Empire contends that the district court erred in granting the preliminary injunction which bars it from completing the ITU process by filing a factually supported statement of use.

We agree. Empire does not contend that the filing of its ITU application empowered it to seek affirmative or offensive relief precluding WarnerVision's use of the Real Wheels mark. It seeks instead to assert the ITU filing as a defense to WarnerVision's efforts to prevent it from completing the ITU registration process. In substance, Empire requests that the normal principles of preliminary injunction law be applied in the instant case. This accords with the stated intent of Congress that the Lanham Act would be governed by equitable principles, which Congress described as "the core of U.S. trademark jurisprudence." *See* S. Rep. No. 515, 100th Cong., 2d Sess. 30 (1988), *reprinted in* 1988 U.S.C.C.A.N. 5577, 5592.

Thirty years ago, the author of a note in 78 Harv. L. Rev. 994 (1965) made the following cogent observation concerning preliminary injunctions:

> A court hearing a request for a preliminary order must determine how best to create or preserve a state of affairs such that it will be able upon conclusion of the full trial to render a meaningful decision for either party.

This concept—the preservation of the court's power to render a meaningful decision after trial on the merits—has been, and continues to be, a basic principle of preliminary injunction law. The purpose of a preliminary injunction is not to give the plaintiff the ultimate relief it seeks. It is "to prevent irreparable injury so as to preserve the court's ability to render a meaningful decision on the merits," *Meis v. Sanitas Serv. Corp.*, 511 F.2d 655, 656 (5th Cir. 1975); "to keep the parties, while the suit goes on, as far as possible in the respective positions they occupied when the suit began," *Hamilton Watch Co. v. Benrus Watch Co.*, 206 F.2d 738, 742 (2d Cir. 1953). *See* 11A WRIGHT, MILLER AND KANE, FEDERAL PRACTICE AND PROCEDURE § 2947 at 121. As a general rule, therefore, a temporary injunction "ought not to be used to give final relief before trial," *United States v. Adler's Creamery, Inc.*, 107 F.2d 987, 990 (2d Cir. 1939). Neither should it "permit[ ] one party to obtain an advantage by acting, while the hands of the adverse party are tied by the writ." *Corica v. Ragen*, 140 F.2d 496, 499 (7th Cir. 1944).

As the International Trademark Association ("ITA") correctly notes at page 9 of its amicus brief, if Empire's ITU application cannot be used to defend against WarnerVision's application for a preliminary injunction, Empire will effectively be prevented from undertaking the use required to obtain registration. In short, granting a preliminary injunction to WarnerVision would prevent Empire from ever achieving use, registration and priority and would thus effectively and permanently terminate its rights as the holder of the ITU application. Quoting 2 McCarthy on Trademarks and Unfair Competition § 19.08[1][d] at 19–59 (3d ed. 1992), the ITA said "this result 'would encourage unscrupulous entrepreneurs to look in the record for new [intent-to-use] applications by large companies, rush in to make a few sales under the same mark and sue the large company, asking for a large settlement to permit the [intent-to-use] applicant to proceed on its plans for use of the mark.' " This vulnerability to pirates is precisely what the ITU enactments were designed to eliminate. *See* S. Rep. No. 515, *supra*, at 5592.

The Trademark Trial and Appeal Board believes that an ITU applicant should be able to defend against such piratical acts despite the fact that full registration has not yet been given. *See Larami Corp. v. Talk to Me Programs Inc.*, 36 U.S.P.Q.2D (BNA) 1840 (T.T.A.B. 1995); *Zirco Corp. v. American Tel. & Tel. Co.*, 21 U.S.P.Q.2D (BNA) 1542 (T.T.A.B. 1992). When the foregoing authorities were cited to the district court, the court correctly stated that it was not bound by them. 919 F. Supp. at 721. However, the district court was bound not to construe and apply the ITU provisions in such a manner as to effectively convert a preliminary injunction based largely on disputed affidavits into a final adjudication on the merits.

The ITU provisions permit the holder of an ITU application to use the mark in commerce, obtain registration, and thereby secure priority retroactive to the date of filing of the ITU application. Of course, this right or privilege is not indefinite; it endures only for the time allotted by the statute. But as long as an ITU applicant's privilege has not expired, a court may not enjoin it from making the use necessary for registration on the grounds that another party has used the mark subsequent to the filing of the ITU application. To permit such an injunction would eviscerate the ITU provisions and defeat their very purpose.

This is not to say that a holder of a "live" ITU application may never be enjoined from using its mark. If another party can demonstrate that it used the mark before the holder filed its ITU application or that the filing was for some reason invalid, then it may be entitled to an injunction. WarnerVision says that it made analogous use of the Real Wheels mark before TLV filed its ITU application and also that the assignment to Empire of TLV's ITU application was invalid. But the district court did not pass on these contentions, and we will not consider them in the first instance.

The district court based its grant of preliminary relief on the proposition that "the first party to adopt and use a mark in commerce obtains ownership rights," and held that "WarnerVision made prior use of the mark in commerce and is the senior user." 915 F. Supp. at 645. On the basis of the present record, that decision cannot stand. WarnerVision also contends that TLV's ITU application was not properly assigned to Empire because Empire did not succeed to a portion of TLV's business. See 15 U.S.C. § 1060. Like the claims of analogous use, this contention raises fact issues which should not be addressed in the first instance by this Court. We vacate that portion of the district court's orders that grants WarnerVision preliminary injunctive relief and remand to the district court for further proceedings not inconsistent with this opinion.

We affirm the district court's denial of Empire's application for a preliminary injunction enjoining WarnerVision from using the Real Wheels mark for toys outside the video cassette market. Empire does not claim that it may use TLV's ITU application offensively to obtain this injunction, and we express no opinion on this subject. Empire says only that Buddy L, a company it acquired in a bankruptcy sale, made analogous use of the mark prior to WarnerVision's first use of the mark. On the record before us, we cannot say that the district court abused its discretion in denying a preliminary injunction on this ground.

NOTES FOR DISCUSSION

1.   *The Basic Principles of ITUs.* Let's make sure that we understand the issues presented in the case. First, assume that there had been no intent-to-use applications filed in this case. Who would win the priority battle? Would WarnerVision have been entitled to a preliminary injunction against Empire and/or TLV? Would Empire have been entitled to a preliminary injunction against WarnerVision? Why or why not?

Second, assume that Empire had already begun use and that its ITU application had matured into a registration. Further assume that both of the assignments to Empire, the one from TLV and the one from Buddy L, are valid. Who would win the priority battle? Would WarnerVision have been entitled to a preliminary injunction against Empire and/or TLV? Would Empire have been entitled to a preliminary injunction against WarnerVision? Why or why not?

The actual facts fell in between these two cases. Is the court's resolution required by the statutory language? Is it authorized by the statutory language? Section 1057(c) provides, in relevant part:

> Contingent on the registration of a mark on the principal register provided by this chapter, the filing of the application to register such mark shall constitute constructive use of the mark, conferring a right of priority, nationwide in effect, on or in connection with the goods or services specified in the registration against any other person except for a person whose mark had not been abandoned and who, prior to such filing—(1) has used the mark; [or] (2) has filed an application to register the mark which is pending or has resulted in registration of the mark. . . .

15 U.S.C. § 1057(c).

2. *Sensible Result?* Given that Congress did not specifically address the issue, is the court's resolution a sensible one? One possibility is that WarnerVision, knowing that it could lose the rights to the Real Wheels mark in the future, rebrands its products sufficiently quickly that few, if any, consumers associate the Real Wheels mark with WarnerVision. Thereafter, Empire introduces its Real Wheels products, obtains its registration, and begins to establish consumer recognition of its Real Wheels brand, writing on an essentially blank slate. However, consider two other possible scenarios:

(a) After the case, Empire or its licensee, TLV, begins use, files the appropriate paperwork, and successfully registers the mark Real Wheels on the principal register. However, in the meantime, WarnerVision had continued to use Real Wheels as a mark for its products, and Real Wheels becomes strongly and uniquely associated with WarnerVision as a result of this use. Despite that, when Empire obtains its registration, section 1057(c)'s constructive priority will apply, and Empire will be able to enjoin WarnerVision's continued use of the Real Wheels mark. Once it has its registration, only Empire will have the legal right to use Real Wheels for its products going forward. As a result, in the marketplace, consumers will continue to find Real Wheels products, but where they were accustomed to those products coming from WarnerVision, now they will come from Empire, and will potentially have quite different quality (and qualities). As a result of the transition from WarnerVision's use to Empire's use, will consumer confusion result?

(b) After the case, WarnerVision, knowing that it could lose the rights to the Real Wheels mark in the future, re-brands its products at some expense. Thereafter, Empire abandons its plans to bring Real Wheels products to market and never uses the mark.

To determine whether the court's ruling is sensible, do you need to have some sense for which of these three scenarios is most common, not only in this particular case, but for ITU applications generally? Did the court have any evidence before it as to the relative frequency of these scenarios? If Congress had felt that scenarios (a) and (b) were, by far, the most likely result in this type of case, would it have omitted the sort of priority rule from the statute that the court here adds to it?

3. *The Role of Preliminary Injunctions.* In reversing the trial court, the Second Circuit emphasized that preliminary injunctions, as a general rule, should be used not to resolve the case, but to preserve the status quo until a full trial can be held. While this is a central principle of preliminary injunction jurisprudence, does the appellate court use this rule to achieve exactly the opposite result? Consider the circumstances under which the preliminary injunction was granted. The facts suggest that WarnerVision was actually using the mark, but that Empire had not yet begun use nor filed its statement of use. By granting the preliminary injunction, did the trial

court preserve this status quo for trial? Does granting the injunction also avoid the risk of confusion that would otherwise arise? Consider that in the absence of a preliminary injunction, both parties may use the same mark on similar goods until trial. Is that good for consumers? Under what circumstances would the preliminary injunction constitute a final resolution of the case?

By overturning the injunction, will that change the status quo? Will the Second Circuit's decision allow Empire to begin use, file its statement of use, obtain a registration, and thereby backdate its priority in order to defeat WarnerVision's claims—effectively changing the status quo and ensuring that Empire will prevail before the trial can be held? Doesn't the Second Circuit's decision effectively amount to a final resolution of the case in favor of Empire?

Alternatively, is this principle of "preserving the status quo for trial" simply irrelevant to this case? Is the key issue a factual one that needs to be reserved for trial, or is the key issue the legal question whether filing an ITU provides the applicant with a corresponding legal right to use the mark in order to complete the application process? Do we need to preserve such a legal issue for trial or is a preliminary injunction motion an appropriate means to resolve such an issue?

4. *Establishing Priority on Remand.* Compared to a use-based priority regime, a registration-based priority regime has one clear advantage: when a party's trademark is registered, there is very little dispute about the date it was registered. The ITU process shares this advantage. If a party obtains a certificate of registration, we need only look at the party's filing date to determine when their constructive use began. If, on remand in *WarnerVision*, the only issue was who filed first, there would be no question as to which party would have priority in the Real Wheels mark. On the other hand, if the trial court on remand has to compare a filing date to a first use date, there may be somewhat more room for dispute as to when first actual use began, as *Blue Bell* and *Zazu* both illustrate.

As difficult as resolving questions of first actual use can be, however, resolving priority disputes based upon analogous use are even more difficult. As the Second Circuit notes, both WarnerVision and Empire assert that they begin analogous use before the first ITU application was filed. What is the legal standard that either must satisfy to show priority based upon analogous use? Would it be enough to show that the party began advertising its Real Wheels products before TLV's application was filed? Or would WarnerVision or Empire have to show that it had advertised sufficiently to establish secondary meaning in Real Wheels before TLV's application was filed? If WarnerVision or Empire has to establish secondary meaning, what sort of evidence could either company use at a trial in 1997 or 1998 to show that consumers uniquely associated Real Wheels with WarnerVision or Empire back in September 1994?

5. *Contractual Solutions?* In a situation where more than one party wants to use the same, or a confusingly similar, mark on the same or related goods, can the parties contract around any problems that might otherwise arise? Some contracting took place in this case. Empire bought two ITU applications, one from Buddy L and a second from TLV. Empire then licensed TLV to use Real Wheels as a mark for its scale toy vehicles. (This form of transaction is fairly standard in trademark law, and is known as an assignment and license-back.) However, there are practical and legal limitations on the ability of parties to contract around all of the problems the court's ruling potentially creates. Two legal doctrines in particular may limit a contractual solution. First, trademark law's assignment-in-gross doctrine prohibits the sale of a mark in gross, separate from "the goodwill of the business in which the mark is used." 15 U.S.C. § 1060(a). For ITU applications, where use has not yet begun, Congress prohibited assignment altogether, except to "a successor to the business of the applicant." *Id.* Second, trademark law's naked license doctrine prohibits a trademark owner from licensing a mark unless the trademark owner controls "the nature and quality of the goods or services on or in connection with which the mark is used." 15 U.S.C. § 1127 (definition of "related company").

Although we shall save a complete discussion of these doctrines until Chapter 6, both rules potentially limit the options for Empire and WarnerVision to resolve their dispute contractually. For example, if WarnerVision were willing to license the mark from Empire, it could do so only by agreeing to allow Empire to control the quality of its products sold under the Real Wheels mark. This requirement of quality control can sometimes prove a stumbling block, even when both parties can agree on all other licensing issues. Moreover, if both parties are looking to sell similar products under the Real Wheels mark, a licensing agreement may be impractical. If WarnerVision wanted to sell inexpensive children's toys, for example, and Empire wanted to sell more expensive, higher quality scale reproductions, allowing both to be sold under the same Real Wheels mark would likely prove a poor business decision. Consumers would have a difficult time relying on the trademark as a guarantee of product quality when the quality of the authorized uses differs significantly.

If instead WarnerVision simply wanted to buy rights to the Real Wheels mark from Empire, and was willing to pay a price Empire was willing to accept, until Empire used the mark, the assignment-in-gross doctrine would seemingly prohibit Empire from selling its ITU applications to WarnerVision. Indeed, as the court notes in its opinion, WarnerVision challenged the assignment of TLV's ITU application on precisely these grounds.

Sometimes, but not always, creative lawyering may work around these two doctrines. For example, if WarnerVision wanted the Real Wheels mark to itself and was willing to pay a price for the mark that Empire would accept, could WarnerVision simply pay Empire to abandon, rather than assign, its ITU applications? With Empire's earlier filed ITU application abandoned, WarnerVision's ITU application would advance to the front of the line, and assuming it otherwise complied with the requirements of section 2, would be positioned to mature into a registration. Compared to purchasing Empire's ITU applications, such an approach would push WarnerVision's constructive use date under section 1057(c) back from September 1994 to January 3, 1995. This creates a potentially problematic window of time during which a third party could have developed rights in Real Wheels. However, given that WarnerVision filed its ITU application only four months later, this window is fairly short. Would such an approach otherwise achieve WarnerVision's goals?

6. *INTA and the Bad Faith Interloper.* The court cites an amicus brief from the International Trademark Association, which usually goes by the acronym "INTA." INTA is an association of trademark owners and their attorneys that plays an active and important role in trademark law, usually pushing for broader and more extensive protection for trademark owners. In *WarnerVision*, INTA quoted the leading treatise writer in trademark law, Thomas McCarthy, for the argument that failing to protect the right of an ITU applicant to use the mark would leave room for bad-faith interlopers to jump in, use a mark for which someone else had earlier filed an ITU, and then hold-up the ITU applicant for a monetary payment. Was WarnerVision such a bad-faith interloper with respect to Real Wheels? Could you devise a rule that would separate such a bad-faith interloper from a good-faith user such as WarnerVision?

Moreover, while the bad-faith interloper story may sound persuasive, how plausible is it? If the court had stuck with the language Congress had provided and affirmed the district court, that leaves open the hold-up possibility that McCarthy and INTA articulate, but what would an interloper have to do to extract such a hold-up payment? First, the interloper would have to identify those ITU applications that are in fact valuable. Statistically, most are abandoned. Second, the interloper would actually have to begin use of the mark in connection with the products or services specified in the ITU application. Moreover, such use could not be a token use, but would have to be a "bona fide" use "in the ordinary course of trade" "not made merely to reserve a right in a mark." Third, the interloper would then have to file suit against the ITU applicant and obtain a preliminary injunction against the ITU applicant to prevent the applicant from beginning use of the mark. Otherwise, the ITU applicant could just begin use, file the necessary paperwork, and obtain its registration and backdate its priority pursuant to section 1057(c). Only after taking those three expensive steps would the interloper be in a position to extract a hold-up payment. Of course, even after all this, the ITU applicant could simply switch to some other mark rather than pay the interloper. Would you expect an entity who adopted the role of ITU-interloper as a business model to be profitable? Would you invest your money in such a business?

Compare the plausibility of the ITU-interloper hold-up story with the cybersquatting problem that arose as commerce moved onto the Internet. In the Internet context, during the early 1990s, individuals registered as domain names the trademarks of others in order to extract hold-up payments for the release of the domain name to the trademark owner. Cybersquatting arose, however, because it was far easier to set up a profitable hold-up. First, identifying those domain names that would prove valuable on the Internet was relatively easy. As a general rule, the more valuable a trademark was in the brick-and-mortar world, typically the more valuable the corresponding domain name would be on the Internet. Second, in order to hold up the trademark owner, the cybersquatter did not need to begin commercial use, file a lawsuit, and obtain a preliminary injunction as in the ITU interloper case. All a cybersquatter had to do was register the desired domain name with Netscape Solutions, Inc.—InterNIC—the domain name registry service, for a token fee. Third, because the trademarks at issue were typically well-established in the brick-and-mortar world, avoiding the hold-up demands of the cybersquatter by switching to a different domain name was more difficult for a trademark owner. Of course, the trademark owner could switch to a longer version of its trademark as its Internet domain name. Instead of paying off a cybersquatter who first registered www.pepsi.com, for example, Pepsi could have registered www.pepsicola.com. However, given the token fee entailed for domain name registrations, cybersquatters often registered the obvious variations on a trademark as well. Moreover, trademark owners typically preferred to register www."trademark".com, rather than something longer in order to make it easier for their consumers to find the site. As we shall see in Chapter 10, Congress believed that the risks cybersquatting presented for trademark owners were sufficiently serious that it added in 1999 a specific provision to the Trademark Act to prohibit the practice. *See* The Anticybersquatting Consumer Protection Act of 1999, Pub. L. No. 113, 106 Cong., 1st Sess., 113 Stat. 1501A–545, *codified at* 15 U.S.C. § 1125(d).

Do you think the hold-up risks facing ITU applicants justify the court's ruling?

7. *Solving the Problem of Competing Priority*. We began this chapter with the *Blue Bell* case where two entities both in good faith adopted the same mark for the same products and began marketing campaigns for their respective Time Out products. Under the common law rules, we have to wait until actual sales to determine trademark ownership. As we have discussed, waiting for actual sales to determine ownership can lead to both waste and confusion. Most of the world bases trademark rights on registration to avoid these problems, but the United States has so far rejected that approach. Instead, we have now seen the three approaches that the United States has tried in an attempt to deal with the competing priority problem.

Compare and contrast a registration-based rights system with the three solutions trademark law has adopted to solve this problem: (i) the token use doctrine for federal registration; (ii) the ITU application process; and (iii) the analogous use doctrine. As you consider how well each of these deals with the *Blue Bell* problem, consider as well how each addresses the risk that allowing people to claim trademark rights too readily might allow someone to reserve all of the good marks—the risk that keeps us from following the rest of the world and adopting a simple registration-based priority system.

8.   *Using ITU Applications to Reserve Marks.* How different is the ITU process from a pure registration-based system? There are two principal differences between the ITU process and a pure registration-based system. First, under the ITU process, no substantive rights attach to an ITU unless the applicant actually begins using the mark within the notice of allowance period. If a notice of allowance issues and a statement of use is not timely filed, then the application is abandoned. A person seeking to hold a large portfolio of as-yet unused marks would have to restart the ITU process for each such mark, with respect to each product or service for which she wants to reserve rights, every few years. Moreover, when a given ITU application is abandoned, priority goes to the next filed ITU application and our person attempting to reserve a given mark may lose her place in line. In *WarnerVision*, for example, we have three ITU applications for the same mark on similar products. In such a case, the PTO will suspend processing of the second and third applications filed, until the first application either matures into a registration or is abandoned.[1] If the first application matures into a registration, then the PTO will issue final rejections with respect to the second- and third-filed applications. If, on the other hand, the first-filed application is abandoned, the PTO will resume processing with respect to the second-filed application. The third-filed application will remain suspended until the second-filed application either matures into a registration or is abandoned, and so on. Even in the absence of any other rules, this line-keeping approach, together with the requirement that a mark actually be used for an ITU to mature into a registration, limits the ability to use the ITU process as a way of reserving a wide array of potentially valuable marks.

Second, although the use requirement limits the potential of the ITU process for reserving rights, Congress also added language to the statute to address this risk directly. Specifically, section 1(b)(1) requires not only a bona fide intention to use a trademark in commerce, but also imposes the further limitation that the "circumstances show[ ] the good faith of such person." 15 U.S.C. § 1051(b)(1). In the legislative history accompanying the ITU provisions, Congress indicated that filing and then repeatedly abandoning a large number of ITU applications would reflect a bad faith intent to reserve the marks, and would thus not satisfy the good faith and bona fide intent requirements. As Congress explained in the Senate Report accompanying the ITU amendments:

> [O]ther circumstances may cast doubt on the bona fide nature of the intent or even disprove it entirely. For example, the applicant may have filed numerous intent-to-use applications to register the same

---

[1]   In the case itself, the PTO followed this rule with respect to the second- and third-filed applications, suspending the third-filed application and processing the second-filed. Why didn't the PTO suspend the second-filed application in the light of the first-filed? That is not clear. Perhaps, the PTO examiner considered the products specified in the first- and second-filed applications sufficiently dissimilar that even with identical marks the public would not be confused. Perhaps, the PTO simply missed the issue.

mark for many more new products than are contemplated, numerous intent-to-use applications for a variety of desirable trademarks intended to be used on single new product, numerous intent-to-use applications to register marks consisting of or incorporating descriptive terms relating to a contemplated new product, numerous intent-to-use applications to replace applications which have lapsed because no timely declaration of use has been filed, an excessive number of intent-to-use applications to register marks which ultimately were not actually used, an excessive number of intent-to-use applications in relation to the number of products the applicant is likely to introduce under the applied-for marks during the pendency of the applications, or applications unreasonably lacking in specificity in describing the proposed goods. Other circumstances may also indicate the absence of genuine bona fide intent to actually use the mark.

S. Rep. No. 515, 100th Cong., 2d Sess. 23–24, *reprinted in* 1988 U.S.C.C.A.N. 5577, 5586.

9. *The ITU Process and Descriptive Marks.* An ITU application provides time for an applicant to begin use, while reserving the applicant's priority date. Can it be used to achieve the same result for a descriptive mark? With a descriptive mark, priority attaches not when use begins, but when secondary meaning is achieved. Can a person file an ITU application for a descriptive mark, and then use the time allowed to develop secondary meaning? In theory, the answer is no. The statute provides for the same examination process and standards for both ITU and use applications. Thus, if a mark is descriptive, the PTO should reject the application unless the applicant can show secondary meaning, without regard to whether the application is a use or an ITU application. *See In re Bayer Akt.*, 488 F.3d 960 (Fed. Cir. 2007).

In practice, however, there may be some difference in treatment between the two types of applications. In *Eastman Kodak Co. v. Bell & Howell Document Management Prods. Co.*, Bell & Howell filed a series of ITU applications seeking "to register the numbers '6200,' '6800' and '8100' on the Principal Register as trademarks for microfilm reader/printers." 994 F.2d 1569, 1570 (Fed. Cir. 1993). After the Patent and Trademark Office examined the marks and published them, Eastman Kodak filed an opposition contending that Bell & Howell intended to use the marks as model numbers and that the numbers were therefore merely descriptive. The Federal Circuit held, however, that because Bell & Howell had not yet used the marks, the court could not be certain whether Bell & Howell would use them in a manner that would be merely descriptive. *Id.* at 1576. So long as there was a possibility that the marks could be used in an inherently distinctive manner, the PTO could properly issue the notice of allowance. *Id.* If the marks were in fact used in a manner that was merely descriptive, then the PTO could consider that when Bell & Howell filed its statement of use, or if the PTO failed to do so, Eastman Kodak could petition for cancellation of the resulting registrations when they issued.

Is the opportunity to consider the issue at the statement of use stage, or through a cancellation proceeding, adequate protection against the use of the ITU procedures to register merely descriptive marks? Under section 2 of the Trademark Act, descriptive words may not be registered on the principal register unless the applicant can demonstrate secondary meaning. In *Eastman Kodak*, Bell & Howell filed its ITU applications in October 1990. The Federal Circuit rejected Eastman Kodak's opposition in June 1993, and presumably, Bell & Howell received its notice of allowances shortly thereafter. After the notice of allowances issued, Bell & Howell, assuming it filed for the necessary extensions, would have up to three years to file its statement of use. Assume that Bell & Howell files for the necessary extensions, and then timely files statements of use for its three applications in June 1996. Following the Federal Circuit's suggestion, the PTO rejects the statements, however, on the grounds that they demonstrate that Bell & Howell is using the marks in a merely descriptive manner. Can Bell & Howell respond to that rejection by offering proof that it has not only used the marks, but used them sufficiently to establish secondary meaning within the notice of allowance period?

CHAPTER 3

THE GEOGRAPHIC SCOPE OF
TRADEMARK RIGHTS

■ ■ ■

A. THE COMMON LAW APPROACH

UNITED DRUG CO. V. THEODORE RECTANUS CO.
248 U.S. 90 (1918)

PITNEY, J.

This was a suit in equity brought September 24, 1912, in the United States District Court for the Western District of Kentucky, by the present petitioner, a Massachusetts corporation, against the respondent, a Kentucky corporation, together with certain individual citizens of the latter State, to restrain infringement of trade-mark and unfair competition.

The District Court granted an injunction against the corporation defendant pursuant to the prayer of the bill. 206 Fed. Rep. 570. The Circuit Court of Appeals reversed the decree and remanded the case with directions to dismiss the bill. 226 Fed. Rep. 545. An appeal was allowed by one of the judges of that court, and afterwards we allowed a writ of certiorari. . . .

The essential facts are as follows: About the year 1877 Ellen M. Regis, a resident of Haverhill, Massachusetts, began to compound and distribute in a small way a preparation for medicinal use in cases of dyspepsia and some other ailments, to which she applied as a distinguishing name the word "Rex"—derived from her surname. The word was put upon the boxes and packages in which the medicine was placed upon the market, after the usual manner of a trade-mark. At first alone, and afterwards in partnership with her son under the firm name of "E. M. Regis & Company," she continued the business on a modest scale; in 1898 she recorded the word "Rex" as a trademark under the laws of Massachusetts (Acts 1895, p. 519, c. 462, § 1); in 1900 the firm procured its registration in the United States Patent Office under the Act of March 3, 1881, c. 138, 21 Stat. 502; in 1904 the Supreme Court of Massachusetts sustained their trade-mark right under the state law as against a concern that was selling medicinal preparations of the present petitioner under the designation of "Rexall remedies" (*Regis* v. *Jaynes*, 185 Massachusetts,

458); afterwards the firm established priority in the mark as against petitioner in a contested proceeding in the Patent Office; and subsequently, in the year 1911, petitioner purchased the business with the trade-mark right, and has carried it on in connection with its other business, which consists in the manufacture of medicinal preparations, and their distribution and sale through retail drug stores, known as "Rexall stores," situate in the different States of the Union, four of them being in Louisville, Kentucky.

Meanwhile, about the year 1883, Theodore Rectanus, a druggist in Louisville, familiarly known as "Rex," employed this word as a trade-mark for a medicinal preparation known as a "blood purifier." He continued this use to a considerable extent in Louisville and vicinity, spending money in advertising and building up a trade, so that—except for whatever effect might flow from Mrs. Regis' prior adoption of the word in Massachusetts, of which he was entirely ignorant—he was entitled to use the word as his trade-mark. In the year 1906 he sold his business, including the right to the use of the word, to respondent; and the use of the mark by him and afterwards by respondent was continuous from about the year 1883 until the filing of the bill in the year 1912.

Petitioner's first use of the word "Rex" in connection with the sale of drugs in Louisville or vicinity was in April, 1912, when two shipments of "Rex Dyspepsia Tablets," aggregating 150 boxes and valued at $22.50, were sent to one of the "Rexall" stores in that city. Shortly after this the remedy was mentioned by name in local newspaper advertisements published by those stores. In the previous September, petitioner shipped a trifling amount—five boxes—to a drug store in Franklin, Kentucky, approximately 120 miles distant from Louisville. There is nothing to show that before this any customer in or near Kentucky had heard of the Regis remedy, with or without the description "Rex," or that this word ever possessed any meaning to the purchasing public in that State except as pointing to Rectanus and the Rectanus Company and their "blood purifier." That it did and does convey the latter meaning in Louisville and vicinity is proved without dispute. Months before petitioner's first shipment of its remedy to Kentucky, petitioner was distinctly notified (in June, 1911,) by one of its Louisville distributors that respondent was using the word "Rex" to designate its medicinal preparations, and that such use had been commenced by Mr. Rectanus as much as 16 or 17 years before that time.

There was nothing to sustain the allegation of unfair competition, aside from the question of trade-mark infringement. As to this, both courts found, in substance, that the use of the same mark upon different but somewhat related preparations was carried on by the parties and their respective predecessors contemporaneously, but in widely separated localities, during the period in question—between 25 and 30 years—in perfect good faith, neither side having any knowledge or notice of what was being done by the other. The District Court held that because the adoption of the mark by Mrs. Regis antedated its adoption by Rectanus, petitioner's right to the exclusive use of the word in connection with medicinal preparations intended for dyspepsia and kindred diseases of the stomach and digestive organs must be sustained, but without accounting for profits or assessment of damages for unfair trade; citing *McLean* v. *Fleming*, 96 U.S. 245; *Menendez* v. *Holt*, 128 U.S. 514; *Saxlehner* v. *Eisner & Mendelson Co.*, 179 U.S. 19, 39; *Saxlehner* v. *Siegel-Cooper Co.*, 179 U.S. 42. The Circuit Court of Appeals held that in view of the fact that Rectanus had used the mark for a long period of years in entire ignorance of Mrs. Regis' remedy or of her trade-mark, had expended money in making his mark well known, and had established a considerable though local business under it in Louisville and vicinity, while on the other hand during the same long period Mrs. Regis had done nothing, either by sales agencies or by advertising, to make her medicine or its mark known outside of the New England States, saving sporadic sales in territory adjacent to those States, and had made no effort whatever to extend the trade to Kentucky, she and her successors were bound to know that, misled by their silence and inaction, others might act, as Rectanus and his successors did act, upon the assumption that the field was open, and therefore were estopped to ask for an injunction against the continued use of the mark in Louisville and vicinity by the Rectanus Company.

The entire argument for the petitioner is summed up in the contention that whenever the first user of a trade-mark has been reasonably diligent in extending the territory of his trade, and as a result of such extension has in good faith come into competition with a later user of the same mark who in equal good faith has extended his trade locally before invasion of his field by the first user, so that finally it comes to pass that the rival traders are offering competitive merchandise in a common market under the same trade-mark, the later user should be enjoined at the suit of the prior adopter, even though the latter be the last to enter the competitive field and the former have already established a trade there. Its application to the case is based upon the hypothesis that the record shows that Mrs. Regis and her firm, during the entire period of limited and local trade in her medicine under the Rex mark, were making efforts to extend their trade so far as they were able to do with the means at their disposal. There is little in the record to support this hypothesis; but, waiving this, we will pass upon the principal contention.

The asserted doctrine is based upon the fundamental error of supposing that a trade-mark right is a right in gross or at large, like a statutory copyright or a patent for an invention, to either of which, in truth, it has little or no analogy. *Canal Co.* v. *Clark*, 13 Wall. 311, 322; *McLean* v. *Fleming*, 96 U.S. 245, 254. There is no such thing as property in a trade-mark except as a right appurtenant to an established business or trade in connection with which the mark is employed. The law of trade-marks is but a part of the broader law of unfair competition; the right to a particular mark grows out of its use, not its mere adoption; its function is simply to designate the goods as the product of a particular trader and to protect his good will against the sale of another's product as his; and it is not the subject of property except in connection with an existing business. *Hanover Star Milling Co. v. Metcalf*, 240 U.S. 403, 412–414.

The owner of a trade-mark may not, like the proprietor of a patented invention, make a negative and merely prohibitive use of it as a monopoly. *See United States* v. *Bell Telephone Co.*, 167 U.S. 224, 250; *Bement* v. *National Harrow Co.*, 186 U.S. 70, 90; *Paper Bag Patent Case*, 210 U.S. 405, 424.

In truth, a trade-mark confers no monopoly whatever in a proper sense, but is merely a convenient means for facilitating the protection of one's good-will in trade by placing a distinguishing mark or symbol—a commercial signature—upon the merchandise or the package in which it is sold.

It results that the adoption of a trade-mark does not, at least in the absence of some valid legislation enacted for the purpose, project the right of protection in advance of the extension of the trade, or operate as a claim of territorial rights over areas into which it thereafter may be deemed desirable to extend the trade. And the expression, sometimes met with, that a trade-mark right is not limited in its enjoyment by territorial bounds, is true only in the sense that wherever the trade goes, attended by the use of the mark, the right of the trader to be protected against the sale by others of their wares in the place of his wares will be sustained.

Property in trade-marks and the right to their exclusive use rest upon the laws of the several States, and depend upon them for security and protection; the power of Congress to legislate on the subject being only such as arises from the authority to regulate commerce with foreign nations and among the several States and with the Indian tribes. *Trade-Mark Cases*, 100 U.S. 82, 93.

Conceding everything that is claimed in behalf of the petitioner, the entire business conducted by Mrs. Regis and her firm prior to April, 1911, when petitioner acquired it, was confined to the New England States with inconsiderable sales in New York, New Jersey, Canada, and Nova Scotia. There was nothing in all of this to give her any rights in Kentucky, where the principles of the common law obtain. *Hunt* v. *Warnicke's Heirs*, 3 Kentucky (Hardin), 61, 62; *Lathrop* v. *Commercial Bank*, 8 Dana (Ky.), 114, 121; *Ray* v. *Sweeney*, 14 Bush (Ky.), 1, 9; *Aetna Ins. Co. v. Commonwealth*, 106 Kentucky, 864, 881; *Nider* v. *Commonwealth*, 140 Kentucky, 684, 687. . . .

Undoubtedly, the general rule is that, as between conflicting claimants to the right to use the same mark, priority of appropriation determines the question. *See Canal Co. v. Clark,* 13 Wall. 311, 323; *McLean* v. *Fleming*, 96 U.S. 245, 251; *Manufacturing Co. v. Trainer*, 101 U.S. 51, 53; *Columbia Mill Co. v. Alcorn*, 150 U.S. 460, 463. But the reason is that purchasers have come to understand the mark as indicating the origin of the wares, so that its use by a second producer amounts to an attempt to sell his goods as those of his competitor. The reason for the rule does not extend to a case where the same trade-mark happens to be employed simultaneously by two manufacturers in different markets separate and remote from each other, so that the mark means one thing in one market, an entirely different thing in another. It would be a perversion of the rule of priority to give it such an application in our broadly extended country that an innocent party who had in good faith employed a trade-mark in one State, and by the use of it had built up a trade there, being the first appropriator in that jurisdiction, might afterwards be prevented from using it, with consequent injury to his trade and good-will, at the instance of one who theretofore had employed the same mark but only in other and remote jurisdictions, upon the ground that its first employment happened to antedate that of the first-mentioned trader.

. . . The same point was involved in *Hanover Milling Co. v. Metcalf*, 240 U.S. 403, 415, where we said: "In the ordinary case of parties competing under the same mark in the same market, it is correct to say that prior appropriation settles the question. But where two parties independently are employing the same mark upon goods of the same class, but in separate markets wholly remote the one from the other, the question of prior appropriation is legally insignificant, unless at least it appear that the second adopter has selected the mark with some design inimical to the interests of the first user, such as to take the benefit of the reputation of his goods, to forestall the extension of his trade, or the like."

In this case, as already remarked, there is no suggestion of a sinister purpose on the part of Rectanus or the Rectanus Company; hence the passage quoted correctly defines the status of the parties prior to the time when they came into competition in the Kentucky market. And it results, as a necessary inference from what we have said, that petitioner, being the newcomer in that market, must enter it subject to whatever rights had previously been acquired there in good faith by the Rectanus Company and its predecessor. To hold otherwise—to require Rectanus to retire from the field upon the entry of Mrs. Regis' successor—would be to establish the right of the latter as a right in gross, and to extend it to territory wholly remote from the furthest reach of the trade to which it was annexed, with the effect not merely of depriving Rectanus of the benefit of the good-will resulting from his long-continued use of the mark in Louisville and vicinity, and his substantial expenditures in building up his trade, but of enabling petitioner to reap substantial benefit from the publicity that Rectanus has thus given to the mark in that locality, and of confusing if not misleading the public as to the origin of goods thereafter sold in Louisville under the Rex mark, for, in that market, until petitioner entered it, "Rex" meant the Rectanus product, not that of Regis.

. . . Mrs. Regis and her firm, having during a long period of years confined their use of the "Rex" mark to a limited territory wholly remote from that in controversy, must be held to have taken the risk that some innocent party might in the meantime hit upon the same mark, apply it to goods of similar character, and expend money and effort in building up a trade under it; and since it appears that Rectanus in good faith, and without notice of any prior use by others, selected and used the "Rex" mark, and by the expenditure of money and effort succeeded in building up a local but valuable trade under it in Louisville and vicinity before petitioner entered that field, so that "Rex" had come to be recognized there as the "trade signature" of Rectanus and of respondent as his successor, petitioner is estopped to set up their continued use of the mark in that territory as an infringement of the Regis trade-mark. Whatever confusion may have arisen from conflicting use of the mark is attributable to petitioner's entry into the field with notice of the situation; and petitioner cannot complain of this. As already stated, respondent is not complaining of it.

Decree affirmed.

NOTES FOR DISCUSSION

1. *Trademark Ownership.* Which entity owns the trademark Rex for these types of "medicinal" preparations? As the Court holds, United Drug is not entitled to enjoin the Theodore Rectanus Co.'s use of the mark in Kentucky. The Theodore Rectanus Co. did not ask to enjoin United Drug's use of Rex in Kentucky, but had it done so, would it have been entitled to such an injunction?

2. *The Common Law Rule.* In trademark practice, we refer to the party who begins use of a mark on a given product first as the senior user, and the party who begins use of the same mark on a similar product as the junior user. Can you state the basic rule that the Court establishes for when a junior user can obtain rights with respect to a mark where the senior user has already used the same mark on related goods elsewhere? There are two concepts that the *United Drug* Court seems to emphasize: (i) that the junior user begin its use in good faith; and (ii) that the junior user begin its use in a separate and remote geographic area. *See also Hanover Star Milling Co. v. Metcalf*, 240 U.S. 403, 413–16 (1916). Because the *Hanover Star Milling Co.* case concerned concurrent ownership of the trademark Tea Rose for flour, courts often refer to the common law's remote junior user doctrine as the "Tea Rose-Rectanus" doctrine.

3. *Good Faith, Bad Faith.* To establish rights in a mark, the junior user must have begun use in good faith. The *United Drug* Court, at different points in its opinion, seems to suggest two different interpretations of this requirement. Early in the opinion, the Court states that both parties adopted and began using the mark "in perfect good faith, neither side having any knowledge or notice of what was being done by the other." This language suggests that the junior user satisfies the "good faith" requirement if the junior user begins use without knowledge of the senior user's prior use. However, later in the opinion, the Court seems to suggest that a junior user is in good faith so long as the junior user is not actively in bad faith. Quoting its earlier decision in *Hanover Star Milling Co.*, the Court states that so long as the use begins in a separate and remote geographic area, the junior user can acquire rights " 'unless at least it appear that the second adopter has selected the mark with some design inimical to the interests of the first user, such as to take the benefit of the reputation of his goods, to forestall the extension of his trade, or the like.' " Under this interpretation of the good faith element, a junior user may establish rights, even if aware of the senior user, so long as the junior user is not attempting to confuse consumers or forestall the senior user's expansion.

Most courts have interpreted good faith in this context to require that the junior user lack knowledge of the senior user, and as we shall see, Congress implicitly endorsed this interpretation when it enacted the Trademark Act of 1946. Nevertheless, some courts have embraced the second, "good faith unless in active bad faith" perspective. *See GTE Corp. v. Williams*, 904 F.2d 536, 541 (10th Cir. 1990) ("While a subsequent user's adoption of a mark with knowledge of another's use can certainly support an inference of bad faith, mere knowledge should not foreclose further inquiry.") (internal citations omitted); *ACCU Personnel v. AccuStaff, Inc.*, 846 F.Supp. 1191, 1211 (D. Del. 1994) (holding that prior knowledge of senior user's use is "probative of, but not dispositive of, the question whether the junior user acted in bad faith").

Which interpretation makes more sense? In attempting to resolve this issue, consider the policy objectives that the good faith requirement might serve. Does it ensure that the junior user's use will not confuse consumers when it begins or is that the role of the "separate and remote geographic area" requirement? Is it intended to protect trademark owners in certain cases? From the trademark owner's perspective, why does it make sense to protect trademark owners against some junior users, but not others?

4. *Separate and Remote Geographic Area.* To determine whether a geographic area is "separate and remote," the key issue "is whether the party's mark is sufficiently known there, or whether its sales there are of sufficient volume, to create a likelihood of confusion among consumers, should a second user enter the same territory." *Thrifty Rent-A-Car System, Inc. v. Thrift Cars, Inc.*, 639 F.Supp. 750, 753 (D. Mass. 1986), *aff'd*, 831 F.2d 1177 (1st Cir. 1987).

5. *Zone of Expansion.* What if a junior user begins use in good faith in a separate and remote geographic area, but the senior user has been steadily expanding towards that area and will soon reach it? In *Hanover Star Milling Co.*, the Court specifically left that question for future resolution: "We are not dealing with a case where the junior appropriator of a trade-mark is occupying territory that would probably be reached by the prior user in the natural expansion of his trade, and need pass no judgment upon such a case." *Hanover Star Milling Co. v. Metcalf*, 240 U.S. 403, 420 (1916). Should the senior user have presumptive rights to its natural or probable zone of expansion, or should a good faith junior user prevail if it can otherwise satisfy the remote junior user doctrine?

Some courts have flatly rejected the zone of expansion doctrine. *See, e.g., Raxton Corp. v. Anania Assocs., Inc.*, 635 F.2d 924 (1st Cir. 1980) (rejecting the zone of natural expansion for senior users as a matter of federal rights under section 43(a) and under Massachusetts law). Other courts have recognized the doctrine, but have found that the facts before them did not support its application. *See, e.g., Tally-Ho, Inc. v. Coast Community College Dist.*, 889 F.2d 1018, 1028 (11th Cir. 1989). Still others have recognized the doctrine and used it as an alternate basis for awarding rights to the senior user, where the facts also established that the junior user began its use with knowledge of the senior user or that the senior user and its marks were already known to consumers in the geographic area at issue. *See, e.g., Burger King of Florida, Inc. v. Brewer*, 244 F.Supp. 293, 298 (W.D. Tenn. 1965) (enjoining the defendant's use of Burger King's trademarks in Memphis even though Burger King did not have a franchise in Memphis because that was within Burger King's natural zone of expansion, and also finding that the defendant had knowledge of Burger King's prior use at the time it adopted the marks at issue).

As Judge Goldberg of the Fifth Circuit once exclaimed: " 'Zone of expansion' represents a conundrum within the conundrum of trademark law." *Union Nat'l Bank v. Union Nat'l Bank*, 909 F.2d 839, 843 n.9 (5th Cir. 1990).

B. FEDERAL REGISTRATION AND GEOGRAPHIC SCOPE

DAWN DONUT CO. v. HART'S FOOD STORES, INC.
267 F.2d 358 (2d Cir. 1959)

LUMBARD, CIRCUIT JUDGE

The principal question is whether the plaintiff, a wholesale distributor of doughnuts and other baked goods under its federally registered trademarks "Dawn" and "Dawn Donut," is entitled under the provisions of the Lanham Trade-Mark Act to enjoin the defendant from using the mark "Dawn" in connection with the retail sale of doughnuts and baked goods entirely within a six county area of New York State surrounding the city of Rochester. The primary difficulty arises from the fact that although plaintiff licenses purchasers of its mixes to use its trademarks in connection with the retail sales of food products made from the mixes, it has not licensed or otherwise exploited the mark at the retail level in defendant's market area for some thirty years.

We hold that because no likelihood of public confusion arises from the concurrent use of the mark in connection with retail sales of doughnuts and other baked goods in separate trading areas, and because there is no present likelihood that plaintiff will expand its retail use of the mark into defendant's market area, plaintiff is not now entitled to any relief under the Lanham Act, 15 U.S.C. § 1114. Accordingly, we affirm the district court's dismissal of plaintiff's complaint.

This is not to say that the defendant has acquired any permanent right to use the mark in its trading area. On the contrary, we hold that because of the effect of the constructive notice provision of the Lanham Act, should the plaintiff expand its retail activities into the six county area, upon a proper application and showing to the district court, it may enjoin defendant's use of the mark.

With respect to defendant's counterclaim to cancel plaintiff's registration on the ground that its method of licensing its trademarks violates the Lanham Act, a majority of the court holds that the district court's dismissal of defendant's counterclaim should be affirmed. They conclude that the district court's finding that the plaintiff exercised the degree of control over the nature and quality of the products sold by its licensees required by the Act was not clearly erroneous, particularly in view of the fact that the defendant had the burden of proving its claim for cancellation. I dissent from this conclusion because neither the finding of the trial judge nor the undisputed evidence in the record indicates the extent of supervision and control actually exercised by the plaintiff.

We are presented here with cross-appeals from a judgment entered by the District Court for the Western District of New York dismissing both plaintiff's complaint for infringement of its federally registered trademarks and defendant's counterclaim to cancel plaintiff's federal registrations.

Plaintiff, Dawn Donut Co., Inc., of Jackson, Michigan since June 1, 1922 has continuously used the trademark "Dawn" upon 25 to 100 pound bags of doughnut mix which it sells to bakers in various states, including New York, and since 1935 it has similarly marketed a line of sweet dough mixes for use in the baking of coffee cakes, cinnamon rolls and oven goods in general under that mark. In 1950 cake mixes were added to the company's line of products. Dawn's sales representatives call upon bakers to solicit orders for mixes and the orders obtained are filled by shipment to the purchaser either directly from plaintiff's Jackson, Michigan plant, where the mixes are manufactured, or from a local warehouse within the customer's state. For some years plaintiff maintained a warehouse in Jamestown, New York, from which shipments were made, but sometime prior to the commencement of this suit in 1954 it discontinued this warehouse and has since then shipped its mixes to its New York customers directly from Michigan.

Plaintiff furnishes certain buyers of its mixes, principally those who agree to become exclusive Dawn Donut Shops, with advertising and packaging material bearing the trademark "Dawn" and permits these bakers to sell goods made from the mixes to the consuming public under that trademark. These display materials are supplied either as a courtesy or at a moderate price apparently to stimulate and promote the sale of plaintiff's mixes.

The district court found that with the exception of one Dawn Donut Shop operated in the city of Rochester, New York during 1926–27, plaintiff's licensing of its mark in connection with the retail sale of doughnuts in the state of New York has been confined to areas not less than 60 miles from defendant's trading area. The court also found that for the past eighteen years plaintiff's present New York state representative has, without interruption, made regular calls upon bakers in the city of Rochester, N.Y., and in neighboring towns and cities, soliciting orders for plaintiff's mixes and that throughout this period orders have been filled and shipments made of plaintiff's mixes from Jackson, Michigan into the city of Rochester. But it does not appear that any of these purchasers of plaintiff's mixes employed the plaintiff's mark in connection with retail sales.

The defendant, Hart Food Stores, Inc., owns and operates a retail grocery chain within the New York counties of Monroe, Wayne, Livingston, Genesee, Ontario and Wyoming. The products of defendant's bakery, Starhart Bakeries, Inc., a New York corporation of which it is the sole stockholder, are distributed through these stores, thus confining the distribution of defendant's product to an area within a 45 mile radius of Rochester. Its advertising of doughnuts and other baked products over television and radio and in newspapers is also limited to this area. Defendant's bakery corporation was formed on April 13, 1951 and first used the imprint "Dawn" in packaging its products on August 30, 1951. The district court found that the defendant adopted the mark "Dawn" without any actual knowledge of plaintiff's use or federal registration of the mark, selecting it largely because of a slogan "Baked at midnight, delivered at Dawn" which was originated by defendant's president and used by defendant in its bakery operations from 1929 to 1935. Defendant's president testified, however, that no investigation was made prior to the adoption of the mark to see if anyone else was employing it. Plaintiff's marks were registered federally in 1927, and their registration was renewed in 1947. Therefore by virtue of the Lanham Act, 15 U.S.C. § 1072, the defendant had constructive notice of plaintiff's marks as of July 5, 1947, the effective date of the Act.

Defendant's principal contention is that because plaintiff has failed to exploit the mark "Dawn" for some thirty years at the retail level in the Rochester trading area, plaintiff should not be accorded the exclusive right to use the mark in this area.

We reject this contention as inconsistent with the scope of protection afforded a federal registrant by the Lanham Act.

Prior to the passage of the Lanham Act courts generally held that the owner of a registered trademark could not sustain an action for infringement against another who, without knowledge of the registration, used the mark in a different trading area from that exploited by the registrant so that public confusion was unlikely. By being the first to adopt a mark in an area without knowledge of its prior registration, a junior user of a mark could gain the right to exploit the mark exclusively in that market.

But the Lanham Act, 15 U.S.C. § 1072, provides that registration of a trademark on the principal register is constructive notice of the registrant's claim of ownership. Thus, by eliminating the defense of good faith and lack of knowledge, § 1072 affords nationwide protection to registered marks, regardless of the areas in which the registrant actually uses the mark.

That such is the purpose of Congress is further evidenced by 15 U.S.C. § 1115(a) and (b) which make the certificate of registration evidence of the registrant's "exclusive right to use the * * * mark in commerce." "Commerce" is defined in 15 U.S.C. § 1127 to include all the commerce which may lawfully be regulated by Congress. These two provisions of the Lanham Act make it plain that the fact that the defendant employed the mark "Dawn," without actual knowledge of plaintiff's registration, at the retail level in a limited geographical area of New York state before the plaintiff used the mark in that market, does not entitle it either to exclude the plaintiff from using the mark in that area or to use the mark concurrently once the plaintiff licenses the mark or otherwise exploits it in connection with retail sales in the area.

Plaintiff's failure to license its trademarks in defendant's trading area during the thirty odd years that have elapsed since it licensed them to a Rochester baker does not work an abandonment of the rights in that area. We hold that 15 U.S.C. § 1127, which provides for abandonment in certain cases of non-use, applies only when the registrant fails to use his mark, within the meaning of § 1127, anywhere in the nation. Since the Lanham Act affords a registrant nationwide protection, a contrary holding would create an insoluble problem of measuring the geographical extent of the abandonment. Even prior to the passage of the Lanham Act, when trademark protection flowed from state law and therefore depended on use within the state, no case, as far as we have been able to ascertain, held that a trademark owner abandoned his rights within only part of a state because of his failure to use the mark in that part of the state.

Accordingly, since plaintiff has used its trademark continuously at the retail level, it has not abandoned its federal registration rights even in defendant's trading area. . . .

Accordingly, we turn to the question of whether on this record plaintiff has made a sufficient showing to warrant the issuance of an injunction against defendant's use of the mark "Dawn" in a trading area in which the plaintiff has for thirty years failed to employ its registered mark.

The Lanham Act, 15 U.S.C. § 1114, sets out the standard for awarding a registrant relief against the unauthorized use of his mark by another. It provides that the registrant may enjoin only that concurrent use which creates a likelihood of public confusion as to the origin of the products in connection with which the marks are used. Therefore if the use of the marks by the registrant and the unauthorized user are confined to two sufficiently distinct and geographically separate markets, with no likelihood that the registrant will expand his use into defendant's market, so that no public confusion is possible, then the registrant is not entitled to enjoin the junior user's use of the mark.

As long as plaintiff and defendant confine their use of the mark "Dawn" in connection with the retail sale of baked goods to their present separate trading areas it is clear that no public confusion is likely.

The district court took note of what it deemed common knowledge, that "retail purchasers of baked goods, because of the perishable nature of such goods, usually make such purchases reasonably close to their homes, say within about 25 miles, and retail purchases of such goods beyond that distance are for all practical considerations negligible." No objection is made to this finding and nothing appears in the record which contradicts it as applied to this case.

Moreover, we note that it took plaintiff three years to learn of defendant's use of the mark and bring this suit, even though the plaintiff was doing some wholesale business in the Rochester area. This is a strong indication that no confusion arose or is likely to arise either from concurrent use of the marks at the retail level in geographically separate trading areas or from its concurrent use at different market levels, viz. retail and wholesale in the same area.

The decisive question then is whether plaintiff's use of the mark "Dawn" at the retail level is likely to be confined to its current area of use or whether in the normal course of its business, it is likely to expand the retail use of the mark into defendant's trading area. If such expansion were probable, then the concurrent use of the marks would give rise to the conclusion that there was a likelihood of confusion.

The district court found that in view of the plaintiff's inactivity for about thirty years in exploiting its trademarks in defendant's trading area at the retail level either by advertising directed at retail purchasers or by retail sales through authorized licensed users, there was no reasonable expectation that plaintiff would extend its retail operations into defendant's trading area. There is ample evidence in the record to support this conclusion and we cannot say that it is clearly erroneous.

We note not only that plaintiff has failed to license its mark at the retail level in defendant's trading area for a substantial period of time, but also that the trend of plaintiff's business manifests a striking decrease in the number of licensees employing its mark at the retail level in New York state and throughout the country. In the 1922–1930 period plaintiff had 75 to 80 licensees across the country with 11 located in New York. At the time of the trial plaintiff listed only 16 active licensees not one of which was located in New York.

The normal likelihood that plaintiff's wholesale operations in the Rochester area would expand to the retail level is fully rebutted and overcome by the decisive fact that plaintiff has in fact not licensed or otherwise exploited its mark at retail in the area for some thirty years.

Accordingly, because plaintiff and defendant use the mark in connection with retail sales in distinct and separate markets and because there is no present prospect that plaintiff will expand its use of the mark at the retail level into defendant's trading area, we conclude that there is no likelihood of public confusion arising from the concurrent use of the marks and therefore the issuance of an injunction is not warranted. A fortiori plaintiff is not entitled to any accounting or damages. However, because of the effect we have attributed to the constructive notice provision of the Lanham Act, the plaintiff may later, upon a proper showing of an intent to use the mark at the retail level in defendant's market area, be entitled to enjoin defendant's use of the mark. . . .

The final issue presented is raised by defendant's appeal from the dismissal of its counterclaim for cancellation of plaintiff's registration on the ground that the plaintiff failed to exercise the control required by the Lanham Act over the nature and quality of the goods sold by its licensees.

We are all agreed that the Lanham Act places an affirmative duty upon a licensor of a registered trademark to take reasonable measures to detect and prevent misleading uses of his mark by his licensees or suffer cancellation of his federal registration. The Act, 15 U.S.C. § 1064, provides that a trademark registration may be cancelled because the Trademark has been "abandoned." And "abandoned" is defined in 15

U.S.C. § 1127 to include any act or omission by the registrant which causes the trademark to lose its significance as an indication of origin.

Prior to the passage of the Lanham Act many courts took the position that the licensing of a trademark separately from the business in connection with which it had been used worked an abandonment. *Reddy Kilowatt, Inc. v. MidCarolina Electric Cooperative, Inc.*, 4th Cir., 1957, 240 F.2d 282, 289; *American Broadcasting Co. v. Wahl Co.*, 2d Cir., 1941, 121 F.2d 412, 413; *Everett O. Fisk & Co. v. Fisk Teachers' Agency, Inc.*, 8th Cir., 1924, 3 F.2d 7, 9. The theory of these cases was that:

> A trade-mark is intended to identify the goods of the owner and to safeguard his good will. The designation if employed by a person other than the one whose business it serves to identify would be misleading. Consequently, 'a right to the use of a trade-mark or a trade-name cannot be transferred in gross.'

American Broadcasting Co. v. Wahl Co., supra, 121 F.2d at 413.

Other courts were somewhat more liberal and held that a trademark could be licensed separately from the business in connection with which it had been used provided that the licensor retained control over the quality of the goods produced by the licensee. *E. I. DuPont de Nemours & Co. v. Celanese Corporation of America*, C.C.P.A., 1948, 167 F.2d 484; see also 3 A.L.R.2d 1226, 1277–1282 (1949) and cases there cited. But even in the *DuPont* case the court was careful to point out that naked licensing, viz. the grant of licenses without the retention of control, was invalid. *E. I. DuPont de Nemours & Co. v. Celanese Corporation of America, supra*, 167 F.2d at page 489.

The Lanham Act clearly carries forward the view of these latter cases that controlled licensing does not work an abandonment of the licensor's registration, while a system of naked licensing does. 15 U.S.C. § 1055 provides:

> 'Where a registered mark or a mark sought to be registered is or may be used legitimately by related companies, such use shall inure to the benefit of the registrant or applicant for registration, and such use shall not affect the validity of such mark or of its registration, provided such mark is not used in such manner as to deceive the public.'

And 15 U.S.C. § 1127 defines "related company" to mean "any person who legitimately controls or is controlled by the registrant or applicant for registration in respect to the nature and quality of the goods or services in connection with which the mark is used."

Without the requirement of control, the right of a trademark owner to license his mark separately from the business in connection with which it has been used would create the danger that products bearing the same trademark might be of diverse qualities. See *American Broadcasting Co. v. Wahl Co., supra*; *Everett O. Fisk & Co. v. Fisk Teachers' Agency, Inc., supra*. If the licensor is not compelled to take some reasonable steps to prevent misuses of his trademark in the hands of others the public will be deprived of its most effective protection against misleading uses of a trademark. The public is hardly in a position to uncover deceptive uses of a trademark before they occur and will be at best slow to detect them after they happen. Thus, unless the licensor exercises supervision and control over the operations of its licensees the risk that the public will be unwittingly deceived will be increased and this is precisely what the Act is in part designed to prevent. *See* Sen. Report No. 1333, 79th Cong., 2d Sess. (1946). Clearly the only effective way to protect the public where a trademark is used by licensees is to place on the licensor the affirmative duty of policing in a reasonable manner the activities of his licensees.

The critical question on these facts therefore is whether the plaintiff sufficiently policed and inspected its licensees' operations to guarantee the quality of the products they sold under its trademarks to the public. The trial court found that: "By reason of its contacts with its licensees, plaintiff exercised legitimate control over the nature and quality of the food products on which plaintiff's licensees used the trademark 'Dawn.' Plaintiff and its licensees are related companies within the meaning of Section 45 of the Trademark Act of 1946." It is the position of the majority of this court that the trial judge has the same leeway in determining what constitutes a reasonable degree of supervision and control over licensees under the facts and circumstances of the particular case as he has on other questions of fact; and particularly because it is the defendant who has the burden of proof on this issue they hold the lower court's finding not clearly erroneous.

I dissent from the conclusion of the majority that the district court's findings are not clearly erroneous because while it is true that the trial judge must be given some discretion in determining what constitutes reasonable supervision of licensees under the Lanham Act, it is also true that an appellate court ought not to accept the conclusions of the district court unless they are supported by findings of sufficient facts. It seems to me that the only findings of the district judge regarding supervision are in such general and conclusory terms as to be meaningless. In the absence of supporting findings or of undisputed evidence in the record indicating the kind of supervision and inspection the plaintiff actually made of its licensees, it is impossible for us to pass upon whether there was such supervision as to satisfy the statute. There was evidence before the district court in the matter of supervision, and more detailed findings thereon should have been made.

Plaintiff's licensees fall into two classes: (1) those bakers with whom it made written contracts providing that the baker purchase exclusively plaintiff's mixes and requiring him to adhere to plaintiff's directions in using the mixes; and (2) those bakers whom plaintiff permitted to sell at retail under the "Dawn" label doughnuts and other baked goods made from its mixes although there was no written agreement governing the quality of the food sold under the Dawn mark.

The contracts that plaintiff did conclude, although they provided that the purchaser use the mix as directed and without adulteration, failed to provide for any system of inspection and control. Without such a system plaintiff could not know whether these bakers were adhering to its standards in using the mix or indeed whether they were selling only products made from Dawn mixes under the trademark "Dawn."

The absence, however, of an express contract right to inspect and supervise a licensee's operations does not mean that the plaintiff's method of licensing failed to comply with the requirements of the Lanham Act. Plaintiff may in fact have exercised control in spite of the absence of any express grant by licensees of the right to inspect and supervise.

The question then, with respect to both plaintiff's contract and non-contract licensees, is whether the plaintiff in fact exercised sufficient control.

Here the only evidence in the record relating to the actual supervision of licensees by plaintiff consists of the testimony of two of plaintiff's local sales representatives that they regularly visited their particular customers and the further testimony of one of them, Jesse Cohn, the plaintiff's New York representative, that "in many cases" he did have an opportunity to inspect and observe the operations of his customers. The record does not indicate whether plaintiff's other sales representatives made any similar efforts to observe the operations of licensees.

Moreover, Cohn's testimony fails to make clear the nature of the inspection he made or how often he made one. His testimony indicates that his opportunity to observe a licensee's operations was limited to "those cases where I am able to get into the shop" and even casts some doubt on whether he actually had sufficient technical knowledge in the use of plaintiff's mix to make an adequate inspection of a licensee's operations.

The fact that it was Cohn who failed to report the defendant's use of the mark "Dawn" to the plaintiff casts still further doubt about the extent of the supervision Cohn exercised over the operations of plaintiff's New York licensees.

Thus I do not believe that we can fairly determine on this record whether plaintiff subjected its licensees to periodic and thorough inspections by trained personnel or whether its policing consisted only of chance, cursory examinations of licensees' operations by technically untrained salesmen. The latter system of inspection hardly constitutes a sufficient program of supervision to satisfy the requirements of the Act.

Therefore it is appropriate to remand the counterclaim for more extensive findings on the relevant issues rather than hazard a determination on this incomplete and uncertain record. I would direct the district court to order the cancellation of plaintiff's registrations if it should find that the plaintiff did not adequately police the operations of its licensees.

But unless the district court finds some evidence of misuse of the mark by plaintiff in its sales of mixes to bakers at the wholesale level, the cancellation of plaintiff's registration should be limited to the use of the mark in connection with sale of the finished food products to the consuming public. Such a limited cancellation is within the power of the court. Section 1119 of 15 U.S.C. specifically provides that "In any action involving a registered mark the court may * * * order the cancellation of registrations, in whole or in part, * * * 'Moreover, partial cancellation is consistent with § 1051(a)(1) of 15 U.S.C., governing the initial registration of trademarks which requires the applicant to specify 'the goods in connection with which the mark is used and the mode or manner in which the mark is used in connection with such goods * * *.' "

The district court's denial of an injunction restraining defendant's use of the mark "Dawn" on baked and fried goods and its dismissal of defendant's counterclaim are affirmed.

NOTES FOR DISCUSSION

1.   *A Note on Nomenclature.* When we mix together the different timings that can arise between use and registration, we find three basic fact patterns for cases involving geographic priority and federal registration. In the first, illustrated by *Dawn Donuts*, the junior user begins use after the senior user has both begun use of the mark and federally registered the mark. This is known as the "pure junior user" case. In the second type of case, the junior user begins use between the time at which the senior user: (i) begins use; and (ii) obtains a federal registration. Because the junior user's use begins between the senior user's use and registration, this type of case is known as the "junior intermediate user" case. In the third type of case, the junior user, while beginning use second, actually registers the mark first. This fact pattern is known as the senior unregistered user case.

2.   *The Role of Federal Registration: The Pure Junior User Case.* In both *Dawn Donuts* and *United Drug*, the senior user was unsuccessful in enjoining the junior user's use of the same mark for similar goods. Given that common result, what good did it do Dawn Donuts to obtain a federal registration before Hart Foods' use began? How do Dawn Donuts' trademark rights differ from those of United Drug? If Dawn Donuts were to try and open a franchise in Rochester that would use the plaintiff's trademark Dawn

Donuts at the retail level, would Dawn Donuts have the right to enjoin Hart Foods' continued use of the mark at that time? Or would Hart Foods have the right to enjoin Dawn Donuts' use in the area where Hart Foods began use first? Why?

Under the common law rule, Hart Foods would have rights to the Dawn mark in the Rochester area if it began use in good faith and if Rochester constituted a separate and remote geographic area. Once Dawn Donuts has registered its trademark on the principal register, can Hart Foods satisfy this common law rule? Given the court's resolution of the likelihood of confusion issue, we can safely assume that Rochester would qualify as a separate and remote geographic area. Do you see why?

Nevertheless, Hart Foods will not be able to satisfy the common law's good faith requirement. To understand why, we must start by assuming that "good faith" means that Hart Foods must not know of Dawn Donuts' prior rights when Hart Foods begins its use. Generally, in the law, a party's knowledge can be shown in three ways. First, the party can have actual knowledge. Simply put, the party knows the fact at issue. Second, the party can have inquiry knowledge. With inquiry knowledge, the party is actually unaware of the fact at issue, but it has knowledge of other facts that would lead a reasonable person to investigate and such investigation would reveal the fact at issue. *See Pagan-Lewis Motors, Inc. v. Superior Pontiac, Inc.*, 216 U.S.P.Q. 897 (T.T.A.B. 1982) (finding that applicant had not begun use of a mark in good faith where it had notice of facts that would have led a reasonable person to discover another party's prior use and claim of ownership in the mark). Third, the party can have constructive notice of the relevant fact. In such a case, knowledge is conclusively presumed.

When Congress enacted the Trademark Act in 1946, it was familiar with the common law's rules regarding geographic scope, and so enacted section 22 to defeat a junior user's remote geographic use claim if its use began after the federal registration. Section 22 provides:

> Registration of a mark on the principal register ... shall be constructive notice of the registrant's claim of ownership thereof.

15 U.S.C. § 1072 (2015).

Given section 22, even if Hart Foods did not actually know of Dawn Donuts' use, once Dawn Donuts registered its mark federally, Hart Foods had constructive knowledge of Dawn Donuts' prior rights. Because Hart Foods began its use after the federal registration, Hart Foods could not demonstrate the "good faith" necessary to acquire rights under the common law's rules regarding geographic priority. As a result, once Dawn Donuts registers, Hart Foods may not acquire rights to the mark Dawn for donuts even if Rochester constitutes a separate and remote geographic area.

3. *Factual Plausibility.* The key factual assumption underpinning the court's finding with respect to likelihood of confusion is that consumers do not drive very far for donuts. Is that true in your experience? Even if consumers do not specifically drive very far for donuts, is it possible that consumers from

a geographic area where a Dawn Donuts franchise is located might move to Rochester? Is a mere possibility of confusion enough?

How would you resolve the following:

In 1961, B & B Corporation opened a hotel in St. Thomas, in the Virgin Islands, and used the marks Holiday Inn and Holiday Inn of St. Thomas for the hotel. By that time, Holiday Inn of America, Inc. already had a national reputation and operated more than 150 hotels under the mark Holiday Inn within the continental United States and was rapidly expanding. Holiday Inn of America had federally registered Holiday Inn as a service mark for hotel services in 1954. By the time of trial, Holiday Inn of America was operating some 830 motels, both domestically and internationally, and its nearest hotel was in San Juan, Puerto Rico, approximately 70 miles from the B&B Corporation's hotel. Holiday Inn of America sues, alleging trademark infringement and unfair competition. Should Holiday Inn of America be entitled to injunctive relief now, or only when it takes concrete steps towards opening its own location in St. Thomas?

The Third Circuit held that Holiday Inn of America was entitled to injunctive relief only "upon a showing that Holiday actually has begun the development or construction of a motel in the U.S. Virgin Islands." *See Holiday Inns of America, Inc. v. B&B Corp.*, 409 F.2d 614, 619 (3d Cir. 1969). Do you agree with the court that there is no likelihood of confusion unless and until such development or construction begins? Does it matter whether B & B's customers are primarily locals from St. Thomas or travelers from the United States? Compare *Ritz Carlton Hotel Co. v. Ritz Carlton Hotel Corp.*, 66 F.Supp. 720 (S.D. Fla. 1946) (enjoining the defendant's use of the mark Ritz Carlton for a hotel in Miami, even though the plaintiffs did not have a hotel there, on the grounds that the plaintiffs had established secondary meaning throughout the country).

4. *Implications and Alternative Solutions.* One of the necessary implications of the *Dawn Donuts* decision is that Dawn Donuts will be able to enjoin Hart Foods' use of Dawn should it ever move into Rochester at the retail area. If Dawn Donuts waits twenty years before moving into Rochester, would it still have the right to enjoin Hart Foods' use? Would it have the right even if consumers in Rochester have come to associate Dawn uniquely with Hart Foods? The answer appears to be yes.

Hart Foods might try to argue that, because Dawn Donuts has not used Dawn for donuts in Rochester for more than two decades, that Dawn Donuts has abandoned its rights with respect to Dawn in that geographic area. Does the *Dawn Donuts* court address this issue of partial geographic abandonment? What does the court say?

Alternatively, Hart Foods might argue that Dawn Donuts' long delay in bringing suit to enjoin Hart Foods' use bars the lawsuit under an equitable doctrine such as laches, acquiescence, or estoppel. While we shall study these doctrines in more detail in Chapter 9, the short answer is that Dawn Donuts did not have a cause of action on which it could prevail until it moved into the

Rochester area. Only at that point would an actionable likelihood of confusion arise. Thus, so long as Dawn Donuts brings the lawsuit just before, or soon after, it moves into Rochester, there has been no undue delay.

If Dawn Donuts moves in to Rochester twenty years later, and persuades a court to enjoin Hart Foods' use, will the donut consumers of Rochester be confused? Will they purchase Dawn donuts expecting to receive Hart Foods' donuts, but receive Dawn Donuts' donuts instead? How can we address this risk of consumer confusion?

There are two approaches we might try. First, we could keep the legal rules set forth in *Dawn Donuts* and rely on the parties to address, between themselves, the risk of confusion a late entry by Dawn Donuts into Rochester would create. There are several ways the parties could address the risk. Most obviously, knowing that it could lose the rights to Dawn at any time, Hart Foods could switch to some other trademark. Alternatively, Dawn Donuts could forego entry into the Rochester market to avoid the confusion that would result, or simply because it never manages to grow enough to expand into Rochester. Dawn Donuts and Hart Foods could also enter into a license, under which Hart Foods could continue to use Dawn for donuts in Rochester in return for payment to Dawn Donuts. To be valid, such a license would require Dawn Donuts to control the quality of the donuts Hart Foods was selling under the mark. While the quality control requirement is largely a formality, as the *Dawn Donuts* court's resolution of that issue reflects, allowing Dawn Donuts to control, even at a merely formal level, the quality of Hart Foods' donuts may nonetheless prove a sticking point for Hart Foods. Rather than a license, Hart Foods could purchase a "covenant not to enter" from Dawn Donuts, similar to the "covenant not to sue" that we saw in *Zazu Designs* in Chapter 2. This would achieve the same practical effect as a license, but would avoid the quality control requirement.

Second, and alternatively, we could reject the legal rules regarding geographic use set forth in *Dawn Donuts*. In the first case to interpret the effect of the Trademark Act of 1946 on geographic rights, a district court in *Sterling Brewing, Inc. v. Cold Spring Brewing Corp.*, 100 F.Supp. 412 (D. Mass. 1951), enjoined a remote junior user. In granting the injunction, the district court stated "that the provisions of the Act of 1946 negative the defense of 'territorial limitation' of the protection accorded to a registered trade-mark, and that the plaintiff is entitled to injunctive relief irrespective of the plaintiff's 'expansion situation'." *Id.* at 418. The issue whether the plaintiff had proven a likelihood of confusion, given the junior user's geographic remoteness, was not separately addressed. The district court seemingly combined the issues of who owned the trademark rights in a particular geographic area with the issue whether that owner had shown a likelihood of confusion and thus infringement with respect to the defendant's use.

Dawn Donuts separated these two issues. Giving effect to the constructive notice provision in section 1072, the *Dawn Donuts* court held that the registered user "owns" the trademark rights nationwide, at least vis-à-vis those whose use begins after the federal registration. But, to obtain injunctive relief, the registrant must also and separately prove that the defendant's use creates a likelihood of confusion. As purely a factual matter, unless the registered user is using the mark or is otherwise known to consumers in a given area, there is no likelihood that consumers in that area will mistakenly connect another party's use to the registrant. In short, no one in Rochester would buy Hart Foods' Dawn donuts thinking they were from Dawn Donuts because no one in Rochester was familiar with Dawn Donuts. Until the registrant can prove that its entry into the area is "imminent" or that a likelihood of confusion is otherwise present, the registrant is not entitled to enjoin the junior user's use.

The *Dawn Donuts* approach is the majority approach to the junior use issue today. It is not the only approach to the issue, however. The Sixth Circuit embraced a different approach in *Circuit City Stores, Inc. v. CarMax, Inc.*, 165 F.3d 1047 (6th Cir. 1999). In its decision, the Sixth Circuit agreed with *Dawn Donuts* that ownership and infringement were separate issues. But on the infringement issue, it held that geographic remoteness does not foreclose a finding of infringement. Like most circuits, the Sixth Circuit uses an "eight point test for infringement liability under the Lanham Act." Under this eight point test, the court held that "[l]ikelihood of entry is just one of the eight factors . . . , and it is not dispositive of liability." *Id.* at 1056. As a result, once the district court found a likelihood of confusion under the eight point test as a whole, granting injunctive relief was appropriate even without a showing that "[the plaintiff] was about to enter the defendants' market. . . ."

Should we reject the *Dawn Donuts* approach and adopt in its stead either the *Sterling Brewing* or the *Circuit City Stores, Inc.* approach to the pure junior case? Allowing Dawn Donuts to enjoin Hart Foods' use in 1959 would certainly foreclose the possibility of consumer confusion were Dawn Donuts to enter the Rochester market twenty years later. Does it create other problems, however?

5. *Section 1057(c) and Geographic Priority.* As part of the amendments adding the ITU provisions in 1988, Congress provided in section 1057(c) that "[c]ontingent on the registration of a mark . . . , the filing of the application to register such mark shall constitute constructive use of the mark, conferring a priority, nationwide in effect, on or in connection with the goods or services specified in the registration." 15 U.S.C. § 1057(c) (2015). As we saw in Chapter 2, the purpose of this language was to provide "constructive use" for ITU applications where the applicant had not begun use at the time of filing, so as to satisfy the common law's use requirement.

It has two possible implications for the *Dawn Donuts* situation. First, if the *Dawn Donuts* fact pattern arose today, a plaintiff could argue that although it may not actually be using the mark in a given geographic area, it is constructively using its federally registered mark in that area pursuant to section 1057(c). Given that Congress intended constructive use to count as use, a plaintiff could argue that its registration should today provide a sufficient basis to award the plaintiff injunctive relief. If, as the *Dawn Donuts* court held, relief is not available until the plaintiff enters a given geographic market, a plaintiff today could insist that, given section 1057(c), it has already entered the market, at least constructively. What do you think of this argument? If you were a judge, would you accept it? Does Congress's decision to establish a conclusive presumption of constructive use resolve the issue of whether consumers in a given geographic area will be confused? Is it relevant to it?

Second, section 1057(c) grants constructive use retroactively, as of the date of filing, once an application matures into a registration. In contrast, section 1072 provides constructive notice as of the date of registration. Assume that DD files an ITU application on January 3, 2005; DD begins use of the mark in a given geographic area on January 5, 2006; and its application matures into a registration on January 10, 2008. If a second entity, HFS, begins use of the same mark on the same goods on January 7, 2007, in good faith and in an area that is separate and remote from the area in which DD is using the mark, who will have rights to the mark in HFS's trading area once DD's application matures into a registration? Should we treat HFS as a pure junior user like Hart Foods in the *Dawn Donuts* case, or as a junior intermediate user, as we shall see in the next case?

The intended interaction between section 1072 and the common law rules of geographic priority was clear. The common law rules require good faith. If we interpret that as a lack of knowledge of the senior user, then constructive notice precludes a lack of knowledge. How does constructive use interact with the common law rules? Should we restrict the reach of section 1057(c) to its intended domain of providing constructive use in order to satisfy the common law's use requirement for ITU applications?

6. *Implications, Redux.* So far we have considered the implications of the *Dawn Donuts* rule as between the Dawn Donuts and Hart Foods. But the rule also has potential implications in another scenario. Specifically, what if Dawn Donuts itself has not yet moved into Rochester, and an unrelated third party begins using Dawn for donuts in competition with Hart Foods in the Rochester area? Even if Hart Foods has no rights vis-à-vis Dawn Donuts, may Hart Foods nonetheless obtain an injunction against the unrelated third party?

7. *Constructive Notice and Good Faith.* As we discussed in connection with the *United Drug* case, courts have given the "good faith" element of the common law's rules regarding geographic priority two different interpretations: (i) the junior user did not know of the senior user's prior rights; or (ii) the junior user both knew of the senior user and intended to confuse consumers or to forestall the senior user's geographic expansion. Congress intended section 22's constructive notice provision to establish nationwide rights, but it will accomplish that result only if courts follow the first interpretation of good faith. If they follow the second, then constructive notice alone will not be sufficient to show the active bad faith necessary to prevent a junior user in a separate and remote geographic area from obtaining rights with respect to its use of the trademark. If a court adopted

the second interpretation, what more would Dawn Donuts have to show to defeat a claim by Hart Foods to the mark Dawn in the Rochester area? If it could not show that Hart Foods adopted the mark in bad faith, such as intending to trade on Dawn Donuts' goodwill or to forestall Dawn Donuts' expansion, what would the parties' respective rights to Dawn be?

8. *The Naked License Rule.* In addition to establishing the basic rules still followed today on the relation between federal registration and remote geographic users, the *Dawn Donuts* court also establishes the approach most courts still follow with respect to the naked license issue. What is Hart Foods' argument with respect to Dawn Donuts' licensing of the use of its mixes? If Hart Foods prevailed on its argument, how would that change the outcome in the case? Why does Hart Foods' argument fail? Does the court hold that trademark licenses are permissible with or without control of the quality of the associated goods or services? Or does it hold that quality control is required, but find that Dawn Donuts exercised sufficient quality control? What quality control measures did Dawn Donuts implement?

While we shall study the quality control requirement in more detail in Chapter 6, the *Dawn Donuts* court's *laissez faire* approach to the level of quality control judicially required is fairly typical. Given that Congress expressly required quality control in the Trademark Act, why doesn't the court examine more closely, as Judge Lumbard suggests, the quality control measures Dawn Donuts has in place? Two reasons probably account for the judicial reluctance. First, it is usually in the trademark owner's own economic self-interest to implement effective quality control. If a trademark owner licenses a number of independent entities to use its mark, and fails to control the quality of the associated goods or services, that is likely, as the court notes, to harm consumers. Having made a satisfactory purchase from one trademark licensee, a consumer may see the same trademark elsewhere and, expecting the same quality, purchase from another licensee, only to be disappointed. But that harm to consumers will generally translate directly into lower sales and profits for the trademark licensor. Consumers will not rely on the mark, and as a result, would-be licensees will not offer the licensor very much for using it.

Second, not only are trademark licensors likely to have sufficient incentive from the market directly to implement appropriate quality control, courts and juries are poorly situated to second-guess the trademark owner's decisions with respect to quality control. As quality control improves, a mark may become more valuable, but how much quality control will prove sensible may vary from market-to-market. If the goal is to keep prices low, a lower level of quality control may make economic sense. If the goal is to establish a reputation for exceptional quality, more stringent quality controls will be required, but prices will be correspondingly higher. So long as there is some degree of quality control, should we let a court or jury second-guess the owner's judgment as to what level of quality control it wants to maintain?

Apply these principles to the facts in *Dawn Donuts*. Does Dawn Donuts need to have stringent quality supervision over its licensees? Or do those licensees already have sufficient incentive of their own to ensure that their customers are satisfied? Was there any evidence that the quality of the goods provided varied considerably among the licensees? Was there any evidence that one of the licensees was selling much lower quality goods in an attempt to free ride off of the goodwill the other licensees had created by selling high quality products in connection with the mark? If that were occurring, do you think that Dawn Donuts would learn of and address the situation? Or should we leave that for a court or jury to address through the naked license doctrine? Was there any evidence that consumers purchased from one Dawn Donuts licensee, and when they went back to purchase more from another licensee, were disappointed with the second licensee's quality? Should we require proof of such confusion, or proof of affirmative variations in the quality provided, before finding a violation of the naked license doctrine? We will explore these issues again in Chapter 6.

BURGER KING OF FLORIDA, INC. V. HOOTS
403 F.2d 904 (7th Cir. 1968)

KILEY, C.J.

Defendants' appeal presents a conflict between plaintiffs' right to use the trade mark "Burger King," which plaintiffs have registered under the Federal Trade Mark Act, and defendants' right to use the same trade mark which defendants have registered under the Illinois Trade Mark Act. The district court resolved the conflict in favor of plaintiffs in this case of first impression in this Circuit. We affirm the judgment restraining the defendants from using the name "Burger King" in any part of Illinois except in their Mattoon, Illinois, market, and restraining plaintiffs from using their trade mark in the market area of Mattoon, Illinois.

Defendants do not challenge the district court's findings of fact and have not included testimony of witnesses at the trial in the record on appeal.

Plaintiff Burger King of Florida, Inc. opened the first "Burger King" restaurant in Jacksonville, Florida, in 1953. By 1955, fifteen of these restaurants were in operation in Florida, Georgia and Tennessee; in 1956 the number operating in Alabama, Kentucky and Virginia was twenty-nine; by 1957, in these states, thirty-eight restaurants were in operation.

In July, 1961, plaintiffs opened their first Illinois "Burger King" restaurant in Skokie, and at that time had notice of the defendants' prior registration of the same mark under the Illinois Trade Mark Act. Thereafter, on October 3, 1961, plaintiffs' certificate of federal registration of the mark was issued. Subsequently, plaintiffs opened a restaurant in Champaign, Illinois, and at the time of the trial in November, 1967, were operating more than fifty "Burger King" restaurants in the state of Illinois.

In 1957 the defendants, who had been operating an ice cream business in Mattoon, Illinois, opened a "Burger King" restaurant there. In July, 1959, they registered that name under Illinois law as their trade mark, without notice of plaintiffs' prior use of the same mark. On September 26, 1962, the defendants, with constructive knowledge of plaintiffs' federal trade mark, opened a second similar restaurant, in Charleston, Illinois.

Both parties have used the trade mark prominently, and in 1962 they exchanged charges of infringement in Illinois. After plaintiffs opened a restaurant in Champaign, Illinois, defendants sued in the state court to restrain plaintiffs' use of the mark in Illinois. Plaintiffs then brought the federal suit, now before us, and the defendants counter-claimed for an injunction, charging plaintiffs with infringement of their Illinois trade mark.

The district court concluded, from the unchallenged findings, that plaintiffs' federal registration is prima facie evidence of the validity of the registration and ownership of the mark; that plaintiffs have both a common-law and a federal right in the mark superior to defendants' in the area of natural expansion of plaintiffs' enterprise which "logically included" all of Illinois, except where defendants had actually adopted and used the mark, innocently, i.e., without notice and in good faith; and that the defendants had adopted and continuously used the mark in the Mattoon area innocently and were entitled to protection in that market.

We hold that the district court properly decided that plaintiffs' federal registration of the trade mark "Burger King" gave them the exclusive right to use the mark in Illinois except in the Mattoon market area in Illinois where the defendants, without knowledge of plaintiffs' prior use, actually used the mark before plaintiffs' federal registration. The defendants did not acquire the exclusive right they would have acquired by their Illinois registration had they actually used the mark throughout Illinois prior to the plaintiffs' federal registration.

We think our holding is clear from the terms of the Federal Trade Mark Act. Under 15 U.S.C. § 1065 of the Act, plaintiffs, owners of the federally registered trade mark "Burger King," have the "incontestable" right to use the mark in commerce, except to the extent that such use infringes what valid right the defendants have acquired by their continuous use of the same mark prior to plaintiffs' federal registration.

Under 15 U.S.C. § 1115(b), the federal certificate of registration is "conclusive evidence" of plaintiffs' "exclusive right" to use the mark. This Section, however, also provides a defense to an exclusive right to use a trade mark: If a trade mark was adopted without knowledge of the federal registrant's prior use, and has been continuously used, then such use "shall" constitute a defense to infringement, provided that this defense applies only for the area in which such continuous prior use is proved. Since the defendants have established that they had adopted the mark "Burger King" without knowledge of plaintiffs' prior use and that they had continuously used the mark from a date prior to plaintiffs' federal registration of the mark, they are entitled to protection in the area which that use appropriated to them.

Plaintiffs agree that the defendants as prior good faith users are to be protected in the area that they had appropriated. Thus, the question narrows to what area in Illinois the defendants have appropriated by virtue of their Illinois registration.

At common law, defendants were entitled to protection in the Mattoon market area because of the innocent use of the mark prior to plaintiffs' federal registration. They argue that the Illinois Trade Mark Act was designed to give more protection than they already had at common law, and that various provisions of the Illinois Act indicate an intention to afford Illinois registrants exclusive rights to use trade marks throughout the state, regardless of whether they actually used the marks throughout the state or not. However, the Act itself does not express any such intention. And no case has been cited to us, nor has our research disclosed any case in the Illinois courts deciding whether a registrant is entitled to statewide protection even if he has used the mark only in a small geographical area.

Two decisions of this court, however, shed light on the defendants' argument. In *Philco Corp. v. Phillips Mfg. Co.,* 133 F.2d 663, 148 A.L.R. 125 (7th Cir. 1943), this court, through Judge Kerner, discussed the 1905 and 1920 Trade Mark Acts, and decided that Congress had the constitutional power to legislate on "merits of trade mark questions," *supra* at 670 of 133 F.2d. It then stated that the policy of the Acts, to provide protection of federally registered marks used in interstate commerce, "may not be defeated or obstructed by State law" and that if state law conflicts with the policy it "must yield to the superior federal law." The court held that Philco's federal-registration rendered all questions of use and protection in interstate commerce questions of federal law, not state law. And in *John Morrell & Co. v. Reliable Packing Co.,* 295 F.2d 314 (7th Cir. 1961), Judge Duffy states, at 317, "However, the Illinois registration carries no presumption of validity"—thus attributing greater value to a federal registration because of its "incontestability" feature, which is prima facie evidence of exclusivity in interstate commerce. *See also Hot Shoppes, Inc. v. Hot Shoppe, Inc.,* 203 F. Supp. 777, 781–782. (M.D.N.C.1962).

The competing federal and state statutes confirm the correctness of this court's statements. Under 15 U.S.C. § 1115(b) of the Lanham Act, the federal certificate can be "conclusive evidence" of registrant's "exclusive right." And 15 U.S.C. § 1127 of the Act provides that "The intent of this chapter is * * * to protect registered marks used in such commerce from interference by State * * * legislation." The Illinois Act, however, provides only that a certificate of registration "shall be admissible * * * evidence as competent and sufficient proof of the registration * * *." Ill.Rev.Stat. Ch. 140, § 11 (1967).

Moreover, we think that whether or not Illinois intended to enlarge the common law with respect to a right of exclusivity in that state, the Illinois Act does not enlarge its right in the area where the federal mark has priority. See Hot Shoppes, *supra*, 782. Congress expanded the common law, however, by granting an exclusive right in commerce to federal registrants in areas where there has been no offsetting use of the mark. Congress intended the Lanham Act to afford nation-wide protection to federally-registered marks, and that once the certificate has issued, no person can acquire any additional rights superior to those obtained by the federal registrant. *See John R. Thompson Co. v. Holloway*, 366 F.2d 108 (5th Cir. 1966); *Dawn Donut Co. v. Hart's Food Stores, Inc.*, 267 F.2d 358 (2d Cir. 1959).

. . . We conclude that if we were to accept the defendants' argument we would be fostering, in clear opposition to the express terms of the Lanham Act, an interference with plaintiffs' exclusive right in interstate commerce to use its federal mark.

The undisputed continuous market for the defendants' "Burger King" products was confined to a twenty mile radius of Mattoon. There is no evidence before us of any intention or hope for their use of their Illinois mark beyond that market. Yet they seek to exclude plaintiffs from expanding the scope of their national exclusive right, and from operating fifty enterprises already begun in Illinois. This result would clearly burden interstate commerce.

The defendants argue also that unless they are given the right to exclusive use throughout Illinois, many persons from all parts of Illinois in our current mobile society will come in contact with the defendants' business and will become confused as to whether they are getting the defendants' product, as they intended.

We are not persuaded by this argument. Defendants have not shown that the Illinois public is likely to confuse the products furnished by plaintiffs and by defendants. *John R. Thompson Co. v. Holloway*, 366 F.2d 108 (5th Cir. 1966), and cases cited therein. We are asked to infer that confusion will exist from the mere fact that both trade marks co-exist in the state of Illinois. However, the district court found that the defendants' market area was limited to within twenty miles of their place of business. The court's decision restricted the use of the mark by plaintiffs and defendants to sufficiently distinct and geographically separate markets so that public confusion would be reduced to a minimum. The mere fact that some people will travel from one market area to the other does not, of itself, establish that confusion will result.

Since the defendants have failed to establish on the record any likelihood of confusion or any actual confusion, they are not entitled to an inference that confusion will result.

For the reasons given, the judgment of the district court is affirmed.

NOTES FOR DISCUSSION

1. *The Junior Intermediate User Case.* Under our naming convention, Hoots is a junior intermediate user. He began using the mark in good faith in a separate and remote geographic area after the senior user's use but before the senior user federally registered the mark at issue. As a junior intermediate user, how do Hoots' rights in the Burger King mark differ from those of our pure junior user, Hart Foods? How do they differ from the rights of a junior user, such as the Theodore Rectanus Co., where there is no federal registration at all?

Burger King has not only registered its trademark federally, it has also filed an affidavit under section 15 of the Trademark Act, 15 U.S.C. § 1065 (2015), verifying use in commerce of the trademark for five consecutive years following the registration. Once a registrant files a section 15 affidavit and the PTO accepts it, the evidentiary presumptions associated with the registration change. Prior to that point, the registration provides "prima facie" evidence of the registration's validity, and of the registrant's ownership and exclusive right to use the trademark for the products or services specified. 15 U.S.C. § 1057(b) (2015). After the section 15 affidavit is filed and accepted, the registration becomes "conclusive evidence of the validity of the registered mark and of the registration of the mark, of the registrant's ownership of the mark, and of the registrant's exclusive right to use the registered mark in commerce." 15 U.S.C. § 1115(b) (2015). These enhanced evidentiary presumptions are referred to as "incontestability."

Even with such incontestability, however, the registrant's exclusive right to use the mark "shall be subject to proof of infringement" and to nine enumerated defenses. One of these nine is subsection (b)(5), which provides that the registrant's exclusive right to use is subject to the following defense:

> [t]hat the mark whose use by a party is charged as infringement was adopted without knowledge of the registrant's prior use and has been continuously used by such party . . . from a date prior to (A) the date of the constructive use of the mark established pursuant to section 1057(c) of this title, (B) the registration of the mark under this Act if the application for registration is filed before the effective date of the Trademark Law Revision Act of 1988, or (C) publication of the registered mark under subsection (c) of section 1062 of this title: *Provided, however,* That this defense or defect shall apply only for the area in which such continuous prior use is proved . . .

15 U.S.C. § 1115(b)(5) (2015).

This provision codifies, to some extent, the common law's remote junior user doctrine, but it also raises a few questions. First, subsection (b)(5) does not expressly require that the junior user begin use in a separate and remote geographic area. Is that nonetheless a requirement that a junior intermediate user such as Hoots must establish to defeat Burger King's claim of infringement? Second, it states that the junior user must begin use "without knowledge of the registrant's prior use." Does this effectively codify the "without knowledge" interpretation of good faith for the common law's remote junior user doctrine?

The answer to both questions is not necessarily. While we shall study this in more detail in Chapter 4, the key to understanding why is that Congress intended the enumerated defenses in section 33(b), if established, merely to rebut the conclusive evidentiary presumptions that incontestability otherwise establishes. *See Park 'N Fly, Inc. v. Dollar Park & Fly, Inc.*, 469 U.S. 189, 199 n.6 (1985) ("Representative Lanham made his remarks to clarify that the . . . defenses enumerated in § 33(b) are not substantive rules of law which go to the validity or enforceability of an incontestable mark. 92 Cong. Rec. 7524 (1946). Instead, the defenses affect the evidentiary status of registration where the owner claims the benefit of a mark's incontestable status."). Once the evidentiary presumptions are rebutted, a junior intermediate user, such as Hoots, would presumably still need to establish its rights under the common law's remote junior user doctrine in order to defeat Burger King's infringement claim. Under this approach, the difference between the statutory language and the common law remote junior user doctrine is irrelevant, because the junior user will need to establish the elements of both in order to prevail.

Some courts, however, have suggested that satisfying section 33(b)(5) does more than merely rebut the registration's associated evidentiary presumptions; they have suggested that satisfying section 33(b)(5) establishes a substantive defense to a charge of infringement. *See, e.g., Members First Fed. Credit Union v. Members 1st Fed. Credit Union*, 54 F.2d Supp. 393, 408–09 (M.D. Pa. 1999) (suggesting that section 33(b) constitutes a substantive defense to infringement independent of the common law's remote junior user defense, but finding that the defendant lacked good faith in any event). Under such an approach, the differences between section 33(b)(5) and the common law doctrine become crucial.

2. *The Senior Unregistered User Case.* In *Burger King v. Hoots*, the senior user was also the first to register the mark federally, but this is not always the case. Sometimes, the junior user registers the mark first. We refer to such a fact pattern as a senior unregistered user. In such a case, where the registration has become incontestable, subsection (b)(5) does not, by its express language, apply. Can you see why? One court that could not was *Natural Footwear Ltd. v. Hart, Schaffner & Marx*, 760 F.2d 1383 (3d Cir.) (mistakenly resolving the rights of a senior unregistered user under section 33(b)(5)), *cert. denied*, 474 U.S. 920 (1985). In addition to falling outside the language of section 33(b)(5), a defense allowing continued use by a senior

unregistered user is not otherwise set forth as one of the nine enumerated defenses in section 33(b). Does this mean that a senior unregistered user may not successfully challenge the conclusive presumption of an exclusive right to use otherwise held by a junior, but incontestably registered user?

The answer is no. In addition to the nine enumerated defenses set forth in section 33(b), section 33(b) also incorporates by reference limitations on incontestability set forth in section 15. *See* 15 U.S.C. § 1115(b) (2015) ("To the extent that the right to use has become incontestable under section 1065 of this title, the registration shall be conclusive evidence of the . . . registrant's exclusive right to use. . . ."). Under section 15 of the Act, codified as section 1065 in Title 15 of the United States Code, the junior user's registration is not incontestable "to the extent, if any, to which the use of a mark registered on the principal register infringes a valid right acquired under the law of any State or Territory by use of a mark or trade name continuing from a date prior to the date of registration . . . of such registered mark." 15 U.S.C. § 1065 (2015). How does this provision, and the corresponding rights of the senior unregistered user, differ from section 1115(b)(5) and the rights of the junior intermediate user?

Both provisions effectively confine the unregistered party to a given territory once another's federal registration becomes incontestable. However, the statutory language creates two possible distinctions between the two cases. First, in terms of timing, once the junior party's registration becomes incontestable, the senior unregistered user is confined to a given territory as of the junior user's registration date. When Congress added the ITU provisions to the Act, Congress did not amend the timing rule in the senior unregistered user case to account for section 1057(c)'s backdated constructive use. In contrast, Congress did amend the timing rule for the junior intermediate user. Thus, for cases involving use that begins after the effective date of the 1988 amendments, when the senior user's registration becomes incontestable, the junior intermediate user will be confined to its area of use as of the senior user's application date.

Second, in addition to this timing difference, the two provisions also define the territory of the unregistered user in somewhat different terms. For the junior intermediate user, section 33(b)(5) defines the territory as "that area in which such continuous prior use is proved." 15 U.S.C. § 1115(b)(5) (2015). In contrast, section 15 defines the senior unregistered user's territory as the area in which the junior registrant's use would infringe the senior unregistered user's preexisting state law trademark rights. 15 U.S.C. § 1065 (2015). Given the difference in language, several potential differences in geographic scope arise.

For example, does an unregistered user have rights to an area in which it advertised, but had no, or only limited, sales before the critical date? Similarly, does an unregistered user have rights to an area in which it has only intermittent or occasional sales before the critical date? As we saw in Chapter 2, advertising alone ordinarily does not count as use for purposes of priority. Moreover, section 33(b)(5) requires "continuous prior use." As a result, neither advertising alone, nor occasional sales, may count as use for purposes of section 33(b)(5). For example, in *Thrifty Rent-A-Car System, Inc. v. Thrift Cars, Inc.*, a junior intermediate user operated a custom rental car service from its owner's home in East Taunton, Massachusetts. 639 F.Supp. 750, 751–52 (D. Mass. 1986), *aff'd*, 831 F.2d 1177 (1st Cir. 1987). The junior intermediate user advertised both in local Taunton papers, as well as newspapers with a broader geographic circulation. The junior intermediate user also delivered rental cars, on occasion, to customers in Boston, Providence, and Nantucket. *Id.* Yet, the district court defined the junior intermediate user's area of use to encompass only East Taunton, Massachusetts. *Id.* at 756. In reaching that conclusion, the district court held that advertising alone did not establish use for purposes of section 33(b)(5), and further held that occasional rentals did not constitute "continuous use." *Id.* Nonetheless, the district court held that the junior intermediate user could continue advertising in the newspapers it had been advertising as of the senior user's registration date, even though some of those papers circulated beyond the East Taunton area. Is allowing such advertising to continue consistent with the court's definition of the junior intermediate user's area?

In contrast, the senior unregistered user does not have to demonstrate use in a given area. It only has to demonstrate that allowing use by the junior user in a given area would infringe the senior unregistered user's state law rights. The key issue under section 15 then is whether the senior user is sufficiently well-known in a given area that allowing the junior user to use the mark in that area would create a likelihood of confusion. Advertising in an area, together with sales in a nearby area, or sporadic sales in an area will therefore establish a senior unregistered user's rights to a given so long as there is enough of either to create a likelihood of confusion. In addition, even in the absence of a likelihood of confusion, a senior unregistered user may also be able to claim a given geographic area if it falls within her reasonable zone of expansion, if the state law at issue recognizes that doctrine.

3. *The Timing of Good Faith.* What if a junior user begins use in good faith in a separate and remote geographic area, but then subsequently learns of a senior user? May the junior user expand its business operations into territory as yet unoccupied by either party, or is any expansion after the junior user learns of the senior user in bad faith? *See Weiner King, Inc. v. Wiener King Corp.*, 615 F.2d 512, 523 (C.C.P.A. 1980) (holding that so long as junior user begins use in good faith, it may expand its operations into open territory even after it learns of senior user).

4. *Concurrent Use Proceedings.* The confining effects of both section 1065 for the senior unregistered user and section 1115(b)(5) for the junior intermediate user come into play only if the registration at issue has become incontestable. To avoid these provisions and the resulting confinement, a party may seek a concurrent registration. The right to a concurrent registration arises under section 1052(d) where two parties both have valid rights to a trademark, but in different geographic areas. Where one of the

parties has already registered the mark federally, the other may initiate a concurrent use proceeding by applying for its own registration. Under section 1052(d), concurrent registrations are permissible if the second applicant alleges first use prior to the effective date of the other party's registration or with the written consent of the first registrant.

In a concurrent use proceeding, rather than confine the second registrant to its preexisting territory, the Patent and Trademark Office will consider *inter alia* "each party's (1) previous business activity; (2) previous expansion or lack thereof; (3) dominance of contiguous areas; (4) presently-planned expansion; and, where applicable (5) possible market penetration by means of products brought in from other areas" in determining the respective geographic scope of the concurrent registrations. *Weiner King, Inc. v. Wiener King Corp.*, 615 F.2d 512, 523 (C.C.P.A. 1980). Courts follow a similar approach to allocating geographic territories in cases where neither party has registered its mark federally, or where the federal registrations are not yet incontestable.

C. INTERNATIONAL USE AND DOMESTIC RIGHTS

1. FOREIGN USE AND RIGHTS WITHIN THE UNITED STATES

PERSON'S CO., LTD. v. CHRISTMAN
900 F.2d 1565 (Fed. Cir. 1990)

SMITH, CIRCUIT JUDGE

Person's Co., Ltd. appeals from the decision of the Patent and Trademark Office Trademark Trial and Appeal Board (Board) which granted summary judgment in favor of Larry Christman and ordered the cancellation of appellant's registration for the mark "PERSON'S" for various apparel items. Appellant Person's Co. seeks cancellation of Christman's registration for the mark "PERSON'S" for wearing apparel on the following grounds: likelihood of confusion based on its prior foreign use, abandonment, and unfair competition within the meaning of the Paris Convention. We affirm the Board's decision.

Background

The facts pertinent to this appeal are as follows: In 1977, Takaya Iwasaki first applied a stylized logo bearing the name "PERSON'S" to clothing in his native Japan. Two years later Iwasaki formed Person's Co., Ltd., a Japanese corporation, to market and distribute the clothing items in retail stores located in Japan.

In 1981, Larry Christman, a U.S. citizen and employee of a sportswear wholesaler, visited a Person's Co. retail store while on a business trip to Japan. Christman purchased several clothing items bearing the "PERSON'S" logo and returned with them to the United States. After consulting with legal counsel and being advised that no one had yet established a claim to the logo in the United States, Christman developed designs for his own "PERSON'S" brand sportswear line based on appellant's products he had purchased in Japan. In February 1982, Christman contracted with a clothing manufacturer to produce clothing articles with the "PERSON'S" logo attached. These clothing items were sold, beginning in April 1982, to sportswear retailers in the northwestern United States. Christman formed Team Concepts, Ltd., a Washington corporation, in May 1983 to continue merchandising his sportswear line, which had expanded to include additional articles such as shoulder bags. All the sportswear marketed by Team Concepts bore either the mark "PERSON'S" or a copy of appellant's globe logo; many of the clothing styles were apparently copied directly from appellant's designs.

In April 1983, Christman filed an application for U.S. trademark registration in an effort to protect the "PERSON'S" mark. Christman believed himself to be the exclusive owner of the right to use and register the mark in the United States and apparently had no knowledge that appellant soon intended to introduce its similar sportswear line under the identical mark in the U.S. market. Christman's registration issued in September 1984 for use on wearing apparel.

In the interim between Christman's first sale and the issuance of his registration, Person's Co., Ltd. became a well known and highly respected force in the Japanese fashion industry. The company, which had previously sold garments under the "PERSON'S" mark only in Japan, began implementing its plan to sell goods under this mark in the United States. According to Mr. Iwasaki, purchases by buyers for resale in the United States occurred as early as November 1982. This was some seven months subsequent to Christman's first sales in the United States. Person's Co. filed an application for U.S. trademark registration in the following year, and, in 1985, engaged an export trading company to introduce its goods into the U.S. market. The registration for the mark "PERSON'S" issued in August 1985 for use on luggage, clothing and accessories. After recording U.S. sales near 4 million dollars in 1985, Person's Co. granted California distributor Zip Zone International a license to manufacture and sell goods under the "PERSON'S" mark in the United States.

In early 1986, appellant's advertising in the U.S. became known to Christman and both parties became aware of confusion in the marketplace. Person's Co. initiated an action to cancel Christman's registration on the following grounds: (1) likelihood of confusion; (2) abandonment; and (3) unfair competition within the meaning of the Paris Convention. Christman counterclaimed and asserted prior use and likelihood of confusion as grounds for cancellation of the Person's Co. registration.

After some discovery, Christman filed a motion with the Board for summary judgment on all counts. In a well reasoned decision, the Board held for Christman on the grounds that Person's use of the mark in Japan could not be used to establish priority against a "good faith" senior user in U.S. commerce. The Board found no evidence to suggest that the "PERSON'S" mark had acquired any notoriety in this country at the time of its adoption by Christman. Therefore, appellant had no reputation or goodwill upon which Christman could have intended to trade, rendering the unfair competition provisions of the Paris Convention inapplicable. . . .

The Board held in its opinion on reconsideration that Christman had not adopted the mark in bad faith despite his appropriation of a mark in use by appellant in a foreign country. The Board adopted the view that copying a mark in use in a foreign country is not in bad faith unless the foreign mark is famous in the United States or the copying is undertaken for the purpose of interfering with the prior user's planned expansion into the United States. Person's Co. appeals and requests that this court direct the Board to enter summary judgment in its favor.

Issues

1.   Does knowledge of a mark's use outside U.S. commerce preclude good faith adoption and use of the identical mark in the United States prior to the entry of the foreign user into the domestic market?

. . .

Priority

The first ground asserted for cancellation in the present action is § 2(d) of the Lanham Act; each party claims prior use of registered marks which unquestionably are confusingly similar and affixed to similar goods. *See* 15 U.S.C. § 1052(d) (1987).

Section 1 of the Lanham Act states that "the owner of a trademark *used in commerce* may register his trademark. . . ." 15 U.S.C. § 1051 (1976) (emphasis added). The term "commerce" is defined in Section 45 of the Act as ". . . all commerce which may be lawfully regulated by Congress." 15 U.S.C. § 1127 (1982). No specific Constitutional language gives Congress power to regulate trademarks, so the power of the federal government to provide for trademark registration comes only under its commerce power. The term "used in commerce" in the Lanham Act refers to a sale or transportation of goods bearing the mark in or having an effect on: (1) United States interstate commerce; (2) United States commerce with foreign nations; or (3) United States commerce with the Indian Tribes. U.S. Const. art. I, § 8, cl. 3; *The Trademark Cases*, 100 U.S.

82 (1879); 1 J. McCarthy, *Trademarks and Unfair Competition* § 5:3 (1973).

In the present case, appellant Person's Co. relies on its use of the mark in Japan in an attempt to support its claim for priority in the United States. Such foreign use has no effect on U.S. commerce and cannot form the basis for a holding that appellant has priority here. *See, e.g., Fuji Photo Film Co. v. Shinohara Shoji Kabushiki Kaisha*, 754 F.2d 591, 599 (5th Cir. 1985); *Scholastic, Inc. v. Macmillan, Inc.*, 650 F. Supp. 866, 873 n. 6 (S.D.N.Y. 1987); *Techex, Ltd. v. Dvorkovitz*, 220 U.S.P.Q. (BNA) 81, 83 (TTAB 1983). The concept of territoriality is basic to trademark law; trademark rights exist in each country solely according to that country's statutory scheme. *Fuji Photo Film*, 754 F.2d at 599 (*citing Ingenohl v. Olsen & Co.*, 273 U.S. 541, 544 (1927)). Christman was the first to use the mark in United States commerce and the first to obtain a federal registration thereon. Appellant has no basis upon which to claim priority and is the junior user under these facts.[16]

Bad Faith

Appellant vigorously asserts that Christman's adoption and use of the mark in the United States subsequent to Person's Co.'s adoption in Japan is tainted with "bad faith" and that the priority in the United States obtained thereby is insufficient to establish rights superior to those arising from Person's Co.'s prior adoption in a foreign country. Relying on *Woman's World Shops, Inc. v. Lane Bryant, Inc.*, 5 U.S.P.Q. 2D (BNA) 1985 (TTAB 1988), Person's Co. argues that a "remote junior user" of a mark obtains no right superior to the "senior user" if the "junior user" has adopted the mark with knowledge of the "senior user's" prior use.[18] In *Woman's World*, the senior user utilized the mark within a limited geographical area. A junior user from a different geographical area of the United States sought unrestricted federal registration for a nearly identical mark, with the exception to its virtually exclusive rights being those of the known senior user. The Board held that such an appropriation with knowledge failed to satisfy the good faith requirements of the Lanham Act and denied the concurrent use rights

---

[16] Section 44 of the Lanham Act, 15 U.S.C. § 1126 (1982), permits qualified foreign applicants who own a registered mark in their country of origin to obtain a U.S. trademark registration without alleging actual use in U.S. commerce. If a U.S. application is filed within six months of the filing of the foreign application, such U.S. registration will be accorded the same force and effect as if filed in the United States on the same date on which the application was first filed in the foreign country. The statutory scheme set forth in § 44 is in place to lower barriers to entry and assist foreign applicants in establishing business goodwill in the United States. Person's Co. does not assert rights under § 44, which if properly applied, might have been used to secure priority over Christman.

[18] Appellant repeatedly makes reference to a "world economy" and considers Christman to be the remote junior user of the mark. Although Person's did adopt the mark in Japan prior to Christman's use in United States commerce, the use in Japan cannot be relied upon to acquire U.S. trademark rights. Christman is the senior user as that term is defined under U.S. trademark law.

sought by the junior user. *Id.* at 1988. Person's Co. cites *Woman's World* for the proposition that a junior user's adoption and use of a mark with knowledge of another's prior use constitutes bad faith. It is urged that this principle is equitable in nature and should not be limited to knowledge of use within the territory of the United States.

While the facts of the present case are analogous to those in *Woman's World*, the case is distinguishable in one significant respect. In *Woman's World*, the first use of the mark by both the junior and senior users was in United States commerce. In the case at bar, appellant Person's Co., while first to adopt the mark, was not the first user in the United States. Christman is the senior user, and we are aware of no case where a senior user has been charged with bad faith. The concept of bad faith adoption applies to remote junior users seeking concurrent use registrations; in such cases, the likelihood of customer confusion in the remote area may be presumed from proof of the junior user's knowledge. *See* 2 J. McCarthy, *Trademarks and Unfair Competition* § 26:4 (2d ed. 1984); Restatement of Torts § 732 comment a (1938). In the present case, when Christman initiated use of the mark, Person's Co. had not yet entered U.S. commerce. The Person's Co. had no goodwill in the United States and the "PERSON'S" mark had no reputation here. Appellant's argument ignores the territorial nature of trademark rights.

Appellant next asserts that Christman's knowledge of its prior use of the mark in Japan should preclude his acquisition of superior trademark rights in the United States. The Board found that, at the time of registration, Christman was not aware of appellant's intention to enter the U.S. clothing and accessories market in the future. Christman obtained a trademark search on the "PERSON'S" mark and an opinion of competent counsel that the mark was "available" in the United States. Since Appellant had taken no steps to secure registration of the mark in the United States, Christman was aware of no basis for Person's Co. to assert superior rights to use and registration here. Appellant would have us infer bad faith adoption because of Christman's awareness of its use of the mark in Japan, but an inference of bad faith requires something more than mere knowledge of prior use of a similar mark in a foreign country. *Cf. Sweats Fashions, Inc. v. Pannill Knitting Co.*, 833 F.2d 1560, 1565 (Fed.Cir. 1987).

As the Board noted below, Christman's prior use in U.S. commerce cannot be discounted solely because he was aware of appellant's use of the mark in Japan. While adoption of a mark with knowledge of a prior actual *user* in U.S. commerce may give rise to cognizable equities as between the parties, no such equities may be based upon knowledge of a similar mark's existence or on a problematical intent to use such a similar mark in the future. *Sweats Fashions*, 833 F.2d at 1565; *Selfway, Inc. v. Travelers Petroleum, Inc.*, 579 F.2d 75, 79 (CCPA 1978). Knowledge of a foreign use does not preclude good faith adoption and use in the United States. While there is some case law supporting a finding of bad faith where (1) the foreign mark is famous here or (2) the use is a nominal one made solely to block the prior foreign user's planned expansion into the United States, as the Board correctly found, neither of these circumstances is present in this case. *See, e.g., Vaudable v. Montmartre, Inc.*, 20 Misc. 2d 757 (N.Y.Sup.Ct. 1959); *Mother's Restaurants, Inc. v. Mother's Other Kitchen, Inc.*, 218 U.S.P.Q. (BNA) 1046 (TTAB 1983); *See also Davidoff Extension, S.A. v. Davidoff Int'l*, 221 U.S.P.Q. (BNA) 465 (S.D.Fla. 1983).

We agree with the Board's conclusion that Christman's adoption and use of the mark were in good faith. Christman's adoption of the mark occurred at a time when appellant had not yet entered U.S. commerce; therefore, no prior user was in place to give Christman notice of appellant's potential U.S. rights. Christman's conduct in appropriating and using appellant's mark in a market where he believed the Japanese manufacturer did not compete can hardly be considered unscrupulous commercial conduct. *See Bulk Mfg. Co. v. Schoenbach Prod. Co.*, 208 U.S.P.Q. (BNA) 664, 667–68 (S.D.N.Y. 1980). Christman adopted the trademark being used by appellant in Japan, but appellant has not identified any aspect of U.S. trademark law violated by such action. Trademark rights under the Lanham Act arise solely out of use of the mark in U.S. commerce or from ownership of a foreign registration thereon; "the law pertaining to registration of trademarks does not regulate all aspects of business morality." *Selfway*, 579 F.2d at 79, 198 USPQ at 275. When the law has been crafted with the clarity of crystal, it also has the qualities of a glass slipper: it cannot be shoe-horned onto facts it does not fit, no matter how appealing they might appear.

The Paris Convention

Appellant next claims that Christman's adoption and use of the "PERSON'S" mark in the United States constitutes unfair competition under Articles 6*bis* and 10*bis* of the Paris Convention. *Paris Convention for the Protection of Industrial Property*, 21 U.S.T. 1628, T.I.A.S. No. 6923 (1967). It is well settled that the Trademark Trial and Appeal Board cannot adjudicate unfair competition issues in a cancellation or opposition proceeding. *See Knickerbocker Toy Co. v. Faultless Starch Co.*, 467 F.2d 501, 509 (CCPA 1972). The Board's function is to determine whether there is a right to secure or to maintain a registration. *Wallpaper Mfrs., Ltd. v. Crown Wallcovering Corp.*, 680 F.2d 755, 767 (CCPA 1982). . . .

Conclusion

In *United Drug Co. v. Rectanus Co.*, 248 U.S. 90 (1918), the Supreme Court of the United States determined that "there is no such thing as property in a trademark except as a right appurtenant to an established business or trade in connection with which the mark is employed. . . . Its function is simply to designate the goods as the product of a particular trader and to protect his goodwill against the sale of another's product as his; and it is not the subject of property except in connection with an existing business." *Id.* at 97. In the present case, appellant failed to secure protection for its mark through use in U.S. commerce; therefore, no established business or product line was in place from which trademark rights could arise. Christman was the first to use the mark in U.S. commerce. This first use was not tainted with bad faith by Christman's mere knowledge of appellant's prior foreign use, so the Board's conclusion on the issue of priority was correct. Appellant also raises no factual dispute which is material to the resolution of the issue of abandonment. Accordingly, the grant of summary judgment was entirely in order, and the Board's decision is affirmed.

AFFIRMED.

NOTES FOR DISCUSSION

1.   *The Territoriality Principle.* Judge Leval of the Southern District of New York has offered the following explanation of, and for, the territoriality principle:

> [A] trademark has a separate legal existence under each country's laws, and that its proper lawful function is not necessarily to specify the origin or manufacture of a good (although it may incidentally do that), but rather to symbolize the domestic goodwill of the domestic markholder so that the consuming public may rely with an expectation of consistency on the domestic reputation earned for the mark by its owner, and the owner of the mark may be confident that his goodwill and reputation (the value of the mark) will not be injured through use of the mark by others in domestic commerce.

Osawa & Co. v. B & H Photo, 589 F.Supp. 1163, 1171–72 (S.D.N.Y. 1984).

As traditionally applied, the territoriality principle would mean that the Person's Co. could not sue Christman for his use in the United States based upon the Person's Co.'s prior use and ownership of the same trademark in Japan. What are the justifications for the traditional territoriality principle?

The simplest justification for the rule historically is the same justification that we saw in *United Drug*. We protect and recognize ownership of trademarks when a person has used the mark with respect to specific goods in a given geographic area because consumers in that area have come to rely on the mark to identify a product's source. If a person is using a mark in Massachusetts, but not in Kentucky, then she has rights in the mark in Massachusetts, where consumers have come to know the mark, but not in Kentucky, where the consumers have not. If someone else is the first to use in Kentucky and build up consumer recognition of the mark in that state, then he has rights to the mark in that state.

If that principle holds within the United States, indeed even within a single state, why shouldn't it hold with respect to foreign uses as well? If the same mark can mean different things to consumers in Massachusetts and Kentucky based upon who has used it in each state, it can certainly mean different things in Japan and the United States, based upon who has used it in each.

2.   *Application or Extension of the Doctrine?* Does the *Person's Co.* court merely apply the territoriality principle or does it extend it? Person's is not suing to stop Christman's use in the United States based upon Person's prior use in Japan. Rather, it is arguing that Christman cannot acquire rights to the mark because he began his use with knowledge of Person's prior use. How does the court address this argument? If Person's had prevailed on its argument, that would have barred Christman from registering, or otherwise obtaining ownership rights in, the mark. Would it have enabled Person's to sue to enjoin Christman's use as well?

In *United Drug*, if the Theodore Rectanus Co. had known of United Drug's prior use in Massachusetts, could it have acquired rights in Rexall in Kentucky? Why do we treat these two situations differently? Is it that the borders of the United States mark, in some sense, the reach of its law? Or is it that both Kentucky and Massachusetts are states within a union, while the United States and Japan are not? In answering these questions, keep in mind that there was no "United States" law on trademarks for unregistered marks at the time of the *United Drug* decision. As the Court notes, the applicable law was that of the states of Kentucky and Massachusetts. If the law of the state of Kentucky, which presumably extends only to its borders, can recognize knowledge of a mark's use in Massachusetts as relevant to ownership of the mark in Kentucky, why can't the law of the United States recognize similar knowledge of a mark's use in Japan as relevant to ownership of the mark in the United States? In either case, we are not looking at the extraterritorial enforcement of a given state's law, so presumably principles of international comity and jurisdiction do not come into play. Neither Massachusetts nor Japan is trying to tell Kentucky or the United States, respectively, who should own a given trademark within Kentucky or the United States. Rather, in each case, the relevant jurisdiction, whether the law of Kentucky in *United Drug* or that of the United States in *Person's Co.*, is deciding for itself whether to consider the junior user's knowledge of a use outside its borders as relevant in assigning ownership of the trademark within its borders. Why should the law of Kentucky consider knowledge of a use outside its borders as relevant, while the law of the United States does not?

3.   *Inroads on the Territoriality Principle: Use.* While the territoriality principle remains important, as world markets have become more integrated, courts have sought to narrow the principle's reach. For example, what if an individual is using the mark only in foreign countries, but advertises its goods or services in the United States? Does that count as a domestic use? *See International Bancorp, L.L.C. v. Societe des Bains de Mer et du Cercle des*

Estrangers a Monaco, 329 F.3d 359 (4th Cir. 2003) (yes), *cert. denied*, 540 U.S. 1106 (2004).

4. *Further Inroads: The "Well-Known" or Famous Marks Doctrine.* The first major international treaty that covered trademarks was the Paris Convention of 1883. In article 6*bis*, the Convention requires each signatory nation to "refuse or to cancel the registration, and prohibit the use, of a trademark" which creates confusion with a foreign mark, which while not in use domestically, is nonetheless already well-known in that country. Paris Convention for the Protection of Industrial Property, art. 6*bis* (1883). While the United States is a signatory of the Paris Convention, the Convention is not self-executing. We must therefore look to the Trademark Act, at the federal level, and to the common and statutory law of the states to determine the extent to which the United States has implemented its obligations under the Convention.

In this regard, in *Person's Co.*, the Federal Circuit holds that, despite the language of article 6*bis*, Congress has not authorized the Patent and Trademark Office to deny registration for a domestic mark even if the mark is already well-known in the United States as a result of another party's foreign use. The Federal Circuit suggests that Person's may have a remedy against Christman for his use of the mark under principles of unfair competition, but holds that the availability of an unfair competition claim is not relevant to determining whether Christman is entitled to registration.

Both the Ninth and Second Circuits have addressed whether the unfair competition provision found in section 43(a) of the Lanham Trademark Act incorporates protection for "well-known" or famous foreign marks, but they have reached differing conclusions. In 2004, the Ninth Circuit in *Grupo Gigante S.A. De C.V. v. Dallo & Co.*, 391 F.3d 1088 (9th Cir. 2004), held that the Trademark Act of 1946 incorporated protection in section 43(a) for foreign marks that were famous within the United States, even if not in actual use in the United States. However, three years later, in *ITC Ltd. v. Punchgini, Inc.*, 482 F.3d 135 (2d Cir.), *cert. denied*, 552 U.S. 827 (2007), the Second Circuit held that the Trademark Act did not. Section 43(a) of the Trademark Act, the Second Circuit explained, extends protection only to marks that are "use[d] in commerce" within the United States.

Although the Second Circuit refused to protect well-known, foreign marks under the Trademark Act, it certified to the New York Court of Appeals the question whether New York state law provided such protection. The New York court held that it did. *See ITC Ltd. v. Punchgini, Inc.*, 9 N.Y.3d 467, 850 N.Y.S.2d 366, 880 N.E.2d 852 (2007). Can you think of any foreign marks, where the associated goods or services are not for sale in the United States, but the mark is nonetheless well known here?

5. *Federal Registration Based upon Foreign Registration: Section 44.* As the *Person's Co.* court notes, section 44 of the Trademark Act allows a foreign trademark owner to seek registration in the United States based upon a foreign registration. Section 44(e) expressly permits such registration even

where the foreign owner has not used the mark in commerce within the United States. 15 U.S.C. § 1126(e) (2015). Section 44(e) does require, however, that the applicant have a "bona fide intention to use the mark in commerce." 15 U.S.C. § 1126(e) (2015).

While section 44 allows for the registration of foreign marks, the foreign owner must begin use within the United States within a few years to maintain its registration. Section 44(f) expressly provides that "the duration, validity or transfer . . . of such registration shall be governed by the provisions of this chapter." 15 U.S.C. § 1126(f) (2015). As we shall study in more detail in Chapter 9, ownership of a trademark will end under the Act if the owner abandons the mark. Under the Trademark Act, "[a] mark shall be deemed 'abandoned' . . . when its use has been discontinued with intent not to resume such use." 15 U.S.C. § 1127 (2015). The Act further provides that "[n]onuse for 3 consecutive years shall be prima facie evidence of abandonment." *Id.* While a foreign trademark owner can rebut this prima facie evidence, by proving that it intends to begin use in the United States, if it does not begin actual use in the United States within a reasonable time period, then sooner or later, a section 44 registration will be deemed abandoned for lack of domestic use. *See Rivard v. Linville*, 133 F.3d 1446 (Fed. Cir. 1998) (affirming cancellation of mark registered under section 44 where owner did not begin use of mark within the United States for five years and could not demonstrate intent to begin such use). As a result, section 44, while it allows for the domestic registration of foreign marks, effectively provides only a few years' grace period in which domestic use must begin.

6   *The Madrid Protocol.* In 2002, the United States also became a signatory to a second treaty intended to facilitate the international protection of trademarks, the Madrid Protocol. Implemented through the Madrid Protocol Implementation Act in November 2002, Pub. L. No. 273, 107th Cong., 1st Sess., §§ 13401–13403, 116 Stat. 1758, *codified at* 15 U.S.C. §§ 1141–1141n (2015), the Madrid Protocol simplifies the process of obtaining protection for a mark in other countries. It establishes an International Register for trademarks under the auspices of the World Intellectual Property Organization ("WIPO"). Rather than require a trademark owner to register a mark in each country in which protection is sought, the Protocol allows natural and juristic persons who own a registered trademark in any one signatory country to register such trademarks on the International Register. With such an international registration, the trademark owner may then request an extension of protection for its trademark to any other Madrid Protocol country.

While this simplifies the process of obtaining protection in other countries, a foreign trademark owner who seeks rights in the United States will still need to use its mark in the United States in order to maintain protection. Just as under section 44, a foreign trademark owner who requests an extension of protection to the United States under the Madrid Protocol must verify that it has a "bona fide intention to use the mark in commerce" within the United States. 15 U.S.C. § 1141f(a) (2015). Similarly, just as under section 44, a request for extension of protection "shall not be refused on the ground that the mark has not been used in commerce." 15 U.S.C. § 1141h(a)(3) (2015). Through these two provisions, the Madrid Protocol, just like section 44, allows foreign trademark owners to extend protection of their marks to the United States, without having used their marks in the United States.

However, just as under section 44, an extension of protection under the Madrid Protocol "shall have the same effect and validity as a registration on the principal register." 15 U.S.C. § 1141i (2015). As a result, while a foreign owner can obtain an extension of protection under the Madrid Protocol without use in the United States, if it does not begin such use, sooner or later, its extension of protection under the Madrid Protocol will be deemed abandoned.

2.   PARALLEL IMPORTS

K MART CORP. v. CARTIER, INC.
486 U.S. 281 (1988)

KENNEDY, J.

A gray-market good is a foreign-manufactured good, bearing a valid United States trademark, that is imported without the consent of the United States trademark holder. These cases present the issue whether the Secretary of the Treasury's regulation permitting the importation of certain gray-market goods, 19 CFR § 133.21 (1987), is a reasonable agency interpretation of § 526 of the Tariff Act of 1930 (1930 Tariff Act), 46 Stat. 741, as amended, 19 U.S.C. § 1526.

I

A

The gray market arises in any of three general contexts. The prototypical gray-market victim (case 1) is a domestic firm that purchases from an independent foreign firm the rights to register and use the latter's trademark as a United States trademark and to sell its foreign-manufactured products here. Especially where the foreign firm has already registered the trademark in the United States or where the product has already earned a reputation for quality, the right to use that trademark can be very valuable. If the foreign manufacturer could import the trademarked goods and distribute them here, despite having sold the trademark to a domestic firm, the domestic firm would be forced into sharp intrabrand competition involving the very trademark it purchased. Similar intrabrand competition could arise if the foreign manufacturer markets its wares outside the United States, as is often the case, and a third party who purchases them abroad could legally import them. In either event, the parallel importation, if permitted to proceed, would create a gray market that could jeopardize the trademark holder's investment.

The second context (case 2) is a situation in which a domestic firm registers the United States trademark for goods that are manufactured abroad by an affiliated manufacturer. In its most common variation (case 2a), a foreign firm wishes to control distribution of its wares in this country by incorporating a subsidiary here. The subsidiary then registers under its own name (or the manufacturer assigns to the subsidiary's name) a United States trademark that is identical to its parent's foreign trademark. The parallel importation by a third party who buys the goods abroad (or conceivably even by the affiliated foreign manufacturer itself) creates a gray market. Two other variations on this theme occur when an American-based firm establishes abroad a manufacturing subsidiary corporation (case 2b) or its own unincorporated manufacturing division (case 2c) to produce its United States trademarked goods, and then imports them for domestic distribution. If the trademark holder or its foreign subsidiary sells the trademarked goods abroad, the parallel importation of the goods competes on the gray market with the holder's domestic sales.

In the third context (case 3), the domestic holder of a United States trademark *authorizes* an independent foreign manufacturer to use it. Usually the holder sells to the foreign manufacturer an exclusive right to use the trademark in a particular foreign location, but conditions the right on the foreign manufacturer's promise not to import its trademarked goods into the United States. Once again, if the foreign manufacturer or a third party imports into the United States, the foreign-manufactured goods will compete on the gray market with the holder's domestic goods.

B

Until 1922, the Federal Government did not regulate the importation of gray-market goods, not even to protect the investment of an independent purchaser of a foreign trademark, and not even in the extreme case where the independent foreign manufacturer breached its agreement to refrain from direct competition with the purchaser. That year, however, Congress was spurred to action by a Court of Appeals decision declining to enjoin the parallel importation of goods bearing a trademark that (as in case 1) a domestic company had purchased from an independent foreign manufacturer at a premium. See *A. Bourjois & Co.* v. *Katzel*, 275 F. 539 (CA2 1921), *rev'd*, 260 U.S. 689, 43 S.Ct. 244, 67 L.Ed. 464 (1923).

In an immediate response to *Katzel*, Congress enacted § 526 of the Tariff Act of 1922, 42 Stat. 975. That provision, later reenacted in identical form as § 526 of the 1930 Tariff Act, 19 U.S.C. § 1526, prohibits importing

> into the United States any merchandise of foreign manufacture if such merchandise . . . bears a trademark owned by a citizen of, or by a corporation or association created or organized within, the United States, and registered in the Patent and Trademark Office by a person domiciled in the United States . . . , unless written consent of the owner of such trademark is produced at the time of making entry.

19 U.S.C. § 1526(a).

The regulations implementing § 526 for the past 50 years have not applied the prohibition to all gray-market goods. The Customs Service regulation now in force provides generally that "foreign-made articles bearing a trademark identical with one owned and recorded by a citizen of the United States or a corporation or association created or organized within the United States are subject to seizure and forfeiture as prohibited importations." But the regulation furnishes a "common-control" exception from the ban, permitting the entry of gray-market goods manufactured abroad by the trademark owner or its affiliate:

> "(c) *Restrictions not applicable.* The restrictions . . . do not apply to imported articles when:

>> "(1) Both the foreign and the U.S. trademark or trade name are owned by the same person or business entity; [or]

>> "(2) The foreign and domestic trademark or trade name owners are parent and subsidiary companies or are otherwise subject to common ownership or control. . . ."

The Customs Service regulation further provides an "authorized-use" exception, which permits importation of gray-market goods where

>> "(3) the articles of foreign manufacture bear a recorded trademark or trade name applied under authorization of the U.S. owner. . . ."

19 CFR § 133.21(c) (1987).

Respondents, an association of United States trademark holders and two of its members, brought suit in Federal District Court in February 1984, seeking both a declaration that the Customs Service regulation, 19 CFR §§ 133.21(c)(1)–(3) (1987), is invalid and an injunction against its enforcement. *Coalition to Preserve the Integrity of American Trademarks* v. *United States*, 598 F. Supp. 844 (DC 1984). They asserted that the common-control and authorized-use exceptions are inconsistent with § 526 of the 1930 Tariff Act. Petitioners K mart and 47th Street Photo intervened as defendants.

The District Court upheld the Customs Service regulation, 598 F. Supp. at 853, but the Court of Appeals reversed, *Coalition to Preserve the Integrity of American Trademarks* v. *United States*, 252 U.S. App. D.C. 342, 790 F.2d 903 (1986) (hereinafter *COPIAT*), holding that the Customs Service regulation was an unreasonable administrative interpretation of § 526. We granted certiorari, 479 U.S. 1005 (1986), to resolve a conflict among the Courts of Appeals. *Compare Vivitar Corp.* v. *United States*, 761 F.2d 1552, 1557–1560 (CA Fed. 1985), aff'g 593 F. Supp. 420 (Ct. Int'l Trade 1984), cert. denied, 474 U.S. 1055 (1986); and *Olympus Corp.* v. *United States*, 792 F.2d 315, 317–319 (CA2 1986), *aff'g* 627 F. Supp. 911 (EDNY 1985), cert. pending, No. 86–757, with *COPIAT, supra*, at 346–355, 790 F.2d at 907–916. In an earlier opinion, we affirmed the Court of Appeals' conclusion that the District Court had jurisdiction, and set the cases for reargument on the merits. 485 U.S. 176 (1988).

A majority of this Court now holds that the common-control exception of the Customs Service regulation, 19 CFR §§ 133.21(c)(1)–(2) (1987), is consistent with § 526. *See post*, at 309–310 (opinion of Brennan, J.). A different majority, however, holds that the authorized-use exception, 19 CFR § 133.21(c)(3) (1987), is inconsistent with § 526. See *post*, at 328–329 (opinion of Scalia, J.). We therefore affirm the Court of Appeals in part and reverse in part.

II

A

In determining whether a challenged regulation is valid, a reviewing court must first determine if the regulation is consistent with the language of the statute. "If the statute is clear and unambiguous 'that is the end of the matter, for the court, as well as the agency, must give effect to the unambiguously expressed intent of Congress.' . . . The traditional deference courts pay to agency interpretation is not to be applied to alter the clearly expressed intent of Congress." *Board of Governors, FRS* v. *Dimension Financial Corp.*, 474 U.S. 361, 368, 88 L.Ed.2d 691, 106 S.Ct. 681 (1986), *quoting Chevron U.S.A. Inc.* v. *Natural Resources Defense Council, Inc.*, 467 U.S. 837, 842–843, 81 L.Ed.2d 694, 104 S.Ct. 2778 (1984). In ascertaining the plain meaning of the statute, the court must look to the particular statutory language at issue, as well as the language and design of the statute as a whole. If the statute is silent or ambiguous with respect to the specific issue addressed by the regulation, the question becomes whether the agency regulation is a permissible construction of the statute. If the agency regulation is not in conflict with the plain language of the statute, a reviewing court must give deference to the agency's interpretation of the statute.

B

Following this analysis, I conclude that subsections (c)(1) and (c)(2) of the Customs Service regulation, 19 CFR §§ 133.21 (c)(1) and (c)(2) (1987), are permissible constructions designed to resolve statutory ambiguities. All Members of the Court are in agreement that the agency may interpret the statute to bar importation of gray-market goods in what we have denoted case 1 and to permit the imports under case 2a. As these writings state, "owned by" is sufficiently ambiguous, in the context of the statute, that it applies to situations involving a foreign parent, which is case 2a. This ambiguity arises from the inability to discern, from the statutory language, which of the two entities involved in case 2a can be said to "own" the United States trademark if, as in some instances, the domestic subsidiary is wholly owned by its foreign parent.

A further statutory ambiguity contained in the phrase "merchandise of foreign manufacture," suffices to sustain the regulations as they apply to cases 2b and 2c. This ambiguity parallels that of "owned by," which sustained case 2a, because it is possible to interpret "merchandise of foreign manufacture" to mean (1) goods manufactured in a foreign country, (2) goods manufactured by a foreign company, or (3) goods manufactured in a foreign country by a foreign company. Given the imprecision in the statute, the agency is entitled to choose any reasonable definition and to interpret the statute to say that goods manufactured by a foreign subsidiary or division of a domestic company are not goods "of foreign manufacture."

C

(1) Subsection (c)(3), 19 CFR § 133.21(c)(3) (1987), of the regulation, however, cannot stand. The ambiguous statutory phrases that we have already discussed, "owned by" and "merchandise of foreign manufacture," are irrelevant to the proscription contained in subsection (3) of the regulation. This subsection of the regulation denies a domestic trademark holder the power to prohibit the importation of goods made by an independent foreign manufacturer where the domestic trademark holder has authorized the foreign manufacturer to use the trademark. Under no reasonable construction of the statutory language can goods made in a foreign country by an independent foreign manufacturer be removed from the purview of the statute.

(2) The design of the regulation is such that the subsection of the regulation dealing with case 3, § 133.21(c)(3), is severable. The severance and invalidation of this subsection will not impair the function of the statute as a whole, and there is no indication that the regulation would not have been passed but for its inclusion. Accordingly, subsection (c)(3) of § 133.21 must be invalidated for its conflict with the unequivocal language of the statute.

III.

We hold that the Customs Service regulation is consistent with § 526 insofar as it exempts from the importation ban goods that are manufactured abroad by the "same person" who holds the United States trademark, 19 CFR § 133.21(c) (1) (1987), or by a person who is "subject to common . . . control" with the United States trademark holder, § 133.21(c)(2). Because the authorized-use exception of the regulation, § 133.21(c)(3), is in conflict with the plain language of the statute, that provision cannot stand. The judgment of the Court of Appeals is therefore reversed insofar as it invalidated §§ 133.21(c)(1) and (c)(2), but affirmed with respect to § 133.21(c)(3).

It is so ordered.

NOTES FOR DISCUSSION

1. *The Economics of Parallel Importation.* We begin with a basic question: Why does parallel importation occur? As a systematic activity, it occurs because there is a difference between the price for a trademarked good in one country and that in another, and that difference is sufficiently large that a person can purchase the goods at the lower price in one country, pay to ship the goods, and then resell them at the higher price in the other country, while still earning a profit. Why would such a large price differential exist? There are three possible reasons. First, the goods are identical in the two countries, but they are manufactured locally in each case and the costs of manufacturing them in each country are different. For example, labor or raw materials in one country may cost far less than in another, and so the price of the finished product is lower in that country. Second, although the same brand is used for the goods in both countries, the goods sold in the two countries are actually different. As a result of differences between consumers in the two countries, a firm may alter the taste, quality, or characteristics of its product to better match the preferences of the local consumers in each. As a result of these differences, the product may be less expensive in one country.

While these first two reasons may generate a sufficiently large price differential to make parallel importation profitable in some cases, the predominant reason for large price differentials between countries is price discrimination. In the general absence of perfect competition, a producer will, to the extent it can, charge those consumers who are willing and able to pay more for its product, a higher price. This is difficult to accomplish within a small geographic area, as the wealthier consumers can just drive a few extra miles in order to purchase the lower-priced version of the goods intended for less wealthy consumers. However, as the physical distance, and the associated shipping costs, increase, a large differential becomes easier to maintain. Moreover, if the law bars the parallel importation or reimportation of goods across certain boundaries, then large price differentials can be maintained without regard to shipping costs.

What are the policy implications of parallel importation? Should we allow parallel importation generally? How will companies respond to the legal rules that we establish? Consider the following scenario:

A company manufactures and distributes a medicine used to treat HIV/AIDS. It distributes the medicine throughout the world, charging a very high price for the medicine in the United States, a somewhat lower price in Canada and Europe (largely because of government price controls), and a much lower price in much of Africa (because of the population's inability to afford any higher price). If a third party wants to purchase the medicine in Africa at a low price, and ship it to the United States for resale at a higher price, should we allow the third party to do so?

Should it matter whether the company holds a patent on the medicine or its use? What if the company uses a trademark for the medicine? Should the third party be allowed to bring it into the United States and call it by its trademark? Should it matter whether the medicine is all manufactured in one place? What if that place is the United States? What if that place is China? What if the medicine is manufactured in different locations around the world? Should it matter whether the company itself owns each of the manufacturing plants? What if each of the manufacturing plants is owned by a separate, but affiliated corporate entity (i.e. parent-subsidiaries)? What if each of the manufacturing plants is a separate entity, but is licensed to manufacture the medicine by the company? In policy terms, what should a coherent parallel importation rule or set of rules look like? Who should we protect and to what extent?

2. *The Law.* If we focus on the Court's resolution of the parallel importation issue under the Tariff Act, the Court identifies three cases:

Case 1. A foreign firm has been using a given mark in its own country, and perhaps in the United States as well, for products that it manufactures in its own country. At some point, the foreign firm assigns rights with respect to the mark for use in the United States to a separate entity. The separate entity then registers the mark in the United States, and sells products purchased from the foreign firm under the trademark in the United States. At some point thereafter, an unrelated third party begins purchasing the same goods directly from the foreign firm and reselling them in the United States. Permissible under the Tariff Act?

Case 2. Again a domestic company has registered a mark in the United States and is importing and selling goods manufactured abroad under the mark, but there is now an affiliation (or common corporate ownership) between the domestic company and the foreign manufacturer. In Case 2a, the domestic company is a subsidiary of the foreign manufacturer. In Case 2b, the foreign manufacturer is a subsidiary of, or otherwise affiliated to, the domestic firm. In Case 2c, the foreign manufacturer is a unincorporated division of the domestic firm. For each variation, assume that an unrelated third party begins purchasing the goods abroad and seeks to import them into the United States. Permissible under the Tariff Act?

Case 3. Again a domestic company has registered a mark in the United States and is importing and selling goods from an unaffiliated company abroad who is manufacturing and branding the goods under a license from the domestic company. If an unrelated third party begins purchasing the goods abroad and seeks to import them into the United States, will such importation be permissible under the Tariff Act?

What sort of sensible policy arguments can you advance that would justify distinguishing Cases 1 and 3 from Case 2?

3. *Administrative Agencies and* Chevron *Deference.* In *K Mart*, the Court determines whether the Custom Services' regulations are permissible interpretations of the Tariff act using the now standard two-step process set forth in *Chevron U.S.A. Inc.* v. *Natural Resources Defense Council, Inc.*, 467 U.S. 837, 842–843 (1984). Under the *Chevron* approach, the first step is to determine if the regulation is inconsistent with the statute. This entails a determination of the statute's meaning using the traditional tools of statutory construction. If the statute is unambiguous and the regulation is inconsistent with the statute, then the regulation is struck down. In this step, no deference is paid to the administrative agency's interpretation of the statute. If, as part of this first step, a court determines that the statute is ambiguous, then the second step is to determine whether the regulation is a permissible interpretation of the statute. In this step, a court should defer to the administrative agency's interpretation so long as it is reasonable. *Id.*

Before the Court's decision, the Customs Service's regulation permitted parallel importation in Cases 2 and 3, but not in Case 1. How does the Court resolve whether the regulation allowing parallel importation in Case 2(a)–(c) is a permissible interpretation of the Tariff Act? Is the statute ambiguous? Can the words of the statute be reasonably interpreted in different ways, and if so, how? Did the administrative agency's regulations adopt one of those permissible interpretations? How does the Court resolve whether the regulation allowing parallel importation in Case 3 is a permissible interpretation of the statute? Is the statute ambiguous? Was the regulation consistent with the statute's unambiguous meaning? When Congress originally adopted the Tariff Act in 1992, which of the three cases was it expressly trying to address? Do you think any individual legislators actually considered and intended to address Case 3 as well? How then can the Court find an unambiguous expression of Congress' intent with respect to Case 3 in the statute?

4. *Adapting to the Law.* ABC Co., a Delaware firm with its headquarters and manufacturing plant in Illinois, has come to you for legal advice. It is currently manufacturing and selling a popular product under a well-known trademark within the United States and is looking to expand its distribution activities to Canada and Mexico. It plans to sell its products for a lower price in Mexico, and is concerned about possibility of a grey market developing, particularly in Texas and California, which are two of its biggest markets. It is also considering moving its manufacturing facilities to Mexico. Focusing solely on the Tariff Act, how should ABC structure its business operations in order to have the legal right to bar imports of goods bearing its trademark from Mexico?

Aside from the parallel importation issue, the choice whether to expand into Mexico either internally through vertical integration (creating new subsidiaries or unincorporated divisions within its existing corporate structure) or externally through contracts with unrelated companies also implicates other business and legal considerations, including tax and control. If these other considerations suggest that an internal, vertically integrated expansion makes more sense, and the firm goes that route, will the firm be able to control parallel importation under the Tariff Act? If not, why do we force a firm to make that choice, balancing these other considerations against the problem of parallel importation? Why should vertical integration be the touchstone that determines whether parallel importation is permissible?

5. *Are Old Mistakes Law?* As the Court notes, the Customs Service's rule allowing parallel importation in Case 3 had been in place for more than fifty years before the Court overturned it. Even if the rule was inconsistent with the statute, as the Court holds, should the rule's longstanding nature insulate it from reversal? After all, Congress was presumably well aware of the Customs Service's interpretation of the Tariff Act of 1930, and yet did not revise the statute or otherwise overturn the agency's interpretations. In addition, parties on both sides of the parallel importation issue presumably relied on the rule in establishing their business models. Similarly, should the Court hesitate to overturn the administrative agency's contemporaneous interpretation of the statute based upon the Court's reading fifty years later? From the Court's decision, it appears that the answer to these questions is no. Why?

The answer to the first question is found in Justice Frankfurter's caution: "[W]e walk on quicksand when we try to find in the absence of corrective legislation a controlling legal principle." *Helvering v. Hallock*, 309 U.S. 106, 121 (1940). Or as the Court has said in other contexts: "Congress' silence is just that—silence." *Alaska Airlines, Inc. v. Brock*, 480 U.S. 678, 686 (1987). Should we infer congressional approval of the Customs Service's regulation allowing parallel importation from Congress' long silence? Should we infer approval of the Court's rejection of the regulation, given that Congress has not overruled *K Mart*?

LEVER BROS. CO. v. UNITED STATES
981 F.2d 1330 (D.C. Cir. 1993)

SENTELLE, J.

The District Court entered a judgment invalidating the "affiliate exception" of 19 C.F.R. § 133.21(c)(2) (1988) as inconsistent with the statutory mandate of the Lanham Act of 1946, 15 U.S.C. § 1124 (1988), prohibiting importation of goods which copy or simulate the mark of a domestic manufacturer, and issued a nationwide injunction barring enforcement of the regulation with respect to *any* foreign goods bearing a valid United States trademark but materially and physically differing from the United States version of the goods. The United States appeals. We conclude that the District Court, obedient to our limited remand in a prior decision in this same cause, properly determined that the regulation is inconsistent with the statute. However, because we conclude that the remedy the District Court provided is overbroad, we vacate the judgment and remand for entry of an injunction against allowing the importation of the foreign-produced Lever Brothers brand products at issue in this case.

I. BACKGROUND

Lever Brothers Company ("Lever US" or "Lever"), an American company, and its British affiliate, Lever Brothers Limited ("Lever UK"), both manufacture deodorant soap under the "Shield" trademark and hand dishwashing liquid under the "Sunlight" trademark. The trademarks are registered in each country. The products have evidently been formulated differently to suit local tastes and circumstances. The U.S. version lathers more, the soaps smell different, the colorants used in American "Shield" have been certified by the FDA whereas the colorants in British "Shield" have not, and the U.S. version contains a bacteriostat that enhances the deodorant properties of the soap. The British version of "Sunlight" dishwashing soap produces less suds, and the American version is formulated to work best in the "soft water" available in most American cities, whereas the British version is designed for "hard water" common in Britain.

The packaging of the U.S. and U.K. products is also somewhat different. The British "Shield" logo is written in script form and is packaged in foil wrapping and contains a wave motif, whereas the American "Shield" logo is written in block form, does not come in foil wrapping and contains a grid pattern. There is small print on the packages indicating where they were manufactured. The British "Sunlight" comes in a cylindrical bottle labeled "Sunlight Washing Up Liquid." The American "Sunlight" comes in a yellow, hourglass-shaped bottle labeled "Sunlight Dishwashing Liquid."

Lever asserts that the unauthorized influx of these foreign products has created substantial consumer confusion and deception in the United

States about the nature and origin of this merchandise, and that it has received numerous consumer complaints from American consumers who unknowingly bought the British products and were disappointed.

Lever argues that the importation of the British products was in violation of section 42 of the Lanham Act, 15 U.S.C. § 1124 which provides that with the exception of goods imported for personal use:

> No article of imported merchandise which shall copy or simulate the name of the [sic] any domestic manufacture, or manufacturer . . . or which shall copy or simulate a trademark registered in accordance with the provisions of this chapter . . . shall be admitted to entry at any customhouse of the United States.

Id. The United States Customs Service ("Customs"), however, was allowing importation of the British goods under the "affiliate exception" created by 19 C.F.R. § 133.21(c)(2), which provides that foreign goods bearing United States trademarks are not forbidden when "the foreign and domestic trademark or tradename owners are parent and subsidiary companies or are otherwise subject to common ownership or control."

In *Lever I,* we concluded that "the natural, virtually inevitable reading of section 42 is that it bars foreign goods bearing a trademark identical to the valid U.S. trademark but physically different," without regard to affiliation between the producing firms or the genuine character of the trademark abroad. In so concluding, we applied the teachings of *Chevron U.S.A. Inc. v. NRDC,* 467 U.S. 837 (1984). Under the *Chevron* analysis, if Congress has clearly expressed an intent on a matter, we give that intent full effect (Step One of *Chevron*). If there is any ambiguity, we accept Customs' interpretation, provided only that it is reasonable (Step Two of *Chevron*). The *Lever I* panel found the present controversy to survive barely *Chevron* Step One and "provisionally" concluded that the affiliate exception is inconsistent with section 42 with respect to physically different goods. The "provisional" qualifier on our determination of the invalidity of the exception was a very limited one. Noting that "neither party has briefed the legislative history nor administrative practice in any detail," we adopted the apparently controlling reading of section 42 only "tentatively" and remanded the case to the District Court to allow the parties to "join issue on those points." The panel in *Lever I* thus created a very small window of opportunity for the government to establish that the affiliate exception regulation was consistent with section 42 of the Lanham Act. At that time we said, "subject to some persuasive evidence running against our tentative conclusion, we must say that Lever's probability of success on its legal argument is quite high."

Our task today is clearly circumscribed. Under the "law of the case" doctrine, any determination as to an issue in the case which has previously been determined is ordinarily binding upon us. . . .

After reviewing the submissions of the parties, the District Court found that Customs' administrative practice was "at best inconsistent" and, in any event, had "never addressed the specific question of physically different goods that bear identical trademarks." The District Court concluded that "section 42 . . . prohibits the importation of foreign goods that . . . are physically different, regardless of the validity of the foreign trademark or the existence of an affiliation between the U.S. and foreign markholders." The court accordingly concluded that "neither the legislative history of the statute nor the administrative practice of the Customs Service clearly contradicts the plain meaning of section 42" and granted summary judgment against the government.

By way of remedy, the District Court enjoined Customs "from enforcing 19 C.F.R. § 133.21(c)(2) as to foreign goods that bear a trademark identical to a valid United States trademark but which are materially, physically different."

II. ANALYSIS

Here the specific question at Step Two of *Chevron* is whether the intended prohibition of section 42 admits of an exception for materially different goods manufactured by foreign affiliates. We apply a very limited Step Two *Chevron* analysis because we previously concluded that the intent of Congress is virtually plain. The government bears a heavy burden in attempting to overcome the apparent meaning of the statute. In *Griffin v. Oceanic Contractors, Inc.,* 458 U.S. 564 (1982), the Supreme Court held that when Congress's "will has been expressed in reasonably plain terms, 'that language must ordinarily be regarded as conclusive,'" A presumption in favor of reasonably clear statutory language will be disrupted only if there is a "'clearly expressed legislative intention' contrary to that language." *INS v. Cardoza-Fonseca,* 480 U.S. 421, 432 (1987) (quoting *United States v. James,* 478 U.S. 597, 606 (1986)). When we remanded this case, we indicated that the Government could not prevail unless it produced "persuasive evidence" rebutting our tentative reading of the statute, *Lever I,* 877 F.2d at 111, because the affiliate exception appears to contradict the clear implication of the language of section 42. The legislative history and administrative practice before us, as before the District Court, will not perform that onerous task. . . .

Customs' main argument from the legislative history is that section 42 of the Lanham Act applies only to imports of goods bearing trademarks that "copy or simulate" a registered mark. Customs thus draws a distinction between "genuine" marks and marks that "copy or simulate." A mark applied by a foreign firm subject to ownership and control common to that of the domestic trademark owner is by definition "genuine," Customs urges, regardless of whether or not the goods are identical. Thus, any importation of goods manufactured by an affiliate of a U.S. trademark owner cannot "copy or simulate" a registered mark because those goods are *ipso facto* "genuine."

This argument is fatally flawed. It rests on the false premise that foreign trademarks applied to foreign goods are "genuine" in the United States. Trademarks applied to physically different foreign goods are not genuine from the viewpoint of the American consumer. As we stated in *Lever I:*

> On its face ... section [42] appears to aim at deceit and consumer confusion; when identical trademarks have acquired different meanings in different countries, one who imports the foreign version to sell it under that trademark will (in the absence of some specially differentiating feature) cause the confusion Congress sought to avoid. The fact of affiliation between the producers in no way reduces the probability of that confusion; it is certainly not a constructive consent to importation.

Id.

There is a larger, more fundamental and ultimately fatal weakness in Customs' position in this case. Section 42 on its face appears to forbid importation of goods that "copy or simulate" a United States trademark. Customs has the burden of adducing evidence from the legislative history of section 42 and its administrative practice of an exception for materially different goods whose similar foreign and domestic trademarks are owned by affiliated companies. At a minimum, this requires that the specific question be addressed in the legislative history and administrative practice. The bottom line, however, is that the issue of materially different goods was not addressed either in the legislative history or the administrative record. It is not enough to posit that silence implies authorization, when the authorization sought runs counter to the evident meaning of the governing statute. Therefore, we conclude that section 42 of the Lanham Act precludes the application of Customs' affiliate exception with respect to physically, materially different goods. . . .

IV. CONCLUSION

For the foregoing reasons, we affirm the District Court's ruling that section 42 of the Lanham Act, 15 U.S.C. § 1124, bars the importation of physically different foreign goods bearing a trademark identical to a valid U.S. trademark, regardless of the trademark's genuine character abroad or affiliation between the producing firms. Injunctive relief, however, is limited to the two products which were the subject of this action. We therefore vacate the District Court's prior order to the extent that it renders global relief and remand for the entry of an injunction consistent with this opinion.

So ordered.

NOTES FOR DISCUSSION

1.   *The Statutory Language.* Section 42 of the Lanham Trademark Act, in relevant part, provides:

> [N]o article of imported merchandise which shall copy or simulate the name of any domestic manufacture, or manufacturer, . . . or which shall copy or simulate a trademark registered in accordance with the provisions of this chapter . . . shall be admitted to entry at any customhouse of the United States. . . .

15 U.S.C. § 1124 (2015).

Whether you are sympathetic to the result in *Lever Bros.* or not, is there any possible way to reconcile the *Lever Bros.* rule with the statutory language? Soap or dishwashing liquid from England is undoubtedly an "article of imported merchandise." The key issue given the statutory language is whether the use of the Shield or Sunlight marks on the UK-Lever Bros.'s products should be considered to "copy or simulate" the federally registered trademark of the US-Lever Bros. The Customs Service argued that, so long as the UK-Lever Bros. and the US-Lever Bros. are related, the Shield or Sunlight marks on the UK-Lever Bros.'s products do not "copy or simulate" the US-Lever Bros.'s registered marks. They are not copies or simulations; they are the same as the domestically registered marks. The Second Circuit panel rejects that argument and concludes that even if the two entities are affiliated, the marks on the UK-Lever Bros. products "copy or simulate" the federally registered marks of the US-Lever Bros. if and only if the characteristics of the associated products "differ materially" from the corresponding US-Lever Bros.'s products. How does the *Lever Bros.* court attempt to reconcile this rule with the statutory language? Do the words "genuine goods" appear in the statutory language?

What is the paradigm case that Congress intended to address with this provision? If Congress specifically intended the provision to address the importation of black market or counterfeit goods, and as the court admits, did not address, one way or the other, the case of materially different, gray market goods, should the court fill the gap that Congress left or wait for Congress to decide whether the gap should be filled? Is the complaint of "judicial activism" fully answered by noting that if Congress feels that the court misjudged the issue and extended the statute inappropriately, Congress can act to correct the court's misjudgment?

2.   *Consumer Protection or Trademark Owner Protection.* Protecting consumers plays a central role in the *Lever Bros.* court's willingness to re-write the statute. Consider the following cases and discuss whether the *Lever Bros.* rule, once established, remained true to its consumer protection origins:

a.   Original Appalachian Artworks ("OAA") created, makes, and licenses others to make Cabbage Patch Dolls. It also owns and has registered the corresponding United States trademarks. OAA has licensed a Spanish company, Jesmar, S.A., to make and sell Cabbage Patch Dolls, but the license limits such sales to Spain. An unrelated third party, Granada Electronics, has purchased some of the Jesmar Cabbage Patch Dolls in Spain and seeks to bring them into the United States for resale. Except for the Cabbage Patch Dolls mark itself, which is in English, the Jesmar dolls' packaging and associated materials, including the dolls' birth certificate and adoption papers, are in Spanish. When an OAA doll is purchased in the United States, the consumer can complete the adoption papers and submit them to OAA, and receive in return a certificate of adoption and a birthday card on the doll's first "birthday." OAA is unwilling to provide this service for Jesmar dolls sold in the United States. OAA sues Granada, alleging that its importation of the Jesmar dolls constitutes trademark infringement. How should the court rule? *See Original Appalachian Artworks, Inc. v. Granada Electronics, Inc.*, 816 F.2d 68 (2d Cir. 1987) (extending the *Lever Bros.* "materially different" standard from section 44 to trademark's traditional infringement standard of likelihood of confusion under section 32, and finding a likelihood of confusion because the Jesmar dolls were materially different).

b.   Davidoff & Cie, S.A., a Swiss corporation manufacture and sell expensive perfumes, and also owns and has registered the corresponding United States trademarks. An unrelated third party, PLD International, purchases cases of the perfume intended for overseas sales and resells them to discount retail stores in the United States. To make it more difficult for Davidoff & CIE to identify and control contractually the sources through which PLD obtains the perfume, PLD etches the batch codes off the bottom of each bottle of perfume. This leaves a mark approximately one and one-eighth inches long and one-eighth inch wide. Davidoff & Cie sues, contending that such resales are a violation of section 44. How should the court rule? *See Davidoff & CIE, S.A. v. PLD Int'l, Corp.*, 263 F.3d 1297, 1302–03 (11th Cir. 2001) (affirming grant of preliminary injunction on grounds that scratching the codes off creates a materially different product).

c.   Matrix Essentials manufactures and sells high-end hair care products, and owns and has registered the corresponding trademarks. It sells its line of hair care products exclusively through salons and licensed cosmetologists to ensure that each consumer receives the Matrix product appropriate for his or her hair care needs. Emporium Drug Mart, a discount drug store, procured and stocked on its shelves a large quantity of Matrix. Many of the Matrix products Emporium stocked bore the label "Guaranteed Only When Purchased in Professional Salons." Matrix sues, alleging Emporium is infringing Matrix's trademarks by selling its products outside of professional salons and thereby rendering its product materially different. How should the court rule? *See Matrix Essentials, Inc. v. Emporium Drug Mart, Inc.*, 988 F.2d 587 (5th Cir. 1993) (granting summary judgment to the defendant).

3.   *Business Models Revisited.* Revisit our ABC Company hypothetical. Does the *Lever Bros.* rule provide ABC Co. with any additional options to address the risks of parallel importation if it expands into Mexico?

CHAPTER 4

PREREQUISITES FOR TRADEMARK PROTECTION: DISTINCTIVENESS

■ ■ ■

The second prerequisite for trademark protection is distinctiveness. In today's advertising intensive world, sellers evoke a variety of words, symbols, and imagery in an attempt to persuade consumers to purchase one product rather than another. While these words and symbols may play a variety of informational roles, they will receive protection as trademarks if they are distinctive. Distinctiveness has two aspects. First, the words or symbols claimed as a trademark must play a specific informational role. They must convey to consumers, and consumers must rely on them, to identify the source of, or otherwise to convey brand-specific information with respect to, the associated goods or services. Second, in addition to this positive requirement of playing a source-identifying role, there is also a negative requirement. The words or symbols at issue must also not play a more important informational role that is not source-identifying or brand-specific for the associated goods or services.

With respect to this second requirement, there are three types of non-brand informational roles that will potentially preclude trademark protection. First, rather than, or in addition to, conveying brand-specific information to consumers, the words or symbols at issue may also convey other *accurate* information about the associated goods or services that is not brand-specific. For example, rather than tell them who made the product, consumers may rely on the words claimed as a trademark to tell them what kind of product it is. The word "beer," for example, on a bottle of beer tells a consumer that the product in the bottle is beer; it does not tell the consumer who made it. Alternatively, they may rely on the words for information concerning characteristics or features of the associated products or services that are not uniquely associated with a particular brand. The words "Lone Star" used in connection with beer made in Texas may have brand-specific connotations, but may also be taken as a representation as to where the beer was made. In either case, competitors may need to use the same word or words to identify or describe their products. As Judge Cudahy of the Seventh Circuit has explained: "It is no purpose of trademark protection to allow a firm to prevent its competitors from informing consumers about the attributes of the competitors' brands." *Spraying Sys. Co. v. Delavan, Inc.*, 975 F.2d 387, 392 (7th Cir. 1992).

Second, rather than, or in addition to, conveying brand-specific information to consumers, the words or symbols at issue may also convey other information about the associated goods or services, but that other information is in fact *inaccurate.* Consumers may interpret the words claimed as a trademark as a representation that the goods or services come from, or were made in, a particular geographic area. They may take the claimed trademark as a representation that the associated goods will have certain characteristics or are made from certain materials. Yet, in either case, the goods were not or do not.

Third, in addition to conveying brand-specific information, some consumers may find the claimed trademarks *objectionable.* Consumers may find the claimed trademarks immoral or scandalous. The words claimed as a trademark may disparage or bring into disrepute a particular group of people. Or they may "falsely suggest a connection to a person, living or dead." 15 U.S.C. § 1052(a) (2015).

To determine whether a word, name, symbol or device should receive protection, we must consider all of the informational roles the claimed trademark is serving. To receive trademark protection, the claimed trademark must, as a minimum, serve to identify source or otherwise convey brand-specific information. Yet, while playing the role of source-identifier is a necessary condition for trademark protection, it is not sufficient. We must also consider whether the claimed trademark plays some other informational role(s) as well. If it does, and if that other informational role militates against protection, then we must balance the relative importance of the competing informational roles to determine whether, and if so, how extensively to protect the word, name, symbol, or device at issue as a trademark.

We begin our examination of this balancing process with trademark law's spectrum of distinctiveness and the protection available under trademark law for descriptive words.

A. DESCRIPTIVE MARKS AND THE SPECTRUM OF DISTINCTIVENESS

ZATARAINS, INC. V. OAK GROVE SMOKEHOUSE, INC.
698 F.2d 786 (5th Cir. 1983)

GOLDBERG, CIRCUIT JUDGE

This appeal of a trademark dispute presents us with a menu of edible delights sure to tempt connoisseurs of fish and fowl alike. At issue is the alleged infringement of two trademarks, "Fish-Fri" and "Chick-Fri," held by appellant Zatarain's, Inc. ("Zatarain's"). The district court held that the alleged infringers had a "fair use" defense to any asserted infringement of the term "Fish-Fri" and that the registration of the term "Chick-Fri" should be cancelled. We affirm.

I.   FACTS AND PROCEEDINGS BELOW

A.   THE TALE OF THE TOWN FRIER

Zatarain's is the manufacturer and distributor of a line of over one hundred food products. Two of these products, "Fish-Fri" and "Chick-Fri," are coatings or batter mixes used to fry foods. These marks serve as the entree in the present litigation.

Zatarain's "Fish-Fri" consists of 100% corn flour and is used to fry fish and other seafood. "Fish-Fri" is packaged in rectangular cardboard boxes containing twelve or twenty-four ounces of coating mix. The legend "Wonderful FISH-FRI®" is displayed prominently on the front panel, along with the block Z used to identify all Zatarain's products. The term "Fish-Fri" has been used by Zatarain's or its predecessor since 1950 and has been registered as a trademark since 1962.

Zatarain's "Chick-Fri" is a seasoned corn flour batter mix used for frying chicken and other foods. The "Chick-Fri" package, which is very similar to that used for "Fish-Fri," is a rectangular cardboard container labelled "Wonderful CHICK-FRI." Zatarain's began to use the term "Chick-Fri" in 1968 and registered the term as a trademark in 1976.

Zatarain's products are not alone in the marketplace. At least four other companies market coatings for fried foods that are denominated "fish fry" or "chicken fry." Two of these competing companies are the appellees here, and therein hangs this fish tale.

Appellee Oak Grove Smokehouse, Inc. ("Oak Grove") began marketing a "fish fry" and a "chicken fry" in March 1979. Both products are packaged in clear glassine packets that contain a quantity of coating mix sufficient to fry enough food for one meal. The packets are labelled with Oak Grove's name and emblem, along with the words "FISH FRY" OR "CHICKEN FRY." Oak Grove's "FISH FRY" has a corn flour base seasoned with various spices; Oak Grove's "CHICKEN FRY" is a seasoned coating with a wheat flour base.

Appellee Visko's Fish Fry, Inc. ("Visko's") entered the batter mix market in March 1980 with its "fish fry." Visko's product is packed in a cylindrical eighteen-ounce container with a resealable plastic lid. The words "Visko's FISH FRY" appear on the label along with a photograph of a platter of fried fish. Visko's coating mix contains corn flour and added spices.

Other food manufacturing concerns also market coating mixes. Boochelle's Spice Co. ("Boochelle's"), originally a defendant in this lawsuit, at one time manufactured a seasoned "FISH FRY" packaged in twelve-ounce vinyl plastic packets. Pursuant to a settlement between Boochelle's and Zatarain's, Boochelle's product is now labelled "FISH AND VEGETABLE FRY." Another batter mix, "YOGI Brand® OYSTER SHRIMP and FISH FRY," is also available. Arnaud Coffee Corporation ("Arnaud") has manufactured and marketed "YOGI Brand" for ten to twenty years, but was never made a party to this litigation. A product called "Golden Dipt Old South Fish Fry" has recently entered the market as well.

B.   OUT OF THE FRYING PAN, INTO THE FIRE

Zatarain's first claimed foul play in its original complaint filed against Oak Grove on June 19, 1979, in the United States District Court for the Eastern District of Louisiana. The complaint alleged trademark infringement and unfair competition under the Lanham Act §§ 32(1), 43(a), 15 U.S.C. §§ 1114(1), 1125(a) (1976), and La.Rev.Stat.Ann. § 51:1405(A) (West Supp.1982). . . . The defendants . . . counterclaimed for cancellation of the trademarks "Fish-Fri" and "Chick-Fri" under section 37 of the Lanham Act, 15 U.S.C. § 1119 (1976), and for damages under section 38 of the Lanham Act, 15 U.S.C. § 1120 (1976).

The case was tried to the court without a jury. Treating the trademark claims first, the district court classified the term "Fish-Fri" as a descriptive term identifying a function of the product being sold. The court found further that the term "Fish-Fri" had acquired a secondary meaning in the New Orleans geographical area and therefore was entitled to trademark protection, but concluded that the defendants were entitled to fair use of the term "fish fry" to describe characteristics of their goods. Accordingly, the court held that Oak Grove and Visko's had not infringed Zatarain's trademark "Fish-Fri."

With respect to the alleged infringement of the term "Chick-Fri," the court found that "Chick-Fri" was a descriptive term that had not acquired a secondary meaning in the minds of consumers. Consequently, the court held that Zatarain's claim for infringement of its trademark "Chick-Fri" failed and ordered that the trademark registration of "Chick-Fri" should be cancelled.

Turning to Zatarain's unfair competition claims, the court observed that the evidence showed no likelihood of or actual confusion on the part of the buying public. Additionally, the court noted that the dissimilarities in trade dress of Zatarain's, Oak Grove's, and Visko's products diminished any possibility of buyer confusion. For these reasons, the court found no violations of federal or state unfair competition laws. . . .

II.   ISSUES ON APPEAL

. . . Battered, but not fried, Zatarain's appeals from the adverse judgment on several grounds. First, Zatarain's argues that its trademark

"Fish-Fri" is a suggestive term and therefore not subject to the "fair use" defense. Second, Zatarain's asserts that even if the "fair use" defense is applicable in this case, appellees cannot invoke the doctrine because their use of Zatarain's trademarks is not a good faith attempt to describe their products. Third, Zatarain's urges that the district court erred in cancelling the trademark registration for the term "Chick-Fri" because Zatarain's presented sufficient evidence to establish a secondary meaning for the term. For these reasons, Zatarain's argues that the district court should be reversed.

Oak Grove and Visko's also present an appeal to this court, contending that the district court erred in dismissing their counterclaims against Zatarain's. In particular, Oak Grove and Visko's again urge that Zatarain's conduct has violated the Sherman Act, the Lanham Act, the federal regulations governing product identity labelling, and Louisiana law prohibiting restraint of trade; Oak Grove and Visko's also pray for an award of attorneys' fees. We now turn to an appraisal of these issues.

III. THE TRADEMARK CLAIMS

A. *BASIC PRINCIPLES*

1. *Classifications of Marks*

The threshold issue in any action for trademark infringement is whether the word or phrase is initially registerable or protectable. *Vision Center v. Opticks, Inc.*, 596 F.2d 111, 115 (5th Cir. 1979); *American Heritage Life Insurance Co. v. Heritage Life Insurance Co.*, 494 F.2d 3, 10 (5th Cir. 1974). Courts and commentators have traditionally divided potential trademarks into four categories. A potential trademark may be classified as (1) generic, (2) descriptive, (3) suggestive, or (4) arbitrary or fanciful. These categories, like the tones in a spectrum, tend to blur at the edges and merge together. The labels are more advisory than definitional, more like guidelines than pigeonholes. Not surprisingly, they are somewhat difficult to articulate and to apply. *Soweco, Inc. v. Shell Oil Co.*, 617 F.2d 1178, 1183 (5th Cir. 1980); *Vision Center*, 596 F.2d at 115.

A *generic* term is "the name of a particular genus or class of which an individual article or service is but a member." *Vision Center*, 596 F.2d at 115; *Abercrombie & Fitch Co. v. Hunting World, Inc.*, 537 F.2d 4, 9 (2d Cir. 1976). A generic term connotes the "basic nature of articles or services" rather than the more individualized characteristics of a particular product. *American Heritage*, 494 F.2d at 11. Generic terms can never attain trademark protection. *William R. Warner & Co. v. Eli Lilly & Co.*, 265 U.S. 526, 528, 44 S.Ct. 615, 616, 68 L.Ed. 1161 (1924); *Soweco*, 617 F.2d at 1183; *Vision Center*, 596 F.2d at 115. Furthermore, if at any time a registered trademark becomes generic as to a particular product or service, the mark's registration is subject to cancellation. Lanham Act § 14, 15 U.S.C. § 1064(c) (1976). Such terms as aspirin and cellophane have been held generic and therefore unprotectable as trademarks. *See Bayer Co. v. United Drug Co.*, 272 F. 505 (S.D.N.Y.1921) (aspirin); *DuPont Cellophane Co. v. Waxed Products Co.*, 85 F.2d 75 (2d Cir. 1936) (cellophane).

A *descriptive* term "identifies a characteristic or quality of an article or service," *Vision Center*, 596 F.2d at 115, such as its color, odor, function, dimensions, or ingredients. *American Heritage*, 494 F.2d at 11. Descriptive terms ordinarily are not protectable as trademarks, Lanham Act § 2(e)(1), 15 U.S.C. § 1052(e)(1) (1976); they may become valid marks, however, by acquiring a secondary meaning in the minds of the consuming public. *See id.* § 2(f), 15 U.S.C. § 1052(f). Examples of descriptive marks would include "Alo" with reference to products containing gel of the aloe vera plant, *Aloe Creme Laboratories, Inc. v. Milsan, Inc.*, 423 F.2d 845 (5th Cir. 1970), and "Vision Center" in reference to a business offering optical goods and services, *Vision Center*, 596 F.2d at 117. As this court has often noted, the distinction between descriptive and generic terms is one of degree. *Soweco*, 617 F.2d at 1184; *Vision Center*, 596 F.2d at 115 n. 11 (citing 3 R. Callman, *The Law of Unfair Competition, Trademarks and Monopolies* § 70.4 (3d ed. 1969)); *American Heritage*, 494 F.2d at 11. The distinction has important practical consequences, however; while a descriptive term may be elevated to trademark status with proof of secondary meaning, a generic term may never achieve trademark protection. *Vision Center*, 596 F.2d at 115 n.11.

A *suggestive* term suggests, rather than describes, some particular characteristic of the goods or services to which it applies and requires the consumer to exercise the imagination in order to draw a conclusion as to the nature of the goods and services. *Soweco*, 617 F.2d at 1184; *Vision Center*, 596 F.2d at 115–16. A suggestive mark is protected without the necessity for proof of secondary meaning. The term "Coppertone" has been held suggestive in regard to sun tanning products. *See Douglas Laboratories, Corp. v. Copper Tan, Inc.*, 210 F.2d 453 (2d Cir. 1954).

Arbitrary or *fanciful* terms bear no relationship to the products or services to which they are applied. Like suggestive terms, arbitrary and fanciful marks are protectable without proof of secondary meaning. The term "Kodak" is properly classified as a fanciful term for photographic supplies, *see Eastman Kodak Co. v. Weil*, 137 Misc. 506, 243 N.Y.S. 319 (1930) ("Kodak"); "Ivory" is an arbitrary term as applied to soap. *Abercrombie & Fitch*, 537 F.2d at 9 n.6.

2.   *Secondary Meaning*

As noted earlier, descriptive terms are ordinarily not protectable as trademarks. They may be protected, however, if they have acquired a secondary meaning for the consuming public. The concept of secondary meaning recognizes that words with an ordinary and primary meaning of their own "may by long use with a particular product, come to be known by the public as specifically designating that product." *Volkswagenwerk Aktiengesellschaft v. Rickard*, 492 F.2d 474, 477 (5th Cir. 1974). In order to establish a secondary meaning for a term, a plaintiff "must show that the primary significance of the term in the minds of the consuming public is not the product but the producer." *Kellogg Co. v. National Biscuit Co.*, 305 U.S. 111, 118, 59 S.Ct. 109, 113, 83 L.Ed. 73 (1938). The burden of proof to establish secondary meaning rests at all times with the plaintiff; this burden is not an easy one to satisfy, for " '[a] high degree of proof is necessary to establish secondary meaning for a descriptive term.' " *Vision Center*, 596 F.2d at 118 (quoting 3 R. Callman, *supra*, § 77.3, at 359). Proof of secondary meaning is an issue only with respect to descriptive marks; suggestive and arbitrary or fanciful marks are automatically protected upon registration, and generic terms are unprotectable even if they have acquired secondary meaning. *See Soweco*, 617 F.2d at 1185 n.20.

3. The "Fair Use" Defense

Even when a descriptive term has acquired a secondary meaning sufficient to warrant trademark protection, others may be entitled to use the mark without incurring liability for trademark infringement. When the allegedly infringing term is "used fairly and in good faith only to describe to users the goods or services of [a] party, or their geographic origin," Lanham Act § 33(b)(4), 15 U.S.C. § 1115(b)(4) (1976), a defendant in a trademark infringement action may assert the "fair use" defense. The defense is available only in actions involving descriptive terms and only when the term is used in its descriptive sense rather than its trademark sense. *Soweco*, 617 F.2d at 1185; *see Venetianaire Corp. v. A & P Import Co.*, 429 F.2d 1079, 1081–82 (2d Cir. 1970). In essence, the fair use defense prevents a trademark registrant from appropriating a descriptive term for its own use to the exclusion of others, who may be prevented thereby from accurately describing their own goods. *Soweco*, 617 F.2d at 1185. The holder of a protectable descriptive mark has no legal claim to an exclusive right in the primary, descriptive meaning of the term; consequently, anyone is free to use the term in its primary, descriptive sense so long as such use does not lead to customer confusion as to the source of the goods or services. *See* 1 J. MCCARTHY, TRADEMARKS AND UNFAIR COMPETITION § 11.17, at 379 (1973).

4. Cancellation of Trademarks

Section 37 of the Lanham Act, 15 U.S.C. § 1119 (1976), provides as follows:

> In any action involving a registered mark the court may determine the right to registration, order the cancelation of registrations, in whole or in part, restore canceled registrations, and otherwise rectify the register with respect to the

registrations of any party to the action. Decrees and orders shall
be certified by the court to the Commissioner, who shall make
appropriate entry upon the records of the Patent Office, and
shall be controlled thereby.

This circuit has held that when a court determines that a mark is either a
generic term or a descriptive term lacking secondary meaning, the
purposes of the Lanham Act are well served by an order cancelling the
mark's registration. *American Heritage*, 494 F.2d at 14.

We now turn to the facts of the instant case.

B.   *"FISH-FRI"*

1.   *Classification*

Throughout this litigation, Zatarain's has maintained that the term
"Fish-Fri" is a suggestive mark automatically protected from infringing
uses by virtue of its registration in 1962. Oak Grove and Visko's assert
that "fish fry" is a generic term identifying a class of foodstuffs used to fry
fish; alternatively, Oak Grove and Visko's argue that "fish fry" is merely
descriptive of the characteristics of the product. The district court found
that "Fish-Fri" was a descriptive term identifying a function of the
product being sold. Having reviewed this finding under the appropriate
"clearly erroneous" standard, we affirm. *See Vision Center*, 596 F.2d at
113.

We are mindful that "the concept of descriptiveness must be
construed rather broadly." 3 R. Callman, *supra*, § 70.2. Whenever a word
or phrase conveys an immediate idea of the qualities, characteristics,
effect, purpose, or ingredients of a product or service, it is classified as
descriptive and cannot be claimed as an exclusive trademark. *Id.* § 71.1;
see Stix Products, Inc. v. United Merchants & Manufacturers, Inc., 295 F.
Supp. 479, 488 (S.D.N.Y.1968). Courts and commentators have
formulated a number of tests to be used in classifying a mark as
descriptive.

A suitable starting place is the dictionary, for "the dictionary
definition of the word is an appropriate and relevant indication 'of the
ordinary significance and meaning of words' to the public." *American
Heritage*, 494 F.2d at 11 n.5; *see also Vision Center*, 596 F.2d at 116.
Webster's Third New International Dictionary 858 (1966) lists the
following definitions for the term "fish fry": "1. a picnic at which fish are
caught, fried, and eaten;.... 2. fried fish." Thus, the basic dictionary
definitions of the term refer to the preparation and consumption of fried
fish. This is at least preliminary evidence that the term "Fish-Fri" is
descriptive of Zatarain's product in the sense that the words naturally
direct attention to the purpose or function of the product.

The "imagination test" is a second standard used by the courts to identify descriptive terms. This test seeks to measure the relationship between the actual words of the mark and the product to which they are applied. If a term "requires imagination, thought and perception to reach a conclusion as to the nature of goods," *Stix Products*, 295 F. Supp. at 488, it is considered a suggestive term. Alternatively, a term is descriptive if standing alone it conveys information as to the characteristics of the product. In this case, mere observation compels the conclusion that a product branded "Fish-Fri" is a prepackaged coating or batter mix applied to fish prior to cooking. The connection between this merchandise and its identifying terminology is so close and direct that even a consumer unfamiliar with the product would doubtless have an idea of its purpose or function. It simply does not require an exercise of the imagination to deduce that "Fish-Fri" is used to fry fish. *See Vision Center*, 596 F.2d at 116–17; *Stix Products*, 295 F. Supp. at 487–88. Accordingly, the term "Fish-Fri" must be considered descriptive when examined under the "imagination test."

A third test used by courts and commentators to classify descriptive marks is "whether competitors would be likely to need the terms used in the trademark in describing their products." *Union Carbide Corp. v. Ever-Ready, Inc.*, 531 F.2d 366, 379 (7th Cir. 1976). A descriptive term generally relates so closely and directly to a product or service that other merchants marketing similar goods would find the term useful in identifying their own goods. *Vision Center*, 596 F.2d at 116–17; *Stix Products*, 295 F. Supp. at 488. Common sense indicates that in this case merchants other than Zatarain's might find the term "fish fry" useful in describing their own particular batter mixes. While Zatarain's has argued strenuously that Visko's and Oak Grove could have chosen from dozens of other possible terms in naming their coating mix, we find this position to be without merit. As this court has held, the fact that a term is not the only or even the most common name for a product is not determinative, for there is no legal foundation that a product can be described in only one fashion. *Vision Center*, 596 F.2d at 117 n.17. There are many edible fish in the sea, and as many ways to prepare them as there are varieties to be prepared. Even piscatorial gastronomes would agree, however, that frying is a form of preparation accepted virtually around the world, at restaurants starred and unstarred. The paucity of synonyms for the words "fish" and "fry" suggests that a merchant whose batter mix is specially spiced for frying fish is likely to find "fish fry" a useful term for describing his product.

A final barometer of the descriptiveness of a particular term examines the extent to which a term actually has been used by others marketing a similar service or product. *Vision Center*, 596 F.2d at 117; *Shoe Corp. of America v. Juvenile Shoe Corp.*, 46 C.C.P.A. 868, 266 F.2d 793, 796 (C.C.P.A.1959). This final test is closely related to the question whether competitors are likely to find a mark useful in describing their products. As noted above, a number of companies other than Zatarain's have chosen the word combination "fish fry" to identify their batter mixes. Arnaud's product, "Oyster Shrimp and Fish Fry," has been in competition with Zatarain's "Fish-Fri" for some ten to twenty years. When companies from A to Z, from Arnaud to Zatarain's, select the same term to describe their similar products, the term in question is most likely a descriptive one.

The correct categorization of a given term is a factual issue, *Soweco*, 617 F.2d at 1183 n.12; consequently, we review the district court's findings under the "clearly erroneous" standard of Fed.R.Civ.P. 52. *See Vision Center*, 596 F.2d at 113; *Volkswagenwerk*, 492 F.2d at 478. The district court in this case found that Zatarain's trademark "Fish-Fri" was descriptive of the function of the product being sold. Having applied the four prevailing tests of descriptiveness to the term "Fish-Fri," we are convinced that the district court's judgment in this matter is not only not clearly erroneous, but clearly correct.

2. Secondary Meaning

Descriptive terms are not protectable by trademark absent a showing of secondary meaning in the minds of the consuming public. To prevail in its trademark infringement action, therefore, Zatarain's must prove that its mark "Fish-Fri" has acquired a secondary meaning and thus warrants trademark protection. The district court found that Zatarain's evidence established a secondary meaning for the term "Fish-Fri" in the New Orleans area. We affirm.

The existence of secondary meaning presents a question for the trier of fact, and a district court's finding on the issue will not be disturbed unless clearly erroneous. *American Heritage*, 494 F.2d at 13; *Volkswagenwerk*, 492 F.2d at 477. The burden of proof rests with the party seeking to establish legal protection for the mark—the plaintiff in an infringement suit. *Vision Center*, 596 F.2d at 118. The evidentiary burden necessary to establish secondary meaning for a descriptive term is substantial. *Id.; American Heritage*, 494 F.2d at 12; 3 R. CALLMAN, *supra*, § 77.3, at 359.

In assessing a claim of secondary meaning, the major inquiry is the consumer's attitude toward the mark. The mark must denote to the consumer "a single thing coming from a single source," *Coca-Cola Co. v. Koke Co.*, 254 U.S. 143, 146, 41 S.Ct. 113, 114, 65 L.Ed. 189 (1920); *Aloe Creme Laboratories*, 423 F.2d at 849, to support a finding of secondary meaning. Both direct and circumstantial evidence may be relevant and persuasive on the issue.

Factors such as amount and manner of advertising, volume of sales, and length and manner of use may serve as circumstantial evidence relevant to the issue of secondary meaning. *See, e.g., Vision Center*, 596 F.2d at 119; *Union Carbide Corp.*, 531 F.2d at 380; *Aloe Creme Laboratories*, 423 F.2d at 849–50. While none of these factors alone will prove secondary meaning, in combination they may establish the necessary link in the minds of consumers between a product and its source. It must be remembered, however, that "the question is not the *extent* of the promotional efforts, but their *effectiveness* in altering the meaning of [the term] to the consuming public." *Aloe Creme Laboratories*, 423 F.2d at 850.

Since 1950, Zatarain's and its predecessor have continuously used the term "Fish-Fri" to identify this particular batter mix. Through the expenditure of over $400,000 for advertising during the period from 1976 through 1981, Zatarain's has promoted its name and its product to the buying public. Sales of twelve-ounce boxes of "Fish-Fri" increased from 37,265 cases in 1969 to 59,439 cases in 1979. From 1964 through 1979, Zatarain's sold a total of 916,385 cases of "Fish-Fri." The district court considered this circumstantial evidence of secondary meaning to weigh heavily in Zatarain's favor.

In addition to these circumstantial factors, Zatarain's introduced at trial two surveys conducted by its expert witness, Allen Rosenzweig. In one survey, telephone interviewers questioned 100 women in the New Orleans area who fry fish or other seafood three or more times per month. Of the women surveyed, twenty-three percent specified *Zatarain's* "Fish-Fri" as a product they "would buy at the grocery to use as a coating" or a "product on the market that is especially made for frying fish." In a similar survey conducted in person at a New Orleans area mall, twenty-eight of the 100 respondents answered "*Zatarain's* 'Fish-Fri' " to the same questions.

The authorities are in agreement that survey evidence is the most direct and persuasive way of establishing secondary meaning. *Vision Center*, 596 F.2d at 119; *Aloe Creme Laboratories*, 423 F.2d at 849; 1 J. McCarthy, *supra*, § 15.12(D). The district court believed that the survey evidence produced by Zatarain's, when coupled with the circumstantial evidence of advertising and usage, tipped the scales in favor of a finding of secondary meaning. Were we considering the question of secondary meaning *de novo*, we might reach a different conclusion than did the district court, for the issue is close. Mindful, however, that there is evidence in the record to support the finding below, we cannot say that the district court's conclusion was clearly erroneous. Accordingly, the finding of secondary meaning in the New Orleans area for Zatarain's descriptive term "Fish-Fri" must be affirmed.

3. The "Fair Use" Defense

Although Zatarain's term "Fish-Fri" has acquired a secondary meaning in the New Orleans geographical area, Zatarain's does not now prevail automatically on its trademark infringement claim, for it cannot prevent the fair use of the term by Oak Grove and Visko's. The "fair use" defense applies only to descriptive terms and requires that the term be "used fairly and in good faith only to describe to users the goods or services of such party, or their geographic origin." Lanham Act § 33(b), 15 U.S.C. § 1115(b)(4) (1976). The district court determined that Oak Grove and Visko's were entitled to fair use of the term "fish fry" to describe a characteristic of their goods; we affirm that conclusion.

Zatarain's term "Fish-Fri" is a descriptive term that has acquired a secondary meaning in the New Orleans area. Although the trademark is valid by virtue of having acquired a secondary meaning, only that penumbra or fringe of secondary meaning is given legal protection. Zatarain's has no legal claim to an exclusive right in the original, descriptive sense of the term; therefore, Oak Grove and Visko's are still free to use the words "fish fry" in their ordinary, descriptive sense, so long as such use will not tend to confuse customers as to the source of the goods. *See* 1 J. MCCARTHY, *supra*, § 11.17.

The record contains ample evidence to support the district court's determination that Oak Grove's and Visko's use of the words "fish fry" was fair and in good faith. Testimony at trial indicated that the appellees did not intend to use the term in a trademark sense and had never attempted to register the words as a trademark. Record on Appeal, Vol. II at 28, 33, 226–30, 243–47. Oak Grove and Visko's apparently believed "fish fry" was a generic name for the type of coating mix they manufactured. *Id.* at 28, 226, 244. In addition, Oak Grove and Visko's consciously packaged and labelled their products in such a way as to minimize any potential confusion in the minds of consumers. *Id.* at 244–45, 251–52. The dissimilar trade dress of these products prompted the district court to observe that confusion at the point of purchase—the grocery shelves—would be virtually impossible. Our review of the record convinces us that the district court's determinations are correct. We hold, therefore, that Oak Grove and Visko's are entitled to fair use of the term "fish fry" to describe their products; accordingly, Zatarain's claim of trademark infringement must fail.

C. *"CHICK-FRI"*

1. *Classification*

Most of what has been said about "Fish-Fri" applies with equal force to Zatarain's other culinary concoction, "Chick-Fri." "Chick-Fri" is at least as descriptive of the act of frying chicken as "Fish-Fri" is descriptive of frying fish. It takes no effort of the imagination to associate the term "Chick-Fri" with Southern fried chicken. Other merchants are likely to want to use the words "chicken fry" to describe similar products, and others have in fact done so. Sufficient evidence exists to support the district court's finding that "Chick-Fri" is a descriptive term; accordingly, we affirm.

2. Secondary Meaning

The district court concluded that Zatarain's had failed to establish a secondary meaning for the term "Chick-Fri." We affirm this finding. The mark "Chick-Fri" has been in use only since 1968; it was registered even more recently, in 1976. In sharp contrast to its promotions with regard to "Fish-Fri," Zatarain's advertising expenditures for "Chick-Fri" were mere chickenfeed; in fact, Zatarain's conducted no direct advertising campaign to publicize the product. Thus the circumstantial evidence presented in support of a secondary meaning for the term "Chick-Fri" was paltry.

Allen Rosenzweig's survey evidence regarding a secondary meaning for "Chick-Fri" also "lays an egg." The initial survey question was a "qualifier:" "Approximately how many times in an average month do you, yourself, fry *fish or other seafood?*" Only if respondents replied "three or more times a month" were they asked to continue the survey. This qualifier, which may have been perfectly adequate for purposes of the "Fish-Fri" questions, seems highly unlikely to provide an adequate sample of potential consumers of "Chick-Fri." This survey provides us with nothing more than some dates regarding fish friers' perceptions about products used for frying chicken. As such, it is entitled to little evidentiary weight.

It is well settled that Zatarain's, the original plaintiff in this trademark infringement action, has the burden of proof to establish secondary meaning for its term. *Vision Center*, 596 F.2d at 118; *American Heritage*, 494 F.2d at 12. This it has failed to do. The district court's finding that the term "Chick-Fri" lacks secondary meaning is affirmed.

3. Cancellation

Having concluded that the district court was correct in its determination that Zatarain's mark "Chick-Fri" is a descriptive term lacking in secondary meaning, we turn to the issue of cancellation. The district court, invoking the courts' power over trademark registration as provided by section 37 of the Lanham Act, 15 U.S.C. § 1119 (1976), ordered that the registration of the term "Chick-Fri" should be cancelled. The district court's action was perfectly appropriate in light of its findings that "Chick-Fri" is a descriptive term without secondary meaning. We affirm. *See American Heritage*, 494 F.2d at 13–14. . . .

V. CONCLUSION

And so our tale of fish and fowl draws to a close. We need not tarry long, for our taster's choice yields but one result, and we have other fish to fry. Accordingly, the judgment of the district court is hereby and in all things AFFIRMED.

NOTES FOR DISCUSSION

1. *The Spectrum of Distinctiveness.* We can think of distinctiveness along a spectrum. At one end are words or symbols that serve to convey information that is not brand specific. The word "beer," for example, if used with respect to beer, tells us nothing about any specific brand of beer. Rather, it tells us only the general class of product at issue. At the other end are words or symbols that serve to convey information that is only brand-specific or source-identifying. Coined words, for example, such as Exxon and Kodak, have no meaning independent of their brand significance. As we move from either end of the spectrum, we move from words that serve only one information role or the other to words that serve a mixture of informational roles. In trademark practice, we refer to the generic-descriptive-suggestive-arbitrary-fanciful spectrum of distinctiveness that the *Zatarains* court enuciates as the *Abercrombie* spectrum, after Judge Friendly's opinion in Abercrombie & Fitch Co. v. Hunting World, Inc., 537 F.2d 4 (2d Cir. 1976).

As the *Zatarains* opinion illustrates, in trademark law, we divide potential marks into three legally-significant categories. First, we classify words that fall near the "only brand-specific information" end of the spectrum as inherently distinctive. Given their nature and manner of use, these words are likely to play an important source-identification role from the outset. At the same time, they are also unlikely to play any other important informational role. As we saw in Chapter 2, Time Out for men's sportswear and Zazu for hair coloring products fall into this category of inherently distinctive marks. As a general rule, we protect such inherently distinctive words or symbols as trademarks from their first use. In *Zatarain's*, the court identifies three classes of word marks that qualify as inherently distinctive. What are they? How do we define each?

Second, as we move towards the middle of the spectrum, we find words that convey a mixture of brand-specific information and non-brand information given the products or services with which they are associated. Recognizing this mixed informational role, we exclude such words from the category of inherently distinctive marks, but recognize that they may become distinctive with time. For words in this middle ground, we will extend trademark protection only when a party can establish that the words have acquired distinctiveness or developed a secondary meaning. Requiring proof of secondary meaning allows us to determine: (i) whether the words at issue have come to play a brand-specific information role; and (ii) whether the importance of that brand-specific informational role has come to outweigh the importance of the words' other informational roles for the products or services at issue. Only when the words' importance for conveying brand-specific information begins to outweigh their other informational roles will we extend trademark protection. We use the label descriptive to cover words that fall into this category. In *Zatarian's*, the court identifies Fish Fri and Chick Fri as words that are descriptive. How does the court define the category of descriptive words? What guidelines or tests do we use to separate descriptive word marks from inherently distinctive marks?

Third, as we move towards the other end of the distinctiveness spectrum, we reach our final category: generic words. These words may never receive protection as trademarks. In part, this is because such words seldom play a brand-specific informational role. That is not the only reason, however. Even where these words have come to play a brand-specific role in a particular case, we still refuse to protect them as trademarks. We refuse to protect them because the words also play other informational roles and those other roles are too important to allow any one entity to claim an exclusive right to use them.

If we put the court's categories to one side, what are the different informational roles that the words "fish fri" or "chick fri" might play for the products at issue in *Zatarain's*? Do you agree with the court that these words should be classified as descriptive for the products at issue? Or should they be classified as generic? What is the generic name for the products at issue? If you were asking your spouse or a roommate to pick up this type of product at the store, and you wanted to use a generic rather than a brand name, what would you ask for? If you were walking through a grocery store and saw the words Fish Fry or Chick Fry on a package, what meaning would you attribute to those words?

2. *Word Marks versus Design Marks.* The *Abercrombie* spectrum applies primarily to word marks. How do we determine whether a design mark, such as an emblem or figure, is inherently distinctive? For example, assume that an entity has long used a five-pointed star in a circle on its business premises. Is that "star symbol" inherently distinctive or must secondary meaning first be proven? Attempting to label the star symbol as either generic, descriptive, suggestive, arbitrary, or fanciful labels is not particularly helpful. Unlike a word, a design or symbol may have no literal meaning. For such design marks, the Court of Customs and Patent Appeals developed an alternative approach to identifying inherently distinctive designs. Rather than try and fit a design into one of the *Abercrombie* categories, the court instead identified four factors as relevant to determining whether a design was inherently distinctive:

> [1] whether it was a "common" basic shape or design, [2] whether it was unique or unusual in a particular field, [3] whether it was a mere refinement of a commonly-adopted and well-known form of ornamentation for a particular class of goods viewed by the public as a dress or ornamentation for the goods, or [4] whether it was capable of creating a commercial impression distinct from the accompanying words.

Seabrook Foods, Inc. v. Bar-Well Foods Ltd., 568 F.2d 1342, 1344 (C.C.P.A. 1978).

3. *Policy and Doctrine: Deny Protection or Limit Its Scope.* If we are concerned that the protection of descriptive words as trademarks may limit competitors' ability to use them, there are two basic approaches through which we can ensure that these words remain availability to competitors.

First, we can deny trademark protection altogether for such words. Second, we can protect them as trademarks, but limit the scope of protection provided.

Through either approach, we are attempting to use doctrine to implement our underlying policy concerns. The separation of words into the inherently distinctive, descriptive, and generic categories represents a first rough cut at this attempt. Through this first cut, we label as inherently distinctive and protect as trademarks words where we believe the policy balance reflecting the relative importance of the words' different informational roles will almost always tilt in favor of such protection; we label as generic and bar protection for words where we believe the policy balance will almost always tilt against such protection; and we label as descriptive words for which the policy balance requires a closer look.

To improve the fit between policy and outcomes, we can also protect a word as a trademark, but then vary the scope of protection provided. We can vary the scope of protection provided either generally by considering where a mark falls on the spectrum of distinctiveness as part of our standard for infringement, as we shall see in Chapter 7. We can also vary the scope of protection in specific factual contexts, through doctrines such as fair use.

In *Zatarain's*, the court relies on the fair use doctrine to ensure that the defendants can continue to use fish fry in its descriptive sense. Why does the defendants' use constitute fair use? In terms of our policy analysis, a finding of fair use in this case represents a conclusion that on balance consumers are more likely to rely on the words "Fish Fry" on the defendants' boxes as a non-brand description of the associated product, rather than as a statement that the associated product was made by Zatarain's. Do you agree with the court that consumers are more likely to interpret "Fish Fry" as a description of the nature, rather than the source, of the defendants' product? What other words could the defendants use to tell consumers what their products are?

Given the court's conclusion that Zatarain's had established secondary meaning and was therefore entitled to trademark protection for the words "Fish Fri," presumably that finding means that Zatarain's is entitled to some protection for its mark. Given that the court treats the defendants' actual use as fair, how would you have to change the facts for the defendants' use to be infringing?

While we shall study fair use in more detail in Chapter 9, one statement by the *Zatarain's* court deserves correction. In describing the nature and scope of fair use, the *Zatarain's* court states: "Oak Grove and Visko's are still free to use the words 'fish fry' in their ordinary, descriptive sense, *so long as such use will not tend to confuse customers as to the source of the goods.*" 698 F.2d at 796 (emphasis added). This statement, if taken too literally, would mean that the fair use defense would never apply. If the defendant's use is not confusing, then the defendant may assert the fair use defense. However, in such a case, the defense is unnecessary because without confusion there is no trademark infringement in any event. On the other hand, if the use is confusing and hence constitutes actionable trademark infringement, then the fair use defense becomes necessary but, according to the *Zatarain's* court, is not available.

In *KP Permanent Make-Up, Inc. v. Lasting Impression I, Inc.*, the Court addressed this paradox and held that a use may be fair even if it creates some likelihood of confusion. 543 U.S. 111, 124 (2004). However, the Court left open the question whether a court could consider the degree of confusion created in determining whether a particular use was fair. *Id.* at 123.

4.   *The Legal Recognition of Descriptive Words as Trademarks.* Before the Trademark Act of 1946, only inherently distinctive marks were eligible for protection as trademarks. Descriptive words could not receive protection as trademarks, even with proof of secondary meaning. However, although not technically trademarks, with proof of secondary meaning, descriptive words could receive protection under the rubric of unfair competition and the doctrine of passing off. In the Trademark Act of 1946, Congress expressly allowed for the registration of descriptive words as trademarks on the principal register so long as secondary meaning was shown. 15 U.S.C. § 1052(e)(1), (f) (2015).

What substantive difference did this shift from "unfair competition" to "trademark" make in terms of the protection available to descriptive words? Not much in terms of the substantive law. Under either approach, secondary meaning had to be shown. Under either approach, the general scope of protection was defined by the likelihood of confusion standard. Under either approach, this general scope of protection was specifically limited by the fair use doctrine. While courts may have become somewhat more lenient in terms of the proof required to demonstrate secondary meaning or infringement after Congress formally recognized descriptive words with secondary meaning as trademarks, the basic doctrinal requirements for obtaining protection and showing infringement remained the same.

However, by recognizing descriptive words with secondary meaning as trademarks, Congress extended the substantial procedural advantages federal registration offered to such words. These advantages include: (i) prima facie evidence of ownership, validity, and exclusive right to use, 15 U.S.C. § 1057(b) (2015); (ii) conclusive evidence of ownership, validity, and exclusive right to use, subject only to a limited set of defenses, once the trademark has been registered for five years and a section 15 affidavit is filed and accepted, 15 U.S.C. §§ 1065, 1115(b) (2015); (iii) nationwide priority as of the trademark's registration date, 15 U.S.C. § 1072 (2015); and (iv) the availability of enhanced remedies against counterfeit marks, 15 U.S.C. §§ 1116(d), 1117(b) (2015).

5.   *Misspellings, Initials, and Foreign Equivalents.* What significance did the court give to Zatarain's misspelling of the word "fry" as "fri"? The general rule is that phonetic equivalents of a generic or descriptive word are treated as the word itself. Had the defendants in *Zatarain's* used the misspelling, "Fish Fri," on their packages, how would the case have come out?

What if Zatarain's had used the initials "FF" or "CF" on its boxes? When dealing with initials, the key question is how consumers will understand them. If consumers will understand the initials as the corresponding descriptive or generic words, then generally we treat them accordingly in trademark law. For example, in National Conference of Bar Examiners v. Multistate Legal Studies, Inc., 692 F.2d 478 (7th Cir. 1982), *cert. denied*, 464 U.S. 814 (1983), the court considered whether the phrase "Multistate Bar Examination" and its initials "MBE" were descriptive. The Seventh Circuit reversed the district court's finding of inherent distinctiveness, and held both descriptive. As the court explained:

> [U]nder settled trademark law if the components of a trade name are common descriptive terms, a combination of such terms retains that quality. We note further that [the fact that] plaintiffs also use the initials "MBE" to designate their test is of no consequence. Abbreviations for generic or common descriptive phrases must be treated similarly.

Id. at 488.

On the other hand, if the relevant consumers will not equate the initials with the corresponding descriptive terms, then the initials may qualify as inherently distinctive. For example, in *Modern Optics, Inc. v. Univis Lens Co.*, 234 F.2d 504 (C.C.P.A. 1956), the Court of Customs and Patent Appeals allowed the registration of the initials CV for trifocal lenses without proof of secondary meaning. Even if the relevant consumers recognized the corresponding phrase "continuous vision" as generic or descriptive for trifocal lenses, the evidence did not establish that consumers would automatically associate the initials with the corresponding phrase. *Id.* at 506.

With respect to foreign language words, as a general rule, courts treat foreign words as their English equivalent. In *Enrique Bernat F., S.A. v. Guadalajara, Inc.*, 210 F.3d 439 (5th Cir. 2000), the plaintiff sued alleging infringement of its trademark "Chupa Chups" for lollipops based upon the defendants use of the mark "Chupa Gurts" for its lollipops. Although the district court granted a preliminary injunction enjoining the defendant's use, the Fifth Circuit held that this constituted an abuse of discretion. The evidence established that the word "chupa" was Spanish for lollipop, and under the "foreign equivalents" doctrine, it was therefore generic. As a result, the Fifth Circuit vacated and remanded for further proceedings focusing on whether the non-generic portions of the two marks, "Chups" versus "Gurts," created a likelihood of confusion.

5.   *The Line Between Suggestive and Descriptive.* One treatise describes the difference between suggestive marks and descriptive words as follows: "Generally speaking, if the mark imparts information directly, it is descriptive. If it stands for an idea which requires some operation of the imagination to connect it with the goods, it is suggestive." A. SEIDEL, S. DALROFF, AND E. GONDA, TRADEMARK LAW AND PRACTICE § 4.06, at 77 (1963). Yet, as the Seventh Circuit has noted, the "line between descriptive and

suggestive marks is scarcely 'pikestaff plain.' " *Union Carbide Corp. v. Ever-Ready Inc.*, 531 F.2d 366, 379 (7th Cir.), *cert. denied*, 429 U.S. 830 (1976). Often, the determination seems to be "made on an intuitive basis rather than as the result of a logical analysis susceptible of articulation." *Id.* How would you classify the following words?

a. "Coppertone" for tanning oils and sunscreen. *See Douglas Labs. Corp. v. Copper Tan, Inc.*, 210 F.2d 453, 455 (2d Cir. 1954) (reversing trial court and finding that Coppertone was "not descriptive, but fanciful").

b. "Brown-in-Bag" for transparent plastic film bags used to bake foods and brown meats. *See In re Reynolds Metals Co.*, 480 F.2d 902, 903 (C.C.P.A. 1973) (suggestive).

c. "Chicken of the Sea" for canned tuna. *Compare Van Camp Sea Food Co. v. Westgate Sea Prods. Co.*, 28 F.2d 957 (9th Cir. 1928) (descriptive), *cert. denied*, 279 U.S. 841 (1929), *with Van Camp Sea Food Co. v. Alexander B. Stewart Orgs.*, 50 F.2d 976 (C.C.P.A. 1931) ("While 'Chicken of the Sea' is somewhat suggestive, we cannot conclude that it is descriptive. We think it is an arbitrary and fanciful mark.").

d. "The Money Store" for a check cashing and payday loan store. *See Money Store v. Harriscorp Finance, Inc.*, 689 F.2d 666 (7th Cir. 1982) (suggestive).

6. *What is Secondary Meaning?* The *Zatarain's* court quotes from the Supreme Court's decision in *Kellogg Co. v. National Biscuit Co.* for its definition of secondary meaning: "In order to establish a secondary meaning for a term, a plaintiff 'must show that the primary significance of the term in the minds of the consuming public is not the product but the producer.' " *Zatarain's*, 698 F.2d at 791 (*quoting Kellogg Co. v. National Biscuit Co.*, 305 U.S. 111, 118 (1938)). What does the phrase "not the product but the producer" mean? Is the Court's definition in *Coca-Cola Co. v. Koke Co.*, more helpful, asking whether the mark denotes "a single thing coming from a single source"? 254 U.S. 143, 146 (1920).

As amended, the Trademark Act of 1946 defines a trademark to "include[ ] any word, name, symbol, or device, or any combination thereof [used] . . . to identify and distinguish his or her goods . . . from those manufactured or sold by others and to indicate the source of the goods, even if that source is unknown." 15 U.S.C. § 1127 (2015). Congress added the last phrase, "even if that source is unknown," to the definition in 1988, and thereby gave its approval to the anonymous source doctrine. The anonymous source doctrine recognizes that even though consumers may understand a word as denoting "a single thing coming from a single source," they may not know who that source is. For example, can you name the source of the following well-known brands?

(a) Braun razors;

(b) Ivory dishwashing liquid;

(c) Old Spice deodorant; and

(d) Iams pet food.

7. *Secondary Meaning: Second-In-Time, First-In-Mind.* The *Kellogg Co.* Court also required a showing that the "*primary* significance of the term in the minds of the consuming public" is the brand rather than the descriptive meaning. If the brand meaning has to be the primary meaning, why then do we refer to this concept as "secondary" meaning? The difference is to recognize that primary and secondary can have two different meanings. We can refer to things as primary and secondary based upon when they occur in time, and can also refer to things as primary and secondary in importance. Thus, we refer to the development of a "second-in-time" meaning that comes to displace the primary, original, or "first-in-time" meaning of the word or phrase. But to count legally, this second-in-time meaning (or secondary meaning) must become first in importance in the minds of consumers. The brand meaning of the word or phrase must come to displace, at least as applied to the particular products or services at issue, the original descriptive connotation of the word or phrase. In the most clear cut cases of secondary meaning, the secondary meaning becomes the only meaning of the words at issue to the typical consumer. See if you know the original descriptive significance of some now well-known trademarks:

(a) Budweiser;

(b) Coca-Cola; or

(c) Gatorade.

8. *Proving Secondary Meaning.* As with any fact at issue in litigation, a party can offer two types of evidence to establish the existence of secondary meaning: (i) circumstantial evidence; and (ii) direct evidence. Circumstantial evidence includes such things as advertising, sales, and length and manner of use. As the *Zatarain's* court recognizes, evidence regarding these issues is relevant only to the extent that it tends to establish that consumers have come to understand the words at issue as a trademark. Have we seen any other types of evidence used to establish secondary meaning? How was secondary meaning established by the Baltimore Orioles in the *Maryland Stadium Authority* case in Chapter 2?

Congress has expressly recognized the use of circumstantial evidence to establish secondary meaning for purposes of registering a descriptive mark. In relevant part, section 2(f) provides:

> The Director may accept as prima facie evidence that the mark has become distinctive, as used on or in connection with the applicant's goods in commerce, proof of substantially exclusive and continuous use thereof as a mark by the applicant in commerce for the five years before the date on which the claim of distinctiveness is made.

15 U.S.C. § 1052(f) (2015).

The *Zatarain's* court neither cited nor relied on this provision. Should it have relied on this provision as prima facie evidence of Chick Fri's secondary meaning?

Alternatively, a party can seek to establish secondary meaning through direct evidence. Direct evidence includes consumer testimony and surveys that seek to establish how consumers understand the word(s) at issue.

Do you agree with the court that Zatarain's has proven that for Fish Fri the brand-specific informational role has come to outweigh the non-brand informational role for the consumers at issue? Do you agree with the court that Zatarain's has failed to prove such a shift in the balance for Chick Fri?

9. *Establishing Secondary Meaning with Surveys.* Surveys are commonly introduced as evidence of secondary meaning. The first step in creating a proper survey is to draw the survey sample—the individuals who participate in the survey—from the correct survey universe. The legal principles of trademark law define the relevant survey universe. Courts have defined secondary meaning in various ways, but the key question is whether consumers of the trademarked product have come to associate the trademark with a unique, albeit perhaps anonymous, source. Given this definition, a survey of secondary meaning should draw its sample from individuals who have bought or who are likely to buy the specific goods or services for which a party is claiming secondary meaning in an associated trademark or trade dress. A preliminary question or set of questions, known as screener questions, is typically used in surveying to ensure that the survey sample is drawn from the correct universe. What were the screener questions used for the Fish Fri and Chick Fri surveys in *Zatarain's*? Was the screener question effective for both products to ensure that the survey drew a sample from the correct universe? What was the consequence of failing to draw the sample from the correct universe?

Once a correct sample is drawn, the next step is formulating a question or series of questions that probes the issue of secondary meaning. What substantive questions were the survey respondents asked in *Zatarain's* in an attempt to examine the issue of secondary meaning? Does a response of "Zatarain's Fish Fri" or "Zatarain's Chick Fri" to these questions provide evidence one way or the other on whether "Fish Fri" or "Chick Fri" has developed secondary meaning? (Incidentally, given that the respondents answer verbally, how we will we know if they were saying "fish fry" or "Fish Fri"?) If we asked a similar survey question, but for beer instead, and consumers responded that they would purchase "budweiser beer," would that establish secondary meaning for "budweiser"? Would it establish secondary meaning for "beer"?

A more typical secondary meaning survey format asks consumers: "Do you associate [claimed trademark] with [product identification] of one or more than one companies?" and then asks them to explain their answers. *See* Vincent N. Palladino, *Surveying Secondary Meaning*, 84 TRADEMARK REP. 155, 165 (1994). The percentage of respondents who associate the claimed mark with only one company is then calculated, and if sufficiently large, is proffered as evidence of secondary meaning. How would you apply this survey format to the *Zatarain's* case? What question(s) would you ask the survey respondents? Do you see any flaws inherent in this format? Is it possible that two respondents might both respond "one company," yet be thinking of entirely different companies? *See, e.g., Test Masters Educational Servs., Inc. v. Robin Singh Educational Servs., Inc.*, ___ F.3d ___, 2015 WL 4997705, at *5 (5th Cir. 2015) (discounting results from secondary meaning survey that asked respondents if they associated claimed trademark with "one company" because it was unclear if respondents who said yes associated mark uniquely with plaintiff, uniquely with defendant, or uniquely with some other company). What additional questions would you ask to address this possibility?

In *Storck U.S.A., L.P. v. Farley Candy Co.*, 797 F.Supp. 1399 (N.D. Ill. 1992), the plaintiff offered a variation on this survey format in an attempt to establish secondary meaning in the white-on-gold wrapper of individual Werther's Original candy pieces. The survey asked: "Do you think pieces of butterscotch or buttery-flavored hard candy with wrappings that look like these are put out by one company or by more than one company?" *Id.* at 1411. Note the subtle changes in phrasing. How, if at all, do you think those changes affected the responses? Although forty-six percent of the survey respondents answered "one company," the trial court found that the survey "is not probative of secondary meaning" because *inter alia* it failed to distinguish between inherent distinctiveness and secondary meaning. *Id.* at 1412.

In *Sunbeam Corp. v. Equity Industries Corp.*, 635 F.Supp. 625 (E.D. Va. 1986), *aff'd w/o op.*, 811 F.2d 1505 (4th Cir. 1987), the plaintiff and the defendant offered competing surveys on the issue of whether the shape of a food processor had developed secondary meaning. After being shown a food processor with the brand names covered, the plaintiff's survey asked three substantive questions:

Q4: What company do you think puts out this food processor?

Q5: What is the name of this food processor?

Q6: Do you associate the appearance of this food processor with one company or more than one company?

Sunbeam Corp., 635 F.Supp. at 630. Although fifty-eight percent of the survey respondents answered question six with "one company," the district court found that the survey results were of "little, if any, value to the Court's secondary meaning analysis" for two reasons. *Id.* at 631. First, questions four and five both either stated or suggested that only one company manufactured the food processor and thus may have biased responses to question six. (This sort of bias, which arises from ordering questions so that earlier questions suggest the answer to later questions, is known as an "order effect.") Second, the use of the phrase "this food processor" in question six may have led respondents to believe that they were being asked whether one or more than one company made the particular food processor they were being shown. *Id.*

The trial court found the defendant's survey flawed as well. As in the plaintiff's survey, the defendant's expert showed the survey respondents the food processor with the brand names covered, and then asked two relevant questions:

Q1a: Do you have a belief as to what company or companies put out this food processor?

Q1b: What company or companies do you believe put out this food processor?

Only 9.2 percent of the respondents correctly identified the food processor's manufacturer or brand name, and the defendant therefore offered the survey to show a lack of secondary meaning. However, the trial court accorded the defendant's survey little weight, finding that it also suffered from two serious flaws. First, it failed to direct the survey respondents specifically to the plaintiff's claimed trade dress—the design or overall configuration of the food processor, as distinct from the food processor itself. Second, by asking for a specific company name, the survey overlooked respondents who associated the product's overall appearance with a unique, but anonymous source. *Id.*

How should the surveys in these cases be modified to address these concerns?

B. GENERIC WORDS

ANTI-MONOPOLY, INC. V. GENERAL MILLS FUN GROUP, INC.

684 F.2d 1316 (9th Cir. 1982)

WALLACE, CIRCUIT JUDGE

This is the second appeal in this case. Our first opinion is reported in *Anti-Monopoly, Inc. v. General Mills Fun Group*, 9 Cir., 1979, 611 F.2d 296 (*Anti-Monopoly I*). On remand the district court again found that the "Monopoly" trademark was valid and had been infringed by *Anti-Monopoly, Inc. Anti-Monopoly, Inc. v. General Mills Fun Group, Inc.*, N.D.Cal., 1981, 515 F. Supp. 448 (*Anti-Monopoly II*). We reverse and remand for further proceedings.

I. *Prior Proceedings.*

General Mills is the successor to Parker Brothers, Inc., which had produced and sold a game it called Monopoly since 1935. Parker Brothers registered "Monopoly" as a trademark in that year. In 1973 Anti-Monopoly, Inc. was established to produce and sell a game it called Anti-Monopoly. General Mills claimed that this infringed its trademark. This action was then brought by Anti-Monopoly, seeking a declaratory judgment that the registered trademark "Monopoly" was invalid, and cancelling its registration. In a counterclaim, General Mills sought declaratory and injunctive relief upholding its trademark, and the dismissal of the action. The case was tried without a jury in 1976. The court entered a judgment for General Mills. We reversed and remanded for further consideration of (i) the validity of the trademark, (ii) infringement of the trademark, if it is valid, by Anti-Monopoly, and (iii) state law claims concerning unfair competition and dilution. We also chose to defer consideration of (iv) Anti-Monopoly's defense that General Mills had unclean hands. On remand, after hearing further evidence, the district court again entered a judgment for General Mills.

II. *The Standard of Review.*

We state the standard of review at the beginning of this opinion, lest we be charged with not applying it because our "acknowledgement [of it] came late in [our] opinion." *Pullman-Standard v. Swint*, 102 S.Ct. 1781, at 1791 (1982); *id*. Marshall, J., dissenting 102 S.Ct. at 1784–85.

We must apply the standard stated in Rule 52(a), F.R.Civ.P., the case having been tried without a jury: "Findings of fact shall not be set aside unless clearly erroneous. . . ." This has been interpreted to mean that the trial judge's finding of fact cannot be set aside unless, "although there is evidence to support it, the reviewing court on the entire evidence is left with the definite and firm conviction that a mistake has been committed." *United States v. United States Gypsum Co.*, 333 U.S. 364, 395 (1948).

The Supreme Court has recently reminded us of the importance of the rule and of our duty to abide by it. *Pullman-Standard, supra*, 102 S.Ct. at 1789. In that case, the Court held that the rule applies equally to "ultimate" facts and to "subsidiary" facts. *Id*. The Court also held that, when a finding is based on an erroneous view of the law, it may be set aside, but that in such a case the appellate court cannot make a contrary finding, but must remand to the trial court for new findings, to be made in the light of the correct rule of law. *Id*. at 1791–92. To this there is one exception: A remand is unnecessary if "the record permits only one resolution of the factual issue." *Id. citing Kelley v. Southern Pacific Co.*, 1974, 419 U.S. 318, 331–332. . . .

III. *The Burden of Proof.*

The district court ruled that Anti-Monopoly had the burden of showing genericness "by convincing evidence." *Anti-Monopoly II*, 515 F. Supp. at 451–452. The case cited for that proposition, *Feathercombs, Inc. v. Solo Products Corp.*, 306 F.2d 251 (2d Cir. 1962), does not announce such a rule. The only reference to "convincing evidence" is at 306 F.2d at 256, and says nothing about burden of proof. There is a presumption in favor of a registered trademark, and the burden of proof is upon one who attacks the mark as generic, but the presumption can be overcome by a showing by a preponderance of the evidence that the term was or has become generic. *See Vuitton Et Fils S.A. v. J. Young Enterprises*, 644 F.2d 769, 775–776 (9th Cir. 1981).

IV. *Generic Terms—The Law.*

Our opinion in *Anti-Monopoly I* binds both this court and the district court. There, we set out the law about generic terms and explained how it was to be applied to the particular facts of this case. *Anti-Monopoly I*, 611 F.2d at 300–306. In this opinion, we assume that the reader will be familiar with that opinion. Here, we emphasize what we consider to be its essence. A word used as a trademark is not generic if "the primary significance of the term in the minds of the consuming public is not the product but the producer." *Id.* at 302. "When a trademark primarily denotes a product, not the product's producer, the trademark is lost." *Id.* at 301. A registered mark is to be cancelled if it has become "the common descriptive name of an article," 15 U.S.C. § 1064(c), and no incontestable right can be acquired in such a mark. 15 U.S.C. § 1065(4). We said "Even if only one producer—Parker Brothers—has ever made the MONOPOLY game, so that the public necessarily associates the product with that particular producer, the trademark is invalid unless source indication is its primary significance." *Anti-Monopoly I*, 611 F.2d at 302. "It is the source-denoting function which trademark laws protect, and nothing more." *Id.* at 301. "One competitor will not be permitted to impoverish the language of commerce by preventing his fellows from fairly describing their own goods." *Id. quoting Bada Co. v. Montgomery Ward & Co.*, 426 F.2d 8, 11 (9th Cir. 1970). "When members of the consuming public use a game name to denote the game itself, and not its producer, the trademark is generic and, therefore, invalid." *Id.* at 304. . . .

VI. *Has "Monopoly" Become Generic Since It Was Registered?*

This question is discussed, and the trial court's findings of fact appear in *Monopoly II*, 515 F. Supp. at 452–455. Under the heading "FINDINGS OF FACT," the following appears:

> 1. The court again finds as fact each fact found in this Opinion as set forth in the foregoing.

> 2. As a game trademark, MONOPOLY primarily denotes its producer, Parker Brothers, and primarily denoted its producer when registered.

Id. at 455. We consider finding 2 to be one of ultimate fact, and subject to the "clearly erroneous" standard of Rule 52(a). *See Pullman-Standard, supra*, 102 S.Ct. at 1789.

The district court also said " 'Primary significance' logically implies a hierarchical priority over a competing alternative." 515 F. Supp. at 454. Dictionary definitions are in accord. Funk & Wagnalls' New Standard Dictionary gives "primary 1. First in . . . thought or intention, 2. First in degree, rank or importance, most fundamental, chief. . . ." Webster's New International Dictionary (2d Ed.) gives "1. First in . . . intention; 2. First in . . . importance; chief, principal. . . ." We are not sure what the district court meant by a "competing alternative." To us, this carries some suggestion of "either, or." Yet it is nearly always the case, as the district court recognized, that a trademark will identify both the product and its producer. *Anti-Monopoly II*, 515 F. Supp. at 454. Indeed, its value lies in its identification of the product with its producer.

In its opinion, the district court supports its finding 2 as follows:

> The difficulty in this regard arises due to the public's dual usage of the trade name, denoting both product and source. For example, the mark "Ford" to the average consumer denotes *both* car and motor car company. However, to demonstrate "primary significance" it is necessary to show more than a high percentage of the consuming public who recognize MONOPOLY as a brand name (as defendant has done: 63% of those polled recognized MONOPOLY as a "brand name"). It is necessary to show more than a public awareness that Parker Brothers is the sole manufacturer of MONOPOLY (55% correctly identified Parker Brothers in defendant's survey). "Primary significance" logically implies a hierarchical priority over a competing alternative.

> Yet the cumulative weight of the evidence does satisfy this court that the primary significance of MONOPOLY in the public's eye is to denote a "Parker Brothers' Game" (*i.e.*, source) in contradistinction to that "popular game of MONOPOLY" (product). Parker Brothers has expended substantial time, energy, and money in promoting and policing their trademark, expending over $4 million in advertising expenditures. One result of these diligent efforts has been the extraordinary success Parker Brothers has achieved in creating public source awareness. Over 55% of the American public correctly identified Parker Brothers as the producer of the game. *Cf. Selchow & Righter Co. v. Western Printing & Lithographing Co.*, D.C., 47 F. Supp. 322, 326 (court finding it "very evident that any ordinary customer, going into a store, and asking for the game "PARCHEESI" had no information as to who might have manufactured and produced the game.") An even more impressive display of the amount of goodwill which Parker Brothers has imbued through its various games—especially MONOPOLY—*is the finding of plaintiff's survey that one out of three MONOPOLY purchasers do so primarily because "they like Parker Brothers' products."* Hence, source attribution is a dominant perceived effect of the MONOPOLY trademark. This court cannot say from the facts before it that it is not the "primary significance" of the mark.

Id. at 454–455 (emphasis in the original).

In considering whether these findings, and finding 2, are clearly erroneous, we have in mind an obvious proposition. The word "Monopoly," while not in its ordinary meaning descriptive of the game "Monopoly," is an ordinary English word, and it does describe the objective of the game. This was recognized in the rules of the game published by Parker Brothers in 1935. They begin with:

BRIEF IDEA OF THE GAME

THE IDEA OF THE GAME is to BUY and RENT or SELL properties so profitably that one becomes the wealthiest player and eventual MONOPOLIST.

A Monopolist has a monopoly. By choosing the word as a trademark, Parker Brothers subjected itself to a considerable risk that the word would become so identified with the game as to be "generic."

In *Anti-Monopoly II* the district court also said this: "Unless the Ninth Circuit standard is meant to foreclose the possibility of trademark protection for any producer of a unique game whose corporate name does not appear in the title of the game (e.g., 'SCRABBLE,' 'TOWER OF BABBLE'), then its test cannot be used here to thwart MONOPOLY's trademark rights." 515 F. Supp. at 455. Nothing in our opinion in *Anti-Monopoly I* even hints at the relevance of whether or not the corporate name of the producer of a game appears in the title of the game, and our opinion does not foreclose the possibility of trademark protection of the name of a game that does not embody the corporate name of its producer. But our opinion does squarely hold as follows: "Even if only one producer—Parker Brothers—has ever made the MONOPOLY game, so that the public necessarily associates the product with that particular producer, the trademark is invalid unless source identification is its primary significance." 611 F.2d at 302.

The district court obviously felt that our opinion in *Anti-Monopoly I* gave Anti-Monopoly an easier task in trying to show that "Monopoly" has become generic than the district court would give. Nevertheless, both we and the district court are bound by our decision in *Anti-Monopoly I.*

We now consider whether finding 2 of the district court is clearly erroneous. We conclude that it is.

As we have seen, the district court relied in part upon the fact that General Mills and its predecessor have spent time, energy, and money in promoting and policing use of the term "Monopoly." That fact, however, is not of itself sufficient to create legally protectable rights. *HMH Publishing Co. v. Brincat*, 504 F.2d 713, 719 (9th Cir. 1974). It is not, of itself, enough that over 55% of the public has come to associate the product, and as a consequence the name by which the product is generally known, with Parker Brothers. *Anti-Monopoly I*, 611 F.2d at 302. *See also Kellogg Co. v. National Biscuit Co.*, 305 U.S. 111, 118 (1938) (the

"Shredded Wheat" case). Even if one third of the members of the public who purchased the game did so because they liked Parker Brothers' products, that fact does not show that "Monopoly" is primarily source indicating. The very survey on which the district court placed emphasis by italicizing its result shows that two thirds of the members of the public who purchased the game wanted "Monopoly" and did not care who made it.

The real question is what did Parker Brothers and General Mills get for their money and efforts? To us, the evidence overwhelmingly shows that they very successfully promoted the game of Monopoly, but that in doing it they so successfully promoted "Monopoly" as "the name of the game," that it became generic in the sense in which we use that term in trademark law. We recognize that "there is evidence to support" the trial court's findings, *United States Gypsum Co., supra*, 333 U.S. at 395, but "on the entire evidence [we are] left with the definite and firm conviction that a mistake has been committed." *Id*.

The principal evidence in the case was in the form of consumer surveys, and to these we now turn.

A.   *The Brand-name Survey.*

General Mills conducted a survey based upon a survey approved by a district court in the "Teflon" case, *E.I. Du Pont de Nemours & Co. v. Yoshida International, Inc.*, 393 F. Supp. 502 (E.D.N.Y. 1975). In the survey conducted by General Mills, people were asked whether "Monopoly" is a "brand-name," and were told: "By *brand* name, I mean a name like *Chevrolet*, which is made by *one* company; by common name, I mean 'automobile,' which is made by a number of different companies." (Emphasis in the original.) The results of this survey had no relevance to the question in this case. Under the survey definition, "Monopoly" would have to be a "brand name" because it is made by only one company. This tells us nothing at all about the *primary* meaning of "Monopoly" in the minds of consumers.

It is true that the witness through whom the survey was introduced testified on direct examination that as a result of it his opinion was that "Monopoly" primarily denotes source or producer. However, on cross-examination and redirect examination it became clear that this witness had done no more than reduplicate the "Teflon" survey (with appropriate substitutions and slight additions) and had no opinion on the relevance of this survey to any issue in the present case. The brand-name survey is not even some evidence to support finding 2; it is no evidence to support it.

B.   *The "Thermos" Survey.*

Anti-Monopoly's first survey was based upon that used in the "Thermos" case, *American Thermos Co. v. Aladdin Industries, Inc.*, 207 F.

Supp. 9, 20–21 (D.Conn. 1962), *aff'd*, 321 F.2d 577 (2d Cir. 1963). In Anti-Monopoly's survey people were asked the question: "Are you familiar with business board games of the kind in which players buy, sell, mortgage and trade city streets, utilities and railroads, build houses, collect rents and win by bankrupting all other players, or not"? About 53% said they were. Those people were then asked: "If you were going to buy this kind of game, what would you ask for, that is, what would you tell the sales clerk you wanted"? About 80% said: "Monopoly."

The witness through whom this survey was introduced testified that Anti-Monopoly gave his firm the questions used in the "Thermos" survey and asked it to conduct a similar one. Anti-Monopoly provided the wording of the questions in the present survey as well. The research firm was responsible for deciding how to reach a sample that would adequately represent the population of the United States. The witness gave no testimony as to the relevance of the results of the survey to the issues in the case.

In one of its briefs, General Mills points out that the survey used in the "Thermos" case was described as "generally corroborative of the court's conclusions drawn from other evidence," and that the district court which decided the "Teflon" case found a "Thermos"-like survey defective because "the design of the questions more often than not [focused] on supplying the inquirer a 'name,' without regard to whether the principal significance of the name supplied was 'its indication of the nature or class of an article, rather than an indication of its origin,' *King-Seeley Thermos Co., supra*, 321 F.2d at 580." *E.I. Du Pont de Nemours & Co., supra*, 393 F. Supp. at 527. Be that as it may, we think that the results of this survey are compelling evidence of a proposition that is also dictated by common sense: an overwhelming proportion of those who are familiar with the game would ask for it by the name "Monopoly."

C.   *The Motivation Survey.*

After the remand to the district court, Anti-Monopoly commissioned a further survey. This survey was based upon the following language from our opinion in *Anti-Monopoly I*:

> It may be that when a customer enters a game store and asks for MONOPOLY, he means: "I would like Parker Brothers' version of a real estate trading game, because I like Parker Brothers' products. Thus, I am not interested in board games made by Anti-Monopoly, or anyone other than Parker Brothers." On the other hand, the consumer may mean: "I want a 'Monopoly' game. Don't bother showing me Anti-Monopoly, or EASY MONEY, or backgammon. I am interested in playing the game of Monopoly. I don't much care who makes it."

In the first example, the consumer differentiates between MONOPOLY and other games according to source-particular criteria. In the second example, source is not a consideration. The relevant genus, or product category, varies accordingly. At the urging of Parker Brothers, the district court erred by first defining the genus, and then asking the "primary significance" question about the wrong genus-species dichotomy. The proper mode of analysis is to decide but one question: whether the primary significance of a term is to denote product, or source. In making this determination, the correct genus-species distinction, that is, the correct genericness finding, follows automatically.

611 F.2d at 305–306.

The wording of the questions was provided by Dr. Anspach, Anti-Monopoly's president, and by the expert who testified at trial. The expert had studied our first opinion. The survey was designed to ascertain the use of the term "Monopoly" by those who had purchased the game in the past or intended to do so in the near future. It was conducted by telephone. The results were as follows: 92% were aware of "Monopoly," the business board game produced by Parker Brothers. Of that 92%, 62% either had "purchased 'Monopoly' within the last couple of years" or intended to purchase it in the near future. Those people were asked why they had bought or would buy monopoly. The answers exhibited the following pattern: 82% mentioned some aspect of the playing of the game (e.g., that they played it as a kid, it was a family game, it was enjoyable, it was fun to play, it was interesting), 14% mentioned some educational aspect of the game, 7% mentioned the equipment (e.g., saying it was durable) or said they were replacing a set, 1% spoke of price, 34% gave other reasons neutral to the issues in this case (e.g., it was for a gift, the game was a classic, people like the game). The percentages total more than 100 because respondents often gave more than one reason.

The people who said that they had purchased the game within the last couple of years or would purchase it in the near future were then given a choice of two statements and were asked which best expressed their reasons. Sixty-five percent chose: "I want a 'Monopoly' game primarily because I am interested in playing 'Monopoly,' I don't much care who makes it." Thirty-two percent chose: "I would like Parker Brothers' 'Monopoly' game primarily because I like Parker Brothers' products."

A very similar "intercept survey" was conducted by face to face interviews. The results were very close to those of the telephone survey, but the expert did not claim that the intercept study was validly projectable.

The district court indicated its reasons for rejecting this survey. Insofar as these are findings of fact they must be accorded the deference required by Rule 52(a), and, giving them that deference, we hold them to be clearly erroneous. The district court's major objection to the survey was that it sought an explanation of an actual purchaser's motivation in purchasing the game rather than the primary significance of the word. *Anti-Monopoly, Inc.,* 515 F. Supp. at 453. This objection cannot stand. In our earlier opinion we made it clear that what was relevant was the sense in which a purchaser used the word "Monopoly" when asking for the game by that name. The survey was a reasonable effort to find that out and was modeled closely on what we said in our opinion.

The district court thought that the survey was invalidated by the fact that in the first question people were asked if they were "aware of 'Monopoly,' the business board game *produced* by *Parker Brothers*" (emphasis supplied). It supposed that the presence of the emphasized words somehow inhibited those who might otherwise have responded to later questions that they bought the game because it was produced by Parker Brothers. No evidence or expert opinion was given to support this view and it has no inherent plausibility.

In a footnote the district court said of this survey that "other methodological deficiencies abound." *Id.* 515 F. Supp. at 453 n.4. One suggested deficiency is that Professor Anspach suggested the language that was used. This is taken to be evidence of "inherent bias." General Mills argues to us that little weight should be given to this survey because it was devised by Dr. Anspach and the survey firm without the mediation of a trademark attorney. We find no merit in these objections.

The district court found that the study was "overwhelmingly prone to errors of subjective grading." *Id.* No doubt it was referring to the process by which responses were categorized as, for example, education, enjoyable, "played it as a kid," or equipment. This process of categorization was not purely mechanical, and did involve some use of human judgment. However, we are not prepared to dismiss every process that includes the operation of human judgment as "overwhelmingly prone to errors of subjective grading." Nor do we find any special reasons to suspect the exercise of judgment in the case of this survey. The categories that were listed strike us as reasonable ones.

Neither the district court nor General Mills claims that there were *in fact* errors of judgment, but only that there might have been. The raw responses to the survey were at one point offered in evidence by Anti-Monopoly, but the offer was withdrawn after General Mills objected, citing F.R. Evidence 705, 1005 and 1006, and the district judge said: "if [counsel for General Mills had] asked for them, he could have received them. If he received them, he could have turned them over to his expert to check them out and see if they give a reliable or non-reliable basis for the opinion. But since he didn't ask for them, I don't think they should go into evidence." Under these circumstances, General Mills cannot now argue that the raw responses were not in fact correctly categorized.

Finally, in the same footnote, the district court suggested that the result that 82% of monopoly purchasers buy for "product related" reasons *cannot be reconciled* with the other result that 32% of actual or potential buyers chose the statement "I would buy Parker Brothers' 'monopoly' game primarily because I like Parker Brothers' products." This is a misconception of the survey results. The comparable figure to the 32% is the 65% who chose the statement "I want a 'monopoly' game primarily because I am interested in playing 'monopoly,' I don't much care who makes it." The 82% who gave "product related" answers no doubt had both product related and source related reasons for buying, and, with some, enough to reduce 82% to 65%, the source related reason was stronger when the person had to choose. But it is still true that 65% chose product, rather than source.

We conclude that the findings regarding the survey are clearly erroneous, and that it does support the conclusion that the primary significance of "Monopoly" is product rather than source.

D.   *The Tide Survey.*

General Mills introduced a survey that was intended as a *reductio ad absurdum* of the motivation survey. It showed that when asked to supply a reason for buying Tide about 60% of those who might buy it now or in the future said that they would buy Tide because it does a good job. However, when asked "Would you buy Tide primarily because you like Procter and Gamble's products, or primarily because you like Tide detergent?" about 68% indicated the latter reason. There were various respects in which this survey was different from the motivation survey used by Anti-Monopoly, but we shall not suddenly attach great importance to technical considerations. We suspect that these results tend to show that the general public regards "Tide" as the name of a particular detergent, having particular qualities, rather than as one producer's brand name for the same detergent which is available from a variety of sources. We do not know whether the general public thinks this, or if it does, is correct in thinking this, or whether Procter and Gamble intend them to think it. If the general public does think this, and if the test formulated in *Anti-Monopoly I* could be mechanically extended to the very different subject of detergents, then Procter and Gamble might have cause for alarm. The issue is not before us today. The motivation survey conducted by Anti-Monopoly, Inc. was in accordance with the views we expressed in *Anti-Monopoly I*. The results in the Tide Survey are of no relevance to this case.

E. *Conclusion.*

We hold that Finding 2 is clearly erroneous because, although there is some evidence to support it, our examination of the evidence leaves us with the definite and firm conviction that a mistake has been committed. We hold that, as applied to a board game, the word "Monopoly" has become "generic," and the registration of it as a trademark is no longer valid.

VII. *Other Issues.*

The district court must determine whether Anti-Monopoly is taking reasonable care to inform the public of the source of its product, and if it finds that this is not so may enjoin the sale of anti-monopoly save upon appropriate conditions. *Anti-Monopoly I,* 611 F.2d at 307.

We remand the case. The district court shall enter judgment for Anti-Monopoly, Inc. on the question of trademark validity and take whatever actions are necessary and consistent with this opinion.

NOTES FOR DISCUSSION

1. *The Firestorm.* The *Anti-Monopoly* decision generated a firestorm of criticism among trademark owners and commentators. Chief among the academic commentary was Hans Zeisel's article, *The Surveys that Broke Monopoly,* 50 U. CHI. L. REV. 896 (1983), who argued: "The genericness doctrine marks the only place in the law of intellectual property in which success is punished rather than rewarded." The argument was not new. The Second Circuit had considered it and rejected it twenty years earlier in *King-Seeley Thermos Co. v. Aladdin Indus., Inc.*:

> No doubt, the Aspirin and Cellophane doctrine can be a harsh one for it places a penalty on the manufacturer who has made skillful use of advertising and has popularized his product. *See* 3 Callman, Unfair Competition and Trademarks 1149–50 (2d ed. 1950). However, King-Seeley has enjoyed a commercial monopoly of the word "thermos" for over fifty years. During that period, despite its efforts to protect the trademark, the public has virtually expropriated it as its own. The word having become part of the public domain, it would be unfair to unduly restrict the right of a competitor of King-Seeley to use the word.

321 F.2d 577, 581 (2d Cir. 1963).

Nevertheless, Congress responded to the criticism by amending the Lanham Trademark Act in two ways in the Trademark Clarification Act of 1984. Pub. L. No. 620, 98th Cong., 2d Sess., §§ 102–103, 98 Stat. 3335, 3335. First, to section 14(3), Congress added two sentences: "A registered mark shall not be deemed to be the generic name of goods or services solely because such mark is also used as a name of or to identify a unique product or service. The primary significance of the registered mark to the relevant public rather than purchaser motivation shall be the test for determining whether the registered mark has become the generic name of goods or services on or in connection with which it has been used." 15 U.S.C. § 1064(3). Second, to the definition of "abandonment" in section 45, Congress added the sentence: "Purchaser motivation shall not be a test for determining abandonment under this paragraph." 15 U.S.C. § 1127. In the Trademark Law Revision Act of 1988, Congress also amended the language of section 14(3) to replace the phrase "the common descriptive name of an article" with the phrase "the generic name for the goods . . . for which it is registered." Pub. L. No. 667, 100th Cong., 2d Sess., § 15, 102 Stat. 3935, 3940.

If the *Anti-Monopoly* case arose today, would these amendments change the outcome? Are the results of the "purchaser motivation" survey still relevant to the post-amendment legal standard of "the primary significance of the registered mark to the relevant public"? The term "Monopoly" on a board game box can signify to consumers either: (i) the nature of the game in the box, in terms of the board layout, equipment included, and the rules of the game; or (ii) the maker of the product. Given that a defendant may no longer use the purchaser motivation survey after the congressional amendments, could the defendant nevertheless use a survey that asked consumers whether the primary significance of the term "Monopoly" on a board game box was the nature of the game or the maker of the product? Would such a question correspond to the *Kellogg* Court's rule that consumers must rely on a claimed trademark to identify "not the product but the producer"? Could a survey ask consumers whether the term "Monopoly" primarily identified the product or the producer?

Should the genericness doctrine be seen as a penalty on those who have so successfully marketed their products or services that their mark becomes synonymous with the good or service itself? Or is it simply recognition that consumers would be better off if competitors were also allowed to use the word at issue to inform consumers of the nature of their products?

2. *Genericide.* Because of their antagonism towards the doctrine, trademark plaintiffs' attorneys—which is pretty much the entire trademark bar—coined the term "genericide" to capture their sense that finding a trademark generic unfairly punishes successful trademark owners. By relabeling a court's decision that a term is or has become generic as genericide, the trademark bar attempted to link findings that a claimed trademark is generic with homicide or genocide, and other "-cides" that are inherently wrong.

In the debates leading to the enactment of the Trademark Act, the trademark bar took the position that genericness should not focus on consumer understanding, but on the trademark owner's actions or inactions with respect to the asserted trademark. Indeed, the 1944 bill contained no separate genericness provision. Rather, the bill allowed for loss of trademark protection only where the actions or inaction of the trademark owner caused the mark to become generic.

Only at the insistence of the Department of Justice did Congress add a separate and independent genericness doctrine that focused on consumer understanding to sections 14(3) and 15(4). 15 U.S.C. §§ 1064(3) (allowing a registered trademark that is or has become the generic name for the goods or services, or a portion thereof, for which it is registered to be cancelled at any time), 1065(4) (providing that a registration shall not become incontestable to the extent the mark is or becomes generic for its associated goods or services) (2015); *see also* Glynn S. Lunney, Jr., *Trademark Monopolies*, 48 Emory L.J. 367, 421–22 & nn. 214–215 (1999).

3. *Genericness and Federal Registration.* Look at section 2 of the Trademark Act. May the Patent and Trademark Office refuse to register on the principal register a generic term for a given product or service as a mark for that product or service? Presumably, the answer to that question has to be yes. Is there any language in section 2 that would provide a basis for such a rejection? As mentioned, in response to the Department of Justice's concerns, Congress amended sections 14 and 15 to incorporate a separate genericness doctrine just before the Trademark Act's enactment in 1946. However, there was no parallel amendment made to section 2. As a result, the precise statutory basis for denying a generic term registration on the principal register is not clear. Yet, the alternative of registering such terms, and then allowing them to be cancelled at any time under section 14, makes little sense.

Courts have universally held that generic terms may not be registered, but have differed on the legal basis for such exclusion. The Federal Circuit has simply asserted that the Patent and Trademark Office may, and indeed, shall deny registration to a generic term, without citing specific statutory language. *See, e.g., In re Dial-A-Mattress Operating Corp.*, 240 F.3d 1341, 1341 (Fed. Cir. 2001). Other courts have found the authority to deny registration as a necessary implication of section 14. *See, e.g., CES Pub. Corp. v. St. Regis Pubs.*, 531 F.2d 11, 13 (2d Cir. 1975) ("Although the Act does not explicitly say that a generic word cannot be validly registered even if there is proof of secondary meaning, this is the necessary implication from the contrast between § 14(c) and § 15(4) on the one hand, which provide that a registered mark may be cancelled at any time if it becomes 'the common descriptive name of an article or substance,' and that 'No incontestable right shall be acquired in a mark which is the common descriptive name of any article or substance, patented or otherwise,' and §§ 2(e), (f) and § 15 on the other, which permit registration of 'merely descriptive' marks if they have 'become distinctive of the applicant's goods in commerce' and 'allow such marks to achieve incontestability.'"). Another possibility is the preamble of section 2. Because consumers understand generic terms, by definition, to refer primarily to the genus of goods or services at issue, rather than to a particular source of those goods or services, a generic term is not a "trademark by which the goods of the applicant may be distinguished from the good of others. . . ." 15 U.S.C. § 1052 (2015). In any event, whatever the precise statutory basis, the authority of the Patent and Trademark Office to deny registration to a generic term is unquestioned.

4.   *The Policy Basis of Genericness.* What are the consumer interests at stake in the *Anti-Monopoly* case? Did the decision benefit consumers in any way? The *Anti-Monopoly* case provides fertile ground for considering these issues because the court's finding of genericness led to a sharp change in the associated market. So long as Monopoly remained a trademark, no one else offered a similar game. Once the Ninth Circuit declared the term generic, competition in the Monopoly market exploded, as other companies jumped in with a vast array of variations on the basic Monopoly game. In response, General Mills sharply expanded its own offerings of the game, as well. Today, consumers can pick and choose among these offerings, whereas before the Ninth Circuit's decision, they had only one option. There can be little doubt that this sharp increase in competition in the field of -opoly games generated a corresponding increase in consumer welfare.

Did the Ninth Circuit's decision harm consumers in any way? In terms of consumer welfare, the central concern is increased confusion or search costs. If a consumer wants a genuine General Mills-brand Monopoly game, can a consumer readily find such a game? Does the proliferation of other companies' versions of the game make that unduly difficult? The answer here might appear to be a simple no, but think about the issue carefully. What brand-specific information are consumers concerned about in choosing between a General Mills Monopoly game and one from some other company? Brand-specific information might include such things as whether all of the pieces are in fact included in each game sold, the quality of manufacture of the pieces, and the quality of the printing on the board, cards, and other materials. If a person plays a General Mills Monopoly game at a friend's house, and is satisfied with both the game play and the quality of the game's manufacture, when that person goes to purchase their own Monopoly game, does finding Monopoly generic create a risk that that person may purchase some other company's lower quality Monopoly game by mistake and be dissatisfied? With the lower quality pieces, cards, or board? In an ordinary genericness case, this trade-off between the benefits from increased competition against the costs from the possibility of increased confusion, or higher search costs generally, in the original product market balances the relevant consumer interests at stake and defines whether consumers are better or worse off from a finding of genericness.

The *Anti-Monopoly, Inc.* case was not, however, an ordinary genericness case. Anti-Monopoly did not want to market its own version of the Monopoly game, but a different game with a similar name. If we focus on the defendant directly, the question becomes whether consumers are better or worse off allowing this defendant to use "Anti-Monopoly" as the name of its game. How does allowing such use make consumers' better-off? True, the name describes to some extent the nature of the original Anti-Monopoly game, where the players take the role of lawyers working for the Antitrust Department of the United States government and seek to break the monopolies found on the game board. Are there other names that would convey the nature of the game just as well?

On the other side, how does allowing such use make consumers worse off? Here the concern is that the similar names will lead some consumers to buy the Anti-Monopoly game as a result of their positive associations from playing the Monopoly game. Do you think that's likely? Before you reject such a possibility out-of-hand, I must confess that when we heard of the Anti-Monopoly game, my brothers and I begged our parents to buy it. We believed that it was a sequel to, or otherwise affiliated with the Monopoly game, in a way that meant that we would enjoy the Anti-Monopoly game as much as we enjoyed Monopoly. Perhaps my experience was unique in that regard, but if that perception was widespread, is that a type of confusion that trademark law can and should address?

To resolve the *Anti-Monopoly* case, should we focus solely on the consumer welfare balance solely with respect to the defendant's actual use? Or should we consider the broader implications that a finding of genericness will have for the Monopoly game market? If, on balance, we found that consumers would be better off if Monopoly were generic for the Monopoly market, but at the same time, we also found that consumers were on balance worse off if the defendant's use were permitted, is there some way to find Monopoly generic for one use, but a brand for the other? Or is it an all-or-nothing choice? And if it is all-or-nothing, how do we decide which?

Moreover, we should not analyze these issues as if they were static. Even if the Ninth Circuit had ruled the other way, competitors could, in theory at least, offer their own versions of the Monopoly game. They would simply have to use a different name for it and then spend money on advertising to inform consumers that their game was the same game as Monopoly, though perhaps in a different setting. If that seems impractical, consider that the generally accepted name for the class of truck-like, multi-use, multi-passenger vehicles back in the 1980s was "jeep." It did not matter if the truck at issue was a Chevy Blazer or a Ford Bronco II; they were all "jeeps." As the popularity of this class of vehicle increased in the 1990s, and as Jeep became a little more sensitive about the status of its claimed trademark, a different name for this class of vehicles was popularized. What is the generally accepted name for that class of vehicles today? Is there some other way that would-be competitors could have informed consumers of the nature of their board games without calling them Monopoly? How much would it have cost to develop and popularize such an alternative? Would incurring the costs of developing an alternative have made sense given the expected profits available from entering the Monopoly market? Is the fact that no one else offered their own version of the Monopoly game before the Ninth Circuit's decision sufficient evidence that popularizing an alternative name was impractical?

Similarly, the Ninth Circuit's ruling does not mean that General Mills is unable to brand its Monopoly games. It simply has to use something other than the name Monopoly itself as its brand designator. It can popularize a unique character, such as Mr. Moneybags, and use that as its brand designator. It can include a house mark, or its company name, or phrases such as, "the Original" or "Genuine," as ways to identify its versions of the Monopoly game. Will such alternative brandings eliminate the risk that the proliferation of sources of Monopoly games will confuse consumers?

This suggests that in resolving a question of genericness, we must balance consumers' interest in competition against the risks of confusion both over the short-term and over the long-run. However the court rules, we should expect both the would-be trademark owner and would-be competitors to respond and adapt to that ruling, and as they do, we should expect consumers to come to understand the resulting markets that are created. Thus, as part of our genericness determination, we should consider whether it would cost less: (i) for competitors to find or develop some other way to inform consumers that they are offering a competing product; or (ii) for the would-be trademark owner to find or develop some other way to brand its version of the product. For a similar approach, see Ralph H. Folsom & Larry L. Teply, *Trademarked Generic Words*, 89 YALE L.J. 1323 (1980).

5. *Rewarding General Mills?* From a producer-centric, or property-based, view of trademarks, Professor Zeisel's "punishment" argument presumably reflects a view that the Ninth Circuit's decision reduced General Mills' profits from the Monopoly market, compared to what it would have been had the term Monopoly remained a trademark. Should we use trademark law to "reward" General Mills for its, or its predecessor-in-interest's, creation, or perhaps popularization, of the Monopoly game? If so, how much of a reward does General Mills deserve? How long and how broad should General Mills' protection be based upon such a theory? Would such an approach necessarily make trademark protection "a mutant species of copyright" as Justice Scalia warned in *Dastar*, 539 U.S. 23, 34 (2003).

6. *Genericness and Competition.* Courts often refer to a two-part test for identifying generic terms. First, what is the relevant genus of goods or services at issue? And second, does the consuming public understand the term at issue to refer primarily to that genus of goods or services? *See, e.g., H. Marvin Ginn Corp. v. International Ass'n of Fire Chiefs, Inc.*, 782 F.2d 987, 990 (Fed. Cir. 1986). But how do we define a relevant "genus" of goods or services? For example, in the *Anti-Monopoly, Inc.* case, is the relevant genus the specific game Monopoly, real estate trading games, board games, games, entertainment, or something else?

If we conclude that the relevant genus is the specific game Monopoly, then the word Monopoly is almost necessarily generic. Do you see why? If, on the other hand, we conclude that the relevant genus is the class of real estate trading games or board games, then Monopoly is presumably a brand. Or as courts sometimes say, Monopoly would be a species of the broader genus of, for example, board games. So how do we define the genus?

Courts say surprisingly little about this process. Instead, they usually just identify the genus that strikes them as appropriate or that supports the conclusion they have already reached. Is there some more coherent and objectively consistent way of identifying a relevant genus?

In antitrust analysis, we identify a "market" by examining the willingness of consumers to switch from one product to another in response to a price increase. Economists refer to this willingness to switch as the cross-elasticity of demand. Consider a simple example. In a student lounge, there are two vending machines, side-by-side, each of which sells cold drinks in 12 ounce aluminum cans. Assume that Coca-Cola is available in both. If the two vending machines are independently owned, and both presently sell Coke for $0.60 per can, would it be profitable for one of the vending machine owners to raise her price a nontrivial amount, say to $0.65? The answer presumably is no. Consumers would simply purchase Coke at the adjacent vending machine for $0.60, and our price-raiser would lose all of her sales. The competition, in such a case involving independent sellers offering identical goods in close geographic proximity, is perfect. Any price increase by one of the vendors will lead enough of the relevant consumers to switch to the other vending machine that the price increase would prove unprofitable.

Now what if instead of both vending machines offering Coke, one offers Coke and one offers Pepsi. If you were a Coke drinker and the price on the Coke machine went up to $0.65, would you buy the Pepsi instead? What if the Coke price went up to $0.70 or to $1.00? At what point would you switch to the Pepsi? Each Coke consumer will answer this question for himself, but as the price for Coke continues to increase, eventually enough consumers would switch to Pepsi (or do without) so that any further price increase would not be profitable. While we can certainly debate how much prices could profitably be increased, to the extent that enough consumers prefer Coke to Pepsi, there is likely some level of price increase that could be profitably achieved. Unlike the Coke vs. Coke situation, Coke and Pepsi do not compete perfectly.

Moreover, if we assume that rather than Pepsi, the second vending machine offers only a generic cola, or Dr. Pepper, or Seven-Up, or juice, or water, then the owner of the Coke vending machine could likely increase her price more before further price increases became unprofitable. At the end of the day, the extent to which products compete with Coke sufficiently to preclude the possibility of a nontrivial price increase is not a question that can be answered in the abstract, but is a function of actual consumer preferences and behavior in the marketplace. Given the alternatives available, at what point will enough consumers actually switch so that a further price increase becomes unprofitable?

While this is an empirical question, if we could answer it, then we could define a "market" to include those products that compete, in the sense that their presence in the market would preclude a nontrivial price increase, and exclude those products the availability of which would not preclude such a price increase. Using such an approach, how would you define the relevant market in which Coke is marketed? Is it only Coke? Is it only brand-name colas? Is it colas generically? Is it sodas? Is it liquid refreshment? Now assume that we had the empirical evidence necessary to define the relevant market in which Coke is traded and further assume that only Coke is in that market. Should we use that market definition to define product genus for purposes of trademark law?

F.M. Scherer has reported that leading brands charge prices four to sixty-seven percent above the average price for private-label or generic items of comparable quality. *See* F.M. SCHERER, INDUSTRIAL MARKET STRUCTURE AND ECONOMIC PERFORMANCE 330–32 (1972). Does that price difference suggest that most leading brands constitute their own market in an economic sense? Does it suggest that leading brands should generally constitute their own genus?

More generally, what does the genus approach add to the genericness analysis? Is it better to ask whether Coke constitutes its own genus, or to ask whether consumers would be better or worse off by allowing competitors to use Coke in naming their own products?

7.   *Dual-Use Marks.* Consumers routinely use and recognize some popular trademarks as both trademarks and as generic terms. If you ask for a rum-and-Coke at a bar, do you want a rum-and-Coke brand cola, or a rum-and-cola? If you are at the drug store and ask for Kleenex, are you asking for facial tissue generically or for Kleenex-brand facial tissue specifically? If you ask for a rum-and-Coke, and the bartender serves you a rum-and-Pepsi, does that constitute trademark infringement? If you ask for Kleenex, and the drug store sells you some other brand of facial tissues, does that constitute trademark infringement?

What should we do with these dual use marks? Should we address the differing informational roles these marks play through an all-or-nothing doctrine such as genericness? If so, how do we approach the genericness issue? Should we ask which meaning is primary? What does primary mean in this context—more important, more commonly used, or something else? Should we focus on consumer welfare and ask how, if at all, a finding of genericness would change the associated markets? In more practical terms, should we place the burden on the bartender to inform the customer that Coke is not available and to ask if Pepsi is acceptable? (As John Belushi famously exclaimed in a Saturday Night Live skit for the Olympia Café which served only cheeseburgers, chips, and Pepsi: "No Coke, Pepsi.") Should we place the burden on the customer to make plain her preference for a rum-and-Coke-brand-cola? Or, as a third possibility, should we place the burden on Coca-Cola to develop some other trademark to enable consumers to convey more clearly what they want?

In ordinary language, many common words have multiple meanings and we discern which meaning was intended through context and other conversational clues. Can you think of any? If we are accustomed to dealing with words with dual meanings in ordinary language, is there any way to preserve the dual roles that some marks play? For example, can we adapt the likelihood of confusion test for infringement or the fair use doctrine to accommodate dual use?

8. *Abandonment and Genericness.* As previously noted, in the original bills that became the Trademark Act, genericness was treated solely as a question of abandonment. Before enactment, however, Congress added language to sections 14 and 15 of the Trademark Act recognizing genericness as a separate doctrine that focused on consumer understanding. 15 U.S.C. §§ 1064(3) (allowing cancelling of a registration "[a]t any time if the registered mark become the generic name for the goods or services, or a portion thereof, for which it is registered"), 1065(4) (providing that "no incontestable right shall be acquired in a mark which is the generic name for the goods or services or a portion thereof, for which it is registered") (2015).

Because these additions occurred at the last minute in the legislative process, Congress also retained the language dealing with genericness as a question of abandonment. Thus, section 45 of the Trademark Act, as amended, continues to define a mark as abandoned, *inter alia*:

> (2) When any course of conduct of the owner, including act of omission as well as commission, causes the mark to become the generic name for the goods or services on or in connection with which it is used. . . .

15 U.S.C. § 1127 (2015).

Both of these approaches can be used to deny protection to a given word or phrase when it is or has become generic. With an abandonment approach, however, the mark must not only be generic, it must be the trademark owner's fault. Only if the mark became generic as a result of the trademark owner's actions, whether using the mark itself as the generic name for the associated goods or services, or failing to police (or stop) such generic uses by others, will abandonment result.

In contrast, under the genericness approach codified in sections 14 and 15, the reasons why a mark becomes generic are irrelevant. If the "primary significance" of the claimed trademark is or becomes generic, then the trademark is no longer protected. Whether the trademark owner has contributed to that, or indeed, even if the trademark owner has done everything possible to prevent it, is immaterial.

As Judge Learned Hand once explained in finding aspirin to be generic:

> The single question, as I view it, in all these cases, is merely one of fact: What do the buyers understand by the word for whose use the parties are contending? If they understand by it only the kind of goods sold, then, I take it, it makes no difference whatever what efforts the plaintiff has made to get them to understand more.

Bayer Co. v. United Drug Co., 272 F. 505, 509 (S.D.N.Y. 1921); see also *Illinois High School Ass'n v. GTE Vantage, Inc.*, 99 F.3d 244, 247 (7th Cir. 1996) ("When a trademark becomes generic, such as 'aspirin' or 'thermos,' and so loses trademark protection, because the public, perhaps egged on by the omnipresent media, decides to use the trademark to designate not the particular manufacturer's brand but the entire product comprising all the competing brands, the trademark is dead no matter how vigorously the holder has tried to prevent this usage.").

9. *Is Consumer Understanding the Sole Question?* As codified, the test for genericness is the "primary significance" of the mark to the consuming public. 15 U.S.C. § 1064(3) (2015). However, what if as a result of a patent or for other reasons, there has only been one manufacturer of a given product for a long time, as in the *Anti-Monopoly* case itself. In such a case, consumers may well associate the common name for the product with that manufacturer uniquely. In terms of our tests for secondary meaning, the term may well connote "a single thing coming from a single source." *Coca-Cola Co. v. Koke Co.*, 254 U.S. 143, 146 (1920). Should the existence of such *de facto* secondary meaning entitle the term to legal protection as a trademark?

The answer courts consistently give to this question is no. If would-be competitors need the term to inform consumers that they are now offering competing products, the harm from any short-term confusion that may result is outweighed by the long-term advantages competition will bring to the market for the product in question.

10. *Surveying Genericness.* Given Judge Hand's definition of genericness, codified in the "primary significance" test found in section 14(3), how consumers understand a term is the central issue in determining whether a mark is or has become generic. For that reason, courts will often look to survey evidence to help them determine a mark's "primary significance." The first standard survey format on the issue of genericness appeared in *American Thermos Co. v. Aladdin Industries, Inc.*, 207 F.Supp. 9, 20–21 (D. Conn. 1962), *aff'd*, 321 F.2d 577 (2d Cir. 1963). Known as a *Thermos*-style format, this survey asks respondents if they are familiar with the product or service at issue generically described. For those respondents who are familiar with the product or services at issue, the survey then asks: "If you wanted to purchase this kind of product, how would you ask for it in a store?" If a respondent answers this question with the claimed trademark, that response is interpreted as evidence that the primary significance of the claimed trademark is generic for that respondent. After the survey is completed, the survey expert totals all of the survey responses and then proffers the percentage of respondents who used the claimed trademark as their response to this first question as evidence that the primary significance of the mark for those respondents is generic.

Do you see any problems with this interpretation of the responses? In *E.I. Du Pont de Nemours & Co. v. Yoshida International, Inc.*, the court faced the question whether Teflon was generic for nonstick surfaces on cooking pans. 393 F.Supp. 502 (E.D.N.Y. 1975). Faced with the results from several *Thermos*-style surveys purporting to demonstrate that consumers understood Teflon generically, the district court rejected the survey format. *Id.* at 527. In the district court's view, one could not tell whether a respondent answering "Teflon" to the question "how would you ask for it," was using Teflon in its generic or brand sense. *Id.* In the court's view, the survey responses did not therefore address the relevant question. Do you agree? How did the Ninth Circuit treat the *Thermos*-style survey used in the *Anti-Monopoly* case?

As an alternative to the *Thermos*-style surveys, E.I. Du Pont proffered results from a different format. Known as the *Teflon*-style or format survey, the plaintiff's survey began with a general description of the differences between brand and generic words. It then proceeded through a list of terms, asking the respondent with respect to each, whether the term was brand or generic. With respect to the word Teflon, 68 percent of the survey respondents identified it as a brand. In finding that Teflon was a brand, and not generic, the district court relied heavily on the survey. *Id.* ("It stands unrebutted as evidence that, to the extent it accurately reflects public opinion, a substantial majority of the public continues to believe that TEFLON is a brand name.").

Do you see any problems with this survey format? Do you agree with the court's interpretation of its results? If consumers use and understand a mark, such as Teflon, in both a brand and generic sense, and the survey format forces them to classify it as one or the other, which one will they choose? Will their answer reflect the mark's "primary significance" to them? In what sense? Or does the survey format lead respondents to identify such dual use marks as a "brand" even if they primarily use or understand the mark generically? In the *Teflon* survey itself, Thermos was one of the words included in the list and 51 percent of the respondents identified it as a brand more than ten years after a court held it to be generic. Does that suggest that the *King-Seeley Thermos Co.* court reached the wrong factual conclusion? Does it suggest a problem with the *Teflon* format?

Why did the *Anti-Monopoly* court reject the *Teflon* format survey General Mills proffered? Could that portion of the survey have been rewritten to address the court's concern? Do you think such a rewriting would have changed the percentage of respondents who identified Monopoly as a brand very much?

Can we improve the relevance of the *Thermos* format, and perhaps address the *Teflon* court's concerns, by asking follow-up questions? Such follow-up questions are common with *Thermos*-style surveys. Follow-up questions might include: (i) "Does the 'Word(s)-at-Issue' have a trademark significance?"; or (ii) "Is there any other word(s) you might use to ask for this kind of product?" The last question focuses on an issue other than a mark's primary significance to consumers, but it turns out to be an excellent predictor of how cases are resolved. If a properly conducted survey shows that a substantial majority of the respondents do not know of any words, other than the trademark at issue, to ask for the kind of product in question, courts almost invariably find the mark generic. Can you see why? Is that consistent with Congress's codification of the "primary significance" test? Consider the next case.

GENESEE BREWING CO. v. STROH BREWING CO.

124 F.3d 137 (2d Cir. 1997)

CALABRESI, CIRCUIT JUDGE

This trademark case concerns the right of a brewer to identify its beer with the words "Honey Brown." Beer can be either lager or ale, and in this case, the plaintiff uses the words "Honey Brown" (and others) on its lager product, while the defendant uses the same words (and others) on its ale product. In resolving the appeal, we explicitly endorse the rule that, when a producer creates a new product that differs from an established product class in a particular characteristic, the law of trademark will not grant the producer the exclusive right to label its product with words that are necessary to describe that new characteristic. Applying that rule, we find that the phrase "Honey Brown" is generic as applied to ales—such as the beer produced by the defendant—since those words are needed to describe a beer in the traditional category of "brown ale" that is brewed with the addition of honey. Because the plaintiff's beer is a lager, and not an ale, and "brown lager" is not a traditional category of beer, it is perhaps possible that the phrase "Honey Brown" may not be generic as applied to the plaintiff's own product. But that is a question we need not decide today. It is enough for us to hold that since the words "Honey Brown" are generic as applied to the defendant's product, the defendant has a right to use them and the plaintiff cannot recover for trademark infringement. The plaintiff may be able to recover for unfair competition, but the particular preliminary relief sought is inappropriate given the generic nature of the words "Honey Brown" as used by the defendant on its product. We therefore affirm the district court's denial of a preliminary injunction.

BACKGROUND

In this era of renewed interest in quality beers, sometimes dubbed the "Renaissance of Beer," MICHAEL JACKSON, MICHAEL JACKSON'S BEER COMPANION 8 (1993) [hereinafter, JACKSON, BEER COMPANION] many large brewing companies have attempted to cash in on the growing consumer demand for unique, well-made beers, by brewing specialty beers of their own. See Thomas H. Walters, Note, *Michigan's New Brewpub License: Regulation of Zymurgy for the Twenty-First Century*, 71 U. DET. MERCY L. REV. 621, 668 & n.416 (1994). In order to conceal the identity of the producer—beer connoisseurs are typically wary of mass-produced beers—these companies market specialty beers under small-town names. See Bill McDowell, *In Craft Beer, It's "Style" over Brand Substance*, ADVERTISING AGE, Mar. 10, 1997, at 20 (noting that "major breweries have been . . . criticized for building marketing cachet by hiding their own specialty beer efforts behind subsidiaries with faux-microbrand names"). And so it is with this case, a dispute between two of America's largest brewing companies—the Genesee Brewing Company ("Genesee") and the Stroh Brewing Company ("Stroh")—doing business as Highfalls Brewing Company and Northern Plains Brewing Company, respectively.

Despite extensive efforts, many large brewers have had little success in the craft-brewing business. Occasionally, however, a large brewer develops a specialty beer that becomes a popular favorite. A recent example is plaintiff Genesee's "JW Dundee's Honey Brown Lager." Sales of that brew, which was introduced in January 1994, have climbed to over 2.5 million cases a year, making it one of the four best-selling specialty beers in the country.

Genesee refers to this beer simply as "Honey Brown." Apparently, prior to Genesee's product, no beer had been marketed with a brand name that included those words. Genesee's labeling and advertising emphasize "Honey Brown," and Genesee chose that title as the beer's "bar call." Consumers have followed suit. The record is flooded with menus, fliers, and unsolicited letters that confirm 1) that a large number of beer drinkers refer to Genesee's product using only the words "Honey Brown," and 2) that many menus list "Honey Brown" among brands of beer, like "Budweiser" and "Coors."

Genesee filed in the United States Patent and Trademark Office for a trademark for its entire product name—"JW Dundee's Honey Brown Lager." The trademark examiner initially rejected Genesee's application, requiring that Genesee disclaim any trademark in the words "Honey Brown." Genesee refused to do so, and appealed to the Trademark Trial and Appeal Board. While that application was pending, the trademark examiner backed down and sent Genesee's trademark application to publication without requiring Genesee to disclaim the right to "Honey Brown." Although it has been published, Genesee's trademark has encountered opposition and has yet to be registered.

In early 1996, defendant Stroh began to market "Red River Valley Honey Brown Ale," with the conceded purpose of competing with Genesee. Stroh's label and advertising, like Genesee's, place emphasis on the words "Honey Brown." Aware of Genesee's attempts to secure exclusive use of those words, Stroh intervened in Genesee's trademark application proceeding, which is now before the Trademark Trial and Appeal Board on Stroh's opposition. That body has stayed the proceedings pending the outcome of this case.

Once Stroh began to produce its "Honey Brown," other brewers introduced products with these words in their names. There are now numerous beers in the marketplace with brand names that contain the words "Honey Brown," including "J.J. Wainwright's Evil Eye Honey Brown," "Bank Draft Honey Brown Ale," "Tivoli Honey Brown Lager," and "Algonquin Honey Brown Lager."

In October 1996, alleging that Stroh had violated § 43(a) of the Lanham Act, 15 U.S.C. § 1125(a), by appropriating Genesee's unregistered trademark and engaging in unfair competition, Genesee filed suit in the United States District Court for the Western District of New York seeking to enjoin Stroh from using the words "Honey Brown" on its product, and to require Stroh to recall and destroy any bottles of Red River Valley Honey Brown Ale currently on the market. In an unpublished opinion dated November 19, 1996, the district court (Michael A. Telesca, Judge) denied Genesee's motion for a preliminary injunction, concluding 1) that Genesee was not likely to succeed on the merits of its trademark claim, because "Honey Brown" is a generic term that cannot be trademarked; 2) that Genesee was not likely to succeed on the merits of its unfair competition claim, because Stroh had not acted in bad faith; and 3) that the balance of the hardships favored Stroh.

This appeal followed.

DISCUSSION

In order to obtain a preliminary injunction, a party must demonstrate: 1) that it is subject to irreparable harm; and 2) either a) that it will likely succeed on the merits or b) that there are sufficiently serious questions going to the merits of the case to make them a fair ground for litigation, and that a balancing of the hardships tips "decidedly" in favor of the moving party. *See Warner-Lambert Co. v. Northside Dev. Corp.*, 86 F.3d 3, 6 (2d Cir. 1996) (citing *Jackson Dairy v. H.P. Hood & Sons*, 596 F.2d 70, 72 (2d Cir. 1979) (per curiam)). We review a district court's decision to grant or deny a preliminary injunction for abuse of discretion, which occurs, *inter alia*, when the district court applies the wrong legal standard or bases its decision on clearly erroneous findings of fact. *See id.*

I.   *Irreparable Harm*

In the context of trademark and unfair competition injunctions, the requirement of irreparable harm carries no independent weight, as we have held that a showing of likelihood of confusion (a requirement of both trademark infringement and unfair competition claims) establishes irreparable harm. *See Hasbro, Inc. v. Lanard Toys, Ltd.*, 858 F.2d 70, 73 (2d Cir. 1988).

II.   *Likelihood of Success on the Merits*

Section 43(a) of the Lanham Act, 15 U.S.C. § 1125(a), creates a federal private cause of action for injunctive relief and damages against a manufacturer who "uses in commerce any word, term, name, symbol, or device" or "any false designation of origin" that is "likely to cause confusion" as to the origin of its product. Section 43(a) may protect unregistered trademarks from infringement, and even offers a degree of protection from unfair competition for "unregistrable marks," such as generic words that have acquired significant secondary meaning.

A. Unregistered Trademark Infringement

Section 43(a) may "protect[ ] an unregistered trademark . . . against infringement." *Grupke v. Linda Lori Sportswear, Inc.*, 921 F. Supp. 987, 994 (E.D.N.Y. 1996) (citing *Coach Leatherware Co. v. AnnTaylor, Inc.*, 933 F.2d 162, 168 (2d Cir. 1991)). "The general principles qualifying a mark for registration under § 2 of the Lanham Act are for the most part applicable in determining whether an unregistered mark is entitled to protection under § 43(a)." *Two Pesos, Inc. v. Taco Cabana, Inc.*, 505 U.S. 763, 768 (1992).

Thus, Genesee will prevail on the merits of its unregistered trademark infringement claim if it can show that "it has a valid trademark entitled to protection and that the defendant's use of it is likely to cause confusion." *Arrow Fastener Co. v. Stanley Works*, 59 F.3d 384, 390 (2d Cir. 1995) (citation and internal quotation marks omitted). We agree with the district court that Genesee does not have a trademark in the words "Honey Brown" that can be protected against appropriation by Stroh. Accordingly, we affirm without reaching the question of likelihood of confusion.

A trademark is "any word, name, symbol, or device, or any combination thereof" used by a person "to identify and distinguish his or her goods, including a unique product, from those manufactured or sold by others and to indicate the source of the goods, even if that source is unknown." 15 U.S.C. § 1127. "Following the classic formulation set out by Judge Friendly," trademarks are divided into five general categories of distinctiveness: 1) generic; 2) descriptive; 3) suggestive; 4) arbitrary; and 5) fanciful. *Two Pesos, Inc.*, 505 U.S. at 768 (citing *Abercrombie & Fitch Co. v. Hunting World, Inc.*, 537 F.2d 4, 9 (2d Cir. 1976)). "A generic mark is generally a common description of goods," *W.W.W. Pharm. Co. v. Gillette Co.*, 984 F.2d 567, 572 (2d Cir. 1993), "one that refers, or has come to be understood as referring, to the genus of which the particular product is a species," *Abercrombie & Fitch Co. v. Hunting World, Inc.*, 537 F.2d 4, 9 (2d Cir. 1976). . . .

The district court found that "Honey Brown" is generic, and hence automatically ineligible for protection. That classification is a fact-bound determination, and so long as the district court utilized the correct legal standard, *see, e.g., Hasbro*, 858 F.2d at 74 (reversing a district court's classification because the court had misapplied the law), it will be upheld unless clearly erroneous, *see Bristol-Myers Squibb Co. v. McNeil-P.P.C., Inc.*, 973 F.2d 1033, 1039–40 (2d Cir. 1992).

Genesee argues that the district court, by basing its conclusion that "Honey Brown" is generic solely on the framework laid out in the Third

Circuit's opinion in *A.J. Canfield Co. v. Honickman*, 808 F.2d 291 (3d Cir. 1986) (Becker, J.), rather than on the "primary significance test" used in this circuit, employed the wrong legal standard. We reject this contention.

The "primary significance test" is the law of the land; it was adopted by the Supreme Court in *Kellogg Co. v. National Biscuit Co.*, 305 U.S. 111, 118 (1938), and subsequently codified by Congress in the Trademark Clarification Act of 1984, Pub. L. No. 98–620, § 102, 98 Stat. 3335 (codified at 15 U.S.C. § 1064). Under this familiar test, a plaintiff seeking to establish a valid trademark "must show that the primary significance of the term in the minds of the consuming public is not the product but the producer." *Kellogg*, 305 U.S. at 118. To satisfy this requirement, a trademark need not only and exclusively indicate the producer (the "source"), but may, instead, serve a " 'dual function—that of identifying a product while at the same time indicating its source,' " *Canfield*, 808 F.2d at 300 (quoting S. Rep. No. 98–627, 98th Cong. 5 (1984)). "[A] mark is not generic merely because it has *some* significance to the public as an indication of the nature or class of an article. In order to become generic the *principal* significance of the word must be its indication of the nature or class of an article, rather than an indication of its origin." *King-Seeley Thermos Co. v. Aladdin Indus., Inc.*, 321 F.2d 577, 580 (2d Cir. 1963) (citation and internal quotation marks omitted).

The Third Circuit did not disregard the primary significance test in *Canfield*. Rather, it explained that the test—of itself—is of limited usefulness when the operative question is whether a new product name, even if it does tend to indicate the producer or source of the product, *must nonetheless* be considered a product genus or type, rather than merely a product brand. *See Canfield*, 808 F.2d at 299–301. For, as Judge Becker noted in *Canfield*, the "primary significance" test suffers from a potential weakness: it does not tell us how to deal with situations in which, while "a term signifies a product that emanates from a single source," that term is needed also to designate "not only a product brand but . . . also a product genus." *Id.* at 301.

In confronting these situations, courts must remember that the genericness doctrine prevents trademarks from serving as the substitutes for patents, and protects the public right to copy any non-patented, functional characteristic of a competitor's product. Trademark law seeks to provide a producer neither with a monopoly over a functional characteristic it has originated nor with a monopoly over a particularly effective marketing phrase. Instead the law grants a monopoly over a phrase only if and to the extent it is necessary to enable consumers to distinguish one producer's goods from others and even then only if the grant of such a monopoly will not substantially disadvantage competitors by preventing them from describing the nature of their goods. Accordingly, if a term is necessary to describe a product characteristic that a competitor has a right to copy, a producer may not effectively preempt competition by claiming that term as its own.

Id. at 305 (citations omitted).

Thus, explained Judge Becker,

to be consistent with the primary significance test, whether a product brand with a name used by one producer constitutes its own genus must turn on the extent to which the brand name communicates functional characteristics that differentiate the brand from the products of other producers. In making these calculations, consumer understanding will determine the extent to which a term communicates functional characteristics and the significance of a term's role in doing so because of a dearth or abundance of alternative terms that effectively communicate the same functional information.

Id.

With these principles in mind, the *Canfield* court . . . promulgated a test to determine if a new product name must be deemed also to refer to a product genus or type, rather than simply to an individual product brand:

If a producer introduces a product that differs from an established product class in a particular characteristic, and uses a common descriptive term of that characteristic as the name of the product, then the product should be considered its own genus. Whether the term that identifies the product is generic then depends on the competitors' need to use it. At the least, if no commonly used alternative effectively communicates the same functional information, the term that denotes the product is generic. If we held otherwise, a grant of trademark status could effectively prevent a competitor from marketing a product with the same characteristic despite its right to do so under the patent laws.

Canfield, 808 F.2d at 305–06 (citation and footnote omitted). We adopt that test today, and conclude that *Canfield* is based on long-standing and integral principles of trademark law. As such, it is a useful complement to, rather than a rejection of, the primary significance test.

The case before us is appropriate for analysis under *Canfield*. Like *Canfield* (which concerned "Diet Chocolate Fudge Soda"), the case involves, in Judge Telesca's words, "a relatively new product that . . . differs from an established product class in a significant, functional characteristic," and "uses the common descriptive term for that characteristic as its name." As such, although "Honey Brown" is clearly descriptive of Genesee's product—the beer is sweet, flavored with honey, and deep brown in color—it still might, of necessity, signify a generic category (or subcategory) of beer. *Cf. Anheuser-Busch, Inc. v. John Labatt Ltd.*, 89 F.3d 1339, 1346 (8th Cir. 1996) (upholding a jury's verdict that "ice was and always had been the name of a beer category"), *cert. denied*, 136 L.Ed.2d 833 (1997); *Miller Brewing Co. v. G. Heileman Brewing Co.*, 561 F.2d 75, 80–81 (7th Cir. 1977) (holding that "light" beer is a generic category of beer).

Employing the *Canfield* analysis, the district court had little trouble concluding that Genesee's mark is generic as applied to Stroh's product. We find the issue somewhat more complicated than did the district court, but we reach the same result.

The district court accepted Stroh's assertion that "brown beer" is a category of beer, and found that "Honey Brown" differs from this category by the addition of the descriptive word "honey"—which is not an ordinary ingredient of brown beers—and that "the word 'honey' is a commonly used descriptive term for which there is no effective equivalent." Accordingly, the district court concluded that "Honey Brown" is a generic mark not entitled to protection.

The problem with the district court's analysis is that, as Genesee correctly argues, there is no such category of beer as "brown beer." Beers have traditionally been divided into two general categories: 1) ales, which are fermented at high temperatures for short periods of time; and 2) lagers, which are fermented at low temperatures for longer periods of time. Until the development of lagering techniques in the 19th century, all beers were made with ale yeasts. Today, most English, Irish, Scottish, and Belgian beers are ales, while most German, Czech, Austrian, and Dutch beers are lagers.

The category of ales is further divided into numerous subcategories (*e.g.*, pale ale, porter, stout), as is the category of lagers (*e.g.*, pilsner, bock, Oktoberfest). Thus, "ale" and "lager" are to zymurgy what "plant" and "animal" are to biology—the primary taxonomic divisions, each of which is further subdivided into numerous more specific but still generic classifications.

One traditional subcategory of ale is brown ale. There is no comparable subcategory of "brown lager." Nor is there a general category of "brown beer" that somehow encompasses both lagers and ales. Such a category would be antithetical to the fundamental notion that, absent a handful of hybrid and miscellaneous styles, all barley-based beer styles represent subcategories of the general categories of lager and ale.

Stroh asserts first that "brown ale" is a category of beer, and then that any beer that is brown and includes honey can be placed in a "honey brown" subcategory of "brown ales." The problem with this analysis is that many beers that are using the name "Honey Brown"—including Genesee's—are not brown ales at all. They are not even ales; they are lagers. As such, it is simply not the case that Genesee's and Stroh's products both fall into the same subcategory of beer: brown ales brewed with honey. It follows that the district court's conclusion "that there is a category of 'brown' beers in the market place, and both plaintiff's and defendant's beers are distinct from that category in that they contain honey," was clearly erroneous.

This does not solve the problem, however. It merely complicates it. It is well-established that "[a] word may be generic of some things and not of others." *Soweco, Inc. v. Shell Oil Co.*, 617 F.2d 1178, 1183 (5th Cir. 1980). "To take a familiar example, 'Ivory' would be generic when used to describe a product made from the tusks of elephants but arbitrary as applied to soap." *Abercrombie & Fitch*, 537 F.2d at 9 n.6. Accordingly, "in various cases a word [has been] found to be generic in one application but not in another." *Expoconsul Int'l, Inc. v. A/E Sys., Inc.*, 755 F. Supp. 1237, 1243 (S.D.N.Y. 1991). For instance, in *Abercrombie & Fitch*, we found that the word "safari" was generic as applied to hats, jackets, and "expeditions into the African wilderness," but fanciful as applied to shorts, scarves, portable grills, and other items. *See Abercrombie & Fitch*, 537 F.2d at 11–14. And in *Polo Fashions, Inc. v. Extra Special Prods., Inc.*, 451 F. Supp. 555 (S.D.N.Y. 1978), the court found it "clear that 'polo' is generic to polo shirts and coats, descriptive as to other shirts and coats and fanciful as it is applied to other articles of wearing apparel." *Id.* at 559; *see also Comic Strip, Inc. v. Fox Television Stations, Inc.*, 710 F. Supp. 976, 978 (S.D.N.Y. 1989) ("As applied to a serial in the funny pages, the words 'comic strip' might be deemed . . . generic. As applied to a nightclub providing live comedy entertainment, however, the terms take on another meaning" and are "at least suggestive."); *Five Platters, Inc. v. Purdie*, 419 F. Supp. 372, 381 & n.6 (D. Md. 1976) (noting that, "as the name of a singing and entertainment group," the name "The Platters" is "arbitrary and distinctive," even though "platter is a generic term as applied to dishes").

This same principle applies to the *Canfield* analysis. A mark that is descriptive, suggestive, arbitrary, or fanciful when applied to some products may nonetheless be generic when applied to certain other products, namely those products that require the use of the mark in order to convey their nature to the consumer. "Rosemary Fried Surfboards" would be an arbitrary mark entitled to protection. But "Rosemary Fried Chicken" would probably be generic, since "fried chicken" is clearly a product genus, and the words "rosemary fried chicken" are necessary for a chef effectively to communicate the fact that her fried chicken differs from most fried chicken in that it is flavored with rosemary. Similarly, "Dry White" is probably descriptive as applied to confetti or toothpaste, but would perhaps be generic as applied to wine. Or finally, the owner of the "Red Hot Dating Service" would not be able to recover from the maker of "Acme Red Hot Dogs" for trademark infringement.

So it is with this case. It is conceivable—though we certainly do not suggest, let alone decide—that Genesee's mark—"Honey Brown"—when applied to a *lager* (like its own beer) might be deemed descriptive, rather than generic. For this to be so, a court would have to find that there were ways to convey the fact that a lager is brown in color and flavored with honey without using the words "Honey Brown" (at least in the order or way that Genesee has used them to identify its lager), and that consumers at large (as opposed to the beer *cognoscenti*) did not understand "brown beer" (or "brown lager") to be a generic category of beer. *Cf. Eagle Snacks, Inc. v. Nabisco Brands, Inc.*, 625 F. Supp. 571, 580–82 (D.N.J. 1985) (finding the term "Honey Roast" to be descriptive as applied to nuts); *Schmidt v. Quigg*, 609 F. Supp. 227, 230–31 (E.D. Mich. 1985) (finding the term "Honey Baked Ham" descriptive, and protectable because of secondary meaning).

But when applied to an *ale*, the mark is generic. There are numerous styles of beer in the marketplace, the names of which consist of a time-honored beer category modified by a new, creative ingredient or flavor. Examples include maple porter, pumpkin ale, nut brown ale, raspberry wheat, cranberry lambic, and oatmeal stout. In some of these new beer styles, the innovative ingredient is honey. As a result, there are honey wheats, honey porters, and honey cream ales on the market. Under the *Canfield* reasoning, which we have adopted, none of these names may be trademarked. Someone is always the first to sell these products, and if that brewer were granted a monopoly on the name, subsequent producers would lose the right to "describe [their] goods as what they are." *CES Publ'g Corp.*, 531 F.2d at 13.

Of course, the availability of alternative means of describing the product does not automatically preclude a finding that a trademark is generic. *See Thompson Med. Co. v. Pfizer Inc.*, 753 F.2d 208, 217 (2d Cir. 1985); *King-Seeley Thermos Co.*, 321 F.2d at 580. But the inverse proposition—that the lack of alternatives will render a mark generic—must be true, at least where a producer who has introduced a product that differs from an established class in one significant way attempts to trademark the only effective means of conveying that distinction.

That principle controls this case. There is a recognized category of beers in the marketplace known as "brown ales." And Stroh's product, Red River Valley Honey Brown Ale (but not Genesee's product, JW Dundee's Honey Brown Lager) can be placed within that category, or more precisely, within a new subcategory of that category—brown ales made with honey: "honey brown ales." Indeed, Stroh developed Red River Valley Honey Brown Ale by altering its "brown ale recipe to include honey and brown sugar which created a smoother and sweeter brown ale." Declaration of Joseph Hertrich, Vice President, Brewing, Stroh Brewing Co., Joint Appendix at 185. Because the addition of the word "honey" is necessary to indicate a brown ale that is brewed with honey, Stroh has the right to call its beer a "Honey Brown Ale." *Cf. Miller Brewing Co.*, 561 F.2d at 81 ("[Miller] could not acquire the exclusive right to use the common descriptive word 'light' as a trademark for that beer. Other brewers whose beers have qualities that make them 'light' as that word has commonly been used remain free to call their beer 'light.' Otherwise a manufacturer could remove a common descriptive word from the public domain by investing his goods with an additional quality, thus gaining the exclusive right to call his wine 'rose', his whiskey 'blended', or his bread 'white.' ").

We therefore affirm the district court's conclusion that Genesee is not likely to succeed on the merits of its trademark infringement claim.

B. Unfair Competition Involving Unregistrable Marks

Genesee also alleges that, even if "Honey Brown" is generic, an injunction is justified to prevent Stroh from engaging in unfair competition. The district court rejected this contention summarily: "To establish a claim of unfair competition, plaintiff must demonstrate, *inter alia*, bad faith on the part of the defendant in appropriating the plaintiff's mark. I note only that plaintiff has failed to establish bad faith, and thus has not established an unfair competition claim."

The district court was correct that Genesee's *state law* claim of unfair competition is not viable without a showing of bad faith. *See Jeffrey Milstein, Inc. v. Greger, Lawlor, Roth, Inc.*, 58 F.3d 27, 34–35 (2d Cir. 1995). But a plaintiff may recover for unfair competition in violation of *federal law* without a showing of bad faith. *See Johnson & Johnson v. Carter-Wallace, Inc.*, 631 F.2d 186, 189 (2d Cir. 1980) (noting that § 43(a) of the Lanham Act "does not require proof of intent to deceive" in order to sustain a claim of unfair competition); *Girl Scouts v. Bantam Doubleday Dell Publ'g Group, Inc.*, 808 F. Supp. 1112, 1131 (S.D.N.Y. 1992) ("Under New York law, common law unfair competition claims closely resemble Lanham Act claims except insofar as the state law claim may require an additional element of bad faith or intent.") (internal quotation marks omitted), *aff'd*, 996 F.2d 1477 (2d Cir. 1993). The lack of bad faith is therefore not dispositive of Genesee's federal unfair competition claim.

The fact that Genesee's mark is generic as applied to Stroh's product also does not preclude a finding that Stroh has violated the Lanham Act by engaging in unfair competition. While a mark "may be generic and not entitled to trademark protection, [a] claim of unfair competition is not foreclosed." *Murphy Door Bed Co. v. Interior Sleep Systems*, 874 F.2d 95, 102 (2d Cir. 1989).

> Regardless of whether a term is trademarked, a plaintiff may show that the term name is so associated with its goods that use of the same or similar term by another company

constitutes a representation that its goods come from the same source.

Courts typically grant relief, injunctive or otherwise, for misrepresentations as to the source of a product where a formerly exclusive trademark is no longer protectible because it has become generic. However, as the Supreme Court's decision in *Kellogg Co. v. National Biscuit Co.* demonstrates, relief is also available when the misrepresentation of source arises through the use of a phrase (like Swiss Army knife) that is generic *ab initio.*

Forschner Group, Inc. v. Arrow Trading Co., 30 F.3d 348, 358–59 (2d Cir. 1994) (citations omitted); *see also Metric & Multistandard Components Corp. v. Metric's Inc.*, 635 F.2d 710, 714 (8th Cir. 1980).

In *Kellogg*, the Supreme Court held that, while subsequent producers have the right to use generic product names that have traditionally been associated with one manufacturer, those users have an obligation "to use every reasonable means to prevent confusion" as to the source of the products. *Kellogg*, 305 U.S. at 121. Relying on *Kellogg*, we have explained that if

"the consumer associates '[Honey Brown]' with a particular manufacturer, perhaps because that manufacturer enjoyed a de facto (or de jure) monopoly for many years, there is a risk that the consumer may erroneously assume that any product entitled "[Honey Brown]" comes from that manufacturer. *A second manufacturer may increase the risk of confusion by, for example, using a similar label, similar packaging, misleading advertisements, or simply by failing to state the product's source. . . . When there is a likelihood that the newcomer might thus pass its product off as the original manufacturer's . . . a court [may] require the newcomer to distinguish its product or to notify consumers explicitly that its product does not come from the original manufacturer.*"

Forschner, 30 F.3d at 359 (quoting *Blinded Veterans Ass'n v. Blinded Am. Veterans Found.*, 277 U.S. App. D.C. 65, 872 F.2d 1035, 1045 (D.C. Cir. 1989)) (emphasis in *Forschner*).

In other words—even though "Honey Brown" is a generic mark at least as to ales—if "Honey Brown" is closely associated with Genesee's product, then Stroh's use of those words "is permissible only to the extent that such use does not engender a likelihood of confusion as to the source of [Stroh]'s product." *Id.* at 360.

Thus, to recover for unfair competition, Genesee must show: 1) "an association of origin by the consumer between the mark and the first user," *Forschner Group, Inc. v. Arrow Trading Co., Inc.*, 904 F. Supp.

1409, 1417 (S.D.N.Y. 1995), that is, secondary meaning; and 2) "a likelihood of consumer confusion when the mark is applied to the second user's good," *id.* And Stroh will, nonetheless, escape liability if it has "used every reasonable means to prevent confusion" as to the source of the products, *Kellogg*, 305 U.S. at 121. The district court did not consider whether these factors had been shown.

Genesee has, in fact, proffered evidence that might, if believed and not sufficiently countered by Stroh's evidence, support a finding at trial of both secondary meaning and a likelihood of confusion that Stroh has not taken all reasonable steps to prevent. Specifically, Genesee has attempted to show that, intentionally or not, Stroh is marketing its beer in such a way as to lead consumers to believe that they are getting Genesee's product. *Cf. Miller Brewing Co. v. Jos. Schlitz Brewing Co.*, 605 F.2d 990, 997 (7th Cir. 1979) (explaining that, notwithstanding the lack of trademark protection for "light beer," Miller could have sustained an unfair competition claim if it could have shown: a "failure of Schlitz adequately to identify itself as the source of its beer; . . . a confusingly similar dress used by Schlitz for its beer, which might result from such factors as the label's style, [or] the relative size of words in the label . . . ; [or] Schlitz' use of advertising calculated to lead to confusion"); *American Footwear Corp. v. General Footwear Co.*, 609 F.2d 655, 662 (2d Cir. 1979) (noting that unfair competition liability can arise when a defendant "confuses the public into mistakenly purchasing the product in the belief that the product is the product of the competitor").

Genesee's beer has become the fourth best selling specialty brew in the country, and consumers and bartenders refer to it simply as "Honey Brown"—a phrase that had apparently never been used to describe a beer before Genesee introduced its product. The words "Honey Brown" dominate Genesee's labeling and advertising materials, and according to Genesee, consumers expect to get Genesee's product when they order a "Honey Brown."

Stroh has also chosen to emphasize the words "Honey Brown" on its label, rather than the words "Red River Valley" or "Honey Brown Ale." Stroh's marketing memoranda to distributors emphasize the need to compete with Genesee's product, and to beat Genesee into certain untapped markets, even though the two products are not, in fact, examples of the same subcategory of beer. And Stroh has arranged to have Safeway Food Stores counter-coupon Genesee's product. (This means that Safeway gives coupons for Red River Valley Honey Brown Ale to any person who purchases JW Dundee's Honey Brown Lager.) Moreover, according to Genesee, many of the restaurants and bars that list Genesee's product simply as "Honey Brown" on their menus and tap lists—which list brands of beer, not kinds of beer-have switched from

Genesee's product to Stroh's less-expensive product without changing their menus.

All of this evidence could potentially support a finding that there is a likelihood of confusion and that Stroh has not "taken every reasonable precaution to prevent confusion or the practice of deception in the sale of its product." *Kellogg*, 305 U.S. at 122. If Genesee can establish this at trial, along with secondary meaning, it may be granted an injunctive remedy that, while allowing Stroh to continue to market its beer and sell it as a "honey brown ale," would require Stroh to make more of an effort to ensure that its product is not confused with Genesee's.

Nevertheless, the district court did not err in denying the preliminary injunction. For the preliminary relief that Genesee requested—an injunction forbidding Stroh from using the words "Honey Brown" on its product—is inappropriate in a claim of unfair competition with respect to a generic mark. Where a generic mark is involved, "the relief granted should go only so far as to alleviate the source confusion caused by [Stroh] and no further." *Forschner*, 904 F. Supp. at 1428. While a court may therefore "require the newcomer to distinguish its product or to notify consumers explicitly that its product does not come from the original manufacturer," *Forschner*, 30 F.3d at 359 (emphasis altered, internal quotation marks omitted), or otherwise "to use every reasonable means to prevent confusion," *Kellogg*, 305 U.S. at 121, it may not prevent the defendant from using the plaintiff's mark altogether, *see id.* As such, even if Genesee was likely to prevail on this claim, the preliminary injunction sought could not have been granted. Hence, the district court did not abuse its discretion in denying it.

CONCLUSION

Stroh has the right to add honey to its brown ale, and it has the right to call its beer what it is: a honey brown ale. Accordingly, Genesee may not recover for trademark infringement, and the district court properly refused to enjoin Stroh from using those words to label its beer. While Genesee has stated a claim for unfair competition, the specific preliminary injunctive relief that Genesee has sought is not available to it. We therefore affirm the district court's order without considering whether at trial Genesee is likely to succeed on the merits of its unfair competition claim.

NOTES FOR DISCUSSION

1.   *Genus Revisited.* The court quotes the Third Circuit's approach to defining product genus:

> to be consistent with the primary significance test, whether a
> product brand with a name used by one producer constitutes its own
> genus must turn on the extent to which the brand name

communicates functional characteristics that differentiate the brand from the products of other producers.

Genesee Brewing Co. v. Stroh Brewing Co., 124 F.3d 137, 144–45 (2d Cir. 1997) (*quoting* A.J. Canfield Co. v. Honickman, 808 F.2d 291, 305 (3d Cir. 1986)).

Does this test improperly combine two separate inquiries: (i) what is the relevant genus; and (ii) are the words at issue the generic name for products in that genus? What is the relevant genus in this case? Why is honey brown ale a separate genus, rather than a species within the broader genus of ales or brown ales? If Genesee Brewing had chosen a fanciful mark for its new honey brown ale, would that change the genus?

2.   *"Not the Product, but the Producer."* In *Zatarain's*, the Fifth Circuit quoted this phrase from *Kellogg* as the standard for secondary meaning. In *Genesee Brewing*, the Second Circuit quoted this phrase as the standard for genericness. Which is it? Can it be both?

3.   *Generic Words and Unfair Competition.* The court affirms the district court finding that Honey Brown is generic with respect to the defendant's ale, yet holds that the plaintiff may nonetheless be entitled to relief under unfair competition if it can establish secondary meaning in Honey Brown. Recall that before the Trademark Act, descriptive words were not technically considered trademarks, yet with proof of secondary meaning, they received essentially the same protection as if they were trademarks under the rubric of unfair competition. Is the court replicating that approach here? If so, what is left of the generic words category?

The Second Circuit, quoting *Kellogg Co. v. National Biscuit Co.*, 305 U.S. 111, 121 (1938), requires Stroh's "to use every reasonable means to prevent confusion." *Genesee Brewing Co.*, 124 F.3d at 150. Is not the easiest way to prevent confusion for Stroh's to stop marketing a honey brown beer altogether, or at the very least for Stroh's to not use the words "honey brown" at all? Does the court require Stroh's to take such steps? Why not? What does that suggest that "reasonable" means in the court's standard?

What must Stroh's do to comply with this "every reasonable means" requirement? When we studied *Dastar* in Chapter 1, one of our concerns was that, if the Court recognized a right of attribution, the plaintiff would nitpick the labeling on the defendant's product, not to protect consumers, but to protect itself from competition, by delaying and increasing the cost and uncertainty associated with competitive entry. Is there a similar risk here? Instead of requiring Stroh's to use "every reasonable means to prevent confusion," should we focus on prohibiting Stroh's from taking affirmative steps, beyond the mere use of a generic phrase, to confuse consumers?

What if a customer asks a bartender for a "Honey Brown"? Is the bartender liable for trademark infringement or passing off if he serves a Stroh's instead of a Genesee? Must a bartender use "every reasonable means" to prevent confusion as well?

4. *Bar Calls and Abandonment.* As a general rule, companies would like their brands to be both the generic name consumers routinely use for the product and protected as a trademark. The common use of their brand as the generic name is a form of free advertising, yet so long as the brand remains protected as a trademark, their bottom line remains secure. Thus, Genesee popularized "Honey Brown" as the bar call for its beer, rather than the more distinctive "JW Dundee." Should we blame Genesee for any confusion that results from Stroh's entry because it emphasized the descriptive, rather than the more distinctive, aspects of its brand name as its bar call? Does this constitute a "course of conduct" by Genesee that causes the mark to become generic within the meaning of the Trademark Act's definition of abandonment? Should we impose on Genesee the same obligation that the court imposes on Stroh's and require Genesee to use "every reasonable means" to prevent confusion?

5. *A "Unique Product or Service."* When Congress amended the Trademark Act in response to the *Anti-Monopoly* firestorm, it added the sentence: "A registered mark shall not be deemed to be the generic name of goods or services solely because such mark is also used as a name of or to identify a unique product or service." 15 U.S.C. § 1064(3) (2015). Is Genesee's Honey Brown ale a "unique product"? Was Monopoly? Did the courts at issue deem either "Honey Brown" or "Monopoly" generic "solely because [it was] also used [as the] name of . . . a unique product"? If the "unique product" language does not govern in these cases, when will it govern?

6. *Extending the Genericness Doctrine: Common Laudatory Phrases.* Boston Beer Co. seeks to register the phrase "The Best Beer in America," as a trademark, for its beers. It proffers circumstantial evidence of secondary meaning, including eight years of continuous use, annual advertising expenditures of ten million dollars, and annual sales of eighty-five million dollars. Assuming that this circumstantial evidence is sufficient to establish secondary meaning, may Boston Beer register the phrase on the principal register or otherwise obtain trademark protection for it?

In *In re Boston Beer Co.*, the Federal Circuit held that the phrase was generic. 198 F.3d 1370, 1373–74 (Fed. Cir. 1999). In reaching that conclusion, the court wrote:

> As in this case, a phrase or slogan can be so highly laudatory and descriptive as to be incapable of acquiring distinctiveness as a trademark. The proposed mark is a common, laudatory advertising phrase which is merely descriptive of Boston Beer's goods. Indeed, it is so highly laudatory and descriptive of the qualities of its product that the slogan does not and could not function as a trademark to distinguish Boston Beer's goods and serve as an indication of origin.

Id.

Do you agree with the court? Why?

7. *Preliminary Injunctions and Irreparable Harm.* In discussing what is required to obtain a preliminary injunction, the court required no independent showing of irreparable harm. As the court explained:

> In the context of trademark and unfair competition injunctions, the requirement of irreparable harm carries no independent weight, as we have held that a showing of likelihood of confusion (a requirement of both trademark infringement and unfair competition claims) establishes irreparable harm.

Genesee Brewing Co., 124 F.3d at 142.

While it was common at the time to presume or infer irreparable harm once a plaintiff had shown trademark infringement, or a likelihood thereof, the Supreme Court's subsequent decisions in *eBay Inc. v. Merc Exchange, LLC*, 547 U.S. 388 (2006) and *Winter v. Natural Resources Defense Council, Inc.*, 555 U.S. 7 (2008) cast doubt on the practice. As we shall discuss in more detail in Chapter 11, some circuits now require that a plaintiff independently prove irreparable harm.

C. PRIMARY MERELY A SURNAME

Both before and after the Trademark Act of 1946, the legal protection available for proper names under trademark and unfair competition law has paralleled that available for descriptive words. Before the Trademark Act of 1946, courts would not extend trademark protection to proper names, even with proof of secondary meaning. However, although not recognized as technical trademarks, names received essentially equivalent protection under the rubric of unfair competition where secondary meaning and a likelihood of confusion were shown. As it did with descriptive terms, Congress formally recognized names as eligible for registration on the principal register as trademarks in the Trademark Act. 15 U.S.C. § 1052(e)(4), (f) (2015). As codified, Congress prohibited the registration of a mark which "is primarily merely a surname," unless and until secondary meaning could be shown. *Id.*

In the 1913 poem, *Sacred Emily,* Gerturde Stein wrote "Rose is a rose is a rose is a rose." We examine the issue of proper names within trademark law by asking a corollary question: When is a name a name?

PEACEABLE PLANET, INC. V. TY, INC.
362 F.3d 986 (7th Cir. 2004)

POSNER, C.J.

In the most common type of suit for trademark infringement, the plaintiff complains that the defendant is passing off his (inferior) product as the plaintiff's. But here we have the converse case of "reverse passing off," in which the plaintiff complains that the defendant is trying to pass off the plaintiff's product as the defendant's. Why would anyone want to do such a thing? One reason might be to obliterate the plaintiff's corporate identity and prevent him from entering new markets, where the defendant, having appropriated the plaintiff's trademark, would claim that the plaintiff was the infringer. Such would be a case of deliberate reverse passing off, and terms like "passing off" and "reverse passing off" are sometimes reserved for deliberate efforts to confuse the consuming public, but either form of confusion can be actionable without proof of intent to confuse.

The trademark infringement claim is federal, and there is also a claim for false advertising, also under the Lanham Act, plus several claims governed by Illinois law, including one for product disparagement. All the claims were rejected on summary judgment.

The disappointed plaintiff is Peaceable Planet. Like the defendant, the much larger and better known Ty Inc. . . , Peaceable Planet makes plush toys in the shape of animals, filled with bean-like materials to give the toys a soft and floppy feel. Ty's plush toys are, of course, the famous "Beanie Babies."

In the spring of 1999, Peaceable Planet began selling a camel that it named "Niles." The name was chosen to evoke Egypt, which is largely desert except for the ribbon of land bracketing the Nile. The camel is a desert animal, and photos juxtaposing a camel with an Egyptian pyramid are common. The price tag fastened to Niles's ear contains information both about camels and about Egypt, and the Egyptian flag is stamped on the animal.

A small company, Peaceable Planet sold only a few thousand of its camels in 1999. In March of the following year, Ty began selling a camel also named "Niles." It sold a huge number of its "Niles" camels—almost two million in one year—precipitating this suit. The district court ruled that "Niles," being a personal name, is a descriptive mark that the law does not protect unless and until it has acquired secondary meaning, that is, until there is proof that consumers associate the name with the plaintiff's brand. Peaceable Planet did not prove that consumers associate the name "Niles" with its camel.

The general principle that formed the starting point for the district court's analysis was unquestionably sound. A descriptive mark is not legally protected unless it has acquired secondary meaning. 15 U.S.C. §§ 1052(e), (f); *Two Pesos, Inc. v. Taco Cabana, Inc.*, 505 U.S. 763, 769 (1992); *Ty Inc. v. Perryman*, 306 F.3d 509, 513–14 (7th Cir. 2002); *Platinum Home Mortgage Corp. v. Platinum Financial Group, Inc.*, 149 F.3d 722, 727 (7th Cir. 1998); *Abercrombie & Fitch Co. v. Hunting World, Inc.*, 537 F.2d 4, 10 (2d Cir. 1976). An example is "All Bran." The name describes the product. If the first firm to produce an all-bran cereal could obtain immediate trademark protection, and thus prevent all other producers of all-bran cereal from describing their product as all bran, it would be difficult for competitors to gain a foothold in the market. They would be as if speechless. Had Peaceable Planet named its camel "Camel," that would be a descriptive mark in a relevant sense, because it would make it very difficult for Ty to market its own camel—it wouldn't be satisfactory to have to call it "Dromedary" or "Bactrian."

Although cases and treatises commonly describe personal names as a subset of descriptive marks, *Perini Corp. v. Perini Construction, Inc.*, 915 F.2d 121, 125 (4th Cir. 1990); *Marker Int'l v. DeBruler*, 844 F.2d 763, 764 (10th Cir. 1988); *Yarmuth-Dion, Inc. v. D'ion Furs, Inc.*, 835 F.2d 990, 993 (2d Cir. 1987); 4 Callmann, *Unfair Competition, Trademarks & Monopolies* § 22:42 (4th ed. 2003), it is apparent that the rationale for denying trademark protection to personal names without proof of secondary meaning can't be the same as the rationale just sketched for marks that are "descriptive" in the normal sense of the word. Names, as distinct from nicknames like "Red" or "Shorty," are rarely descriptive. "Niles" may evoke but it certainly does not describe a camel, any more than "Pluto" describes a dog, "Bambi" a fawn, "Garfield" a cat, or "Charlotte" a spider. (In the *Tom and Jerry* comics, "Tom," the name of the cat, could be thought descriptive, but "Jerry," the name of the mouse, could not be.) So anyone who wanted to market a toy camel, dog, fawn, cat, or spider would not be impeded in doing so by having to choose another name.

The reluctance to allow personal names to be used as trademarks reflects valid concerns (three such concerns, to be precise), but they are distinct from the concern that powers the rule that descriptive marks are not protected until they acquire secondary meaning. One of the concerns is a reluctance to forbid a person to use his own name in his own business. . . . Supposing a man named Brooks opened a clothing store under his name, should this prevent a second Brooks from opening a clothing store under his own (identical) name even though consumers did not yet associate the name with the first Brooks's store? It should not. . . .

Another and closely related concern behind the personal-name rule is that some names are so common—such as "Smith," "Jones," "Schwartz," "Wood," and "Jackson"—that consumers will not assume that two products having the same name therefore have the same source, and so they will not be confused by their bearing the same name. . . . If there are two bars in a city that are named "Steve's," people will not infer that they are owned by the same Steve.

The third concern, which is again related but brings us closest to the rule regarding descriptive marks, is that preventing a person from using his name to denote his business may deprive consumers of useful information. Maybe "Steve" is a well-known neighborhood figure. If he can't call his bar "Steve's" because there is an existing bar of that name, he is prevented from communicating useful information to the consuming public. . . .

The scope of a rule is often and here limited by its rationale. Or, to make the same point differently, one way of going astray in legal analysis is to focus on the semantics of a rule rather than its purpose. Case 1 might say that a personal name could not be trademarked in the circumstances of that case without proof of secondary meaning. Case 2 might say that personal names cannot be trademarked without proof of secondary meaning but might leave off the qualifications implicit in the circumstances of the case. And then in Case 3 the court might just ask, is the trademark at issue a personal name? As we observed in *AM Int'l, Inc. v. Graphic Management Associates, Inc.*, 44 F.3d 572, 575 (7th Cir. 1995), "rules of law are rarely as clean and strict as statements of them make them seem. So varied and unpredictable are the circumstances in which they are applied that more often than not the summary statement of a rule—the terse formula that judges employ as a necessary shorthand to prevent judicial opinions from turning into treatises—is better regarded as a generalization than as the premise of a syllogism." The "rule" that personal names are not protected as trademarks until they acquire secondary meaning is a generalization, and its application is to be guided by the purposes that we have extracted from the case law. When none of the purposes that animate the "personal name" rule is present, and application of the "rule" would impede rather than promote competition and consumer welfare, an exception should be recognized. And will be; for we find cases holding, very sensibly—and with inescapable implications for the present case—that the "rule" does not apply if the public is unlikely to understand the personal name as a personal name. *Lane Capital Management, Inc. v. Lane Capital Management, Inc.*, 192 F.3d 337, 345–46 (2d Cir. 1999); *Circuit City Stores, Inc. v. CarMax, Inc.*, 165 F.3d 1047, 1054 (6th Cir. 1999).

The personal-name "rule," it is worth noting, is a common law rather than statutory doctrine. All that the Lanham Act says about personal names is that a mark that is "primarily merely a surname" is not registrable in the absence of secondary meaning. 15 U.S.C. §§ 1052(e)(4), (f). There is no reference to first names. The reason for the surname provision is illustrated by the Brooks example. The extension of the rule to first names is a judicial innovation and so needn't be pressed further than its rationale, as might have to be done if the rule were codified in inflexible statutory language. Notice too the limitation implicit in the statutory term "primarily."

In thinking about the applicability of the rationale of the personal-name rule to the present case, we should notice first of all that camels, whether real or toy, do not go into business. Peaceable Planet's appropriation of the name "Niles" for its camel is not preventing some hapless camel in the Sahara Desert who happens to be named "Niles" from going into the water-carrier business under its own name. The second thing to notice is that "Niles" is not a very common name; in fact it is downright rare. And the third thing to notice is that if it were a common name, still there would be no danger that precluding our hypothetical Saharan water carrier from using its birth name "Niles" would deprive that camel's customers of valuable information. In short, the rationale of the personal-name rule is wholly inapplicable to this case.

What is more, if one wants to tie the rule in some fashion to the principle that descriptive marks are not protectable without proof of second meaning, then one must note that "Niles," at least when affixed to a toy camel, is a suggestive mark, like "Microsoft" or *Business Week*," or—coming closer to this case—like "Eor" used as the name of a donkey, or the proper names in *Circuit City Stores, Inc. v. CarMax, Inc., supra*, 165 F.3d at 1054, rather than being a descriptive mark. Suggestive marks are protected by trademark law without proof of secondary meaning.... Secondary meaning is not required because there are plenty of alternatives to any given suggestive mark. There are many more ways of suggesting than of describing. Suggestive names for camels include "Lawrence [of Arabia]" (one of Ty's other Beanie Babies *is* a camel named "Lawrence"); "Desert Taxi," "Sopwith" (the Sopwith Camel was Snoopy's World War I fighter plane), "Camelia," "Traveling Oasis," "Kamelsutra," "Cameleon," and "Humpy-Dumpy."

If "Niles" cannot be a protected trademark, it must be because to give it legal protection would run afoul of one of the purposes of the common law rule that we have identified rather than because it is a descriptive term, which it is not. But we have seen that it does not run afoul of any of those purposes. "Niles" is not the name of the defendant—it's not as if Peaceable Planet had named its camel "Ty Inc." or "H. Ty Warner." It also is not a common name, like "Smith" or "Jackson." And making Ty use a different name for its camel would not deprive the consumer of valuable information about Ty or its camel.

Treating the personal-name rule as a prohibition against ever using a personal name as a trademark (in the absence of secondary meaning) would lead to absurd results, which is a good reason for hesitating to press a rule to its logical limit, its semantic outer bounds. It would mean that the man who invented "Kitty Litter" could not trademark the name ("Kitty" is a more common first name than "Niles") until it had acquired secondary meaning. So as soon as "Kitty Litter" hit the market, a much larger producer of cat litter could appropriate the name, flood the market with its product, and eventually obtain an enforceable trademark in the name by dint of having invested it with secondary meaning, squashing the originator. This is not an entirely fanciful example. Kitty Litter was invented (and named) in 1947 by a young man, Ed Lowe, in Cassopolis,

Michigan, a town of notable obscurity. (As recently as July 2002, its population was only 1,703. We do not know what it was in 1947.) At first he sold the new product mainly to neighbors. On Ty's conception of the personal-name rule, without a patent Lowe could not have prevented a large company from selling the same product under the same name, thus squashing him. We cannot see what purpose of trademark law would be served by encouraging such conduct. Ty marks its "Niles" camel with the trademark symbol, and given the ratio of its sales to those of Peaceable Planet's "Niles," the Ty Niles may be well on its way to acquiring secondary meaning—at which point it will be able to enjoin Peaceable Planet from using the name on Peaceable's camel even though Peaceable thought of naming a camel "Niles" before Ty did. For all we know, Ty may have copied the idea from Peaceable, though Peaceable has not proved that.

Ty argues (we are quoting from its brief) that "one competitor should not be allowed to impoverish the language of commerce by monopolizing descriptive names," and "there are a limited number of personal names that are recognized as such by the public." All true. But the suggestion that "Niles" belongs to the limited class of "recognized" names or that "Niles" is the only way to name a camel is ridiculous.

And there is more: as both *Lane Capital Management, Inc. v. Lane Capital Management, Inc.*, and *Circuit City Stores, Inc. v. CarMax, Inc.*, which we cited earlier, point out, a word that is used as a person's name can be understood as something else ("Kitty," again), in which event the personal-name rule falls by the wayside. On the question whether "Niles" is likely to be understood by the plush-toy consuming public as a personal name rather than as a play on "Nile" the river, Ty conducted a survey in which about half the respondents indicated that they consider "Niles" a personal name. That is not an impressive fraction; imagine the response if one asked whether "William" is a personal name, or "Michael" or "Judith." Moreover, the survey was limited to adults even though Ty's primary market is children, and the questions posed to the respondents were slanted by obsessive repetition of the term "person's name," as in (we are quoting from the survey) "Do you think of the word on this card mainly as a person's name, mainly as something other than a person's name, or as both a person's name and as something else, or don't you have an opinion?" The intention doubtless was to create a subliminal association between "Niles" and "person's name." But the survey was not merely devoid of probative value, unprofessional, and probably inadmissible under the *Daubert* standard; it was irrelevant. If people were asked what came to mind when they saw the word "Niles" and they said a camel, there would be an argument that "Niles" was a descriptive mark, and Peaceable Planet would be sunk. The fact that "Niles" can be a person's name (as can almost any combination of letters)—although according to Ty's own statistics only about one resident of Illinois in

50,000 is named "Niles"—does not bear on whether "Niles" is a descriptive mark as applied to a plush toy camel. It is not.

There is a town named "Niles" in Illinois and another one in Michigan, and this is a reminder of the importance of context in characterizing a trademark. "Apple" is a generic term when used to denote the fruit, but a fanciful mark (the kind that receives the greatest legal protection) when used to denote a computer. If a gas station in Niles, Michigan, calls itself the "Niles Gas Station," it cannot before acquiring secondary meaning enjoin another firm from opening the "Niles Lumber Yard" in the town, on the ground that people will think that the firms are under common ownership. . . . In a town named Niles, firms bearing the name are sharing a name that is too common to be appropriable without proof of secondary meaning. That is not the case when the name is applied to a camel. And while both Niles, Illinois, and Niles, Michigan, are fine towns, neither is the place of origin of the camel or identified with that animal in some other way.

We conclude that Peaceable Planet has a valid trademark in the name "Niles" as applied to its camel, and so the case must be returned to the district court, where Peaceable Planet, to prove infringement of its trademark ("reverse confusion"), will have to show that a substantial number of consumers think that its camel is actually Ty's. For in that event Peaceable Planet will have suffered injury by losing "the value of the trademark—its product identity, corporate identity, control over its goodwill and reputation, and ability to move into new markets," *Sands, Taylor & Wood Co. v. Quaker Oats Co., supra*, 978 F.2d at 957, quoting *Ameritech, Inc. v. American Information Technologies Corp.*, 811 F.2d 960, 964 (6th Cir. 1987), and so will be entitled to a remedy. But we agree with Ty that Peaceable Planet cannot prove its case by showing that consumers will think it pirated Ty's product. . . . That is a charge of defamation rather than of reverse passing off. The purpose of trademark law (setting to one side dilution cases) is to prevent confusion by consumers concerning the sources of the products they buy. Knowing or thinking that a producer is a pirate is not a confusion about source; you know who the source is, whether you think him a good guy or a bad guy.

It is true that some cases say, contrary to *DeCosta*, that being thought a pirate is one of the harms that the prohibition of reverse passing off is intended to prevent. *Sands, Taylor & Wood Co. v. Quaker Oats Co., supra*, 978 F.2d at 958; *W.W.W. Pharmaceutical Co. v. Gillette Co.*, 984 F.2d 567, 571 (2d Cir. 1993); *Banff, Ltd. v. Federated Dep't Stores, Inc.*, 841 F.2d 486, 490 (2d Cir. 1988). But we think that what these cases mean—this is explicit in our opinion in *Sands*—is that the junior user (Ty) might injure the senior user (Peaceable Planet) by suing for trademark infringement if the latter tried to enter a new market in which the junior was already operating. That would be a case in which reverse passing off had engendered confusion as to source. But that is not argued here, and so if there is reverse passing off here it has to be grounded in evidence other than that of perceived piracy.

Ty contends that there is no other evidence of reverse passing off; and, as is its right, it urges us to affirm the dismissal of the trademark count on this alternative ground, which the district court did not reach because it didn't think Peaceable Planet had a trademark on which to base a suit in the first place. Ty urges the alternative ground in spare and conclusional terms, however, and we think that Peaceable Planet did present enough admissible evidence, though barely, to create a triable issue. The similarity of the products, the identity of the marks, the disparity in the fame of the respective producers, and the fact that Ty flooded the market—selling 1.8 million of its Niles camels in only a year— and advertised the camel on its popular website, and that traffic on Peaceable Planet's website soared 600 percent after Ty announced the launching of its Niles, taken together, enable though they do not compel an inference that a substantial number of consumers thought that Peaceable's Niles was actually Ty's. It is an issue for trial.

But we think the district judge was right to dismiss the product-disparagement count in Peaceable Planet's complaint. It is conceivable that some consumers, mistakenly thinking that Ty must have been the inventor of "Niles" the camel, would think Peaceable Planet a pirate and think worse of it on that account, though most consumers would probably not care a whit. But product disparagement and defamation are distinct torts. *Brown & Williamson Tobacco Corp. v. Jacobson*, 713 F.2d 262, 269 (7th Cir. 1983) (Illinois law); *Crinkley v. Dow Jones & Co.*, 385 N.E.2d 714, 719 (Ill. App. 1978); *Boule v. Hutton*, 328 F.3d 84, 94 n. 8 (2d Cir. 2003); W. Page Keeton, et al., *Prosser and Keeton on the Law of Torts* § 128, p. 964 (5th ed. 1984). A pirated product is not necessarily inferior to the lawful original; it may indeed be identical to it. So an accusation of piracy is not, as Peaceable Planet appears to think, product disparagement per se. *Fedders Corp. v. Elite Classics*, 279 F. Supp. 2d 965, 972 (S.D. Ill. 2003); see *Curtis-Universal, Inc. v. Sheboygan Emergency Medical Services, Inc.*, 43 F.3d 1119, 1124 (7th Cir. 1994); *Allcare, Inc. v. Bork*, 531 N.E.2d 1033, 1037–38 (Ill. App. 1988); *American Pet Motels, Inc. v. Chicago Veterinary Medical Ass'n*, 435 N.E.2d 1297, 1302–03 (Ill. App. 1982), overruled on other grounds in *Kuwik v. Starmark Star Marketing & Administration, Inc.*, 156 619 N.E.2d 129, 133 (Ill. 1993). Highly ethical consumers may think worse of the pirate and turn away from his goods; but if so, and if the junior user is responsible for the false impression that the senior is a pirate, the junior is guilty of defamation. See *Brown & Williamson Tobacco Corp. v. Jacobson, supra*, 713 F.2d at 269 (Illinois law); *Gardner v. Senior Living Systems, Inc.*, 731 N.E.2d 350, 355–56 (Ill. App. 2000); *Allcare, Inc. v. Bork, supra*, 531 N.E.2d at 1037 (Ill. App. 1988); *Crinkley v. Dow Jones and Co., supra*, 385 N.E.2d at 719. There is no evidence of that here; indeed, the complaint contains no defamation count. . . .

To summarize, the dismissal of the product-disparagement count is affirmed, but the dismissal of the remaining counts is reversed and the case is remanded for further proceedings consistent with this opinion.

AFFIRMED IN PART, REVERSED IN PART, AND REMANDED.

NOTES FOR DISCUSSION

1. *When is a Name a Name?* What rule or rules does Chief Judge Posner set forth for determining when a name is a name? Should the court require secondary meaning if a party seeks trademark protection in the following cases:

(a) Bird for radio components, including electrical filters, electrical switches, and electrical meters, manufactured by Bird Electronic Corp., the president of which is Bruce Bird. *See Fisher Radio Corp. v. Bird Electronic Corp.*, 162 U.S.P.Q. 265, 266–67 (T.T.A.B. 1969) (allowing registration without proof of secondary meaning given that primary meaning of "bird" is not as a surname).

(b) Hutchinson Technology for computer-related components. *See In re Hutchinson Technology, Inc.*, 852 F.2d 552, 554 (Fed. Cir. 1988) (holding that mark must be considered as a whole, and given that Technology is neither generic for nor merely descriptive of applicant's goods, finding that mark was not primarily merely a surname).

2. *History of the Personal Names Doctrine.* In the 19th century, courts generally recognized an individual's right to use his own name in business, even if some confusion resulted. Only if a defendant went further than simply using his own name, for example, by imitating the plaintiff's packaging or labels, would the court step in, and only then to stop the trade dress imitation, not to enjoin the use of the name. For example, in *Brown Chemical Co. v. Meyer*, 139 U.S. 540 (1891), the maker of "Brown's Iron Bitters" sued the makers of "Brown's Iron Tonic" for trademark infringement and unfair competition. The Court rejected the claim. As the Court explained:

> A man's name is his own property, and he has the same right to its use and enjoyment as he has to that of any other species of property. If such use be a reasonable, honest and fair exercise of such right, he in no more liable for the incidental damage he may do a rival in trade than he would be for injury to his neighbor's property by the smoke issuing from his chimney, or for the fall of his neighbor's house by reason of necessary excavations upon his own land. These and similar instances are cases of damnum absque injuria.

Brown Chemical Co., 139 U.S. at 544.

In the 20th century, abuses of this right, particularly in the context of naming a corporation, led courts to abandon it and to focus instead on a balancing on whether consumers would be confused by the defendant's use of his name and whether the defendant's use was in good faith. As an example of the sort of abuse that occurred, consider the facts in *De Nobili Cigar Co. v. Nobile Cigar Co.*, 56 F.2d 324 (1st Cir. 1932). The plaintiff had been selling cigars under the mark "De Nobili" since 1906 and its cigars had become very popular. In 1928, two cigar manufacturers, Felice and Biagio Melaragno formed a corporation to make and sell cigars with a third individual who was not a cigar manufacturer, but whose name happened to be Francesco G. Nobile. *Id.* at 326. They named the corporation the Nobile Cigar Co. and marketed their cigars as F.G. Nobile cigars. When the plaintiff sued alleging trademark infringement, the defendant took refuge in Mr. Nobile's right to use his own name in his business. The First Circuit rejected the defense, however. As the court explained:

> We find that this prominent display of trade-name so near in sound and appearance to the trade-name on complainant's product makes it clear that the defendant's product as put on the market does deceive (Celluloid Mfg. Co. v. Cellonite Mfg. Co. [C.C.] 32 F. 94, 101), and we are unable to get away from the conviction that the defendant was induced to go into the cigar business for the purpose of obtaining such advantages as it could from the fact that the surname of one of its incorporators was "Nobile."

> ... While it is true that every man has a right to use his own name in his own business, it is also true that he has no right to use it for the purpose of stealing the good will of his neighbor's business, nor to commit a fraud upon his neighbor, nor to trespass upon his neighbor's rights or property. It has been held, with reference to trade-marks, that a man has not the right to use even his own name so as to deceive the public, and cause a belief that he is selling the goods of another of the same name.

Id. at 327. The court therefore enjoined the defendant's use of the "Nobile" name.

When Congress enacted the Trademark Act of 1946, it expressly allowed for the registration and protection of surnames as trademarks upon proof of secondary meaning. *See* 15 U.S.C. 1052(e)(4), (f) (2015). Surnames today are thus treated identically with other descriptive word marks. They receive protection when they have acquired a secondary meaning. Infringement is judged using the same likelihood of confusion standard. Even if there is some likelihood of confusion, a defendant may assert a fair use defense, just as the defendants did in the *Zatarain's* case.

D. DECEPTIVE MARKS: MATERIALLY FALSE INFORMATION

IN RE BUDGE MFG. CO., INC.

857 F.2d 773 (Fed. Cir. 1988)

NIES, C.J.

Budge Manufacturing Co., Inc., appeals from the final decision of the United States Trademark Trial and Appeal Board refusing registration of LOVEE LAMB for "automotive seat covers," application Serial No. 507,974 filed November 9, 1984. The basis for rejection is that the term LAMB is deceptive matter within the meaning of section 2(a) of the Lanham Act, 15 U.S.C. § 1052(a) (1982), as applied to Budge's goods which are made wholly from synthetic fibers. We affirm.

Opinion

Section 2(a) of the Lanham Act bars registration of a mark which: "Consists of or comprises . . . deceptive . . . matter. . . ." As stated in *In re Automatic Radio Mfg. Co.*, 404 F.2d 1391, 1396 (CCPA 1969): "The proscription [of section 2(a)] is not against misdescriptive terms unless they are also deceptive." Thus, that a mark or part of a mark may be inapt or misdescriptive as applied to an applicant's goods does not make it "deceptive." *Id.* (AUTOMATIC RADIO not a deceptive mark for air conditioners, ignition systems, and antennas). Recognizing that premise, the Trademark Trial and Appeal Board has sought to articulate a standard by which "deceptive matter" under section 2(a) can be judged. In this case, the board applied the three-part test which was stated in *In re Shapely, Inc.*, 231 USPQ 72, 73 (TTAB 1986): (1) whether the term is misdescriptive as applied to the goods, (2) if so, whether anyone would be likely to believe the misrepresentation, and (3) whether the misrepresentation would materially affect a potential purchaser's decision to buy the goods.

Budge argues that the board was bound to follow the standard articulated in *In re Simmons, Inc.*, 192 USPQ 331 (TTAB 1976). Per Budge, *Simmons* sets forth a different standard in that it requires as a minimum that "the mark convey some information, upon which an intended customer may reasonably rely, concerning something about the character, quality, function, composition or use of the goods to induce the purchase thereof, but which information, in fact, is misleadingly false." *Id.* at 332.

. . . [W]hile phrased differently, we discern no material difference between the standard set forth in *Shapely* and that in *Simmons*. . . . Where the issue relates to deceptive misdescriptiveness within the meaning of 2(a), we are in general agreement with the standard set out by the board in *Shapely*, with the following amplification in part drawn from *Simmons*:

> (1) Is the term misdescriptive of the character, quality, function, composition or use of the goods?

> (2) If so, are prospective purchasers likely to believe that the misdescription actually describes the goods?

> (3) If so, is the misdescription likely to affect the decision to purchase?

In *ex parte* prosecution, the burden is initially on the Patent and Trademark Office (PTO) to put forth sufficient evidence that the mark for which registration is sought meets the above criteria of unregistrability. Mindful that the PTO has limited facilities for acquiring evidence—it cannot, for example, be expected to conduct a survey of the marketplace or obtain consumer affidavits—we conclude that the evidence of record here is sufficient to establish a *prima facie* case of deceptiveness. That evidence shows with respect to the three-pronged test:

> (1) Budge admits that its seat covers are not made from lamb or sheep products. Thus, the term LAMB is misdescriptive of its goods.

> (2) Seat covers for various vehicles can be and are made from natural lambskin and sheepskin. Applicant itself makes automobile seat covers of natural sheepskin. Lambskin is defined, *inter alia*, as fine-grade sheep skin. The board's factual inference is reasonable that purchasers are likely to believe automobile seat covers denominated by the term LAMB or SHEEP are actually made from natural sheep or lamb skins.

> (3) Evidence of record shows that natural sheepskin and lambskin is more expensive than simulated skins and that natural and synthetic skins have different characteristics. Thus, the misrepresentation is likely to affect the decision to purchase.

Faced with this *prima facie* case against registration, Budge had the burden to come forward with countering evidence to overcome the rejection. It wholly failed to do so.

Budge argues that its use of LAMB as part of its mark is not misdescriptive when considered in connection with the text in its advertising, which states that the cover is of "simulated sheepskin." Some, but not all, of Budge's specimen labels also have this text. This evidence is unpersuasive. In *R. Neumann & Co. v. Overseas Shipments, Inc.*, 326 F.2d 786 (CCPA 1964), a similar argument was made that the mark DURA-HYDE on shoes was not deceptive as an indication of leather because of tags affixed to the shoes proclaiming the legend "Outwears leather." In discounting the evidence, the court stated: "The legends constitute advertisement material separate and apart from any trademark significance." *Id.* at 790. To the same effect is *In re Bonide Chemical Co.*, 46 F.2d 705 (CCPA 1931). There the court held, with respect to a clarifying statement made in advertising circulars, which the applicant urged negated the deceptive nature of the mark, "This argument is beside the issue. It is the word of the mark, not the statement of an advertising circular which appellant seeks to register. . . ." *Id.* at 708.

Thus, we conclude that the board properly discounted Budge's advertising and labeling which indicate the actual fabric content. Misdescriptiveness of a term may be negated by its meaning in the context of the whole mark inasmuch as the combination is seen together and makes a unitary impression. *A.F. Gallun & Sons Corp. v. Aristocrat Leather Prods., Inc.*, 135 USPQ 459, 460 (TTAB 1962) (COPY CALF not misdescriptive, but rather suggests *imitation* of calf skin). The same is not true with respect to explanatory statements in advertising or on labels which purchasers may or may not note and which may or may not always be provided. The statutory provision bars registration of *a mark* comprising deceptive matter. Congress has said that the advantages of registration may not be extended to a mark which deceives the public. Thus, the mark standing alone must pass muster, for that is what the applicant seeks to register, not extraneous explanatory statements.

Budge next argues that no reasonable purchaser would expect to purchase lambskin automobile seat covers because none made of lambskin are on the market. Only sheepskin automobile seat covers are being made, per Budge. Not only was no evidence submitted on the point Budge seeks to make, only statements of Budge's attorney, but also the argument is without substance. The board properly equated sheepskin and lambskin based on the dictionary definition which indicates that the terms may be used interchangeably. In addition, while Budge would discount the evidence presented that bicycle and airline seat coverings are made of lambskin, we conclude that it does support the board's finding that there is nothing incongruous about automobile seat covers being made from lambskin. We also agree with the board's conclusion that any differences between sheepskin and lambskin would not be readily apparent to potential purchasers of automobile seat covers. The board's finding here that purchasers are likely to believe the misrepresentation is not clearly erroneous.

. . . Finally, we note the evidence of Budge's extensive sales since 1974 under the mark. However, it is too well established for argument that a mark which includes deceptive matter is barred from registration and cannot acquire distinctiveness.

Conclusion

None of the facts found by the board have been shown to be clearly erroneous nor has the board erred as a matter of law. Accordingly, we affirm the board's decision that Budge's mark LOVEE LAMB for automobile seat covers made from synthetic fibers is deceptive within the meaning of 15 U.S.C. § 1052(a) and is, thus, barred from registration.

AFFIRMED.

E. PRIMARILY GEOGRAPHICALLY DECEPTIVELY MISDESCRIPTIVE MARKS

IN RE CALIFORNIA INNOVATIONS, INC.
329 F.3d 1334 (Fed. Cir. 2003)

RADER, CIRCUIT JUDGE

California Innovations, Inc. (CA Innovations), a Canadian-based corporation, appeals the Trademark Trial and Appeal Board's refusal to register its mark—CALIFORNIA INNOVATIONS. Citing section 2(e)(3) of the Lanham Act, 15 U.S.C. § 1052(e)(3) (2000), the Board concluded that the mark was primarily geographically deceptively misdescriptive. Because the Board applied an outdated standard in its analysis under § 1052(e)(3), this court vacates the Board's decision and remands.

CA Innovations filed an intent-to-use trademark application, Serial No. 74/650,703, on March 23, 1995, for the composite mark CALIFORNIA INNOVATIONS and Design. The application sought registration for the following goods:

> automobile visor organizers, namely, holders for personal effects, and automobile trunk organizers for automotive accessories in International Class 12; backpacks in International Class 18; thermal insulated bags for food and beverages, thermal insulated tote bags for food or beverages, and thermal insulated wraps for cans to keep the containers cold or hot in International Class 21; and nylon, vinyl, polyester and/or leather bags for storage and storage pouches in International Class 22.

The United States Patent and Trademark Office (PTO) initially refused registration based on an alleged likelihood of confusion with some prior registrations. At the PTO's request, applicant disclaimed the CALIFORNIA component of the mark. Applicant also amended its identification and classification of goods to conform to the examiner's suggestions. Thereafter, the PTO issued a notice of publication. The mark was published for opposition on September 29, 1998. No opposition was ever filed.

In July 1999, the PTO reasserted jurisdiction over the application under 37 C.F.R. § 2.84(a) and refused registration under § 1052(e)(3), concluding that the mark was primarily geographically deceptively misdescriptive. Applicant filed a timely notice for reconsideration with the PTO and a notice of appeal to the Board in November 2000. After the PTO refused to reconsider its decision, CA Innovations renewed its appeal to the Board. On February 20, 2002, the Board upheld the PTO's refusal to register applicant's mark and concluded that the mark was primarily geographically deceptively misdescriptive.

This court reviews the Board's "legal conclusions, such as its interpretations of the Lanham Act," without deference. *In re Hiromichi Wada*, 194 F.3d 1297, 1299 (Fed. Cir. 1999). Under a proper legal standard, the Board's determination of geographic misdescription is a factual finding. *See In re Compagnie Generale Maritime*, 993 F.2d 841, 845 (Fed. Cir. 1993). This court upholds the Board's factual findings "unless they are unsupported by substantial evidence." *Recot, Inc. v. M.C. Becton*, 214 F.3d 1322, 1327 (Fed. Cir. 2000). . . .

II.

The Lanham Act addresses geographical marks in three categories. The first category, § 1052(a), identifies geographically deceptive marks:

> No trademark by which the goods of the applicant may be distinguished from the goods of others shall be refused registration on the principal register on account of its nature unless it—(a) Consists of or comprises immoral, deceptive, or scandalous matter; or matter which may disparage or falsely suggest a connection with persons, living or dead, institutions, beliefs, or national symbols, or bring them into contempt, or disrepute.

15 U.S.C. § 1052(a) (2000) (emphasis added).

Although not expressly addressing geographical marks, § 1052(a) has traditionally been used to reject geographic marks that materially deceive the public. A mark found to be deceptive under § 1052(a) cannot receive protection under the Lanham Act. To deny a geographic mark protection under § 1052(a), the PTO must establish that (1) the mark misrepresents or misdescribes the goods, (2) the public would likely believe the misrepresentation, and (3) the misrepresentation would materially affect the public's decision to purchase the goods. This test's central point of analysis is materiality because that finding shows that the misdescription deceived the consumer.

The other two categories of geographic marks are (1) "primarily geographically descriptive" marks and (2) "primarily geographically deceptively misdescriptive" marks under § 1052(e). The North American Free Trade Agreement, as implemented by the NAFTA Implementation

Act in 1993, has recently changed these two categories. Before the NAFTA changes, § 1052(e) and (f) stated:

> No trademark by which the goods of the applicant may be distinguished from the goods of others shall be refused registration on the principal register on account of its nature unless it—

> (e) Consists of a mark which . . .

> (2) when used on or in connection with the goods of the applicant is primarily geographically descriptive or deceptively misdescriptive of them.

>   * * *

> (f) Except as expressly excluded in paragraphs (a)–(d) of this section, nothing in this chapter shall prevent the registration of a mark used by the applicant which has become distinctive of the applicant's goods in commerce.

15 U.S.C. § 1052(e)(2) and (f) (1988).

The law treated these two categories of geographic marks identically. Specifically, the PTO generally placed a "primarily geographically descriptive" or "deceptively misdescriptive" mark on the supplemental register. Upon a showing of acquired distinctiveness, these marks could qualify for the principal register.

Thus, in contrast to the permanent loss of registration rights imposed on deceptive marks under § 1052(a), pre-NAFTA § 1052(e)(2) only required a temporary denial of registration on the principal register. Upon a showing of distinctiveness, these marks could acquire a place on the principal register. As permitted by pre-NAFTA § 1052(f), a mark could acquire distinctiveness or "secondary meaning" by showing that "in the minds of the public, the primary significance of a product feature or term is to identify the source of the product rather than the product itself."

In the pre-NAFTA era, the focus on distinctiveness overshadowed the deceptiveness aspect of § 1052(e)(2) and made it quite easy for the PTO to deny registration on the principal register to geographically deceptively misdescriptive marks under § 1052(e)(2). On the other hand, the deception requirement of § 1052(a) protected against fraud and could not be overlooked. Therefore, the PTO had significantly more difficulty denying registration based on that higher standard.

Before NAFTA, in *In re Nantucket*, 209 USPQ 868, 870 (TTAB 1981), the Board used a three-prong test to detect either primarily geographically descriptive or deceptively misdescriptive marks. Under the Board's test, the only substantive inquiry was whether the mark conveyed primarily a geographical connotation. On appeal in *In re Nantucket*, this court's predecessor rejected that test:

> The board's test rests mechanistically on the one question of whether the mark is recognizable, at least to some large segment of the public, as the name of a geographical area. NANTUCKET is such. That ends the board's test. Once it is found that the mark is the name of a known place, i.e., that it has "a readily recognizable geographic meaning," the next question, whether applicant's goods do or do not come from that place, becomes irrelevant under the board's test, for if they do, the mark is "primarily geographically descriptive"; if they don't, the mark is "primarily geographically deceptively misdescriptive." Either way, the result is the same, for the mark must be denied registration on the principal register unless resort can be had to § 2(f).

In re Nantucket, Inc., 677 F.2d 95, 97–98 (CCPA 1982).

Thus *In re Nantucket*, for the first time, set forth a goods-place association requirement. In other words, this court required a geographically deceptively misdescriptive mark to have more than merely a primary geographic connotation. Specifically, the public must also associate the goods in question with the place identified by the mark—the goods-place association requirement. However, this court did not require a showing that the goods-place association was material to the consumer's decision before rejection under § 1052(e).

In *In re Loew's Theatres, Inc.*, 769 F.2d 764, 767–69 (Fed. Cir. 1985), this court expressly permitted a goods-place association without any showing that the place is "well-known" or "noted" for the goods in question. The Loew's court explained: "If the place is noted for the particular goods, a mark for such goods which do not originate there is likely to be deceptive under § 2(a) and not registrable under any circumstances." Clarifying that pre-NAFTA § 1052(e)(2) does not require a "well-known" place, this court noted:

> The PTO's burden is simply to establish that there is a reasonable predicate for its conclusion that the public would be likely to make the particular goods/place association on which it relies. . . . The issue is not the fame or exclusivity of the place name, but the likelihood that a particular place will be associated with particular goods.

Id.

As noted, the Lanham Act itself does not expressly require different tests for geographically misleading marks. In order to implement the Lanham Act prior to the NAFTA amendments, the PTO used a low standard to reject marks for geographically deceptive misdescriptiveness under pre-NAFTA § 1052(e), which was relatively simple to meet. In contrast, the PTO required a much more demanding finding to reject for geographical deception under § 1052(a). This distinction was justified because rejection under subsection (a) was final, while rejection under pre-NAFTA subsection (e)(2) was only temporary, until the applicant could show that the mark had become distinctive. The more drastic consequence establishes the propriety of the elevated materiality test in the context of a permanent ban on registration under § 1052(a).

NAFTA and its implementing legislation obliterated the distinction between geographically deceptive marks and primarily geographically deceptively misdescriptive marks. Article 1712 of NAFTA provides:

> 1.   Each party [United States, Mexico, Canada] shall provide, in respect of geographical indications, the legal means for interested persons to prevent:
>
>> (a) the use of any means in the designation or presentation of a good that indicates or suggests that the good in question originates in a territory, region or locality other than the true place of origin, in a manner that misleads the public as to the geographical origin of the good. . . .

See NAFTA, Dec. 17, 1992, art. 1712, 32 I.L.M. 605, 698.

This treaty shifts the emphasis for geographically descriptive marks to prevention of any public deception. Accordingly, the NAFTA Act amended § 1052(e) to read:

> No trademark by which the goods of the applicant may be distinguished from the goods of others shall be refused registration on the principal register on account of its nature unless it—
>
>> (e) Consists of a mark which (1) when used on or in connection with the goods of the applicant is merely descriptive or deceptively misdescriptive of them, (2) when used on or in connection with the goods of the applicant is primarily geographically descriptive of them, except as indications of regional origin may be registrable under section 4 [15 USCS § 1054], (3) when used on or in connection with the goods of the applicant is primarily geographically deceptively misdescriptive of them, (4) is primarily merely a surname, or (5) comprises any matter that, as a whole, is functional.
>
>> (f) Except as expressly excluded in subsections (a), (b), (c), (d), (e)(3), and (e)(5) of this section, nothing herein shall prevent the registration of a mark used by the applicant which has become distinctive of the applicant's goods in commerce.

15 U.S.C. § 1052(e)–(f) (2000).

Recognizing the new emphasis on prevention of public deception, the NAFTA amendments split the categories of geographically descriptive and geographically deceptively misdescriptive into two subsections (subsections (e)(2) and (e)(3) respectively). Under the amended Lanham Act, subsection (e)(3)—geographically deceptive misdescription—could no longer acquire distinctiveness under subsection (f). Accordingly, marks determined to be primarily geographically deceptively misdescriptive are permanently denied registration, as are deceptive marks under § 1052(a).

Thus, § 1052 no longer treats geographically deceptively misdescriptive marks differently from geographically deceptive marks. Like geographically deceptive marks, the analysis for primarily geographically deceptively misdescriptive marks under § 1052(e)(3) focuses on deception of, or fraud on, the consumer. The classifications under the new § 1052 clarify that these two deceptive categories both receive permanent rejection. Accordingly, the test for rejecting a deceptively misdescriptive mark is no longer simple lack of distinctiveness, but the higher showing of deceptiveness. . . .

Before NAFTA, the PTO identified and denied registration to a primarily geographically deceptively misdescriptive mark with a showing that (1) the primary significance of the mark was a generally known geographic location, and (2) "the public was likely to believe the mark identified the place from which the goods originate and that the goods did not come from there." *In re Loew's*, 769 F.2d at 768. The second prong of the test represents the "goods-place association" between the mark and the goods at issue. This test raised an inference of deception based on the likelihood of a goods-place association that did not reflect the actual origin of the goods. A mere inference, however, is not enough to establish the deceptiveness that brings the harsh consequence of non-registrability under the amended Lanham Act. As noted, NAFTA and the amended Lanham Act place an emphasis on actual misleading of the public.

Therefore, the relatively easy burden of showing a naked goods-place association without proof that the association is material to the consumer's decision is no longer justified, because marks rejected under § 1052(e)(3) can no longer obtain registration through acquired distinctiveness under § 1052(f). To ensure a showing of deceptiveness and misleading before imposing the penalty of non-registrability, the PTO may not deny registration without a showing that the goods-place association made by the consumer is material to the consumer's decision to purchase those goods. This addition of a materiality inquiry equates this test with the elevated standard applied under § 1052(a). This also properly reflects the presence of the deceptiveness criterion often overlooked in the "primarily geographically deceptively misdescriptive" provision of the statute.

The shift in emphasis in the standard to identify primarily geographically deceptively misdescriptive marks under § 1052(e)(3) will bring that section into harmony with § 1052(a). Both sections involve proof of deception with the consequence of non-registrability. The adherence to the pre-NAFTA standard designed to focus on distinctiveness would almost read the term "deceptively" out of § 1052(e)(3), which is the term that the NAFTA amendments to the Lanham Act has reemphasized. Accordingly, under the amended Lanham Act, both subsection (a) and subsection (e)(3) share a similar legal standard. . . .

Thus, due to the NAFTA changes in the Lanham Act, the PTO must deny registration under § 1052(e)(3) if (1) the primary significance of the mark is a generally known geographic location, (2) the consuming public is likely to believe the place identified by the mark indicates the origin of the goods bearing the mark, when in fact the goods do not come from that place, and (3) the misrepresentation was a material factor in the consumer's decision. . . .

III.

CA Innovations unequivocally states in its opening brief that its "petition seeks review only of that portion of the [Board's] decision that pertains to 'thermal insulated bags for food and beverages and thermal insulated wraps for cans'" as identified in International Class 21 in the application. Therefore, because of applicant's decision not to challenge the Board's judgment with respect to all goods other than those identified in class 21, that part of the Board's decision is not affected by this opinion.

As a preliminary issue, this court may affirm or reverse a rejection of an application with respect to only a portion of the goods identified. This court discerns no legal limitation on an appeal with respect to a portion of the goods listed in the application. In fact, the Board also perceives no legal restrictions on narrowing the issues in an application.

The parties agree that CA Innovations' goods do not originate in California.

Under the first prong of the test—whether the mark's primary significance is a generally known geographic location—a composite mark such as the applicant's proposed mark must be evaluated as a whole. . . . It is not erroneous, however, for the examiner to consider the significance of each element within the composite mark in the course of evaluating the mark as a whole.

The Board found that "the word CALIFORNIA is a prominent part of applicant's mark and is not overshadowed by either the word INNOVATIONS or the design element." Although the mark may also convey the idea of a creative, laid-back lifestyle or mindset, the Board properly recognized that such an association does not contradict the primary geographic significance of the mark. Even if the public may associate California with a particular life-style, the record supports the Board's finding that the primary meaning remains focused on the state of California. Nonetheless, this court declines to review at this stage the Board's finding that CA Innovations' composite mark CALIFORNIA INNOVATIONS and Design is primarily geographic in nature. Rather the PTO may apply the entire new test on remand.

The second prong of the test requires proof that the public is likely to believe the applicant's goods originate in California. The Board stated that the examining attorney submitted excerpts from the Internet and the NEXIS database showing "some manufacturers and distributors of backpacks, tote bags, luggage, computer cases, and sport bags ... headquartered in California." The Board also acknowledged articles "which make reference to companies headquartered in California which manufacture automobile accessories such as auto organizers," as well as the "very serious apparel and sewn products industry" in California.

A great deal of the evidence cited in this case relates to the fashion industry, which is highly prevalent in California due to Hollywood's influence on this industry. However, clothing and fashion have nothing to do with the products in question. At best, the record in this case shows some general connection between the state of California and backpacks and automobile organizers. However, because CA Innovations has limited its appeal to insulated bags and wraps, the above referenced evidence is immaterial. Therefore, this opinion has no bearing on whether the evidence of record supports a rejection of the application with regard to any goods other than those identified in CA Innovations' application under International Class 21, namely insulated bags and wraps.

CA Innovations argues that the examining attorney provided no evidence at all concerning insulated bags for food and wraps for cans in California. The Government contends that the evidence shows some examples of a lunch bag, presumed to be insulated, and insulated backpacks. According to the government, the evidence supports a finding of a goods-place association between California and insulated bags and wraps. This court has reviewed the publications and listings supplied by the examining attorney. At best, the evidence of a connection between California and insulated bags and wraps is tenuous. Even if the evidence supported a finding of a goods-place association, the PTO has yet to apply the materiality test in this case. This court declines to address that issue and apply the new standard in the first instance. Accordingly, this court vacates the finding of the Board that CA Innovations' mark is primarily geographically deceptively misdescriptive, and remands the case for further proceedings. On remand, the Board shall apply the new three-prong standard.

COSTS

Each party shall bear its own costs.

VACATED and REMANDED

NOTES FOR DISCUSSION

1. *Pre-NAFTA Amendments Framework.* Before *In re California Innovations* and the NAFTA Amendments, the same basic framework controlled the determination whether representations concerning geographic origin, or some other factual characteristic or feature, of the product or service at issue, were descriptive, deceptively misdescriptive, or deceptive:

1(a). Are consumers likely to perceive the mark at issue as making a representation regarding the nature, characteristics, feature, or geographic origin of the good?

If yes, go to question 1(b). If no, then the mark at issue is either arbitrary or suggestive and may be registered without proof of secondary meaning.

1(b). Is the representation true or false?

If true, the mark is merely descriptive and requires proof of secondary meaning to be registered. If false, then the mark is misdescriptive; proceed to question 2.

2. Are consumers likely to believe the representation?

If yes, then the mark is either deceptive or deceptively misdescriptive. Go to question 3 to determine which. If no, then the mark at issue is either arbitrary or suggestive and may be registered without proof of secondary meaning.

3. Is the representation likely to be material to consumer purchasing decisions?

If yes, then the mark is deceptive, under section 1052(a), and may not be registered. Moreover, if such a mark is registered improperly, a petition to cancel the registration may be filed at any time under section 1064(3) and the mark's validity may be challenged even if it has become incontestable under sections 1065 and 1115(b). Further, not only will use of such a deceptive term never establish trademark rights, it may also constitute false advertising under section 43(a)(1)(B) of the Lanham Act, as we shall see in Chapter 12.

If no, then the mark is deceptively misdescriptive, whether primarily geographically or otherwise, and prior to the NAFTA Amendments could be registered, but only with a showing of secondary meaning.

Note that in *In re Budge Manufacturing*, the court combines questions 1(a) and 1(b) into a single "Is the term misdescriptive ..." inquiry. Does separating that single inquiry into its component parts change the analysis with respect to LOVEE LAMB for artificial sheepskin seat covers?

In *In re California Innovations*, the court summarizes the pre-NAFTA Amendments test as a two-part standard: (1) the primary meaning of the term is geographic; and (2) consumers are likely to believe the representation and it is false. Such an approach separates questions 1(a) and 1(b), but adds question 1(b) regarding falsity or misdescriptiveness into question 2 which deals with whether consumers will believe the representation.

2. *"Primarily Geographically Deceptively Misdescriptive."* The statutory language labeling this category of marks is a mouthful, but each of the words addresses a specific issue. The first phrase "primarily geographic" corresponds to question 1(a) in our framework. Under this phrase, courts separate marks that consumers would understand primarily in a geographic sense, such as Nantucket, from words, such as Ivory, that have a geographic meaning, but also have other non-geographic meanings. The word "deceptively" corresponds to question (2) in our framework, and asks whether consumers would believe the representation of geographic origin. The word "misdescriptive" corresponds to question 1(b) in our framework, and asks whether the representation is true of false. What word in the statutory language encompasses question 3?

3. *The NAFTA Amendments.* In 1993, Congress amended the Lanham Act with respect to primarily geographically deceptively misdescriptive marks. It did not change the structure of the analysis, or the statutory catchphrase, set forth above, but it barred registration of primarily geographically deceptively misdescriptive terms unless secondary meaning could be established prior to the effective date of the NAFTA Amendments, December 8, 1993. Congress did not, however, fully equate primarily geographically deceptively misdescriptive terms in section 1052(e)(3) with geographically deceptive terms in section 1052(a), as Judge Rader suggested in *In re California Innovations*. Even after the NAFTA Amendments, some important differences remain. First, another party can seek to cancel the improper registration of a primarily geographically deceptively misdescriptive mark only within five years of the mark's registration under section 1064(1). In contrast, the registration of a deceptive term, whether deceptive with respect to geographic origin or otherwise, can be challenged at any time under section 1064(3). Second, if a mark that is primarily geographically deceptively misdescriptive is improperly registered and becomes incontestable under sections 1065 and 1115(b), then the registration may no longer be challenged on the grounds that it is primarily geographically deceptively misdescriptive. In contrast, an improperly registered deceptive mark can be challenged even after it becomes incontestable under sections 1065 and 1115(b).

4. *Rewriting the Test for Geographic Misdescriptiveness.* As a result of the NAFTA amendments, Judge Rader rewrote the test for finding words primarily geographically deceptively misdescriptive. How does his opinion change the framework for such marks? Specifically, if a mark makes an

untrue representation of geographic origin that consumers are likely to believe—what the case law historically referred to as a "goods-place association"—but the false representation is not material, may the mark be registered? Does registration of a mark that creates such a false goods-place association require proof of secondary meaning under Judge Rader's reasoning? Did such a mark require proof of secondary meaning before it could be registered in the pre-NAFTA Amendments era?

5.   *Counting the Flaws.* There are numerous flaws in Judge Rader's reasoning in *In re California Innovations* and Professor Mary LaFrance has catalogued them in her article, *Innovation Palpitations: The Confusing Status of Geographically Misdescriptive Trademarks*, 12 J. INTELL. PROP. L. 125 (2004). Let's review them:

(a) Bowing to pressure from our trading partners who tend to care more about misleading use of geographical indications (known in international trademark circles as "GIs"), Congress's intent in the NAFTA Amendments was to make it more difficult to register GIs that were potentially misleading. After Judge Rader's opinion, is it more difficult or easier to register misleading GIs? For example, before the NAFTA Amendments, could the applicant have registered the mark at issue in *California Innovations*, and if so, what would the applicant have had to show? What about after the NAFTA Amendments and Judge Rader's opinion?

(b) Under Judge Rader's interpretation, will all marks that qualify as primarily geographically deceptively misdescriptive also qualify as deceptive? If so, does Judge Rader's opinion render 1052(e)(3) superfluous?

(c) Does Judge Rader's opinion interpret the words "deceptively misdescriptive" for representations concerning geographic origin under section 1052(e)(3) differently from the same words "deceptively misdescriptive" for other types of factual representations under section 1052(e)(1)?

(d) If Congress intended primarily geographically deceptively misdescriptive under section 1052(e)(3) to have the same meaning as deceptive under section 1052(a) for false representations of geographic origin, why did Congress use different words in the two sections?

6.   *Pathways to Reversal.* Given that Judge Rader's interpretation of the statute fails to reflect Congress's intent, if you represent a client concerned about the misleading use of GIs, how can you seek reversal of *In re California Innovations*? First, you can petition Congress to enact a clarifying amendment, perhaps adding a provision that expressly states that materiality is not required to establish that a term is primarily geographically deceptively misdescriptive. Second, assuming that your client believes they would be damaged by the registration of a misleading GI, you could file an opposition or cancellation petition with the Trademark Trial and

Appeal Board ("TTAB"). Both the TTAB and later panels of the Federal Circuit are bound, however, to follow Judge Rader's incorrect interpretation absent intervening congressional or Supreme Court action. *See, e.g., In re Spirits Int'l*, 563 F.3d 1347 (Fed. Cir. 2009) (following *California Innovations* despite its manifest flaws). So you would have to be prepared to lose at the TTAB and at the Federal Circuit initially, and hope that you could persuade either: (i) the Federal Circuit to rehear the case *en banc* or (ii) the Supreme Court to grant *certiorari*, and in either case, reverse *In re California Innovations*.

As you can readily surmise, none of these options is particularly attractive. Are there any others? The Trademark Act provides at least one important alternative. Under section 1071(b) of the Act, after losing at the TTAB, instead of appealing to the Federal Circuit, a party dissatisfied with a decision of the TTAB may file a civil action in a federal district court for resolution of the issues. 15 U.S.C. § 1071(b) (2015). In such a district court action, while Judge Rader's opinion would still provide persuasive authority on the proper interpretation of the phrase "primarily geographically deceptively misdescriptive," it would not be binding. Moreover, any appeal from the district court decision would go to the district court's regional circuit, and that regional circuit would again not be bound to follow *In re California Innovations*. We shall see an example of a party taking advantage of this alternative in the next section.

F. OBJECTIONABLE MARKS

Section 1052 prohibits federal registration for marks that are objectionable. In relevant part, subsection (a) prohibits federal registration for a mark that "consists of or comprises immoral, deceptive, or scandalous matter; or matter which may disparage of falsely suggest a connection with persons, living or dead, institutions, beliefs, or national symbols, or bring them into contempt, or disrepute. . . ." 15 U.S.C. § 1052(a) (2015). Subsection (b) prohibits federal registration for a mark that "consists of or comprises the flag or coat of arms or other insignia of the United States, or of any State or municipality, or of any foreign nation, or any simulation thereof." 15 U.S.C. § 1052(b) (2015). Subsection (c) prohibits the federal registration of a mark that "consists of or comprises a name, portrait, or signature identifying a particular living individual except by his written consent, or the name, signature, or portrait of a deceased President of the United States during the life of his widow, if any, except by the written consent of the widow." 15 U.S.C. § 1052(c) (2015).

These provisions do not prohibit an entity from using such objectionable marks in commerce; they merely prohibit their registration on the principal register. Nonetheless, by prohibiting the registration of objectionable marks, these provisions deny such marks the advantages of federal registration, including the evidentiary presumptions, the nationwide priority, and the enhanced remedies that come with registration. The next case reflects the importance of these advantages and a party's willingness to fight for them.

PRO-FOOTBALL, INC. V. BLACKHORSE

___ F.Supp.3d ___, 2015 WL 4096277 (E.D. Va. 2015)

GERALD BRUCE LEE, J.

THIS MATTER is before the Court on two sets of cross-motions for summary judgment. First, Plaintiff Pro-Football, Inc. ("PFI"), Defendants Amanda Blackhorse, Marcus Briggs-Cloud, Phillip Gover, Jillian Pappan, and Courtney Tsotigh ("Blackhorse Defendants"), and the United States of America filed cross-motions for summary judgment on PFI's claims challenging the constitutionality of Section 2(a) of the Lanham Act (Counts III–VI) (Docs. 54, 105, and 108). Second, Blackhorse Defendants and PFI filed cross-motions for summary judgment on PFI's claims contesting the Trademark Trial and Appeal Board's ("TTAB") Order cancelling the registrations of six of PFI's trademarks on the grounds that they consisted of matter that "may disparage" Native Americans and bring them into contempt or disrepute, and that the defense of laches does not bar the claims (Counts I, II, and VII) (Docs. 69 and 79). This case concerns Blackhorse Defendants' petition to cancel the registration of six trademarks owned by PFI on the grounds that the marks consisted of matter that "may disparage" a substantial composite of Native Americans and bring them into contempt or disrepute under Section 2(a) of the Lanham Act, 15 U.S.C. § 1052(a), at the time of their registrations (1967, 1974, 1978, and 1990). . . .

BACKGROUND

The "Washington Redskins" are a well-known professional football team. The "Redskins" mark was first used by the "Washington Redskins" National Football League ("NFL") franchise in 1933 when then-owner George Preston Marshall selected the name while the team was located in Boston, Massachusetts. "Redskins" was chosen to distinguish the football team from the Boston Braves professional baseball team. The team has used the name ever since. The United States Patent and Trademark Office ("PTO") approved and registered the mark in 1967. Five additional variations of "Redskins" trademarks were approved and registered between 1974 and 1990 (collectively "Redskins Marks"). The registrations of the Redskins Marks have been renewed repeatedly since 1967, with the most recent renewal occurring in 2015. PFI owns, and has always owned, the Redskins Marks. . . .

The Redskins Marks have not evaded controversy. For example, in 1971 and 1972, there were a host of newspaper articles detailing opposition to the name "Redskins" by some Native Americans. Similarly, in 1972 Leon Cook, President of the National Congress of American Indians ("NCAI"), among others, met with Edward Bennett Williams, the president of PFI, to explain that the team name was a slur; Williams reported the meeting to the NFL Commissioner the following day. Also, a 1972 official game program referenced the controversy surrounding the team's name.

The registrability of the Redskins Marks has been litigated for over two decades. In 1992, Susan Harjo and six other Native Americans filed a petition to cancel the registrations of the Redskins Marks under Section 2(a) of the Lanham Act. Seven years later, the TTAB ruled that the Redskins Marks "may disparage" Native Americans when registered and ordered that the registrations of the marks be cancelled. *Harjo v. Pro-Football, Inc.*, 50 U.S.P.Q.2d (BNA) 1705. On appeal, the United States District Court for the District of Columbia reversed the TTAB, holding that (1) the TTAB's finding of disparagement was unsubstantiated, and (2) the doctrine of laches precluded consideration of the case.

The case traversed back and forth between the district court and the D.C. Circuit, with the final outcome being that D.C. Circuit affirmed the district court's ruling that laches barred the claim. *Pro-Football, Inc. v. Harjo*, 565 F.3d 880 (D.C. Cir. 2009). The D.C. Circuit never addressed the TTAB's finding of disparagement on the merits.

On August 11, 2006, while Harjo was pending, Amanda Blackhorse, Marcus BriggsCloud, Phillip Cover, Jillian Pappan, and Courtney Tsotigh ("Blackhorse Defendants") filed a petition to cancel the same six registrations of the Redskins Marks. The TTAB suspended action in the Blackhorse case until the Harjo litigation concluded in 2009. The parties here have agreed that the entire Harjo record could be entered into evidence in the case before the TTAB. The parties also waived all non-relevance evidentiary objections to that evidence.

On June 18, 2014, the TTAB scheduled the cancellation of the registrations of the Redskins Marks under Section 2(a) of the Lanham Act, 15 U.S.C. § 1052(a), finding that at the time of their registrations the marks consisted of matter that both "may disparage" a substantial composite of Native Americans and bring them into contempt or disrepute. See *Blackhorse v. Pro-Football, Inc.*, 111 U.S.P.Q.2d (BNA) 1080 (T.T.A.B. 2014). This action seeks a de novo review, pursuant to 15 U.S.C. § 1071(b), of the TTAB's decision, based on the TTAB Blackhorse record and the additional evidence the parties have submitted to this Court. . . .

STANDARDS OF REVIEW

A. Summary Judgment

Under Federal Rule of Civil Procedure 56, the Court must grant summary judgment if the moving party demonstrates that there is no genuine issue as to any material fact, and that the moving party is entitled to judgment as a matter of law. Fed.R.Civ.P. 56(c). . . .

B.   Review of TTAB Decision

15 U.S.C. § 1071(b)(1) "permits a party in a trademark suit to initiate a civil action in the place of an appeal of the TTAB's determination to the Federal Circuit." *Swatch AG v. Beehive Wholesale, LLC*, 739 F.3d 150, 155 (4th Cir. 2014). "In a § 1071(b) action, the district court reviews the record de novo and acts as the finder of fact. The district court has authority independent of the PTO to grant or cancel registrations and to decide any related matters such as infringement and unfair competition claims." *Id.* (*citing* 15 U.S.C. § 1071(b)(1); *Durox Co. v. Duron Paint Mfg. Co.*, 320 F.2d 882, 883–84 (4th Cir. 1963)). Where a party to such an action exercises its right to supplement the TTAB record, the Court gives no deference to the TTAB's findings. *Swatch*, 739 F.3d at 156.

ANALYSIS

. . .

A.   Trademark Registration vs. Trademarks Themselves

As a threshold matter, throughout the pleadings the parties conflated the legal principles surrounding trademarks with those surrounding trademark registration. . . . It is the registrations of the Redskins Marks that were scheduled for cancellation by the TTAB's decision, not the trademarks. In fact, the TTAB itself pointed out that it is only empowered to cancel the statutory registration of the marks under Section 2(a); it cannot cancel the trademarks themselves. *See Blackhorse v. Pro-Football, Inc.*, 111 U.S.P.Q.2d (BNA) 1080, 2014 WL 2757516, at *1 (T.T.A.B. 2014) (citation omitted). Thus, regardless of this Court's ruling, PFI can still use the Redskins Marks in commerce.

It is also important to identify the effect of federal trademark registration. . . . Registration confers several benefits upon the owner of a mark in addition to those available at common law:

> (1) constructive notice of the registrant's claim of ownership of the trademark; (2) prima facie evidence of the validity of the registration, of the registrant's ownership of the mark, and of his exclusive right to use the mark in commerce as specified in the certificate; (3) the possibility that, after five years, registration will become [incontestable] and constitute conclusive evidence of the registrant's right to use the mark; (4) the right to request customs officials to bar the importation of goods bearing infringing trademarks; (5) the right to institute trademark actions in federal courts without regard to diversity of citizenship or the amount in controversy; and (6) treble damage actions against infringing trademarks and other remedies.

Georator Corp. v. United States, 485 F.2d 283, 285 (4th Cir. 1973) (*citing* 15 U.S.C. § 1051 et seq.), *abrogated on other grounds by NCNB Corp. v. United States*, 684 F.2d 285 (4th Cir. 1982). Incontestability and proof of ownership are among the most significant advantages of registration. *See Brittingham v. Jenkins*, 914 F.2d 447, 452 (4th Cir. 1990).

What is at issue here is the registration of the Redskins Marks and the benefits associated with registration, not the use of the marks.

B.   Constitutional Challenges

1.   PFI's First Amendment Challenge Fails

With regard to PFI's First Amendment challenge (Count III), the Court DENIES PFI's Motion for Summary Judgment on Constitutional Claims and GRANTS the cross-motions for summary judgment filed by Blackhorse Defendants and the United States of America for two reasons. First, Section 2(a) of the Lanham Act does not implicate the First Amendment. Second, under the Supreme Court's decision in *Walker v. Tex. Div., Sons of Confederate Veterans, Inc.*, ___ U.S. ___, 135 S.Ct. 2239 (2015), the Fourth Circuit's mixed/hybrid speech test, and *Rust v. Sullivan*, 500 U.S. 173 (1991), the federal trademark registration program is government speech and is therefore exempt from First Amendment scrutiny.

a.   Cancellation of Trademark Registration Does Not Implicate PFI's First Amendment Rights

The Court GRANTS Blackhorse Defendants and the United States' cross-motions for summary judgment on the constitutional claims and DENIES PFI's Motion for Summary Judgment on Constitutional Claims as to PFI's First Amendment claim (Count III) because Section 2(a) of the Lanham Act does not implicate the First Amendment. Section 2(a) provides, in pertinent part, that a trademark shall be refused registration if it "consists of or comprises immoral, deceptive, or scandalous matter; or matter which may disparage or falsely suggest a connection with persons, living or dead, institutions, beliefs, or national symbols, or bring them into contempt, or disrepute. . . ." 15 U.S.C. § 1052(a) (emphasis added).

The Federal Circuit and Fifth Circuit have both held that the PTO's refusal to register an applicant's mark does not infringe upon the mark owner's First Amendment rights as "[no] conduct is proscribed[ ] and no tangible form of expression is suppressed." *In re McGinley*, 660 F.2d 481, 484 (C.C.P.A. 1981); *see Test Masters Educ. Servs. v. Singh*, 428 F.3d 559, 578 n.9 (5th Cir. 2005).

Nothing about Section 2(a) impedes the ability of members of society to discuss a trademark that was not registered by the PTO. Simply put, the Court holds that cancelling the registrations of the Redskins Marks under Section 2(a) of the Lanham Act does not implicate the First

Amendment as the cancellations do not burden, restrict, or prohibit PFI's ability to use the marks. . . .

Cancelling the registration of a mark under Section 2(a) of the Lanham Act does not restrict the public debate on public issues as the mark owner is still able to use the mark in commerce. Accordingly, the Court agrees with the Federal Circuit and Fifth Circuit and holds that Section 2(a) of the Lanham Act does not implicate the First Amendment. . . .

b. The Federal Trademark Registration Program is Government Speech and is Exempt from First Amendment Scrutiny

The Court GRANTS Blackhorse Defendants and the United States' cross-motions for summary judgment on the constitutional claims and DENIES PFI's Motion for Summary Judgment on Constitutional Claims as to PFI's First Amendment claim (Count III) because the federal trademark registration program is government speech and is thus exempt from First Amendment scrutiny. [The court analogized registration of a trademark on the principal register to a state's approval and adoption of specialty license plate designs.]

c. Lanham Act Challenges

With regard to PFI's "may disparage" claim (Count I), the Court DENIES PFI's Cross-Motion for Summary Judgment on Claims I, II, and VII, and GRANTS Blackhorse Defendants' Motion for Summary Judgment on Counts I, II, and VII of Complaint because the (1) dictionary evidence, (2) literary, scholarly, and media references, and (3) statements of individuals and groups in the referenced group show that the Redskins Marks consisted of matter that "may disparage" a substantial composite of Native Americans during the relevant time period (1967, 1974, 1978, and 1990).

Section 2(a) of the Lanham Act, 15 U.S.C. § 1052(a), provides that registration should be denied to any mark that "[c]onsists of or comprises immoral, deceptive, or scandalous matter; or matter which may disparage or falsely suggest a connection with persons, living or dead, institutions, beliefs, or national symbols, or bring them into contempt or disrepute. . . ." *Id.* The TTAB has established a two-part test to determine whether a mark contains matter that "may disparage." The parties agree that the test in this case is as follows:

1. What is the meaning of the matter in question, as it appears in the marks and as those marks are used in connection with the goods and services identified in the registrations?

2. Is the meaning of the marks one that may disparage Native Americans?

See Blackhorse v. Pro-Football, Inc., 111 U.S.P.Q.2d 1080, 2014 WL 2757516, at *4 (T.T.A.B. 2014) (citations omitted); *see also In re Geller*, 751 F.3d 1355, 1358 (Fed. Cir. 2014). This inquiry focuses on the registration dates of the marks at issue. *Blackhorse*, 2014 WL 2757516, at *4 (citations omitted). Here, the registration dates are 1967, 1974, 1978, and 1990.

When answering the second question, whether the term "redskins" "may disparage" Native Americans, courts should look to the views of Native Americans, not those of the general public. *Id.* Moreover, Blackhorse Defendants are only required to show that the marks "may disparage" a "substantial composite" of Native Americans. *See Geller*, 751 F.3d at 1358 (citations omitted). A substantial composite is not necessarily a majority. *See In re Boulevard Ent., Inc.*, 334 F.3d 1336, 1340 (Fed. Cir. 2003).

Courts consider dictionary evidence when determining whether a term "may disparage" a substantial composite of the referenced group. In *In re Boulevard*, the Federal Circuit held that when a mark has only "one pertinent meaning[,] a standard dictionary definition and an accompanying editorial designation alone sufficiently demonstrate[ ] that a substantial composite of the general public" considers a term scandalous. 334 F.3d 1336, 1340–41 (Fed. Cir. 2003) (emphasis added) (citing 15 U.S.C. § 1052(a)) (finding that a mark had one "pertinent meaning" when all of the dictionaries consulted contained usage labels characterizing a term as "vulgar").

Courts can use usage labels to decide whether a term "may disparage" a specific referenced group, as opposed to the general public in Section 2(a) "scandalous" actions, because usage labels denote when words are disparaging or offensive to the group referenced in the underlying term. *See, e.g.*, Symbols and Labels Used in Oxford Learner's Dictionaries, Oxford Learner's Dictionaries, http://www.oxfordlearners dictionaries.com/us/about/labels (last visited July 6, 2015) ("offensive expressions are used by some people to address or refer to people in a way that is very insulting, especially in connection with their race, religion, sex or disabilities").

Thus, using a dictionary's usage labels to determine whether a term "may disparage" a substantial composite of Native Americans during the relevant time period is consistent with the Federal Circuit's holding in *Boulevard. See In re Fox*, 702 F.3d 633, 635 (Fed. Cir. 2012) ("But where it is clear from dictionary evidence that the mark as used by the applicant in connection with the products described in the application invokes a vulgar meaning to a substantial composite of the general public, the mark is unregistrable." (citation and internal quotation marks omitted)).

However, when dictionaries are not unanimous in their characterization of a term, additional evidence must be adduced to satisfy the PTO's burden. . . .

1.   The Meaning of the Matter in Question is a Reference to Native Americans

The Court finds that the meaning of the matter in question in all six Redskins Marks—the term "redskins" and derivatives thereof—is a reference to Native Americans. PFI admits that "redskins" refers to Native Americans. . . .

2.   The Redskins Marks "May Disparage" a Substantial Composite of Native Americans During the Relevant Time Period

The Court finds that the meaning of the marks is one that "may disparage" a substantial composite of Native Americans in the context of the "Washington Redskins" football team. The relevant period for the disparagement inquiry is the time at which the marks were registered. *Blackhorse*, 2014 WL 2757516, at *4 (citations omitted). Here, the Court focuses on the time period between 1967 and 1990. When reviewing whether a mark "may disparage," the PTO does not, and practically cannot, conduct a poll to determine the views of the referenced group. *See In re Loew's Theatres, Inc.*, 769 F.2d 764, 768 (Fed. Cir. 1985). Instead, three categories of evidence are weighed to determine whether a term "may disparage": (1) dictionary definitions and accompanying editorial designations; (2) scholarly, literary, and media references; and (3) statements of individuals or group leaders of the referenced group regarding the term.

Furthermore, by using the term "may disparage," Section 2(a) does not require that the mark holder possess an intent to disparage in order to deny or cancel a registration. *See Harjo*, 284 F. Supp. 2d at 125. Also, in order to be cancelled or denied registration, the marks must consist of matter that "may disparage" in the context of the goods and services provided. *See In re McGinley*, 660 F.2d 481, 485 (C.C.P.A. 1981).

a.   Dictionary Evidence

First, the record evidence contains dictionary definitions and accompanying designations of "redskins" that weigh in favor of finding that the Redskins Marks consisted of matter that "may disparage" a substantial composite of Native Americans when each of the six marks was registered. . . .

The record contains several dictionaries defining "redskins" as a term referring to North American Indians and characterizing "redskins" as offensive or contemptuous:

1.   Webster's Collegiate Dictionary 682 (1898) ("often contemptuous");

2. The Random House Dictionary of the English Language 1204 (1966) ("Often Offensive");

3. Random House Dictionary of the English Language 1204 (1967) ("Often Offensive");

4. Random House Dictionary of the English Language 1204 (1973) ("Often Offensive");

5. Thorndike-Barnhart Intermediate Dictionary 702 (2d ed.1974) ("a term often considered offensive");

6. Oxford American Dictionary 564 (1980) ("contemptuous");

7. The American Heritage Dictionary of the English Language: Second College Edition 1037 (1982) ("Offensive Slang");

8. Webster's Ninth New Collegiate Dictionary 987 (1983) ("usu[ally] taken to be offensive");

9. Merriam-Webster Collegiate Dictionary (1983) ("usu[ally] taken to be offensive");

10. Collier's Dictionary (1986) ("considered offensive"); and

11. Oxford English Dictionary 429 (2d ed. 1989) ("Not the preferred term").

PFI attempts to rebut Blackhorse Defendants' dictionary evidence by arguing that (1) that the usage label evidence is not relevant because none of the usage labels use the word "disparage"; (2) the modifiers "usually" or "often" make the labels conditional and thus irrelevant under Section 2(a); (3) usage labels are chosen at the dictionary editor-in-chief's discretion with no industry standards for selection; and (4) many dictionaries considered "redskin" a neutral term and only began affixing negative usage labels to it within the last few decades. These arguments fail as they ignore the great weight the Federal Circuit affords to dictionary usage labels.

The Court finds that PFI's argument that dictionary usage labels such as "offensive" and "contemptuous" do not implicate Section 2(a) because they do not label the term "disparaging" is unpersuasive for two reasons. First, the Federal Circuit and the TTAB use "offensive" and "disparage" interchangeably when deciding whether a mark consists of matter that "may disparage." *See, e.g., In re Geller*, 751 F.3d 1355 (Fed. Cir. 2014). Furthermore, because the parties conceded that the test for "contempt or disrepute" under Section 2(a) is the same as the "may disparage" test, the distinction between "disparage" and "contemptuous" is one without a difference.

Second, the Court rejects PFI's argument that the modifiers on the usage labels made them conditional and thus irrelevant. In *In re Tinseltown, Inc.*, 212 U.S.P.Q. 863, 1981 WL 40474 (T.T.A.B. 1981), an applicant attempted to register the mark BULLSHIT for personal accessories. The Examiner relied on dictionaries unanimously characterizing the mark as "usu[ally] considered vulgar" to conclude that it consisted of scandalous matter under Section 2(a). The TTAB affirmed the Examiner's decision.

The Federal Circuit cited *Tinseltown* with approval on the unanimous usage label issue in *In re Mavety Media Grp.*, 33 F.3d 1367 (Fed. Cir. 1994). Notably, that case involved Section 2(a)'s scandalous provision, which requires a showing that the mark consists of or comprises immoral or scandalous matter. Section 2(a)'s "may disparage" prohibition sets a lower bar as it only requires a showing that the mark consists of or comprises matter that "may disparage." Because the Federal Circuit cited *Tinseltown* with approval in *Mavety Media Grp.* and Section 2(a) only requires that a mark "may disparage," the Court finds PFI's argument regarding the relevance of usage labels unpersuasive. . . .

b.   Scholarly, Literary, and Media References

Second, the record evidence contains scholarly, literary, and media references that weigh in favor of finding that "redskins" "may disparage" a substantial composite of Native Americans when each of the six Redskins Marks was registered. . . . Here, there are several examples of scholarly, literary, and media references, including:

1.   Encyclopedia Britannica 452 (1911) ("Other popular terms for the American Indians which have more or less currency are 'red race,' 'Red man,' 'Redskin,' the last not in such good repute as the corresponding German Routhaüte, or French Peaux-rouges, which have scientific standing.");

2.   Erdman B. Palmore, Ethnophaulisms and Ethnocentrism, 67 Am. J. Soci. 442, 442 (1962) (noting that "redskin" is an ethnophaulism used for Native Americans);

3.   Alan Dundes and C. Fayne Porter, American Indian Student Slang, 38 Am. Speech 270, 271 (1963) (stating that "[a]lmost all the students" at the Haskell Institute, a federally-operated post-secondary coeducational vocational training school for Native Americans, "resent being called redskins"). . . . [The court lists an additional twenty-three scholarly, literary, and media references that show the disparaging nature of "redskins," published from 1971 through 1990.]

Prior to the first mark's registration in 1967, there were two renowned journals and an Encyclopedia Britannica reference that illustrate the term's disfavor among Native Americans. Taken altogether, the Court finds that these three pieces of evidence establish that in 1967, the date of the first registration, evidence existed that showed that the Redskins Marks consisted of matter that "may disparage" a substantial composite of Native Americans during the relevant time period.

c. Statements of Individuals or Group Leaders

Third, the record evidence contains statements of Native American individuals or leaders of Native American groups that weigh in favor of finding that the Redskins Marks consisted of matter that "may disparage" a substantial composite of Native Americans during the relevant time period.

Blackhorse Defendants reference a 1972 meeting between PFI's president and a few major Native American organizations about the "Washington Redskins" team name to show that it "may disparage." In March 1972, a delegation of Native American leaders met with the then President of PFI, Edward Bennett Williams, to demand that the team change its name. . . . The next day, Williams wrote to NFL Commissioner Pete Rozelle to inform him about the meeting, noting that the "delegation of American Indian leaders . . . vigorously object[ed] to the continued use of the name Redskins." Although Williams did not change the team name after the meeting, he did change the fight song and altered the cheerleaders' outfits so that they were less stereotypical.

The Court finds this meeting probative on the issue of whether the mark consisted of matter that "may disparage" a substantial composite of Native Americans during the relevant time period. Representatives of several prominent Native American organizations protesting the "Redskins" name is strong evidence that the term "may disparage." Williams himself regarded the Native Americans he met with as "leaders," rather than a group of individuals representing their own interests.

In support of their argument that prominent Native American organizations and leaders in the Native American community have long opposed the use of the term "redskins" as the name of an NFL football team name, Blackhorse Defendants have submitted several declarations. Below are quotes from the declarations of four prominent Native Americans: Raymond Apodaca (former Area Vice President of NCAI and Governor for the Yselta Del Sur Pueblo); Leon Cook (former NCAI President and former Council Member and Tribal Administrator for the Red Lake Nation); Kevin Gover (prominent attorney, former Assistant Secretary of the Interior for Indian Affairs, and current Director of the Smithsonian Institution's National Museum of the American Indian); and Suzanne Harjo (former Executive Director of the NCAI and 2014 recipient of the Presidential Medal of Freedom for her work on behalf of Native Americans). Each declaration affirms Blackhorse Defendants' argument that from 1967 to 1990, the Redskins Marks consisted of matter that "may disparage" a substantial composite of Native Americans.

Raymond Apodaca was born in 1946 and is a member of the Yselta Del Sur Pueblo. Apodaca is a former Executive Director of the Texas Indian Commission, serving in that capacity from 1982–1989. From

1991–1992, he was the Tribal Administrator for the Yselta Del Sur Pueblo. At the time, Tribal Administrator was the highest administrative role within the tribe. He also served as Tribal Governor for the same pueblo from 1990–1992. Apodaca has been an active member of the NCAI since 1973. Apodaca declared that "NCAI is the oldest and the preeminent Native American organization, representing the majority of Native Americans on a variety of political, cultural, and social policy issues."

He further stated that because NCAI represents the majority of Native Americans in federally recognized tribes, NCAI is the best organization to consult to discern an understanding of Native Americans' position on an issue. He held several leadership positions in NCAI, including Area Vice President. Apodaca has thought that "redskin," both the term and the professional football team name, was a racial slur against Native Americans since the 1960s. [The other three individuals provide similar declarations stating their belief that the term "redskin" was disparaging to Native Americans before 1967.]

The Court finds that the declarations from these prominent Native American individuals and leaders, replete with the actions of groups concerning the "Washington Redskins" football team and anecdotes of personal experiences with the term "redskin," show that the Redskins Marks consisted of matter that "may disparage" a substantial composite of Native Americans during the relevant time period.

Additional evidence that the marks consisted of matter that "may disparage" is found in the NCAI Resolution. In 1993, the Executive Council of the NCAI passed a resolution on the "Washington Redskins" team name. Founded in 1944, NCAI bills itself as "the oldest and largest intertribal organization nationwide representative of, and advocate for national, regional, and local tribal concerns." The resolution provided, in pertinent part, that, "[T]he term REDSKINS is not and has never been one of honor or respect, but instead it has always been and continues to be a pejorative, derogatory, denigrating, offensive, scandalous, contemptuous, disreputable, disparaging and racist designation for Native American[s]." The Court finds that this resolution is probative of NCAI's constituent members' collective opinion of the term "redskin" and PFI's marks for many years, including when the last Redskins Mark was registered. See In re Heeb Media LLC, 89 U.S.P.Q.2d (BNA) 1071, 2008 WL 5065114, at *1 (T.T.A.B. 2008) (affirming denial of registration of a mark based in part on excerpts from "individuals representing Jewish groups or in their individual capacity," which provided that they "consider the term HEEB to be a disparaging").

PFI objects to this evidence on relevancy grounds because the resolution was passed outside of the relevant time period. However, as suggested by the TTAB in Blackhorse, this is just like any other testimony from individuals that was taken after the fact: witnesses testify about what they perceived in the past. PFI may challenge the weight this evidence is afforded but the words of the resolution are indisputable: this national organization of Native Americans declared that the term "REDSKINS" has always been derogatory, offensive, and disparaging. Because this evidence tends to prove or disprove a matter, *see* Fed. R. Evid. 401, the Court overrules PFI's objection and finds that the resolution is probative of whether a substantial composite of Native Americans thought "redskin" "may disparage" them during the relevant time period.

Throughout PFI's briefs it appears to suggest that the evidence of the 1972 meeting with former-PFI president Williams, NCAI's 1993 resolution on the team name, and any other evidence of Native American opposition is immaterial because "mainstream Native Americans" support the team name "Washington Redskins." Respondents in *In re Hoob Media, LLC*, 89 U.S.P.Q.2d (BNA) 1071, 2008 WL 5065114 (T.T.A.B. 2008), and *In re Squaw Valley Dev. Co.*, 80 U.S.P.Q.2d (BNA) 1264, 2006 WL 1546500 (T.T.A.B. 2006), also tried to dismiss the views of those finding a term offensive as out of the mainstream. The TTAB rejected this argument both times. The Court agrees with the TTAB's approach and similarly rejects PFI's attempted characterization of some of Blackhorse Defendants' witnesses and their respective testimony. That a "substantial composite" is not necessarily a majority further compels this result. Assuming the Court accepted PFI's proffered dichotomy of "mainstream" versus "avant-garde" members of a referenced group, as a matter of principle it is indisputable that those with "non-mainstream" views on whether a term is disparaging can certainly constitute a substantial composite of a referenced group. The Court finds that to be the case here.

PFI sought to rebut Blackhorse Defendants' evidence multiple ways. First, PFI relies upon the 1977 All-Indian Half-Time Marching Band and Pageant and Native Americans naming their own sports teams "Redskins" to argue that the term is not disparaging. Hundreds of Native Americans participated in the half-time program and several-hundred more applied but were ultimately not able to partake in the event. PFI contends that the "positive tone" of the Native American press reports on the event, among other things, shows that the mark did not consist of matter that "may disparage" a substantial composite Native Americans during the relevant time period. Additionally, PFI maintains that Native Americans' own extensive use of the term "Redskins" for different nicknames and the names of over twenty local sports teams precludes it from being considered as a term that "may disparage."

The Court finds these arguments unpersuasive because this evidence does not show that there is not a substantial composite of Native Americans who find the matter was one that "may disparage." *Heeb* is again instructive. *Heeb* involved an effort to register the mark HEEB for apparel and the publication of magazines. *In re Heeb Media, LLC*, 89 U.S.P.Q.2d (BNA) 1071, 2008 WL 5065114, at *1 (T.T.A.B. 2008). The TTAB acknowledged that there was a movement within the Jewish community to take command of the term "heeb" and not be offended by it. Id. at *5–*6. However, despite the fact that "many of this country's most established Jewish philanthropies and cultural organizations have openly and actively supported Applicant's magazine," id. at *3, the TTAB held that the evidence showed there was still a substantial composite of Jewish individuals who would find the term "heeb" to be one that "may disparage."

In *Heeb*, the TTAB explained that disparate views within the community of the referenced group countenance reliance on the rule that a substantial composite is not necessarily a majority. The TTAB wrote:

> With regard to applicant's argument that a minority opinion should not veto registration of a particular mark, this is not in keeping with the standard set forth by our primary reviewing court. While case law does not provide a fixed number or percentage, it is well established that a "substantial composite" is not necessarily a majority. Here we have clear evidence that a substantial composite of the referenced group considers HEEB to be a disparaging term. The examining attorney has presented evidence from various segments of the Jewish community, including the Anti-Defamation League, a university professor, rabbis, a talk-show host and ordinary citizens.

Id. at *8.

The current case mirrors the circumstances in *Heeb*. Similar to *Heeb*, segments of the Native American community have decried "redskin" as disparaging, including the NCAI, a former tribal leader, and an author. The Court recognizes PFI's evidence that some members of the Native American community did not ever, and do not now, find "redskin" disparaging, whether in the context of the "Washington Redskins" or not. As reinforced in *Heeb*, the substantial composite rule does not require that a majority of the referenced group find that a mark consists of matter that "may disparage." Id. Accordingly, PFI's argument that the 1977 halftime show and the use of "Redskins" as a nickname by Native Americans means that the term is not one that "may disparage" must fail because, consistent with *Heeb*, the record evidence shows that a substantial composite of Native Americans find that the term is offensive.

Accordingly, the Court finds that the record evidence of statements from Native American leaders and groups weighs in favor of finding that between 1967 and 1990, the Redskins Marks consisted of matter that "may disparage" a substantial composite of Native Americans. . . .

The determination of whether a substantial composite of the referenced group believes that a mark consists of a term that "may disparage" is not a mathematical equation requiring the parties to argue over whether the evidence shows that a specific threshold was met. *See Heeb*, 2008 WL 5065114, at *8 (citation omitted). Instead, courts consider (1) dictionary definitions and accompanying editorial designations; (2) scholarly, literary, and media references; and (3) statements of individuals or group leaders of the referenced group on the term.

Here, the Court finds that the record contains evidence in all three categories demonstrating that between 1967 and 1990, the Redskins Marks consisted of matter that "may disparage" a substantial composite of Native Americans. The dictionary evidence included multiple definitions describing the term "redskin" in a negative fight, including one from 1898—almost seventy years prior to the registration of the first Redskins Mark—characterizing "redskin" as "often contemptuous." The record evidence also included references in renowned scholarly journals and books showing that "redskin" was offensive prior to 1967. Encyclopedia Britannica described its poor repute in 1911. The record evidence also shows that in 1972 NCAI, a national Native American organization founded in 1944, sent its president to accompany leaders of other Native American organizations at a meeting with the president of PFI to demand that the team's named be changed. NCAI also passed a resolution which provided that it has always found the term and team name "Redskins" to be derogatory, offensive, and disparaging.

PFI cites to no cases from either the Federal Circuit or the TTAB where the record contained evidence of (1) multiple dictionary definitions and usage labels showing that a term was "often offensive" and "often contemptuous"; (2) scholarly, literary, and media references in journals, books, newspaper articles and editorials, and encyclopedias referencing a term as "derogatory," "deprecatory," an "ethnophaulism," and a "racial epithet"; and (3) statements from individuals and organizations in the referenced group explaining how a mark consists of matter that is offensive to them, and the mark owner was still permitted to maintain a federal trademark registration. That is because the case law is clear: when all three categories contain evidence that a mark consists of matter that "may disparage" a substantial composite of the referenced group, the TTAB and the Federal Circuit have denied or cancelled the mark's registration.

This remains true even when there is also dictionary evidence that does not characterize the term as offensive, literary references using the term in a non-disparaging fashion, and statements from members of the referenced group demonstrating that they do not think the mark consists of matter that "may disparage." That is because Section 2(a) does not require a finding that every member of the referenced group thinks that the matter "may disparage." Nor does it mandate a showing that a majority of the referenced group considers the mark one that consists of matter that "may disparage." Instead, Section 2(a) allows for the denial or cancellation of a registration of any mark that consists of or comprises matter that "may disparage" a substantial composite of the referenced group.

The Court finds that Blackhorse Defendants have shown by a preponderance of the evidence that there is no genuine issue of material fact as to the "may disparage" claim: the record evidence shows that the term "redskin," in the context of Native Americans and during the relevant time period, was offensive and one that "may disparage" a substantial composite of Native Americans, "no matter what the goods or services with which the mark is used." *In re Squaw Valley Dev. Co.*, 80 U.S.P.Q.2d (BNA) 1264, 2006 WL 1546500, at *16 (T.T.A.B. 2006). "Redskin" certainly retains this meaning when used in connection with PFI's football team; a team that has always associated itself with Native American imagery, with nothing being more emblematic of this association than the use of a Native American profile on the helmets of each member of the football team.

Accordingly, the Court finds that the Redskins Marks consisted of matter that "may disparage" a substantial composite of Native Americans during the relevant time period, 1967–1990, and must be cancelled. Also, consistent with the parties' concession that Section 2(a)'s "may disparage" and "contempt or disrepute" provisions use the same legal analysis, the Court further finds that the Redskins Marks consisted of matter that bring Native Americans into "contempt or disrepute." Thus, Blackhorse Defendants are entitled to summary judgment on Count II.

The Court so holds with the benefit of a supplemented record and post-2003 cases from the Federal Circuit and TTAB applying Section 2(a) of the Lanham Act—items that the district court in Harjo was not privy to when it made its initial ruling. *See Pro-Football, Inc. v. Harjo*, 284 F. Supp. 2d 96 (D.D.C. 2003). Specifically, this record contained the following supplemental evidence:

    1.   Evidence establishing that in 1962, "almost all the students at Haskell Institute resent[ed] being called redskins" (at the time, Haskell was a post-secondary vocational school for American Indians, with 1,000 students);

    2.   Evidence establishing the NCAI, AIM, and other diverse Indian organizations found common ground to fight the team name and met with PFI's President in 1972 to demand that PFI change the team name;

3.   Evidence establishing that in 1972, the University of Utah dropped the name "Redskins" due to concern that the term was offensive;

4.   Evidence establishing further efforts by NCAI over several decades to bring about a change in PFI's team name;

5.   Declarations from prominent Native Americans and representatives of Native American organizations regarding their own experiences with "redskin" used as a slur, their understanding of the term, and the basis of their understanding; and

6.   Additional data analysis by Dr. Nunberg demonstrating the negative connotations of "redskin."

Also, the standard of review here is different than the standard in Harjo. In Harjo, the court applied the APA's "substantial evidence" standard: "the Court will reverse the TTAB's findings of fact only if they are 'unsupported by substantial evidence.'" Harjo, 284 F. Supp. 2d at 114 (citing 5 U.S.C. § 706). In Harjo, the TTAB made only limited findings of fact in two areas: linguists' testimony and survey evidence. Harjo, 284 F. Supp. 2d at 119. Thus, it was only those two areas that were subjected to court scrutiny under the substantial evidence standard. See id. Here, the TTAB made 39 findings of fact in two areas: "General Analysis of the Word" and "Native American Objection to Use of the Word Redskins for Football Teams." Blackhorse, 2014 WL 2757516, at *25–*28. Moreover, because the TTAB review in this case was brought pursuant to 15 U.S.C. § 1071(b), the Court reviews the *entire* record *de novo*—the Court is not restricted to only reviewing the TTAB's findings of fact like the district court in Harjo. Even if that was true, the TTAB's findings of fact in Blackhorse were more thorough than the findings of fact in Harjo. . . .

CONCLUSION

. . . The Court has applied the Lanham Act to the issue presented in this trademark cancellation proceeding: whether a substantial composite of Native Americans deem the term "redskin" as one that "may disparage" in the context of PFI's Redskins Marks during the relevant time period. The evidence before the Court supports the legal conclusion that between 1967 and 1990, the Redskins Marks consisted of matter that "may disparage" a substantial composite of Native Americans. Section 2(a) of the Lanham Act requires cancellation of the registrations of PFI's Redskins Marks, resulting in their removal from the PTO's Principal Register.

To be clear, the Court's judgment is *not* an order that precludes PFI from using the marks in commerce. Nor does the Court's ruling that the Redskins Marks consisted of matter that "may disparage" a substantial composite of Native Americans during the relevant time period preclude sports fans from collecting, wearing, or displaying the Redskins Marks. Courts do not create trademarks; only businesses like PFI control their own destiny with respect to how the public discerns the source and origin of PFI's goods and services. What actions, if any, PFI takes going forward with the marks are a business judgment beyond the purview of this Court's jurisdiction.

Accordingly, it is hereby ... **ORDERED** that the United States Patent and Trademark Office is **DIRECTED** to schedule the cancellation of the registrations for the following six marks: Registration No. 0836122, Registration No. 0978824, Registration No. 098666, Registration No. 0987127, Registration No. 1085092, and Registration No. 1606810.

IT IS SO ORDERED.

NOTES FOR DISCUSSION

1. *Appeal to Federal Circuit versus Action in District Court*. Why did the registrant file its action in federal district court, rather than simply appeal the Trademark Trial and Appeal Board's decision to the Federal Circuit? As mentioned in the previous section, one reason to file an action in a district court, rather than simply appeal, is to avoid adverse Federal Circuit precedent. Did the plaintiff contest any of the legal standards that the Trademark Trial and Appeal Board applied? A second reason is that, unlike appeal, a party who files an action in a district court is allowed to introduce new or additional evidence. Did either party take advantage of that opportunity? If not, then why pursue review of the Trademark Trial and Appeal Board's decision through a district court? Did the plaintiff simply hope that the district court judges sitting on the United States District Court for the Eastern District of Virginia would be bigger Redskin's football fans? Or was there some other reason to pursue review through the district court, rather than appeal to the Federal Circuit?

2. *Standard of Review*. In authorizing a party to file an action in a federal district court, Congress did not specify expressly a standard of review to apply when a party files for review of a Trademark Trial and Appeal Board ruling in a district court. The statutory language merely states that, as an alternative to filing an appeal with the Federal Circuit, a party may "have remedy by a civil action." 15 U.S.C. § 1071(b) (2015). Because a party may introduce additional evidence in the proceeding, courts have often treated the civil action as a separate action, where the court resolves the issues *de novo*, rather than as an appeal, with its more deferential standard for reviewing factual findings. In *Harjo*, given that neither party introduced any additional evidence, the district court decided that it was reviewing the Trademark Trial and Appeal Board's decision. Therefore, rather than consider whether "Redskins" is disparaging *de novo*, the district court adopted the review standard from the Administrative Procedure Act, and asked whether the Trademark Trial and Appeal Board's findings were supported by substantial evidence. What standard did the court apply in *Blackhorse*?

In section 1071(b), the Trademark Act provides:

The court may adjudge that an applicant is entitled to registration upon the application involved, that a registration should be canceled, or such other matter as the issues in the proceedings require, as the facts in the case may appear.

15 U.S.C. § 1071(b)(1) (2015).

Does this language suggest that the role of the district court is more one of reviewing the TTAB's decision or more one of resolving the issues directly?

3. *The Legal Standard of "Disparage."* In approaching the question of whether the trademarks at issue were disparaging, there were three key legal issues. The first is the question of perspective. When one party insults or disparages another, there are three possible perspectives in play. The first is the perspective of the speaker: Did she intend to disparage the other party? The second is the target: Did he feel disparaged? The third is the perspective of bystanders to the exchange: Did they perceive the remarks as disparaging? From which perspective does the court determine whether the trademarks, as used for football, are disparaging? Why? Are you persuaded?

The second key question is the time frame for determining whether the trademarks at issue are disparaging. Do we determine whether the marks were disparaging at the time of their registration? Or may the registrations be cancelled "at any time" if the trademarks become disparaging after they have been registered? Section 1064(3) allows for the cancellation of a registration "[a]t any time if the . . . registration was obtained contrary to the provisions of . . . subsection (a), (b), or (c) of section 1052 of this title. . . ." 15 U.S.C. § 1064(3) (2015). Section 1052 provides in turn that: "No trademark . . . shall be refused registration . . . on account of its nature unless it—(a) Consists of or comprises . . . matter which may disparage . . . persons living or dead. . . ." 15 U.S.C. § 1052(a) (2015). Taken together, does the phrase "registration was obtained" in section 1064(3), along with the phrasing of section 1052, "shall be refused registration," dictate that the issue of disparagement is determined only as of the date of registration? Compare the language with respect to genericness which permits cancellation "[a]t any time if the registered mark becomes the generic name for the goods or services . . . for which it is registered." 15 U.S.C. § 1064(3) (2015).

The third key question is whether all, or only some, Native Americans must find the trademarks at issue disparaging. The court interprets the statutory language "may disparage" to require that only a "substantial composite" of Native Americans find the trademarks at issue disparaging. Do you agree with this interpretation of the statutory language?

4. *Harjo vs. Blackhorse.* As the district court notes, a group of Native Americans had previously sought cancellation of the Redskins trademarks in the *Harjo* case. Although they ultimately lost on laches, the district court in that case found that the trademarks "Redskins" was not disparaging at the relevant times, particularly as applied to the goods or services at issue. What additional or different evidence does the *Blackhorse* district court have to

establish that the marks at issue were disparaging when they were registered? What evidence does the *Blackhorse* court have to establish that the marks at issue were disparaging as applied to football?

5.   *The First Amendment.* The *Blackhorse* court held that the First Amendment did not limit the government's ability to deny registration for a trademark that "may disparage" for two reasons. First, it followed the traditional justification and held that a denial of registration does not restrict speech. A denial of registration does not bar a mark owner from using a mark; it only denies the mark owner the procedural and substantive advantages associated with federal registration. This is a little disingenuous, isn't it? The Blackhorse defendants are suing to cancel the trademark registrations. Presumably, they are doing so to persuade the football team to change its name. How then, can the court pretend that registration has no influence on speech?

This approach to avoiding First Amendment scrutiny of section 2(a) traces back to the Court of Customs and Patent Appeals decision in *In re McGinley*. 600 F.2d 481 (C.C.P.A. 1981). While not a disparaging use case, in *In re McGinley*, the Court of Customs and Patent Appeals held that because a refusal to register did not affect an applicant's right to use the mark, no First Amendment interest was implicated. *Id.* at 383. Although it has stood for more than thirty years, this approach has recently come under more careful scrutiny. In *In re Tam*, the USPTO denied registration to the mark "The Slants" for a musical band on the grounds that it was disparaging to people of Asian descent. On appeal, a panel of the Federal Circuit rejected a First Amendment challenge to the "may disparage" provision in section 2(a), relying on the *McGinley* approach. 785 F.3d 567, 571–72 (Fed. Cir. 2015). On April 27, 2015, the Federal Circuit *sua sponte* ordered a rehearing *en banc* of the case on the following issue: "Does the bar on registration of disparaging marks in 15 U.S.C. § 1052(a) violate the First Amendment?" The central argument that it does is that the restriction on registration constitutes an unconstitutional condition. As the *Blackhorse* court acknowledges, registration offers substantial benefits to a trademark owner, but those benefits are conditioned on the trademark owner's speech satisfying the government. While conditioning benefits on the government's approval of the speech is not the same as barring the speech directly, it does have some tendency to influence what is said, and should therefore have to pass constitutional scrutiny. As Judge Moore stated in her separate opinion in *In re Tam*, "[t]he government cannot hinge the benefits of federal trademark registration on constitutionally protected speech—here, the applicant's selection of a suitable mark—unless the government's actions pass constitutional scrutiny." 785 F.3d at 581.

6.   *"Immoral . . . or Scandalous Matter."* In addition to prohibiting the registration of matter "which may disparage . . . persons living or dead," section 2 of the Trademark Act also prohibits the registration of trademarks that consist of "immoral or scandalous matter." 15 U.S.C. § 1052(a) (2015). A desire to avoid offending potential consumers will usually, but not always,

suffice to ensure that a would-be trademark owner avoids offensive terms. As a result, cases raising the "immoral" or "scandalous" bar are relatively rare, but they do occur. Does this limitation on registration constitute an impermissible governmental restriction on free speech in violation of the First Amendment? This was the actual issue presented in *In re McGinley*, and as just discussed, the Court of Customs and Patent Appeals held that it does not.

As the court explained:

> With respect to appellant's First Amendment rights, it is clear that the PTO's refusal to register appellant's mark does not affect his right to use it. No conduct is proscribed, and no tangible form of expression is suppressed. Consequently, appellant's First Amendment rights would not be abridged by the refusal to register his mark.

660 F.2d 481, 484 (C.C.P.A. 1981).

The court then proceeded to define a "scandalous" use of a mark as a use which would be " 'shocking to the sense of . . . propriety,' would 'give "offense to the conscience or moral feelings," ' or would 'call out condemnation.' " *Id.* at 485. Based upon that definition, are the following marks "scandalous"?

(a) "Queen Mary" for underwear. *See In re* Martha Maid Manufacturing Co., 37 USPQ 156 (Asst. Comm'r 1938) (scandalous).

(b) "Bubby Trap" for brassieres. *See In re* Runsdorf, 171 USPQ 443, 443–44 (T.T.A.B. 1971) (scandalous).

(c) "Week-end Sex" for a magazine. *See In re* Madsen, 180 USPQ 334, 335 (T.T.A.B. 1973) (not scandalous).

G. FEDERAL REGISTRATION AND DISTINCTIVENESS: PRESUMPTIONS OF VALIDITY

Along with establishing nationwide priority and making available a broader range of remedies, federal registration of a trademark on the principal register also establishes certain evidentiary presumptions with respect to the ownership, validity, and exclusive right to use a trademark. Initially, a certificate of registration provides "prima facie evidence of the validity of the registered mark . . . , of the registrant's ownership of the mark, and of the registrant's exclusive right to use the registered mark in commerce on or in connection with the goods or services specified in the certificate." 15 U.S.C. §§ 1057(b), 1115(a) (2015). However, the certificate "shall not preclude another person from proving any legal or equitable defense or defect . . . which might have been asserted if such mark had not been registered." 15 U.S.C. § 1115(a) (2015). Nevertheless, by providing prima facie evidence of the mark's validity, and the registrant's ownership and exclusive right to use, registration serves to shift the burden of production to a party seeking to challenge a registered mark on one of these issues.

Moreover, once a mark has been registered for five years, stronger evidentiary presumptions become available. At that point, a trademark owner can obtain an incontestable right to use the registered mark by filing a section 15 affidavit. 15 U.S.C. § 1065 (2015). In a section 15 affidavit, the registrant must verify that the registered mark "has been in continuous use for five consecutive years subsequent to the date of registration and is still in use in commerce." *Id.* If the PTO accepts the affidavit, then the registrant's right to use the mark becomes incontestable.

With such incontestability, its registration becomes:

conclusive evidence of the validity of the registered mark, . . . of the registrant's ownership of the mark, and of the registrant's exclusive right to use the registered mark in commerce. . . . Such conclusive evidence of the right to use the registered mark shall be subject to proof of infringement as defined in section 1114 of this tile, and shall be subject to the following defenses or defects:

(1) That the registration or the incontestable right to use the mark was obtained fraudulently; or

(2) That the mark has been abandoned by the registrant; or

(3) That the registered mark is being used, by or with the permission of the registrant or a person in privity with the registrant, so as to misrepresent the source of the goods or services on or in connection with which the mark is used; or

(4) That the use of the name, term, or device charged to be an infringement is a use, otherwise than as a mark, of the party's individual name in his own business, or of the individual name of anyone in privity with such party, or of a term or device which is descriptive of and used fairly and in good faith only to describe the goods or services of such party, or their geographic origin; or

(5) That the mark whose use by a party is charged as an infringement was adopted without knowledge of the registrant's prior use and has been continuously used by such party or those in privity with him from a date prior to (A) the date of constructive use of the mark established pursuant to section 7(c) [15 USCS § 1057(c)], (B) the registration of the mark under this Act if the application for registration is filed before the effective date of the Trademark Law Revision Act of 1988, or (C) publication of the registered mark under subsection (c) of section 12 of this Act [15 USCS § 1062(c)]: *Provided, however*, That this

defense or defect shall apply only for the area in which such continuous prior use is proved; or

(6) That the mark whose use is charged as an infringement was registered and used prior to the registration under this Act or publication under subsection (c) of section 12 of this Act [15 USCS § 1062(c)] of the registered mark of the registrant, and not abandoned: *Provided, however*, That this defense or defect shall apply only for the area in which the mark was used prior to such registration or such publication of the registrant's mark; or

(7) That the mark has been or is being used to violate the antitrust laws of the United States; or

(8) That the mark is functional; or

(9) That equitable principles, including laches, estoppel, and acquiescence, are applicable.

15 U.S.C. § 1115(b) (2015).

Along with allowing the registration of descriptive words and surnames as trademarks, where secondary meaning was established, the incontestability provision represented a significant change from the protection provided under the Trademark Act of 1905 or the common law. Taken together, these modifications created a risk that a descriptive word could receive protection as a trademark without ever having to establish secondary meaning. Specifically, if a descriptive word could somehow slip past the Patent and Trademark Office, and then remain on the register for five years, the registrant could file its section 15 affidavit and obtain incontestability. In such a case, the descriptive word would receive protection as a trademark even though secondary meaning was never shown, and indeed, even if it was entirely lacking. In the legislative debates leading to the adoption of the Trademark Act of 1946, proponents of the incontestability measure downplayed the likelihood of such an occurrence. Inevitably, however, given human frailties, mistakes are made, and so the question eventually arose: If a claimed trademark, consisting solely of descriptive words, sneaks past the PTO and becomes incontestably registered, may a defendant sued for infringement of the registered mark challenge the mark on the grounds that the mark is descriptive and lacks secondary meaning? The Court answered that question in the next case.

PARK 'N FLY, INC. v. DOLLAR PARK & FLY, INC.
469 U.S. 189 (1985)

O'CONNOR, J.

In this case we consider whether an action to enjoin the infringement of an incontestable trade or service mark may be defended on the grounds that the mark is merely descriptive. We conclude that neither the language of the relevant statutes nor the legislative history supports such a defense.

I

Petitioner operates long-term parking lots near airports. After starting business in St. Louis in 1967, petitioner subsequently opened facilities in Cleveland, Houston, Boston, Memphis, and San Francisco. Petitioner applied in 1969 to the United States Patent and Trademark Office (Patent Office) to register a service mark consisting of the logo of an airplane and the words "Park 'N Fly." The registration issued in August 1971. Nearly six years later, petitioner filed an affidavit with the Patent Office to establish the incontestable status of the mark. As required by § 15 of the Trademark Act of 1946 (Lanham Act), 60 Stat. 433, as amended, 15 U.S.C. § 1065, the affidavit stated that the mark had been registered and in continuous use for five consecutive years, that there had been no final adverse decision to petitioner's claim of ownership or right to registration, and that no proceedings involving such rights were pending. Incontestable status provides, subject to the provisions of § 15 and § 33(b) of the Lanham Act, "conclusive evidence of the registrant's exclusive right to use the registered mark. . . ." § 33(b), 15 U.S.C. § 1115(b).

Respondent also provides long-term airport parking services, but only has operations in Portland, Oregon. Respondent calls its business "Dollar Park and Fly." Petitioner filed this infringement action in 1978 in the United States District Court for the District of Oregon and requested the court permanently to enjoin respondent from using the words "Park and Fly" in connection with its business. Respondent counterclaimed and sought cancellation of petitioner's mark on the grounds that it is a generic term. See § 14(c), 15 U.S.C. § 1064(c). Respondent also argued that petitioner's mark is unenforceable because it is merely descriptive. *See* § 2(e), 15 U.S.C. § 1052(e). As two additional defenses, respondent maintained that it is in privity with a Seattle corporation that has used the expression "Park and Fly" since a date prior to the registration of petitioner's mark, *see* § 33(b)(5), 15 U.S.C. § 1115(b)(5), and that it has not infringed because there is no likelihood of confusion. See § 32(1), 15 U.S.C. § 1114(1).

After a bench trial, the District Court found that petitioner's mark is not generic and observed that an incontestable mark cannot be challenged on the grounds that it is merely descriptive. App. 75. The District Court also concluded that there was no evidence of privity between respondent and the Seattle corporation. App. 76. Finally, the District Court found sufficient evidence of likelihood of confusion. App. 76. The District Court permanently enjoined respondent from using the words "Park and Fly" and any other mark confusingly similar to "Park 'N Fly." App. 77.

The Court of Appeals for the Ninth Circuit reversed. 718 F.2d 327 (1983). The District Court did not err, the Court of Appeals held, in refusing to invalidate petitioner's mark. *Id.* at 331. The Court of Appeals noted, however, that it previously had held that incontestability provides a defense against the cancellation of a mark, but it may not be used offensively to enjoin another's use. *Ibid.* Petitioner, under this analysis, could obtain an injunction only if its mark would be entitled to continued registration without regard to its incontestable status. Thus, respondent could defend the infringement action by showing that the mark was merely descriptive. Based on its own examination of the record, the Court of Appeals then determined that petitioner's mark is in fact merely descriptive, and therefore respondent should not be enjoined from using the name "Park and Fly." *Ibid.*

The decision below is in direct conflict with the decision of the Court of Appeals for the Seventh Circuit in *Union Carbide Corp.* v. *Ever-Ready, Inc.,* 531 F.2d 366, *cert. denied,* 429 U.S. 830 (1976). We granted certiorari to resolve this conflict, 465 U.S. 1078 (1984), and we now reverse.

II

Congress enacted the Lanham Act in 1946 in order to provide national protection for trademarks used in interstate and foreign commerce. S. Rep. No. 1333, 79th Cong., 2d Sess., 5 (1946). Previous federal legislation, such as the Federal Trademark Act of 1905, 33 Stat. 724, reflected the view that protection of trademarks was a matter of state concern and that the right to a mark depended solely on the common law. S. Rep. No. 1333, at 5. Consequently, rights to trademarks were uncertain and subject to variation in different parts of the country. Because trademarks desirably promote competition and the maintenance of product quality, Congress determined that "a sound public policy requires that trademarks should receive nationally the greatest protection that can be given them." *Id.* at 6. Among the new protections created by the Lanham Act were the statutory provisions that allow a federally registered mark to become incontestable. §§ 15, 33(b), 15 U.S.C. §§ 1065, 1115(b).

The provisions of the Lanham Act concerning registration and incontestability distinguish a mark that is "the common descriptive name of an article or substance" from a mark that is "merely descriptive." §§ 2(e), 14(c), 15 U.S.C. §§ 1052(e), 1064(c). Marks that constitute a common descriptive name are referred to as generic. A generic term is one that refers to the genus of which the particular product is a species. *Abercrombie & Fitch Co.* v. *Hunting World, Inc.,* 537 F.2d 4, 9 (CA2 1976). Generic terms are not registrable, and a registered mark may be canceled at any time on the grounds that it has become generic. *See* §§ 2, 14(c), 15

U.S.C. §§ 1052, 1064(c). A "merely descriptive" mark, in contrast, describes the qualities or characteristics of a good or service, and this type of mark may be registered only if the registrant shows that it has acquired secondary meaning, *i.e.*, it "has become distinctive of the applicant's goods in commerce." §§ 2(e), (f), 15 U.S.C. §§ 1052(e), (f).

This case requires us to consider the effect of the incontestability provisions of the Lanham Act in the context of an infringement action defended on the grounds that the mark is merely descriptive. Statutory construction must begin with the language employed by Congress and the assumption that the ordinary meaning of that language accurately expresses the legislative purpose. *See American Tobacco Co.* v. *Patterson*, 456 U.S. 63, 68 (1982). With respect to incontestable trade or service marks, § 33(b) of the Lanham Act states that "registration shall be conclusive evidence of the registrant's exclusive right to use the registered mark" subject to the conditions of § 15 and certain enumerated defenses. Section 15 incorporates by reference subsections (c) and (e) of § 14, 15 U.S.C. § 1064. An incontestable mark that becomes generic may be canceled at any time pursuant to § 14(c). That section also allows cancellation of an incontestable mark at any time if it has been abandoned, if it is being used to misrepresent the source of the goods or services in connection with which it is used, or if it was obtained fraudulently or contrary to the provisions of § 4, 15 U.S.C. § 1054, or §§ 2(a)–(c), 15 U.S.C. §§ 1052(a)–(c).

One searches the language of the Lanham Act in vain to find any support for the offensive/defensive distinction applied by the Court of Appeals. The statute nowhere distinguishes between a registrant's offensive and defensive use of an incontestable mark. On the contrary, § 33(b)'s declaration that the registrant has an "exclusive right" to use the mark indicates that incontestable status may be used to enjoin infringement by others. A conclusion that such infringement cannot be enjoined renders meaningless the "exclusive right" recognized by the statute. Moreover, the language in three of the defenses enumerated in § 33(b) clearly contemplates the use of incontestability in infringement actions by plaintiffs.

The language of the Lanham Act also refutes any conclusion that an incontestable mark may be challenged as merely descriptive. A mark that is merely descriptive of an applicant's goods or services is not registrable unless the mark has secondary meaning. Before a mark achieves incontestable status, registration provides prima facie evidence of the registrant's exclusive right to use the mark in commerce. § 33(a), 15 U.S.C. § 1115(a). The Lanham Act expressly provides that before a mark becomes incontestable an opposing party may prove any legal or equitable defense which might have been asserted if the mark had not been registered. *Ibid.* Thus, § 33(a) would have allowed respondent to challenge petitioner's mark as merely descriptive if the mark had not become incontestable. With respect to incontestable marks, however, § 33(b) provides that registration is *conclusive* evidence of the registrant's exclusive right to use the mark, subject to the conditions of § 15 and the seven defenses enumerated in § 33(b) itself. Mere descriptiveness is not recognized by either § 15 or § 33(b) as a basis for challenging an incontestable mark.

The statutory provisions that prohibit registration of a merely descriptive mark but do not allow an incontestable mark to be challenged on this ground cannot be attributed to inadvertence by Congress. The Conference Committee rejected an amendment that would have denied registration to any descriptive mark, and instead retained the provisions allowing registration of a merely descriptive mark that has acquired secondary meaning. *See* H. R. Conf. Rep. No. 2322, 79th Cong., 2d Sess., 4 (1946) (explanatory statement of House managers). The Conference Committee agreed to an amendment providing that no incontestable right can be acquired in a mark that is a common descriptive, *i.e.*, generic, term. *Id.* at 5. Congress could easily have denied incontestability to merely descriptive marks as well as to generic marks had that been its intention.

The Court of Appeals in discussing the offensive/defensive distinction observed that incontestability protects a registrant against cancellation of his mark. 718 F.2d, at 331. This observation is incorrect with respect to marks that become generic or which otherwise may be canceled at any time pursuant to §§ 14(c) and (e). Moreover, as applied to marks that are merely descriptive, the approach of the Court of Appeals makes incontestable status superfluous. Without regard to its incontestable status, a mark that has been registered five years is protected from cancellation except on the grounds stated in §§ 14(c) and (e). Pursuant to § 14, a mark may be canceled on the grounds that it is merely descriptive only if the petition to cancel is filed within five years of the date of registration. § 14(a), 15 U.S.C. § 1064(a). The approach adopted by the Court of Appeals implies that incontestability adds nothing to the protections against cancellation already provided in § 14. The decision below not only lacks support in the words of the statute; it effectively emasculates § 33(b) under the circumstances of this case.

III

Nothing in the legislative history of the Lanham Act supports a departure from the plain language of the statutory provisions concerning incontestability. Indeed, a conclusion that incontestable status can provide the basis for enforcement of the registrant's exclusive right to use a trade or service mark promotes the goals of the statute. The Lanham Act provides national protection of trademarks in order to secure to the owner of the mark the goodwill of his business and to protect the ability of consumers to distinguish among competing producers. *See* S. Rep. No. 1333, at 3, 5. National protection of trademarks is desirable, Congress concluded, because trademarks foster competition and the maintenance of quality by securing to the producer the benefits of good reputation. *Id.* at 4. The incontestability provisions, as the proponents of the Lanham Act emphasized, provide a means for the registrant to quiet title in the ownership of his mark. See Hearings on H. R. 82 before the Subcommittee of the Senate Committee on Patents, 78th Cong., 2d Sess., 21 (1944) (remarks of Rep. Lanham); *id.* at 21, 113 (testimony of Daphne Robert, ABA Committee on Trade Mark Legislation); Hearings on H. R. 102 *et al.* before the Subcommittee on Trade-Marks of the House Committee on Patents, 77th Cong., 1st Sess., 73 (1941) (remarks of Rep. Lanham). The opportunity to obtain incontestable status by satisfying the requirements of § 15 thus encourages producers to cultivate the goodwill associated with a particular mark. This function of the incontestability provisions would be utterly frustrated if the holder of an incontestable mark could not enjoin infringement by others so long as they established that the mark would not be registrable but for its incontestable status.

Respondent argues, however, that enforcing petitioner's mark would conflict with the goals of the Lanham Act because the mark is merely descriptive and should never have been registered in the first place. Representative Lanham, respondent notes, explained that the defenses enumerated in § 33(b) were "not intended to enlarge, restrict, amend, or modify the substantive law of trademarks either as set out in other sections of the act or as heretofore applied by the courts under prior laws." 92 Cong. Rec. 7524 (1946). Respondent reasons that because the Lanham Act did not alter the substantive law of trademarks, the incontestability provisions cannot protect petitioner's use of the mark if it were not originally registrable. Moreover, inasmuch as petitioner's mark is merely descriptive, respondent contends that enjoining others from using the mark will not encourage competition by assisting consumers in their ability to distinguish among competing producers.

These arguments are unpersuasive. Representative Lanham's remarks, if read in context, clearly refer to the effect of the *defenses* enumerated in § 33(b). There is no question that the Lanham Act altered existing law concerning trademark rights in several respects. For example, § 22, 15 U.S.C. § 1072, provides for constructive notice of registration and modifies the common-law rule that allowed acquisition of concurrent rights by users in distinct geographic areas if the subsequent user adopted the mark without knowledge of prior use. *See Hanover Star Milling Co.* v. *Metcalf*, 240 U.S. 403, 415–416 (1916) (describing pre-Lanham Act law). Similarly, § 14 cuts off certain grounds for cancellation five years after registration and thereby modifies the previous rule that the validity of a trademark could be attacked at any time. *See White House Milk Products Co.* v. *Dwinell-Wright Co.*, 111 F.2d 490 (1940). Most significantly, Representative Lanham himself observed that incontestability was one of "the valuable new rights created by the act." 92 Cong. Rec. 7524 (1946).

Respondent's argument that enforcing petitioner's mark will not promote the goals of the Lanham Act is misdirected. Arguments similar to those now urged by respondent were in fact considered by Congress in hearings on the Lanham Act. For example, the United States Department of Justice opposed the incontestability provisions and expressly noted that a merely descriptive mark might become incontestable. Hearings on H. R. 82, at 59–60 (statement of the U.S. Dept. of Justice). This result, the Department of Justice observed, would "go beyond existing law in conferring unprecedented rights on trade-mark owners," and would undesirably create an exclusive right to use language that is descriptive of a product. *Id.* at 60; *see also* Hearings on H. R. 102, at 106–107, 109–110 (testimony of Prof. Milton Handler); *id.* at 107, 175 (testimony of attorney Louis Robertson). These concerns were answered by proponents of the Lanham Act, who noted that a merely descriptive mark cannot be registered unless the Commissioner finds that it has secondary meaning. *Id.* at 108, 113 (testimony of Karl Pohl, U.S. Trade Mark Assn.). Moreover, a mark can be challenged for five years prior to its attaining incontestable status. *Id.* at 114 (remarks of Rep. Lanham). The supporters of the incontestability provisions further observed that a generic mark cannot become incontestable and that § 33(b)(4) allows the nontrademark use of descriptive terms used in an incontestable mark. *Id.* at 110–111 (testimony of Wallace Martin, chairman, ABA Committee on Trade Mark Legislation).

The alternative of refusing to provide incontestable status for descriptive marks with secondary meaning was expressly noted in the hearings on the Lanham Act. *Id.* at 64, 69 (testimony of Robert Byerley, New York Patent Law Assn.); Hearings on S. 895 before the Subcommittee of the Senate Committee on Patents, 77th Cong., 2d Sess., 42 (1942) (testimony of Elliot Moyer, Special Assistant to the Attorney General). Also mentioned was the possibility of including as a defense to infringement of an incontestable mark the "fact that a mark is a descriptive, generic, or geographical term or device." *Id.* at 45, 47. Congress, however, did not adopt either of these alternatives. Instead, Congress expressly provided in § 33(b) and 15 that an incontestable mark could be challenged on specified grounds, and the grounds identified by Congress do not include mere descriptiveness.

The dissent echoes arguments made by opponents of the Lanham Act that the incontestable status of a descriptive mark might take from the public domain language that is merely descriptive. *Post*, at 214–216. As we have explained, Congress has already addressed concerns to prevent the "commercial monopolization," *post*, at 214, of descriptive language.

The Lanham Act allows a mark to be challenged at any time if it becomes generic, and, under certain circumstances, permits the nontrademark use of descriptive terms contained in an incontestable mark. Finally, if "monopolization" of an incontestable mark threatens economic competition, § 33(b)(7), 15 U.S.C. § 1115(b)(7), provides a defense on the grounds that the mark is being used to violate federal antitrust laws. At bottom, the dissent simply disagrees with the balance struck by Congress in determining the protection to be given to incontestable marks.

IV

Respondent argues that the decision by the Court of Appeals should be upheld because trademark registrations are issued by the Patent Office after an *ex parte* proceeding and generally without inquiry into the merits of an application. This argument also unravels upon close examination. The facts of this case belie the suggestion that registration is virtually automatic. The Patent Office initially denied petitioner's application because the examiner considered the mark to be merely descriptive. Petitioner sought reconsideration and successfully persuaded the Patent Office that its mark was registrable.

More generally, respondent is simply wrong to suggest that third parties do not have an opportunity to challenge applications for trademark registration. If the Patent Office examiner determines that an applicant appears to be entitled to registration, the mark is published in the Official Gazette. § 12(a), 15 U.S.C. § 1062(a). Within 30 days of publication, any person who believes that he would be damaged by registration of the mark may file an opposition. § 13, 15 U.S.C. § 1063. Registration of a mark provides constructive notice throughout the United States of the registrant's claim to ownership. § 22, 15 U.S.C. § 1072. Within five years of registration, any person who believes that he is or will be damaged by registration may seek to cancel a mark. § 14(a), 15 U.S.C. § 1064(a). A mark may be canceled at any time for certain specified grounds, including that it was obtained fraudulently or has become generic. § 14(c), 15 U.S.C. § 1064(c).

The Lanham Act, as the dissent notes, *post*, at 217, authorizes courts to grant injunctions "according to principles of equity." § 34, 15 U.S.C 1116. Neither respondent nor the opinion of the Court of Appeals relies on this provision to support the holding below. Whatever the precise boundaries of the courts' equitable power, we do not believe that it encompasses a substantive challenge to the validity of an incontestable mark on the grounds that it lacks secondary meaning. To conclude otherwise would expand the meaning of "equity" to the point of vitiating the more specific provisions of the Lanham Act. Similarly, the power of the courts to cancel registrations and "to otherwise rectify the register," §§ 37, 15 U.S.C. § 1119, must be subject to the specific provisions concerning incontestability. In effect, both respondent and the dissent argue that these provisions offer insufficient protection against improper registration of a merely descriptive mark, and therefore the validity of petitioner's mark may be challenged notwithstanding its incontestable status. Our responsibility, however, is not to evaluate the wisdom of the legislative determinations reflected in the statute, but instead to construe and apply the provisions that Congress enacted. . . .

VI

We conclude that the holder of a registered mark may rely on incontestability to enjoin infringement and that such an action may not be defended on the grounds that the mark is merely descriptive. Respondent urges that we nevertheless affirm the decision below based on the "prior use" defense recognized by § 33(b)(5) of the Lanham Act. Alternatively, respondent argues that there is no likelihood of confusion and therefore no infringement justifying injunctive relief. The District Court rejected each of these arguments, but they were not addressed by the Court of Appeals. 718 F.2d, at 331–332 n.4. That court may consider them on remand. The judgment of the Court of Appeals is reversed, and the case is remanded for further proceedings consistent with this opinion.

JUSTICE STEVENS, dissenting.

In trademark law, the term "incontestable" is itself somewhat confusing and misleading because the Lanham Act expressly identifies over 20 situations in which infringement of an allegedly incontestable mark is permitted. Moreover, in § 37 of the Act, Congress unambiguously authorized judicial review of the validity of the registration "in any action involving a registered mark." The problem in this case arises because of petitioner's attempt to enforce as "incontestable" a mark that Congress has plainly stated is inherently unregistrable.

The mark "Park 'N Fly" is at best merely descriptive in the context of airport parking. Section 2 of the Lanham Act plainly prohibits the registration of such a mark unless the applicant proves to the Commissioner of the Patent and Trademark Office that the mark "has become distinctive of the applicant's goods in commerce," or to use the accepted shorthand, that it has acquired a "secondary meaning." See 15 U.S.C. §§ 1052(e), (f). Petitioner never submitted any such proof to the Commissioner, or indeed to the District Court in this case. Thus, the registration plainly violated the Act.

The violation of the literal wording of the Act also contravened the central purpose of the entire legislative scheme. Statutory protection for trademarks was granted in order to safeguard the goodwill that is associated with particular enterprises. A mark must perform the function of distinguishing the producer or provider of a good or service in order to have any legitimate claim to protection. A merely descriptive mark that has not acquired secondary meaning does not perform that function because it simply "describes the qualities or characteristics of a good or service." *Ante*, at 194. No legislative purpose is served by granting anyone a monopoly in the use of such a mark.

Instead of confronting the question whether an inherently unregistrable mark can provide the basis for an injunction against alleged infringement, the Court treats the case as though it presented the same question as *Union Carbide Corp.* v. *Ever-Ready, Inc.*, 531 F.2d 366 (CA7), *cert. denied*, 429 U.S. 830 (1976), a case in which the merely descriptive mark had an obvious and well-established secondary meaning. In such a case, I would agree with the Court that the descriptive character of the mark does not provide an infringer with a defense. In this case, however, the provisions of the Act dealing with incontestable marks do not support the result the Court has reached. . . .

In sum, if petitioner had complied with § 2(f) at the time of its initial registration, or if it had been able to prove secondary meaning in this case, I would agree with the Court's disposition. I cannot, however, subscribe to its conclusion that the holder of a mark which was registered in violation of an unambiguous statutory command "may rely on incontestability to enjoin infringement." *Ante*, at 205; *see also ante*, at 196. Accordingly, I respectfully dissent.

NOTES FOR DISCUSSION

1.   *A Mistake Was Made, but Not by the PTO.* Both the majority and the dissent take the position that the Patent and Trademark Office may have acted improperly in allowing the registration of the Park 'N Fly trademark without proof of secondary meaning. Where they differ is on whether this mistake can be considered and corrected once the registration became incontestable. However, the actual service mark registered was not the words "park 'n fly" alone, but as the Court notes: "the logo of an airplane and the words 'Park 'N Fly.'" How does or should the addition of the airplane logo change the descriptiveness analysis?

U.S. Reg. No. 0919591.

What the plaintiff did here, combining descriptive words with a logo, is one of several techniques commonly used to obtain a federal registration that, at least nominally, covers the descriptive words themselves. Although the mark contains the descriptive words, registration does not require proof of secondary meaning because the mark, taken as a whole, is not *"merely descriptive."* Although the logo is the key element that avoids the secondary meaning requirement, registrants often ignore the logo in their cease-and-desist letters and in litigation, and try to pretend that the registration is for the descriptive words alone, just as the plaintiff did in this case. Whose job is it to bring the logo to the courts' attention? What role does or should the logo play in the litigation?

As time goes by and use continues, a would-be owner of a descriptive mark will become better able to establish secondary meaning, either directly or circumstantially, and will eventually seek registration for the descriptive words alone. For example, the *Park 'N Fly* plaintiff was subsequently able to register the words Park 'N Fly alone. U.S. Reg. No. 1,111,956 (registered Jan. 23, 1979). However, because this registration did not issue until after the infringement lawsuit was filed, it played no role in the litigation.

2.   *Disclaimer Practice Under Section 6.* Section 6 of the Trademark Act states: "The Director may require the applicant to disclaim an unregistrable component of a mark otherwise registrable." 15 U.S.C. § 1056(a) (2015). Under this provision, the Patent and Trademark Office routinely requires a disclaimer of those portions of a mark that are generic or descriptive. Should a disclaimer have been required here? How would a disclaimer have changed the likelihood of confusion analysis?

> A disclaimer does not remove the disclaimed matter from the mark. The mark must still be regarded as a whole, including the disclaimed matter, in evaluating similarity to other marks.

Trademark Manual of Examining Procedure ch. 1213.10 (2007).

3.   *Generic versus Descriptive.* The district court found that "Park 'N Fly" was not generic. Do you agree? What is the generic name or names for offsite airport parking with regular shuttle service to and from the airport?

4.   *Secondary Meaning and Likelihood of Confusion.* The Court's decision means that Dollar Park and Fly cannot argue that the mark is invalid for lack of secondary meaning. Can Dollar Park and Fly raise that same argument in any other way in the litigation? Specifically, if there is no secondary meaning in the phrase, is it likely that people who park at the defendant's airport parking facility will believe that they are actually parking at one of the plaintiff's facilities?

5.   *Remand.* The Court leaves for remand two principal arguments. First, Dollar Park and Fly could demonstrate that it was a good faith junior user in a separate and remote geographic area. Second, Park 'N Fly might not be able to establish that there was a likelihood of confusion. With respect to the first, when would Dollar's use need to have begun for it to satisfy the requirements of section 33(b)(5), which we looked at in Chapter 3?

What about a *Dawn Donuts*-style argument for no likelihood of confusion? The defendant operated in Portland, Oregon, while the plaintiff's nearest location was San Francisco, California. How likely is it that customers looking for offsite airport parking in Portland, Oregon will park at the defendant's believing it to be the plaintiff's because of the similarities in the trademarks?

Are there any other arguments that the defendant might assert? What about a fair use argument similar to that made in *Zatarain's*? *See* 15 U.S.C. 1115(b)(4) (2015) (allowing a defendant to assert fair use as a defense to an infringement claim by the owner of an incontestability registered mark).

6.   *What Difference Did Incontestability Make?* Do you think that Park 'N Fly could have proven secondary meaning had it been required to do so? Did incontestability's conclusive evidentiary presumption change the outcome in this case, or was it just a procedural shortcut that reached the same resolution with respect to secondary meaning that we would almost certainly have reached through a trial, just far more quickly and with far less expense? If we look beyond this particular case, and consider incontestably registered trademarks generally, how often do you think the owner of such a mark would be unable to establish secondary meaning if required to do so?

7.   *Offensive and Defensive Incontestability.* The Court rejects the Ninth Circuit's distinction between offensive and defensive incontestability given that Park 'N Fly has filed its section 15 affidavit. While the Court's rejection of the distinction is proper on the facts before it, the Act expressly creates such a potential distinction if a trademark has been registered for five years, but a section 15 affidavit has not yet been filed. To see this, we begin with section 1064. Under section 1064, a party may petition to cancel a registered trademark for any reason within five years of the registration. 15 U.S.C. § 1064(1) (2015). However, after a trademark has been registered on the principal register for five years, the grounds for seeking cancellation are limited to those set forth in subsections 1064(3) and (5). 15 U.S.C. § 1064(3) (2015). Under subsection (3), once a descriptive mark has been registered for five years, a party may no longer seek cancellation of the registration on the grounds that the mark is descriptive and lacks secondary meaning. Moreover, this limitation arises automatically, as soon as a trademark has been registered for five years.

In contrast, to obtain the conclusive evidentiary presumptions of validity, ownership, and exclusive right to use set forth in section 1115(b), the mere passage of time since registration is not sufficient. A trademark must have been registered for at least five years *and* the registrant must file, and the PTO must accept, a section 15 affidavit verifying that the registered mark "has been in continuous use for five consecutive years subsequent to the date of registration and is still in use in commerce. . . ." 15 U.S.C. § 1065 (2015).

Given these differing requirements, if Park 'N Fly's mark had been registered for five years, but Park 'N Fly had not yet filed its section 15 affidavit, then Dollar Park and Fly could not petition the Trademark Trial and Appeal Board to cancel the mark for lack of secondary meaning. After the mark has been registered for five years, Dollar Park and Fly could petition for cancellation only on one of the grounds set forth in section 1064(3). Descriptiveness together with a lack of secondary meaning is not one of those grounds. Thus, Park 'N Fly's registration would be insulated from cancellation and so-called "defensive incontestability" would arise. At the same time, however, if Park 'N Fly went on the offensive and sued Dollar Park and Fly for trademark infringement, until the section 15 affidavit was filed and accepted, Dollar Park and Fly could raise the lack of secondary meaning as a defense to challenge the validity of Park 'N Fly's mark.

Thus, the Act expressly creates something like the offensive-defensive incontestability distinction the Ninth Circuit recognized. However, it creates that distinction only where a mark has been registered for five years, but the section 15 affidavit has not yet been filed and accepted. This was not the case in *Park 'N Fly*. As the Court notes, Park 'N Fly filed its section 15 affidavit in 1977. As a result, the offensive-defensive distinction that the statute creates did not apply.

In contrast, review the facts in *Zatarain's*. Zatarain's had used the mark "Fish-Fri" since 1950 and federally registered it in 1962. It had first used the mark "Chick-Fri" in 1968 and federally registered the mark in 1976. Although the litigation was not brought until the 1980s, the court allowed the defendants to challenge both marks on the grounds that they were descriptive and lacked secondary meaning. Why? Apparently, Zatarain's had not filed its section 15 affidavits. As a result, while the defendants could not petition to cancel the registrations under section 1064 on the grounds of descriptiveness, they could raise descriptiveness as a defense to the validity of the marks under section 1115(a). Had Zatarain's waited to file the litigation until its section 15 affidavits were filed and accepted, then the defendants would not have been able to challenge either mark on the grounds of descriptiveness.

Would that have changed the outcome in the case? Presumably not with respect to "Fish-Fri." As already noted, fair use is available as a defense even with respect to infringement of an incontestably registered mark. *See* 15 U.S.C. § 1115(b)(4) (2015). Thus, the *Zatarain's* court's ruling that the defendants' use was fair would still apply, even if "Fish Fri" had been incontestably registered. However, if "Chick-Fri" had been incontestably registered, then its validity could not have been challenged for lack of secondary meaning. If the validity of the "Chick-Fri" registration could not have been challenged, would Zatarain's necessarily have won with respect to "Chick-Fri"? Again, the likely answer is no. If the defendants' use of "Fish Fry" was not infringing under the fair use doctrine, presumably their use of "Chick Fry" would have been similarly non-infringing. However, had the section 15 affidavit been filed and accepted, the "Chick-Fri" registration would not have been cancelled. Do you see why?

On a related issue, how could the *Zatarain's* court order the cancellation of the "Chick-Fri" registration in 1983? The cancellation order came more than five years after the mark's date of registration. But under section 1064, once a mark has been registered for five years, a party may no longer petition for cancellation of the registration on the grounds of descriptiveness. The court nevertheless orders the registration's cancellation. On what basis?

8. *Genericness and Incontestability.* Is genericness a defense that can be raised against a federally registered trademark that has become incontestable? It is not expressly listed in section 1115(b) as one of the nine enumerated defenses. It is absent from this section, just as it is absent from section 1052, because the initial drafts of the Trademark Act had omitted genericness as a separate doctrine. As we have previously discussed, the trademark bar wanted genericness treated solely as an issue of abandonment, which was included as one of the enumerated defenses in section 1115(b). When Congress added genericness as a separate doctrine just before enactment, it added it to sections 1064 and 1065, but not to section 1052 or section 1115. Can a defendant nevertheless raise genericness as a defense to a claim that the defendant is infringing an incontestably registered mark?

The answer is yes. While genericness is not one of the nine enumerated defenses in section 1115(b), that section begins with the statement: "To the extent that the right to use the registered mark has become incontestable under section 1065 of this title. . . ." 15 U.S.C. § 1115(b) (2015). As the Court notes, this language incorporates by reference any limitations on incontestability set forth in section 1065. *See Park 'N Fly, Inc.*, 469 U.S. at 194–95.

Section 1065, in turn, expressly provides that "no incontestable right shall be acquired in a mark which is the generic name for the goods or services or a portion thereof, for which it is registered." 15 U.S.C. § 1065(4) (2015). Thus, genericness may be raised in litigation to challenge the validity of even an incontestably registered trademark. *See TE-TA-MA Truth Found.- Family of URI, Inc. v. World Church of the Creator*, 297 F.3d 662, 665 (7th Cir. 2002); *Sunrise Jewelry Mfg. Co. v. Fred S.A.*, 175 F.3d 1322 (Fed. Cir. 1999).

Moreover, if the language in section 1065(4) were not enough, section 1065 also provides that incontestability does not extend to "a ground for which application to cancel may be filed at any time under paragraph (3) and (5) of section 1064 of this title. . . ." 15 U.S.C. § 1065 (2015). Among other grounds, section 1064(3) provides that a petition to cancel may be filed at any time with respect to a "registered mark [which] becomes the generic name for the goods or services, of a portion thereof, for which is registered. . . ." 15 U.S.C. § 1064(3) (2015).

9. *Other Available Defenses.* In addition to genericness, section 1115(b)'s incorporation by reference of the limits on incontestability set forth in section 1065 and subsections 1064(3) and (5) also allows a defendant to challenge an incontestably registered trademark on a number of additional grounds. As we saw in Chapter 3, it allows a senior unregistered user to rebut the registrant's presumptive right to use the mark in the area in which the senior unregistered user had established preexisting state law rights to

the mark at issue. 15 U.S.C. § 1065 (2015). The incorporation of section 1064(3) allows a defendant to challenge an incontestably registered trademark on the grounds that the trademark was abandoned (though that is also expressly enumerated as one of the defenses in section 1115(b)), is functional (also expressly enumerated in section 1115(b)), conveys materially false information and is thus deceptive, or is disparaging, scandalous, or immoral, or otherwise objectionable under subsection 1052(a), (b), or (c). 15 U.S.C. § 1064(3) (2015). In addition, subsection 1064(3) also allows a registered trademark to be challenged at any time if the registration was obtained fraudulently (also expressly enumerated in section 1115(b)), or where the registrant engages in naked licensing or assigns the registered mark in gross (also expressly enumerated in section 1115(b)). 15 U.S.C. § 1064(3) (2015) (permitting cancellation at any time if the "registration was obtained fraudulently" or if the registered trademark "is being used by, or with the permission of, the registrant so as to misrepresent the source of the goods or services on or in connection with which the mark is used.").

CHAPTER 5

THE PROTECTION OF TRADE DRESS

∎ ∎ ∎

In the preceding chapter, we focused on the protection of words as trademarks. However, trademark law has long encompassed more than merely words. In 1878, the Court summarized the subject matter eligible for protection as a trademark as follows:

> [A] trade-mark may consist of a name, symbol, figure, letter, form, or device, if adopted and used by a manufacturer or merchant in order to designate the goods he manufactures or sells to distinguish the same from those manufactured or sold by another, to the end that the goods may be known in the market as his, and to enable him to secure such profits as result from his reputation for skill, industry, and fidelity.

McLean v. Fleming, 96 U.S. 245, 254 (1878).

Despite the potential breadth of this definition, the shape, design, or features of the product itself, or of the product's packaging were not eligible for protection as a trademark under the common law. As courts consistently held, "the symbol, figure, letter, form, or mark, used for a trade-mark, must be a mark, impressed, cut, engraved, stamped, cast upon, or in some way wrapped around, or appended to, the article, or the package, as something independent of the article itself, or the package used to contain it." *Moorman v. Hoge*, 17 F. Cas. 715, 718 (C.C.D. Cal. 1871). Although not technically eligible for protection as a trademark, a product's design or its packaging could receive some degree of protection under the rubric of unfair competition.

In enacting the Trademark Act of 1946, Congress decided to retain this common law framework. Paraphrasing *McLean's* definition of technical trademark subject matter, Congress specifically defined trademarks eligible for registration on the principal register to exclude trade dress. Nevertheless, acting either in deliberate disregard or in ignorance of Congress's express intentions, the Commissioner of the Patent and Trademark Office, and later courts, have recognized a product's configuration and its packaging as subject matter eligible both for registration on the principal register under section 2, and for protection in the absence of registration under section 43(a), of the Trademark Act.

Whether addressed under the rubric of unfair competition or treated as a technical trademark, the argument for extending protection to trade dress is superficially the same as for word marks. Just as consumers may sometimes rely on words to convey brand-specific information, they may sometimes rely on the packaging or design of the product itself to identify the product's source, or otherwise to convey brand-specific information. So there is a plausible argument that trade dress should be protected as if it were a trademark when it serves the informational role of a trademark.

Yet, at the same time, the packaging and design of a product also invariably serve other roles. Unlike words, which at best, may describe or identify a product, a product's design or packaging are an integral aspect of the product itself. Rather than want the packaging or design for what it tells them about who made the product, consumers usually want the packaging or feature for its own sake, because they believe that it makes the product more useful, more convenient, or more attractive.

The question thus becomes whether, and if so, how to protect the brand-specific informational role that trade dress may serve without unduly limiting the ability of would-be competitors to take advantage of the other roles that the packaging, features, or design claimed as trade dress also serve. We have seen this tension before, particularly with respect to generic words. Even with respect to generic words, however, the question was not whether would-be competitors could offer a competing, or even an identical product, but what word(s) they could use to inform consumers that their product was, in fact, competing or identical. Of course, the ability to inform consumers that a product is competing is often necessary to ensure effective competition. Yet, it is distinctly secondary to, and depends entirely upon, the would-be competitor's ability to offer a competing product in the first place. If General Mills can protect the layout, or pieces, or game play of Monopoly, or if Genesee could protect the flavor of its honey brown ale, by arguing that the unique features of the game or the unique taste of the beer were themselves trademarks, the dispute over whether a would-be competitor could use the words "Monopoly" or "Honey Brown" would become far less material.

Unfortunately, nowhere is the line between fair and unfair competition less clear than with respect to imitation of a product's features, design, or packaging. The doctrinal rules are often inconsistently phrased, and even when phrased consistently, are not consistently applied. As a result, case outcomes seem largely dictated by the luck of the draw—quite literally. Some judges have considerable natural sympathy for a plaintiff whose popular product has been copied. Whatever the formal doctrinal rules, these judges manage to find competition unfair readily, and when they find it, grant relief against the imitation broadly. Other judges are inherently more skeptical of such claims. In their view, trade dress claims usually have little real link to protecting consumers from confusion, but reflect an attempt to use trademark and unfair competition law as a "mutant species" of patent or copyright. Again, whatever the formal doctrinal rules, these judges usually find a way either to allow the imitation outright, or to limit the relief available to proper labeling.

Nevertheless, with the hope of bringing, at least, some clarity to the issues, we begin with two foundational cases concerning the protection available to a product's configuration under the common law's doctrine of unfair competition.

A. THE COMMON LAW'S PROTECTION OF TRADE DRESS

KELLOGG CO. v. NATIONAL BISCUIT CO.
305 U.S. 111 (1938)

BRANDEIS, J.

This suit was brought in the federal court for Delaware by National Biscuit Company against Kellogg Company to enjoin alleged unfair competition by the manufacture and sale of the breakfast food commonly known as shredded wheat. The competition was alleged to be unfair mainly because Kellogg Company uses, like the plaintiff, the name shredded wheat and, like the plaintiff, produces its biscuit in pillow-shaped form.

Shredded wheat is a product composed of whole wheat which has been boiled, partially dried, then drawn or pressed out into thin shreds and baked. The shredded wheat biscuit generally known is pillow-shaped in form. It was introduced in 1893 by Henry D. Perky, of Colorado; and he was connected until his death in 1908 with companies formed to make and market the article. Commercial success was not attained until the Natural Food Company built, in 1901, a large factory at Niagara Falls, New York. In 1908, its corporate name was changed to "The Shredded Wheat Company"; and in 1930 its business and goodwill were acquired by National Biscuit Company.

Kellogg Company has been in the business of manufacturing breakfast food cereals since its organization in 1905. For a period commencing in 1912 and ending in 1919 it made a product whose form was somewhat like the product in question, but whose manufacture was different, the wheat being reduced to a dough before being pressed into shreds. For a short period in 1922 it manufactured the article in question. In 1927, it resumed manufacturing the product. In 1928, the plaintiff sued for alleged unfair competition two dealers in Kellogg shredded wheat biscuits. That suit was discontinued by stipulation in 1930. On

June 11, 1932, the present suit was brought. Much evidence was introduced; but the determinative facts are relatively few; and as to most of these there is no conflict.

In 1935, the District Court dismissed the bill. It found that the name "Shredded Wheat" is a term describing alike the product of the plaintiff and of the defendant; and that no passing off or deception had been shown. It held that upon the expiration of the Perky patent No. 548,086 issued October 15, 1895, the name of the patented article passed into the public domain. In 1936, the Circuit Court of Appeals affirmed that decree. Upon rehearing, it vacated, in 1937, its own decree and reversed that of the District Court, with direction "to enter a decree enjoining the defendant from the use of the name 'Shredded Wheat' as its trade-name and from advertising or offering for sale its product in the form and shape of plaintiff's biscuit in violation of its trade-mark; and with further directions to order an accounting for damages and profits." In its opinion the court described the trade-mark as "consisting of a dish, containing two biscuits submerged in milk." 91 F.2d 150, 152. We denied Kellogg Company's petition for a writ of certiorari, 302 U.S. 733; and denied rehearing, 302 U.S. 777.

On January 5, 1938, the District Court entered its mandate in the exact language of the order of the Circuit Court of Appeals, and issued a permanent injunction. Shortly thereafter National Biscuit Company petitioned the Circuit Court of Appeals to recall its mandate "for purposes of clarification." It alleged that Kellogg Company was insisting, contrary to the court's intention, that the effect of the mandate and writ of injunction was to forbid it from selling its product only when the trade name "Shredded Wheat" is applied to a biscuit in the form and shape of the plaintiff's biscuit and is accompanied by a representation of a dish with biscuits in it; and that it was not enjoined from making its biscuit in the form and shape of the plaintiff's biscuit, nor from calling it "Shredded Wheat," unless at the same time it uses upon its cartons plaintiff's trade-mark consisting of a dish with two biscuits in it. On May 5, 1938, the Circuit Court of Appeals granted the petition for clarification and directed the District Court to enter a decree enjoining Kellogg Company (96 F.2d 873):

> "(1) from the use of the name 'SHREDDED WHEAT' as its trade name, (2) from advertising or offering for sale its product in the form and shape of plaintiff's biscuit, and (3) from doing either."

Kellogg Company then filed a petition for a writ of certiorari to review the decree as so clarified, and also sought reconsideration of our denial of its petition for certiorari to review the decree as entered in its original form. In support of these petitions it called to our attention the decision of the British Privy Council in *Canadian Shredded Wheat Co.* v. *Kellogg Co. of Canada*, 55 R. P. C. 125, rendered after our denial of the petition for certiorari earlier in the term. We granted both petitions for certiorari.

The plaintiff concedes that it does not possess the exclusive right to make shredded wheat. But it claims the exclusive right to the trade name "Shredded Wheat" and the exclusive right to make shredded wheat biscuits pillow-shaped. It charges that the defendant, by using the name and shape, and otherwise, is passing off, or enabling others to pass off, Kellogg goods for those of the plaintiff. Kellogg Company denies that the plaintiff is entitled to the exclusive use of the name or of the pillow-shape; denies any passing off; asserts that it has used every reasonable effort to distinguish its product from that of the plaintiff; and contends that in honestly competing for a part of the market for shredded wheat it is exercising the common right freely to manufacture and sell an article of commerce unprotected by patent.

First. The plaintiff has no exclusive right to the use of the term "Shredded Wheat" as a trade name. For that is the generic term of the article, which describes it with a fair degree of accuracy; and is the term by which the biscuit in pillow-shaped form is generally known by the public. Since the term is generic, the original maker of the product acquired no exclusive right to use it. As Kellogg Company had the right to make the article, it had, also, the right to use the term by which the public knows it. . . .

Moreover, the name "Shredded Wheat," as well as the product, the process and the machinery employed in making it, has been dedicated to the public. The basic patent for the product and for the process of making it, and many other patents for special machinery to be used in making the article, issued to Perky. In those patents the term "shredded" is repeatedly used as descriptive of the product. The basic patent expired October 15, 1912; the others soon after. Since during the life of the patents "Shredded Wheat" was the general designation of the patented product, there passed to the public upon the expiration of the patent, not only the right to make the article as it was made during the patent period, but also the right to apply thereto the name by which it had become known. As was said in *Singer Mfg. Co. v. June Mfg. Co.*, 163 U.S. 169, 185:

> "It equally follows from the cessation of the monopoly and the falling of the patented device into the domain of things public, that along with the public ownership of the device there must also necessarily pass to the public the generic designation of the thing which has arisen during the monopoly. . . . To say otherwise would be to hold that, although the public had acquired the device covered by the patent, yet the owner of the patent or the manufacturer of the patented thing had retained the designated name which was essentially necessary to vest the

public with the full enjoyment of that which had become theirs by the disappearance of the monopoly."

It is contended that the plaintiff has the exclusive right to the name "Shredded Wheat," because those words acquired the "secondary meaning" of shredded wheat made at Niagara Falls by the plaintiff's predecessor. There is no basis here for applying the doctrine of secondary meaning. The evidence shows only that due to the long period in which the plaintiff or its predecessor was the only manufacturer of the product, many people have come to associate the product, and as a consequence the name by which the product is generally known, with the plaintiff's factory at Niagara Falls. But to establish a trade name in the term "shredded wheat" the plaintiff must show more than a subordinate meaning which applies to it. It must show that the primary significance of the term in the minds of the consuming public is not the product but the producer. This it has not done. The showing which it has made does not entitle it to the exclusive use of the term shredded wheat but merely entitles it to require that the defendant use reasonable care to inform the public of the source of its product.

The plaintiff seems to contend that even if Kellogg Company acquired upon the expiration of the patents the right to use the name shredded wheat, the right was lost by delay. The argument is that Kellogg Company, although the largest producer of breakfast cereals in the country, did not seriously attempt to make shredded wheat, or to challenge plaintiff's right to that name until 1927, and that meanwhile plaintiff's predecessor had expended more than $17,000,000 in making the name a household word and identifying the product with its manufacture. Those facts are without legal significance. Kellogg Company's right was not one dependent upon diligent exercise. Like every other member of the public, it was, and remained, free to make shredded wheat when it chose to do so; and to call the product by its generic name. The only obligation resting upon Kellogg Company was to identify its own product lest it be mistaken for that of the plaintiff.

Second. The plaintiff has not the exclusive right to sell shredded wheat in the form of a pillow-shaped biscuit—the form in which the article became known to the public. That is the form in which shredded wheat was made under the basic patent. The patented machines used were designed to produce only the pillow-shaped biscuits. And a design patent was taken out to cover the pillow-shaped form. Hence, upon expiration of the patents the form, as well as the name, was dedicated to the public. . .

Where an article may be manufactured by all, a particular manufacturer can no more assert exclusive rights in a form in which the public has become accustomed to see the article and which, in the minds of the public, is primarily associated with the article rather than a particular producer, than it can in the case of a name with similar connections in the public mind. Kellogg Company was free to use the pillow-shaped form, subject only to the obligation to identify its product lest it be mistaken for that of the plaintiff.

Third. The question remains whether Kellogg Company in exercising its right to use the name "Shredded Wheat" and the pillow-shaped biscuit, is doing so fairly. Fairness requires that it be done in a manner which reasonably distinguishes its product from that of plaintiff.

Each company sells its biscuits only in cartons. The standard Kellogg carton contains fifteen biscuits; the plaintiff's twelve. The Kellogg cartons are distinctive. They do not resemble those used by the plaintiff either in size, form, or color. And the difference in the labels is striking. The Kellogg cartons bear in bold script the names "Kellogg's Whole Wheat Biscuit" or "Kellogg's Shredded Whole Wheat Biscuit" so sized and spaced as to strike the eye as being a Kellogg product. It is true that on some of its cartons it had a picture of two shredded wheat biscuits in a bowl of milk which was quite similar to one of the plaintiff's registered trade-marks. But the name Kellogg was so prominent on all of the defendant's cartons as to minimize the possibility of confusion.

Some hotels, restaurants, and lunchrooms serve biscuits not in cartons and guests so served may conceivably suppose that a Kellogg biscuit served is one of the plaintiff's make. But no person familiar with plaintiff's product would be misled. The Kellogg biscuit is about two-thirds the size of plaintiff's; and differs from it in appearance. Moreover, the field in which deception could be practiced is negligibly small. Only 2 1/2 per cent of the Kellogg biscuits are sold to hotels, restaurants and lunchrooms. Of those so sold 98 per cent are sold in individual cartons containing two biscuits. These cartons are distinctive and bear prominently the Kellogg name. To put upon the individual biscuit some mark which would identify it as the Kellogg product is not commercially possible. Relatively few biscuits will be removed from the individual cartons before they reach the consumer. The obligation resting upon Kellogg Company is not to insure that every purchaser will know it to be the maker but to use every reasonable means to prevent confusion.

It is urged that all possibility of deception or confusion would be removed if Kellogg Company should refrain from using the name "Shredded Wheat" and adopt some form other than the pillow-shape. But the name and form are integral parts of the goodwill of the article. To share fully in the goodwill, it must use the name and the pillow-shape. And in the goodwill Kellogg Company is as free to share as the plaintiff. Compare *William R. Warner & Co.* v. *Eli Lilly & Co.*, 265 U.S. 526, 528, 530. Moreover, the pillow-shape must be used for another reason. The evidence is persuasive that this form is functional—that the cost of the biscuit would be increased and its high quality lessened if some other form were substituted for the pillow-shape.

Kellogg Company is undoubtedly sharing in the goodwill of the article known as "Shredded Wheat"; and thus is sharing in a market which was created by the skill and judgment of plaintiff's predecessor and has been widely extended by vast expenditures in advertising persistently made. But that is not unfair. Sharing in the goodwill of an article unprotected by patent or trade-mark is the exercise of a right possessed by all—and in the free exercise of which the consuming public is deeply interested. There is no evidence of passing off or deception on the part of the Kellogg Company; and it has taken every reasonable precaution to prevent confusion or the practice of deception in the sale of its product.

Decrees reversed with direction to dismiss the bill.

MR. JUSTICE MCREYNOLDS and MR. JUSTICE BUTLER are of opinion that the decree of the Circuit Court of Appeals is correct and should be affirmed. To them it seems sufficiently clear that the Kellogg Company is fraudulently seeking to appropriate to itself the benefits of a goodwill built up at great cost by the respondent and its predecessors.

CRESCENT TOOL CO. v. KILBORN & BISHOP CO.

247 F. 299 (2d Cir. 1917)

HAND, L.

The cases of so-called "nonfunctional" unfair competition, starting with the "coffee mill case," *Enterprise Mfg. Co. v. Landers, Frary & Clark*, 131 Fed. 240, 65 C.C.A. 587, are only instances of the doctrine of "secondary" meaning. All of them presuppose that the appearance of the article, like its descriptive title in true cases of "secondary" meaning, has become associated in the public mind with the first comer as manufacturer or source, and, if a second comer imitates the article exactly, that the public will believe his goods have come from the first, and will buy, in part, at least, because of that deception. Therefore it is apparent that it is an absolute condition to any relief whatever that the plaintiff in such cases show that the appearance of his wares has in fact come to mean that some particular person—the plaintiff may not be individually known—makes them, and that the public cares who does make them, and not merely for their appearance and structure. It will not be enough only to show how pleasing they are, because all the features of beauty or utility which commend them to the public are by hypothesis already in the public domain. The defendant has as much right to copy the "nonfunctional" features of the article as any others, so long as they have not become associated with the plaintiff as manufacturer or source. The critical question of fact at the outset always is whether the public is moved in any degree to buy the article because of its source and what are the features by which it distinguishes that source. Unless the plaintiff can answer this question he can take no step forward; no degree of imitation of details is actionable in its absence.

In the case at bar it nowhere appears that before 1910, when the defendant began to make its wrenches, the general appearance of the plaintiff's wrench had come to indicate to the public any one maker as its source, or that the wrench had been sold in any part because of its source, as distinct from its utility or neat appearance. It is not enough to show that the wrench became popular under the name "Crescent"; the plaintiff must prove that before 1910 the public had already established the habit of buying it, not solely because they wanted that kind of wrench, but because they also wanted a Crescent, and thought all such wrenches were Crescents.

Upon the trial the plaintiff may, however, be able to establish this, and it is only fair to indicate broadly the considerations which will then determine the scope of his relief. In such cases neither side has an absolute right, because their mutual rights conflict. Thus the plaintiff has the right not to lose his customers through false representations that those are his wares which in fact are not, but he may not monopolize any design or pattern, however trifling. The defendant, on the other hand, may copy the plaintiff's goods slavishly down to the minutest detail; but he may not represent himself as the plaintiff in their sale. When the appearance of the goods has in fact come to represent a given person as their source, and that person is in fact the plaintiff, it is impossible to make these rights absolute; compromise is essential, exactly as it is with the right to use the common language in cases of "secondary" meaning. We can only say that the court must require such changes in appearance as will effectively distinguish the defendant's wares with the least expense to him; in no event may the plaintiff suppress the defendant's sale altogether. The proper meaning of the phrase "nonfunctional," is only this: That in such cases the injunction is usually confined to nonessential elements, since these are usually enough to distinguish the goods, and are the least burdensome for the defendant to change. Whether changes in them are in all conceivable cases the limit of the plaintiff's right is a matter not before us. If a case should arise in which no effective distinction was possible without change in functional elements, it would demand consideration; but the District Court may well find an escape here from that predicament. Certainly the precise extent and kind of relief must in the first instance be a matter for the discretion of that court.

Order reversed, and motion denied.

NOTES FOR DISCUSSION

1. *Markets and the Law.* We take for granted today the existence of competitive markets in both shredded wheat cereal and crescent wrenches. Yet, a student should note that both the Supreme Court in *Kellogg Co.* and the Second Circuit in *Crescent Tool Co.* reverse lower court decisions that would have barred the defendant from making a similar looking product. Had three more justices in *Kellogg Co.* or two judges in *Crescent Tool Co.* voted the other way, how much different would these markets look today? Would consumers be better or worse off? With word marks, the decision to protect a given word may force would-be competitors to find an alternate way to tell consumers that they are offering a competing product. Can would-be competitors do the same thing with respect to product design? Would the availability of a corn flake cereal constrain Nabisco's ability to increase the price of its shredded wheat cereal as effectively as the availability of another shredded wheat cereal? Would the availability of a shredded wheat cereal that did not use the familiar pillow shape constrain Nabisco's ability to increase the price for its shredded wheat to the same extent as the availability of another pillow-shaped, shredded wheat cereal?

On the other side of the coin, is there any realistic chance that a consumer today is unable to differentiate between Kellogg and Nabisco Shredded Wheat, or between the various brands of crescent wrenches available? Will adequately labeling and the use of word marks always, or almost always, suffice to address the risk of consumer confusion and to minimize search costs? Have you ever purchased one brand of product thinking you were purchasing another because of the products' similar dress?

Even if in theory we could identify cases where protecting trade dress would make sense, should we entrust competition in markets to this sort of judicial oversight? Or given that mistakes are inevitable in any human system of justice, should we simply refuse to protect a product's design under the rubric of trademark and unfair competition law altogether?

2. *The Legal Rules.* Although neither case extends protection to the product shape or design at issue, they both articulate two requirements necessary to obtain trade dress protection. First, the shape of the product must possess secondary meaning. Second, the shape of the product must also not be functional. How does each court define these requirements? Which of these elements is Nabisco unable to prove for the pillow-shaped biscuit? Which is Crescent Tool unable to prove for its wrench?

3. *De Facto Secondary Meaning.* In *Kellogg Co.*, Nabisco contends that both the words "Shredded Wheat" and the pillow-shape of its biscuit have a secondary meaning because it (or its predecessors-in-interest) had been the exclusive manufacturer of shredded wheat for more than thirty years. Given that Nabisco was the sole source of shredded wheat cereal for such a long time, the Court acknowledges that "many people have come to associate the product, and as a consequence the name by which the product is generally

known, with the plaintiff's factory at Niagara Falls." *Kellogg Co.*, 305 U.S. at 118. Is this sufficient to establish secondary meaning? Why or why not?

Following *Kellogg Co.*, courts have remained skeptical of attempts to establish secondary meaning based simply upon the fact that the plaintiff has been the only party making a given product for a long time, usually as a result of a patent. In such a case, consumers may in fact associate both the product's design and common name uniquely with a specific producer. As a result of that association, allowing competitors to sell similar products will almost invariably lead to some confusion, as consumers adjust their expectations from a market with only one company offering the product to a market with multiple companies offering the product. Nevertheless, despite this initial period of confusion, consumer welfare is almost always better served over the long run by allowing competition into such markets than it would be by permanently preserving such markets as monopolies.

To avoid giving legal recognition to such secondary meaning, courts will sometimes refer to the secondary meaning that can in fact develop with respect to a generic word or phrase during a period of exclusive use as *de facto* secondary meaning. Such *de facto* secondary meaning is not legally sufficient to justify protecting a generic word or phrase as a trademark. As one court explained:

> Underlying the genericness doctrine is the principle that some terms so directly signify the nature of the product that interests of competition demand that other producers be able to use them even if terms have or might become identified with a source and so acquire "de facto" secondary meaning. *See, e.g.*, CES Pub. Corp. v. St. Regis Publications, Inc., 531 F.2d 11, 13 (2d Cir. 1975) (Friendly, J.) ("To allow trademark protection for generic terms, i.e., names which describe the genus of goods being sold, even when these have become identified with a first user, would grant the owner of the mark a monopoly, since a competitor could not describe his goods as what they are."). Courts refuse to protect a generic term because competitors need it more to describe their goods than the claimed markholder needs it to distinguish its goods from others.

A.J. Canfield Co. v. Honickman, 808 F.2d 291, 304 (3d Cir. 1986).

4. *Patents, Trademarks, and Trade Dress.* Would the Court have decided *Kellogg Co.* differently if Nabisco's predecessor had not had a patent on the process of making shredded wheat cereal? What difference did the patents make in the Court's analysis? What difference should they make? If we are trying to maximize consumer welfare through trademark and unfair competition, then the Court's holding that the phrase "shredded wheat" and the pillow shape may be used by Kellogg should reflect a conclusion that consumers will be better off with competition in the shredded wheat market than without. Is the fact that the process for making the cereal was patented relevant to the question of consumer welfare? Does it tend to suggest that

consumers would be better off by allowing competition? Or is it irrelevant to that issue?

On the other side of the coin, will the legal rule that we adopt on this issue in trademark law influence the decision whether to seek a patent for companies in Nabisco's situation in the future? Knowing that obtaining a utility patent will limit the availability of trademark protection, will a company choose to forego patent protection in order to increase the trademark protection potentially available? Assuming that the patent was material to the *Kellogg* Court's refusal to provide trademark protection or to find unfair competition, the question for Nabisco would have been whether the expected profits from exclusivity during the patent's twenty-year term would be greater or less than those from protecting the phrase "shredded wheat" and the pillow shape under trademark and unfair competition law perpetually. In making this calculation, Nabisco would need to consider not only the time difference in protection available under patent and trademark, but also the differing scope of and requirements for protection.

Both forms of protection have uncertainties associated with them. Even if the phrase "shredded wheat" and the pillow shape would have been protected under trademark and unfair competition law, a would-be competitor could, at least in theory, popularize some other generic term for the cereal and could offer some other shape of shredded wheat. The question for Nabisco is whether such entry is likely, and if it occurs, to what extent will consumers come to recognize the competitor's offering as a substitute for Nabisco's original. Similar issues arise with a patent. While a patent provides an exclusive right to make, use, sell, or offer for sale the patented invention, it is not ironclad either. Because the patented invention is defined by the patent's written claims, drafting the claims broadly enough to bar all competitive entry is often difficult. For a variety of reasons, claim language will often leave room for would-be competitors to work around a patent and offer an effective substitute.

In terms of prerequisites, the worry on the trademark side is whether, in the absence of a patent, competitive entry will occur before secondary meaning can develop in the phrase "shredded wheat" and the pillow shape. On the patent side, the question is whether, after the patent has issued, a court will nonetheless find the patent invalid for failing to satisfy patent law's nonobviousness standard, or one of patent law's other prerequisites.

While it is difficult to know how this calculation will work out in every case, there will inevitably be cases at the margin, where the rents available from the two forms of protection are roughly comparable. For those marginal cases, adopting the rule that the existence of a utility patent largely forecloses the availability of trademark or trade dress protection will lead parties to forego filing a patent application.

Given this analysis, two questions arise. First, will our rule choice in trademark law influence enough patent filing decisions that patent considerations should predominate? Second, if so, how should we structure our rule regarding the effect of a patent on the availability of trademark protection to minimize the influence the rule exerts on the decision to file for a patent? While the first question is empirical, and so difficult to answer, the second has two possible answers. Most obviously, we can treat the existence, or lack, of a patent, as irrelevant to the availability of protection under trademark and unfair competition law. No court, however, has adopted this approach. As an alternative, we can limit the availability of protection under trademark and unfair competition law either if a party had obtained a patent for the claimed trade dress, as in *Kellogg*, or if a party could have sought a patent for the claimed trade dress. Again, however, courts have focused on whether in fact a patent has been obtained, rather than on whether it could have been obtained, and thus, the risk that our trademark rules may influence a party's decision as to whether to file a patent application remains.

B. THE PREEMPTION OF STATE LAW PROTECTION OF TRADE DRESS

As we saw in *Kellogg*, a party will sometimes seek trade dress protection for a product design or feature that either was or could have been patented. Nominally, the purposes of trade dress and patent protection are different. Trade dress protection is supposed to prevent consumer confusion in the marketplace. Patent protection provides an incentive for invention and innovation. Yet, their legal and economic consequences are similar. If their respective prerequisites are met, both provide an exclusive right to use a given product design. And that exclusive right, in turn, can insulate its holder from competition by making it more difficult, more expensive, and more time consuming for would-be competitors to work around the protection provided in order to enter a given market and offer an effective substitute for the original. The exclusive right can thereby enable the rights holder to charge correspondingly higher prices and earn correspondingly higher profits.

How then should we view the relationship between patent and trade dress protection? Does the additional profit that trade dress protection potentially provides complement, substitute for, or conflict with the incentives for innovation that the patent system seeks to provide? As the decision in *Kellogg* reflects, courts have long been reluctant to allow a patent holder to claim the exclusive right to the common name for the patented article under trademark law, or to the design of the article as trade dress under unfair competition law, once an associated utility patent has expired. Claims for such protection struck courts as an impermissible attempt to use trademark and unfair competition law to extend the statutorily limited term of the patent. Yet, the Court did not address the broader question regarding the fit between patent and trade dress until March 9, 1964, when the Warren Court issued the following pair of decisions.

SEARS, ROEBUCK & CO. V. STIFFEL CO.
376 U.S. 225 (1964)

BLACK, J.

The question in this case is whether a State's unfair competition law can, consistently with the federal patent laws, impose liability for or prohibit the copying of an article which is protected by neither a federal patent nor a copyright. The respondent, Stiffel Company, secured design and mechanical patents on a "pole lamp"—a vertical tube having lamp fixtures along the outside, the tube being made so that it will stand upright between the floor and ceiling of a room. Pole lamps proved a decided commercial success, and soon after Stiffel brought them on the market Sears, Roebuck & Company put on the market a substantially identical lamp, which it sold more cheaply, Sears' retail price being about the same as Stiffel's wholesale price. Stiffel then brought this action against Sears in the United States District Court for the Northern District of Illinois, claiming in its first count that by copying its design Sears had infringed Stiffel's patents and in its second count that by selling copies of Stiffel's lamp Sears had caused confusion in the trade as to the source of the lamps and had thereby engaged in unfair competition under Illinois law. There was evidence that identifying tags were not attached to the Sears lamps although labels appeared on the cartons in which they were delivered to customers, that customers had asked Stiffel whether its lamps differed from Sears', and that in two cases customers who had bought Stiffel lamps had complained to Stiffel on learning that Sears was selling substantially identical lamps at a much lower price.

The District Court, after holding the patents invalid for want of invention, went on to find as a fact that Sears' lamp was "a substantially exact copy" of Stiffel's and that the two lamps were so much alike, both in appearance and in functional details, "that confusion between them is likely, and some confusion has already occurred." On these findings the court held Sears guilty of unfair competition, enjoined Sears "from unfairly competing with [Stiffel] by selling or attempting to sell pole lamps identical to or confusingly similar to" Stiffel's lamp, and ordered an accounting to fix profits and damages resulting from Sears' "unfair competition."

The Court of Appeals affirmed. 313 F.2d 115. That court held that, to make out a case of unfair competition under Illinois law, there was no need to show that Sears had been "palming off" its lamps as Stiffel lamps; Stiffel had only to prove that there was a "likelihood of confusion as to the source of the products"—that the two articles were sufficiently identical that customers could not tell who had made a particular one. Impressed by the "remarkable sameness of appearance" of the lamps, the Court of Appeals upheld the trial court's findings of likelihood of confusion and some actual confusion, findings which the appellate court construed to mean confusion "as to the source of the lamps." The Court of Appeals thought this enough under Illinois law to sustain the trial court's holding of unfair competition, and thus held Sears liable under Illinois law for doing no more than copying and marketing an unpatented article. We granted certiorari to consider whether this use of a State's law of unfair competition is compatible with the federal patent law. 374 U.S. 826.

Before the Constitution was adopted, some States had granted patents either by special act or by general statute, but when the Constitution was adopted provision for a federal patent law was made one of the enumerated powers of Congress because, as Madison put it in *The Federalist* No. 43, the States "cannot separately make effectual provision" for either patents or copyrights. That constitutional provision is Art. I, § 8, cl. 8, which empowers Congress "To promote the Progress of Science and useful Arts, by securing for limited Times to Authors and Inventors the exclusive Right to their respective Writings and Discoveries." Pursuant to this constitutional authority, Congress in 1790 enacted the first federal patent and copyright law, 1 Stat. 109, and ever since that time has fixed the conditions upon which patents and copyrights shall be granted, *see* 17 U.S.C. §§ 1–216; 35 U.S.C. §§ 1–293. These laws, like other laws of the United States enacted pursuant to constitutional authority, are the supreme law of the land. *See Sperry* v. *Florida*, 373 U.S. 379 (1963). When state law touches upon the area of these federal statutes, it is "familiar doctrine" that the federal policy "may not be set at naught, or its benefits denied" by the state law. *Sola Elec. Co.* v. *Jefferson Elec. Co.*, 317 U.S. 173, 176 (1942). This is true, of course, even if the state law is enacted in the exercise of otherwise undoubted state power.

The grant of a patent is the grant of a statutory monopoly; indeed, the grant of patents in England was an explicit exception to the statute of James I prohibiting monopolies. Patents are not given as favors, as was the case of monopolies given by the Tudor monarchs, *see The Case of Monopolies* (*Darcy* v. *Allein*), 11 Co. Rep. 84 b., 77 Eng. Rep. 1260 (K. B. 1602), but are meant to encourage invention by rewarding the inventor with the right, limited to a term of years fixed by the patent, to exclude others from the use of his invention. During that period of time no one may make, use, or sell the patented product without the patentee's authority. 35 U.S.C. § 271. But in rewarding useful invention, the "rights and welfare of the community must be fairly dealt with and effectually guarded." *Kendall* v. *Winsor*, 21 How. 322, 329 (1859). To that end the prerequisites to obtaining a patent are strictly observed, and when the patent has issued the limitations on its exercise are equally strictly enforced. To begin with, a genuine "invention" or "discovery" must be demonstrated "lest in the constant demand for new appliances the heavy hand of tribute be laid on each slight technological advance in an art." *Cuno Engineering Corp.* v. *Automatic Devices Corp.*, 314 U.S. 84, 92 (1941); *see Great Atlantic & Pacific Tea Co.* v. *Supermarket Equipment*

Corp., 340 U.S. 147, 152–153 (1950); *Atlantic Works* v. *Brady*, 107 U.S. 192, 199–200 (1883). Once the patent issues, it is strictly construed, *United States* v. *Masonite Corp.*, 316 U.S. 265, 280 (1942), it cannot be used to secure any monopoly beyond that contained in the patent, *Morton Salt Co.* v. *G. S. Suppiger Co.*, 314 U.S. 488, 492 (1942), the patentee's control over the product when it leaves his hands is sharply limited, *see United States* v. *Univis Lens Co.*, 316 U.S. 241, 250–252 (1942), and the patent monopoly may not be used in disregard of the antitrust laws, *see International Business Machines Corp.* v. *United States*, 298 U.S. 131 (1936); *United Shoe Machinery Corp.* v. *United States*, 258 U.S. 451, 463–464 (1922). Finally, and especially relevant here, when the patent expires the monopoly created by it expires, too, and the right to make the article—including the right to make it in precisely the shape it carried when patented—passes to the public. *Kellogg Co.* v. *National Biscuit Co.*, 305 U.S. 111, 120–122 (1938); *Singer Mfg. Co.* v. *June Mfg. Co.*, 163 U.S. 169, 185 (1896).

Thus the patent system is one in which uniform federal standards are carefully used to promote invention while at the same time preserving free competition. Obviously a State could not, consistently with the Supremacy Clause of the Constitution, extend the life of a patent beyond its expiration date or give a patent on an article which lacked the level of invention required for federal patents. To do either would run counter to the policy of Congress of granting patents only to true inventions, and then only for a limited time. Just as a State cannot encroach upon the federal patent laws directly, it cannot, under some other law, such as that forbidding unfair competition, give protection of a kind that clashes with the objectives of the federal patent laws.

In the present case the "pole lamp" sold by Stiffel has been held not to be entitled to the protection of either a mechanical or a design patent. An unpatentable article, like an article on which the patent has expired, is in the public domain and may be made and sold by whoever chooses to do so. What Sears did was to copy Stiffel's design and to sell lamps almost identical to those sold by Stiffel. This it had every right to do under the federal patent laws. That Stiffel originated the pole lamp and made it popular is immaterial. "Sharing in the goodwill of an article unprotected by patent or trade-mark is the exercise of a right possessed by all—and in the free exercise of which the consuming public is deeply interested." *Kellogg Co.* v. *National Biscuit Co., supra*, 305 U.S., at 122. To allow a State by use of its law of unfair competition to prevent the copying of an article which represents too slight an advance to be patented would be to permit the State to block off from the public something which federal law has said belongs to the public. The result would be that while federal law grants only 14 or 17 years' protection to genuine inventions, *see* 35 U.S.C. §§ 154, 173, States could allow perpetual protection to articles too lacking in novelty to merit any patent at all under federal constitutional standards. This would be too great an encroachment on the federal patent system to be tolerated.

Sears has been held liable here for unfair competition because of a finding of likelihood of confusion based only on the fact that Sears' lamp was copied from Stiffel's unpatented lamp and that consequently the two looked exactly alike. Of course there could be "confusion" as to who had manufactured these nearly identical articles. But mere inability of the public to tell two identical articles apart is not enough to support an injunction against copying or an award of damages for copying that which the federal patent laws permit to be copied. Doubtless a State may, in appropriate circumstances, require that goods, whether patented or unpatented, be labeled or that other precautionary steps be taken to prevent customers from being misled as to the source, just as it may protect businesses in the use of their trademarks, labels, or distinctive dress in the packaging of goods so as to prevent others, by imitating such markings, from misleading purchasers as to the source of the goods. But because of the federal patent laws a State may not, when the article is unpatented and uncopyrighted, prohibit the copying of the article itself or award damages for such copying. Cf. *G. Ricordi & Co.* v. *Haendler*, 194 F.2d 914, 916 (C. A. 2d Cir. 1952). The judgment below did both and in so doing gave Stiffel the equivalent of a patent monopoly on its unpatented lamp. That was error, and Sears is entitled to a judgment in its favor.

Reversed.

HARLAN, J. (concurring)

In one respect I would give the States more leeway in unfair competition "copying" cases than the Court's opinions would allow. If copying is found, other than by an inference arising from the mere act of copying, to have been undertaken with the dominant purpose and effect of palming off one's goods as those of another or of confusing customers as to the source of such goods, I *see* no reason why the State may not impose reasonable restrictions on the future "copying" itself. Vindication of the paramount federal interest at stake does not require a State to tolerate such specifically oriented predatory business practices. Apart from this, I am in accord with the opinions of the Court, and concur in both judgments since neither case presents the point on which I find myself in disagreement.

COMPCO CORP. v. DAY-BRITE LIGHTING, INC.

376 U.S. 234 (1964)

BLACK, J.

As in *Sears, Roebuck & Co.* v. *Stiffel Co., ante,* p. 225, the question here is whether the use of a state unfair competition law to give relief against the copying of an unpatented industrial design conflicts with the federal patent laws. Both Compco and Day-Brite are manufacturers of fluorescent lighting fixtures of a kind widely used in offices and stores. Day-Brite in 1955 secured from the Patent Office a design patent on a reflector having cross-ribs claimed to give both strength and attractiveness to the fixture. Day-Brite also sought, but was refused, a mechanical patent on the same device. After Day-Brite had begun selling its fixture, Compco's predecessor began making and selling fixtures very similar to Day-Brite's. This action was then brought by Day-Brite. One count alleged that Compco had infringed Day-Brite's design patent; a second count charged that the public and the trade had come to associate this particular design with Day-Brite, that Compco had copied Day-Brite's distinctive design so as to confuse and deceive purchasers into thinking Compco's fixtures were actually Day-Brite's, and that by doing this Compco had unfairly competed with Day-Brite. The complaint prayed for both an accounting and an injunction.

The District Court held the design patent invalid; but as to the second count, while the court did not find that Compco had engaged in any deceptive or fraudulent practices, it did hold that Compco had been guilty of unfair competition under Illinois law. The court found that the overall appearance of Compco's fixture was "the same, to the eye of the ordinary observer, as the overall appearance" of Day-Brite's reflector, which embodied the design of the invalidated patent; that the appearance of Day-Brite's design had "the capacity to identify [Day-Brite] in the trade and does in fact so identify [it] to the trade"; that the concurrent sale of the two products was "likely to cause confusion in the trade"; and that "actual confusion has occurred." On these findings the court adjudged Compco guilty of unfair competition in the sale of its fixtures, ordered Compco to account to Day-Brite for damages, and enjoined Compco "from unfairly competing with plaintiff by the sale or attempted sale of reflectors identical to, or confusingly similar to" those made by Day-Brite.

The Court of Appeals held there was substantial evidence in the record to support the District Court's finding of likely confusion and that this finding was sufficient to support a holding of unfair competition under Illinois law. Although the District Court had not made such a finding, the appellate court observed that "several choices of ribbing were apparently available to meet the functional needs of the product," yet Compco "chose precisely the same design used by the plaintiff and followed it so closely as to make confusion likely." A design which identifies its maker to the trade, the Court of Appeals held, is a "protectable" right under Illinois law, even though the design is unpatentable. We granted certiorari.

To support its findings of likelihood of confusion and actual confusion, the trial court was able to refer to only one circumstance in the record. A plant manager who had installed some of Compco's fixtures later asked Day-Brite to service the fixtures, thinking they had been made by Day-Brite. There was no testimony given by a purchaser or by anyone else that any customer had ever been misled, deceived, or "confused," that is, that anyone had ever bought a Compco fixture thinking it was a Day-Brite fixture. All the record shows, as to the one instance cited by the trial court, is that both Compco and Day-Brite fixtures had been installed in the same plant, that three years later some repairs were needed, and that the manager viewing the Compco fixtures—hung at least 15 feet above the floor and arranged end to end in a continuous line so that identifying marks were hidden—thought they were Day-Brite fixtures and asked Day-Brite to service them. Not only is this incident suggestive only of confusion after a purchase had been made, but also there is considerable evidence of the care taken by Compco to prevent customer confusion, including clearly labeling both the fixtures and the containers in which they were shipped and not selling through manufacturers' representatives who handled competing lines.

Notwithstanding the thinness of the evidence to support findings of likely and actual confusion among purchasers, we do not find it necessary in this case to determine whether there is "clear error" in these findings. They, like those in *Sears, Roebuck & Co. v. Stiffel Co., supra*, were based wholly on the fact that selling an article which is an exact copy of another unpatented article is likely to produce and did in this case produce confusion as to the source of the article. Even accepting the findings, we hold that the order for an accounting for damages and the injunction are in conflict with the federal patent laws. Today we have held in *Sears, Roebuck & Co. v. Stiffel Co., supra*, that when an article is unprotected by a patent or a copyright, state law may not forbid others to copy that article. To forbid copying would interfere with the federal policy, found in Art. I, § 8, cl. 8, of the Constitution and in the implementing federal statutes, of allowing free access to copy whatever the federal patent and copyright laws leave in the public domain. Here Day-Brite's fixture has been held not to be entitled to a design or mechanical patent. Under the federal patent laws it is, therefore, in the public domain and can be copied in every detail by whoever pleases. It is true that the trial court found that the configuration of Day-Brite's fixture identified Day-Brite to the trade because the arrangement of the ribbing had, like a trademark, acquired a "secondary meaning" by which that particular design was associated with Day-Brite. But if the design is not entitled to a design patent or other federal statutory protection, then it can be copied at will.

As we have said in *Sears*, while the federal patent laws prevent a State from prohibiting the copying and selling of unpatented articles, they do not stand in the way of state law, statutory or decisional, which requires those who make and sell copies to take precautions to identify their products as their own. A State of course has power to impose liability upon those who, knowing that the public is relying upon an original manufacturer's reputation for quality and integrity, deceive the public by palming off their copies as the original. That an article copied from an unpatented article could be made in some other way, that the design is "nonfunctional" and not essential to the use of either article, that the configuration of the article copied may have a "secondary meaning" which identifies the maker to the trade, or that there may be "confusion" among purchasers as to which article is which or as to who is the maker, may be relevant evidence in applying a State's law requiring such precautions as labeling; however, and regardless of the copier's motives, neither these facts nor any others can furnish a basis for imposing liability for or prohibiting the actual acts of copying and selling. *Cf. Kellogg Co. v. National Biscuit Co.*, 305 U.S. 111, 120 (1938). And of course a State cannot hold a copier accountable in damages for failure to label or otherwise to identify his goods unless his failure is in violation of valid state statutory or decisional law requiring the copier to label or take other precautions to prevent confusion of customers as to the source of the goods.

NOTES FOR DISCUSSION

1.   *Consumer Protection or Producer Protection.* What evidence is there in either *Sears* or *Compco* that suggests that the similarities in the product designs were tricking consumers into purchasing the Sears or Compco product believing it came from Stiffel or Day-Brite? Why did the Court rely on preemption rather than address the problems with the lower court decisions by tightening the secondary meaning requirements, or limiting protection for functional product designs?

2.   *The Trade Dress Cycle.* How did the trial and intermediate appellate courts rule in *Kellogg Co., Sears,* and *Compco*? Every thirty years it seems, courts use the rubric of unfair competition or trade dress to create a regime that generally and effectively forbids the imitation of any new and popular product. The Court then steps in to re-limit trade dress protection. The late-Professor Ralph S. Brown has argued that "[t]he imperfect stabilization of the concept of functionality (and related doctrines) probably stemmed, not from judicial obtuseness . . . [but from] a persistent urge to create some general protection against copiers. That urge has never achieved dominant expression in the cases. But it runs along like the Manichean heresy, forever pitting the forces of light and the alleged forces of darkness." Ralph S. Brown, *Product Simulation: A Right or A Wrong?*, 64 COLUM. L. REV. 1216, 1227 n.382 (1964). As you read through the cases in this Chapter tracing the rise of federal trade dress protection, see if the cycle of broad trade dress protection recurs.

3.   *Preemption: Express and Implied.* Federal preemption of state laws derives from the Supremacy Clause found in Article 6 of the United States Constitution. The second clause of Article 6 provides:

> This Constitution, and the Laws of the United States which shall be made in Pursuance thereof; and all Treaties made, or which shall be made, under the Authority of the United States, shall be the supreme Law of the Land; and the Judges in every State shall be bound thereby, any Thing in the Constitution or Laws of any State to the Contrary notwithstanding.

U.S. Const. Art. 6, cl. 2.

Federal preemption is not uniquely associated with patent and copyright law. Rather, *Sears* and *Compco* are merely one aspect of the Court's jurisprudence on preemption. In 2008 and 2009, for example, the Court held that a New York statute barring its trial courts from hearing claims seeking money for damages from a Corrections officer acting within the scope of his or her employment was inconsistent with and therefore preempted by section 1983, *Haywood v. Drown*, 556 U.S. 729 (2009); that recovery under Vermont product's liability law based upon inadequate labeling was not inconsistent with and therefore not preempted by FDA approval of the product's labeling, *Wyeth v. Levine*, 555 U.S. 555 (2009); that recovery under state Unfair Trade Practices Act based upon warning label on cigarettes was not inconsistent with and therefore not preempted by the Federal Cigarette Labeling and Advertising Act, *Altria Group, Inc. v. Good,* 555 U.S. 70 (2008); and that a California statute which prohibited several classes of employees that received state funds from using the funds to assist, promote, or deter union organizing was inconsistent with and hence preempted by the National Labor Relations Act. *Chamber of Commerce of the United States v. Brown*, 554 U.S. 60 (2008).

In general, federal preemption may be either express or implied. Express preemption arises when a federal statute expressly prohibits state law with respect to a specific issue. While neither the Trademark Act nor the Patent Act include an express preemption provision, the Copyright Act of 1976 does. Section 301(a) of the Copyright Act states:

> On and after January 1, 1978, all legal or equitable rights that are equivalent to any of the exclusive rights within the general scope of copyright as specified by section 106 [17 USCS § 106] in works of authorship that are fixed in a tangible medium of expression and come within the subject matter of copyright as specified by sections 102 and 103 [17 USCS §§ 102 and 103], whether created before or after that date and whether published or unpublished, are governed exclusively by this title. Thereafter, no person is entitled to any such right or equivalent right in any such work under the common law or statutes of any State.

17 U.S.C. § 301(a) (2015).

Whether Congress includes an express preemption provision or not, state law may also be impliedly preempted. Implied preemption arises in three circumstances. First, if the federal and state laws are directly inconsistent, so that it is not possible to obey both, the state law is preempted. Taking an example from copyright, section 204 of the Copyright Act requires that any assignment of a copyright be in writing and signed by the author to be enforceable. Yet, in most states, oral contracts, including oral assignments of personal property, are fully enforceable. As applied to copyrights, however, the state law allowing the enforcement of an oral assignment flatly contradicts the federal provision. As a result, the inconsistent state law is preempted and oral assignments of copyright are not enforceable. *See Valente-Kritzer Video v. Pinckney*, 881 F.2d 772, 774 (9th Cir. 1989), *cert. denied*, 493 U.S. 1062 (1990); *Library Pubs., Inc. v. Medical Economics Co.*, 548 F.Supp. 1231, 1233 (E.D. Pa. 1982), *aff'd*, 714 F.2d 123 (3d Cir. 1983). Is there an argument that the state protection of a product's design under unfair competition directly contradicts the federal Patent Act?

Second, even where state and federal law do not conflict directly, implied preemption also arises where they conflict indirectly. Although phrased in various ways by the Court, the key question here is whether enforcement of the state law would frustrate or impede the purposes of the federal statute. Would the protection of product design under state unfair competition law, as in *Sears* and *Compco*, create such an indirect conflict? What are the purposes of the federal statutes at issue? How would state protection under unfair competition law frustrate those purposes?

Third, federal law will also preempt state law where federal law so pervasively regulates a given area that it leaves no room for state law. *See Schneidewind v. ANR Pipeline Co.*, 485 U.S. 293, 299–300 (1988). In such a case, courts will say that federal law occupies the field, and will preempt any attempt by a state to regulate in the area. *Id.*

4. *Are* Sears *and* Compco *Still Good Law: State Trade Dress Protection?* As a formal matter, the Court has never expressly overruled either *Sears* or *Compco*, yet they are seldom treated as controlling today and, indeed, are often ignored entirely. Even with respect to state trade dress protection, lower courts have re-written *Sears* and *Comco* to stand for the proposition that product design may not receive protection unless secondary meaning and non-functionality were shown. *See, e.g., Ideal Toy Corp. v. Plawner Toy Mfg. Corp.*, 685 F.2d 78, 81 (3d Cir. 1982) (protecting "Rubik's Cube" design from imitation under state unfair competition law). As the Third Circuit said: "*Sears* and *Compco* do not preclude a court from affording protection [under state law] from infringement of a design element that has achieved secondary meaning and is non-functional, notwithstanding the absence of a patent." *Id.* Do you agree? What language in *Sears* or *Compco* supports such an interpretation? What language is inconsistent with such an interpretation? Did the Court in *Sears* and *Compco* reverse the lower court decisions on the factual grounds that the product designs at issue lacked secondary meaning or were functional? Did the Court reverse because the lower courts had failed to make findings on these issues?

Other courts, perhaps feeling not quite so brazen, found ways to distinguish the *Sears* and *Compco* decisions. For example, in *NFL Properties, Inc. v. Consumer Enters. Inc.*, the plaintiff sued to enjoin under state law the defendant's manufacture and sale of sew-on cloth emblems duplicating the emblems of NFL teams. 26 Ill.App.3d 814, 327 N.E.2d 242 (1975). The defendant argued, relying on *Sears* and *Compco*, that it was merely duplicating and selling a product unprotected by either federal patent or copyright law, and that its copying could not therefore be enjoined under state unfair competition law. *Id.* at 246. The court rejected the argument. It held that *Sears* and *Compco* did not apply because the article at issue was the trademark itself. *Id.* The court further held that the plaintiff was entitled to enjoin the sale of such emblems entirely. Ensuring that the defendant's products were properly labeled or included a disclaimer was not sufficient. According to the court, allowing the defendant to continue to sell the emblems, even if properly labeled, would not adequately protect "the property rights built up through the efforts of plaintiff." *Id.* at 247.

Do you agree that the court has adequately distinguished *Sears* and *Compco*? Could the plaintiffs in *Sears* and *Compco* have prevailed had they argued that their products were in fact their trademarks?

5.   Sears, Compco, *and Subsequent Developments in Preemption.* Chief Justice Burger replaced Chief Justice Warren in 1969 and came to the Court with a sharply different perspective regarding the proper relationship between the federal and state governments. In a pair of decisions that he authored, Chief Justice Burger sought to step away from the *Sears* and *Compco* approach to preemption in the field of intellectual property. *See Kewanee Oil Co. v. Bicron Corp.*, 416 U.S. 470 (1974); *Goldstein v. California*, 412 U.S. 546 (1973). In *Kewanee Oil Co.*, the Court held that the protection of a process for growing crystals, although neither patented nor copyrighted, could nevertheless receive protection under state trade secret law. 416 U.S. at 491–92. In *Goldstein*, the Court held that a state law prohibiting the copying of sound recordings, which at the time were not protected by federal copyright law, was also not preempted. 412 U.S. at 569–70. In both cases, Chief Justice Burger distinguished *Sears* and *Compco*, and held that the state law protection available complemented, rather than conflicted with, the protection provided under the federal patent and copyright statutes.

In *Sears* and *Compco*, the Court took the view that the patent and copyright statutes contained an implicit negative. Both statutes grant the inventor or author an exclusive right to make or copy a given invention or work of authorship, so long as certain prerequisites are satisfied. Both statutes thus, at least in the Warren Court's view, implicitly state that such an exclusive right is not available unless the prerequisites of the patent or the copyright statute are satisfied. A state law purporting to provide such an exclusive right, without satisfying the federal prerequisites, thus necessarily frustrates, and arguably directly conflicts, with the federal statutes.

Chief Justice Burger, however, rejected this view. That the federal law makes available an exclusive right in certain circumstances does not itself bar the states from making available an exclusive right in other circumstances. This is particularly true for a state law such as trade secret that has long existed alongside patent law. To the extent that preemption is primarily a question of congressional intent, the fact that Congress has long known about, and yet never indicated an intent to preempt, related state regulation in an area suggests that preemption would be inappropriate. *See Kewanee Oil Co.*, 416 U.S. at 494 (Marshall, J., concurring).

However, following Chief Justice Burger's retirement in 1986, the Court re-embraced the implicit negative view of federal patent law found in *Sears* and *Compco. Bonito Boats, Inc. v. Thunder Craft Boats, Inc.*, 489 U.S. 141 (1989). In *Bonito Boats,* the Court faced the question whether federal patent law preempted a recently enacted Florida statute that prohibited the copying of fiberglass boat hulls using a particular technique, known as plug molding. The Court held that the Florida statute was preempted. *Id.* at 159–62. In reaching that conclusion, the Court explained:

> [Under the Patent Act, t]he applicant whose invention satisfies the requirements of novelty, nonobviousness, and utility, and who is willing to reveal to the public the substance of his discovery and "the best mode . . . of carrying out his invention," 35 U.S.C. § 112, is granted "the right to exclude others from making, using, or selling the invention throughout the United States," for a period of 17 years. 35 U.S.C. § 154. The federal patent system thus embodies a carefully crafted bargain for encouraging the creation and disclosure of new, useful, and nonobvious advances in technology and design in return for the exclusive right to practice the invention for a period of years. . . .

> The attractiveness of such a bargain, and its effectiveness in inducing creative effort and disclosure of the results of that effort, depend almost entirely on a backdrop of free competition in the exploitation of unpatented designs and innovations. The novelty and nonobviousness requirements of patentability embody a congressional understanding, implicit in the Patent Clause itself, that free exploitation of ideas will be the rule, to which the protection of a federal patent is the exception. . . . The offer of federal protection from competitive exploitation of intellectual property would be rendered meaningless in a world where substantially similar state law protections were readily available. To a limited extent, the federal patent laws must determine not only what is protected, but also what is free for all to use.

Id. at 150–51. The Court therefore concluded that the Florida statute was preempted. By providing protection to the boat hull design, in circumstances where it was not entitled to protection under federal law, the Florida statute undermined the purposes of the Patent Act.

Despite embracing the reasoning of *Sears* and *Compco*, the *Bonito Boats* Court did not overrule its decisions in *Kewanee Oil* or *Goldstein*, leaving preemption with respect to intellectual property issues in a somewhat muddled state. Moreover, the *Bonito Boats* Court formally accepted the lower court's re-writing of *Sears* and *Compco* to permit the protection of product design under state unfair competition law where secondary meaning, non-functionality, and a likelihood of confusion were shown. In the Court's words:

> The pre-emptive sweep of our decisions in *Sears* and *Compco* has been the subject of heated scholarly and judicial debate. Read at their highest level of generality, the two decisions could be taken to stand for the proposition that the States are completely disabled from offering any form of protection to articles or processes which fall within the broad scope of patentable subject matter. Since the potentially patentable includes "anything under the sun that is made by man," *Diamond v. Chakrabarty*, 447 U.S. 303, 309 (1980) (citation omitted), the broadest reading of *Sears* would prohibit the States from regulating the deceptive simulation of trade dress or the tortious appropriation of private information.
>
> That the extrapolation of such a broad pre-emptive principle from *Sears* is inappropriate is clear from the balance struck in *Sears* itself. The *Sears* Court made it plain that the States "may protect businesses in the use of their trademarks, labels, or distinctive dress in the packaging of goods so as to prevent others, by imitating such markings, from misleading purchasers as to the source of the goods." *Sears, supra,* at 232 (footnote omitted). Trade dress is, of course, potentially the subject matter of design patents. Yet our decision in *Sears* clearly indicates that the States may place limited regulations on the circumstances in which such designs are used in order to prevent consumer confusion as to source. Thus, while *Sears* speaks in absolutist terms, its conclusion that the States may place some conditions on the use of trade dress indicates an implicit recognition that all state regulation of potentially patentable but unpatented subject matter is not ipso facto pre-empted by the federal patent laws.

Id. at 154 (internal citations omitted). In this discussion, is the Court using the words "dress" to include both a product's packaging and its design, or just its packaging?

6. *Do* Sears *and* Compco *Apply, and if so How, to Federal Trade Dress Protection?* As we shall see in the next section, plaintiffs seeking trade dress protection began asserting claims under section 43(a) of the Trademark Act in the 1970s. Given that the Trademark Act is, like the Patent Act, also a federal statute, what role should *Sears* and *Compco* play in deciding claims under section 43(a)?

Courts that have considered the issue have uniformly recognized that the doctrinal holding of *Sears* and *Compco* with respect to preemption of state law does not formally apply to a co-equal federal statute, such as the Trademark Act. Beyond that general agreement however, courts have sharply disagreed over the question whether the competition policies that animate the Court's decisions in *Sears* and *Compco* should play a role in shaping federal trade dress protection.

On one side, some courts have insisted that *Sears* and *Compco* have no relevance to the protection of trade dress under the Trademark Act. *See, e.g., Ferrari S.P.A. v. Roberts*, 944 F.2d 1235, 1241 (6th Cir. 1991), *cert. denied*, 505 U.S. 1219 (1992); *In re Teledyne Indus., Inc.*, 696 F.2d 968, 971 n.4 (Fed. Cir. 1982); *Dallas Cowboys Cheerleaders, Inc. v. Pussycat Cinema, Ltd.*, 604 F.2d 200, 204 (2d Cir. 1979); *In re Honeywell, Inc.*, 497 F.2d 1344, 1349 (C.C.P.A. 1974); *Rolls-Royce Motors, Ltd. v. A & A Fiberglass, Inc.*, 428 F.Supp. 689, 692 (N.D. Ga. 1976). These courts assert that trademarks and unfair competition serve an entirely different purpose than either patent or copyright, and hence there can be no conflict between them. *See, e.g., Kohler Co. v. Moen Inc.*, 12 F.3d 632, 637–43 (7th Cir. 1993); *W.T. Rogers Co. v. Keene*, 778 F.2d 334, 337 (7th Cir. 1985); *Truck Equip. Serv. Co. v. Fruehauf Corp.*, 536 F.2d 1210 (8th Cir.), *cert. denied*, 429 U.S. 861 (1976); *In re Mogen David Wine Corp.*, 328 F.2d 925, 928 (C.C.P.A. 1964).

On the other side, courts have recognized that overbroad federal trade dress protection can prove problematic in the same ways as the overbroad state trade dress protection at issue in *Sears* and *Compco*. Even if federal trade dress protection is not "preempted" by the patent or copyright statutes, federal trade dress protection should be tailored to avoid potential conflicts between the statutes. *See, e.g., Landscape Forms, Inc. v. Columbia Cascade Co.*, 113 F.3d 373 (2d Cir. 1997); *Versa Prods. Co. v. Bifold Co. (Mfg.) Ltd.*, 50 F.3d 189 (3d Cir. 1995); *Stormy Clime Ltd. v. ProGroup, Inc.*, 809 F.2d 971 (2d Cir. 1987).

In your opinion, which side has the better argument? If state trade dress protection can interfere with federal patent policy, as the Court specifically held in *Sears* and *Compco*, what difference does it make, in terms of the factual interference, as opposed to the legal question of preemption, whether the trade dress protection derives from state or federal law?

C. THE RISE OF FEDERAL TRADE DRESS CLAIMS

As we saw in section A, the common law denied technical trademark status to product features and packaging and relegated claims based upon the imitation of such features to the doctrine of unfair competition. When Congress enacted the Trademark Act of 1946, it considered the question whether it should change this approach and expressly allow protection of product packaging or configuration as trademarks. In the end, however, Congress limited registration on the principal register to traditional trademark subject matter, and relegated trade dress to the supplemental register. *Compare* 15 U.S.C. § 1127 (defining "trademarks" eligible for registration on the principal register to include "any word, name, symbol, or device, or any combination thereof. . . .") *with* 15 U.S.C. § 1091(c) (defining "marks" eligible for registration on the supplemental register to include "any trademark, symbol, label, package, configuration of goods, name, word, slogan, phrase, surname, geographical name, numeral, device, any matter that, as a whole, is not functional, or any combination of any of the foregoing. . . ."). Nevertheless, during the legislative history, the Department of Justice and others expressed the concern that section 2(f), because it used the broader word "mark," rather than the narrower word "trademark," would allow registration of trade dress on the principal register once it had become distinctive. 15 U.S.C. § 1052(f) ("[N]othing in this chapter shall prevent the registration of a mark used by the applicant which has become distinctive of the applicant's goods in commerce."). Proponents of the Trademark Act denied any intention to allow such cross-over registration, where a mark initially registered on the supplemental register would, with proof of secondary meaning, "cross-over" to the principal register, and the Act was specifically amended during the legislative process to foreclose such an interpretation.

Nonetheless, almost immediately after the Trademark Act passed, proponents of broader trade dress protection advanced the cross-over argument as a basis for the registration of product packaging and product design on the principal registration. Daphne Robert, for example, in her book, The New Trademark Manual, published the year after the Trademark Act's enactment, argued as follows:

> Packages and configurations of goods which have become distinctive through use may be registrable on the principal register under Section 2(f). That section provides that nothing in the Act shall prevent the registration of 'marks' which have become distinctive. "Marks" are defined as trade-marks, service-marks, collective marks, and certification marks entitled to registration, whether registered or not. Since packages and configurations of goods are entitled to registration under the Act [on the supplemental register], it would seem to follow that if they become distinctive they are registrable on the principal register.

DAPHNE ROBERT, THE NEW TRADEMARK MANUAL 67 (1947).

Despite these arguments, for the first twelve years following the Trademark Act's enactment, the Patent and Trademark Office uniformly rejected applications to register trade dress on the principal register. For example, in 1947, 3M applied to register the shape of its cellophane tape dispenser as a trademark on the principal register. When the examiner refused to register the tape dispenser, 3M appealed, advancing the cross-over registration argument. The Patent and Trademark Office squarely rejected it. *See In re Minnesota Mining & Mfg. Co.*, 92 U.S.P.Q. (BNA) 74, 75–76 (Comm'r 1952). In doing so, the Patent and Trademark Office confirmed the rule that neither product packaging nor product design were, as a matter of law, eligible for registration on the principal register. *Id.*; *see also Lucien Lelong, Inc. v. Lenel, Inc.*, 181 F.2d 3 (5th Cir. 1950);

In re Boye Needle Co., 100 U.S.P.Q. (BNA) 124, 124 (Comm'r 1953); *In re Mars Signal-Light Co.*, 85 U.S.P.Q. (BNA) 173, 175 (Comm'r 1950); *In re Pulitzer Pub. Co.*, 82 U.S.P.Q. (BNA) 229 (Comm'r 1949).

In 1958, however, a newly appointed Assistant Commissioner of Trademarks decided that the rules needed to be changed. In a case involving Haig & Haig's pinch whiskey bottle, Assistant Commissioner of Trademarks, Daphne Robert Leeds, reversed the longstanding rule barring the registration of trade dress as a trademark and allowed the registration of a product package on the principal register. In her opinion, Assistant Commissioner Leeds made no attempt to explain or justify her departure from established law and Congress's plain intentions. Nor did she advance the cross-over registration argument that she had articulated in her book. Rather, her reasoning, as such, consisted entirely of the strategic placement of dashes in a way meant to suggest that a bottle was a "symbol or device" within the meaning of the Trademark Act:

> The fundamental question, then, is not whether or not containers are registrable on the Principal Register, but it is whether or not what is presented is a trademark—a symbol or device—identifying applicant's goods and distinguishing them from those of others. . . .
>
> [T]he contour or conformation of the container may be a trademark—a symbol or device—which distinguishes the applicant's goods, and it may be registrable on the Principal Register.

In re Haig & Haig Ltd., 118 U.S.P.Q. (BNA) 229, 230, 231 (Comm'r 1958).

Even when Ms. Leeds's actions are viewed in the best possible light, Ms. Leeds simply took advantage of her authority as administrator to rewrite the statute to reflect her personal predilections and to override by fiat Congress's deliberate choice. As an exercise of judicial (or quasi-judicial) reasoning, the decision is an embarrassment, reflecting the sort of naked assertion of agency authority and administrator hubris about which the theories of agency capture and bureaucratic expansion warn.

Following the *In re Haig & Haig* decision in 1958, nearly twenty years passed before a federal appellate court—the Eighth Circuit in *Truck Equipment Service Co. v. Fruehauf Corp.*, 536 F.2d 1210 (8th Cir.), *cert. denied*, 429 U.S. 861 (1976)—first expressly affirmed a finding of liability for infringement of a trade dress claim under section 43(a) of the Trademark Act. In that case, the question whether Congress intended to allow such protection was not even raised. Instead, the defendants argued that *Sears* and *Compco* barred the availability of such protection. In reply, the court wrote: "Neither case is controlling here." The court then continued:

The language relied upon is *dictum*. The law of trademark and the issues of functionality and secondary meaning were not before the Court. The issue before the Court was whether state law could extend the effective term of patent protection granted by the federal statutes. The focus of the Court was the Supremacy Clause of the Constitution.

The protection accorded by the law of trademark and unfair competition is greater than that accorded by the law of patents because each is directed at a different purpose.

Id. at 1214–15. Rejecting the defendant's argument that *Sears* and *Compco* controlled, the Eighth Circuit became the first federal circuit to write trade dress protection into section 43(a). Do you see any problems with the Eighth Circuit's reasoning or its treatment of *Sears* and *Compco*? Other courts could not. Whatever the weaknesses in the Eighth Circuit's reasoning, over the succeeding decade, every other circuit joined with the Eighth and recognized a federal cause of action for trade dress infringement under section 43(a).

By the time that the Court directly addressed the requirements for trade protection under section 43(a) in 1992, nearly a half-century had passed since Congress enacted the Trademark Act of 1946. The fact that Congress intended to exclude so-called trade dress from federal protection entirely had been forgotten. In its place, both judges and lawyers had come to take federal trade dress protection for granted—an assumption that would lead Justice Marshall badly astray in the following case.

1. DISTINCTIVENESS

TWO PESOS, INC. V. TACO CABANA, INC.
505 U.S. 763 (1992)

MARSHALL, J.

The issue in this case is whether the trade dress of a restaurant may be protected under § 43(a) of the Trademark Act of 1946 (Lanham Act), 60 Stat. 441, 15 U.S.C. § 1125(a) (1982 ed.), based on a finding of inherent distinctiveness, without proof that the trade dress has secondary meaning.

I

Respondent Taco Cabana, Inc., operates a chain of fast-food restaurants in Texas. The restaurants serve Mexican food. The first Taco Cabana restaurant was opened in San Antonio in September 1978, and five more restaurants had been opened in San Antonio by 1985. Taco Cabana describes its Mexican trade dress as "a festive eating atmosphere having interior dining and patio areas decorated with artifacts, bright colors, paintings and murals. The patio includes interior and exterior areas with the interior patio capable of being sealed off from the outside patio by overhead garage doors. The stepped exterior of the building is a festive and vivid color scheme using top border paint and neon stripes. Bright awnings and umbrellas continue the theme." 932 F.2d 1113, 1117 (CA5 1991).

In December 1985, a Two Pesos, Inc., restaurant was opened in Houston. Two Pesos adopted a motif very similar to the foregoing description of Taco Cabana's trade dress. Two Pesos restaurants expanded rapidly in Houston and other markets, but did not enter San Antonio. In 1986, Taco Cabana entered the Houston and Austin markets and expanded into other Texas cities, including Dallas and El Paso where Two Pesos was also doing business.

In 1987, Taco Cabana sued Two Pesos in the United States District Court for the Southern District of Texas for trade dress infringement under § 43(a) of the Lanham Act, 15 U.S.C. § 1125(a) (1982 ed.), and for theft of trade secrets under Texas common law. The case was tried to a jury, which was instructed to return its verdict in the form of answers to five questions propounded by the trial judge. The jury's answers were: Taco Cabana has a trade dress; taken as a whole, the trade dress is nonfunctional; the trade dress is inherently distinctive; the trade dress has not acquired a secondary meaning in the Texas market; and the alleged infringement creates a likelihood of confusion on the part of ordinary customers as to the source or association of the restaurant's goods or services. Because, as the jury was told, Taco Cabana's trade dress was protected if it either was inherently distinctive or had acquired a secondary meaning, judgment was entered awarding damages to Taco Cabana. In the course of calculating damages, the trial court held that Two Pesos had intentionally and deliberately infringed Taco Cabana's trade dress.

The Court of Appeals ruled that the instructions adequately stated the applicable law and that the evidence supported the jury's findings. In particular, the Court of Appeals rejected petitioner's argument that a finding of no secondary meaning contradicted a finding of inherent distinctiveness.

In so holding, the court below followed precedent in the Fifth Circuit. In *Chevron Chemical Co. v. Voluntary Purchasing Groups, Inc.*, 659 F.2d 695, 702 (CA5 1981), the court noted that trademark law requires a demonstration of secondary meaning only when the claimed trademark is not sufficiently distinctive of itself to identify the producer; the court held that the same principles should apply to protection of trade dresses. The Court of Appeals noted that this approach conflicts with decisions of other courts, particularly the holding of the Court of Appeals for the Second Circuit in *Vibrant Sales, Inc. v. New Body Boutique, Inc.*, 652 F.2d 299 (1981), *cert. denied*, 455 U.S. 909 (1982), that § 43(a) protects unregistered trademarks or designs only where secondary meaning is shown. *Chevron, supra*, at 702. We granted certiorari to resolve the conflict among the Courts of Appeals on the question whether trade dress that is inherently distinctive is protectible under § 43(a) without a showing that it has acquired secondary meaning. 502 U.S. 1071 (1992). We find that it is, and we therefore affirm.

II

The Lanham Act was intended to make "actionable the deceptive and misleading use of marks" and "to protect persons engaged in . . . commerce against unfair competition." § 45, 15 U.S.C. § 1127. Section 43(a) "prohibits a broader range of practices than does § 32," which applies to registered marks, *Inwood Laboratories, Inc. v. Ives Laboratories, Inc.*, 456 U.S. 844, 858 (1982), but it is common ground that § 43(a) protects qualifying unregistered trademarks and that the general principles qualifying a mark for registration under § 2 of the Lanham Act are for the most part applicable in determining whether an unregistered mark is entitled to protection under § 43(a). *See A. J. Canfield Co. v. Honickman*, 808 F.2d 291, 299, n.9 (CA3 1986); *Thompson Medical Co. v. Pfizer Inc.*, 753 F.2d 208, 215–216 (CA2 1985).

A trademark is defined in 15 U.S.C. § 1127 as including "any word, name, symbol, or device or any combination thereof" used by any person "to identify and distinguish his or her goods, including a unique product, from those manufactured or sold by others and to indicate the source of the goods, even if that source is unknown." In order to be registered, a mark must be capable of distinguishing the applicant's goods from those of others. § 1052. Marks are often classified in categories of generally increasing distinctiveness; following the classic formulation set out by Judge Friendly, they may be (1) generic; (2) descriptive; (3) suggestive; (4) arbitrary; or (5) fanciful. *See Abercrombie & Fitch Co. v. Hunting World, Inc.*, 537 F.2d 4, 9 (CA2 1976). The Court of Appeals followed this classification and petitioner accepts it. Brief for Petitioner 11–15. The latter three categories of marks, because their intrinsic nature serves to identify a particular source of a product, are deemed inherently distinctive and are entitled to protection. In contrast, generic marks— those that "refer to the genus of which the particular product is a species," *Park 'N Fly, Inc. v. Dollar Park & Fly, Inc.*, 469 U.S. 189, 194 (1985), citing *Abercrombie & Fitch, supra*, at 9—are not registrable as trademarks. *Park 'N Fly, supra*, at 194.

Marks which are merely descriptive of a product are not inherently distinctive. When used to describe a product, they do not inherently identify a particular source, and hence cannot be protected. However, descriptive marks may acquire the distinctiveness which will allow them to be protected under the Act. Section 2 of the Lanham Act provides that a descriptive mark that otherwise could not be registered under the Act may be registered if it "has become distinctive of the applicant's goods in commerce." §§ 2(e), (f), 15 U.S.C. §§ 1052(e), (f). *See Park 'N Fly, supra*, at 194, 196. This acquired distinctiveness is generally called "secondary meaning." *See ibid.; Inwood Laboratories, supra*, at 851, n.11; *Kellogg Co. v. National Biscuit Co.*, 305 U.S. 111, 118 (1938). The concept of secondary meaning has been applied to actions under § 43(a). *See, e.g., University of Georgia Athletic Assn. v. Laite*, 756 F.2d 1535 (CA11 1985); *Thompson Medical Co. v. Pfizer Inc., supra*.

The general rule regarding distinctiveness is clear: An identifying mark is distinctive and capable of being protected if it *either* (1) is inherently distinctive *or* (2) has acquired distinctiveness through secondary meaning. Restatement (Third) of Unfair Competition § 13, pp. 37–38, and Comment *a* (Tent. Draft No. 2, Mar. 23, 1990). Cf. *Park 'N Fly, supra*, at 194. It is also clear that eligibility for protection under § 43(a) depends on nonfunctionality. *See, e.g., Inwood Laboratories, supra*, at 863 (WHITE, J., concurring in result); *see also, e.g., Brunswick Corp. v. Spinit Reel Co.*, 832 F.2d 513, 517 (CA10 1987); *First Brands Corp. v. Fred Meyer, Inc.*, 809 F.2d 1378, 1381 (CA9 1987); *Stormy Clime Ltd. v. ProGroup, Inc.*, 809 F.2d 971, 974 (CA2 1987); *Ambrit, Inc. v. Kraft, Inc.*, 812 F.2d 1531, 1535 (CA11 1986); *American Greetings Corp. v. Dan-Dee Imports, Inc.*, 807 F.2d 1136, 1141 (CA3 1986). It is, of course, also undisputed that liability under § 43(a) requires proof of the likelihood of confusion. *See, e.g., Brunswick Corp., supra*, at 516–517; *AmBrit, supra*, at 1535; *First Brands, supra*, at 1381; *Stormy Clime, supra*, at 974; *American Greetings, supra*, at 1141.

The Court of Appeals determined that the District Court's instructions were consistent with the foregoing principles and that the evidence supported the jury's verdict. Both courts thus ruled that Taco Cabana's trade dress was not descriptive but rather inherently distinctive, and that it was not functional. None of these rulings is before us in this case, and for present purposes we assume, without deciding, that each of them is correct. In going on to affirm the judgment for respondent, the Court of Appeals, following its prior decision in *Chevron*, held that Taco Cabana's inherently distinctive trade dress was entitled to protection despite the lack of proof of secondary meaning. It is this issue that is before us for decision, and we agree with its resolution by the Court of Appeals. There is no persuasive reason to apply to trade dress a general requirement of secondary meaning which is at odds with the principles generally applicable to infringement suits under § 43(a). Petitioner devotes much of its briefing to arguing issues that are not before us, and we address only its arguments relevant to whether proof of secondary meaning is essential to qualify an inherently distinctive trade dress for protection under § 43(a).

Petitioner argues that the jury's finding that the trade dress has not acquired a secondary meaning shows conclusively that the trade dress is not inherently distinctive. Brief for Petitioner 9. The Court of Appeals' disposition of this issue was sound:

> "Two Pesos' argument—that the jury finding of inherent distinctiveness contradicts its finding of no secondary meaning in the Texas market—ignores the law in this circuit. While the necessarily imperfect (and often prohibitively difficult) methods for assessing secondary meaning address the empirical question of current consumer association, the legal recognition of an inherently distinctive trademark or trade dress acknowledges the owner's legitimate proprietary interest in its unique and valuable informational device, regardless of whether substantial consumer association yet bestows the additional empirical protection of secondary meaning." 932 F.2d at 1120, n.7.

Although petitioner makes the above argument, it appears to concede elsewhere in its brief that it is possible for a trade dress, even a restaurant trade dress, to be inherently distinctive and thus eligible for protection under § 43(a). Brief for Petitioner 10–11, 17–18; Reply Brief for Petitioner 10–14. Recognizing that a general requirement of secondary meaning imposes "an unfair prospect of theft [or] financial loss" on the developer of fanciful or arbitrary trade dress at the outset of its use, petitioner suggests that such trade dress should receive limited protection without proof of secondary meaning. *Id.*, at 10. Petitioner argues that such protection should be only temporary and subject to defeasance when over time the dress has failed to acquire a secondary meaning. This approach is also vulnerable for the reasons given by the Court of Appeals. If temporary protection is available from the earliest use of the trade dress, it must be because it is neither functional nor descriptive, but an inherently distinctive dress that is capable of identifying a particular source of the product. Such a trade dress, or mark, is not subject to copying by concerns that have an equal opportunity to choose their own inherently distinctive trade dress. To terminate protection for failure to gain secondary meaning over some unspecified time could not be based on the failure of the dress to retain its fanciful, arbitrary, or suggestive nature, but on the failure of the user of the dress to be successful enough in the marketplace. This is not a valid basis to find a dress or mark ineligible for protection. The user of such a trade dress should be able to maintain what competitive position it has and continue to seek wider identification among potential customers.

This brings us to the line of decisions by the Court of Appeals for the Second Circuit that would find protection for trade dress unavailable absent proof of secondary meaning, a position that petitioner concedes would have to be modified if the temporary protection that it suggests is to be recognized. Brief for Petitioner 10–14. In *Vibrant Sales, Inc. v. New Body Boutique, Inc.*, 652 F.2d 299 (1981), the plaintiff claimed protection under § 43(a) for a product whose features the defendant had allegedly copied. The Court of Appeals held that unregistered marks did not enjoy the "presumptive source association" enjoyed by registered marks and hence could not qualify for protection under § 43(a) without proof of secondary meaning. *Id.*, at 303, 304. The court's rationale seemingly denied protection for unregistered, but inherently distinctive, marks of all kinds, whether the claimed mark used distinctive words or symbols or distinctive product design. The court thus did not accept the arguments that an unregistered mark was capable of identifying a source and that copying such a mark could be making any kind of a false statement or representation under § 43(a).

This holding is in considerable tension with the provisions of the Lanham Act. If a verbal or symbolic mark or the features of a product design may be registered under § 2, it necessarily is a mark "by which the goods of the applicant may be distinguished from the goods of others," 60 Stat. 428, and must be registered unless otherwise disqualified. Since § 2 requires secondary meaning only as a condition to registering descriptive marks, there are plainly marks that are registrable without showing secondary meaning. These same marks, even if not registered, remain inherently capable of distinguishing the goods of the users of these marks. Furthermore, the copier of such a mark may be seen as falsely claiming that his products may for some reason be thought of as originating from the plaintiff.

Some years after *Vibrant*, the Second Circuit announced in *Thompson Medical Co. v. Pfizer Inc.*, 753 F.2d 208 (1985), that in deciding whether an unregistered mark is eligible for protection under § 43(a), it would follow the classification of marks set out by Judge Friendly in *Abercrombie & Fitch*, 537 F.2d at 9. Hence, if an unregistered mark is deemed merely descriptive, which the verbal mark before the court proved to be, proof of secondary meaning is required; however, "suggestive marks are eligible for protection without any proof of secondary meaning, since the connection between the mark and the source is presumed." 753 F.2d at 216. The Second Circuit has nevertheless continued to deny protection for trade dress under § 43(a) absent proof of secondary meaning, despite the fact that § 43(a) provides no basis for distinguishing between trademark and trade dress. *See, e.g., Stormy Clime Ltd. v. ProGroup, Inc.*, 809 F.2d at 974; *Union Mfg. Co. v. Han Baek Trading Co.*, 763 F.2d 42, 48 (1985); *LeSportsac, Inc. v. K Mart Corp.*, 754 F.2d 71, 75 (1985).

The Fifth Circuit was quite right in *Chevron*, and in this case, to follow the *Abercrombie* classifications consistently and to inquire whether trade dress for which protection is claimed under § 43(a) is inherently distinctive. If it is, it is capable of identifying products or services as coming from a specific source and secondary meaning is not required. This is the rule generally applicable to trademarks, and the protection of trademarks and trade dress under § 43(a) serves the same statutory purpose of preventing deception and unfair competition. There is no persuasive reason to apply different analysis to the two. The "proposition that secondary meaning must be shown even if the trade dress is a distinctive, identifying mark, [is] wrong, for the reasons explained by Judge Rubin for the Fifth Circuit in *Chevron*." *Blau Plumbing, Inc. v. S. O. S. Fix-It, Inc.*, 781 F.2d 604, 608 (CA7 1986). The Court of Appeals for the Eleventh Circuit also follows *Chevron, AmBrit, Inc. v. Kraft, Inc.*, 805 F.2d 974, 979 (1986), and the Court of Appeals for the Ninth Circuit appears to think that proof of secondary meaning is superfluous if a trade dress is inherently distinctive, *Fuddruckers, Inc. v. Doc's B. R. Others, Inc.*, 826 F.2d 837, 843 (1987).

It would be a different matter if there were textual basis in § 43(a) for treating inherently distinctive verbal or symbolic trademarks differently from inherently distinctive trade dress. But there is none. The section does not mention trademarks or trade dress, whether they be called generic, descriptive, suggestive, arbitrary, fanciful, or functional. Nor does the concept of secondary meaning appear in the text of § 43(a). Where secondary meaning does appear in the statute, 15 U.S.C. § 1052 (1982 ed.), it is a requirement that applies only to merely descriptive marks and not to inherently distinctive ones. We see no basis for requiring secondary meaning for inherently distinctive trade dress protection under § 43(a) but not for other distinctive words, symbols, or devices capable of identifying a producer's product.

Engrafting onto § 43(a) a requirement of secondary meaning for inherently distinctive trade dress also would undermine the purposes of the Lanham Act. Protection of trade dress, no less than of trademarks, serves the Act's purpose to "secure to the owner of the mark the goodwill of his business and to protect the ability of consumers to distinguish among competing producers. National protection of trademarks is desirable, Congress concluded, because trademarks foster competition and the maintenance of quality by securing to the producer the benefits of good reputation." *Park 'N Fly*, 469 U.S. at 198, citing S. Rep. No. 1333, 79th Cong., 2d Sess., 3–5 (1946) (citations omitted). By making more difficult the identification of a producer with its product, a secondary meaning requirement for a nondescriptive trade dress would hinder improving or maintaining the producer's competitive position.

Suggestions that under the Fifth Circuit's law, the initial user of any shape or design would cut off competition from products of like design and shape are not persuasive. Only nonfunctional, distinctive trade dress is protected under § 43(a). The Fifth Circuit holds that a design is legally functional, and thus unprotectible, if it is one of a limited number of equally efficient options available to competitors and free competition would be unduly hindered by according the design trademark protection. *See Sicilia Di R. Biebow & Co. v. Cox*, 732 F.2d 417, 426 (1984). This serves to assure that competition will not be stifled by the exhaustion of a limited number of trade dresses.

On the other hand, adding a secondary meaning requirement could have anticompetitive effects, creating particular burdens on the startup of small companies. It would present special difficulties for a business, such as respondent, that seeks to start a new product in a limited area and then expand into new markets. Denying protection for inherently distinctive nonfunctional trade dress until after secondary meaning has been established would allow a competitor, which has not adopted a distinctive trade dress of its own, to appropriate the originator's dress in other markets and to deter the originator from expanding into and competing in these areas.

As noted above, petitioner concedes that protecting an inherently distinctive trade dress from its inception may be critical to new entrants to the market and that withholding protection until secondary meaning has been established would be contrary to the goals of the Lanham Act. Petitioner specifically suggests, however, that the solution is to dispense with the requirement of secondary meaning for a reasonable, but brief, period at the outset of the use of a trade dress. Reply Brief for Petitioner 11–12. If § 43(a) does not require secondary meaning at the outset of a business' adoption of trade dress, there is no basis in the statute to support the suggestion that such a requirement comes into being after some unspecified time.

III

We agree with the Court of Appeals that proof of secondary meaning is not required to prevail on a claim under § 43(a) of the Lanham Act where the trade dress at issue is inherently distinctive, and accordingly the judgment of that court is affirmed.

JUSTICE STEVENS and JUSTICE THOMAS concurred in separate opinions.

NOTES FOR DISCUSSION

1. *Imitation and Exact Duplication.* Just how similar were the two restaurants in *Two Pesos?* Although not appealed to the Supreme Court, the jury also found Two Pesos liable under a trade secret theory for misappropriating Taco Cabana's architectural plans and kitchen equipment

layout and design. *Taco Cabana Int'l v. Two Pesos, Inc.*, 932 F.2d 1113, 1123 (5th Cir. 1991), *aff'd on other grounds*, 505 U.S. 763 (1992). So the two restaurants were about as similar as one might expect given that they were both built from the same set of plans.

2. *Is "Not Descriptive" the Same as Inherently Distinctive?* In his *Two Pesos* opinion, Justice Marshall stated that the jury found that Taco Cabana's trade dress was inherently distinctive. This is not quite true. The jury was not asked if the trade dress was inherently distinctive. Instead, the jury interrogatory asked whether Taco Cabana's trade dress was "merely descriptive." Not knowing how to make sense of this non-sensical question, the jury answered it "no." Using the *Abercrombie* spectrum of distinctiveness, and the fact that neither party argued that the trade dress was generic, the Fifth Circuit re-interpreted this finding of "not merely descriptive" as a finding of "was inherently distinctive." *Taco Cabana Int'l*, 932 F.2d at 1120 n.8 ("As no one contends that Taco Cabana's trade dress is generic, the jury finding that the trade dress is not merely descriptive means that the dress is arbitrary, fanciful, or suggestive."). Do you agree with the Fifth Circuit's and Justice Marshall's re-interpretation of the jury's findings? Do you think the jury's answering "no" to a "merely descriptive" question means that the jury would necessarily have answered "yes" to an interrogatory asking whether the trade dress was "arbitrary, fanciful, or suggestive"? If we have to stick with the *Abercrombie* categories, which is the right question to ask? As an attorney for Taco Cabana, which question would you prefer? For Two Pesos? Alternatively, should we ask juries a question that focuses on the underlying meaning of inherent distinctiveness more directly? For example, how do you think a jury would have answered: "Do you find that consumers will rely on the 'festive eating atmosphere' of Taco Cabana's restaurants immediately and inherently to identify restaurants with such an atmosphere as Taco Cabana?"

3. *Alternate Interpretations of Congress's Failure to Include a Secondary Meaning Requirement in Section 2.* Justice Marshall reasons that because Congress omitted a specific secondary meaning requirement for trade dress from section 2 and included a secondary meaning requirement only for, *inter alia,* descriptive trademarks, Congress must have intended to limit the secondary meaning requirement to descriptive trade dress. What other explanation is there for Congress's failure in section 2 to state whether trade dress requires secondary meaning before it can be registered on the principal register? If Congress had intended to exclude trade dress from registration on the principal register altogether, would Congress have detailed the secondary meaning requirements for trade dress in section 2 or would it have omitted any such discussion? For a careful and thorough review of the historical record that demonstrates the Congress intended in 1946 to bar the registration of trade dress on the principal register altogether, see Glynn S. Lunney, Jr., *The Trade Dress Emperor's New Clothes: Why Trade Dress Does Not Belong on the Principal Register*, 52 HASTINGS L. REV. 1131 (2000).

4.   *Trade Dress Protection and Consumer Welfare.* Are consumers better off as a result of the *Two Pesos* decision? Given the difference in restaurant names prominently displayed, is there any real likelihood of consumer confusion? I lived in Houston when both Two Pesos and Taco Cabana restaurants operated there. Although I preferred Two Pesos to Taco Cabana, as I was driving around the I-610 loop near the Galleria area one day, I saw the characteristic shape that both restaurants shared. Being hungry and thinking it was a Two Pesos, I pulled off the freeway and only realized as I pulled into the restaurant that it was a Taco Cabana. Disappointed, but still hungry, I had Taco Cabana for lunch that day. So I can attest that consumer confusion did occur. Does that mean consumers are better off as a result of the *Two Pesos* decision?

Unfortunately, the *Two Pesos* decision forced Two Pesos out-of-business, so today when I drive through Houston, I no longer have a choice at all. Is this a situation where even though there may be some incidental confusion, consumers are still better off having competition and a choice?

5.   *Abercrombie versus Seabrook.* If we are going to allow some trade dress to be inherently distinctive, does it make more sense to identify inherently distinctive trade dress using the *Abercrombie* spectrum or the *Seabrook* approach. As discussed in Chapter 4, courts primarily use the *Abercrombie* spectrum for word marks, while they primarily use the *Seabrook* approach for designs or symbols. The *Seabrook* approach determines whether designs or symbols are inherently distinctive by looking at four factors:

> [1] whether it was a "common" basic shape or design, [2] whether it was unique or unusual in a particular field, [3] whether it was a mere refinement of a commonly-adopted and well-known form of ornamentation for a particular class of goods viewed by the public as a dress or ornamentation for the goods, or [4] whether it was capable of creating a commercial impression distinct from the accompanying words.

Seabrook Foods, Inc. v. Bar-Well Foods Ltd., 568 F.2d 1342, 1344 (C.C.P.A. 1978).

Would Taco Cabana's restaurant décor by inherently distinctive under the *Seabrook* approach?

6.   *Descriptive Trade Dress?* If we must apply the *Abercrombie* spectrum to trade dress, as the Court holds, what exactly would a descriptive restaurant décor look like? Perhaps, one example would be Oscar Meyer's wienermobile—a hot dog shaped vehicle from which they sell hot dogs. Can you think of any other examples?

7.   *Copyright: Real and Mutant.* Why didn't Taco Cabana seek protection for its restaurant design and décor under copyright law? Before 1990, copyright extended protection to architectural plans, but not to the buildings themselves. Congress changed this rule with the Architectural Works Copyright Protection Act, Pub. L. No. 101–650, 104 Stat. 5089 (1990). Unfortunately for Taco Cabana, the Act was not retroactive, but extended

protection only to those architectural works created on or after December 1, 1990. The Act did not therefore extend protection to Taco Cabana's restaurant, which first opened in San Antonio in 1978. Does the fact that Congress added architectural works to the Copyright Act support or undercut Justice Marshall's majority opinion?

Moreover, even if copyright protection had been available, the architect, and not Taco Cabana, would in all likelihood have been the copyright owner with respect to the plans for the restaurants. Are the interests of Taco Cabana and the architect the same or do they differ in important respects? For example, if, instead of misappropriating the plans from one of Taco Cabana's subcontractors, Two Pesos had purchased them from the architect, should the copyright interests of the architect prevail over the branding interests of Taco Cabana? Or should the branding interests of Taco Cabana prevail over the architect?

8. *Unthinking Judicial Activism.* In his concurrence, Justice Thomas recognizes that courts, and not Congress, added trade dress to section 43(a), but he argues that this is okay because the courts carefully considered whether and under what circumstances trade dress protection would be desirable. If only that were true. For the most part, courts have said very little about why trade dress protection makes sense. Most have pretended, just as Justice Marshall did with respect to the secondary meaning issue, that Congress has already resolved the issue. Others have simply taken trade dress protection for granted. At best, courts have suggested that protecting trade dress implicates concerns similar to those implicated by protecting trademarks and have therefore argued that trade dress protection is desirable by analogy. But the analogy is a poor one in that it overstates the benefits and understates the costs of trade dress protection.

On the benefit side, even where trade dress serves a source identification role, trade dress ordinarily is not the only means for conveying that information to consumers. So long as a producer can properly label her goods and receive protection for her traditional word and symbol trademarks, the producer has alternative means to convey source-related information to consumers. Although a second source for the same information has value, because some inattentive consumers may miss the first, the benefits consumers derive from the protection of trade dress is sharply less than the benefit from the protection of word marks because the trade dress simply duplicates information already available to consumers from the word marks. For trade dress to offer a real benefit to consumers requires evidence that purchasers or prospective purchasers of a product: (1) are relying on the dress to distinguish a product's or service's source; (2) have no other means available for distinguishing its source; and (3) are unlikely over time to develop the ability to distinguish between similar or similarly dressed products. Can you think of any products where you routinely rely on trade dress to identify a brand? Can you think of any products where you would be unable to find the brand you are looking for if others could freely copy its dress?

On the cost side, protecting trade dress almost always poses a more serious threat to competition than protecting a traditional word mark. Is Justice Marshall correct in his assertion that the functionality doctrine will forestall any threat to competition or eliminate any anticompetitive costs of trade dress protection? Keep in mind that before the *Two Pesos* decision, there were two, upscale drive-in Mexican restaurants in Houston. After the decision, there was only one. Of course, in theory, Two Pesos could re-open; it only needed to rebuild its restaurants entirely to do so. Which is less expensive and otherwise easier to do, changing a word mark associated with a product or changing the product's design or packaging? Even now, a new Two Pesos could arise to compete with Taco Cabana. All that *Two Pesos* requires is that the new challenger not copy Taco Cabana's appearance too closely. And yet, more than fifteen years after the *Two Pesos* decision, no such challenger has arisen. Should consumers take comfort in the fact that, at least theoretically, competition is not foreclosed, even though in reality, it has been?

Although we apply the same balance of costs and benefits to word marks, it is trivially easy to think of real-world examples where protection of a word as a trademark generates an unambiguous increase in consumer welfare. Can you think of any similar examples where protecting a product's packaging or design creates a similarly unambiguous increase? Would consumers be better off had the courts protected the pillow shape of shredded wheat or the shape of a crescent wrench as so-called trade dress? Were consumers looking for upscale drive-through Mexican food in Texas better off as a result of the *Two Pesos* decision? As you read through the remaining cases in this Chapter, see if you can identify even one where protecting a product's packaging or design as if it were a trademark unambiguously increases consumer welfare.

9. *Functionality.* Because Congress excluded trade dress from federal protection when it enacted the Trademark Act of 1946, Congress did not address functionality in the original statute. Despite this silence, courts universally followed the common law approach and held, just as Justice Marshall recognized in *Two Pesos*, that functional aspects of a product's design, features, or packaging could not receive protection. How can Justice Marshall recognize functionality as a limitation on federal trade dress protection when Congress, at the time of the decision, was silent on the issue, yet refuse to require proof of secondary meaning because Congress was silent on the issue?

Congress eventually added functionality to the Trademark Act as a limitation on registration under section 2 in 1998, and as a limitation on protection under section 43(a) in 1999. *See* Trademark Law Treaty Implementation Act, Pub. L. No. 330, 105th Cong., 2d Sess., § 201(a)(2)(A)(ii), 112 Stat. 3064, 3069 (1998), *codified at* 15 U.S.C. § 1052(e)(5) (2015); Trademark Amendments Act of 1999, Pub. L. No. 43, 106th Cong., 1st Sess., § 5, 113 Stat. 218, 220, *codified at* 15 U.S.C. § 1125(a)(3) (2015).

While we shall examine the issue of functionality in more detail in the next section, the Court set forth the present-day standard for functionality in *Inwood Labs. v. Ives Labs.*, 456 U.S. 844 (1982). In that case, the Court considered whether the blue-red coloring Ives Laboratories adopted for its Cyclospasmol brand of cyclandelate—a vasodilator used for long-term therapy for peripheral and cerebral vascular diseases—could be protected against imitation by generic manufacturers under section 43(a). The Court held that the coloring could not be protected because it served to differentiate this particular medicine, whether in brand or generic formulation, from other medicines. Can a similar argument be made that Taco Cabana's restaurant appearance served to differentiate the genus of upscale, drive-in Mexican restaurants from other drive-in Mexican restaurants? If consumers used the restaurant appearance to differentiate upscale drive-ins from others, would that render the appearance functional or generic?

10. *Ethics and the Trademark Defense Attorney.* Why didn't the attorneys for *Two Pesos* argue that Congress did not intend to provide protection for trade dress at all in the Lanham Act? Having failed to make that argument, did the attorneys argue for the Second Circuit's position that secondary meaning is always required? What did the attorneys for Two Pesos argue with respect to the secondary meaning requirement? Was there any support in the statute for their position? Why did the Two Pesos attorneys acknowledge that there was a prospect of "unfair theft or unfair financial loss" if secondary meaning were required? Too often, defendants in trademark litigation are represented by lawyers who usually represent trademark plaintiffs. This practice raises both ethical and practical questions.

Ethically, may an attorney represent a trade dress defendant in one case, when the attorney is actively seeking trade dress protection for other clients? The American Bar Association Model Rules of Professional Conduct state that "[a] lawyer shall not represent a client if the representation of that client may be materially limited by the lawyer's responsibilities to another client or to a third person, or by the lawyer's own interests. . . ." Rule 1.7(b). The Rules leave a lawyer some room to take contrary positions for different clients on a legal issue, *see* Rule 1.7, cmt. 9, and if the question is purely factual, such as whether particular trade dress satisfies a well-established legal requirement, such as functionality, the ethical issues are not insurmountable. However, when it is the legal requirements themselves that are at issue, may an attorney argue in one case that Congress did not intend to provide federal trade dress protection, while simultaneously arguing that Congress intended to provide such protection in another?

Moreover, even if an attorney may ethically represent both clients, often as a practical matter, the attorney will prove ineffective as an advocate for one position or the other. Long practice from the plaintiff's side of the bar may lead an attorney to develop blinders that handicap and constrain an attorney's ability to recognize and articulate the most compelling arguments from the other side. Had Two Pesos' attorneys looked at the historical genesis of federal trade protection, they could have answered Justice Marshall's question as to why Congress did not mention a secondary meaning requirement in section 2. Yet, they did not. Having missed the opportunity to set the record straight in *Two Pesos*, it now becomes far more difficult, although not impossible, for the rest of us to raise the issue in later cases.

QUALITEX CO. V. JACOBSON PRODS. CO.
514 U.S. 159 (1995)

BREYER, J.

The question in this case is whether the Trademark Act of 1946 (Lanham Act), 15 U.S.C. §§ 1051–1127 (1988 ed. and Supp. V), permits the registration of a trademark that consists, purely and simply, of a color. We conclude that, sometimes, a color will meet ordinary legal trademark requirements. And, when it does so, no special legal rule prevents color alone from serving as a trademark.

I

The case before us grows out of petitioner Qualitex Company's use (since the 1950's) of a special shade of green-gold color on the pads that it makes and sells to dry cleaning firms for use on dry cleaning presses. In 1989, respondent Jacobson Products (a Qualitex rival) began to sell its own press pads to dry cleaning firms; and it colored those pads a similar green-gold. In 1991, Qualitex registered the special green-gold color on press pads with the Patent and Trademark Office as a trademark. Registration No. 1,633,711 (Feb. 5, 1991). Qualitex subsequently added a trademark infringement count, 15 U.S.C. § 1114(1), to an unfair competition claim, § 1125(a), in a lawsuit it had already filed challenging Jacobson's use of the green-gold color.

Qualitex won the lawsuit in the District Court. 21 U.S.P.Q.2D (BNA) 1457 (CD Cal. 1991). But, the Court of Appeals for the Ninth Circuit set aside the judgment in Qualitex's favor on the trademark infringement claim because, in that Circuit's view, the Lanham Act does not permit Qualitex, or anyone else, to register "color alone" as a trademark. 13 F.3d 1297, 1300, 1302 (1994).

The Courts of Appeals have differed as to whether or not the law recognizes the use of color alone as a trademark. Compare *NutraSweet Co. v. Stadt Corp.*, 917 F.2d 1024, 1028 (CA7 1990) (absolute prohibition against protection of color alone), with *In re Owens-Corning Fiberglas Corp.*, 774 F.2d 1116, 1128 (CA Fed. 1985) (allowing registration of color pink for fiberglass insulation), and *Master Distributors, Inc. v. Pako Corp.*, 986 F.2d 219, 224 (CA8 1993) (declining to establish *per se* prohibition against protecting color alone as a trademark). Therefore, this Court granted certiorari. 512 U.S. 1287 (1994). We now hold that there is no rule absolutely barring the use of color alone, and we reverse the judgment of the Ninth Circuit.

II

The Lanham Act gives a seller or producer the exclusive right to "register" a trademark, 15 U.S.C. § 1052 (1988 ed. and Supp. V), and to prevent his or her competitors from using that trademark, § 1114(1). Both the language of the Act and the basic underlying principles of trademark law would seem to include color within the universe of things that can qualify as a trademark. The language of the Lanham Act describes that universe in the broadest of terms. It says that trademarks "include any word, name, symbol, or device, or any combination thereof." § 1127. Since human beings might use as a "symbol" or "device" almost anything at all that is capable of carrying meaning, this language, read literally, is not restrictive. The courts and the Patent and Trademark Office have authorized for use as a mark a particular shape (of a Coca-Cola bottle), a particular sound (of NBC's three chimes), and even a particular scent (of plumeria blossoms on sewing thread). *See, e.g.,* Registration No. 696,147 (Apr. 12, 1960); Registration Nos. 523,616 (Apr. 4, 1950) and 916,522 (July 13, 1971); *In re Clarke,* 17 U.S.P.Q.2D (BNA) 1238, 1240 (TTAB 1990). If a shape, a sound, and a fragrance can act as symbols why, one might ask, can a color not do the same?

A color is also capable of satisfying the more important part of the statutory definition of a trademark, which requires that a person "use" or "intend to use" the mark

> "to identify and distinguish his or her goods, including a unique product, from those manufactured or sold by others and to indicate the source of the goods, even if that source is unknown." 15 U.S.C. § 1127.

True, a product's color is unlike "fanciful," "arbitrary," or "suggestive" words or designs, which almost *automatically* tell a customer that they refer to a brand. *Abercrombie & Fitch Co. v. Hunting World, Inc.,* 537 F.2d 4, 9–10 (CA2 1976) (Friendly, J.); *see Two Pesos, Inc. v. Taco Cabana, Inc.,* 505 U.S. 763, 768 (1992). The imaginary word "Suntost," or the words "Suntost Marmalade," on a jar of orange jam immediately would signal a brand or a product "source"; the jam's orange color does not do so. But, over time, customers may come to treat a particular color on a product or its packaging (say, a color that in context seems unusual, such as pink on a firm's insulating material or red on the head of a large industrial bolt) as signifying a brand. And, if so, that color would have come to identify and distinguish the goods—*i.e.,* "to indicate" their "source"—much in the way that descriptive words on a product (say, "Trim" on nail clippers or "Car-Freshner" on deodorizer) can come to indicate a product's origin. *See, e.g., J. Wiss & Sons Co. v. W. E. Bassett Co.,* 462 F.2d 567 (Pat.), 462 F.2d 567, 569 (1972); *Car-Freshner Corp. v.*

Turtle Wax, Inc., 268 F. Supp. 162, 164 (SDNY 1967). In this circumstance, trademark law says that the word (*e.g.*, "Trim"), although not inherently distinctive, has developed "secondary meaning." *See Inwood Laboratories, Inc. v. Ives Laboratories, Inc.*, 456 U.S. 844, 851, n. 11 (1982) ("Secondary meaning" is acquired when "in the minds of the public, the primary significance of a product feature . . . is to identify the source of the product rather than the product itself"). Again, one might ask, if trademark law permits a descriptive word with secondary meaning to act as a mark, why would it not permit a color, under similar circumstances, to do the same?

We cannot find in the basic objectives of trademark law any obvious theoretical objection to the use of color alone as a trademark, where that color has attained "secondary meaning" and therefore identifies and distinguishes a particular brand (and thus indicates its "source"). In principle, trademark law, by preventing others from copying a source-identifying mark, "reduce[s] the customer's costs of shopping and making purchasing decisions," 1 J. McCarthy, McCarthy on Trademarks and Unfair Competition § 2.01[2], p. 2–3 (3d ed. 1994) (hereinafter McCarthy), for it quickly and easily assures a potential customer that *this* item—the item with this mark—is made by the same producer as other similarly marked items that he or she liked (or disliked) in the past. At the same time, the law helps assure a producer that it (and not an imitating competitor) will reap the financial, reputation-related rewards associated with a desirable product. The law thereby "encourage[s] the production of quality products," *ibid.*, and simultaneously discourages those who hope to sell inferior products by capitalizing on a consumer's inability quickly to evaluate the quality of an item offered for sale. *See, e.g.,* 3 L. Altman, Callmann on Unfair Competition, Trademarks and Monopolies § 17.03 (4th ed. 1983); Landes & Posner, The Economics of Trademark Law, 78 T. M. Rep. 267, 271–272 (1988); *Park 'N Fly, Inc. v. Dollar Park & Fly, Inc.*, 469 U.S. 189, 198 (1985); S. Rep. No. 100–515, p. 4 (1988). It is the source-distinguishing ability of a mark—not its ontological status as color, shape, fragrance, word, or sign—that permits it to serve these basic purposes. *See* Landes & Posner, Trademark Law: An Economic Perspective, 30 J. Law & Econ. 265, 290 (1987). And, for that reason, it is difficult to find, in basic trademark objectives, a reason to disqualify absolutely the use of a color as a mark.

Neither can we find a principled objection to the use of color as a mark in the important "functionality" doctrine of trademark law. The functionality doctrine prevents trademark law, which seeks to promote competition by protecting a firm's reputation, from instead inhibiting legitimate competition by allowing a producer to control a useful product feature. It is the province of patent law, not trademark law, to encourage invention by granting inventors a monopoly over new product designs or functions for a limited time, 35 U.S.C. §§ 154, 173, after which competitors are free to use the innovation. If a product's functional features could be used as trademarks, however, a monopoly over such features could be obtained without regard to whether they qualify as patents and could be extended forever (because trademarks may be renewed in perpetuity). *See Kellogg Co. v. National Biscuit Co.*, 305 U.S. 111, 119–120 (1938) (Brandeis, J.); *Inwood Laboratories, Inc., supra*, at 863 (White, J., concurring in result) ("A functional characteristic is 'an important ingredient in the commercial success of the product,' and, after expiration of a patent, it is no more the property of the originator than the product itself") (citation omitted). Functionality doctrine therefore would require, to take an imaginary example, that even if customers have come to identify the special illumination-enhancing shape of a new patented light bulb with a particular manufacturer, the manufacturer may not use that shape as a trademark, for doing so, after the patent had expired, would impede competition—not by protecting the reputation of the original bulb maker, but by frustrating competitors' legitimate efforts to produce an equivalent illumination-enhancing bulb. *See, e.g., Kellogg Co., supra*, at 119–120 (trademark law cannot be used to extend monopoly over "pillow" shape of shredded wheat biscuit after the patent for that shape had expired). This Court consequently has explained that, "in general terms, a product feature is functional," and cannot serve as a trademark, "if it is essential to the use or purpose of the article or if it affects the cost or quality of the article," that is, if exclusive use of the feature would put competitors at a significant non-reputation-related disadvantage. *Inwood Laboratories, Inc., supra*, at 850, n. 10. Although sometimes color plays an important role (unrelated to source identification) in making a product more desirable, sometimes it does not. And, this latter fact—the fact that sometimes color is not essential to a product's use or purpose and does not affect cost or quality—indicates that the doctrine of "functionality" does not create an absolute bar to the use of color alone as a mark. *See Owens-Corning*, 774 F.2d at 1123 (pink color of insulation in wall "performs no non-trademark function").

It would seem, then, that color alone, at least sometimes, can meet the basic legal requirements for use as a trademark. It can act as a symbol that distinguishes a firm's goods and identifies their source, without serving any other significant function. *See* U.S. Dept. of Commerce, Patent and Trademark Office, Trademark Manual of Examining Procedure § 1202.04(e), p. 1202–13 (2d ed. May, 1993) (hereinafter PTO Manual) (approving trademark registration of color alone where it "has become distinctive of the applicant's goods in commerce," provided that "there is [no] competitive need for colors to remain available in the industry" and the color is not "functional"); *see also* 1 McCarthy §§ 3.01[1], 7.26, pp. 3–2, 7–113 ("requirements for qualification of a word or symbol as a trademark" are that it be (1) a "symbol," (2) "used ... as a mark," (3) "to identify and distinguish the seller's goods from goods made or sold by others," but that it not be "functional"). Indeed, the District Court, in this case, entered findings (accepted by the Ninth Circuit) that show Qualitex's green-gold press pad color has met these requirements. The green-gold color acts as a symbol. Having developed secondary meaning (for customers identified the green-gold color as Qualitex's), it identifies the press pads' source. And, the green-gold color serves no other function. (Although it is important to use *some* color on press pads to avoid noticeable stains, the court found "no competitive need in the press pad industry for the green-gold color, since other colors are equally usable." 21 U.S.P.Q.2D (BNA) at 1460.) Accordingly, unless there is some special reason that convincingly militates against the use of color alone as a trademark, trademark law would protect Qualitex's use of the green-gold color on its press pads.

III

Respondent Jacobson Products says that there are four special reasons why the law should forbid the use of color alone as a trademark. We shall explain, in turn, why we, ultimately, find them unpersuasive.

First, Jacobson says that, if the law permits the use of color as a trademark, it will produce uncertainty and unresolvable court disputes about what shades of a color a competitor may lawfully use. Because lighting (morning sun, twilight mist) will affect perceptions of protected color, competitors and courts will suffer from "shade confusion" as they try to decide whether use of a similar color on a similar product does, or does not, confuse customers and thereby infringe a trademark. Jacobson adds that the "shade confusion" problem is "more difficult" and "far different from" the "determination of the similarity of words or symbols." Brief for Respondent 22.

We do not believe, however, that color, in this respect, is special. Courts traditionally decide quite difficult questions about whether two words or phrases or symbols are sufficiently similar, in context, to confuse buyers. They have had to compare, for example, such words as "Bonamine" and "Dramamine" (motion-sickness remedies); "Huggies" and "Dougies" (diapers); "Cheracol" and "Syrocol" (cough syrup); "Cyclone" and "Tornado" (wire fences); and "Mattres" and "1-800-Mattres" (mattress franchisor telephone numbers). *See, e.g., G. D. Searle & Co. v. Chas. Pfizer & Co.*, 265 F.2d 385, 389 (CA7 1959); *Kimberly-Clark Corp. v. H. Douglas Enterprises, Ltd.*, 774 F.2d 1144, 1146–1147 (CA Fed. 1985); *Upjohn Co. v. Schwartz*, 246 F.2d 254, 262 (CA2 1957); *Hancock v. American Steel & Wire Co. of N.J.*, 40 C.C.P.A. 931, 935, 203 F.2d 737, 740–741 (1953); *Dial-A-Mattress Franchise Corp. v. Page*, 880 F.2d 675, 678 (CA2 1989). Legal standards exist to guide courts in making such comparisons. *See, e.g.*, 2 McCarthy § 15.08; 1 McCarthy §§ 11.24–11.25 ("Strong" marks, with greater secondary meaning, receive broader protection than "weak" marks). We do not see why courts could not apply those standards to a color, replicating, if necessary, lighting conditions under which a colored product is normally sold. *See* Ebert, Trademark Protection in Color: Do It By the Numbers!, 84 T. M. Rep. 379, 405 (1994). Indeed, courts already have done so in cases where a trademark consists of a color plus a design, *i.e.*, a colored symbol such as a gold stripe (around a sewer pipe), a yellow strand of wire rope, or a "brilliant yellow" band (on ampules). *See, e.g., Youngstown Sheet & Tube Co. v. Tallman Conduit Co.*, 149 U.S.P.Q. (BNA) 656, 657 (TTAB 1966); *Amsted Industries, Inc. v. West Coast Wire Rope & Rigging Inc.*, 2 U.S.P.Q.2D (BNA) 1755, 1760 (TTAB 1987); *In re Hodes-Lange Corp.*, 167 U.S.P.Q. (BNA) 255, 256 (TTAB 1970).

Second, Jacobson argues, as have others, that colors are in limited supply. *See, e.g., NutraSweet Co.*, 917 F.2d at 1028; *Campbell Soup Co. v. Armour & Co.*, 175 F.2d 795, 798 (CA3 1949). Jacobson claims that, if one of many competitors can appropriate a particular color for use as a trademark, and each competitor then tries to do the same, the supply of colors will soon be depleted. Put in its strongest form, this argument would concede that "hundreds of color pigments are manufactured and thousands of colors can be obtained by mixing." L. Cheskin, Colors: What They Can Do For You 47 (1947). But, it would add that, in the context of a particular product, only some colors are usable. By the time one discards colors that, say, for reasons of customer appeal, are not usable, and adds the shades that competitors cannot use lest they risk infringing a similar, registered shade, then one is left with only a handful of possible colors. And, under these circumstances, to permit one, or a few, producers to use colors as trademarks will "deplete" the supply of usable colors to the point where a competitor's inability to find a suitable color will put that competitor at a significant disadvantage.

This argument is unpersuasive, however, largely because it relies on an occasional problem to justify a blanket prohibition. When a color serves as a mark, normally alternative colors will likely be available for similar use by others. *See, e.g., Owens-Corning*, 774 F.2d at 1121 (pink insulation). Moreover, if that is not so—if a "color depletion" or "color scarcity" problem does arise—the trademark doctrine of "functionality" normally would seem available to prevent the anticompetitive consequences that Jacobson's argument posits, thereby minimizing that argument's practical force.

The functionality doctrine, as we have said, forbids the use of a product's feature as a trademark where doing so will put a competitor at a significant disadvantage because the feature is "essential to the use or purpose of the article" or "affects [its] cost or quality." *Inwood Laboratories, Inc.*, 456 U.S. at 850, n. 10. The functionality doctrine thus protects competitors against a disadvantage (unrelated to recognition or reputation) that trademark protection might otherwise impose, namely their inability reasonably to replicate important non-reputation-related product features. For example, this Court has written that competitors might be free to copy the color of a medical pill where that color serves to identify the kind of medication (*e.g.*, a type of blood medicine) in addition to its source. *See id.*, at 853, 858, n. 20 ("Some patients commingle medications in a container and rely on color to differentiate one from another"); *see also* J. Ginsburg, D. Goldberg, & A. Greenbaum, Trademark and Unfair Competition Law 194–195 (1991) (noting that drug color cases "have more to do with public health policy" regarding generic drug substitution "than with trademark law"). And, the federal courts have demonstrated that they can apply this doctrine in a careful and reasoned manner, with sensitivity to the effect on competition. Although we need not comment on the merits of specific cases, we note that lower courts have permitted competitors to copy the green color of farm machinery (because customers wanted their farm equipment to match) and have barred the use of black as a trademark on outboard boat motors (because black has the special functional attributes of decreasing the apparent size of the motor and ensuring compatibility with many different boat colors). *See Deere & Co. v. Farmhand, Inc.*, 560 F. Supp. 85, 98 (SD Iowa 1982), aff'd, 721 F.2d 253 (CA8 1983); *Brunswick Corp. v. British Seagull Ltd.*, 35 F.3d 1527, 1532 (CA Fed. 1994), cert. pending, No. 94–1075; *see also Nor-Am Chemical* v. *O. M. Scott & Sons Co.*, 4 U.S.P.Q.2D (BNA) 1316, 1320 (ED Pa. 1987) (blue color of fertilizer held functional because it indicated the presence of nitrogen). The Restatement (Third) of Unfair Competition adds that, if a design's "aesthetic value" lies in its ability to "confer a significant benefit that cannot practically be duplicated by the use of alternative designs," then the design is "functional." Restatement (Third) of Unfair Competition § 17, Comment *c*, pp. 175–176 (1993). The "ultimate test of aesthetic functionality," it explains, "is whether the recognition of trademark rights would significantly hinder competition."

The upshot is that, where a color serves a significant nontrademark function—whether to distinguish a heart pill from a digestive medicine or to satisfy the "noble instinct for giving the right touch of beauty to common and necessary things," G. Chesterton, Simplicity and Tolstoy 61 (1912)—courts will examine whether its use as a mark would permit one competitor (or a group) to interfere with legitimate (nontrademark-related) competition through actual or potential exclusive use of an important product ingredient. That examination should not discourage firms from creating esthetically pleasing mark designs, for it is open to their competitors to do the same. *See, e.g., W.T. Rogers Co. v. Keene*, 778 F.2d 334, 343 (CA7 1985) (Posner, J.). But, ordinarily, it should prevent the anticompetitive consequences of Jacobson's hypothetical "color depletion" argument, when, and if, the circumstances of a particular case threaten "color depletion."

Third, Jacobson points to many older cases—including Supreme Court cases—in support of its position. In 1878, this Court described the common-law definition of trademark rather broadly to "consist of a name, symbol, figure, letter, form, or device, if adopted and used by a manufacturer or merchant in order to designate the goods he manufactures or sells to distinguish the same from those manufactured or sold by another." *McLean* v. *Fleming*, 96 U.S. 245, 254. Yet, in interpreting the Trademark Acts of 1881 and 1905, 21 Stat. 502, 33 Stat. 724, which retained that common-law definition, the Court questioned "whether mere color can constitute a valid trade-mark," *A. Leschen & Sons Rope Co. v. Broderick & Bascom Rope Co.*, 201 U.S. 166, 171 (1906), and suggested that the "product including the coloring matter is free to all who make it," *Coca-Cola Co. v. Koke Co. of America*, 254 U.S. 143, 147 (1920). Even though these statements amounted to dicta, lower courts interpreted them as forbidding protection for color alone. *See, e.g., Campbell Soup Co.*, 175 F.2d at 798, and n. 9; *Life Savers Corp. v. Curtiss Candy Co.*, 182 F.2d 4, 9 (CA7 1950) (*Campbell Soup, supra*, at 798).

These Supreme Court cases, however, interpreted trademark law as it existed *before* 1946, when Congress enacted the Lanham Act. The Lanham Act significantly changed and liberalized the common law to "dispense with mere technical prohibitions," S. Rep. No. 1333, 79th Cong., 2d Sess., 3 (1946), most notably, by permitting trademark registration of descriptive words (say, "U-Build-It" model airplanes) where they had acquired "secondary meaning." *See Abercrombie & Fitch Co.*, 537 F.2d at 9 (Friendly, J.). The Lanham Act extended protection to descriptive marks by making clear that (with certain explicit exceptions not relevant here)

> "nothing . . . shall prevent the registration of a mark used by the applicant which has become distinctive of the applicant's goods in commerce." 15 U.S.C. § 1052(f) (1988 ed., Supp. V).

This language permits an ordinary word, normally used for a nontrademark purpose (*e.g.*, description), to act as a trademark where it has gained "secondary meaning." Its logic would appear to apply to color as well. Indeed, in 1985, the Federal Circuit considered the significance of the Lanham Act's changes as they related to color and held that trademark protection for color was consistent with the

> "jurisprudence under the Lanham Act developed in accordance with the statutory principle that if a mark is capable of being or becoming distinctive of [the] applicant's goods in commerce, then it is capable of serving as a trademark." *Owens-Corning*, 774 F.2d at 1120.

In 1988, Congress amended the Lanham Act, revising portions of the definitional language, but left unchanged the language here relevant. § 134, 102 Stat. 3946, 15 U.S.C. § 1127. It enacted these amendments against the following background: (1) the Federal Circuit had decided *Owens-Corning;* (2) the Patent and Trademark Office had adopted a clear policy (which it still maintains) permitting registration of color as a trademark, *see* PTO Manual § 1202.04(e) (at p. 1200–12 of the January 1986 edition and p. 1202–13 of the May 1993 edition); and (3) the Trademark Commission had written a report, which recommended that "the terms 'symbol, or device' . . . not be deleted or narrowed to preclude registration of such things as a color, shape, smell, sound, or configuration which functions as a mark," The United States Trademark Association Trademark Review Commission Report and Recommendations to USTA President and Board of Directors, 77 T. M. Rep. 375, 421 (1987); *see also* 133 Cong. Rec. 32812 (1987) (statement of Sen. DeConcini) ("The bill I am introducing today is based on the Commission's report and recommendations"). This background strongly suggests that the language "any word, name, symbol, or device," 15 U.S.C. § 1127, had come to include color. And, when it amended the statute, Congress retained these terms. Indeed, the Senate Report accompanying the Lanham Act revision explicitly referred to this background understanding, in saying that the "revised definition intentionally retains . . . the words 'symbol or device' so as not to preclude the registration of colors, shapes, sounds or configurations where they function as trademarks." S. Rep. No. 100–515, at 44. (In addition, the statute retained language providing that "no trademark by which the goods of the applicant may be distinguished from the goods of others shall be refused registration . . . on account of its nature" (except for certain specified reasons not relevant here). 15 U.S.C. § 1052 (1988 ed., Supp. V).)

This history undercuts the authority of the precedent on which Jacobson relies. Much of the pre-1985 case law rested on statements in Supreme Court opinions that interpreted pre-Lanham Act trademark law and were not directly related to the holdings in those cases. Moreover, we believe the Federal Circuit was right in 1985 when it found that the 1946 Lanham Act embodied crucial legal changes that liberalized the law to permit the use of color alone as a trademark (under appropriate circumstances). At a minimum, the Lanham Act's changes left the courts free to reevaluate the preexisting legal precedent which had absolutely forbidden the use of color alone as a trademark. Finally, when Congress reenacted the terms "word, name, symbol, or device" in 1988, it did so against a legal background in which those terms had come to include color, and its statutory revision embraced that understanding.

Fourth, Jacobson argues that there is no need to permit color alone to function as a trademark because a firm already may use color as part of a trademark, say, as a colored circle or colored letter or colored word, and may rely upon "trade dress" protection, under § 43(a) of the Lanham Act, if a competitor copies its color and thereby causes consumer confusion regarding the overall appearance of the competing products or their packaging, *see* 15 U.S.C. § 1125(a) (1988 ed., Supp. V). The first part of this argument begs the question. One can understand why a firm might find it difficult to place a usable symbol or word on a product (say, a large industrial bolt that customers normally see from a distance); and, in such instances, a firm might want to use color, pure and simple, instead of color as part of a design. Neither is the second portion of the argument convincing. Trademark law helps the holder of a mark in many ways that "trade dress" protection does not. *See* 15 U.S.C. § 1124 (ability to prevent importation of confusingly similar goods); § 1072 (constructive notice of ownership); § 1065 (incontestible status); § 1057(b) (prima facie evidence of validity and ownership). Thus, one can easily find reasons why the law might provide trademark protection in addition to trade dress protection.

IV

Having determined that a color may sometimes meet the basic legal requirements for use as a trademark and that respondent Jacobson's arguments do not justify a special legal rule preventing color alone from serving as a trademark (and, in light of the District Court's here undisputed findings that Qualitex's use of the green-gold color on its press pads meets the basic trademark requirements), we conclude that the Ninth Circuit erred in barring Qualitex's use of color as a trademark. For these reasons, the judgment of the Ninth Circuit is

Reversed.

NOTES FOR DISCUSSION

1.   *A "Word, Name, Symbol, or Device."* Section 43(a) reaches in part "any person who . . . uses . . . any word, term, name, symbol, or device, or any combination thereof . . . which is likely to cause confusion." 15 U.S.C. § 1125(a)(1)(A). Section 45 defines a trademark eligible for registration on the principal register to include "any word, name, symbol, or device, or any combination thereof." 15 U.S.C. § 1127. Justice Breyer tells us that the word "symbol" in these sections means "almost anything at all that is capable of carrying meaning." While that is one possible meaning of the word "symbol," the word also has narrower meanings, such as "emblem or insignia," that would encompass only things such as the Ralph Lauren polo player or the Izod alligator. If we were philosopher kings, monks, or Ph.D. students in English Literature, then we could pick whatever meaning of "symbol" strikes our fancy. But as lawyers and judges interpreting a statute in order to determine Congress's intent, that path is presumably not open to us. Instead, there are rules that guide our choice between two possible interpretations of statutory language. Consider the following rules and see whether they point to a narrow or broad definition of the word "symbol" in section 43(a) and the statutory definition of a trademark in section 45.

a.   In statutory language, we give words with a recognized legal meaning their legal rather than their ordinary meaning. Before the enactment of the Trademark Act in 1946, the words "symbol" and "device" had long been part of the common law's definition of a technical trademark. *See, e.g., McLean v. Fleming*, 96 U.S. 245, 254 (1878). Yet, as cases such as *Kellogg Co.* and *Crescent Tool Co.* reflect, these words, when used in the common law's definition of a trademark, did not encompass trade dress. Instead, as terms of art in the field of trademark law, they carried their narrower meaning of emblem or insignia. Should the Court have followed the narrower legal definition of "symbol" or a broader, ordinary language meaning in interpreting the Trademark Act?

b.   In interpreting a statute, "[i]t is the duty of the Court to give effect, if possible, to every clause and word of a statute." *Tabor v. Ulloa*, 323 F.2d 823, 824 (9th Cir. 1963). Interpreting "symbol" as "anything at all that is capable of carrying meaning" violates this rule by rendering the other parts of the definition of a trademark—"word, name, symbol, or device, or any combination thereof"—redundant and superfluous. Moreover, as a matter of ordinary English grammar, how likely is it that Congress would put a catch-all category in the middle of its list, particularly when there was already a catch-all category at the end of the list? Substituting the Court's definition for "symbol" into the statutory list directly, how sensible is the resulting phrase "word, name, anything at all that is capable of carrying meaning, or device, or any combination thereof"? How sensible is the list if we substitute the traditional definition of symbol as "emblem" into the list, "word, name, emblem, or device, or any combination thereof"?

c.   In interpreting a statute, we should not interpret words to ignore differences in statutory language that Congress has deliberately adopted. In the Trademark Act, Congress defines a "trademark" and "service mark" eligible for registration on the principal register to include "any word, name, symbol, or device, or any combination thereof". 15 U.S.C. § 1127 (definition of trademark and service mark). In contrast, Congress defined "marks" eligible for registration on the supplemental register to include "any trademark, symbol, label, package, configuration of goods, name, word, slogan, phrase, surname, geographical name, numeral device, any matter that, as a whole, is not functional, or any combination of any of the foregoing." 15 U.S.C. § 1091(c). By defining trademarks and marks differently, Congress plainly intended to define a broader class of subject matter as eligible for registration on the supplemental register. Further, Congress specifically included trade dress—"package, configuration of goods"—on the list of marks eligible for registration on the supplemental register, but omitted them from the list of trademarks eligible for registration on the principal register. Should we give effect to this difference or should we interpret "symbol" so broadly as to eliminate it?

d.   Where Congress amends statutory language during the legislative process, we should interpret the resulting statutory language in a way that gives effect to the amendment. From its first introduction in 1924 until 1943, the bills that would eventually become the Trademark Act of 1946 defined "trademark" in broad fashion. For example, S. 2679, introduced in 1924, defined trademarks registrable on the principal register as follows: "The term 'trade-mark' includes any mark so used as to distinguish the source or origin of the user's goods. . . ." S. 2679, 68th Cong., 1st Sess. § 31 (1924). H.R. 9041, introduced in 1938, provided: "The term 'trade-mark' includes any mark so used as to distinguish the user's goods from the goods of others. . . ." H.R. 9041, 75th Cong., 3d Sess. § 43 (1938), *reprinted in Trade-marks: Hearings on H.R. 9041 Before the Subcomm. on Trade-marks of the House Comm. on Patents,* 75th Cong., 3d Sess. 9 (1938). Similarly, H.R. 102 and H.R. 4744, introduced in 1941 and 1939, respectively, provided that "[t]he terms 'trade-mark' and 'mark' include any mark which is entitled to registration under the terms of this Act and whether registered or not." H.R. 102, 77th Cong., 1st Sess. § 45 (1941), *reprinted in Trade-marks: Hearings on H.R. 102, H.R. 5461, and S. 895 Before the Subcomm. on Trade-marks of the House Comm. on Patents,* 77th Cong., 1st Sess. 13 (1941); H.R. 4744, 76th Cong., 1st Sess. § 46 (1939), *reprinted in Trade-marks: Hearings on H.R. 4744 Before the Subcomm. on Trade-marks of the House Comm. on Patents,* 76th Cong., 1st Sess. 172 (1939) ("The term 'trade-mark' includes any mark which is entitled to registration under the terms of this Act and whether registered or not."). All of these bills expressly defined "trademarks" as "any mark" and may thereby have incorporated by reference the broad definition of "marks" eligible for registration on the supplemental register. The 1924 and 1938 bills also focused eligibility for registration exclusively on whether the thing claimed as a trademark was being "so used as to distinguish" the applicant's goods, implicitly suggesting that distinguishing use was the sole test for registrability.

In 1943, just three years before final enactment, Congress amended the definition of "trademark" in the proposed bill and replaced it with the language eventually adopted, defining a trademark to include "any word, name, symbol, or device." By doing so, didn't Congress make clear, contrary to Justice Breyer's suggestion, that in determining what is eligible for protection as a trademark, ontological status matters?

2. *Functionality, Aesthetic Functionality, and Colors.* When is a color functional? For trademark purposes, when we talk about functionality, is it a question of whether the color makes the product work better or is it a question of consumer acceptance? Consider two examples. First, is the color blue functional for a toilet bowl cleanser? Does it make the product work better? Will consumers accept some other color? What other colors would consumers accept? A nice golden yellow? A rich, chocolate brown? What does it mean for a product to "work better"? Even if a product is, in some sense, functionally identical, if consumers will not actually switch to it in response to a price increase on some other product, do the two products compete?

Second, how about the color brown for colas? Is that functional? The natural color of cola when it is made is clear; the brown is simply dye that the manufacturer adds to the product. Does that mean the color brown is not functional? In the early 1990s, Pepsi marketed a clear cola product, Crystal Pepsi. Its market stay was short-lived. Consumers refused to accept a clear cola. Why? While I can't say for sure, part of the reason certainly had to do with conditioned consumer response. After years of associating clear, carbonated beverages with a lemon-lime flavor, such as Sprite or Seven-Up, there was simply too much conflict when the brain was saying "lemon-lime" and the taste buds were saying "cola."

What about the examples that the Court cites? Why is a particular shade of green, so commonly associated with John Deere that it is generally known as John Deere green, functional for tractors? Do you really believe that farmers, given their well-known aesthetic sensibilities, were concerned about the extent to which their new farm equipment would color coordinate with their old? It is undoubtedly true that copying John Deere's green color scheme facilitated market entry for foreign tractor manufacturers. Farmers preferred to purchase foreign tractors that were colored John Deere green. That's why the foreign manufacturers chose the color. Of course, the green coloring—camouflage of sorts—doesn't fool the farmers purchasing the foreign tractors; they know exactly which tractor store they went to and from whom they were buying. Whom does it fool? In 1988, the Trademark Trial and Appeal Board rejected the Iowa district court's finding of functionality and allowed Deere & Co. to register a color scheme consisting of a uniform green color for the body and yellow wheels for farm equipment on the principal register. *See In re* Deere & Co., 7 U.S.P.Q.2d (BNA) 1401, 1404 (T.T.A.B. 1988). Which court's decision better balances consumers' competing interests? If you believe that we should allow other farm equipment manufacturers to use John Deere green because it facilitates competitive entry against an entrenched and dominant market player, can a similar argument be made to allow Jacobson to copy the green-gold coloring of the dominant player in its industry in order to facilitate competitive entry? Are consumers better or worse off, on balance, if we protect John Deere green as if it were a trademark?

Is the color black functional for an outboard motor? The Court cites with approval a Federal Circuit decision saying that it was. In its opinion, the Federal Circuit gave two reasons why black is functional for outboard motors. First, it makes the outboard motor appear smaller. Is that a feature that consumers of outboard motors are looking for? Do they want their outboards to appear smaller? Or is this just rationalizing a result that is plainly sensible for other reasons? The second reason for finding black functional is that black readily matches many other color schemes. What about blue or silver or green? Can you give some specific reasons why each of those colors might be functional as applied to outboard motors? Do we have to invent some clever, but transparently disingenuous argument as to why these colors are functional, such as blue matching the color of the sky?

Should we have to give some specific reason why a particular color is better before competitors should be allowed to use it? Are there consumers who might prefer a blue or silver or green or black boat motor—not for what it may tell them about who made it, but just because they like the color? Is that enough to show functionality? Should it be? Does it make more sense to leave manufacturers free to compete in every color so long as they plainly label their motors, or should we leave it to the courts to determine whether we will have competition or monopoly in boat motors of a given color based upon the court's assessment of whether that particular color serves some "substantial non-reputation related" purpose?

3. *Secondary Meaning and Colors.* Justice Breyer requires proof of secondary meaning before a uniform color can receive protection as a trademark. What statutory basis is there for this requirement? How would you prove it in any event? Is circumstantial evidence such as long and exclusive use or extensive advertising or sales enough to establish secondary meaning? How does such evidence show that consumers have moved from primarily perceiving a color aesthetically to primarily perceiving the color as a brand? For example, if the walls of a retail store have been painted a uniform shade of lilac for twenty years, does that establish that consumers have come to rely upon the wall color as a source identifier?

Consider three statements that a consumer might make with respect to a color:

a. As a consumer, I prefer green-gold dry-cleaning pads because I associate the green-gold color with Qualitex, and I believe that pads made by Qualitex are better.

b. As a consumer, I prefer green-gold dry-cleaning pads because I believe green-gold pads are better.

c. I've always used green-gold dry-cleaning pads, and they have worked great for me. I intend to keep using them.

Are any or all of these statements evidence of secondary meaning? *See Huston v. Buckeye Bait Corp.*, 145 F.Supp. 600, 607 (S.D. Ohio 1955) ("There must be an established identity so that one looks at the product externally and says 'That is the article I want because I know the source of its production and I want the article made by that manufacturer.' "). Which statement most naturally represents how a consumer might think about the issue? If a plaintiff can show that the color does not in fact affect the performance of the product, that the color, for example, is just a dye added to the final product, does that make the second statement equivalent to the first? If a plaintiff can show that it is the only company that has marketed green-gold dry-cleaning pads, does that make the second statement equivalent to the first? Can circumstantial evidence of long use or extensive sales distinguish between these statements? Could you devise a survey that would distinguish between these statements?

Which statements suggest that Jacobson would face a more difficult time persuading consumers to use its dry cleaning pads if it cannot color them green-gold? Which statements, if any, suggest that the color is functional in that Jacobson would face a "significant non-reputation related disadvantage" if it could not use the color green-gold for its dry cleaning pads?

4.   *Trade Dress and Competitive Entry.* As in *Two Pesos*, the ultimate issue for consumers is a balancing of the benefits they can obtain from Jacobson's competitive entry against the potential confusion and higher search costs if the copying is permitted. While secondary meaning and functionality are both on-off legal results, in the real world, they are more questions of degree: How much more difficult will it be for Jacobson to enter this market if it can't use the green-gold color? Is it none, some, or a lot given that the long use of the color by the dominant market player may have conditioned customers to look for green-gold dry-cleaning pads? At the very least, if Jacobson can't use the green-gold pads, it will likely face somewhat more difficulty entering the dry-cleaning pad market. Depending on the market conditions, it's possible that the difficulty may increase enough to persuade Jacobson not to enter the market at all.

On the infringement side, the legal question is again on-off: Is there or is there not a likelihood of confusion? For consumers, however, the reality will again be a question of degree: How much more difficult for consumers would it be to find the precise brand they want if both Qualitex and Jacobson pads are green-gold? Depending on marketplace conditions, how the goods are purchased, and what other means are available to distinguish the two manufacturers' pads, that the pads are the same color may increase the costs of distinguishing the two brands not at all, some, or a lot.

Given that both sides of the balance are questions of degree, is there a way to combine these two questions to reflect a true balancing of the consumer's concerns, rather than try to answer them separately? For example, under one set of market conditions, allowing Jacobson to copy the color might increase consumer search costs only a little. Granting protection to the color as a trademark would thus yield little benefit to consumers. In such a case, the harms to consumers of protecting the color would outweigh its benefits so long as protection entails even a small threat to competition by slightly increasing the costs for Jacobson to enter the market or by slightly increasing the risk that Jacobson will decide not to enter the market. In other cases, allowing Jacobson to copy the color might increase consumer search costs considerably. Granting protection would therefore yield more substantial benefits to consumers. These more substantial benefits might still be outweighed if protection posed a correspondingly substantial threat to competition or eliminated it entirely, but the threat to competition would have to be more serious than in the first case to outweigh the more substantial consumer benefit.

Ideally, doctrines such as functionality, secondary meaning, and likelihood of confusion should be tailored to incorporate this balance, so that courts extend protection and find infringement more readily where the defendant's behavior generates only slight or trivial benefits for consumers, on the one hand, and on the other, extend protection and find infringement less readily where the defendant's behavior advances consumers interests more directly. While the Court in both *Two Pesos* and *Qualitex* shows almost no awareness of the need to incorporate such sensitivity into trademark doctrine, the Court in other cases, such as *Kellogg Co.*, does a much better job balancing the competing interests trademark and unfair competition law are supposed to serve.

5. *Consumer Confusion?* Given the nature of the customers for dry cleaning pads, how likely is it that dry cleaning businesses will purchase the Jacobson dry cleaning pads believing that they are receiving the Qualitex pads because of the pads' similar coloring?

6. *Results and Reasoning.* In what way or ways does the Court follow the path it set in *Two Pesos*? In what way or way does the Court blaze a new path?

The Aftermath of *Two Pesos*

Following the *Two Pesos* decision, several things occurred. First, the trickle of trade dress infringement cases filed under the federal Trademark Act which only began in the 1970s became a flood. Essentially every time a new and successful product, service, or business format was introduced and then imitated, a suit for trade dress infringement inevitably followed. For example, plaintiffs asserted that copying golf course holes constituted trade dress infringement, *see Pebble Beach, Co. v. Tour 18 I Ltd.*, 155 F.3d 526 (5th Cir. 1998); that copying furniture designs constituted trade dress infringement, *see, e.g., Ashley Furniture Indus., Inc. v. SanGiamo N.A., Ltd.*, 187 F.3d 363 (4th Cir. 1999); *Landscape Forms, Inc. v. Columbia Cascade Co.*, 113 F.3d 373 (2d Cir. 1997); that copying the design of a cable tie used to bundle wires constituted trade dress infringement, *see Thomas & Betts Corp. v. Panduit Corp.*, 138 F.3d 277 (7th Cir.), *cert. denied*, 525 U.S. 929 (1998); that copying the profile of a steel deck used in construction constituted trade dress infringement, *see Epic Metals Corp. v. Souliere*, 99 F.3d 1034 (11th Cir. 1996); and that copying a toilet-shaped coin bank constituted trade dress infringement. *See Fun-Damental Too v. Gemmy Indus. Corp.*, 111 F.3d 993 (2d Cir. 1997).

Second, a split developed in applying the *Two Pesos* decision. By the nature of judicial authority, the *Two Pesos* decision resolved the question whether trade dress could be inherently distinctive only for restaurant decor. When the question arose whether the generic-descriptive-suggestive-arbitrary-fanciful spectrum should be applied to other forms of trade dress, some lower courts refused to extend *Two Pesos* to cases where a party claimed the design, configuration, or particular features of its product as trade dress. Arguing that the *Ambercrombie* spectrum was non-sensical as applied to such product design trade dress (though, in practice, it was equally non-sensical as applied to product packaging), some lower courts developed alternative approaches to separating product design trade dress that was inherently distinctive from product design that required proof of secondary meaning. For example, the Third Circuit in *Duraco Prods. v. Joy Plastic Enters.* held that "to be inherently distinctive, a product configuration— comprising a product feature or some particular combination or arrangement of product features—for which Lanham Act protection is sought must be (i) unusual and memorable; (ii) conceptually separable from the product; and (iii) likely to serve primarily as a designator of origin of the product." 40 F.3d 1431, 1448–49 (3d Cir. 1994). In *Knitwaves, Inc. v. Lollytogs Ltd.*, the Second Circuit also refused to extend *Two Pesos* to product designs. Instead, the court asked "whether [the feature at issue] is 'likely to serve primarily as a designator of origin of the product.'" 71 F.3d 996, 1008 (2d Cir. 1995) (*quoting Duraco Prods.*, 40 F.3d at 1449). Other circuits refused to limit *Two Pesos* to its factual context and extended the generic-descriptive-suggestive-arbitrary-fanciful rubric to product design, as well as product packaging, trade dress claims. *See, e.g., Stuart Hall Co. v. Ampad Corp.*, 51 F.3d 780, 787–88 (8th Cir. 1995).

To resolve this split, the Court granted *certiorari* in *Wal-Mart Stores, Inc. v. Samara Bros.* As set forth in Wal-Mart's opening brief, the question presented on certiorari was: "What must be shown to establish that a product's design is inherently distinctive for purposes of Lanham Act trade dress protection?"

WAL-MART STORES, INC. V. SAMARA BROS., INC.

529 U.S. 205 (2000)

SCALIA, J.

In this case, we decide under what circumstances a product's design is distinctive, and therefore protectible, in an action for infringement of unregistered trade dress under § 43(a) of the Trademark Act of 1946 (Lanham Act), 60 Stat. 441, as amended, 15 U.S.C. § 1125(a).

I

Respondent Samara Brothers, Inc., designs and manufactures children's clothing. Its primary product is a line of spring/summer one-piece seersucker outfits decorated with appliques of hearts, flowers, fruits, and the like. A number of chain stores, including JCPenney, sell this line of clothing under contract with Samara.

Petitioner Wal-Mart Stores, Inc., is one of the nation's best known retailers, selling among other things children's clothing. In 1995, Wal-Mart contracted with one of its suppliers, Judy-Philippine, Inc., to manufacture a line of children's outfits for sale in the 1996 spring/summer season. Wal-Mart sent Judy-Philippine photographs of a number of garments from Samara's line, on which Judy-Philippine's garments were to be based; Judy-Philippine duly copied, with only minor modifications, 16 of Samara's garments, many of which contained copyrighted elements. In 1996, Wal-Mart briskly sold the so-called knockoffs, generating more than $1.15 million in gross profits.

In June 1996, a buyer for JCPenney called a representative at Samara to complain that she had seen Samara garments on sale at Wal-Mart for a lower price than JCPenney was allowed to charge under its contract with Samara. The Samara representative told the buyer that Samara did not supply its clothing to Wal-Mart. Their suspicions aroused, however, Samara officials launched an investigation, which disclosed that Wal-Mart and several other major retailers—Kmart, Caldor, Hills, and Goody's—were selling the knockoffs of Samara's outfits produced by Judy-Philippine.

After sending cease-and-desist letters, Samara brought this action in the United States District Court for the Southern District of New York against Wal-Mart, Judy-Philippine, Kmart, Caldor, Hills, and Goody's for copyright infringement under federal law, consumer fraud and unfair competition under New York law, and—most relevant for our purposes—infringement of unregistered trade dress under § 43(a) of the Lanham Act, 15 U.S.C. § 1125(a). All of the defendants except Wal-Mart settled before trial.

After a weeklong trial, the jury found in favor of Samara on all of its claims. Wal-Mart then renewed a motion for judgment as a matter of law, claiming, *inter alia*, that there was insufficient evidence to support a conclusion that Samara's clothing designs could be legally protected as distinctive trade dress for purposes of § 43(a). The District Court denied the motion, 969 F. Supp. 895 (SDNY 1997), and awarded Samara damages, interest, costs, and fees totaling almost $1.6 million, together with injunctive relief, *see* App. to Pet. for Cert. 56–58. The Second Circuit affirmed the denial of the motion for judgment as a matter of law, 165 F.3d 120 (1998), and we granted certiorari, 528 U.S. 808 (1999).

II

The Lanham Act provides for the registration of trademarks, which it defines in § 45 to include "any word, name, symbol, or device, or any combination thereof [used or intended to be used] to identify and distinguish [a producer's] goods . . . from those manufactured or sold by others and to indicate the source of the goods. . . ." 15 U.S.C. § 1127. Registration of a mark under § 2 of the Act, 15 U.S.C. § 1052, enables the owner to sue an infringer under § 32, 15 U.S.C. § 1114; it also entitles the owner to a presumption that its mark is valid, *see* § 7(b), 15 U.S.C. § 1057(b), and ordinarily renders the registered mark incontestable after five years of continuous use, *see* § 15, 15 U.S.C. § 1065. In addition to protecting registered marks, the Lanham Act, in § 43(a), gives a producer a cause of action for the use by any person of "any word, term, name, symbol, or device, or any combination thereof . . . which . . . is likely to cause confusion . . . as to the origin, sponsorship, or approval of his or her goods. . . ." 15 U.S.C. § 1125(a). It is the latter provision that is at issue in this case.

The breadth of the definition of marks registrable under § 2, and of the confusion-producing elements recited as actionable by § 43(a), has been held to embrace not just word marks, such as "Nike," and symbol marks, such as Nike's "swoosh" symbol, but also "trade dress"—a category that originally included only the packaging, or "dressing," of a product, but in recent years has been expanded by many courts of appeals to encompass the design of a product. *See, e.g., Ashley Furniture Industries, Inc. v. Sangiacomo N. A., Ltd.*, 187 F.3d 363 (CA4 1999) (bedroom furniture); *Knitwaves, Inc. v. Lollytogs, Ltd.*, 71 F.3d 996 (CA2 1995) (sweaters); *Stuart Hall Co., Inc. v. Ampad Corp.*, 51 F.3d 780 (CA8 1995) (notebooks). These courts have assumed, often without discussion, that trade dress constitutes a "symbol" or "device" for purposes of the relevant sections, and we conclude likewise. "Since human beings might use as a 'symbol' or 'device' almost anything at all that is capable of carrying meaning, this language, read literally, is not restrictive." *Qualitex Co. v. Jacobson Products Co.*, 514 U.S. 159, 162 (1995). This reading of § 2 and § 43(a) is buttressed by a recently added subsection of § 43(a), § 43(a)(3), which refers specifically to "civil actions for trade dress infringement under this chapter for trade dress not registered on the principal register." 15 U.S.C. § 1125(a)(3) (Oct. 1999 Supp.).

The text of § 43(a) provides little guidance as to the circumstances under which unregistered trade dress may be protected. It does require that a producer show that the allegedly infringing feature is not "functional," *see* § 43(a)(3), and is likely to cause confusion with the product for which protection is sought, *see* § 43(a)(1)(A), 15 U.S.C. § 1125(a)(1)(A). Nothing in § 43(a) explicitly requires a producer to show that its trade dress is distinctive, but courts have universally imposed that requirement, since without distinctiveness the trade dress would not "cause confusion . . . as to the origin, sponsorship, or approval of [the] goods," as the section requires. Distinctiveness is, moreover, an explicit prerequisite for registration of trade dress under § 2, and "the general principles qualifying a mark for registration under § 2 of the Lanham Act are for the most part applicable in determining whether an unregistered mark is entitled to protection under § 43(a)." *Two Pesos, Inc. v. Taco Cabana, Inc.*, 505 U.S. 763, 768 (1992) (citations omitted).

In evaluating the distinctiveness of a mark under § 2 (and therefore, by analogy, under § 43(a)), courts have held that a mark can be distinctive in one of two ways. First, a mark is inherently distinctive if "[its] intrinsic nature serves to identify a particular source." *Ibid.* In the context of word marks, courts have applied the now-classic test originally formulated by Judge Friendly, in which word marks that are "arbitrary" ("Camel" cigarettes), "fanciful" ("Kodak" film), or "suggestive" ("Tide" laundry detergent) are held to be inherently distinctive. *See Abercrombie & Fitch Co. v. Hunting World, Inc.*, 537 F.2d 4, 10–11 (CA2 1976). Second, a mark has acquired distinctiveness, even if it is not inherently distinctive, if it has developed secondary meaning, which occurs when, "in the minds of the public, the primary significance of a [mark] is to identify the source of the product rather than the product itself." *Inwood*

Laboratories, Inc. v. Ives Laboratories, Inc., 456 U.S. 844, 851, n. 11 (1982).

The judicial differentiation between marks that are inherently distinctive and those that have developed secondary meaning has solid foundation in the statute itself. Section 2 requires that registration be granted to any trademark "by which the goods of the applicant may be distinguished from the goods of others"—subject to various limited exceptions. 15 U.S.C. § 1052. It also provides, again with limited exceptions, that "nothing in this chapter shall prevent the registration of a mark used by the applicant which has become distinctive of the applicant's goods in commerce"—that is, which is not inherently distinctive but has become so only through secondary meaning. § 2(f), 15 U.S.C. § 1052(f). Nothing in § 2, however, demands the conclusion that *every* category of mark necessarily includes some marks "by which the goods of the applicant may be distinguished from the goods of others" *without* secondary meaning—that in every category some marks are inherently distinctive.

Indeed, with respect to at least one category of mark—colors—we have held that no mark can ever be inherently distinctive. *See Qualitex*, 514 U.S. at 162–163. In *Qualitex*, petitioner manufactured and sold green-gold dry-cleaning press pads. After respondent began selling pads of a similar color, petitioner brought suit under § 43(a), then added a claim under § 32 after obtaining registration for the color of its pads. We held that a color could be protected as a trademark, but only upon a showing of secondary meaning. Reasoning by analogy to the *Abercrombie & Fitch* test developed for word marks, we noted that a product's color is unlike a "fanciful," "arbitrary," or "suggestive" mark, since it does not "almost *automatically* tell a customer that [it] refers to a brand," *ibid.*, and does not "immediately . . . signal a brand or a product 'source,' " 514 U.S. at 163. However, we noted that, "over time, customers may come to treat a particular color on a product or its packaging . . . as signifying a brand." 514 U.S. at 162–163. Because a color, like a "descriptive" word mark, could eventually "come to indicate a product's origin," we concluded that it could be protected *upon a showing of secondary meaning. Ibid.*

It seems to us that design, like color, is not inherently distinctive. The attribution of inherent distinctiveness to certain categories of word marks and product packaging derives from the fact that the very purpose of attaching a particular word to a product, or encasing it in a distinctive packaging, is most often to identify the source of the product. Although the words and packaging can serve subsidiary functions—a suggestive word mark (such as "Tide" for laundry detergent), for instance, may invoke positive connotations in the consumer's mind, and a garish form of packaging (such as Tide's squat, brightly decorated plastic bottles for its liquid laundry detergent) may attract an otherwise indifferent consumer's attention on a crowded store shelf—their predominant function remains source identification. Consumers are therefore predisposed to regard those symbols as indication of the producer, which is why such symbols "almost *automatically* tell a customer that they refer to a brand," 514 U.S. at 162–163, and "immediately . . . signal a brand or a product 'source,'" 514 U.S. at 163. And where it is not reasonable to assume consumer predisposition to take an affixed word or packaging as indication of source—where, for example, the affixed word is descriptive of the product ("Tasty" bread) or of a geographic origin ("Georgia" peaches)—inherent distinctiveness will not be found. That is why the statute generally excludes, from those word marks that can be registered as inherently distinctive, words that are "merely descriptive" of the goods, § 2(e)(1), 15 U.S.C. § 1052 (e)(1), or "primarily geographically descriptive of them," *see* § 2(e)(2), 15 U.S.C. § 1052(e)(2). In the case of product design, as in the case of color, we think consumer predisposition to equate the feature with the source does not exist. Consumers are aware of the reality that, almost invariably, even the most unusual of product designs—such as a cocktail shaker shaped like a penguin—is intended not to identify the source, but to render the product itself more useful or more appealing.

The fact that product design almost invariably serves purposes other than source identification not only renders inherent distinctiveness problematic; it also renders application of an inherent-distinctiveness principle more harmful to other consumer interests. Consumers should not be deprived of the benefits of competition with regard to the utilitarian and esthetic purposes that product design ordinarily serves by a rule of law that facilitates plausible threats of suit against new entrants based upon alleged inherent distinctiveness. How easy it is to mount a plausible suit depends, of course, upon the clarity of the test for inherent distinctiveness, and where product design is concerned we have little confidence that a reasonably clear test can be devised. Respondent and the United States as *amicus curiae* urge us to adopt for product design relevant portions of the test formulated by the Court of Customs and Patent Appeals for product packaging in *Seabrook Foods, Inc. v. Bar-Well Foods, Ltd.*, 568 F.2d 1342 (1977). That opinion, in determining the inherent distinctiveness of a product's packaging, considered, among other things, "whether it was a 'common' basic shape or design, whether it was unique or unusual in a particular field, [and] whether it was a mere refinement of a commonly-adopted and well-known form of ornamentation for a particular class of goods viewed by the public as a dress or ornamentation for the goods." (footnotes omitted). Such a test would rarely provide the basis for summary disposition of an anticompetitive strike suit. Indeed, at oral argument, counsel for the United States quite understandably would not give a definitive answer as to whether the test was met in this very case, saying only that "this is a very difficult case for that purpose."

It is true, of course, that the person seeking to exclude new entrants would have to establish the nonfunctionality of the design feature, *see* § 43(a)(3), 15 U.S.C. § 1125(a)(3) (Oct. 1999 Supp.)—a showing that may involve consideration of its esthetic appeal, *see Qualitex*, 514 U.S. at 170. Competition is deterred, however, not merely by successful suit but by the plausible threat of successful suit, and given the unlikelihood of inherently source-identifying design, the game of allowing suit based upon alleged inherent distinctiveness seems to us not worth the candle. That is especially so since the producer can ordinarily obtain protection for a design that *is* inherently source identifying (if any such exists), but that does not yet have secondary meaning, by securing a design patent or a copyright for the design—as, indeed, respondent did for certain elements of the designs in this case. The availability of these other protections greatly reduces any harm to the producer that might ensue from our conclusion that a product design cannot be protected under § 43(a) without a showing of secondary meaning.

Respondent contends that our decision in *Two Pesos* forecloses a conclusion that product-design trade dress can never be inherently distinctive. In that case, we held that the trade dress of a chain of Mexican restaurants, which the plaintiff described as "a festive eating atmosphere having interior dining and patio areas decorated with artifacts, bright colors, paintings and murals," 505 U.S. at 765 (internal quotation marks and citation omitted), could be protected under § 43(a) without a showing of secondary meaning, *see* 505 U.S. at 776. *Two Pesos* unquestionably establishes the legal principle that trade dress can be inherently distinctive, *see, e.g.*, 505 U.S. at 773, but it does not establish that *product-design* trade dress can be. *Two Pesos* is inapposite to our holding here because the trade dress at issue, the decor of a restaurant, seems to us not to constitute product *design*. It was either product packaging—which, as we have discussed, normally *is* taken by the consumer to indicate origin—or else some *tertium quid* that is akin to product packaging and has no bearing on the present case.

Respondent replies that this manner of distinguishing *Two Pesos* will force courts to draw difficult lines between product-design and product-packaging trade dress. There will indeed be some hard cases at the margin: a classic glass Coca-Cola bottle, for instance, may constitute packaging for those consumers who drink the Coke and then discard the bottle, but may constitute the product itself for those consumers who are bottle collectors, or part of the product itself for those consumers who buy Coke in the classic glass bottle, rather than a can, because they think it more stylish to drink from the former. We believe, however, that the frequency and the difficulty of having to distinguish between product design and product packaging will be much less than the frequency and the difficulty of having to decide when a product design is inherently distinctive. To the extent there are close cases, we believe that courts should err on the side of caution and classify ambiguous trade dress as product design, thereby requiring secondary meaning. The very closeness will suggest the existence of relatively small utility in adopting an inherent-distinctiveness principle, and relatively great consumer benefit in requiring a demonstration of secondary meaning. . . .

We hold that, in an action for infringement of unregistered trade dress under § 43(a) of the Lanham Act, a product's design is distinctive, and therefore protectible, only upon a showing of secondary meaning. The judgment of the Second Circuit is reversed, and the case is remanded for further proceedings consistent with this opinion.

It is so ordered.

NOTES FOR DISCUSSION

1. *Preliminary Issue.* How did the Court answer the question presented for *certiorari*?

2. *Statutory Basis?* What basis is there in the Trademark Act to support Justice Scalia's distinction between product design and product packaging trade dress?

3. *Packaging or Design?* What test does the Court provide to separate product packaging from product design? Does the Court provide any guidance on the issue at all? Is there anything, after *Wal-Mart*, which still falls under the rule of *Two Pesos*? Consider two possible approaches to separating product design from product packaging:

a. A feature is product packaging if it is thrown away by the typical consumer after consumption of the good or service.

b. A feature is product design if it makes the product or service more appealing to consumers for a non-reputation related reason. In other words, a feature is product design if some consumers desire the feature for its own sake rather than for what it tells them about who made the product.

Is there language in the Court's opinion that supports either of these rules for separating product packaging from product design? Consider the Coke bottle example. Why is the glass bottle product design for the collector? Why is it product design for the Coke consumer who believes that the glass bottle is more stylish than a can? Is it product design for consumers who prefer the taste of Coke from a glass bottle? If the bottle is design for some consumers and packaging for others, which is it for purposes of trademark law? Does it depend upon the proportion of consumers who consider it design or packaging?

Which rule is more consistent with the purposes of the secondary meaning requirement as articulated by the Court? How would each rule classify a restaurant's décor? What about the tube in which toothpaste is customarily distributed? Packaging or design? How was toothpaste distributed before manufacturers began using tubes? If consumers prefer the new distribution technology—tubes from which you squeeze the toothpaste—to the old—jars into which you dipped your toothbrush—how does that factor into the packaging versus design divide? Which costs the manufacturer more: the toothpaste or the tube? Should that matter in determining whether the tube is packaging or design? Keep in mind that while most toothpaste manufacturers use tubes today, for every product commonly marketed or packaged in some form today, there was some company that was the first to market or package it that way. Assuming that the tube is not functional or generic (which it may well be), should trademark law extend to the company that was first to distribute toothpaste in tubes exclusive rights to the tube "packaging" at the moment it begins offering toothpaste in tubes or only after it has established a secondary meaning in the use of tubes?

4. *Secondary Meaning and Trade Dress.* What is the Court's reason for requiring proof of secondary meaning? Will requiring evidence of secondary meaning achieve that purpose? Is there sufficient evidence in this case, given the facts recited by the Court, to establish a triable case of secondary meaning with respect to Samara Brothers' clothing designs?

If we use the same approach to secondary meaning for product design that we use for word marks, Samara Brothers probably can offer sufficient circumstantial evidence to support a finding of secondary meaning. Although we do not have all of the relevant evidence, at the very least, we know that Samara Brothers' clothing line has proven both sufficiently popular and attractive that Wal-Mart decided to copy it. Should that be sufficient to create a genuine issue with respect to secondary meaning? If so, will the Court's ruling enable Wal-Mart to obtain "summary disposition of an anticompetitive strike suit"?

More generally, should we rely on the same kinds of evidence to establish secondary meaning with respect to trade dress as we do with respect to word and symbol trademarks? Some courts are skeptical of the use of circumstantial evidence to establish secondary meaning in trade dress cases, particularly with respect to product design. As Judge Becker has explained:

> Sales success by itself will typically not be as probative of secondary meaning in a product configuration case as in a trademark case, since the product's market success may well be attributable to the desirability of the product configuration rather than the source-designating capacity of the supposedly distinguishing feature or combination of features. And unlike with a trademark, where repeated purchases of a product support an inference that consumers have associated the mark with the producer or source, one can much less confidently presume that a consumer's repeated purchase of a product has created an association between a particular product configuration and the source.

The very fact that a consumer could identify the source based on the product's configuration implies that the configuration is at least somewhat unusual, and this "distinctiveness" of the product itself may be the source of the motivation to purchase if a consumer does not care about who the source is. In this respect product configuration again differs dramatically from trademark and from product packaging, since the success of a particular product—especially if similar competing products exist—does not readily lead to the inference of source identification and consumer interest in the source; it may well be that the product, inclusive of the product configuration, is itself inherently desirable, in a way that product packagings and trademarks are not.

Duraco Prods., Inc. v. Joy Plastics Enters., Ltd., 40 F.3d 1431, 1452–53 (3d Cir. 1994). Adopting similar reasoning, some courts have held that circumstantial evidence alone is insufficient to establish secondary meaning with respect to product design trade dress. *See, e.g., Yankee Candle Co. v. Bridgewater Candle Co.*, 259 F.3d 25, 45 (1st Cir. 2001) ("Although it has introduced some of the circumstantial evidence often used to support such a finding, the lack of any evidence that actual consumers associated the claimed trade dress with Yankee, as well as the lack of evidence as to confusion on the part of actual consumers, renders this circumstantial evidence insufficient for a reasonable juror to find that the trade dress had acquired a secondary meaning.").

Other courts have disagreed, however, and have relied on evidence of sales and advertising alone to establish secondary meaning. *See, e.g., Clamp Mfg. Co. v. Enco Mfg. Co.*, 870 F.2d 512, 517 (9th Cir. 1989) (finding secondary meaning in design of a patented clamp based upon exclusive use and advertising alone).

Courts have also disagreed as to how we should deal with proof of intentional copying. Should we treat the copying of a product's design or packaging as proof of secondary meaning in the same way that we treated the copying in the Baltimore Orioles case in Chapter 2 as proof of secondary meaning? Some courts consider intentional copying irrelevant to the question of secondary meaning where a defendant has copied in order to compete rather than to confuse consumers. *See Duraco Prods., Inc.*, 40 F.3d at 1453. Other courts have considered evidence of intentional copying relevant, but insufficient on its own to establish secondary meaning. *See GMC v. Lanard Toys, Inc.*, 468 F.3d 405, 419 (6th Cir. 2006), *cert. denied*, 552 U.S. 819 (2007). Still others have held that, in the absence of other evidence, proof of intentional copying is sufficient to establish secondary meaning for trade dress, just as it would be for word marks. *See Abercrombie & Fitch Stores, Inc. v. American Eagle Outfitters, Inc.*, 280 F.3d 619, 639 (6th Cir. 2002). Going even further, the Fourth Circuit has held that intentional copying creates a presumption of secondary meaning, at least with respect to product packaging. *See Osem Food Indus. Ltd. v. Sherwood Foods, Inc.*, 917 F.2d 161, 163–64 (4th Cir. 1990).

5. *Is Trade Dress Protection a "Mutant Species" of Patent and Copyright?* Courts have recognized the central role that imitation plays in ensuring competitive markets. Consider, for example, Judge Medina's statement in *American Safety Table Co. v. Schreiber*:

> [I]mitation is the life blood of competition. It is the unimpeded availability of substantially equivalent units that permits the normal operation of supply and demand to yield the fair price society must pay for a given commodity.

269 F.2d 255, 272 (2d Cir.), *cert. denied*, 361 U.S. 915 (1959).

As previously noted, some courts have insisted that trade dress does not amount to a mutant species of patent or copyright because it serves (or, at least, is supposed to serve) a fundamentally different purpose. Yet, in addition to permitting mere imitation of a popular product to create a triable issue with respect to both secondary meaning, some, but not all, courts also permit mere imitation to create a triable issue with respect to infringement. *Compare Nora Beverages, Inc. v. Perrier Group of America, Inc.*, 269 F.3d 114, 124 (2d Cir. 2001) (holding that " 'the intent to compete by imitating the successful features of another's product is vastly different from the intent to deceive purchasers as to the source of the product' ") (*quoting Streetwise Maps, Inc. v. VanDam, Inc.*, 159 F.3d 739, 745 (2d Cir. 1998)); *with Perfect Fit Indus., Inc. v. Acme Quilting Co.*, 618 F.2d 950, 954 (2d Cir. 1980) ("In assessing the likelihood of confusion to the public, an important factor is whether or not the second comer created the similar trade dress intentionally. If there was intentional copying the second comer will be presumed to have intended to create a confusing similarity of appearance and will be presumed to have succeeded.").

If a triable claim of unfair competition or trade dress infringement can be established merely by showing the copying of a popular product, does such protection have the same economic consequences as a patent or copyright? If so, what difference does it make that unfair competition purports to serve a different purpose?

2. FUNCTIONALITY AND THE ROAD TO *TRAFFIX*

Percolating alongside the distinctiveness requirement in *Two Pesos*, *Qualitex*, and *Wal-mart*, the functionality doctrine received periodic asides in each of these cases, but no definitive statement. In the absence of specific direction from the Court, a number of different interpretations of functionality sprung up. Historically, as set forth in the Restatement (First) of Torts, a product feature was functional for purposes of trademark and unfair competition law if it "affects their purpose, action or performance, or the facility or economy of processing, handling or using them." Restatement of Torts § 742 (1938).

In 1952, the Ninth Circuit considered whether the design pattern of hotel china could be protected under unfair competition law in *Pagliero v.*

Wallace China Co., 198 F.2d 339, 343–44 (9th Cir. 1952). The key issue was whether the china pattern was functional. Finding that the pattern was an essential selling feature, the court concluded that the pattern was functional and could be freely copied. In explaining its decision, the court wrote:

> "Functional" in this sense might be said to connote other than a trade-mark purpose. If the particular feature is an important ingredient in the commercial success of the product, the interest in free competition permits its imitation in the absence of a patent or copyright. On the other hand, where the feature or, more aptly, design, is a mere arbitrary embellishment, a form of dress for the goods primarily adopted for purposes of identification and individuality and, hence, unrelated to basic consumer demands in connection with the product, imitation may be forbidden where the requisite showing of secondary meaning is made.

Id. at 343; *see also International Order of Job's Daughters v. Lindeburg & Co.*, 633 F.2d 912, 917 (9th Cir. 1980) (defining functional features as features "which constitute the actual benefit that the consumer wishes to purchase, as distinguished from an assurance that a particular entity made, sponsored, or endorsed a product").

While the *Pagliero* court acknowledged that the defendant could compete by creating its own attractive designs, the court held that this was irrelevant. As the court explained:

> Of course, Tepco can also compete by developing designs even more aesthetically satisfying, but the possibility that an alternative product might be developed has never been considered a barrier to permitting imitation competition in other types of cases. The law encourages competition not only in creativeness but in economy of manufacture and distribution as well.

Id. at 344.

Although the Ninth Circuit subsequently clarified the *Pagliero* standard to distinguish between features that were an important ingredient in a product's success because they were source identifying and those that were an important ingredient because they were desired by consumers for their own sake, *see Vuitton Et Fils S.A. v. J. Young Enters., Inc.*, 644 F.2d 769, 773 (9th Cir. 1981), the Ninth Circuit has generally given a broad reach to the functionality limitation in trademark law. As the Ninth Circuit explained in *Disc Golf Ass'n v. Champion Discs*:

> A product feature need only have some utilitarian advantage to be considered functional. This court has never held, as DGA suggests, that the product feature must provide superior

utilitarian advantages. To the contrary, this court has suggested that "in order to establish nonfunctionality the party with the burden must demonstrate that the product feature serves no purpose other than identification."

158 F.3d 1002, 1007 (9th Cir. 1998).

Other circuits have disagreed. They worry that the *Pagliero* approach "provides a disincentive for development of imaginative and attractive design. The more appealing the design, the less protection it would receive." *Keene Corp. v. Paraflex Indus., Inc.,* 653 F.2d 822, 825 (3d Cir. 1981). Does such an argument necessarily convert trademark law into "a mutant species" of copyright? In cases decided before Justice Scalia's cautionary opinion in *Dastar,* some courts expressly embraced trade dress as a desirable supplement to copyright and patent. For example, in *Hartford House, Ltd. v. Hallmark Cards, Inc.,* the plaintiff had developed an attractive new style of greeting cards, which the defendant copied. 647 F.Supp. 1533 (D. Colo. 1986), *aff'd,* 846 F.2d 1268 (10th Cir.), *cert. denied,* 488 U.S. 908 (1988). When the plaintiff sued, claiming the card design as trade dress and alleging unfair competition under section 43(a), the defendant asserted that the card design was functional, just as the china design was functional in *Pagliero.* Both the district court and the Tenth Circuit rejected the argument, however. In justifying its decision to protect the card design from imitation under section 43(a), the district court expressly embraced trademark protection as a mutant species of copyright. "One salutary purpose of the Lanham Act in this context," the court wrote, "is to protect a creative artists' rights in his or her creation and thus provide incentive to be creative." *Id.* at 1540.

Even where courts were not willing to go quite so far, some courts nevertheless sharply narrowed the reach of the functionality doctrine by focusing on the availability of alternative designs. If the purpose of the functionality doctrine is to protect the ability of competitors to compete, they reasoned, then the availability of alternative designs that served the same purpose should be a critical consideration. So long as there were other equally effective or attractive designs available or that could be developed, it was not really necessary or essential to copy the plaintiff's design in order to compete. Thus, the plaintiff's design should not be considered functional.

Reasoning from this perspective and without responding to the *Pagliero* court's point that we want competition in economy of manufacture, as well as in creating alternative designs, Judge Rich of the Court of Customs and Patent Appeals held that it was not enough that a given design was the reason a product worked, *i.e.* was functional in fact or *de facto* functionality, the design had to be the best or one of the few best way of achieving a given result before it would be functional for purposes of trademark law, *i.e. de jure* functional. *See, e.g., In re Morton-*

Norwich Prods., Inc., 671 F.2d 1332, 1341 (C.C.P.A. 1982). To determine whether a feature was functional in both fact and law, Judge Rich identified four relevant factors: (1) the existence of a utility patent disclosing the utilitarian advantages of the design; (2) advertising materials in which the originator of the design touts the design's utilitarian advantages; (3) the availability to competitors of functionally equivalent designs; and (4) facts indicating that the design results in a comparatively simple or cheap method of manufacturing the product. *Id.* at 1340–41. As a practical matter, Judge Rich's approach significantly narrowed the functionality doctrine, and gave a consequently wider range for claims of trade dress infringement.

While the appellate courts battled over the proper interpretation of functionality, the Court dithered. When the Court offered, in passing, a definition of functionality in a footnote in *Inwood Labs. v. Ives Labs.*, 456 U.S. 844 (1982), it paraphrased the Restatement standard and wrote: "In general terms, a product feature is functional if it is essential to the use or purpose of the article or if it affects the cost or quality of the article." *Id.* at 850 n.10. As authority for this definition, the Court cited its earlier decisions in *Sears* and *Kellogg Co.* Review those decisions and see how, if at all, they define functionality. In applying its definition, the Court held that the blue-red coloring of a medication was functional because it served important non-brand purposes. Specifically, the coloring identified the medicine's formulation, whether brand or generic, and thereby differentiated this kind of medicine from other medicines. Citing the findings of the district court, the Court wrote that "many elderly patients associate color with therapeutic effect; some patients commingle medications in a container and rely on color to differentiate one from another; colors are of some, if limited, help in identifying drugs in emergency situations; and use of the same color for brand name drugs and their generic equivalents helps avoid confusion on the part of those responsible for dispensing drugs." *Inwood Labs.*, 456 U.S. at 853.

Although the Court's application of its standard was entirely consistent with the traditionally broad reading of the functionality doctrine, the application was difficult to reconcile with the words the Court had used to define functionality. Specifically, while the district court's findings certainly indicate that the pill's coloring served a non-brand purpose, it is a little harder to say how the coloring was *"essential to the use or purpose"* of the medicine or *"affected the cost or quality"* of the medicine. As a result, both the traditional broad reading, and the revisionist narrow reading, of functionality found support in *Inwood Labs.* Traditionalists pointed to the Court's application of the functionality doctrine, while the revisionists pointed to the Court's use of the word "essential" in its statement of the standard.

In *Qualitex*, the Court again addressed the issue, but only added further uncertainty. In addition to citing *Inwood Labs.'* definition of functionality, *Qualitex Co.*, 514 U.S. at 165, Justice Breyer's majority opinion also cited with approval Justice White's statement in his *Inwood Labs.* concurrence that a product feature was functional if it was " 'an important ingredient in the commercial success of the product.' " *Id.* (*quoting Ives Labs. v. Darby Drug Co.*, 601 F.2d 631, 643 (2d Cir. 1979) (*quoting Pagliero*, 198 F.2d at 343)). In *Qualitex*, Justice Breyer also added his own gloss by defining features as functional "if exclusive use of the feature would put competitors at a significant non-reputation-related disadvantage." *Id.*

None of these pronouncements narrowed the increasingly sharp gap between those courts that interpreted functionality broadly and those that interpreted it narrowly.

In addition to the general split over the proper meaning and application of the functionality doctrine, a further split developed over what role an expired utility patent should play in determining a feature's or design's functionality. Could a party claim a feature as trade dress that had formerly been protected by a now-expired (or invalid) utility patent? Some courts saw this as a plainly improper attempt to leverage the 20-year period of exclusivity given by a patent—a period during which secondary meaning could easily develop—into a perpetual exclusive right over a product's feature and design. Purporting to follow *Kellogg Co.*, these courts held that the existence of a prior utility patent on the specific feature now claimed as trade dress established *per se* functionality and barred a trade dress claim. *See, e.g., Vornado Air Circulation Systems, Inc. v. Duracraft Corp.*, 58 F.3d 1498, 1500 (10th Cir. 1995) ("Where a product configuration is a significant inventive component of an invention covered by a utility patent . . . it cannot receive trade dress protection").

Other circuits disagreed. While they recognized that the existence of a prior utility patent was relevant to the functionality determination, it was not conclusive. A utility patent provided evidence that a feature or design was *a* way of achieving a given result, but not that it was *the only* way, or even *one of the best* ways. As a result, these courts applied their standard approach to functionality and would protect the feature as trade dress, even if previously patented, unless there was no alternative design available. In *TrafFix Devices, Inc. v. Marketing Displays, Inc.*, the Sixth Circuit followed precisely such an approach. When Marketing Displays' patent on a dual-spring traffic construction sign expired, Marketing Displays asserted that the dual springs constituted protectible trade dress. On the functionality issue, Marketing Displays presented evidence that alternative designs using three or four springs were available and, on that basis, the Sixth Circuit held, as a matter of law, that the dual spring design was not functional.

To resolve the conflict between the circuits over both the general standard for functionality and the role that an expired utility patent should play in it, the Court granted *certiorari*.

TrafFix Devices, Inc. v. Marketing Displays, Inc.

532 U.S. 23 (2001)

KENNEDY, J.

Temporary road signs with warnings like "Road Work Ahead" or "Left Shoulder Closed" must withstand strong gusts of wind. An inventor named Robert Sarkisian obtained two utility patents for a mechanism built upon two springs (the dual-spring design) to keep these and other outdoor signs upright despite adverse wind conditions. The holder of the now-expired Sarkisian patents, respondent Marketing Displays, Inc. (MDI), established a successful business in the manufacture and sale of sign stands incorporating the patented feature. MDI's stands for road signs were recognizable to buyers and users (it says) because the dual-spring design was visible near the base of the sign.

This litigation followed after the patents expired and a competitor, TrafFix Devices, Inc., sold sign stands with a visible spring mechanism that looked like MDI's. MDI and TrafFix products looked alike because they were. When TrafFix started in business, it sent an MDI product abroad to have it reverse engineered, that is to say copied. Complicating matters, TrafFix marketed its sign stands under a name similar to MDI's. MDI used the name "WindMaster," while TrafFix, its new competitor, used "WindBuster."

MDI brought suit under the Trademark Act of 1964 (Lanham Act), 60 Stat. 427, as amended, 15 U.S.C. § 1051 *et seq.*, against TrafFix for trademark infringement (based on the similar names), trade dress infringement (based on the copied dual-spring design) and unfair competition. TrafFix counterclaimed on antitrust theories. After the United States District Court for the Eastern District of Michigan considered cross-motions for summary judgment, MDI prevailed on its trademark claim for the confusing similarity of names and was held not liable on the antitrust counterclaim; and those two rulings, affirmed by the Court of Appeals, are not before us.

I

We are concerned with the trade dress question. The District Court ruled against MDI on its trade dress claim. 971 F. Supp. 262 (ED Mich. 1997). After determining that the one element of MDI's trade dress at issue was the dual-spring design, *id.* at 265, it held that "no reasonable trier of fact could determine that MDI has established secondary meaning" in its alleged trade dress, *id.* at 269. In other words, consumers did not associate the look of the dual-spring design with MDI. As a second, independent reason to grant summary judgment in favor of TrafFix, the District Court determined the dual-spring design was functional. On this rationale secondary meaning is irrelevant because there can be no trade dress protection in any event. In ruling on the functional aspect of the design, the District Court noted that Sixth Circuit precedent indicated that the burden was on MDI to prove that its trade dress was nonfunctional, and not on TrafFix to show that it was functional (a rule since adopted by Congress, *see* 15 U.S.C. § 1125(a)(3) (1994 ed., Supp. V)), and then went on to consider MDI's arguments that the dual-spring design was subject to trade dress protection. Finding none of MDI's contentions persuasive, the District Court concluded MDI had not "proffered sufficient evidence which would enable a reasonable trier of fact to find that MDI's vertical dual-spring design is *non*-functional.".". Summary judgment was entered against MDI on its trade dress claims.

The Court of Appeals for the Sixth Circuit reversed the trade dress ruling. 200 F.3d 929 (1999). The Court of Appeals held the District Court had erred in ruling MDI failed to show a genuine issue of material fact regarding whether it had secondary meaning in its alleged trade dress, 200 F.3d at 938, and had erred further in determining that MDI could not prevail in any event because the alleged trade dress was in fact a functional product configuration, 200 F.3d at 940. The Court of Appeals suggested the District Court committed legal error by looking only to the dual-spring design when evaluating MDI's trade dress. Basic to its reasoning was the Court of Appeals' observation that it took "little imagination to conceive of a hidden dual-spring mechanism or a tri or quad-spring mechanism that might avoid infringing [MDI's] trade dress." *Ibid.* The Court of Appeals explained that "if TrafFix or another competitor chooses to use [MDI's] dual-spring design, then it will have to find *some other way* to set its sign apart to avoid infringing [MDI's] trade dress." *Ibid.* It was not sufficient, according to the Court of Appeals, that allowing exclusive use of a particular feature such as the dual-spring design in the guise of trade dress would "hinder competition somewhat." Rather, "exclusive use of a feature must 'put competitors at a *significant* non-reputation-related disadvantage' before trade dress protection is denied on functionality grounds." *Ibid.* (quoting *Qualitex Co. v. Jacobson Products Co.,* 514 U.S. 159, 165 (1995)). In its criticism of the District Court's ruling on the trade dress question, the Court of Appeals took note of a split among Courts of Appeals in various other Circuits on the issue whether the existence of an expired utility patent forecloses the possibility of the patentee's claiming trade dress protection in the product's design. 200 F.3d at 939. Compare *Sunbeam Products, Inc. v. West Bend Co.,* 123 F.3d 246 (CA5 1997) (holding that trade dress protection is not foreclosed), *Thomas & Betts Corp. v. Panduit Corp.,* 138 F.3d 277 (CA7 1998) (same), and *Midwest Industries, Inc. v. Karavan Trailers, Inc.,* 175 F.3d 1356 (CA Fed 1999) (same), with *Vornado Air*

Circulation Systems, Inc. v. Duracraft Corp., 58 F.3d 1498, 1500 (CA10 1995) ("Where a product configuration is a significant inventive component of an invention covered by a utility patent . . . it cannot receive trade dress protection"). To resolve the conflict, we granted certiorari. 530 U.S. 1260 (2000).

II

It is well established that trade dress can be protected under federal law. The design or packaging of a product may acquire a distinctiveness which serves to identify the product with its manufacturer or source; and a design or package which acquires this secondary meaning, assuming other requisites are met, is a trade dress which may not be used in a manner likely to cause confusion as to the origin, sponsorship, or approval of the goods. In these respects protection for trade dress exists to promote competition. As we explained just last Term, *see Wal-Mart Stores, Inc. v. Samara Brothers, Inc.*, 529 U.S. 205 (2000), various Courts of Appeals have allowed claims of trade dress infringement relying on the general provision of the Lanham Act which provides a cause of action to one who is injured when a person uses "any word, term name, symbol, or device, or any combination thereof . . . which is likely to cause confusion . . . as to the origin, sponsorship, or approval of his or her goods." 15 U.S.C. § 1125(a)(1)(A). Congress confirmed this statutory protection for trade dress by amending the Lanham Act to recognize the concept. Title 15 U.S.C. § 1125(a)(3) (1994 ed., Supp. V) provides: "In a civil action for trade dress infringement under this chapter for trade dress not registered on the principal register, the person who asserts trade dress protection has the burden of proving that the matter sought to be protected is not functional." This burden of proof gives force to the well-established rule that trade dress protection may not be claimed for product features that are functional. *Qualitex*, 514 U.S. at 164–165; *Two Pesos, Inc. v. Taco Cabana, Inc.*, 505 U.S. 763, 775 (1992). And in *Wal-Mart, supra*, we were careful to caution against misuse or over-extension of trade dress. We noted that "product design almost invariably serves purposes other than source identification." 529 U.S. at 213.

Trade dress protection must subsist with the recognition that in many instances there is no prohibition against copying goods and products. In general, unless an intellectual property right such as a patent or copyright protects an item, it will be subject to copying. As the Court has explained, copying is not always discouraged or disfavored by the laws which preserve our competitive economy. *Bonito Boats, Inc. v. Thunder Craft Boats, Inc.*, 489 U.S. 141, 160 (1989). Allowing competitors to copy will have salutary effects in many instances. "Reverse engineering of chemical and mechanical articles in the public domain often leads to significant advances in technology." *Ibid*.

The principal question in this case is the effect of an expired patent on a claim of trade dress infringement. A prior patent, we conclude, has vital significance in resolving the trade dress claim. A utility patent is strong evidence that the features therein claimed are functional. If trade dress protection is sought for those features the strong evidence of functionality based on the previous patent adds great weight to the statutory presumption that features are deemed functional until proved otherwise by the party seeking trade dress protection. Where the expired patent claimed the features in question, one who seeks to establish trade dress protection must carry the heavy burden of showing that the feature is not functional, for instance by showing that it is merely an ornamental, incidental, or arbitrary aspect of the device.

In the case before us, the central advance claimed in the expired utility patents (the Sarkisian patents) is the dual-spring design; and the dual-spring design is the essential feature of the trade dress MDI now seeks to establish and to protect. The rule we have explained bars the trade dress claim, for MDI did not, and cannot, carry the burden of overcoming the strong evidentiary inference of functionality based on the disclosure of the dual-spring design in the claims of the expired patents.

The dual springs shown in the Sarkisian patents were well apart (at either end of a frame for holding a rectangular sign when one full side is the base) while the dual springs at issue here are close together (in a frame designed to hold a sign by one of its corners). As the District Court recognized, this makes little difference. The point is that the springs are necessary to the operation of the device. The fact that the springs in this very different-looking device fall within the claims of the patents is illustrated by MDI's own position in earlier litigation. In the late 1970's, MDI engaged in a long-running intellectual property battle with a company known as Winn-Proof. Although the precise claims of the Sarkisian patents cover sign stands with springs "spaced apart," U.S. Patent No. 3,646,696, col. 4; U.S. Patent No. 3,662,482, col. 4, the Winn-Proof sign stands (with springs much like the sign stands at issue here) were found to infringe the patents by the United States District Court for the District of Oregon, and the Court of Appeals for the Ninth Circuit affirmed the judgment. *Sarkisian* v. *Winn-Proof Corp.*, 697 F.2d 1313 (1983). Although the Winn-Proof traffic sign stand (with dual springs close together) did not appear, then, to infringe the literal terms of the patent claims (which called for "spaced apart" springs), the Winn-Proof sign stand was found to infringe the patents under the doctrine of equivalents, which allows a finding of patent infringement even when the accused product does not fall within the literal terms of the claims. 697 F.2d at 1321–1322; *see generally Warner-Jenkinson Co. v. Hilton Davis Chemical Co.*, 520 U.S. 17 (1997). In light of this past ruling—a ruling procured at MDI's own insistence—it must be concluded the products here at issue would have been covered by the claims of the expired patents.

The rationale for the rule that the disclosure of a feature in the claims of a utility patent constitutes strong evidence of functionality is well illustrated in this case. The dual-spring design serves the important purpose of keeping the sign upright even in heavy wind conditions; and, as confirmed by the statements in the expired patents, it does so in a unique and useful manner. As the specification of one of the patents recites, prior art "devices, in practice, will topple under the force of a strong wind." U.S. Patent No. 3,662,482, col. 1. The dual-spring design allows sign stands to resist toppling in strong winds. Using a dual-spring design rather than a single spring achieves important operational advantages. For example, the specifications of the patents note that the "use of a pair of springs . . . as opposed to the use of a single spring to support the frame structure prevents canting or twisting of the sign around a vertical axis," and that, if not prevented, twisting "may cause damage to the spring structure and may result in tipping of the device." U.S. Patent No. 3,646,696, col. 3. In the course of patent prosecution, it was said that "the use of a pair of spring connections as opposed to a single spring connection . . . forms an important part of this combination" because it "forces the sign frame to tip along the longitudinal axis of the elongated ground-engaging members." App. 218. The dual-spring design affects the cost of the device as well; it was acknowledged that the device "could use three springs but this would unnecessarily increase the cost of the device." App. 217. These statements made in the patent applications and in the course of procuring the patents demonstrate the functionality of the design. MDI does not assert that any of these representations are mistaken or inaccurate, and this is further strong evidence of the functionality of the dual-spring design.

III

In finding for MDI on the trade dress issue the Court of Appeals gave insufficient recognition to the importance of the expired utility patents, and their evidentiary significance, in establishing the functionality of the device. The error likely was caused by its misinterpretation of trade dress principles in other respects. As we have noted, even if there has been no previous utility patent the party asserting trade dress has the burden to establish the nonfunctionality of alleged trade dress features. MDI could not meet this burden. Discussing trademarks, we have said " 'in general terms, a product feature is functional,' and cannot serve as a trademark, 'if it is essential to the use or purpose of the article or if it affects the cost or quality of the article.' " *Qualitex*, 514 U.S. at 165 (quoting *Inwood Laboratories, Inc. v. Ives Laboratories, Inc.*, 456 U.S. 844, 850, n. 10 (1982)). Expanding upon the meaning of this phrase, we have observed that a functional feature is one the "exclusive use of [which] would put competitors at a significant non-reputation-related disadvantage." 514 U.S. at 165. The Court of Appeals in the instant case seemed to interpret this language to mean that a necessary test for functionality is "whether the particular product configuration is a competitive necessity." 200 F.3d at 940. *See* also *Vornado,* 58 F.3d at 1507 ("Functionality, by contrast, has been defined both by our circuit, and more recently by the Supreme Court, in terms of competitive need"). This was incorrect as a comprehensive definition. As explained in *Qualitex, supra,* and *Inwood, supra,* a feature is also functional when it is essential to the use or purpose of the device or when it affects the cost or quality of the device. The *Qualitex* decision did not purport to displace this traditional rule. Instead, it quoted the rule as *Inwood* had set it forth. It is proper to inquire into a "significant non-reputation-related disadvantage" in cases of aesthetic functionality, the question involved in *Qualitex.* Where the design is functional under the *Inwood* formulation there is no need to proceed further to consider if there is a competitive necessity for the feature. In *Qualitex,* by contrast, aesthetic functionality was the central question, there having been no indication that the green-gold color of the laundry press pad had any bearing on the use or purpose of the product or its cost or quality.

The Court has allowed trade dress protection to certain product features that are inherently distinctive. *Two Pesos,* 505 U.S. at 774. In *Two Pesos,* however, the Court at the outset made the explicit analytic assumption that the trade dress features in question (decorations and other features to evoke a Mexican theme in a restaurant) were not functional. 505 U.S. at 767, n. 6. The trade dress in those cases did not bar competitors from copying functional product design features. In the instant case, beyond serving the purpose of informing consumers that the sign stands are made by MDI (assuming it does so), the dual-spring design provides a unique and useful mechanism to resist the force of the wind. Functionality having been established, whether MDI's dual-spring design has acquired secondary meaning need not be considered.

There is no need, furthermore, to engage, as did the Court of Appeals, in speculation about other design possibilities, such as using three or four springs which might serve the same purpose. 200 F.3d at 940. Here, the functionality of the spring design means that competitors need not explore whether other spring juxtapositions might be used. The dual-spring design is not an arbitrary flourish in the configuration of MDI's product; it is the reason the device works. Other designs need not be attempted.

Because the dual-spring design is functional, it is unnecessary for competitors to explore designs to hide the springs, say by using a box or framework to cover them, as suggested by the Court of Appeals. *Ibid.* The dual-spring design assures the user the device will work. If buyers are assured the product serves its purpose by seeing the operative mechanism that in itself serves an important market need. It would be at cross-purposes to those objectives, and something of a paradox, were we to require the manufacturer to conceal the very item the user seeks.

In a case where a manufacturer seeks to protect arbitrary, incidental, or ornamental aspects of features of a product found in the patent claims, such as arbitrary curves in the legs or an ornamental pattern painted on the springs, a different result might obtain. There the manufacturer could perhaps prove that those aspects do not serve a purpose within the terms of the utility patent. The inquiry into whether such features, asserted to be trade dress, are functional by reason of their inclusion in the claims of an expired utility patent could be aided by going beyond the claims and examining the patent and its prosecution history to see if the feature in question is shown as a useful part of the invention. No such claim is made here, however. MDI in essence seeks protection for the dual-spring design alone. The asserted trade dress consists simply of the dual-spring design, four legs, a base, an upright, and a sign. MDI has pointed to nothing arbitrary about the components of its device or the way they are assembled. The Lanham Act does not exist to reward manufacturers for their innovation in creating a particular device; that is the purpose of the patent law and its period of exclusivity. The Lanham Act, furthermore, does not protect trade dress in a functional design simply because an investment has been made to encourage the public to associate a particular functional feature with a single manufacturer or seller. The Court of Appeals erred in viewing MDI as possessing the right to exclude competitors from using a design identical to MDI's and to require those competitors to adopt a different design simply to avoid copying it. MDI cannot gain the exclusive right to produce sign stands using the dual-spring design by asserting that consumers associate it with the look of the invention itself. Whether a utility patent has expired or there has been no utility patent at all, a product design which has a particular appearance may be functional because it is "essential to the use or purpose of the article" or "affects the cost or quality of the article." *Inwood*, 456 U.S. at 850, n. 10.

TrafFix and some of its *amici* argue that the Patent Clause of the Constitution, Art. I, § 8, cl. 8, of its own force, prohibits the holder of an expired utility patent from claiming trade dress protection. Brief for Petitioner 33–36; Brief for Panduit Corp. as *Amicus Curiae* 3; Brief for Malla Pollack as *Amicus Curiae* 2. We need not resolve this question. If, despite the rule that functional features may not be the subject of trade dress protection, a case arises in which trade dress becomes the practical equivalent of an expired utility patent, that will be time enough to consider the matter. The judgment of the Court of Appeals is reversed, and the case is remanded for further proceedings consistent with this opinion.

It is so ordered.

NOTES FOR DISCUSSION

1.   *Functionality After* TrafFix. How did the Court resolve the split over the proper functionality standard? Did it change the standard? The Federal Circuit has said that it did not. *See Valu Eng'g, Inc. v. Rexnord Corp.*, 278 F.3d 1268, 1276 (Fed. Cir. 2002) ("We do not understand the Supreme Court's decision in *TrafFix* to have altered the *Morton-Norwich* analysis"). Do you agree?

What is the functionality standard after *TrafFix*? Are the *Inwood Labs.* standard and the *Qualitex* standard overlapping definitions of a single, unified functionality standard? *See Eppendorf-Netheler-Hinz GMBH v. Ritter GMBH*, 289 F.3d 351 (5th Cir.) (yes), *cert. denied*, 537 U.S. 1071 (2002). Or does the first govern functionality with respect to useful features, while the second governs aesthetic features? *See Abercrombie & Fitch Stores, Inc. v. American Eagle Outfitters, Inc.*, 280 F.3d 619, 641 (6th Cir. 2002) (yes). Given that the Court holds that the dual spring design is "essential to the use" of the signs at issue, what does that result necessarily suggest regarding the proper interpretation of the word "essential" in the *Inwood Labs.* formulation? In what sense are the dual springs "essential" to the use of the sign?

Following *TrafFix*, a number of circuits have continued to evaluate functionality using the four factors Judge Rich identified in *In re Morton-Norwich*: "(1) whether the design yields a utilitarian advantage, (2) whether alternative designs are available, (3) whether advertising touts the utilitarian advantages of the design, and (4) whether the particular design results from a comparatively simple or inexpensive method of manufacture." *See, e.g., McAirlaids, Inc. v. Kimberly-Clark Corp.*, 756 F.3d 307, 313 (4th Cir. 2014); *In re Becton, Dickinson & Co.*, 675 F.3d 1368, 1371–72 (Fed. Cir. 2012); *Secalt S.A. v. Wuxi Shenxi Const. Machinery Co.*, 668 F.3d 677, 685 (9th Cir. 2012); *Georgia-Pacific Consumer Prods. LP v. Kimberly-Clark Corp.*, 647 F.3d 723, 728–31 (7th Cir. 2011); *Fuji Kogyo Co. v. Pacific Bay Int'l, Inc.*, 461 F.3d 675, 685 (6th Cir. 2006).

Although the circuits today generally recite the same standard and formulaic language for functionality, the circuit split that gave rise to *TrafFix* remains. The Ninth Circuit, for example, applies the *Morton-Norwich* factors strictly. In asking whether the design at issue yields a utilitarian advantage, under the first factor, the question is not whether the design offers superior utilitarian advantages; rather the question is whether the design "serves no purpose other than identification." *Apple, Inc. v. Samsung Electronics Co.*, 786 F.3d 983, 992 (Fed. Cir. 2015) (applying Ninth Circuit law). Moreover, under the second factor, alternative designs are relevant only if they "offer *exactly* the same features." *Id.* at 993. That there are alternative designs that offer a different set of advantages and disadvantages is not sufficient. *Id.*

In *Apple, Inc. v. Samsung Electronics Co.*, Apple sued Samsung for copying the appearance of its iPhone. Along with design patent and other claims, Apple claimed that the appearance of the iPhone constituted trade dress. Apple identified the elements of its trade dress as:

a rectangular product with four evenly rounded corners;

a flat, clear surface covering the front of the product;

a display screen under the clear surface;

substantial black borders above and below the display screen and narrower black borders on either side of the screen; and

when the device is on, a row of small dots on the display screen, a matrix of colorful square icons with evenly rounded corners within the display screen, and an unchanging bottom dock of colorful square icons with evenly rounded corners set off from the display's other icons.

Samsung countered that the claimed trade dress was functional. Can you identify how each of these features is functional? What about the combination of features? How would you resolve the case? Would consumers be better or worse off if Samsung is allowed to copy the iPhone's appearance? For the court's resolution, see *Apple, Inc. v. Samsung Electronics Co.*, 786 F.3d at 996 (reversing jury's finding that trade dress was functional and holding that product's design was functional as a matter of law).

2. *Functionality and Patents*. How did the Court resolve the split between the circuits over the role of an expired utility patent? If an expired utility patent covers a given product feature or design, but that feature or design represents only one of many ways to achieve a given result, is that feature or design functional for purposes of trademark law?

How would you resolve the following case: Georgia-Pacific holds a patent on a process for making toilet paper. The process prints a diamond pattern on the paper to increase the apparent softness of the toilet paper. Georgia-Pacific markets the resulting toilet paper under the name "Quilted Northern." After more than ten years of success on the market, a competitor, Kimberly-Clark, redesigns two of its toilet paper lines to incorporate a similar quilted diamond design. However, in making its toilet papers, Kimberly-Clark uses a different process and does not therefore infringe Georgia-Pacific's patent. Instead of asserting patent infringement, Georgia-Pacific alleges that the quilted diamond design constitutes trade dress and that Kimberly-Clark's pattern is confusingly similar. Kimberly-Clark counters that the quilted diamond design is functional. Is the diamond design functional? *Compare Georgia-Pacific Consumer Prods. LP v. Kimberly-Clark Corp.*, 647 F.3d 723, 731 (7th Cir. 2011) ("Georgia-Pacific, whether intentionally or not, patented their Quilted Diamond Design and claimed it to be functional. They must now live with that choice and can benefit only under the protection of a patent, not that of a trademark."), *with McAirlaids, Inc. v. Kimberly-Clark Corp.*, 756 F.3d 307, 313 (4th Cir. 2014) ("McAirlaids's fiber-fusion process and resulting material are patented; however, as we have pointed out, the patents do not extend to any specific embossing pattern or the shapes used therein"; finding that functionality presents a genuine issue of material fact and remanding for trial).

3. *The Role of Alternative Designs.* If there was one thing that was clear in the Court's decision it is that the availability of alternative designs does not preclude a finding of functionality. The Court specifically reversed the Sixth Circuit's holding that the availability of three-or four-spring designs meant that the dual-spring design was not functional. Moreover, in doing so, the Court expressly held that once one design is shown to serve the function at issue, "[o]ther designs need not be attempted." *TrafFix Devices, Inc.*, 532 U.S. at 34.

Following *TrafFix*, however, trial and appellate courts have had trouble letting go of the alternative design theory. Consider the Federal Circuit's reading of *TrafFix*'s seemingly straightforward language:

> Nothing in *TrafFix* suggests that consideration of alternative designs is not properly part of the overall mix, and we do not read the Court's observations in *TrafFix* as rendering the availability of alternative designs irrelevant. Rather, we conclude that the Court merely noted that once a product feature is found functional based on other considerations there is no need to consider the availability of alternative designs, because the feature cannot be given trade dress protection merely because there are alternative designs available. But that does not mean that the availability of alternative designs cannot be a legitimate source of evidence to determine whether a feature is functional in the first place.

Valu Eng'g, Inc. v. Rexnord Corp., 278 F.3d 1268, 1276 (Fed. Cir. 2002).

Before rejecting the Federal Circuit's reading as mere sophistry, consider the following question: Is the shape of the Coke bottle functional? Or does the clear availability of alternative designs preclude such a result? Is the difference that we know that there are alternative bottle shapes that work perfectly well for soda, but we only had a paid expert's testimony (or as the Court labeled it, "speculation") that one might be able to use an equally-effective three- or four-spring design for road signs?

4. *Aesthetic Functionality.* Justice Kennedy asserts that "[i]n *Qualitex*, by contrast, aesthetic functionality was the central question. . . ." Is that true? Was there any evidence that dry cleaners in *Qualitex* wanted green-gold pads because they found the color attractive and wanted aesthetically attractive pads for their dry cleaning machines?

More generally, do we need an alternative standard for aesthetic functionality, or can we analyze the issue under the general *Inwood Labs.* standard? If consumers purchase a product because it is aesthetically attractive, and such attractiveness is in fact the purpose of the article from the consumer's perspective, can we say that the article's aesthetic appeal is "essential to the use or purpose of the article"?

As Chief Judge Posner once explained:

> It would be arbitrary as well as puritanical and even philistine to deny that one function of modern consumer packaging is to be beautiful, the motivation being sometimes a hope that the consumer will infer the quality of the product from the beauty of the package and sometimes a hope that the consumer will derive utility (and so be willing to pay more) from the packaging directly, as when a consumer displays a shapely bottle of champagne to his dinner guests. A producer cannot in the name of trade dress prevent his competitors from making their products as visually entrancing as his own. Ordinarily there is a sufficient variety of pleasing shapes, sizes, colors, and ornamentation to enable beauty without sacrificing differentiation. But if consumers derive a value from the fact that a product looks a certain way that is distinct from the value of knowing at a glance who made it, then it is a nonappropriable feature of the product.

Publications Int'l, Ltd. v. Landoll, Inc., 164 F.3d 337, 339 (7th Cir. 1998), *cert. denied*, 526 U.S. 1088 (1999).

Were the clothing designs at issue in *Wal-Mart* functional? In *Knitwaves, Inc. v. Lollytogs Ltd.*, Knitwaves sued Lollytogs under section 43(a) for copying two of its sweater designs—"its 'Leaf Sweater,' a multicolored striped sweater with puffy leaf appliques, and its 'Squirrel Cardigan,' which has a squirrel and leaves appliqued onto its multipaneled front." 71 F.3d 996, 999 (2d Cir. 1995). Applying the alternative design approach common before *TrafFix*, the Second Circuit held that, although the primary purpose of the design was to enhance the aesthetic appeal of the sweaters, rather than to identify source, the design was nevertheless not functional. Because there were other attractive designs that could be developed, protecting Knitwaves' specific designs under trademark law would not foreclose effective competition. *Id.* at 1006. Should a court reach the same conclusion on functionality today, after *TrafFix*? How would the reasoning of *TrafFix* apply to such a case? In *TrafFix,* if we removed the dual springs, the sign would no longer function as intended. Do we apply similar reasoning to the sweaters? If we removed the design, would the sweater still clothe the body? Would it still have the same aesthetic appeal? Which is the relevant question?

5.   *Aesthetic Functionality and Ornamental Use*. In *Pagliero*, the plaintiff developed an attractive design for china, and once it became popular, sought to protect it from imitation by claiming that it constituted trade dress. As noted, the Ninth Circuit rejected the claim, and held that the design was functional. In reaching that conclusion, the Ninth Circuit held that a feature was functional if "it constituted an important ingredient in the commercial success of the product." *Pagliero v. Wallace China Co.*, 198 F.2d 339, 343 (9th Cir. 1952). What if the attractive design on a product was also a trademark? For example, some Louis Vuitton handbags have a repeating pattern of the familiar LV logo and fleur-de-lis insignia. Assume that a would-be competitor offers similar looking handbags, and that Louis Vuitton sues for trademark

infringement. As its defense, the would-be competitor insists that the features copied are functional—they represent the very design consumers are looking for. How should the case be resolved? *See Vuitton Et Fils S.A. v. J. Young Enters., Inc.*, 644 F.2d 769, 775 (9th Cir. 1981) (allowing protection and holding that "a trademark which identifies the source of goods and incidentally serves another function may still be entitled to protection").

What if an individual wants to sell t-shirts bearing Louisiana State University's team name and colors, or wants to sell key chains or license plate brackets bearing the word Audi or Volkswagen? If the respective trademark owners sue for infringement, can the defendant successfully argue that, as applied to his products, the trademarks constitute the commercial appeal of his products and hence are functional? *See Board of Supervisors v. Smack Apparel Co.*, 550 F.3d 465, 488 (5th Cir. 2008) (holding that "alleged competitive disadvantage in the ability to sell game day apparel relates solely to an inability to take advantage of the Universities' reputation and the public's desired association with the Universities that its shirts create"), *cert. denied*, 556 U.S. 1268 (2009); *Au-Tomotive Gold, Inc. v. Volkswagen of America, Inc.*, 457 F.3d 1062, 1074 (9th Cir. 2006) (holding that "Audi" or "Volkswagen" on key chains or license plate brackets were not functional; any disadvantage that arose from not being able to sell products bearing "Audi" or "Volkswagen" "is tied to the reputation and association with Volkswagen and Audi"), *cert. denied*, 549 U.S. 1282 (2007).

Are consumers better or worse off as a result of these three decisions? Are their interests in the three cases the same? If we allow others to sell handbags with the same repeating LV, fleur-de-lis pattern, what will allowing such "competition" do to the market for such handbags? Will it enable consumers to obtain what they are looking for at a lower price? What if we allow others to market LSU t-shirts, or Audi key chains?

One key difference between these products is that the first is a prestige good. Consumers purchase a Louis Vuitton handbag, in part, precisely because it is more expensive. By paying more for the product, consumers can signal their wealth to others. If we allow others to sell imitations that are indistinguishable from the original Louis Vuitton handbags, the cheap imitations will prevent Louis Vuitton handbags from serving this signaling function. Thus, in contrast to the markets for ordinary goods, for prestige goods, high prices, which require in turn a corresponding real or legally-maintained scarcity, are arguably essential. In that light, would allowing LV imitators introduce competition into the market for Louis Vuitton handbags or would it destroy that market? If low-price imitations became commonplace, would anyone purchase the original? Would anyone purchase the imitations?

In contrast, is there any argument that consumers would be worse off by allowing unauthorized sales of LSU t-shirts or Audi key chains? Do these products serve a wealth signaling function? If not, why should we use trademark law to maintain artificial scarcity and correspondingly higher prices?

Assume, for the moment, that we could maximize consumer welfare by prohibiting the Louis Vuitton imitations, while allowing the LSU t-shirts and the Audi key chains. Is there any chance that courts will have the information necessary both to recognize that such a line should be drawn and to draw the line appropriately? If courts are unable to draw and enforce a line distinguishing between these uses, and so must choose between allowing all three or prohibiting all three, which way should the courts go if the sole concern is maximizing consumer welfare?

Is there a concern other than consumer welfare that we ought to consider in defining the availability and scope of trademark protection? Should we extend trademark protection to these three uses merely because it enables the trademark owner to earn more money or because the trademark owner created the demand for the associated product? If either of those concerns is a sufficient justification for protection, was *Pagliero* wrongly decided?

6.   *Does the Functionality Doctrine Apply to Word Marks?* While there can be a question with respect to whether a particular word or phrase as used in a specific context is best dealt with under the rubric of functionality, genericness, or descriptiveness, the general rule is that a word or phrase may be functional. In *Smith v. Krause*, for example, the owner of a federally registered trademark for the words "Merrie Christmas" woven into a ribbon sued to enjoin another for selling ribbon bearing the same words. 160 F. 270 (C.C.S.D.N.Y. 1908). The court rejected the claim, finding that "the fact that it has "Merrie Christmas' inscribed upon it adds a value to it over the value of a plain ribbon." *Id.* at 271.

How would you resolve the following case:

> Plaintiff, Damn I'm Good Inc., has . . . [since 1976] been in the mail order business selling bracelets inscribed across their face in large capital letters with the phrase DAMN I'M GOOD. . . . The bracelets are smooth-surfaced with a high-gloss finish, approximately 3/4 inches in width, flexible to fit all sized wrists, and may be purchased in brass or copper, and at one time in sterling silver or 14-karat gold. As of May 1980, plaintiff also sells pendants, umbrellas and gold ball markers inscribed with the DAMN I'M GOOD phrase. . . . Beginning in December 1978, defendant Sakowitz, Inc., a former major retailer of plaintiff's bracelets, sold money clips, ties, bath towels and bath rugs of its own manufacture bearing the phrase DAMN I'M GOOD. Beginning in its Christmas 1979 catalog, defendant Hanover sold bracelets that appear similar to those of plaintiff which also bear the DAMN I'M GOOD inscription.

> The plaintiff has sued the defendants alleging that their use of the phrase DAMN I'M GOOD on their products is a violation of section 43(a).

See Damn I'm Good, Inc. v. Sakowitz, Inc., 514 F.Supp. 1357 (S.D.N.Y. 1981) (finding that the "primary appeal of the plaintiff's bracelet is the message inscribed on them" and that the phrase was therefore functional); *see also In re Schwauss*, 217 U.S.P.Q. (BNA) 361 (T.T.A.B. 1983) (denying registration to "Fragile" for labels and bumper stickers as functional).

7.   *Generic Trade Dress.* Just as the functionality doctrine applies to word marks in appropriate cases, so too does the genericness doctrine apply to product design and packaging, as the Court recognized in *Two Pesos.* As a general rule, a product design or packaging claimed as trade dress will be generic if it is "well-known or common, a mere refinement of a commonly-adopted and well-known form of ornamentation, or a common basic shape or design, even if it has not before been refined in precisely the same way." *Ale House Management v. Raleigh Ale House,* 205 F.3d 137, 142 (4th Cir. 2000). In *Ale House Management v. Raleigh Ale House,* the plaintiff claimed the interior layout of its Ale House as trade dress. The trade dress consisted of a "centrally located rectangular bar with two types of seating on either side and television monitors, arcades, and pool tables, decorated generally in wood and brass." *Id.* at 142. Finding that there was no evidence that the plaintiff's interior layout was "unique or unusual," the court concluded that the claimed trade dress was generic. *Id.* Would such a layout also be functional?

8.   *The Relationship Between Functionality and Distinctiveness.* As a legal matter, functionality and distinctiveness are independent requirements for protection. If the claimed feature is functional, then it is unprotectible, even if distinctive. Similarly, if the feature is not distinctive, then it is unprotectible even if not functional. However, the *Wal-Mart* Court suggested that there is also a factual relationship between the two. Specifically, the *Wal-Mart* Court wrote: "Consumers are aware of the reality that, almost invariably, even the most unusual of product designs—such as a cocktail shaker shaped like a penguin—is intended not to identify the source, but to render the product itself more useful or more appealing." *Wal-Mart, Stores Inc.,* 529 U.S. at 213.

This implicitly suggests that product features are likely to serve one predominant purpose. Either consumers will take them as features of the product itself or as source identifiers, but not both. Taking that as simply a factual assertion regarding consumer behavior, do you agree? Even if the assertion is not factually accurate, does it nonetheless make good policy sense?

As we have discussed before with respect to genericness, functionality and distinctiveness for trade dress are legally on-off categories. The feature is either legally functional or not; it is distinctive or not. If it is both distinctive and non-functional, then it is protectable. Yet, in the marketplace, these may be questions of degree. A product feature may increase the inherent appeal of the associate product none, a little, some, or a lot. At some point, the feature will become such a central part of the product's inherent appeal that every court will agree that it is *de jure* functional. Yet, even before reaching that point, the feature may still play some role, perhaps even an important role, as an aspect of the product itself. From a consumer welfare perspective, as the product feature at issue becomes more functional, the costs of protecting that feature increase, and we may therefore want to see a stronger showing of distinctiveness before protecting the feature as trade dress.

Although not perfectly formalized in the law, numerous cases recognize this insight and hence consider the extent to which the feature claimed as trade dress is *de facto* functional in determining whether the trade dress is distinctive or source-identifying. For example, in the *Knitwaves, Inc.* case discussed in note 3, *supra*, the court held that the availability of alternative designs for fall sweaters precluded a finding that the particular sweater designs at issue were *de jure* functional. 71 F.3d at 1006. Nevertheless, the fact that the design was primarily intended to enhance the sweaters' aesthetic appeal established that the designs were not distinctive.

As the court explained:

> [Because of the potential availability of alternative designs,] Lollytogs ... cannot meet the market foreclosure requirement of functionality. The arguments it raises under the rubric of functionality, however, support a related (and more successful) argument: since the primary purpose of Knitwaves' sweater designs is aesthetic rather than source-identifying, Knitwaves' sweater designs do not meet the first requirement of an action under § 43(a) of the Lanham Act—that they be used as a mark to identify or distinguish the source.

Id.

9. *Is Trade Dress Protectible Under the Trademark Act?* As noted, Congress intended to exclude trade dress from federal protection when it enacted the Trademark Act of 1946. First Daphne Leeds, as Assistant Commissioner of Trademarks, and later courts, either disregarded or ignored Congress' intent in this regard. In *Two Pesos*, the Court took this mistake a step further and interpreted Congress' silence with respect to secondary meaning as an intent to abolish this traditional common law requirement for trade dress protection. In *Qualitex*, Justice Breyer creatively read the word "symbol" in section 43(a) and in the definition of a "trademark" to encompass trade dress. In *Wal-Mart*, the Court began to recognize that the federal protection of trade dress is entirely a creature of judicial, and not legislative, decision-making. In *TrafFix*, Justice Kennedy, writing for the majority, frankly acknowledges that federal trade dress protection is a judicial creation. Having added trade dress to the statute in disregard of Congress' express intent, is it too late for courts simply to remove trade dress from the ambit of federal protection altogether?

In the majority opinion in *TrafFix*, Justice Kennedy suggests that Congress has sanctioned federal trade dress protection by adding section 43(a)(3) to the Act. Added in 1999, section 43(a)(3) provides:

> In a civil action for trade dress infringement under this Act for trade dress not registered on the principal register, the person who

asserts trade dress protection has the burden of proving that the matter sought to be protected is not functional.

15 U.S.C. § 1125(a)(3) (2015).

Does the addition of section 43(a)(3) represent Congress' approval of federal trade dress protection? Should the fact that Congress acted to correct one judicial mistake, with respect to how the burden of proof with respect to functionality should be assigned, preclude the courts from correcting another, with respect to whether trade dress should receive protection at all? Does it represent Congress' approval of the PTO's decision to allow trade dress on the principal register? Or is an implicit negative insufficient to overcome the express language by which Congress relegated trade dress to the supplemental register?

As part of the amendments to the Trademark Act in 1998, Congress expressly considered adding language that would have defined trade dress as eligible for registration on the principal register. H.R. 3163, 105th Cong., 2d Sess., § 2(a)(3) (1998) (proposing to add subsection (g) to section 2 of the Trademark Act and expressly authorize the registration of trade dress on the principal register). However, Congress refused to adopt the proposed language. Is that relevant?

CHAPTER 6

TRADEMARK OWNERSHIP

■ ■ ■

A. INITIAL OWNERSHIP

As a general rule, we assign initial ownership of a trademark to the entity that is using the mark in commerce. The use requirement resolves many potential ownership disputes. For example, as we discussed in Chapter 2, the use requirement dictates that as between the advertising agency who coins a mark and prepares the associated ad campaign, and the agency's client who takes the mark and uses the mark to sell its products, the client owns the trademark. In some cases, however, two or more parties may be involved in a single use. For example, one party may design a product, but contract with a second firm to build the product. If the parties do not address the issue contractually, who owns the trademark associated with the product? The next case considers that issue.

SENGOKU WORKS LTD. v. RMC INT'L, LTD.
96 F.3d 1217 (9th Cir. 1996)

HALL, C.J.

RMC International Ltd., and its officers Michael Resmo and Joseph Malaga, appeal the district court's judgment, following a jury trial, in favor of Sengoku Works Ltd. for trademark and trade dress infringement under the Lanham Act, 15 U.S.C. §§ 1051–1127, and breach of contract under California law. RMC had served since 1985 as exclusive United States distributor of kerosene heaters manufactured by Sengoku, a Japanese corporation, and these charges arose in connection with RMC's decision to market kerosene heaters from another source.

In this opinion we address only the issue of ownership of the Keroheat trademark. All the other issues are disposed of in a separate unpublished disposition.

I

RMC is an importer of portable kerosene heaters. From 1985 to 1994, it imported and sold exclusively heaters manufactured by Sengoku, pursuant to yearly contracts signed by the parties. These contracts included exclusivity provisions, under which Sengoku appointed RMC its exclusive U.S. distributor, and RMC agreed to distribute only Sengoku-manufactured heaters. As part of this arrangement, Sengoku sold the heaters to an independent trading company, Zenith & Co., who then sold them to RMC. The RMC/Zenith/Sengoku heaters bore the trademark "Keroheat."

Under the agreement, RMC handled all of the marketing and advertising for the heaters, and arranged for all of the retailer purchases of the heaters. Only RMC's name appeared on the product and packaging, and RMC dealt with all consumer complaints and returns. RMC claims that in the early 1990s it began to experience increasing quality problems with the Sengoku heaters, and increasing customer complaints. When Sengoku did not take satisfactory steps to remedy the problems, in 1993 RMC began to negotiate with Wooshin, a Korean corporation, to manufacture and supply kerosene heaters to RMC.

RMC maintains that they had no valid contract with Sengoku for 1994. For the first quarter of 1994, RMC performed as it had for the previous nine years. But in late March Sengoku became aware that RMC was selling heaters to Sengoku's largest U.S. customer that were manufactured by Wooshin, and that bore the Keroheat trademark and closely resembled Sengoku's heaters. Sengoku filed suit against RMC for breaching the exclusivity provision of their contract, and for trademark and trade dress infringement.

Sengoku and RMC each claim ownership of the Keroheat trademark. From 1982 to 1985, prior to the Sengoku/RMC agreements, Sengoku heaters bearing the Keroheat mark were sold to a trading company called Imarflex, and were then sold in the U.S. by C.C.I., a company partially owned by Cort Clark. In 1985, Clark sued Imarflex for breach of contract and trademark infringement, claiming that he owned the Keroheat trademark. After the Sengoku/Imarflex/Clark deal ended, Clark then founded RMC, with Michael Resmo and Joseph Malaga. RMC began selling Sengoku heaters under the Keroheat mark in 1985, and obtained a federal registration of the mark. Clark left RMC in 1992, and now works for Sengoku.

In July 1994 the district court granted Sengoku a preliminary injunction to enjoin RMC from selling the Wooshin heater bearing the Keroheat mark. After a seven day jury trial, the jury found for Sengoku on all claims. The jury awarded Sengoku only $1.00 in damages on the trademark infringement claim. The district court then ordered the cancellation of RMC's federal trademark registration for Keroheat, and entered a permanent injunction barring RMC from using the mark. The district court also denied RMC's post-trial motions for judgment as a matter of law and for a new trial. This appeal followed.

II

Both parties agree that RMC did distribute heaters bearing the Keroheat trademark that were not manufactured by Sengoku. However, they both claim ownership of the Keroheat trademark, and this issue is central to the finding for Sengoku on trademark infringement.

Challenges to the sufficiency of the evidence and the denial of a motion for judgment notwithstanding the verdict are reviewed de novo to determine if the plaintiff's claims were supported by substantial evidence. *Erickson v. Pierce County*, 960 F.2d 801, 804 (9th Cir.), *cert. denied,* 506 U.S. 1035 (1992). Substantial evidence is such relevant evidence as reasonable minds might accept as adequate to support the jury's verdict. *Murray v. Laborers Union Local No. 324,* 55 F.3d 1445, 1452 (9th Cir. 1995).

It is axiomatic in trademark law that the standard test of ownership is priority of use. To acquire ownership of a trademark it is not enough to have invented the mark first or even to have registered it first; the party claiming ownership must have been the first to actually use the mark in the sale of goods or services. *See generally* J. Thomas McCarthy, 2 *McCarthy on Trademarks and Unfair Competition* § 16.03 (3d ed. 1996) (hereinafter *McCarthy*). When proving ownership of a trademark, federal registration of the mark is prima facie evidence that the registrant is the owner of the mark. Lanham Act § 7(b), 15 U.S.C. § 1057(b); Lanham Act § 33(a), 15 U.S.C. § 1115(a). Therefore, the registrant is granted a presumption of ownership, dating to the filing date of the application for federal registration, and the challenger must overcome this presumption by a preponderance of the evidence. *Vuitton Et Fils S.A. v. J. Young Enterprises,* 644 F.2d 769, 775–76 (9th Cir. 1981); *Rolley, Inc. v. Younghusband,* 204 F.2d 209 (9th Cir. 1953). However, the non-registrant can rebut this presumption by showing that the registrant had not established valid ownership rights in the mark at the time of registration—in other words, if the non-registrant can show that he used the mark in commerce first, then the registration may be invalidated.

Disputes over trademark ownership often arise when the mark is used on goods that are manufactured by one company, but are marketed by another pursuant to an exclusive distributorship agreement. These relationships usually arise in one of two factual situations: either (1) the manufacturer licenses the distributor to use a trademark owned by the manufacturer, or (2) the distributor owns its own mark, sometimes called a "private label," which it affixes to the manufacturer's product before delivery. In either case, the ownership of the mark turns on which party was the initial owner.

Unfortunately, not every distribution agreement fits clearly into one of these two categories. When disputes arise between a manufacturer and distributor, courts will look first to any agreement between the parties regarding trademark rights. *Premier Dental Products v. Darby Dental Supply Co.,* 794 F.2d 850, 854 (3d Cir.), *cert. denied,* 479 U.S. 950 (1986). But in the absence of an agreement between the parties, the manufacturer is presumed to own the trademark. *Energy Jet, Inc. v. Forex Corp.,* 589 F. Supp. 1110, 1116 (E.D. Mich. 1984); *Wrist-Rocket Mfr. Co. v. Saunders,* 379 F. Supp. 902, 909 (D. Neb. 1974) ("*Wrist-Rocket I*"), *aff'd in part and rev'd in part on other grounds,* 516 F.2d 846 (8th Cir.) ("*Wrist-Rocket II*"), *cert. denied,* 423 U.S. 870 (1975); *Automated Productions Inc. v. FMB Maschinenbaugesellschaft mbH & Co.,* 36 U.S.P.Q.2D (BNA) 1714, 1716 (N.D. Ill. 1995). That presumption applies with equal force to cases involving foreign manufacturers. *See, e.g., Energy Jet,* 589 F. Supp. at 1116; *Hank Thorp, Inc. v. Minilite, Inc.,* 474 F. Supp. 228, 236 (D. Del. 1979). Although some courts have suggested that the presumption may be different in the case of foreign manufacturers, frequently the identical standard has in fact been applied, and we see no reason for doing otherwise.

The presumption in favor of the manufacturer is rebuttable, however, and a long-standing line of precedent holds that an exclusive distributor may acquire trademark rights superior to those of the manufacturer. *See Menendez v. Holt,* 128 U.S. 514 (1888); *Omega Nutrition v. Spectrum Marketing,* 756 F. Supp. 435, 438 (N.D. Cal. 1991) (granting [an injunction] to the exclusive distributor against the manufacturer for trademark infringement); *see also* 2 *McCarthy,* § 16.15[1] n.3 (citing a long list of cases following this principle). Therefore, the distributor may rebut the presumption in favor of the manufacturer, and courts look to various factors when determining which party has the superior right of ownership, including:

(1) which party invented and first affixed the mark onto the product;

(2) which party's name appeared with the trademark;

(3) which party maintained the quality and uniformity of the product; and

(4) with which party the public identified the product and to whom purchasers made complaints.

Omega Nutrition, 756 F. Supp. at 438–49.

Furthermore, courts will also consider which party possesses the goodwill associated with the product, or which party the public believes stands behind the product. *Premier Dental,* 794 F.2d at 854.

On appeal (and at trial), Sengoku seemed to argue that once it was established that Sengoku was the manufacturer and RMC was the exclusive distributor, then the issue of trademark ownership is resolved— in other words, if this was a manufacturer/exclusive distributor relationship, then Sengoku is entitled to the presumption in favor of the manufacturer and has therefore established its ownership of the trademark. This is, however, an oversimplification of the law.

The determinative issue is not which label is placed upon the relationship, but rather which party can establish priority of ownership. *See Wrist-Rocket II,* 516 F.2d at 850 (When the issue "is who, as between the manufacturer and distributor, has ownership of a trademark created *after* formation of the business relationship . . . the dispositive question [is] which party has priority of appropriation and use of the trademark."). The court must first look to any agreement or acknowledgment between the parties regarding trademark rights. There was no such agreement between Sengoku and RMC; thus, if neither party can prove that it initially owned the trademark, then Sengoku is entitled to claim the presumption in favor of the manufacturer. In that case, RMC may rebut this presumption by addressing the factors set forth above.

While this is a close question, we find that there is substantial evidence in the record to support a finding that Sengoku owned the trademark. Sengoku first affixed the Keroheat mark to its heaters in 1982, at least two years before RMC began distributing Keroheat heaters. RMC's federal registration of the mark was not acquired until 1992, and RMC claimed it first used the mark in commerce in 1985. Although RMC claims that CCI, the exclusive distributor before RMC, owned the trademark, there is no evidence that ownership was transferred to RMC. Thus, the jury could reasonably have found that Sengoku established prior use.

Furthermore, when considering the factors that go to trademark ownership, some support Sengoku's argument, and some support RMC's. Only RMC's name appears on the product and packaging, and RMC handles all customer complaints and returns. However, Sengoku exercises control over the product quality and uniformity, and Sengoku apparently first affixed the trademark to its heaters. Also, other dealers in the business testified that they attribute the heaters bearing the Keroheat mark to Sengoku.

In determining whether substantial evidence supports a jury verdict, we cannot simply substitute our judgment for that of the jury. We must consider whether the record contains substantial evidence upon which reasonable minds could base the verdict. In this case, we find that the jury could reasonably have found that Sengoku owned the trademark. Therefore, we affirm the jury's verdict for Sengoku on trademark infringement. . . .

IV

For the foregoing reasons, we hold that the jury's verdict for Sengoku on trademark infringement is supported by substantial evidence, and is therefore AFFIRMED.

NOTES FOR DISCUSSION

1. *Consumer Protection.* How should trademark law assign ownership in the manufacturer-distributor context in order to ensure that consumers continue to find what they expect from heaters bearing the Keroheat mark? Is that the purpose that the court's approach is intended to serve? If it is not, what is the purpose of the court's approach? In your view, to which party should we assign ownership of the trademark in order to ensure that consumers continue to receive what they expect from heaters bearing the Keroheat mark?

2. *Clarity and Justice.* Why did the parties fail to address trademark ownership contractually? Was it because the parties did not think about trademark ownership at the outset of their relationship? Or was it because the ambiguity in the trademark ownership rules afforded each a reasonable basis to believe that it was the trademark owner? Would a simpler rule, such as irrebuttable presumption of ownership in favor of the manufacturer, be better? If our sole underlying policy concern is ensuring that consumers continue to receive what they expect from the trademark, would such a simpler rule usually assign ownership to the "right" party? If the simpler rule would sometimes assign ownership to the "wrong" party, can we reasonably expect the parties to address that mistake contractually?

3. *Musical Groups.* The manufacturer-distributor context is one of the few areas where trademark ownership disputes arise. Another is music. If there are four or five members of a musical group, and the group disbands, who, if anyone, owns the band's name as a trademark? If a band has a producer, who owns the trademark, the band members or the producer? As in the manufacturer-distributor context, courts will usually, but not always, abide by the trademark ownership to which band members contractually agree. *Compare Brother Records, Inc. v. Jardine*, 318 F.3d 900 (9th Cir. 2003) (recognizing assignment of trademark "Beach Boys" to corporation formed by band members), *with Robi v. Five Platters, Inc.*, 838 F.2d 318 (9th Cir. 1988) (giving effect to a California Superior Court judgment holding that manager's attempt to assign ownership of "The Platters" trademark to a corporation he controlled was ineffective).

Absent a contractual agreement, how should we assign ownership of a band's name? The Ninth Circuit has set forth the following general principles:

> Neither the Supreme Court nor the Ninth Circuit has directly discussed the status of a trademark for the name of a musical group when one of its members departs and continues to perform under the group's name. Courts that have confronted this problem have

determined that members of a group do not retain rights to use the group's name when they leave the group.

On the other hand, it has also been held that a person who remains continuously involved with the group and is in a position to control the quality of its services retains the right to use of the mark, even when that person is a manager rather than a performer.

Robi v. Reed, 173 F.3d 736, 739–40 (9th Cir.), *cert. denied*, 528 U.S. 952 (1999).

Should trademark law seek to assign ownership of a band's name to the person or persons best placed to ensure that consumers continue to receive the quality and type of music that they have come to expect from the band? How would you resolve the following case:

> Lynn Easton, Michael Mitchell, Norman Sundholm, Richard Peterson and Barry Curtis, the plaintiffs, claim that they comprise a rock and roll band known as The Kingsmen. The original Kingsmen were formed in 1962. While the members of the band were still in high school, they recorded a demonstration tape of a song entitled "Louie, Louie." The lead vocalist on that recording was Jack Ely who, along with Easton, was an original member of the group.

> Ely left the group in 1964 after his recording of Louie, Louie but before it became popular on the record charts. In 1964, Louie, Louie became the second best selling record in the United States, and The Kingsmen were off to a successful music career. They recorded a number of albums after their initial success with Louie, Louie, and made numerous concert tours and television appearances. The five named plaintiffs comprised The Kingsmen during this period. Although Ely had originally recorded Louie, Louie, he did not tour with the band, did not perform on their subsequent albums, and did not participate in any fashion with the other members of the band after his 1964 departure. The Kingsmen ceased performing and disbanded in 1967 after three years of relative success.

> In 1976, after nearly a decade in which no member of the group performed as The Kingsmen, S.J. Productions ... communicated with Ely and made a proposal to "re-record" Louie, Louie. The recording was to be included on records produced by the defendant highlighting the most popular dance songs of the 1960's. Ely recorded Louie, Louie. The original members of The Kingsmen (except for Ely) did not participate in the recording sessions.

> Ely's re-recording now appears on ERA Records, Inc.'s "60's Dance Party" album, which was released in October, 1982. This record contains songs identified with a number of groups popular during the 1960's. The title "Louie, Louie ... The Kingsmen" appears in bold black letters on the back of the album cover. In

small print below the listing of the contents of the album is the notation, "These selections are re-recordings by the original artists."

The plaintiffs have sued Ely, ERA Records, and S.J. Productions alleging trademark infringement.

See Kingsmen v. K-Tel Int'l, Ltd., 557 F.Supp. 178 (S.D.N.Y. 1983) (granting preliminary injunction to the plaintiffs and enjoining the defendants' sale of the album).

B. OWNING TRADEMARKS BY PURCHASE: ASSIGNMENTS

SUGAR BUSTERS LLC V. BRENNAN
177 F.3d 258 (5th Cir. 1999)

KING, CHIEF JUDGE

This appeal challenges the district court's grant of a preliminary injunction prohibiting defendants-appellants from selling or distributing a book entitled "SUGAR BUST For Life!" as infringing plaintiff-appellee's federally registered service mark, "SUGARBUSTERS." Plaintiff-appellee is an assignee of a registered "SUGARBUSTERS" service mark and the author of a best-selling diet book entitled "SUGAR BUSTERS! Cut Sugar to Trim Fat." We determine that the assignment of the registered "SUGARBUSTERS" service mark to plaintiff-appellee was in gross and was therefore invalid, and we vacate the injunction. However, because plaintiff-appellee might still obtain protection for its book title from unfair competition under § 43(a) of the Lanham Act, 15 U.S.C. § 1125(a), we remand to the district court to consider plaintiff-appellee's unfair competition claims.

I.   FACTUAL AND PROCEDURAL HISTORY

Plaintiff-appellee Sugar Busters, L.L.C. (plaintiff) is a limited liability company organized by three doctors and H. Leighton Steward, a former chief executive officer of a large energy corporation, who co-authored and published a book entitled "SUGAR BUSTERS! Cut Sugar to Trim Fat" in 1995. In "SUGAR BUSTERS! Cut Sugar to Trim Fat," the authors recommend a diet plan based on the role of insulin in obesity and cardiovascular disease. The authors' premise is that reduced consumption of insulin-producing food, such as carbohydrates and other sugars, leads to weight loss and a more healthy lifestyle. The 1995 publication of "SUGAR BUSTERS! Cut Sugar to Trim Fat" sold over 210,000 copies, and in May 1998 a second edition was released. The second edition has sold over 800,000 copies and remains a bestseller.

Defendant-appellant Ellen Brennan was an independent consultant employed by plaintiff to assist with the sales, publishing, and marketing of the 1995 edition. In addition, Ellen Brennan wrote a foreword in the 1995 edition endorsing the diet plan, stating that the plan "has proven to be an effective and easy means of weight loss" for herself and for her friends and family. During her employment with plaintiff, Ellen Brennan and Steward agreed to co-author a cookbook based on the "SUGAR BUSTERS!" lifestyle. Steward had obtained plaintiff's permission to independently produce such a cookbook, which he proposed entitling "Sugar Busting is Easy." Plaintiff reconsidered its decision in December 1997, however, and determined that its partners should not engage in independent projects. Steward then encouraged Ellen Brennan to proceed with the cookbook on her own, and told her that she could "snuggle up next to our book, because you can rightly claim you were a consultant to Sugar Busters!"

Ellen Brennan and defendant-appellant Theodore Brennan then co-authored "SUGAR BUST For Life!," which was published by defendant-appellant Shamrock Publishing, Inc. in May 1998. "SUGAR BUST For Life" states on its cover that it is a "cookbook and companion guide by the famous family of good food," and that Ellen Brennan was "Consultant, Editor, Publisher, [and] Sales and Marketing Director for the original, best-selling 'Sugar Busters!TM Cut Sugar to Trim Fat.'" The cover states that the book contains over 400 recipes for "weight loss, energy, diabetes and cholesterol control and an easy, healthful lifestyle." Approximately 110,000 copies of "SUGAR BUST For Life!" were sold between its release and September 1998.

Plaintiff filed this suit in the United States District Court for the Eastern District of Louisiana on May 26, 1998, asserting causes of action for trademark infringement and dilution under 15 U.S.C. §§ 1114 and 1125(c), unfair competition and trade dress infringement under § 43(a) of the Lanham Act, 15 U.S.C. § 1125(a), and trademark dilution, misrepresentation, unfair competition and misappropriation of trade secrets under Louisiana state law. Plaintiff sought to enjoin defendants-appellants Ellen Brennan, Theodore Brennan and Shamrock Publishing, Inc. (collectively, defendants) from selling, displaying, advertising or distributing "SUGAR BUST For Life!," to destroy all copies of the cookbook, and to recover damages and any profits derived from the cookbook.

The mark that is the subject of plaintiff's infringement claim is a service mark that was registered in 1992 by Sugarbusters, Inc., an Indiana corporation operating a retail store named "Sugarbusters" in Indianapolis that provides products and information for diabetics. The "SUGARBUSTERS" service mark, registration number 1,684,769, is for "retail store services featuring products and supplies for diabetic people; namely, medical supplies, medical equipment, food products, informational literature and wearing apparel featuring a message regarding diabetes." Sugarbusters, Inc. sold "any and all rights to the mark" to Thornton-Sahoo, Inc. on December 19, 1997, and Thornton-Sahoo, Inc. sold these rights to Elliott Company, Inc. (Elliott) on January 9, 1998. Plaintiff obtained the service mark from Elliott pursuant to a "servicemark purchase agreement" dated January 26, 1998. Under the terms of that agreement, plaintiff purchased "all the interests [Elliott] owns" in the mark and "the goodwill of all business connected with the use of and symbolized by" the mark. Furthermore, Elliott agreed that it "will cease all use of the mark, name and trademark interests within one hundred eighty (180) days."

In support of its request for a preliminary injunction, plaintiff argued to the district court that the recipes in the cookbook did not comport with the "SUGAR BUSTERS!" lifestyle and that consumers were being misled into believing that defendants' cookbook was affiliated with, or otherwise approved by, plaintiff. Plaintiff asserted that even if its purported service mark is found invalid, plaintiff is still entitled to a preliminary injunction under § 43(a) of the Lanham Act because its title "SUGAR BUSTERS! Cut Sugar to Trim Fat!" has developed a "secondary meaning" in the minds of customers, plaintiff has developed a common law service mark through the seminars it holds regarding the "SUGAR BUSTERS!" lifestyle, and defendants infringed plaintiff's trade dress.

Defendants argued to the district court that plaintiff's service mark is invalid because: (1) it was purchased "in gross," (2) the term "SUGARBUSTERS" has become generic through third-party use, and (3) plaintiff abandoned the mark by licensing it back to Elliott without any supervision or control over the retail store in Indiana that continues to operate under the "Sugarbusters" name. Defendants argued that, even if the service mark is valid, their cookbook could not infringe it because the mark is limited to a retail store and a trademark may not be obtained for a book title. Finally, defendants asserted that their use of the title was a "fair use" and that plaintiff is not entitled to an injunction under equitable principles because Stewart breached his agreement with Ellen Brennan and invited her to write the cookbook that is now the subject of this case.

The district court heard evidence relating to the preliminary injunction for three days beginning on June 30, 1998 and entered a preliminary injunction on September 22, 1998 that prohibits defendants from engaging in the sale and distribution of their cookbook, "SUGAR BUST For Life!" *See Sugar Busters, L.L.C. v. Brennan*, 48 U.S.P.Q.2D (BNA) 1511, 1512 (E.D. La. 1998). The district court found that plaintiff is the owner of the registered service mark, "SUGARBUSTERS," and that the mark is registered in International Class 16, "information, literature, and books." 48 U.S.P.Q.2D (BNA) at 1514. The district court found that the mark is valid and that the transfer of the mark to plaintiff was not "in gross" because

> the plaintiff has used the trademark to disseminate information through its books, seminars, the Internet, and the cover of plaintiff's recent book, which reads "Help Treat Diabetes and Other Diseases." Moreover, the plaintiff is moving forward to market and sell its own products and services, which comport with the products and services sold by the Indiana corporation. There has been a full and complete transfer of the good will related to the mark, and the plaintiff has licensed the Indiana corporation to use the mark for only six months to enable it to wind down its operations.

The district court then considered whether defendants' use of the mark " 'creates a likelihood of confusion in the minds of potential customers as to the source, affiliation, or sponsorship' " of the cookbook using the factors we outlined in *Elvis Presley Enterprises, Inc. v. Capece*, 141 F.3d 188, 194 (5th Cir. 1998). *Sugar Busters*, 48 U.S.P.Q.2D (BNA) at 1513 (quoting *Elvis Presley Enters.*, 141 F.3d at 193).

The district court found that "plaintiff has established that there is a likelihood of confusion in the minds of customers," that there is a substantial threat plaintiff will suffer irreparable injury without a preliminary injunction, that this threatened injury outweighs any damage that an injunction may cause defendants, and that an injunction will not disserve the public interest. 48 U.S.P.Q.2D (BNA) at 1516. The court refused to consider defendants' fair-use argument because it was raised for the first time in defendants' post-hearing brief, found defendants' equitable argument insufficient to prevent an injunction, and enjoined defendants from engaging in the sale and distribution of "SUGAR BUST For Life!" *See id.* at 1517. Because the district court entered the injunction based on plaintiff's trademark infringement claim, the court declined to analyze or discuss plaintiff's remaining claims. *See id.* at 1516. Defendants timely appeal.

II. DISCUSSION

Defendants argue that the district court erroneously concluded that plaintiff's purported service mark in "SUGARBUSTERS" is valid and that their cookbook infringes the mark. Defendants also argue that plaintiff's unfair competition claims under § 43(a) of the Lanham Act fail because that section cannot protect a single book title or, alternatively, that remand is necessary because the district court did not consider whether the book title has acquired secondary meaning. Defendants assert that remand is also necessary on plaintiff's claim that it has an unregistered service mark in "SUGAR BUSTERS!" as a result of the seminars it held promoting the book because the district court did not consider this argument or make any factual finding regarding likelihood of confusion.

Finally, defendants argue that the district court erred by rejecting their arguments regarding fair use and equitable principles. We address each of these arguments in turn.

A. Standard of Review

We review a district court's ultimate decision to grant a preliminary injunction for an abuse of discretion. *See Affiliated Prof'l Home Health Care Agency v. Shalala*, 164 F.3d 282, 284 (5th Cir. 1999); *Sunbeam Prods., Inc. v. West Bend Co.*, 123 F.3d 246, 250 (5th Cir. 1997), cert. denied, 523 U.S. 1118 (1998). A preliminary injunction is an extraordinary equitable remedy that may be granted only if plaintiff establishes the following four elements: (1) a substantial likelihood of success on the merits, (2) a substantial threat that plaintiff will suffer irreparable injury if the injunction is denied, (3) that the threatened injury outweighs any damage that the injunction might cause defendants, and (4) that the injunction will not disserve the public interest. *See Hoover v. Morales*, 164 F.3d 221, 224 (5th Cir. 1998); *Sunbeam Prods.*, 123 F.3d at 250. Defendants' arguments challenging the preliminary injunction focus only on the first element—the likelihood that plaintiff will succeed on the merits of its claims. Because this element "presents a mixed question of law and fact, this court must uphold the district court's subsidiary fact findings unless clearly erroneous; conclusions of law and the ultimate application of the law to the facts, however, are freely reviewable." *Byrne v. Roemer*, 847 F.2d 1130, 1133 (5th Cir. 1988). Finally, plaintiff reminds us that we may "affirm a judgment of the district court if the result is correct, even if our affirmance is upon grounds not relied upon by the district court." *Foreman v. Babcock & Wilcox Co.*, 117 F.3d 800, 804 (5th Cir. 1997), *cert. denied*, 522 U.S. 1115 (1998); *see Herwald v. Schweiker*, 658 F.2d 359, 362–63 (5th Cir. Unit A Oct. 1981) (applying rule to preliminary injunction).

B. Plaintiff's Registered Service Mark

A trademark is merely a symbol of goodwill and has no independent significance apart from the goodwill that it symbolizes. *See Marshak v. Green*, 746 F.2d 927, 929 (2d Cir. 1984); 2 McCarthy, *Trademarks and Unfair Competition,* § 18:2 (4th ed. 1999) [hereinafter McCarthy]. "A trade mark only gives the right to prohibit the use of it so far as to protect the owner's good will. . . ." *Prestonettes, Inc. v. Coty*, 264 U.S. 359, 368 (1924) (Holmes, J.). Therefore, a trademark cannot be sold or assigned apart from the goodwill it symbolizes. *See* 15 U.S.C. § 1060 ("A registered mark or a mark for which application to register has been filed shall be assignable with the goodwill of the business in which the mark is used, or with that part of the goodwill of the business connected with the use of and symbolized by the mark."); *Marshak*, 746 F.2d at 929. The sale or assignment of a trademark without the goodwill that the mark represents is characterized as in gross and is invalid. *See PepsiCo, Inc. v. Grapette Co.*, 416 F.2d 285, 287 (8th Cir. 1969); 2 McCarthy § 18:3.

The purpose of the rule prohibiting the sale or assignment of a trademark in gross is to prevent a consumer from being misled or confused as to the source and nature of the goods or services that he or she acquires. *See Visa, U.S.A., Inc. v. Birmingham Trust Nat'l Bank*, 696 F.2d 1371, 1375 (Fed. Cir. 1982). "Use of the mark by the assignee in connection with a different goodwill and different product would result in a fraud on the purchasing public who reasonably assume that the mark signifies the same thing, whether used by one person or another." *Marshak*, 746 F.2d at 929. Therefore, " 'if consumers are not to be misled from established associations with the mark, [it must] continue to be associated with the same or similar products after the assignment.' " *Visa*, U.S.A., 696 F.2d at 1375 (quoting *Raufast S.A. v. Kicker's Pizzazz, Ltd.*, 208 U.S.P.Q. 699, 702 (E.D.N.Y. 1980)).

Plaintiff's purported service mark in "SUGARBUSTERS" is valid only if plaintiff also acquired the goodwill that accompanies the mark; that is, "the portion of the business or service with which the mark is associated." *Id.* Defendants claim that the transfer of the "SUGARBUSTERS" mark to plaintiff was in gross because "none of the assignor's underlying business, including its inventory, customer lists, or other assets, were transferred to [plaintiff]." Defendants' view of goodwill, however, is too narrow. Plaintiff may obtain a valid trademark without purchasing any physical or tangible assets of the retail store in Indiana—"the transfer of goodwill requires only that the services be sufficiently similar to prevent consumers of the service offered under the mark from being misled from established associations with the mark." 696 F.2d at 1376 (internal quotation marks omitted); *see Marshak*, 746 F.2d at 930 ("The courts have upheld such assignments if they find that the assignee is producing a product or performing a service substantially similar to that of the assignor and that the consumers would not be deceived or harmed."); *PepsiCo*, 416 F.2d at 288 ("Basic to this concept [of protecting against consumer deception] is the proposition that any assignment of a trademark and its goodwill (with or without tangibles or intangibles assigned) requires the mark itself be used by the assignee on a product having substantially the same characteristics."); *cf. Money Store v. Harriscorp Fin., Inc.*, 689 F.2d 666, 678 (7th Cir. 1982) ("In the case of a service mark . . . confusion would result if an assignee offered a service different from that offered by the assignor of the mark.").

The district court found, without expressly stating the applicable legal standard, that "there has been a full and complete transfer of the good will related to the mark." *Sugar Busters*, 48 U.S.P.Q.2D (BNA) at 1514. The proper standard, as discussed above, is whether plaintiff's book and the retail store in Indiana are sufficiently similar to prevent consumer confusion or deception when plaintiff uses the mark previously associated with the store as the title of its book. We conclude that even if the district court applied this standard, its finding that goodwill was transferred between Elliott and plaintiff is clearly erroneous.

In concluding that goodwill was transferred, the district court relied in part on its finding that the mark at issue is registered in International Class 16, "information, literature, and books." However, the registration certificate issued by the United States Patent and Trademark Office states that the service mark is "in class 42" and is "for retail store services featuring products and supplies for diabetic people." The district court also relied on its finding that "plaintiff is moving forward to market and sell its own products and services, which comport with the products and services sold by the Indiana corporation." *Id.* Steward testified, however, that plaintiff does not have any plans to operate a retail store, and plaintiff offered no evidence suggesting that it intends to market directly to consumers any goods it licenses to carry the "SUGAR BUSTERS!" name. Finally, we are unconvinced by plaintiff's argument that, by stating on the cover of its diet book that it may "help treat diabetes and other diseases" and then selling some of those books on the Internet, plaintiff provides a service substantially similar to a retail store that provides diabetic supplies. *See PepsiCo*, 416 F.2d at 286–89 (determining that pepper-flavored soft drink and cola-flavored soft drink are not substantially similar and therefore purported assignment was in gross and invalid). We therefore must conclude that plaintiff's purported service mark is invalid. Thus, its trademark infringement claim under 15 U.S.C. § 1114 cannot succeed on the merits and the district court improperly relied on this ground in granting plaintiff's request for a preliminary injunction.

C.   Unfair Competition Claims

Plaintiff argues that we must still uphold the preliminary injunction because it has demonstrated a likelihood of success on the merits of its claims under § 43(a) of the Lanham Act. The Supreme Court has recognized that § 43(a) " 'prohibits a broader range of practices than does § 32,' which applies to registered marks," and that § 43(a) protects qualifying unregistered marks. *Two Pesos, Inc. v. Taco Cabana, Inc.*, 505 U.S. 763, 768 (1992) (quoting *Inwood Lab., Inc. v. Ives Lab., Inc.*, 456 U.S. 844, 858 (1982)). Plaintiff asserts that the district court could have granted the preliminary injunction on the basis of its claim that defendants' use of the title "SUGAR BUST For Life!" is likely to cause confusion or deceive consumers as to its connection with plaintiff's book, "SUGAR BUSTERS! Cut Sugar to Trim Fat." Additionally, plaintiff argues that it has developed a common law service mark in "SUGAR BUSTERS!" based on seminars it has held promoting its book, and that defendants' title is likely to cause confusion with respect to those seminars. We consider plaintiff's arguments in turn.

1. Plaintiff's Book Title

As a preliminary matter, we must consider defendants' contention that a book title may not receive protection under § 43(a). Defendants contend that "titles of single literary works are not registerable" as trademarks, and therefore that § 43(a) cannot protect plaintiff's title because the Supreme Court has held "that the general principles qualifying a mark for registration under § 2 of the Lanham Act are for the most part applicable in determining whether an unregistered mark is entitled to protection under § 43(a)." *Id.*; *see Thompson Med. Co. v. Pfizer Inc.*, 753 F.2d 208, 215 (2d Cir. 1985) ("The starting point of our examination [under § 43(a)] is determining whether a mark is eligible for protection."). Defendants argue that just as generic marks can be neither registered as trademarks nor protected under § 43(a), *see Union National Bank of Texas, Laredo, Texas v. Union National Bank of Texas, Austin, Texas*, 909 F.2d 839, 844 (5th Cir. 1990) ("Generic terms are never eligible for trademark protection."); *A.J. Canfield Co. v. Honickman*, 808 F.2d 291, 297 (3d Cir. 1986) (stating that "if we hold a designation generic, it is never protectable"), a single book title is ineligible for trademark registration or § 43(a) protection.

In order to be registered as a trademark, a mark must be capable of distinguishing the applicant's goods from those of others. *See* 15 U.S.C. § 1052; *Two Pesos*, 505 U.S. at 768. "Marks are often classified in categories of generally increasing distinctiveness; following the classic formulation set out by Judge Friendly, they may be (1) generic; (2) descriptive; (3) suggestive; (4) arbitrary; or (5) fanciful." *Two Pesos*, 505 U.S. at 768 (citing *Abercrombie & Fitch Co. v. Hunting World, Inc.*, 537 F.2d 4, 9 (2d Cir. 1976)). The latter three categories of marks are entitled to trademark protection because they are inherently distinctive—they serve to identify a particular source of a product. *See id.* Generic marks, in contrast, " 'refer to the genus of which the particular product is a species' " and are neither registerable as trademarks, *id.* (quoting *Park 'N Fly, Inc. v. Dollar Park & Fly, Inc.*, 469 U.S. 189, 194 (1985)) (alteration in original), nor protectable under § 43(a), *see Thompson Medical*, 753 F.2d at 212. The final category, consisting of marks that describe a product, "do not inherently identify a particular source, and hence cannot be protected" unless they acquire distinctiveness through secondary meaning. *Two Pesos*, 505 U.S. at 769. Such secondary meaning is achieved when, " 'in the minds of the public, the primary significance of a product feature or term is to identify the source of the product rather than the product itself.' " *Id.* at 766 n.4 (quoting *Inwood Lab.*, 456 U.S. at 851 n.11); *see Sunbeam Prods.*, 123 F.3d at 252 (recognizing that "descriptive marks are entitled to protection only if they have come to be uniquely associated with a particular source"); Restatement (3d), *Unfair Competition,* § 13 (1995) [hereinafter Restatement] (describing secondary meaning as "acquired distinctiveness").

Over forty years ago, the Court of Customs and Patent Appeals (the predecessor to the current Federal Circuit) considered whether the title of a single book may be the subject of a trademark. *See In re Cooper,* 45 C.C.P.A. 923, 254 F.2d 611, 613–16 (C.C.P.A. 1958). The court determined that, "however arbitrary, novel or nondescriptive of contents the name of a book—its title—may be, it nevertheless describes the book." 254 F.2d at 615. As the court explained,

> The purchaser of a book is not asking for a "kind" or "make" of book. He is pointing out which one out of millions of distinct titles he wants, designating the book by its name. It is just as though one walked into a grocery store and said "I want some food" and in response to the question "What kind of food?" said, "A can of chicken noodle soup."

See also International Film Serv. Co. v. Associated Producers, Inc., 273 F. 585, 587 (S.D.N.Y. 1921) ("A title is, if not strictly descriptive, at least suggestive, and not an arbitrary sign. . . . The title is the proper name of a specific thing, not the differential of a species, as in the case of fungibles.") (Hand, J.).

The Trademark Trial and Appeal Board has consistently interpreted *Cooper* as prohibiting the registration of single book titles as trademarks. *See, e.g., In re Posthuma,* 45 U.S.P.Q.2D (BNA) 2011, 2012–13 (T.T.A.B. 1998); *In re Scholastic Inc.,* 23 U.S.P.Q.2D (BNA) 1774, 1776–77 (T.T.A.B. 1992); *In re Hal Leonard Publ'g Co.,* 15 U.S.P.Q.2D (BNA) 1574, 1576 (T.T.A.B. 1990); *In re Nat'l Council Books, Inc.,* 121 U.S.P.Q. 198, 198–99 (T.T.A.B. 1959).

The descriptive nature of a literary title does not mean, however, that such a title cannot receive protection under § 43(a). In fact, the *Cooper* decision itself recognized that "it is well known that the rights in book titles are afforded appropriate protection under the law of unfair competition." 254 F.2d at 617. If the title of such a single work has acquired secondary meaning, "the holder of the rights to that title may prevent the use of the same or confusingly similar titles by other authors." *Rogers v. Grimaldi,* 875 F.2d 994, 998 (2d Cir. 1989); *see also Trapani v. CBS Records, Inc.,* 857 F.2d 1475, No. 87–6034 (6th Cir. Sept. 2, 1988) (unpublished opinion) ("It is clear that the title to a song cannot be copyrighted as such, or registered as a trademark. However, a title may be protected as a common law trademark if two elements are satisfied: the title has acquired 'secondary meaning,' and the allegedly infringing use of the title creates a substantial likelihood of confusion.") (citations omitted); 2 McCarthy, §§ 10:1–:5. Thus, for plaintiff to prevail under § 43(a), it must demonstrate (1) that its title has secondary meaning, and (2) that defendants' title is likely to confuse or mislead consumers under the factors set forth in *Elvis Presley Enterprises*, 141 F.3d at 194.

Plaintiff must demonstrate a high degree of proof to establish secondary meaning. *See Vision Ctr. v. Opticks, Inc.*, 596 F.2d 111, 118 (5th Cir. 1979); *Thompson Med.*, 753 F.2d at 217. Plaintiff must show that "the title is sufficiently well known that consumers associate it with a particular author's work." Rogers, 875 F.2d at 998; *see also Sunbeam Prods.*, 123 F.3d at 253 (stating that "the primary element of secondary meaning is a mental association in buyer[s'] minds between the alleged mark and a single source of the product") (internal quotation marks omitted). Because the determination of whether a mark has acquired secondary meaning is primarily an empirical inquiry, "survey evidence is the most direct and persuasive evidence." *Sunbeam Prods.*, 123 F.3d at 253–54. Survey evidence is not the only relevant evidence, however—"in addition, the court may consider the length and manner of the use of a mark, the nature and extent of advertising and promotion of the mark, the sales volume of the product, and instances of actual confusion." *See Pebble Beach Co. v. Tour 18 I Ltd.*, 155 F.3d 526, 541 (5th Cir. 1998); *Thompson Med.*, 753 F.2d at 217; 2 McCarthy, § 10.13.

Plaintiff asserts that the record is "replete with evidence sufficient to support a ruling [on secondary meaning] by this court," including evidence that plaintiff sold over 210,000 copies of its book prior to May 1998, received unsolicited media coverage, used the title exclusively for thirty months, and was intentionally copied by defendants. Furthermore, plaintiff argues that the district court found secondary meaning in plaintiff's book title when it stated that it "finds that the trademark, SUGARBUSTERS, has gained strength, not only locally, but nationally due to its use in conjunction with the success of the book." *Sugar Busters*, 48 U.S.P.Q.2D (BNA) at 1514. We disagree with plaintiff's contention that the district court has already considered and found secondary meaning with respect to plaintiff's book title. The language that plaintiff cites from the district court's opinion pertains to the strength of the registered "SUGARBUSTERS" service mark—a mark we have already determined was not validly assigned to plaintiff—and the opinion states explicitly that the district court did not consider plaintiff's unfair competition arguments. Accordingly, we decline plaintiff's invitation to make such factual findings on our own, and we remand plaintiff's unfair competition claim to the district court so that it can determine whether the book title "SUGAR BUSTERS! Cut Sugar to Trim Fat" had obtained secondary meaning in May 1998 and, if so, whether defendants' book title is so likely to confuse consumers that it outweighs any First Amendment interests defendants have in the title of their book. . . .

D.   Fair Use

Defendants argue that plaintiff cannot prevail on its § 43(a) claims because defendants' use of their book title "SUGAR BUST For Life!" is protected by the fair-use doctrine. *See Soweco, Inc. v. Shell Oil Co.*, 617 F.2d 1178, 1190 (5th Cir. 1980) (applying fair-use defense to § 43(a) claim). The fair-use defense allows a party to use a term in good faith to describe its goods or services, but only in actions involving descriptive terms and only when the term is used in its descriptive sense rather than in its trademark sense. *See* 15 U.S.C. § 1115(b)(4); *Zatarains, Inc. v. Oak Grove Smokehouse, Inc.*, 698 F.2d 786, 791 (5th Cir. 1983); Restatement, § 28 & cmt. c; *see also* 2 McCarthy, § 10:14 ("Since the use of a descriptive title cannot serve to prevent others from using the title in a descriptive, non-trademark sense, others may be able to use the title as the only term available."). The fair-use defense does not apply if a term is used as a mark to identify the markholder's goods or services, but the fair use of a term may be protected even if some residual confusion is likely. *See Pebble Beach*, 155 F.3d at 545 n.12; *Soweco*, 617 F.2d at 1189 n.30 ("We are convinced that even if there were a likelihood of confusion, the defendant would still be entitled to its fair-use defense, so long as it had met the requirements of § 1115(b)(4). To hold otherwise would effectively eviscerate the fair-use defense."); Restatement, § 28 cmt. b. The fair-use defense thus prevents a markholder from "appropriating a descriptive term for his exclusive use and so prevent others from accurately describing a characteristic of their goods." *Soweco*, 617 F.2d at 1185.

The district court declined to consider defendants' fair-use argument, stating that it was raised for the first time in defendants' post-hearing brief. *See Sugar Busters*, 48 U.S.P.Q.2D (BNA) at 1517. Fair use is an affirmative defense that is usually waived if not affirmatively pled under Federal Rule of Civil Procedure 8(c). *See Car-Freshner Corp. v. S.C. Johnson & Son, Inc.*, 70 F.3d 267, 268 (2d Cir. 1995); *Dakota Indus., Inc. v. Ever Best Ltd.*, 28 F.3d 910, 912–13 (8th Cir. 1994). We have recognized, however, that if "a defendant raises [an] issue at a 'pragmatically sufficient time,' and if the plaintiff is not prejudiced in its ability to respond, there is no waiver of the defense." *Simon v. United States*, 891 F.2d 1154, 1157 (5th Cir. 1990) (quoting *Lucas v. United States*, 807 F.2d 414, 418 (5th Cir. 1986)); *see Allied Chem. Corp. v. Mackay*, 695 F.2d 854, 855–56 (5th Cir. 1983) ("Where the matter is raised in the trial court in a manner that does not result in unfair surprise . . . technical failure to comply precisely with Rule 8(c) is not fatal."). We find no such waiver here. Defendants pled fair use as an affirmative defense in their answer to plaintiff's complaint, presented relevant evidence at the preliminary injunction hearing, and argued the issue in their post-hearing brief. Furthermore, plaintiff filed a rebuttal brief in September 1998, addressing explicitly the fair-use argument and claiming that the defense was "refuted in plaintiff's original brief." We therefore remand defendants' fair-use argument to the district court so that it may properly consider this potential defense to plaintiff's unfair competition claims.

E. Equitable Considerations

Defendants' final argument is that plaintiff is not entitled to a preliminary injunction under principles of equity. *See* 15 U.S.C. § 1116(a) ("The several courts vested with jurisdiction of civil actions arising under this chapter shall have power to grant injunctions, according to the principles of equity and upon such terms as the court may deem reasonable, to prevent . . . a violation under section 1125(a) of this title."). Defendants assert that plaintiff engaged in inequitable conduct because Steward breached an agreement with Ellen Brennan to co-author a cookbook, Steward invited Ellen Brennan to "snuggle up" to plaintiff's book, plaintiff terminated Ellen Brennan's employment after she retained counsel, and plaintiff refused to abide by a purported settlement of the claims at issue in this case.

The district court found that defendants' asserted "equitable considerations based on the arguments of 'inequitable behavior' and 'improper purpose' are inadequate to present a defense based on equitable relief." *Sugar Busters*, 48 U.S.P.Q.2D (BNA) at 1517. The court apparently relied on the omission of these terms from the statement in 15 U.S.C. § 1069 that "in all inter parties proceedings equitable principles of laches, estoppel, and acquiescence, where applicable may be considered and applied." We do not agree with the district court's assessment that the equitable considerations relevant to a preliminary injunction of unfair competition are so limited as to exclude consideration of inequitable conduct or purpose. *See Levi Strauss & Co. v. Shilon*, 121 F.3d 1309, 1313 (9th Cir. 1997) ("'Unclean hands is a defense to a Lanham Act infringement suit.' . . . In its claim for equitable relief, 'the defendant must demonstrate that the plaintiff's conduct is inequitable and that the conduct relates to the subject matter of its claims.'") (quoting *Fuddruckers, Inc. v. Doc's B.R. Others, Inc.*, 826 F.2d 837, 847 (9th Cir. 1987)) (citations omitted); Restatement, § 32 & cmt. a ("The doctrine of unclean hands is applicable in actions for the infringement of registered trademarks . . . and in actions involving unregistered marks under § 43(a) of the [Lanham Act] and at common law."); 5 McCarthy, §§ 31:44–:58. Without expressing any opinion as to the merit of defendants' arguments that plaintiff has engaged in inequitable conduct and that such conduct is sufficient to preclude an equitable remedy, we remand this issue so that the district court may properly consider this potential defense.

III. CONCLUSION

For the foregoing reasons, we VACATE the preliminary injunction and REMAND to the district court for further proceedings consistent with this opinion.

NOTES FOR DISCUSSION

1. *The Assignment-in-Gross Doctrine: Early Judicial Development.* Under the common law, trademarks were assignable only as part of a sale of the associated business as a going concern. *See, e.g., Mulhens & Kropff, Inc. v. Ferd Muelhens, Inc.*, 43 F.2d 937 (2d Cir. 1930); *Bulte v. Igleheart Bros.*, 137 F. 492, 499 (7th Cir. 1905). Under this test, the Court upheld an assignment of the word mark "S.N. Pike's Magnolia Whiskey" for whiskey when Pike sold the mark along with the premises and distillery where the whiskey was made. *Kidd v. Johnson*, 100 U.S. 617 (1880). However, courts refused to recognize assignments that transferred a trademark without the associated business. *See, e.g., Bulte*, 137 F. at 498–99. As the *Bulte* court explained:

> A trade-mark or trade-name is of no virtue in and of itself. It becomes of value only through use, and because by use it is an assurance to purchasers of the excellence of the article to which it is affixed as manufactured by the one whose name appears as the producer. The fanciful or arbitrary trade-mark, by association with the name of the producer, becomes, therefore, valuable, because it is a sign and symbol to the purchaser, an assurance to him of the genuineness of the article and of its manufacture by the proprietor of the trade-mark or trade-name. Dissociated from such manufacture, it is not an assurance of genuineness. When used by another, its use works a fraud upon the purchaser. A trade-mark is analogous to the good will of a business. Whoever heard of a good will being sold to one while the original owner continues the business as before? The good will is inseparable from the business itself. So, likewise, is a trade-mark or trade-name that gives assurance to a purchaser that the article upon which is stamped the trade-mark or trade-name is the genuine production of the manufacturer to whom the trade-name or trade-mark points by association as the maker of the article. Therefore it is that it is a necessary qualification to the assignability of a trade-mark that there goes with it the transfer of the business and good will of the owner of the symbol.

Id. Importantly, courts specifically rejected the proposition that an assignment was valid so long as the assignee continued to use the assigned mark "in connection with the same class of manufacture." *Id.* at 498.

2. *Statutory Codification of the Assignment-in-Gross Doctrine.* Congress initially codified the common law's prohibition on assignments in gross in section 10 of the Trademark Act of 1905. Act of Feb. 20, 1905, § 10, 33 Stat. 727 ("Every registered trade-mark ... shall be assignable in connection with the good will of the business in which the mark is used."). During the debates leading to the Trademark Act of 1946, trademark owners proposed eliminating the assignment-in-gross doctrine. The initial draft of what would become the Trademark Act of 1946 provided that "a registered trade-mark ... shall be assignable either with or without the good will of the business in which the mark is used." H.R. 9041, 75th Cong., § 10 (1938).

Congress eventually rejected the proposal to eliminate the doctrine, and in the final version of the Act, retained the 1905 Act's statutory phrasing. Section 10 today provides:

> A registered mark . . . shall be assignable with the good will of the business in which the mark is used, or with that part of the good will of the business connected with the use of and symbolized by the mark.

15 U.S.C. § 1060 (2015).

Retaining the statutory phrasing of the 1905 Act presumably reflected Congress's intent to retain the traditional assignment-in-gross rule. The last phrase represented the only concession to a more liberal approach to assignments. Through it, Congress intended to allow a corporation with different divisions or product lines, each with its own trademark, to spin them off separately, along with their associated trademarks, without having to sell the entire company.

3. *The Assignment-in-Gross Doctrine: Modern Judicial Development.* Unable to persuade Congress to liberalize the assignment rules, trademark owners took their arguments to the courts. In 1962, the Court of Customs and Patent Appeals in *Hy-Cross Hatchery, Inc. v. Osborne* accepted the free assignability arguments and moved to eliminate the assignment-in-gross doctrine. 303 F.2d 947 (C.C.P.A. 1962). The facts in the case were simple. For one hundred dollars, the trademark owner assigned to another the exclusive right to use the mark "American Whites" for chicks. No part of the trademark owner's own chicken business was transferred along with the trademark. The assignment did contain a goodwill recital—words stating that the mark was assigned "together with that part of the good will of the business connected with the use and symbolized by the mark." Yet, words alone would not suffice to satisfy the traditional assignment-in-gross doctrine. Nevertheless, the court upheld the assignment. Reasoning that the trademark's goodwill was its selling power, the court held that it was sufficient that before the assignment the assignor had the exclusive right to use the mark and exploit its selling power, while after the assignment, the assignee had the exclusive right. *Id.* at 950.

Taken literally, the decision largely abolishes the assignment-in-gross doctrine. Can you see why? Are there any assignments that would fail to satisfy the *Hy-Cross Hatchery* court's interpretation of the assignment-in-gross doctrine?

Subsequent decisions rejected such a literal reading of *Hy-Cross Hatchery* and eventually settled on the "continuity" test set forth in *SugarBusters*. While courts have phrased the test using slightly different language, an assignment will satisfy the continuity test so long as the assignee continues to use the mark in connection with the "same or similar goods." Note that historically courts, such as the *Bulte* court, specifically rejected such an interpretation of the assignment-in-gross doctrine.

Although the governing test changed, courts continue to propound the traditional policy justification for the assignment-in-gross doctrine. The central concern remains the risk of consumer deception or confusion that an assignment creates. Having come to associate a given level of quality or particular characteristics with the trademark as a result of the assignor's use, consumers will expect the same quality or characteristics from the trademarked goods after an assignment. Indeed, many consumers will be entirely unaware that an assignment has occurred. If the quality or characteristics of the associated product or service changes after the assignment, consumers will be deceived.

How well does the modern formulation of the assignment-in-gross doctrine serve that purpose? Assume that a given trademark has long been associated with high quality women's shoes. After an assignment, the assignee continues to use the mark in connection with women's shoes, but in order to increase its profit margin, the assignee makes and sells much lower quality shoes under the mark. Does such an assignment create a risk of consumer deception? Would the assignment be valid or invalid under the continuity test? If the assignment is valid under the continuity test, does the continuity test validate precisely those assignments most likely to create the risk of consumer deception?

In a related vein, what does a trademark tell consumers—the general category of goods to which the product belongs or the precise quality or characteristic a consumer can expect from these specific goods? If a word tells consumer only the general category of the associated goods, can it be a trademark or is it generic? Should the continuity test focus on whether the goods are of the same general kind, or whether they have the same specific characteristics and quality?

One of the principal arguments for abandoning the assignment-in-gross doctrine is that trademark law permits a trademark owner to change the quality of its products without losing the associated trademark. Given that, why can't an assignee? In *Muhlens & Kropff, Inc.*, the court considered and rejected this argument in deciding the validity of an assignment of a trademark used in connection with cologne, where the secret formula for the associated cologne was not transferred. Here's what the court said:

> Logic will hardly solve the problem. On the one hand, it is said that to allow one who does not know the recipe to seize the good will dependent on marketing the product of the secret formula runs counter to the admitted principle that good will cannot be assigned in gross; on the other, that, since Muelhens would have had the privilege of somewhat changing the formula and still applying to the modified product the old mark, his successor in business should have the same privilege, and the right to prevent Muelhens' user. While the question is very doubtful, a majority of the court believe that assignment of the recipe is essential to give the assignee the exclusive right to a mark which denotes a product manufactured thereunder. Otherwise the public will be unable to procure the

genuine product under the name by which it has always been known.

43 F.2d at 939.

4. *Policing Costs and Proxies.* Is there any way to design an assignment-in-gross doctrine that precisely matches, in the sense that it is neither over-nor under-inclusive with respect to, our policy objective? Why should we police quality changes when an assignment occurs, but not otherwise? As the *SugarBusters* court notes, under the modern formulation of the assignment-in-gross doctrine, an assignment of physical assets is not required. Should it be? Would requiring the simultaneous transfer of the physical plant, and other tangible assets, associated with a trademark product, make deceptive trademark assignments less likely?

In attempting to answer these questions, consider the economics of a quality change. Where a trademark connotes high quality to consumers, lowering the quality of the associated product offers the trademark owner a one-time profit-making opportunity. If consumers have come to expect high quality from the trademarked goods based upon past experience, consumers may pay a high-quality price for the goods, even after the quality is lowered. However, this profit-making opportunity will last only until consumers adjust their expectations to the new, lower quality. Moreover, to exploit this opportunity, the trademark owner will have to forego the stream of future profits associated with the high quality goods. The owner will continue to earn whatever profits are available from the low quality goods, but the expected value of the profit stream from the high quality goods was likely higher than the expected value of the profit stream from the low quality goods. Simply as an exercise in profit maximization, the question becomes whether the short-term profits from the quality reduction exceed the loss in the expected value of future profits.

Assuming that a quality change will generate a net profit, is there a reason to believe that a preexisting trademark owner might forego the opportunity, while an assignee would take it? Would requiring a transfer of the physical assets associated with the trademarked product reduce the opportunity for a profitable quality change in the assignment context? If the assignee pays a large price for the assignment, should that weigh in favor of, or against, or be irrelevant to the assignment-in-gross issue?

5. *Other Purposes: Policing Priority and Ownership.* Why did SugarBusters obtain the assignment at issue in the case? Although courts continue to recite the traditional consumer protection rationale for the assignment-in-gross doctrine, the actual application of the continuity rule seems to reflect a different set of policy concerns. Specifically, courts appear to use the rule to police priority and ownership rules. Thus, SugarBusters "purchased" the trademark for a diabetic goods store in order to circumvent the longstanding prohibition on trademarks in book titles, and the court invalidated the assignment as a means of enforcing that prohibition. Is this a more plausible explanation for the *SugarBusters* outcome than consumer

confusion? If the court upheld the assignment, how many consumers would have purchased a diet book entitled SugarBusters believing it came from the Indiana diabetic goods store?

Similarly, in *PepsiCo, Inc. v. Grapette Co.*, the Eighth Circuit invalidated an assignment of the mark "Peppy" that had been used by the assignor in connection with a cola-flavored syrup. 416 F.2d 285, 287 (8th Cir. 1969). Although the court focused on the assignee's intent to change the nature of the associated product to a "pepper type bottled beverage," the assignee, Grapette, purchased the Peppy trademark in order to avail itself of a laches defense against Pepsico's claims of trademark infringement. The prior owner of the Peppy mark had used it for decades, and thus would likely have had a laches defense had Pepsico sued it directly. Should Grapette be able to step into its assignor's shoes and assert laches against Pepsico if it continues to make the same product, but not if it changes the nature of the associated product? Can we address that issue more sensibly by focusing on the implications of the change in the product's nature in terms of the applicability of laches or through manipulation of the assignment-in-gross doctrine?

6.   *Assignments and License-Backs.* To enable assignments that are *de facto* in gross, yet nevertheless satisfy the assignment-in-gross doctrine, lawyers developed the practice of assigning the trademark and then having the assignee license the mark back to the assignor. We saw this technique in Chapter 2 in connection with the *WarnerVision* intent-to-use case involving the mark Real Wheels, and it also occurred in *SugarBusters*. By licensing the mark back to the assignor, the assignor continues using the mark for precisely the same goods or services in connection with which it had been used before the assignment. In that sense, any risk of consumer deception is minimized. Because the assignor will continue using the mark under the license-back, consumers can find precisely the same goods or services in connection with the mark both before and after the assignment. The assignment is thereby validated, leaving the assignee free to use the trademark for new or additional products or services while claiming rights, the priority and validity of which, tie back to the assignor's initial use of the mark.

Trademark law polices the use of such assignment and license-back arrangements in part through the naked licensing doctrine that we shall study in the next section. As we shall see, for any trademark license, including a license-back arrangement, to be valid, the licensor must control the quality of the goods or products sold in connection with the mark. However, as we saw in *Dawn Donuts*, courts have held that minimal, even token, quality control measures will suffice. As a result, the naked license doctrine does not limit very much the availability of assignment and license-back arrangements.

If SugarBusters had licensed the continued use of the mark back to the Indiana diabetic goods store and had sufficient quality control in place, would the assignment have been valid? If the assignment was valid, would that give

SugarBusters a trademark in its book title? Would the priority in the mark for a diabetic goods store automatically become the priority for the mark in a book title? In resolving the likelihood of confusion issue, would we treat the plaintiff's product as the SugarBusters book or the underlying diabetic goods store?

7. *Book Titles.* The *SugarBusters* case also introduces us to some of the special rules applicable to book titles. As the court notes, the title of an individual book is the generic name for that book and hence may not receive protection as a trademark. As the *SugarBusters* court explained, book titles may receive protection under unfair competition and section 43(a) against confusingly similar imitations where they have established secondary meaning. Book titles are denied trademark status for two reasons. First, as a general rule, consumers simply do not consider book titles to be trademarks. Consumers think of Gone with the Wind as the name of a specific book, not as a brand of southern romance novel. Second, there is a First Amendment interest in allowing authors to title their works in a manner intended to convey the nature and content of their books to their audience. In this regard, is Ellen Brennan entitled to write a cook book that follows the dietary precepts laid out in the SugarBusters diet book? If she is, is she also entitled to use a title for her cook book that effectively conveys to her audience that her book follows those precepts? By denying titles trademark status, trademark law denies book titles the procedural and substantive advantages registration offers and thereby leaves subsequent authors more leeway to title their books as they feel appropriate.

Yet, at the same time, allowing a later author to use an identical or nearly identical title can lead to consumer confusion. If a subsequent author were permitted to use the title Gone with the Wind for her book, a consumer looking for Gone with the Wind, based, for example, upon a friend's recommendation of the book by title alone, might not know which author's to purchase. Thus, courts have long provided book titles with some protection under unfair competition where secondary meaning has been shown.

Even where secondary meaning has been shown, however, not every confusingly similar book title will prove infringing. Even with secondary meaning, the First Amendment interest in the communicative aspect of a title remains, and as the *SugarBusters* court notes, courts have both narrowed the infringement standard and used the fair use doctrine to leave later authors room to title their works appropriately. For example, in *Rogers v. Grimaldi*, Ginger Rogers sued the producers and distributors of a film entitled "Ginger and Fred" alleging a violation of section 43(a) and her common law rights of publicity. 875 F.2d 994 (2d Cir. 1989). The film portrayed a fictional pair of Italian dancers who imitated Ginger Rogers and Fred Astaire and became known in Italy as "Ginger and Fred." Although the Second Circuit acknowledged Ginger Rogers's fame, it nonetheless held that the title did not infringe her rights under section 43(a) or the common law right of publicity. In the light of the First Amendment, the court held that a title would violate section 43(a) only if "the title has no artistic relevance to the underlying work whatsoever, or . . . explicitly misleads as to the source or the content of the work." *Rogers*, 875 F.2d at 999. Although survey evidence in the case tended to prove "that some members of the public would draw the incorrect inference that Rogers had some involvement with the film," *id.* at 1001, the court nevertheless affirmed a grant of summary judgment for the defendants. In the court's words, "th[e] risk of [consumer] misunderstanding, not engendered by any overt claim in the title, is so outweighed by the interests in artistic expression as to preclude application of the Lanham Act." *Id. See also Twin Peaks Prods. v. Publications Int'l, Ltd.*, 996 F.2d 1366, 1379 (2d Cir. 1993) (holding that for book titles, "the finding of likelihood of confusion must be particularly compelling to outweigh the First Amendment interest recognized in *Rogers*").

C.   LICENSING OF TRADEMARKS AND THE NAKED LICENSE DOCTRINE

BARCAMERICA INT'L USA TRUST V. TYFIELD IMPORTERS, INC.

289 F.3d 589 (9th Cir. 2002)

O'SCANNLAIN, C.J.

We must decide whether a company engaged in "naked licensing" of its trademark, thus resulting in abandonment of the mark and ultimately its cancellation.

I

This case involves a dispute over who may use the "Leonardo Da Vinci" trademark for wines.

A

Barcamerica International USA Trust ("Barcamerica") traces its rights in the Leonardo Da Vinci mark to a February 14, 1984 registration granted by the United States Patent and Trademark Office ("PTO"), on an application filed in 1982. On August 7, 1989, the PTO acknowledged the mark's "incontestability." *See* 15 U.S.C. § 1115(b). Barcamerica asserts that it has used the mark continuously since the early 1980s. In the district court, it produced invoices evidencing two sales per year for the years 1980 through 1993: one to a former employee and the other to a barter exchange company. Barcamerica further produced invoices evidencing between three and seven sales per year for the years 1994 through 1998. These include sales to the same former employee, two barter exchange companies, and various sales for "cash." The sales volume reflected in the invoices for the years 1980 through 1988 range from 160 to 410 cases of wine per year. Barcamerica also produced sales summaries for the years 1980 through 1996 which reflect significantly higher sales volumes; these summaries do not indicate, however, to whom the wine was sold.

In 1988, Barcamerica entered into a licensing agreement with Renaissance Vineyards ("Renaissance"). Under the agreement, Barcamerica granted Renaissance the nonexclusive right to use the "Da Vinci" mark for five years or 4,000 cases, "whichever comes first," in exchange for $2,500. The agreement contained no quality control provision. In 1989, Barcamerica and Renaissance entered into a second agreement in place of the 1988 agreement. The 1989 agreement granted Renaissance an exclusive license to use the "Da Vinci" mark in the United States for wine products or alcoholic beverages. The 1989 agreement was drafted by Barcamerica's counsel and, like the 1988 agreement, it did not contain a quality control provision. In fact, the only evidence in the record of any efforts by Barcamerica to exercise "quality control" over Renaissance's wines comprised (1) Barcamerica principal George Gino Barca's testimony that he occasionally, informally tasted of the wine, and (2) Barca's testimony that he relied on the reputation of a "world-famous winemaker" employed by Renaissance at the time the agreements were signed.[3] (That winemaker is now deceased, although the record does not indicate when he died.) Nonetheless, Barcamerica contends that Renaissance's use of the mark inures to Barcamerica's benefit. *See* 15 U.S.C. § 1055.

B

Cantine Leonardo Da Vinci Soc. Coop. a.r.l. ("Cantine"), an entity of Italy, is a wine producer located in Vinci, Italy. Cantine has sold wine products bearing the "Leonardo Da Vinci" tradename since 1972; it selected this name and mark based on the name of its home city, Vinci. Cantine began selling its "Leonardo Da Vinci" wine to importers in the United States in 1979. Since 1996, however, Tyfield Importers, Inc. ("Tyfield") has been the exclusive United States importer and distributor of Cantine wine products bearing the "Leonardo Da Vinci" mark. During the first eighteen months after Tyfield became Cantine's exclusive importer, Cantine sold approximately 55,000 cases of wine products

---

[3] [Note from Opinion] After the commencement of this litigation, Barcamerica proposed a new agreement to Renaissance. The proposed agreement included a quality control provision, and the letter from Barcamerica's attorney proposing this new agreement acknowledged that the agreement "addresses requirements of trademark law that the licensor maintain some control over the licensed product." Renaissance never accepted Barcamerica's invitation to enter into this new agreement. In 1999, Barcamerica again acknowledged it had an obligation to perform quality control for the licensed product and requested that Renaissance execute a declaration stating, *inter alia*, that Barcamerica had been involved in the quality control of the licensed product. Renaissance refused to execute this declaration, because it was "neither truthful nor accurate." Indeed, in a letter to Barcamerica, Renaissance's counsel stated:

> Never at any time, to [Renaissance's] knowledge, has Mr. Barca ever had any involvement of any kind whatsoever regarding quality, quality control, the use of the *Da Vinci* label, or the marketing of the *Da Vinci* label wines, nor has he ever "examined" Renaissance's wine, "sampled" it, or had any involvement whatsoever regarding the quality of the wine and maintaining it at any level.

bearing the "Leonardo Da Vinci" mark to Tyfield. During this same period, Tyfield spent between $250,000 and $300,000 advertising and promoting Cantine's products, advertising in *USA Today*, and such specialty magazines as *The Wine Spectator*, *Wine and Spirits*, and *Southern Beverage Journal*.

Cantine learned of Barcamerica's registration of the "Leonardo Da Vinci" mark in or about 1996, in the course of prosecuting its first trademark application in the United States. Cantine investigated Barcamerica's use of the mark and concluded that Barcamerica was no longer selling any wine products bearing the "Leonardo Da Vinci" mark and had long since abandoned the mark. As a result, in May 1997, Cantine commenced a proceeding in the PTO seeking cancellation of Barcamerica's registration for the mark based on abandonment. Barcamerica responded by filing the instant action on January 30, 1998, and thereafter moved to suspend the proceeding in the PTO. The PTO granted Barcamerica's motion and suspended the cancellation proceeding.

Although Barca has been aware of Cantine's use of the "Leonardo Da Vinci" mark since approximately 1993, Barcamerica initiated the instant action only after Tyfield and Cantine commenced the proceeding in the PTO. A month after Barcamerica filed the instant action, it moved for a preliminary injunction enjoining Tyfield and Cantine from any further use of the mark. The district court denied the motion, finding, among other things, that "there is a serious question as to whether [Barcamerica] will be able to demonstrate a bona fide use of the Leonardo Da Vinci mark in the ordinary course of trade and overcome [the] claim of abandonment." *Barcamerica Int'l U.S.A. Trust v. Tyfield Importers, Inc.*, No. CV–98–00206–FCD, at 4–5 (E.D. Cal. 2000).

Thereafter, Tyfield and Cantine moved for summary judgment on various grounds. The district court granted the motion, concluding that Barcamerica abandoned the mark through naked licensing. The court further found that, in any event, the suit was barred by laches because Barcamerica knew several years before filing suit that Tyfield and Cantine were using the mark in connection with the sale of wine. This timely appeal followed. . . .

III

We now turn to the merits of the appeal. Barcamerica first challenges the district court's conclusion that Barcamerica abandoned its trademark by engaging in naked licensing. It is well-established that "[a] trademark owner may grant a license and remain protected provided quality control of the goods and services sold under the trademark by the licensee is maintained." *Moore Bus. Forms, Inc. v. Ryu*, 960 F.2d 486, 489 (5th Cir. 1992). But "uncontrolled or 'naked' licensing may result in the trademark ceasing to function as a symbol of quality and controlled source." McCarthy, *Trademarks and Unfair Competition*, § 18:48, at 18–79 (4th ed. 2001). Consequently, where the licensor fails to exercise adequate quality control over the licensee, "a court may find that the trademark owner has abandoned the trademark, in which case the owner would be estopped from asserting rights to the trademark." *Moore*, 960 F.2d at 489. Such abandonment "is purely an 'involuntary' forfeiture of trademark rights," for it need not be shown that the trademark owner had any subjective intent to abandon the mark. McCarthy § 18:48, at 18–79. Accordingly, the proponent of a naked license theory "faces a stringent standard" of proof. *Moore*, 960 F.2d at 489.

A

Judge Damrell's analysis of this issue in his memorandum opinion and order is correct and well-stated, and we adopt it as our own. As that court explained,

> In 1988, [Barcamerica] entered into an agreement with Renaissance in which [Barcamerica] granted Renaissance the non-exclusive right to use the "Da Vinci" mark for five years or 4,000 cases, "whichever comes first." There is no quality control provision in that agreement. In 1989, [Barcamerica] and Renaissance entered into a second agreement in place of the 1998 agreement. The 1989 agreement grants Renaissance an exclusive license to use the "Da Vinci" mark in the United States for wine products or alcoholic beverages. The 1989 agreement was to "continue in effect in perpetuity," unless terminated in accordance with the provisions thereof. The 1989 agreement does not contain any controls or restrictions with respect to the quality of goods bearing the "Da Vinci" mark. Rather, the agreement provides that Renaissance is "solely responsible for any and all claims or causes of action for negligence, breach of contract, breach of warranty, or products liability arising from the sale or distribution of Products using the Licensed Mark" and that Renaissance shall defend and indemnify plaintiff against such claims.
>
> The lack of an express contract right to inspect and supervise a licensee's operations is not conclusive evidence of lack of control. "There need not be formal quality control where 'the particular circumstances of the licensing arrangement [indicate] that the public will not be deceived.'" *Moore Bus. Forms, Inc.*, 960 F.2d at 489 (quoting *Taco Cabana Int'l, Inc.*, 932 F.2d 1113, 1121 (5th Cir. 1991)). Indeed, "courts have upheld licensing agreements where the licensor is familiar with and relies upon the licensee's own efforts to control quality." *Morgan Creek Prods., Inc. v. Capital Cities/ABC Inc.*, 22 U.S.P.Q. 2d 1881, 1884 (C.D. Cal. 1991) (citing *Transgo, Inc. v. Ajac*

Transmission Parts Corp., 768 F.2d 1001, 1017–18 (9th Cir. 1985)).

Here, there is no evidence that [Barcamerica] is familiar with or relied upon Renaissance's efforts to control quality. Mr. Barca represents that Renaissance's use of the mark is "controlled by" plaintiff "with respect to the nature and quality of the wine sold under the license," and that "the nature and quality of Renaissance wine sold under the trademark is good." [Barcamerica]'s sole evidence of any such control is Mr. Barca's own apparently random tastings and his reliance on Renaissance's reputation. According to Mr. Barca, the quality of Renaissance's wine is "good" and at the time plaintiff began licensing the mark to Renaissance, Renaissance's winemaker was Karl Werner, a "world famous" winemaker.

Mr. Barca's conclusory statements as to the existence of quality controls is insufficient to create a triable issue of fact on the issue of naked licensing. While Mr. Barca's tastings perhaps demonstrate a minimal effort to monitor quality, Mr. Barca fails to state when, how often, and under what circumstances he tastes the wine. Mr. Barca's reliance on the reputation of the winemaker is no longer justified as he is deceased. Mr. Barca has not provided any information concerning the successor winemaker(s). While Renaissance's attorney, Mr. Goldman, testified that Renaissance "strives extremely hard to have the highest possible standards," he has no knowledge of the quality control procedures utilized by Renaissance with regard to testing wine. Moreover, according to Renaissance, Mr. Barca never "had any involvement whatsoever regarding the quality of the wine and maintaining it at any level." [Barcamerica] has failed to demonstrate any knowledge of or reliance on the actual quality controls used by Renaissance, nor has it demonstrated any ongoing effort to monitor quality.

[Barcamerica] and Renaissance did not and do not have the type of close working relationship required to establish adequate quality control in the absence of a formal agreement. *See, e.g., Taco Cabana Int'l, Inc.*, 932 F.2d at 1121 (licensor and licensee enjoyed close working relationship for eight years); *Transgo*, 768 F.2d at 1017–18 (licensor manufactured 90% of components sold by licensee, licensor informed licensee that if he chose to use his own parts "[licensee] wanted to know about it," licensor had ten year association with licensee and was familiar with his ability and expertise); *Taffy Original Designs, Inc. v. Taffy's Inc.*, 161 U.S.P.Q. 707, 713 (N.D. Ill. 1966) (licensor and licensee were sisters in business together for seventeen years, licensee's business was a continuation of the licensor's and licensee's prior business, licensor visited licensee's store from time to time and was satisfied with the quality of the merchandise offered); *Arner v. Sharper Image Corp.*, 39 U.S.P.Q.2d 1282 (C.D. Cal. 1995) (licensor engaged in a close working relationship with licensee's employees and license agreement provided that license would terminate if certain employees ceased to be affiliated with licensee). No such familiarity or close working relationship ever existed between [Barcamerica] and Renaissance. Both the terms of the licensing agreements and the manner in which they were carried out show that [Barcamerica] engaged in naked licensing of the "Leonardo Da Vinci" mark. Accordingly, [Barcamerica] is estopped from asserting any rights in the mark.

Barcamerica, No. CV–98–00206–FCD, at 9–13 (E.D. Cal. 2000) (record citations and footnote omitted).

B

On appeal, Barcamerica does not seriously contest any of the foregoing. Instead, it argues essentially that because Renaissance makes good wine, the public is not deceived by Renaissance's use of the "Da Vinci" mark, and thus, that the license was legally acceptable. This novel rationale, however, is faulty. Whether Renaissance's wine was objectively "good" or "bad" is simply irrelevant. What matters is that Barcamerica played no meaningful role in holding the wine to a standard of quality—good, bad, or otherwise. As McCarthy explains,

> It is important to keep in mind that "quality control" does not necessarily mean that the licensed goods or services must be of "high" quality, but merely of equal quality, whether that quality is high, low or middle. *The point is that customers are entitled to assume that the nature and quality of goods and services sold under the mark at all licensed outlets will be consistent and predictable.*

McCarthy § 18:55, at 18–94 (emphasis added) (footnotes omitted).

And "it is well established that where a trademark owner engages in naked licensing, without any control over the quality of goods produced by the licensee, such a practice is *inherently deceptive* and constitutes abandonment of any rights to the trademark by the licensor." *First Interstate Bancorp v. Stenquist*, 16 U.S.P.Q. 2d 1704, 1706 (N.D. Cal. 1990).

Certainly, "it is difficult, if not impossible to define in the abstract exactly how much control and inspection is needed to satisfy the requirement of quality control over trademark licensees." McCarthy, § 18:55, at 18–94. And we recognize that "the standard of quality control and the degree of necessary inspection and policing by the licensor will vary with the wide range of licensing situations in use in the modern marketplace." *Id.*, at 18–95. But in this case we deal with a relatively simple product: wine. Wine, of course, is bottled by season. Thus, at the very least, one might have expected Barca to sample (or to have some designated wine connoisseur sample) on an annual basis, in some organized way, some adequate number of bottles of the Renaissance wines which were to bear Barcamerica's mark to ensure that they were of sufficient quality to be called "Da Vinci." But Barca did not make even this minimal effort.

C

We therefore agree with Judge Damrell, and hold that Barcamerica engaged in naked licensing of its "Leonardo Da Vinci" mark—and that by so doing, Barcamerica forfeited its rights in the mark. We also agree that cancellation of Barcamerica's registration of the mark was appropriate. *See* McCarthy, § 18:48, at 18–82 (explaining that " 'naked' licensing can result in such a loss of significance of a trademark that its federal registration should be cancelled").

IV

For the foregoing reasons, the decision of the district court is AFFIRMED.

NOTES FOR DISCUSSION

1. *The Evolution of the Naked License Doctrine.* As we saw back in Chapter 3, in *Dawn Donuts*, before the enactment of the Trademark Act of 1946, courts divided on the question whether trademark licensing was permissible. Some courts held that any licensing of a trademark to a separate and independent entity constituted abandonment. *See, e.g., American Broadcasting Co. v. Wahl Co.*, 121 F.2d 412, 413 (2d Cir. 1941); *Everett O. Fisk & Co. v. Fisk Teachers' Agency, Inc.*, 3 F.2d 7, 9 (8th Cir. 1924). Other courts disagreed and permitted licensing so long as the licensor controlled the quality of the goods sold under the mark. *See E. I. DuPont De Nemours & Co. v. Celanese Corporation of America*, 167 F.2d 484 (C.C.P.A. 1948). In the Trademark Act, Congress resolved the split and permitted licensing of a mark through section 5 and the definition of a related company. Section 5 of the Act provides:

> Where a registered mark or a mark sought to be registered is or may be used legitimately by related companies, such use shall inure to the benefit of the registrant or applicant for registration, and such use shall not affect the validity of such mark or of its registration, provided such mark is not used in such manner as to deceive the public. If first use of a mark by a person is controlled by the registrant or applicant for registration of the mark with respect to the nature and quality of the goods or services, such use shall

inure to the benefit of the registrant or applicant, as the case may be.

15 U.S.C. § 1055 (2015).

In section 45, Congress then defined "related companies" as follows:

> The term "related company" means any person whose use of a mark is controlled by the owner of the mark with respect to the nature and quality of the goods or services on or in connection with which the mark is used.

15 U.S.C. § 1127 (2015). Note that "related company" is defined as "any person," and thus includes actual people—a reversal of our usual practice of treating companies as people.

Having decided to allow trademark licensing with quality control, the question became how much or what sort of quality control is required. The ultimate goal, of course, is to ensure that consumers find a consistent quality from the goods sold under a mark. Was there any evidence that the quality of the wine Renaissance was offering under the "Da Vinci" mark was varying because of a lack of supervision from Barcamerica? If not, why should Barcamerica lose its trademark? Is there any language in the statute that suggests courts should focus on the fact of inconsistent quality, and the associated harm to consumers, directly? Is there any language in the statute that suggests courts should focus on the presence or absence of quality control by the licensor, irrespective of the actual quality of the associated goods?

2. *Justifying the Quality Control Requirement.* Do we need a quality control requirement in trademark law? Since the Trademark Act of 1946 formally allowed licensing, a number of franchising arrangements have sprung up. Some of these arrangements include very tight quality control by the licensor. McDonald's, for example, is famous for its efforts at maintaining a consistent level of quality for all of its restaurants, both those owned directly, as well as those independently owned. Do you happen to know whether your local McDonald's is a company-owned or independently-owned franchise? Other franchise operations have less stringent quality control requirements. Just to take an example, have you experienced different quality in the products or services offered at different locations of the same restaurant? How do you, as a consumer, respond to such quality variation? Do we need a legal rule to minimize such quality variations and to ensure that consumers receive the quality they expect? Do we need such a legal rule so long as the differing locations are independently-owned franchises but not if they are owned by a single entity? *See* 15 U.S.C. § 1064(3), 1115(b)(3) (2015) (allowing cancellation of a registration at any time where a mark is "being used by, or with the permission of, the registrant so as to misrepresent the source of the goods or services on or in connection with which the mark is used").

3. *Satisfying the Quality Control Requirement.* What is the minimum that Barcamerica could have done to satisfy the quality control requirement?

Would it have been enough to include a right to control the quality of the wine in the licensing agreement with Renaissance, even if no actual quality control was ever undertaken? Did the lawyer who prepared the license commit malpractice by failing to include such a quality control provision? If Barca had testified to annual wine tastings, would that have been sufficient? What if Barcamerica simply monitored the sales of, or consumer complaints concerning, or returns of, "Da Vinci" wine, relying on one of these as a proxy for consumer satisfaction and thus quality?

4. *Consequences of a Naked License.* Who owns the "Leonardo Da Vinci" trademark for wine? If Barcamerica does not, does that mean that Renaissance owns it? May Renaissance enjoin Cantine's use? If not, does that mean that Cantine owns the trademark rights in "Da Vinci" for wine in the United States? If so, may Cantine enjoin Renaissance's continued use? If a third party begins selling a wine with a "Da Vinci" mark, may either Renaissance or Cantine enjoin the use?

5. *Priority of Use?* As between Cantine and Renaissance, who began use in commerce of the "Da Vinci" mark on wine first?

D. LOSS OF TRADEMARK RIGHTS: ABANDONMENT BY NONUSE

SILVERMAN V. CBS INC.
870 F.2d 40 (2d Cir. 1989)

NEWMAN, C.J.

This appeal presents somewhat novel issues of both copyright and trademark law arising from the efforts of appellant Stephen M. Silverman to develop a musical based on the "Amos 'n' Andy" characters. The attempt to transport Amos, Andy, Kingfish, Algonquin J. Calhoun, and all the others from the well-known radio and television shows of earlier decades to Broadway (possibly in a cab of the Fresh Air Taxi Co.) has thus far been stymied by the assertion of copyright and trademark infringement claims by appellee CBS Inc. Silverman appeals from a judgment of the District Court for the Southern District of New York (Gerard L. Goettel, Judge) awarding CBS damages, declaratory relief, and an injunction. Because some "Amos 'n' Andy" materials are in the public domain while others remain subject to CBS copyrights, and because CBS has elected not to make commercial use of its "Amos 'n' Andy" radio and television programs, nor create new ones, since 1966, the issues primarily raised on this appeal are the extent of copyright protection available to CBS with respect to the "Amos 'n' Andy" characters and whether CBS has abandoned through non-use whatever trademarks it might have. We conclude that to a limited extent copyright infringement has occurred, that the declaratory and injunctive relief awarded CBS should be modified to avoid extension of copyright protection to public domain materials, that Silverman is entitled to limited declaratory relief, and that CBS's trademarks, if valid, have been abandoned.

Facts

The "Amos 'n' Andy" characters were created in 1928 by Freeman F. Gosden and Charles J. Correll, who wrote and produced for radio broadcasting "The Amos 'n' Andy Show." The show became one of the country's most popular radio programs. The characters in the Amos 'n' Andy programs were Black. Gosden and Correll, who were White, portrayed Amos and Andy on radio. The authors appeared in blackface in publicity photos. Black actors played the parts in the subsequent television programs.

Gosden and Correll assigned all of their rights in the "Amos 'n' Andy Show" scripts and radio programs to CBS Inc. in 1948. Gosden and Correll continued to create new "Amos 'n' Andy" scripts, which formed the basis for CBS radio programs. The radio programs continued until 1955. Beginning in 1951 CBS also broadcast an "Amos 'n' Andy" television series. The television series was aired on CBS affiliate stations until 1953 and continued in reruns and non-network syndication until 1966. CBS has not aired or licensed for airing any of the radio or television programs since 1966.

In 1981, Silverman began writing a script for a Broadway musical based on the "Amos 'n' Andy" characters. The title of this work was originally "Amos 'n' Andy Go To The Movies." A revision was titled "Amos 'n' Andy In Hollywood," and a more extensive revision was titled "Fresh Air Taxi." Silverman sought a license to use the "Amos 'n' Andy" characters, but CBS refused.

Silverman filed this lawsuit seeking a declaration that the "Amos 'n' Andy" radio programs broadcast from March 1928 through March 1948 (the "pre-1948 radio programs") are in the public domain and that he is therefore free to make use of the content of the programs, including the characters, character names, and plots. He also sought a declaration that CBS has no rights in these programs under any body of law, including statutory and common law copyright law and trademark law. CBS asserted five counterclaims: (1) that Silverman's scripts infringed CBS's copyrights in the scripts for three post-1948 radio programs; (2) that the Silverman scripts violated section 43(a) of the Lanham Act, 15 U.S.C. § 1125(a) (1982), by infringing various CBS trademarks, including "AMOS 'N' ANDY", the names of various characters such as "George ('Kingfish') Stevens," "Madame Queen," and "Lightnin'," and various phrases such as "Scuse me for protruding," "splain dat," and "Holy mackral" (perhaps Amos's best-known contribution to the language); (3) that the infringement of CBS's trademarks also violated CBS's rights under state unfair competition and anti-dilution law; (4) that Silverman had misappropriated CBS's goodwill associated with the "Amos 'n' Andy" programs and trademarks; and (5) that Silverman had obtained improper copyright registration of his first movie script, claiming it to be an original work, whereas it used protected material from scripts in which CBS held copyrights.

District Court Decisions

Judge Goettel adjudicated the plethora of issues before him in three stages, writing thoughtful opinions at each stage. The initial decision granted in part and denied in part CBS's motion for summary judgment. *Silverman v. CBS*, 632 F. Supp. 1344 (S.D.N.Y. 1986) (hereafter *"Silverman I"*). Judge Goettel ruled initially that since all of the works in which CBS claims a statutory copyright were created long before January 1, 1978, the effective date of the 1976 Copyright Act, 17 U.S.C. §§ 101–914 (1982 and Supp. IV 1986), the copyright issues were primarily governed by the Copyright Act of 1909. Act of March 4, 1909, ch. 320, 35 Stat. 1075. The District Judge then considered CBS's copyright claims with respect to the pre-1948 radio programs, the post-1948 radio programs, and the television programs.

With respect to the pre-1948 radio programs, Judge Goettel ruled that the scripts for these programs were in the public domain because the copyrights in these scripts, originally obtained by Gosden and Correll, had not been renewed. He also ruled that the broadcasts of these programs (presumably the audiotapes of the broadcasts) were entitled to common law copyright protection because the broadcasts did not constitute publication, and publication had not otherwise occurred. That ruling, however, does not appear to have affected the judgment that was ultimately entered. The District Judge did not rule that Silverman's scripts infringed CBS's rights in the pre-1948 broadcasts, nor did he rule that Silverman was entitled to a declaration of the right to use material from these broadcasts. Judge Goettel expressed the view that though CBS had the right to prevent copying of "the sound recordings of the radio shows," CBS's rights in the pre-1948 programs were "immaterial" because Silverman did not plan to use recordings of these programs in his musical.

Turning next to the post-1948 radio programs, Judge Goettel ruled that CBS had common law copyrights in the scripts for these programs, which became statutory copyrights pursuant to the 1976 Act when CBS registered these scripts with the Copyright Office in early 1985. The District Judge then found that Silverman had had access to the scripts and had listened to the broadcasts, that the first script for his musical indisputably contained substantial portions of dialogue from at least one of the post-1948 radio scripts, and that Silverman was therefore liable for copyright infringement. Summary judgment was granted to CBS on its first and fifth counterclaims.

Turning next to the television programs, the District Judge noted that CBS had obtained copyright registrations and renewals for the televised programs (which were fixed in the tangible medium of film or videotape). He then rejected Silverman's claim that CBS had placed these telecasts in the public domain by publishing them without copyright notice. Recognizing that broadcasting the television programs was not publication, Silverman had nevertheless contended that CBS had made a sufficiently broad distribution of the programs to constitute publication by reason of the distribution of copies of the programs to affiliate and non-affiliate stations. Silverman relied primarily on the practice known as "bicycling," whereby one television station forwards the program to another. Judge Goettel expressed some doubt that the record assembled on summary judgment supported the claim, but ruled in any event that distribution of copies for "synchronized national broadcast" was not a general publication.

Then, facing the issue of the scope of copyright protection for the television programs, Judge Goettel focused on the graphic representation of the "Amos 'n' Andy" characters in the telecasts. Mindful that the pre-1948 radio scripts were in the public domain, he framed the key question to be "are characters that are in the public domain in a literary work protectable by copyright in an audiovisual presentation?" The District Judge answered "yes" and ruled that "duplication of the characters as they appeared on television would infringe CBS's copyrights." Reaching the issue of infringement, Judge Goettel then ruled that substantial similarity could not be determined until the characters in Silverman's musical were seen on stage, and he therefore dismissed the counterclaim as unripe to the extent that it sought relief for infringement of the television programs.

On the trademark side of the case, Judge Goettel ruled that the name "Amos 'n' Andy," as well as the names and appearances of "Amos 'n' Andy" characters and "other distinctive features of the . . . radio and television shows" are protectable marks. He then set down for trial the issue of whether CBS's non-use of the marks constituted abandonment. Finally, he ruled that the issue of trademark infringement, as well as the related issues of unfair competition and dilution, were premature in the absence of a staging of Silverman's musical.

After a bench trial on the issue of abandonment, Judge Goettel concluded that CBS had not abandoned its trademarks. *Silverman v. CBS*, 666 F. Supp. 575 (S.D.N.Y. 1987) (*Silverman II*). Finally, upon CBS's motion for damages and an award of attorney's fees, the District Judge ordered Silverman to pay damages of $9,403.07 (representing the difference between $20,000 of revenue received from backers of his musical and expenses of $10,596.93), plus an attorney's fee of $10,000. *Silverman v. CBS*, 675 F. Supp. 870 (S.D.N.Y. 1988) (*Silverman III*).

The final judgment entered in the District Court included several provisions. Silverman was enjoined from "creating . . . distributing . . . or offering for sale any script, or permitting the display or performance publicly of any musical play based thereon, bearing or containing any substantial copy or derivative work based upon any episode of an Amos 'n' Andy radio or television program created by or for CBS in or after August 1948. . . ." He was also ordered to recall and deliver to CBS copies of the scripts titled "Amos 'n' Andy in Hollywood" and "Amos 'n' Andy Go To The Movies." The judgment declared that Silverman's copyright registration in his first script was void, that CBS's copyright registrations in episodes of the "Amos 'n' Andy" radio and television programs are valid, that the "characters' names and appearances and other distinctive features" of the "Amos 'n' Andy" radio and television shows are trademarks of CBS, and that CBS has not abandoned such marks. CBS was awarded damages and attorney's fees totaling $19,403.07. Finally, the judgment dismissed with prejudice all claims and counterclaims except CBS's second, third, and fourth counterclaims, which were dismissed without prejudice. This dismissal of all claims resulted in the denial of Silverman's claim for a declaration of his right to use any of the component parts of the pre-1948 radio programs, including the programs' titles, characters, characters' names, and plots. Though *Silverman I* had determined that the scripts for the pre-1948 radio programs were in the public domain, Silverman obtained no rights to their use because of the District Court's ruling that "AMOS 'N' ANDY" and the "Amos 'n' Andy" characters and phrases were protected trademarks of CBS.

Discussion

We consider first the trademark side of this case because our conclusion on the trademark issues significantly alters the context in which the copyright issues arise.

1. *Trademark Issues.* Silverman challenges the District Court's rulings that CBS has protectable trademarks in the "Amos 'n' Andy" names, characters, and other features of the radio and television programs, including phrases of dialogue, and that CBS has not abandoned these marks. We find it unnecessary to decide which features of the programs might give rise to protectable marks because we agree with Silverman that CBS has abandoned the marks.

Section 45 of the Lanham Act provides:

A mark shall be deemed to be "abandoned"—

(a) When its use has been discontinued with intent not to resume. Intent not to resume may be inferred from circumstances. Nonuse for two consecutive years shall be prima facie abandonment.

15 U.S.C. § 1127 (1982).

There are thus two elements for abandonment: (1) non-use and (2) intent not to resume use. *See Saratoga Vichy Spring Co. v. Lehman*, 625 F.2d 1037, 1043 (2d Cir. 1980). Two years of non-use creates a rebuttable presumption of abandonment. *Id.* at 1044.

On the undisputed facts of this case, CBS made a considered decision to take the "Amos 'n' Andy" television programs off the air. It took this action in response to complaints by civil rights organizations, including the NAACP, that the programs were demeaning to Blacks. By the time the abandonment issue came before the District Court, non-use of the AMOS 'N' ANDY marks had continued for 21 years. Although CBS has no current plans to use the marks within the foreseeable future, CBS asserts that it has always intended to resume using them at some point in the future, should the social climate become more hospitable.

Ordinarily, 21 years of non-use would easily surpass the non-use requirement for finding abandonment. *See, e.g., I.H.T. Corp. v. Saffir Publishing Corp.*, 444 F. Supp. 185 (S.D.N.Y. 1978) (denying preliminary injunction to protect trademark after 12 years of non-use). The District Court concluded, however, that CBS had successfully rebutted the presumption of abandonment arising from its prolonged non-use by offering a reasonable explanation for its decision to keep the programs off the air and by asserting its intention to resume use at some indefinite point in the future. This conclusion raises a question as to the proper interpretation of the statutory phrase "intent not to resume": Does the phrase mean intent *never* to resume use or does it merely mean intent not to resume use within the reasonably foreseeable future?

We conclude that the latter must be the case. The statute provides that intent not to resume may be inferred from circumstances, and two consecutive years of non-use is prima facie abandonment. Time is thereby made relevant. Indeed, if the relevant intent were intent never to resume use, it would be virtually impossible to establish such intent circumstantially. Even after prolonged non-use, and without any concrete plans to resume use, a company could almost always assert truthfully that at some point, should conditions change, it would resume use of its mark.

We do not think Congress contemplated such an unworkable standard. More likely, Congress wanted a mark to be deemed abandoned once use has been discontinued with an intent not to resume within the reasonably foreseeable future. This standard is sufficient to protect against the forfeiture of marks by proprietors who are temporarily unable to continue using them, while it also prevents warehousing of marks, which impedes commerce and competition.

We are buttressed in this conclusion by the fact that the statute requires proof of "intent not to resume," rather than "intent to abandon." The statute thus creates no state of mind element concerning the ultimate issue of abandonment. On the contrary, it avoids a subjective inquiry on this ultimate question by setting forth the circumstances under which a mark shall be "deemed" to be abandoned. Of course, one of those circumstances is intent not to resume use, which is a matter of subjective inquiry. But we think the provision, by introducing the two concepts of "deemed" abandonment and intent not to resume use, contemplates a distinction, and it is a distinction that turns at least in part on duration of the contemplated non-use.

Congress's choice of wording appears to have been deliberate. One early version of what became section 45 of the Lanham Act had provided that "intent to *abandon* may be inferred from the circumstances." H.R. Rep. 4744, 76th Cong., 1st Sess. (1939) (emphasis added). However, shortly thereafter a new bill modified this phrase by substituting "intent not to resume" for "intent to abandon." H.R. Rep. 6618, 76th Cong., 1st Sess. (1939). Though it has been suggested that the phrases are interchangeable, *see* Note, 56 Fordham L. Rev. 1003, 1020 n. 113 (1988), we agree with the Fifth Circuit that the phrases are better understood as having distinct meanings. *See Exxon Corp. v. Humble Exploration Co.*, 695 F.2d 96, 102, 103 n. 7 (5th Cir. 1983). "Abandonment" connotes permanent relinquishment. *See Webster's Third New International Dictionary* 2 (1981) (defining "abandon" to mean "to cease to assert . . . an interest . . . esp. with the intent of *never* again resuming or reasserting it") (emphasis added). We think that Congress, by speaking of "intent not to resume" rather than "intent to abandon" in this section of the Act meant to avoid the implication that intent never to resume use must be shown.

This approach is consistent with our recent decisions concerning trademark abandonment. In *Saratoga Vichy Spring Co. v. Lehman, supra*, we rejected a claim of abandonment based on seven years of non-use where the initial decision to cease use resulted from a decision of the state legislature and the state, which was the trademark owner, continuously sought to sell the mark along with the mineral water business to which it applied. Similarly, in *Defiance Button Machine Co. v. C & C Metal Products Corp.*, 759 F.2d 1053 (2d Cir.), *cert. denied*, 474 U.S. 844 (1985), we rejected an abandonment claim where, during a brief period of non-use, the proprietor tried to sell the mark, its associated goodwill, and some other assets and, upon failing to find a buyer, became a subsidiary of a company in its original line of trade and prepared to resume its business. In both cases, the proprietor of the mark had an intention to exploit the mark in the reasonably foreseeable future by resuming its use or permitting its use by others.

The undisputed facts of the pending case are entirely different. Unlike the proprietors in *Saratoga Vichy* and *Defiance Button*, CBS has not been endeavoring to exploit the value of its marks, failing to do so only because of lack of business opportunities. Instead, it has decided, albeit for socially commendable motives, to forgo whatever business opportunities may currently exist in the hope that greater opportunities, unaccompanied by adverse public reaction, will exist at some undefined time in the future.

A proprietor who temporarily suspends use of a mark can rebut the presumption of abandonment by showing reasonable grounds for the suspension and plans to resume use in the reasonably foreseeable future when the conditions requiring suspension abate. *See, e.g., Star-Kist Foods, Inc. v. P.J. Rhodes & Co.*, 769 F.2d 1393 (9th Cir. 1985); *Chandon Champagne Corp. v. San Marino Wine Corp.*, 335 F.2d 531, 535 (2d Cir. 1964); *Continental Distilling Corp. v. Old Charter Distillery Co.*, 188 F.2d 614, 619–20 (D.C. Cir. 1950). But a proprietor may not protect a mark if he discontinues using it for more than 20 years and has no plans to use or permit its use in the reasonably foreseeable future. A bare assertion of possible future use is not enough.

We recognize the point, forcefully made by Judge Goettel, when he wrote:

> It would be offensive to basic precepts of fairness and justice to penalize CBS, by stripping it of its trademark rights, merely because it succumbed to societal pressures and pursued a course of conduct that it reasonably believes to be in the best interests of the community.

Silverman II, 666 F. Supp. at 581.

Nonetheless, we believe that however laudable one might think CBS's motives to be, such motives cannot overcome the undisputed facts that CBS has not used its marks for more than 20 years and that, even now, it has no plans to resume their use in the reasonably foreseeable future. Though we agree with Judge Goettel that CBS should not be penalized for its worthy motive, we cannot adjust the statutory test of abandonment to reward CBS for such motive by according it protection where its own voluntary actions demonstrate that statutory protection has ceased. Moreover, we see nothing in the statute that makes the consequence of an intent not to resume use turn on the worthiness of the motive for holding such intent.

We are also mindful of the facts, relied on by the District Court, that show some minor activities by CBS regarding its properties, allegedly sufficient to rebut abandonment of the marks. These are CBS's actions in licensing the programs for limited use in connection with documentary and educational programs, challenging infringing uses brought to its attention, renewing its copyrights, and periodically reconsidering whether to resume use of the programs. But challenging infringing uses is not use, and sporadic licensing for essentially non-commercial uses of a mark is not sufficient use to forestall abandonment. *Cf. Exxon Corp. v. Humble Exploration Co., supra*, 695 F.2d at 102 (use must be "commercial use" to avoid abandonment). Such uses do not sufficiently rekindle the public's identification of the mark with the proprietor, which is the essential condition for trademark protection, nor do they establish an intent to resume commercial use. CBS's minor activities, like worthy motives for non-use, cannot dispel the legal consequence of prolonged non-use coupled with an intent not to resume use in the reasonably foreseeable future. *See Kirkland v. National Broadcasting Co.*, 425 F. Supp. 1111, 1117–18 (E.D. Pa. 1976), *aff'd mem.*, 565 F.2d 152 (3d Cir. 1977) (abandonment after 23-year period without commercial exploitation).

An adjudication of trademark rights often involves a balancing of competing interests. *See La Societe Anonyme des Parfums Le Galion v. Jean Patou, Inc.*, 495 F.2d 1265, 1274 n. 11 (2d Cir. 1974). In weighing the competing interests and reaching our conclusion concerning abandonment, we are influenced in part by the context in which this dispute arises—one in which the allegedly infringing use is in connection with a work of artistic expression. Just as First Amendment values inform application of the idea/expression dichotomy in copyright law, *see Harper & Row Publishers, Inc. v. Nation Enterprises*, 471 U.S. 539, 556 (1985), in similar fashion such values have some bearing upon the extent of protection accorded a trademark proprietor against use of the mark in works of artistic expression.

Ordinarily, the use of a trademark to identify a commodity or a business "is a form of commercial speech and nothing more." *Friedman v. Rogers*, 440 U.S. 1, 11 (1979). Requiring a commercial speaker to choose words and labels that do not confuse or deceive protects the public and does not impair expression. *See, e.g., United States v. Ninety Five Barrels, More or Less, Alleged Cider Vinegar*, 265 U.S. 438, 443 (1924) ("It is not difficult to choose statements, designs and devices which will not deceive."); *cf. Vidal Sassoon, Inc. v. Bristol-Myers Co.*, 661 F.2d 272, 276 n. 8 (2d Cir. 1981) (First Amendment concerns do not justify alteration of normal standard of preliminary injunctive relief on Lanham Act claim involving shampoo advertisements).

In the area of artistic speech, however, enforcement of trademark rights carries a risk of inhibiting free expression, *cf. L.L. Bean, Inc. v. Drake Publishers, Inc.*, 811 F.2d 26, 28–29 (1st Cir.), *cert. denied*, 483 U.S. 1013 (1987), not only in the case at hand but in other situations where authors might contemplate use of trademarks in connection with works of artistic expression. These risks add some weight to Silverman's claims.

From the standpoint of the proprietor of a mark in a work of artistic expression, there is also an interest in expression, along with the traditional trademark interest in avoiding public confusion as to source.

Trademark law can contribute to a favorable climate for expression by complementing the economic incentive that copyright law provides to create and disseminate artistic works, *see Harper & Row Publishers, Inc. v. Nation Enterprises, supra*, 471 U.S. at 558. In this case, however, the expression interest on CBS's side is markedly diminished by its decision to withhold dissemination of the works with which its marks are associated.

The interest of CBS, and the public, in avoiding public confusion, an interest obviously entitled to weight in every trademark case, is also somewhat diminished in the context of this case. This interest is not as weighty as in a case involving a non-artistic product whose trademark is associated with high quality or other consumer benefits. Though Silverman undoubtedly hopes that some of his audience will be drawn from those who favorably recall the "Amos 'n' Andy" programs, we doubt if many who attend Broadway musicals are motivated to purchase tickets because of a belief that the musical is produced by the same entity responsible for the movie, book, or radio or television series on which it is based. That is not to say that the musical is in a sufficiently distinct line of commerce to preclude all protection; the holder of a mark associated with a television series would normally be entitled to "bridge the gap" and secure some protection against an infringing use of the mark in connection with a Broadway musical. It is to say, however, that most theater-goers have sufficient awareness that the quality of a musical depends so heavily on a combination of circumstances, including script, score, lyrics, cast, and direction, that they are not likely to be significantly influenced in their ticket-purchasing decision by an erroneous belief that the musical emanated from the same production source as the underlying work.

The point must not be overstated. Trademark protection is not lost simply because the allegedly infringing use is in connection with a work of artistic expression. But in determining the outer limits of trademark protection—here, concerning the concept of abandonment—the balance of risks just noted is relevant and in some cases may tip the scales against trademark protection. These considerations are especially pertinent in the pending case where some aspects of the material claimed to be protected by trademark are in the public domain as far as copyright law is concerned.

For all of these reasons, we conclude that the undisputed facts establish abandonment of the AMOS 'N' ANDY marks. . . .

Affirmed in part, vacated in part, and remanded. No costs.

NOTES FOR DISCUSSION

1. *Abandonment.* The statutory definition of abandonment actually contains two alternative provisions. The first encompasses "nonuse"

abandonment, and requires proof of: (i) cessation of use; and (ii) an intent not to resume use. The second, which we saw in Chapter 4, encompasses genericness, assignments-in-gross, and naked licensing and occurs when "any course of conduct of the owner, including acts of omission as well as commission, causes the mark to become the generic name for the goods or services on or in connection with which it is used or otherwise to lose its significance as a mark." 15 U.S.C. § 1127 (2015) (definition of "abandoned").

In its opinion, the court distinguishes between the statutorily required "intent not to resume use" and an "intent to abandon"—the general standard for abandonment of personal property. What is the difference between these two intents?

How may a party prove that a trademark owner has the requisite "intent not to resume use"? The statute provides that such intent may be presumed from a period of nonuse. At the time of the decision, two years of nonuse created a rebuttable presumption of an intent not to resume use. Congress amended the statute in 1994, and it presently requires three years of nonuse to create such a presumption. Uruguay Round Agreements Act, Pub. L. No. 465, 103d Cong., 2d Sess., § 521, 108 Stat. 4809, 4982 (1994). Aside from this presumption, what other evidence could be used to demonstrate an intent not to resume use?

2.   *Residual Consumer Recognition.* In its opinion, the court discounts the risk that the defendant's use of Amos 'n Andy in the title of its musical will mislead many consumers. Do you agree? Or do you believe that some not insubstantial number of ordinarily prudent consumers will purchase tickets for the musical with an expectation concerning its quality based upon their memories of the original Amos 'n Andy programs?

While many of trademark law's key doctrines, from distinctiveness to infringement, focus entirely on consumer understanding of a word or mark, the statute defines nonuse abandonment entirely from the trademark owner's perspective. According to the statute, the only two questions are whether the trademark owner has stopped using the mark and done so with the intent not to resume use. If a mark retains considerable consumer recognition and the defendant's use is likely to create consumer confusion, is there some way that trademark law can remedy that risk?

In *Indianapolis Colts, Inc. v. Metropolitan Baltimore Football Club Ltd. Partnership,* Chief Judge Posner of the Seventh Circuit found a way. 34 F.3d 410 (7th Cir. 1994). Beginning in 1952, a NFL team, the Baltimore Colts, played in Baltimore. However, in 1984, literally, in the middle of the night, the team moved to Indianapolis and changed its name to the Indianapolis Colts. Some ten years later, in 1994, the Canadian Football League decided to establish a team in Baltimore and call it the Baltimore CFL Colts. In response, the Indianapolis Colts sued for trademark infringement and unfair competition. The Seventh Circuit held that the Indianapolis Colts had abandoned its trademark rights in "Baltimore Colts," when it had moved from Baltimore to Indianapolis and ceased using the mark. Nonetheless, the court held that the team still had valid trademark rights in the mark "Indianapolis Colts," and further held that there was a likelihood of confusion between the defendant's mark "Baltimore CFL Colts" and the plaintiff's mark "Indianapolis Colts." In affirming the district court's finding of a likelihood of confusion, the court specifically accepted survey results showing confusion between "Baltimore CFL Colts" and "Baltimore Colts" even though the mark "Baltimore Colts" had been abandoned. *Id.* at 415. As for why the court could rely on a survey showing confusion between the defendant's mark and an abandoned mark, the court explained:

> We also do not think it was improper for Jacoby to inquire about confusion between "Baltimore CFL Colts" and "Baltimore Colts," even though the Indianapolis Colts have abandoned "Baltimore Colts." If consumers believe that the new Baltimore team is the old Baltimore Colts, and the Indianapolis Colts some sort of upstart . . . , they will be less likely to buy merchandise stamped "Indianapolis Colts."

Id.

Does the Seventh Circuit's reasoning suggest that the fact of confusion trumps abandonment? For a different result on similar facts, see *Major League Baseball Properties, Inc. v. Sed Non Olet Denarius, Ltd.*, 817 F. Supp. 1103, 1128 (S.D.N.Y. 1993) (finding that Los Angeles Dodgers had abandoned the trademark Brooklyn Dodgers and allowing the defendant's restaurant to continue to operate in New York City under Brooklyn Dodger mark). What if the NFL team, in moving from Baltimore to Indianapolis, had changed its name from the Baltimore Colts to the Indianapolis Racers, would the outcome have been the same? Should it have been? *See American Motors Corp. v. Action-Age, Inc.*, 178 U.S.P.Q. (BNA) 377 (T.T.A.B.1973) (denying registration to mark "Scrambler" based upon confusing similarity to famous mark "Rambler" even though American Motors had ceased making Ramblers); *Lyon Metal Prods., Inc. v. Lyon Inc.*, 134 U.S.P.Q. (BNA) 31 (T.T.A.B. 1962) (denying registration to mark "Lyoncraft" based upon confusing similarity to mark "Lyon" even though "Lyon" no longer used in retail channels based in part on residual consumer recognition).

We have already seen that courts have recognized a section 43(a) cause of action for generic terms and book titles—neither of which may be owned as a trademark—where secondary meaning exists and consumer confusion is likely. Should we recognize a similar cause of action for abandoned trademarks? The Fifth Circuit has specifically rejected such an argument. *See Exxon Corp. v. Humble Exploration Co.*, 695 F.2d 96, 103–04 (5th Cir. 1983). According to the Fifth Circuit, "[i]t would be incongruous to hold that Exxon had abandoned the mark, . . . and thus that appellant had a right to use that mark because of Exxon's abandonment, and then to hold that appellant had engaged in false designation or representation of origin [under section 43(a)]." *Id.* (citation omitted). Is that any more incongruous than finding a word or book title to be generic, yet holding that its use by the defendant violates section 43(a)?

3.   *Trademark Maintenance Programs.* Where a trademark owner ceased commercial use of a trademark, but did not want to lose the trademark, some resorted to token uses of the sort that we saw in Chapter 2 to avoid abandonment. These trademark maintenance programs, as they became known, took different guises, but generally they entailed attaching the trademark at issue to one of the company's other products and shipping them out. Customers receiving the dual-labeled products were typically warned in advance of the nature of, and the reasons for, the dual labeling.

Courts generally greeted such maintenance programs with considerable skepticism. For example, in *Exxon Corp. v. Humble Exploration Co.*, the Fifth Circuit faced the issue whether Exxon had abandoned the trademark "Humble." 695 F.2d 96 (5th Cir. 1983). Beginning in 1917, Humble Oil & Refining Co. had extensively used the "Humble" mark, along with two other trade names, "Esso" and "Enco," for its products and service stations. Concerned that consumers were confused by the use of three different marks, in 1973, Humble Oil & Refining became Exxon Company, U.S.A. and adopted "Exxon" as its sole primary brand name. Exxon sold off its remaining supply of Humble-branded products by mid-1974. From mid-1974 until 1977, Exxon made a few token sales of dual-labeled "Exxon" and "Humble" products, and also used the name "Humble" on the invoices of a few bulk sales. Exxon argued that these token uses were sufficient to stave off abandonment of the "Humble" mark. The Fifth Circuit disagreed. *Id.* at 100–01.

At the court explained:

> In this case, the mark HUMBLE was used only on isolated products or selected invoices sent to selected customers. No sales were made that depended upon the HUMBLE mark for identification of source. To the contrary, purchasers were informed that the selected shipments would bear the HUMBLE name or be accompanied by an HUMBLE invoice but were the desired Exxon products. That is, the HUMBLE mark did not with these sales play the role of a mark. That casting, however, is central to the plot that the Lanham Act rests on the idea of registration of marks otherwise born of use rather than the creation of marks by the act of registration. That precept finds expression in the Lanham Act requirement that to maintain a mark in the absence of use there must be an intent to resume use. That expression is plain. The Act does not allow the preservation of a mark solely to prevent its use by others. Yet the trial court's reasoning allows precisely that warehousing so long as there is residual goodwill associated with the mark. Exxon makes the same argument here. While that may be good policy, we cannot square it with the language of the statute. In sum, these arranged sales in which the mark was not allowed to play its basic role of identifying source were not "use" in the sense of section 1127 of the Lanham Act.

Id.

As we saw in Chapter 2, Congress amended the definition of "use" in section 1127 in 1988 to mean "the bona fide use of a mark in the ordinary course of trade, and not made merely to reserve a right in a mark." 15 U.S.C. § 1127 (2015) (definition of "use in commerce"). This amendment effectively forecloses the token use option as a means to stave off abandonment.

If General Motors came to you today and asked how it could maintain rights in the mark Oldsmobile, what advice would you give? Would it be enough to continue to sell parts for, and service, Oldsmobile-brand automobiles? *Compare Emergency One, Inc. v. American FireEagle, Ltd.*, 228 F.3d 531, 536 (4th Cir. 2000) ("Exclusive repair and recycling services like those offered by E-One might be sufficient commercial use of the mark to prevent abandonment, but only if E-One used the mark on the repaired or remanufactured goods or 'on documents associated with the goods or their sale.' "); *with American Motors Corp. v. Action-Age, Inc.*, 178 U.S.P.Q. (BNA) 377, 378 (T.T.A.B.1973) (finding no abandonment of "Rambler" mark for cars based in part upon "opposer's activities in supplying 'RAMBLER' parts and accessories to owners of these vehicles"). Would it be enough to sell promotional items, such as t-shirts and caps, bearing the Oldsmobile mark? *See Emergency One, Inc.*, 228 F.3d at 536–37 (holding that such promotional efforts do not count as use for fire engines, but provide some evidence of an intent to resume use of the mark for fire engines); Imperial Tobacco, Ltd. v. Philip Morris, Inc., 899 F.2d 1575, 1582–83 (Fed. Cir. 1990) (holding that promotional use of mark in sales of whiskey, pens, watches, sunglasses, and food did not constitute use of mark for cigarettes)

4. *Resumption of Use.* How would you resolve the following case:

> From 1927 to 1932, Kraft manufactured and sold an ice cream novelty under the name "Polar B'ar" with an image of a polar bear on it. From 1932 until 1980, it made no sales under the Polar B'ar mark. In 1978, Islay began selling an ice cream novelty under the name "Klondike Bar" with a picture of a polar bear on it. In 1980, Kraft began offering an ice cream novelty under the name "Polar B'ar" with an image of a polar bear on it. Kraft and Islay sue each other, both claiming exclusive right to the polar bear image as a trademark for ice cream novelties.

See AmBrit, Inc. v. Kraft, Inc., 812 F.2d 1531, 1550–51 (11th Cir. 1986) (holding that Kraft had abandoned polar bear image as trademark and that Islay had acquired rights in the trademark through his use which began before Kraft's new use).

Would or should the outcome change if Kraft's use had occurred from 1967 through 1972? What if it had occurred from 1972 through 1976?

CHAPTER 7

TRADEMARK INFRINGEMENT

■ ■ ■

A. THE BASIC STANDARD: LIKELIHOOD OF CONFUSION

At the turn of the twentieth century, the scope of trademark and unfair competition protection was limited to the use of an identical or near-identical mark on the same product. Both the 1881 and 1905 Trademark Acts incorporated this common law standard and prohibited the infringement of a registered trademark using identical language:

> Any person who shall, without the consent of the owner thereof, reproduce, counterfeit, copy, or colorably imitate any registered trade-mark under this act and affix the same to merchandise of substantially the same descriptive properties as those described in the registration shall be liable to an action of the case for damages for the wrongful use of said trade-mark. . . .

Act of Mar. 3, 1881, 46 Cong., 3d Sess., § 7, 21 Stat. 502, 503–04; Trademark Act of 1905, Pub. L. No. 84, 58th Cong., 3d Sess., § 16, 33 Stat. 724, 728.

Under this standard, the use of the same mark on a different product did not constitute trademark infringement. For example, in 1912, Borden's Condensed Milk, which had long used Borden as the brand name for its condensed milk, sued another company that began using the name "Borden's" for ice cream. Although the district court granted relief, the Seventh Circuit reversed and rejected the claim. *Borden Ice Cream Co. v. Borden's Condensed Milk Co.*, 201 F. 510 (7th Cir. 1912). The court held that because milk and ice cream were not competing products, there could be no unfair competition. *Id.* at 514. Recognizing that ice cream and milk did not share the "same descriptive properties," the plaintiff nevertheless argued that it should be entitled to relief for two reasons. First, it intended to enter the ice cream market. Second, it was selling its condensed milk to ice cream manufacturers, and so the markets were close enough that some ice cream dealers would mistakenly believe that the plaintiff had made the defendant's product. The court rejected both arguments, however. With respect to the first, the court insisted that the law " 'deals with acts and not intentions.' " *Id.* at 515 (*quoting George v. Smith*, 52 F. 830, 832 (C.C.S.D.N.Y. 1892)). Because the defendant actually began selling ice cream under the Borden's name first, the defendant held the rights to that name for ice cream, and the plaintiff's intent to enter that market was simply irrelevant. With respect to the second, the court said the specter of confusion was simply too "speculative and remote" to justify relief. *Borden's Ice Cream Co.*, 201 F. at 515.

Just five years later, however, the Second Circuit considered a similar claim in *Aunt Jemima Mills Co. v. Rigney & Co.*, 247 F. 407 (2d Cir. 1917). In this case, the plaintiff had used the phrase Aunt Jemima's for self-rising flour for years, when the defendant began using Aunt Jemima's for syrup. As the two goods did not have "substantially the same descriptive properties," the district court dismissed the complaint. On appeal, the Second Circuit reversed. Although the court acknowledged the traditional limits of trademark law, it nonetheless felt that the two products were sufficiently related that consumers were likely to believe that the plaintiff had made the defendant's product. It therefore granted relief and enjoined the defendant's use. As the court explained:

> It is said that even a technical trade-mark may be appropriated by any one in any market for goods not in competition with those of the prior user. This was the view of the court below in saying that no one wanting syrup could possibly be made to take flour. But we think that goods, though different, may be so related as to fall within the mischief which equity should prevent. Syrup and flour are both food products, and food products commonly used together. Obviously the public, or a large part of it, seeing this trade-mark on a syrup, would conclude that it was made by the complainant. Perhaps they might not do so, if it were used for flatirons. In this way the complainant's reputation is put in the hands of the defendants. It will enable them to get the benefit of the complainant's reputation and advertisement. These we think are property rights which should be protected in equity.

Aunt Jemima Mills Co., 247 F. at 409–10.

Although the case law proceeded in fits and starts, sometimes embracing the *Aunt Jemima* approach, and sometimes the traditional "same descriptive properties" approach, gradually the courts began to focus on a single question: Was the defendant's use of a similar mark likely to confuse consumers and lead them to believe (mistakenly) that the plaintiff had manufactured (*e.g.* was the source of) the defendant's goods? This approach to the issue was plainly inconsistent with the statutory language of the Trademark Act of 1905. Yet, this did not appear to trouble courts much, and eventually, the courts simply started pretending that Congress had intended to adopt the likelihood of confusion test when it used the "same descriptive properties" language in the 1905 Act. *See Yale Electric Corp. v. Robertson*, 26 F.2d 972 (2d Cir. 1928) (L. Hand, J.).

The need for such pretense evaporated, however, when Congress expressly embraced the likelihood of confusion standard as the infringement standard in the Trademark Act of 1946. As codified and amended, section 32 of the Trademark Act of 1946 currently provides, in relevant part:

15 U.S.C. § 1114. Remedies; infringement; innocent infringement by printers and publishers

(1) Any person who shall, without the consent of the registrant—

(a) use in commerce any reproduction, counterfeit, copy, or colorable imitation of a registered mark in connection with the sale, offering for sale, distribution, or advertising of any goods or services on or in connection with which such use is likely to cause confusion, or to cause mistake, or to deceive; or

(b) reproduce, counterfeit, copy, or colorably imitate a registered mark and apply such reproduction, counterfeit, copy, or colorable imitation to labels, signs, prints, packages, wrappers, receptacles or advertisements intended to be used in commerce upon or in connection with the sale, offering for sale, distribution, or advertising of goods or services on or in connection with which such use is likely to cause confusion, or to cause mistake, or to deceive,

shall be liable in a civil action by the registrant for the remedies hereinafter provided.

Following the Trademark Act of 1946, the likelihood of confusion standard became the standard for determining liability for trademark infringement, but questions remained over how to apply it to particular cases. For years, as the likelihood of confusion standard took hold in the courts, and even after Congress expressly adopted it, courts struggled to develop sensible rules to define when consumers were likely to be confused by the defendant's use of a similar mark. How closely related did the goods have to be? How similar did the marks have to be? Did it matter how well-known the plaintiff's mark was? Did it matter whether the plaintiff intended to enter the defendant's product market?

Eventually, the courts threw up their hands at attempting to draw any definitive lines, and simply acknowledged that a variety of factors might be relevant to the ultimate question of whether consumer confusion was likely. Chief Judge Friendly of the Second Circuit helpfully summarized these factors in *Polaroid Corp. v. Polarad Electronics Corp.*:

Where the products are different, the prior owner's chance of success is a function of many variables: the strength of his mark, the degree of similarity between the two marks, the proximity of the products, the likelihood that the prior owner will bridge the gap, actual confusion, and the reciprocal of defendant's good faith in adopting its own mark, the quality of defendant's product, and the sophistication of the buyers. Even this extensive catalogue does not exhaust the possibilities—the court may have to take still other variables into account.

287 F.2d 492, 495 (2d Cir.), *cert. denied*, 368 U.S. 820 (1961).

Today, every circuit uses its own version of the *Polaroid* factors as a guide to help resolve the likelihood of confusion issue. To get a sense for how these factors work, consider the following case.

ESTEE LAUDER, INC. V. OLD NAVY CLOTHING CO.
108 F.3d 1503 (2d Cir. 1997)

KEARSE, C.J.

Defendant The Gap, Inc. d/b/a Old Navy Clothing Company ("Gap"), appeals from a final judgment of the United States District Court for the Southern District of New York, Lewis A. Kaplan, *Judge*, permanently enjoining Gap from using the term "100%" alone or with other terms as a trademark in connection with the manufacture, promotion, or distribution of its personal care products and bathroom furnishings and implements. The district court found that Gap's use of terms such as "100% BODY CARE" on its products was likely to cause consumers to confuse Gap's products with a moisturizer product manufactured by plaintiff Estee Lauder Inc. ("Lauder") and marketed under Lauder's trademark "100%." On appeal, Gap contends principally that the district court erred in finding Lauder's "100%" mark protectable and in finding that Gap's use of a mark that includes "100%" in conjunction with other terms would create a likelihood of consumer confusion. We agree that the district court erred in its likelihood-of-confusion analysis, and we accordingly reverse.

I.   BACKGROUND

Lauder is an international cosmetics company that manufactures skin care, makeup, and fragrance products. The company distributes its products through cosmetics specialty stores and "upscale" department stores that, in its view, complement the image of quality it cultivates. Gap is an international retailer of apparel and other products. Gap owns and operates Old Navy Clothing Company ("Old Navy"), whose stores are located primarily in strip malls and shopping centers and cater to the mass middle market. All Old Navy products, and virtually no others, are distributed through Old Navy stores.

In December 1994, Gap developed a line of personal care products to be distributed through Old Navy, intending to market, *inter alia*, shampoo, soap, and body lotion under the label "100% BODY CARE." In September 1995, Gap began a search into the availability of a trademark containing the term "100%." In the meantime, Lauder was developing a facial moisturizer, and in December 1995 it began its own investigation into the availability of the term "100%" as the trademark for its moisturizer.

Both companies eventually learned that a third company, Les Parfums de Dana, Inc. ("Dana"), was the record owner of the trademark "100% HUNDRED PER CENT," but that Dana had abandoned use of its trademark. Lauder obtained an assignment of the "100%" trademark and registration from Dana, and in December 1995 Lauder filed an intent-to-use ("ITU") application with the United States Patent and Trademark Office seeking to register "100%" as a trademark. In January 1996, Gap filed a similar application to register "100%" alone; it also filed applications to register "100% BODY CARE" and "100% BODY CARE AND DESIGN." Thereafter, it filed numerous additional applications to register "100%" in combination with other terms such as "100% SPORT," "100% BODY CARE FOR KIDS," and "100% HOME SCENT."

In March 1996, Gap contacted Lauder to discuss the two companies' conflicting ITU applications. In light of Lauder's intent to use "100%" as the mark for its moisturizer, Gap offered assurance that for Gap's own products it would not use the term "100%" alone, and it abandoned its ITU application for the mark "100%" alone. Gap subsequently modified its planned "100% BODY CARE" mark to increase emphasis on the words "BODY CARE" and to decrease emphasis on the number "100." The parties failed to reach agreement.

Lauder began to distribute its moisturizer in April 1996, packaged in a 1.7-ounce aquamarine glass bottle, as part of its "blue line" of products that are typically marketed in aquamarine packaging. Lauder's moisturizer has a suggested retail price of $32.50. As the packaging is shown in Appendix A to this opinion, Lauder's "EL" logo is prominently displayed at the top of the bottle, and the company's "ESTEE LAUDER" house mark appears immediately below that. Near the bottom, the following lines appear:

100% Time Release Moisturizer with BioMineral Water

The back of the bottle contains the notation: "C ESTEE LAUDER, DIST."

Gap's "100% BODY CARE" products are packaged principally in plastic bottles that range in size from .15 to 33 fluid ounces. At the top of each bottle appears a generic designation of its contents (*e.g.*, "bubble bath," "shampoo," "body lotion") in large, lower case letters. The suggestion of a fragrance for each product (*e.g.*, "Groovy Grapefruit," "Some Are Pink," "Positively Purple") is printed in an elongated oval just above the center of the bottle. The bottles themselves are translucent, presenting the various colors of their respective contents. The logo

100% BODY CARE

appears towards the bottom of the bottle. As illustrated in Appendix B, the "%"sign is oversized, approximately three times the height of "100."

The back of the bottle contains the Old Navy house mark, followed by the notation, "A division of Gap, Inc." Gap planned to release this line of products on a test basis in August 1996. The planned prices for each type and quantity of these products were small fractions of the suggested retail price of Lauder's product.

In June 1996, Lauder commenced the present action seeking preliminary and permanent injunctions against the use of "100%" as part of Gap's marks, alleging principally that such use would lead consumers to believe that Gap's products were associated with Lauder and would thereby violate Lauder's rights under § 43(a) of the Lanham Act (the "Act"), 15 U.S.C. § 1125(a) (1994). Gap disputed Lauder's assertions and counterclaimed for declaratory and injunctive relief against interference by Lauder with Gap's efforts to register various marks incorporating the term "100%." The district court ordered expedited discovery and conducted a two-day bench trial in July 1996.

In a post trial Opinion dated July 22, 1996, reported at 932 F. Supp. 595, the court ruled that Lauder was entitled to a permanent injunction prohibiting Gap from including the term "100%" in trademarks on Gap's personal care and other products. The court found that Lauder's "100%" mark was suggestive and, therefore, protectable. . . .

Having noted Lauder's concession that its mark had not acquired secondary meaning, *see, e.g., id.* at 606, the court proceeded to address the factors set forth in *Polaroid Corp. v. Polarad Electronics Corp.*, 287 F.2d 492, 495 (2d Cir.), *cert. denied*, 368 U.S. 820 (1961), in order to determine whether there was a likelihood of consumer confusion. First the court found that Lauder's mark was of "moderate strength" because it was "inherently distinctive[ ]," 932 F. Supp. at 612, and that the "prominent use of '100%' by both parties—particularly in view of the fact that each of the parties uses '100%' to convey the same idea in conjunction with closely related personal care products—makes the similarity factor weigh in Lauder's favor," *id.* at 613.

The court saw some obvious differences between Lauder's product and those of Gap. . . . But the court found these differences to be outweighed by the fact that the products are closely related, *i.e.*, that they are "all used for personal care," *id.* The court also found that, although there was some overlap in clientele, the two companies' products were sold through markedly different channels of distribution. . . . However, the court found these differences outweighed by the fact that "not all customers are knowledgeable, and even knowledgeable customers could be misled into thinking that Lauder is associated with the '100% BODY

CARE' products, either as producer or licensor of an off-price line." *Id.*
The court also found that although there was no suggestion that Gap's
products were not inherently of good quality for what they were, there
was a "genuine risk that consumers who purchase the Gap product in the
belief that it is associated in some way with Lauder will be disappointed
and that the disappointment will rub off on Lauder." *Id.* at 616.

Although the court also found that Lauder had no plans to enter the
mass middle market in which Old Navy normally operates, *see id.* at 615,
that there was "no evidence of actual confusion," *id.*, and that in seeking
to use "100%" as part of its own marks, "Gap acted in good faith," *id.* at
616, all of which were factors that did not favor Lauder's claim, the court
concluded, weighing all the factors, that Gap's use of "100%" in its marks
would create a likelihood of consumer confusion. . . .

A final judgment was entered dismissing Gap's counterclaim and
permanently enjoining Gap from using the term "100%" alone or with
other terms as a trademark in connection with the manufacture,
promotion, or distribution of its personal care products and bathroom
furnishings and implements. This appeal followed.

II. DISCUSSION

In order to prevail on a claim of trademark infringement in violation
of the Lanham Act, a plaintiff must show (1) that it has a valid mark that
is entitled to protection under the Act, and (2) that use of the defendant's
mark infringes, or is likely to infringe, the mark of the plaintiff. The
degree to which a mark is entitled to protection under the Act depends on
whether the mark is classified as (a) generic, (b) descriptive, (c)
suggestive, or (d) fanciful or arbitrary. "The test for infringement is
whether the actor's use of a designation as a trademark . . . creates a
likelihood of confusion. . . ." *Restatement (Third) of Unfair Competition*
§ 21 comment *a* (1995) ("*Restatement*").

There is no contention in the present case that Lauder's mark is
generic, arbitrary, or fanciful. It is also undisputed that Lauder's mark
had not acquired secondary meaning. Gap contends that the district court
erred (1) in finding Lauder's mark suggestive rather than descriptive, and
hence protectable in the absence of secondary meaning, and (2) in finding
that there was a likelihood of consumer confusion in the absence of
secondary meaning. We agree with the latter contention.

. . . The issue of likelihood of confusion turns on whether "numerous
ordinarily prudent purchasers are likely to be misled or confused as to the
source of the product in question because of the entrance in the
marketplace of defendant's mark." *Gruner + Jahr USA Publishing v.
Meredith Corp.*, 991 F.2d 1072, 1077 (2d Cir. 1993). Likelihood of
confusion means a probability of confusion; "it is not sufficient if

confusion is merely 'possible'." 3 J. McCarthy, *McCarthy on Trademarks and Unfair Competition* § 23:2, at 23–10, 11 (1996).

"Courts deciding whether a plaintiff has established likelihood of confusion must consider the eight factors elaborated" in *Polaroid Corp. v. Polarad Electronics Corp.*, 287 F.2d 492, 495 (2d Cir.), *cert. denied*, 368 U.S. 820 (1961). *Arrow Fastener Co. v. Stanley Works*, 59 F.3d at 391; *see, e.g., Gruner + Jahr USA Publishing v. Meredith Corp.*, 991 F.2d at 1077. Those factors are: "1) the strength of the plaintiff's mark; 2) the similarity of plaintiff's and defendant's marks; 3) the competitive proximity of the products; 4) the likelihood that plaintiff will 'bridge the gap' and offer a product like defendant's; 5) actual confusion between products; 6) good faith on the defendant's part; 7) the quality of defendant's product; and 8) the sophistication of buyers." *Id.*; *see, e.g., Arrow Fastener Co. v. Stanley Works*, 59 F.3d at 391. As to the first factor,

> the distinctiveness or "strength" of a mark measures its capacity to indicate the source of the goods or services with which it is used. The greater the distinctiveness of the mark, the greater the likelihood that prospective purchasers will associate the same or a similar designation found on other goods, services, or businesses with the prior user. . . .
>
> "Strength" . . . ultimately depends on the degree to which the designation is associated by prospective purchasers with a particular source.

Restatement § 21 comment *i.*

No one of the *Polaroid* factors is dispositive, and the list is not exhaustive; "the analysis of the factors is not a mechanical process." *Arrow Fastener Co. v. Stanley Works*, 59 F.3d at 391 (internal quotation marks omitted); *see, e.g., Gruner + Jahr USA Publishing v. Meredith Corp.*, 991 F.2d at 1077. A trial court's finding as to each individual factor is one of fact, subject to review under the clearly erroneous standard. *See, e.g., id.*; *Arrow Fastener Co. v. Stanley Works*, 59 F.3d at 391. The ultimate weighing of the factors, however, is reviewed *de novo. See, e.g., id.* at 391, 400 (reversing after a *de novo* review of the court's weighing of the *Polaroid* factors); *Plus Products v. Plus Discount Foods, Inc.*, 722 F.2d at 1004, 1005 (partial reversal based on conclusion that the district "court's balancing of the *Polaroid* factors was incorrect").

In the present case, the main *Polaroid* factors relied on by the district court in concluding that Gap's use of "100%" as part of its marks would create a likelihood of confusion were (1) the strength of Lauder's mark, (2) the similarity of the two companies' marks, and (3) the competitive proximity of the products. We have difficulty principally with the court's findings as to the first of these factors and with its weighing of the third against all other factors. First, the court found that Lauder's mark, though neither at the weakest nor at the strongest end of the range for suggestiveness, was moderately strong. The district court made this finding on the ground that Lauder's mark was "inherently distinctive[ ]." 932 F. Supp. at 612. These findings are unsupported by any evidence that consumers associated the term "100%" or the phrase "100% Time Release Moisturizer" with Lauder; indeed, they are undercut by Lauder's concession that its mark had not acquired secondary meaning, *see id.* at 606, 611–12. And while the absence of secondary meaning does not preclude the court from finding that a mark is strong if it is otherwise distinctive, *see, e.g., W.W.W. Pharmaceutical Co. v. Gillette Co.*, 984 F.2d 567, 573 (2d Cir. 1993), the court's finding of distinctiveness here is undermined by its own finding that Lauder's use of "100%" in a suggestive sense "is not wholly original," *id.* at 612. The latter finding is amply supported by the trial evidence that, prior to Lauder's ITU application, there were more than 70 trademark registrations, pending applications for registration or renewal, or publications-for-opposition that incorporated the term "100%," and that some of those marks were for cosmetic products.

Given the principle that a mark's " 'strength' . . . ultimately depends on the degree to which the designation is associated by prospective purchasers with a particular source," *Restatement* § 21 comment *i*, plus the court's finding that Lauder's use of the term "100%" was not original and Lauder's concession that prospective purchasers did not associate that term with Lauder, we conclude that the court's finding that Lauder's mark is moderately strong is clearly erroneous.

Second, we think the court erred in weighing the similarity of the products against their differences and the disparate channels through which they are distributed. The court found that although the two lines of products are to be sold in mutually exclusive types of stores and "no one knowledgeable about the sort of places in which Lauder sells its upscale products would be likely to think that the very same products would be available in an Old Navy store," confusion "may be" likely because some customers are not knowledgeable, and even knowledgeable customers "could" be misled, as the products are closely related. 932 F. Supp. at 614. The test, however, is not whether confusion is possible; nor is it whether confusion is probable among customers who are not knowledgeable. Rather, the test, correctly stated by the district court elsewhere in its opinion, is whether confusion is probable among numerous customers who are ordinarily prudent. Especially given the concession that consumers do not associate "100%" with Lauder, and the fact that each product is labeled to show which company is its source, we see no support for a finding that an appreciable number of ordinarily prudent consumers would likely think that Lauder, whose product costs $32.50 for less than two ounces in an upscale store, is the source of products that at Old Navy cost a small fraction of that price for 10 or 20 times that quantity.

The predominant element of the district court's conclusion that the use of "100%" by Gap would result in the likelihood of confusion seems to have been that Lauder's moisturizer and some of the products to be marketed by Gap are "closely related products." Having reviewed *de novo* the district court's weighing of the factors, we conclude that the close relationship between Lauder's moisturizer and some of Gap's products, and the fact that some consumers shop in both types of stores, do not outweigh the facts that the rendering of "100%" in the two sets of marks is different in appearance; that the appearance of the packaging overall is quite different in graphic design; that on each package the purveyor of that product is expressly identified; that the use of "100%" is not original; that the companies' products are sold in disparate types of stores; that the per-ounce price of Gap's body care products would likely be less than five percent of the per-ounce price of Lauder's product; that Lauder does not plan to enter Gap's market; that Gap did not act in bad faith; and that, as the district court found, no knowledgeable consumer would be likely to buy one product thinking it was the other. In sum, weighing all of the factors, we conclude that Gap's use of "100%" as part of its planned marks would not create a likelihood of confusion among ordinarily prudent consumers.

CONCLUSION

We have considered all of Lauder's arguments on this appeal and have found in them no basis for upholding the decision below. The judgment of the district court is reversed, and the matter is remanded for entry of an amended judgment dismissing the complaint.

NOTES FOR DISCUSSION

1. *Issue of Fact or Law.* In the *Estee Lauder* case, the Second Circuit treats the individual *Polaroid* factors as factual, but the ultimate weighing of the factors to determine whether consumers are likely to be confused as a legal issue. Other circuits have disagreed and have treated both the individual factors and the ultimate weighing as factual issues. *See, e.g., Levi Strauss & Co. v. Blue Bell, Inc.*, 778 F.2d 1352, 1355–56 & n.5 (9th Cir. 1985) (en banc) (holding that likelihood of confusion is a mixed question of fact and law "which appears to be predominantly factual in nature"). The decision whether to label likelihood of confusion as one of fact or one of law has important implications, both, for the standard of review on appeal, and for the grant of summary judgment.

With respect to appeal, if the ultimate question of whether consumers are likely to be confused is considered a legal issue, as in *Estee Lauder*, the appellate court reviews that issue *de novo*, giving no deference to the trial court or jury. If, on the other hand, the question of confusion is treated as a factual issue, then the appellate court may not substitute its own judgment for that of the trial court, but may reverse only if the appellate court is left

with "the definite and firm conviction that a mistake has been committed."
United States v. United States Gypsum Co., 333 U.S. 364, 395 (1948).

With respect to summary judgment, summary judgment may only be
granted if there is no genuine dispute as to a material fact. If there is a
factual dispute with respect to one of the underlying *Polaroid* factors, such as
whether actual confusion did or did not occur, and that dispute is material to
the resolution of the question whether consumer confusion is likely, then
summary judgment would not be appropriate under either approach.
However, what if the facts for each of the underlying *Polaroid* factors are
undisputed? Although the facts relevant to each factor may be undisputed,
the factors may cut in different directions, some weighing in favor of
infringement, some weighing against. May summary judgment be granted if
the facts pertaining to each of the underlying factors are undisputed but
there is a dispute as to how to weigh and balance the various factors? If we
treat the ultimate question as a legal issue, then the answer to that question
is yes—summary judgment is appropriate, and the court should itself weigh
and balance the factors in order to reach a conclusion as to whether there is a
likelihood of confusion. In contrast, if we treat the ultimate question as a
factual issue, then the process of weighing and balancing the competing
factors to determine whether there was a likelihood of confusion is itself a
factual issue that may not be resolved on summary judgment.

So how should we treat the ultimate question of whether consumers are
likely to be confused? Usually, we label an issue as factual where the trial
court or jury is better positioned to resolve the issue. The trial court actually
sits through the entire trial, can observe the witnesses directly, and is likely
better positioned to resolve those disputes that call for credibility
determinations or otherwise require the reconciliation of conflicting stories.
The appellate court, reviewing the case based solely on the cold, written
record is not as well positioned to resolve the issue of who is telling the truth.
On the other hand, we usually label an issue as law where it involves the
resolution of some underlying policy considerations that we want to see
resolved consistently. Do you think that the ultimate question as to whether
consumers are likely to be confused should be legal or factual?

2. *Will the Real Infringement Standard Please Stand Up?* As the
statutory language expressly states, the legal standard for liability is
whether the defendant's use creates a likelihood of confusion. The *Polaroid*
factors are not the infringement standard. They are simply a collection of
factual considerations that historically courts have found helpful in
particular contexts to determine whether confusion is likely. As the *Estee
Lauder* court notes, the factors are not meant to be applied mechanically or
as if they were a check-list. In appropriate cases, other factors may be
relevant or even decisive.

Recall the *Dawn Donuts* case from Chapter 3. If you simply applied the
Polaroid factors to that case, how do you think it would come out? How many
factors weigh in favor of finding a likelihood of confusion? How many against?
Yet, in that case, a single consideration—a consideration that is not one of

the *Polaroid* factors—was decisive. Specifically, because the plaintiff did not operate in the same area as the defendant, none of the defendant's customers would be familiar with the plaintiff, and hence none would mistakenly believe that the defendant was the plaintiff. Consumer confusion was therefore unlikely even though the defendant was using the same mark on the same products.

Courts sometimes have trouble, though, maintaining the gap between the *Polaroid* factors and the standard for liability. Thus, on facts similar to those in *Dawn Donuts*, the Sixth Circuit found liability in *Circuit City Stores, Inc. v. CarMax, Inc.*, 165 F.3d 1047 (6th Cir. 1999). As in *Dawn Donuts*, the geographic remoteness of the plaintiff's and the defendant's operations made consumer confusion unlikely. Nonetheless, the court affirmed a finding of infringement. According to the court, geographic remoteness was just one of the relevant factors, and so long as the other factors weighed in favor of infringement, then there was infringement. As the court attempted to explain: "If a plaintiff can otherwise demonstrate a likelihood of confusion by a strong showing on the other seven factors, it seems an odd result that the same plaintiff cannot obtain an injunction against an infringer simply because the parties operate in different geographical regions." *Id.* at 1057. But why should such a result seem "odd"? If the parties operate in different geographic regions, are the defendant's customers likely to be familiar with the plaintiff? If not, why, when they shop at the defendant's store, would they believe that they were at the plaintiff's?

3. *Forums: Registration and Infringement.* There are two forums in which likelihood of confusion issues may be resolved. The *Estee Lauder* case illustrates the first: infringement litigation in federal or state courts. The second is registration proceedings before the United States Patent and Trademark Office. Although federal registration is not a requirement for trademark protection, it offers certain substantive and procedural advantages. As a result, trademark owners routinely seek to register their trademarks on the principal register. As we saw in Chapter 4, there are a number of bars to registration, including, for example, section 2(a)'s prohibition on the registration of marks that consist of "immoral, deceptive, or scandalous matter." Section 2(d) of the Trademark Act prohibits the registration of a trademark that is likely to cause confusion with a previously registered or previously used trademark. 15 U.S.C. § 1052(d) (2015). Thus, when a trademark owner applies for registration, the examiner may reject the application on the grounds that the trademark at issue is confusingly similar to a previously registered trademark. An applicant may appeal such a rejection initially to the Trademark Trial and Appeal Board (or TTAB), and if still unsatisfied, to the Federal Circuit. Alternatively, if the examiner finds no likelihood of confusion and approves the application, a private party may initiate an opposition proceeding before the TTAB seeking to block the registration on the grounds that the applied-for mark is likely to cause confusion with its previously registered or used mark. The statutory language setting forth the likelihood of confusion standard for registration in section 2(d) and the statutory language setting forth the likelihood of

confusion standard for infringement in section 32 are nearly identical, and have been since Congress amended the Act in 1962 to make them so. There are significant differences, however, in the practice and procedure of the TTAB, and some differences in the actual implementation of the legal standard. For example, registration proceedings focus on the likelihood of confusion between the marks as they are sought to be registered, where infringement litigation focuses on the marks as they are actually used in the marketplace.

In any event, trademark practitioners had long thought of the two issues, registration and infringement, as distinct. In particular, the refusal of the United States Patent and Trademark Office to register a mark on the grounds that it was confusingly similar to a previously registered trademark did not, of itself, bar use of that mark in commerce. Such an adverse registration decision might be relevant evidence should infringement litigation subsequently commence, but it was not controlling. This allowed trademark practitioners to treat registration proceedings as a nonbinding, test or trial run of potential infringement issues.

In *B & B Hardware, Inc. v. Hargis Indus., Inc.*, the Supreme Court put an end to this practice. 135 S.Ct. 1293 (2015). The case concerned two companies, both of which manufacture and sell metal fasteners. Although both sell metal fasteners, they are not exactly competitors. B & B's fasteners are intended for the aerospace industry, while Hargis's fasteners are intended for the construction trade. Both have long used similar trademarks. B & B has used the mark Sealtight for its fasteners. Hargis has used the mark Sealtite for its fasteners. B & B won the race to the PTO, and registered its trademark first in 1993. Hargis applied to register its trademark in 1996. When the mark was approved by the PTO and published in 2002, B & B opposed the mark's registration. B & B prevailed before the TTAB, and Hargis did not appeal. While the opposition proceeding was pending, B & B had also sued Hargis in federal district court for trademark infringement. When the TTAB ruled against Hargis, B & B argued to the district court that the TTAB's decision should have preclusive effect in the infringement litigation. The district court rejected this argument on the grounds that the TTAB was not an Article III court, and allowed a jury to decide the likelihood of confusion issue. The jury found no likelihood of confusion. B & B appealed, but the Eighth Circuit affirmed. So B & B petitioned the Court to grant *certiorari*. The Court granted *certiorari* and reversed. The Court held that despite the differences between the TTAB proceeding and infringement litigation, the likelihood of confusion was essentially the same. Unless there was some material difference between the marks as registered or applied for, and the marks as used in commerce, issue preclusion should apply.

In reaching this conclusion, the Court changed, perhaps radically, the relationship between registration proceedings and infringement litigation. Parties will have to think far more carefully before applying for registration, and will have to take registration proceedings before the TTAB far more seriously, than they had previously.

4. *Strength of the Mark.* Courts usually evaluate the strength of the plaintiff's mark along two dimensions. First, courts look at where the mark falls along the spectrum of distinctiveness. Second, courts also look at how well known a mark is among the relevant consumers. As the *Estee Lauder* court notes, the second of these dimensions—how well known a mark is—is the more important because, in most cases, it provides more persuasive circumstantial evidence that defendant's use of a similar mark will lead consumers to believe (mistakenly) that the defendant's products come from the plaintiff.

Nevertheless, where the mark falls along the spectrum of distinctiveness is also relevant to the question of consumer confusion. As the mark moves down the spectrum towards descriptive or suggestive, it becomes more plausible that a defendant wants to use a similar mark to describe or suggest the characteristics of its own products. In contrast, there is less excuse for similarity when the plaintiff's mark is arbitrary or fanciful. Why do you think the Gap wanted to use the phrase "100%" on its products?

5. *Similarity of the Marks.* Similarity of the marks is usually judged by a tripartite standard that asks whether the marks are similar either by sight, sound, or meaning. Similarity along any one of these dimensions will weigh in favor of finding infringement. The words "cyclone" and "tornado" neither look nor sound alike. Yet, they have related meanings. As a result, when one company sought to register "tornado" as the brand name for its chain-link fencing, the Court of Customs and Patent Appeals found it confusingly similar to the well-known "Cyclone" mark for fencing and refused registration. *See Hancock v. American Steel & Wire Co.*, 203 F.2d 737 (C.C.P.A. 1953).

In judging the marks, courts sometimes emphasize that the marks are not to be dissected, but are to be compared as a whole. At the same time, they will also sometimes focus on the dominant aspects of the mark, particularly where portions of the marks are generic or otherwise unprotectible. Thus, in *Boston Duck Tours, LP v. Super Duck Tours, LLC*, 531 F.3d 1 (1st Cir. 2008), the district court found a likelihood of confusion and emphasized the fact that both marks contained the words "duck tours." On appeal, the First Circuit reversed. *Id.* at 24. The defendant conceded that the mark as a whole, "Boston Duck Tours," was a valid mark, but argued that the words "duck tours" alone were generic. The First Circuit agreed. *Id.* at 17–23.

Because a portion of the mark, standing alone, was generic, in evaluating similarity for determining whether confusion is likely, the marks as a whole are compared, but similarities in the generic aspects of the marks are given less weight. As the court stated: "we compare the nongeneric components of a mark . . . in the context of the overall composite mark." *Id.* at 24 (internal quotations and citations omitted). Applying this standard, the court rejected the district court's conclusion with respect to similarity:

Analyzing the similarities ourselves with the correct genericism conclusion in mind, we focus our inquiry, albeit not exclusively, on the similarities and differences between the words "Boston" and "Super," the non-generic elements of each mark. Allowing "duck tours" to largely drop out of the analysis, we conclude that the parties' marks are reasonably, although not completely, dissimilar.

Id. at 25.

What if a defendant includes a family or house mark along with the disputed mark at issue? Some courts find that including a house mark reduces the similarity of the mark and therefore weighs against finding a likelihood of confusion. *See, e.g., Playtex Prods. v. Georgia-Pacific Corp.*, 390 F.3d 158, 164–65 (2d Cir. 2004). Other courts take the opposite approach and state that including a house mark represents a bad faith attempt to claim ownership of the mark at issue. *See, e.g., A.T. Cross Co. v. Jonathan Bradley Pens, Inc.*, 470 F.2d 689, 692 (2d Cir. 1972). Having characterized the inclusion of a house mark in such a way, they find that including a house mark weighs in favor of finding a likelihood of confusion. *Id.* (finding that the inclusion of a house mark made confusion more likely as "a purchaser could well think plaintiff had licensed defendant as a second user").

6. *Actual Confusion.* Taken literally, the likelihood of confusion test is a prediction concerning the future: If the defendant's use continues, is it probable that "numerous ordinarily prudent consumers" would actually purchase the defendant's product believing it to be the plaintiff's? Courts nevertheless insist that evidence of actual confusion is not necessary to prevail on a trademark infringement claim. *See, e.g., W. E. Bassett Co. v. Revlon, Inc.*, 435 F.2d 656, 662 (2d Cir. 1970). Why is this? First, sometimes actual confusion exists but obtaining evidence of the confusion can be difficult. Recall from Chapter 1 that a trademark works as an informal guarantee of quality. To play that role, consumers need not complain to producers when they are dissatisfied with their products; they need only switch to some other product. If a consumer purchases defendant's product believing it to be plaintiff's, is dissatisfied with it, and therefore switches to another producer's product, that is actionable actual confusion. But many such consumers will switch without ever writing or otherwise informing the plaintiff as to the reasons for their switch. *Id.* Second, just as in *Estee Lauder*, a plaintiff will often pursue a trademark infringement claim as soon as it learns of the defendant's intentions to market a similarly branded product. When a plaintiff sues promptly, the defendant's product may not have been on the market at all or, alternatively, not long enough for actual confusion to develop.

Proof of actual confusion is not therefore essential to prevail on a trademark claim. At the same time, however, courts also routinely hold that where the plaintiff and defendant's products have co-existed in the same markets for "a significant period of time," the absence of any evidence of actual confusion will weigh against a finding that confusion is likely. *See, e.g., McGregor-Doniger, Inc. v. Drizzle, Inc.*, 599 F.2d 1126, 1136 (2d Cir. 1979).

7.   *Good Faith.* Good faith is a one-way street. If a defendant intends to confuse consumers through its adoption of a similar mark, and is thus acting in bad faith, that factor alone may be sufficient to establish infringement. *See, e.g., Sun-Fun Products, Inc. v. Suntan Research & Development Inc.*, 656 F.2d 186, 190 (5th Cir. Unit B Sept. 1981) ("Proof that a defendant chose a mark with the intent of copying plaintiff's mark, standing alone, may justify an inference of confusing similarity."). Proof of good faith, on the other hand, does not weigh against a finding of likelihood of confusion. Rather, if a defendant did not intend to cause confusion, then a court must evaluate the remaining *Polaroid* factors to determine whether confusion is likely.

Defining the intent necessary to establish bad faith is therefore critical. Yet, courts often disagree about what sort of intent will establish the requisite bad faith. Classically, the question was whether the defendant intended to trick consumers into purchasing its product believing it to be the plaintiff's. *See, e.g., Starbucks Corp. v. Wolfe's Borough Coffee, Inc.*, 588 F.3d 97, 117 (2d Cir. 2009) ("[T]he 'only relevant intent is intent to confuse. There is a considerable difference between an intent to copy and an intent to deceive.' 4 McCarthy on Trademarks § 23.113."). Not all courts will follow this definition, though. As we discussed in Chapter 2, trademark law uses the good faith-bad faith line in a number of areas, and sometimes courts will apply the standard for bad faith developed in one context, such as likelihood of confusion, and (mis)apply it to another, such as the remote junior user defense. *See, e.g., GTE Corp. v. Williams*, 904 F.2d 536, 541–42 (10th Cir. 1990). In addition, some courts define bad faith for purposes of the likelihood of confusion analysis more broadly, to encompass, for example, cases where the court believes the defendant is free riding on the reputation of the plaintiff or otherwise reaping where another has sown. *See, e.g., Sicilia Di R. Biebow & Co. v. Cox*, 732 F.2d 417, 431 (5th Cir. 1984) ("The proper focus is whether the defendant had the intent to derive benefit from the reputation or goodwill of the plaintiff.").

Should a court infer bad faith based upon a defendant's adoption of a similar mark, at least, when other marks were available? *Compare Beer Nuts, Inc. v. Clover Club Foods Co.*, 805 F.2d 920, 928 (10th Cir. 1986) (finding that marks were similar and holding that "intent should have been inferred from that similarity"), *with Holiday Inns, Inc. v. Holiday Out In America*, 481 F.2d 445, 449 (5th Cir. 1973) ("The obvious flaw in this argument [that intent should be inferred from similarity] is that it requires the court to assume that which is to be proved.").

8.   *Quality of the Defendant's Product.* Relative to the quality of the plaintiff's branded product, the defendant's quality can be either: (i) the same; (ii) lower; or (iii) higher. If the defendant's quality is the same, a consumer is most likely to make the mistake of purchasing the defendant's believing it to be the plaintiff's. Yet, if the defendant's quality is the same, there is no harm from such confusion. Should we require a plaintiff to prove that the defendant's quality is lower and that the confusion is thus harmful

to consumers in order to prevail on a trademark or unfair competition cause of action?

If the defendant's quality and associated price are both visibly lower, then it is somewhat less likely that a consumer will purchase the defendant's product believing it to be the plaintiff's. Nevertheless, the harm from any confusion that does result will be greater, both for the confused consumers and for the plaintiff. Courts therefore typically weigh lower product quality as a factor in favor of finding infringement.

What if the defendant's quality and associated price are both visibly higher? Here, logic suggests that confusion is both less likely and less harmful should it occur. You might therefore rationally expect that a higher product quality would weigh against infringement. Sometimes it does, but not always. For example, in *Lois Sportswear, U.S.A., Inc. v. Levi Strauss & Co.*, Levi Strauss sued, alleging trademark infringement, when Lois Sportswear offered an upscale designer line of jeans with stitching on the back pockets similar to that found on the back pockets of Levi's jeans. 799 F.2d 867, 869 (2d Cir. 1986). Levi conceded that the Lois designer jeans were "not of an inferior quality," and the court recognized that this "arguably reduc[ed] appellee's interest in protecting its reputation from debasement." *Id.* at 875. Nevertheless, the court went on:

> . . . under the circumstances of this case the good quality of the appellants' products may increase the likelihood of confusion as to source. Particularly in the post-sale context, consumers easily could assume that quality jeans bearing what is perceived as appellee's trademark stitching pattern to be a Levi's product. The fact that appellants have produced a quality copy suggests that the possibility of their profiting from appellee's goodwill is still likely.

Id.

9. *Consumer Sophistication.* Consumer sophistication is a proxy for the extent to which consumers are likely to rely on the trademark in making a purchasing decision. For relatively inexpensive, impulse purchases, consumers are likely to rely heavily on the product's trademarks both to find the product they are looking for and as an implicit and informal guarantee of the product's quality and other unobservable characteristics, such as taste. On the other hand, for very expensive purchases, trademarks are likely to play a less important role both in finding the right product and guaranteeing the product's quality. As a result, courts will tolerate greater similarity in trademarks for expensive goods than for inexpensive goods.

Compare Beer Nuts, Inc. v. Clover Club Foods Co., 805 F.2d 920, 926 (10th Cir. 1986) (finding that consumers purchasing nuts are more easily confused because they are "inexpensive snack foods" "purchased as impulse items" and hence with "little care"), *with McGregor-Doniger, Inc. v. Drizzle, Inc.*, 599 F.2d 1126, 1137 (2d Cir. 1979) (finding that "the relevant purchasing group [for women's overcoats and raincoats priced from $100 to $900] tends to be sophisticated and knowledgeable about women's apparel").

10. *Survey Methodology.* Because likelihood of confusion focuses on whether consumers will be confused, courts have emphasized the desirability of presenting survey evidence on the issue. While surveys are not mandatory, where a plaintiff has adequate time and resources to conduct a survey on likelihood of confusion, yet fails to do so, a jury may infer that the results of the survey would have been adverse to the plaintiff. *See Charles Jacquin Et Cie, Inc. v. Destileria Serralles, Inc.*, 921 F.2d 467, 476 (3d Cir. 1990).

In a typical likelihood of confusion survey, respondents are shown the defendant's product, as it is actually marketed, and asked: "Who makes this product?" Courts sometimes insist on a follow-up question, such as "Why do you think so?," in order to ensure that the confusion is caused by the similarity in the protected aspects of the marks at issue. *See Holiday Inns, Inc. v. Holiday Out In America*, 481 F.2d 445, 448 (5th Cir. 1973) (rejecting survey results where respondents were shown a placard with "Holiday Out" on it "because the format failed to account for the number of responses attributable to use of the word "Holiday" as distinguished from the service mark HOLIDAY OUT"). The percentage of respondents who are confused because of the similarity in the marks is then tallied. For such a single-question, source confusion survey, depending on the number of consumers surveyed and other factors that affect the survey's reliability, courts will usually weigh a confusion result in excess of ten percent of the respondents in favor of finding a likelihood of confusion, and will weigh a confusion result below ten percent against. *See Henri's Food Prods. Co., Inc. v. Kraft, Inc.*, 717 F.2d 352, 358–59 (7th Cir. 1983).

While this survey format works well in many instances, courts have approved other survey formats as well. For example, what if the plaintiff's brand is popular, but consumers do not know the name of the plaintiff itself? In the 1970s, Union Carbide made and sold Eveready batteries, as well as flashlights and miniature bulbs for automobile and marine use. Although the Eveready brand was very popular, many consumers were not aware that it was Union Carbide that made the brand. Given the anonymous source doctrine, the inability of consumers to name "Union Carbide" as the source of Eveready products does not limit Union Carbide's trademark rights. However, it can make surveying confusion more difficult. If another company, the Ever-Ready Company began to sell Ever-Ready miniature bulbs for high intensity lamps, how could Union Carbide design a survey to test for consumer confusion? Showing consumers the defendant's products and asking them "who makes this" and "why do you think that" would not likely prove helpful. Do you see why? Can you show the respondents the defendant's product and ask: "Do you believe that the company that makes this product also makes any other products?" And then ask those who respond "yes" to that question: "What other products?" What answers to these additional questions would reflect confusion and why? *See Union Carbide Corp. v. Ever-Ready, Inc.*, 531 F.2d 366, 387–88 (7th Cir. 1976) (approving such a survey and relying on it to find a likelihood of confusion). *But see Amstar Corp. v. Domino's Pizza, Inc.*, 615 F.2d 252, 264 (5th Cir. 1980) (characterizing such a survey as a mere "word association" test and holding that it was not probative of the issue of likelihood of confusion).

Both of these survey approaches attempt to answer the question whether consumers are likely to purchase the defendant's products believing that it was made by or comes from the plaintiff. But as we shall see in the next sections, such confusion, known as confusion as to source, does not represent the limits of trademark infringement. Confusion as to endorsement or sponsorship, initial interest confusion, post-sale confusion, and reverse confusion are all actionable in appropriate cases. To be relevant, a survey must address the type of confusion the plaintiff contends is present.

B. EXPANDING THE REACH OF "LIKELIHOOD OF CONFUSION"

Although the *Aunt Jemima* case broadened the standard for trademark infringement, it still required proof that consumers were likely to be confused as to the source of the defendant's products. This standard focuses on whether "numerous ordinarily prudent consumers" would purchase the defendant's goods believing, because of the defendant's use of an unduly similar mark, that the plaintiff had manufactured them, if the defendant's use were to continue. Although such confusion as to source was once essential to obtain relief under trademark or unfair competition law, it is no longer.

Today, a trademark owner can succeed on a claim of trademark infringement on a variety of confusion theories. Today, it is enough to show a likelihood of confusion, not just to source, but to sponsorship, endorsement, or association. Under these theories, consumers need not believe that the plaintiff has manufactured the defendant's goods. It is sufficient if consumers mistakenly believe that the plaintiff sponsored or endorsed the defendant's goods, or that the plaintiff and the defendant are affiliated. Similarly, where trademark law once focused on whether consumers purchased the defendant's goods based upon their mistaken impressions, now confusion that arises post-sale, or that arises initially, but is dispelled before purchase, is sufficient to sustain a cause of action for infringement.

We will explore each of these theories of liability in turn. As we do so, consider the following questions: Are consumers better off as a result of these broadenings of the infringement standard? Is the trademark owner better off? What are the limits to these new theories of liability?

1. LIKELIHOOD OF CONFUSION AND PROMOTIONAL GOODS

Following the move towards a likelihood of confusion approach in the 1917 *Aunt Jemima* case, courts quickly recognized endorsement confusion as actionable. In *Vogue Co. v. Thompson-Hudson Co.*, a plaintiff who had long used the mark Vogue for its fashion magazine sued a defendant that had thereafter adopted the mark Vogue for its hats. 300 F. 509 (6th Cir. 1924). The district court dismissed the complaint on the grounds that no reasonable consumer would believe that Vogue magazine had begun manufacturing the defendant's hats. Although the Sixth Circuit agreed that such confusion as to source was unlikely, it nonetheless reversed. In the Sixth Circuit's view, the defendant's use would likely lead consumers to believe that the plaintiff had sponsored or endorsed the defendant's hats and this was sufficient to sustain the cause of action.

As the court explained:

> Plaintiff's magazine is so far an arbiter of style, and the use of plaintiff's trade-mark upon defendants' hats so far indicates that the hats were at least sponsored and approved by the plaintiff, that the same considerations which make the misrepresentation so valuable to defendants make it pregnant with peril to plaintiff.

Vogue Co. v. Thompson-Hudson Co., 300 F. at 512.

Even if we approach trademark and unfair competition law from a consumer-centric, deception-based perspective, the *Vogue Co.* decision makes good sense. Consumers are likely to be confused, and that confusion is likely to prove material to their purchasing decisions. But having recognized sponsorship confusion as actionable, courts seemed to have trouble confining it. Consider the following case.

BOSTON PROF'L HOCKEY ASS'N, INC. V. DALLAS CAP & EMBLEM MFG., INC.

510 F.2d 1004 (5th Cir.), *cert. denied*, 423 U.S. 868 (1975)

RONEY, C.J.

Nearly everyone is familiar with the artistic symbols which designate the individual teams in various professional sports. The question in this case of first impression is whether the unauthorized, intentional duplication of a professional hockey team's symbol on an embroidered emblem, to be sold to the public as a patch for attachment to clothing, violates any legal right of the team to the exclusive use of that symbol. Contrary to the decision of the district court, we hold that the team has an interest in its own individualized symbol entitled to legal protection against such unauthorized duplication.

The National Hockey League (NHL) and thirteen of its member hockey teams brought this action to enjoin Dallas Cap & Emblem Manufacturing, Inc., from manufacturing and selling embroidered emblems depicting their trademarks. All plaintiffs assert a cause of action for common law unfair competition. The NHL and twelve of the plaintiff teams have secured federal registration of their team symbols as service marks for ice hockey entertainment services and seek relief under both provisions of the Lanham Act, 15 U.S.C. §§ 1114, 1125, which give statutory protection to such marks. . . . None of the symbols of the various teams have been copyrighted.

The district court denied Lanham Act relief and granted only limited relief for unfair competition, requiring solely that defendant place on the emblems or the package a notice that the emblems are not authorized by or have not emanated from the plaintiffs. The claim for damages was denied.

The Facts

The controlling facts of the case at bar are relatively uncomplicated and uncontested. Plaintiffs play ice hockey professionally. In producing and promoting the sport of ice hockey, plaintiffs have each adopted and widely publicized individual team symbols. . . .

Plaintiffs have authorized National Hockey League Services, Inc. (NHLS) to act as their exclusive licensing agent. NHLS has licensed various manufacturers to use the team symbols on merchandise and has granted to one manufacturer, Lion Brothers Company, Inc., the exclusive license to manufacture embroidered emblems depicting the marks in question. . . .

Defendant Dallas Cap & Emblem Manufacturing, Inc., is in the business of making and selling embroidered cloth emblems. In August of 1968 and June of 1971, defendant sought to obtain from NHLS an exclusive license to make embroidered emblems representing the team motifs. Although these negotiations were unsuccessful, defendant went ahead and manufactured and sold without authorization emblems which were substantial duplications of the marks. During the month of April 1972, defendant sold approximately 24,603 of these emblems to sporting goods stores in various states. Defendant deliberately reproduced plaintiffs' marks on embroidered emblems and intended the consuming public to recognize the emblems as the symbols of the various hockey teams and to purchase them as such.

The Law

The complaint alleged that defendant's manufacture and sale of the team symbols constitutes (1) an infringement of the plaintiffs' registered marks in violation of 15 U.S.C. § 1114; (2) false designation of origin in violation of 15 U.S.C. § 1125; and (3) common law unfair competition.

The statutory cause of action emanates from what is commonly called the Lanham Act. 15 U.S.C. § 1051 et seq. The Lanham Act defines a service mark as "a mark used in the sale or advertising of services to identify the services of one person and distinguish them from the services of others" and a trademark as "any word, name, symbol, or device or any combination thereof adopted and used by a manufacturer or merchant to identify his goods and distinguish them from those manufactured or sold by others." 15 U.S.C. § 1127. Service mark infringement and trademark infringement are governed by identical standards. The terms can be used interchangeably when the marks are both service marks and trademarks. For convenience we use the word trademark in this opinion to designate both service mark and trademark use of the symbols involved.

A cause of action for the infringement of a registered mark in violation of 15 U.S.C. § 1114 exists where a person uses (1) any reproduction, counterfeit, copy or colorable imitation of a mark; (2) without the registrant's consent; (3) in commerce; (4) in connection with the sale, offering for sale, distribution or advertising of any goods; (5) where such use is likely to cause confusion, or to cause mistake or to deceive. A broadening of the protection afforded by the statute occurred by amendment in 1962 which deleted the previously existing requirement that the confusion or deception must relate to the "source of origin of such goods or service." Pub.L. 87–772, § 17, 76 Stat. 773 (1962). *Continental Motors Corp. v. Continental Aviation Corp.*, 375 F.2d 857, 860 (5th Cir. 1967). . . .

The Case

The difficulty with this case stems from the fact that a reproduction of the trademark itself is being sold, unattached to any other goods or services. The statutory and case law of trademarks is oriented toward the use of such marks to sell something other than the mark itself. The district court thought that to give plaintiffs protection in this case would be tantamount to the creation of a copyright monopoly for designs that were not copyrighted. The copyright laws are based on an entirely different concept than the trademark laws, and contemplate that the copyrighted material, like patented ideas, will eventually pass into the public domain. The trademark laws are based on the needed protection of the public and business interests and there is no reason why trademarks should ever pass into the public domain by the mere passage of time.

Although our decision here may slightly tilt the trademark laws from the purpose of protecting the public to the protection of the business interests of plaintiffs, we think that the two become so intermeshed when viewed against the backdrop of the common law of unfair competition that both the public and plaintiffs are better served by granting the relief sought by plaintiffs.

Underlying our decision are three persuasive points. *First*, the major commercial value of the emblems is derived from the efforts of plaintiffs. *Second*, defendant sought and ostensibly would have asserted, if obtained, an exclusive right to make and sell the emblems. *Third*, the sale of a reproduction of the trademark itself on an emblem is an accepted use of such team symbols in connection with the type of activity in which the business of professional sports is engaged. We need not deal here with the concept of whether every artistic reproduction of the symbol would infringe upon plaintiffs' rights. We restrict ourselves to the emblems sold principally through sporting goods stores for informal use by the public in connection with sports activities and to show public allegiance to or identification with the teams themselves.

As to 15 U.S.C. § 1114.

Plaintiffs indisputably have established the first three elements of a § 1114 cause of action. Plaintiffs' marks are validly registered and defendant manufactured and sold emblems which were (1) substantial duplications of the marks, (2) without plaintiffs' consent, and (3) in interstate commerce. The issue is whether plaintiffs have proven elements four and five of an action for mark infringement under the Lanham Act, i.e., whether the symbols are used in connection with the sale of goods and whether such use is likely to cause confusion, mistake or deception.

The fourth requisite of a § 1114 cause of action is that the infringing use of the registered mark must be in connection with the sale, offering for sale, distribution or advertising of any goods. Although the district court did not expressly find that plaintiffs had failed to establish element four, such a finding was implicit in the court's statement that "in the instant case, the registered trade mark is, in effect, the product itself."

Defendant is in the business of manufacturing and marketing emblems for wearing apparel. These emblems are the products, or goods, which defendant sells. When defendant causes plaintiffs' marks to be embroidered upon emblems which it later markets, defendant uses those marks in connection with the sale of goods as surely as if defendant had embroidered the marks upon knit caps. *See Boston Professional Hockey Association, Inc. v. Reliable Knitting Works, Inc.*, 178 U.S.P.Q. (BNA) 274 (E.D. Wis. 1973). The fact that the symbol covers the entire face of defendant's product does not alter the fact that the trademark symbol is used in connection with the sale of the product. The sports fan in his local sporting goods store purchases defendant's fabric and thread emblems because they are embroidered with the symbols of ice hockey teams. Were defendant to embroider the same fabric with the same thread in other designs, the resulting products would still be emblems for wearing apparel but they would not give trademark identification to the customer. The conclusion is inescapable that, without plaintiffs' marks, defendant would not have a market for his particular product among ice hockey fans desiring to purchase emblems embroidered with the symbols of their favorite teams. It becomes clear that defendant's use of plaintiffs' marks is in connection with the sale, offering for sale, distribution, or advertising of goods and that plaintiffs have established the fourth element of a § 1114 cause of action.

The fifth element of a cause of action for mark infringement under 15 U.S.C. § 1114 is that the infringing use is likely to cause confusion, or to cause mistake or to deceive. The district court decided that there was no likelihood of confusion because the usual purchaser, a sports fan in his local sporting goods store, would not be likely to think that defendant's emblems were manufactured by or had some connection with plaintiffs. *Cf. Sun-Maid Raisin Growers of California v. Sunaid Food Products, Inc.*, 356 F.2d 467 (5th Cir. 1966). This court has held that the findings of a district court as to likelihood of confusion are factual and not to be overturned unless clearly erroneous. *Hang Ten International v. Sherry Manufacturing Co.*, 498 F.2d 326 (5th Cir. 1974); *American Foods, Inc. v. Golden Flake, Inc.*, 312 F.2d 619 (5th Cir. 1963). In this case, however, the district court overlooked the fact that the act was amended to eliminate the source of origin as being the only focal point of confusion. The confusion question here is conceptually difficult. It can be said that the public buyer *knew* that the emblems portrayed the teams' symbols. Thus, it can be argued, the buyer is not confused or deceived. This argument misplaces the purpose of the confusion requirement. The confusion or deceit requirement is met by the fact that the defendant duplicated the protected trademarks and sold them to the public knowing that the public would identify them as being the teams' trademarks. The certain knowledge of the buyer that the source and origin of the trademark symbols were in plaintiffs satisfies the requirement of the act. The argument that confusion must be as to the source of the manufacture of the emblem itself is unpersuasive, where the trademark, originated by the team, is the triggering mechanism for the sale of the emblem.

. . . Plaintiffs are entitled to an injunction permanently enjoining defendant from the manufacture and sale, in interstate commerce, of emblems embroidered with substantial duplications of plaintiffs' marks without plaintiffs' consent, and such other relief as might flow from the facts.

Reversed and remanded.

NOTES FOR DISCUSSION

1. *Confusion as a Factual Issue: Then.* In the 1970s, the professional sports leagues, as well as some college teams, had exclusive licensing arrangements with a particular entity or entities to manufacture and sell official merchandise bearing the team names and logos. Yet, except perhaps for NFL-related merchandise, the sale of unauthorized merchandise bearing team names and logos was commonplace. If a consumer wanted the official merchandise, he or she knew where to buy it. You would shop at the team's official store, usually located in the stadium. If you wanted lower prices or

higher quality, and hence preferred unauthorized merchandise, it was readily available pretty much everywhere else. Thus, as a factual matter, the district court was plainly right, and the appellate court admits as much: consumers who bought Dallas Cap emblems were not confused as to the source or sponsorship of those emblems. When they bought the emblems from Dallas Cap, they knew the emblem was unauthorized.

How then does the court find infringement? What is the nature of the confusion that the court identifies? Is it confusion as to source of the emblems in the traditional sense? In other words, do consumers mistakenly believe that the defendant's emblems were manufactured by the plaintiffs? Is it confusion as to sponsorship or endorsement? At a minimum, confusion presumably requires that a consumer holds a belief that is not true. On this key issue, the court simply asserts:

> The confusion or deceit requirement is met by the fact that the defendant duplicated the protected trademarks and sold them to the public knowing that the public would identify them as being the teams' trademarks. The certain knowledge of the buyer that the source and origin of the trademark symbols were in plaintiffs satisfies the requirement of the act.

Boston Prof'l Hockey Ass'n, Inc., 510 F.2d at 1012.

Does this reasoning demonstrate that a consumer holds a belief with respect to the emblem that is not true? Is there consumer confusion here, or is it just the court's confusion?

2. *Confusion as a Legal Issue.* The confusion over confusion in *Boston Prof'l Hockey* did not go unnoticed, and the decision was heavily criticized. The Ninth Circuit went so far as to say: "We reject the reasoning of *Boston Hockey.*" *International Order of Job's Daughters v. Lindeburg & Co.*, 633 F.2d 912, 918 (9th Cir. 1980). As a general rule, courts insisted that, going forward, a likelihood of confusion as to sponsorship or endorsement was essential to demonstrate infringement. Consistent with this approach, the Fifth Circuit itself re-interpreted the *Boston Prof'l Hockey* decision to incorporate the requirement of consumer confusion as to sponsorship or endorsement:

> *Boston Hockey* also reiterated our unbroken insistence on a showing of confusion, and we believe that our opinion must be read in that context. Under the circumstances there—involving sales to the consuming public of products bearing trademarks universally associated with Boston Hockey—the fact that the buyers knew the *symbols* originated with Boston Hockey supported the inescapable inference that many would believe that the *product itself* originated with or was somehow endorsed by Boston Hockey.

Kentucky Fried Chicken Corp. v. Diversified Packaging Corp., 549 F.2d 368, 389 (5th Cir. 1977).

Do you agree with the Fifth Circuit that just because the name or logo were uniquely related to a given sports team consumers would necessarily believe that the merchandise was officially licensed? Does the *Kentucky Fried Chicken* court establish this as a presumption? Is it rebuttable?

Unfortunately, at least for professional sports fans, the damage was already done. Today, the notion that professional and amateur sports have exclusive control over their associated merchandise is virtually unchallenged. *But see* Stacey L. Dogan & Mark A. Lemley, *The Merchandising Right: Fragile Theory or Fait Accompli?*, 54 EMORY L.J. 461 (2005) (arguing that the Court's recognition of a narrower role for trademarks in some of its recent decisions, such as *Wal-mart*, *TrafFix*, and *Dastar*, opens the door to reexamining and narrowing the scope of sponsorship and endorsement liability).

3.   *Confusion as a Factual Issue: Now.* Accepting that consumers were not confused as to either source or sponsorship with respect to this type of unauthorized merchandise in the 1970s, is that still true today? Or would a consumer today who is purchasing merchandise or apparel bearing a team name or logo believe that the team had licensed or sponsored the merchandise? *See, e.g., National Football League Props., Inc. v. New Jersey Giants, Inc.*, 637 F.Supp. 507, 515 (D.N.J. 1986) (citing a survey showing that up to 67% of football fans were confused as to the NFL's sponsorship of GIANTS merchandise); *National Football League v. Governor of Del.*, 435 F.Supp. 1372, 1381 (D. Del. 1977) ("Apparently, in this day and age when professional sports teams franchise pennants, tee-shirts, helmets, drinking glasses and a wide range of other products, a substantial number of people believe, if not told otherwise, that one cannot conduct an enterprise of this kind without NFL approval."); *cf. National Football League Props., Inc. v. Wichita Falls Sportswear, Inc.*, 532 F.Supp. 651 (W.D. Wash. 1982) (finding that up to 53.6% of consumers who saw defendant's replicas of NFL jerseys believed that the use required permission from the NFL).

If ordinarily prudent consumers today really do believe that all merchandise bearing a team's name or logo is endorsed or authorized by the team, where did that belief come from? Is it simply the result of the legal rules that have been in place? By forbidding the sale of unlicensed merchandise, did we create markets where, as a general rule, only licensed merchandise was available, so that consumers came to believe that all merchandise bearing team names or logos is or should be licensed? If *Boston Prof'l Hockey* had come out the other way, would consumers be confused by the sale of unlicensed merchandise today? Is the issue simply circular? Does confusion result from consumers' experience in the market which is in turn shaped by the legal rules? If so, how can we use confusion to determine the legal rules?

4.   *Consumer Welfare.* Going forward, are consumers better or worse off as a result of courts' creating an exclusive merchandising right for team apparel? Consider the following hypothetical. In 2010, for the first time since their founding in 1966, the New Orleans Saints made it to and won the NFL

Superbowl. During the play-off run, a number of local merchants began selling t-shirts and other merchandise bearing the phrase "Who Dat," as a shorthand expression for the slogan "Who Dat Say Dey Gonna Beat Dem Saints." The NFL sent cease-and-desist letters to the merchants, asserting trademark rights under section 43(a) in the slogan and the phrase. Viewing the issue exclusively from the perspective of consumer welfare, would consumers be better or worse off if courts were to give the NFL exclusive rights over the slogan, the phrase, and merchandise bearing either?

If courts were to recognize such exclusive rights, then consumers looking for authorized merchandise would face lower search costs as they would not need to sort through as much unauthorized merchandise to find the authorized merchandise. Also, consumers who wanted to purchase authorized merchandise would not run the risk of purchasing unauthorized merchandise by mistake. Are there any other consumer welfare gains from recognizing the NFL's claims? What about an argument that restricting the sale of unauthorized merchandise will increase the NFL's revenue, which the NFL can then reinvest in improving the quality of its product, *i.e.* NFL games?

At the same time, however, recognizing such rights would also diminish consumer welfare in three ways. First, consumers looking for lower-priced unauthorized merchandise would have a harder time finding it. Second, unauthorized merchandise, because it would be subject to seizure by the NFL, would be lower quality than it would be if unauthorized merchandise were legal. Third, consumers would lose much of the diversity and creativity that an open market in "Who Dat" merchandise would otherwise create. If anyone can make such merchandise, merchants will compete with each other to develop the best, most popular, most creative uses of the phrase and slogan. If the NFL is given control over the phrase, this creativity must operate through the narrow gate of the NFL's permission. For all practical purposes, that means much of it will never occur.

On balance, then, would consumers be better or worse off if the NFL was given exclusive rights over "Who Dat"? Does your analysis differ in any way if the issue is whether the NFL should be given exclusive rights over team jerseys or other merchandise? Why or why not?

5. *Is It Simply a Question of Confusion?* Consider two cases, both involving the Boston Marathon. In the first, an individual wants to sell t-shirts bearing the words "The Boston Marathon." In the second, a television station wants to broadcast the Boston Marathon live as it is run on the public streets in and around Boston and wants to add the words "The Boston Marathon" at the bottom of the picture. Both want to use the words "The Boston Marathon" without the consent of the Boston Athletic Association, which puts on the race and owns the trademark, "The Boston Marathon." In fact, with respect to both types of uses, the Boston Athletic Association has entered into an exclusive licensing agreement with another party either to make apparel bearing the words "The Boston Marathon," or to broadcast the race live. In both cases, the money made from these licenses is funneled back into the race. Should both unauthorized uses constitute trademark

infringement? Should neither? Should only one? If so, which one and why? *Compare Boston Athletic Ass'n v. Sullivan*, 867 F.2d 22 (1st Cir. 1989) (finding that the t-shirt use would create a likelihood of consumer confusion), *with WCVB-TV v. Boston Athletic Ass'n*, 926 F.2d 42 (1st Cir. 1991) (finding that the television broadcast does not create a likelihood of consumer confusion).

Do you agree with the First Circuit that we can differentiate these two cases based purely on factual differences in the likelihood that consumers will be confused? Assume that we surveyed 400 random consumers in the Boston area, and showed half of them Sullivan's t-shirt, and the other half the WCVB-TV broadcast, and then asked each consumer: Do you believe that [Sullivan, WCVB-TV] obtained permission for this use from the Boston Athletic Association? How much difference between the percentages who said yes with respect to the t-shirt and the television broadcast do you think we would find? If there were no difference in the percentages who were confused with respect to the two uses, should the two cases be resolved in the same way?

Which use creates a greater likelihood that a consumer will purchase the unauthorized merchandise or watch the unauthorized broadcast believing it to be authorized? As a serious runner, I can tell you than no runner of the Boston Marathon would mistakenly purchase unauthorized apparel by mistake. There is a special store reserved for the athletes competing in and finishing the Marathon. Runners who want the authorized apparel would have no trouble finding it, even if unauthorized apparel were rampant. Is there any way for a television viewer to distinguish between the authorized broadcast and an unauthorized broadcast? Moreover, which unauthorized use will more greatly reduce the revenue from the Boston Marathon?

6.   *Is It Simply a Question of Confusion: The Stopper Hypo.* James Johnson has some to you for legal advice. He is tired of all of the excesses that seem to accompany rich sports players, and wants to hit them where it hurts—their wallets. He therefore wants to start marketing apparel and merchandise with team names, colors, and logos on them. His marketing scheme is officially centered on the fact that he will pay no licensing fees to the leagues whatsoever. All of his merchandise will be sold with tags explaining that he is not paying any fees to the leagues or the players' unions. Instead, his merchandise will be cheaper than the official gear in order both to save the average fan money and to reduce the money available to "overpaid, whiners" for playing a kids' game. All of his merchandise, in addition to the team names, logos, and colors, will also prominently bear Jim's own trademark, a red stop sign with the word "Stopper" emblazoned across it. In order to obtain funding for his venture, Jim needs a legal opinion that his proposed use will not constitute trademark infringement. Would you be willing to give him a written opinion of counsel on the issue?

7.   *Vogue Hats and Ball Caps.* Does the recognition of exclusive merchandising rights for professional sports teams logically follow from the *Vogue* hat case? How are they similar? How do they differ? Would you say

consumers were better or worse off as a result of the *Vogue* hat case? Would you say consumers were better or worse off as a result of *Boston Prof'l Hockey*? If your answers differ, why? Why does Vogue's endorsement change the value of a garment? Does the Boston Bruins' endorsement of a particular jersey bearing its team name and logo change the value of that garment in similar ways and for similar reasons? Can another magazine or clothing designer realistically compete with Vogue? Can another entity realistically compete with Boston Bruins' merchandise for those consumers who want it? What does it mean to compete? Is it realistic to insist that a would-be competitor set up a competing hockey league?

8.   *Other Hurdles to Recognition of a Merchandising Rights for Sports Teams.* The likelihood of confusion issue was not the only hurdle facing sports league in trying to control the sales of apparel and merchandise bearing team names and logos. The widespread sale of such apparel and merchandise, without authorization, had been going on for decades in some cases, raising serious questions with respect to laches and estoppel. In addition, in some instances, it was not even the team or the league that began using a nickname or logo for the team first. Another entity, such as a local bookstore, would create the nickname or logo, companies would begin manufacturing and selling apparel and merchandise bearing the nickname or logo, and then many years later when the nickname and logo had become popular, the college would try to step in and claim exclusive rights in the nickname and logo, raising issues of genericness and first use. Although these hurdles might have seemed insurmountable, courts had little trouble helping plaintiffs leap them. *See University of Pittsburgh v. Champion Products Inc.*, 686 F.2d 1040 (3d Cir.) (rejecting laches argument despite long delay in enforcing claimed trademark rights), *cert. denied*, 459 U.S. 1087 (1982); *University Book Store v. Board of Regents of the University of Wisconsin*, 33 U.S.P.Q.2d (BNA) 1385 (T.T.A.B. 1994) (allowing the University of Wisconsin to register a Bucky Badger trademark even though others had developed and initially used the nickname in connection with the University on apparel and merchandise). Indeed, in the Bucky Badger case, the Trademark Trial and Appeal Board brushed off the argument that long and unauthorized use by others somehow limited the University's rights to register Bucky, with the response that the University was just being a good citizen: "Applicant, like numerous other colleges and universities, permitted others to sell imprinted merchandise as expressions of community support and goodwill." *Id.* at 1395.

Defendants have also argued in these cases that the logo or team name on the merchandise is aesthetically functional. Courts have squarely rejected this line of argument, however. For example, in *Board of Supervisors v. Smack Apparel, Co.*, Smack Apparel had marketed t-shirts using the color scheme of Louisiana State and Ohio State Universities when the two teams faced each other in the 2004 Sugar Bowl. 550 F.3d 465, 472–73 (5th Cir. 2008), *cert. denied*, 556 U.S. 1268 (2009). Smack argued that the color schemes served a functional purpose and that it would be:

placed at a significant non-reputation-related disadvantage if it 'is unable to satisfy consumer demand for game day clothing that allows fans to conform to the crowd, or satisfy consumer demand for game day clothing that matches other items of clothing worn by the consumer.'

Id. at 488.

The Fifth Circuit was not persuaded. In the court's view, "any demand for Smack's t-shirts is inextricably tied to the Universities' trademarks themselves." *Id.* It was therefore a "reputation related disadvantage."

9.   *The 1962 Amendments.* As the *Boston Prof'l Hockey* court noted, Congress amended the infringement standard for registered trademarks in 1962. Specifically, Congress deleted the italicized phrase from section 32(a):

> (1) Any person who shall, without the consent of the registrant—(a) use in commerce any reproduction, counterfeit, copy, or colorable imitation of a registered mark in connection with the sale, offering for sale, distribution, or advertising of any goods or services on or in connection with which such use is likely to cause confusion, or to cause mistake, or to deceive *purchasers as to the source or origin of such products or services.*

More than a decade later, some courts, such as the *Boston Prof'l Hockey* court, read this amendment as congressional license to treat confusion of any sort as actionable trademark infringement. *See, e.g., James Burrough Ltd. v. Sign of the Beefeater, Inc.*, 540 F.2d 266, 274 (7th Cir. 1976); *Rolex Watch U.S.A. v. Canner*, 645 F.Supp. 484, 492–93 & n.2 (S.D. Fla. 1986).

Read in isolation the deletion of the italicized phrase does seem to suggest an intention to expand the infringement standard. Yet, the notion that this "Housekeeping Amendment," as it was denominated, represents congressional intent to expand the infringement standard to encompass any sort of confusion is almost certainly flawed. *See* Glynn S. Lunney, Jr., *Trademark Monopolies*, 48 Emory L.J. 367, 470–75 (1999). As the legislative history accompanying the Act explains, Congress modified the statutory language in this way for two reasons—one a matter of form and one a matter of substance. As a matter of form, Congress intended to reconcile the language in four different sections that each invoked the likelihood of confusion standard. In addition to the likelihood of confusion language in section 32, section 1(a)(1)(A) of the Act requires an application seeking registration to state that the mark for which registration is sought does not create a likelihood of confusion with a valid, prior mark. Section 2(d) authorizes the Patent and Trademark Office to refuse to register a mark that creates a likelihood of confusion with a previously registered mark. Section 16 authorizes the Commissioner to declare an interference where a mark for which registration is sought creates a likelihood of confusion with a previously registered mark. Before the 1962 Amendments, these four sections, although they each used the same likelihood of confusion standard, expressed that standard in three different ways. Thus, Congress's first reason for the amendment was simply a matter of form; Congress wanted to use identical language to invoke the same likelihood of confusion standard in all four sections. Because only section 32 contained the phrase "as to the source or origin of such products or services," Congress deleted that language simply to make section 32 identical to the other three sections.

In terms of substance, Congress also deleted the word "purchaser" which appeared in three of the sections. In the legislative history, Congress expressly stated that it deleted this language to make clear that the likelihood of confusion standard extended to confusion among prospective purchasers as well as actual purchasers. *See* S. Rep. No. 87–2107 (1962), *reprinted in* 1962 U.S.C.C.A.N. 2844, 2847. While this demonstrates Congress's intent to expand the infringement standard in a particular way through the 1962 Amendment, it is a far cry from the radical expansion some courts have suggested Congress intended by the Amendment.

10. *Association Confusion.* In 1968, a federal district court extended the endorsement theory to situations where a defendant's use of an unduly similar mark causes consumer confusion with respect to an association or affiliation between the plaintiff and the defendant. As the court explained:

> Given the general situation where the public is generally unaware of the specific corporate structure of those whose products it buys, but is aware that corporate diversification, mergers, acquisitions and operation through subsidiaries is a fact of life, it is reasonable to believe that the appearance of "Black Label" on cigarettes could lead to some confusion as to the sponsorship of EITHER or both the cigarettes and the beer. Whether the public concludes (if it really draws a specific conclusion) that plaintiff's Black Label beer may have become connected with Philip Morris, or that Carling may now be putting out cigarettes is immaterial.

Carling Brewing Co. v. Philip Morris Inc., 297 F.Supp. 1330, 1337 (N.D. Ga. 1968).

What do you think of this association or affiliation confusion? Do you think consumers are often or ever confused about these issues? If a consumer somehow mistakenly comes to believe that there is a parent-subsidiary relationship between two firms, do you think that belief will prove material to the consumer's purchasing decisions? Chevrolet, Cadillac, and Corvette are all brands within the General Motors Corp. family. If you had a bad experience with a Chevy, would you attribute that bad experience to Cadillacs and Corvettes as well? Empirical research suggests that such carry-over is unlikely. *See* Rebecca Tushnet, *Gone in 60 Milliseconds: Trademark Law and Cognitive Science*, 86 TEX. L. REV. 507, 543 (2008) ("[C]onsumers have robust mental concepts of strong brands. If consumers are given a reason to distinguish an authorized extension or cobranded product from the core brand—for example, a name like Courtyard by Marriott instead of Marriott or Coke BlaK instead of Coke—they will do so, and negative opinions about the extension will not return to harm opinions of the core brand.").

11. *The 1988 Amendments to the Trademark Act.* In 1988, Congress amended section 43(a) to incorporate sponsorship and association confusion. After the amendment, the likelihood of confusion standard in section 43(a) now reaches the use of a mark that "is likely to cause confusion, or to cause mistake, or to deceive as to the affiliation, connection, or association of such person with another person, or as to the origin, sponsorship, or approval of his or her goods, services, or commercial activities by another person." 15 U.S.C. § 1125(a)(1)(A). Although Congress has not yet expressly amended section 32(a) to encompass association and endorsement confusion, courts have continued to read the section as incorporating both. *See, e.g., Team Tires Plus, Ltd. v. Tires Plus, Inc.*, 394 F.3d 831, 835 (10th Cir. 2005) (holding that for infringement of a registered trademark under section 32(a) "the relevant confusion under trademark law is not limited to confusion of consumers as to the source of the goods, but also includes confusion as to sponsorship or affiliation, such as a consumer's mistaken belief that a retailer is part of a larger franchising operation").

Does this amendment amount to a congressional endorsement of the *Vogue* hat case? The *Boston Prof'l Hockey* case?

2. PROTECTING PRESTIGE GOODS: POST-SALE CONFUSION

FERRARI S.P.A. V. ROBERTS
944 F.2d 1235 (6th Cir. 1991)

RYAN, C.J.

This is a trademark infringement action brought pursuant to the Lanham Act, 15 U.S.C. § 1051, *et seq.* The principal issue is whether the district court correctly concluded that plaintiff Ferrari enjoyed unregistered trademark protection in the exterior shape and appearance of two of its automobiles and, if so, whether defendant Roberts' replicas of Ferrari's designs infringed that protection, in violation of section 43(a) of the Lanham Act. More narrowly focused, the issues are:

— Whether Ferrari's automobile designs have acquired secondary meaning;

— Whether there is a likelihood of confusion between Ferrari's cars and Roberts' replicas;

— Whether the appropriated features of Ferrari's designs are nonfunctional; and

— Whether the injunction granted by the district court is excessively broad.

We must also decide whether the district court, 739 F. Supp. 1138, properly rejected Roberts' request for a jury trial.

We hold that the district court properly decided all of the issues and, therefore, we shall affirm.

I.   The Facts

Ferrari is the world famous designer and manufacturer of racing automobiles and upscale sports cars. Between 1969 and 1973, Ferrari produced the 365 GTB/4 Daytona. Because Ferrari intentionally limits production of its cars in order to create an image of exclusivity, only 1400 Daytonas were built; of these, only 100 were originally built as Spyders, soft-top convertibles. Daytona Spyders currently sell for one to two million dollars. Although Ferrari no longer makes Daytona Spyders, they have continuously produced mechanical parts and body panels, and provided repair service for the cars.

Ferrari began producing a car called the Testarossa in 1984. To date, Ferrari has produced approximately 5000 Testarossas. Production of these cars is also intentionally limited to preserve exclusivity: the entire anticipated production is sold out for the next several years and the waiting period to purchase a Testarossa is approximately five years. A new Testarossa sells for approximately $230,000.

Roberts is engaged in a number of business ventures related to the automobile industry. One enterprise is the manufacture of fiberglass kits that replicate the exterior features of Ferrari's Daytona Spyder and Testarossa automobiles. Roberts' copies are called the Miami Spyder and the Miami Coupe, respectively. The kit is a one-piece body shell molded from reinforced fiberglass. It is usually bolted onto the undercarriage of another automobile such as a Chevrolet Corvette or a Pontiac Fiero, called the donor car. Roberts marketed the Miami Spyder primarily through advertising in kit-car magazines. Most of the replicas were sold as kits for about $8,500, although a fully accessorized "turnkey" version was available for about $50,000.

At the time of trial, Roberts had not yet completed a kit-car version of the Miami Coupe, the replica of Ferrari's Testarossa, although he already has two orders for them. He originally built the Miami Coupe for the producers of the television program "Miami Vice" to be used as a stunt car in place of the more expensive Ferrari Testarossa.

The district court found, and it is not disputed, that Ferrari's automobiles and Roberts' replicas are virtually identical in appearance.

Ferrari brought suit against Roberts in March 1988 alleging trademark infringement, in violation of section 43(a) of the Lanham Act, and obtained a preliminary injunction enjoining Roberts from manufacturing the replica cars. The injunction was later amended to permit Roberts to recommence production of the two models.

Five months later, Roberts filed a voluntary petition in bankruptcy. Despite the Chapter 11 proceedings, the bankruptcy court, in a carefully limited order, lifted the automatic stay and permitted Ferrari to continue to prosecute this action. Prior to trial, the district court denied Roberts' request for a jury, and the case was tried to the court resulting in a verdict for Ferrari and a permanent injunction enjoining Roberts from producing the Miami Spyder and the Miami Coupe.

II.

Section 43(a) of the Lanham Act creates a civil cause of action for trademark infringement. In relevant part, section 43(a) provides:

> Any person who, on or in connection with any goods or services, or any container for goods, uses in commerce any word, term, name, symbol, or device, or any combination thereof, or any false designation of origin, false or misleading description of fact, or false or misleading representation of fact, which—
>
> > (1) is likely to cause confusion, or to cause mistake, or to deceive as to the affiliation, connection, or association of such person with another person, or as to the origin, sponsorship, or approval of his or her goods, services, or commercial activities by another person. . . .
>
> shall be liable in a civil action by any person who believes that he or she is or is likely to be damaged by such act.

The protection against infringement provided by section 43(a) is not limited to "goods, services or commercial activities" protected by registered trademarks. It extends as well, in certain circumstances, to the unregistered "trade dress" of an article. "Trade dress" refers to "the image and overall appearance of a product." *Allied Mktg. Group, Inc. v. CDL Mktg., Inc.*, 878 F.2d 806, 812 (5th Cir. 1989). It embodies "that arrangement of identifying characteristics or decorations connected with a product, whether by packaging or otherwise, intended to make the source of the product distinguishable from another and to promote its sale." *Mr. Gasket Co. v. Travis*, 35 Ohio App. 2d 65, 72 n. 13 (1973).

Ferrari's Lanham Act claim in this case is a "trade dress" claim. Ferrari charges, and the district court found, that the unique and distinctive exterior shape and design of the Daytona Spyder and the Testarossa are protected trade dress which Roberts has infringed by copying them and marketing his replicas.

Roberts asserts that . . . there is no actionable likelihood of confusion between Ferrari's vehicles and Roberts' replicas at the point of sale.

III.

To prove a violation of section 43(a), Ferrari's burden is to show, by a preponderance of the evidence: . . . that there is a likelihood of confusion based on the similarity of the exterior shape and design of Ferrari's vehicles and Roberts' replicas. . . .

B.   Likelihood of Confusion

1.   *District Court's Findings*

. . . The district court found, based upon an evaluation of the eight *Frisch* factors, that the similarity of the exterior design of the Ferrari vehicles and the Roberts replicas was likely to confuse the public. The court noted that while no evidence was offered on two of the factors, evidence of actual confusion and likelihood of expansion of the product lines, two others, marketing channels and purchaser care, favored Roberts and the remaining factors "radically favor[ed] Ferrari."

. . . Roberts disagrees with the legal significance of the district court's findings of likelihood of confusion. He argues that for purposes of the Lanham Act, the requisite likelihood of confusion must be confusion at the point of sale—purchaser confusion—and not the confusion of nonpurchasing, casual observers. The evidence is clear that Roberts assured purchasers of his replicas that they were not purchasing Ferraris and that his customers were not confused about what they were buying. . . .

a.   *Confusion as to Source*

Roberts is correct that, for the most part, similarity of products alone is not actionable; there must also be confusion as to the origin of the product. *West Point Mfg.*, 222 F.2d at 589; *see also Fisher Stoves, Inc. v. All Nighter Stove Works, Inc.*, 626 F.2d 193, 195 (1st Cir. 1980). Similarity of products, however, does become actionable when the similarity leads to confusion as to source and the public cares who the source of the product is.

. . . Because consumers care that they are purchasing a Ferrari as opposed to a car that looks like a Ferrari, and because Roberts' replicas look like Ferraris, Ferrari presented an actionable claim as to confusion of source.

b.   *Confusion at Point of Sale*

Roberts argues that his replicas do not violate the Lanham Act because he informed his purchasers that his significantly cheaper cars and kits were not genuine Ferraris and thus there was no confusion at the point of sale. The Lanham Act, however, was intended to do more than protect consumers at the point of sale. When the Lanham Act was enacted in 1946, its protection was limited to the use of marks "likely to cause confusion or mistake or to deceive purchasers as to the source of origin of such goods or services." In 1967, [*sic,* 1962] Congress deleted this language and broadened the Act's protection to include the use of marks "likely to cause confusion or mistake or to deceive." Thus, Congress intended "to regulate commerce within [its control] by making actionable the deceptive and misleading use of marks in such commerce; [and] . . . to protect persons engaged in such commerce against unfair competition. . . ." 15 U.S.C. § 1127. Although, as the dissent points out, Congress rejected an anti-dilution provision when recently amending the Lanham Act, it made no effort to amend or delete this language clearly protecting the confusion of goods *in commerce*. The court in *Rolex Watch* explicitly recognized this concern with regulating commerce:

> The real question before this Court is whether the alleged infringer has placed a product *in commerce* that is "likely to cause confusion, or to cause mistake, or to deceive." . . . The fact that an immediate buyer of a $25 counterfeit watch does not entertain any notions that it is the real thing has no place in this analysis. Once a product is injected into commerce, there is no bar to confusion, mistake, or deception occurring at some future point in time.

Rolex Watch, 645 F. Supp. at 492–93 (emphasis in original).

The *Rolex Watch* court noted that this interpretation was necessary to protect against the cheapening and dilution of the genuine product, and to protect the manufacturer's reputation. *Id.* at 495; *see also Mastercrafters*, 221 F.2d at 466. As the court explained:

> Individuals examining the counterfeits, believing them to be genuine Rolex watches, might find themselves unimpressed with the quality of the item and consequently be inhibited from purchasing the real time piece. Others who see the watches bearing the Rolex trademarks on so many wrists might find themselves discouraged from acquiring a genuine because the items have become too common place and no longer possess the prestige once associated with them.

Rolex Watch, 645 F. Supp. at 495; *see also Mastercrafters*, 221 F.2d at 466.

Such is the damage which could occur here. As the district court explained when deciding whether Roberts' former partner's Ferrari replicas would be confused with Ferrari's cars:

> Ferrari has gained a well-earned reputation for making uniquely designed automobiles of quality and rarity. The DAYTONA SPYDER design is well-known among the relevant public and exclusively and positively associated with Ferrari. If the country is populated with hundreds, if not thousands, of replicas of rare, distinct, and unique vintage cars, obviously they are no longer unique. Even if a person seeing one of these

replicas driving down the road is not confused, Ferrari's exclusive association with this design has been diluted and eroded. If the replica Daytona looks cheap or in disrepair, Ferrari's reputation for rarity and quality could be damaged. . . .

Ferrari, 11 U.S.P.Q.2d at 1848.

The dissent argues that the Lanham Act requires proof of confusion at the point of sale because the eight factor test used to determine likelihood of confusion focuses on the confusion of the purchaser, not the public. The dissent submits that three of the factors, marketing channels used, likely degree of purchaser care and sophistication, and evidence of actual confusion, specifically relate to purchasers. However, evidence of actual confusion is not limited to purchasers. The survey evidence in this case showed that members of the public, but not necessarily purchasers, were actually confused by the similarity of the products. Moreover, the other five factors, strength of the mark, relatedness of the goods, similarity of the marks, defendant's intent in selecting the mark, and likelihood of product expansion, do not limit the likelihood of confusion test to purchasers.

Since Congress intended to protect the reputation of the manufacturer as well as to protect purchasers, the Act's protection is not limited to confusion at the point of sale. Because Ferrari's reputation in the field could be damaged by the marketing of Roberts' replicas, the district court did not err in permitting recovery despite the absence of point of sale confusion. . . .

IV.

For the foregoing reasons, the judgment of the district court is AFFIRMED.

KENNEDY, CIRCUIT JUDGE, dissenting.

I respectfully dissent because the majority opinion does more than protect consumers against a likelihood of confusion as to the source of goods; it protects the source of the goods, Ferrari, against plaintiff's copying of its design even if the replication is accompanied by adequate labeling so as to prevent consumer confusion. I believe the majority commits two errors in reaching this result. The majority first misconstrues the scope of protection afforded by the Lanham Act by misapplying the "likelihood of confusion" test and reading an anti-dilution provision into the language of section 43(a). The majority then affirms an injunction that is overbroad. The product of these errors is a remedy that provides defendant with absolute protection in perpetuity against copying its unpatented design. This remedy is contrary to the language and purpose of the Lanham Act and runs afoul of Supreme Court precedent. *Bonito Boats, Inc. v. Thunder Craft Boats, Inc.*, 489 U.S. 141 (1989);

Compco Corp. v. Day-Brite Lighting, Inc., 376 U.S. 234 (1964); *Sears, Roebuck & Co. v. Stiffel Co.*, 376 U.S. 225 (1964). . . .

NOTES FOR DISCUSSION

1. *Consumer Welfare.* Are consumers better or worse off as a result of this decision? Are some consumers better off, while others are worse off? If so, how do we balance the competing consumer interests at stake? Why do consumers purchase a prestige good such as a Ferrari, rather than a less expensive car? There are three possible reasons. First, a consumer may feel satisfaction from owning the Ferrari directly. Second, a consumer may derive satisfaction from being able to communicate or signal others that he has sufficient wealth to purchase a Ferrari. Third, a consumer may derive satisfaction from making others feel dissatisfaction because they do not have sufficient wealth to afford a Ferrari. Should the law protect all three of these interests?

Prestige goods are often called Veblen goods, after Thorstein Veblen who first analyzed them. *See* T.B. VEBLEN, THE THEORY OF THE LEISURE CLASS (1899). He theorized that for such goods, consumer demand for the good will increase, rather than decrease as it does for ordinary goods, with price. An increased price will increase the perception of status and exclusivity associated with the good and thereby increase demand for the good. For such goods, one might argue that the ordinary consumer interest in competition is lessened, if not absent altogether. Are you persuaded that such prestige goods really exist? Keep in mind that a positive correlation between price and demand can only hold over some limited price ranges. Even for a Ferrari, and even if we assume that some degree of exclusivity is desirable, at some point, further price increases will reduce, not increase demand. Otherwise, Ferrari would charge an infinite price for its vehicles. Similarly, even for Ferraris, if their price fell radically, so that a consumer could purchase either a Ferrari or a Ford for the same price, many consumers would gladly purchase the Ferrari, even if a few Veblen consumers might decide to look elsewhere. Thus, even for Ferraris, consumers' general preference for competition probably still holds.

In any event, even if prestige goods exist, should we use trademark law to insulate such goods from competition? Should we limit the theory of post-sale confusion to cases involving prestige goods? Courts have not. For example, in *Lois Sportswear, U.S.A., Inc. v. Levi Strauss & Co.*, 799 F.2d 867 (2d Cir. 1986), the Second Circuit found actionable confusion in the post-sale market when a defendant used a back pocket stitching pattern on its upscale, designer jeans strikingly similar to that found on Levi's jeans. As the court explained: "In the post-sale context, this striking similarity no doubt will cause consumers to transfer the goodwill they feel for appellee to appellants, at least initially. This misuse of goodwill is at the heart of unfair competition." *Id.* at 873. Do you agree that consumers are harmed by such a use? How?

Can you think of any real world, non-trademark prestige goods that face "competition" from lower-cost, lower-quality imitators? What about diamonds and cubic zirconias (or "CZs")? Has the availability of CZs destroyed the market for diamonds? Have consumers been harmed by the availability of CZs? Why should diamond miners have to face competition from fake diamonds, while Ferrari does not have to face competition from fake Ferraris? From a consumer welfare perspective, are the two cases the same or different? Are there any other perspectives that we should consider?

2. *Confusion as to Source.* Are consumers likely to purchase Roberts' kit cars under the mistaken belief that they are in fact purchasing a real Ferrari? How does the court resolve this issue?

3. *Post-Sale Confusion.* With respect to post-sale confusion, there are two issues. First, is such confusion actionable as a legal matter? How does the court rule on this first issue? Are the policy concerns implicated by recognizing post-sale confusion identical to those implicated by recognizing confusion as to source at the point of sale? In what ways are they similar? In what ways are they different? As in the *Boston Prof'l Hockey* case, the court once again cites the 1962 Housekeeping Amendments to the Trademark Act. Do you agree that Congress intended those amendments to recognize the sort of confusion that the court here finds actionable?

Second, is such confusion present as a factual matter? How does the court rule on this second issue? Has the court established that an appreciable number of ordinarily prudent consumers will be confused post-sale or has it merely offered a story about how such consumers might be confused post-sale? What evidence is there that ordinarily prudent consumers are in fact actually confused post-sale? Can you tell the difference between an authentic antique car and a kit car made to resemble the antique? Can you tell the difference between a diamond and a CZ? Can you tell the difference between a real Fendi handbag and a fake?

4. Sears *and* Compco *Revisited.* We discussed the implications of the Court's decisions in *Sears* and *Compco* for the protection of trade dress under the federal Trademark Act. As we saw there, the holdings in *Sears* and *Compco* with respect to preemption of state law trade dress protection do not directly apply to trade dress protection under the Lanham Trademark Act because it is a coequal federal statute and hence not subject to preemption. Nevertheless, although the *Sears* and *Compco* holdings do not control, their reasoning may remain persuasive. Courts are split on this issue, however. Some courts, like the majority in the *Ferrari* case, reason that patent and trademark laws serve different purposes and hence no conflict can arise. Other courts, and the dissent in the *Ferrari* case, disagree. Trade dress law, whether it arises under state or federal law, can frustrate the purposes of the Patent Act to the extent that it provides patent-like protection to things that have not satisfied the prerequisites for a patent. Does protecting the Ferrari car shape under trademark law insulate Ferrari cars from competition more broadly, less broadly, or to the same extent as would a patent?

5.   *Defining Trade Dress.* The court states: " 'Trade dress' refers to 'the image and overall appearance of a product.' " Is that a satisfactory definition of trade dress? Is "the image and overall appearance of a product" always trade dress, or is it trade dress only in those cases when consumers rely on "the image and overall appearance" to identify the product's source? Should we require evidence that consumers are relying on the overall appearance as a brand-identifier before addressing the secondary meaning issue, or should we jump directly into secondary meaning? What about the layout of a golf course hole? Should we conduct a preliminary inquiry into whether consumers are relying on the hole's layout as a brand-identifier or simply focus on whether there is sufficient circumstantial evidence to establish secondary meaning?

3. INITIAL INTEREST CONFUSION

MOBIL OIL CORP. v. PEGASUS PETROLEUM CORP.
818 F.2d 254 (2d Cir. 1987)

LUMBARD, CIRCUIT JUDGE

Mobil Oil Corporation brought this action in the Southern District charging Pegasus Petroleum Corporation with trademark infringement and unfair competition, 15 U.S.C. § 1114(1); false designation of origin, 15 U.S.C. § 1125(a); and trademark dilution, N.Y. Gen. Bus. Law § 368–d. On July 8, 1986, after a three-day bench trial, Judge MacMahon entered judgment for Mobil on each of its claims, dismissed Pegasus Petroleum's counterclaims seeking to cancel Mobil's trademark registration, and enjoined Pegasus Petroleum from using the mark "Pegasus" in connection with the petroleum industry or related businesses. We affirm.

Mobil, one of the world's largest corporations, manufactures and sells a vast array of petroleum products to industrial consumers and to the general public. Since 1931, Mobil has made extensive use of its well known "flying horse" symbol—representing Pegasus, the winged horse of Greek mythology—in connection with its petroleum business. Mobil displays this registered trademark, usually in red, but occasionally in blue, black, white, or outline form, at virtually all its gasoline service stations (usually on an illuminated disk four feet in diameter); in connection with all petroleum products sold at its service stations; in connection with the sale of a variety of its other petroleum products; on its oil tankers, barges, and other vehicles; and on its letterhead. As the district court explained, it is "undisputed that Mobil's extensive use of the flying horse symbol for such a long period of time in connection with all of Mobil's commercial activity has rendered it a very strong mark. Indeed, counsel for [Pegasus Petroleum] could think of few trademarks, if any, that were stronger trademarks in American commerce today."

As part of its petroleum business, Mobil buys and sells crude and refined petroleum products in bulk, an activity known as oil trading, to insure a continuous flow of oil to its refineries, and ultimately to its customers. The oil trading market is tight-knit and sophisticated: It encompasses a select group of professional buyers and brokers, representing approximately 200 oil companies, wholesalers, and oil traders; deals are in the hundreds of thousands, or millions of dollars, and in tens of tons; and, oil traders do not consummate deals with strangers except after a thorough credit check. Mobil does not use its flying horse symbol in connection with its oil trading business.

Pegasus Petroleum, incorporated in 1981, confines its activities to oil trading, and does not sell directly to the general public. Its founder, Gregory Callimanopulos, testified that he selected the name "Pegasus Petroleum" because he wanted a name with both mythical connotations and alliterative qualities. Callimanopulos admitted that he knew of Mobil's flying horse symbol when he picked the name, but claimed that he did not know that the symbol represented Pegasus or that Mobil used the word "Pegasus" in connection with its petroleum business. Shortly after the genesis of Pegasus Petroleum, Ben Pollner, then president of the company, sent a letter to 400–500 people in the oil trading business informing them about Pegasus Petroleum's formation. The letter stated that Pegasus Petroleum was part of the "Callimanopulos group of companies," and used an interlocking double P as a letterhead. Pegasus Petroleum has never used a flying horse symbol and sells no products with the name "Pegasus" on them.

In 1982, Mobil approached Pegasus Petroleum after learning of its use of the mark "Pegasus." When attempts to reach an agreement failed, Mobil filed the instant suit. The case proceeded to trial before Judge MacMahon, without a jury. After examining the criteria set forth in *Polaroid Corp. v. Polarad Electronics Corp.*, 287 F.2d 492, 495 (2d Cir.), *cert. denied*, 368 U.S. 820 (1961), Judge MacMahon concluded that "there is a sufficient likelihood of confusion between [Mobil's flying horse symbol] and [Pegasus Petroleum's use of the 'Pegasus' mark] to grant [Mobil] relief under the Lanham Act." Judge MacMahon also held for Mobil on its unfair competition, false designation, and antidilution claims; and enjoined Pegasus Petroleum's further use of the mark "Pegasus" in connection with the oil industry. With Mobil's consent, the injunction has been stayed, pending resolution of this appeal.

The Lanham Act prohibits the use of "any reproduction, counterfeit, copy, or colorable imitation of a registered mark" where "such use is likely to cause confusion, or to cause mistake, or to deceive." 15 U.S.C. § 1114(1)(a). To state a claim under this section, a plaintiff must show a "likelihood that an appreciable number of ordinarily prudent purchasers are likely to be misled, or indeed simply confused, as to the source of the goods in question." *Mushroom Makers, Inc. v. R. G. Barry Corp.*, 580 F.2d 44, 47 (2d Cir. 1978) (per curiam) (citing cases), *cert. denied*, 439 U.S. 1116 (1979). A nonexclusive list of eight factors, articulated by Judge Friendly in *Polaroid, supra*, 287 F.2d at 495, helps guide this inquiry: (1) the strength of the plaintiff's mark: (2) the degree of similarity between the two marks; (3) the competitive proximity of the products or services; (4) the existence of actual confusion; (5) the likelihood that the plaintiff will "bridge the gap" between the two markets; (6) the defendant's good faith in adopting its mark; (7) the quality of the defendant's product; and (8) the sophistication of the purchasers. We agree with both the district court's determination of each of the *Polaroid* factors and its balancing of those factors to arrive at its conclusion that Pegasus Petroleum infringed upon Mobil's senior mark—the flying horse.

Pegasus Petroleum does not dispute the district court's conclusion that the strength of Mobil's flying horse mark is "without question, and perhaps without equal." As an arbitrary mark—there is nothing suggestive of the petroleum business in the flying horse symbol—Mobil's symbol deserves "the most protection the Lanham Act can provide." *Lois Sportswear, U.S.A., Inc. v. Levi Strauss & Co.*, 799 F.2d 867, 871 (2d Cir. 1986). On the other hand, Pegasus Petroleum vigorously attacks the district court's finding of similarity between the two marks. Pegasus Petroleum argues that the district court erred by blindly equating the word "Pegasus" with its pictorial representation—Mobil's flying horse. While we agree that words and their pictorial representations should not be equated as a matter of law, a district court may make such a determination as a factual matter. *See, e.g., Beer Nuts, Inc. v. King Nut Co.*, 477 F.2d 326, 329 (6th Cir.) ("It is well settled that words and their pictorial representation are treated the same in determining the likelihood of confusion between two marks."), *cert. denied*, 414 U.S. 858 (1973). . . . Judge MacMahon made such a determination here.

> We find that the similarity of the mark exists in the strong probability that prospective purchasers of defendant's product will equate or translate Mobil's symbol for "Pegasus" and vice versa.

> We find that the word "Pegasus" evokes the symbol of the flying red horse and that the flying horse is associated in the mind with Mobil. In other words, the symbol of the flying horse and its name "Pegasus" are synonymous.

That conclusion finds support in common sense as well as the record.

The third *Polaroid* factor addresses the competitive proximity between the two marks. Pegasus Petroleum points out that while Judge MacMahon correctly found that Mobil and Pegasus Petroleum both compete in the oil trading business, Mobil does not use its flying horse trademark in that field. However, "direct competition between the products is not a prerequisite to relief. . . . Confusion, or the likelihood of confusion, not competition, is the real test of trademark infringement." *Continental Motors Corp. v. Continental Aviation Corp.*, 375 F.2d 857, 861 (5th Cir. 1967) (citations omitted). Both Mobil and Pegasus Petroleum use their marks in the petroleum industry. *See, e.g., AMF, Inc. v. Sleekcraft Boats*, 599 F.2d 341, 350 (9th Cir. 1979) (competitive proximity may be found where goods are similar in use and function). . . .

Moreover, competitive proximity must be measured with reference to the first two *Polaroid* factors: The unparalleled strength of Mobil's mark demands that it be given broad protection against infringers. *See, e.g., James Burrough Ltd. v. Sign of Beefeater, Inc.*, 540 F.2d 266, 276 (7th Cir. 1976) ("A mark that is strong because of its fame or its uniqueness, is more likely to be remembered and more likely to be associated in the public mind with a greater breadth of products or services than is a mark that is weak. . . .") . . . . Mobil's ubiquitous presence throughout the petroleum industry further increases the likelihood that a consumer will confuse Pegasus Petroleum with Mobil. *See Armco, Inc. v. Armco Burglar Alarm Co.*, 693 F.2d 1155, 1161 (5th Cir. 1982) ("Diversification makes it more likely that a potential customer would associate the non-diversified company's services with the diversified company, even though the two companies do not actually compete."). Finally, the great similarity between the two marks—the district court concluded that they were "synonymous"—entitles Mobil's mark to protection over a broader range of related products. We agree with the district court's finding of competitive proximity.

Our evaluation of the first three *Polaroid* factors, perhaps the most significant in determining the likelihood of confusion, strongly supports the district court's conclusion that such a likelihood exists. The district court's finding under the fourth *Polaroid* factor that Pegasus Petroleum did not innocently select its potentially confusing mark reinforces this conclusion: Intentional copying gives rise to a presumption of a likelihood of confusion. *Perfect Fit Industries v. Acme Quilting Co.*, 618 F.2d 950, 954 (2d Cir. 1980) (citing cases). The district court discredited Gregory Callimanopulos's testimony that "he did not intentionally choose the tradename 'Pegasus' with either the symbol of Mobil's flying horse or Mobil's wordmark in mind." The court explained:

> Mr. Callimanopulos is obviously an educated, sophisticated man who, from his prior shipping business, was familiar with the flying horse and from his own background and education and awareness of Greek mythology could not have escaped the conclusion that the use of the word "Pegasus" would infringe the tradename and symbol of the plaintiff.

In response, Pegasus Petroleum first contends that this finding is clearly erroneous given the objective evidence before the court, specifically pointing to its letter to the trade of June, 1982, which stated that it was a member of the Callimanopulos group of companies. While this correspondence was one piece of evidence for the district court to consider, it falls far short of establishing, by itself, Pegasus Petroleum's good faith. Pegasus Petroleum also notes that "actual and constructive notice of another company's prior registration of the mark . . . [is] not *necessarily* indicative of bad faith, because the presumption of an exclusive right to use a registered mark extends only so far as the goods or services noted in the registration certificate." *McGregor-Doniger, Inc. v. Drizzle, Inc.*, 599 F.2d 1126, 1137 (2d Cir. 1979) (emphasis added). However, actual or constructive knowledge *may* signal bad faith. Indeed, "in this circuit and others, numerous decisions have recognized that the second comer has a duty to so name and dress his product as to avoid all likelihood of consumers confusing it with the product of the first comer." *Harold F. Ritchie Inc. v. Chesebrough-Pond's, Inc.*, 281 F.2d 755, 758 (2d Cir. 1960) (footnote omitted). . . . We believe the record clearly substantiates Judge MacMahon's inference of bad faith.

The existence of some evidence of actual confusion, the fifth *Polaroid* factor, further buttresses the finding of a likelihood of confusion. *See, e.g., World Carpets, Inc. v. Dick Littrell's New World Carpets*, 438 F.2d 482, 489 (5th Cir. 1971) ("While . . . it is not necessary to show actual confusion . . . there can be no more positive or substantial proof of the likelihood of confusion than proof of actual confusion.") (footnotes omitted). Both Mobil and Pegasus Petroleum offered surveys of consumers and of members of the oil trading industry as evidence relating to the existence of actual confusion between the two marks. The district court properly admitted these surveys into evidence, despite claims of statistical imperfections by both sides, as those criticisms affected the weight accorded to the evidence rather than its admissibility. *See, e.g., Grotrian, Helfferich, Schulz, Th. Steinweg Nachf. v. Steinway & Sons*, 523 F.2d 1331, 1341 (2d Cir. 1975). After reviewing these surveys, Judge MacMahon concluded that there was "evidence of actual confusion." His decision was not clearly erroneous. *Id.*

Pegasus Petroleum argues that the absence of misdirected mail and telephone calls between the parties, and the fact that Pegasus Petroleum must post a letter of credit as security during its oil trading deals while Mobil need not, prove that no actual confusion between the two firms existed. This argument misunderstands the district court's opinion. Judge MacMahon found a likelihood of confusion not in the fact that a third party would do business with Pegasus Petroleum believing it related to Mobil, but rather in the likelihood that Pegasus Petroleum would gain crucial credibility during the initial phases of a deal. For example, an oil trader might listen to a cold phone call from Pegasus Petroleum—an admittedly oft used procedure in the oil trading business—when otherwise he might not, because of the possibility that Pegasus Petroleum is related to Mobil. The absence of misdirected phone calls and the difference in the letter of credit requirements are other matters.

Pegasus Petroleum never rebutted the inference of a likelihood of confusion. The district court did not examine the sixth *Polaroid* factor—whether Mobil would "bridge the gap" by expanding its use of the flying horse symbol into the oil trading market (Mobil presently competes, but does not use its flying horse trademark, in the oil trading field). Nevertheless, "sufficient likelihood of confusion may be established although likelihood of bridging the gap is not demonstrated." *McGregor-Doniger, supra*, 599 F.2d at 1136. The absence of an intent to bridge the gap does not negate a finding of a likelihood of confusion in the market as presently constituted. *See Scarves by Vera, Inc. v. Todo Imports, Ltd.*, 544 F.2d 1167, 1174 (2d Cir. 1976). The Lanham Act extends trademark protection to related goods in order to guard against numerous evils in addition to restraints on the possible expansion of the senior user's market, including consumer confusion, tarnishment of the senior user's reputation, and unjust enrichment of the infringer. 2 J. McCarthy, *supra*, § 24:5 at 177–81.

The seventh *Polaroid* factor suggests that the court examine the quality of Pegasus Petroleum's product. The district court made no findings on this issue. Pegasus Petroleum argues that its product—oil—does not differ from that sold by Mobil. However, a senior user may sue to protect his reputation even where the infringer's goods are of top quality. *See, e.g., Wesley-Jessen Div. of Schering Corp. v. Bausch & Lomb Inc.*, 698 F.2d 862, 867 (7th Cir. 1983) ("Even if the infringer's goods are of high quality, the victim has the right to insist that its reputation not be imperiled by another's actions."). . . .

We finally turn to the eighth *Polaroid* factor, the sophistication of purchasers. The district court concluded that, "even though defendant's business is transacted in large quantities only with sophisticated oil traders, there is still and nevertheless a likelihood of confusion." We agree. As explained above, the district court's concerns focused upon the probability that potential purchasers would be misled into an initial interest in Pegasus Petroleum. Such initial confusion works a sufficient trademark injury. *Steinway & Sons, supra*, 523 F.2d at 1342. The district court's concerns had a sufficient basis in fact despite the sophistication of the oil trading market: Pegasus Petroleum admits that it solicits business through telephone calls to potential customers. Pegasus Petroleum also acknowledges that "trust, in the oil industry, is of paramount importance." Finally, Mobil's Oil Trading Department executive, Thomas Cory, testified that he did not undertake an investigation of a new company before initially dealing with it. Such an investigation was undertaken only prior to the culmination of a deal.

For the foregoing reasons, we agree with the district court's finding that Pegasus Petroleum infringed on Mobil's registered flying horse trademark and therefore affirm its judgment. Mobil's "unfair competition claim is governed by essentially the same considerations as its infringement claim." *Steinway & Sons, supra*, 523 F.2d at 1342 n.21. Therefore, we also affirm the district court on Mobil's unfair competition claim. As the judgment finds full support in the district court's findings on Mobil's first two claims, we need not consider Mobil's other two claims—false designation of origin, and trademark dilution under New York law.

Affirmed.

NOTES FOR DISCUSSION

1.   *Consumer Welfare.* Are consumers better off or worse off as a result of the judicial recognition of initial interest confusion as actionable? What is the harm to consumers from initial interest confusion? Is it the same harm that arises from traditional confusion? On the other side of the coin, is there any benefit to consumers from allowing the defendant to call itself Pegasus Petroleum? Are the consumer interests at stake in *Mobil Oil* the same in kind and degree as in *Steinway & Sons*? Do you agree with the court's decision to extend the reasoning in *Steinway & Sons* to cover the defendant's conduct in *Mobil Oil*?

2.   *Marks, Confusion, and Selling Power.* One potential difference between the cases is that whatever selling power the mark "Steinway" generated for pianos was entirely the result of the plaintiff's efforts. Is that equally true for the "Pegasus" mark? Did it have value only because of Mobil Oil's use? Or does the mark, because of its historical origins, have its own unique appeal or inherent selling power?

3.   *Initial Interest Confusion and the Factor Test.* Does the initial interest confusion substitute for the traditional *Polaroid* factor test? Or does it modify it in some respect? What role does initial interest confusion play?

4.   *Product Design and Initial Interest Confusion.* Should we extend initial interest confusion to product designs claimed as trade dress? How would you resolve the following case? Gibson Guitars has long marketed a single-cutaway guitar with an unusual appearance under the word mark "Les Paul." A single-cutaway guitar:

> is a traditionally shaped guitar with a portion removed from [the] body of the guitar where the lower section of the fingerboard meets the body of the guitar. The term "cutaway guitar" denotes that portion of the guitar between the neck and its lower[ ] part, that appears to be missing from the natural, rounded body contour. The removal of this portion forms what is often referred to as the "horn." One aspect of this horn design is that the musician can access higher strings [and] positions.

A competing guitar company, Paul Reed Smith Guitars, begins offering a similar-looking single-cutaway guitar. Although plainly labeled with its own word marks, the competing guitars look sufficiently similar that from across the room in a guitar store, a consumer will initially mistake one for the other. It is also likely that people will mistake one for the other from a distance post sale, for example when one of the guitars is held by a rock star on a concert stage or in a music video. Gibson sues alleging trade dress infringement. Assuming that the design is nonfunctional, how should the court rule on the question of likelihood of confusion? *See Gibson Guitar Corp. v. Paul Reed Smith Guitars, LP,* 423 F.3d 539, 549 (6th Cir. 2005) ("We conclude that neither initial-interest confusion, nor post-sale confusion, nor any combination of two, is applicable in this case."). Do you agree with the court's decision? Why or why not?

4. REVERSE CONFUSION

A & H SPORTSWEAR, INC. V. VICTORIA'S SECRET STORES, INC.

237 F.3d 198 (3d Cir. 2000)

BECKER, CHIEF JUDGE

The critical question in this trademark infringement case, before us for the second time, is whether a typical consumer is likely to confuse MIRACLESUIT swimwear with THE MIRACLE BRA swimwear. The former is a product of Plaintiff A & H Sportswear Company ("A & H"), which manufactures ten percent of all swimsuits made in the United States. The latter is a product of Defendant Victoria's Secret, the lingerie leviathan that recently entered the swimwear market. A & H filed suit in the District Court for the Eastern District of Pennsylvania claiming that The Miracle Bra swimwear mark violates the Lanham Act because it is confusingly similar to the Miraclesuit swimwear mark, which A & H registered first. A & H contends that: (1) consumers are likely to wrongly associate The Miracle Bra with A & H (the direct confusion claim); or, in the alternative, (2) consumers are likely to think that Miraclesuit is a product of Victoria's Secret (the reverse confusion claim).

During an extensive bench trial, A & H argued that Victoria's Secret should be enjoined from using The Miracle Bra mark for swimwear. Finding a "possibility of confusion," the District Court granted relief to A & H. Following an appeal to this Court that clarified that likelihood of confusion (instead of possibility of confusion) was the correct standard, the District Court concluded that A & H had failed to show by a preponderance of the evidence that Victoria's Secret's The Miracle Bra swimwear mark created a likelihood of either direct or reverse confusion with the Miraclesuit product.

. . . [A & H has appealed, challenging the district court's findings with respect to both the direct and the reverse confusion claims. With respect to the direct confusion claim,] we conclude that neither the District Court's fact-finding nor its balancing of factors warrants reversal, and hence we will affirm its judgment on the direct confusion claim.

As for the reverse confusion claim, A & H challenges the District Court's treatment as inadequate, and inconsistent with the method laid out in our leading reverse confusion case, *Fisons Horticulture, Inc. v. Vigoro Industries, Inc.*, 30 F.3d 466 (3d Cir. 1994). *Fisons* adopted the doctrine of reverse confusion, and used the *Lapp* factors to assess the likelihood of such confusion, with a few minor modifications. The District Court interpreted our precedents to require a two-step inquiry, engaging the *Lapp* factors only after an initial assessment that the disparity in commercial strength reached a high threshold. Because the threshold degree of commercial disparity that the court believed was required was not met, the court did not even examine whether there existed a likelihood of confusion.

After reviewing *Fisons* and our precedent, we are persuaded that the District Court erred in fashioning a two-step inquiry, and in failing to consider the *Lapp* factors as they apply to reverse confusion claims. We will demonstrate that the application of some of the factors changes in the reverse confusion context, and we conclude that, on the record before us, the judgment must be vacated with respect to the reverse confusion claim and the case remanded for further proceedings.

I.   Facts

The Miraclesuit bathing suit is made by A & H, which manufactures ten percent of all swimwear in the United States. . . . The Miraclesuit is advertised as having a slimming effect on the wearer without using uncomfortable girdle-like binds. Its material purportedly smooths out middle body bulges and works with a flattering design to confuse the eye such that the wearer is advised, in advertising and in tags that generally accompany the product, that she will "look ten pounds lighter in 10 seconds[:] The ten seconds it takes to slip it on." Miraclesuits also include tags indicating that they are Swim Shaper products.

Miraclesuits, which sell for between $50 and $100, come in both single pieces and bikinis. Many are equipped with push up bras, shaping or underwire bras, or simple, unshaped bras. They are typically sold to trade buyers for department store sales and national mail-order catalogues, and, on two occasions, they were featured in the Victoria's Secret catalogue. A & H received a trademark registration for the mark Miraclesuit in the fall of 1992. The District Court found that A & H has spent over $1.2 million to advertise the Miraclesuit in magazines and trade papers, and has received the equivalent of $1.5 million of advertising in "free publicity," i.e., publicity in trade magazines, consumer columns, and the general press. The advertising and publicity campaign has been a success, and Miraclesuits constitute approximately ten percent of all of A & H's sales.

While A & H is busy selling skinny waists and midriffs, Victoria's Secret, the nation's premier lingerie seller, has focused on instant enlargements of the bust. In 1993, Victoria's Secret released The Miracle Bra, a padded push-up bra. Victoria's Secret filed an application to register its The Miracle Bra trademark, and unleashed an avalanche of advertising and publicity, ultimately spending over $13 million on The Miracle Bra products. The campaign succeeded, and sales of The Miracle Bra products have topped $140 million since they were first introduced.

In 1994, Victoria's Secret's trademark application for The Miracle Bra mark on lingerie was approved. Later that year, Victoria's Secret moved The Miracle Bra mark into swimwear, and The Miracle Bra swimsuit and The Miracle Bra bikini started appearing in Victoria's Secret catalogues. (The Miracle Bra lingerie and swimwear are sold only in Victoria's Secret stores and catalogues.). The cost of The Miracle Bra swimwear varies, but it is typically in the neighborhood of $70, and The Miracle Bra and Victoria's Secret tags are prominently featured on all swimwear. This product also succeeded: The total sales of The Miracle Bra swimsuits reached $28 million by summer 1997. The last critical fact regarding this swimwear is that, as a result of this litigation, Victoria's Secret has committed itself to using the following disclaimer with all promotion, advertising, and sales of The Miracle Bra: "The Miracle Bra Swimwear Collection is exclusive to Victoria's Secret and is not associated with Miraclesuit by Swimshaper."

In 1995, after this litigation began, Victoria's Secret applied to the PTO for a trademark for The Miracle Bra for swimsuits, bathing suits, and bikinis. Because it had previously conducted a search for The Miracle Bra as applied to lingerie, which had led it to the conclusion that The Miracle Bra did not threaten to infringe on other trademarks, Victoria's Secret had not conducted a separate trademark search of The Miracle Bra trademark as it applied to swimwear. However, the PTO examining attorney denied Victoria's Secret's application due to its similarity to Miraclesuit because he determined that: (1) "Miracle" was the dominant feature of each mark; and (2) the product lines overlap. The denial was not appealed.

II. Procedural History

In December 1994, A & H filed a complaint against Victoria's Secret, alleging direct and reverse trademark infringement, unfair competition, dilution, and unjust enrichment. The District Court held a bench trial on liability in the fall of 1995, and a damages and relief trial in 1996. The court found that Victoria's Secret's use of The Miracle Bra on its lingerie created no likelihood of confusion with A & H's Miraclesuit. *See A & H*

Sportswear Co. v. Victoria's Secret Stores, Inc., 926 F. Supp. 1233, 1264 (E.D. Pa. 1996) ("A & H I"). However, with regard to Victoria's Secret's use of The Miracle Bra mark on swimwear, the District Court found a "possibility of confusion" with A & H's Miraclesuit swimwear. *See id.* at 1269. Based upon this finding, it ordered Victoria's Secret not to use The Miracle Bra tag with swimwear unless it was accompanied by the disclaimer: "The Miracle Bra (TM) swimwear collection is exclusive to Victoria's Secret and not associated with Miraclesuit® by Swim Shaper (R)." *A & H Sportswear Co. v. Victoria's Secret Stores, Inc.*, 967 F. Supp. 1457, 1482 (E.D. Pa. 1997) ("A & H II"). The District Court also ordered that royalties on past and future sales of The Miracle Bra swimsuits be paid to A & H. *See id.* at 1483. Both parties appealed. Although the District Court granted a stay of its order pending appeal, Victoria's Secret has continued to use the disclaimer voluntarily and has represented to us at oral argument that it will continue to do so regardless of the outcome of this litigation.

During the prior appeal, we heard the case *en banc* to consider the viability of the "possibility of confusion" standard originally used by the District Court. We rejected that standard, and remanded the case to the District Court to apply the traditional "likelihood of confusion" standard to the swimsuits' marks. *See A & H Sportswear, Inc. v. Victoria's Secret Stores, Inc.*, 166 F.3d 197, 206 (3d Cir. 1999) ("A & H III"). . . .

Following our mandate, the District Court applied the "likelihood of confusion" test and found that there was no likelihood of direct confusion and no grounds for consideration of reverse confusion. It therefore denied the request for injunctive relief. *See A & H Sportswear Co. v. Victoria's Secret Stores, Inc.*, 57 F. Supp. 2d 155, 178–79 (E.D. Pa. 1999) ("A & H IV"). A & H appeals. . . .

III. The Direct Confusion Claim

. . . [After reviewing the evidence and the district court's analysis, the court affirmed the district court's finding that there was no likelihood of forward or, in the court's words, "direct" confusion.] . . .

V.   The Reverse Confusion Claim

A.   Introduction

We recently recognized the doctrine of "reverse confusion" as a distinct basis for a claim under § 43(a) of the Lanham Act. *See Fisons*, 30 F.3d at 475. While the essence of a direct confusion claim is that a junior user of a mark is said to free-ride on the "reputation and good will of the senior user by adopting a similar or identical mark," *id.*, reverse confusion occurs when "the junior user saturates the market with a similar trademark and overwhelms the senior user." *Id.* (quoting *Ameritech, Inc. v. American Info. Techs. Corp.*, 811 F.2d 960, 964 (6th Cir. 1987)). The harm flowing from reverse confusion is that the public comes to assume the senior user's products are really the junior user's or that the former has become somehow connected to the latter. . . . The senior user loses the value of the trademark—its product identity, corporate identity, control over its goodwill and reputation, and ability to move into new markets.

Ameritech, Inc., 811 F.2d at 964. As we explained in *Fisons*, reverse confusion protects "smaller senior users . . . against larger, more powerful companies who want to use identical or confusingly similar trademarks." 30 F.3d at 475. Absent reverse confusion, "a company with a well established trade name and with the economic power to advertise extensively [would be immunized from suit] for a product name taken from a competitor." *Big O Tire Dealers, Inc.*, 561 F.2d at 1372 (citation omitted).

The doctrine of reverse confusion—or, at least, some of its applications—is not without its critics. *See, e.g.*, Thad G. Long & Alfred M. Marks, *Reverse Confusion: Fundamentals and Limits*, 84 TRADEMARK REP. 1, 2–3 (1994); Daniel D. Domenico, Note, *Mark Madness: How Brent Musburger and the Miracle Bra May Have Led to a More Equitable and Efficient Understanding of the Reverse Confusion Doctrine in Trademark Law*, 86 VA. L. REV. 597, 613–14, 621–24 (2000).

The chief danger inherent in recognizing reverse confusion claims is that innovative junior users, who have invested heavily in promoting a particular mark, will suddenly find their use of the mark blocked by plaintiffs who have not invested in, or promoted, their own marks. *See Weiner King, Inc. v. Wiener King Corp.*, 615 F.2d 512, 522 (C.C.P.A. 1980). Further, an overly-vigorous use of the doctrine of reverse confusion could potentially inhibit larger companies with established marks from expanding their product lines—for instance, had Victoria's Secret thought, at the outset, that it would not be permitted to carry over its popular The Miracle Bra mark from lingerie to swimwear, it might have chosen not to enter the swimsuit market at all.

This would be an undesirable result; in fact, it is precisely to allow a certain amount of "space" for companies to expand their product lines under established marks that we allow infringement suits against suppliers of noncompeting goods. *See Interpace Corp. v. Lapp, Inc.*, 721 F.2d 460, 464 (3d Cir. 1983). This is not to say that the reverse confusion doctrine does not have its proper place; as has been recognized, without the existence of such a claim, smaller business owners might not have any incentive to invest in their marks at all, for fear the mark could be usurped at will by a larger competitor. *See SK & F, Co. v. Premo Pharm. Labs., Inc.*, 625 F.2d 1055, 1067 (3d Cir. 1980) ("Permitting piracy of . . . identifying trade dress can only discourage other manufacturers from making a similar individual promotional effort."). However, these concerns do sensitize us to the potential untoward effects of an overenthusiastic enforcement of reverse confusion claims, although they cannot supersede our judicial recognition of the doctrine.

B. The Test for Reverse Confusion

As in a direct confusion claim, the ultimate question in a reverse confusion claim is whether there is a likelihood of consumer confusion as to the source or sponsorship of a product. *See Fisons*, 30 F.3d at 475. Although it would seem somewhat counter-intuitive to posit that the likelihood of confusion analysis changes from the direct confusion to the reverse confusion context, there are differences between the two situations that bear mentioning. Therefore, to clarify the test for reverse confusion that has developed in our jurisprudence, we will walk through the factors that a district court should consider (where relevant) in assessing such a claim.

1. The Factors that are the Same

As an initial matter, there are several factors that should generally be analyzed in the same way for a reverse confusion claim as they are for a direct confusion claim. First, the attentiveness of consumers does not change (factor (3)); in both direct and reverse confusion, the question is whether this is the kind of product that consumers will care enough about to notice the differences, or purchase hastily with only a limited impression. *See Fisons*, 30 F.3d at 476 n.12 (considering this factor in the same manner as it would for direct confusion). Second, and similarly, the degree to which the channels of trade and advertisement overlap (factor (7)) should be analyzed in the same fashion. *See id.* at 475–76 (analyzing the channels of trade in the same manner). Finally, *Lapp* factors (8) and (9), considering the similarity of the targets of the parties' sales efforts and the similarity of products, are also analyzed no differently in the reverse confusion context. *See id.* at 475, 481 (treating these factors in the same way for reverse confusion as they would have been treated for direct confusion).

2. Similarity of the Marks

Generally speaking, the similarity of the marks themselves is necessarily analyzed in the same way in direct and reverse confusion claims; the court looks to sight, sound, and meaning, and compares whether these elements combine to create a general commercial impression that is the same for the two marks. *See, e.g., Fisons*, 30 F.3d at 478–79 (analyzing the commercial impression of the marks in light of direct confusion principles). Therefore, a district court would not need to examine these in a different manner than it would in a direct confusion claim.

On the other hand, the direct confusion claim in this case was rejected by the District Court in considerable measure because the court felt that the Victoria's Secret housemark, coupled with the disclaimer, alleviated any confusion that might otherwise result. *See A & H IV*, 57 F. Supp. 2d at 168–69. Yet in the reverse confusion context, the presence of housemarks or disclaimers must obviously be treated differently than in the direct confusion context. It is the essence of the reverse confusion claim that, when consumers come across the Miraclesuit in the stream of commerce, they will confuse it with The Miracle Bra and think that it is a Victoria's Secret product. Therefore, the weight of a disclaimer on the Victoria's Secret product is necessarily lessened. Because A & H puts no disclaimer on its product to distinguish it from The Miracle Bra, the consumer considering a purchase of the Miraclesuit will not have the same handy reminder that Miraclesuit is not associated with The Miracle Bra or Victoria's Secret. This is not to say that such a disclaimer may not, in fact, mitigate confusion in some cases; if consumers are faced with the disclaimer every time they flip through the Victoria's Secret catalogue, they are less likely to forget that Miraclesuit is unrelated to The Miracle Bra swimwear.

As to the presence of the housemark on the Victoria's Secret product, not only is there the possibility that consumers will fail to remember the mark when encountering A & H's swimwear, but there is also the possibility that the mark will aggravate, rather than mitigate, reverse confusion, by reinforcing the association of the word "miracle" exclusively with Victoria's Secret. *See, e.g., Sands, Taylor & Wood Co. v. Quaker Oats Co.*, 978 F.2d 947, 960 (7th Cir. 1992). Of course, we do not suggest that this actually occurred in this particular case; after all, the District Court observed that A & H typically includes its own housemark on Miraclesuits, *see A & H IV*, 57 F. Supp. 2d at 160, but, because the court only conducted a likelihood of confusion analysis for the direct confusion claim, it only briefly addressed the significance of the A & H housemark, *see id.* at 168 n.17.

Clearly, the proper significance to be accorded these facts is a matter best suited for the determination of the trial court. Instead, we merely highlight the questions raised by the use of the housemarks and disclaimers in order to emphasize that a district court must separately examine the similarity factor to determine whether there are any aspects of the analysis that should be different for a reverse confusion claim, and, if so, alter its examination accordingly.

3. Strength of the Marks

An important difference between reverse and direct confusion manifests in the analysis of the strength of the marks. As we explained *supra*, this factor requires consideration both of the mark's commercial and conceptual strength. For ease of understanding, we will explain the appropriate treatment of commercial strength first, and the treatment of conceptual strength second.

a.   Commercial Strength

It has been observed that a consumer first encountering a mark with one set of goods is likely to continue to associate the mark with those goods, and whether any subsequent confusion is "direct" or "reverse" will depend on whether the consumer's first experience was with the junior or the senior user of the mark. *See Banff, Ltd. v. Federated Dep't Stores, Inc.*, 841 F.2d 486, 490 (2d Cir. 1988) (acknowledging such a possibility); Long & Marks, *supra*, at 5. The greater the commercial disparity between the manufacturers, the more likely it is that a consumer's first experience with a mark will be with one particular manufacturer. That is, if one manufacturer—junior or senior—expends tremendous sums in advertising while the other does not, consumers will be more likely to encounter the heavily advertised mark first. Where the greater advertising originates from the senior user, we are more likely to see a case of direct confusion; if the greater advertising originates from the junior user, reverse confusion is more likely. . . .

Logically, then, in a direct confusion claim, a plaintiff with a commercially strong mark is more likely to prevail than a plaintiff with a commercially weak mark. Conversely, in a reverse confusion claim, a plaintiff with a commercially weak mark is more likely to prevail than a plaintiff with a stronger mark, and this is particularly true when the plaintiff's weaker mark is pitted against a defendant with a far stronger mark. McCarthy has written that "the relatively large advertising and promotion of the junior user . . . is the hallmark of a reverse confusion case." 3 McCarthy, *supra*, § 23:10, at 23–37. "The lack of commercial strength of the smaller senior user's mark is to be given less weight in the analysis because it is the strength of the larger, junior user's mark which results in reverse confusion." *Commerce Nat'l Ins. Servs., Inc. v. Commerce Ins. Agency, Inc.*, 214 F.3d 432, 444 (3d Cir. 2000). As we explained in *Fisons,* "the evidence of commercial strength is different from what we expect in a case of forward confusion, where the junior user tries to palm off his goods as those of the senior user." 30 F.3d at 479.

Therefore, in a reverse confusion claim, a court should analyze the "commercial strength" factor in terms of (1) the commercial strength of the junior user as compared to the senior user; and (2) any advertising or marketing campaign by the junior user that has resulted in a saturation in the public awareness of the junior user's mark. *See Fisons*, 30 F.3d at 474, 479.

b.   Distinctiveness or Conceptual Strength

In *Fisons* we remanded the case for the district court to "reevaluate[ ] . . . distinctiveness as well as [the mark's] commercial strength" for the reverse confusion claim. *Fisons*, 30 F.3d at 479. Although we explained that the evaluation of commercial strength would have to be altered for reverse confusion claims, we did not discuss how distinctiveness, or conceptual strength, should be re-weighed in light of our adoption of the reverse confusion doctrine. Nor did we clarify this aspect of our jurisprudence in *Commerce National Insurance Services, Inc. v. Commerce Insurance Agency, Inc.*, 214 F.3d 432 (3d Cir. 2000), where we referred to the different test for "commercial strength," in a reverse confusion context, without reference to "conceptual strength."

As stated above, in the paradigmatic reverse confusion case, the senior user has a commercially weak mark when compared with the junior user's commercially strong mark. When it comes to conceptual strength, however, we believe that, just as in direct confusion cases, a strong mark should weigh in favor of a senior user. Our decision is supported by the fact that those courts that have clearly distinguished conceptual from commercial strength in the reverse confusion context have weighed a conceptually strong mark in the senior user's favor, in the same manner as they would in direct confusion cases. *See, e.g., Worthington Foods, Inc. v. Kellogg Co.*, 732 F. Supp. 1417, 1456 (S.D. Ohio 1990). . . .

4.   The Intent of the Defendant

In the direct confusion context, the intent of the defendant is relevant to the extent that it bears on the likelihood of confusion analysis. As we have said:

> In the likelihood of confusion inquiry . . . we do not focus on a defendant's bare intent to adopt a mark . . . substantially identical to a plaintiff's mark . . . , since there is little basis in fact or logic for supposing from a defendant's intent to copy without more that the defendant's actions will in fact result in confusion. Thus, what we have held is that a defendant's intent to confuse or deceive consumers as to the product's source may be highly probative of likelihood of confusion.

Versa Prods. Co., Inc. v. Bifold Co. (Mfg.) Ltd., 50 F.3d 189, 205 (3d Cir. 1995) (emphasis omitted).

When reverse, rather than direct, confusion is alleged, "intent to confuse" is unlikely to be present. *Cf. Fisons*, 30 F.3d at 480. However, though perhaps unusual, should an intent to confuse exist, it would be relevant to the likelihood of confusion analysis in the same manner as it would for a direct confusion claim. For instance, in *Commerce National Insurance Services, Inc. v. Commerce Insurance Agency, Inc.*, 214 F.3d 432 (3d Cir. 2000), we were confronted with a situation in which the litigants had used very similar marks in noncompetitive industries for a number of years, each fully aware of the other and with no incidents of actual confusion. Eventually, however, the larger company expanded into the smaller company's line of business, deliberately choosing to promote its services under an almost identical mark. In holding that the smaller company could maintain its claim against the larger for reverse confusion, we specifically highlighted the possibility that the larger company had adopted the mark with the deliberate intent of pushing its rival out of the market, and that it was this sort of usurpation of business identity that the reverse confusion doctrine was designed to prevent. *See id.* at 445.

As we have noted in our two prior cases on this issue, the defendant's intent may be discovered through such inquiries as whether the defendant was aware of the senior user's mark when it adopted its own mark, and whether the defendant considered that its adoption of the mark might result in confusion. *See id.* at 444; *Fisons*, 30 F.3d at 480. If such an intent to confuse does, in fact, exist in a reverse confusion case, it should weigh against the defendant in the same manner as it would in a direct confusion case. . . .

Although we recognize that our opinion in *Fisons* perhaps implied that mere carelessness, as opposed to deliberate intent to confuse, would weigh in a plaintiff's favor in a reverse confusion case, we are reluctant to adopt such an interpretation, as it would be manifestly out of step with our prior holdings regarding the relevance of "intent" in trademark infringement claims. . . . Ultimately, all of the *Lapp* factors are meant only to determine whether confusion is likely; mere carelessness, like deliberate copying, does not shed any light on this inquiry. Further, to the extent that the intent inquiry in the likelihood of confusion analysis carries with it the attribution of fault, there is no reason to ascribe higher penalties to a lower degree of fault because a particular case involves reverse, rather than direct, confusion. Finally, in light of the policy concerns implicated by the reverse confusion doctrine, it would be troubling indeed to hold that a lesser degree of culpability would weigh in the plaintiff's favor for a reverse confusion claim than it would for a direct confusion claim.

5.   Factors Relating to Actual Confusion

As a matter of intuition, one would expect that in a reverse confusion claim, evidence of actual confusion would be as important as in a direct confusion claim, though the nature of the confusion that would be probative would be quite different. *See Lang v. Retirement Living Publ'g Co.*, 949 F.2d 576, 583 (2d Cir. 1991) (holding that evidence of "actual confusion" in which the public thought the senior user was the origin of the junior user's products was irrelevant for a reverse confusion claim). As applied to this case, for example, evidence that consumers thought that The Miracle Bra was an A & H product would be probative on a direct confusion claim, but not on a reverse confusion claim. Conversely, evidence that consumers thought that Miraclesuit was a Victoria's Secret product would support a reverse confusion claim, but not a direct confusion claim. This was apparently the District Court's intuition;

although it declined to consider A & H's reverse confusion claim, it did observe that most of the evidence A & H had put forth with regard to "actual confusion" related to direct, rather than reverse, confusion. *See A & H IV*, 57 F. Supp. 2d at 178 n.32.

However, marshalling evidence of actual confusion is often difficult. *See, e.g., Liquid Glass Enters., Inc. v. Dr. Ing. h.c.F. Porsche AG*, 8 F. Supp. 2d 398, 403 (D.N.J. 1998). In our view, if we were to create a rigid division between "direct" and "reverse" confusion evidence, we would run the risk of denying recovery to meritorious plaintiffs. For example, if a plaintiff alleged theories of both direct and reverse confusion and was able to prove a few instances of "actual" confusion in each direction, we might conclude that the plaintiff did not have enough evidence of either type to succeed on either of its claims, even though, taken together, all of the evidence of actual confusion would be probative of a real problem. As we explained in Part V.B.3, *supra*, the manifestation of consumer confusion as "direct" or "reverse" may merely be a function of the context in which the consumer first encountered the mark. Isolated instances of "direct" confusion may occur in a reverse confusion case, and vice-versa. See Long & Marks, *supra*, at 5. Though we might expect that, in most instances, the consumer's first encounter will be with the mark that has greater commercial strength, this will not invariably be the case.

Given the problems litigants typically encounter in locating evidence of actual confusion, then, we decline to create a strict bar to the use of "direct" confusion evidence in a "reverse" confusion case, or vice versa. However, evidence working in the same direction as the claim is preferred, and "misfitting" evidence must be treated carefully, for large amounts of one type of confusion in a claim for a different type may in fact work against the plaintiff. For instance, the existence of reverse confusion might disprove a plaintiff's claim that its descriptive mark has secondary meaning, thus resulting in no recovery at all. *See Jefferson Home Furniture Co., Inc. v. Jefferson Furniture Co., Inc.*, 349 So. 2d 5, 8 (Ala. 1977).

It follows that the other factor relating to actual confusion, *Lapp* factor (4), examining the time the mark has been used without evidence of actual confusion, should be approached similarly.

6. Other Relevant Facts

The final factor of the *Lapp* test directs courts to look at "other facts suggesting that the consuming public might expect the prior owner to manufacture both products, or expect the prior owner to manufacture a product in the defendant's market, or expect that the prior owner is likely to expand into the defendant's market." This factor is necessarily transformed in the reverse confusion context to an examination of other facts suggesting that the consuming public might expect the larger, more powerful company to manufacture both products, or expect the larger company to manufacture a product in the plaintiff's market, or expect that the larger company is likely to expand into the plaintiff's market. *See Fisons*, 30 F.3d at 480 (directing the district court to examine facts suggesting that the public might think that the junior user would expand into the senior user's market).

7.   Summary of the Test for Reverse Confusion

In sum, in the typical case in which there is a claim of reverse confusion, a court should examine the following factors as aids in its determination whether or not there is a likelihood of such confusion:

(1) the degree of similarity between the owner's mark and the alleged infringing mark;

(2) the strength of the two marks, weighing both a commercially strong junior user's mark and a conceptually strong senior user's mark in the senior user's favor;

(3) the price of the goods and other factors indicative of the care and attention expected of consumers when making a purchase;

(4) the length of time the defendant has used the mark without evidence of actual confusion arising;

(5) the intent of the defendant in adopting the mark;

(6) the evidence of actual confusion;

(7) whether the goods, competing or not competing, are marketed through the same channels of trade and advertised through the same media;

(8) the extent to which the targets of the parties' sales efforts are the same;

(9) the relationship of the goods in the minds of consumers, whether because of the near-identity of the products, the similarity of function, or other factors;

(10) other facts suggesting that the consuming public might expect the larger, more powerful company to manufacture both products, or expect the larger company to manufacture a product in the plaintiff's market, or expect that the larger company is likely to expand into the plaintiff's market.

As with the test for direct confusion, no one factor is dispositive, and in individual cases, particular factors may not be probative on the issue of likelihood of confusion. "The weight given to each factor in the overall picture, as well as its weighing for plaintiff or defendant, must be done on an individual fact-specific basis." *Fisons*, 30 F.3d at 476 n.11.

C. The District Court's Opinion

The District Court approached the reverse confusion claim in a different manner from that described in the foregoing section. It held that before engaging the reverse confusion factors, A & H needed to demonstrate, as a threshold matter, that Victoria's Secret "used their economic power to overwhelm the market with advertising" of their product. *A & H IV*, 57 F. Supp. 2d at 178. The opinion therefore focused only on a comparison between the commercial strengths of the Miraclesuit and The Miracle Bra, i.e., only on one aspect of the "mark strength" inquiry. The District Court found that Victoria's Secret had saturated the market with $13 million in The Miracle Bra advertising, and that a "meaningful portion" of the advertising went towards promoting The Miracle Bra swimwear. It then compared Victoria's Secret's effort to A & H's effort to promote Miraclesuit swimwear; A & H spent over $1.2 million on advertising, and received $1.5 million in free publicity.

The court noted that A & H did not dispute—even heralded—the fact that its campaign was widely successful. Therefore, it found that "plaintiffs' [sic] are not entirely without market power in the swimwear industry" and that "in light of Plaintiffs' advertising campaign, we find that, in comparison, Defendants did not saturate the marketplace with its advertising to promote The Miracle Bra swimwear." *Id.* at 177. Consequently, the District Court concluded that the doctrine of reverse confusion was not even implicated, and "declined to examine whether a likelihood of reverse confusion exists." *Id.* at 178.

In *A & H III*, we began our discussion of reverse confusion with an explanation of the phenomenon: "Reverse confusion occurs when a larger more powerful company uses the trademark of a smaller, less powerful senior owner and thereby causes likely confusion as to the source of the senior user's goods or services." 166 F.3d at 207 (*quoting Fisons*, 30 F.3d at 474.). In *Fisons*, we stated that it would be necessary to recognize the reverse confusion doctrine to provide protection to "smaller, senior users" against "larger, more powerful companies." 30 F.3d at 475. While these are accurate statements about the doctrine of reverse confusion, the District Court appears to have interpreted them as establishing a separate, threshold step that must be examined prior to engaging the *Lapp* test, and, finding the threshold not met, concluded that A & H's power to advertise extensively precluded it from bringing a reverse confusion claim. The District Court was correct to note that commercial disparity is, in fact, a factor to consider (factor (2), to be specific); however, it erred in applying a threshold commercial disparity requirement, in effect making this sole factor determinative and treating the reverse confusion inquiry as requiring a two-step process.

The quoted statements are understandably confusing, and the method of applying the doctrine of reverse confusion is admittedly still developing. However, a close examination of *Fisons*, from which the quotes hail, reveals that they are nothing more than descriptions of the phenomenon of reverse confusion, and do not establish an initial inquiry that a court needs to make in order to apply the reverse confusion analysis. In *Fisons* we held that the *Lapp* factors constitute the method courts should use in order to determine if a likelihood of reverse confusion exists. We made no mention of a threshold requirement, nor did we direct the District Court, on remand, to use one.

The District Court further explained its choice not to apply the reverse confusion factors by reference to the fact that several reverse confusion cases involve enormous junior companies pitted against tiny senior companies; it cited these cases and concluded that the same degree of economic disparity was non-existent in this case. *See A & H IV*, 57 F. Supp. 2d at 178. The difficulty with this conclusion is that in *Fisons* itself, in which we found a viable reverse confusion claim, Fisons had fully 25% of the peat moss market, greater than A & H's 10% of the swimwear market. This suggests that a company need not be all that weak within its market in order to bring a viable reverse confusion claim. *See Fisons*, 30 F.3d at 479; *see also Fuji Photo Film v. Shinohara Shoji Kabushiki Kaisha*, 754 F.2d 591 (5th Cir. 1985) (finding a viable reverse confusion claim where the plaintiff had spent millions of dollars). In fact, in stating that "in reverse confusion, the junior user is typically a wealthier, more powerful company who can overwhelm the market with advertising," 30 F.3d at 479 (emphasis added), we implied that there might be the rare case in which reverse confusion exists where the junior company overwhelms the senior user with advertisements although it is not wealthier and more powerful.

In short, we hold that, although economic disparity between the companies and the marks is an important consideration in the evaluation of the marks' commercial strength, the District Court legally erred in fashioning a threshold "economic disparity" requirement before a reverse confusion claim will even be considered. Because the District Court failed to undertake the Lapp analysis with respect to A & H's reverse confusion claim, we must vacate the judgment with respect to that claim and remand to the District Court for a redetermination of those factors that receive different treatment under direct and reverse confusion theories, and for a reweighing of all of the factors once those redeterminations have been made. . . .

VI. Conclusion

We will affirm the District Court's judgment for Victoria's Secret on the direct confusion claim. However, we will vacate the judgment with respect to the reverse confusion claim, and remand to the District Court for further proceedings consistent with this opinion. The District Court may wish to hear and consider additional evidence from the parties on reverse confusion. The parties shall bear their own costs.

NOTES FOR DISCUSSION

1. *Reverse Confusion and Consumer Welfare.* What is the harm of reverse confusion? Is it harm to consumers? Or is it harm to the senior, but less well known user? Are consumers better or worse off as a result of Victoria Secret's entry into the swimwear market? Does the court's decision in this case make that entry more expensive? If so, does it make such entry in similar circumstances less likely in the future? Is that good for consumers? Did Victoria Secret have a legitimate reason for seeking to enter the swimwear market with its existing "Miracle Bra" trademark? Would consumers be better off if Victoria Secret could enter the swimwear market, but not with its "Miracle Bra" trademark?

2. *Reverse Confusion: Easier to Prove?* Is reverse confusion easier or harder to prove than traditional forward confusion? Which type of confusion is more likely to harm consumers? If reverse confusion is less harmful to consumers, should we make it easier to establish?

C. PARODY: A SPECIAL CASE?

ANHEUSER-BUSCH, INC. v. L & L WINGS, INC.
962 F.2d 316 (4th Cir. 1992)

WILKINSON, C.J.

In this case, plaintiff Anheuser-Busch sued defendants for selling souvenir T-shirts that plaintiff claimed infringed its Budweiser beer trademarks. The jury returned a verdict in favor of defendants, finding that defendants' T-shirt design did not create a likelihood of consumer confusion, but the district judge granted plaintiff's motion for judgment notwithstanding the verdict. We reverse. The record reveals sufficient differences between the T-shirt design and plaintiff's trademarks to permit the jury to conclude that consumer confusion was unlikely. Accordingly, we think the district judge improperly substituted his judgment as to likelihood of confusion for that of the jury, and we remand with instructions to reinstate the jury verdict in favor of defendants.

I.

In 1987, Michael Berard was a student at the University of North Carolina at Chapel Hill. In order to supplement his income, Berard decided to go into the business of designing and selling T-shirts. During 1987, Berard devised a T-shirt design that he planned to sell as a souvenir of Myrtle Beach. That design depicted a beer can with a red, white and blue label. The words on the can did not refer to beer, however, but only to Myrtle Beach.

In 1988, Berard incorporated Venture Marketing, Inc., (Venture) in order to manufacture and wholesale his T-shirts. Venture marketed the Myrtle Beach T-shirts through L & L Wings, Inc., (Wings) which operates a number of retail beach stores at Myrtle Beach, South Carolina and at other beaches. Wings purchased over 20,000 shirts from Venture.

In 1989 Anheuser-Busch, Inc., brought this trademark infringement action against Venture and Wings. Anheuser-Busch alleged that the T-shirt design was confusingly similar to the Budweiser beer label, a registered trademark which Anheuser-Busch had used on its own line of T-shirts and other apparel. Anheuser-Busch complained that the Myrtle Beach T-shirt infringed its trademarks because consumers were likely to believe the T-shirt was sold or sponsored by Anheuser-Busch. The case was tried before a jury for three days, and the jury returned a verdict in favor of the defendants. Anheuser-Busch filed a motion for j.n.o.v. or, in the alternative, for a new trial. After briefing and argument, the district judge granted the j.n.o.v. motion, holding that the evidence before the jury permitted only one reasonable conclusion: that the T-shirt created a likelihood of confusion and thus infringed Anheuser-Busch's trademarks. Accordingly, the district court entered judgment on the question of liability in favor of Anheuser-Busch, and took the motion for a new trial under advisement pending appeal. Venture and Wings then brought this appeal.

II.

Under the Lanham Act, a registered trademark holder has a right to prevent another's use of a trademark that is "likely to cause confusion, or to cause mistake, or to deceive." 15 U.S.C. § 1114(1)(a). *See Shell Oil Co. v. Commercial Petroleum, Inc.*, 928 F.2d 104, 108 (4th Cir. 1991). In other words, an unauthorized use of a trademark infringes the trademark holder's rights if it is likely to confuse an "ordinary consumer" as to the source or sponsorship of the goods. *Ford Motor Co. v. Summit Motor Products, Inc.*, 930 F.2d 277, 293 (3d Cir. 1991); 2 J. McCarthy, *Trademarks and Unfair Competition* § 23:28 (1984). This pivotal trademark issue is particularly amenable to resolution by a jury for two reasons. First, the jury, which represents a cross-section of consumers, is well-suited to evaluating whether an "ordinary consumer" would likely be confused. Second, the likelihood of consumer confusion is an "inherently factual" issue that depends on the unique facts and circumstances of each case. *Levi Strauss & Co. v. Blue Bell, Inc.*, 778 F.2d 1352, 1356 n.5 (9th Cir. 1985). Likelihood of confusion is "frequently a fairly disputed issue of fact on which reasonable minds may differ," *Warner Bros., Inc. v. American Broadcasting Cos.*, 720 F.2d 231, 246 (2d Cir. 1983), and has long been recognized to be "a matter of varying human reactions to situations incapable of exact appraisement." *Colburn v. Puritan Mills, Inc.*, 108 F.2d 377, 378 (7th Cir. 1939).

A district judge may overturn a jury verdict on a motion for j.n.o.v. only if "there is no legally sufficient evidentiary basis for a reasonable jury to have found for [the prevailing] party." Fed. R. Civ. P. 50(a)(1). In making this determination, the judge is not to weigh the evidence or appraise the credibility of witnesses, but must view the evidence in the light most favorable to the non-moving party and draw legitimate inferences in its favor. *Mays v. Pioneer Lumber Corp.*, 502 F.2d 106, 107 (4th Cir. 1974). Our review of the district court's action is de novo. Here we believe the district judge improperly assumed the jury's role of determining whether an ordinary consumer would likely be confused by the T-shirt, and we reverse the court's entry of j.n.o.v.

The jury was entitled to conclude that consumer confusion was unlikely based on a number of conspicuous differences between the T-shirt design and the Budweiser label. First, the T-shirt design makes no reference of any sort to Anheuser-Busch or Budweiser. By contrast, the Budweiser label displays a number of prominent indications of the product's source or sponsor: the name "Budweiser" flanked on either side by the word "genuine"; the geographic designation "Anheuser-Busch, Inc., St. Louis, Mo."; the letters "AB" for Anheuser-Busch; and the Anheuser-Busch trademark depicting an eagle in the middle of the letter "A." With respect to all of these, the T-shirt design either omits them entirely or replaces them with references to the beach. The T-shirt design replaces the Budweiser name with the words "Myrtle Beach"; substitutes the words "Myrtle Beach, S.C." for "Anheuser-Busch, Inc., St. Louis, Mo."; and replaces the letters "AB" with "SC." In addition, the T-shirt eliminates the Anheuser-Busch trademark "A" and omits the word "genuine."

Second, the T-shirt replaces the Budweiser label's descriptions of the beer with analogous language descriptive of the beach. The Budweiser label reads as follows:

> This is the famous Budweiser beer. We know of no brand produced by any other brewer which costs so much to brew and age. Our exclusive Beechwood Aging produces a taste, a smoothness, and a drinkability you will find in no other beer at any price.

On the Venture Marketing T-shirt design, these sentences are replaced with a description of the beach:

> This is the famous beach of Myrtle Beach, S.C. We know of no other resort in any state which lays claim to such a rich history. The unspoiled beaches, natural beauty, and southern

hospitality compose a mixture you will find on no other beach in any state.

Similarly, the descriptive words at the bottom of the Budweiser label—announcing that the beer is "Brewed by our original process from the Choicest Hops, Rice and Best Barley Malt"—are replaced in the T-shirt design with words proclaiming that "Myrtle Beach contains the Choicest Surf, Sun, and Sand."

Third, the T-shirt design incorporates its own beach slogans in place of the Budweiser beer slogans. The Budweiser label includes the slogan "King of Beers" under the Budweiser name. On the T-shirt, this is replaced with the words "King of Beaches." In addition, the T-shirt mimics another Budweiser slogan, "This Bud's for You," with its own slogan, "This Beach is for You."

Together, we think these differences are sufficient at least to create a reasonable jury question on the issue of likelihood of confusion. The jury had the opportunity to visually examine the T-shirt and to compare it with the Anheuser-Busch trademarks. We cannot say that the jury's conclusion was the only one it could have reached, but neither are we able to say that its verdict was unreasonable. In this regard, our dissenting brother faithfully presents Anheuser-Busch's side of the jury argument. To believe that the jury should have heard this argument is not to say that the jury was required to accept it.

III.

Anheuser-Busch suggests two reasons why we should disregard the jury verdict in this case. First, it contends that a judgment in its favor was compelled because the T-shirt incorporated a beer label design that intentionally imitated the non-verbal portion of the Budweiser label. At trial, Michael Berard admitted that he had patterned the T-shirt's beer label after the basic Budweiser format, and it is undisputed that he was successful in that endeavor. In Anheuser-Busch's view, this similarity of format by itself infringes its registered trademark in the Budweiser beer label design.

We disagree. Anheuser-Busch would have us isolate the non-verbal portion of the T-shirt design, while ignoring the substantial verbal differences that set it apart from the Budweiser label. Under the Lanham Act, however, a holder of a registered trademark is entitled to protection only from uses of the mark that create a likelihood of consumer confusion. 15 U.S.C. § 1114(1)(a). The statutory standard for infringement does not depend on how closely a fragment of a given use duplicates the trademark, but on whether the use in its entirety creates a likelihood of confusion. In making that determination, we must examine the allegedly infringing use in the context in which it is seen by the ordinary consumer; we must look not only at the portion of the T-shirt that duplicates the

Budweiser label design, but at the T-shirt as a whole as sold in the marketplace. *See Homeowners Group, Inc. v. Home Marketing Specialists, Inc.*, 931 F.2d 1100, 1109 (6th Cir. 1991); *Franklin Mint Corp. v. Master Mfg. Co.*, 667 F.2d 1005, 1007 (C.C.P.A. 1981). The jury examined the T-shirt as a whole and reasonably concluded that consumer confusion was unlikely.

Second, Anheuser-Busch argues that the jury verdict must be overturned because there was insufficient evidence to support it under the factors announced in *Pizzeria Uno Corp. v. Temple*, 747 F.2d 1522, 1527 (4th Cir. 1984). In that case, this court identified seven factors that have been considered in determining whether there is a likelihood of confusion: the strength of the plaintiff's mark, the degree of similarity between the two marks, the similarity of the goods they identify, the similarity of the facilities used in the businesses, the similarity of the advertising, the defendant's intent, and the presence of actual confusion. *Id.* The district judge evaluated the evidence presented to the jury under these seven factors, and found that although there was no evidence of actual confusion, other factors favored the plaintiff: plaintiff's trademarks were unquestionably strong, the T-shirt design was similar to the Budweiser label, the goods the marks identify were identical, and the facilities and advertising used by the parties were similar.

We believe, however, that the district judge misconstrued the nature of the *Pizzeria Uno* factors in overturning the jury's verdict. The "factors" announced in *Pizzeria Uno* are not meant to be a "rigid formula" for infringement. *Murphy v. Provident Mut. Life Ins. Co.*, 923 F.2d 923, 928 (2d Cir. 1990). *See also Lois Sportswear, U.S.A., Inc. v. Levi Strauss & Co.*, 799 F.2d 867, 872 (2d Cir. 1986). Rather, the *Pizzeria Uno* factors are only a guide—a catalog of various considerations that may be relevant in determining the ultimate statutory question of likelihood of confusion. As this circuit recognized in *Pizzeria Uno*, not all of the factors are of equal importance, nor are they always relevant in any given case. 747 F.2d at 1527.

In this case, we think the jury was entitled to give decisive weight to the predominant differences between the T-shirt design and the Budweiser label. Where there is no evidence of actual confusion and a jury reasonably concludes that there is no likelihood of confusion because of the differences between the marks, consideration of the remaining *Pizzeria Uno* factors is unnecessary. We recognize, of course, that the likelihood of consumer confusion may be affected not only by the intrinsic similarity of two trademarks, but also by certain extrinsic factors such as the strength of the plaintiff's mark and the similarity of the products, sales outlets, and advertising. At the same time, however, these extrinsic factors are insufficient by themselves to establish likelihood of confusion absent some threshold of intrinsic similarity between the plaintiff's trademark and the defendant's alleged infringement. *Sun-Fun Products, Inc. v. Suntan Research & Development, Inc.*, 656 F.2d 186, 189 (5th Cir. 1981). The Lanham Act was obviously not intended to create a barrier to competition by preventing the use of distinguishable trademarks to market similar goods through identical channels. *See Anti-Monopoly, Inc. v. General Mills Fun Group*, 611 F.2d 296, 300–01 (9th Cir. 1979) (trademarks are designed to protect consumers from being misled, not to "further or perpetuate product monopolies"). Indeed, the marketing of commodities would be impaired if these external factors were assigned controlling weight in cases where the subject trademarks are readily distinguishable. In this case, the extrinsic factors—including the fact that the T-shirt competed with Anheuser-Busch's own product line—were appropriate for the jury to consider. We think, however, that there were sufficient intrinsic differences between the T-shirt and the Anheuser-Busch trademarks to permit a reasonable jury to find that consumer confusion was unlikely irrespective of the evidence under those extrinsic considerations.

In short, the most important factor in this particular case was whether plaintiff's mark and defendant's T-shirt design looked alike in the eyes of the ordinary consumer. We think the jury was uniquely positioned to make the critical determination in that regard.

IV.

At trial, Michael Berard testified that his intent in creating the T-shirt design was to parody the Budweiser beer label. The crux of his defense was that the T-shirt—as parody—was especially unlikely to create confusion in the minds of ordinary consumers. We think that a reasonable jury could find that the T-shirt was readily recognizable as parody, and that such a finding provides additional support for the jury's verdict.

Anheuser-Busch, however, insists that appellants' T-shirt design has no element of parody because its purpose was to make money and not to make any commentary about Budweiser beer. We disagree. The T-shirt design fits a conventional definition of trademark parody—it is "a simple form of entertainment conveyed by juxtaposing the irreverent representation of the trademark with the idealized image created by the mark's owner." *L.L. Bean, Inc. v. Drake Publishers, Inc.*, 811 F.2d 26, 34 (1st Cir. 1987). The T-shirt design mimics the characteristic turns of phrase on the Budweiser label by applying them to the beach: the "taste," "smoothness," and "drinkability" found "in no other beer at any price" become the"unspoiled beaches, natural beauty, and southern hospitality" composing a "mixture you will find on no other beach in any state"; the beer's ingredients—the "Choicest Hops, Rice and Best Barley Malt"—are imitated by the "Choicest Surf, Sun, and Sand"; "King of Beers" is changed to "King of Beaches"; and "This Bud's For You" is mimicked by

"This Beach is For You." Berard testified that this "irreverent representation" was calculated to parody or satirize the Budweiser label, and we think the jury was entitled to agree that it had that effect.

The district court unfortunately ignored the issue of parody in evaluating the sufficiency of the evidence to support the jury's verdict. In so doing, the judge failed to recognize that the multi-factored inquiry under *Pizzeria Uno* "is at best awkward in the context of parody." *Cliffs Notes*, 886 F.2d at 495 n.3. Outside the context of parody, for example, intentional similarities between trademarks may lead to a presumption of a likelihood of confusion. *Osem Food Industries Ltd. v. Sherwood Foods, Inc.*, 917 F.2d 161, 164–65 (4th Cir. 1990). In cases of parody, however, courts have concluded that intentional similarity is unavoidable: "The keystone of parody is imitation. It is hard to imagine, for example, a successful parody of Time magazine that did not reproduce Time's trademarked red border." *Cliffs Notes*, 886 F.2d at 494. *See also Jordache Enterprises, Inc. v. Hogg Wyld, Ltd.*, 828 F.2d 1482, 1485 (10th Cir. 1987).

Courts have further recognized that although parody necessarily evokes the original trademark, effective parody also diminishes any risk of consumer confusion. *See Jordache*, 828 F.2d at 1486; *Universal City Studios, Inc. v. Nintendo Co.*, 746 F.2d 112, 116 (2d Cir. 1984). Successful trademark takeoffs dispel consumer confusion by conveying just enough of the original design to allow the consumer to appreciate the point of the parody. *Cliffs Notes*, 886 F.2d at 494. Here the T-shirt necessarily adopts the basic format of the Budweiser label, but we think the similarities merely convey the message that the T-shirt is a parody of the original, and are not indicative of consumer confusion. The substantial differences detailed above would at least permit a jury to conclude that the T-shirt design was nothing more than a commentary on the pleasures of beach life that effectively parodied the Budweiser label but could hardly be confused with it.

Anheuser-Busch would also have us give substantial weight to defendants' intent to draw on the "commercial magnetism" of the Budweiser label. It is true that appellants' primary motive in creating the T-shirt design was to make a profit, but the relevant intent in trademark cases is not merely an intent to profit, which would condemn all commercial parody, but an "intent to confuse the buying public." *Pizzeria Uno*, 747 F.2d at 1535. Ordinarily, an intent to profit from the original is the same thing as an intent to confuse—the infringer benefits only if consumers confuse his trademark with the original. But that equation does not hold in the context of parody. An alleged infringer may intend to benefit from the original trademark without ever intending or causing consumer confusion:

> In one sense, a parody is an attempt "to derive benefit from the reputation" of the owner of the mark, if only because no

parody could be made without the initial mark. The benefit to
the one making the parody, however, arises from the humorous
association, not from public confusion as to the source of the
marks. A parody relies upon a difference from the original mark,
presumably a humorous difference, in order to produce its
desired effect.

Jordache, 828 F.2d at 1486, quoting *Sicilia Di R. Biebow & Co. v. Cox*,
732 F.2d 417, 431 (5th Cir. 1984).

An intent to parody, then, is an intent to benefit from the original
trademark, but such an intent is not necessarily probative of a likelihood
of consumer confusion. We cannot assume that the commercial success of
the Myrtle Beach T-shirt resulted from consumer confusion; consumers
may have been moved to buy the T-shirt by the simple fact that they were
amused by the cleverness of its design.

Throughout this litigation, Anheuser-Busch has invited the court to
place dispositive weight upon factors which are at best proxies for the
ultimate statutory standard—whether the T-shirt is "likely to cause
confusion." 15 U.S.C. § 1114(1)(a). Similarity of format and intent to
profit, however, are not precise equivalents of the dispositive statutory
language. The jury was entitled to find that the statutory standard did
not condemn appellants' humorous takeoff on the Budweiser label. The
purpose of the Lanham Act is to eliminate consumer confusion, not to
banish all attempts at poking fun or eliciting amusement. *Elsmere Music,
Inc. v. National Broadcasting Co.*, 623 F.2d 252, 253 (2d Cir. 1980). The
statute is designed to protect consumers from product misinformation,
not to deprive the commercial world of all humor and levity. In this case,
the ordinary consumers who served as jurors reason ably concluded that
the T-shirt eliminated any risk of confusion, and we refuse to interfere
with that verdict.

V.

Our dissenting brother's standard is so broad that it would banish
virtually all attempts at humorous takeoffs on trademarks as a matter of
law. The dissent would establish a zone of immunity for any trademark
that could lay claim to strength and familiarity—the very marks for
which parody is most likely. Its view is that almost any imitation of
design, no matter how humorous or distinct the accompanying lyrics or
verbiage, will run afoul of the Lanham Act. We think the evident tensions
in the trademark field between commercial piracy and discouragement of
competition, as well as between permissible parody and impermissible
imitation, are often best resolved by a jury on a case-by-case basis. The
balance established by the Lanham Act risks serious disturbance when
courts too readily assume the roles of ordinary consumers and interpose
sweeping pronouncements of law.

In sum, this was a jury verdict that should have been sustained. We thus reverse the district court's entry of j.n.o.v. and instruct it to reinstate the jury verdict.

REVERSED

POWELL, ASSOCIATE JUSTICE, dissenting:

The issue presented in this case is whether defendants' T-shirts infringe federally registered trademarks owned by Anheuser-Busch. A jury found no infringement. But the district court, finding insufficient evidence to support the jury's decision, entered judgment notwithstanding the verdict. The court today reverses, reinstating the jury verdict.

The court rests its decision on three related grounds: (i) the jury's finding of no likelihood of confusion is supported by differences between defendants' T-shirt design and the Budweiser label; (ii) defendants' T-shirt design withstands scrutiny under *Pizzeria Uno Corp. v. Temple*, 747 F.2d 1522 (4th Cir. 1984); and (iii) defendants' parody defense also supports the verdict. I disagree with this assessment of the evidence and in certain respects with the characterization of the law that precedes it.

I

Few can disclaim familiarity with the Budweiser label design. It has been used by Anheuser-Busch as a trademark on beer cans since 1876 and on clothing since 1967. It has been the subject of extensive advertising. And it has been used to market several thousand products, including T-shirts sold in seaside stores. In short, it is, as the district court observed, "one of the strongest marks in this country, indeed in the world."

Not surprisingly, defendants concede that the strength of the trademark, the "paramount" consideration in the seven-factor analysis, *Pizzeria Uno*, 747 F.2d at 1527, favors Anheuser-Busch. Defendants further admit that three other factors support Anheuser-Busch's claim: (a) the similarity of the parties' goods (T-shirts), (b) the similarity of the outlets where such goods are sold (beach-front stores), and (c) the similarity of the parties' advertising.

That leaves a trio of considerations to support the jury verdict in favor of defendants—actual confusion, defendants' intent, and design similarities. I will consider each in turn.

Agreeing with the district court, the court in this case finds no proof of actual confusion between the Budweiser label design and defendants' T-shirt. That is a mistaken view. Anheuser-Busch did present evidence of actual confusion. Michael Kroshinsky, one of defendant Wings' wholesale purchasers, testified that his initial reaction to the T-shirt was that it "was a copy of a Budweiser shirt." Such proof is "substantial evidence" of likely confusion, *AMP Inc. v. Foy*, 540 F.2d 1181, 1186 (4th Cir. 1976), particularly when it is a professional buyer who has been confused. This consideration thus also helps Anheuser-Busch.

There also was evidence of intentional copying. Michael Berard, the founder of Venture Marketing and the designer of defendants' T-shirt, admitted that he intended to copy the Budweiser label design. This evidence creates a presumption of likelihood of confusion. *Osem Food Indus., Ltd. v. Sherwood Foods, Inc.*, 917 F.2d 161, 165 (4th Cir. 1990). The court does not discuss this factor in its application of *Pizzeria Uno*. Instead, in Part IV of the opinion, it suggests that an exception to the presumption should apply when a defendant asserts that he intended to parody a particular trademark. I am not persuaded that such an exception is applicable here. It is true that parody requires a degree of imitation. But the burden of disproving infringement should rest on one who intentionally uses another's trademark-even as parody. If the parody is strong, the burden will be light. If it is not, then a heavy burden is appropriate since the junior user is likely to benefit from its continuing affiliation with the "drawing power," *Mishawaka Rubber & Woolen Mfg. Co. v. S.S. Kresge Co.*, 316 U.S. 203, 205 (1942), of the senior user's mark. In short, I would not jettison this presumption in the parody context, and would find that this consideration favors Anheuser-Busch.

II

The court today relies, as it must, on the final factor—the similarity between the senior user's mark and the junior user's design. It gives "decisive weight" to the "predominant differences" between the T-shirt design and Anheuser-Busch's mark. In emphasizing this consideration, the court extends precedent and ignores the facts of this case.

To be sure, the court is correct in the abstract: that is, design differences can be determinative. "Some threshold of intrinsic similarity" between marks is required before the "extrinsic" factors come into play. But I know of no precedent that allows conclusive weight to be given to this factor when a party has borrowed a distinctive mark, without making any discernible changes to it, and placed that mark on identical products marketed through identical commercial channels.

Even if as a legal matter the *Pizzeria Uno* analysis could be configured in such a manner, the evidentiary foundation for such an analysis is lacking here. In the court's view, what sustains the imitation are the words added to the Budweiser design. These words dispel confusion, the court maintains, in two ways: (i) the words are different from the language ordinarily appearing on a Budweiser beer can (i.e., "Myrtle Beach" is substituted for "Budweiser") and (ii) the words parody the Budweiser slogans and beer can (i.e., "This Beach Is For You" is substituted for "This Bud Is For You"). Neither argument is persuasive.

The court begins its "different words" analysis by emphasizing that defendants' T-shirt design makes "no reference of any sort to Anheuser-Busch or Budweiser." That by itself is of no importance. It is enough that the T-shirt adopts the Budweiser label design. This symbol needs no verbal cue to call Budweiser to mind. The symbol characterizes the name as much as the name does the symbol. It also is a separately registered trademark. For that reason, T-shirts bearing the non-verbal Budweiser label design, and nothing more, would infringe Anheuser-Busch's trademark.

True, defendants did not simply refrain from mentioning Budweiser or Anheuser-Busch by name; they also added language descriptive of the beach. Putting aside consideration of this language as a matter of parody, I suggest that the added words still fail to eliminate the connection to Anheuser-Busch that follows from use of the Budweiser label. First, the subject matter of the substituted words is not foreign to Anheuser-Busch, Budweiser, or even to beer. To the contrary, the "beach" is a familiar theme in Budweiser advertisements. Second, the substituted words do not rid the T-shirt of a Budweiser connection. Neither "Myrtle Beach," which is a location not a company name, nor any of the other words establishes that a corporation other than Anheuser-Busch sponsors the T-shirt. Anheuser-Busch in fact has used its label frequently to endorse non-beer items. Nor does the fine-print reference to "Venture Marketing, Inc." tend to eliminate confusion. Anheuser-Busch requires its licensees' names to appear on their products.

That brings me to the question of parody. Parody is not an affirmative defense to an infringement claim.

> Rather, it is merely a way of phrasing the argument that confusion is unlikely. Because the purpose of trademark law is to protect the public from confusion, it would make no sense to say that a "parody" which is likely to confuse is permitted merely because it is a "parody."

McCarthy, *Trademarks and Unfair Competition*, § 31:38, at 671 (2d ed. 1984).

In this instance, the "parody" does little to prevent consumer confusion as to the sponsor of defendants' T-shirt. It does not ridicule Budweiser or offer social commentary on the evils of alcohol.

Nor could it be deemed "so obvious and heavy handed that a clear distinction was preserved in the viewer's mind between the source of the actual product and the source of the parody." *Mutual of Omaha Ins. Co. v. Novak*, 648 F.Supp. 905, 910 (D. Neb. 1986), *aff'd*, 836 F.2d 397 (8th Cir. 1987), *cert. denied*, 488 U.S. 933 (1988).

All that it does is play on the words of the Budweiser label, adopting a theme (the beach) and a method (humor) that is fully consistent with

Anheuser-Busch's marketing efforts. *See Cliffs Notes*, 886 F.2d at 494 (requiring two marks to send "contradictory" "messages"). Moreover, since the attempted parody does not dissociate defendants' T-shirt from Anheuser-Busch's products, consumers will be just as likely to buy the T-shirt because of its continuing affiliation with Anheuser-Busch as because of its humor. That danger is particularly acute here since Anheuser-Busch and defendants compete in the same market. The parody here thus amounts to nothing more than a "merchandising short-cut," *S.S. Kresge Co.*, 316 U.S. at 205. I conclude that the parody defense falls far short of supporting the verdict. . . .

I agree with the district court that defendants' use of the Budweiser label design in the manner depicted in the Appendix establishes infringement as a matter of law.

I respectfully dissent.

ANHEUSER-BUSCH, INC. V. BALDUCCI PUBS.

28 F.3d 769 (8th Cir. 1994)

GIBSON, C.J.

Anheuser-Busch, Inc., appeals from the judgment of the district court dismissing its federal and state trademark infringement, trademark dilution, and unfair competition claims against Balducci Publications and its publishers, Richard and Kathleen Balducci, for the use of registered Anheuser-Busch trademarks in a fictitious advertisement for "Michelob Oily." *See* 15 U.S.C. §§ 1114(1), 1125(a) (1988); Mo. Rev. Stat. §§ 417.056, 417.061 (1986). We have carefully reviewed the record before us, and we reverse.

Anheuser-Busch operates a brewery in St. Louis. Its products include the Michelob family of beers: Michelob, Michelob Dry, Michelob Light and Michelob Classic Dark. For use in its marketing of these products, Anheuser-Busch owns several federally-registered trademarks: (1) Michelob; (2) Michelob Dry; (3) A & Eagle Design; (4) Bottle and Label Configuration; (5) Bottle Configuration; (6) Vertical Stripe Design; (7) the phrase "ONE TASTE AND YOU'LL DRINK IT DRY;" and (8) Vertical Stripe and A & Eagle Design. Of these, (1) and (3) are also registered Missouri trademarks.

Balducci Publications is a publishing business owned by Richard and Kathleen Balducci, also defendants in this case. Balducci Publications has published Snicker, a humor magazine, since April 1987. The back cover of issue 5–1/2, published in April 1989, contains a mock advertisement for the fictitious product "Michelob Oily." A reduced copy of the advertisement is attached as Appendix A. The advertisement states in bold type, "ONE TASTE AND YOU'LL DRINK IT OILY" immediately above "MICHELOB OILY (R)." The accompanying graphics include a partially-obscured can of Michelob Dry pouring oil onto a fish, an oil-soaked rendition of the A & Eagle design (with the eagle exclaiming "Yuck!") below a Shell Oil symbol, and various "Michelob Oily" products bearing a striking resemblance to appellants' Michelob family. This resemblance was quite intentional, as evidenced by the admitted use of actual Anheuser-Busch "clip-art" in replicating several of the protected trademarks. In smaller text the ad opines, "At the rate it's being dumped into our oceans, lakes and rivers, you'll drink it oily sooner or later, anyway." Finally, the following disclaimer is found in extremely small text running vertically along the right side of the page: "Snicker Magazine Editorial by Rich Balducci. Art by Eugene Ruble. Thank goodness someone still cares about quality (of life)." A full-size reproduction of this part of the ad is contained in Appendix B.

Balducci continues to sell back issues of Snicker—including Issue 5–1/2. Advertising for back issues of the magazine has included the words "Michelob Oily" and a blue ribbon design associated with Anheuser-Busch.

Mr. Balducci stated at trial that he used the parody to comment on: (1) the effects of environmental pollution, including a specific reference to the then-recent Shell oil spill in the Gasconade River—a source of Anheuser-Busch's water supply; (2) Anheuser-Busch's subsequent decision to temporarily close its St. Louis brewery; and (3) the proliferation of Anheuser-Busch beer brands and advertisements. The defendants concede they possessed no knowledge that any Anheuser-Busch product actually contained oil.

Anheuser-Busch, displeased with Balducci's extensive use of its trademarks and the possible implication that its products were tainted with oil, brought this suit in May 1989. It asserted five causes of action: (1) infringement of federally-registered trademarks, 15 U.S.C. § 1114(1); (2) federal unfair competition, 15 U.S.C. § 1125(a); (3) state trademark infringement, Mo. Rev. Stat. § 417.056; (4) common law unfair competition; and (5) state law trademark dilution, Mo. Rev. Stat. § 417.061. It sought one dollar in nominal damages and injunctive relief.

Other than the Balducci ad itself, the primary evidence offered by Anheuser-Busch was a study designed by Jacob Jacoby, Ph.D., and conducted under the supervision of Leon B. Kaplan, Ph.D. This survey, conducted in St. Louis shopping malls, involved 301 beer drinkers or purchasers who claimed to periodically review magazines or newspapers. The surveyors showed the Balducci ad to 200 participants and a Michelob Dry ad to the remaining 101. Of those viewing the Balducci ad, many expressed an impression of Anheuser-Busch's role in its creation. For example, fifty-eight percent felt the creators "did have to get permission to use the Michelob name." Fifty-six percent believed permission would be required for the various symbols and logos. Six percent of the classified responses construed the Balducci ad to be an actual Anheuser-Busch advertisement. Almost half (45%) found nothing about the parody which suggested it was an editorial, and seventy-five percent did not perceive it as satirical. Virtually none (3.5%) noticed the tiny disclaimer on the side of the ad. Fifty-five percent construed the parody as suggesting that Michelob beer is or was in some way contaminated with oil. As a result, twenty-two percent stated they were less likely to buy Michelob beer in the future.

After a bench trial, the district court ruled in favor of Balducci on each of the five theories. Although the court found that "Defendants clearly used Plaintiff's marks in their ad parody, they used some of those marks without alteration, and they did so without Plaintiff's permission," it dismissed the trademark claims because "Defendants' use of [the] marks did not create a likelihood of confusion in the marketplace." Balducci, 814 F.Supp. 791 at 793. In reaching this decision, the court expressed the need to give "special sensitivity" to the First Amendment aspects of the case. *Id.* at 796. Accordingly, the court concluded that although "Plaintiff's statistical evidence [might] well be persuasive in the context of a classic trademark infringement case, ... where the allegedly infringing use occurs in an editorial context," more persuasive evidence of confusion is required. *Id.* at 797. The court similarly dismissed the state law dilution claim, stating that "because Defendant's use of Plaintiff's marks occurred in an editorial context, there is no threat of tarnishment through association with shoddy or disharmonious products." *Id.* at 799. Finally, the court rejected the unfair competition claims because the "parody was not in any way connected with the sale of a product and because Plaintiff has failed to establish a likelihood of confusion in the marketplace." *Id.* at 798.

On appeal, Anheuser-Busch contends the district court gave inordinate weight to Balducci's First Amendment claims and erred in finding no likelihood of confusion. Balducci contends the court correctly found no likelihood of confusion and, furthermore, argues the ad parody is absolutely protected by the First Amendment.

I.

This case involves the tension between the protection afforded by the Lanham Act to trademark owners and the competing First Amendment rights of the parodist. Our analysis of the district court's decision encompasses two related, but distinct steps. We begin by considering whether the district court erred in finding no likelihood of confusion. Since a trademark infringement action requires a likelihood of confusion, this finding, if upheld, decides this case. If we conclude the court erred in finding no likelihood of confusion, we must consider Balducci's additional argument that the First Amendment protects it from liability.

Section 32(1) of the Lanham Act protects owners of registered trademarks from uses "likely to cause confusion, or to cause mistake, or to deceive." 15 U.S.C. § 1114(1). The determination of whether "likelihood of confusion" exists is a factual determination which we review under the clearly erroneous standard. *Mutual of Omaha Ins. Co. v. Novak*, 836 F.2d 397, 398 (8th Cir. 1987); *SquirtCo v. Seven-Up Co.*, 628 F.2d 1086, 1091 (8th Cir. 1980). However, our review is not so limited when, as here, the district court's "conclusions are inextricably bound up in its view of the law." *Calvin Klein Cosmetics Corp. v. Lenox Labs.*, 815 F.2d 500, 504 (8th Cir. 1987). Rather than first considering whether Balducci's ad parody was likely to confuse the public and then considering the scope of First Amendment protection, the district court conflated the two. The court essentially skewed its likelihood of confusion analysis in an attempt to give "special sensitivity" to the First Amendment, holding Anheuser Busch to a higher standard than required in a "classic trademark infringement case." Balducci, 814 F.Supp. at 796–97. Since we cannot separate the court's factual finding of confusion from its legal conclusions, we conduct a de novo review of the well-developed record before us. Calvin Klein, 815 F.2d at 504.

Many courts have applied, we believe correctly, an expansive interpretation of likelihood of confusion, extending "protection against use of [plaintiff's] mark on any product or service which would reasonably be thought by the buying public to come from the same source, or thought to be affiliated with, connected with, or sponsored by, the trademark owner." McCarthy, Trademarks and Unfair Competition § 24.03, at 24–13 (3d ed. 1992); *Novak*, 836 F.2d at 398; *Nike, Inc. v. "Just Did It" Enters.*, 6 F.3d 1225, 1228 (7th Cir. 1993); *Dallas Cowboys Cheerleaders, Inc. v. Pussycat Cinema, Ltd.*, 604 F.2d 200, 204–05 (2d Cir. 1979); *Jordache Enters., Inc. v. Levi Strauss*, 841 F.Supp. 506 (S.D.N.Y. 1993). This approach seems consistent with congressional intent, as evidenced by the express inclusion during the 1989 revision of the Lanham Act of protection against confusion as to "origin, sponsorship, or approval." 15 U.S.C. § 1125(a). This court enumerated several factors pertinent to the finding of likelihood of confusion in *SquirtCo*, 628 F.2d at 1091: (1) the strength of the trademark; (2) the similarity between the plaintiff's and defendant's marks; (3) the competitive proximity of the parties' products'; (4) the alleged infringer's intent to confuse the public; (5) evidence of any actual confusion; and (6) the degree of care reasonably expected of the plaintiff's potential customers. These factors are not a distinct test, but represent the sort of considerations which a court should consider in determining whether likelihood of confusion exists. We briefly consider the application of these factors to this case.

Anheuser-Busch possessed several very strong trademarks that Balducci displayed virtually unaltered in the ad parody. Thus, the first two *SquirtCo* factors weigh heavily in favor of Anheuser-Busch. The third factor, competitive proximity, is less one-sided. Balducci does not directly compete with Anheuser-Busch. Confusion, however, may exist in the absence of direct competition. *SquirtCo*, 628 F.2d at 1091. Moreover, Balducci published the parody on the back cover of a magazine—a location frequently devoted to real ads, even in Snicker. This location threatens to confuse consumers accustomed to seeing advertisements on the back cover of magazines.

According to Richard Balducci, he sought to comment on certain social conditions through parody. "An intent to parody is not an intent to confuse." *Jordache Enters., Inc. v. Hogg Wyld, Ltd.*, 828 F.2d 1482, 1486 (10th Cir. 1987). Other factors, however, suggest Balducci had, if not an intent to confuse, at least an indifference to the possibility that some consumers might be misled by the parody. For example, no significant steps were taken to remind readers that they were viewing a parody and not an advertisement sponsored or approved by Anheuser-Busch. Balducci carefully designed the fictitious ad to appear as authentic as possible. Several of Anheuser-Busch's marks were used with little or no alteration. The disclaimer is virtually undetectable. Balducci even included a (R) symbol after the words Michelob Oily. These facts suggest that Balducci sought to do far more than just "conjure up" an image of Anheuser-Busch in the minds of its readers. Cf. *Walt Disney Productions v. Air Pirates*, 581 F.2d 751, 758 (9th Cir. 1978), *cert. denied*, 439 U.S. 1132 (1979) (in copyright context, "fair use" doctrine does not entitle parodist to copy everything needed to create the "best parody;" rather, the parodist may copy only that portion of the protected work necessary to "conjure up the original"). These factors limit the degree to which Balducci's intent to parody weighs in favor of a finding of no likelihood of confusion.

Balducci's desired message, or humor, presumably hinged on consumers' ultimate realization that although this "advertisement" was based on the painstaking duplication of Anheuser-Busch's marks, it was in fact a parody or editorial parody. We have significant doubt as to whether many consumers would develop this understanding of Balducci's true purpose. There is a distinct possibility, accepted by the district court, "that a superficial observer might believe that the ad parody was approved by Anheuser-Busch." *Balducci*, 814 F. Supp. at 797. The back cover of magazines is frequently used for advertisements and cannot be expected to command the thoughtful deliberation of all or even most of the viewing public. The district court downplayed this fact, observing that "once again . . . the First Amendment concerns at issue in this litigation require a closer examination of Plaintiff's claims." *Id*. When objectively viewed, the fourth and sixth *SquirtCo* factors (i.e., intent and degree of care) may not fully support Anheuser-Busch, but they are consistent with a finding that the parody presented a significant likelihood of confusing consumers.

The survey evidence, whether considered as direct or indirect evidence of actual confusion, tilts the analysis in favor of Anheuser-Busch. Over half of those surveyed thought Balducci needed Anheuser-Busch's approval to publish the ad. Many of these presumably felt that such approval had in fact been obtained. Six percent thought that the parody was an actual Anheuser-Busch advertisement. Other courts have accepted similar survey findings. *See Novak*, 836 F.2d at 400; *Nat'l Football League Props., Inc. v. New Jersey Giants, Inc.*, 637 F. Supp. 507, 517 (D.N.J. 1986) (citing decisions relying on surveys showing 8.5% to 15% confusion); *Schieffelin & Co. v. Jack Company of Boca*, 850 F. Supp. 232 (S.D.N.Y. 1994). In Novak, for example, "approximately ten percent of all the persons surveyed thought that Mutual 'goes along' with Novak's product." 836 F.2d at 400. The court found this persuasive despite the existence of "some ambiguity" in the survey question. *Id.* Thus, we are left with evidence, obtained by means of a valid consumer survey, that strongly indicates actual consumer confusion.

Our review of the record before the district court, including the Balducci ad and the survey evidence, convinces us that the court erred in finding no likelihood of confusion. The court reached its finding only after it mistakenly weighted its analysis in favor of Balducci in an effort to satisfy the limits set by the First Amendment. We believe the better course would have been to analyze the likelihood of confusion first and then proceed to an analysis of the First Amendment issues.

Having determined that a likelihood of confusion exists, we must next consider Balducci's argument that the First Amendment protects it from liability for its ad parody. Parody does implicate the First Amendment's protection of artistic expression. *Cliffs Notes, Inc. v. Bantam Doubleday Dell Pub. Group*, 886 F.2d 490, 493 (2d Cir. 1989). Based on this, Balducci argues it has an absolute First Amendment right to use plaintiff's trademarks in its parody. No such absolute right exists. *See id.* at 493–94 ("Trademark protection is not lost simply because the allegedly infringing use is in connection with a work of artistic expression.") (quoting *Silverman v. CBS Inc.*, 870 F.2d 40, 49 (2d Cir.), *cert. denied*, 492 U.S. 907 (1989)); *Nike*, 6 F.3d at 1228; *Dallas Cowboys Cheerleaders*, 604 F.2d at 206 (defendant liable for using cheerleader uniform in X-rated film); *Pillsbury Co. v. Milky Way Productions, Inc.*, 215 U.S.P.Q. 124, 135 (N.D. Ga. 1981) (defendant liable for dilution for publishing cartoon of "Poppin' Fresh" and "Poppie Fresh" doughpersons engaging in sexual intercourse and fellatio); *Edgar Rice Burroughs, Inc. v. Manns Theatres*, 195 U.S.P.Q. (BNA) 159, 162 (C.D. Cal. 1976) (defendant liable for using TARZAN mark in X-rated film).

In arguing against the reasoning of these many cases, Balducci relies on this court's opinion in *Mutual of Omaha Ins. Co. v. Novak*, 836 F.2d 397 (8th Cir. 1987), *cert. denied*, 488 U.S. 933 (1988). In *Novak*, a panel of this court upheld an injunction against Novak's continued sale of anti-war T-shirts, coffee mugs and other products containing words such as "Mutants of Omaha" and bearing symbols with a likeness to plaintiff's Indian head logo. *Id.* at 398. In dicta, the court stated that the injunction "in no way infringes upon the constitutional protection the First Amendment would provide were Novak to present an editorial parody in a book, magazine, or film." *Id.* at 402. This language does not support absolute protection for editorial parody, but merely reflects the fact that a parody contained in an obvious editorial context is less likely to confuse, and thus more deserving of protection than those displayed on a product. *See Nike*, 6 F.3d at 1228; *Jordache Enters., Inc. v. Hogg Wyld, Ltd.*, 625 F. Supp. 48, 55 (D.N.M. 1985), *aff'd*, 828 F.2d 1482 (10th Cir. 1987); 3 J.T. McCarthy § 31:38 at 31–213. A parody creating a likelihood of confusion may be subject to a trademark infringement action. *Cliffs Notes*, 886 F.2d at 494 (confusing parodies are "vulnerable under trademark law"); *L.L. Bean, Inc. v. Drake Publishers, Inc.*, 811 F.2d 26, 32 n.3 (1st Cir.) (confusing parodies "implicate[ ] the legitimate commercial and consumer protection objectives of trademark law"), *cert. denied and appeal dismissed*, 483 U.S. 1013 (1987).

There is no simple, mechanical rule by which courts can determine when a potentially confusing parody falls within the First Amendment's protective reach. Thus, "in deciding the reach of the Lanham Act in any case where an expressive work is alleged to infringe a trademark, it is appropriate to weigh the public interest in free expression against the public interest in avoiding consumer confusion." *Cliffs Notes*, 886 F.2d at 494. "This approach takes into account the ultimate test in trademark law, namely, the likelihood of confusion as to the source of the goods in question." *Id.* at 495 (internal quotations omitted).

In applying this balancing test, we begin with the recognition that parody serves as a "humorous form of social commentary and literary criticism that dates back as far as Greek antiquity." *Bean*, 811 F.2d at 28. Balducci purports to comment on several matters, including environmental pollution and Anheuser-Busch's brand proliferation. The First Amendment's protection of social commentary generally, and parody in particular, is certainly implicated in this case. "The fact that parody can claim legitimacy for some appropriation does not, of course, tell either parodist or judge much about where to draw the line." *Campbell v. Acuff-Rose Music, Inc.*, 114 S.Ct. 1164, 1172 (1994). "The benefit to the one making the parody . . . arises from the humorous association, not from public confusion as to the source of the marks." *Jordache Enters.*, 828 F.2d at 1486. Thus, we must weigh the public interest in protecting Balducci's expression against the public interest in avoiding consumer confusion.

Applying this standard, we are convinced that the First Amendment places no bar to the application of the Lanham Act in this case. As we have discussed, Balducci's ad parody was likely to confuse consumers as to its origin, sponsorship or approval. This confusion might have to be tolerated if even plausibly necessary to achieve the desired commentary— a question we need not decide. In this case, the confusion is wholly unnecessary to Balducci's stated purpose. By using an obvious disclaimer, positioning the parody in a less-confusing location, altering the protected marks in a meaningful way, or doing some collection of the above, Balducci could have conveyed its message with substantially less risk of consumer confusion. Other courts have upheld the use of obvious variations of protected marks. *See, e.g., Cliffs Notes*, 886 F.2d at 496 ("Spy Notes" held not to infringe "Cliffs Notes" mark); Jordache Enters., 828 F.2d at 1485–88 (comparing "Jordache" and "Lardashe" jeans). The First Amendment does not excuse Balducci's failure to do so. . . .

Balducci's ad, developed through the nearly unaltered appropriation of Anheuser-Busch's marks, conveys that it is the original, but the ad founders on its failure to convey that it is not the original. Thus, it is vulnerable under trademark law since the customer is likely to be confused, as the record before the district court demonstrated.

We believe it is important to acknowledge the limits of our holding today. We do not hold that Balducci's extensive borrowing of Anheuser-Busch's trademarks amounts to a per se trademark violation. Unlike copyright and patent owners, trademark owners have no right in gross. *See* McCarthy § 24.03[4][d]; *Jordache*, 625 F. Supp. at 56 (trademark owner "does not own in gross the penumbral customer awareness of its name, nor the fallout from its advertising"). By taking steps to insure that viewers adequately understood this was an unauthorized editorial, Balducci might have avoided or at least sharply limited any confusion, and thereby escaped from liability. Absent such measures, Balducci's ad parody was likely to confuse consumers and fall subject to federal trademark law. . . .

III.

The final question presented in this case involves the proper remedy. Anheuser-Busch seeks one dollar in damages and an injunction against further infringement. The requested nominal damages seem proper given the survey evidence suggesting actual confusion. *See Brunswick Corp. v. Spirit Reel Co.*, 832 F.2d 513, 525 (10th Cir. 1987) (awarding damages based on survey evidence); *PPX Enters., Inc. v. Audiofidelity Enters., Inc.*, 818 F.2d 266, 271 (2d Cir. 1987) (same).

Injunctive relief is also appropriate and, under the Missouri anti-dilution statute, required. The injunction sought by Anheuser-Busch, however, is quite broad. It would permanently enjoin Balducci from publishing any "false description" of Anheuser-Busch products or

482   TRADEMARK INFRINGEMENT   CH. 7

"publishing [the protected marks in] . . . any documents or material." This relief seems to encompass a great number of uses which might amount to no infringement at all. Courts should tread cautiously when considering injunctive relief against future publication. The proponent of prior restraint " 'carries a heavy burden of showing justification for the imposition of such a restraint.' " *New York Times Co. v. United States*, 403 U.S. 713, 714 (1971) (quoting *Bantam Books, Inc. v. Sullivan*, 372 U.S. 58, 70 (1963)). The parties have not developed a satisfactory record or fully briefed this issue. Thus, we decline to delineate the precise limits which the First Amendment might place on the scope of the injunctive relief available to Anheuser-Busch.

We reverse the district court's dismissal of Anheuser-Busch's trademark infringement (15 U.S.C. § 1114(1)) and dilution (Mo. Rev. Stat. § 417.061) claims and instruct the district court to enter judgment for Anheuser-Busch on these claims and award appropriate relief.

NOTES FOR DISCUSSION

1. *Difference in Facts; Difference in Outcomes?* Why do the two cases come out differently? Is there a material difference in their facts? Is it simply a difference in the judges who decided the case? Having lost in the *L & L Wings* case, what did Anheuser-Busch do differently in the *Balducci Pubs.* case? In *L & L Wings*, a jury decided the factual issues; in *Balducci Pubs.*, a judge was the fact-finder. Why? In *Balducci Pubs.*, Anheuser-Busch also had a survey that purportedly demonstrated consumer confusion. If it had had such a survey in *L & L Wings* and it demonstrated a similar level of confusion, would that have changed the outcome in *L & L Wings*?

In the Boston Marathon cases, the First Circuit found that a defendant who used the Boston Marathon trademark without authorization on t-shirts created a likelihood of confusion, while a television station that used the trademark without authorization on a broadcast of the marathon did not. *Compare Boston Athletic Ass'n v. Sullivan*, 867 F.2d 22 (1st Cir. 1989) *with WCVB-TV v. Boston Athletic Ass'n*, 926 F.2d 42 (1st Cir. 1991). These decisions suggest that consumer confusion is more likely for unauthorized use of a mark on merchandise, rather than a television broadcast. They also leave more room for a traditional press activity, such as a television broadcast, rather than a simple commercial product, such as a t-shirt. Are the two *Anheuser-Busch* cases consistent with the First Circuit's resolution of the Boston Marathon cases?

2. *Likelihood of Confusion Factors.* The *Polaroid* eight-factor likelihood of confusion test arose in cases where the key issue was whether the defendant was trying to persuade consumers to purchase its products by implicitly suggesting that its products not only were like the plaintiff's, but were in fact the plaintiff's. Does it make any sense to apply the eight-factor test in cases involving parody or satire? What additional factors might we

add to the list in order to address more directly the confusion concerns that arise in these cases?

In traditional trademark infringement cases, the harm to the plaintiff is that consumers will purchase the defendant's products, thinking they come from the plaintiff, and being dissatisfied with the defendant's products, will stop buying from the plaintiff. What is the harm to the plaintiff in these two cases? Why is Anheuser-Busch trying to stop these uses? Had Balducci included a more plain disclaimer that prevented a likelihood of confusion, would Anheuser-Busch have been content with that or would it have sued anyway?

3. *Sponsorship or Endorsement Confusion?* As previously discussed, courts first recognized sponsorship or endorsement confusion in cases where consumers would likely both perceive an endorsement, irrespective of the legal rules of trademark law, and would rely on that in making their purchasing decisions. Do you think both elements are present if a consumer mistakenly believes that a given use requires a plaintiff's permission? Assume that Justice Powell was right and that consumers will believe that the Anheuser-Busch gave permission for the Myrtle Beach t-shirts. Would that affect consumers' decision to purchase the t-shirts in the same way that a mistaken belief that Vogue had endorsed a particular line of hats would?

4. *Surveys and Confusion.* What did the survey in *Balducci Pubs.* ask? The court states that "fifty-eight percent [of the respondents] felt that the [editorial] creators 'did have to get permission to use the Michelob name.'" *Balducci Pubs.*, 28 F.3d at 772. Does the survey improperly ask consumers to guess what the legal rule is? *See, e.g., NFL Props. v. ProStyle, Inc.*, 16 F. Supp. 2d 1012, 1018 (E.D. Wis. 1998) (rejecting survey that asked: "Do you think that, in order to put out this shirt, the company that put it out did need to get permission, did not need to get permission, or you have no thoughts about this?" on the grounds that it improperly asked respondents for a legal conclusion). How should the question have been phrased?

5. *Consumer Welfare.* Which decision better advances consumer welfare? What are the relevant consumer interests at stake? Are the consumer interests materially different in the two cases? In which case do you think it more likely that consumers will perceive an implicit endorsement that will affect their decision to purchase the defendant's product or the plaintiff's product in the future? If courts extend trademark law to give Anheuser-Busch, and other trademark owners, rights over these uses, will Anheuser-Busch ever license them? Will eliminating these uses improve consumer welfare? How? Will it reduce consumer welfare? How? Would you prefer to live in a society where people can use another's trademark to make fun of them or in a society where people cannot?

6. *Summary Disposition.* In his opinion in *Wal-Mart Stores, Inc. v. Samara Brothers*, found in Chapter 5, Justice Scalia cautioned: "Competition is deterred, however, not merely by successful suit but by the plausible threat of successful suit. . . ." 529 U.S. 205, 214 (2000). Given that risk, the Court

adopted a bright-line rule requiring proof of acquired distinctiveness for all product design trade dress, rather than a rule that attempted to identify inherently distinctive product designs from non-inherently distinctive product designs. In the Court's view, anything other than the Court's bright-line rule would "rarely provide the basis for summary disposition of an anticompetitive strike suit." *Id.* Is there any way to provide a similarly bright-line rule for parody? Was either defendant able to escape liability in these two cases before trial? Do these two cases provide much clear guidance for would-be parodist as to what uses will be permissible under trademark law?

D. SECONDARY LIABILITY

HARD ROCK CAFÉ LICENSING CORP. v. CONCESSION SERVS., INC.
955 F.2d 1143 (7th Cir. 1992)

CUDAHY, C.J.

The Hard Rock Cafe Licensing Corporation (Hard Rock) owns trademarks on several clothing items, including t-shirts and sweatshirts and apparently attempts to exploit its trademark monopoly to the full. In the summer of 1989, Hard Rock sent out specially trained private investigators to look for counterfeit Hard Rock Cafe merchandise. The investigators found Iqbal Parvez selling counterfeit Hard Rock t-shirts from stands in the Tri-State Swap-O-Rama and the Melrose Park Swap-O-Rama, flea markets owned and operated by Concession Services Incorporated (CSI). The investigators also discovered that Harry's Sweat Shop (Harry's) was selling similar items. Hard Rock brought suit against Parvez, CSI, Harry's and others not relevant to this appeal under the Lanham Trademark Act, 15 U.S.C. §§ 1051 *et seq.* (1988). Most of the defendants settled, including Parvez, who paid Hard Rock some $30,000. CSI and Harry's went to trial.

After a bench trial, the district court found that both remaining defendants violated the Act and entered permanent injunctions forbidding Harry's to sell merchandise bearing Hard Rock's trademarks (whether counterfeit or genuine) and forbidding CSI to permit the sale of such merchandise at its flea markets. . . .

All of the parties who participated in the trial appealed. CSI believes that it is not liable and that, in any event, entry of the injunction was inappropriate. . . . Finding errors of law and a fatal ambiguity in the findings of fact, we vacate the judgment against CSI . . . and remand for further proceedings.

I.

Most of the facts are undisputed. The following account draws from the district court's findings, the record on appeal and the submissions of the parties. Where there are disputes of fact we will note them and defer to the district court's resolution unless clearly erroneous. *Anderson v. Bessemer City,* 470 U.S. 564, 573, 84 L.Ed.2d 518, 105 S.Ct. 1504 (1985).

A. *The Parties and Their Practices*

1. *Concession Services, Inc.*

In the summer of 1989, CSI owned and operated three "Swap-O-Rama" flea markets in the Chicago area: the Tri-State, in Alsip, Illinois; the Melrose Park, in Melrose Park, Illinois; and the Brighton Park, in Chicago itself. Although Parvez sold counterfeits at the Tri-State Swap-O-Rama and at Melrose Park, testimony at trial concentrated on the operations at the Tri-State. We too will refer mainly to the Tri-State Swap-O-Rama, although CSI's operations are apparently similar at all three flea markets.

CSI generates revenue from a flea market in four ways. First, it rents space to vendors for flat fees that vary by the day of the week and the location of the space. Second, CSI charges a reservation and storage fee to those vendors who want to reserve the same space on a month-to-month basis. Third, CSI charges shoppers a nominal 75 cents admission charge. Fourth, CSI runs concession stands inside the market. To promote its business, CSI advertises the markets, announcing "BARGAINS" to be had, but does not advertise the presence of any individual vendors or any particular goods.

Supervision of the flea markets is minimal. CSI posts a sign at the Tri-State prohibiting vendors from selling "illegal goods." It also has "Rules For Sellers" which prohibit the sale of food or beverages, alcohol, weapons, fireworks, live animals, drugs and drug paraphernalia and subversive or un-American literature. Other than these limitations, vendors can, and do, sell almost any conceivable item. Two off-duty police officers provide security and crowd control (an arrangement that does not apply to the other markets). These officers also have some duty to ensure that the vendors obey the Sellers' Rules. The manager of the Tri-State, Albert Barelli, walks around the flea market about five times a day, looking for problems and violations of the rules. No one looks over the vendors' wares before they enter the market and set up their stalls, and any examination after that is cursory. Moreover, Barelli does not keep records of the names and addresses of the vendors. The only penalty for violating the Seller's Rules is expulsion from the market.

James Pierski, the vice president in charge of CSI's flea markets, testified that CSI has a policy of cooperating with any trademark owner that notifies CSI of possible infringing activity. But there is no evidence that this policy has ever been carried into effect. Before this case, there have been a few seizures of counterfeit goods at Swap-O-Rama flea markets. In no case was CSI informed of a pending seizure, involved in a seizure or notified as to the ultimate disposition of the seized goods. On the other hand, CSI did not investigate any of the seizures, though it knew they had occurred.

2. *Harry's Sweat Shop*

Harry's is a small store in Darien, Illinois, owned and operated by Harry Spatero. The store sells athletic shoes, t-shirts, jackets with the names of professional sports teams and the like. Spatero testified that the store contains over 20,000 different items. When buying t-shirts, Harry's is somewhat indiscriminate. The store buys seconds, overruns and closeouts from a variety of sources. Harry's buys most of its t-shirts from Supply Brokers of Pennsylvania, a firm which specializes in buying up stocks from stores going out of business. Spatero testified that Supply Brokers sends him largely unidentified boxes of shirts which he may choose to return after looking them over. But Spatero testified that Harry's also bought shirts from people who came around in unmarked vans, offering shirts at a discount. The store kept no records of the sources of its inventory.

3. *Hard Rock Licensing Corp.*

Hard Rock owns the rights to a variety of Hard Rock trademarks. The corporation grants licenses to use its trademarks to the limited partnerships that own and operate the various Hard Rock Cafe restaurants. These restaurants are the only authorized distributors of Hard Rock Cafe merchandise, but apparently this practice of exclusivity is neither publicized nor widely known. The shirts themselves are produced by Winterland Productions, which prints logos on blank, first quality t-shirts that it buys from Hanes, Fruit-of-the-Loom and Anvil. According to the manager of the Chicago Hard Rock Cafe, Scott Floersheimer, Winterland has an agreement with Hard Rock to retain all defective Hard Rock shirts. Thus, if Winterland performs as agreed, all legitimate Hard Rock shirts sold to the public are well-made and cleanly printed.

The Chicago Hard Rock Cafe has done very well from its business. Since 1986, it has sold over 500,000 t-shirts at an average gross profit of $10.12 per shirt.

B. *The Investigation*

National Investigative Services Corporation (NISCOR) carried out the search for counterfeit merchandise on Hard Rock's behalf. Another firm, Trademark Facts, Inc., trained NISCOR's investigators to recognize counterfeit merchandise. Recognizing counterfeit Hard Rock goods was apparently easy. Any shirt not sold in a Hard Rock Cafe restaurant was, unless second-hand, counterfeit. Other than this, the investigators were instructed to check for the manufacturer of the t-shirt, a registration or trademark symbol, the quality of the printed design, the color of the design, the quality of the shirt stock and the price. But as to these latter factors (except for the price), Floersheimer testified that even he would have trouble distinguishing a good counterfeit from a legitimate t-shirt.

The investigators visited both the Melrose Park and the Tri-State Swap-O-Ramas and observed Iqbal Parvez (or his employees) offering more than a hundred Hard Rock t-shirts for sale. Cynthia Myers, the chief investigator on the project, testified that these shirts were obviously counterfeit. The shirts were poor quality stock, with cut labels and were being sold for $3 apiece (a legitimate Hard Rock shirt, we are told, goes for over $14). Harry's had four Hard Rock shirts for sale, sitting on a discount table for $3.99 each. The district court found that these too were of obviously low quality, with cut labels and cracked and worn designs. Nonetheless, both Parvez and Harry's were selling t-shirts made by approved manufacturers. Parvez was selling Hanes t-shirts, and Harry's was selling Fruit-of-the-Loom.

At no point before filing suit did Hard Rock warn Harry's or CSI (or Parvez, whose supplier Hard Rock was trying to track down) that the shirts were counterfeits.

C. *The District Court Proceedings*

Hard Rock brought suit against the defendants in September 1989, alleging violations of sections 32 and 43 of the Lanham Act. 15 U.S.C. §§ 1114 & 1125 (1988). Pending trial, the court entered temporary restraining orders and then preliminary injunctions against both CSI and Harry's. Harry's got rid of its remaining Hard Rock t-shirts, and CSI told any vendors selling Hard Rock merchandise in its flea markets to get rid of their stock as well. There have been no more violations.

After a bench trial, the district court entered permanent injunctions against both defendants and ordered Harry's to pay treble damages based on Hard Rock's lost profits on four t-shirts (in sum, $120). Findings of Fact, Conclusions of Law and Order at 8 (Sept. 12, 1990) (hereinafter Mem. Op.). The court denied Hard Rock's request for attorney's fees. *Id.*

The court's reasoning is crucial to the resolution of this appeal. Accordingly, we think it appropriate to quote from it at some length. The court concluded that both defendants were "guilty of willful blindness that counterfeit goods were being sold on [their] premises." *Id.* at 7. Another sentence follows, however, which somewhat dilutes the impact of the preceding finding: "Neither defendant took reasonable steps to detect or prevent the sale of Hard Rock Cafe counterfcit T-shirts on its premise [sic]." *Id.* This suggests mere negligence.

Willful blindness, the court said, "is a sufficient basis for a finding of violation of the Lanham Act. *Louis Vuitton S.A. v. Lee,* 875 F.2d 584, 590 (7th Cir. 1989)." *Id.* As to CSI's argument that it did not actually sell the offending goods, the court observed that CSI is not "merely a landlord; it also advertises and promoted the activity on its premises, sells admission tickets to buyers and supervises the premises. Under these circumstances it must also take reasonable precautions against the sale of counterfeit products." *Id.*

II.

The Lanham Trademark Act protects consumers from deceptive claims about the nature and origin of products. 15 U.S.C. § 1114(1)(a) & (b) (use of mark violates Act if "likely to cause confusion, or to cause mistake, or to deceive"); 15 U.S.C. § 1125(a)(1) (false designation of origin violates Act if "likely to cause confusion, or to cause mistake, or to deceive"). But the Lanham Act also protects trademarks as a form of intellectual property. In this case, the Act protects Hard Rock's investment in a fashionable image and a reputation for selling high quality goods. *See Inwood Laboratories, Inc. v. Ives Laboratories, Inc.,* 456 U.S. 844, 854, 72 L.Ed.2d 606, 102 S.Ct. 2182 n.14 (1982) (citing S. Rep. No. 1333, 79th Cong., 2d Sess. 3 (1946)).

A. *Secondary Liability*

The most interesting issue in this case is CSI's liability for Parvez's sales. Hard Rock argues that CSI has incurred both contributory and vicarious liability for the counterfeits, and we take the theories of liability in that order.

It is well established that "if a manufacturer or distributor intentionally induces another to infringe a trademark, or if it continues to supply its product to one whom it knows or has reason to know is engaging in trademark infringement, the manufacturer or distributor is contributorially responsible for any harm done as a result of the deceit." *Id.* at 854 (footnote omitted). Despite this apparently definitive statement, it is not clear how the doctrine applies to people who do not actually manufacture or distribute the good that is ultimately palmed off as made by someone else. A temporary help service, for example, might not be liable if it furnished Parvez the workers he employed to erect his stand, even if the help service knew that Parvez would sell counterfeit goods. Thus we must ask whether the operator of a flea market is more like the manufacturer of a mislabeled good or more like a temporary help service supplying the purveyor of goods. To answer questions of this sort, we have treated trademark infringement as a species of tort and have turned to the common law to guide our inquiry into the appropriate boundaries of liability. *David Berg & Co. v. Gatto Int'l Trading Co.,* 884 F.2d 306, 311 (7th Cir. 1989).

CSI characterizes its relationship with Parvez as that of landlord and tenant. Hard Rock calls CSI a licensor, not a landlord. Either way, the Restatement of Torts tells us that CSI is responsible for the torts of those it permits on its premises "knowing or having reason to know that the other is acting or will act tortiously. . . ." Restatement (Second) of Torts § 877(c) & cmt. d (1979). The common law, then, imposes the same duty on landlords and licensors that the Supreme Court has imposed on manufacturers and distributors. In the absence of any suggestion that a trademark violation should not be treated as a common law tort, we believe that the Inwood Labs. test for contributory liability applies. CSI may be liable for trademark violations by Parvez if it knew or had reason to know of them. But the factual findings must support that conclusion.

The district court found CSI to be willfully blind. Since we have held that willful blindness is equivalent to actual knowledge for purposes of the Lanham Act, *Lee,* 875 F.2d at 590, this finding should be enough to hold CSI liable (unless clearly erroneous). But we very much doubt that the district court defined willful blindness as it should have. To be willfully blind, a person must suspect wrongdoing and deliberately fail to investigate. *Id.* The district court, however, made little mention of CSI's state of mind and focused almost entirely on CSI's failure to take precautions against counterfeiting. Mem. Op. at 5–6. In its conclusions of law, the court emphasized that CSI had a duty to take reasonable precautions. Mem. Op. at 7. In short, it looks as if the district court found CSI to be negligent, not willfully blind.

This ambiguity in the court's findings would not matter if CSI could be liable for failing to take reasonable precautions. But CSI has no affirmative duty to take precautions against the sale of counterfeits. Although the "reason to know" part of the standard for contributory liability requires CSI (or its agents) to understand what a reasonably prudent person would understand, it does not impose any duty to seek out and prevent violations. Restatement (Second) of Torts § 12(1) & cmt. a (1965). We decline to extend the protection that Hard Rock finds in the common law to require CSI, and other landlords, to be more dutiful guardians of Hard Rock's commercial interests. Thus the district court's findings do not support the conclusion that CSI bears contributory liability for Parvez's transgressions.

Before moving on, we should emphasize that we have found only that the district court applied an incorrect standard. We have not found that the evidence cannot support the conclusion that CSI was in fact willfully blind. At the Tri-State, Barelli saw Parvez's shirts and had the opportunity to note that they had cut labels and were being sold cheap. Further, Barelli testified that he did not ask vendors whether their goods were counterfeit because they were sure to lie to him. One might infer from these facts that Barelli suspected that the shirts were counterfeits but chose not to investigate.

On the other hand, we do not wish to prejudge the matter. For it is undisputed that Hard Rock made no effort to broadcast the information that legitimate Hard Rock t-shirts could only be found in Hard Rock Cafes. Moreover, there does not seem to be any particular reason to believe that inexpensive t-shirts with cut labels are obviously counterfeit, no matter what logo they bear. *Cf. Lee,* 875 F.2d at 590 (genuine Vuitton and Gucci bags unlikely to display poor workmanship or purple vinyl linings). The circumstantial evidence that Barelli suspected the shirts to be counterfeit is, at best, thin. On remand, the district court may choose to develop this issue more fully.

Perhaps recognizing that the district court's opinion is unclear, Hard Rock urges us to find CSI vicariously liable for Parvez's sales, regardless of its knowledge of the counterfeiting. Indeed, if we accept this theory, CSI is liable for Parvez's sales even if it was not negligent. *See, e.g., Shapiro, Bernstein & Co. v. H.L. Green Co.,* 316 F.2d 304, 309 (2d Cir. 1963).

We have recognized that a joint tortfeasor may bear vicarious liability for trademark infringement by another. *David Berg,* 884 F.2d at 311. This theory of liability requires a finding that the defendant and the infringer have an apparent or actual partnership, have authority to bind one another in transactions with third parties or exercise joint ownership or control over the infringing product. *Id.* The case before us does not fit into the joint tortfeasor model, and Hard Rock does not argue that it does.

Instead, Hard Rock wants us to apply the more expansive doctrine of vicarious liability applicable to copyright violations. Under the test developed by the Second Circuit, a defendant is vicariously liable for copyright infringement if it has "the right and ability to supervise the infringing activity and also has a direct financial interest in such activities." *Gershwin Publishing Corp. v. Columbia Artists Management, Inc.,* 443 F.2d 1159, 1162 (2d Cir. 1971) (hereinafter CAMI); *F.E.L. Publications, Ltd. v. National Conf. of Catholic Bishops,* 466 F. Supp. 1034, 1040 (N.D. Ill. 1978); *see also Dreamland Ball Room, Inc. v. Shapiro, Bernstein & Co.,* 36 F.2d 354, 355 (7th Cir. 1929) (owner of dance hall liable for copyright violations by band hired to entertain paying customers); *Famous Music Corp. v. Bay State Harness Horse Racing & Breeding Ass'n,* 554 F.2d 1213, 1215 (1st Cir. 1977) (owner of racetrack liable for copyright violations by company hired to supply music over public address system). The purpose of the doctrine is to prevent an entity that profits from infringement from hiding behind undercapitalized "dummy" operations when the copyright owner eventually sues. *Shapiro, Bernstein,* 316 F.2d at 309.

The parties have argued vigorously about the application of this doctrine to the facts. But we need not decide the question; for the Supreme Court tells us that secondary liability for trademark infringement should, in any event, be more narrowly drawn than secondary liability for copyright infringement. *Sony Corp. of America v. Universal City Studios, Inc.,* 464 U.S. 417, 439, 78 L.Ed.2d 574, 104 S.Ct. 774 n.19 (1984) (citing "fundamental differences" between copyright and trademark law). If Hard Rock referred us to some principle of common law that supported its analogy to copyright, we would be more understanding of its claims. But it has not. Further, there is no hint that CSI is playing at the sort of obfuscation that inspired the Second Circuit to develop its more expansive form of vicarious copyright liability. Hard Rock must look to Congress to provide the level of protection it demands of CSI here.

In sum, we find that CSI may bear contributory liability for Parvez's unlawful sales, but we see no evidence on the record that would support a finding that CSI is vicariously liable. Accordingly, because the district court's findings fall to establish that CSI knew or had reason to know that Parvez was selling counterfeits, we must vacate the judgment against CSI and remand for further proceedings. . . .

III.

For the foregoing reasons, we VACATE the finding of liability as to CSI . . . and REMAND for further proceedings consistent with this opinion.

NOTES FOR DISCUSSION

1. *Origins.* The Supreme Court first recognized third party liability for trademark infringement or unfair competition in *William R. Warner & Co. v. Eli Lilly & Co.,* 265 U.S. 526 (1924). In that case, Eli Lilly had popularized a chocolate and quinine mixture, called Coco-Quinine. When William Warner introduced a competing chocolate and quinine product, named Quin-Coco, Eli Lilly sued for trademark infringement and unfair competition. The Court rejected the infringement claim on the grounds that William Warner's name accurately described its product, and was thus a truthful or fair use. *Id.* at 528.

With respect to the unfair competition claim, Eli Lilly argued, not that William Warner was seeking to confuse the druggists who purchased the product directly, but the ultimate consumers, by persuading druggists to substitute William Warner's product for Eli Lilly's. While William Warner denied the accusation, the Court agreed with Eli Lilly's characterization of the facts:

It is apparent, from a consideration of the testimony, that the efforts of petitioner to create a market for Quin-Coco were directed not so much to showing the merits of that preparation as they were to demonstrating its practical identity with Coco-Quinine, and, since it was sold at a lower price, inducing the purchasing druggist, in his own interest, to substitute, as far as he could, the former for the latter. . . . The evidence establishes by a fair preponderance that some of petitioner's salesmen suggested that, without danger of detection, prescriptions and orders for Coco-Quinine could be filled by substituting Quin-Coco. More often, however, the feasibility of such a course was brought to the mind of the druggist by pointing out the identity of the two preparations and the enhanced profit to be made by selling Quin-Coco because of its lower price.

Id. at 529–30.

The Court held that such inducement was sufficient to establish William Warner's liability for the actions of the druggists who had competed unfairly by substituting William Warner's product when a customer requested Eli Lilly's. *Id.* at 530–31 ("One who induces another to commit a fraud and furnishes the means of consummating it is equally guilty and liable for the injury.").

2.   *William R. Warner Revisited.* Some sixty years later, in *Inwood Labs., Inc. v. Ives Labs., Inc.*, history repeated itself and the facts in *William Warner* arose again. This time, Inwood had popularized a heart medication, and sold it exclusively in a blue and red capsule. 456 U.S. 844 (1982). When the patent on the medication expired, generic manufacturers began offering a generic version of the medication and copied the red-blue coloring. As Eli Lilly had some sixty years previously, Ives alleged that, by copying the coloring of Ives' brand name pharmaceutical, Inwood had induced some pharmacists to substitute the generic when a customer had requested the brand name. *Id.* at 849–50. Agreeing with its earlier decision, the Court held that the generic manufacturers could be secondarily liable for this unfair substitution. However, the Court held that to establish secondary liability, it was not enough that the generic manufacturers, by copying the coloration of Ives' medication, had made the substitution possible; nor was it enough that the generic manufacturers "could reasonably anticipate" such substitution. *Id.* at 854 n.13. Rather, Ives had to show that the generic manufacturers had gone further and either "intentionally induced the pharmacists to mislabel generic drugs or, in fact, continued to supply cyclandelate to pharmacists whom the petitioners knew were mislabeling generic drugs." *Id.* at 855. After reviewing the evidence, the Court held that Ives had not made the requisite showing. *Id.* at 857–58.

3.   *Modern Applications.* Most modern applications of trademark's secondary liability arise in resale markets, such as the flea market at issue in *Hard Rock Café. See also Fonovisa, Inc. v. Cherry Auction, Inc.*, 76 F.3d 259 (9th Cir. 1996). How should the secondary liability standard apply to electronic flea markets, such as eBay? What legal rights does a jewelry company, such as Tiffany, for example, have against eBay for sales of counterfeit jewelry through eBay's website? Consider the following. Tiffany has determined that 73% of the sterling silver Tiffany merchandise sold

through eBay during 2003 was counterfeit. Based upon this finding, counsel for Tiffany wrote eBay in May 2004, "demanding that eBay should '(i) ban any eBay seller from listing five (5) or more "Tiffany" jewelry items at any given time; (ii) ban the sale of silver "Tiffany" jewelry, the vast majority of which our analysis has shown to be counterfeit; (iii) ban the sale of any "Tiffany" item that is advertised as being counterfeit (as some currently are) or as being "inspired by Tiffany" (as is often the case now); (iv) not advertise the sale of "Tiffany" merchandise and (v) remove sponsored links to "Tiffany" on any search engine.'" If you represented eBay, what advice would you give eBay with respect to each of these requests? Is eBay potentially liable? If Tiffany sued, could eBay prevail on a Rule 12(b)(6) motion, or on a summary judgment, or would the dispute have to be resolved through a trial? *See Tiffany (NJ) Inc. v. eBay, Inc.*, 600 F.3d 93 (2d Cir. 2010) (on appeal following a bench trial, holding that generalized knowledge of counterfeit activity is not sufficient to establish secondary liability; holding instead, that Tiffany must prove that eBay " 'knew or had reason to know of specific instances of actual infringement"; finding *inter alia* that eBay was not secondarily liable so long as eBay removed listings where the goods were known to be counterfeit; but remanding for further consideration of the false advertising claims).

4. *Judicial versus Legislative Authority.* In *Central Bank of Denver, N.A. v. First Interstate Bank of Denver, N.A.,* 511 U.S. 164 (1994), the Court refused to recognize aiding and abetting liability for violations of § 10(b) of the Securities Exchange Act of 1934. *Id.* at 191. As grounds for its decision, the Court held that the text of the statute did not "reach those who aid and abet a § 10(b) violation." *Id.* at 177. For the Court, "that conclusion resolves the case." *Id.* Because the cause of action at issue was statutory, Congress's decision not to recognize aiding and abetting liability in the statute meant that no such liability existed. The Lanham Trademark Act similarly creates statutory causes of action for trademark infringement and unfair competition, and also does not expressly provide for third-party liability, whether for aiding and abetting, contributory liability, or vicarious liability. Should courts therefore limit liability under the Trademark Act to the direct liability the statute expressly creates?

5. *Secondary Liability and the Least-Cost Avoider.* In the secondary liability cases, the trademark owner is often trying to shift part of the costs of policing and enforcing its trademarks to another, such as the flea market operator in the *Hard Rock Café Licensing* case. Who can control the distribution of counterfeit or unauthorized merchandise at a flea market at a lower cost, the trademark owner or the flea market operator? Both presumably would face similar costs to hire personnel to look for and identify counterfeit goods. The trademark owner would have a clear cost advantage though in distinguishing authorized from unauthorized merchandise. Why then shift the legal duty to detect and stop the sale of unauthorized merchandise to the flea market operator? Is it that the flea market operator has a lower cost enforcement mechanism available? After all, the flea market operator can simply exclude a merchant who repeatedly offers counterfeit goods from the market altogether. In contrast, the trademark owner's only

remedy is to repeatedly sue such a repeat offender in court. Is the flea market operator's remedy of complete exclusion always appropriate? What if the merchant in question sells some counterfeit goods, but primarily sells legitimate goods? Is the flea market operator the lower cost enforcer of the trademark rights in that case?

In any event, if the flea market operator can enforce the trademark owner's rights at a lower cost, is the fact alone sufficient to justify imposing a legal obligation on the flea market operator to do so? Can the trademark owner hire, or otherwise contract with, the flea market operator to enforce its trademark rights? When should the law impose the legal obligation on a flea market operator to police the trademark owner's rights without compensation? When should the law force the trademark owner, if it wants the flea market operator to enforce its rights, to pay the flea market operator for those enforcement services?

CHAPTER 8

DILUTION

■ ■ ■

As discussed in the previous chapter, the scope of trademark protection steadily expanded over the course of the twentieth century. At least in theory, though not so much in practice, all of this expansion is supposed to relate to the protection of consumers from confusion and deception, as the phrase "likelihood of confusion" inherently suggests. In 1927, before much of this expansion took place, Professor Frank Schechter wrote a law review article arguing for broader protection of famous trademarks on a different ground. He argued "that the preservation of the uniqueness of a trademark should constitute the only rational basis for its protection." Frank Schechter, *Rational Basis of Trademark Protection*, 40 HARV. L. REV. 813, 831. He worried that widespread use of a famous trademark by others on unrelated goods— goods sufficiently unrelated that consumers would not be confused— would gradually whittle away the fame and selling power of the initial mark until it was altogether gone. In the latter half of the twentieth century, this concern, known as dilution, gradually gained statutory recognition.

Twenty years after Schechter's article, Massachusetts became the first state to adopt a specific anti-dilution statute. Its statute provided:

> Likelihood of injury to business reputation or of dilution of the distinctive quality of a trade name or trade-mark shall be a ground for injunctive relief in cases of trade-mark infringement or unfair competition notwithstanding the absence of competition between the parties or of confusion as to the source of goods or services.

1947 Mass. Acts, p. 300, ch. 307.

There were several key differences between Schechter's proposal and the Massachusetts statute, however. First, Schechter had proposed dilution protection only for famous marks; the Massachusetts statute did not require fame. Second, Schechter specifically defined his concept of dilution as the use of an identical mark; the Massachusetts statute did not limit dilution to the use of an identical mark. Third, Schechter limited dilution to the use of the mark on unrelated goods; the Massachusetts statute included such use, but did not limit dilution to use on unrelated goods. Dilution might arise under the Massachusetts statute even where the parties were competing. Fourth, at the time Schechter wrote, only inherently distinctive marks could be trademarks. Descriptive words that had gained a secondary meaning were not protected as technical trademarks, but under the general rubric of unfair competition. By 1947, when the Massachusetts statute was enacted, Congress had made descriptive words eligible for registration as trademarks so long as secondary meaning could be shown. The question thus arose whether dilution should apply only to inherently distinctive marks, or to marks whether protected as a result of inherent or acquired distinctiveness. Fifth, Schechter focused solely on the risk that a mark could be whittled away by use on unrelated goods, which became known as "blurring." In contrast, the Massachusetts statute, with its "injury to business reputation" language, was broad enough to encompass a second form of dilution, known as "tarnishment," where the use of the mark on unrelated good is likely to generate not merely unfavorable, but affirmatively offensive, associations. Between 1947 and 1995, at least twenty-five states adopted similar anti-dilution statutes. *See* Restatement (Third) of Unfair Competition § 25, Statutory Note (1995).

As you read the following materials involving the theory of dilution, the key question for you as a trademark practitioner is: What conduct does the theory of dilution reach that ordinary trademark infringement does not? When Schechter wrote his article in 1927, the trademark infringement standard was extremely narrow, reaching only the use of a near identical mark on competing, or as the *Aunt Jemima* case illustrates, closely related goods. At that time, there was a plausible need for broader protection for famous marks in at least some contexts. Following the steady expansion of the trademark infringement standard, however, what role is left for dilution today?

A. STATE APPROACHES TO DILUTION

MEAD DATA CENTRAL, INC. V. TOYOTA MOTOR SALES, U.S.A., INC.
875 F.2d 1026 (2d Cir. 1989)

VAN GRAAFEILAND, J.

Toyota Motor Sales, U.S.A., Inc. and its parent, Toyota Motor Corporation, appeal from a judgment of the United States District Court for the Southern District of New York (Edelstein, J.) enjoining them from using LEXUS as the name of their new luxury automobile and the division that manufactures it. The district court held that, under New York's antidilution statute, N.Y. Gen. Bus. Law § 368–d, Toyota's use of LEXUS is likely to dilute the distinctive quality of LEXIS, the mark used by Mead Data Central, Inc. for its computerized legal research service. 702 F. Supp. 1031 (1988). On March 8, 1989, we entered an order of reversal, stating that an opinion would follow. This is the opinion.

THE STATUTE

Section 368–d of New York's General Business Law, which has counterparts in at least twenty other states, reads as follows:

> Likelihood of injury to business reputation or of dilution of the distinctive quality of a mark or trade name shall be a ground for injunctive relief in cases of infringement of a mark registered or not registered or in cases of unfair competition, notwithstanding the absence of competition between the parties or the absence of confusion as to the source of goods or services.

THE PARTIES AND THEIR MARKS

Mead and Lexis

Mead is a corporation organized under the laws of Delaware with its principal place of business in Miamisburg, Ohio. Since 1972, Mead has provided a computerized legal research service under the trademark LEXIS. Mead introduced evidence that its president in 1972 "came up with the name LEXIS based on Lex which was Latin for law and I S for information systems." In fact, however, the word "lexis" is centuries old. It is found in the language of ancient Greece, where it had the meaning of "phrase", "word", "speaking" or "diction". Pinkerton, *Word for Word*, 179 (1982). "Lexis" subsequently appeared in the Latin where it had a substantially similar meaning, *i.e.*, "word", "speech", or "language". Oxford Latin Dictionary (1983); Lewis and Short, *A Latin Dictionary* (1980); Lewis, *An Elementary Latin Dictionary* (1979).

Like many other Latin words, "lexis" has been incorporated bodily into the English. It can be found today in at least sixty general dictionaries or other English word books, including Webster's Ninth New Collegiate Dictionary and Webster's New World Dictionary. Moreover, its meaning has not changed significantly from that of its Latin and Greek predecessors; *e.g.*, "Vocabulary, the total set of words in a language" (American Heritage Illustrated Encyclopedic Dictionary); "A vocabulary of a language, a particular subject, occupation, or activity" (Funk & Wagnalls Standard Dictionary). The district court's finding that "to establish that LEXIS is an English word required expert testimony at trial" is clearly erroneous. Anyone with a rudimentary knowledge of English can go to a library or bookstore and find the word in one of the above-mentioned standard dictionaries.

Moreover, the record discloses that numerous other companies had adopted "Lexis" in identifying their business or its product, *e.g.*, Lexis Ltd., Lexis Computer Systems Ltd., Lexis Language and Export Information Service, Lexis Corp., Maxwell Labs Lexis 3. In sum, we reject Mead's argument that LEXIS is a coined mark which originated in the mind of its former president and, as such, is entitled per se to the greater protection that a unique mark such as "Kodak" would receive. *See*

Esquire, Inc. v. Esquire Slipper Mfg. Co., 243 F.2d 540, 543 (1st Cir. 1957); *Intercontinental Mfg. Co. v. Continental Motors Corp.*, 230 F.2d 621, 623 (C.C.P.A. 1956).

Nevertheless, through its extensive sales and advertising in the field of computerized legal research, Mead has made LEXIS a strong mark in that field, and the district court so found. In particular, the district court accepted studies proffered by both parties which revealed that 76 percent of attorneys associated LEXIS with specific attributes of the service provided by Mead. However, among the general adult population, LEXIS is recognized by only one percent of those surveyed, half of this one percent being attorneys or accountants. The district court therefore concluded that LEXIS is strong only within its own market.

As appears in the Addendum to this opinion, the LEXIS mark is printed in block letters with no accompanying logo.

Toyota and Lexus

Toyota Motor Corp. has for many years manufactured automobiles, which it markets in the United States through its subsidiary Toyota Motor Sales, U.S.A. On August 24, 1987 Toyota announced a new line of luxury automobiles to be called LEXUS. The cars will be manufactured by a separate LEXUS division of Toyota, and their marketing pitch will be directed to well-educated professional consumers with annual incomes in excess of $50,000. Toyota had planned to spend $18 million to $20 million for this purpose during the first nine months of 1989.

Before adopting the completely artificial name LEXUS for its new automobile, Toyota secured expert legal advice to the effect that "there is absolutely no conflict between 'LEXIS' and 'LEXUS.'" Accordingly, when Mead subsequently objected to Toyota's use of LEXUS, Toyota rejected Mead's complaints. The district court held correctly that Toyota acted without predatory intent in adopting the LEXUS mark.

> The absence of predatory intent by the junior user is a relevant factor in assessing a claim under the antidilution statute, . . . since relief under the statute is of equitable origin, ...

Sally Gee, Inc. v. Myra Hogan, Inc., 699 F.2d 621, 626 (2d Cir. 1983) (citations omitted).

However, the district court erred in concluding that Toyota's refusal to acknowledge that its use of LEXUS might harm the LEXIS mark, deprived it of the argument that it acted in good faith. If, as we now hold, Toyota's mark did not dilute Mead's, it would be anomalous indeed to hold Toyota guilty of bad faith in proceeding in reliance on its attorney's correct advice to that effect. *See Sweats Fashions, Inc. v. Pannill Knitting Co.*, 833 F.2d 1560, 1565 (Fed.Cir. 1987); *E.S. Originals Inc. v. Stride Rite*

Corp., 656 F. Supp. 484, 490 (S.D.N.Y. 1987); *Inc. Publishing Corp. v. Manhattan Magazine, Inc.*, 616 F. Supp. 370, 394–96 (S.D.N.Y. 1985), *aff'd*, 788 F.2d 3 (2d Cir. 1986); *Procter & Gamble Co. v. Johnson & Johnson, Inc.*, 485 F. Supp. 1185, 1201–02 (S.D.N.Y. 1979), *aff'd*, 636 F.2d 1203 (2d Cir. 1980). Indeed, even if the attorney's professional advice had been wrong, it does not follow that Toyota's reliance on that advice would have constituted bad faith. *Information Clearing House, Inc. v. Find Magazine*, 492 F. Supp. 147, 161–62 (S.D.N.Y. 1980).

The LEXUS mark is in stylized, almost script-like lettering and is accompanied by a rakish L logo. *See* Addendum.

THE LAW

The brief legislative history accompanying section 368–d describes the purpose of the statute as preventing "the whittling away of an established trade-mark's selling power and value through *its* unauthorized use by others upon dissimilar products." 1954 N.Y. Legis. Ann. 49 (emphasis supplied). If we were to interpret literally the italicized word "its", we would limit statutory violations to the unauthorized use of the identical established mark. This is what Frank Schechter, the father of the dilution theory, intended when he wrote *The Rational Basis of Trademark Protection*, 40 Harv. L. Rev. 813 (1927). *See id.* at 830–33; *see also* Shire, *Dilution Versus Deception—Are State Antidilution Laws an Appropriate Alternative to the Law of Infringement*, 77 Trademark Rep. 273–76 (1987). However, since the use of obvious simulations or markedly similar marks might have the same diluting effect as would an appropriation of the original mark, the concept of exact identity has been broadened to that of substantial similarity. *Community Federal Savings and Loan Ass'n v. Orondorff*, 678 F.2d 1034 (11th Cir. 1982) (quoting *Pro-phy-lac-tic Brush Co. v. Jordan Marsh Co.*, 165 F.2d 549, 553 (1st Cir. 1948)); *Dreyfus Fund, Inc. v. Royal Bank of Canada*, 525 F. Supp. 1108, 1124 (S.D.N.Y. 1981); 2 J. McCarthy, *Trademarks and Unfair Competition* § 24:13 at 215 (2d ed. 1984). Nevertheless, in keeping with the original intent of the statute, the similarity must be substantial before the doctrine of dilution may be applied. *See Alberto-Culver Co. v. Andrea Dumon, Inc.*, 466 F.2d 705, 709 (7th Cir. 1972); *Consolidated Cosmetics v. Neilson Chemical Co.*, 109 F. Supp. 300, 310 (E.D. Mich. 1952); Ehrlich, *Anti-Dilution Laws Give Plaintiffs Powerful Weapon Against Copiers*, Nat'l L.J., May 16, 1983, at 28.

Indeed, some courts have gone so far as to hold that, although violation of an antidilution statute does not require confusion of product or source, the marks in question must be sufficiently similar that confusion may be created as between the marks themselves. *See Holiday Inns, Inc. v. Holiday Out in America*, 481 F.2d 445, 450 (5th Cir. 1973); *King Research, Inc. v. Shulton, Inc.*, 324 F. Supp. 631, 638 (S.D.N.Y. 1971), *aff'd*, 454 F.2d 66 (2d Cir. 1972). We need not go that far. We hold only that the marks must be "very" or "substantially" similar and that, absent such similarity, there can be no viable claim of dilution.

The district court's opinion was divided into two sections. The first section dealt with Toyota's alleged violation of the Lanham Act, and the second dealt with the alleged dilution of Mead's mark under New York's antidilution statute. The district court made several findings on the issue of similarity in its Lanham Act discussion; it made none in its discussion of section 368–d. Assuming that the district court's finding of lack of physical similarity in the former discussion was intended to carry over into the latter, we would find ourselves in complete accord with it since we would make the same finding. *See* Addendum; *see also Blue Bell, Inc. v. Jaymar-Ruby, Inc.*, 497 F.2d 433, 435 (2d Cir. 1974). However, if the district court's statement in its Lanham Act discussion that "in everyday spoken English, LEXUS and LEXIS are virtually identical in pronunciation" was intended to be a finding of fact rather than a statement of opinion, we question both its accuracy and its relevance. The word LEXUS is not yet widely enough known that any definitive statement can be made concerning its pronunciation by the American public. However, the two members of this Court who concur in this opinion use "everyday spoken English", and we would not pronounce LEXUS as if it were spelled LEXIS. Although our colleague takes issue with us on this point, he does not contend that if LEXUS and LEXIS are pronounced correctly, they will sound the same. We liken LEXUS to such words as "census", "focus" and "locus", and differentiate it from such words as "axis", "aegis" and "iris". If we were to substitute the letter "i" for the letter "u" in "census", we would not pronounce it as we now do. Likewise, if we were to substitute the letter "u" for the letter "i" in "axis", we would not pronounce it as we now do. In short, we agree with the testimony of Toyota's speech expert, who testified:

> Of course, anyone can pronounce "lexis" and "lexus" the same, either both with an unstressed I or both with an unstressed U, or schwa—or with some other sound in between. But, properly, the distinction between unstressed I and unstressed U, or schwa, is a standard one in English; the distinction is there to be made in ordinary, reasonably careful speech.

In addition, we do not believe that "everyday spoken English" is the proper test to use in deciding the issue of similarity in the instant case. Under the Constitution, there is a " 'commonsense' distinction between speech proposing a commercial transaction, which occurs in an area traditionally subject to government regulation, and other varieties of speech." *Central Hudson Gas & Electric Corp. v. Public Service Comm'n*, 447 U.S. 557, 562 (1980) (quoting *Ohralik v. Ohio State Bar Ass'n*, 436 U.S. 447, 455–56 (1978)). "The legitimate aim of the anti-dilution statute is to prohibit the unauthorized use of another's trademark in order to market incompatible products or services", and this constitutes a "legitimate regulation of commercial speech." *L.L. Bean, Inc. v. Drake Publishers, Inc.*, 811 F.2d 26, 32–33 (1st Cir.), *cert. denied*, 483 U.S. 1013 (1987). "Advertising is the primary means by which the connection between a name and a company is established ...", *Beneficial Corp. v. Beneficial Capital Corp.*, 529 F. Supp. 445, 448 (S.D.N.Y. 1982), and oral advertising is done primarily on radio and television. When Mead's speech expert was asked whether there were instances in which LEXUS and LEXIS would be pronounced differently, he replied "Yes, although a deliberate attempt must be made to do so. ... They can be pronounced distinctly but they are not when they are used in common parlance, in everyday language or speech." We take it as a given that television and radio announcers usually are more careful and precise in their diction than is the man on the street. Moreover, it is the rare television commercial that does not contain a visual reference to the mark and product, which in the instant case would be the LEXUS automobile. We conclude that in the field of commercial advertising, which is the field subject to regulation, there is no substantial similarity between Mead's mark and Toyota's.

There are additional factors that militate against a finding of dilution in the instant case. Such a finding must be based on two elements. First, plaintiff's mark must possess a distinctive quality capable of dilution. *Allied Maintenance Corp. v. Allied Mechanical Trades, Inc.*, 42 N.Y.2d 538, 545 (1977). Second, plaintiff must show a likelihood of dilution, *Sally Gee, Inc. v. Myra Hogan, Inc., supra*, 699 F.2d at 625. As section 368–d expressly states, a plaintiff need not show either competition between its product or service and that of the defendant or a likelihood of confusion as to the source of the goods or services. *Allied Maintenance Corp. v. Allied Mechanical Trades, Inc., supra*, 42 N.Y.2d at 543.

Distinctiveness for dilution purposes often has been equated with the strength of a mark for infringement purposes. *P.F. Cosmetique, S.A. v. Minnetonka, Inc.*, 605 F. Supp. 662, 672 (S.D.N.Y. 1985); *Allied Maintenance Corp. v. Allied Mechanical Trades, Inc., supra*, 42 N.Y.2d at 545. It also has been defined as uniqueness or as having acquired a secondary meaning. *Allied Maintenance, supra*, 42 N.Y.2d at 545. A trademark has a secondary meaning if it "has become so associated in the mind of the public with that entity [Allied] or its product that it identifies the goods sold by that entity and distinguishes them from goods sold by others." *Id.* In sum, the statute protects a trademark's "selling power." *Sally Gee, Inc. v. Myra Hogan, Inc., supra*, 699 F.2d at 624–25. However, the fact that a mark has selling power in a limited geographical or commercial area does not endow it with a secondary meaning for the public generally. *See Hartman v. Hallmark Cards, Inc.*, 833 F.2d 117, 121 (8th Cir. 1987); *Truck Equipment Service Co. v. Fruehauf Corp.*, 536 F.2d 1210, 1219 (8th Cir.), *cert. denied*, 429 U.S. 861,(1976) (quoting *Shoppers*

Fair of Arkansas, Inc. v. Sanders Co., 328 F.2d 496, 499 (8th Cir. 1964));
Restaurant Lutece, Inc. v. Houbigant, Inc., 593 F. Supp. 588, 596 (D.N.J.
1984); *Scott v. Mego International, Inc.*, 519 F. Supp. 1118, 1138 (D.
Minn. 1981).

The strength and distinctiveness of LEXIS is limited to the market
for its services—attorneys and accountants. Outside the market, LEXIS
has very little selling power. Because only one percent of the general
population associates LEXIS with the attributes of Mead's service, it
cannot be said that LEXIS identifies that service to the general public
and distinguishes it from others. Moreover, the bulk of Mead's advertising
budget is devoted to reaching attorneys through professional journals.

This Court has defined dilution as either the blurring of a mark's
product identification or the tarnishment of the affirmative associations a
mark has come to convey. *Sally Gee, Inc. v. Myra Hogan, Inc., supra*, 699
F.2d at 625 (quoting 3A Callman, *The Law of Unfair Competition,
Trademarks and Monopolies* § 84.2 at 954–55). Mead does not claim that
Toyota's use of LEXUS would tarnish affirmative associations engendered
by LEXIS. The question that remains, therefore, is whether LEXIS is
likely to be blurred by LEXUS.

Very little attention has been given to date to the distinction between
the confusion necessary for a claim of infringement and the blurring
necessary for a claim of dilution. Shire, *supra*, 77 Trademark Rep. at 293.
Although the antidilution statute dispenses with the requirements of
competition and confusion, it does not follow that every junior use of a
similar mark will dilute the senior mark in the manner contemplated by
the New York Legislature.

As already stated, the brief legislative history accompanying section
368–d described the purpose of the statute as preventing "the whittling
away of an established trademark's selling power and value through its
unauthorized use by others upon dissimilar products." The history
disclosed a need for legislation to prevent such "hypothetical anomalies"
as "Dupont shoes, Buick aspirin tablets, Schlitz varnish, Kodak pianos,
Bulova gowns, and so forth", and cited cases involving similarly famous
marks, *e.g., Tiffany & Co. v. Tiffany Productions, Inc.*, 147 Misc. 679, 264
N.Y.S. 459 (1932), *aff'd*, 237 A.D. 801, 260 N.Y.S. 821, *aff'd*, 262 N.Y. 482,
188 N.E. 30 (1933); *Philadelphia Storage Battery Co. v. Mindlin*, 163
Misc. 52, 296 N.Y.S. 176 (1937). 1954 N.Y. Legis. Ann. 49–50.

It is apparent from these references that there must be some mental
association between plaintiff's and defendant's marks.

If a reasonable buyer is not at all likely to link the two uses of
the trademark in his or her own mind, even subtly or
subliminally, then there can be no dilution. . . . Dilution theory

presumes *some kind of mental association* in the reasonable buyer's mind between the two party's [sic] uses of the mark.

2 J. McCarthy, *supra*, § 24.13 at 213–14.

This mental association may be created where the plaintiff's mark is very famous and therefore has a distinctive quality for a significant percentage of the defendant's market. *Sally Gee, Inc. v. Myra Hogan, Inc., supra*, 699 F.2d at 625. However, if a mark circulates only in a limited market, it is unlikely to be associated generally with the mark for a dissimilar product circulating elsewhere. *See, e.g., Estee Lauder, Inc. v. Cinnabar 2000 Haircutters, Inc.*, 218 U.S.P.Q. (BNA) 191 (S.D.N.Y.), *aff'd*, 714 F.2d 112 (2d Cir. 1982); *Markel v. Scovill Mfg. Co.*, 471 F. Supp. 1244 (W.D.N.Y.), *aff'd*, 610 F.2d 807 (2d Cir. 1979). As discussed above, such distinctiveness as LEXIS possesses is limited to the narrow market of attorneys and accountants. Moreover, the process which LEXIS represents is widely disparate from the product represented by LEXUS. For the general public, LEXIS has no distinctive quality that LEXUS will dilute.

The possibility that someday LEXUS may become a famous mark in the mind of the general public has little relevance in the instant dilution analysis since it is quite apparent that the general public associates nothing with LEXIS. On the other hand, the recognized sophistication of attorneys, the principal users of the service, has substantial relevance. *See Sally Gee, Inc. v. Myra Hogan, Inc., supra*, 699 F.2d at 626. Because of this knowledgeable sophistication, it is unlikely that, even in the market where Mead principally operates, there will be any significant amount of blurring between the LEXIS and LEXUS marks.

For all the foregoing reasons, we hold that Toyota did not violate section 368–d. We see no need therefore to discuss Toyota's remaining arguments for reversal.

SWEET, J. (concurring):

I concur, but write separately because I disagree with the majority's conclusion that LEXIS is not a strong mark capable of dilution and that LEXIS and LEXUS differ significantly in pronunciation, and I have a different view of the factors that are necessary to a finding of dilution.

It has become talismanic in the New York courts and in this Circuit that a cause of action under section 368–d involves two elements: 1) an extremely strong mark—either because of the mark's distinctive quality or because it has acquired secondary meaning—and 2) a likelihood of dilution. *See Allied Maintenance Corp. v. Allied Mechanical Trades, Inc.*, 42 N.Y.2d 538,(1977); *Miss Universe, Inc. v. Patricelli*, 753 F.2d 235, 238 (2d Cir. 1985); *Universal City Studios, Inc. v. Nintendo Co.*, 746 F.2d 112, 120 (2d Cir. 1984); *Sally Gee, Inc. v. Myra Hogan, Inc.*, 699 F.2d 621, 625 (2d Cir. 1983). No showing of competition between the parties or confusion about the source of products is required. *See Allied*, 42 N.Y.2d 538, at 632; *Sally Gee*, 699 F.2d at 624.

Extremely Strong Trademark

The first element of a dilution cause of action requires the plaintiff to establish that it possesses an extremely strong mark—one "which is 'truly of *distinctive* quality' or which has 'acquired a secondary meaning in the mind of the public.' " *Sally Gee*, 699 F.2d at 625 (quoting *Allied*, 42 N.Y.2d 538, at 633) (emphasis in original). A trademark has a distinctive quality if it is "distinctive, arbitrary, fanciful or coined" rather than "generic or descriptive." *Allied*, 42 N.Y.2d 538, at 632. Courts have analyzed distinctiveness for antidilution purposes in much the same way they assess the strength of the mark when evaluating likelihood of confusion. *See McDonald's Corp. v. McBagel's, Inc.*, 649 F. Supp. 1268, 1281 (S.D.N.Y. 1986); *P.F. Cosmetique, S.A. v. Minnetonka Inc.*, 605 F. Supp. 662, 672 (S.D.N.Y. 1985). "To establish secondary meaning it must be shown that through exclusive use and advertising by one entity, a name or mark has become so associated in the mind of the public with that entity or its product that it identifies the goods sold by that entity and distinguishes them from goods sold by others." *Allied*, 42 N.Y.2d 538, at 633.

The majority concludes that LEXIS is not a strong mark capable of dilution, noting that "the fact that a mark has selling power in a limited geographical or commercial area does not endow it with a secondary meaning for the public generally." Op. at 1030 (citations omitted). The majority adds:

> The strength and distinctiveness of LEXIS is limited to the market for its services—attorneys and accountants. Outside that market, LEXIS has very little selling power. Because only one percent of the general population associates LEXIS with the attributes of Mead's service, it cannot be said that LEXIS identifies that service to the general public and distinguishes it from others. Moreover, the bulk of Mead's advertising is devoted to reaching attorneys through professional journals.

Id. at 11.

This conclusion limits section 368–d's protection to nationally famous marks, because a strong mark capable of dilution is an element of a section 368–d cause of action and a plaintiff can lose on this ground alone. *See, e.g., Allied Maintenance Corp. v. Allied Mechanical Trades, Inc.*, 42 N.Y.2d 538, 632–33 (1977).

However, "the interest protected by § 368–d is . . . the *selling power* that a distinctive mark or name with favorable associations has engendered for a product in the mind of the *consuming* public." *Sally Gee, Inc. v. Myra Hogan, Inc.*, 699 F.2d 621, 624 (2d Cir. 1983) (emphasis added). The LEXIS mark has "selling power" among its consuming public—attorneys and accountants. Its lack of selling power among the general public—*i.e.*, the nonconsuming public—should not deprive the company of section 368–d's protection against dilution. *See Dreyfus Fund Inc. v. Royal Bank of Canada*, 525 F. Supp. 1108, 1125 (S.D.N.Y. 1981) ("The statute should not be read to deprive marks from protection against dilution in limited areas of use, since otherwise it would afford protection only to the most notorious of all marks."); *Wedgwood Homes, Inc. v. Lund*, 659 P.2d 377, 381 (1983) ("We see no reason why marks of national renown should enjoy protection while local marks should not. A small local firm may expend efforts and money proportionately as great as those of a large firm in order to establish its mark's distinctive quality."). The renown of a senior mark is a factor a court should assess when evaluating the likelihood of dilution, not the strength of the mark.

Further, the district court as a matter of fact found LEXIS to be a very strong mark capable of dilution. Because imagination, thought, and perception are required to associate LEXIS with a computerized legal research service, the district court ruled that the mark is at least suggestive or arbitrary. *See* Dist. Ct. Op. at 10, 26. Moreover, the district court found the mark to possess secondary meaning because it "distinguishes the LEXIS service from other products and it is uniquely associated by the consuming public with the source of the product." *Id.* at 26. It added:

> Mead has expended considerable time, effort, and money to promote the LEXIS mark. In 1987, Mead spent $3.8 million in advertising and promotion. This advertising has proven effective, judging from the LEXIS-related revenues, which exceeded $200 million in 1987. These revenues are even more impressive when viewed in light of their growth since 1984, when revenues totalled $400,000.

Id. at 27. These findings cannot be set aside as arbitrary or capricious and amply support a conclusion that LEXIS is a strong mark capable of dilution.

Likelihood of Dilution

Several definitions of dilution exist. The legislative history defined the concept as "unlawful injury caused by the whittling away of an established trade-mark's selling power and value through its unauthorized use by others upon dissimilar products." 1954 N.Y. Leg. Ann. 49. The New York Court of Appeals offered the following definition:

> The harm that section 398–d is designed to prevent is the gradual whittling away of a firm's distinctive trade-mark or name. It is not difficult to imagine the possible effect which the proliferation of various non-competitive businesses utilizing the

name Tiffany's would have upon the public's association of the name Tiffany's solely with fine jewelry. The ultimate effect has been appropriately termed dilution.

Allied, 42 N.Y.2d 538, at 632. In *Sally Gee*, this Court refined these general definitions by describing dilution as "an act which 'threatens two separable but related components of advertising value. Junior uses may blur a mark's product identification or they may tarnish the affirmative associations a mark has come to convey.'" 699 F.2d at 625 (quoting 3 R. Callman, *The Law of Unfair Competition, Trademarks, and Monopolies* § 84.2, at 954–55 (footnote omitted)).

By treating similarity of the marks as a separate element of a dilution cause of action and by evaluating the dilution claim without developing an analytical framework, the majority threatens to muddy the already murky waters of antidilution analysis. *See, e.g., Sally Gee, Inc. v. Myra Hogan, Inc.*, 699 F.2d 621, 625 (2d Cir. 1983) (dilution "remains a somewhat nebulous concept"); *Home Box Office v. Showtime/The Movie Channel*, 665 F. Supp. 1079, 1087 (S.D.N.Y.) ("a claim for dilution differs markedly from a federal trademark claim and appears less well defined"), *aff'd in part, vacated in part*, 832 F.2d 1311 (2d Cir. 1987); *see also* Shire, *Dilution Versus Deception—Are State Antidilution Laws an Appropriate Alternative to the Law of Infringement*, 77 Trademark Rep. 273, 293 (1987) [hereinafter cited as "Shire"] (courts "have consistently failed to analyze how a specific defendant's use has diluted a mark or its selling power when there is no likelihood of confusion"); Greiwe, *Antidilution Statutes: A New Attack on Comparative Advertising*, 72 Trademark Rep. 178, 183–84 (1982) ("Analysis of the process of dilution . . . has been largely superficial.").

Applying *Sally* Gee's definition, the majority finds little likelihood of dilution because LEXIS circulates in a limited market, the products covered by the LEXIS and LEXUS marks differ substantially, and Mead's principal consumers—attorneys—are sophisticated. Although I agree with these findings, I believe the majority has failed adequately to define the likelihood of dilution concept.

Defining likelihood of dilution as "tarnishing" is helpful because that principle can be applied in practice. *See, e.g., Dallas Cowboys Cheerleaders, Inc. v. Pussycat Cinema, Ltd.*, 604 F.2d 200 (2d Cir. 1979) (plaintiff's distinctive uniform diluted by defendant's use of a similar uniform in an X-rated movie); *Coca-Cola Co. v. Gemini Rising, Inc.*, 346 F. Supp. 1183 (E.D.N.Y. 1972) (plaintiff's "Coca-Cola" mark diluted by defendant's use of similar lettering in printing "Cocaine" on poster). "Blurring," however, offers practitioners and courts only marginally more guidance than "likelihood of dilution."

There is much to be gained by defining a general concept like "blurring" more specifically. As in this instance, confusion in the doctrine has created problems for trademark attorneys advising their clients about adopting trademarks, for potential litigants assessing their chances of pursuing or defending against dilution claims, and for courts attempting to apply the statute. *See* Shire, 77 Trademark Rep. at 288. In the trademark infringement context, Judge Friendly defined a similarly broad standard—likelihood of confusion—by articulating a multi-factor balancing test that considers:

> the strength of [plaintiff's] mark, the degree of similarity between the two marks, the proximity of the products, the likelihood that the prior owner will bridge the gap, actual confusion, and the reciprocal of defendant's good faith in adopting its own mark, the quality of defendant's product, and the sophistication of the buyers.

Polaroid Corp. v. Polarad Elecs. Corp., 287 F.2d 492, 495 (2d Cir.), *cert. denied*, 368 U.S. 820 (1961). This test has provided practitioners and district courts a helpful framework for assessing likelihood of confusion. *See, e.g., Lobo Enters., Inc. v. Tunnel, Inc.*, 693 F. Supp. 71, 76–79 (S.D.N.Y. 1988); *Toys "R" Us, Inc. v. Canarsie Kiddie Shop, Inc.*, 559 F. Supp. 1189, 1195–1200 (E.D.N.Y. 1983).

Like likelihood of confusion, blurring sufficient to constitute dilution requires a case-by-case factual inquiry. A review of the anti-dilution cases in this Circuit indicates that courts have articulated the following factors in considering the likelihood of dilution caused by blurring:

1) similarity of the marks

2) similarity of the products covered by the marks

3) sophistication of consumers

4) predatory intent

5) renown of the senior mark

6) renown of the junior mark

The application of these factors here requires reversal of the decision below, although on a basis that I believe differs from that stated by the majority. . . .

Balancing the Factors

The district court found a likelihood of dilution, reasoning that Toyota's promotional campaign for its LEXUS automobile "will dwarf the LEXIS mark," Dist. Ct. Op. at 30, and that Toyota acted in bad faith—although without predatory intent—by launching its LEXUS line "without any regard for its effect on the LEXIS mark." *Id.* at 31. The district court's dilution analysis did not refer to the other factors discussed above, nor did it conduct a balancing test.

It is the rule in this Circuit that a district court's findings regarding each of the *Polaroid* factors are findings of fact to which the clearly erroneous standard applies, but that the balancing of those factors to assess the likelihood of confusion is a legal conclusion subject to *de novo* appellate review. *See Hasbro, Inc. v. Lanard Toys, Ltd.*, 858 F.2d 70, 75–76 (2d Cir. 1988); *Plus Prods. v. Plus Discount Foods, Inc.*, 722 F.2d 999, 1004–05 (2d Cir. 1983). Because I discern no legitimate distinction between the district court's role in assessing each of the *Polaroid* factors and its evaluation of those factors to determine the likelihood of confusion, I believe that the clearly erroneous standard should apply to both findings and that this Court should not employ *Plus* Product's approach in its dilution analysis.

Either approach, however, would support a reversal in this case. Although the district court did not use a balancing test, its findings on the various factors demonstrate that it would have found little likelihood of dilution had it done so. LEXIS and LEXUS are pronounced the same, but the marks differ in physical appearance, they will appear in different contexts, and the products bearing the marks are dissimilar. Moreover, Mead's consumers are sophisticated, Toyota adopted the LEXUS mark without predatory intent, and LEXIS enjoys no national renown.

The only finding that supports a likelihood of dilution is the district court's conclusion that LEXUS eventually may become so famous that members of the general public who now associate LEXIS or LEXUS with nothing at all may associate the terms with Toyota's automobiles and that Mead's customers may think first of Toyota's car when they hear LEXIS. *See* Dist. Ct. Op. at 30–31. This analysis is problematic. First, section 368–d protects a mark's selling power among the consuming public. *Allied Maintenance Corp. v. Allied Mechanical Trades, Inc.*, 42 N.Y.2d 538, 630 (1977); *Sally Gee, Inc. v. Myra Hogan, Inc.*, 699 F.2d 621, 624–25 (2d Cir. 1983). Because the LEXIS mark possesses selling power only among lawyers and accountants, it is irrelevant for dilution analysis that the general public may come to associate LEXIS or LEXUS with Toyota's automobile rather than nothing at all. Second, the district court offered no evidence for its speculation that LEXUS's fame may cause Mead customers to associate "lexis" with Toyota's cars. It seems equally plausible that no blurring will occur—because many lawyers and accountants use Mead's services regularly, their frequent association of LEXIS with those services will enable LEXIS's mark to withstand Toyota's advertising campaign.

Therefore, even if we accept the district court's finding regarding the renown of the LEXUS mark, however, reversal still is required. The differences in the marks and in the products covered by the marks, the sophistication of Mead's consumers, the absence of predatory intent, and the limited renown of the LEXIS mark all indicate that blurring is unlikely.

For the reasons set forth above, I concur.

NOTES FOR DISCUSSION

1. *Dilution, Likelihood of Confusion, and the "Sweet" Factors.* The majority's reasoning in the case, idiosyncratic as it was, has never gained much traction in the subsequent development of dilution law, but the six factors that Judge Sweet identified in his concurrence for determining whether there is a likelihood of dilution became known as the "Sweet factors" and were widely adopted as a useful approach to the issue. Examine the factors. How are they similar to, and how do they differ from, the *Polaroid* factors used to determine the likelihood of confusion?

2. *Dilution and Likelihood of Confusion: Redundant or Different?* Despite the differences between the factors used for the two tests, the outcome in *Mead Data Central* reflects the reality that dilution is almost always merely redundant to the standard trademark infringement analysis. In virtually all of the cases, state and federal, that have been litigated since Massachusetts first adopted a dilution statute in 1947, the two causes of action, dilution and trademark infringement, are resolved identically. If a jury or the court finds trademark infringement, it will also find dilution. If the jury or court finds no likelihood of confusion, it will also find no dilution. Over the past sixty years, there are only a relative handful of cases where the two causes of action are resolved differently.

To see why this might be the case, consider the following questions: Why did Mead Data lose on its dilution claim? Was its mark insufficiently famous? Is fame required by the New York statute? Was it that the goods were too unrelated? But isn't reaching unrelated goods the point of dilution? Now compare your answer to those questions with your answer to the following question: Why did Mead Data lose on its likelihood of confusion claim?

3. *Three Practical Approaches to Dilution.* Consider three approaches to dilution. The first, just discussed, is that dilution is entirely redundant to the ordinary standard of infringement. Under this view, dilution does not change the outcome of any case. It merely reinforces, and to some extent, represents *ex post* legislative approval, of the judicial expansion of the likelihood of confusion standard.

Second, if we were really serious about protecting the trademark owner's interest in her mark, without regard to other considerations, we could interpret dilution to provide property-like rights to the mark in gross—that is entirely divorced from the goods or services to which the mark is attached. Under this approach, once a mark becomes sufficiently distinctive or famous, then any commercial use of the same or sufficiently similar mark will create actionable dilution. Although rare, occasionally courts suggest that dilution amounts to such property-like protection. For example, in *Ringling Bros.-Barnum & Bailey Combined Shows, Inc. v. Celozzi-Ettelson Chevrolet, Inc.,* the circus sued a used car dealer for using the slogan THE GREATEST USED CAR SHOW ON EARTH. 855 F.2d 480 (7th Cir. 1988). Applying Illinois's dilution statute, the Seventh Circuit held that such use constituted dilution on the grounds that the plaintiff's mark was famous and that the defendant's mark was too similar. *Id.* at 482–83.

The central difficulty with this approach, from a statutory construction perspective, is that Congress knows how to provide such property-like protection in marks. In the Amateur Sports Act, Congress expressly provided such property-like protection for the word Olympics, and related words, to the United States Olympic Committee (the "USOC"). 36 U.S.C. § 220506 (stating that the USOC shall have "the exclusive right to use . . . the word[ ] 'Olympics' "); *see also San Francisco Arts & Athletics, Inc. v. United States Olympic Committee*, 483 U.S. 522, 531 (1987) (holding that Congress gave the USOC the exclusive right to use the words OLYMPICS without regard to the presence or absence of a likelihood of confusion and without regard to trademark's traditional defenses, such as fair use). Both Congress and the state legislatures before it used quite different language in crafting protection against dilution.

A third approach is to treat dilution as some sort of "likelihood of confusion-plus" analysis. Here, the notion is that whatever scope of protection the traditional likelihood of confusion test supplies, dilution adds just a little bit more. Particularly by deemphasizing those factors in the likelihood of confusion analysis that focus on the similarity of products and marketing channels, dilution allows a trademark owner to reach some conduct that would not create a likelihood of confusion. But why would such a penumbra of protection be desirable? Professor Robert Bone argues that we may need to provide such "surplus" protection, compared to the theoretical ideal protecting consumers would require, because in the real world trademark protection entails enforcement costs. Robert G. Bone, *Enforcement Costs and Trademark Puzzles*, 90 VA. L. REV. 2099 (2004). Recall, for example, from our previous discussion of actual confusion that just because there is actual confusion does not mean a plaintiff will be able to prove it in court. Not every confused consumer will complain to the trademark owner; in fact, the vast majority of confused consumers probably do not. Even where confusion is widespread, converting that fact into a witness prepared to testify in court is not easy. These enforcement costs create the possibility that there are cases where consumer confusion is occurring, but the enforcement costs will preclude proof of that in a judicial proceeding. One way to address such cases, assuming they exist, would be to provide a penumbra around the likelihood of confusion standard. *Id.* at 2144–55 (attempting to justify the recognition of sponsorship confusion using a similar analysis).

The central difficulty with such a justification, however, is that the standard infringement inquiry already includes considerable wiggle room. Is there any reasonable argument that we need dilution in order to be sure to catch all of the cases where actual confusion will occur if a defendant's use is allowed to continue? Why do you think that Mead Data Central wanted to stop Toyota from using the mark Lexus for its luxury-line of cars?

4. *Theory and Reality: Does Dilution Exist?* As a theory, the notion that a mark might be "whittled away" to nothing by others' use of an identical or near-identical mark on unrelated goods is perfectly coherent, but as a matter of reality, does such whittling away ever occur? In this regard, note that the New York legislature in enacting the statute refers primarily to hypothetical cases, "Dupont shoes, Buick aspirin tablets, Schlitz varnish, Kodak pianos, Bulova gowns, and so forth." None of these cases actually occurred. We'll see this reliance on hypotheticals again when Congress enacted the Federal Trademark Dilution Act. Should hypotheticals justify state or congressional action? Why not point to real world instances where an initially famous mark has been whittled away to nothing because of others' use of the mark on unrelated goods?

To be fair, as the court notes, the New York legislature also cited two cases, *Tiffany & Co. v. Tiffany Productions, Inc.*, 147 Misc. 679, 264 N.Y.S. 459 (1932), *aff'd*, 237 A.D. 801, 260 N.Y.S. 821, *aff'd*, 262 N.Y. 482, 188 N.E. 30 (1933); *Philadelphia Storage Battery Co. v. Mindlin*, 163 Misc. 52, 296 N.Y.S. 176 (1937), as justification for the dilution provision. Ironically, however, both of the plaintiffs in those two cases prevailed, and the defendants' use of TIFFANY in the first case, and PHILCO in the second, were enjoined under the ordinary infringement standard even though the defendants' use was on unrelated services or goods. Does the citation to these cases reinforce the notion that dilution is merely redundant to the broader likelihood of confusion infringement standard that developed over the twentieth century?

Given that the federal protection against dilution was not available until 1995, and that before that, only roughly half the states provided such protection, surely we can identify at least one real world instance where dilution occurred over the course of the twentieth century. Can you name one famous mark that has been whittled away through widespread use on unrelated goods? Remember dilution does not override the genericness doctrine, so identifying initially famous brands that became the generic name for the associated good or service does not count. Moreover, it's also not enough to identify a once-famous mark that has faded over time. You must also show that the fading was caused by the diluting uses of the mark, rather than some other factors, such as the ups-and-downs of the marketplace.

Despite years of asking, no one has yet to identify even a single such case to me. The closest I can come are instances where famous marks have entered the popular vocabulary as adjectives with either positive, negative or potentially mixed, context-dependent, connotations. For example, I have heard the following trademarks used as such adjectives in ordinary conversation: MICKEY MOUSE; CADILLAC and ROLLS ROYCE; and BARBIE. Can you think of any additional ones? Is this what we mean by dilution?

Of course, this is not the classic blurring of the hypothetical "Buick aspirin tablets." Indeed, in many of these cases, it is consumers rather than the producers of unrelated goods that have adopted, rewritten, or expanded the meanings of these marks. If this is what we mean by dilution, has the widespread use of these marks as ordinary adjectives "whittled away" the brand significance of these marks? Or, to the contrary, would you say that the common use of these marks in ordinary speech has reinforced the fame and distinctiveness of the original? Even if you feel this should be actionable dilution, who would the trademark owners sue to stop such use?

Another real world example that may help understand whether dilution ever occurs is the practice of reusing city names. For example, there is a Rome in every state in this country. Has that widespread use "whittled away" the connection between the word Rome and a city in Italy which made the name initially famous? If I told you that I went to Paris this summer, would you ask me if I saw the Eiffel Tower or the Paris Texas Eiffel Tower? (Yes, Paris, Texas not only took Paris, France's name, it also has a replica of the Eiffel Tower. It proudly proclaims itself the second largest Paris with the second largest Eiffel Tower.)

On the other hand, would you say that New York has whittled away the significance of York? Has the fame of York faded because the city and state of New York adopted similar names or for other reasons?

5. *Marketing Research and Dilution.* Market researchers have investigated whether a third party's use of a mark on an unrelated good can cause dilution in various experimental settings. For example, Maureen Morrin and Jacob Jacoby tested a group of sixty-four undergraduates to determine whether their ability to link a famous mark to its associated product or characteristics was slowed, or rendered less accurate, as a result of exposure to potentially blurring or tarnishing advertisements. *See* Maureen Morrin & Jacob Jacoby, *Trademark Dilution: Empirical Measures for an Elusive Concept,* 19 J. PUB. POL'Y & MARKETING 265 (2000). They tested three marks, Godiva, Heineken, and Hyatt, that they considered famous. They exposed one group of the students to reinforcing ads—that is ads for these marks in connection with the products or services for which they are famous. They exposed a second group to unrelated ads. They exposed a third group to potentially diluting ads, such as Dogiva for dog biscuits, Hyatt for legal services, and Heineken for popcorn. They then tested participants in each group using a computer program to see how quickly and accurately the subjects could determine whether a given connection between the mark and a product or product quality were true or false. For example, the word "Godiva" will flash on the screen followed shortly by "chocolate," and the students were asked to indicate either yes or no as to whether that was a correct connection as quickly as possible.

The researchers found that the students exposed to the potentially diluting ads were somewhat less accurate in identifying connections between a mark and its meaning, than those who had been exposed to reinforcing or neutral ads, with a mean accuracy of 73.1 percent for the students shown diluting ads compared with mean accuracies of 88.9 percent and 84.3 percent for the students shown reinforcing or neutral ads, respectively. Similarly, where they identified the correct associations, students shown the potentially diluting ads were also slightly slower to respond than the students shown reinforcing or neutral ads, with a mean response time of 836 milliseconds for the diluting ads group, compared with 672 milliseconds and 713 milliseconds for the reinforcing and neutral ads groups respectively. *Id.* at 269. Other researchers have obtained similar experimental results. *See* Chris Pullig *et al., Brand Dilution: When Do New Brands Hurt Existing Brands?*, J. MARKETING, Spring 2006, at 52, 61–62.

Do these studies provide proof that dilution is not merely a theoretical concept? Or are the results simply a construct of the artificial setting in which the questions were asked? In answering these questions, think about how important context is to interpreting what a speaker has said. If a single word, such as Paris, has several meanings, or if different words, such as to, too, and two, all sound alike, how does a listener determine which meaning to attach? In the Morrin and Jacoby study, they offered the students in one of the groups different meanings for the same or similar words. Then they asked them which meaning was intended, but used a computer program to explore meanings that divorced the word entirely from any broader conversational context. Given this set-up, isn't it inevitable that the students exposed to different meanings will be less certain which meaning the researchers were looking for in the computer questionnaire? Is that all these experiments effectively demonstrate—that context matters? Would one of these students, who may have been momentarily uncertain when trying to respond to questions on a computer screen, remain even momentarily uncertain if they were in the mall looking for chocolate, or driving down a freeway looking for a hotel to spend the night, or in the beer aisle looking for a six-pack? For more on this, see Rebecca Tushnet, *Gone in 60 Milliseconds: Trademark Law and Cognitive Science*, 86 TEX. L. REV. 507 (2008). Chris Brown, *A Dilution Delusion: The Unjustifiable Protection of Similar Marks*, 72 U. CIN. L. REV. 1023, 1038–39 (2004) (citing psychological evidence that the mental processing of related uses may actually strengthen rather than blur the brand in some cases).

B. THE RISE OF FEDERAL DILUTION CLAIMS

Not satisfied with the somewhat patchwork nature of state dilution protection, trademark owners repeatedly attempted to add anti-dilution protection to the Lanham Trademark Act. Indeed, proposals for dilution protection were included in some of the bills in the 1930s and 1940s during the legislative process leading to the enactment of the Trademark Act of 1946. Proponents tried again in the 1950s, and yet again in the 1980s, as part of the Trademark Law Revision Act of 1988. None of these efforts bore fruit, however, until 1995, when President Bill Clinton signed the Federal Trademark Dilution Act (the "FTDA"), and added section 43(c) to the Trademark Act.

Although enacted in part to replace the varying state law approaches to dilution with a uniform federal standard, the act has so far failed to achieve uniformity for two reasons. First, for the most part, it did not preempt state dilution law, and as a result, for plaintiffs unable to satisfy the federal standards, pursuing a state law claim for dilution remains a viable option. Second, in addition to the continuing availability of state dilution law, the federal courts disagreed as to what was required to establish dilution under the federal statute.

These disagreements covered a range of issues. For example, in contrast to many of the state dilution statutes, the FTDA expressly required a mark to be famous. Yet, some federal courts held that fame in a particular product market (so-called "niche" fame) or in a particular geographic region was sufficient. *See, e.g., Everest Capital Ltd. v. Everest Funds Mgmt., L.L.C.*, 393 F.3d 755, 763 (8th Cir. 2005). Other courts held that the FTDA extended dilution protection only to inherently distinctive marks. *See, e.g., New York Stock Exchange, Inc. v. New York, New York Hotel, LLC*, 293 F.3d 550, 557 (2d Cir. 2002); *TCPIP Holding, Inc. v. Haar Communications*, 244 F.3d 88, 98 (2d Cir. 2001). Yet others suggested that the FTDA reached only blurring and not tarnishment. *See, e.g., Moseley v. V Secret Catalogue, Inc.*, 537 U.S. 418, 432 (2003) (questioning whether the specific language of the FTDA could be read to encompass a claim based upon tarnishment). The most significant disagreement among the federal courts, however, concerned the standard for liability. One group of courts, led by the Second Circuit, held that a plaintiff could establish liability by showing that dilution was likely in the future; proof that dilution had already occurred was not required. However, a second group, led by the Fourth Circuit, held that the language of the FTDA did not encompass a mere likelihood of dilution, but required proof of actual dilution. In *Moseley v. V Secret Catalogue, Inc.*, 537 U.S. 418 (2003), the Court resolved this conflict between the circuits and held that the FTDA required proof of actual dilution.

Proponents of broad dilution protection complained to Congress that the *Moseley* decision had inappropriately narrowed the availability of dilution protection. Responding to these concerns, and attempting to resolve the other conflicts which had arisen concerning the proper interpretation of the federal dilution statute, Congress made significant amendments to section 43(c) in the Trademark Dilution Revision Act of 2006, Pub. L. No. 312, 109th Cong., 2d Sess., 120 Stat. 1730, and it currently reads, in relevant part:

Section 43(c). Dilution by blurring; dilution by tarnishment.

(1) *Injunctive relief.* Subject to the principles of equity, the owner of a famous mark that is distinctive, inherently or through acquired distinctiveness, shall be entitled to an injunction against another person who, at any time after the owner's mark has become famous, commences

use of a mark or trade name in commerce that is likely to cause dilution by blurring or dilution by tarnishment of the famous mark, regardless of the presence or absence of actual or likely confusion, of competition, or of actual economic injury.

(2) *Definitions.*

(A) For purposes of paragraph (1), a mark is famous if it is widely recognized by the general consuming public of the United States as a designation of source of the goods or services of the mark's owner. In determining whether a mark possesses the requisite degree of recognition, the court may consider all relevant factors, including the following:

(i) The duration, extent, and geographic reach of advertising and publicity of the mark, whether advertised or publicized by the owner or third parties.

(ii) The amount, volume, and geographic extent of sales of goods or services offered under the mark.

(iii) The extent of actual recognition of the mark.

(iv) Whether the mark was registered under the Act of March 3, 1881, or the Act of February 20, 1905, or on the principal register.

(B) For purposes of paragraph (1), "dilution by blurring" is association arising from the similarity between a mark or trade name and a famous mark that impairs the distinctiveness of the famous mark. In determining whether a mark or trade name is likely to cause dilution by blurring, the court may consider all relevant factors, including the following:

(i) The degree of similarity between the mark or trade name and the famous mark.

(ii) The degree of inherent or acquired distinctiveness of the famous mark.

(iii) The extent to which the owner of the famous mark is engaging in substantially exclusive use of the mark.

(iv) The degree of recognition of the famous mark.

(v) Whether the user of the mark or trade name intended to create an association with the famous mark.

(vi) Any actual association between the mark or trade name and the famous mark.

(C) For purposes of paragraph (1), "dilution by tarnishment" is association arising from the similarity between a mark or trade name and a famous mark that harms the reputation of the famous mark.

(3) *Exclusions.* The following shall not be actionable as dilution by blurring or dilution by tarnishment under this subsection:

(A) Any fair use, including a nominative or descriptive fair use, or facilitation of such fair use, of a famous mark by another person other than as a designation of source for the person's own goods or services, including use in connection with—

> (i) advertising or promotion that permits consumers to compare goods or services; or

> (ii) identifying and parodying, criticizing, or commenting upon the famous mark owner or the goods or services of the famous mark owner.

(B) All forms of news reporting and news commentary.

(C) Any noncommercial use of a mark.

(4) *Burden of proof.* In a civil action for trade dress dilution under this Act for trade dress not registered on the principal register, the person who asserts trade dress protection has the burden of proving that—

(A) the claimed trade dress, taken as a whole, is not functional and is famous; and

(B) if the claimed trade dress includes any mark or marks registered on the principal register, the unregistered matter, taken as a whole, is famous separate and apart from any fame of such registered marks.

* * *

(7) *Savings clause.* Nothing in this subsection shall be construed to impair, modify, or supersede the applicability of the patent laws of the United States.

NOTES FOR DISCUSSION

1. *Federal Dilution: Post-2006.* How did Congress resolve each of the disputes that led to the 2006 Amendments? Following the amendments, is niche or regional fame sufficient to support a federal claim for dilution? Are only inherently distinctive marks eligible for dilution protection or does the statute protect marks that have acquired distinctiveness as well? Does the federal statute encompass both blurring and tarnishment, or only blurring? Must a plaintiff prove actual dilution or is a likelihood of dilution sufficient?

2. *Federal Dilution and Professor Schechter.* How does the federal statute compare to Professor Schechter's original vision? Does it contain the limitations Professor Schechter articulated? For example, does the federal statute reach only the use of identical marks by a defendant? Does it reach a defendant's use only if it is on unrelated goods?

3. *Practical Differences?* Although Congress enacted dilution protection, the key question remains: In practice, what conduct does dilution reach that likelihood of confusion does not? The legislative history does not provide much useful guidance on this issue. In an attempt to differentiate the two, the House Report which accompanied the FTDA offered the following

distinction: "Confusion leads to immediate injury, while dilution is an infection, which if allowed to spread, will inevitably destroy the advertising value of the mark." H.R. Rep. No. 104–374, p. 1030 (1995). Powerful imagery, but does this provide a workable test for identifying when dilution is likely?

In addition, just like the state legislatures before it, the House Report also offered some (indeed, the same) hypothetical examples of dilution. It stated that "the use of DUPONT shoes, BUICK aspirin, and KODAK pianos would be actionable under this legislation." *Id.* Does this suggest that Congress intended dilution to create property-like rights in famous marks, so that the owner of a famous mark can enjoin a junior user's use of an identical mark on unrelated goods as a matter of course? *Cf. Moseley v. V Secret Catalogue*, 537 U.S. 418 (2003) (suggesting that actual dilution could be proven through circumstantial evidence and then stating that "the obvious case is one where the junior and senior marks are identical").

Following the 2006 amendments, the statute defines dilution by blurring as an "association arising from the similarity between a mark or trade name and a famous mark that impairs the distinctiveness of the famous mark." 15 U.S.C. § 1125(c)(2)(A). Should we interpret that language in the same way as the language in the Amateur Sports Act (providing that the Olympics Committee "shall have the exclusive right to use . . . the word[ ] 'Olympics' ")? What does the word "distinctiveness" mean in the statute? Does it mean "uniqueness"? Or does it mean the mark's capacity for source identification? Are these the same? Is the word "American" in American Airlines unique? Is it source-identifying? For an argument that a lack of uniqueness should constitute a complete defense to a claim for dilution, see Sara K. Stadler, *The Wages of Ubiquity in Trademark Law*, 88 IOWA L. REV. 731 (2003).

1. DILUTION: CONCEPT AND POLICY

TY INC. V. PERRYMAN

306 F.3d 509 (7th Cir. 2002)

POSNER, J.

Ty Inc., the manufacturer of Beanie Babies, the well-known beanbag stuffed animals, brought this suit for trademark infringement against Ruth Perryman. Perryman sells second-hand beanbag stuffed animals, primarily but not exclusively Ty's Beanie Babies, over the Internet. Her Internet address ("domain name"), a particular focus of Ty's concern, is bargainbeanies.com. She has a like-named Web site (http://www.bargain beanies.com) where she advertises her wares. Ty's suit is based on the federal antidilution statute, 15 U.S.C. § 1125(c), which protects "famous" marks from commercial uses that cause "dilution of the distinctive quality of the mark." See *Nabisco, Inc. v. PF Brands, Inc.*, 191 F.3d 208, 214–16 (2d Cir. 1999). The district court granted summary judgment in favor of Ty and entered an injunction that forbids the defendant to use "BEANIE or BEANIES or any colorable imitation thereof (whether alone or in connection with other terms) within any business name, Internet domain name, or trademark, or in connection with any non-Ty products." Perryman's appeal argues primarily that "beanies" has become a generic term for beanbag stuffed animals and therefore cannot be appropriated as a trademark at all, and that in any event the injunction (which has remained in effect during the appeal) is overbroad.

The fundamental purpose of a trademark is to reduce consumer search costs by providing a concise and unequivocal identifier of the particular source of particular goods. The consumer who knows at a glance whose brand he is being asked to buy knows whom to hold responsible if the brand disappoints and whose product to buy in the future if the brand pleases. This in turn gives producers an incentive to maintain high and uniform quality, since otherwise the investment in their trademark may be lost as customers turn away in disappointment from the brand. A successful brand, however, creates an incentive in unsuccessful competitors to pass off their inferior brand as the successful brand by adopting a confusingly similar trademark, in effect appropriating the goodwill created by the producer of the successful brand. The traditional and still central concern of trademark law is to provide remedies against this practice.

Confusion is not a factor here, however, with a minor exception discussed at the end of the opinion. Perryman is not a competing producer of beanbag stuffed animals, and her Web site clearly disclaims any affiliation with Ty. But that does not get her off the hook. The reason is that state and now federal law also provides a remedy against the "dilution" of a trademark, though as noted at the outset of this opinion the federal statute is limited to the subset of "famous" trademarks and to dilutions of them caused by commercial uses that take place in interstate or foreign commerce. "Beanie Babies," and "Beanies" as the shortened form, are famous trademarks in the ordinary sense of the term: "everybody has heard of them"; they are "truly prominent and renowned," in the words of Professor McCarthy, 4 *McCarthy on Trademarks and Unfair Competition* § 24: 109, p. 24–234 (2001), as distinguished from having a merely local celebrity. *TCPIP Holding Co. v. Haar Communications Inc.*, 244 F.3d 88, 98–99 (2d Cir. 2001). And while both this court and the Third Circuit have held, in opposition to the Second Circuit's *TCPIP* decision, that "fame," though it cannot be local, may be limited to "niche" markets, *Syndicate Sales, Inc. v. Hampshire Paper Corp.*, 192 F.3d 633, 640–41 (7th Cir. 1999); *Times Mirror Magazines, Inc. v. Las Vegas Sports News, L.L.C.*, 212 F.3d 157, 164 (3d Cir. 2000), this is not a conflict to worry over here; Ty's trademarks are household words. And Perryman's use of these words was commercial in nature and took place in interstate commerce, and doubtless, given the reach of the aptly named World Wide Web, in foreign commerce as well.

But what is "dilution"? There are (at least) three possibilities relevant to this case, each defined by a different underlying concern. First, there is concern that consumer search costs will rise if a trademark becomes associated with a variety of unrelated products. Suppose an upscale restaurant calls itself "Tiffany." There is little danger that the consuming public will think it's dealing with a branch of the Tiffany jewelry store if it patronizes this restaurant. But when consumers next see the name "Tiffany" they may think about both the restaurant and the jewelry store, and if so the efficacy of the name as an identifier of the store will be diminished. Consumers will have to think harder—incur as it were a higher imagination cost—to recognize the name as the name of the store. *Exxon Corp. v. Exxene Corp.*, 696 F.2d 544, 549–50 (7th Cir. 1982); cf. *Mead Data Central, Inc. v. Toyota Motor Sales, U.S.A., Inc.*, 875 F.2d 1026, 1031 (2d Cir. 1989) ("The [legislative] history [of New York's antidilution statute] disclosed a need for legislation to prevent such 'hypothetical anomalies' as 'Dupont shoes, Buick aspirin tablets, Schlitz varnish, Kodak pianos, Bulova gowns' "); 4 *McCarthy on Trademarks and Unfair Competition, supra*, § 24: 68, pp. 24–120 to 24–121. So "blurring" is one form of dilution.

Now suppose that the "restaurant" that adopts the name "Tiffany" is actually a striptease joint. Again, and indeed even more certainly than in the previous case, consumers will not think the striptease joint under common ownership with the jewelry store. But because of the inveterate tendency of the human mind to proceed by association, every time they think of the word "Tiffany" their image of the fancy jewelry store will be tarnished by the association of the word with the strip joint. *Hormel Foods Corp. v.* Jim Henson Productions, Inc., 73 F.3d 497, 507 (2d Cir. 1996); 4 *McCarthy on Trademarks and Unfair Competition, supra*, § 24: 95, pp. 24–195, 24–198. So "tarnishment" is a second form of dilution. Analytically it is a subset of blurring, since it reduces the distinctiveness of the trademark as a signifier of the trademarked product or service.

Third, and most far-reaching in its implications for the scope of the concept of dilution, there is a possible concern with situations in which, though there is neither blurring nor tarnishment, someone is still taking a free ride on the investment of the trademark owner in the trademark. Suppose the "Tiffany" restaurant in our first hypothetical example is located in Kuala Lumpur and though the people who patronize it (it is upscale) have heard of the Tiffany jewelry store, none of them is ever going to buy anything there, so that the efficacy of the trademark as an identifier will not be impaired. If appropriation of Tiffany's aura is nevertheless forbidden by an expansive concept of dilution, the benefits of the jewelry store's investment in creating a famous name will be, as economists say, "internalized"—that is, Tiffany will realize the full benefits of the investment rather than sharing those benefits with others—and as a result the amount of investing in creating a prestigious name will rise.

This rationale for antidilution law has not yet been articulated in or even implied by the case law, although a few cases suggest that the concept of dilution is not exhausted by blurring and tarnishment, see *Panavision Int'l, L.P. v. Toeppen*, 141 F.3d 1316, 1326 (9th Cir. 1998); *Intermatic, Inc. v. Toeppen*, 947 F. Supp. 1227, 1238–39 (N.D. Ill. 1996); *Rhee Bros., Inc. v. Han Ah Reum Corp.*, 178 F. Supp. 2d 525, 530 (D. Md. 2001), and the common law doctrine of "misappropriation" might conceivably be invoked in support of the rationale that we have sketched. See Rochelle Cooper Dreyfuss & Roberta Rosenthal Kwall, *Intellectual Property: Cases and Materials on Trademark, Copyright and Patent Law* 137–38 (1996). The validity of the rationale may be doubted, however. The number of prestigious names is so vast (and, as important, would be even if there were no antidilution laws) that it is unlikely that the owner of a prestigious trademark could obtain substantial license fees if commercial use of the mark without his consent were forbidden despite the absence of consumer confusion, blurring, or tarnishment. Competition would drive the fee to zero since, if the name is being used in an unrelated market, virtually every prestigious name will be a substitute for every other in that market.

None of the rationales we have canvassed supports Ty's position in this case. Perryman is not producing a product, or a service, such as dining at a restaurant, that is distinct from any specific product; rather, she is selling the very product to which the trademark sought to be defended against her "infringement" is attached. You can't sell a branded product without using its brand name, that is, its trademark. Supposing that Perryman sold *only* Beanie Babies (a potentially relevant qualification, as we'll see), we would find it impossible to understand how she could be thought to be blurring, tarnishing, or otherwise free riding to any significant extent on Ty's investment in its mark. To say she was would amount to saying that if a used car dealer truthfully advertised that it sold Toyotas, or if a muffler manufacturer truthfully advertised that it specialized in making mufflers for installation in Toyotas, Toyota would have a claim of trademark infringement. Of course there can be no aftermarket without an original market, and in that sense sellers in a trademarked good's aftermarket are free riding on the trademark. But in that attenuated sense of free riding, almost everyone in business is free riding. . . .

We do not think that by virtue of trademark law producers own their aftermarkets and can impede sellers in the aftermarket from marketing the trademarked product. In this respect the case parallels our most recent decision dealing with Ty's intellectual property, in which we found that Ty was attempting to control the market in collectors' guides to

Beanie Babies by an overly expansive interpretation of its copyrights. *Ty, Inc. v. Publications Int'l Ltd.*, 292 F.3d 512 (7th Cir. 2002).

We surmise that what Ty is seeking in this case is an extension of antidilution law to forbid commercial uses that accelerate the transition from trademarks (brand names) to generic names (product names). Words such as "thermos," "yo-yo," "escalator," "cellophane," and "brassiere" started life as trademarks, but eventually lost their significance as source identifiers and became the popular names of the product rather than the name of the trademark owner's brand, and when that happened continued enforcement of the trademark would simply have undermined competition with the brand by making it difficult for competitors to indicate that they were selling the same product—by rendering them in effect speechless. Ty is doubtless cognizant of a similar and quite real danger to "Beanie Babies" and "Beanies." Notice that the illustrations we gave of trademarks that became generic names are all descriptive or at least suggestive of the product, which makes them better candidates for genericness than a fanciful trademark such as "Kodak" or "Exxon." Ty's trademarks likewise are descriptive of the product they denote; its argument that "Beanies" is "inherently distinctive" (like Kodak and Exxon), and therefore protected by trademark law without proof of secondary meaning, is nonsense. A trademark that describes a basic element of the product, as "Beanies" does, is not protected unless the owner can establish that the consuming public accepts the word as the designation of a brand of the product (that it has acquired, as the cases say, secondary meaning). *Two Pesos, Inc. v. Taco Cabana, Inc.*, 505 U.S. 763, 769 (1992); *Platinum Home Mortgage Corp. v. Platinum Financial Group, Inc.*, 149 F.3d 722, 727 (7th Cir. 1998). As the public does with regard to "Beanies"—for now. But because the word is catchier than "beanbag stuffed animals," "beanbag toys," or "plush toys," it may someday "catch on" to the point where the mark becomes generic, and then Ty will have to cast about for a different trademark.

Although there is a social cost when a mark becomes generic—the trademark owner has to invest in a new trademark to identify his brand—there is also a social benefit, namely an addition to ordinary language. A nontrivial number of words in common use began life as trademarks. See, e.g., Shawn M. Clankie, "Brand Name Use in Creative Writing: Genericide or Language Right?" in *Perspectives on Plagiarism and Intellectual Property in a Postmodern World* 253 (Lisa Buranen and Alice M. Roy eds. 1999); Monroe Friedman, "The Changing Language of a Consumer Society: Brand Name Usage in Popular American Novels in the Postwar Era," 11 *Journal of Consumer Research* 927 (1985). An interpretation of antidilution law as arming trademark owners to enjoin uses of their mark that, while not confusing, threaten to render the mark generic may therefore not be in the public interest. Moreover, the vistas of litigation that such a theory of dilution opens up are staggering. Ty's counsel at argument refused to disclaim a right to sue the publishers of dictionaries should they include an entry for "beanie," lowercased and defined as a beanbag stuffed animal, thus accelerating the transition from trademark to generic term. He should have disclaimed such a right. See *Illinois High School Ass'n v. GTE Vantage Inc.*, 99 F.3d 244, 246 (7th Cir. 1996); 2 *McCarthy on Trademarks and Unfair Competition, supra*, § 12: 28, pp. 12–79 to 12–81.

We reject the extension of antidilution law that Ty beckons us to adopt, but having done so we must come back to the skipped issue of confusion. For although 80 percent of Perryman's sales are of Ty's products, this means that 20 percent are not, and on her Web page after listing the various Ty products under such names as "Beanie Babies" and "Teenie Beanies" she has the caption "Other Beanies" and under that is a list of products such as "Planet Plush" and "Rothschild Bears" that are not manufactured by Ty. This is plain misdescription, in fact false advertising, and supports the last prohibition in the injunction, the prohibition against using "Beanie" or "Beanies" "in connection with any non-Ty products." That much of the injunction should stand. But Ty has not demonstrated any basis for enjoining Perryman from using the terms in "any business name, Internet domain name, or trademark." . . .

So the judgment must be vacated and the case remanded for the formulation of a proper injunction. But is more open on remand? The judge merely granted summary judgment for Ty, and we are merely reversing (in part) that ruling. Ordinarily this would mean that Ty would have a shot at a trial in which it might try to convince the judge (as there is no jury in trademark cases) that its rights under antidilution law really were violated. But this case is unusual because, given Perryman's status as a seller in the secondary market created as a result of Ty's marketing strategy, we cannot imagine a state of facts consistent with the extensive record compiled in the summary judgment proceeding that could possibly justify an injunction against Perryman's representing in her business name and Internet and Web addresses that she is doing what she has a perfect right to do, namely sell Beanie Babies. We therefore direct that the proceedings on remand be limited to the reformulation of the injunction in conformity with this opinion.

VACATED AND REMANDED WITH INSTRUCTIONS.

NOTES FOR DISCUSSION

1. *Dilution versus Confusion.* How did the court resolve the dilution claim? How did it resolve the likelihood of confusion claim? What, if anything, did the dilution claim address that likelihood of confusion did not?

2. *Theories of Dilution.* The court lays out the two accepted theories of dilution: (i) blurring; and (ii) tarnishment. The court also articulates a third: (iii) free-riding. Should courts recognize "free riding" on the goodwill or

reputation of a famous brand to be actionable dilution? Does this category have any sensible limits? What is free riding? Is Perryman "free riding"? Certainly, she is making money on the popularity of Beanie Babies and is not paying Ty for that privilege. Is that free riding? The court admits that it might be, but then insists that in that broad sense "almost everyone in business is free riding." Do you agree? Does that provide a meaningful limit to a concept of dilution based upon free riding? If everyone is engaging in the type of free riding at issue, does that suggest that the free riding at issue is or should be permissible?

Admittedly, allowing others to earn money based upon one entity's creation, through hard work and investment, of a famous brand creates an external benefit. Will this externality lead to an insufficient supply of famous brands or leave businesses with too little incentive to invest in making their brands famous? Do we have any empirical evidence on this issue? Did companies invest sufficiently to create famous brands before the advent of dilution protection? Would society be better off with more investment in creating such brands? Where would the extra money to invest in making a brand famous come from? What would society have to give up in order to get more famous brands? How do we know which use of the available resources would be more valuable to society?

Alternatively, should a trademark owner have the legal right to control every valuable use of its mark, something akin to the "full and despotic" dominion Blackstone once attributed to English landowners over their land?

3. *Justifications: Dilution by Blurring.* How does the court justify a cause of action against dilution by blurring? Do you think Congress enacted the FTDA in order to prevent uses that increase consumer search costs?

4. *Control of Second-Hand Markets.* As we shall see in Chapter 9, Ty is not the first trademark owner to seek control of the sale of its used products based upon trademark law. Indeed, the original drafts of the bill that would become the Trademark Act in 1946 included a provision, section 33(c), that would have prohibited the sale of used and repaired goods bearing a trademark without the trademark owner's permission. After the Department of Justice objected to the provision, Congress removed it before enacting the Lanham Trademark Act. Should a trademark owner have the legal right to control the sale of its used goods?

5. *Preventing a Mark from Becoming Generic.* The court states that Ty is seeking "an extension of antidilution law to forbid commercial uses that accelerate the transition from trademarks (brand names) to generic names (product names)." Did the court find that an appropriate use of dilution law? Why not? Did the court's ruling on the likelihood of confusion issue effectively provide Ty with the right to forbid such uses? What sort of uses would accelerate the transition from trademark to generic name? Did the court bar such uses under the likelihood of confusion doctrine? Didn't the court say that allowing a plaintiff to interfere with a word's or phrase's transitions from mark to generic was bad policy?

2. DILUTION BY BLURRING

JADA TOYS, INC. V. MATTEL, INC.

518 F.3d 628 (9th Cir. 2008)

SANDOVAL, J.

Defendant-Appellant Mattel, Inc. ("Mattel") appeals the grant of summary judgment in favor of Jada Toys, Inc. ("Jada") on Mattel's federal and state trademark infringement counterclaims. Mattel also challenges the district court's entry of summary judgment in favor of Jada as to its dilution and copyright claims.

We hold that because the district court erred in its application of the relevant infringement test, the district court's entry of summary judgment in Jada's favor as to those claims is reversed. We also hold that genuine issues of material fact exist as to Mattel's copyright and dilution claims and, therefore, the district court's entry of summary judgment as to those claims in favor of Jada is also reversed.

I. FACTUAL AND PROCEDURAL BACKGROUND

Jada Toys is a California corporation that specializes in the distribution and sale of miniature diecast toy cars, trucks, and other vehicles. Generally, these vehicles are scale model replicas of actual vehicles. From 2001 to 2004, Jada produced a line of toy trucks called HOT RIGZ.

In 2001, Jada filed an application for a trademark registration of the term HOT RIGZ with the United States Patent and Trademark Office ("U.S. PTO"). The trademark was issued by and registered with the U.S. PTO in 2002, though Jada used its HOT RIGZ trademark in advertising material and on its toys and their packaging from 2001 to 2004.

Mattel is also a toy company. Among its many lines of toys is its familiar HOT WHEELS miniature vehicle brand, which it has been marketing since 1968. The HOT WHEELS vehicle line includes small scale versions of big rig trucks. Since 1968, Mattel has employed the use of a flame logo ("68 logo") to identify the HOT WHEELS brand. In 1982 Mattel developed a complementary version of the 68 logo, this one incorporating the Mattel seal, to be used in conjunction with the sale of its product. Mattel owns U.S. federal trademark registrations for both of these flame logos.

On April 20, 2004, Jada filed an action against Mattel, asserting claims for trademark infringement, false designation of origin, and unfair competition. Jada's allegations, however, were not related to its HOT RIGZ mark; rather, Jada claimed that Mattel's advertising and sale of its OLD SCHOOL and NEW SCHOOL lines infringed on Jada's use of its registered trademark OLD SKOOL. Mattel asserted various affirmative defenses and counterclaims. Among the counterclaims were allegations that Jada's HOT RIGZ mark infringed on Mattel's HOT WHEELS mark. Mattel also counterclaimed for copyright infringement and dilution. Ultimately, each party submitted motions for summary judgment.

On March 15, 2005, the district court issued its ruling regarding the parties' motions for summary judgment. As to Jada's claims relating to Mattel's OLD SCHOOL and NEW SCHOOL marks, the court granted summary judgment in Mattel's favor. And as to Mattel's counterclaims for infringement, copyright, and dilution, relating to Jada's use of its HOT RIGZ logo, the court granted summary judgment in Jada's favor. In granting summary judgment as to Mattel's infringement claims, the district court relied on the dissimilarity of the marks alone to determine that no likelihood of confusion existed. Mattel timely appealed the grant of summary judgment as to its counterclaims.

II. STANDARD OF REVIEW

The review of a grant of summary judgment as to an infringement claim is *de novo. Surfvivor Media, Inc. v. Survivor Prods.*, 406 F.3d 625, 630 (9th Cir. 2005). As such, we "must determine whether, 'viewing the evidence in the light most favorable to the nonmoving party, . . . there are any genuine issues of material fact, and whether the district court correctly applied the relevant substantive law.' " *Entrepreneur Media, Inc. v. Smith*, 279 F.3d 1135, 1140 (9th Cir. 2002) (quoting *Wendt v. Host Int'l, Inc.*, 125 F.3d 806, 809–10 (9th Cir. 1997)). "Because of the intensely factual nature of trademark disputes, summary judgment is generally disfavored in the trademark arena." *Id.* (quoting *Interstellar Starship Servs., Ltd. v. Epix, Inc.*, 184 F.3d 1107, 1109 (9th Cir. 1999)). The Court may affirm a judgment on any ground fairly supported by the record. *Narell v. Freeman*, 872 F.2d 907, 910 (9th Cir. 1989) (citing *De Nardo v. Murphy*, 781 F.2d 1345, 1347 (9th Cir. 1986), *cert. denied*, 476 U.S. 1111 (1986)).

III. ANALYSIS

A. MATTEL'S TRADEMARK CLAIMS

All of Mattel's infringement claims are subject to the same test. *See Century 21 Real Estate Corp. v. Sandlin*, 846 F.2d 1175, 1178 (9th Cir. 1988) (citing *Rodeo Collection, Ltd. v. W. Seventh,* 812 F.2d 1215, 1217 (9th Cir. 1987)); *see also Vuitton Et Fils S.A. v. J. Young Enter.*, 644 F.2d 769, 777 (9th Cir. 1981) (noting that if a product is marketed in such a way so as to cause a likelihood of confusion, the defendant might be guilty of "palming off"). Therefore, the critical determination is " 'whether an alleged trademark infringer's use of a mark creates a likelihood that the consuming public will be confused as to who makes what product.' " *Brother Records, Inc. v. Jardine*, 318 F.3d 900, 908 (9th Cir. 2003) (quoting *Thane Int'l, Inc. v. Trek Bicycle Corp.*, 305 F.3d 894, 901 (9th Cir. 2002)).

We employ an eight factor test ("*Sleekcraft* factors") in determining the likelihood of confusion. *Brookfield Communs., Inc. v. West Coast Entm't Corp.*, 174 F.3d 1036, 1053–54 (9th Cir. 1999). These factors include: (1) strength of the mark; (2) proximity of the goods; (3) similarity of the marks; (4) evidence of actual confusion; (5) marketing channels used; (6) type of goods and the degree of care likely to be exercised by the purchaser; (7) defendant's intent in selecting the mark; and (8) likelihood of expansion of the product lines. *AMF Inc. v. Sleekcraft Boats*, 599 F.2d 341, 348–49 (9th Cir. 1979) (citations omitted).

We have previously noted that the test for likelihood of confusion is "pliant," and that "[s]ome factors are much more important than others, ..." *Brookfield*, 174 F.3d at 1054. Jada seizes on such language as an indication that the district court's consideration of the dissimilarity of the marks alone was sufficient to support its conclusion. We disagree.

Though the language we have used warns against "excessive rigidity" in applying the test, *see id.*, we have never countenanced a likelihood of confusion determination based on a consideration of dissimilarity alone or, indeed, on the consideration of any single factor. Instead, we have regularly applied all the relevant factors, noting that a final likelihood of confusion determination may rest on those factors that are of the most relative importance in any particular case. *See, e.g., Surfvivor*, 406 F.3d at 631–34 (applying all eight factors and noting that "the test is a fluid one and the plaintiff need not satisfy every factor, provided that strong showings are made with respect to some of them."). Thus, while a likelihood of confusion determination may ultimately rest on a sub-set of factors, evidence of relatively important factors must be considered as part of that set. In the context of two subjectively dissimilar marks, evidence of actual confusion and evidence defining the context in which the goods are sold are particularly relevant.

To hold otherwise would allow the possibility that persuasive evidence of a particular factor may be considered at the expense of relevant evidence of others. This problem is particularly acute where, as here, a court relies on the dissimilarity of the marks to conclude that no likelihood of confusion exists. In such a case, the potential for a judge to elevate his or her own subjective impressions of the relative dissimilarity of the marks over evidence of, for example, actual confusion, is great. And where the subjective impressions of a particular judge are weighed at the expense of other relevant evidence, the value of the multi-factor approach sanctioned by this Court is undermined.

Today's holding is consistent with our prior decisions. For while Jada accurately cites language from the case law of this Circuit suggesting that dissimilarity alone may be a sufficient basis upon which to judge the likelihood of confusion, *Brookfield*, 174 F.3d at 1054; *Sleeper Lounge Co. v. Bell Mfg Co.*, 253 F.2d 720, 723 (9th Cir. 1958), we conclude that the language employed in those cases constitutes dicta and, therefore, we are not bound by it. *See Inlandboatmens Union of Pac. v. Dutra Group*, 279 F.3d 1075, 1081 (9th Cir. 2002) (holding that a panel is not bound by dicta in prior decisions).

In *Brookfield*, for example, we stated that "[w]here the two marks are entirely dissimilar, there is no likelihood of confusion. 'Pepsi' does not infringe Coca-Cola's 'Coke.' Nothing further need be said." *Brookfield*, 174 F.3d at 1054. In *Brookfield*, however, we did not conclude that the marks in question were so dissimilar that no likelihood of confusion could exist. *Id.* at 1054–55. To the contrary, we found that the marks were quite similar. *Id.* Moreover, there is no indication that in *Brookfield* we ignored evidence of other important factors in determining that dissimilarity could be determinative. *See id.* at 1054–60. And, beyond that, there was no evidence of actual confusion presented in the case. *Id.* at 1060. Thus, in *Brookfield* we were not confronted with a situation where, as here, strong evidence of other important factors existed to counter the conclusion that dissimilarity alone could be dispositive. Consequently, in *Brookfield* we were not afforded the opportunity to consider fully the ramifications of our comment.

The same is true of our decision in *Sleeper Lounge*. There, we noted that "[similarity of the marks] is the one essential feature, without which the others have no probative value." *Sleeper Lounge*, 253 F.2d at 723. But as was the case in *Brookfield*, in *Sleeper Lounge* we expressly noted that no evidence of actual confusion had been presented. *Id.* Thus, in *Sleeper Lounge* we were no more able to consider fully the impact of our statement than we were in *Brookfield*.

While the *Brookfield* and *Sleeper Lounge* decisions offer important insight into the persuasiveness of dissimilarity, we must, nonetheless, conclude that though it may be true that very dissimilar marks will rarely present a significant likelihood of confusion, dissimilarity alone does not obviate the need to inquire into evidence of other important factors. Only upon such an inquiry may a court ensure that its judgment as to the likelihood of confusion is fully informed and without error. Therefore, because the district court considered only the dissimilarity of the marks in question, we reverse its grant of summary judgment in favor of Jada.

B. MATTEL'S DILUTION CLAIM

Mattel brought dilution claims under both federal and California state law. The analysis under each is the same. *Panavision Int'l, L.P. v. Toeppen*, 141 F.3d 1316, 1324 (9th Cir. 1998). In order to prove a violation, a plaintiff must show that (1) the mark is famous and distinctive; (2) the defendant is making use of the mark in commerce; (3)

the defendant's use began after the mark became famous; and (4) the defendant's use of the mark is likely to cause dilution by blurring or dilution by tarnishment. 15 U.S.C. § 1125(c)(1); California Business and Professions Code section 14330. . . .

Neither federal law nor California state law requires a showing of competition or likelihood of confusion to succeed on a dilution claim. *Nissan Motor Co. v. Nissan Computer Corp.*, 378 F.3d 1002, 1011 (9th Cir. 2004) (citing 15 U.S.C. § 1127).; Cal. Bus. & Prof. Code § 14330. However, for a plaintiff to establish that the mark is being used in commerce (as per step two),"the mark used by the alleged diluter must be identical, or nearly identical, to the protected mark." *Thane Int'l*, 305 F.3d at 905 (noting that this circuit's description of dilution by blurring and by tarnishment requires a defendant to use the plaintiff's actual mark) (citation omitted). In order to be nearly identical, two marks "must be 'similar enough that a significant segment of the target group of customers sees the two marks as essentially the same.' " *Id.* at 906 (quoting *Playboy Enters. Inc. v. Welles*, 279 F.3d 796, 806 n.41 (9th Cir. 2002)).

Here, the district court granted summary judgment in favor of Jada on Mattel's dilution claims because the marks at issue were not identical or nearly identical. Mattel claims that because it has shown a likelihood of confusion, that finding was inappropriate.

Jada claims, on the other hand, that the district court's determination that the marks were not identical is supported by the record and, therefore, summary judgment was appropriate. Jada also contends that Mattel has not made a showing of actual dilution sufficient to support its claim under federal law. And as to Mattel's state law claim, Jada argues that Mattel is barred from such a claim because Jada owns a valid federal registration mark, which acts as a complete bar to a dilution claim under state law. 15 U.S.C. § 1125(c)(6).

Turning first to the district court's determination that the marks in question were not sufficiently identical, we conclude that a reasonable trier of fact could find that the HOT WHEELS and HOT RIGZ marks are nearly identical. They both contain the word "hot," they both are accompanied by a flame, and they use similar colors; they also convey a similar meaning and connotation *vis a vis* their use of the modifier "hot." *Cf. Thane Int'l*, 305 F.3d at 907 (holding that a reasonable trier of fact could conclude that the marks "OrbiTrek" and "TREK" were nearly identical).

In determining the degree of fame a mark retains, 15 U.S.C. § 1125(c)(2)(A) provides a non-exclusive list of four factors that a court may consider. . . .

Here, a reasonable trier of fact could conclude that the HOT WHEELS mark is famous: it has been in use for over thirty-seven years; 350 million dollars have been expended in advertising the mark; three billion HOT WHEELS units have been sold since the inception of the mark; and HOT WHEELS are sold in all fifty states and throughout the world.

A reasonable trier of fact could also conclude that Jada began using its mark after HOT WHEELS became famous. The HOT WHEELS mark has been in use since 1968, but it was only in 2001 that Jada began to employ the use of HOT RIGZ. Thus, the HOT WHEELS mark had been acquiring recognition for over thirty years before HOT RIGZ entered the market.

The federal dilution statute also requires a showing of likelihood of dilution either by blurring or by tarnishment. 15 U.S.C. § 1125(c)(1). Where, as here, a plaintiff's claim is based on a dilution by blurring theory, the question is whether the "association arising from the similarity between a mark or trade name and a famous mark . . . impairs the distinctiveness of the famous mark." *Id.* § 1125(c)(2)(B). A court may consider all relevant factors in making this determination, including the six identified by the statute. . . .

As has been stated, in this case a reasonable trier of fact could conclude that the marks at issue are quite similar. Moreover, there is significant evidence of actual association between the alleged diluting mark and the famous mark. As evidence of such, Mattel has submitted two surveys. In the first, respondents were exposed to the HOT RIGZ name and asked who they believed "puts out or makes" a toy vehicle with that name. Twenty-eight percent of respondents thought that the toy vehicle put out under that name was either made by Mattel or by the same company that produced HOT WHEELS, or that whatever company did produce it required permission from Mattel to sell the product.

In a separate survey, respondents were shown a HOT RIGZ package and asked who they thought put out that product. Of the respondents, 7% believed it was either made by Mattel or by the same company that produced HOT WHEELS, or that whatever company did produce it required permission from Mattel to sell the product.

Not only do these surveys indicate that consumers associate one mark with the other; they suggest, too, that Mattel's HOT WHEELS mark does not adequately identify its product because Jada is able to convey, through the use of its HOT RIGZ mark, the impression that Mattel either produces or allows the production of HOT RIGZ. *See Moseley*, 537 U.S. at 433–34 (holding that such evidence is sufficient to meet the heightened standard of actual dilution). Thus, a reasonable trier of fact could conclude that this evidence was sufficient to establish the existence of a likelihood of dilution. The district court's entry of summary judgment is, therefore, reversed. . . .

IV. CONCLUSION

The district court's reliance on a single *Sleekcraft* factor—dissimilarity of the marks—in its likelihood of confusion determination was in error; therefore, its entry of summary judgment in Jada's favor as to Mattel's trademark claims is reversed. Those claims are hereby remanded for consideration consistent with this opinion. The district court must analyze Mattel's copyright claim under the *Apple Computer* framework. In addition, Mattel raised a genuine issue of material fact as to its dilution and copyright claims; thus, the district court's entry of summary judgment in favor of Jada as to those claims is also reversed.

REVERSED AND REMANDED FOR FURTHER PROCEEDINGS CONSISTENT WITH THIS OPINION.

NOTES FOR DISCUSSION

1. *Dilution versus Confusion.* How did the court resolve the dilution claim? How did it resolve the likelihood of confusion claim? Did the dilution claim provide the plaintiff with any additional rights?

2. *Survey Evidence.* In discussing the likelihood of dilution claim, the court cites two surveys that show that respondents believed that Jada's cars were either made or endorsed by Mattel. Are these surveys evidence of a likelihood of dilution or a likelihood of confusion? While the court cites the surveys as evidence of an association, do the surveys actually refute the court's conclusion? The first survey indicated that twenty-eight percent of the respondents were confused when exposed to Jada's work mark "Hot Rigz" alone. The second survey indicated that only seven percent were confused when shown the "Hot Rigz" packaging. Which survey result is more reliable? As a general rule, surveys should duplicate as closely as possible the marketplace conditions in which a consumer will encounter the defendant's product. *See, e.g., AmBrit, Inc. v. Kraft, Inc.*, 812 F.2d 1531, 1544 (11th Cir. 1986) (affirming district court's decision to give survey little weight when it failed to "duplicate the circumstances confronting an actual consumer in the marketplace"); *see also Beneficial Corp. v. Beneficial Capital Corp.*, 529 F.Supp. 445, 451 (S.D.N.Y. 1982) ("The survey establishes no more than that the names are similar, a factor as to which there can be little genuine dispute in any event, and that portions of the general public will make the reasonable assumption, that, in the absence of any other information, two companies with similar names are likely to have a business connection. However, this proposition provides no indication of public reaction under actual market conditions."). Which of the two surveys more closely duplicates the circumstances under which an actual consumer would encounter Jada's product?

Although courts vary in their interpretation of survey results, a seven percent confusion response rate is usually too low to support a finding of likelihood of confusion, and indeed, generally weighs against such a finding. *See, e.g., Sara Lee Corp. v. Kayser-Roth Corp.*, 81 F.3d 455, 467 n.15 (4th Cir. 1996) ("We may infer from the case law that survey evidence clearly favors the defendant when it demonstrates a level of confusion much below ten percent."). The reason for this is two-fold. First, every survey will generate some level of false positives. If you ask two hundred consumers virtually any question, you can expect some incorrect responses. Some consumers will not properly hear the question; some will not be paying attention; some will simply answer perversely. As a result, every likelihood of confusion survey will indicate some level of confusion. Second, even if we could eliminate the false positives, trademark law prohibits a use not when it causes "any" confusion, but as we saw in the *Estee Lauder* case in Chapter 7, only when it leads "numerous ordinarily prudent consumers" to become confused. As a result, even a properly conducted survey must typically indicate that at least ten percent or more of the respondents were confused before the results will support a finding of likelihood of confusion.

Moreover, even the first survey's twenty-eight percent confusion level is not as persuasive as it at first appears. While that level of confusion seems high, it represents the summation of three different types of confusion: (1) confusion as to source: who do you think makes this?; (2) anonymous source confusion: what other products do you think they make?; and (3) sponsorship or endorsement confusion: do you think the entity that makes this product had to get permission from Mattel? While each of these types of confusion are legally actionable, when a survey asks about multiple types of confusion, its error rate increases substantially. Even considered individually, each of these questions will generate their own false positives. Indeed, survey experts know this and often include extra questions in a survey specifically to increase the number of false positives and to inflate the apparent level of confusion. Why, for example, did the survey in this case ask the anonymous source question? As we discussed in Chapter 7, in connection with Union Carbide's Eveready trademark infringement survey, an anonymous source question makes perfect sense when the defendant's name is identical to the plaintiff's brand and consumers are unlikely to know the plaintiff's corporate name. In such a case, survey respondents' likely answers to the question "who makes this?" will not meaningfully distinguish between the plaintiff and the defendant when she answers "Eveready" to the first question. An anonymous source question—"what else does this company make?"—can help clarify whether a respondent is thinking of the plaintiff or the defendant. Why did Mattel include the question in its survey? Even if a respondent didn't know that Mattel was the company that made Hot Wheels, wouldn't the respondent's answer to "who made this" still readily distinguish between Hot Rigz (Jada) and Hot Wheels (Mattel)? Will consumers take the "what other products" question as asking, essentially, "what other toys cars are you familiar with"? Did Mattel add the anonymous source question to its survey simply to inflate the apparent level of confusion?

In addition, multi-question formats are more likely to generate a demand effect. Social science research suggests that survey respondents try to please the surveyor. As a result, if a respondent can determine what answer a surveyor is demanding, they will give it. *See, e.g., Government Employees Ins. Co. v. Google, Inc.*, 77 U.S.P.Q.2d (BNA) 1841 (E.D. Va. 2005) ("A demand effect results when the interviewer's questions or other elements of the survey design influence participants' responses by suggesting what the 'correct' answers might be or by implying associations that might not otherwise occur to participants."). In a multi-question format, a respondent can use trial-and-error in an attempt to determine which answer will please the surveyor. As a result, formats that inquire about two or three or more different types of confusion, like Mattel's, always generate much higher levels of apparent confusion than formats that focus on a single type of confusion.

In an attempt to account for the false positives surveys can generate, courts have increasingly required the use of control surveys before they will admit survey results. *See, e.g., THOIP v. Walt Disney Co.*, 690 F.Supp.2d 218, 240 (S.D.N.Y. 2010) (excluding likelihood of confusion survey because, *inter alia*, it lacked an adequate control). With a control, the surveyor asks the same set of questions to two different groups of consumers. The first group of consumers is asked the relevant survey questions after being shown or exposed to the defendant's allegedly infringing mark or trade dress (the "treatment" survey). The second group of consumers is asked the same questions but is shown or exposed to a mark or dress which is similar, but admittedly non-infringing (the "control" survey). The purpose of the control survey is to identify the level of false positives that the survey format generates, given the market conditions otherwise present. To identify the likely level of false positives accurately, the control stimulus should duplicate as many characteristics of the defendant's allegedly infringing mark or dress as possible, and should differ only with respect to the precise characteristics alleged to constitute infringement. After conducting both the treatment and the control survey, the survey expert subtracts the level of confusion measured in the control survey from the level of confusion measured in the treatment survey to remove (hopefully) the false positives and to generate a net confusion level that better reflects the actual level of confusion likely in the marketplace. *Id.*

Mattel did not perform a control survey. While twenty-eight percent seems like considerable confusion, is there any way to know whether the twenty-eight percent accurately reflects consumer confusion or mere false positives? How many false positives can there be? Control surveys performed in other cases establish that the level of false positives can be quite high, particularly for surveys that ask about multiple types of confusion. For example, in *Sara Lee Corp. v. Kayser-Roth Corp.*, Sara Lee, the manufacturer of "L'Eggs" pantyhose, sued Kayser-Roth for trademark infringement when its rival introduced a new line of pantyhose under the mark "Legs Looks", 81 F.3d 455, 459 (4th Cir.), *cert. denied*, 519 U.S. 976 (1996). Sara Lee also asserted that the packaging of Kayser-Roth's new line was confusingly similar to the packaging of Sara Lee's "L'Eggs" pantyhose. *Id.* To establish a likelihood of confusion, Sara Lee arranged for two surveys. Both surveys included responses from a treatment group and a control group. *See Sara Lee Corp. v. Kayser-Roth Corp.*, 1994 U.S. Dist. LEXIS 19198, at *61–69, *rev'd* 81 F.3d 455 (4th Cir.), *cert. denied*, 519 U.S. 976 (1996). In the first survey, respondents were shown Sara Lee's "L'Eggs" "Sheer Energy" pantyhose, and either the defendant's allegedly infringing "Legs Looks" packaging (for the treatment group) or an admittedly noninfringing pair of "Jaclyn Smith" pantyhose in its packaging (for the control group). Respondents were then asked whether they believed the products were made by the same or different companies and, if so, why. Although the "Jaclyn Smith" packaging and word mark were not remotely similar to Sara Lee's packaging and word mark, nonetheless twelve percent of the control respondents stated that they believed the two were made by the same company. For the second survey, Sara Lee showed the respondents either the allegedly infringing "Legs Looks" packaging (for the treatment group) or the "Jaclyn Smith" packaging (for the control group). Respondents were then asked questions both with respect to source confusion—"Who do you think makes this?"—and anonymous source confusion—"What other brands of pantyhose do you think the company that makes this also makes?" Again, although the "Jaclyn Smith" packaging and word mark were not similar in any way to Sara Lee's word marks or its trade dress, of the participants shown the Jaclyn Smith® package, thirty-seven percent made some association between it and Plaintiff's companies or products. Although this is only one example, it suggests that surveys can generate a significant level of false positives, even surveys that focus on a single type of confusion. It also suggests that the level of false positives tends to increase substantially, from twelve to thirty-seven percent in this case, when a survey moves from asking about one to multiple types of confusion.

If the second *Sara Lee* generated a false positive rate of thirty-seven percent by asking about two types of confusion, what do you think the false positive rate would be for the *Mattel* survey given that it asks about three types of confusion (source confusion, anonymous source confusion, and endorsement or approval confusion)? Absent a control survey, is there any way to know? Should the *Mattel* survey be admissible absent an appropriate control? What would a proper control survey in the *Mattel* case ask? If the treatment group of survey respondents would be shown Jada's packaging and product, what should the control group be shown?

3. *Consumer Welfare.* Are consumers better or worse off as a result of the court's decision? Does the court's decision increase the costs to Jada of entering this market? Is there any excuse for Jada using "hot" as part of its trademark? Is all of the selling power of "hot" in this market attributable to Mattel's development of the "Hot Wheels" brand? Or does the word "hot" have its own, inherent selling power? Does it describe, suggest, or connote a desirable feature of this kind of product? If you believe that "hot" has value to the relevant consumers for its own sake, is there any way to allow Jada to share in the word's inherent selling power without interfering with that portion of the word's selling power attributable to Mattel's reputation?

4. *Blurring and Dilution: Property-Like Rights in Trademarks?* One of the most difficult issues in dilution is when the trademark at issue is also a word with a common descriptive meaning. In such cases, a conflict arises between the brand and ordinary meanings of the word. How would you resolve the following case:

> Joseph Orr runs eVisa, a "multilingual education and information business that exists and operates exclusively on the Internet," at www.evisa.com. . . . Orr traces the name eVisa back to an English language tutoring service called "Eikaiwa Visa" that he ran while living in Japan. "Eikaiwa" is Japanese for English conversation, and the "e" in eVisa is short for Eikaiwa. The use of the word "visa" in both eVisa and Eikaiwa Visa is meant to suggest "the ability to travel, both linguistically and physically, through the English-speaking world." Orr founded eVisa shortly before his return to America, where he started running it out of his apartment in Brooklyn, New York.
>
> Visa International Service Association [owner of the mark VISA for credit card services] sued JSL Corporation, through which Orr operates eVisa, claiming that eVisa is likely to dilute the Visa trademark.

See *Visa Int'l Serv. Ass'n v. JSL Corp.*, 610 F.3d 1088 (9th Cir. 2010).

The Ninth Circuit affirmed the district court's summary judgment and held that JSL's use created a likelihood of dilution. Writing for the court, Judge Kozinski explained the outcome as follows:

> It's true that the word visa is used countless times every day for its common English definition, but the prevalence of such non-trademark use does not undermine the uniqueness of Visa as a trademark. "The significant factor is not whether the word itself is common, but whether the way the word is used in a particular context is unique enough to warrant trademark protection." *Wynn Oil Co. v. Thomas*, 839 F.2d 1183, 1190 n.4 (6th Cir. 1988). In the context of anti-dilution law, the "particular context" that matters is use of the word in commerce to identify a good or service. There are, for instance, many camels, but just one Camel; many tides, but just one Tide. Camel cupcakes and Tide calculators would dilute the value of those marks. Likewise, despite widespread use of the word visa for its common English meaning, the introduction of the eVisa mark to the marketplace means that there are now two products, and not just one, competing for association with that word. This is the quintessential harm addressed by anti-dilution law.

Id. at 1091.

Do you agree with Judge Kozinski's reasoning? Does the reasoning essentially create a property-like, exclusive right to any trademark use of a famous mark? Does Judge Kozinski's reasoning reduce the relevant factors in a likelihood of dilution analysis from the six Congress identified to two: (i) fame and (ii) similarity?

In sharp contrast to Judge Kozinski's ruling in the *Visa* case is the Federal Circuit's ruling in *Coach Servs., Inc. v. Triumph Learning LLC*, 668 F.3d 1356 (Fed. Cir. 2012). In that case, the owner of the COACH trademark for luxury handbags opposed the registration of the mark COACH with a design for computer software used to prepare students for taking standardized tests. The applicant's mark included the word COACH along with an image of a coach, and was using COACH in its ordinary sense to suggest coaching a student to success. Nonetheless, the owner of the COACH trademark for luxury handbags argued that the applicant's mark created a likelihood of confusion and a likelihood of dilution. With respect to the likelihood of confusion issue, the Federal Circuit affirmed the Trademark Trial and Appeal Board's findings that the applicant used the word COACH in a different sense than opposer and that the parties' goods or services were too unrelated to create a likelihood of confusion. *Id.* at 1370. With respect to the dilution issue, the Federal Circuit affirmed the Trademark Trial and Appeal Board's finding that the opposer's mark COACH for luxury handbags was not famous and thus could not support dilution claim. *Id.* at 1374–75. Opposer's mark COACH for luxury handbags was not famous even though opposer had sixteen federal trademark registrations, its sales exceeded $1 billion per year, and its mark had achieved a substantial degree of recognition among women ages 13–24. *Id.*

These two cases illustrate two possible ways to resolve dilution claims when the trademark at issue entails both a brand-specific and an ordinary meaning. In the *Visa* case, the Ninth Circuit finds the mark VISA to be famous and essentially prohibits all use of the word as a mark by others. It protects the brand-specific meaning at the expense of the ordinary meaning. In the *Coach* case, the Federal Circuit refuses to find the mark COACH to be famous in order to preserve others' freedom to use the word in its ordinary sense. It protects the ordinary meaning of the word at the expense of the brand-specific meaning. Which approach is better? Are there other approaches that might be better yet?

3.   DILUTION BY TARNISHMENT

DEERE & COMPANY V. MTD PRODUCTS, INC.

41 F.3d 39 (2d Cir. 1994)

NEWMAN, J.

This appeal in a trademark case presents a rarely litigated issue likely to recur with increasing frequency in this era of head-to-head comparative advertising. The precise issue, arising under the New York anti-dilution statute, N.Y. Gen. Bus. Law § 368–d (McKinney 1984), is whether an advertiser may depict an altered form of a competitor's trademark to identify the competitor's product in a comparative ad. The issue arises on an appeal by defendant-appellant MTD Products, Inc. ("MTD") from the August 9, 1994, order of the United States District Court for the Southern District of New York (Lawrence M. McKenna, Judge) granting a preliminary injunction to plaintiff-appellee Deere & Company ("Deere") and Deere's cross-appeal to broaden the scope of the injunction beyond New York State. The injunction prevents MTD from airing a television commercial that shows an animated version of the leaping deer that has become appellee's well-known logo.

Although a number of dilution cases in this Circuit have involved use of a trademark by a competitor to identify a competitor's products in comparative advertising, as well as use by a noncompetitor in a humorous variation of a trademark, we have not yet considered whether the use of an altered version of a distinctive trademark to identify a competitor's product and achieve a humorous effect can constitute trademark dilution. Though we find MTD's animated version of Deere's deer amusing, we agree with Judge McKenna that the television commercial is a likely violation of the anti-dilution statute. We therefore affirm the preliminary injunction.

Background

Deere, a Delaware corporation with its principal place of business in Illinois, is the world's largest supplier of agricultural equipment. For over one hundred years, Deere has used a deer design ("Deere Logo") as a trademark for identifying its products and services. Deere owns numerous trademark registrations for different versions of the Deere Logo. Although these versions vary slightly, all depict a static, two-dimensional silhouette of a leaping male deer in profile. The Deere Logo is widely recognizable and a valuable business asset.

MTD, an Ohio company with its principal place of business in Ohio, manufactures and sells lawn tractors. In 1993, W.B. Doner & Company ("Doner"), MTD's advertising agency, decided to create and produce a commercial—the subject of this litigation—that would use the Deere Logo, without Deere's authorization, for the purpose of comparing Deere's line of lawn tractors to MTD's "Yard-Man" tractor. The intent was to identify Deere as the market leader and convey the message that Yard-Man was of comparable quality but less costly than a Deere lawn tractor.

Doner altered the Deere Logo in several respects. For example, as Judge McKenna found, the deer in the MTD version of the logo ("Commercial Logo") is "somewhat differently proportioned, particularly with respect to its width, than the deer in the Deere Logo." Doner also removed the name "John Deere" from the version of the logo used by Deere on the front of its lawn tractors, and made the logo frame more sharply rectangular.

More significantly, the deer in the Commercial Logo is animated and assumes various poses. Specifically, the MTD deer looks over its shoulder, jumps through the logo frame (which breaks into pieces and tumbles to the ground), hops to a pinging noise, and, as a two-dimensional cartoon, runs, in apparent fear, as it is pursued by the Yard-Man lawn tractor and a barking dog. Judge McKenna described the dog as "recognizable as a breed that is short in stature," and in the commercial the fleeing deer appears to be even smaller than the dog. Doner's interoffice documents reflect that the animated deer in the commercial was intended to appear "more playful and/or confused than distressed."

MTD submitted the commercial to ABC, NBC, and CBS for clearance prior to airing, together with substantiation of the various claims made regarding the Yard-Man lawn tractor's quality and cost relative to the corresponding Deere model. Each network ultimately approved the commercial, though ABC reserved the right to re-evaluate it "should there be [a] responsible complaint," and CBS demanded and received a letter of indemnity from Doner. The commercial ran from the week of March 7, 1994, through the week of May 23, 1994.

Deere filed a complaint, along with an order to show cause seeking a preliminary injunction and a temporary restraining order, alleging violations of the New York anti-dilution statute and section 43(a) of the Lanham Act, 15 U.S.C. § 1125(a) (1988), as well as common law claims of unfair competition and unjust enrichment. Following a hearing, the District Court denied Deere's application for a temporary restraining order, but subsequently found that Deere had demonstrated a likelihood of prevailing on its dilution claim and granted preliminary injunctive relief limited to activities within New York State. In its August 11, 1994, Supplemental Findings of Fact, Conclusions of Law, and Order ("Supplemental Order"), the Court concluded that Deere had not shown a likelihood of success on the merits of its Lanham Act claim.

On appeal, MTD argues that the anti-dilution statute does not prohibit commercial uses of a trademark that do not confuse consumers or result in a loss of the trademark's ability to identify a single manufacturer, or tarnish the trademark's positive connotations. Deere cross-appeals, contending that injunctive relief should not have been limited to New York State. We affirm both the finding of likely dilution and the scope of the injunction.

Discussion

Section 368–d, which has counterparts in more than twenty states, reads as follows:

> Likelihood of injury to business reputation or of dilution of the distinctive quality of a mark or trade name shall be a ground for injunctive relief in cases of infringement of a mark registered or

not registered or in cases of unfair competition, notwithstanding the absence of competition between the parties or the absence of confusion as to the source of goods or services.

N.Y. Gen. Bus. Law § 368–d (McKinney 1984). The anti-dilution statute applies to competitors as well as noncompetitors, *see Nikon Inc. v. Ikon Corp.*, 987 F.2d 91, 96 (2d Cir. 1993), and explicitly does not require a plaintiff to demonstrate a likelihood of consumer confusion, *see Sally Gee, Inc. v. Myra Hogan, Inc.*, 699 F.2d 621, 624 (2d Cir. 1983).

In order to prevail on a section 368–d dilution claim, a plaintiff must prove, first, that its trademark either is of truly distinctive quality or has acquired secondary meaning, and, second, that there is a "likelihood of dilution." *Sally Gee*, 699 F.2d at 625. A third consideration, the predatory intent of the defendant, may not be precisely an element of the violation, but, as we discuss below, is of significance, especially in a case such as this, which involves poking fun at a competitor's trademark.

MTD does not dispute that the Deere Logo is a distinctive trademark that is capable of dilution and has acquired the requisite secondary meaning in the marketplace. *See Allied Maintenance Corp. v. Allied Mechanical Trades, Inc.*, 42 N.Y.2d 538, 545 (1977). Therefore, the primary question on appeal is whether Deere can establish a likelihood of dilution of this distinctive mark under section 368–d.

Likelihood of Dilution. Traditionally, this Court has defined dilution under section 368–d "as either the blurring of a mark's product identification or the tarnishment of the affirmative associations a mark has come to convey." *See Mead Data Central, Inc. v. Toyota Motor Sales, U.S.A., Inc.*, 875 F.2d 1026, 1031 (2d Cir. 1989) (citing *Sally Gee*, 699 F.2d at 625 (quoting 3 R. Callman, *The Law of Unfair Competition, Trademarks and Monopolies* § 84.2, at 954–55)).

In previous cases, "blurring" has typically involved "the whittling away of an established trademark's selling power through its unauthorized use by others upon dissimilar products." *Mead Data*, 875 F.2d at 1031 (describing such " 'hypothetical anomalies' as 'DuPont shoes, Buick aspirin tablets, Schlitz varnish, Kodak pianos, Bulova gowns, and so forth' ") (quoting legislative history of section 368–d) (citation omitted). Thus, dilution by "blurring" may occur where the defendant uses or modifies *the plaintiff's trademark* to identify *the defendant's goods and services*, raising the possibility that the mark will lose its ability to serve as a unique identifier of the plaintiff's product.

"Tarnishment" generally arises when the plaintiff's trademark is linked to products of shoddy quality, or is portrayed in an unwholesome or unsavory context likely to evoke unflattering thoughts about the owner's product. In such situations, the trademark's reputation and commercial value might be diminished because the public will associate the lack of quality or lack of prestige in the defendant's goods with the plaintiff's unrelated goods, or because the defendant's use reduces the trademark's reputation and standing in the eyes of consumers as a wholesome identifier of the owner's products or services.

At the hearing on Deere's application for a temporary restraining order, the District Court initially suggested that there was neither blurring nor tarnishment as those terms have been used, and consequently no dilution of the Deere Logo. The Court observed that MTD's commercial "makes it clear that Deere is a distinct product coming from a different source than Yard-Man," and does not "bring the plaintiff's mark into disrepute." However, in its preliminary injunction ruling, the Court found that Deere would probably be able to establish a likelihood of dilution by blurring under section 368–d; tarnishment was not discussed.

The District Court noted that "the instant case was one of first impression" because it involved a defendant's use of a competitor's trademark to refer to the competitor's products rather than to identify the defendant's products. For this reason, the traditional six-factor test for determining whether there has been dilution through blurring of a trademark's product identification was not fully applicable. Focusing only on the alteration of the static Deere Logo resulting from MTD's animation, the Court concluded that MTD's version constituted dilution because it was likely to diminish the strength of identification between the original Deere symbol and Deere products, and to blur the distinction between the Deere Logo and other deer logos in the marketplace, including those in the insurance and financial markets. Although we agree with the District Court's finding of a likelihood of dilution, we believe that MTD's commercial does not fit within the concept of "blurring," but, as we explain below, nonetheless constitutes dilution.

The District Court's analysis endeavored to fit the MTD commercial into one of the two categories we have recognized for a section 368–d claim. However, the MTD commercial is not really a typical instance of blurring, *see, e.g., Toys "R" Us, Inc. v. Canarsie Kiddie Shop, Inc.*, 559 F. Supp. 1189, 1208 (E.D.N.Y. 1983) (finding blurring of "Toys 'R' Us" mark by "Kids 'r' Us" mark), because it poses slight if any risk of impairing the identification of Deere's mark with its products. Nor is there tarnishment, which is usually found where a distinctive mark is depicted in a context of sexual activity, obscenity, or illegal activity. *See, e.g., Coca-Cola*, 346 F. Supp. at 1191 (relying on dilution by tarnishment as alternative basis for issuance of preliminary injunction against defendant's "Enjoy Cocaine" poster); *Pillsbury Co. v. Milky Way Productions, Inc.*, 8 Media L. Rep. 1016, 215 U.S.P.Q. 124, 135 (N.D. Ga. 1981) (concluding that defendant's sexually-oriented variation tarnished plaintiff's mark). But the blurring/tarnishment dichotomy does not necessarily represent the full range of uses that can dilute a mark under New York law. *See Allied Maintenance*, 42 N.Y.2d at 545, at 632 (defining dilution simply as "the gradual whittling away of a firm's distinctive trade-mark or name"); *Shadow Box, Inc. v. Drecq*, 336 N.Y.S.2d 801, 802 (N.Y. Sup. Ct. 1972) (stating that section 368–d "protects . . . against any use of the symbol that may drain off any of the potency of the mark").

In giving content to dilution beyond the categories of blurring or tarnishment, however, we must be careful not to broaden section 368–d to prohibit all uses of a distinctive mark that the owner prefers not be made. Several different contexts may conveniently be identified. Sellers of commercial products may wish to use a competitor's mark to identify the competitor's product in comparative advertisements. *See, e.g., R.G. Smith v. Chanel, Inc.*, 402 F.2d 562, 567 (9th Cir. 1968) (perfume manufacturer used competitor's mark in comparative advertisements; injunction denied). As long as the mark is not altered, such use serves the beneficial purpose of imparting factual information about the relative merits of competing products and poses no risk of diluting the selling power of the competitor's mark. Satirists, selling no product other than the publication that contains their expression, may wish to parody a mark to make a point of social commentary, *see, e.g., Stop the Olympic Prison v. United States Olympic Committee*, 489 F. Supp. 1112, 1123 (S.D.N.Y. 1980) (poster used defendant's trademark to criticize trademark owner's involvement with proposed prison; injunction denied), to entertain, *see, e.g., L.L. Bean v. Drake Publishers, Inc.*, 811 F.2d 26 (1st Cir.) (satiric magazine parodying L.L. Bean catalogue; injunction denied), *cert. denied*, 483 U.S. 1013 (1987), or perhaps both to comment and entertain, *see, e.g., Girl Scouts of USA v. Personality Posters Manufacturing Co.*, 304 F. Supp. 1228, 1233 (S.D.N.Y. 1969) (poster depicting pregnant Girl Scout to suggest humorously that trademark owner's traditional image of chastity and wholesomeness was somewhat illusory; injunction denied). Such uses risk some dilution of the identifying or selling power of the mark, but that risk is generally tolerated in the interest of maintaining broad opportunities for expression. *Cf. Rogers v. Grimaldi*, 875 F.2d 994, 1000 (2d Cir. 1989) (risk that film title might mislead and violate Lanham Act outweighed by danger of restricting artistic expression).

Sellers of commercial products who wish to attract attention to their commercials or products and thereby increase sales by poking fun at widely recognized marks of noncompeting products, *see, e.g., Eveready Battery Co., Inc. v. Adolph Coors Co.*, 765 F. Supp. 440 (N.D. Ill. 1991) (beer manufacturer spoofed Energizer Bunny trademark; preliminary injunction under Lanham Act and state dilution statute denied), risk diluting the selling power of the mark that is made fun of. When this occurs, not for worthy purposes of expression, but simply to sell products, that purpose can easily be achieved in other ways. The potentially diluting effect is even less deserving of protection when the object of the joke is the mark of a directly competing product. *See, e.g., Wendy's International, Inc. v. Big Bite, Inc.*, 576 F. Supp. 816 (S.D. Ohio 1983) ("fast-food" chain made fun of "fast-food" competitors' trademarks; preliminary injunction granted under Lanham Act). The line-drawing in this area becomes especially difficult when a mark is parodied for the dual purposes of making a satiric comment and selling a somewhat competing product. *See, e.g., Yankee Publishing Inc. v. News America Publishing Inc.*, 809 F. Supp. 267 (S.D.N.Y. 1992) (magazine satirized another magazine; injunction denied).

Whether the use of the mark is to identify a competing product in an informative comparative ad, to make a comment, or to spoof the mark to enliven the advertisement for a noncompeting or a competing product, the scope of protection under a dilution statute must take into account the degree to which the mark is altered and the nature of the alteration. Not every alteration will constitute dilution, and more leeway for alterations is appropriate in the context of satiric expression and humorous ads for noncompeting products. But some alterations have the potential to so lessen the selling power of a distinctive mark that they are appropriately proscribed by a dilution statute. Dilution of this sort is more likely to be found when the alterations are made by a competitor with both an incentive to diminish the favorable attributes of the mark and an ample opportunity to promote its products in ways that make no significant alteration.

We need not attempt to predict how New York will delineate the scope of its dilution statute in all of the various contexts in which an accurate depiction of a distinctive mark might be used, nor need we decide how variations of such a mark should be treated in different contexts. Some variations might well be *de minimis*, and the context in which even substantial variations occur may well have such meritorious purposes that any diminution in the identifying and selling power of the mark need not be condemned as dilution.

Wherever New York will ultimately draw the line, we can be reasonably confident that the MTD commercial challenged in this case crosses it. The commercial takes a static image of a graceful, full-size deer—symbolizing Deere's substance and strength—and portrays, in an animated version, a deer that appears smaller than a small dog and scampers away from the dog and a lawn tractor, looking over its shoulder in apparent fear. Alterations of that sort, accomplished for the sole purpose of promoting a competing product, are properly found to be within New York's concept of dilution because they risk the possibility that consumers will come to attribute unfavorable characteristics to a mark and ultimately associate the mark with inferior goods and services. *See Merriam-Webster, Inc. v. Random House, Inc.*, 35 F.3d 65, 73 (2d Cir. 1994) (injunction under section 368–d appropriate where there is likelihood that distinctive trademark will be "'weakened, blurred or diluted'" in its value or quality) (quoting *Miss Universe, Inc. v. Patricelli*, 753 F.2d 235, 238 (2d Cir. 1985)); *Sally Gee*, 699 F.2d at 624–25 ("The interest protected by § 368–d is not simply commercial goodwill, but the selling power that a distinctive mark or name with favorable associations has engendered for a product in the mind of the consuming public.").

Significantly, the District Court did not enjoin accurate reproduction of the Deere Logo to identify Deere products in comparative advertisements. MTD remains free to deliver its message of alleged product superiority without altering and thereby diluting Deere's trademarks. The Court's order imposes no restriction on truthful advertising properly comparing specific products and their "objectively measurable attributes." *FTC Policy Statement on Comparative Advertising*, 16 C.F.R. § 14.15 n.1 (1993). In view of this, the District Court's finding of a likelihood of dilution was entirely appropriate, notwithstanding the fact that MTD's humorous depiction of the deer occurred in the context of a comparative advertisement. . . .

The order of the District Court granting a preliminary injunction as to activities within New York State is affirmed.

NOTES FOR DISCUSSION

1. *Dilution versus Confusion.* How did the court resolve the dilution claim? How did it resolve the likelihood of confusion claim? Did the dilution cause of action provide the plaintiff with any additional rights?

2. *Tarnishment: Origins.* The tarnishment theory of dilution is usually traced to a trilogy of cases. In the first, the Fifth Circuit enjoined a company's use of "Where there's life, there's bugs" for a floor wax containing an insecticide, finding it confusingly similar to Anheuser-Busch's slogan "Where there's life, there's Bud." *Chemical Corp. v. Anheuser-Busch, Inc.*, 306 F.2d 433 (5th Cir. 1962). In the second, a New York district court enjoined a company's sale of posters which bore the slogan "Enjoy Cocaine" in the same script and colors as Coca-Cola's slogan "Enjoy Coca-Cola." *Coca-Cola Co. v. Gemini Rising, Inc.*, 346 F.Supp. 1183 (E.D.N.Y. 1972). In the third, the Dallas Cowboys Cheerleaders sued the defendant over an X-rated film, *Debbie Does Dallas*, alleging unfair competition and dilution due to a scene in which the movie's star appeared dressed, albeit briefly, in a Dallas Cowboys Cheerleaders uniform. *Dallas Cowboys Cheerleaders, Inc. v. Pussycat Cinema, Ltd.*, 604 F.2d 200 (2d Cir. 1979). The Second Circuit affirmed the district court's finding of a likelihood of confusion and enjoined the use. *Id.* at 205.

In each case, the court insisted that the association between the plaintiff's trademark and the unwholesome aspects of the defendant's product or use would linger in consumer's minds, and thereby harm the plaintiff. In the *Dallas Cowboys Cheerleaders* case, for example, the Second Circuit said:

In the instant case, the uniform depicted in "Debbie Does Dallas" unquestionably brings to mind the Dallas Cowboys Cheerleaders. Indeed, it is hard to believe that anyone who had seen defendants' sexually depraved film could ever thereafter disassociate it from plaintiff's cheerleaders. This association results in confusion which has "a tendency to impugn (plaintiff's services) and injure plaintiff's business reputation."

Dallas Cowboys Cheerleaders, Inc., 604 F.2d at 204 (*quoting Coca-Cola Co. v. Gemini Rising, Inc.*, 346 F.Supp. at 1189).

Although tarnishment is now usually associated with dilution, each of these courts enjoined the use at issue based upon unfair competition or a likelihood of confusion. Two of them, *Coca-Cola Co.* and *Dallas Cowboys Cheerleaders, Inc.*, offered New York's antidilution statutes as an alternative basis for their decisions. *Dallas Cowboys Cheerleaders, Inc.*, 604 F.2d at 205 n.8; *Coca-Cola Co. v. Gemini Rising, Inc.*, 346 F.Supp. at 1191–92. Should tarnishment be actionable under a likelihood of confusion theory?

In any event, following the lead of these three courts, later courts readily accepted the factual assumption that blame for a defendant's unauthorized use of a mark in an unwholesome context would somehow attach to the mark's owner. Courts have therefore repeatedly enjoined the use of a plaintiff's mark in an obscene or illegal context. *See, e.g., Pillsbury Co. v. Milky Way Productions, Inc.*, 215 U.S.P.Q. 124, 135 (N.D. Ga. 1981) (enjoining use of "Poppin' Fresh" and "Poppie Fresh" doughpersons shown engaging in sexual intercourse and fellatio); *Edgar Rice Burroughs, Inc. v. Manns Theatres*, 195 U.S.P.Q. (BNA) 159, 162 (C.D. Cal. 1976) (finding defendant liable for using TARZAN mark in X-rated film).

What evidence supports the factual supposition that a defendant's use of a mark in an unwholesome setting will somehow injure the mark's owner? Why would the public blame the plaintiff for such an unauthorized use? If you liked Pillsbury's products and heard that someone else had drawn sexual cartoons featuring the Pillsbury doughboy, would that make you less likely to buy Pillsbury products the next time that you go to the store? If you see an "Enjoy Cocaine" poster, would you switch from Coke to Pepsi?

Even if you agree that the Dallas Cowboys Cheerleaders should be able to enjoin the porn film, because it puts ideas in its audience's heads, should we extend that rationale to prohibit MTD's advertisements? Would you enjoin a poster that showed a girl, visibly pregnant, in a girl scout uniform with the Boy Scout motto "Be Prepared" next to her. *See Girl Scouts of United States of America v. Personality Posters Mfg. Co.*, 304 F.Supp. 1228 (S.D.N.Y. 1969) (finding no likelihood of confusion and denying relief).

3.   *Competition: Entry and Equilibrium.* The *John Deere & Co.* court distinguishes ridicule for its own sake from ridicule to sell products, particularly competing products, because "that purpose can easily be achieved in other ways." *Deere & Co.*, 41 F.3d at 45. Is that true? What evidence does the court offer in support of its factual supposition? If it is true,

then why are the parties each spending hundreds of thousands, if not millions, of dollars litigating this particular advertising campaign?

Assume that MTD plans to enter the lawn tractor market in order to compete against the dominant brand, John Deere. MTD can use two different advertising campaigns. The first is the one discussed in the case, which ridicules John Deere through the distorted or "scared" deer logo. The second is one that uses the John Deere logo in unaltered form and compares the parties' specific products and "their objectively measurable attributes." Assume further that the parties know the truth better than the court and that they are fighting this case because the first campaign will prove far more effective than the second. With the first campaign, MTD will achieve a 15 percent share of the lawn tractor market in two years for a given investment in advertising. To achieve that same level of penetration over the same time period with the second campaign, MTD would have to spend twice as much on advertising. Is society, including consumers, MTD, and John Deere, better off by forcing MTD to undertake the second campaign? Why or why not? What if MTD will find it profitable to enter the market only if it can use the first marketing campaign? Should we bar the use of that campaign and hence bar MTD's competitive entry altogether?

4. *Humor and Ridicule as Marketing Techniques.* Why would the first campaign, that employs the distorted "scared deer" mark, be more effective than the second campaign that relies on objective comparison of the respective products? Is it simply that humor is memorable, and so will stick with the consumer? Or is it more than that? Does an advertising campaign based upon "objective" facts have to pass through the careful and skeptical scrutiny of the consumer's conscious mind? Will ridicule, on the other hand, jump somehow right past the conscious mind and its filters, and disrupt directly the consumer's subconscious link between John Deere's actual trademark and desirable products? Is that what the court meant when it wrote that MTD's alterations "risk the possibility that consumers will come to attribute unfavorable characteristics to a mark and ultimately associate the mark with inferior goods and services." *Deere & Co.*, 41 F.3d at 45. Does the court cite any evidence or social science research to support this possibility? Whose burden is it to show that this "possibility" actually exists? By analogy to the likelihood of confusion standard, isn't the standard a likelihood, and hence probability, of dilution, not a possibility of dilution?

5. *Breaking a Habit.* In dissent in *Triangle Pubs., Inc. v. Rohrlich,* Judge Frank wrote:

> The trade-name doctrine, this court has said per Judge Learned Hand, enables one to acquire a vested interest in a demand 'spuriously' stimulated through 'the art of advertising' by 'the power of reiterated suggestion' which creates stubborn habits. *See Shredded Wheat Co. v. Humphrey Cornell Co.*, 2 Cir., 250 F. 960, 962, 963. This poses an important policy question: Should the courts actively lend their aid to the making of profits derived from the

building of such habits so dominate buyers that they pay more for a product than for an equally good competing product?

167 F.2d 969, 980 n.13 (2d Cir. 1948) (Frank, J., dissenting). Modern social science research confirms that purchasing a given brand can become a habit with consumers, and a habit that is hard to break.

If John Deere, through its advertising and other promotional efforts, has created in consumers the habit of John Deere, should courts "lend their aid" to John Deere's efforts to protect that habit, and thereby make additional profits, by barring MTD's use? Is it sensible policy to encourage John Deere to invest resources in creating such habits? Or does it matter where the preference for John Deere tractors came from? Once established, should we protect it?

While much of this is uncertain and might reasonably be debated, one thing that is clear is that it is hard to enter a market long-dominated by one company. Given the benefits of competition, should we make such entry easier or harder for a would-be competitor?

4.   TRADE DRESS DILUTION?

I.P. LUND TRADING APS V. KOHLER CO.
163 F.3d 27 (1st Cir. 1998)

LYNCH, J.

This is an appeal from the district court's issuance of a preliminary injunction enjoining defendants Kohler Company and Robern, Inc. from selling the Kohler Falling Water faucet, a faucet resembling plaintiff Lund's VOLA faucet. The VOLA faucet mounts on a wall, has been in the design collection at the Museum of Modern Art, and has a certain cachet among those who enjoy bathrooms and kitchens beautiful. Kohler intended to produce a faucet like Lund's, but not identical to it, and hence designed the now-enjoined Falling Water faucet. There were two basic claims before the trial court: that the Falling Water faucet "diluted" the VOLA faucet's trade dress within the meaning of the Federal Trademark Dilution Act of 1995 ("FTDA"), 15 U.S.C. § 1125(c), and that the Falling Water faucet infringed the VOLA's trade dress. Lund won a preliminary injunction on the first ground, but not on the second. *See I.P. Lund Trading ApS v. Kohler Co.*, 11 F. Supp. 2d 112, 127 (D. Mass. 1998) (*"Lund I"*).

This difference in results was not anomalous. The district court found, as to the infringement claim, that while the VOLA faucet was not inherently distinctive, it had acquired secondary meaning and thus was protectable, but that there was no infringement because there was no confusion on the part of consumers. In contrast, under the FTDA, where no confusion need be shown, the court found the VOLA faucet was famous and that Kohler's faucet diluted the identity of the VOLA faucet.

This case presents complex issues arising in areas of intellectual property law recently extended and not yet well demarcated. Few courts of appeals have yet interpreted the FTDA and this court has never addressed certain key issues, under both the infringement and FTDA claims, necessary to the resolution of the case. The district court wrote thoughtfully, and, particularly as to the FTDA issues, without much appellate guidance. The claim for protection here comes not from traditional marks such as names but from the very design of the faucet itself—that design is said to give the faucet its identity and distinctiveness. Although Lund may have been able to obtain a design patent and so protect its VOLA faucet in that way, at least for a period of fourteen years, *see* 35 U.S.C. § 173, it chose not to. Rather, it chose to turn for protection to legal doctrines of trademark and trade dress, originally crafted without product designs in mind. The trade dress of product designs, unlike other forms of trade dress, cannot be separated from the product itself. Kohler has raised serious constitutional concerns, saying that this use of the FTDA against a competing product essentially gives a perpetual monopoly to product design, a perpetual monopoly prohibited by the Patent Clause.

Kohler and Robern (collectively "Kohler") argue that the district court erred in its determination that plaintiffs I.P. Lund Trading ApS and Kroin Incorporated (collectively "Lund") demonstrated a likelihood of success on the merits of their claim under the FTDA that the Falling Water faucet dilutes the trade dress of Lund's VOLA faucet. Lund cross-appeals, arguing that the district court erred in determining that Lund was unlikely to succeed on the merits of its infringement claim. We affirm the denial of the preliminary injunction on the infringement claim. We vacate the grant of the injunction on the FTDA claim.

Under the FTDA, we hold that a party who wishes to establish fame of the trade dress for which protection is sought bears a significantly greater burden than the burden of establishing distinctiveness for infringement purposes. The FTDA creates an exceptional anti-dilution remedy for truly famous marks. Once this greater burden of establishing fame has been met under the FTDA, the issue of dilution must be addressed. We reject the use of the "Sweet factors" as the test for dilution and instead require an inquiry into whether target customers will perceive the products as essentially the same. We hold that the dilution standard is a rigorous one, and Lund has not shown that it is likely to succeed. While we acknowledge serious constitutional concerns about application of the FTDA to a dilution claim against a competing product which does not confuse consumers, the resolution of the case obviates the as applied constitutional issue, and we decline to address any residual facial challenge.

II. *Facts and Procedural History*

Lund, a Danish corporation, manufactures bathroom and kitchen fixtures and accessories, including faucets. Lund has been a family-owned corporation since its establishment in 1873. In 1969, Lund introduced the VOLA faucet, designed by the noted architect Arne Jacobsen. The faucet, which has received numerous awards over the past quarter-century, is Lund's principal revenue-producing product. Lund has sold a total of more than 600,000 VOLA faucets. The faucet has been regularly advertised and featured in numerous magazines. Kroin Incorporated is the sole United States distributor of the VOLA.

Kohler is the largest supplier of plumbing fixtures in this country, selling hundreds of types of kitchen and bathroom fixtures. In 1994, Kohler contacted Lund regarding the possibility of selling the VOLA faucet under Kohler's name. In 1995, Kohler purchased eight VOLA faucets from Lund for the purpose of testing the faucets to see if they fit in a sink that Kohler planned to introduce and to ensure that the faucets complied with United States regulations. Kohler claims that it tested the faucets and found that they did not meet U.S. regulations regarding water flow capacity and resistance to hydrostatic pressure, a contention Lund contests, and as to which there was conflicting evidence.

Kohler gave a VOLA faucet to Erich Slothower, an industrial designer employed by Kohler. Slothower then designed the Falling Water faucet, which Kohler introduced for sale at a price lower than that of the VOLA faucet. Slothower testified that he examined the VOLA carefully prior to designing the Falling Water, but that he attempted to make the Falling Water faucet different from the VOLA. Kohler's large size and well-established distribution channels mean that the Falling Water is likely to be more easily available, in addition to being less expensive.

The district court found a number of similarities between the VOLA and the Falling Water faucets. Both are "single-control, wall-mounted faucets" with handles that "utilize a thin cylindrical lever to adjust water temperature and volume"; both have "spouts and aerator holders . . . of uniform diameter," with the spouts "bending downward at right angles softened by a curve"; and "both faucets offer spouts in almost exactly the same three lengths." *Lund I*, 11 F. Supp. 2d at 116. Both faucets fit no-hole sinks. In contrast, most sinks sold in the United States are "three-hole" sinks, with one hole each for the water spout and the hot and cold spigots. However, the district court also found dissimilarities between the faucets, including differences in the faucets' handles, a rounded lever on the Falling Water faucet compared to a flat lever on the VOLA, and a rounded bonnet—a piece that connects the faucet to the wall—on the mounting end of the Falling Water spout, compared to no bonnet on the

VOLA. *See id.* The court also found that the housemarks, "VOLA" and "Kohler," are clearly dissimilar and are prominently displayed on the faucets. *See id.* at 123.

Co-defendant Robern, which Kohler acquired in August 1995, also purchased a number of VOLA faucets. Before being acquired by Kohler, Robern purchased 218 VOLA faucets from Kroin for use in a sink module. Robern apparently promoted its sink module pictured with the VOLA faucets. At approximately the same time as Kohler acquired Robern, Kroin refused to sell additional VOLA faucets to Robern, claiming that Robern was selling the faucets to Kroin's customers at prices below those Kroin was charging. One year later, Robern announced plans to market its sink module with the Falling Water faucet. Lund produced evidence that Robern has continued to use pictures of the VOLA in promotional materials, despite the fact that it has replaced the VOLA with the Falling Water faucet in its sink modules.

Kohler introduced the Falling Water faucet to the market in 1996. Lund filed suit on February 27, 1997, alleging trade dress infringement under Section 43(a) of the Lanham Act and trade dress dilution under the FTDA. Kohler denied any violations and argued that the FTDA was unconstitutional as applied to product designs. The district court held an evidentiary hearing on April 16 and 30, 1997.

The court ruled on the motion for a preliminary injunction in three stages. In a February 5, 1998 Memorandum and Order, the court found that Lund had demonstrated a substantial likelihood of success on its dilution claim, and so enjoined Kohler from selling its Falling Water faucet. *See Lund I*, 11 F. Supp. 2d at 127. At the same time, the court found that Lund had failed to show likelihood of success on its claim of trade dress infringement, and it reserved decision on the question of the constitutionality of the FTDA pending additional briefing. *See id.*

On February 12, 1998, the district court stayed the preliminary injunction pending resolution of Kohler's claim that application of the FTDA to product designs violates the Patent Clause.

In an order dated March 31, 1998 and a memorandum dated April 2, 1998, the district court found that Kohler's constitutional argument was unlikely to succeed on the merits, lifted the stay on the injunction, and ordered Lund to post a bond of $250,000. See I.P. Lund Trading ApS v. *Kohler Co.*, 11 F. Supp. 2d 127, 134–35 (D. Mass. 1998) ("*Lund II*").

The district court also denied Kohler's request to stay the injunction pending appeal to this court. On April 29, 1998, this court rejected Kohler's request for a stay pending appeal.

III. *Purposes of Trademark and Trade Dress Protection*

The basic building blocks of the analysis are worth reiterating. Section 43(a) of the Lanham Act provides protection against the use of "any word, term, name, symbol, or device" that "is likely to cause confusion, or to cause mistake, or to deceive" as to the source of a product. 15 U.S.C. § 1125(a). Trade dress includes "the design and appearance of [a] product together with the elements making up the overall image that serves to identify the product presented to the consumer." *Chrysler Corp. v. Silva*, 118 F.3d 56, 58 (1st Cir. 1997) (alteration in original) (quoting *Fun-Damental Too, Ltd. v. Gemmy Indus. Corp.*, 111 F.3d 993, 999 (2d Cir. 1997)) (internal quotation marks omitted). The new law, the FTDA, Lanham Act section 43(c), grants protection to "famous" marks against any use of the mark that "causes dilution of the distinctive quality of the mark." 15 U.S.C. § 1125(c).

. . .

A primary purpose of trade dress or trademark protection is to protect that which identifies a product's source. *See Qualitex Co. v. Jacobson Prods. Co.*, 514 U.S. 159, 162 (1995) (noting that "the statutory definition of a trademark . . . requires that a person 'use' or 'intend to use' the mark 'to identify and distinguish his or her goods, including a unique product, from those manufactured or sold by others and to indicate the source of the goods, even if that source is unknown'" (alterations in original) (quoting 15 U.S.C. § 1127)). "The purpose of trademark laws is to prevent the use of the same or similar marks in a way that confuses the public about the actual source of the goods or service." *Star Fin. Servs., Inc. v. Aastar Mortgage Corp.*, 89 F.3d 5, 9 (1st Cir. 1996). Traditional trademark and trade dress law thus encourages production of products of high quality "and simultaneously discourages those who hope to sell inferior products by capitalizing on a consumer's inability quickly to evaluate the quality of an item offered for sale." *Qualitex*, 514 U.S. at 164. More importantly for our purposes, trademark and trade dress protection serves to protect both the trademark or trade dress owner and the public by avoiding confusion or mistake.

In contrast, dilution statutes, and the FTDA in particular, protect only the trademark or trade dress owner and are not concerned with possible confusion on the part of consumers. *See* J. Gilson, *Trademark Protection and Practice* § 5.12 (1998). Any protection of the public intended by the FTDA is indirect at best. "Anti-dilution statutes have developed to fill a void left by the failure of trademark infringement law to curb the unauthorized use of marks where there is no likelihood of confusion between the original use and the infringing use." *L.L. Bean, Inc. v. Drake Publishers, Inc.*, 811 F.2d 26, 30 (1st Cir. 1987). Filling this void, Congress passed the FTDA in 1995 both to provide uniform national protection against dilution and to bring this country's law into conformity with international agreements. *See* H.R. Rep. No. 104–374, at 3–4 (1995), *reprinted in* 1995 U.S.C.C.A.N 1029, 1030–31.

IV. *Prerequisites for Protection from Infringement and Dilution*

Despite different purposes being served, claims for protection against trademark and trade dress infringement, on the one hand, and dilution, on the other, share three common elements before the analyses diverge. Those elements are that marks (a) must be used in commerce, (b) must be non-functional, and (c) must be distinctive. While all such marks may be protected against infringement, under the FTDA only *famous* and distinctive marks are eligible for protection against dilution. No requirement for fame is present in trademark and trade dress infringement.

[The court discussed these requirements. It found that the trade dress was used in commerce, but was not certain that the trade dress was non-functional or distinctive. Rather than resolve the case on these grounds, however, the court proceeded to consider whether Lund had shown a likelihood of success on the trademark infringement and dilution claims.]

V. *Infringement*

Establishing trademark infringement requires a showing that prospective buyers of the product in question—here, high-end faucets—are likely to be confused as to the product's source. *See* 15 U.S.C. § 1125(a); *Two Pesos*, 505 U.S. at 769; *TEC Eng'g Corp.*, 82 F.3d at 545; *Purolator, Inc. v. EFRA Distribs., Inc.*, 687 F.2d 554, 559 (1st Cir. 1982); cf. *International Ass'n of Machinists & Aerospace Workers v. Winship Green Nursing Ctr.*, 103 F.3d 196, 201 (1st Cir. 1996) ("The law has long demanded a showing that the allegedly infringing conduct carries with it a likelihood of confounding an appreciable number of reasonably prudent purchasers exercising ordinary care."). Establishing infringement also requires a showing that the plaintiff uses, and thus owns, the mark in question, and that the defendant's mark is similar to or the same as the plaintiff's mark. *See DeCosta*, 981 F.2d at 605. A plaintiff is not entitled to a preliminary injunction on a trademark infringement claim unless it can persuade the district court that it is likely to be able to demonstrate consumer confusion. *See WCVB-TV v. Boston Athletic Ass'n*, 926 F.2d 42, 44 (1st Cir. 1991).

This court has identified eight factors to be weighed in determining likelihood of confusion:

(1) the similarity of the marks; (2) the similarity of the goods; (3) the relationship between the parties' channels of trade; (4) the relationship between the parties' advertising; (5) the classes of prospective purchasers; (6) evidence of actual confusion; (7) the defendant's intent in adopting its mark; and (8)

the strength of the plaintiff's mark. . . . No one factor is necessarily determinative, but each must be considered.

Boston Athletic Ass'n, 867 F.2d at 29 (quoting *Volkswagenwerk Aktiengesellschaft v. Wheeler*, 814 F.2d 812, 817 (1st Cir. 1987)) (citations and internal quotation marks omitted). The factors are non-exclusive, however, and are not always apt to the particular facts of a case. *See Winship Green*, 103 F.3d at 201. In addition, the first factor, similarity, "is determined on the basis of the total effect of the designation, rather than a comparison of individual features." *Pignons S.A. de Mecanique de Precision v. Polaroid Corp.*, 657 F.2d 482, 487 (1st Cir. 1981) (internal quotation marks omitted).

The district court applied these eight factors and determined that, taken together, the factors weighed against a finding of a likelihood of consumer confusion. The court found that the strength of the VOLA's mark and the similarity of the VOLA and the Falling Water products were factors that favored the plaintiffs, but that the class of prospective purchasers, the channels of trade, the defendant's intent, and the dissimilarity of the VOLA and Falling Water marks all favored the defendants. The court found that the two remaining factors did not weigh in favor of either party.

· · ·

Review of factual determinations is for clear error. We have carefully considered each of Lund's arguments, and are unpersuaded that the district court's determination as to the probability of success on each of these points was erroneous.

· · ·

The district court correctly found that Lund was unlikely to prevail on the merits of its infringement claim, and so correctly denied the preliminary injunction on those grounds.

VI. *Dilution*

Lund obtained the preliminary injunction against Kohler's distribution and promotion of the Falling Water faucet based on the district court's finding of likelihood of success under the new federal anti-dilution statute, the FTDA, which became effective in 1996. The injunction rested on the conclusion that Lund had established a likelihood of success of showing two essential elements. The first is that the "mark," that is, the VOLA product design as an identifying mark, was "famous." The second is that Kohler's Falling Water faucet "diluted" Lund's mark. Both the terms "famous" and "dilution" are terms of art given specific rigorous meanings by the FTDA.

We start with the language of the Act. The FTDA provides:

> The owner of a famous mark shall be entitled, subject to the principles of equity and upon such terms as the court deems reasonable, to an injunction against another person's commercial use in commerce of a mark or trade name, if such use begins after the mark has become famous and causes dilution of the distinctive quality of the mark, and to obtain such other relief as is provided in this subsection.

15 U.S.C. § 1125(c)(1).

The FTDA created a new "federal cause of action to protect famous marks from unauthorized users that attempt to trade upon the goodwill and established renown of such marks and, thereby, dilute their distinctive quality." H.R. Rep. No. 104–374, at 3, *reprinted in* 1995 U.S.C.C.A.N at 1030. Congress acted against a "patch-quilt system" of state law protection in which approximately twenty-five states had laws prohibiting trademark dilution. *Id.* While creating a federal cause of action, Congress expressly did not preempt state law, but attempted to create uniformity through the availability of a federal cause of action. A second consideration—protection of famous marks of U.S. companies abroad—also motivated Congress. *See id.* at 4, *reprinted in* 1995 U.S.C.C.A.N at 1031. Enactment of the FTDA was consistent with agreements which were part of the Uruguay Round of the General Agreement on Tariffs and Trade (specifically, the Agreement on Trade-Related Aspects of Intellectual Property Rights, including Trade in Counterfeit Goods ("TRIPS")) and the Paris Convention. Enactment of the law was also thought to be of value to the U.S. in bilateral and multilateral trade negotiations. *See id.*

Sponsors of the bill articulated the type of problem the Act was meant to solve:

> This bill is designed to protect famous trademarks from subsequent uses that blur the distinctiveness of the mark or tarnish or disparage it, even in the absence of a likelihood of confusion. Thus, for example, the use of DuPont shoes, Buick aspirin, and Kodak pianos would be actionable under this bill.

141 Cong. Rec. S19306, S19310 (daily ed. Dec. 29, 1995) (statement of Sen. Hatch). Thus the archetypal problems involved non-competing products as to which there could, by definition, be no confusion and a world-famous brand name which was either tarnished or blurred by its application to a different product which was obviously trading on the good will of that name.

The language of the FTDA itself is, however, not limited to addressing these archetypal problems. A few observations are in order. First, the Act applies to products which are competitors (as is true of the faucets here) as well as to products which are totally dissimilar and are not competitors. Second, the Act applies to a famous "mark" and does not restrict the definition of that term to names or traditional marks. In the absence of such a restriction, the Act applies to all types of marks recognized by the Lanham Act, including marks derived from product designs. Kohler's argument that the Act cannot, as a matter of statutory interpretation, be applied to product design is rejected. Third, the Act applies even where there is no customer confusion, a point with consequences discussed later. Fourth, the additional protection afforded by the Act requires that a mark go beyond what is required for ordinary Lanham Act protection. Only those marks which are "distinctive and famous" are protected. 15 U.S.C. § 1125(c)(1). As set forth in the 1987 Trademark Review Commission Report, the precursor of the 1996 Act, this language reflected "the policy goal that to be protected, a mark had to be truly prominent and renowned." 3 McCarthy § 24.91 (citing *The United States Trademark Association Trademark Review Commission Report and Recommendations to USTA President and Board of Directors*, 77 Trademark Rep. 375, 459–60 (1987)). With this background, we turn to the district court's two essential conclusions.

A. *Fame and Distinctiveness*

The requirements of commercial use, non-functionality, and distinctiveness are common to both the infringement claim and the FTDA dilution claim. In order to fall within the sphere of protection against dilution the FTDA adds an additional requirement: the FTDA grants protection only to famous marks. *See* 15 U.S.C. § 1125(c); *cf.* Gilson § 5.12[1][a] (calling the FTDA "a major breakthrough for an elite category of trademark owners"). The FTDA provides a non-exclusive list of eight factors that courts should consider in determining whether a mark is "distinctive and famous." 15 U.S.C. § 1125(c)(1). . . .

The district court found likelihood of success on the claim that the VOLA's design was a famous mark. Kohler challenges this finding.

Both the text and legislative history of the original bill in 1988 and the FTDA itself indicate a congressional intent that courts should be discriminating and selective in categorizing a mark as famous. For example, the Senate Judiciary Committee Report on the 1988 precursor bill said the Committee wished "to underscore its determination that the new dilution provisions should apply only to . . . very unique marks." 3 McCarthy § 24:92 n.6 (quoting S. Rep. No. 100–515, at 41–42) (internal quotation marks omitted). The Trademark Review Commission noted that the showing of fame required employment of a "higher standard" than fame among an "appreciable number of persons" in order to be "eligible for this extraordinary remedy." *Id.* n.8 (quoting *The United States Trademark Association Trademark Review Commission Report*, 77 Trademark Rep. at 461) (internal quotation marks omitted). Onc commentator has referred to this category of famous marks as "Supermarks." *See* Gilson § 5.12[1][a]. As the Restatement (Third) of Unfair Competition notes:

> A mark that evokes an association with a specific source only when used in connection with the particular goods or services that it identifies is ordinarily not sufficiently distinctive to be protected against dilution.

Restatement (Third) of Unfair Competition § 25 cmt. e (1995).

The record here reflects that there was not sufficient attention paid to the heightened fame standard that the FTDA establishes. The district court found that "in its market, the VOLA's design is famous and distinctive" based on its prior analysis under the infringement claim that "the VOLA mark is strong, and has acquired secondary meaning in its market; and it has been used for some twenty years in this country." *Lund I*, 11 F. Supp. 2d at 125. Both the Restatement (Third) of Unfair Competition and the state anti-dilution statutes against the background of which Congress enacted the FTDA make clear that the standard for fame and distinctiveness required to obtain anti-dilution protection is more rigorous than that required to seek infringement protection. *See* Restatement (Third) of Unfair Competition § 25 cmt. e. As one commentator has stated:

> Certainly, the mere acquisition of secondary meaning to achieve trademark status in a non-inherently distinctive designation is nowhere near sufficient to achieve the status of "famous mark" under the anti-dilution statute. The acquisition of secondary meaning merely establishes the minimum threshold necessary for trademark status: section 43(c) requires a great deal more.

3 McCarthy § 24:91; *see also* Gilson § 5.12[1][c][ii] ("A trademark can certainly be distinctive without being famous, but it cannot be famous without being distinctive.").

We do not understand the district court's conclusion about fame, despite some ambiguity, to have rested solely on its conclusion that the VOLA faucet was distinctive (because it had acquired secondary meaning); any such per se analysis would be erroneous. But it appears that the district court did not apply the more rigorous definition of fame under the FTDA. While one can posit a case having very strong facts which support a distinctiveness finding based on secondary meaning and then using those facts to support the separate, more rigorous analysis of fame, the facts in this case do not have such strength. Lund has a difficult case to establish fame through the product design of the VOLA faucet, and this record is not strong. There has been no use by Kohler of the VOLA name, or any other name by which the faucet is known. Kohler's use, if any, is of a like product design. There is little to suggest that this product design, itself unregistered and not inherently distinctive, is so strong a mark and so well publicized and known that it has achieved the level of fame Congress intended under the Act. Consumer surveys could be used as evidence of such fame, but consumer surveys are absent from this case. Additionally, although some marks, such as COCA-COLA, may be so famous as to be judicially noticed, *see* Gilson § 5.12[1][c][iii], the VOLA faucet is far from being a candidate for such judicial notice.

Further, national renown is an important factor in determining whether a mark qualifies as famous under the FTDA. Although the district court found that "in the world of interior design and high-end bathroom fixtures, the VOLA is renowned," *Lund I*, 11 F. Supp. 2d at 126, and that the faucet has been featured and advertised in national magazines and displayed in museums, whether the VOLA's identifying design is sufficiently famous to qualify for the FTDA's protection is far from clear. In light of the rigorous standard for fame, we find that Lund has not met its burden of showing likelihood of success.

B. *Dilution*

Under the FTDA, even if a mark is famous there is no relief unless that mark has been diluted. As the district court noted, there are two types of dilution recognized: blurring and tarnishing. This case involves no claim of tarnishing, an area in which Congress expressed a strong interest. Further, in light of the finding of no customer confusion, only a particular type of blurring may be involved.

The intellectual origins of the dilution doctrine are traced to a 1927 Harvard Law Review article, which urged protection against "the gradual whittling away or dispersion of the identity and hold upon the public mind of the mark or name by its use upon non-competing goods." Schecter, *The Rational Basis of Trademark Protection*, 40 Harv. L. Rev. 813, 825 (1927). Although the origins of the doctrine are concerned with non-competing goods, Congress used language in the FTDA which extends dilution protection even to competing goods. "Dilution" is defined as "the lessening of the capacity of a famous mark to identify and distinguish good or services." 15 U.S.C. § 1127; *see also* H.R. Rep. No. 104–374, at 3, *reprinted in* 1995 U.S.C.C.A.N at 1030 (stating that dilution "applies when the unauthorized use of a famous mark reduces the public's perception that the mark signifies something unique, singular, or particular"); 3 McCarthy § 24:93 ("The crux is whether this particular challenged use lessens the capacity of the famous mark to carry out its role as a trademark—namely, to identify and distinguish.").

This case differs in several respects from usual dilution cases. First, unlike most claims of dilution by tarnishment or blurring, the aspect of its product that Lund seeks to protect—the design of the VOLA faucet—likely could have been protected by a design patent. The possibility of obtaining a design patent is not dispositive of the availability of trade dress protection: more than one form of intellectual property protection may simultaneously protect particular product features. Moreover, design patent protection would not have provided protection identical to that sought here. Nevertheless, the availability of design patent protection does suggest that the claim in this case differs fundamentally from the claims the drafters of the FTDA had in mind—cases where dilution protection is the only form of protection available for a famous mark threatened by unauthorized use of the mark that lessens the mark's capacity to identify its source. Congress's intent to provide protection where none previously existed is evidenced by the House Report's statement that "[a] federal dilution statute is necessary because famous marks ordinarily are used on a nationwide basis and dilution protection is currently only available on a patch-quilt system of protection, in that only approximately 25 states have laws that prohibit trademark dilution." H.R. Rep. No. 104–374, at 3, *reprinted in* 1995 U.S.C.C.A.N. at 1030.

Second, Lund is seeking protection against a direct competitor. Although the FTDA states that dilution protection is available against unauthorized use of a famous mark that lessens the mark's ability "to identify and distinguish goods or services, *regardless of the presence or absence of . . . competition between the owner of the famous mark and other parties,*" 15 U.S.C. § 1127 (emphasis added), dilution protection has most often been extended to non-competing uses of a mark, *see, e.g.,* H.R. Rep. No. 104–374, at 3, *reprinted in* 1995 U.S.C.C.A.N. at 1030 (giving examples of "DUPONT shoes, BUICK aspirin, and KODAK pianos"); 3 McCarthy § 24.72 (noting "split of authority under . . . state statutes as to whether the anti-dilution rule is applicable where the parties are in competition"). The FTDA recognizes the possibility that dilution may occur in some circumstances where, although some consumers are not confused as to the products' sources, a competitor's use of a mark tarnishes or blurs a senior mark. Nevertheless, such cases are likely to be exceptions to the more common cases of dilution by non-competing marks. Dilution laws are intended to address specific harms; they are not intended to serve as mere fallback protection for trademark owners unable to prove trademark infringement.

While there may be a tendency to think of dilution in terms of confusion, Congress made it clear that dilution can occur even in the absence of confusion. It is simple to see why that should be so when non-competing goods are at issue. No one would confuse Kodak pianos with Kodak film, but the use of the name on the piano could dilute its effectiveness as a mark for the film. But Congress did not say that there can be dilution without confusion only among non-competing goods. As the district court aptly noted, the analysis becomes complicated when the concept of blurring is applied to competing similar products.

We deal first with the approach taken by the district court, an approach which had support in precedent. The district court articulated the standard for determining blurring as follows: "Lund must demonstrate that 'the use of a junior mark has caused a lessening of demand for the product or services bearing the famous mark.'" *Lund I*, 11 F. Supp. 2d at 126 (quoting *Ringling Bros.-Barnum & Bailey Combined Shows, Inc. v. Utah Div. of Travel Dev.*, 955 F. Supp. 605, 616 (E.D. Va. 1997)). This, we think, is not the correct standard. As Kohler observes, demand for one product is almost always lessened whenever a competing product achieves a measurable degree of success. Further, blurring has to do with the identification of a product and that is not the same thing as a lessening of demand.

In addressing the dilution claim, the district court used the "Sweet factors," named after the six factors set forth in Judge Sweet's concurrence in *Mead Data Central, Inc. v. Toyota Motor Sales, U.S.A., Inc.*, 875 F.2d 1026, 1035 (2d Cir. 1989) (Sweet, J., concurring), which involved a claim brought under a New York dilution statute. Some district courts have used these factors to examine whether dilution exists under the FTDA. *See, e.g., Ringling Bros.-Barnum & Bailey Combined Shows, Inc. v. B.E. Windows Corp.*, 937 F. Supp. 204, 211–14 (S.D.N.Y. 1996); *WAWA, Inc. v. Haaf*, 1996 U.S. Dist. LEXIS 11494, 40 U.S.P.Q.2D (BNA) 1629, 1632–33 (E.D. Pa. Aug. 7, 1996), *aff'd*, 116 F.3d 471 (3d Cir. 1997); *Clinique Lab., Inc. v. Dep Corp.*, 945 F. Supp. 547, 562 (S.D.N.Y. 1996).

Kohler argues that Judge Sweet's six-factor test is inappropriate in determining whether dilution has occurred for purposes of the FTDA. We agree. The Sweet factors have been criticized by both courts and commentators for introducing factors that "are the offspring of classical likelihood of confusion analysis and are not particularly relevant or helpful in resolving the issues of dilution by blurring." 3 McCarthy § 24:94.1. The six Sweet factors are: "1) similarity of the marks 2) similarity of the products covered by the marks 3) sophistication of consumers 4) predatory intent 5) renown of the senior mark [and] 6) renown of the junior mark." *Mead Data*, 875 F.2d at 1035 (Sweet, J., concurring). McCarthy urges that only the first and fifth of Judge Sweet's factors—the similarity of the marks and the renown of the senior mark—are relevant to determining whether dilution has occurred. *See* 3 McCarthy § 24:94.1; *see also Hershey Foods Corp. v. Mars, Inc.*, 998 F. Supp. 500, 520 (M.D. Pa. 1998) (stating that "whether the products are similar or not adds nothing to the analysis" because "dilution can apply to competitors"); Klieger, *Trademark Dilution: The Whittling Away of the Rational Basis for Trademark Protection*, 58 U. Pitt. L. Rev. 789, 826–27 (1997) (noting that "few of these factors bear any relation to whether a particular junior use will debilitate the selling power of a mark" and that "so long as a mark qualifies for dilution protection and the senior and junior uses of the mark are not so unrelated as to foreclose the possibility of a mental connection, blurring ... is a foregone conclusion"). These criticisms are well taken.

The district court's finding of likelihood of dilution by blurring depended on its use of inappropriate Sweet factors. As McCarthy points out, use of factors such as predatory intent, similarity of products, sophistication of customers, and renown of the junior mark work directly contrary to the intent of a law whose primary purpose was to apply in cases of widely differing goods, i.e. Kodak pianos and Kodak film. *See* 3 McCarthy § 24:94.1.

There are difficulties with the Sweet factors even when used with competing goods. Blurring occurs in the minds of potential customers. Predatory intent tells little about how customers in fact perceive products. That customers are sophisticated may well mean less likelihood of blurring. That customers knowingly choose to pay less to get a similar product, and trade lower price against having a product of greater fame, does not, contrary to Lund's argument, establish blurring. Indeed, the district court's findings, in the infringement context, of dissimilarity and sophistication of the customers tend to cut against any finding of blurring. "The familiar test of similarity used in the traditional likelihood of confusion test cannot be the guide [for dilution analysis], for likelihood of confusion is not the test of dilution." *Id.* § 24:90.1. Instead, the inquiry is into whether target customers are likely to view the products "as essentially the same." *Id.*

There is a more fundamental problem here in attempting to apply the dilution analysis to the design itself of the competing product involved. We doubt that Congress intended the reach of the dilution concept under the FTDA to extend this far and our doubts are heightened by the presence of constitutional constraints. Where words are the marks at issue it is easy to understand that there can be blurring and tarnishment when there is a completely different product to which the words are applied. The congressional history described earlier gives such examples. What is much more difficult is to see how dilution is to be shown where some of a design is partially replicated and the result is largely dissimilar and does not create consumer confusion. If that is so, as is true here, then it is difficult to see that there has been dilution of the source signaling function of the design (even assuming that such a function has been established through secondary meaning).

Instead, it appears that an entirely different issue is at stake—not interference with the source signaling function but rather protection from an appropriation of or free riding on the investment Lund has made in its design. That investment is usually given protection by patents, which have a limited duration. *See W.T. Rogers Co.*, 778 F.2d at 348. But again, that free riding or appropriation appears to be of the beauty of the object and not of the source, and may in fact be good for consumers. As the district court observed, these sophisticated buyers know a different source is involved and are, accordingly, most likely purchasing because of the aesthetics. And even if there is some appropriation or free riding, the extent of it here is not clear. Certainly it is not plausible to think that Congress intended to protect aesthetic characteristics by simply assuming harm or damages based on the fact that the plaintiff will sell less if the defendant sells more. What is clear is that the interests here are not the interests at the core of what Congress intended to protect in the FTDA.

It is possible that Congress did not really envision protection for product design from dilution by a competing product under the FTDA, but the language it used does not permit us to exclude such protection categorically and rare cases can be imagined. But a broad reading of dilution would bring us close to the constitutional edge, and we decline to attribute such brinksmanship to Congress, and so insist on rigorous review.

Under the interpretation of the fame and dilution requirements for the FTDA set forth today, the requirements for granting the preliminary injunction have not been met.

VII. *Constitutionality of the FTDA*

Kohler argues that the FTDA may never constitutionally be applied to enjoin a competitor in a product design trade dress case. Kohler's constitutional challenge involves two steps. First, Kohler argues that applying the FTDA to product designs grants patent-like protections for an unlimited period of time. Second, Kohler argues that Congress's Commerce Clause power—the basis of Congress's regulation of trademarks and trade dress—cannot be used to trump the Patent Clause. Lund responds that federal anti-dilution legislation is fully consistent with Congress's Commerce Clause power, and that patent and trademark laws protect different interests and serve different goals.

The district court correctly noted that Kohler faced a "very high preliminary injunction standard on their [constitutional] claim," and that the statute was "presumptively constitutional." Lund II, 11 F. Supp. 2d at 134. The court concluded that defendant Kohler was unlikely to succeed with its argument that the FTDA is unconstitutional in all product design contexts.

Kohler's constitutional attack on application of the FTDA here is mooted by our resolution of the injunction issue. To the extent Kohler is mounting something akin to a facial attack, we think it better not to address constitutional issues in the abstract. The resolution of any conflict between the Patent Clause and the FTDA is better handled on specific facts which present the issues with clarity, and not on the basis of theoretical impacts.

VIII. *Conclusion*

Both the parties and the district court labored through this case without the benefit of binding precedent on a number of key and difficult issues, particularly the interpretation of the FTDA. The denial of the preliminary injunction on the infringement claim is affirmed. The grant of the injunction on the FTDA claim is vacated inasmuch as there were no findings on functionality and standards for determining both fame and dilution under the FTDA were used which are different from those announced today and the evidence does not show probability of success under those standards. The case is remanded for further proceedings not inconsistent with this opinion. No costs are awarded.

The separate, concurring opinion of JUDGE BOUDIN is omitted.

NOTES FOR DISCUSSION

1.   *Dilution versus Confusion.* How did the court resolve the dilution claim? How did it resolve the likelihood of confusion claim? What additional rights did the dilution cause of action give the plaintiff?

2.   *Goldfish Crackers.* The year after the First Circuit decided *I.P. Lund*, the Second Circuit faced a similar case. In *Nabisco, Inc. v. PF Brands, Inc.*, 191 F.3d 208 (2d Cir. 1999), Pepperidge Farms sued alleging trade dress infringement and dilution when Nabisco began offering snack crackers in association with the Cat-Dog television show, a popular children's cartoon. Nabisco's product included three cracker shapes. Half of the crackers were in the shape of the two-headed Cat-Dog character. The remaining crackers were split evenly between a bone shape, representing the favorite food of the Dog half of the main character, and a fish shape, representing Cat's favorite food. The district court concluded that Pepperidge Farms had not shown a likelihood of success on the merits with respect to trademark infringement, but found a likelihood of success on the dilution claim and therefore granted a preliminary injunction. Nabisco appealed. How should the Second Circuit rule? *See Nabisco, Inc. v. PF Brands, Inc.*, 191 F.3d 208, 222 (2d Cir. 1999) ("Considering the reasonable distinctiveness of the Goldfish mark, the very close proximity of the products, the degree of similarity between the two goldfish crackers, the low level of sophistication of many consumers, the occurrence of adjudication at the start of the junior use (and consequent absence of injury to the junior user's accumulated goodwill in its mark), we conclude that Pepperidge Farm has demonstrated a high likelihood of success in proving that Nabisco's commercial use of its goldfish shape will dilute the distinctiveness of Pepperidge Farm's nearly identical famous senior mark.").

3.   *Trade Dress and the 2006 Amendments.* In 2006, Congress added section 43(c)(4) to the Trademark Act. Review that language. Does that dictate a different outcome in the *I.P. Lund* case? Does it expressly reflect Congress's intention to provide dilution protection for trade dress? What is the effect of the savings clause Congress added in section 43(c)(7)? Does this language reflect Congress's determination that dilution protection for product

design trade dress does not interfere with the purposes of the Patent Act? Does it direct courts to make a separate inquiry into whether providing dilution protection in a particular case would frustrate or impede the purposes of the Patent Act?

4. *The Sweet Factors and the 2006 Amendments.* In the 2006 Amendments, Congress also adopted a set of factors for courts to use in determining whether dilution was likely. While not identical to the Sweet factors, they are very similar. How would the *I.P. Lund* case come out under those factors?

5. *Sears/Compco: Redux.* In Chapter 5, we discussed the implications of the Court's decisions in *Sears* and *Compco* for federal trade dress protection. Courts generally agree that the specific preemption holdings of *Sears* and *Compco* do not directly apply to federal trade dress protection. As a co-equal federal statute, trade dress protection under the Lanham Trademark Act, unlike state unfair competition law, is not subject to preemption. Courts differ, however, on whether the reasoning of the *Sears* and *Compco* decisions suggests a need to limit federal trade dress protection. Some courts argue that it does not because patent and trade dress law serve fundamentally different purposes: patent serves to encourage innovation, while trade dress serves to protect consumers from confusion. What is the purpose of federal dilution protection? If we extend it to product design, does that create a mutant species of patent or copyright? May Congress create federal dilution protection for product designs under the Commerce Clause and thereby avoid the "limited times" proviso of the Patent and Copyright Clause?

In *I.P. Lund,* the First Circuit recognized these issues but did not resolve them. The court held that these issues were mooted by its resolution of the dilution claims. When these issues arise and are ripe in a subsequent case, how should a court rule?

C. PARODY AND DILUTION

LOUIS VUITTON MALLETIER S.A. V. HAUTE DIGGITY DOG, LLC

507 F.3d 252 (4th Cir. 2007)

NIEMEYER, J.

Louis Vuitton Malletier S.A., a French corporation located in Paris, that manufactures luxury luggage, handbags, and accessories, commenced this action against Haute Diggity Dog, LLC, a Nevada corporation that manufactures and sells pet products nationally, alleging trademark infringement under 15 U.S.C. § 1114(1)(a), trademark dilution under 15 U.S.C. § 1125(c), copyright infringement under 17 U.S.C. § 501, and related statutory and common law violations. Haute Diggity Dog manufactures, among other things, plush toys on which dogs can chew, which, it claims, parody famous trademarks on luxury products, including those of Louis Vuitton Malletier. The particular Haute Diggity Dog chew toys in question here are small imitations of handbags that are labeled "Chewy Vuiton" and that mimic Louis Vuitton Malletier's LOUIS VUITTON handbags.

On cross-motions for summary judgment, the district court concluded that Haute Diggity Dog's "Chewy Vuiton" dog toys were successful parodies of Louis Vuitton Malletier's trademarks, designs, and products, and on that basis, entered judgment in favor of Haute Diggity Dog on all of Louis Vuitton Malletier's claims.

On appeal, we agree with the district court that Haute Diggity Dog's products are not likely to cause confusion with those of Louis Vuitton Malletier and that Louis Vuitton Malletier's copyright was not infringed. On the trademark dilution claim, however, we reject the district court's reasoning but reach the same conclusion through a different analysis. Accordingly, we affirm.

I

Louis Vuitton Malletier S.A. ("LVM") is a well known manufacturer of luxury luggage, leather goods, handbags, and accessories, which it markets and sells worldwide. In connection with the sale of its products, LVM has adopted trademarks and trade dress that are well recognized and have become famous and distinct. Indeed, in 2006, *BusinessWeek* ranked LOUIS VUITTON as the 17th "best brand" of all corporations in the world and the first "best brand" for any fashion business. . . .

LVM has registered trademarks for "LOUIS VUITTON," in connection with luggage and ladies' handbags (the "LOUIS VUITTON mark"); for a stylized monogram of "LV," in connection with traveling bags and other goods (the "LV mark"); and for a monogram canvas design consisting of a canvas with repetitions of the LV mark along with four-pointed stars, four-pointed stars inset in curved diamonds, and four-pointed flowers inset in circles, in connection with traveling bags and other products (the "Monogram Canvas mark"). In 2002, LVM adopted a brightly-colored version of the Monogram Canvas mark in which the LV mark and the designs were of various colors and the background was white (the "Multicolor design"), created in collaboration with Japanese artist Takashi Murakami. For the Multicolor design, LVM obtained a copyright in 2004. In 2005, LVM adopted another design consisting of a canvas with repetitions of the LV mark and smiling cherries on a brown background (the "Cherry design"). . . .

During the period 2003–2005, LVM spent more than $48 million advertising products using its marks and designs, including more than $4 million for the Multicolor design. It sells its products exclusively in LVM stores and in its own in-store boutiques that are contained within department stores such as Saks Fifth Avenue, Bloomingdale's, Neiman Marcus, and Macy's. LVM also advertises its products on the Internet through the specific websites www.louisvuitton.com and www.eluxury. com.

Although better known for its handbags and luggage, LVM also markets a limited selection of luxury pet accessories—collars, leashes, and dog carriers—which bear the Monogram Canvas mark and the Multicolor design. These items range in price from approximately $200 to $1600. LVM does not make dog toys.

Haute Diggity Dog, LLC, which is a relatively small and relatively new business located in Nevada, manufactures and sells nationally— primarily through pet stores—a line of pet chew toys and beds whose names parody elegant high-end brands of products such as perfume, cars, shoes, sparkling wine, and handbags. These include—in addition to Chewy Vuiton (LOUIS VUITTON)—Chewnel No. 5 (Chanel No. 5), Furcedes (Mercedes), Jimmy Chew (Jimmy Choo), Dog Perignonn (Dom Perignon), Sniffany & Co. (Tiffany & Co.), and Dogior (Dior). The chew toys and pet beds are plush, made of polyester, and have a shape and design that loosely imitate the signature product of the targeted brand. They are mostly distributed and sold through pet stores, although one or two Macy's stores carries Haute Diggity Dog's products. The dog toys are generally sold for less than $20, although larger versions of some of Haute Diggity Dog's plush dog beds sell for more than $100.

Haute Diggity Dog's "Chewy Vuiton" dog toys, in particular, loosely resemble miniature handbags and undisputedly evoke LVM handbags of similar shape, design, and color. In lieu of the LOUIS VUITTON mark, the dog toy uses "Chewy Vuiton"; in lieu of the LV mark, it uses "CV"; and the other symbols and colors employed are imitations, but not exact ones, of those used in the LVM Multicolor and Cherry designs.

In 2002, LVM commenced this action, naming as defendants Haute Diggity Dog; Victoria D.N. Dauernheim, the principal owner of Haute Diggity Dog; and Woofies, LLC, a retailer of Haute Diggity Dog's products, located in Asburn, Virginia, for trademark, trade dress, and copyright infringement. Its complaint includes counts for trademark counterfeiting, under 15 U.S.C. § 1114(1)(a); trademark infringement, under 15 U.S.C. § 1114(1)(a); trade dress infringement, under 15 U.S.C. § 1125(a)(1); unfair competition, under 15 U.S.C. § 1125(a)(1); trademark dilution, under 15 U.S.C. § 1125(c); trademark infringement, under Virginia common law; trade dress infringement, under Virginia common law; unfair competition, under Virginia common law; copyright infringement of the Multicolor design, under 17 U.S.C. § 501; and violation of the Virginia Consumer Protection Act, under Virginia Code § 59.1–200. On cross-motions for summary judgment, the district court granted Haute Diggity Dog's motion and denied LVM's motion, entering judgment in favor of Haute Diggity Dog on all of the claims. It rested its analysis on each count principally on the conclusion that Haute Diggity Dog's products amounted to a successful parody of LVM's marks, trade dress, and copyright. See *Louis Vuitton Malletier S.A. v. Haute Diggity Dog, LLC*, 464 F. Supp. 2d 495 (E.D. Va. 2006).

LVM appealed and now challenges, as a matter of law, virtually every ruling made by the district court.

II

LVM contends first that Haute Diggity Dog's marketing and sale of its "Chewy Vuiton" dog toys infringe its trademarks because the advertising and sale of the "Chewy Vuiton" dog toys is likely to cause confusion. *See* 15 U.S.C. § 1114(1)(a). . . .

Haute Diggity Dog contends that there is no evidence of confusion, nor could a reasonable factfinder conclude that there is a likelihood of confusion, because it successfully markets its products as parodies of famous marks such as those of LVM. It asserts that "precisely because of the [famous] mark's fame and popularity . . . confusion is avoided, and it is this lack of confusion that a parodist depends upon to achieve the parody." . . .

Concluding that Haute Diggity Dog did not create any likelihood of confusion as a matter of law, the district court granted summary judgment to Haute Diggity Dog. *Louis Vuitton Malletier*, 464 F. Supp. 2d at 503, 508. We review its order *de novo. See CareFirst of Md., Inc. v. First Care, P.C.*, 434 F.3d 263, 267 (4th Cir. 2006).

To prove trademark infringement, LVM must show (1) that it owns a valid and protectable mark; (2) that Haute Diggity Dog uses a "reproduction, counterfeit, copy, or colorable imitation" of that mark in commerce and without LVM's consent; and (3) that Haute Diggity Dog's use is likely to cause confusion. 15 U.S.C. § 1114(1)(a); *Care-First*, 434 F.3d at 267. The validity and protectability of LVM's marks are not at issue in this case, nor is the fact that Haute Diggity Dog uses a colorable imitation of LVM's mark. Therefore, we give the first two elements no further attention. To determine whether the "Chewy Vuiton" product line creates a likelihood of confusion, we have identified several nonexclusive factors to consider: (1) the strength or distinctiveness of the plaintiff's mark; (2) the similarity of the two marks; (3) the similarity of the goods or services the marks identify; (4) the similarity of the facilities the two parties use in their businesses; (5) the similarity of the advertising used by the two parties; (6) the defendant's intent; and (7) actual confusion. *See Pizzeria Uno Corp. v. Temple*, 747 F.2d 1522, 1527 (4th Cir. 1984). These *Pizzeria Uno* factors are not always weighted equally, and not all factors are relevant in every case. *See CareFirst*, 434 F.3d at 268.

Because Haute Diggity Dog's arguments with respect to the *Pizzeria Uno* factors depend to a great extent on whether its products and marks are successful parodies, we consider first whether Haute Diggity Dog's products, marks, and trade dress are indeed successful parodies of LVM's marks and trade dress.

For trademark purposes, "[a] 'parody' is defined as a simple form of entertainment conveyed by juxtaposing the irreverent representation of the trademark with the idealized image created by the mark's owner." *People for the Ethical Treatment of Animals v. Doughney* ("*PETA*"), 263 F.3d 359, 366 (4th Cir. 2001) (internal quotation marks omitted). "A parody must convey two simultaneous—and contradictory—messages: that it is the original, but also that it is *not* the original and is instead a parody." *Id.* (internal quotation marks and citation omitted). This second message must not only differentiate the alleged parody from the original but must also communicate some articulable element of satire, ridicule, joking, or amusement. Thus, "[a] parody relies upon a difference from the original mark, presumably a humorous difference, in order to produce its desired effect." *Jordache Enterprises, Inc. v. Hogg Wyld, Ltd.*, 828 F.2d 1482, 1486 (10th Cir. 1987) (finding the use of "Lardashe" jeans for larger women to be a successful and permissible parody of "Jordache" jeans).

When applying the *PETA* criteria to the facts of this case, we agree with the district court that the "Chewy Vuiton" dog toys are successful parodies of LVM handbags and the LVM marks and trade dress used in connection with the marketing and sale of those handbags. First, the pet chew toy is obviously an irreverent, and indeed intentional, representation of an LVM handbag, albeit much smaller and coarser. The dog toy is shaped roughly like a handbag; its name "Chewy Vuiton" sounds like and rhymes with LOUIS VUITTON; its monogram CV mimics LVM's LV mark; the repetitious design clearly imitates the design on the LVM handbag; and the coloring is similar. In short, the dog toy is a small, plush imitation of an LVM handbag carried by women, which invokes the marks and design of the handbag, albeit irreverently and incompletely. No one can doubt that LVM handbags are the target of the imitation by Haute Diggity Dog's "Chewy Vuiton" dog toys.

At the same time, no one can doubt also that the "Chewy Vuiton" dog toy is not the "idealized image" of the mark created by LVM. The differences are immediate, beginning with the fact that the "Chewy Vuiton" product is a dog toy, not an expensive, luxury LOUIS VUITTON handbag. The toy is smaller, it is plush, and virtually all of its designs differ. Thus, "Chewy Vuiton" is not LOUIS VUITTON ("Chewy" is not "LOUIS" and "Vuiton" is not "VUITTON," with its two Ts); CV is not LV; the designs on the dog toy are simplified and crude, not detailed and distinguished. The toys are inexpensive; the handbags are expensive and marketed to be expensive. And, of course, as a dog toy, one must buy it with pet supplies and cannot buy it at an exclusive LVM store or boutique within a department store. In short, the Haute Diggity Dog "Chewy Vuiton" dog toy undoubtedly and deliberately conjures up the famous LVM marks and trade dress, but at the same time, it communicates that it is not the LVM product.

Finally, the juxtaposition of the similar and dissimilar—the irreverent representation and the idealized image of an LVM handbag—immediately conveys a joking and amusing parody. The furry little "Chewy Vuiton" imitation, as something to be *chewed by a dog*, pokes fun at the elegance and expensiveness of a LOUIS VUITTON handbag, which must *not* be chewed by a dog. The LVM handbag is provided for the most elegant and well-to-do celebrity, to proudly display to the public and the press, whereas the imitation "Chewy Vuiton" "handbag" is designed to mock the celebrity and be used by a dog. The dog toy irreverently presents haute couture as an object for casual canine destruction. The satire is unmistakable. The dog toy is a comment on the rich and famous, on the LOUIS VUITTON name and related marks, and on conspicuous consumption in general. This parody is enhanced by the fact that "Chewy Vuiton" dog toys are sold with similar parodies of other famous and expensive brands—"Chewnel No. 5" targeting "Chanel No. 5"; "Dog Perignonn" targeting "Dom Perignon"; and "Sniffany & Co." targeting "Tiffany & Co."

We conclude that the *PETA* criteria are amply satisfied in this case and that the "Chewy Vuiton" dog toys convey "just enough of the original design to allow the consumer to appreciate the point of parody," but stop well short of appropriating the entire marks that LVM claims. *PETA*, 263 F.3d at 366 (quoting *Jordache*, 828 F.2d at 1486).

Finding that Haute Diggity Dog's parody is successful, however, does not end the inquiry into whether Haute Diggity Dog's "Chewy Vuiton" products create a likelihood of confusion. *See* 6 J. Thomas McCarthy, *Trademarks and Unfair Competition* § 31:153, at 262 (4th ed. 2007) ("There are confusing parodies and non-confusing parodies. All they have in common is an attempt at humor through the use of someone else's trademark"). The finding of a successful parody only influences the way in which the *Pizzeria Uno* factors are applied. *See, e.g., Anheuser-Busch, Inc. v. L & L Wings, Inc.*, 962 F.2d 316, 321 (4th Cir. 1992) (observing that parody alters the likelihood-of-confusion analysis). Indeed, it becomes apparent that an effective parody will actually diminish the likelihood of confusion, while an ineffective parody does not. We now turn to the *Pizzeria Uno* factors.

A

As to the first *Pizzeria Uno* factor, the parties agree that LVM's marks are strong and widely recognized. They do not agree, however, as to the consequences of this fact. LVM maintains that a strong, famous mark is entitled, as a matter of law, to broad protection. While it is true that finding a mark to be strong and famous usually favors the plaintiff in a trademark infringement case, the opposite may be true when a legitimate claim of parody is involved. As the district court observed, "In cases of parody, a strong mark's fame and popularity is precisely the mechanism by which likelihood of confusion is avoided." *Louis Vuitton Malletier*, 464 F. Supp. 2d at 499 (citing *Hormel Foods Corp. v. Jim Henson Prods., Inc.*, 73 F.3d 497, 503–04 (2d Cir. 1996); *Schieffelin & Co. v. Jack Co. of Boca, Inc.*, 850 F. Supp. 232, 248 (S.D.N.Y. 1994)). "An intent to parody is not an intent to confuse the public." *Jordache*, 828 F.2d at 1486.

We agree with the district court. It is a matter of common sense that the strength of a famous mark allows consumers immediately to perceive the target of the parody, while simultaneously allowing them to recognize the changes to the mark that make the parody funny or biting. *See Tommy Hilfiger Licensing, Inc. v. Nature Labs, LLC*, 221 F. Supp. 2d 410, 416 (S.D.N.Y. 2002) (noting that the strength of the "TOMMY HILFIGER" fashion mark did not favor the mark's owner in an infringement case against "TIMMY HOLEDIGGER" novelty pet perfume). In this case, precisely because LOUIS VUITTON is so strong a mark and so well recognized as a luxury handbag brand from LVM, consumers readily recognize that when they see a "Chewy Vuiton" pet toy, they see a parody. Thus, the strength of LVM's marks in this case does not help LVM establish a likelihood of confusion.

B

With respect to the second *Pizzeria Uno* factor, the similarities between the marks, the usage by Haute Diggity Dog again converts what might be a problem for Haute Diggity Dog into a disfavored conclusion for LVM.

Haute Diggity Dog concedes that its marks are and were designed to be somewhat similar to LVM's marks. But that is the essence of a parody—the invocation of a famous mark in the consumer's mind, so long as the distinction between the marks is also readily recognized. While a trademark parody necessarily copies enough of the original design to bring it to mind as a target, a successful parody also distinguishes itself and, because of the implicit message communicated by the parody, allows the consumer to appreciate it. *See PETA*, 263 F.3d at 366 (citing *Jordache*, 828 F.2d at 1486); *Anheuser-Busch*, 962 F.2d at 321.

In concluding that Haute Diggity Dog has a successful parody, we have impliedly concluded that Haute Diggity Dog appropriately mimicked a part of the LVM marks, but at the same time sufficiently distinguished its own product to communicate the satire. The differences are sufficiently obvious and the parody sufficiently blatant that a consumer encountering a "Chewy Vuiton" dog toy would not mistake its source or sponsorship on the basis of mark similarity.

This conclusion is reinforced when we consider how the parties actually use their marks in the marketplace. *See CareFirst*, 434 F.3d at 267 (citing *What-A-Burger of Va., Inc. v. Whataburger, Inc.*, 357 F.3d 441, 450 (4th Cir. 2004)); *Lamparello v. Falwell*, 420 F.3d 309, 316 (4th Cir. 2005); *Hormel Foods*, 73 F.3d at 503. The record amply supports Haute Diggity Dog's contention that its "Chewy Vuiton" toys for dogs are generally sold alongside other pet products, as well as toys that parody other luxury brands, whereas LVM markets its handbags as a top-end luxury item to be purchased only in its own stores or in its own boutiques within department stores. These marketing channels further emphasize that "Chewy Vuiton" dog toys are not, in fact, LOUIS VUITTON products.

C

Nor does LVM find support from the third *Pizzeria Uno* factor, the similarity of the products themselves. It is obvious that a "Chewy Vuiton" plush imitation handbag, which does not open and is manufactured as a dog toy, is not a LOUIS VUITTON handbag sold by LVM. Even LVM's most proximate products—dog collars, leashes, and pet carriers—are fashion accessories, not dog toys. As Haute Diggity Dog points out, LVM does not make pet chew toys and likely does not intend to do so in the future. Even if LVM were to make dog toys in the future, the fact remains that the products at issue are not similar in any relevant respect, and this factor does not favor LVM.

D

The fourth and fifth *Pizzeria Uno* factors, relating to the similarity of facilities and advertising channels, have already been mentioned. LVM products are sold exclusively through its own stores or its own boutiques within department stores. It also sells its products on the Internet through an LVM-authorized website. In contrast, "Chewy Vuiton" products are sold primarily through traditional and Internet pet stores, although they might also be sold in some department stores. The record demonstrates that both LVM handbags and "Chewy Vuiton" dog toys are sold at a Macy's department store in New York. As a general matter, however, there is little overlap in the individual retail stores selling the brands.

Likewise with respect to advertising, there is little or no overlap. LVM markets LOUIS VUITTON handbags through high-end fashion magazines, while "Chewy Vuiton" products are advertised primarily through pet-supply channels.

The overlap in facilities and advertising demonstrated by the record is so minimal as to be practically nonexistent. "Chewy Vuiton" toys and LOUIS VUITTON products are neither sold nor advertised in the same way, and the *de minimis* overlap lends insignificant support to LVM on this factor.

E

The sixth factor, relating to Haute Diggity Dog's intent, again is neutralized by the fact that Haute Diggity Dog markets a parody of LVM products. As other courts have recognized, "An intent to parody is not an intent to confuse the public." *Jordache*, 828 F.2d at 1486. Despite Haute Diggity Dog's obvious intent to profit from its use of parodies, this action does not amount to a bad faith intent to create consumer confusion. To the contrary, the intent is to do just the opposite—to evoke a humorous, satirical association that *distinguishes* the products. This factor does not favor LVM.

F

On the actual confusion factor, it is well established that no actual confusion is required to prove a case of trademark infringement, although the presence of actual confusion can be persuasive evidence relating to a likelihood of confusion. *See CareFirst*, 434 F.3d at 268.

While LVM conceded in the district court that there was no evidence of actual confusion, on appeal it points to incidents where retailers misspelled "Chewy Vuiton" on invoices or order forms, using two Ts instead of one. Many of these invoices also reflect simultaneous orders for multiple types of Haute Diggity Dog parody products, which belies the notion that any actual confusion existed as to the source of "Chewy Vuiton" plush toys. The misspellings pointed out by LVM are far more likely in this context to indicate confusion over how to spell the product name than any confusion over the source or sponsorship of the "Chewy Vuiton" dog toys. We conclude that this factor favors Haute Diggity Dog.

In sum, the likelihood-of-confusion factors substantially favor Haute Diggity Dog. But consideration of these factors is only a proxy for the ultimate statutory test of whether Haute Diggity Dog's marketing, sale, and distribution of "Chewy Vuiton" dog toys is likely to cause confusion. Recognizing that "Chewy Vuiton" is an obvious parody and applying the *Pizzeria Uno* factors, we conclude that LVM has failed to demonstrate any likelihood of confusion. Accordingly, we affirm the district court's grant of summary judgment in favor of Haute Diggity Dog on the issue of trademark infringement.

III

LVM also contends that Haute Diggity Dog's advertising, sale, and distribution of the "Chewy Vuiton" dog toys dilutes its LOUIS VUITTON, LV, and Monogram Canvas marks, which are famous and distinctive, in violation of the Trademark Dilution Revision Act of 2006 ("TDRA"), 15 U.S.C. § 1125(c) (West Supp. 2007). It argues, "Before the district court's decision, Vuitton's famous marks were unblurred by any third party trademark use." "Allowing defendants to become the first to use similar marks will obviously blur and dilute the Vuitton Marks." It also contends that "Chewy Vuiton" dog toys are likely to tarnish LVM's marks because they "pose a choking hazard for some dogs."

Haute Diggity Dog urges that, in applying the TDRA to the circumstances before us, we reject LVM's suggestion that a parody "automatically" gives rise to "actionable dilution." Haute Diggity Dog contends that only marks that are "identical or substantially similar" can give rise to actionable dilution, and its "Chewy Vuiton" marks are not identical or sufficiently similar to LVM's marks. It also argues that "[its] spoof, like other obvious parodies," " 'tends to increase public identification' of [LVM's] mark with [LVM]," quoting *Jordache*, 828 F.2d at 1490, rather than impairing its distinctiveness, as the TDRA requires. As for LVM's tarnishment claim, Haute Diggity Dog argues that LVM's position is at best based on speculation and that LVM has made no showing of a likelihood of dilution by tarnishment. . . .

A

We address first LVM's claim for dilution by blurring.

The first three elements of a trademark dilution claim are not at issue in this case. LVM owns famous marks that are distinctive; Haute Diggity Dog has commenced using "Chewy Vuiton," "CV," and designs and colors that are allegedly diluting LVM's marks; and the similarity between Haute Diggity Dog's marks and LVM's marks gives rise to an association between the marks, albeit a parody. The issue for resolution is whether the association between Haute Diggity Dog's marks and LVM's marks is likely to impair the distinctiveness of LVM's famous marks.

In deciding this issue, the district court correctly outlined the six factors to be considered in determining whether dilution by blurring has been shown. *See* 15 U.S.C. § 1125(c)(2)(B). But in evaluating the facts of the case, the court did not directly apply those factors it enumerated. It held simply:

> [The famous mark's] strength is not likely to be blurred by a parody dog toy product. Instead of blurring Plaintiff's mark, the success of the parodic use depends upon the continued association with LOUIS VUITTON.

Louis Vuitton Malletier, 464 F. Supp. 2d at 505. The amicus supporting LVM's position in this case contends that the district court, by not applying the statutory factors, misapplied the TDRA to conclude that simply because Haute Diggity Dog's product was a parody meant that "there can be no *association* with the famous mark as a matter of law." Moreover, the amicus points out correctly that to rule in favor of Haute

Diggity Dog, the district court was required to find that the "association" did not impair the distinctiveness of LVM's famous mark.

LVM goes further in its own brief, however, and contends . . . that any use by a third person of an imitation of its famous marks dilutes the famous marks as a matter of law. This contention misconstrues the TDRA.

The TDRA prohibits a person from using a junior mark that is likely to dilute (by blurring) the famous mark, and blurring is defined to be an impairment to the famous mark's distinctiveness. "Distinctiveness" in turn refers to the public's recognition that the famous mark identifies a single source of the product using the famous mark.

To determine whether a junior mark is likely to dilute a famous mark through blurring, the TDRA directs the court to consider all factors relevant to the issue, including six factors that are enumerated in the statute. . . . Not every factor will be relevant in every case, and not every blurring claim will require extensive discussion of the factors. But a trial court must offer a sufficient indication of which factors it has found persuasive and explain why they are persuasive so that the court's decision can be reviewed. The district court did not do this adequately in this case. Nonetheless, after we apply the factors as a matter of law, we reach the same conclusion reached by the district court.

We begin by noting that parody is not automatically a complete *defense* to a claim of dilution by blurring where the defendant uses the parody as its own designation of source, i.e., *as a trademark*. Although the TDRA does provide that fair use is a complete defense and allows that a parody can be considered fair use, it does not extend the fair use defense to parodies used as a trademark. . . . Under the statute's plain language, parodying a famous mark is protected by the fair use defense only if the parody is *not* "a designation of source for the person's own goods or services."

The TDRA, however, does not require a court to ignore the existence of a parody that is used as a trademark, and it does not preclude a court from considering parody as part of the circumstances to be considered for determining whether the plaintiff has made out a claim for dilution by blurring. Indeed, the statute permits a court to consider "all relevant factors," including the six factors supplied in § 1125(c)(2)(B).

Thus, it would appear that a defendant's use of a mark as a parody is relevant to the overall question of whether the defendant's use is likely to impair the famous mark's distinctiveness. Moreover, the fact that the defendant uses its marks as a parody is specifically relevant to several of the listed factors. For example, factor (v) (whether the defendant intended to create an association with the famous mark) and factor (vi) (whether there exists an actual association between the defendant's mark and the famous mark) directly invite inquiries into the defendant's intent in using the parody, the defendant's actual use of the parody, and the effect that its use has on the famous mark. While a parody intentionally creates an association with the famous mark in order to be a parody, it also intentionally communicates, if it is successful, that it is *not* the famous mark, but rather a satire of the famous mark. *See PETA*, 263 F.3d at 366. That the defendant is using its mark as a parody is therefore relevant in the consideration of these statutory factors.

Similarly, factors (i), (ii), and (iv)—the degree of similarity between the two marks, the degree of distinctiveness of the famous mark, and its recognizability—are directly implicated by consideration of the fact that the defendant's mark is a successful parody. Indeed, by making the famous mark an object of the parody, a successful parody might actually enhance the famous mark's distinctiveness by making it an icon. The brunt of the joke becomes yet more famous. *See Hormel Foods*, 73 F.3d at 506 (observing that a successful parody "tends to increase public identification" of the famous mark with its source); *see also Yankee Publ'g Inc. v. News Am. Publ'g Inc.*, 809 F. Supp. 267, 272–82 (S.D.N.Y. 1992) (suggesting that a sufficiently obvious parody is unlikely to blur the targeted famous mark).

In sum, while a defendant's use of a parody as a mark does not support a "fair use" defense, it may be considered in determining whether the plaintiff-owner of a famous mark has proved its claim that the defendant's use of a parody mark is likely to impair the distinctiveness of the famous mark.

In the case before us, when considering factors (ii), (iii), and (iv), it is readily apparent, indeed conceded by Haute Diggity Dog, that LVM's marks are distinctive, famous, and strong. The LOUIS VUITTON mark is well known and is commonly identified as a brand of the great Parisian fashion house, Louis Vuitton Malletier. So too are its other marks and designs, which are invariably used with the LOUIS VUITTON mark. It may not be too strong to refer to these famous marks as icons of high fashion.

While the establishment of these facts satisfies essential elements of LVM's dilution claim, *see* 15 U.S.C. § 1125(c)(1), the facts impose on LVM an increased burden to demonstrate that the distinctiveness of its famous marks is likely to be impaired by a successful parody. Even as Haute Diggity Dog's parody mimics the famous mark, it communicates simultaneously that it is not the famous mark, but is only satirizing it. *See PETA*, 263 F.3d at 366. And because the famous mark is particularly strong and distinctive, it becomes more likely that a parody will not impair the distinctiveness of the mark. In short, as Haute Diggity Dog's "Chewy Vuiton" marks are a successful parody, we conclude that they will not blur the distinctiveness of the famous mark as a unique identifier of its source. . . .

In a similar vein, when considering factors (v) and (vi), it becomes apparent that Haute Diggity Dog intentionally associated its marks, but only partially and certainly imperfectly, so as to convey the simultaneous message that it was not in fact a source of LVM products. Rather, as a parody, it separated itself from the LVM marks in order to make fun of them.

In sum, when considering the relevant factors to determine whether blurring is likely to occur in this case, we readily come to the conclusion, as did the district court, that LVM has failed to make out a case of trademark dilution by blurring by failing to establish that the distinctiveness of its marks was likely to be impaired by Haute Diggity Dog's marketing and sale of its "Chewy Vuiton" products.

B

LVM's claim for dilution by tarnishment does not require an extended discussion. To establish its claim for dilution by tarnishment, LVM must show, in lieu of blurring, that Haute Diggity Dog's use of the "Chewy Vuiton" mark on dog toys harms the reputation of the LOUIS VUITTON mark and LVM's other marks. LVM argues that the possibility that a dog could choke on a "Chewy Vuiton" toy causes this harm. LVM has, however, provided no record support for its assertion. It relies only on speculation about whether a dog could choke on the chew toys and a logical concession that a $10 dog toy made in China was of "inferior quality" to the $1190 LOUIS VUITTON handbag. The speculation begins with LVM's assertion in its brief that "defendant Woofie's admitted that 'Chewy Vuiton' products pose a choking hazard for some dogs. Having prejudged the defendant's mark to be a parody, the district court made light of this admission in its opinion, and utterly failed to give it the weight it deserved," citing to a page in the district court's opinion where the court states:

> At oral argument, plaintiff provided only a flimsy theory that a pet may some day choke on a Chewy Vuiton squeak toy and incite the wrath of a confused consumer against LOUIS VUITTON.

Louis Vuitton Malletier, 464 F. Supp. 2d at 505. The court was referring to counsel's statement during oral argument that the owner of Woofie's stated that "she would not sell this product to certain types of dogs because there is a danger they would tear it open and choke on it." There is no record support, however, that any dog has choked on a pet chew toy, such as a "Chewy Vuiton" toy, or that there is any basis from which to conclude that a dog would likely choke on such a toy.

We agree with the district court that LVM failed to demonstrate a claim for dilution by tarnishment. *See Hormel Foods*, 73 F.3d at 507. . . .

The judgment of the district court is *AFFIRMED*.

NOTES FOR DISCUSSION

1. *Dilution versus Confusion.* How did the court resolve the dilution claim? How did it resolve the likelihood of confusion claim? What additional rights did the dilution cause of action give the plaintiff?

2. *Comparison with Deere & Co.* Why did this case come out differently from *Deere & Co. v. MTD Products, Inc.*? Both are making fun of the plaintiffs, both are modifying the plaintiffs' trademarks to do so, and both intend to make money, but the *LVM* court allows the use here, while the *Deere & Co.* prohibits the use by MTD. Is it because MTD is manufacturing competing products while Haute Diggity Dog's goods are unrelated? Isn't dilution intended to provide protection primarily against use on unrelated goods? Is it because MTD can compete without distorting John Deere's trademark, while Haute Diggity Dog's products would not exist without distorting Louis Vuitton's marks?

3. *Factual Presumptions and Evidence.* The court asserts that the defendant's use "might actually enhance the famous mark's distinctiveness by making it an icon." What evidence supports the court's assertion in this regard? Back at the beginning of this Chapter, we discussed social science research that found that the use of a famous mark on an unrelated good slowed the test subjects' ability to associate quickly and accurately a famous mark with its goods or services. If Louis Vuitton had introduced such a study in this case, demonstrating that Haute Diggity Dog had impaired respondents' ability to associate the LVM mark with its products quickly and accurately, would such evidence require a different outcome on the dilution issue?

4. *Parody and Whittling Away.* If parodies of LVM, such as the defendants, were to become extremely commonplace, would that whittle away the selling power of the LVM mark? Or would the mark retain its present prestige value? Is there any possibility that such widespread parodic use would enhance the mark's prestige value by making it into an icon, as the court suggests?

CHAPTER 9

TRADEMARK DEFENSES

■ ■ ■

A. FAIR USE

Recall that before the enactment of the Trademark Act of 1946, descriptive terms were not considered trademarks, and received protection, if at all, only under the rubric of unfair competition. Although some uses by a competitor of an unduly similar descriptive term could constitute unfair competition, there were sharp limits on the availability of relief where the descriptive term at issue was accurate as applied to the defendant's goods or services. When Congress allowed registration of descriptive terms on the principal register with proof of secondary meaning, it also codified the common law's limitation on such protection in the fair use defense. The following two cases illustrate the common law and statutory fair use defenses.

CANAL CO. V. CLARK
80 U.S. 311 (1872)

STRONG, J.

The first and leading question presented by this case is whether the complainants have an exclusive right to the use of the words "Lackawanna coal," as a distinctive name or trade-mark for the coal mined by them and transported over their railroad and canal to market.

The averments of the bill are supported by no inconsiderable evidence. The complainants were undoubtedly, if not the first, among the first producers of coal from the Lackawanna Valley, and the coal sent to market by them has been generally known and designated as Lackawanna coal. Whether the name "Lackawanna coal" was devised or adopted by them as a trade-mark before it came into common use is not so clearly established. On the contrary the evidence shows that long before the complainants commenced their operations, and long before they had any existence as a corporation, the region of country in which their mines were situated was called "The Lackawanna Valley;" that it is a region of large dimensions, extending along the Lackawanna River to its junction with the Susquahanna, embracing within its limits great bodies of coal lands, upon a portion of which are the mines of the complainants, and upon other portions of which are the mines of The Pennsylvania Coal Company, those of The Delaware, Lackawanna, and Western Railroad

Company, and those of other smaller operators. The word "Lackawanna," then, was not devised by the complainants. They found it a settled and known appellative of the district in which their coal deposits and those of others were situated. At the time when they began to use it, it was a recognized description of the region, and of course of the earths and minerals in the region.

The bill alleges, however, not only that the complainants devised, adopted, and appropriated the word, as a name or trade-mark for their coal, but that it had never before been used, or applied in combination with the word "coal," as a name or trade-mark for any kind of coal, and it is the combination of the word Lackawanna with the word coal that constitutes the trade-mark to the exclusive use of which they assert a right.

It may be observed there is no averment that the other coal of the Lackawanna Valley differs at all in character or quality from that mined on the complainants' lands. On the contrary, the bill alleges that it cannot easily be distinguished therefrom by inspection. The bill is therefore an attempt to secure to the complainants the exclusive use of the name "Lackawanna coal," as applied, not to any manufacture of theirs, but to that portion of the coal of the Lackawanna Valley which they mine and send to market, differing neither in nature or quality from all other coal of the same region.

Undoubtedly words or devices may be adopted as trade-marks which are not original inventions of him who adopts them, and courts of equity will protect him against any fraudulent appropriation or imitation of them by others. Property in a trade-mark, or rather in the use of a trade-mark or name, has very little analogy to that which exists in copyrights, or in patents for inventions. Words in common use, with some exceptions, may be adopted, if, at the time of their adoption, they were not employed to designate the same, or like articles of production. The office of a trade-mark is to point out distinctively the origin, or ownership of the article to which it is affixed; or, in other words, to give notice who was the producer. This may, in many cases, be done by a name, a mark, or a device well known, but not previously applied to the same article.

But though it is not necessary that the word adopted as a trade-name should be a new creation, never before known or used, there are some limits to the rights of selection. This will be manifest when it is considered that in all cases where rights to the exclusive use of a trade-mark are invaded, it is invariably held that the essence of the wrong consists in the sale of the goods of one manufacturer or vendor as those of another; and that it is only when this false representation is directly or indirectly made that the party who appeals to a court of equity can have relief. . . . The trade-mark must therefore be distinctive in its original signification, pointing to the origin of the article, or it must have become such by association. And there are two rules which are not to be overlooked. No one can claim protection for the exclusive use of a trade-mark or trade-name which would practically give him a monopoly in the sale of any goods other than those produced or made by himself. If he could, the public would be injured rather than protected, for competition would be destroyed. Nor can a generic name, or a name merely descriptive of an article of trade, of its qualities, ingredients, or characteristics, be employed as a trade-mark and the exclusive use of it be entitled to legal protection. . . .

And it is obvious that the same reasons which forbid the exclusive appropriation of generic names or of those merely descriptive of the article manufactured and which can be employed with truth by other manufacturers, apply with equal force to the appropriation of geographical names, designating districts of country. Their nature is such that they cannot point to the origin (personal origin) or ownership of the articles of trade to which they may be applied. They point only at the place of production, not to the producer, and could they be appropriated exclusively, the appropriation would result in mischievous monopolies. Could such phrases, as "Pennsylvania wheat," "Kentucky hemp," "Virginia tobacco," or "Sea Island cotton," be protected as trade-marks; could any one prevent all others from using them, or from selling articles produced in the districts they describe under those appellations, it would greatly embarrass trade, and secure exclusive rights to individuals in that which is the common right of many. It can be permitted only when the reasons that lie at the foundation of the protection given to trade marks are entirely overlooked. It cannot be said that there is any attempt to deceive the public when one sells as Kentucky hemp, or as Lehigh, coal, that which in truth is such, or that there is any attempt to appropriate the enterprise or business reputation of another who may have previously sold his goods with the same description. It is not selling one man's goods as and for those of another. Nothing is more common than that a manufacturer sends his products to market, designating them by the name of the place where they were made. But we think no case can be found in which other producers of similar products in the same place, have been restrained from the use of the same name in describing their goods. . . .

It must then be considered as sound doctrine that no one can apply the name of a district of country to a well-known article of commerce, and obtain thereby such an exclusive right to the application as to prevent others inhabiting the district or dealing in similar articles coming from district, from truthfully using the same designation. It is only when the adoption or imitation of what is claimed to be a trade-mark amounts to a false representation, express or implied, designed or incidental, that there is any title to relief against it. True it may be that the use by a second producer, in describing truthfully his product, of a name or a combination of words already in use by another, may have the effect of causing the public to mistake as to the origin or ownership of the product, but if it is just as true in its application to his goods as it is to those of another who first applied it, and who therefore claims an exclusive right to use it, there is no legal or moral wrong done. Purchasers may be mistaken, but they are not deceived by false representations, and equity will not enjoin against telling the truth.

These principles, founded alike on reason and authority, are decisive of the present case, and they relieve us from the consideration of much that was pressed upon us in the argument. The defendant had advertised for sale and he is selling coal not obtained from the plaintiffs, not mined or brought to market by them, but coal which he purchased from the Pennsylvania Coal Company, or from the Delaware, Lackawanna, and Western Railroad Company. He has advertised and sold it as Lackawanna coal. It is in fact coal from the Lackawanna region. It is of the same quality and of the same general appearance as that mined by the complainants. It is taken from the same veins or strata. It is truly described by the term Lackawanna coal, as is the coal of plaintiffs. The description does not point to its origin or ownership, nor indicate in the slightest degree the person, natural or artificial, who mined the coal or brought it to market. All the coal taken from that region is known and has been known for years by the trade, and rated in public statistics as Lackawanna coal. True the Delaware, Lackawanna, and Western Railroad Company have sometimes called their coal Scranton coal, and sometimes Scranton coal from the Lackawanna, and the Pennsylvania Coal Company have called theirs Pittston coal, thus referring to the parts of the region in which they mine. But the generic name, the comprehensive name for it all is Lackawanna coal. . . . We are therefore of opinion that the defendant has invaded no right to which the plaintiffs can maintain a claim. By advertising and selling coal brought from the Lackawanna Valley as Lackawanna coal, he has made no false representation, and we see no evidence that he has attempted to sell his coal as and for the coal of the plaintiffs. If the public are led into mistake, it is by the truth, not by any false pretense. If the complainants' sales are diminished, it is because they are not the only producers of Lackawanna coal, and not because of any fraud of the defendant. The decree of the Circuit Court dismissing the bill must, therefore, be AFFIRMED.

KP PERMANENT MAKE-UP, INC. V. LASTING IMPRESSION I, INC.

543 U.S. 111 (2004)

SOUTER, J.

The question here is whether a party raising the statutory affirmative defense of fair use to a claim of trademark infringement, 15

U.S.C. § 1115(b)(4), has a burden to negate any likelihood that the practice complained of will confuse consumers about the origin of the goods or services affected. We hold it does not.

I

Each party to this case sells permanent makeup, a mixture of pigment and liquid for injection under the skin to camouflage injuries and modify nature's dispensations, and each has used some version of the term "micro color" (as one word or two, singular or plural) in marketing and selling its product. Petitioner KP Permanent Make-Up, Inc., claims to have used the single-word version since 1990 or 1991 on advertising flyers and since 1991 on pigment bottles. Respondents Lasting Impression I, Inc., and its licensee, MCN International, Inc. (Lasting, for simplicity), deny that KP began using the term that early, but we accept KP's allegation as true for present purposes; the District and Appeals Courts took it to be so, and the disputed facts do not matter to our resolution of the issue. In 1992, Lasting applied to the United States Patent and Trademark Office (PTO) under 15 U.S.C. § 1051 for registration of a trademark consisting of the words "Micro Colors" in white letters separated by a green bar within a black square. The PTO registered the mark to Lasting in 1993, and in 1999 the registration became incontestable. § 1065.

It was also in 1999 that KP produced a 10-page advertising brochure using "microcolor" in a large, stylized typeface, provoking Lasting to demand that KP stop using the term. Instead, KP sued Lasting in the Central District of California, seeking, on more than one ground, a declaratory judgment that its language infringed no such exclusive right as Lasting claimed. Lasting counterclaimed, alleging, among other things, that KP had infringed Lasting's "Micro Colors" trademark.

KP sought summary judgment on the infringement counterclaim, based on the statutory affirmative defense of fair use, 15 U.S.C. § 1115(b)(4). After finding that Lasting had conceded that KP used the term only to describe its goods and not as a mark, the District Court held that KP was acting fairly and in good faith because undisputed facts showed that KP had employed the term "microcolor" continuously from a time before Lasting adopted the two-word, plural variant as a mark. Without inquiring whether the practice was likely to cause confusion, the court concluded that KP had made out its affirmative defense under § 1115(b)(4) and entered summary judgment for KP on Lasting's infringement claim. See Case No. SA CV 00–276–GLT (EEx) (May 16, 2001), pp. 8–9, App. to Pet. for Cert. 29a–30a.

On appeal, 328 F.3d 1061 (9th Cir. 2003), the Court of Appeals for the Ninth Circuit thought it was error for the District Court to have addressed the fair use defense without delving into the matter of possible confusion on the part of consumers about the origin of KP's goods. The reviewing court took the view that no use could be recognized as fair where any consumer confusion was probable, and although the court did not pointedly address the burden of proof, it appears to have placed it on KP to show absence of consumer confusion. *Id.*, at 1072 ("Therefore, KP can only benefit from the fair use defense if there is no likelihood of confusion between KP's use of the term 'micro color' and Lasting's mark"). Since it found there were disputed material facts relevant under the Circuit's eight-factor test for assessing the likelihood of confusion, it reversed the summary judgment and remanded the case.

We granted KP's petition for certiorari, 540 U.S. 1099, 157 L.Ed.2d 811, 124 S.Ct. 981 (2004), to address a disagreement among the Courts of Appeals on the significance of likely confusion for a fair use defense to a trademark infringement claim, and the obligation of a party defending on that ground to show that its use is unlikely to cause consumer confusion. Compare 328 F.3d at 1072 (likelihood of confusion bars the fair use defense); *PACCAR Inc.* v. *TeleScan Technologies, L.L.C.*, 319 F.3d 243, 256 (CA6 2003) ("[A] finding of a likelihood of confusion forecloses a fair use defense"); and *Zatarains, Inc.* v. *Oak Grove Smokehouse, Inc.*, 698 F.2d 786, 796 (CA5 1983) (alleged infringers were free to use words contained in a trademark "in their ordinary, descriptive sense, so long as such use [did] not tend to confuse customers as to the source of the goods"), with *Cosmetically Sealed Industries, Inc.* v. *Chesebrough-Pond's USA Co.*, 125 F.3d 28, 30–31 (CA2 1997) (the fair use defense may succeed even if there is likelihood of confusion); *Shakespeare Co.* v. *Silstar Corp. of Am., Inc.*, 110 F.3d 234, 243 (CA4 1997) ("[A] determination of likely confusion [does not] preclud[e] considering the fairness of use"); *Sunmark, Inc.* v. *Ocean Spray Cranberries, Inc.*, 64 F.3d 1055, 1059 (CA7 1995) (finding that likelihood of confusion did not preclude the fair use defense). We now vacate the judgment of the Court of Appeals.

II

A

The Trademark Act of 1946, known for its principal proponent as the Lanham Act, 60 Stat. 427, as amended, 15 U.S.C. § 1051 *et seq.*, provides the user of a trade or service mark with the opportunity to register it with the PTO, §§ 1051, 1053. If the registrant then satisfies further conditions including continuous use for five consecutive years, "the right . . . to use such registered mark in commerce" to designate the origin of the goods specified in the registration "shall be incontestable" outside certain listed exceptions. § 1065.

The holder of a registered mark (incontestable or not) has a civil action against anyone employing an imitation of it in commerce when "such use is likely to cause confusion, or to cause mistake, or to deceive." § 1114(1)(a). Although an incontestable registration is "conclusive evidence . . . of the registrant's exclusive right to use the . . . mark in commerce," § 1115(b), the plaintiff's success is still subject to "proof of infringement as defined in section 1114," *ibid*. And that, as just noted, requires a showing that the defendant's actual practice is likely to produce confusion in the minds of consumers about the origin of the goods or services in question. See *Two Pesos, Inc.* v. *Taco Cabana, Inc.*, 505 U.S. 763, 780, 120 L.Ed.2d 615, 112 S.Ct. 2753 (1992) (Stevens, J., concurring); *Lone Star Steakhouse & Saloon, Inc.* v. *Alpha of Virginia, Inc.*, 43 F.3d 922, 935 (CA4 1995); Restatement (Third) of Unfair Competition § 21, Comment *a* (1995) (hereinafter Restatement). This plaintiff's burden has to be kept in mind when reading the relevant portion of the further provision for an affirmative defense of fair use, available to a party whose

> "use of the name, term, or device charged to be an infringement is a use, otherwise than as a mark, . . . of a term or device which is descriptive of and used fairly and in good faith only to describe the goods or services of such party, or their geographic origin. . . ." § 1115(b)(4).

Two points are evident. Section 1115(b) places a burden of proving likelihood of confusion (that is, infringement) on the party charging infringement even when relying on an incontestable registration. And Congress said nothing about likelihood of confusion in setting out the elements of the fair use defense in § 1115(b)(4).

Starting from these textual fixed points, it takes a long stretch to claim that a defense of fair use entails any burden to negate confusion. It is just not plausible that Congress would have used the descriptive phrase "likely to cause confusion, or to cause mistake, or to deceive" in § 1114 to describe the requirement that a markholder show likelihood of consumer confusion, but would have relied on the phrase "used fairly" in § 1115(b)(4) in a fit of terse drafting meant to place a defendant under a burden to negate confusion. " '[W]here Congress includes particular language in one section of a statute but omits it in another section of the same Act, it is generally presumed that Congress acts intentionally and purposely in the disparate inclusion or exclusion.' " *Russello* v. *United States*, 464 U.S. 16, 23 (1983) (quoting *United States* v. *Wong Kim Bo*, 472 F.2d 720, 722 (CA5 1972)) (alteration in original).

Nor do we find much force in Lasting's suggestion that "used fairly" in § 1115(b)(4) is an oblique incorporation of a likelihood-of-confusion test developed in the common law of unfair competition. Lasting is certainly correct that some unfair competition cases would stress that use of a term by another in conducting its trade went too far in sowing confusion, and would either enjoin the use or order the defendant to include a disclaimer. See, *e.g.*, *Baglin* v. *Cusenier Co.*, 221 U.S. 580, 602 (1911) ("[W]e are unable to escape the conclusion that such use, in the manner shown, was to serve the purpose of simulation . . ."); *Herring-Hall-Marvin Safe Co.* v. *Hall's Safe Co.*, 208 U.S. 554, 559 (1908) ("[T]he rights of the two parties have been reconciled by allowing the use, provided that an explanation is attached"). But the common law of unfair competition also tolerated some degree of confusion from a descriptive use of words contained in another person's trademark. See, *e.g., William R. Warner & Co.* v. *Eli Lilly & Co.*, 265 U.S. 526, 528 (1924) (as to plaintiff's trademark claim, "[t]he use of a similar name by another to truthfully describe his own product does not constitute a legal or moral wrong, even if its effect be to cause the public to mistake the origin or ownership of the product"); *Canal Co.* v. *Clark*, 80 U.S. (13 Wall.) 311 (1872) ("Purchasers may be mistaken, but they are not deceived by false representations, and equity will not enjoin against telling the truth"); see also 3 L. Altman, Callmann on Unfair Competition, Trademarks and Monopolies § 18:2, pp. 18–8 to 18–9, n. 1 (4th ed. 2004) (citing cases). While these cases are consistent with taking account of the likelihood of consumer confusion as one consideration in deciding whether a use is fair, see Part II-B, *infra*, they do not stand for the proposition that an assessment of confusion alone may be dispositive. Certainly one cannot get out of them any defense burden to negate it entirely.

Finally, a look at the typical course of litigation in an infringement action points up the incoherence of placing a burden to show nonconfusion on a defendant. If a plaintiff succeeds in making out a prima facie case of trademark infringement, including the element of likelihood of consumer confusion, the defendant may offer rebutting evidence to undercut the force of the plaintiff's evidence on this (or any) element, or raise an affirmative defense to bar relief even if the prima facie case is sound, or do both. But it would make no sense to give the defendant a defense of showing affirmatively that the plaintiff cannot succeed in proving some element (like confusion); all the defendant needs to do is to leave the factfinder unpersuaded that the plaintiff has carried its own burden on that point. A defendant has no need of a court's true belief when agnosticism will do. Put another way, it is only when a plaintiff has shown likely confusion by a preponderance of the evidence that a defendant could have any need of an affirmative defense, but under Lasting's theory the defense would be foreclosed in such a case. "[I]t defies logic to argue that a defense may not be asserted in the only situation where it even becomes relevant." *Shakespeare Co.* v. *Silstar Corp.*, 110 F.3d at 243. Nor would it make sense to provide an affirmative defense of no confusion plus good faith, when merely rebutting the plaintiff's case on confusion would entitle the defendant to judgment, good faith or not. . . .

B

Since the burden of proving likelihood of confusion rests with the plaintiff, and the fair use defendant has no free-standing need to show confusion unlikely, it follows (contrary to the Court of Appeals's view) that some possibility of consumer confusion must be compatible with fair use, and so it is. The common law's tolerance of a certain degree of confusion on the part of consumers followed from the very fact that in cases like this one an originally descriptive term was selected to be used as a mark, not to mention the undesirability of allowing anyone to obtain a complete monopoly on use of a descriptive term simply by grabbing it first. *Canal Co.* v. *Clark*, 13 Wall., at 323–324, 327. The Lanham Act adopts a similar leniency, there being no indication that the statute was meant to deprive commercial speakers of the ordinary utility of descriptive words. "If any confusion results, that is a risk the plaintiff accepted when it decided to identify its product with a mark that uses a well known descriptive phrase." *Cosmetically Sealed Industries, Inc.* v. *Chesebrough-Pond's USA Co.*, 125 F.3d at 30. See also *Park 'N Fly, Inc.* v. *Dollar Park & Fly, Inc.*, 469 U.S. 189, 201 (1985) (noting safeguards in Lanham Act to prevent commercial monopolization of language); *Car-Freshner Corp.* v. *S.C. Johnson & Son, Inc.*, 70 F.3d 267, 269 (CA2 1995) (noting importance of "protect[ing] the right of society at large to use words or images in their primary descriptive sense"). This right to describe is the reason that descriptive terms qualify for registration as trademarks only after taking on secondary meaning as "distinctive of the applicant's goods," 15 U.S.C. § 1052(f), with the registrant getting an exclusive right not in the original, descriptive sense, but only in the secondary one associated with the markholder's goods, 2 McCarthy, *supra*, § 11:45 ("The only aspect of the mark which is given legal protection is that penumbra or fringe of secondary meaning which surrounds the old descriptive word").

While we thus recognize that mere risk of confusion will not rule out fair use, we think it would be improvident to go further in this case, for deciding anything more would take us beyond the Ninth Circuit's consideration of the subject. It suffices to realize that our holding that fair use can occur along with some degree of confusion does not foreclose the relevance of the extent of any likely consumer confusion in assessing whether a defendant's use is objectively fair. Two Courts of Appeals have found it relevant to consider such scope, and commentators and *amici* here have urged us to say that the degree of likely consumer confusion bears not only on the fairness of using a term, but even on the further question whether an originally descriptive term has become so identified as a mark that a defendant's use of it cannot realistically be called descriptive. See *Shakespeare Co.* v. *Silstar Corp.*, 110 F.3d, at 243 ("[T]o the degree that confusion is likely, a use is less likely to be found fair . . ." (emphasis deleted)); *Sunmark, Inc.* v. *Ocean Spray Cranberries, Inc.*, 64 F.3d at 1059; Restatement § 28; Brief for American Intellectual Property Law Association as *Amicus Curiae* 13–18; Brief for Private Label Manufacturers Association as *Amicus Curiae* 16–17; Brief for Society of Permanent Cosmetic Professionals et al. as *Amici Curiae* 8–11.

Since we do not rule out the pertinence of the degree of consumer confusion under the fair use defense, we likewise do not pass upon the position of the United States, as *amicus*, that the "used fairly" requirement in § 1115(b)(4) demands only that the descriptive term describe the goods accurately. Tr. of Oral Arg. 17. Accuracy of course has to be a consideration in assessing fair use, but the proceedings in this case so far raise no occasion to evaluate some other concerns that courts might pick as relevant, quite apart from attention to confusion. The Restatement raises possibilities like commercial justification and the strength of the plaintiff's mark. Restatement § 28. As to them, it is enough to say here that the door is not closed.

III

In sum, a plaintiff claiming infringement of an incontestable mark must show likelihood of consumer confusion as part of the prima facie case, 15 U.S.C. § 1115(b), while the defendant has no independent burden to negate the likelihood of any confusion in raising the affirmative defense that a term is used descriptively, not as a mark, fairly, and in good faith, § 1115(b)(4).

Because we read the Court of Appeals as requiring KP to shoulder a burden on the issue of confusion, we vacate the judgment and remand the case for further proceedings consistent with this opinion.

It is so ordered.

NOTES FOR DISCUSSION

1. *Evolving Treatment of Descriptive Terms.* As we discussed in Chapter 4, under the common law, descriptive terms were not eligible for protection as technical trademarks. Instead, they received protection, if at all, under the rubric of unfair competition. Congress retained this rule in the Trademark Act of 1905. However, in the Trademark Act of March 19, 1920, Congress provided a separate register for marks that were not eligible for registration under the 1905 Act. Under the 1920 Act, a descriptive term that had been used in commerce for more than one year could be registered. While registration under the 1920 Act provided no substantive rights domestically, it gave the registrant, first, a domestic registration that could be used to obtain trademark registration in other countries; and, second, it allowed a registrant to pursue its common law claims for unfair competition in federal court. *See Armstrong Paint & Varnish Works v. Nu-Enamel Corp.*, 305 U.S. 315 (1938). Whether pursued in federal or state court, however, to establish unfair competition, a plaintiff had to establish secondary meaning and passing off. However, even with evidence of secondary meaning, the plaintiff could not prevent another from using the term truthfully.

In the Trademark Act of 1946, Congress expressly allowed the registration of descriptive terms as trademarks on the principal register provided that secondary meaning was shown. 15 U.S.C. § 1052(e)(1), (f)

(2015). However, it also codified the common law's truthful or fair use defense in section 33(b)(4). Thus, Congress moved descriptive terms from the rubric of unfair competition into the category of technical trademarks. Aside from the name, did any of the applicable legal rules change? The *Armstrong* Court suggested not. 305 U.S. at 325 ("The facts supporting a suit for infringement and one for unfair competition are substantially the same.").

How would *Canal Co. v. Clark* come out under the 1946 Act? Could Canal Co. register on the principal register "Lackawanna Coal" as a trademark for coal from the Lackawanna Valley? The first question is whether the term is generic or descriptive. When is a term of geographic origin generic rather than descriptive? Do we need to define the relevant product genus? If so, would it be coal generally, or coal from the Lackawanna Valley? Why? Assume that a court determines that Lackawanna coal is primarily geographically descriptive, rather than generic. Reading together sections section 2(e)(2) and 2(f) of the 1946 Act, such terms may be registered on the principal register if secondary meaning is shown. Based upon the facts given, can Canal Co. establish secondary meaning? Assume that Canal Co. established secondary meaning and obtained a federal registration, could Clark establish the elements of the statutory fair use defense? Is Clark's use "otherwise than as a mark"? Did he use Lackawanna "fairly and in good faith"? Under the common law, the fact that Lackawanna was descriptively accurate as applied to Clark's coal was a complete defense. Does it remain such under the 1946 Act?

2.   *"Otherwise Than as a Mark."* Section 1115(b)(4) of the 1946 Trademark Act allows for third-party use of a trademarked name or term if it is used "otherwise than as a mark." This leaves the question of what constitutes use as a mark. Courts are split on how to interpret this statutory language. As we saw in *Zatarain's* in Chapter 4, some have taken the approach that a use is "otherwise than as a mark" when the descriptive terms are used in conjunction with a brand-name or "house mark." Courts in such cases reason that the house mark is serving as the relevant trademark, leaving the descriptive terms to be merely descriptive. Not all courts agree, however. Other courts reason that any prominent or attention getting use of a descriptive term will constitute use as a trademark that bars the availability of the fair use defense. Thus, in *Sands, Taylor & Wood Co. v. Quaker Oats Co.*, 978 F.2d 947 (7th Cir. 1992), reproduced in Chapter 11, the court faced the question whether Quaker Oats's use of the plaintiff's trademark "thirst aid" in the advertising slogan "Gatorade is thirst aid for that deep down body thirst" was a fair use. The court rejected the defense, however, and ruled that Quaker Oats' use was not "otherwise than as a mark." *Id.* at 954. The court emphasized that: (i) the words "thirst aid" were used as an "attention-getting symbol"; (ii) they appeared "more prominently and in larger type" in the advertising copy than the word Gatorade; and (iii) they also rhyme with Gatorade, and their use would therefore tend to create a mnemonic that would associate "thirst aid" uniquely with Gatorade. *Id.*

In *KP Permanent Make-Up*, the district court found that Lasting Impressions conceded that KP was using the term "microcolor" "otherwise than as a mark." Had Lasting Impressions contested the issue, would KP's use have been "otherwise than as a mark"?

3.   *Confusion and Fair Use: "Used Fairly and In Good Faith Only to Describe."* In *KP Permanent Make-Up*, the Court granted certiorari to resolve a split between the circuits on whether a defendant could establish fair use if the defendant's use created a likelihood of confusion. Did the Court resolve the split, and if so, how?

Because of the procedural context in which the case arose, the Court did not resolve the split. In the case, the defendant had moved for summary judgment on its fair use defense. While the defendant bore the burden of proof with respect to fair use, the plaintiff would have the burden at trial of proving a likelihood of confusion. In the summary judgment context, the burden of producing evidence sufficient to create a genuine issue on a material fact rests on the party who will ultimately have the burden of proof on that issue at trial. As a result, the Court ruled that a defendant does not have the burden of disproving a likelihood of confusion when moving for summary judgment on a fair use defense. The Court was therefore able to avoid resolving the split.

When the split is more plainly presented to the Court, how should the Court rule? What is the relationship between likelihood of confusion and fair use? Should a particularly strong showing on likelihood of confusion preclude a fair use defense? Should a particularly strong showing of fair use preclude liability even if considerable confusion arises?

Consider the following hypothetical: Joe Smith is a student of the historic art of brewing beer. He has studied extensively various European brewing techniques, and has discovered one particular method associated with the town of Budweis in what is now the Czech Republic. Beers brewed according to that method were known historically and are still known in Europe as "budweisers." Assume that is also the original descriptive significance of Anheuser-Busch's "Budweiser" trademark. Joe wants to brew a beer according to this method, sell it in the United States, and call it Joe's Original Budweiser. Is such a use fair? Does it depend on the relative type size and type fonts that Joe uses on his labels?

4.   *Consumer Welfare: Competition and Confusion.* In dealing with descriptive terms, consumers have two, potentially conflicting interests. They want competition. In order to have competition, consumers need to be able to identify competing products easily. To ensure such ease in identifying competing products, competitors will often need to use descriptive terms. How will consumers know that products compete if competitors cannot use descriptive words to tell them? At the same time, consumers want to avoid confusion; they do not want to purchase the goods of one company believing that they are the goods of another company. One could argue that the easiest way to avoid any conflict between these two interests is to protect only non-

descriptive trademarks. This will avoid the problem from the outset by encouraging companies to pick non-descriptive terms as their marks. Should trademark and unfair competition law only protect inherently distinctive marks? The *Canal Co.* decision and other pre-1946 common law decisions, while not fully adopting that perspective, had considerable sympathy for it. As one court explained:

> It is settled, beyond all controversy, that a manufacturer has no right to the exclusive use of a descriptive word in connection with his goods, and if nevertheless he adopts such a trade-mark, he himself is largely to blame for the confusion which ensues when other manufacturers, with equal right, adopt similar terms to describe their products.

Bliss, Fabyan & Co. v. Aileen Mills, 25 F.2d 370, 372 (4th Cir. 1928).

With Congress's formal recognition of trademark status for descriptive terms, presumably a court could not deny protection to a descriptive term altogether. Nonetheless, the secondary meaning requirement, the conceptual strength factor in the likelihood of confusion analysis, and the fair use doctrine all reflect a continuing concern for ensuring that descriptive terms remain available in their descriptive sense. Given the limitations on the protection afforded a descriptive mark, why would a company select a descriptive term as its trademark in the first place? Do these reasons suggest any welfare gains for consumers from allowing companies to select a descriptive term as their trademark? Does protecting the first company to develop secondary meaning in a descriptive term give that company an unfair advantage?

Alternatively, could we improve the fair use analysis in this area by focusing on consumer welfare directly, balancing the descriptive or informational value that allowing a competitor to use a term in a particular context generates against the confusion that such use will likely create? Should we consider whether the defendant could use some other term to convey the same information just as effectively? Should we consider that the plaintiff could adopt, or could have adopted, some non-descriptive term for its trademark? Should we refuse to consider the possibility that plaintiff could have developed an alternative trademark if the plaintiff has invested considerable time and resources in developing the originally descriptive term into a brand?

5. *Fair Use and Suggestive Marks?* Can a defendant argue fair use if the plaintiff's mark is suggestive as applied to the plaintiff's products or services? The express language of section 1115(b)(4) focuses on whether the use is descriptive as applied to the defendant's goods or services. Thus, a defendant may use a mark descriptively and claim fair use, even if the mark is suggestive or arbitrary as applied to the plaintiff's products or services, just as an apple seller may use the word apple generically despite Apple's trademark on the term for computers. *See Car-Freshner Corp. v. S.C. Johnson & Son*, 70 F.3d 267, 269 & n.1 (2d Cir. 1995).

6. *Priority?* Returning to the facts in *KP Permanent Make-Up*, who was the first to use "microcolor" or "micro color" with respect to their products, KP Permanent or Lasting Impressions? Why didn't KP argue that it first used "microcolor" as a mark and therefore owned rights in the mark? True, Lasting Impression has an incontestable federal registration, but as we saw in Chapter 3, an unregistered senior user can overcome even an incontestable federal registration by state law rights in the trademark arising from use which began before the date of junior user's registration. 15 U.S.C. § 1065 (2015).

B. DESCRIPTIVE USE AND NOMINATIVE FAIR USE

CHAMPION SPARK PLUG CO. V. SANDERS
331 U.S. 125 (1947)

MR. JUSTICE DOUGLAS

Petitioner is a manufacturer of spark plugs which it sells under the trade mark "Champion." Respondents collect the used plugs, repair and recondition them, and resell them. Respondents retain the word "Champion" on the repaired or reconditioned plugs. The outside box or carton in which the plugs are packed has stamped on it the word "Champion," together with the letter and figure denoting the particular style or type. They also have printed on them "Perfect Process Spark Plugs Guaranteed Dependable" and "Perfect Process Renewed Spark Plugs." Each carton contains smaller boxes in which the plugs are individually packed. These inside boxes also carry legends indicating that the plug has been renewed. But respondent company's business name or address is not printed on the cartons. It supplies customers with petitioner's charts containing recommendations for the use of Champion plugs. On each individual plug is stamped in small letters, blue on black, the word "Renewed," which at times is almost illegible.

Petitioner brought this suit in the District Court, charging infringement of its trade mark and unfair competition. See Judicial Code § 24(1), (7), 28 U.S.C. § 41(1), (7). The District Court found that respondents had infringed the trade mark. It enjoined them from offering or selling any of petitioner's plugs which had been repaired or reconditioned unless (a) the trade mark and type and style marks were removed, (b) the plugs were repainted with a durable grey, brown, orange, or green paint, (c) the word "REPAIRED" was stamped into the plug in letters of such size and depth as to retain enough white paint to display distinctly each letter of the word, (d) the cartons in which the plugs were packed carried a legend indicating that they contained used spark plugs originally made by petitioner and repaired and made fit for use up to

10,000 miles by respondent company. The District Court denied an accounting. See 56 F.Supp. 782, 61 F.Supp. 247.

The Circuit Court of Appeals held that respondents not only had infringed petitioner's trade mark but also were guilty of unfair competition. It likewise denied an accounting but modified the decree in the following respects: (a) it eliminated the provision requiring the trade mark and type and style marks to be removed from the repaired or reconditioned plugs; (b) it substituted for the requirement that the word "REPAIRED" be stamped into the plug, etc., a provision that the word "REPAIRED" or "USED" be stamped and baked on the plug by an electrical hot press in a contrasting color so as to be clearly and distinctly visible, the plug having been completely covered by permanent aluminum paint or other paint or lacquer; and (c) it eliminated the provision specifying the precise legend to be printed on the cartons and substituted therefor a more general one. 156 F.2d 488. The case is here on a petition for certiorari which we granted because of the apparent conflict between the decision below and *Champion Spark Plug Co.* v. *Reich*, 121 F.2d 769, decided by the Circuit Court of Appeals for the Eighth Circuit.

There is no challenge here to the findings as to the misleading character of the merchandising methods employed by respondents, nor to the conclusion that they have not only infringed petitioner's trade mark but have also engaged in unfair competition. The controversy here relates to the adequacy of the relief granted, particularly the refusal of the Circuit Court of Appeals to require respondents to remove the word "Champion" from the repaired or reconditioned plugs which they resell.

We put to one side the case of a manufacturer or distributor who markets new or used spark plugs of one make under the trade mark of another. See *Bourjois & Co.* v. *Katzel*, 260 U.S. 689; *Old Dearborn Co.* v. *Seagram Corp.*, 299 U.S. 183, 194. Equity then steps in to prohibit defendant's use of the mark which symbolizes plaintiff's good will and "stakes the reputation of the plaintiff upon the character of the goods." *Bourjois & Co.* v. *Katzel, supra*, p. 692.

We are dealing here with second-hand goods. The spark plugs, though used, are nevertheless Champion plugs and not those of another make. There is evidence to support what one would suspect, that a used spark plug which has been repaired or reconditioned does not measure up to the specifications of a new one. But the same would be true of a second-hand Ford or Chevrolet car. And we would not suppose that one could be enjoined from selling a car whose valves had been reground and whose piston rings had been replaced unless he removed the name Ford or Chevrolet. *Prestonettes, Inc.* v. *Coty*, 264 U.S. 359, was a case where toilet powders had as one of their ingredients a powder covered by a trade mark and where perfumes which were trade marked were rebottled and sold in smaller bottles. The Court sustained a decree denying an injunction where the prescribed labels told the truth. Mr. Justice Holmes stated, "A trade mark only gives the right to prohibit the use of it so far as to protect the owner's good will against the sale of another's product as his. . . . When the mark is used in a way that does not deceive the public we see no such sanctity in the word as to prevent its being used to tell the truth. It is not taboo." P. 368.

Cases may be imagined where the reconditioning or repair would be so extensive or so basic that it would be a misnomer to call the article by its original name, even though the words "used" or "repaired" were added. Cf. *Ingersoll* v. *Doyle*, 247 F. 620. But no such practice is involved here. The repair or reconditioning of the plugs does not give them a new design. It is no more than a restoration, so far as possible, of their original condition. The type marks attached by the manufacturer are determined by the use to which the plug is to be put. But the thread size and size of the cylinder hole into which the plug is fitted are not affected by the reconditioning. The heat range also has relevance to the type marks. And there is evidence that the reconditioned plugs are inferior so far as heat range and other qualities are concerned. But inferiority is expected in most second-hand articles. Indeed, they generally cost the customer less. That is the case here. Inferiority is immaterial so long as the article is clearly and distinctly sold as repaired or reconditioned rather than as new. The result is, of course, that the second-hand dealer gets some advantage from the trade mark. But under the rule of *Prestonettes, Inc.* v. *Coty, supra*, that is wholly permissible so long as the manufacturer is not identified with the inferior qualities of the product resulting from wear and tear or the reconditioning by the dealer. Full disclosure gives the manufacturer all the protection to which he is entitled. . . .

Affirmed.

NOTES FOR DISCUSSION

1. *Competition and Confusion.* The rule that the Court recognizes in *Champion Spark Plug Co.* inevitably strikes a balance between confusion and competition. Courts have not always struck that balance consistently, however. With which of the following cases does the *Champion Spark Plug Co.* ruling most closely accord?

a) *Dastar Corp.* v. *Twentieth Century Fox*, 539 U.S. 23 (2003), reproduced in Chapter 1; or

b) *Kellogg Co.* v. *National Biscuit Co.*, 305 U.S. 111 (1938), reproduced in Chapter 5.

Recall that in *Dastar*, 20th Century Fox had failed to renew its copyright on the television series *Crusade in Europe*. When Dastar copied the series and released it at Dastar's own work under the title, *Campaigns in Europe*, 20th Century Fox sued alleging misattribution under section 43(a) of the Trademark Act. The Court rejected the claim, however. Although there was clearly some risk of consumer confusion in that case, the Court refused to recognize a right against misattribution. The Court feared that recognizing such a right would convert trademark law into a mutant species of copyright. If a right were recognized, no matter what attribution or credit Dastar gave 20th Century Fox, 20th Century Fox could sue and argue that it was not enough or not in the right form. Through such nitpicking of the attribution provided, 20th Century Fox could convert a legal right against misattribution into a *de facto* prohibition on copying.

In *Kellogg Co.*, National Biscuit Co. sued to enjoin Kellogg from making shredded wheat cereal in the pillow-shaped biscuit form that National Biscuit Co. had popularized. National Biscuit Co. argued that because of the similar shape, some consumers might mistake Kellogg's cereal for National Biscuit Co.'s. While the Court refused to require Kellogg to change the shape of its cereal, it did require Kellogg "to use every reasonable means to prevent confusion." *Id.* at 121.

2.   *Striking the Right Balance.* How should the Court strike the balance in the *Champion Spark Plug* case? Which of the following facts, if true, would or should change the outcome?

a) Assume that Clark can show that the additional cost he would incur to stamp or burn the word "Used" or "Repaired" on the spark plug itself would, given marketplace conditions, render his process unprofitable. He is willing to include an appropriate legend on the packaging accompanying his repaired spark plugs, but if the court requires him to mark each plug, he will not offer repaired plugs at all.

b) Assume that there are two makers of spark plugs in the economy, Champion and Brand X. When new, Champion spark plugs are high-quality and high-priced, while Brand X are medium-quality and medium-priced. Once they have been used and refurbished using Clark's process, the two brands are now of equally low quality.

3.   *Section 32(c).* During the legislative debates leading up to the enactment of the Trademark Act in 1946, some of the bills included section 33(c) that would have barred the sale of repaired or second-hand goods, bearing a trademark, without the trademark owner's permission. The Department of Justice opposed section 33(c), arguing that it was anticompetitive. *See* Trade-Marks: Hearings Before the Subcomm. of the Senate Comm. on Patents, 78th Cong. 58–71 (1944) ("1944 Trade-Mark Hearings"). In response to these concerns, Congress removed section 33(c) from the bill and did not enact it as part of the Trademark Act of 1946.

4.   *Relabeling.* What if Sanders had completely repainted all of the used sparkplugs and labeled them with his own trademark? Could he have thereby avoided the lawsuit from Champion? Or could Champion sue him for reverse passing off? Recall, as we saw in Chapter 1, that in *Dastar Corp. v. 20th Century Fox*, Justice Scalia rejected 20th Century Fox's claim for reverse passing off based upon Dastar taking the content of 20th Century Fox's television series, *Crusade in Europe*. 539 U.S. 23, 38 (2003). However, in

doing so, Justice Scalia, writing for the Court, stated: "That claim would undoubtedly be sustained if Dastar had bought some of New Line's Crusade videotapes and merely repackaged them as its own." 539 U.S. at 31.

SMITH V. CHANEL, INC.
402 F.2d 562 (9th Cir. 1968)

BROWNING, CIRCUIT JUDGE

Appellant R. G. Smith, doing business as Ta'Ron, Inc., advertised a fragrance called "Second Chance" as a duplicate of appellees' "Chanel No. 5," at a fraction of the latter's price. Appellees were granted a preliminary injunction prohibiting any reference to Chanel No. 5 in the promotion or sale of appellants' product. This appeal followed.

The action rests upon a single advertisement published in "Specialty Salesmen," a trade journal directed to wholesale purchasers. The advertisement offered "The Ta'Ron Line of Perfumes" for sale. It gave the seller's address as "Ta'Ron Inc., 26 Harbor Cove, Mill Valley, Calif." It stated that the Ta'Ron perfumes "duplicate 100% perfect the exact scent of the world's finest and most expensive perfumes and colognes at prices that will zoom sales to volumes you have never before experienced!" It repeated the claim of exact duplication in a variety of forms.

The advertisement suggested that a "Blindfold Test" be used "on skeptical prospects," challenging them to detect any difference between a well known fragrance and the Ta'Ron "duplicate." One suggested challenge was, "We dare you to try to detect any difference between Chanel #5 (25.00) and Ta'Ron's 2nd Chance. $7.00."

In an order blank printed as part of the advertisement each Ta'Ron fragrance was listed with the name of the well known fragrance which it purportedly duplicated immediately beneath. Below "Second Chance" appeared " *(Chanel #5)." The asterisk referred to a statement at the bottom of the form reading "Registered Trade Name of Original Fragrance House."

Appellees conceded below and concede here that appellants "have the right to copy, if they can, the unpatented formula of appellees' products." Moreover, for the purposes of these proceedings, appellees assume that "the products manufactured and advertised by [appellants] are *in fact* equivalents of those products manufactured by appellees." (Emphasis in original.) Finally, appellees disclaim any contention that the packaging or labeling of appellants' "Second Chance" is misleading or confusing.

I

The principal question presented on this record is whether one who has copied an unpatented product sold under a trademark may use the trademark in his advertising to identify the product he has copied. We hold that he may, and that such advertising may not be enjoined under either the Lanham Act, 15 U.S.C. § 1125(a) (1964), or the common law of unfair competition, so long as it does not contain misrepresentations or create a reasonable likelihood that purchasers will be confused as to the source, identity, or sponsorship of the advertiser's product. . . .

. . . Appellees argue that protection should also be extended to the trademark's commercially more important function of embodying consumer good will created through extensive, skillful, and costly advertising. The courts, however, have generally confined legal protection to the trademark's source identification function for reasons grounded in the public policy favoring a free, competitive economy.

Preservation of the trademark as a means of identifying the trademark owner's products, implemented both by the Lanham Act and the common law, serves an important public purpose. It makes effective competition possible in a complex, impersonal marketplace by providing a means through which the consumer can identify products which please him and reward the producer with continued patronage. Without some such method of product identification, informed consumer choice, and hence meaningful competition in quality, could not exist.

On the other hand, it has been suggested that protection of trademark values other than source identification would create serious anti-competitive consequences with little compensating public benefit. This is said to be true for the following reasons.

The object of much modern advertising is "to impregnate the atmosphere of the market with the drawing power of a congenial symbol." *Mishawaka Rubber & Woolen Mfg. Co. v. S.S. Kresge Co.*, 316 U.S. 203, 205, 62 S.Ct. 1022, 1024, 86 L.Ed. 1381 (1942), rather than to communicate information as to quality or price. The primary value of the modern trademark lies in the "conditioned reflex developed in the buyer by imaginative or often purely monotonous selling of the mark itself." Derring, *Trademarks on Noncompetitive Products*, 36 Or.L.Rev. 1, 2 (1956). To the extent that advertising of this type succeeds, it is suggested, the trademark is endowed with sales appeal independent of the quality or price of the product to which it is attached; economically irrational elements are introduced into consumer choices; and the trademark owner is insulated from the normal pressures of price and quality competition. In consequence the competitive system fails to perform its function of allocating available resources efficiently.

Moreover, the economically irrelevant appeal of highly publicized trademarks is thought to constitute a barrier to the entry of new competition into the market. "The presence of irrational consumer allegiances may constitute an effective barrier to entry. Consumer allegiances built over the years with intensive advertising, trademarks, trade names, copyrights and so forth extend substantial protection to firms already in the market. In some markets this barrier to entry may be insuperable." Papandreou, *The Economic Effects of Trademarks*, 44 Calif.L.Rev. 503, 508–09 (1956). High barriers to entry tend, in turn, to produce "high excess profits and monopolistic output restriction" and "probably * * * high and possibly excessive costs of sales promotion." J. Bain, Barriers to New Competition 203 (1955).

A related consideration is also pertinent to the present case. Since appellees' perfume was unpatented, appellants had a right to copy it, as appellees concede. There was a strong public interest in their doing so, "for imitation is the life blood of competition. It is the unimpeded availability of substantially equivalent units that permits the normal operation of supply and demand to yield the fair price society must pay for a given commodity." *American Safety Table Co. v. Schreiber*, 269 F.2d 255, 272 (2d Cir. 1959). But this public benefit might be lost if appellants could not tell potential purchasers that appellants' product was the equivalent of appellees' product. "A competitor's chief weapon is his ability to represent his product as being equivalent and cheaper * *." Alexander, *Honesty and Competition*, 39 So. Cal. L. Rev. 1, 4 (1966). The most effective way (and, where complex chemical compositions sold under trade names are involved, often the only practical way) in which this can be done is to identify the copied article by its trademark or trade name. To prohibit use of a competitor's trademark for the sole purpose of identifying the competitor's product would bar effective communication of claims of equivalence. Assuming the equivalence of "Second Chance" and "Chanel No. 5," the public interest would not be served by a rule of law which would preclude sellers of "Second Chance" from advising consumers of the equivalence and thus effectively deprive consumers of knowledge that an identical product was being offered at one third the price.

As Justice Holmes wrote in *Saxlehner v. Wagner*. [216 U.S. 375 (1910),] the practical effect of such a rule would be to extend the monopoly of the trademark to a monopoly of the product. The monopoly conferred by judicial protection of complete trademark exclusivity would not be preceded by examination and approval by a governmental body, as is the case with most other government-granted monopolies. Moreover, it would not be limited in time, but would be perpetual.

Against these considerations, two principal arguments are made for protection of trademark values other than source identification.

The first of these, as stated in the findings of the district court, is that the creation of the other values inherent in the trademark require "the expenditure of great effort, skill and ability," and that the competitor should not be permitted "to take a free ride" on the trademark owner's "widespread goodwill and reputation."

A large expenditure of money does not in itself create legally protectable rights. Appellees are not entitled to monopolize the public's desire for the unpatented product, even though they themselves created that desire at great effort and expense. As we have noted, the most effective way (and in some cases the only practical way) in which others may compete in satisfying the demand for the product is to produce it and tell the public they have done so, and if they could be barred from this effort appellees would have found a way to acquire a practical monopoly in the unpatented product to which they are not legally entitled.

Disapproval of the copyist's opportunism may be an understandable first reaction, "but this initial response to the problem has been curbed in deference to the greater public good." American Safety Table Co. v. Schreiber, 269 F.2d at 272. By taking his "free ride," the copyist, albeit unintentionally, serves an important public interest by offering comparable goods at lower prices. On the other hand, the trademark owner, perhaps equally without design, sacrifices public to personal interests by seeking immunity from the rigors of competition.

Moreover, appellees' reputation is not directly at stake. Appellants' advertisement makes it clear that the product they offer is their own. If it proves to be inferior, they, not appellees, will bear the burden of consumer disapproval. Cf. Prestonettes, Inc. v. Coty, 264 U.S. 359, 369 (1924).

The second major argument for extended trademark protection is that even in the absence of confusion as to source, use of the trademark of another "creates a serious threat to the uniqueness and distinctiveness" of the trademark, and "if continued would create a risk of making a generic or descriptive term of the words" of which the trademark is composed.

The contention has little weight in the context of this case. Appellants do not use appellees' trademark as a generic term. They employ it only to describe appellees' product, not to identify their own. They do not label their product "Ta'Ron's Chanel No. 5," as they might if appellees' trademark had come to be the common name for the product to which it is applied. Appellants' use does not challenge the distinctiveness of appellees' trademark, or appellees' exclusive right to employ that trademark to indicate source or sponsorship. For reasons already discussed, we think appellees are entitled to no more. The slight tendency to carry the mark into the common language which even this use may have is outweighed by the substantial value of such use in the maintenance of effective competition.

We are satisfied, therefore, that both authority and reason require a holding that in the absence of misrepresentation or confusion as to source or sponsorship a seller in promoting his own goods may use the trademark of another to identify the latter's goods. The district court's contrary conclusion cannot support the injunction. . . .

Reversed and remanded for further proceedings.

NOTES FOR DISCUSSION

1.   *Comparative Advertising and the Limits of Confusion.* Until this case, it was not clear whether one company could use another company's trademarks for the purpose of comparative advertising. The result in *Chanel Co.* expressly approves Smith's comparative use, at least, absent any false or misleading representations of fact. Does the *Chanel Co.* decision establish that the use of another's mark for purposes of comparative advertising does not create confusion as a matter of law or does it simply find that such confusion was not present in this case? What if a properly conducted survey found that twenty percent of the relevant consumers believed that Chanel had given Smith permission to use its trademarks in his advertisements? Should his use become actionable as trademark infringement?

2.   *Prestige Goods and Economic Value.* Recall our discussion of prestige goods from Chapter 7. A prestige good is a good where demand rises, rather than falls as we usually expect, as price increases. While the question whether such goods really exist remains an open one, it is readily apparent that some goods market themselves at a high price in return for perceived exclusivity. Chanel No. 5 is arguably such a good, and Chanel expressly asked the court to use trademark law to protect its economic investment in creating the status and prestige associated with Chanel No. 5. The court refused. However, when we discussed this issue in Chapter 7, courts willingly embraced a vision of trademark law that extended protection to such prestige value. For example, in *Ferrari S.P.A. v. Roberts*, 944 F.2d 1235 (6th Cir. 1991), the court recognized post-sale confusion as actionable, at least, in part to enable Ferrari to preserve the prestige value of its cars. Why shouldn't we protect that value here? Are consumers better or worse off as a result of the *Chanel Co.* decision?

If Chanel cannot protect its exclusivity by restricting Smith's ability to compare his fragrance to Chanel's using Chanel's word mark, can Chanel assert that its scent constitutes a trademark, and that its duplication by Smith creates actionable post-sale confusion? Or is the scent of Chanel No. 5 functional? What if a properly conducted survey found that twenty percent of the relevant consumers believed that Smith "had to get" Chanel's permission to duplicate its perfume? Should we recognize such confusion as actionable under trademark law? Or would that convert trademark law's likelihood of confusion standard into a "mutant species of" patent or copyright? Would your answer differ if the survey asked if consumers believed that Smith "had gotten" Chanel's permission? What is the difference between "had to get" and "had gotten"? Putting to one side the relevant legal doctrine, why should Ferrari be able to use trademark law to ensure the exclusivity of its prestige good, when Chanel may not?

3.   *Remand.* What is left for the district court on remand? In footnote 25, the Ninth Circuit stated, in relevant part:

> [I]f appellants' specific claims of equivalence are false, appellees may have a remedy under § 43(a) of the Lanham Act, 15 U.S.C. § 1125(a) (1964), which provides a civil remedy to a person injured by "any false description or representation, including words or other symbols * * *." of goods in interstate commerce.

On remand, some five years after the Ninth Circuit's decision, the district court found that the defendant was guilty of false advertising with respect to three statements it made in marketing its smell-alike fragrance. The three statements were: (i) that " 'Ta'Ron, Inc.' duplicated 100% perfect the exact scent of "Chanel No. 5"; (ii) that "defendant performed a masterful breakdown of plaintiff's perfume and cologne"; and (iii) that "it took years to find the secret of positive duplication of plaintiff's perfume and cologne bearing the name 'Chanel No. 5.' " *See Chanel, Inc. v. Smith*, 178 U.S.P.Q. (BNA) 630 (N.D. Cal. 1973), *aff'd*, 528 F.2d 284 (9th Cir. 1976). What remedies should be given with respect to this false advertising? Should Smith be barred from using Chanel's trademark in his advertisements? Should he be barred from offering his smell-alike perfumes?

4.   *Alternative Phrasings.* Do the following phrasings create a likelihood of confusion as to sponsorship? Do they create potentially actionable factual representations?

a) A smell-alike competitor offers its Confess body fragrance with the following slogan: "If you like OBSESSION by CALVIN KLEIN, you'll love CONFESS." *See Calvin Klein Cosmetics Corp. v. Parfums de Coeur, Ltd.*, 824 F.2d 665 (8th Cir. 1987) (affirming denial of preliminary injunction on the grounds that as used slogan was not likely to create confusion); *see also Saxony Products, Inc. v. Guerlain, Inc.*, 513 F.2d 716 (9th Cir. 1975) (affirming summary judgment on likelihood of confusion with respect to "like/love" phrasing, but reversing and remanding with respect to false advertising claim given disputed facts regarding whether defendant's perfume in fact was similar to the plaintiff's perfume). *But see Charles of the Ritz Group Ltd. v. Quality King Distributors, Inc.*, 636 F.Supp. 433, 438 (S.D.N.Y. 1986) (finding a likelihood of confusion and enjoining defendant's use of slogan "If you like OPIUM, you'll love OMNI" on its product packaging).

b) Alexander, a low-cost, discount retailer in New York, makes copies of Christian Dior dresses and attaches a hang tag to them that states: " 'Original by Christian Dior—Alexander's Exclusive—Paris—Adaptation.' " *See Societe Comptoir De L'Industrie v. Alexander's Department Stores, Inc.*, 299 F.2d 33, 36 (2d Cir. 1962) ("The Lanham Act does not prohibit a commercial rival's truthfully denominating his goods a copy of a design in the public domain, though he uses the name of the designer to do so. Indeed it is difficult to see any other means that might be employed to inform the consuming public of the true origin of the design.").

c) NEXxUS offers high-end, professional quality line of hair care products, sold exclusively through salons. Gentle Concepts imitates their hair care products and offers them for sale at a much lower price. Initially, Gentle Concepts labels their bottles as "FORMULA N/1" a "VERSION OF NEXxUS ASSURE." When NEXxUS complains, Gentle Concepts changes its labels to "FORMULA N/1" a "SALON EQUIVALENT TO NEXxUS ASSURE." *See NEXxUS Prods. Co. v. Gentle Concepts*, 28 U.S.P.Q.2D (BNA) 1257 (M.D. Fla. 1993) (finding a likelihood of confusion). *But see G.D. Searle & Co. v. Hudson Pharmaceutical Corp.*, 715 F.2d 837, 842–43 (3d Cir. 1983) (upholding district court's injunction that allowed competitor to label its product as "Equivalent to Metamucil®").

THE NEW KIDS ON THE BLOCK V. NEWS AMERICA PUBLISHING, INC.
971 F.2d 302 (9th Cir. 1992)

KOZINSKI, CIRCUIT JUDGE.

The individual plaintiffs perform professionally as The New Kids on the Block, reputedly one of today's hottest musical acts. This case requires us to weigh their rights in that name against the rights of others to use it in identifying the New Kids as the subjects of public opinion polls.

Background

No longer are entertainers limited to their craft in marketing themselves to the public. This is the age of the multi-media publicity blitzkrieg: Trading on their popularity, many entertainers hawk posters, T-shirts, badges, coffee mugs and the like—handsomely supplementing their incomes while boosting their public images. The New Kids are no exception; the record in this case indicates there are more than 500 products or services bearing the New Kids trademark. Among these are services taking advantage of a recent development in telecommunications: 900 area code numbers, where the caller is charged a fee, a portion of which is paid to the call recipient. Fans can call various New Kids 900 numbers to listen to the New Kids talk about themselves, to listen to other fans talk about the New Kids, or to leave messages for the New Kids and other fans.

The defendants, two newspapers of national circulation, conducted separate polls of their readers seeking an answer to a pressing question: Which one of the New Kids is the most popular? *USA Today's* announcement contained a picture of the New Kids and asked, "Who's the best on the block?" The announcement listed a 900 number for voting, noted that "any USA Today profits from this phone line will go to charity," and closed with the following:

New Kids on the Block are pop's hottest group. Which of the five is your fave? Or are they a turn off? . . . Each call costs 50 cents. Results in Friday's Life section.

The Star's announcement, under a picture of the New Kids, went to the heart of the matter: "Now which kid is the sexiest?" The announcement, which appeared in the middle of a page containing a story on a New Kids concert, also stated:

Which of the New Kids on the Block would you most like to move next door? Star wants to know which cool New Kid is the hottest with our readers.

Readers were directed to a 900 number to register their votes; each call cost 95 cents per minute.

Fearing that the two newspapers were undermining their hegemony over their fans, the New Kids filed a shotgun complaint in federal court raising no fewer than ten claims: (1) common law trademark infringement; (2) Lanham Act false advertising; (3) Lanham Act false designation of origin; (4) Lanham Act unfair competition; (5) state trade name infringement; (6) state false advertising; (7) state unfair competition; (8) commercial misappropriation; (9) common-law misappropriation; and (10) intentional interference with prospective economic advantage. The two papers raised the First Amendment as a defense, on the theory that the polls were part and parcel of their "news-gathering activities." The district court granted summary judgment for defendants. 745 F. Supp. 1540 (C.D. Cal. 1990).

Discussion

While the district court granted summary judgment on First Amendment grounds, we are free to affirm on any ground fairly presented by the record. *Jackson* v. *Southern Cal. Gas Co.,* 881 F.2d 638, 643 (9th Cir. 1989); *Pelleport Inv., Inc.* v. *Budco Quality Theatres, Inc.,* 741 F.2d 273, 278 (9th Cir. 1984). Indeed, where we are able to resolve the case on nonconstitutional grounds, we ordinarily must avoid reaching the constitutional issue. *In re Snyder,* 472 U.S. 634, 642–43 (1985); *Schweiker* v. *Hogan,* 457 U.S. 569, 585 (1982). Therefore, we consider first whether the New Kids have stated viable claims on their various causes of action.

I

A. Since at least the middle ages, trademarks have served primarily to identify the source of goods and services, "to facilitate the tracing of 'false' or defective wares and the punishment of the offending craftsman." F. Schechter, *The Historical Foundations of the Law Relating to Trade-marks* 47 (1925). The law has protected trademarks since the early seventeenth century, and the primary focus of trademark law has been misappropriation—the problem of one producer's placing his rival's

mark on his own goods. See, e.g., *Southern* v. *How,* 79 Eng. Rep. 1243
(K.B. 1618). The law of trademark infringement was imported from
England into our legal system with its primary goal the prevention of
unfair competition through misappropriated marks. See, e.g., *Taylor* v.
Carpenter, 23 F. Cas. 742 (C.C.D. Mass. 1844) (Story, J.). Although an
initial attempt at federal regulation was declared unconstitutional, see
the *Trade-Mark Cases,* 100 U.S. 82, 25 L.Ed. 550 (1879), trademarks have
been covered by a comprehensive federal statutory scheme since the
passage of the Lanham Act in 1946.

Throughout the development of trademark law, the purpose of
trademarks remained constant and limited: Identification of the
manufacturer or sponsor of a good or the provider of a service. And the
wrong protected against was traditionally equally limited: Preventing
producers from free-riding on their rivals' marks. Justice Story outlined
the classic scenario a century and a half ago when he described a case of
"unmitigated and designed infringement of the rights of the plaintiffs, for
the purpose of defrauding the public and taking from the plaintiffs the
fair earnings of their skill, labor and enterprise." *Taylor,* 23 F. Cas. at
744. The core protection of the Lanham Act remains faithful to this
conception. See 15 U.S.C. § 1114 (prohibiting unauthorized use in
commerce of registered marks). Indeed, this area of the law is generally
referred to as "unfair competition"—unfair because, by using a rival's
mark, the infringer capitalizes on the investment of time, money and
resources of his competitor; unfair also because, by doing so, he obtains
the consumer's hard-earned dollar through something akin to fraud. See
Paul Heald, *Federal Intellectual Property Law and the Economics of
Preemption,* 76 Iowa L. Rev. 959, 1002–03 (1991).

A trademark is a limited property right in a particular word, phrase
or symbol. And although English is a language rich in imagery, we need
not belabor the point that some words, phrases or symbols better convey
their intended meanings than others. See *San Francisco Arts & Athletics,
Inc.* v. *U.S.O.C.,* 483 U.S. 522, 569 (1987) (Brennan, J., dissenting) ("[A]
jacket reading 'I Strongly Resent the Draft' would not have conveyed
Cohen's message."). Indeed, the primary cost of recognizing property
rights in trademarks is the removal of words from (or perhaps non-
entrance into) our language. Thus, the holder of a trademark will be
denied protection if it is (or becomes) generic, i.e., if it does not relate
exclusively to the trademark owner's product. See, e.g., *Kellogg Co.* v.
National Biscuit Co., 305 U.S. 111 (1938) ("shredded wheat"); *Eastern Air
Lines, Inc.* v. *New York Air Lines, Inc.,* 559 F. Supp. 1270 (S.D.N.Y. 1983)
("air-shuttle" to describe hourly plane service). This requirement allays
fears that producers will deplete the stock of useful words by asserting
exclusive rights in them. When a trademark comes to describe a class of
goods rather than an individual product, the courts will hold as a matter

of law that use of that mark does not imply sponsorship or endorsement of the product by the original holder.

A related problem arises when a trademark also describes a person, a place or an attribute of a product. If the trademark holder were allowed exclusive rights in such use, the language would be depleted in much the same way as if generic words were protectable. Thus trademark law recognizes a defense where the mark is used only "to describe the goods or services of [a] party, or their geographic origin." 15 U.S.C. § 1115(b)(4). "The 'fair-use' defense, in essence, forbids a trademark registrant to appropriate a descriptive term for his exclusive use and so prevent others from accurately describing a characteristic of their goods." *Soweco, Inc.* v. *Shell Oil Co.,* 617 F.2d 1178, 1185 (5th Cir. 1980). Once again, the courts will hold as a matter of law that the original producer does not sponsor or endorse another product that uses his mark in a descriptive manner. See, e.g., *Schmid Laboratories* v. *Youngs Drug Products Corp.,* 482 F. Supp. 14 (D.N.J. 1979) ("ribbed" condoms).

With many well-known trademarks, such as Jell-O, Scotch tape and Kleenex, there are equally informative non-trademark words describing the products (gelatin, cellophane tape and facial tissue). But sometimes there is no descriptive substitute, and a problem closely related to genericity and descriptiveness is presented when many goods and services are effectively identifiable only by their trademarks. For example, one might refer to "the two-time world champions" or "the professional basketball team from Chicago," but it's far simpler (and more likely to be understood) to refer to the Chicago Bulls. In such cases, use of the trademark does not imply sponsorship or endorsement of the product because the mark is used only to describe the thing, rather than to identify its source.

Indeed, it is often virtually impossible to refer to a particular product for purposes of comparison, criticism, point of reference or any other such purpose without using the mark. For example, reference to a large automobile manufacturer based in Michigan would not differentiate among the Big Three; reference to a large Japanese manufacturer of home electronics would narrow the field to a dozen or more companies. Much useful social and commercial discourse would be all but impossible if speakers were under threat of an infringement lawsuit every time they made reference to a person, company or product by using its trademark.

A good example of this is *Volkswagenwerk Aktiengesellschaft* v. *Church,* 411 F.2d 350 (9th Cir. 1969), where we held that Volkswagen could not prevent an automobile repair shop from using its mark. We recognized that in "advertising [the repair of Volkswagens, it] would be difficult, if not impossible, for [Church] to avoid altogether the use of the word 'Volkswagen' or its abbreviation 'VW,' which are the normal terms which, to the public at large, signify appellant's cars." *Id.* at 352. Church did not suggest to customers that he was part of the Volkswagen organization or that his repair shop was sponsored or authorized by VW; he merely used the words "Volkswagen" and "VW" to convey information about the types of cars he repaired. Therefore, his use of the Volkswagen trademark was not an infringing use.

The First Circuit confronted a similar problem when the holder of the trademark "Boston Marathon" tried to stop a television station from using the name:

> The words "Boston Marathon" . . . do more than call attention to Channel 5's program; they also *describe* the event that Channel 5 will broadcast. Common sense suggests (consistent with the record here) that a viewer who sees those words flash upon the screen will believe simply that Channel 5 will show, or is showing, or has shown, the marathon, not that Channel 5 has some special approval from the [trademark holder] to do so. In technical trademark jargon, the use of words for descriptive purposes is called a "fair use," and the law usually permits it even if the words themselves also constitute a trademark.

WCVB-TV v. *Boston Athletic Ass'n,* 926 F.2d 42, 46 (1st Cir. 1991). Similarly, competitors may use a rival's trademark in advertising and other channels of communication if the use is not false or misleading. See, e.g., *Smith* v. *Chanel, Inc.,* 402 F.2d 562 (9th Cir. 1968) (maker of imitation perfume may use original's trademark in promoting product).

Cases like these are best understood as involving a non-trademark use of a mark—a use to which the infringement laws simply do not apply, just as videotaping television shows for private home use does not implicate the copyright holder's exclusive right to reproduction. See *Sony Corp.* v. *Universal City Studios, Inc.,* 464 U.S. 417, 447–51 (1984). Indeed, we may generalize a class of cases where the use of the trademark does not attempt to capitalize on consumer confusion or to appropriate the cachet of one product for a different one. Such *nominative use* of a mark— where the only word reasonably available to describe a particular thing is pressed into service—lies outside the strictures of trademark law: Because it does not implicate the source-identification function that is the purpose of trademark, it does not constitute unfair competition; such use is fair because it does not imply sponsorship or endorsement by the trademark holder. "When the mark is used in a way that does not deceive the public we see no such sanctity in the word as to prevent its being used to tell the truth." *Prestonettes, Inc.* v. *Coty,* 264 U.S. 359, 368 (1924) (Holmes, J.).

To be sure, this is not the classic fair use case where the defendant has used the plaintiff's mark to describe the defendant's *own* product. Here, the New Kids trademark is used to refer to the New Kids themselves. We therefore do not purport to alter the test applicable in the paradigmatic fair use case. If the defendant's use of the plaintiff's trademark refers to something other than the plaintiff's product, the traditional fair use inquiry will continue to govern. But, where the defendant uses a trademark to describe the plaintiff's product, rather than its own, we hold that a commercial user is entitled to a nominative fair use defense provided he meets the following three requirements: First, the product or service in question must be one not readily identifiable without use of the trademark; second, only so much of the mark or marks may be used as is reasonably necessary to identify the product or service; and third, the user must do nothing that would, in conjunction with the mark, suggest sponsorship or endorsement by the trademark holder.

B. The New Kids do not claim there was anything false or misleading about the newspapers' use of their mark. Rather, the first seven causes of action, while purporting to state different claims, all hinge on one key factual allegation: that the newspapers' use of the New Kids name in conducting the unauthorized polls somehow implied that the New Kids were sponsoring the polls. It is no more reasonably possible, however, to refer to the New Kids as an entity than it is to refer to the Chicago Bulls, Volkswagens or the Boston Marathon without using the trademark. Indeed, how could someone not conversant with the proper names of the individual New Kids talk about the group at all? While plaintiffs' trademark certainly deserves protection against copycats and those who falsely claim that the New Kids have endorsed or sponsored them, such protection does not extend to rendering newspaper articles, conversations, polls and comparative advertising impossible. The first nominative use requirement is therefore met.

Also met are the second and third requirements. Both *The Star* and *USA Today* reference the New Kids only to the extent necessary to identify them as the subject of the polls; they do not use the New Kids' distinctive logo or anything else that isn't needed to make the announcements intelligible to readers. Finally, nothing in the announcements suggests joint sponsorship or endorsement by the New Kids. The *USA Today* announcement implies quite the contrary by asking whether the New Kids might be "a turn off." *The Star's* poll is more effusive but says nothing that expressly or by fair implication connotes endorsement or joint sponsorship on the part of the New Kids.

The New Kids argue that, even if the newspapers are entitled to a nominative fair use defense for the announcements, they are not entitled to it for the polls themselves, which were money-making enterprises separate and apart from the newspapers' reporting businesses. According to plaintiffs, defendants could have minimized the intrusion into their rights by using an 800 number or asking readers to call in on normal telephone lines which would not have resulted in a profit to the newspapers based on the conduct of the polls themselves.

The New Kids see this as a crucial difference, distinguishing this case from *Volkswagenwerk, WCBV-TV* and other nominative use cases. The New Kids' argument in support of this distinction is not entirely implausible: They point out that their fans, like everyone else, have limited resources. Thus a dollar spent calling the newspapers' 900 lines to express loyalty to the New Kids may well be a dollar not spent on New Kids products and services, including the New Kids' own 900 numbers. In short, plaintiffs argue that a nominative fair use defense is inapplicable where the use in question competes directly with that of the trademark holder.

We reject this argument. While the New Kids have a limited property right in their name, that right does not entitle them to control their fans' use of their own money. Where, as here, the use does not imply sponsorship or endorsement, the fact that it is carried on for profit and in competition with the trademark holder's business is beside the point. See, e.g., *Universal City Studios, Inc.* v. *Ideal Publishing Corp.,* 195 U.S.P.Q. 761 (S.D.N.Y. 1977) (magazine's use of TV program's trademark "Hardy Boys" in connection with photographs of show's stars not infringing). Voting for their favorite New Kid may be, as plaintiffs point out, a way for fans to articulate their loyalty to the group, and this may diminish the resources available for products and services they sponsor. But the trademark laws do not give the New Kids the right to channel their fans' enthusiasm (and dollars) only into items licensed or authorized by them. See *International Order of Job's Daughters* v. *Lindeburg & Co.,* 633 F.2d 912 (9th Cir. 1980) (no infringement where unauthorized jewelry maker produced rings and pins bearing fraternal organization's trademark). The New Kids could not use the trademark laws to prevent the publication of an unauthorized group biography or to censor all parodies or satires which use their name. We fail to see a material difference between these examples and the use here.

Summary judgment was proper as to the first seven causes of action because they all hinge on a theory of implied endorsement; there was none here as the uses in question were purely nominative. . . .

Conclusion

The district court's judgment is *AFFIRMED.*

NOTES FOR DISCUSSION

1. *Nominative Fair Use: An Unnecessary Defense?* In justifying the nominative fair use defense, Judge Kozinski cites three earlier cases, *Volkswagenwerk Aktiengesellschaft* v. *Church,* 411 F.2d 350 (9th Cir. 1969), *WCVB-TV* v. *Boston Athletic Ass'n,* 926 F.2d 42, 46 (1st Cir. 1991), and *Smith*

v. *Chanel, Inc.,* 402 F.2d 562 (9th Cir. 1968). Yet, in each of those three cases, the courts resolved the issue by finding no likelihood of confusion. Why doesn't the court follow that path here?

Presumably, part of the reason is the expansion in the likelihood of confusion test that took place between the 1960s and the 1990s. With decisions such as *Mutual of Omaha Ins. Co. v. Novak,* 836 F.2d 397 (8th Cir. 1987), recognizing liability based upon survey results in which 10 percent of the relevant consumers believed that the plaintiff "went along with" the defendant's use, it became far more difficult for defendants to prevail at trial on the grounds that a likelihood of confusion did not exist. Persuading a court to grant summary judgment on the grounds of no likelihood of confusion, particular in circuits where likelihood of confusion is treated as a factual issue, became nearly impossible.

Consider the facts in *New Kids on the Block.* Of the people likely to participate in the USA Today or Star poll, how many do you think believed that the New Kids on the Block had endorsed or sponsored the polls? Absent a trial, is there any way to be sure? Would there inevitably be disputed issues of material fact with respect to the likelihood of confusion inquiry? Did the district court grant summary judgment finding that no reasonable jury could find a likelihood of confusion with respect to the defendants' uses? Could the district court have granted summary judgment on that basis?

Judge Kozinski's formulation of the nominative fair use defense was intended to provide defendants an alternative avenue for obtaining an early resolution of a trademark case. Is this a sensible approach? If the court felt that the likelihood of confusion doctrine had extended potential liability for trademark infringement too far, why not address that directly, perhaps by limiting the scope of "approval" confusion, rather than indirectly, by creating a new "nominative" fair use defense?

2.   *Nominative Fair Use and the Likelihood of Confusion.* In *KP Permanent Make-Up,* the Court left open the precise relationship between descriptive fair use and the likelihood of confusion. What is the relationship between nominative fair use and the likelihood of confusion? Will a strong showing of likely confusion preclude the availability of the nominative fair use defense? Will a strong showing of nominative fair use bar liability even if confusion is otherwise likely? In other words, is nominative fair use a defense in cases where there is otherwise actionable confusion?

Alternatively, is nominative fair use a substitute for the ordinary *Polaroid*-style factor analysis on likelihood of confusion that does a better job of determining whether confusion is likely when a nominative use is made? *See Playboy Enters. v. Welles,* 279 F.3d 796, 801 (9th Cir. 2002) ("In cases in which the defendant raises a nominative use defense, the above three-factor test should be applied instead of the test for likelihood of confusion set forth in *Sleekcraft.*").

Moreover, to establish a nominative fair use, the third element in Judge Kozinski's formulation requires that "the user must do nothing that would, in conjunction with the mark, suggest sponsorship or endorsement by the trademark holder." Is this simply a restatement of the likelihood of confusion test? *See Brother Records, Inc. v. Jardine*, 318 F.3d 900, 908 n.5 (9th Cir. 2003) ("In reaching this conclusion, we note that the third requirement of the nominative fair use defense—the lack of anything that suggests sponsor-ship or endorsement—is merely the other side of the likelihood-of-confusion coin."). If so, does the defendant have to negate a likelihood of confusion to prevail on a nominative fair use defense? Is such a result contrary to the Court's ruling in *KP Permanent Make-Up*? In any event, if a defendant satisfies the third factor by showing no likelihood of confusion, isn't that enough for a defendant to prevail without any need for a nominative fair use defense? Why should a defendant also have to prove the first two factors?

Because of these uncertainties, other circuits have approached nominative fair use with caution. The Sixth Circuit, for example, has rejected it altogether. *See PACCAR Inc. v. TeleScan Technologies, L.L.C.*, 319 F.3d 243, 256 (6th Cir. 2003). The Third Circuit has adopted it, with modifications. *See Century 21 Real Estate Corporation v. Lending Tree, Inc.*, 425 F.3d 211 (3d Cir. 2005).

3. *Confusion: Factual Assumptions and Legal Presumptions*. The *New Kids on the Block* court repeatedly insists that "the [defendants'] use does not imply sponsorship or endorsement." Is the court asserting that as a factual assumption or as a legal presumption? In either case, may the factual assumption or legal presumption be rebutted? For example, if a properly conducted survey found that twenty percent of the relevant consumers believed that USA Today or The Star had obtained permission from the New Kids on the Block to perform the surveys, would that change the outcome in the case? What if a survey showed that twenty percent of the relevant consumers believed that the New Kids on the Block had endorsed the surveys? What is the difference between permission and endorsement? Should that difference matter in trademark law, or should confusion as to either be actionable?

In the field of book and movie titles, for example, as we discussed in Chapter 6, courts have held that a title does not create actionable confusion unless it "has no artistic relevance to the underlying work whatsoever, or . . . explicitly misleads as to the source or the content of the work." *Rogers v. Grimaldi*, 875 F.2d 994, 999 (2d Cir. 1989). Even if surveys demonstrate that some confusion will occur, no liability will accrue for consumers mistaken inferences of implied endorsement. *Id.* at 1001. Should we interpret Judge Kozinski's language in the third nominative fair use factor—that a defendant "must *do nothing* . . . that would suggest sponsorship or endorsement"—as adopting a similar "explicitly misleads" standard? In other words, should a defendant be able to claim nominative fair use unless the defendant does something, beyond merely using the mark, that affirmatively suggests sponsorship or endorsement?

However we might read Judge Kozinski's language, would it have made more sense to extend the *Rogers v. Grimaldi* approach to encompass the surveys by USA Today and The Star? Should we limit the circumstances under which consumers' interpretation of use as implied endorsement is actionable, and if so, what limitation would make sense?

For example, how would you resolve the following case? Liquid Glass sells car cleaners and waxes, and in one of its television commercials, "portrays a provocatively-dressed woman applying Liquid Glass car polish to a Porsche 911 with the trademark 'PORSCHE' prominently displayed on the car." *Liquid Glass Enters., Inc. v. Dr. Ing. h.c.F. Porsche AG*, 8 F. Supp. 2d 398, 399 (D.N.J. 1998). May Porsche reasonably pursue a claim for trademark infringement, asserting the consumers will believe that Porsche has endorsed Liquid Glass's products based upon the use of its car and trademark in the commercial? If so, and if Porsche moves for a summary judgment, should it be granted? May Liquid Glass reasonably assert nominative fair use in this context?

4. *Nominative Fair Use versus Descriptive Fair Use.* One question that Judge Kozinski leaves open is when we should apply descriptive fair use and when we should apply nominative fair use. The Ninth Circuit addressed these issues in a subsequent case involving Alan Jardine, one of the original members of the band, The Beach Boys. *Brother Records, Inc. v. Jardine*, 318 F.3d 900 (9th Cir. 2003). After the Beach Boys stopped touring, Jardine started performing concerts under the name "The Beach Boys Family and Friends." In response, the three other original members of the band sued, alleging trademark infringement. In response, Jardine asserted both descriptive and nominative fair use. Do both apply or just one? If only one applies, which one? In any event, how should each defense be resolved?

In the case, the court held that the descriptive fair use did not apply because Jardine was not using "beach boy" in its original descriptive sense of "boys who frequent a stretch of sand beside the sea." *Id.* at 907. The court also found that nominative fair use applied, but Jardine's use failed the third element of the nominative fair use inquiry. In the court's view, Jardine's use suggested sponsorship because his "promotional materials display 'The Beach Boys' more prominently and boldly than 'Family and Friends,'" and created actual consumer confusion. *Id.* at 908. Although the nominative fair use defense was available, Jardine could not therefore establish its elements and was liable for the confusion his use created. *Id.*

5. *Applying Nominative Fair Use.* In footnote seven of its opinion, the court explained its rule that, to constitute a nominative fair use, a defendant could use no more of the plaintiff's trademark than necessary:

> Thus, a soft drink competitor would be entitled to compare its product to Coca-Cola or Coke, but would not be entitled to use Coca-Cola's distinctive lettering.

The New Kids on the Block v. News America Publishing, Inc., 971 F.2d 302, 308 n.7 (9th Cir. 1992).

Does this requirement allow a plaintiff to nitpick the defendant's precise use in a way that will likely chill the defendant's legitimate use of a plaintiff's trademark? Consider the facts in *Playboy Enterprises, Inc. v. Welles*, 279 F.3d 796 (9th Cir. 2002). In the case, Terri Welles was Playboy Playmate of the Year in 1981. When she and Playboy parted ways, Welles set up her own website and prominently proclaimed her status as Playmate of the Year. She used the word Playboy, Playmate of the Year, and the abbreviation PMOY on her website and in her metatags associated with the site. The court held that the model's identification of her past affiliation with Playboy and her status as "Playboy Playmate of the Year 1981" satisfied the nominative fair use defense. *Id.* at 802–04. However, the court held that Welles' repeated use of "PMOY" on her background wallpaper was excessive and was more than necessary to explain her past status as Playmate of the Year. *Id.* at 804–05. With respect to that use, Welles could not satisfy the second prong of the *New Kids on the Block* nominative fair use test. As a result, the court remanded the case to the district court to determine whether that use otherwise created a likelihood of confusion. *Id.* at 805.

Would we be better served with the common law's traditional formulation as set forth by Justice Homes: "When the mark is used in a way that does not deceive the public we see no such sanctity in the word as to prevent its being used to tell the truth"? *Prestonettes, Inc. v. Coty,* 264 U.S. 359, 368 (1924). How would Welles' wallpaper fare under that standard?

C. LACHES, ESTOPPEL, AND ACQUIESCENCE

CONAN PROPERTIES, INC. V. CONANS PIZZA, INC.

752 F.2d 145 (5th Cir. 1985)

JERRE S. WILLIAMS, CIRCUIT JUDGE

Conan Properties, Inc. (CPI) owns the literary property rights in the fictional character "CONAN THE BARBARIAN" and licenses others to use the character in various commercial and entertainment works. CPI sued Conans Pizza, Inc. (Conans) for infringement of its federal trademark and for unfair competition and misappropriation of its property under Texas common law. By a special verdict, the jury found trademark infringement and unfair competition but refused to award damages, concluding that CPI had unreasonably delayed instituting this suit and had acquiesced in Conans' conduct. After the trial, CPI moved for injunctive relief, but the district court denied the motion. CPI appeals from that judgment, claiming that it was entitled to injunctive relief notwithstanding the jury's findings of laches and acquiescence. Conans asserts that the jury's implicit finding of likelihood of confusion was unsupported by the evidence. We affirm in part but we find the district court's denial of all injunctive relief was in error and we reverse to that extent. In all other respects, the judgment of the district court is affirmed.

I.

The CONAN character was created in 1929 by Robert Howard. But the character remained relatively dormant until the 1950's when L. Sprague deCamp, a contemporary author, rediscovered and began writing books featuring CONAN THE BARBARIAN. As the title might suggest, deCamp's *CONAN THE BARBARIAN* series told the tales of a gigantic, sword and battle-ax wielding barbarian adventurer who roamed the world in search of foes. Many of deCamp's works were illustrated by Frank Frazetta, an artist famous for his "sword and sorcery" style artwork. In 1970, the Howard estate licensed Marvel Comics to publish a series of comic books featuring CONAN THE BARBARIAN. To avoid litigation over who had rights in CONAN THE BARBARIAN, the Howard estate and deCamp united their interests in the CONAN character in 1976 and formed CPI. deCamp is one of the two 50% shareholders of CPI. In that same year the United States Patent and Trademark Office (USPTO) granted CPI a federally registered trademark for the title "CONAN THE BARBARIAN" for comic books.

Also in this same year, Scott Leist and Jerry Strader opened "Conans Pizza", a restaurant in Austin, Texas. The restaurant's menus, signs, promotional material, specialty items, and general decor featured a barbarian-like man who closely resembled CPI's CONAN character. For example, Conans Pizza's menus depicted a loincloth-clad, sword wielding, sandal wearing, barbarian-like muscle man, and they described one of the featured pizzas as the "Savage, Barbaric, All the Way Pizza." The owners decorated the restaurant with dozens of reproductions of Frank Frazetta's artwork, although only a few of the reproductions actually represented CONAN THE BARBARIAN.

While visiting relatives in Austin approximately one month after Conans Pizza opened, deCamp noticed the restaurant. He stopped by the restaurant, spoke with Jerry Strader, and identified himself as one of the creators of the CONAN character. He wished Strader success with his business and had a photograph taken of Strader and himself in front of one of the restaurant's signs. Later, deCamp sent Strader a copy of the photograph, on which he wrote: "With best wishes to Jerry Stader and Scott Leist from one of Conan's creators—L. Sprague deCamp."

At trial deCamp testified that he informed CPI's attorney about the existence of Conans Pizza in late 1976 and that the CPI board of directors from time to time at meetings discussed the trademark issue raised by the existence of Conans Pizza. In January 1981, CPI wrote Conans Pizza and for the first time objected to Conans' use of CPI's mark. CPI demanded Conans cease using the mark. Later in 1981, Conans discontinued using much, but certainly not all, of the CONAN THE BARBARIAN indicia. It continued using "Conan" in its trade name and describing the featured pizza as "The Savage". It removed only those

Frazetta prints that actually depicted CONAN, though the remaining prints closely resembled those few that featured CONAN. CPI filed this suit in March 1982, approximately 5 1/2 years after deCamp first saw Conans Pizza.

From 1976 to 1980, Conans had opened four additional "Conans Pizza" restaurants in the Austin area. In April 1980, before CPI had sent its letter objecting to the use of the name "Conans Pizza", Conans filed with the USPTO an application for the service mark "CONANS PIZZA" for restaurant services. That application was granted by the USPTO in July 1982, after this suit had been filed. In the meantime, in January 1982, before this suit was filed but after Conans had received CPI's letter of objection, Conans opened a Conans Pizza restaurant in San Antonio, Texas. This restaurant was the sixth in of the chain and the first outside the Austin area. Conans' combined sales from its six restaurants increased thirty-fold from 1976 to 1982, accounting for gross annual sales exceeding $3,000,000.

In its suit CPI sought injunctive relief, damages, and an accounting for profits. CPI alleged that the name Conans Pizza and Conans' activities infringed CPI's federally registered trademark under section 32(1) of the Lanham Trademark Act, 15 U.S.C. § 1114(1) (1982), created a false designation of origin under section 43(a) of the Lanham Act, 15 U.S.C. § 1125(a) (1982), and constituted unfair competition and misappropriation of its merchandising property under Texas common law. Conans denied each of CPI's allegations and asserted the equitable defenses of laches and acquiescence.

Prior to trial Conans moved for partial summary judgment on CPI's common law claim for misappropriation of a merchandising property. The district court granted the motion and dismissed this claim. The remaining issues were tried and submitted to the jury. By a special verdict, the jury found that CPI had proved all of the elements of both a trademark infringement claim under the Lanham Act and an unfair competition claim under Texas common law. The jury found, however, that CPI had not proved all of the elements under the Lanham Act of its false designation of origin claim. In response to other special interrogatories, the jury determined that Conans' acquiescence and laches defenses were valid and precluded either the recovery of damages or an accounting for profits by CPI. After the trial CPI moved for injunctive relief, seeking to prevent Conans from using the mark CONANS PIZZA both locally and nationally. A nationwide injunction was particularly important to CPI because Conans was tentatively planning a national franchising scheme. The district court denied CPI's post-trial motion for injunctive relief.

II.

A. *The Jury's Findings of Trademark Infringement and Unfair Competition*

The initial issue in this appeal is whether the jury's findings of trademark infringement under 15 U.S.C. § 1114(1) and unfair competition under Texas common law can stand against the claim that they were in error as a matter of law. Conans Pizza argues that the jury's implicit finding of likelihood of confusion for both the trademark infringement and the unfair competition claims was against the great weight of evidence and must be reversed.

The standard of an appellate court's review of a jury's verdict is narrow and exacting. The verdict must be upheld unless the facts and inferences point so strongly and so overwhelmingly in favor of one party that reasonable persons could not arrive at a contrary verdict. *Western Co. of North America v. United States*, 699 F.2d 264, 276 (5th Cir.), *cert. denied*, 464 U.S. 892 (1983). Even if the jury's verdict was based on sharply conflicting evidence and the court of appeals determines that reasonable persons might reach a contrary result, the jury verdict must be upheld. *Slavin v. Curry*, 690 F.2d 446, 449 (5th Cir. 1982); *United States v. 6,162.78 Acres of Land*, 680 F.2d 396, 398 (5th Cir. 1982). Our task, therefore, is limited to determining whether the jury had before it any competent and substantial evidence that fairly supports the verdict. *Stewart v. Thigpen*, 730 F.2d 1002, 1007 (5th Cir. 1984).

To prevail on its trademark infringement and unfair competition claims, CPI needed to demonstrate that Conans' use of the CONAN THE BARBARIAN mark and image was likely to create confusion in the mind of the ordinary consumer as to the source, affiliation, or sponsorship of Conans' service and product. *See, e.g., Amstar Corp. v. Domino's Pizza, Inc.*, 615 F.2d 252, 258 (5th Cir.) (likelihood of confusion test applies to common law unfair competition claims as well as to claims under 15 U.S.C. §§ 1114(1), 1125(a)), *cert. denied*, 449 U.S. 899 (1980). A nonexhaustive list of factors to be considered in determining whether a likelihood of confusion exists include: (1) the type of trademark alleged to have been infringed, (2) the similarity of design between the two marks, (3) similarity of the products or services, (4) the identity of the retail outlets and purchasers, (5) the identity of the advertising medium utilized, (6) the defendant's intent, and (7) evidence of actual confusion. *Armco, Inc. v. Armco Burglar Alarm Co.*, 693 F.2d 1155, 1159 (5th Cir. 1982). The absence or presence of any one factor ordinarily is not dispositive; indeed, a finding of likelihood of confusion need not be supported by even a majority of the seven factors. *Id.* at 1159.

We conclude that CPI presented sufficient evidence related to these seven factors to permit the jury to find that Conans' conduct created a likelihood of confusion as to the source, sponsorship, or affiliation of its service and product. The evidence adduced at trial revealed that Conans was aware of the CONAN THE BARBARIAN character prior to its adoption of the name Conans Pizza. Additionally, Conans' menus, advertising material, specialty items, and general decor featured a character unmistakably similar if not identical to CONAN THE BARBARIAN.

Conans answers that no reasonable person could have believed that its restaurants were related to CPI's CONAN THE BARBARIAN, since the products and services each provided were different. We must disagree. Although CPI never licensed any entity to use its mark in connection with restaurant services, ordinary consumers may well believe that Conans was in fact licensed by CPI. At the trial CPI presented evidence of numerous cartoon and other characters whose names, marks, or images were used in extensive licensing programs to promote everything from children's toys to fast-food restaurants. These characters included SNOOPY, POPEYE, DICK TRACY, PETER PAN, E.T., and ROY ROGERS. Many of today's consumers expect such endorsements and act favorably toward them. It is reasonable to assume, as the jury found, that ordinary consumers who patronized Conans Pizza and experienced the pervasive, inescapable aura of CONAN THE BARBARIAN in those restaurants were likely to believe that the restaurants were in some way licensed by or affiliated with CPI. We therefore leave undisturbed the jury's findings of trademark infringement and unfair competition. . . .

C.   *CPI's Motion for Injunctive Relief*

CPI next argues that the jury's findings of laches and acquiescence properly barred its request for damages but should not have precluded it from securing an injunction preventing Conans from continuing to infringe its mark both locally and nationally. With respect to Conans' infringement of CPI's mark locally, in Austin, we must conclude that the district court correctly denied CPI's request for injunctive relief after considering the jury's findings of laches and acquiescence. We emphasize, however, that Austin is the only area in which CPI waived its right to protect its mark, CONAN THE BARBARIAN. Conans received CPI's cease and desist letter prior to opening the San Antonio restaurant. Conans therefore opened that restaurant at its own peril, without the defenses of laches and acquiescence. *See, e.g.*, 2 J. McCarthy, *supra*, § 26:3; *James Burrough Ltd. v. Sign of the Beefeater, Inc.*, 572 F.2d 574, 578 (7th Cir. 1978); *Big O Tire Dealers, Inc. v. Goodyear Tire & Rubber Co.*, 561 F.2d 1365 (10th Cir. 1977) (even assuming defendant's first use of the infringing mark was in good faith, it could not execute a planned national advertising campaign using that mark after it had received the plaintiff's objection), *cert. dismissed*, 434 U.S. 1052 (1978).

A finding of laches alone ordinarily will not bar the plaintiff's request for injunctive relief, although it typically will foreclose a demand for an accounting or damages. *Menendez v. Holt*, 128 U.S. 514, 524 (1888); *McLean v. Fleming*, 96 U.S. 245, 258, 24 L.Ed. 828 (1877); *James Burrough Ltd. v. Sign of the Beefeater, Inc.*, 572 F.2d 574, 578 (7th Cir. 1978); *Grotrian, Helfferich, Schulz, Th. Steinweg Nachf. v. Steinway & Sons*, 523 F.2d 1331, 1344 (2d Cir. 1975). This is because courts construe the plaintiff's unreasonable delay to imply consent to the defendant's conduct, which amounts to nothing more than a revocable license; the license is revoked once the plaintiff objects to the defendant's infringement. *Menendez*, 128 U.S. at 524, 9 S.Ct. at 145; *University of Pittsburgh v. Champion Products, Inc.*, 686 F.2d 1040, 1045 (3d Cir.), *cert. denied*, 459 U.S. 1087 (1982). In cases where the defendant actually relies upon the plaintiff's affirmative act, however, the fiction of implied consent is inapplicable and an injunction may not issue. *See, e.g., Saratoga Vichy Spring Co. v. Lehman*, 625 F.2d 1037, 1041 (2d Cir. 1980) (the plaintiff's unreasonable delay and the defendant's actual reliance upon that delay precluded the issuance of an injunction).

In this case CPI unreasonably delayed in protecting its rights in Austin, and its dilatoriness prejudiced Conans. Moreover, through the affirmative acts of L. Sprague deCamp, one of its agents, CPI implicitly if not explicitly authorized Conans to continue using the CONAN THE BARBARIAN name and image in connection with restaurant services in Austin. Responding to the special interrogatories, the jury found that Conans had proven all of the elements of the defense of laches and acquiescence. The jury's affirmative finding of acquiescence establishes the reliance necessary to preclude the issuance of an injunction, and the record supports the jury's implicit conclusion that Conans relied upon deCamp's conduct. We therefore hold that the district court properly denied CPI's post-trial request for injunctive relief related to the Austin area.

A more difficult question is whether CPI's laches and acquiescence in one locale eternally forecloses it from asserting its rights if Conans expands beyond that area. CPI instituted this suit after it learned that Conans had applied with the USPTO for a service mark for "Conans Pizza" and was contemplating a national franchising scheme. In rejecting CPI's post-trial request for injunctive relief, the district court implicitly determined that laches in one locale resulted in laches everywhere. We conclude that CPI's laches and acquiescence in Austin did not constitute an eternal abandonment nationwide. We reverse, therefore, the judgment of the district court insofar as the judgment denied an injunction for any geographical area other than Austin.

The respective definitions of laches and acquiescence offer the most compelling reason for concluding that CPI did not forfeit it rights nationally. Laches is commonly defined as an inexcusable delay that results in prejudice to the defendant. *Matter of Bohart*, 743 F.2d 313, 325

(5th Cir. 1984); *Armco*, 693 F.2d at 1161; *Environmental Defense Fund, Inc. v. Alexander*, 614 F.2d 474, 478 (5th Cir.), *cert. denied*, 449 U.S. 919 (1980). Similarly, acquiescence involves the plaintiff's implicit or explicit assurances to the defendant which induces reliance by the defendant. *Dwinell-Wright Co. v. White House Milk Co.*, 132 F.2d 822, 825 (2d Cir. 1943); *Golden West Brewing Co. v. Milonas & Sons, Inc.*, 104 F.2d 880, 882, 42 U.S.P.Q. (BNA) 185 (9th Cir. 1939); *Procter & Gamble Co. v. J.L. Prescott Co.*, 102 F.2d 773, 780, 40 U.S.P.Q. (BNA) 434 (3d Cir.), *cert. denied*, 308 U.S. 557 (1939). As affirmative defenses, the defendant must prove how it will be prejudiced by the plaintiff's unreasonable delay and implicit or explicit assurances. *Bohart*, 743 F.2d at 326 n. 13; *Environmental Defense Fund*, 614 F.2d at 479. An injunction against future infringement in a particular locale when laches and acquiescence have been found, as in this case, is properly denied if the plaintiff's delay or other conduct either induced reliance on the defendant's part or will result in substantial prejudice to the defendant if the plaintiff is permitted to enforce its rights in the trademark. Whether phrased as "reliance" or "prejudice", the effect is the same—the defendant has done something it otherwise would not have done absent the plaintiff's conduct.

The result is different, however, when the asserted future infringement would occur in a geographical area other than the one in which the plaintiff waived its right to protect its mark. In the new geographical area where the defendant has not yet expanded its business, the defendant is hard pressed to demonstrate how it could have relied to its detriment upon the plaintiff's inactivity or other conduct. Stated simply, the defendant at best can show only that the plaintiff acquiesced or unreasonably delayed in protecting its mark in the local area. Since a showing of mere delay will not support a finding of laches or acquiescence, *Bohart*, 743 F.2d at 326, the defenses are invalid. In this case we conclude that Conans has made sufficient showings of reliance and prejudice in the Austin area to justify denying an injunction, but has failed to offer any evidence, let alone carry its burden of demonstrating that it would be prejudiced if barred from infringing CPI's mark in any area other than Austin.

Three other practical considerations guide our determination that CPI's laches and acquiescence should not have barred its post-trial request for injunctive relief outside Austin. First, allowing Conans, which has been found to have infringed CPI's mark and violated Texas unfair competition laws, to expand its trademark violation and unfair competition would be inequitable and unworthy of judicial protection. Second, permitting Conans to expand its infringement into geographical areas it has never penetrated would grant Conans an unjustified windfall. Finally, creating a risk that CPI may be barred from asserting its rights nationwide because of its failure to challenge what it may have considered a *de minimis*, local infringement may spur litigation where litigation otherwise would not be necessary, since CPI would be forced to bring infringement suits in local *de minimis* situations.

Having concluded that CPI is entitled to an injunction prohibiting Conans from infringing its mark in CONAN THE BARBARIAN in areas outside Austin, Texas, we now turn to the scope of the injunction. As previously stated, the conduct in which Conans currently engages that CPI alleges constitutes an infringement of its mark includes (1) using the service mark "CONANS PIZZA" as its restaurants' name, (2) describing one of the featured pizzas as "The Savage", and (3) decorating the restaurants with Frank Frazetta's artwork which is commonly associated with *CONAN THE BARBARIAN* books and the CONAN THE BARBARIAN character. In 1981, Conans discontinued using all other indicia of CPI's trademark, including its use of the barbarian man on T-shirts, advertising material, and signs.

When fashioning an injunction in a suit such as this, the court must give careful consideration to the possibility that a defendant found to have either infringed the plaintiff's mark or unfairly competed with the plaintiff will modify his behavior ever so slightly and attempt to skirt the line of permissible conduct. Courts have responded to this problem by issuing broad injunctions that prohibit conduct that clearly infringes the plaintiff's mark as well as conduct that ordinarily would not justify any relief. For example, in *Chevron Chemical Co. v. Voluntary Purchasing Groups, Inc.*, 659 F.2d 695 (5th Cir. 1981), *cert. denied*, 457 U.S. 1126, 102 S.Ct. 2947, 73 L.Ed.2d 1342 (1982), we stated that:

> [A] competitive business, once convicted of unfair competition in a given particular, should thereafter be required to keep a safe distance away from the margin line—even if that requirement involves a handicap as compared with those who have not disqualified themselves.

Id. at 705 (quotation omitted). Similarly, in *Kentucky Fried Chicken Corp. v. Diversified Packaging Corp.*, 549 F.2d 368 (5th Cir. 1977), a case in which the defendant had engaged in an elaborate and calculated scheme of unfair competition, we declined to modify the scope of a permanent injunction that prohibited the defendant from using certain marks that the plaintiff had alleged were likely to cause confusion with its trademarks. In upholding the broad injunction, we assumed without deciding that absent its other conduct the defendant would have been entitled to use the allegedly confusing marks but that its history of improper behavior justified a broad injunction. We reasoned that "an injunction can be therapeutic as well as protective. In fashioning relief against a party who has transgressed the governing legal standards, a court of equity is free to proscribe activities that, standing alone, would have been unassailable." *Id.* at 390.

These standards justify the issuance of an injunction in this case prohibiting Conans from ever using any semblance of the CONAN THE BARBARIAN theme in its current and future restaurants outside Austin. This includes using the barbarian name or theme on menus, specialty items, signs, etc. Specifically, Conans must not be permitted to use "The Savage" or any similar phrase to describe its food items. Further, the printing of the name "Conans" must be in a form which does not resemble in any way the manner in which CPI prints the name CONAN. The writing of the name "Conans" in script form as Conans is now doing is a reasonable and proper presentation of the name. Finally, Conans must not display either the familiar Frazetta prints or any other artwork that even remotely suggests a connection between it and CONAN THE BARBARIAN. Because Conans opened the San Antonio restaurant after it had notice of CPI's objection to its use of CPI's mark, this injunction must apply with equal force to that restaurant.

We perceive no need to invoke the full breadth of the court's powers to prohibit Conans from using its name, "Conans Pizza", or the word "Conan" in the San Antonio restaurant or in any future restaurant outside Austin. This case is unlike the *Chevron Chemical* and *Kentucky Fried Chicken* cases, where the defendants' conduct was egregious, and this Court was concerned that any relief other than broad injunctions would permit the defendants to retain part of the goodwill they had originally misappropriated from the plaintiffs. In view of CPI's laches and acquiescence, we view Conans' conduct as significantly different from the defendants' conduct in *Chevron Chemical* and *Kentucky Fried Chicken*. In addition, we see no likelihood that Conans will retain any goodwill which may have been misappropriated from CPI by merely using the names "Conans Pizza" or "Conans" without any indicia of CONAN THE BARBARIAN.

Another reason compels our conclusion that Conans should not be enjoined from using these names if it expands beyond Austin. CPI's argument reduced to its core is that it has exclusive rights in the name Conan in any form and in connection with any product or service. We reject this argument. Although we conclude that CPI has protectable rights in the CONAN THE BARBARIAN name and character, we hold that CPI lacks similar rights in merely the name Conan. "Conan" is a surname and can be regarded as a descriptive term rather than an inherently distinctive mark. *Amstar Corp. v. Domino's Pizza, Inc.*, 615 F.2d 252, 260 (5th Cir.), (the name "Domino" is a surname and warrants less protection than an arbitrary mark), *cert. denied*, 449 U.S. 899 (1980). Descriptive terms may acquire trademark protection only with a showing that through usage the name has acquired distinctiveness (the so-called secondary meaning requirement) in the minds of ordinary consumers. *L.E. Waterman Co. v. Modern Pen Co.*, 235 U.S. 88, 94 (1914); *Herring-Hall-Marvin Safe Co. v. Hall's Safe Co.*, 208 U.S. 554, 559 (1908); *Amstar*,

615 F.2d at 260; *John R. Thompson Co. v. Holloway*, 366 F.2d 108, 113 (5th Cir. 1966); *Hanover Mfg. Co. v. Ed Hanover Trailers, Inc.*, 434 S.W.2d 109, 111 (Tex. 1968); *In re Glen Raven Knitting Mills, Inc.*, 153 U.S.P.Q. (BNA) 134 (T.T.A.B. 1967); *Dunfey Hotels Corp. v. Meridien Hotels Investments Group, Inc.*, 504 F. Supp. 371, 378, 380 (S.D.N.Y. 1980) (plaintiff established that the name "Parker House" is a well-known service mark for hotel services but failed to establish that merely the name "Parker" triggered the same public recognition). One noted commentator has stated that this test requires the plaintiff to show that "the public has come to recognize the personal name as a symbol which identifies and distinguishes the goods or services of only one seller." 1 J. McCarthy, *supra*, § 13:2 at 446 (footnote omitted).

At trial CPI failed to introduce any evidence, testimonial, statistical, or otherwise, demonstrating that its use of merely the name Conan established the requisite distinctiveness in the minds of ordinary consumers. CPI's failure to introduce any evidence establishing secondary meaning in the name Conan mandates denying the extraordinarily broad injunction it seeks. We conclude, therefore, that Conans' use of its trade name on existing and future restaurants outside Austin poses no legally significant threat to CPI's mark. . . .

AFFIRMED in part; REVERSED AND REMANDED in part.

CLARK, CHIEF JUDGE, dissenting:

I concur in all of Judge Williams' opinion for the court except that part which permits defendant to continue its use of the name CONAN outside of the city of Austin. Since this court has chosen to frame a proper injunction, we are bound to balance the equities in ordering its terms.

It could be true in some abstract setting that use of the name CONAN becomes innocuous when it is disembodied from THE BARBARIAN and other associated trappings adopted by the plaintiff. I think it is unlikely here. CONAN does not refer to Arthur Conan Doyle or his family. Nor does it refer to Scott Leist or Gerald Strader. It is not descriptive of defendant's restaurant by style or product.

The majority says that once CONAN has been civilized by isolating it from its creation, it carries none of the good will defendants appropriated from plaintiff's intellectual property. That being so, the name alone can be of no business significance to defendant either. This leaves but two possible effects to its continued use: One, no one will know what CONAN means. Two, those who are familiar with plaintiff's property will continue to associate CONAN with THE BARBARIAN.

Defendant's use of CONAN originated in infringement, albeit innocent. As the majority observes, this gives defendant no right to expand that original use and the likelihood of confusion which this jury found it carried. Continued use of CONAN outside of Austin creates a distinct hazard that plaintiff will be injured. That use is of no established benefit to defendants. Balancing the equities between the parties in framing the injunctive relief granted clearly indicates we should wipe the slate clean outside of Austin.

KELLOGG CO. V. EXXON CORP.

209 F.3d 562 (6th Cir. 2000)

ALICE M. BATCHELDER, CIRCUIT JUDGE

Plaintiff-Appellant Kellogg Company appeals the district court's order granting summary judgment to Defendant-Appellee Exxon Corporation on Kellogg's complaint alleging federal and state law claims of trademark infringement, false designation of origin, false representation, dilution, and unfair competition. Because we conclude that the district court erred in (1) holding that Kellogg had acquiesced in Exxon's use of the challenged mark, (2) dismissing Kellogg's dilution claim, and (3) holding that no genuine issues of fact material to Kellogg's claim of abandonment remain for trial, we reverse the judgment of the district court and remand the case for further proceedings.

BACKGROUND

In 1952, Kellogg began using a cartoon tiger in connection with "Kellogg's Frosted Flakes" cereal and registered its "Tony The Tiger" name and illustration in the United States Patent and Trademark Office ("PTO"). Today, Kellogg owns a number of federal trademark registrations for the name and appearance of its "Tony The Tiger" trademark; those trademark registrations cover, among other things, "cereal-derived food product to be used as a breakfast food, snack food or ingredient for making food."

In 1959, Exxon began using a cartoon tiger to promote motor fuel products, and in 1965, Exxon registered federally its "Whimsical Tiger" for use in connection with the sale of petroleum products. Exxon used its cartoon tiger in its "Put A Tiger In Your Tank" advertising campaign, which ran between 1964 and 1968. In 1968, Kellogg acknowledged Exxon's use of its cartoon tiger when it requested Exxon not to oppose Kellogg's application to register its "Tony The Tiger" trademark in Germany. Exxon's "Whimsical Tiger" trademark, obtained with no opposition from Kellogg, became incontestable in 1970.

In 1972, Exxon changed its name from Standard Oil Company to Exxon Corporation and changed its primary trademarks from "Esso," "Enco", and "Humble" to "Exxon." Exxon submitted into evidence numerous newspaper and magazine articles and other promotional materials demonstrating its extensive and costly advertising campaign to promote its new "Exxon" mark using the cartoon tiger and to launch its "Energy For A Strong America" campaign, which ran in the latter half of the 1970s. For example, an article in a 1973 issue of *Advertising Age* called Exxon's advertising campaign "the classic 'name change' campaign of all time, with approximately $100,000,000 involved in the face lift!" Harry Wayne McMahan, *McMahan Picks the 100 Best TV Commercials of the Year*, Advertising Age, Feb. 19, 1973.

In the early 1980s, Exxon's advertising agency, McCann-Erickson ("McCann"), suggested that Exxon phase out the use of its cartoon tiger and begin using a live tiger, opining that the cartoon tiger was too whimsical and, hence, inappropriate in light of prevalent oil shortages. In 1981, Exxon began to adopt a new look for its gas stations, implementing a program to modernize the gas pumps and to eliminate its cartoon tiger on the pump panels. At that time, Exxon had between 16,000 and 18,000 gas stations in the United States. Over 11,000 of these gas stations were owned and operated by independent distributors ("distributor stations"), and the rest were owned and operated by Exxon ("company operated retail stores" or "CORS") or owned by Exxon and operated by independent dealers ("dealer stations"). The modernization program to bring about this "new look" entailed removal of the cartoon tiger head design from the lower panels or "pump skirts" on its Exxon "Extra" gasoline dispensers. In a letter dated August 12, 1982, Exxon instructed its regional managers to begin phasing out their use of the cartoon tiger:

> The purpose of this memo is to communicate new guidelines pertaining to the application of the Exxon Tiger and the Exxon Emblem in all advertising, point-of-sale material, Company publications, etc.

> Exxon Tiger—Effective immediately, the use of the cartoon tiger is to be discontinued.

Exxon explored possible ways to protect its cartoon tiger trademark while shifting toward a live tiger. For example, a 1984 internal office memo suggested:

> Since the only way to protect the Trademark is to use it, it might be wise for us to explore ways that the Cartoon Tiger can be used in marketing on a limited basis. This is not a hot item, but one that we can't forget about and be embarrassed later.

A 1985 internal office memo, which listed the subject as "Trademarks," stated:

> Advertising discontinued use of the "Cartoon Tiger" in all advertising, point-of-sale material and company publications on August 12, 1982. Regions were advised at that time to do the same (see letter attached). To my knowledge, there has been no use of the "Cartoon Tiger" by advertising or [in] the areas other than the tiger head which appears on the pre-RID Trimline Exxon Extra gasoline pumps/dispensers.

We have asked McCann to explore ways that the "Cartoon Tiger" could be used to protect the mark. In reviewing possible station applications, two general areas seem to afford the most opportunities. . . .

This memo discussed possible strategic placement of cartoon tiger decals around the pump islands and sales rooms/kiosks. Other correspondence between Exxon's attorneys, Exxon's marketing department, and McCann reveals Exxon's efforts to reduce its use of the cartoon tiger while ensuring trademark protection. Exxon ultimately decided to use its cartoon tiger as a graphic display on its stations' pump toppers.

Many Exxon stations were slow to remove the cartoon tiger from their pumps. In late 1985 and early 1986, Exxon was using its cartoon tiger on pump toppers at approximately 2,500 gas stations. In 1987, Exxon photographed every distributor station in the United States. Thousands of photographs were taken and stored at Exxon, but most of them were destroyed in a 1994 routine file room clean-up. Based upon those photographs that remain, Exxon estimates that approximately 10% of the 11,000 distributor stations still displayed the cartoon tiger in 1987. In 1993, Exxon contractually obligated its distributors to comply with the modernization program and to convert their stations to the "new look," threatening to remove from the Exxon chain those stations that failed to comply by April 1, 1995.

Exxon submitted evidence in an effort to show that, despite its efforts to convert the look of its gas stations and shift toward the use of a live tiger, its use of the cartoon tiger throughout the 1980s was sufficient to maintain its rights in the mark. In November 1985, Exxon had renewed its federal trademark registration for its cartoon tiger; this renewal would last an additional 20 years. From 1985 to 1990, some Exxon stations used a costumed version of the cartoon tiger for appearances at grand opening events and various promotional activities. In late 1989 and again in 1993, Exxon ran a promotion called "Color to Win," in which over one million contestants submitted entries of a cartoon tiger to hundreds of Exxon stations. In the early 1990s, Exxon used its cartoon tiger to promote the Texas State Fair. Exxon also presented evidence showing that in 1973, an Exxon distributor in Virginia placed a large statue of a cartoon tiger in front of its gas station near the highway, and the statue remains there today.

In the early 1990s, after the *Exxon Valdez* oil spill, Exxon changed the appearance of its cartoon tiger, making it "more endearing, warm, and friendly." In the words of Exxon's principal artist, "Today's tiger is now cast in a more humanitarian role. He is polite to the elderly, plants trees for ecology and has an overall concern for the environment." Exxon also began to expand the use of its cartoon tiger. Although Exxon had opened its first company-operated convenience store in 1984, it was not until the early 1990s that Exxon began to use its cartoon tiger to promote the sale in those stores of certain foods and beverages, such as Domino's Pizza, Coca Cola, Pepsi Cola, Lays Potato Chips, and Dunkin Donuts. Exxon also began using its cartoon tiger to promote its own private label beverage, "Wild Tiger," and its own private label coffee, "Bengal Traders."

Exxon's use of the cartoon tiger to promote food, beverages, and convenience stores increased dramatically from 1992 to 1996. In October 1992, Exxon had about eight "Tiger Mart" stores; by October 1993, there were about 68 "Tiger Mart" stores; by October 1996, there were over 265 "Tiger Mart" stores.

On November 3, 1992, having learned of Exxon's reintroduction of its cartoon tiger in Canada and Argentina, Kellogg's trademark counsel complained about that use in a telephone conversation with an Exxon attorney and was advised that Exxon had been using its cartoon tiger in the United States as well. Kellogg immediately requested examples of such use, and on November 20, 1992, Exxon sent Kellogg a compilation of 14 examples of promotional materials appearing in the United States featuring its cartoon tiger. Not one of those examples disclosed Exxon's use of its cartoon tiger to promote food and beverage items or its new "Tiger Mart" stores.

In 1993, Kellogg challenged Exxon's use of the cartoon tiger in Canada, and in 1994, filed a lawsuit against Exxon's Canadian affiliate. Kellogg was unsuccessful in its attempt to negotiate a global settlement in 1994 and 1995. In March 1996, Exxon published for opposition its application to the PTO to register its cartoon tiger for use with convenience stores, and Kellogg commenced opposition proceedings. On October 7, 1996, Kellogg filed suit against Exxon in the United States District Court for the Western District of Tennessee. Kellogg originally sought actual and punitive damages derived from Exxon's use of its cartoon tiger trademark in connection with the sale of food items, as well as a preliminary and permanent injunction to prohibit Exxon's continued use of its cartoon tiger in connection with the sale of food items on the ground that it unlawfully infringed upon and diluted Kellogg's "Tony The Tiger" mark. Exxon moved for summary judgment on the infringement claim based on its affirmative defense of acquiescence, and for partial summary judgment on Kellogg's claims of abandonment and progressive encroachment. The district court granted these motions and, holding that its decision rendered all remaining motions moot, dismissed Kellogg's bad faith infringement and dilution claims. *See Kellogg Co. v. Exxon Corp.*, 1998 U.S. Dist. LEXIS 22416, 50 U.S.P.Q.2D (BNA) 1499, 1507 (W.D. Tenn. 1998).

Kellogg raises the following assignments of error on appeal: (1) the district court improperly granted summary judgment because Exxon presented no evidence that Kellogg acquiesced in Exxon's use of its cartoon tiger in connection with the sale of non-petroleum products; (2) the district court improperly denied Kellogg's progressive encroachment claim because progressive encroachment is not limited by a requirement of "direct competition" and the district court failed to consider the likelihood of confusion between the marks; (3) the district court improperly denied Kellogg's abandonment claim because there are genuine issues of material fact with regard to whether Exxon's use of its cartoon tiger during the 1980s was bona fide or simply a sham to protect its rights in the mark; and (4) the district court improperly dismissed Kellogg's bad faith infringement and dilution claims as moot. In this appeal, Kellogg has abandoned its claim for damages and pursues only its claim for injunctive relief.

ANALYSIS

* * *

A.   Laches, Acquiescence and Progressive Encroachment

In its motion for summary judgment, Exxon asserted the affirmative defenses of laches and acquiescence. Although laches precludes a plaintiff from recovering damages, it does not bar injunctive relief. *See TWM Mfg. Co., Inc. v. Dura Corp.*, 592 F.2d 346, 349–50 (6th Cir. 1979) ("Laches alone does not foreclose a plaintiff's right in an infringement action to an injunction and damages after the filing of the suit. Only by proving the elements of estoppel may a defendant defeat such prospective relief."); *Tandy Corp. v. Malone & Hyde, Inc.*, 769 F.2d 362, 366 n.2 (6th Cir. 1985) (same). Because Kellogg withdrew its claim for actual and punitive damages, seeking injunctive relief only, the district court properly determined that laches was inapplicable and that Exxon must prove acquiescence.

Acquiescence, like laches, requires a "finding of conduct on the plaintiff's part that amounted to an assurance to the defendant, express or implied, that plaintiff would not assert his trademark rights against the defendant." *Elvis Presley Enter., Inc., v. Elvisly Yours, Inc.*, 936 F.2d 889, 894 (6th Cir. 1991) (quoting *Sweetheart Plastics, Inc. v. Detroit Forming, Inc.*, 743 F.2d 1039, 1046 (4th Cir. 1984)). Although both laches and acquiescence require proof that the party seeking to enforce its trademark rights has unreasonably delayed pursuing litigation and, as a result, materially prejudiced the alleged infringer, acquiescence requires more. *See Elvis*, 936 F.2d at 894 (holding that with acquiescence, "more is necessary than the ordinary requirement of showing unreasonable delay and prejudice to the defendant"); *Tandy*, 769 F.2d at 366 n.2 ("To deny injunctive relief in trademark litigation, . . . some affirmative conduct in the nature of an estoppel, or conduct amounting to 'virtual abandonment,' is necessary.") (internal citations omitted); *Sara Lee Corp. v. Kayser-Roth Corp.*, 81 F.3d 455, 462 (4th Cir. 1996) ("Although the doctrines of acquiescence and laches, in the context of trademark law, both connote consent by the owner to an infringing use of his mark, acquiescence implies active consent, while laches implies a merely passive consent."); *SCI Sys., Inc. v. Solidstate Controls, Inc.*, 748 F. Supp. 1257, 1262 (S.D. Ohio 1990) (same).

In *University of Pittsburgh v. Champion Prod., Inc.*, 686 F.2d 1040, 1044–45 (3d Cir. 1982), a decision relied upon by this Court in *Tandy*, the Third Circuit recognized that although mere delay by an injured party in bringing suit would not bar injunctive relief, "there is that narrow class of cases where the plaintiff's delay has been so outrageous, unreasonable and inexcusable as to constitute a virtual abandonment of its right." (citing *Anheuser-Busch, Inc. v. DuBois Brewing Co.*, 175 F.2d 370, 374 (3d Cir. 1949) ("Mere delay by the injured party in bringing suit would not bar injunctive relief. This doctrine, however, has its limits; for example, had there been a lapse of a hundred years or more, we think it highly dubious that any court of equity would grant injunctive relief against even a fraudulent infringer.")).

Implicit in a finding of laches or acquiescence is the presumption that an underlying claim for infringement existed at the time at which we begin to measure the plaintiff's delay. In *Brittingham v. Jenkins*, 914 F.2d 447 (4th Cir. 1990), the Fourth Circuit held:

> While the operation of laches depends upon the particular facts and circumstances of each case, the following factors ordinarily should be considered: (1) whether the owner of the mark knew of the infringing use; (2) whether the owner's delay in challenging the infringement of the mark was inexcusable or unreasonable; and (3) whether the infringing user was unduly prejudiced by the owner's delay.

Id. at 456. In *Sara Lee*, the Fourth Circuit recognized that a laches analysis "assumes the existence of an infringement for an extended period prior to the commencement of litigation." 81 F.3d at 462 (relying on *Brittingham* and holding that "to the extent that a plaintiff's prior knowledge may give rise to the defense of estoppel by laches, such knowledge must be of a pre-existing, *infringing* use of a mark."). In other words, when a defendant charged with trademark infringement avails itself of an acquiescence defense, we must presume the existence of some underlying infringement to which the plaintiff acquiesced, and any delay attributable to the plaintiff must be measured from the time at which the plaintiff knew or should have known that this infringement had ripened into a provable claim. *See Kason Indus., Inc. v. Component Hardware Group*, 120 F.3d 1199, 1206 (11th Cir. 1997) ("Delay is to be measured from the time at which the plaintiff knows or should know she has a provable claim for infringement."); *Gasser Chair Co. v. Infanti Chair Mfg. Corp.*, 60 F.3d 770, 777 (Fed. Cir. 1995) (holding that the trigger for delay begins when the plaintiff's "right ripens into one entitled to protection") (citation omitted).

Potential plaintiffs in trademark infringement cases steer a hazardous course between the Scylla of laches and acquiescence and the Charybdis of premature litigation. The Fourth Circuit articulated this quandary as follows:

> From the time that [defendant] Kayser-Roth first introduced its Leg Looks (R) products, [plaintiff] Sara Lee has been on the horns of a dilemma: If [the trademark owner] waits for substantial injury and evidence of actual confusion, it may be faced with a laches defense. If it rushes immediately into litigation, it may have little or no evidence of actual confusion and real commercial damage, may appear at a psychological disadvantage as "shooting from the hip" and may even face a counterclaim for overly aggressive use of litigation.

Sara Lee, 81 F.3d at 462 (internal quotation marks and citation omitted) (third alteration in original). This common predicament has given rise to the doctrine of progressive encroachment.

Progressive encroachment is relevant in assessing whether laches or acquiescence may be used to bar a plaintiff's trademark claim; it applies in cases where the defendant has engaged in some infringing use of its trademark—at least enough of an infringing use so that it may attempt to avail itself of a laches or acquiescence defense—but the plaintiff does not bring suit right away because the nature of defendant's infringement is such that the plaintiff's claim has yet to ripen into one sufficiently colorable to justify litigation.

. . .

Because the doctrines of laches and acquiescence must assume some underlying infringement, we recognize progressive encroachment as simply giving the plaintiff some latitude in the timing of its bringing suit, that is, waiting until the "likelihood of confusion looms large" to bring the action. *Sara Lee*, 81 F.3d at 462 (quoting Thomas McCarthy, McCarthy on Trademarks and Unfair Competition, § 31.06[2][a] (3d ed. 1995), renumbered as § 31.19 (4th ed. 1997)); *see also O. & W. Thum Co. v. Dickinson*, 245 F. 609, 623 (6th Cir. 1917) (recognizing that progressive encroachment is "a course [that] does not tend to arouse hostile action until it is fully developed"). Progressive encroachment is an offensive countermeasure to the affirmative defenses of laches and acquiescence; upon a finding of progressive encroachment, the delay upon which those defenses are premised is excused. In other words, progressive encroachment allows the plaintiff to demonstrate that although it might have been justified in bringing suit earlier but did not, certain factors now exist that have prompted it to do so.

. . . In evaluating a plaintiff's claim of progressive encroachment, a court must perform a likelihood of confusion analysis, informed by factors such as whether the defendant has brought itself more squarely into competition with the plaintiff, whether the defendant has made changes to its mark over the years so that it more closely resembles plaintiff's mark, whether the parties market to the same customers or area, and whether the parties sell products interchangeable in use.

In the case before us here, the district court held both that Kellogg had acquiesced in Exxon's use of the cartoon tiger and that Kellogg could not demonstrate progressive encroachment by Exxon on Kellogg's mark. We will address first the district court's holding that Kellogg acquiesced in Exxon's use of the cartoon tiger.

In granting Exxon's motion for summary judgment based on acquiescence, the district court held that Kellogg's remaining silent for a grossly extended period of time and refusing to facilitate the protection of its trademark constituted "conduct amounting to virtual abandonment" such that it acquiesced in Exxon's infringing use of its cartoon tiger. *See SCI*, 748 F. Supp. at 1262; *Tandy*, 769 F.2d at 366 n.2. Relying on the *Anheuser-Busch* decision, the district court found that Kellogg similarly was "grossly remiss" in that Exxon registered its "Whimsical Tiger" in 1965—with no opposition from Kellogg-and Kellogg did not file suit until 31 years later. *See Kellogg*, 50 U.S.P.Q.2D (BNA) at 1505.

We think that the district court erred in this conclusion. The failure to oppose Exxon's registration of its tiger and the lapse of time from that event until the filing of this action are not dispositive here. Although Exxon did in fact register its "Whimsical Tiger" trademark in 1965—with no opposition from Kellogg—Exxon's trademark registration was for use in connection with the sale of petroleum products, a product and product market with which Kellogg had no connection. Exxon had used its cartoon tiger to promote petroleum sales and Kellogg used its trademark to promote food sales; the two marks peaceably co-existed, each catering to its own market. Because proof of the likelihood of confusion is necessary in any trademark infringement claim, Kellogg was not obligated to bring suit at that time in order to protect its trademark. It is undisputed, however, that at some point after registering its cartoon tiger in 1965, Exxon moved into the non-petroleum market of food, beverages, and retail convenience stores and used its cartoon tiger in connection with those sales. The point at which Exxon established itself in this non-petroleum market was the point at which Kellogg knew or should have known that it now had a provable claim for infringement; it was at this point that Kellogg's duty to defend its trademark was triggered, and it is from this point that any delay must be measured for purposes of determining laches or acquiescence. We hold that Exxon's 1965 registration was insufficient to put Kellogg on notice of Exxon's later use of its cartoon tiger in connection with the sale of non-petroleum products. The district court's failure to distinguish between Exxon's sale of petroleum and non-petroleum products resulted in the clearly erroneous conclusion that Kellogg acquiesced in Exxon's use of its cartoon tiger to promote any and all of its products.

Although Kellogg originally challenged Exxon's use of its cartoon tiger in connection with both petroleum and non-petroleum products, Kellogg now seeks injunctive relief only to prohibit Exxon's continued use of its cartoon tiger in connection with food, beverages, and retail convenience stores.

> To defeat a suit for injunctive relief, a defendant must also prove elements of estoppel which requires more than a showing of mere silence on the part of the plaintiff; defendant must show that it had been misled by plaintiff through actual misrepresentations, affirmative acts of misconduct, intentional misleading silence, or conduct amounting to virtual abandonment of the trademark.

SCI, 748 F. Supp. at 1262. The record reflects a genuine factual dispute as to whether Kellogg was put on notice of such use by Exxon in the mid 1980s or the early 1990s; indeed, the evidence suggests that in 1992, when Kellogg requested examples of Exxon's then-current use of its cartoon tiger in the United States, Exxon did not include a single example of its cartoon tiger used in connection with the sale of food items, leading Kellogg to believe that Exxon's use of its cartoon tiger in the United States was limited to the promotion of petroleum products. But even if we were to assume for the sake of argument that Kellogg should have known as early as 1984, when Exxon opened its first convenience store, that Exxon was using the cartoon tiger to promote the sale of food products, Kellogg's failure to bring suit until 1996 was not "so outrageous, unreasonable and inexcusable as to constitute a virtual abandonment of its right" to seek injunctive relief with regard to the sale of non-petroleum products. *See University of Pittsburgh*, 686 F.2d at 1044–45. There simply is no evidence in this record that in waiting until 1996 to file its complaint, Kellogg actively consented to Exxon's use of its cartoon tiger in connection with the sale of non-petroleum products or that it engaged in some "affirmative conduct in the nature of an estoppel, or conduct amounting to 'virtual abandonment.'" *See Tandy*, 769 F.2d at 366 n.2 (internal citations omitted).

We therefore hold that, as a matter of law, Kellogg did not acquiesce in Exxon's use of its cartoon tiger in connection with the sale of non-petroleum products. Accordingly, we reverse the district court's grant of summary judgment to Exxon on the infringement claim and remand this matter for trial on the merits of that claim.

We turn next to the district court's conclusion, based largely on the *Prudential* decision, that "direct competition" was dispositive of Kellogg's progressive encroachment claim:

> Although Exxon has entered into the convenient market food sales arena, Exxon has not become a manufacturer or distributor of food items. Exxon's "product" is a retail convenience store engaged in the business of selling food on the premises of gasoline service stations. Kellogg's "product" for the purposes of this case is cereal. Although, Exxon may sell Kellogg's cereal product in the Tiger Mart or Tiger Express stores, this fact alone does not establish that the parties are competitors in the same or even a related market. Even if there is actual confusion between the Kellogg and Exxon cartoon tiger trademarks, connection between the parties' products and marketing channels for the sale of their products is too attenuated to support Kellogg's claim of progressive encroachment.

Kellogg, 50 U.S.P.Q.2D (BNA) at 1507. In ruling, without engaging in any analysis of the likelihood of confusion, that progressive encroachment requires "direct competition" of identical products, the district court erred as a matter of law. The district court held that (1) a plaintiff who failed to bring suit when it first learned of the defendant's infringing use of plaintiff's mark has acquiesced in the defendant's infringing use, but (2) the plaintiff does not have a meritorious claim of progressive encroachment because the parties' products are dissimilar and the connection between their marketing channels is attenuated. These two propositions are fundamentally irreconcilable. If the second were true, there could be no likelihood of confusion; without a likelihood of confusion, the plaintiff would not have a provable claim of infringement; in the absence of a provable claim of infringement, there would be no basis for the plaintiff's filing suit in the first place, and no infringing conduct in which the plaintiff could have acquiesced. Put another way, if there is sufficient similarity between the products and connection between the marketing channels to start the clock running on the defendant's affirmative defense of acquiescence, then there is sufficient similarity and connection to permit the plaintiff to counter that defense with a showing of progressive encroachment.

Here, we have found as a matter of law that Kellogg did not acquiesce in Exxon's use of the cartoon tiger. Because progressive encroachment has relevance only to counter Exxon's claim of acquiescence, the district court erred in treating progressive encroachment as a claim independent of Exxon's acquiescence defense. Therefore, we will vacate the district court's grant of summary judgment to Exxon with regard to progressive encroachment; we note that the district court need not engage in a progressive encroachment analysis on remand. . . .

CONCLUSION

Accordingly, we REVERSE the judgment of the district court granting summary judgment to Exxon on Kellogg's claims of infringement, dilution, and abandonment, we VACATE the grant of summary judgment to Exxon on Kellogg's claimed grounds of progressive encroachment, and REMAND the case for further proceedings consistent with this opinion.

NOTES FOR DISCUSSION

1. *Limitations and Laches.* Both the Patent Act and the Copyright Act contain express statutes of limitations. The Copyright Act requires civil actions for infringement to be brought within three years after the claim accrued. 17 U.S.C. § 507(b) (2015). The Patent Act requires civil actions for infringement to be brought within six years. 35 U.S.C. § 284 (2015). The Trademark Act, however, contains no statute of limitations. If a defendant's last use of an allegedly infringing mark occurred on March 1, 2009, when is the last date on which a plaintiff may bring an action for infringement? This type of issue does not arise very often in trademark law. Because damages are difficult to prove and therefore rarely awarded, once the alleged infringement has ceased, most plaintiffs are content to let the matter lie. However, if a plaintiff wanted to pursue its claims in this context, the period for filing a complaint would not be governed by laches. Rather, when a federal statute, such as the Trademark Act, lacks its own statute of limitations, courts will apply the most closely analogous state statute of limitations. *See Kason Indus v. Component Hardware Group*, 120 F.3d 1199, 1204 (11th Cir. 1997) (applying analogous state law statute of limitations to section 43(a) claims asserted under the Trademark Act). Thus, if the relevant state's statute of limitations for trademark infringement or unfair competition claims is three years, a plaintiff would need to bring any claims under the Trademark Act within three years of the defendant's last allegedly infringing act.

In contrast, what if a defendant began use of an allegedly infringing mark in 1990 and continues to use that mark to this day? In that case, the statute of limitations would not bar the filing of a complaint. Each use of the allegedly infringing mark would constitute its own act of infringement. The repeated use of the allegedly infringing mark gives rise to a continuing tort. Each use begins a new limitations period. So long as the defendant continued using the allegedly infringing mark, the plaintiff's complaint would not be barred by the statute of limitations. Instead, the issue would be whether the plaintiff's right to relief would be barred by laches, acquiescence, or estoppel.

2. *Laches and Injunctive Relief.* Both the *Conan Properties* court and the *Kellogg* court agree that laches, in the sense of an unreasonable delay in bringing a trademark lawsuit, will preclude an award of damages but will not

bar injunctive relief. This proposition has a long pedigree in trademark law, tracing all the way back to the Supreme Court's decision in *McLean v. Fleming*, 96 U.S. 245 (1878). In that case, the Court expressly found: "Acquiescence of long standing is proved in this case, and inexcusable laches in seeking redress, which show beyond all doubt that the complainant was not entitled to an account nor to a decree for gains or profits; but infringement having been proven, . . . the injunction was properly ordered." *Id.* at 258. Yet, outside of the trademark area, the Court has long held that the presence of laches bars the availability of injunctive relief. *See, e.g., City of Sherrill v. Oneida Indian Nation*, 544 U.S. 197, 217 (2005); *McKnight v. Taylor*, 42 U.S. (1 How.) 161, 168–69 (1843). Indeed, as a historical matter, the doctrine of laches originally developed in the Chancery Courts and applied exclusively to equitable remedies. In a recent copyright case, the Supreme Court relies on this history to hold that laches bars only equitable relief, and not monetary relief. *See Petrella v. Metro-Goldwyn-Meyer, Inc.*, 134 S.Ct. 1962 (2014). As a result, outside of the trademark area, inexcusable delay that prejudices a defendant generally bars the availability of injunctive relief. Moreover, in section 33(b) of the Trademark Act, Congress expressly recognized "laches, estoppels, and acquiescence" as applicable to claims for infringement and referred to them as "equitable principles." 15 U.S.C. § 1115(b)(9) (2015).

Why then is the rule seemingly different, and exactly backwards, in trademark law? Should a showing of unreasonable delay and prejudice be sufficient to bar the availability of injunctive relief in a trademark action? While some courts have followed the traditional laches doctrine in trademark cases, others are reluctant. Part of the reason for that reluctance is undoubtedly that trademark owners who bring claims of infringement are representing not only their own interests, but those of the consumers generally. If a defendant's behavior creates serious consumer confusion, consumers may not bring a claim under the Trademark Act because, as a general matter, they lack standing. *See, e.g., Made in the USA Found. v. Phillips Foods, Inc.*, 365 F.3d 278, 281 (4th Cir. 2004) (noting that "the several circuits that have dealt with the question are uniform in their categorical denial of Lanham Act standing to consumers."). Instead, consumers must rely on the trademark owner to police its marks in a way that protects consumers from confusion. If a plaintiff delays unreasonably in pursuing a claim, that may justify a refusal to vindicate the plaintiff's interests, but does it also justify a refusal to protect the consumers from confusion? Alternatively, in *Petrella*, the Supreme Court distinguished the longstanding interpretation of laches in trademark law on the grounds that Congress did not expressly provide a statute of limitations in the Trademark Act, while it did so in both the Patent and Copyright Acts. *Petrella*, 134 S.Ct. at 1974 n.15.

3. *Acquiescence versus Laches.* While both the *Conan Properties* and *Kellogg* courts state that laches will not bar the availability of injunctive relief, both agree that acquiescence will. What then is the difference between acquiescence and laches? Courts usually emphasize that acquiescence

requires some affirmative statement or conduct by the trademark owner indicating that it would not object to the defendant's use. In contrast, laches reflects mere silence or inaction by the plaintiff in the face of defendant's actions. The line between these is not always clear, however. For example, in *ProFitness Physical Therapy Ctr. v. Pro-Fit Orthopedic and Sports Physical Therapy P.C*, the defendant received a cease and desist letter from the plaintiff. 314 F.3d 62, 69 (2d Cir. 2002). In response, the defendant proposed a good-faith suggestion for a name change to avoid confusion, and stated that if no objection was made, defendant would proceed with the name change. *Id.* at 66. If the plaintiff fails to respond, the defendant adopts the proposed change, and the plaintiff nevertheless sues for infringement after a long delay, is this a case of acquiescence or laches? *Id.* at 68–69 (acquiescence).

4.   *Prejudice or Reliance.* To show laches, acquiescence, or estoppel, a defendant must establish that it was prejudiced by, or relied on, the plaintiff's actions or inaction. What is prejudice? Was Conans Pizza prejudiced by Conan Properties long delay in bringing the lawsuit and by Sprague de Camp's suggestions that its use was acceptable? In *Conan Properties*, the court declined to extend the defense of acquiescence and laches to the defendant's restaurants outside of Austin citing a lack of evidence showing prejudice. 752 F.2d at 153. Is this a justified conclusion? How would things have been different but-for CPI's delay? Assume that CPI had opposed the use of its mark from the onset. Instead of sending a signed picture wishing Conans Pizza good luck, CPI immediately sent a cease and desist letter. Two scenarios would have likely arisen. First, if Conans Pizza felt strongly enough that their use was not infringing, they could have taken the case to court and gotten an early adjudication of their rights. Or, second, if Conans Pizza was fearful of litigation or thought that defending the name and theme of their restaurant against CPI was not worthwhile, they could have picked another name for their restaurant. Had CPI objected promptly, and had Conans Pizza changed its name in response, then Conans Pizza would not be in the situation in which it currently finds itself. It could take its new name and proceed with a national franchising scheme. Because of CPI's delay, it spent years building up its business under the Conans name and now finds its potential growth stunted. So why was no prejudice found? A possible answer once again relates back to the main purpose of trademark law: consumer protection. While consumers in the Austin market were familiar with the Conans Pizza brand because of the restaurants' many years of operation in that city, consumers outside of Austin were not. As a result, if Conans Pizza followed through on its franchising plans, consumers outside of Austin would likely be confused as to the relationship between Conans Pizza and CPI. This suggests a different reason for the court's decision. CPI did delay unreasonably, and allowing CPI to block Conans Pizza's expansion was unfair, at least as between those two parties. But allowing Conans Pizza to expand nationally would be even more unfair to consumers.

5.   *The Scope of Laches and Progressive Encroachment.* In *Conan Properties*, the defendant had a viable laches or acquiescence claim as to Austin and wanted to use that to expand geographically. Similarly, in

Kellogg, the defendant had a viable laches or acquiescence claim as to the use of its cartoon tiger for gasoline and other non-food products, and wanted to use that to expand into food products. In each case, the court permitted the longstanding use to continue, but did not allow the expansion. When should a court allow some expansion in a junior user's use? Is it a function of the equities between the parties? Is it a function of consumer expectations and whether the new use increases the likelihood of confusion?

For example, how would you resolve the following case: Internet Specialties West ("Internet Specialties") and MDE are both internet service providers offering substantially similar services, including Internet access, e-mail, and web-hosting. Internet Specialties uses the domain name "ISWest.com", which it registered in May of 1996. MDE uses the domain name "ISPWest.com", which it registered in July of 1998.

Internet Specialties became aware of ISPWest's existence in late 1998. At that time, the companies did not offer equal services: Internet Specialties offered dial-up, DSL and T-1 Internet access nationwide, whereas MDE offered only dial-up internet access and only in southern California. Internet Specialties' CEO testified that his company was not concerned about competition from MDE at that time, because it did not offer DSL and because the general market for Internet technology start-ups was so volatile that most companies were expected to go out of business.

MDE expanded to nation-wide service in 2002, and began offering DSL in mid-2004. In response, Internet Specialties filed suit alleging trademark infringement in early 2005. Can MDE establish laches or acquiescence? Can Internet Specialties establish progressive encroachment? *See Internet Specialties West, Inc. v. Milon-DiGiorgio Enter., Inc.*, 559 F.3d 985, 992 (9th Cir. 2009) (rejecting progressive encroachment argument—"[o]ffering DSL was not an expansion into a new market, but rather a natural growth of [MDE's] existing business," but also rejecting laches defense for lack of prejudice).

D. THE FIRST AMENDMENT

MATTEL, INC. v. MCA RECORDS, INC.

296 F.3d 894 (9th Cir. 2002)

KOZINSKI, CIRCUIT JUDGE

If this were a sci-fi melodrama, it might be called Speech-Zilla meets Trademark Kong.

I

Barbie was born in Germany in the 1950s as an adult collector's item. Over the years, Mattel transformed her from a doll that resembled a "German street walker," as she originally appeared, into a glamorous, long-legged blonde. Barbie has been labeled both the ideal American woman and a bimbo. She has survived attacks both psychic (from feminists critical of her fictitious figure) and physical (more than 500 professional makeovers). She remains a symbol of American girlhood, a public figure who graces the aisles of toy stores throughout the country and beyond. With Barbie, Mattel created not just a toy but a cultural icon.

With fame often comes unwanted attention. Aqua is a Danish band that has, as yet, only dreamed of attaining Barbie-like status. In 1997, Aqua produced the song Barbie Girl on the album *Aquarium*. In the song, one bandmember impersonates Barbie, singing in a high-pitched, doll-like voice; another bandmember, calling himself Ken, entices Barbie to "go party." (The lyrics are in the Appendix.) Barbie Girl singles sold well and, to Mattel's dismay, the song made it onto Top 40 music charts.

Mattel brought this lawsuit against the music companies who produced, marketed and sold Barbie Girl: MCA Records, Inc., Universal Music International Ltd., Universal Music A/S, Universal Music & Video Distribution, Inc. and MCA Music Scandinavia AB (collectively, "MCA"). MCA in turn challenged the district court's jurisdiction under the Lanham Act and its personal jurisdiction over the foreign defendants, Universal Music International Ltd., Universal Music A/S and MCA Music Scandinavia AB (hereinafter "foreign defendants"); MCA also brought a defamation claim against Mattel for statements Mattel made about MCA while this lawsuit was pending. The district court concluded it had jurisdiction over the foreign defendants and under the Lanham Act, and granted MCA's motion for summary judgment on Mattel's federal and state-law claims for trademark infringement and dilution. The district court also granted Mattel's motion for summary judgment on MCA's defamation claim.

Mattel appeals the district court's ruling that Barbie Girl is a parody of Barbie and a nominative fair use; that MCA's use of the term Barbie is not likely to confuse consumers as to Mattel's affiliation with Barbie Girl or dilute the Barbie mark; and that Mattel cannot assert an unfair competition claim under the Paris Convention for the Protection of Industrial Property. MCA cross-appeals the grant of summary judgment on its defamation claim as well as the district court's jurisdictional holdings.

II

A. All three foreign defendants are affiliated members of Universal Music Group and have an active relationship with each other and with domestic members of the Group. Defendants entered into cross-licensing agreements and developed a coordinated plan to distribute the Barbie Girl song in the United States (including California), and sent promotional copies of the Barbie Girl single and the *Aquarium* album to the United States (including California). This conduct was expressly aimed at, and allegedly caused harm in, California, Mattel's principal place of business. *See Panavision Int'l, L.P.* v. *Toeppen*, 141 F.3d 1316, 1321 (9th Cir. 1998). Mattel's trademark claims would not have arisen "but for" the conduct foreign defendants purposefully directed toward California, and jurisdiction over the foreign defendants, who are represented by the same counsel and closely associated with the domestic defendants, is reasonable. *See id.* at 1321–22. The district court did not err in asserting specific personal jurisdiction over the foreign defendants.

B. Sales of the *Aquarium* album worldwide had a sufficient effect on American foreign commerce, and Mattel suffered monetary injury in the United States from those sales. *See Ocean Garden, Inc.* v. *Marktrade Co.*, 953 F.2d 500, 503 (9th Cir. 1991). Moreover, Mattel's claim is more closely tied to interests of American foreign commerce than it is to the commercial interests of other nations: Mattel's principal place of business is in California, the foreign defendants are closely related to the domestic defendants, and Mattel sought relief only for defendants' sales in the United States. *See Star-Kist Foods, Inc.* v. *P.J. Rhodes & Co.*, 769 F.2d 1393, 1395–96 (9th Cir. 1985). The district court properly exercised extraterritorial jurisdiction under the Lanham Act.

III

A. A trademark is a word, phrase or symbol that is used to identify a manufacturer or sponsor of a good or the provider of a service. *See New Kids on the Block* v. *News Am. Publ'g, Inc.*, 971 F.2d 302, 305 (9th Cir. 1992). It's the owner's way of preventing others from duping consumers into buying a product they mistakenly believe is sponsored by the trademark owner. A trademark "informs people that trademarked products come from the same source." *Id.* at 305 n.2. Limited to this core purpose—avoiding confusion in the marketplace—a trademark owner's property rights play well with the First Amendment. "Whatever first amendment rights you may have in calling the brew you make in your bathtub 'Pepsi' are easily outweighed by the buyer's interest in not being fooled into buying it." *Trademarks Unplugged*, 68 N.Y.U.L. Rev. 960, 973 (1993).

The problem arises when trademarks transcend their identifying purpose. Some trademarks enter our public discourse and become an integral part of our vocabulary. How else do you say that something's "the Rolls Royce of its class?" What else is a quick fix, but a Band-Aid? Does the average consumer know to ask for aspirin as "acetyl salicylic acid?" *See Bayer Co.* v. *United Drug Co.*, 272 F. 505, 510 (S.D.N.Y. 1921). Trademarks often fill in gaps in our vocabulary and add a contemporary flavor to our expressions. Once imbued with such expressive value, the trademark becomes a word in our language and assumes a role outside the bounds of trademark law.

Our likelihood-of-confusion test, see *AMF Inc.* v. *Sleekcraft Boats*, 599 F.2d 341, 348–49 (9th Cir. 1979), generally strikes a comfortable balance between the trademark owner's property rights and the public's expressive interests. But when a trademark owner asserts a right to control how we express ourselves—when we'd find it difficul to describe the product any other way (as in the case of aspirin), or when the mark (like Rolls Royce) has taken on an expressive meaning apart from its source-identifying function—applying the traditional test fails to account for the full weight of the public's interest in free expression.

The First Amendment may offer little protection for a competitor who labels its commercial good with a confusingly similar mark, but "trademark rights do not entitle the owner to quash an unauthorized use of the mark by another who is communicating ideas or expressing points of view." *L.L. Bean, Inc.* v. *Drake Publishers, Inc.*, 811 F.2d 26, 29 (1st Cir. 1987). Were we to ignore the expressive value that some marks assume, trademark rights would grow to encroach upon the zone protected by the First Amendment. *See Yankee Publ'g, Inc.* v. *News Am. Publ'g, Inc.*, 809 F. Supp. 267, 276 (S.D.N.Y. 1992) ("When unauthorized use of another's mark is part of a communicative message and not a source identifier, the First Amendment is implicated in opposition to the trademark right."). Simply put, the trademark owner does not have the right to control public discourse whenever the public imbues his mark with a meaning beyond its source-identifying function. *See Anti-Monopoly, Inc.* v. *Gen. Mills Fun Group*, 611 F.2d 296, 301 (9th Cir. 1979) ("It is the source-denoting function [*901] which trademark laws protect, and nothing more.").

B. There is no doubt that MCA uses Mattel's mark: Barbie is one half of Barbie Girl. But Barbie Girl is the title of a song about Barbie and Ken, a reference that—at least today—can only be to Mattel's famous couple. We expect a title to describe the underlying work, not to identify the producer, and Barbie Girl does just that.

The Barbie Girl title presages a song about Barbie, or at least a girl like Barbie. The title conveys a message to consumers about what they can expect to discover in the song itself; it's a quick glimpse of Aqua's take on their own song. The lyrics confirm this: The female singer, who calls herself Barbie, is "a Barbie girl, in [her] Barbie world." She tells her male counterpart (named Ken), "Life in plastic, it's fantastic. You can brush my hair, undress me everywhere/Imagination, life is your creation." And off they go to "party." The song pokes fun at Barbie and the values that Aqua contends she represents. *See Cliffs Notes, Inc.* v. *Bantam Doubleday Dell Publ'g Group*, 886 F.2d 490, 495–96 (2d Cir. 1989). The female singer explains, "I'm a blond bimbo girl, in a fantasy world/Dress me up, make it tight, I'm your dolly."

The song does not rely on the Barbie mark to poke fun at another subject but targets Barbie herself. *See Campbell* v. *Acuff-Rose Music, Inc.*, 510 U.S. 569, 580, 127 L.Ed.2d 500, 114 S.Ct. 1164 (1994); *see also Dr.*

Seuss Ents., L.P. v. *Penguin Books USA, Inc.*, 109 F.3d 1394, 1400 (9th Cir. 1997). This case is therefore distinguishable from *Dr. Seuss*, where we held that the book *The Cat NOT in the Hat!* borrowed Dr. Seuss's trademarks and lyrics to get attention rather than to mock *The Cat in the Hat!* The defendant's use of the Dr. Seuss trademarks and copyrighted works had "no critical bearing on the substance or style of" *The Cat in the Hat!*, and therefore could not claim First Amendment protection. *Id.* at 1401. *Dr. Seuss* recognized that, where an artistic work targets the original and does not merely borrow another's property to get attention, First Amendment interests weigh more heavily in the balance. *See id.* at 1400–02; *see also Harley-Davidson, Inc.* v. *Grottanelli*, 164 F.3d 806, 812–13 (2d Cir. 1999) (a parodist whose expressive work aims its parodic commentary at a trademark is given considerable leeway, but a claimed parodic use that makes no comment on the mark is not a permitted trademark parody use).

The Second Circuit has held that "in general the [Lanham] Act should be construed to apply to artistic works only where the public interest in avoiding consumer confusion outweighs the public interest in free expression." *Rogers* v. *Grimaldi*, 875 F.2d 994, 999 (2d Cir. 1989); *see also Cliffs Notes*, 886 F.2d at 494 (quoting *Rogers*, 875 F.2d at 999). *Rogers* considered a challenge by the actress Ginger Rogers to the film *Ginger and Fred*. The movie told the story of two Italian cabaret performers who made a living by imitating Ginger Rogers and Fred Astaire. Rogers argued that the film's title created the false impression that she was associated with it.

At first glance, Rogers certainly had a point. Ginger was her name, and Fred was her dancing partner. If a pair of dancing shoes had been labeled Ginger and Fred, a dancer might have suspected that Rogers was associated with the shoes (or at least one of them), just as Michael Jordan has endorsed Nike sneakers that claim to make you fly through the air. But Ginger and Fred was not a brand of shoe; it was the title of a movie and, for the reasons explained by the Second Circuit, deserved to be treated differently.

A title is designed to catch the eye and to promote the value of the underlying work. Consumers expect a title to communicate a message about the book or movie, but they do not expect it to identify the publisher or producer. *See Application of Cooper*, 45 C.C.P.A. 923, 254 F.2d 611, 615–16 (C.C.P.A. 1958) (A "title . . . identifies a specific literary work, . . . and is not associated in the public mind with the . . . manufacturer." (internal quotation marks omitted)). If we see a painting titled "Campbell's Chicken Noodle Soup," we're unlikely to believe that Campbell's has branched into the art business. Nor, upon hearing Janis Joplin croon "Oh Lord, won't you buy me a Mercedes-Benz?," would we suspect that she and the carmaker had entered into a joint venture. A title tells us something about the underlying work but seldom speaks to its origin:

> Though consumers frequently look to the title of a work to determine what it is about, they do not regard titles of artistic works in the same way as the names of ordinary commercial products. Since consumers expect an ordinary product to be what the name says it is, we apply the Lanham Act with some rigor to prohibit names that misdescribe such goods. But most consumers are well aware that they cannot judge a book solely by its title any more than by its cover.

Rogers, 875 F.2d at 1000 (citations omitted).

Rogers concluded that literary titles do not violate the Lanham Act "unless the title has no artistic relevance to the underlying work whatsoever, or, if it has some artistic relevance, unless the title explicitly misleads as to the source or the content of the work." *Id.* at 999 (footnote omitted). We agree with the Second Circuit's analysis and adopt the *Rogers* standard as our own.

Applying *Rogers* to our case, we conclude that MCA's use of Barbie is not an infringement of Mattel's trademark. Under the first prong of *Rogers*, the use of Barbie in the song title clearly is relevant to the underlying work, namely, the song itself. As noted, the song is about Barbie and the values Aqua claims she represents. The song title does not explicitly mislead as to the source of the work; it does not, explicitly or otherwise, suggest that it was produced by Mattel. The *only* indication that Mattel might be associated with the song is the use of Barbie in the title; if this were enough to satisfy this prong of the *Rogers* test, it would render *Rogers* a nullity. We therefore agree with the district court that MCA was entitled to summary judgment on this ground. We need not consider whether the district court was correct in holding that MCA was also entitled to summary judgment because its use of Barbie was a nominative fair use.

IV

Mattel separately argues that, under the Federal Trademark Dilution Act ("FTDA"), MCA's song dilutes the Barbie mark in two ways: It diminishes the mark's capacity to identify and distinguish Mattel products, and tarnishes the mark because the song is inappropriate for young girls. *See* 15 U.S.C. § 1125(c); *see also Panavision Int'l, L.P.* v. *Toeppen*, 141 F.3d 1316, 1324 (9th Cir. 1998).

"Dilution" refers to the "whittling away of the value of a trademark" when it's used to identify different products. 4 J. Thomas McCarthy, *McCarthy on Trademarks and Unfair Competition* § 24.67 at 24–120; § 24.70 at 24–122 (2001). For example, Tylenol snowboards, Netscape sex shops and Harry Potter dry cleaners would all weaken the "commercial magnetism" of these marks and diminish their ability to evoke their original associations. Ralph S. Brown, Jr., *Advertising and the Public Interest: Legal Protection of Trade Symbols*, 57 Yale L.J. 1165, 1187 (1948), *reprinted in* 108 Yale L.J. 1619 (1999). These uses dilute the selling power of these trademarks by blurring their "uniqueness and singularity," Frank I. Schechter, *The Rational Basis of Trademark Protection*, 40 Harv. L. Rev. 813, 831 (1927), and/or by tarnishing them with negative associations.

By contrast to trademark infringement, the injury from dilution usually occurs when consumers *aren't* confused about the source of a product: Even if no one suspects that the maker of analgesics has entered into the snowboard business, the Tylenol mark will now bring to mind two products, not one. Whereas trademark law targets "interference with the source signaling function" of trademarks, dilution protects owners "from an appropriation of or free riding on" the substantial investment that they have made in their marks. *I.P. Lund Trading ApS* v. *Kohler Co.*, 163 F.3d 27, 50 (1st Cir. 1998).

Originally a creature of state law, dilution received nationwide recognition in 1996 when Congress amended the Lanham Act by enacting the FTDA. The statute protects "the owner of a famous mark . . . against another person's commercial use in commerce of a mark or trade name, if such use begins after the mark has become famous and causes dilution of the distinctive quality of the mark." 15 U.S.C. § 1125(c). Dilutive uses are prohibited unless they fall within one of the three statutory exemptions discussed below. *See* pp. 10495–96 *infra*. For a lucid and scholarly discussion of the statutory terms, as well as the purposes of the federal dilution statute, we refer the reader to Judge Leval's opinion in *Nabisco, Inc.* v. *PF Brands, Inc.*, 191 F.3d 208, 214–17 (2d Cir. 1999). Barbie easily qualifies under the FTDA as a famous and distinctive mark, and reached this status long before MCA began to market the Barbie Girl song. The commercial success of Barbie Girl establishes beyond dispute that the Barbie mark satisfies each of these elements.

We are also satisfied that the song amounts to a "commercial use in commerce." Although this statutory language is ungainly, its meaning seems clear: It refers to a use of a famous and distinctive mark to sell goods other than those produced or authorized by the mark's owner. *Panavision*, 141 F.3d at 1324–25. That is precisely what MCA did with the Barbie mark: It created and sold to consumers in the marketplace commercial products (the Barbie Girl single and the *Aquarium* album) that bear the Barbie mark.

MCA's use of the mark is dilutive. MCA does not dispute that, while a reference to Barbie would previously have brought to mind only Mattel's doll, after the song's popular success, some consumers hearing Barbie's name will think of both the doll and the song, or perhaps of the song only. This is a classic blurring injury and is in no way diminished by the fact that the song itself refers back to Barbie the doll. To be dilutive, use of the mark need not bring to mind the junior user alone. The distinctiveness of the mark is diminished if the mark no longer brings to mind the senior user alone.

We consider next the applicability of the FTDA's three statutory exemptions. These are uses that, though potentially dilutive, are nevertheless permitted: comparative advertising; news reporting and commentary; and noncommercial use. 15 U.S.C. § 1125(c)(4)(B). The first two exemptions clearly do not apply; only the exemption for noncommercial use need detain us.

A "noncommercial use" exemption, on its face, presents a bit of a conundrum because it seems at odds with the earlier requirement that the junior use be a "commercial use in commerce." If a use has to be commercial in order to be dilutive, how then can it also be noncommercial so as to satisfy the exception of section 1125(c)(4)(B)? If the term "commercial use" had the same meaning in both provisions, this would eliminate one of the three statutory exemptions defined by this subsection, because any use found to be dilutive would, of necessity, not be noncommercial.

Such a reading of the statute would also create a constitutional problem, because it would leave the FTDA with no First Amendment protection for dilutive speech other than comparative advertising and news reporting. This would be a serious problem because the primary (usually exclusive) remedy for dilution is an injunction. As noted above, tension with the First Amendment also exists in the trademark context, especially where the mark has assumed an expressive function beyond mere identification of a product or service. *See* pp. 10487–89 *supra; New Kids on the Block* v. *News Am. Publ'g, Inc.*, 971 F.2d 302, 306–08 (9th Cir. 1992). These concerns apply with greater force in the dilution context because dilution lacks two very significant limitations that reduce the tension between trademark law and the First Amendment.

First, depending on the strength and distinctiveness of the mark, trademark law grants relief only against uses that are likely to confuse. *See* 5 *McCarthy* § 30:3 at 30–8 to 30–11; *Restatement* § 35 cmt. c at 370. A trademark injunction is usually limited to uses within one industry or several related industries. Dilution law is the antithesis of trademark law in this respect, because it seeks to protect the mark from association in the public's mind with wholly unrelated goods and services. The more remote the good or service associated with the junior use, the more likely it is to cause dilution rather than trademark infringement. A dilution injunction, by contrast to a trademark injunction, will generally sweep across broad vistas of the economy.

Second, a trademark injunction, even a very broad one, is premised on the need to prevent consumer confusion. This consumer protection rationale—averting what is essentially a fraud on the consuming public—is wholly consistent with the theory of the First Amendment, which does not protect commercial fraud. *Cent. Hudson Gas & Elec.* v. *Pub. Serv. Comm'n*, 447 U.S. 557, 566, 65 L.Ed.2d 341, 100 S.Ct. 2343 (1980); *see Thompson* v. *W. States Med. Ctr.*, 535 U.S. 357, 152 L.Ed.2d 563, 122 S.Ct. 1497 (2002) (applying *Central Hudson*). Moreover, avoiding harm to consumers is an important interest that is independent of the senior user's interest in protecting its business.

Dilution, by contrast, does not require a showing of consumer confusion, 15 U.S.C. § 1127, and dilution injunctions therefore lack the built-in First Amendment compass of trademark injunctions. In addition, dilution law protects only the distinctiveness of the mark, which is inherently less weighty than the dual interest of protecting trademark owners and avoiding harm to consumers that is at the heart of every trademark claim.

Fortunately, the legislative history of the FTDA suggests an interpretation of the "noncommercial use" exemption that both solves our interpretive dilemma and diminishes some First Amendment concerns: "Noncommercial use" refers to a use that consists entirely of noncommercial, or fully constitutionally protected, speech. *See* 2 Jerome Gilson et al., *Trademark Protection and Practice* § 5.12[1][c][vi] at 5–240 (this exemption "is intended to prevent the courts from enjoining speech that has been recognized to be [fully] constitutionally protected," "such as parodies"). Where, as here, a statute's plain meaning "produces an absurd, and perhaps unconstitutional, result[, it is] entirely appropriate to consult all public materials, including the background of [the statute] and the legislative history of its adoption." *Green* v. *Bock Laundry Mach. Co.*, 490 U.S. 504, 527, 104 L.Ed.2d 557, 109 S.Ct. 1981 (1989) (Scalia, J., concurring).

The legislative history bearing on this issue is particularly persuasive. First, the FTDA's sponsors in both the House and the Senate were aware of the potential collision with the First Amendment if the statute authorized injunctions against protected speech. Upon introducing the counterpart bills, sponsors in each house explained that the proposed law "will not prohibit or threaten noncommercial expression, such as parody, satire, editorial and other forms of expression that are not a part of a commercial transaction." 141 Cong. Rec. S19306–10, S19310 (daily ed. Dec. 29, 1995) (statement of Sen. Hatch); 141 Cong. Rec. H14317–01, H14318 (daily ed. Dec. 12, 1995) (statement of Rep. Moorhead). The House Judiciary Committee agreed in its report on the FTDA. H.R. Rep. No. 104–374, at 4 (1995), *reprinted in* 1995 U.S.C.C.A.N. 1029, 1031 ("The bill will not prohibit or threaten 'noncommercial' expression, as that term has been defined by the courts.").

The FTDA's section-by-section analysis presented in the House and Senate suggests that the bill's sponsors relied on the "noncommercial use" exemption to allay First Amendment concerns. H.R. Rep. No. 104–374, at 8, *reprinted in* 1995 U.S.C.C.A.N. 1029, 1035 (the exemption "expressly incorporates the concept of 'commercial' speech from the 'commercial speech' doctrine, and proscribes dilution actions that seek to enjoin use of famous marks in 'non-commercial' uses (such as consumer product reviews)"); 141 Cong. Rec. S19306–10, S19311 (daily ed. Dec. 29, 1995) (the exemption "is consistent with existing case law[, which] recognizes that the use of marks in certain forms of artistic and expressive speech is protected by the First Amendment"). At the request of one of the bill's sponsors, the section-by-section analysis was printed in the Congressional Record. 141 Cong. Rec. S19306–10, S19311 (daily ed. Dec. 29, 1995). Thus, we know that this interpretation of the exemption was before the Senate when the FTDA was passed, and that no senator rose to dispute it.

To determine whether Barbie Girl falls within this exemption, we look to our definition of commercial speech under our First Amendment caselaw. *See* H.R. Rep. No. 104–374, at 8, *reprinted in* 1995 U.S.C.C.A.N. 1029, 1035 (the exemption "expressly incorporates the concept of 'commercial' speech from the 'commercial speech' doctrine"); 141 Cong. Rec. S19306–10, S19311 (daily ed. Dec. 29, 1995) (the exemption "is consistent with existing [First Amendment] case law"). "Although the boundary between commercial and noncommercial speech has yet to be clearly delineated, the 'core notion of commercial speech' is that it 'does no more than propose a commercial transaction.'" *Hoffman* v. *Capital Cities/ABC, Inc.*, 255 F.3d 1180, 1184 (9th Cir. 2001) (quoting *Bolger* v. *Youngs Drug Prods Corp.*, 463 U.S. 60, 66, 77 L.Ed.2d 469, 103 S.Ct. 2875 (1983)). If speech is not "purely commercial"—that is, if it does more than propose a commercial transaction—then it is entitled to full First Amendment protection. 255 F.3d at 1185–86 (internal quotation marks omitted).

In *Hoffman*, a magazine published an article featuring digitally altered images from famous films. Computer artists modified shots of Dustin Hoffman, Cary Grant, Marilyn Monroe and others to put the actors in famous designers' spring fashions; a still of Hoffman from the movie "Tootsie" was altered so that he appeared to be wearing a Richard Tyler evening gown and Ralph Lauren heels. Hoffman, who had not given permission, sued under the Lanham Act and for violation of his right to publicity. *Id.* at 1183.

The article featuring the altered image clearly served a commercial purpose: "to draw attention to the for-profit magazine in which it appeared" and to sell more copies. *Id.* at 1186. Nevertheless, we held that the article was fully protected under the First Amendment because it included protected expression: "humor" and "visual and verbal editorial comment on classic films and famous actors." *Id.* at 1185 (internal quotation marks omitted). Because its commercial purpose was "inextricably entwined with [these] expressive elements," the article and accompanying photographs enjoyed full First Amendment protection. *Id.*

Hoffman controls: Barbie Girl is not purely commercial speech, and is therefore fully protected. To be sure, MCA used Barbie's name to sell copies of the song. However, as we've already observed, the song also lampoons the Barbie image and comments humorously on the cultural values Aqua claims she represents. Use of the Barbie mark in the song Barbie Girl therefore falls within the noncommercial use exemption to the FTDA. For precisely the same reasons, use of the mark in the song's title is also exempted. . . .

VI

After Mattel filed suit, Mattel and MCA employees traded barbs in the press. When an MCA spokeswoman noted that each album included a disclaimer saying that Barbie Girl was a "social commentary [that was] not created or approved by the makers of the doll," a Mattel representative responded by saying, "That's unacceptable. . . . It's akin to a bank robber handing a note of apology to a teller during a heist. [It] neither diminishes the severity of the crime, nor does it make it legal." He later characterized the song as a "theft" of "another company's property."

MCA filed a counterclaim for defamation based on the Mattel representative's use of the words "bank robber," "heist," "crime" and "theft." But all of these are variants of the invective most often hurled at accused infringers, namely "piracy." No one hearing this accusation understands intellectual property owners to be saying that infringers are nautical cutthroats with eyepatches and peg legs who board galleons to plunder cargo. In context, all these terms are nonactionable "rhetorical hyperbole," *Gilbrook* v. *City of Westminster*, 177 F.3d 839, 863 (9th Cir. 1999). The parties are advised to chill.

AFFIRMED.

APPENDIX

"Barbie Girl" by Aqua

-Hiya Barbie!

-Hi Ken!

-You wanna go for a ride?

-Sure, Ken!

-Jump in!

-Ha ha ha ha!

(CHORUS:)

I'm a Barbie girl, in my Barbie world

Life in plastic, it's fantastic

You can brush my hair, undress me everywhere

Imagination, life is your creation

Come on Barbie, let's go party!

(CHORUS) I'm a blonde bimbo girl, in a fantasy world

Dress me up, make it tight, I'm your dolly

You're my doll, rock and roll, feel the glamour in pink

Kiss me here, touch me there, hanky-panky

You can touch, you can play

If you say "I'm always yours," ooh ooh

CHORUS)

(BRIDGE:)

Come on, Barbie, let's go party, ah ah ah yeah

Come on, Barbie, let's go party, ooh ooh, ooh ooh

Come on, Barbie, let's go party, ah ah ah yeah

Come on, Barbie, let's go party, ooh ooh, ooh ooh

Make me walk, make me talk, do whatever you please

I can act like a star, I can beg on my knees

Come jump in, be my friend, let us do it again

Hit the town, fool around, let's go party

You can touch, you can play

You can say "I'm always yours"

You can touch, you can play

You can say "I'm always yours"

(BRIDGE)

(CHORUS x2)

(BRIDGE)

-Oh, I'm having so much fun!

-Well, Barbie, we're just getting started!

-Oh, I love you Ken!

NOTES FOR DISCUSSION

1. *The Dilution Revision Act of 2006.* As discussed in Chapter 8, Congress amended the Federal Trademark Dilution Act in 2006 to resolve a number of disputes that had arisen concerning its application. As part of that Act, Congress added section 43(c)(3)(A)(ii) excluding from dilution liability "any fair use, including a nominative or descriptive fair use, . . . identifying and parodying, criticizing, or commenting upon the famous mark owner or the goods or services of the famous mark owner." Does this section effectively codify the outcome in *Mattel v. MCA?* Or does the language "any fair use" impose additional requirements? For example, does the song Barbie Girl use the word Barbie too repetitively to qualify as a nominative fair use?

2. *Parody, Satire, and "Noncommercial Use."* In the 2006 Amendments, Congress retained the language excluding dilution liability for any "noncommercial use of a mark." How did the Ninth Circuit define a "noncommercial use" in *Mattel?* In *Dr. Seuss Enters., L.P. v. Penguin Books USA, Inc.*, an author wrote "a poetic account of the O.J. Simpson double murder trial entitled *The Cat NOT in the Hat! A Parody by Dr. Juice.*" 109 F.3d 1394, 1396 (9th Cir. 1997). When Dr. Seuss Enterprises sued, alleging copyright and trademark infringement, the district court granted a preliminary injunction on both grounds. The Ninth Circuit affirmed the preliminary injunction. With respect to the trademark issues, the *Dr. Seuss* court found that confusion was likely, and rejected the defendant's parody claim, stating that *The Cat NOT in the Hat!* intended "to capitalize on a famous mark's popularity for the defendant's own use." *Id.* at 1406. The *Dr. Seuss* court also rejected the defendant's contention that the First Amendment protected the defendant's use. *Id.* at 1403 n.11.

With respect to the trademark issues, why do the *Dr. Seuss* case and the *Mattel* case come out differently? Judge Kozinski distinguishes the *Dr. Seuss* decision on the grounds that *The Cat NOT in the Hat!* was not making fun of, or parodying, the *The Cat in the Hat*, but using its style to make fun of the OJ Simpson murder trial. In contrast, Aqua was making fun of Barbie herself. Why should this distinction matter in trademark law?

It certainly matters in copyright's fair use analysis. *See Campbell v. Acuff-Rose Music*, 510 U.S. 569, 580–81 (1994) (giving extra fair use leeway to parody—borrowing to comment on the original work, but not for satire— borrowing that has "no critical bearing on the substance or style of the original"). The reasons for granting parody, but not satire, extra fair use leeway in copyright law are two-fold. First, "[p]arody needs to mimic an original to make its point, and so has some claim to use the creation of its victim's (or collective victims') imagination, whereas satire can stand on its own two feet and so requires justification for the very act of borrowing." *Id.* Second, copyright owners are unlikely to license their works for "critical reviews or lampoons of their own productions." *Id.* at 592.

The distinction between parody and satire thus makes reasonable sense in terms of copyright's incentives story and as an attempt to encourage both original works and parodies of those works, but how does the distinction relate to trademark law and its purposes? Are consumers less likely to perceive sponsorship or endorsement in the *Mattel* case, than in the *Dr. Seuss* case, because Aqua is making fun of Barbie herself? Does the *Mattel* court cite survey or other factual evidence that would support such a distinction? If we did an identical survey for the two cases, asking in each whether respondents believed that the defendants had obtained permission to use their titles, or whether the plaintiff "went along" with the defendant's use, do you believe the percentages of confused respondents would differ significantly?

Similarly, in First Amendment terms, is one use more expressive than the other? Does one use merely propose a commercial transaction, while the other does more? As with trademark law, the key question is: Why should the target of a defendant's humor make a difference in the First Amendment analysis? Does the target of the defendant's ridicule determine whether speech is noncommercial?

3. *Balancing Confusion Against Free Speech?* Following *Rogers v. Grimaldi*, the *Mattel* court insists that we must apply a different, heightened standard of confusion, given the First Amendment interests in book, movie, and here, song titles. What is the First Amendment or free speech interest in a song title? Certainly, it is not political speech, which lies at the core of the First Amendment's protection of speech. Is the title of a song more "speech" than the subject of a newspaper poll? Is it more speech than the words "Boston Marathon" on a t-shirt?

Assuming that there is some special free speech interest associated with titles, how do we balance it against the potential confusion a given use creates? Consider the facts in *Rogers v. Grimaldi*. How many consumers do you believe went to see the movie "Ginger and Fred" expecting a movie about Ginger Rogers and Fred Astaire? What free speech interest justifies a court in allowing a defendant to create such confusion? Would requiring Grimaldi to use a different title, such as "Amelia and Pippo: The Italian Ginger and Fred," frustrate Grimaldi's legitimate speech interests? Would it cause fewer consumers to purchase tickets for the movie based upon a mistake as to its subject matter or Ginger Roger's endorsement of the film?

Assume that a movie director wants to create a porn film and have his story revolve around a woman who wants to try out for the Dallas Cowboys Cheerleaders. In the final, climatic scene of the movie, the director has the woman appear, albeit briefly, in the distinctive costume of a Dallas Cowboys Cheerleader. Should such a use constitute trademark infringement? Are consumers more likely to perceive sponsorship or endorsement from such use than from Aqua's use? Is the movie director's use less protected as speech? Does it merely propose a commercial transaction? Is it more expressive or less expressive than Aqua's use? Should the two cases come out the same or differently? *See Dallas Cowboys Cheerleaders, Inc. v. Pussycat Cinema, Ltd.*, 604 F.2d 200, 207 (2d Cir. 1979) (finding a likelihood of confusion and rejecting a First Amendment defense).

With respect to the First Amendment, the *Dallas Cowboys Cheerleaders, Inc.* court offered the following reasoning:

> That defendants' movie may convey a barely discernible message does not entitle them to appropriate plaintiff's trademark in the process of conveying that message. Plaintiff's trademark is in the nature of a property right, and as such it need not "yield to the exercise of First Amendment rights under circumstances where adequate alternative avenues of communication exist." *Lloyd Corp. v. Tanner*, 407 U.S. 551, 567, 92 S.Ct. 2219, 2228, 33 L.Ed.2d 131 (1972). Because there are numerous ways in which defendants may comment on "sexuality in athletics" without infringing plaintiff's trademark, the district court did not encroach upon their first amendment rights in granting a preliminary injunction.

Id. at 208.

If the *Mattel* court had applied this reasoning to Aqua's Barbie Girl song, how would the case have come out? Does the fact that Aqua was making fun of Barbie herself reduce the "alternative avenues of communication"? If so, could the porn director have argued that he was not commenting on "sexuality in athletics," but on the sexuality of Dallas Cowboys Cheerleaders in particular?

4.   *Consistent or Inconsistent Rulings.* As should be apparent by this point, courts do not always apply trademark law consistently. Often, judicial opinions in trademark law seem to reflect more a *post hoc* justification of a judge's gut reaction than a reasoned application of legal principles. Consider the following two examples.

(a)   People for the Ethical Treatment of Animals (or PETA) is an animal rights organization with more than 600,000 members worldwide. PETA "is dedicated to promoting and heightening public awareness of animal protection issues and it opposes the exploitation of animals for food, clothing, entertainment and vivisection."

An unrelated third party, Doughney, registered the domain name www.peta.org. After registering the *peta.org* domain name, Doughney used it to create a website purportedly on behalf of "People Eating Tasty Animals." Doughney claims he created the website as a parody of PETA. A viewer accessing the website would see the title "People Eating Tasty Animals" in large, bold type. Under the title, the viewer would see a statement that the website was a "resource for those who enjoy eating meat, wearing fur and leather, hunting, and the fruits of scientific research." The website contained links to various meat, fur, leather, hunting, animal research, and other organizations, all of which held views generally antithetical to PETA's views. Another statement on the website asked the viewer whether he/she was "Feeling lost? Offended? Perhaps you should, like, *exit immediately*." The phrase *"exit immediately"* contained a hyperlink to PETA's official website.

PETA sued Doughney, alleging likelihood of confusion and dilution. Doughney defended on three grounds; (i) that he had not made a use in connection with the sale of goods or services; (ii) that his use was not likely to cause confusion or dilution; and (iii) that his use was protected by the First Amendment. How should these issues be resolved? *See People for the Ethical Treatment of Animals v. Doughney*, 263 F.3d 359 (4th Cir. 2001) (affirming district court's summary judgment ruling holding: (i) that Doughney had used the PETA mark in connection with the sale of goods or services; (ii) that Doughney had created an actionable likelihood of confusion and dilution; and (iii) that such liability was not foreclosed by the First Amendment).

(b) The National Association for the Advancement of Colored People, better known by its acronym "NAACP," is this country's "oldest and largest civil rights organization," and one that holds a place of honor in our history. It champions "political, educational, social, and economic equality of all citizens" while working to eliminate racial and other forms of prejudice within the United States.

An unrelated third party, Bomberger, authored an article criticizing the NAACP's annual Image Awards, entitled "NAACP: National Association for the Abortion of Colored People." The piece lambasted the NAACP for sponsoring an awards event to recognize Hollywood figures and products that Radiance alleged defied Christian values and perpetuated racist stereotypes. The article then criticized the NAACP for some of its other public stances and actions. It particularly targeted the NAACP's ties to Planned Parenthood and its position on abortion. Though the NAACP has often claimed to be neutral on abortion, Radiance maintains that the NAACP's actions actually demonstrate support for the practice.

The article appeared on three websites: the two owned by Radiance—TheRadianceFoundation.com and TooManyAborted.com—and a third-party site called LifeNews.com. Though the text of the article was identical across the sites, the headlines and presentation varied slightly. On TheRadianceFoundation.com, directly below the headline was an image of a TooManyAborted billboard with the headline "NAACP: National Association for the Abortion of Colored People" repeated next to it. The TooManyAborted.com site posted the headline "The National Association for the Abortion of Colored People" with a graphic below of a red box with the words "CIVIL WRONG" followed by the modified NAACP name. Finally on LifeNews.com, the third-party site, the NAACP's Scales of Justice appeared as a graphic underneath the headline.

The NAACP sued, *inter alia*, Radiance, alleging likelihood of confusion and dilution. Radiance defended on three grounds; (i) that it had not made a use in connection with the sale of goods or services; (ii) that its use was not likely to cause confusion or dilution; and (iii) that its use was protected by the First Amendment. How should these issues be resolved? *See Radiance Foundation, Inc. v. N.A.A.C.P.*, 786 F.3d 316 (4th Cir. 2015) (reversing district court's grant of a preliminary injunction and holding, as a matter of law, that, in the light of the First Amendment's interest in protecting speech, Radiance's use was not made in connection with the sale of goods or services and did not create an actionable likelihood of confusion or dilution).

CHAPTER 10

TRADEMARKS ON THE INTERNET

■ ■ ■

Glynn S. Lunney, Jr., *Trademark on the Internet: the United States Experience*, 97 TRADEMARK REPORTER 931, 938–39 (2007) (footnotes omitted).

The growth of the Internet as a commercial medium can be traced to two developments in 1993. First, on April 30, 1993, the European Organization for Nuclear Research, commonly known as CERN, dedicated the software behind the World Wide Web to the public, making it available for anyone to use on a royalty-free basis. Second, Mark Andreessen's team at the University of Illinois introduced Mosaic, a graphical browser for the Internet. Together, these two developments facilitated the development of web pages with text and integrated graphics, and opened the Internet to ordinary users. With the release of the Netscape Navigator in 1994, the Internet's future as a new venue for commerce was becoming clear.

Nonetheless, while some companies had registered their domain names before the World Wide Web, MIT, for example, in 1985 and IBM in 1986, other companies were slower to act. By May 1994, only one-third of Fortune 500 companies had registered their company names as domain names. Moreover, under [Netscape Solutions, Inc. or, as it was known,] InterNIC's registration policy in effect from April 1993 until July 1995, domain names were registered on a first come-first served basis. As a result, by May 1994, fourteen percent of the Fortune 500 had their names registered by someone else.

Against this background, it didn't take long for the first lawsuits to arise. The first three were, except perhaps for the parties directly involved, more amusing than anything else. In *MTV v. Curry*, 867 F. Supp. 202 (S.D.N.Y. 1994), one of MTV's VJs (video jockey—a play on the traditional radio designation DJ for disk jockey) Adam Curry had registered the domain name "mtv.com" and set up a related website—allegedly with MTV's consent and encouragement. When MTV and Curry parted ways, on not so amicable terms, Curry would not turn the site over to MTV, and so MTV sued. In another instance, Princeton Review registered "kaplan.com"—the domain name corresponding to its chief competitor. Upon arrival at the site, users were immediately informed that they had reached Princeton Review and asked to contribute to a list of complaints about Kaplan Education Centers. Although Princeton

Review claimed to have registered the domain name "as a playful prank" and offered to transfer the domain name to Kaplan for a case of beer, Kaplan sued instead, unwilling to acknowledge its rival's cleverness. In the third case, a writer, Joshua Quittner, registered "mcdonalds.com" to illustrate his point that some well-known businesses were slow to recognize the commercial potential of the Internet. Quittner offered to transfer the domain name to McDonalds if it would pay to provide high-speed Internet access for P.S. 308, a public school in New York. All three cases were eventually resolved without a final judicial resolution, two of them by settlement, and the dispute over "kaplan.com" by arbitration.

Yet, even if they did not contribute to the making of Internet trademark law through the common law adjudicative process, these disputes represented the first trickle of an impending wave of Internet trademark lawsuits.

In this Chapter, we consider some of the key cases applying trademark law to the Internet.

A. TRADEMARK RIGHTS ON THE INTERNET

BROOKFIELD COMMS. v. WEST COAST ENTER. CORP.
174 F.3d 1036 (9th Cir. 1999)

O'SCANNLAIN, J.

We must venture into cyberspace to determine whether federal trademark and unfair competition laws prohibit a video rental store chain from using an entertainment-industry information provider's trademark in the domain name of its web site and in its web site's metatags.

I

Brookfield Communications, Inc. ("Brookfield") appeals the district court's denial of its motion for a preliminary injunction prohibiting West Coast Entertainment Corporation ("West Coast") from using in commerce terms confusingly similar to Brookfield's trademark, "MovieBuff." Brookfield gathers and sells information about the entertainment industry. Founded in 1987 for the purpose of creating and marketing software and services for professionals in the entertainment industry, Brookfield initially offered software applications featuring information such as recent film submissions, industry credits, professional contacts, and future projects. These offerings targeted major Hollywood film studios, independent production companies, agents, actors, directors, and producers.

Brookfield expanded into the broader consumer market with computer software featuring a searchable database containing entertainment-industry related information marketed under the

"MovieBuff" mark around December 1993. Brookfield's "MovieBuff" software now targets smaller companies and individual consumers who are not interested in purchasing Brookfield's professional level alternative, The Studio System, and includes comprehensive, searchable, entertainment-industry databases and related software applications containing information such as movie credits, box office receipts, films in development, film release schedules, entertainment news, and listings of executives, agents, actors, and directors. This "MovieBuff" software comes in three versions—(1) the MovieBuff Pro Bundle, (2) the MovieBuff Pro, and (3) MovieBuff—and is sold through various retail stores, such as Borders, Virgin Megastores, Nobody Beats the Wiz, The Writer's Computer Store, Book City, and Samuel French Bookstores.

Sometime in 1996, Brookfield attempted to register the World Wide Web ("the Web") domain name "moviebuff.com" with Network Solutions, Inc. ("Network Solutions"), but was informed that the requested domain name had already been registered by West Coast. Brookfield subsequently registered "brookfieldcomm.com" in May 1996 and "moviebuffonline.com" in September 1996. Sometime in 1996 or 1997, Brookfield began using its web sites to sell its "MovieBuff" computer software and to offer an Internet-based searchable database marketed under the "MovieBuff" mark. Brookfield sells its "MovieBuff" computer software through its "brookfieldcomm.com" and "moviebuffonline.com" web sites and offers subscribers online access to the MovieBuff database itself at its "inhollywood.com" web site.

On August 19, 1997, Brookfield applied to the Patent and Trademark Office (PTO) for federal registration of "MovieBuff" as a mark to designate both goods and services. Its trademark application describes its product as "computer software providing data and information in the field of the motion picture and television industries." Its service mark application describes its service as "providing multiple-user access to an on-line network database offering data and information in the field of the motion picture and television industries." Both federal trademark registrations issued on September 29, 1998. Brookfield had previously obtained a California state trademark registration for the mark "MovieBuff" covering "computer software" in 1994.

In October 1998, Brookfield learned that West Coast—one of the nation's largest video rental store chains with over 500 stores—intended to launch a web site at "moviebuff.com" containing, *inter alia*, a searchable entertainment database similar to "MovieBuff." West Coast had registered "moviebuff.com" with Network Solutions on February 6, 1996 and claims that it chose the domain name because the term "Movie Buff" is part of its service mark, "The Movie Buff's Movie Store," on which a federal registration issued in 1991 covering "retail store services featuring video cassettes and video game cartridges" and "rental of video cassettes and video game cartridges." West Coast notes further that, since at least 1988, it has also used various phrases including the term "Movie Buff" to promote goods and services available at its video stores in Massachusetts, including "The Movie Buff's Gift Guide"; "The Movie Buff's Gift Store"; "Calling All Movie Buffs!"; "Good News Movie Buffs!"; "Movie Buffs, Show Your Stuff!"; "the Perfect Stocking Stuffer for the Movie Buff!"; "A Movie Buff's Top Ten"; "The Movie Buff Discovery Program"; "Movie Buff Picks"; "Movie Buff Series"; "Movie Buff Selection Program"; and "Movie Buff Film Series."

On November 10, Brookfield delivered to West Coast a cease-and-desist letter alleging that West Coast's planned use of the "moviebuff.com" would violate Brookfield's trademark rights; as a "courtesy" Brookfield attached a copy of a complaint that it threatened to file if West Coast did not desist.

The next day, West Coast issued a press release announcing the imminent launch of its web site full of "movie reviews, Hollywood news and gossip, provocative commentary, and coverage of the independent film scene and films in production." The press release declared that the site would feature "an extensive database, which aids consumers in making educated decisions about the rental and purchase of" movies and would also allow customers to purchase movies, accessories, and other entertainment-related merchandise on the web site.

Brookfield fired back immediately with a visit to the United States District Court for the Central District of California, and this lawsuit was born. In its first amended complaint filed on November 18, 1998, Brookfield alleged principally that West Coast's proposed offering of online services at "moviebuff.com" would constitute trademark infringement and unfair competition in violation of sections 32 and 43(a) of the Lanham Act, 15 U.S.C. §§ 1114, 1125(a). Soon thereafter, Brookfield applied *ex parte* for a temporary restraining order ("TRO") enjoining West Coast "from using . . . in any manner . . . the mark MOVIEBUFF, or any other term or terms likely to cause confusion therewith, including *moviebuff.com*, as West Coast's domain name, . . . as the name of West Coast's website service, in buried code or metatags on their home page or web pages, or in connection with the retrieval of data or information on other goods or services."

On November 27, West Coast filed an opposition brief in which it argued first that Brookfield could not prevent West Coast from using "moviebuff.com" in commerce because West Coast was the senior user. West Coast claimed that it was the first user of "MovieBuff" because it had used its federally registered trademark, "The Movie Buff's Movie Store," since 1986 in advertisements, promotions, and letterhead in connection with retail services featuring videocassettes and video game cartridges. Alternatively, West Coast claimed seniority on the basis that it had garnered common-law rights in the domain name by using "moviebuff.com" before Brookfield began offering its "MovieBuff" Internet-based searchable database on the Web. In addition to asserting seniority, West Coast contended that its planned use of "moviebuff.com" would not cause a likelihood of confusion with Brookfield's trademark "MovieBuff" and thus would not violate the Lanham Act.

The district court heard arguments on the TRO motion on November 30. Later that day, the district court issued an order construing Brookfield's TRO motion as a motion for a preliminary injunction and denying it. The district court concluded that West Coast was the senior user of the mark "MovieBuff" for both of the reasons asserted by West Coast. The court also determined that Brookfield had not established a likelihood of confusion.

Brookfield responded by filing a notice of appeal from the denial of preliminary injunction followed by a motion in the district court for injunction pending appeal, which motion the district court denied. On January 16, 1999, West Coast launched its web site at "moviebuff.com." Fearing that West Coast's fully operational web site would cause it irreparable injury, Brookfield filed an emergency motion for injunction pending appeal with this court a few days later. On February 24, we granted Brookfield's motion and entered an order enjoining West Coast "from using, or facilitating the use of, in any manner, including advertising and promotion, the mark MOVIEBUFF, or any other term or terms likely to cause confusion therewith, including @*moviebuff.com* or *moviebuff.com*, as the name of West Coast's web site service, in buried code or metatags on its home page or web pages, or in connection with the retrieval of data or information on other goods or services." The injunction was to take effect upon the posting of a $25,000 bond in the district court by Brookfield. We scheduled oral argument on an expedited basis for March 10.

West Coast thereupon filed a motion for reconsideration and modification—seeking a stay of the injunction pending appeal and an increase in the bond requirement to $400,000—which we denied. After oral argument on March 10, we ordered that our previously issued injunction remain in effect pending the issuance of this opinion.

II

To resolve the legal issues before us, we must first understand the basics of the Internet and the World Wide Web. Because we will be delving into technical corners of the Internet—dealing with features such as domain names and metatags—we explain in some detail what all these things are and provide a general overview of the relevant technology.

The Internet is a global network of interconnected computers which allows individuals and organizations around the world to communicate and to share information with one another. The Web, a collection of information resources contained in documents located on individual computers around the world, is the most widely used and fastest-growing part of the Internet except perhaps for electronic mail ("e-mail"). *See United States v. Microsoft*, 147 F.3d 935, 939 (D.C. Cir. 1998). With the Web becoming an important mechanism for commerce, *see Reno v. ACLU*, 521 U.S. 844, 850 (1997) (citing an estimate that over 200 million people will use the Internet in 1999), companies are racing to stake out their place in cyberspace. Prevalent on the Web are multimedia "web pages"— computer data files written in Hypertext Markup Language ("HTML")— which contain information such as text, pictures, sounds, audio and video recordings, and links to other web pages. *See* 117 S.Ct. at 2335; *Panavision Int'l, L.P. v. Toeppen*, 141 F.3d 1316, 1318 (9th Cir. 1998).

Each web page has a corresponding domain address, which is an identifier somewhat analogous to a telephone number or street address. Domain names consist of a second-level domain—simply a term or series of terms (e.g., westcoastvideo)—followed by a top-level domain, many of which describe the nature of the enterprise. Top-level domains include ".com" (commercial), ".edu" (educational), ".org" (non-profit and miscellaneous organizations), ".gov" (government), ".net" (networking provider), and ".mil" (military). *See Panavision*, 141 F.3d at 1318. Commercial entities generally use the ".com" top-level domain, which also serves as a catchall top-level domain. *See id.* To obtain a domain name, an individual or entity files an application with Network Solutions listing the domain name the applicant wants. Because each web page must have an unique domain name, Network Solution checks to see whether the requested domain name has already been assigned to someone else. If so, the applicant must choose a different domain name. Other than requiring an applicant to make certain representations, Network Solutions does not make an independent determination about a registrant's right to use a particular domain name. *See id.* at 1318–19.

Using a Web browser, such as Netscape's Navigator or Microsoft's Internet Explorer, a cyber "surfer" may navigate the Web—searching for, communicating with, and retrieving information from various web sites. *See id.*; *Microsoft*, 147 F.3d at 939–40, 950. A specific web site is most easily located by using its domain name. *See Panavision*, 141 F.3d at 1327. Upon entering a domain name into the web browser, the corresponding web site will quickly appear on the computer screen. Sometimes, however, a Web surfer will not know the domain name of the site he is looking for, whereupon he has two principal options: trying to guess the domain name or seeking the assistance of an Internet "search engine."

Oftentimes, an Internet user will begin by hazarding a guess at the domain name, especially if there is an obvious domain name to try. Web users often assume, as a rule of thumb, that the domain name of a particular company will be the company name followed by ".com." *See id.*; *Playboy Enters. v. Universal Tel-a-Talk, Inc.*, No. 96–6961 (E.D. Pa. 1998); *Cardservice Int'l, Inc. v. McGee*, 950 F. Supp. 737, 741 (E.D. Va. 1997), *aff'd by*, 129 F.3d 1258 (4th Cir. 1997). For example, one looking for Kraft Foods, Inc. might try "kraftfoods.com," and indeed this web site contains information on Kraft's many food products. Sometimes, a trademark is better known than the company itself, in which case a Web surfer may assume that the domain address will be " 'trademark'.com." *See Panavision*, 141 F.3d at 1327; *Beverly v. Network Solutions, Inc.*, No. 98–0337 (N.D. Cal. 1998) ("Companies attempt to make the search for their web site as easy as possible. They do so by using a corporate name, trademark or service mark as their web site address."). One interested in today's news would do well visiting "usatoday.com," which features, as one would expect, breaking stories from Gannett's USA Today. Guessing domain names, however, is not a risk-free activity. The Web surfer who assumes that " 'X'.com" will always correspond to the web site of company X or trademark X will, however, sometimes be misled. One looking for the latest information on Panavision, International, L.P., would sensibly try "panavision.com." Until recently, that Web surfer would have instead found a web site owned by Dennis Toeppen featuring photographs of the City of Pana, Illinois. *See Panavision*, 141 F.3d 1316 at 1319. Having registered several domain names that logically would have corresponded to the web sites of major companies such as Panavision, Delta Airlines, Neiman Marcus, Lufthansa, Toeppen sought to sell "panavision.com" to Panavision, which gives one a taste of some of the trademark issues that have arisen in cyberspace. *See id.*; *see also, e.g., Cardservice*, 950 F. Supp. at 740–42.

A Web surfer's second option when he does not know the domain name is to utilize an Internet search engine, such as Yahoo, Altavista, or Lycos. *See ACLU v. Reno*, 31 F. Supp. 2d 473, 484 (E.D. Pa. 1999); *Washington Speakers Bureau, Inc. v. Leading Authorities, Inc.*, 33 F. Supp. 2d 488 (E.D. Va. 1999). When a keyword is entered, the search engine processes it through a self-created index of web sites to generate a (sometimes long) list relating to the entered keyword. Each search engine uses its own algorithm to arrange indexed materials in sequence, so the list of web sites that any particular set of keywords will bring up may differ depending on the search engine used. *See Niton Corp. v. Radiation Monitoring Devices, Inc.*, 27 F. Supp. 2d 102, 104 (D. Mass. 1998); *Intermatic Inc. v. Toeppen*, 947 F. Supp. 1227, 1231–32 (N.D. Ill. 1996); *Shea v. Reno*, 930 F. Supp. 916, 929 (S.D.N.Y. 1996), *aff'd*, 521 U.S. 1113 (1997). Search engines look for keywords in places such as domain names, actual text on the web page, and metatags. Metatags are HTML code intended to describe the contents of the web site. There are different types of metatags, but those of principal concern to us are the "description" and "keyword" metatags. The description metatags are intended to describe the web site; the keyword metatags, at least in theory, contain keywords relating to the contents of the web site. The more often a term appears in the metatags and in the text of the web page, the more likely it is that the web page will be "hit" in a search for that keyword and the higher on the list of "hits" the web page will appear. *See Niton*, 27 F. Supp. 2d at 104.

With this basic understanding of the Internet and the Web, we may now analyze the legal issues before us.

III

We review the district court's denial of preliminary injunctive relief for an abuse of discretion. *See, e.g., Foti v. City of Menlo Park*, 146 F.3d 629, 634–35 (9th Cir. 1998). Under this standard, reversal is appropriate only if the district court based its decision on clearly erroneous findings of fact or erroneous legal principles. *See FDIC v. Garner*, 125 F.3d 1272, 1276 (9th Cir. 1997), *cert. denied*, 523 U.S. 1020 (1998). "A district court would necessarily abuse its discretion if it based its ruling on an erroneous view of the law," *Cooter & Gell v. Hartmarx Corp.*, 496 U.S. 384, 405 (1990), so we review the underlying legal issues injunction de novo, *see, e.g., Barahona-Gomez v. Reno*, 167 F.3d 1228 (9th Cir. 1999); *S.O.C., Inc. v. County of Clark*, 152 F.3d 1136, 1142 (9th Cir. 1998), *amended by*, 160 F.3d 541 (9th Cir. 1998); *Foti*, 146 F.3d at 635; *Garner*, 125 F.3d at 1276; *San Antonio Community Hosp. v. Southern Cal. Dist. Council of Carpenters*, 125 F.3d 1230, 1234 (9th Cir. 1997).

"A plaintiff is entitled to a preliminary injunction in a trademark case when he demonstrates either (1) a combination of probable success on the merits and the possibility of irreparable injury or (2) the existence of serious questions going to the merits and that the balance of hardships tips sharply in his favor." *Sardi's Restaurant Corp. v. Sardie*, 755 F.2d 719, 723 (9th Cir. 1985). To establish a trademark infringement claim under section 32 of the Lanham Act or an unfair competition claim under section 43(a) of the Lanham Act, Brookfield must establish that West Coast is using a mark confusingly similar to a valid, protectable trademark of Brookfield's. n6 *See AMF Inc. v. Sleekcraft Boats*, 599 F.2d 341, 348 (9th Cir. 1979). The district court denied Brookfield's motion for preliminary injunctive relief because it concluded that Brookfield had failed to establish that it was the senior user of the "MovieBuff" mark or that West Coast's use of the "moviebuff.com" domain name created a likelihood of confusion.

We review each of the district court's conclusions in turn.

IV

To resolve whether West Coast's use of "moviebuff.com" constitutes trademark infringement or unfair competition, we must first determine whether Brookfield has a valid, protectable trademark interest in the "MovieBuff" mark. Brookfield's registration of the mark on the Principal Register in the Patent and Trademark Office constitutes prima facie evidence of the validity of the registered mark and of Brookfield's exclusive right to use the mark on the goods and services specified in the registration. *See* 15 U.S.C. §§ 1057(b); 1115(a). Nevertheless, West Coast can rebut this presumption by showing that it used the mark in commerce first, since a fundamental tenet of trademark law is that ownership of an inherently distinctive mark such as "MovieBuff" is governed by priority of use. *See Sengoku Works Ltd. v. RMC Int'l, Ltd.*, 96 F.3d 1217, 1219 (9th Cir. 1996) ("It is axiomatic in trademark law that the standard test of ownership is priority of use. To acquire ownership of a trademark it is not enough to have invented the mark first or even to have registered it first; the party claiming ownership must have been the first to actually use the mark in the sale of goods or services."), *cert. denied*, 521 U.S. 1103 (1997). The first to use a mark is deemed the "senior" user and has the right to enjoin "junior" users from using confusingly similar marks in the same industry and market or within the senior user's natural zone of expansion. *See Union Nat'l Bank of Tex., Laredo, Tex. v. Union Nat'l Bank of Tex., Austin, Tex.*, 909 F.2d 839, 842–43 (5th Cir. 1990); *Tally-Ho, Inc. v. Coast Community College Dist.*, 889 F.2d 1018, 1023 (11th Cir. 1989); *New West Corp. v. NYM Co. of Cal.*, 595 F.2d 1194, 1200–01 (9th Cir. 1979).

It is uncontested that Brookfield began selling "MovieBuff" software in 1993 and that West Coast did not use "moviebuff.com" until 1996. According to West Coast, however, the fact that it has used "The Movie Buff's Movie Store" as a trademark since 1986 makes it the first user for purposes of trademark priority. In the alternative, West Coast claims priority on the basis that it used "moviebuff.com" in commerce before Brookfield began offering its "MovieBuff" searchable database on the Internet. We analyze these contentions in turn.

A

Conceding that the first time that it *actually* used "moviebuff.com" was in 1996, West Coast argues that its earlier use of "The Movie Buff's Movie Store" constitutes use of "moviebuff.com." West Coast has not provided any Ninth Circuit precedent approving of this constructive use theory, but neither has Brookfield pointed us to any case law rejecting it. We are not without guidance, however, as our sister circuits have explicitly recognized the ability of a trademark owner to claim priority in a mark based on the first use date of a similar, but technically distinct, mark—but only in the exceptionally narrow instance where "the previously used mark is 'the legal equivalent of the mark in question or indistinguishable therefrom' such that consumers 'consider both as the same mark.'" *Data Concepts, Inc. v. Digital Consulting, Inc.*, 150 F.3d

620, 623 (6th Cir. 1998) (*quoting Van Dyne-Crotty, Inc. v. Wear-Guard Corp.*, 926 F.2d 1156, 1159 (Fed. Cir. 1991)); *accord Van Dyne-Crotty*, 926 F.2d at 1159.

This constructive use theory is known as "tacking," as the trademark holder essentially seeks to "tack" his first use date in the earlier mark onto the subsequent mark. *See generally* 2 J. Thomas McCarthy, *McCarthy on Trademarks & Unfair Competition* § 17:25–27 (4th ed. 1998) [hereafter "McCarthy"].

We agree that tacking should be allowed if two marks are so similar that consumers generally would regard them as essentially the same. Where such is the case, the new mark serves the same identificatory function as the old mark. Giving the trademark owner the same rights in the new mark as he has in the old helps to protect source-identifying trademarks from appropriation by competitors and thus furthers the trademark law's objective of reducing the costs that customers incur in shopping and making purchasing decisions. *See Qualitex Co. v. Jacobson Prods. Co.*, 514 U.S. 159, 163–64 (1995); *Falcon Rice Mill, Inc. v. Community Rice Mill, Inc.*, 725 F.2d 336, 348 (5th Cir. 1984).

Without tacking, a trademark owner's priority in his mark would be reduced each time he made the slightest alteration to the mark, which would discourage him from altering the mark in response to changing consumer preferences, evolving aesthetic developments, or new advertising and marketing styles.

The standard for "tacking," however, is exceedingly strict: "The marks must create the *same, continuing commercial impression*, and the later mark should not materially differ from or alter the character of the mark attempted to be tacked." *Van Dyne-Crotty*, 926 F.2d at 1159 (emphasis added) (citations and quotation marks omitted). In other words, "the previously used mark must be the *legal equivalent* of the mark in question or indistinguishable therefrom, and the consumer should consider both as the same mark." *Id.* (emphasis added); *see also Data Concepts*, 150 F.3d at 623 (adopting the *Van Dyne-Crotty* test). This standard is considerably higher than the standard for "likelihood of confusion," which we discuss *infra*.

The Federal Circuit, for example, concluded that priority in "CLOTHES THAT WORK. FOR THE WORK YOU DO" could not be tacked onto "CLOTHES THAT WORK." *See Van Dyne-Crotty*, 926 F.2d at 1160 (holding that the shorter phrase was *not* the legal equivalent of the longer mark). The Sixth Circuit held that "DCI" and "dci" were too dissimilar to support tacking. *See Data Concepts*, 150 F.3d at 623–24. And the Trademark Board has rejected tacking in a case involving "American Mobilphone" with a star and stripe design and "American Mobilphone Paging" with the identical design, *see American Paging, Inc. v. American Mobilphone, Inc.*, 13 U.S.P.Q.2D (BNA) 2036 (T.T.A.B. 1989), *aff'd*, 17

U.S.P.Q.2D (BNA) 1726 (Fed. Cir. 1990), as well as in a case involving "PRO-CUTS" and "PRO-KUT," *see Pro-Cuts v. Schilz-Price Enters.*, 27 U.S.P.Q.2D (BNA) 1224, 1227 (T.T.A.B. 1993).

In contrast to cases such as *Van Dyne-Crotty* and *American Paging*, which were close questions, the present case is clear cut: "The Movie Buff's Movie Store" and "moviebuff.com" are very different, in that the latter contains three fewer words, drops the possessive, omits a space, and adds ".com" to the end. Because West Coast failed to make the slightest showing that consumers view these terms as identical, we must conclude that West Coast cannot tack its priority in "The Movie Buff's Movie Store" onto "moviebuff.com." As the Federal Circuit explained, "it would be clearly contrary to well-established principles of trademark law to sanction the tacking of a mark with a narrow commercial impression onto one with a broader commercial impression." *Van Dyne-Crotty*, 926 F.2d at 1160 (noting that prior use of "SHAPE UP" could not be tacked onto "EGO," that prior use of "ALTER EGO" could not be tacked onto "EGO," and that prior use of "Marco Polo could not be tacked onto 'Polo')".

Since tacking does not apply, we must therefore conclude that Brookfield is the senior user because it marketed "MovieBuff" products well before West Coast began using "moviebuff.com" in commerce: West Coast's use of "The Movie Buff's Movie Store" is simply irrelevant.

. . .

West Coast makes a half-hearted claim that "MovieBuff" is confusingly similar to its earlier used mark "The Movie Buff's Movie Store." If this were so, West Coast would undoubtedly be the senior user. *See id.* "Of course, if the symbol or device is already in general use, employed in such a manner that its adoption as an index of source or origin would only produce confusion and mislead the public, it is not susceptible of adoption as a trademark." *Hanover Star Milling Co. v. Metcalf*, 240 U.S. 403, 415 (1916). West Coast, however, essentially conceded that "MovieBuff" and "The Movie Buff's Movie Store" are not confusingly similar when it stated in its pre-argument papers that it does not allege actual confusion between "MovieBuff" and West Coast's federally registered mark. We cannot think of more persuasive evidence that there is no *likelihood* of confusion between these two marks than the fact that they have been simultaneously used for five years without causing any consumers to be confused as to who makes what. *See Libman Co. v. Vining Indus., Inc.*, 69 F.3d 1360, 1361 (7th Cir. 1995) ("Vining sold several hundred thousand of the allegedly infringing brooms, yet there is no evidence that any consumer ever made such an error; if confusion were likely, one would expect at least one person out of this vast multitude to be confused. . . ."). The failure to *prove* instances of actual confusion is *not* dispositive against a trademark plaintiff, because actual confusion is hard to prove; difficulties in gathering evidence of actual confusion make its absence generally unnoteworthy. *See* Eclipse Associates Ltd. v. Data General Corp.*Eclipse Assocs. Ltd. v. Data Gen. Corp.*, 894 F.2d 1114, 1118–19 (9th Cir. 1990); *Sleekcraft*, 599 F.2d at 353. West Coast, however, did not state that it could not *prove* actual confusion; rather, it conceded that there has been none. This is a crucial difference. Although there may be the rare case in which a likelihood of future confusion is possible even where it is conceded that two marks have been used simultaneously for years with no resulting confusion, West Coast has not shown this to be such a case.

Our conclusion comports with the position of the PTO, which effectively announced its finding of no likelihood of confusion between "The Movie Buff's Movie Store" and "MovieBuff" when it placed the latter on the principal register despite West Coast's prior registration of "The Movie Buff's Movie Store." Priority is accordingly to be determined on the basis of whether Brookfield used "MovieBuff" or West Coast used "moviebuff.com" first.

B

West Coast argues that we are mixing apples and oranges when we compare its first use date of "moviebuff.com" with the first sale date of "MovieBuff" *software*. West Coast reminds us that Brookfield uses the "MovieBuff" mark with both computer software and the provision of an Internet database; according to West Coast, its use of "moviebuff.com" can cause confusion only with respect to the latter. West Coast asserts that we should accordingly determine seniority by comparing West Coast's first use date of "moviebuff.com" not with when Brookfield first sold software, but with when it first offered its database online.

As an initial matter, we note that West Coast's argument is premised on the assumption that its use of "moviebuff.com" does not cause confusion between its web site and Brookfield's "MovieBuff" software products. Even though Brookfield's computer software and West Coast's offerings on its web site are not identical products, likelihood of confusion can still result where, for example, there is a likelihood of expansion in product lines. *See Official Airline Guides, Inc. v. Goss*, 6 F.3d 1385, 1394 (9th Cir. 1993). As the leading trademark commentator explains: "When a senior user of a mark on product line A expands later into product line B and finds an intervening user, priority in product line B is determined by whether the expansion is 'natural' in that customers would have been confused as to source or affiliation at the time of the intervening user's appearance." 2 McCarthy § 16:5. We need not, however, decide whether the Web was within Brookfield's natural zone of expansion, because we conclude that Brookfield's use of "MovieBuff" as a service mark preceded West Coast's use.

Brookfield first used "MovieBuff" on its Internet-based products and services in August 1997, so West Coast can prevail only if it establishes first use earlier than that. In the literal sense of the word, West Coast "used" the term "moviebuff.com" when it registered that domain address in February 1996. Registration with Network Solutions, however, does not in itself constitute "use" for purposes of acquiring trademark priority. *See Panavision*, 141 F.3d at 1324–25.

. . .

The district court, while recognizing that mere registration of a domain name was not sufficient to constitute commercial use for purposes of the Lanham Act, nevertheless held that registration of a domain name with the intent to use it commercially was sufficient to convey trademark rights. This analysis, however, contradicts both the express statutory language and the case law which firmly establishes that trademark rights are not conveyed through mere intent to use a mark commercially, *see, e.g., Allard Enters. v. Advanced Programming Resources, Inc.*, 146 F.3d 350, 356 (6th Cir. 1998); *Zazu Designs v. L'Oreal, S.A.*, 979 F.2d 499, 504 (7th Cir. 1992) ("An intent to use a mark creates no rights a competitor is bound to respect."), nor through mere preparation to use a term as a trademark, *see, e.g., Hydro-Dynamics, Inc. v. George Putnam & Co.*, 811 F.2d 1470, 1473–74 (Fed. Cir. 1987); *Computer Food Stores, Inc. v. Corner Store Franchises*, 176 U.S.P.Q. 535, 538 (T.T.A.B. 1973).

West Coast no longer disputes that its use—for purposes of the Lanham Act—of "moviebuff.com" did not commence until after February 1996. It instead relies on the alternate argument that its rights vested when it began using "moviebuff.com" in e-mail correspondence with lawyers and customers sometime in mid-1996. West Coast's argument is not without support in our case law—we have indeed held that trademark rights can vest even before any goods or services are actually sold if "the totality of [one's] prior actions, taken together, [can] establish a right to use the trademark." *New West*, 595 F.2d at 1200. Under *New West*, however, West Coast must establish that its e-mail correspondence constituted " 'use in a way sufficiently public to identify or distinguish the marked goods in an appropriate segment of the public mind as those of the adopter of the mark.' " *Id.* (quoting *New England Duplicating Co. v. Mendes*, 190 F.2d 415, 418 (1st Cir. 1951)); *see also Marvel Comics Ltd. v. Defiant*, 837 F. Supp. 546, 550 (S.D.N.Y. 1993) ("The talismanic test is whether or not the use was sufficiently public to identify or distinguish the marked goods in an appropriate segment of the public mind as those of the adopter of the mark.") (quotation marks and citation omitted).

West Coast fails to meet this standard. Its purported "use" is akin to putting one's mark "on a business office door sign, letterheads, architectural drawings, etc." or on a prototype displayed to a potential buyer, both of which have been held to be insufficient to establish trademark rights. *See Steer Inn Sys., Inc. v. Laughner's Drive-In, Inc.*, 405 F.2d 1401, 1402 (C.C.P.A. 1969); *Walt Disney Prods. v. Kusan, Inc.*, 204

U.S.P.Q. 284, 288 (C.D. Cal. 1979). Although widespread publicity of a company's mark, such as Marvel Comics's announcement to 13 million comic book readers that "Plasma" would be the title of a new comic book, *see Marvel Comics*, 837 F. Supp. at 550, or the mailing of 430,000 solicitation letters with one's mark to potential subscribers of a magazine, *see New West*, 595 F.2d at 1200, may be sufficient to create an association among the public between the mark and West Coast, mere use in limited e-mail correspondence with lawyers and a few customers is not.

West Coast first announced its web site at "moviebuff.com" in a public and widespread manner in a press release of November 11, 1998, and thus it is not until at least that date that it first used the "moviebuff.com" mark for purposes of the Lanham Act. Accordingly, West Coast's argument that it has seniority because it used "moviebuff.com" before Brookfield used "MovieBuff" as a service mark fails on its own terms. West Coast's first use date was *neither* February 1996 when it registered its domain name with Network Solutions as the district court had concluded, *nor* April 1996 when it first used "moviebuff.com" in e-mail communications, but *rather* November 1998 when it first made a widespread and public announcement about the imminent launch of its web site. Thus, West Coast's first use of "moviebuff.com" was preceded by Brookfield's first use of "MovieBuff" in conjunction with its online database, making Brookfield the senior user.

For the foregoing reasons, we conclude that the district court erred in concluding that Brookfield failed to establish a likelihood of success on its claim of being the senior user.

V

Establishing seniority, however, is only half the battle. Brookfield must also show that the public is likely to be somehow confused about the source or sponsorship of West Coast's "moviebuff.com" web site—and somehow to associate that site with Brookfield. *See* 15 U.S.C. § 1114(1); 1125(a). The Supreme Court has described "the basic objectives of trademark law" as follows: "trademark law, by preventing others from copying a source-identifying mark, 'reduces the customer's costs of shopping and making purchasing decisions,' for it quickly and easily assures a potential customer that this item—the item with this mark—is made by the same producer as other similarly marked items that he or she liked (or disliked) in the past. At the same time, the law helps assure a producer that it (and not an imitating competitor) will reap the financial, reputation-related rewards associated with a desirable product." *Qualitex*, 514 U.S. at 163–64 (internal citations omitted). Where two companies each use a different mark and the simultaneous use of those marks does not cause the consuming public to be confused as to who makes what, granting one company exclusive rights over both marks does nothing to further the objectives of the trademark laws; in fact, prohibiting the use of a mark that the public has come to associate with a company would actually contravene the intended purposes of the trademark law by making it *more* difficult to identify and to distinguish between different brands of goods.

"The core element of trademark infringement is the likelihood of confusion, i.e., whether the similarity of the marks is likely to confuse customers about the source of the products." *Official Airline Guides*, 6 F.3d at 1391 (quoting *E. & J. Gallo Winery v. Gallo Cattle Co.*, 967 F.2d 1280, 1290 (9th Cir. 1992)) (quotation marks omitted); *accord International Jensen, Inc. v. Metrosound U.S.A., Inc.*, 4 F.3d 819, 825 (9th Cir. 1993); *Metro Publ'g, Ltd. v. San Jose Mercury News*, 987 F.2d 637, 640 (9th Cir. 1993). We look to the following factors for guidance in determining the likelihood of confusion: similarity of the conflicting designations; relatedness or proximity of the two companies' products or services; strength of Brookfield's mark; marketing channels used; degree of care likely to be exercised by purchasers in selecting goods; West Coast's intent in selecting its mark; evidence of actual confusion; and likelihood of expansion in product lines. *See Dr. Seuss Enters. v. Penguin Books USA, Inc.*, 109 F.3d 1394, 1404 (9th Cir. 1997), *petition for cert. dismissed by*, 118 S.Ct. 27 (1997); *Sleekcraft*, 599 F.2d at 348–49; *see also* Restatement (Third) of Unfair Competition §§ 20–23 (1995). These eight factors are often referred to as the *Sleekcraft* factors.

A word of caution: this eight-factor test for likelihood of confusion is pliant. Some factors are much more important than others, and the relative importance of each individual factor will be case-specific. Although some factors—such as the similarity of the marks and whether the two companies are direct competitors—will always be important, it is often possible to reach a conclusion with respect to likelihood of confusion after considering only a subset of the factors. *See Dreamwerks Prod. Group v. SKG Studio*, 142 F.3d 1127, 1130–32 (9th Cir. 1998). Moreover, the foregoing list does not purport to be exhaustive, and non-listed variables may often be quite important. We must be acutely aware of excessive rigidity when applying the law in the Internet context; emerging technologies require a flexible approach.

A

We begin by comparing the allegedly infringing mark to the federally registered mark. The similarity of the marks will always be an important factor. Where the two marks are entirely dissimilar, there is no likelihood of confusion. "Pepsi" does not infringe Coca-Cola's "Coke." Nothing further need be said. Even where there is precise identity of a complainant's and an alleged infringer's mark, there may be no consumer confusion—and thus no trademark infringement—if the alleged infringer is in a different geographic area or in a wholly different industry. *See Weiner King, Inc. v. Wiener King Corp.*, 615 F.2d 512, 515–16, 521–22

(C.C.P.A. 1980) (permitting concurrent use of "Weiner King" as a mark for restaurants featuring hot dogs in New Jersey and "Wiener King" as a mark for restaurants in North Carolina); *Pinocchio's Pizza Inc. v. Sandra Inc.*, 11 U.S.P.Q.2D (BNA) 1227, 1228 (T.T.A.B. 1989) (permitting concurrent use of "PINOCCHIO'S" as a service mark for restaurants in Maryland and "PINOCCHIOS" as a service mark for restaurants elsewhere in the country). Nevertheless, the more similar the marks in terms of appearance, sound, and meaning, the greater the likelihood of confusion. *See, e.g., Dreamwerks*, 142 F.3d at 1131; *Goss*, 6 F.3d at 1392 ("The court assesses the similarity of the marks in terms of their sight, sound, and meaning."). In analyzing this factor, "the marks must be considered in their entirety and as they appear in the marketplace," *Goss*, 6 F.3d at 1392 (citing *Nutri/System, Inc. v. Con-Stan Indus., Inc.*, 809 F.2d 601, 605–06 (9th Cir. 1987)), with similarities weighed more heavily than differences, *see id.* (citing *Rodeo Collection Ltd. v. West Seventh*, 812 F.2d 1215, 1219 (9th Cir. 1987)).

In the present case, the district court found West Coast's domain name "moviebuff.com" to be quite different than Brookfield's domain name "moviebuffonline.com." Comparison of domain names, however, is irrelevant as a matter of law, since the Lanham Act requires that the allegedly infringing mark be compared with the claimant's *trademark*, *see* 15 U.S.C. § 1114(1), 1125(a), which here is "MovieBuff," not "moviebuffonline.com." Properly framed, it is readily apparent that West Coast's allegedly infringing mark is essentially identical to Brookfield's mark "MovieBuff." In terms of appearance, there are differences in capitalization and the addition of ".com" in West Coast's complete domain name, but these differences are inconsequential in light of the fact that Web addresses are not caps-sensitive and that the ".com" top-level domain signifies the site's commercial nature.

Looks aren't everything, so we consider the similarity of sound and meaning. The two marks are pronounced the same way, except that one would say "dot com" at the end of West Coast's mark. Because many companies use domain names comprised of ".com" as the top-level domain with their corporate name or trademark as the second-level domain, *see Beverly*, 1998 WL 320829, at *1 (unpublished), the addition of ".com" is of diminished importance in distinguishing the mark. The irrelevance of the ".com" becomes further apparent once we consider similarity in meaning. The domain name is more than a mere address: like trademarks, second-level domain names communicate information as to source. As we explained in Part II, many Web users are likely to associate "moviebuff.com" with the trademark "MovieBuff," thinking that it is operated by the company that makes "MovieBuff" products and services. Courts, in fact, have routinely concluded that marks were essentially identical in similar contexts. *See, e.g., Public Serv. Co. v. Nexus Energy Software, Inc.*, 36 F. Supp. 2d 436 (D. Mass. Feb. 24, 1999) (finding "energyplace.com" and "Energy Place" to be virtually identical); *Minnesota Mining & Mfg. Co. v. Taylor*, 21 F. Supp. 2d 1003, 1005 (D. Minn. 1998) (finding "post-it.com" and "Post-It" to be the same); *Interstellar Starship Servs. Ltd. v. Epix, Inc.*, 983 F. Supp. 1331, 1335 (D. Or. 1997) ("In the context of Internet use, ['epix.com'] is the same mark as ['EPIX']."); *Planned Parenthood Federation of America, Inc. v. Bucci*,.97–0629 (S.D.N.Y.1997) (concluding that "plannedparenthood.com" and "Planned Parenthood" were essentially identical), *aff'd by*, 152 F.3d 920 (2d Cir. 1998), *cert. denied*, 119 S.Ct. 90 (1998). As "MovieBuff" and "moviebuff.com" are, for all intents and purposes, identical in terms of sight, sound, and meaning, we conclude that the similarity factor weighs heavily in favor of Brookfield.

The similarity of marks alone, as we have explained, does not necessarily lead to consumer confusion. Accordingly, we must proceed to consider the relatedness of the products and services offered. Related goods are generally more likely than unrelated goods to confuse the public as to the producers of the goods. *See Official Airline Guides*, 6 F.3d at 1392 (citing *Sleekcraft*, 599 F.2d 341 at 350). In light of the virtual identity of marks, if they were used with identical products or services likelihood of confusion would follow as a matter of course. *See Lindy Pen Co. v. Bic Pen Corp.*, 796 F.2d 254, 256–57 (9th Cir. 1986) (reversing a district court's finding of no likelihood of confusion even though the six other likelihood of confusion factors all weighed against a finding of likelihood of confusion); *Interpace Corp. v. Lapp, Inc.*, 721 F.2d 460, 462 (3d Cir. 1983). If, on the other hand, Brookfield and West Coast did not compete to any extent whatsoever, the likelihood of confusion would probably be remote. A Web surfer who accessed "moviebuff.com" and reached a web site advertising the services of Schlumberger Ltd. (a large oil drilling company) would be unlikely to think that Brookfield had entered the oil drilling business or was sponsoring the oil driller. *See, e.g., Toys "R" Us, Inc. v. Feinberg*, 26 F. Supp. 2d 639, 643 (S.D.N.Y. 1998) (no likelihood of confusion between "gunsrus.com" firearms web site and "Toys 'R' Us" trademark); *Interstellar Starship*, 983 F. Supp. at 1336 (finding no likelihood of confusion between use of "epix.com" to advertise the Rocky Horror Picture Show and "Epix" trademark registered for use with computer circuit boards). At the least, Brookfield would bear the heavy burden of demonstrating (through other relevant factors) that consumers were likely to be confused as to source or affiliation in such a circumstance.

The district court classified West Coast and Brookfield as non-competitors largely on the basis that Brookfield is primarily an information provider while West Coast primarily rents and sells videotapes. It noted that West Coast's web site is used more by the somewhat curious video consumer who wants general movie information, while entertainment industry professionals, aspiring entertainment executives and professionals, and highly focused moviegoers are more likely to need or to want the more detailed information provided by "MovieBuff." This analysis, however, overemphasizes differences in principal lines of business, as we have previously instructed that "the relatedness of each company's prime directive isn't relevant." *Dreamwerks*, 142 F.3d at 1131. Instead, the focus is on whether the consuming public is likely somehow to associate West Coast's products with Brookfield. *See id.* Here, both companies offer products and services relating to the entertainment industry generally, and their principal lines of business both relate to movies specifically and are not as different as guns and toys, *see Toys "R" Us*, 26 F. Supp. 2d at 643, or computer circuit boards and the Rocky Horror Picture Show, *see Interstellar Starship*, 983 F. Supp. at 1336. Thus, Brookfield and West Coast are not properly characterized as non-competitors. *See American Int'l Group, Inc. v. American Int'l Bank*, 926 F.2d 829, 832 (9th Cir. 1991) (concluding that although the parties were not direct competitors, they both provided financial services and that customer confusion could result in light of the similarities between the companies' services).

Not only are they not non-competitors, the competitive proximity of their products is actually quite high. Just as Brookfield's "MovieBuff" is a searchable database with detailed information on films, West Coast's web site features a similar searchable database, which Brookfield points out is licensed from a direct competitor of Brookfield. Undeniably then, the products are used for similar purposes. "The rights of the owner of a registered trademark . . . extend to any goods related in the minds of consumers," *E. Remy Martin & Co. v. Shaw-Ross Int'l Imports, Inc.*, 756 F.2d 1525, 1530 (11th Cir. 1985), and Brookfield's and West Coast's products are certainly so related to some extent. The relatedness is further evidenced by the fact that the two companies compete for the patronage of an overlapping audience. The use of similar marks to offer similar products accordingly weighs heavily in favor of likelihood of confusion. *See Sleekcraft*, 599 F.2d at 348 (concluding that high-speed waterskiing racing boats are sufficiently related to family-oriented recreational boats that the public is likely to be confused as to the source of the boats); *Fleischmann Distilling Corp. v. Maier Brewing Co.*, 314 F.2d 149, 153–55 (9th Cir. 1963) (concluding that beer and whiskey are sufficiently similar to create a likelihood of confusion regarding the source of origin when sold under the same trade name); *see also Champions Golf Club, Inc. v. Champions Golf Club, Inc.*, 78 F.3d 1111, 1118 (6th Cir. 1996).

In addition to the relatedness of products, West Coast and Brookfield both utilize the Web as a marketing and advertising facility, a factor that courts have consistently recognized as exacerbating the likelihood of confusion. *See, e.g., Public Serv. Co.*, 1999 WL 98973, at *3 (unpublished); *Washington Speakers Bureau, Inc. v. Leading Auths., Inc.*, 33 F. Supp. 2d

488 (E.D. Va. 1999); *Jews for Jesus v. Brodsky*, 993 F. Supp. 282, 304–05 (D.N.J. 1998), *aff'd*, 159 F.3d 1351 (3d Cir. 1998); *Interstellar Starship Servs.*, 983 F. Supp. at 1336; *Planned Parenthood Fed'n of America*, 1997 WL 133313, at *8 (unpublished). Both companies, apparently recognizing the rapidly growing importance of Web commerce, are maneuvering to attract customers via the Web. Not only do they compete for the patronage of an overlapping audience on the Web, both "MovieBuff" and "moviebuff.com" are utilized in conjunction with Web-based products.

Given the virtual identity of "moviebuff.com" and "MovieBuff," the relatedness of the products and services accompanied by those marks, and the companies' simultaneous use of the Web as a marketing and advertising tool, many forms of consumer confusion are likely to result. People surfing the Web for information on "MovieBuff" may confuse "MovieBuff" with the searchable entertainment database at "moviebuff.com" and simply assume that they have reached Brookfield's web site. *See, e.g., Cardservice Int'l*, 950 F. Supp. at 741. In the Internet context, in particular, entering a web site takes little effort—usually one click from a linked site or a search engine's list; thus, Web surfers are more likely to be confused as to the ownership of a web site than traditional patrons of a brick-and-mortar store would be of a store's ownership. Alternatively, they may incorrectly believe that West Coast licensed "MovieBuff" from Brookfield, *see, e.g., Indianapolis Colts, Inc. v. Metropolitan Baltimore Football Club Ltd.*, 34 F.3d 410, 415–16 (7th Cir. 1994), or that Brookfield otherwise sponsored West Coast's database, *see E. Remy Martin*, 756 F.2d at 1530; *Fuji Photo Film Co. v. Shinohara Shoji Kabushiki Kaisha*, 754 F.2d 591, 596 (5th Cir. 1985). Other consumers may simply believe that West Coast bought out Brookfield or that they are related companies.

Yet other forms of confusion are likely to ensue. Consumers may wrongly assume that the "MovieBuff" database they were searching for is no longer offered, having been replaced by West Coast's entertainment database, and thus simply use the services at West Coast's web site. *See, e.g., Cardservice Int'l*, 950 F. Supp. at 741. And even where people realize, immediately upon accessing "moviebuff.com," that they have reached a site operated by West Coast and wholly unrelated to Brookfield, West Coast will still have gained a customer by appropriating the goodwill that Brookfield has developed in its "MovieBuff" mark. A consumer who was originally looking for Brookfield's products or services may be perfectly content with West Coast's database (especially as it is offered free of charge); but he reached West Coast's site because of its use of Brookfield's mark as its second-level domain name, which is a misappropriation of Brookfield's goodwill by West Coast. *See infra* Part V.B.

The district court apparently assumed that likelihood of confusion exists only when consumers are confused as to the source of a product they actually purchase. It is, however, well established that the Lanham Act protects against the many other forms of confusion that we have outlined. *See Pebble Beach*, 155 F.3d 526 at 544; *Indianapolis Colts*, 34 F.3d at 415–16; *Fuji Photo Film*, 754 F.2d at 596; *HMH Publ'g Co. v. Brincat*, 504 F.2d 713, 716–17 & n.7 (9th Cir. 1974); *Fleischmann Distilling*, 314 F.2d at 155.

The factors that we have considered so far—the similarity of marks, the relatedness of product offerings, and the overlap in marketing and advertising channels—lead us to the tentative conclusion that Brookfield has made a strong showing of likelihood of confusion. Because it is possible that the remaining factors will tip the scale back the other way if they weigh strongly enough in West Coast's favor, we consider the remaining likelihood of confusion factors, beginning with the strength of Brookfield's mark. The stronger a mark—meaning the more likely it is to be remembered and associated in the public mind with the mark's owner—the greater the protection it is accorded by the trademark laws. *See Kenner Parker Toys Inc. v. Rose Art Indus., Inc.*, 963 F.2d 350, 353 (Fed. Cir. 1992); *Nutri/System*, 809 F.2d at 605. Marks can be conceptually classified along a spectrum of generally increasing inherent distinctiveness as generic, descriptive, suggestive, arbitrary, or fanciful. *See Two Pesos*, 505 U.S. at 768. West Coast asserts that Brookfield's mark is "not terribly distinctive," by which it apparently means suggestive, but only weakly so. Although Brookfield does not seriously dispute that its mark is only suggestive, it does defend its (mark's) muscularity.

We have recognized that, unlike arbitrary or fanciful marks which are typically strong, suggestive marks are presumptively weak. *See, e.g., Nutri/Systems*, 809 F.2d at 605. As the district court recognized, placement within the conceptual distinctiveness spectrum is not the only determinant of a mark's strength, as advertising expenditures can transform a suggestive mark into a strong mark, *see id.*, where, for example, that mark has achieved actual marketplace recognition, *see Streetwise Maps, Inc. v. VanDam, Inc.*, 159 F.3d 739, 743–44 (2d Cir. 1998). Brookfield, however, has not come forth with substantial evidence establishing the widespread recognition of its mark; although it argues that its strength is established from its use of "MovieBuff" for over five years, its federal and California state registrations, and its expenditure of $100,000 in advertising its mark, the district court did not clearly err in classifying "MovieBuff" as weak. Some weak marks are weaker than others, and although "MovieBuff" falls within the weak side of the strength spectrum, the mark is not so flabby as to compel a finding of no likelihood of confusion in light of the other factors that we have considered. Importantly, Brookfield's trademark is not descriptive because it does not describe either the software product or its purpose. Instead, it is suggestive—and thus strong enough to warrant trademark protection—because it requires a mental leap from the mark to the product. *See Self-Realization Fellowship Church v. Ananda Church of Self-Realization*, 59 F.3d 902, 910–11 (9th Cir. 1995). Because the products involved are closely related and West Coast's domain name is nearly identical to Brookfield's trademark, the strength of the mark is of diminished importance in the likelihood of confusion analysis. *See* McCarthy Par. 11:76 ("Whether a mark is weak or not is of little importance where the conflicting mark is identical and the goods are closely related.").

We thus turn to intent. "The law has long been established that if an infringer 'adopts his designation with the intent of deriving benefit from the reputation of the trade-mark or trade name, its intent may be sufficient to justify the inference that there are confusing similarities.'" *Pacific Telesis v. International Telesis Comms.*, 994 F.2d 1364, 1369 (9th Cir. 1993) (quoting Restatement of Torts, § 729, Comment on Clause (b)f (1938)). An inference of confusion has similarly been deemed appropriate where a mark is adopted with the intent to deceive the public. *See Gallo*, 967 F.2d at 1293 (citing *Sleekcraft*, 599 F.2d at 354). The district court found that the intent factor favored West Coast because it did not adopt the "moviebuff.com" mark with the specific purpose of infringing Brookfield's trademark. The intent prong, however, is not so narrowly confined.

This factor favors the plaintiff where the alleged infringer adopted his mark with knowledge, actual or constructive, that it was another's trademark. *See Official Airline Guides*, 6 F.3d at 1394 ("When an alleged infringer knowingly adopts a mark similar to another's, courts will presume an intent to deceive the public."); *Fleischmann Distilling*, 314 F.2d 149 at 157. In the Internet context, in particular, courts have appropriately recognized that the intentional registration of a domain name knowing that the second-level domain is another company's valuable trademark weighs in favor of likelihood of confusion. *See, e.g., Washington Speakers*, 1999 WL 51869, at *10 (unpublished). There is, however, no evidence in the record that West Coast registered "moviebuff.com" with the principal intent of confusing consumers. Brookfield correctly points out that, by the time West Coast launched its web site, it *did* know of Brookfield's claim to rights in the trademark "MovieBuff." But when it registered the domain name with Network Solutions, West Coast did not know of Brookfield's rights in "MovieBuff" (at least Brookfield has not established that it did). Although Brookfield asserts that West Coast could easily have launched its web site at its alternate domain address, "westcoastvideo.com," thereby avoiding the infringement problem, West Coast claims that it had already invested considerable sums in developing its "moviebuff.com" web site by the time that Brookfield informed it of its rights in the trademark. Considered as a whole, this factor appears indeterminate.

Importantly, an intent to confuse consumers is not required for a finding of trademark infringement. *See Dreamwerks*, 142 F.3d at 1132 n.12 ("Absence of malice is no defense to trademark infringement"); *Daddy's Junky Music Stores*, 109 F.3d 275 at 287 ("As noted, the presence of intent can constitute strong evidence of confusion. The converse of this proposition, however, is not true: the lack of intent by a defendant is largely irrelevant in determining if consumers likely will be confused as to source.") (internal quotation marks and citations omitted); *Fleischmann Distilling*, 314 F.2d at 157. Instead, this factor is only relevant to the extent that it bears upon the likelihood that consumers will be confused by the alleged infringer's mark (or to the extent that a court wishes to consider it as an equitable consideration). *See Sleekcraft Boats*, 599 F.2d at 348 n.10. Here, West Coast's intent does not appear to bear upon the likelihood of confusion because it did not act with such an intent from which it is appropriate to infer consumer confusion.

The final three *Sleekcraft* factors—evidence of actual confusion, likelihood of expansion in product lines, and purchaser care—do not affect our ultimate conclusion regarding the likelihood of confusion. The first two factors do not merit extensive comment. Actual confusion is not relevant because Brookfield filed suit before West Coast began actively using the "moviebuff.com" mark and thus never had the opportunity to collect information on actual confusion. The likelihood of expansion in product lines factor is relatively unimportant where two companies already compete to a significant extent. *See Official Airline Guides*, 6 F.3d at 1394. In any case, it is neither exceedingly likely nor unlikely that West Coast will enter more directly into Brookfield's principal market, or vice versa.

Although the district court did not discuss the degree of care likely to be exercised by purchasers of the products in question, we think that this issue deserves some consideration. Likelihood of confusion is determined on the basis of a "reasonably prudent consumer." *Dreamwerks*, 142 F.3d at 1129; *Sleekcraft*, 599 F.2d at 353. What is expected of this reasonably prudent consumer depends on the circumstances. We expect him to be more discerning—and less easily confused—when he is purchasing expensive items, *see, e.g., Official Airline Guides*, 6 F.3d at 1393 (noting that confusion was unlikely among advertisers when the products in question cost from $2,400 to $16,000), and when the products being sold are marketed primarily to expert buyers, *see, e.g., Accuride Int'l, Inc. v. Accuride Corp.*, 871 F.2d 1531, 1537 (9th Cir. 1989). We recognize, however, that confusion may often be likely even in the case of expensive goods sold to discerning customers. *See Sleekcraft*, 599 F.3d at 353; *see also, e.g., Daddy's Junky Music Stores*, 109 F.3d at 286; *Banff, Ltd. v. Federated Dep't Stores, Inc.*, 841 F.2d 486, 492 (2d Cir. 1988). On the other hand, when dealing with inexpensive products, customers are likely to exercise less care, thus making confusion more likely. *See, e.g., Gallo,* 967 F.2d at 1293 (wine and cheese).

The complexity in this case arises because we must consider both entertainment professionals, who probably will take the time and effort to find the specific product they want, and movie devotees, who will be more easily confused as to the source of the database offered at West Coast's web site. In addition, West Coast's site is likely to be visited by many casual movie watchers. The entertainment professional, movie devotee, and casual watcher are likely to exercise high, little, and very little care, respectively. Who is the reasonably prudent consumer? Although we have not addressed the issue of purchaser care in mixed buyer classes, another circuit has held that "the standard of care to be exercised by the reasonably prudent purchaser will be equal to that of the least sophisticated consumer." *Ford Motor Co. v. Summit Motor Prods., Inc.,* 930 F.2d 277, 283 (3d Cir. 1991); *see also Omega Importing Corp. v. Petri-Kine Camera Co.,* 451 F.2d 1190, 1195 (2d Cir. 1971) (instructing that, where a product is targeted both to discriminating and casual buyers, a court must consider the likelihood of confusion on the part of the relatively unknowledgeable buyers as well as of the former group); 3 McCarthy § 23:100 (advocating this approach). This is not the only approach available to us, as we could alternatively use a weighted average of the different levels of purchaser care in determining how the reasonably prudent consumer would act. We need not, however, decide this question now because the purchaser confusion factor, even considered in the light most favorable to West Coast, is not sufficient to overcome the likelihood of confusion strongly established by the other factors we have analyzed. . . .

In light of the foregoing analysis, we conclude that Brookfield has demonstrated a likelihood of success on its claim that West Coast's use of "moviebuff.com" violates the Lanham Act. We are fully aware that although the question of "whether confusion is likely is a factual determination woven into the law," we nevertheless must review only for clear error the district court's conclusion that the evidence of likelihood of confusion in this case was slim. *See Levi Strauss & Co. v. Blue Bell, Inc.,* 778 F.2d 1352, 1356 (9th Cir. 1985) (en banc). Here, however, we are "left with the definite and firm conviction that a mistake has been made." *Pacific Telesis Group v. International Telesis Comms.,* 994 F.2d 1364, 1367 (9th Cir. 1993).

B

So far we have considered only West Coast's use of the domain name "moviebuff.com." Because Brookfield requested that we also preliminarily enjoin West Coast from using marks confusingly similar to "MovieBuff" in metatags and buried code, we must also decide whether West Coast can, consistently with the trademark and unfair competition laws, use "MovieBuff" or "moviebuff.com" in its HTML code.

At first glance, our resolution of the infringement issues in the domain name context would appear to dictate a similar conclusion of likelihood of confusion with respect to West Coast's use of "moviebuff.com" in its metatags. Indeed, all eight likelihood of confusion factors outlined in Part V-A—with the possible exception of purchaser care, which we discuss below—apply here as they did in our analysis of domain names; we are, after all, dealing with the same marks, the same products and services, the same consumers, etc. Disposing of the issue so readily, however, would ignore the fact that the likelihood of confusion in the domain name context resulted largely from the associational confusion between West Coast's domain name "moviebuff.com" and Brookfield's trademark "MovieBuff." The question in the metatags context is quite different. Here, we must determine whether West Coast can use "MovieBuff" or "moviebuff.com" in the metatags of its web site at "westcoastvideo.com" or at any other domain address *other than* "moviebuff.com" (which we have determined that West Coast may not use).

Although entering "MovieBuff" into a search engine is likely to bring up a list including "westcoastvideo.com" if West Coast has included that term in its metatags, the resulting confusion is not as great as where West Coast uses the "moviebuff.com" domain name. First, when the user inputs "MovieBuff" into an Internet search engine, the list produced by the search engine is likely to include both West Coast's and Brookfield's web sites. Thus, in scanning such list, the Web user will often be able to find the particular web site he is seeking. Moreover, even if the Web user chooses the web site belonging to West Coast, he will see that the domain name of the web site he selected is "westcoastvideo.com." Since there is no confusion resulting from the domain address, and since West Coast's initial web page prominently displays its own name, it is difficult to say that a consumer is likely to be confused about whose site he has reached or to think that Brookfield somehow sponsors West Coast's web site.

Nevertheless, West Coast's use of "moviebuff.com" in metatags will still result in what is known as initial interest confusion. Web surfers looking for Brookfield's "MovieBuff" products who are taken by a search engine to "westcoastvideo.com" will find a database similar enough to "MovieBuff" such that a sizeable number of consumers who were originally looking for Brookfield's product will simply decide to utilize West Coast's offerings instead. Although there is no source confusion in the sense that consumers know they are patronizing West Coast rather than Brookfield, there is nevertheless initial interest confusion in the sense that, by using "moviebuff.com" or "MovieBuff" to divert people looking for "MovieBuff" to its web site, West Coast improperly benefits from the goodwill that Brookfield developed in its mark. Recently in *Dr. Seuss*, we explicitly recognized that the use of another's trademark in a manner calculated "to capture initial consumer attention, even though no actual sale is finally completed as a result of the confusion, may be still an infringement." *Dr. Seuss*, 109 F.3d at 1405 (citing *Mobil Oil Corp. v. Pegasus Petroleum Corp.*, 818 F.2d 254, 257–58 (2d Cir. 1987)).

The *Dr. Seuss* court, in recognizing that the diversion of consumers' initial interest is a form of confusion against which the Lanham Act protects, relied upon *Mobil Oil*. In that case, Mobil Oil Corporation ("Mobil") asserted a federal trademark infringement claim against Pegasus Petroleum, alleging that Pegasus Petroleum's use of "Pegasus" was likely to cause confusion with Mobil's trademark, a flying horse symbol in the form of the Greek mythological Pegasus. Mobil established that "potential purchasers would be misled into an initial interest in Pegasus Petroleum" because they thought that Pegasus Petroleum was associated with Mobil. *Id.* at 260. But these potential customers would generally learn that Pegasus Petroleum was unrelated to Mobil well before any actual sale was consummated. *See id.* Nevertheless, the Second Circuit held that "such initial confusion works a sufficient trademark injury." *Id.*

Mobil Oil relied upon its earlier opinion in *Grotrian, Helfferich, Schulz, Th. Steinweg Nachf. v. Steinway & Sons*, 523 F.2d 1331, 1341–42 (2d Cir. 1975). Analyzing the plaintiff's claim that the defendant, through its use of the "Grotrian-Steinweg" mark, attracted people really interested in plaintiff's "Steinway" pianos, the Second Circuit explained:

> We decline to hold, however, that actual or potential confusion at the time of purchase necessarily must be demonstrated to establish trademark infringement under the circumstances of this case.

The issue here is not the possibility that a purchaser would buy a Grotrian-Steinweg thinking it was actually a Steinway or that Grotrian had some connection with Steinway and Sons. The harm to Steinway, rather, is the likelihood that a consumer, hearing the "Grotrian-Steinweg" name and thinking it had some connection with "Steinway," would consider it on that basis. The "Grotrian-Steinweg" name therefore would attract potential customers based on the reputation built up by Steinway in this country for many years.*Grotrian*, 523 F.2d at 1342.

Both *Dr. Seuss* and the Second Circuit hold that initial interest confusion is actionable under the Lanham Act, which holdings are bolstered by the decisions of many other courts which have similarly recognized that the federal trademark and unfair competition laws do protect against this form of consumer confusion. *See Green Prods.*, 992 F. Supp. 1070, 1076 (N.D. Iowa 1997) ("In essence, ICBP is capitalizing on the strong similarity between Green Products' trademark and ICBP's domain name to lure customers onto its web page."); *SecuraComm Consulting, Inc. v. Securacom Inc.*, 984 F. Supp. 286, 298 (D.N.J. 1997) (" 'Infringement can be based upon confusion that creates initial customer interest, even though no actual sale is finally completed as a result of the confusion.' ") (citing 3 McCarthy § 23:6), *rev'd on other grounds*, 166 F.3d 182, 186 (3d Cir. 1999) ("In this appeal, [appellant] does not challenge the district court's finding of infringement or order of injunctive relief."); *Kompan A.S. v. Park Structures, Inc.*, 890 F. Supp. 1167, 1180 (N.D.N.Y. 1995) ("Kompan argues correctly that it can prevail by showing that confusion between the Kompan and Karavan lines and names will mistakenly lead the consumer to believe there is some connection between the two and therefore develop an interest in the Karavan line that it would not otherwise have had."); *Blockbuster Entertainment Group v. Laylco, Inc.*, 869 F. Supp. 505, 513 (E.D. Mich. 1994) ("Because the names are so similar and the products sold are identical, some unwitting customers might enter a Video Busters store thinking it is somehow connected to Blockbuster. Those customers probably will realize shortly that Video Busters is not related to Blockbuster, but under [*Ferrari S.P.A. Esercizio v. Roberts*, 944 F.2d 1235 (6th Cir. 1991)] and *Grotrian* that is irrelevant."); *Jordache Enters., Inc. v. Levi Strauss & Co.*, 841 F. Supp. 506, 514–15 (S.D.N.Y. 1993) ("Types of confusion that constitute trademark infringement include where . . . potential consumers initially are attracted to the junior user's mark by virtue of its similarity to the senior user's mark, even though these consumers are not actually confused at the time of purchase."); *Sara Lee Corp. v. Kayser-Roth Corp.*, 1992 No. 92–00460 (W.D.N.C. Dec. 1, 1992) ("That situation offers an opportunity for sale not otherwise available by enabling defendant to interest prospective customers by confusion with the plaintiff's product."); *Television Enter. Network, Inc. v. Entertainment Network, Inc.*, 630 F. Supp. 244, 247 (D.N.J. 1986) ("Even if the confusion is cured at some intermediate point before the deal is completed, the initial confusion may be damaging and wrongful."); *Koppers Co. v. Krupp-Koppers GmbH*, 517 F. Supp. 836, 844 (W.D. Pa. 1981) ("Securing the initial business contact by the defendant because of an assumed association between the parties is wrongful even though the mistake is later rectified."). *See also Forum Corp. of North America v. Forum, Ltd.*, 903 F.2d 434, 442 n.2 (7th Cir. 1990) ("We point out that the fact that confusion as to the source of a product or service is eventually dispelled does not eliminate the trademark infringement which has already occurred."). *But see Astra Pharm. Prods., Inc. v. Beckman Instruments, Inc.*, 718 F.2d 1201, 1206–08 (1st Cir. 1983) (suggesting that only confusion that affects "the ultimate decision of a purchaser whether to buy a particular product" is actionable); *Teletech Customer Care Mgmt. (Cal.), Inc. v. Tele-Tech Co.*, 977 F. Supp. 1407, 1410, 1414 (C.D. Cal. 1997) (finding likelihood of initial interest confusion but concluding that such "brief confusion is not cognizable under the trademark laws").

Using another's trademark in one's metatags is much like posting a sign with another's trademark in front of one's store. Suppose West Coast's competitor (let's call it "Blockbuster") puts up a billboard on a highway reading—"West Coast Video: 2 miles ahead at Exit 7"—where West Coast is really located at Exit 8 but Blockbuster is located at Exit 7. Customers looking for West Coast's store will pull off at Exit 7 and drive around looking for it. Unable to locate West Coast, but seeing the Blockbuster store right by the highway entrance, they may simply rent there. Even consumers who prefer West Coast may find it not worth the trouble to continue searching for West Coast since there is a Blockbuster right there. Customers are not confused in the narrow sense: they are fully aware that they are purchasing from Blockbuster and they have no reason to believe that Blockbuster is related to, or in any way sponsored by, West Coast. Nevertheless, the fact that there is only initial consumer confusion does not alter the fact that Blockbuster would be misappropriating West Coast's acquired goodwill. *See Blockbuster*, 869 F. Supp. at 513 (finding trademark infringement where the defendant, a video rental store, attracted customers' initial interest by using a sign confusingly to its competitor's even though confusion would end long before the point of sale or rental); *see also Dr. Seuss*, 109 F.3d at 1405; *Mobil Oil*, 818 F.2d at 260; *Green Prods.*, 992 F. Supp. at 1076.

The few courts to consider whether the use of another's trademark in one's metatags constitutes trademark infringement have ruled in the affirmative. For example, in a case in which Playboy Enterprises, Inc. ("Playboy") sued AsiaFocus International, Inc. ("AsiaFocus") for trademark infringement resulting from AsiaFocus's use of the federally registered trademarks "Playboy" and "Playmate" in its HTML code, a district court granted judgment in Playboy's favor, reasoning that AsiaFocus intentionally misled viewers into believing that its Web site was connected with, or sponsored by, Playboy. *See Playboy Enters. v. AsiaFocus Int'l, Inc.*, No. 97–734 (E.D. Va. 1998).

In a similar case also involving Playboy, a district court in California concluded that Playboy had established a likelihood of success on the merits of its claim that defendants' repeated use of "Playboy" within "machine readable code in Defendants' Internet Web pages, so that the PLAYBOY trademark [was] accessible to individuals or Internet search engines which attempted to access Plaintiff under Plaintiff's PLAYBOY registered trademark" constituted trademark infringement. *See Playboy Enters. v. Calvin Designer Label*, 985 F. Supp. 1220, 1221 (N.D. Cal. 1997). The court accordingly enjoined the defendants from using Playboy's marks in buried code or metatags. *See id.* at 1221–22.

In a metatags case with an interesting twist, a district court in Massachusetts also enjoined the use of metatags in a manner that resulted in initial interest confusion. *See Niton*, 27 F. Supp. 2d at 102–05.

In that case, the defendant Radiation Monitoring Devices ("RMD") did not simply use Niton Corporation's ("Niton") trademark in its metatags. Instead, RMD's web site directly copied Niton's web site's metatags and HTML code. As a result, whenever a search performed on an Internet search engine listed Niton's web site, it also listed RMD's site. Although the opinion did not speak in terms of initial consumer confusion, the court made clear that its issuance of preliminary injunctive relief was based on the fact that RMD was purposefully diverting people looking for Niton to its web site. *See id.* at 104–05.

Consistently with *Dr. Seuss*, the Second Circuit, and the cases which have addressed trademark infringement through metatags use, we conclude that the Lanham Act bars West Coast from including in its metatags any term confusingly similar with Brookfield's mark. West Coast argues that our holding conflicts with *Holiday Inns*, in which the Sixth Circuit held that there was no trademark infringement where an alleged infringer merely took advantage of a situation in which confusion was likely to exist and did not affirmatively act to create consumer confusion. *See Holiday Inns*, 86 F.3d 619 at 622 (holding that the use of "1-800-405-4329"—which is equivalent to "1-800-HzeroLIDAY"—did not infringe Holiday Inn's trademark, "1-800-HOLIDAY"). Unlike the defendant in *Holiday Inns*, however, West Coast was not a passive figure; instead, it acted affirmatively in placing Brookfield's trademark in the metatags of its web site, thereby *creating* the initial interest confusion. Accordingly, our conclusion comports with *Holiday Inns*.

C

Contrary to West Coast's contentions, we are not in any way restricting West Coast's right to use terms in a manner which would constitute fair use under the Lanham Act. *See New Kids on the Block v. News Amer. Publ'g, Inc.*, 971 F.2d 302, 306–09 (9th Cir. 1992); *see also August Storck K.G. v. Nabisco, Inc.*, 59 F.3d 616, 617–18 (7th Cir. 1995). It is well established that the Lanham Act does not prevent one from using a competitor's mark truthfully to identify the competitor's goods, *see, e.g., Smith v. Chanel, Inc.*, 402 F.2d 562, 563 (9th Cir. 1968) (stating that a copyist may use the originator's mark to identify the product that it has copied), or in comparative advertisements, *see New Kids on the Block*, 971 F.2d at 306–09. This fair use doctrine applies in cyberspace as it does in the real world. *See Radio Channel Networks, Inc. v. Broadcast.Com, Inc.*, No. 98–4799 (S.D.N.Y. 1999); *Bally Total Fitness Holding Corp. v. Faber*, 29 F. Supp. 2d 1161 (C.D. Cal. 1998); *Welles*, 7 F. Supp. 2d at 1103–04; *Patmont Motor Werks, Inc. v. Gateway Marine, Inc.*, No. 96–2703 (N.D. Cal. Dec. 18, 1997); *see also Universal Tel-A-Talk*, 1998 WL 767440, at *9 (unpublished).

In *Welles*, the case most on point, Playboy sought to enjoin former Playmate of the Year Terri Welles ("Welles") from using "Playmate" or

"Playboy" on her web site featuring photographs of herself. *See* 7 F. Supp. 2d at 1100. Welles's web site advertised the fact that she was a former Playmate of the Year, but minimized the use of Playboy's marks; it also contained numerous disclaimers stating that her site was neither endorsed by nor affiliated with Playboy. The district court found that Welles was using "Playboy" and "Playmate" not as trademarks, but rather as descriptive terms fairly and accurately describing her web page, and that her use of "Playboy" and "Playmate" in her web site's metatags was a permissible, good faith attempt to index the content of her web site. It accordingly concluded that her use was permissible under the trademark laws. *See id.* at 1103–04.

We agree that West Coast can legitimately use an appropriate descriptive term in its metatags. But "MovieBuff" is not such a descriptive term. Even though it differs from "Movie Buff" by only a single space, that difference is pivotal. The term "Movie Buff" is a descriptive term, which is routinely used in the English language to describe a movie devotee. "MovieBuff" is not. The term "MovieBuff" is not in the dictionary. *See Merriam-Webster's Collegiate Dictionary* 762 (10th ed. 1998); *American Heritage College Dictionary* 893 (3d ed. 1997); *Webster's New World College Dictionary* 889 (3d ed. 1997); *Webster's Third New Int'l Dictionary* 1480 (unabridged 1993). Nor has that term been used in any published federal or state court opinion. In light of the fact that it is not a word in the English language, when the term "MovieBuff" *is* employed, it is used to refer to Brookfield's products and services, rather than to mean "motion picture enthusiast." The proper term for the "motion picture enthusiast" is "Movie Buff," which West Coast certainly *can* use. It cannot, however, omit the space.

Moreover, West Coast is not absolutely barred from using the term "MovieBuff." As we explained above, that term can be legitimately used to describe Brookfield's product. For example, its web page might well include an advertisement banner such as "Why pay for MovieBuff when you can get the same thing here for FREE?" which clearly employs "MovieBuff" to refer to Brookfield's products. West Coast, however, presently uses Brookfield's trademark not to reference Brookfield's products, but instead to describe its own product (in the case of the domain name and to attract people to its web site in the case of the metatags). That is not fair use.

VI

Having concluded that Brookfield has established a likelihood of success on the merits of its trademark infringement claim, we analyze the other requirement for preliminary injunctive relief inquiry, irreparable injury. Although the district court did not address this issue, irreparable injury may be presumed from a showing of likelihood of success on the merits of a trademark infringement claim. *See Metro Publ'g, Ltd. v. San*

Jose Mercury News, 987 F.2d 637, 640 (9th Cir. 1993) ("Once the plaintiff has demonstrated a likelihood of confusion, it is ordinarily presumed that the plaintiff will suffer irreparable harm if injunctive relief is not granted."). Preliminary injunctive relief is appropriate here to prevent irreparable injury to Brookfield's interests in its trademark "MovieBuff" and to promote the public interest in protecting trademarks generally as well.

VII

As we have seen, registration of a domain name for a Web site does not trump long-established principles of trademark law. When a firm uses a competitor's trademark in the domain name of its web site, users are likely to be confused as to its source or sponsorship. Similarly, using a competitor's trademark in the metatags of such web site is likely to cause what we have described as initial interest confusion. These forms of confusion are exactly what the trademark laws are designed to prevent.

Accordingly, we reverse and remand this case to the district court with instructions to enter a preliminary injunction in favor of Brookfield in accordance with this opinion.

REVERSED and REMANDED.

INTERSTELLAR STARSHIP SERVICES, LTD. V. EPIX, INC.

304 F.3d 936 (9th Cir. 2002)

TROTT, J.

Epix, Inc. ("Epix") sued Interstellar Starship Services ("ISS") and its president Michael Tchou ("Tchou") in district court alleging that their use of the *www.epix.com* domain name infringed Epix's registered EPIX trademark. The district court enjoined ISS and Tchou from future infringing uses of *www.epix.com* but allowed ISS to retain ownership of the domain name. Epix appeals, contesting the district court's failure to find that: (1) ISS's use of epix.com caused initial interest confusion; (2) ISS cybersquatted on epix.com; and (3) ISS diluted the EPIX trademark. Epix appeals also the scope of the injunction imposed by the district court. In the main, Epix argues that the epix.com domain name should be transferred from ISS to Epix or that the injunction should be broadened to include ISS's future successors and assigns of *www.epix.com*. We have jurisdiction pursuant to 28 U.S.C. § 1291 and affirm the district court's decision in all respects.

BACKGROUND

Epix manufactures and sells a wide variety of electronic imaging hardware and software products and provides consulting services associated with these products. Epix markets its products to sophisticated consumers, mainly universities, research laboratories, and photography enthusiasts. It advertises in a variety of trade magazines and sells its products through distributors and on the Internet at *www.epixinc.com*. Its products retail for $395 to $2000.

Epix first used the trademark EPIX in 1984, and registered that mark in 1990 with the Patent and Trademark Office ("PTO") for use with "printed circuit boards and computer programs for image acquisition, processing, display, and transmission." The EPIX trademark acquired incontestable status in December 1996. Epix registered its EPIX mark with the State of Oregon on June 17, 1997.

Tchou is an electrical engineer, with a background in electronic imaging, who has worked for Lattice Corporation and more recently, Intel. Tchou is also the sole founder, officer, director, shareholder and employee of ISS. In 1995, as president of ISS, Tchou registered the domain name *www.epix.com* with Network Solutions. Tchou testified that he registered the domain name epix.com because the catchy name connoted electronic ("e") pictures ("pix").

We have remarked before that "the record does not make crystal clear the precise nature of ISS's business or its use of the 'epix.com' webpage." *Interstellar Starship Servs. v. Epix, Inc.*, 184 F.3d 1107, 1109 (9th Cir. 1999) (*Interstellar I*). As the district court once described: "The site has some characteristics of a serious business venture and some characteristics of a personal scrapbook." *Interstellar Starship Servs. v. Epix, Inc.*, 125 F. Supp. 2d 1269, 1274 (D. Or. 2001). Tchou testified at trial that he hopes to develop the epix.com website into a multimillion dollar Internet portal, like Yahoo, featuring a variety of electronic pictures.

Since its launch, however, ISS's website has not grown to epic proportions. Instead, it has been used mainly to promote the Clinton Street Cabaret, a Portland theater troupe that performs *The Rocky Horror Picture Show*. The website contains numerous digital pictures of the actors and the playhouse, as well as information related to the performance and history of *Rocky Horror*. Several webpages display identification badges that ISS made for members of the Clinton Street Cabaret and a splinter acting group, Sibling Rivalry. A question and answer page provides peculiar information touting Tchou's badge-making abilities.

Initially, the website included uncommonly detailed information about how Tchou transferred the digital pictures onto the Internet and how he touched them up before posting. This information suggested that Tchou prepared the photographs using "proprietary epix.com pixel manipulation (bit-twiddling) tools." In addition, a beta version of the website allegedly hyperlinked to a webpage containing autobiographical information about Tchou. That page purportedly ballyhooed Tchou's technical experience with computer hardware, software, and graphics and also permitted visitors to read about ISS and its consulting services.

The present dispute first erupted when Epix unsuccessfully attempted to register the *www.epix.com* domain name that ISS was already using. Epix demanded that Network Solutions cancel ISS's epix.com registration. When informed by Network Solutions of Epix's demand, ISS filed for a declaratory judgment of non-infringement. Epix counterclaimed, alleging federal unfair competition and trademark infringement, as well as Oregon trademark infringement and dilution. Once Epix counterclaimed, or at some point thereabouts, ISS stripped its site of everything except the Clinton Street Cabaret information.

In the first go-round of this contest, the district court granted summary judgment in favor of ISS, finding no likelihood of confusion between ISS's use of epix.com to support the Clinton Street Cabaret and Epix's business use of the mark EPIX. *Interstellar Starship Servs. v. Epix Inc.*, 983 F. Supp. 1331, 1336–37 (D. Or. 1997). Epix appealed. We held that although the district court "undertook a well-reasoned analysis of the appropriate law," there remained contested issues of material fact concerning whether ISS and Tchou infringed Epix's registration of the EPIX mark by using the epix.com website. *Interstellar I*, 184 F.3d at 1111.

On remand, Epix amended its complaint to include a claim of cybersquatting pursuant to the newly enacted Anticybersquatting Consumer Protection Act ("ACPA"), 15 U.S.C. § 1125(d) (1999). A bench trial ensued, wherein the district court resolved numerous contested factual matters. In the end, the district court held that ISS's *past* use of epix.com to promote Tchou's digital image processing software and computer consulting services *did* infringe Epix's trademark. The district court determined, however, that ISS's *present* use of epix.com to display electronic pictures and other information related to *The Rocky Horror Picture Show did not* infringe Epix's trademark. The district court found no cybersquatting violation under the ACPA and no trademark dilution under Oregon law. To remedy ISS's past infringement, the district court enjoined ISS from further infringing uses of the EPIX mark, including promotion of Tchou's technical services and digital image processing, the use of gray wallpaper, and the use of the EPIX.COM logo without an appropriate annotation disclaiming any affiliation with Epix. Nevertheless, the district court allowed ISS to retain ownership of epix.com. Epix appeals the district court's refusal to transfer to it the epix.com domain name after finding past infringement by ISS.

Epix appeals also the district court's determinations that ISS's use of epix.com did not result in initial interest confusion, that ISS did not cybersquat on epix.com, and that ISS did not dilute the EPIX mark.

Finally, Epix prays that we broaden the district court's injunction to encompass ISS's successors and assigns of the epix.com domain name.

STANDARD OF REVIEW

We review for clear error the district court's legal and factual determination of likelihood of confusion under the trademark laws. *GoTo.Com, Inc. v. Walt Disney Co.*, 202 F.3d 1199, 1204 (9th Cir. 2000). If the district court's account of the evidence is plausible in light of the record viewed in its entirety, we may not reverse even though convinced that had we been sitting as the trier of fact, we would have weighed the evidence differently. *Anderson v. Bessemer City*, 470 U.S. 564, 573–74, 84 L.Ed.2d 518, 105 S.Ct. 1504 (1985). The district court's injunctive relief is reviewed for an abuse of discretion. *Brookfield Communications, Inc. v. W. Coast Entm't Corp.*, 174 F.3d 1036, 1045 (9th Cir. 1999). The grant of a permanent injunction will be reversed only when the district court based its decision on an erroneous legal standard or on clearly erroneous findings of fact. *GoTo.Com*, 202 F.3d at 1204.

DISCUSSION

I.   INITIAL INTEREST CONFUSION

The core element of trademark infringement is whether the similarity of the marks is likely to confuse customers about the source of the products. In this case, Epix argues that ISS's and Tchou's use of epix.com causes a likelihood of initial interest confusion among consumers. *See Brookfield*, 174 F.3d at 1062 (applying initial interest confusion to a domain name case); *Mobil Oil Corp. v. Pegasus Petroleum Corp.*, 818 F.2d 254, 260 (2d Cir. 1987) (recognizing the possibility of initial interest confusion). Initial interest confusion occurs when the defendant uses the plaintiff's trademark "in a manner calculated 'to capture initial consumer attention, even though no actual sale is finally completed as a result of the confusion.'" *Brookfield*, 174 F.3d at 1062 (quoting *Dr. Seuss Enters. v. Penguin Books*, 109 F.3d 1394, 1405 (9th Cir. 1997)); *see also Interstellar I*, 184 F.3d at 1110 ("We recognize a brand of confusion called 'initial interest' confusion, which permits a finding of a likelihood of confusion although the consumer quickly becomes aware of the source's actual identity and no purchase is made as a result of the confusion."). . . .

Epix contends that ISS's use of www.epix.com initially confuses consumers who expect to find Epix at that web address. In the end, however, this dispute arises because while many brick and mortar companies can peacefully coexist using the EPIX mark, there can be only one owner and user of *www.epix.com*.

To evaluate the likelihood of confusion, including initial interest confusion, the so-called *Sleekcraft* factors provide non-exhaustive guidance. *AMF Inc. v. Sleekcraft Boats*, 599 F.2d 341, 346 (9th Cir. 1979);

see also Checkpoint Sys., Inc. v. Check Point Software Tech., Inc., 269 F.3d 270, 297 (3d Cir. 2001) (applying similar factors to initial interest confusion). Those factors are: (1) the similarity of the marks; (2) the relatedness or proximity of the two companies' products or services; (3) the strength of the registered mark; (4) the marketing channels used; (5) the degree of care likely to be exercised by the purchaser in selecting goods; (6) the accused infringers' intent in selecting its mark; (7) evidence of actual confusion; and (8) the likelihood of expansion in product lines. *Sleekcraft*, 599 F.2d at 346. This eight factor test is pliant, and the relative import of each factor is case specific. *Brookfield*, 174 F.3d at 1054.

We have held that "in the context of the Web," the three most important *Sleekcraft* factors in evaluating a likelihood of confusion are (1) the similarity of the marks, (2) the relatedness of the goods or services, and (3) the parties' simultaneous use of the Web as a marketing channel. *GoTo.Com*, 202 F.3d at 1205. When this "controlling troika," *id.* at 1205, or internet trinity, "suggests confusion is . . . likely," *id.* at 1207, the other factors must "weigh strongly" against a likelihood of confusion to avoid the finding of infringement. *Brookfield*, 174 F.3d at 1058. If the internet trinity does not clearly indicate a likelihood of consumer confusion, a district court can conclude the infringement analysis only by balancing all the *Sleekcraft* factors within the unique context of each case.

Epix contends the district court erred as a matter of law in evaluating its claim of initial interest confusion. It argues that the district court erroneously considered all of the *Sleekcraft* factors, rather than just the internet trinity. We disagree.

To the district court's credit, it waded through volumes of evidence and around acrimonious litigants. In making its findings of fact, the district court fastidiously evaluated complex and conflicting testimony. Analyzing the internet trinity, the district court found that the parties' marks (EPIX and epix.com, respectively) were indistinguishable. As for the relatedness of the products, the district court determined that ISS's primary purpose—the promotion of the Clinton Street Cabaret—did not compete with Epix's electronic imaging products, although ISS's incidental purpose—digital image processing and computer-related services—appeared, "at least superficially," the same as services offered by Epix. Finally, the district court determined that both parties maintained an Internet presence, but marketed to a different consumer base. This examination of the "controlling troika" did not clearly indicate that consumer confusion was likely. Thus, the district court appropriately concluded the analysis by balancing all the remaining *Sleekcraft* factors within the unique context of this case.

Considering the remaining *Sleekcraft* factors, the district court determined that Epix's trademark was relatively weak, and that Epix's customers exercised a high degree of care purchasing expensive electronic imaging equipment. Weighing the conflicting evidence, the district court questioned Tchou's veracity, but in the end, found Tchou that adopted epix.com in good faith without knowledge of Epix's mark. Finally, the district court found no evidence of actual confusion and no likelihood that either company would "bridge the gap" to the other company's products or services. The district court did not err in employing this comprehensive likelihood of confusion analysis, and its factual findings were not clearly erroneous.

What Epix really wants from us, it seems, is a holding that, as a matter of law, *any* use of epix.com by ISS creates initial interest confusion with the EPIX mark and that Epix is therefore entitled to ownership of *www.epix.com*. Contrary to Epix's contentions and, as a matter of law, all uses of www.epix.com do *not* generate initial interest confusion with the EPIX mark. In a similar case, the First Circuit rejected Epix's basic contention. It held that use of the domain name *www.clue.com* for computer services did not infringe Hasbro's trademark on the board game Clue. *Hasbro, Inc. v. Clue Computing, Inc.*, 232 F.3d 1, 2 (1st Cir. 2000). The *Clue* court found no initial interest confusion because the companies' products were disparate, and there was no evidence of actual confusion. *Id.*

A series of examples further demonstrate why every use of epix.com does not infringe Epix's trademark EPIX for electronic imaging equipment.

If an apple grower adopts a famous trademark, like *www.DRSEUSS. com*, as a domain name, initial interest confusion probably results, even if that business's goods differ significantly from those of Dr. Seuss. Marks of renown, like DR. SEUSS, describe the source of only one company's products, and the apple grower's adoption of the www.DRSEUSS.com domain name inevitably trades on the favorable cachet associated with that company, its works, and its reputation. Actionable initial interest confusion probably results even if every consumer realizes that DRSEUSS.com is owned by an apple grower, and no consumer ever consummates a Winesap, Delicious, or Granny Smith purchase thinking that Dr. Seuss grows apples or endorses, sponsors, or licenses his name to the apple grower.

In some circumstances, however, the apple grower might adopt a famous trademark without causing initial interest confusion. For example, an apple grower in Washington might register *www.apple.com* to promote his business. Although APPLE is a famous registered trademark of Apple Computer, Inc., many other companies also use the term APPLE to describe a variety of products. Indeed, the apple distributor probably does not infringe Apple Computer's mark because APPLE is also a common noun, used by many companies, and the goods offered by these two companies differ significantly. *See Hasbro*, 232 F.3d at 2 (noting very little similarity between Hasbro's board game CLUE and the products and services of Clue Computing); *Brookfield*, 174 F.3d at 1056 (suggesting Schlumberger Ltd (a large oil drilling company) might advertise at *www.moviebuff.com* without infringing the MOVIEBUFF trademark on movie database software because Schlumberger's oil products differ greatly from software).

If, however, the apple grower adopted the *www.apple.com* domain name, and then competed directly with Apple Computer by selling computers, initial interest confusion probably would result. *See Brookfield*, 174 F.3d at 1056 (finding a likelihood of confusion where a company adopted a competitor's trademark as a domain name and offered similar goods under that name). In that circumstance, the apple grower would have acted in a way which traded on the goodwill of Apple Computer's trademark while preventing Apple Computer from using the APPLE trademark itself. This conduct would be actionable because confusion would inevitably result from the apple grower's actions. For example, a consumer might read about the apple grower's computers on *www.apple.com*, where she expected to find computers sold by Apple Computer, and decide to buy one, thereby permitting the apple grower to capitalize on the goodwill of Apple Computer's APPLE trademark—even if the consumer is never confused about the apple grower's lack of connection with Apple Computer. *See Interstellar I*, 184 F.3d at 1111 (defining initial interest confusion in these terms).

The different legal outcomes envisioned by these examples are predicted by the *Sleekcraft* factors. Consumers expect that owners of famous, fanciful trademarks will own the corresponding domain name, like *www.XEROX.com* or *www.KODAK.com*, for no other companies identify themselves or their products using those marks. Indeed, confusion would abound if anyone other than Xerox owned *www.xerox.com*. Consumers, however, would not be shocked to find an apple grower at *www.apple.com* (although Apple Computer actually owns that domain name), or United Van Lines at www.united.com (although United Airlines happens to own that domain name). Although a consumer might incorrectly guess that United Van Lines would be found at www.united.com, *see Brookfield* 174 F.3d at 1044–45 ("Web users often assume as a rule of thumb that the domain name of a particular company will be company name followed by '.com.' "), such an erroneous guess does not generally amount to a likelihood of initial interest confusion.

As the examples demonstrate, actionable initial interest confusion on the Internet is determined, in large part, by the relatedness of the goods offered and the level of care exercised by the consumer. *See Checkpoint Sys.*, 269 F.3d at 296–97 ("Product relatedness and level of care exercised by consumers are relevant factors in determining initial interest confusion."). If a rogue company adopts as its domain name a protected trademark and proceeds to sell goods similar to those offered by the trademark owner, it necessarily free rides on the trademark owner's goodwill, and that rogue company benefits from increasing initial interest confusion as consumers exercise lower levels of care in making their purchasing decisions. Of course, the remainder of the *Sleekcraft* factors complete the case-by-case inquiry necessary to evaluate initial interest confusion on the Internet.

Applying these principles to our case, we find that it most resembles the example of the apple grower registering *www.apple.com* to sell apples. Like Apple Computer (or Hasbro), Epix has no exclusive claim to its trademark. Indeed, the record reflects that at least eight companies have registered the EPIX mark or a close variation with the PTO, and use the term in connection with on a variety of goods, including men's and women's clothing and medical imaging agents. On the Internet, the use of the EPIX mark is even more widespread. In addition to the brick and mortar companies using the EPIX mark in cyberspace, an Internet service provider, the Eastern Pennsylvania Internet Exchange and a Canadian emergency preparedness information exchange use EPIX to describe themselves. EPIX is also the word used in common Internet parlance to denote electronic pictures. Tchou has even suggested that EPIX is used so often on the Internet to describe electronic pictures that it may have become a generic term. *See Abercrombie & Fitch*, 537 F.2d at 9 (describing how a trademark might shift classifications).

Furthermore, ISS's "products"—the Clinton Street Cabaret and *The Rocky Horror Picture Show*—are extraordinarily different from Epix's digital imaging products. As is obvious by comparing Epix's and ISS's websites, electronic imaging equipment is not *The Rocky Horror Picture Show*, and there is no immediate connection between the products. Upon arriving at ISS's epix.com website, the consumer would not think that Epix licensed, sponsored, or owned the ISS website. *Brookfield*, 174 F.3d at 1057. She would simply come to the inevitable and correct conclusion that more than one company uses the EPIX name and that Epix operates its website at a different address. Indeed, any consumer looking for Epix, who mistakenly guessed that it could be found at *www.epix.com*, would realize in one hot second that she was in the wrong place and either guess again or resort to a search engine to locate the Epix site at *www.epixinc. com*.

We note that although the misdirected consumer might enjoy ISS's digital photography momentarily, ISS could not financially capitalize on that misdirected consumer even if it so desired. Overall, the ISS website had little to do with commerce. The website contained no contact information for ISS or Tchou, and it was otherwise unable to interface with users. Indeed, Epix adduced no evidence that ISS or Tchou ever sold any product or service through its website. Under these circumstances, we discern no likelihood of consumer initial interest confusion.

The district court's additional findings of fact round out the *Sleekcraft* analysis and confirm our conclusion. Epix's mark was weak, even in the field of digital imaging equipment. Moreover, Tchou adopted the name epix.com in good faith because it connoted electronic pictures and no evidence indicated that he sought to trade on the goodwill of Epix or that either company intended to bridge the gap into the other's product line. These findings were not clearly erroneous and they support our conclusion that there was no likelihood of confusion in this case.

II. CYBERSQUATTING

Cybersquatting is the Internet version of a land grab. Cybersquatters register well-known brand names as Internet domain names in order to force the rightful owners of the marks to pay for the right to engage in electronic commerce under their own name. *See Virtual Works, Inc. v. Volkswagen of America Inc.*, 238 F.3d 264, 267 (4th Cir. 2001). Congress enacted the ACPA because cybersquatting "threatened 'the continued growth and vitality of the Internet as a platform' for 'communication, electronic commerce, education, entertainment, and countless yet-to-be-determined uses." *Id.* (quoting S. Rep. No. 106–140, at 8 (1999)).

A cybersquatter is liable under the ACPA to the owner of a protected mark if the cybersquatter has:

> (i) a *bad faith intent* to profit from that mark; and

> (ii) registers, traffics in, or uses a domain name that —

>> (I) in the case of mark that is distinctive . . . , is identical or confusingly similar to that mark that is distinctive.

>> (II) in the case of a famous mark . . . , is identical or confusingly similar to or dilutive of that mark.

See 15 U.S.C. § 1125(d)(1)(A) (emphasis added). A finding of "bad faith" is an essential prerequisite to finding an ACPA violation. Congress enumerated a list of nine factors to consider "in determining whether a person has a bad faith intent." *Id.* Congress did not mean these factors to be an exclusive list; instead, "the most important grounds for finding bad faith are 'the unique circumstances of the case, which do not fit neatly into the specific factors enumerated by Congress.'" *Virtual Works*, 238 F.3d at 271 (4th Cir. 2001) (quoting *Sporty's Farm LLC v. Sportsman's Market, Inc.*, 202 F.3d 489, 495 (2d Cir. 2000)). In addition, the ACPA contains a safe harbor provision: Bad faith "shall not be found in any case in which the court determines that the person believed and had a reasonable grounds to believe that the use of the domain name was fair use or otherwise lawful." 15 U.S.C. § 1125(d)(1)(B)(ii).

In this case, the district court expressly determined only whether ISS violated the ACPA by registering the domain name *www.epix.cc*—a domain name which Epix now owns and which is not at issue on appeal. The district court did not consider Epix's ACPA claim as it related to ISS's use of the *www.epix.com*.

The district court found, however, that Tchou and ISS adopted the *www.epix.com* domain name in good faith. In particular, it determined that Tchou adopted the domain name epix.com as a descriptive term to connote electronic pictures. Evidencing his good faith, Tchou performed a web search on "epix" before registering epix.com, but did not find Epix because it was not yet on the Internet. Furthermore, Tchou engaged in a bona fide use of his website. To transform his website into a "widely known internet portal site," Tchou continuously used the domain name and invested money on hardware and software as well as significant amounts of time on the development of a viable business plan.

The district court rejected Epix's farfetched idea that Tchou registered epix.com in an effort to assist his employer and Epix competitor, Intel. The district court did not, however, comment on Epix's other purported evidence of bad faith—ISS's offer to sell Epix the epix.com domain name for $25,000. While offers to sell a contested domain name may in certain circumstances be probative evidence of bad faith, *see Panavision Int'l L.P. v. Toeppen*, 141 F.3d 1316, 1323 (9th Cir. 1998), here, the offer to sell came from ISS's attorney in the context of settlement negotiations after the commencement of litigation; Tchou was not even present. Epix never established before the district court that the settlement offer was made to extort Epix or for any reason other than to settle the case. Rather, the evidence suggests that ISS offered to sell its investment in hardware, software, and time in an operational website devoted to the Clinton Street Cabaret.

The district court's finding that Tchou adopted *www.epix.com* in good faith was not clearly erroneous considering the "unique circumstances" of this case. Without a finding of bad faith, Epix's cybersquatting claim necessarily fails. . . .

CONCLUSION

The district court's decision is AFFIRMED.

NOTES FOR DISCUSSION

1. *Priority on the Internet.* As in the so-called brick-and-mortar world, the first issue to address in determining trademark rights on the Internet is priority. For inherently distinctive marks, priority turns as in the brick-and-mortar world on first use. The difficulty, though, is determining when, and to what extent, prior use in the brick-and-mortar world establishes trademark rights on the Internet. In *Brookfield*, the court analyzes this issue under the

doctrinal rubric of tacking. After some discussion, the Ninth Circuit ultimately rejects West Coast's tacking claims on the grounds that "moviebuff.com" and "The Movie Buff's Movie Store" did not create the "same, continuing commercial impression." *Id.* at 1049. Do you agree with the court's resolution of that issue? If you were a consumer looking for the Movie Buff's Movie Store online, what terms would you enter into a search engine? Would you type out the full phrase or stop at Movie Buff's? If you were guessing, what would you guess the corresponding domain name for the Movie Buff's Movie Store would be? Moreover, in undertaking this analysis, should we consider the mark as a whole, "Movie Buff's Movie Store," or exclude the generic portions of it? Which words in the mark are generic?

In addition, the court acknowledges that West Coast had used a variety of Movie Buff marks, including: "The Movie Buff's Gift Guide"; "The Movie Buff's Gift Store"; "Calling All Movie Buffs!"; "Good News Movie Buffs!"; "Movie Buffs, Show Your Stuff!"; "the Perfect Stocking Stuffer for the Movie Buff!"; "A Movie Buff's Top Ten"; "The Movie Buff Discovery Program"; "Movie Buff Picks"; "Movie Buff Series"; "Movie Buff Selection Program"; and "Movie Buff Film Series." What is the common element of these marks? Usually, when a company uses a family of marks built on a common suffix, prefix, or phrase, we treat that common element alone as independently worthy of trademark protection. For example, the restaurant McDonalds offers a variety of menu items using "Mc" or "Mac," including, among others, the "Big Mac," the "Egg McMuffin, the "McDouble," the "McChicken," and the "McRib." Given this family of marks built on a common prefix, McDonalds has trademark rights in "Mc" or "Mac" independent of each of these specific uses. *See, e.g., McDonald's Corp. v. Druck and Gerner, DDS., P.C.,* 814 F.Supp. 1127, 1135 (N.D.N.Y. 1993) (enjoining defendant's use of McDental for dental services based upon McDonald's family of "Mc" marks); *Quality Inns International, Inc. v. McDonald's Corp.,* 695 F.Supp. 198, 220 (D.Md. 1988) (enjoining defendant's proposed use of McSleep for a hotel based upon McDonald's family of "Mc" marks). Should West Coast have claimed a family of "Movie Buff" marks? Would that have changed the outcome in the case?

However, even if for one of these reasons, we found that moviebuff.com conveyed the same continuing commercial impression as either the non-generic portions of the "Movie Buff's Movie Store" or the family of "Movie Buff" marks, is tacking the right way to approach priority on the Internet? Tacking ordinarily applies when a trademark owner continues to market the same product through the same marketing and distribution channels, but changes its trademark in some way. Is that what West Coast is doing? Asidefrom tacking, what other rubric could we use?

Consider a brick-and-mortar example. Recall from Chapter 3 that under the common law, absent a federal registration, we could have two different entities using the same trademark for the same goods or services, as long as they operated in separate and remote geographic areas. Assume that there is an Acme Oyster House in Washington, D.C., and a separate and unrelated Acme Oyster House in New York City. As between these two restaurants, which has the right to open an Acme Oyster House in a nearby city, such as Philadelphia? In this context, there are three possible answers. First, it may be that neither existing restaurant is known to consumers in Philadelphia. In this case, Philadelphia is virgin territory and whichever restaurant opens in Philadelphia first will have rights in that market. Second, it may be that one or the other restaurant is already known to consumers in Philadelphia. In this case, only the known restaurant could open in Philadelphia. If the other tried, it would create a likelihood of confusion. Third, it may be that both restaurants are already known to consumers in Philadelphia in that one group of consumers travels routinely to D.C. and is familiar with the D.C. restaurant, while a second group routinely travels to New York and is familiar with the New York restaurant. In this case, neither restaurant can expand to Philadelphia. Do you see why?

Moving from the brick-and-mortar world to the Internet presents the same three choices. First, for a given mark and a given set of facts, we can treat the Internet as virgin territory and give the rights to the first business to use a given mark on the Internet. Second, if consumers on the Internet would already associate a given mark with a given company, based upon its brick-and-mortar operations, then presumably that company should already have priority with respect to use of the mark on the Internet. And, third, if several marks are equally well-known in the real world, so that some consumers would expect Company A to be the company using the mark on the Internet, while others would expect Company B, and still others Company C, then we might bar any of the companies from using the mark on the Internet, at least without some further clarification, such as www.brookfieldmoviebuff.com or www.westcoastmoviebuff.com.

Does the tacking doctrine help us much to decide which of these three choices makes the most sense? How should we determine which of these three approaches to apply? The *Brookfield* court eventually determines that Brookfield had priority on the Internet because it used "MovieBuff" online before West Coast began use of www.moviebuff.com. Is that a sensible resolution of the parties' competing priority claims?

2.   *Likelihood of Confusion on the Internet.* In *Brookfield*, the court uses its *Sleekcraft* factor test to determine whether the domain name, www.moviebuff.com creates a likelihood of confusion with Brookfield's MovieBuff mark for its online database. Disagreeing with the district court, the Ninth Circuit finds a likelihood of confusion. Do you agree with the court's conclusion? The district court found no likelihood of confusion primarily because of the differences in the products each company offered. While both offered databases about movies, Brookfield's was directed at industry professionals; in contrast, West Coast's was directed at ordinary consumers. Did the Ninth Circuit give any deference to the district court's findings on these issues or did it simply substitute its judgment for that of the district court?

3.   *Initial Interest Confusion on the Internet.* The *Brookfield* court also finds that West Coast's use of "MovieBuff" in its metatags creates actionable

initial interest confusion. Given that the court has barred West Coast from using www.moviebuff.com, how does the use of "MovieBuff" in the metatags of West Coast's www.westcoastvideo.com website create initial interest confusion? Won't a consumer see immediately the accurate name of the website? How then can a consumer be confused even initially?

How does the *Brookfield* court justify extending the initial interest confusion doctrine from the brick-and-mortar world into the Internet? In the brick-and-mortar world, initial interest confusion may last long enough that a consumer relies on the initial misimpression to begin negotiations towards an actual purpose. Having started down the path towards a purchase in reliance on an initially mistaken impression, a consumer may continue and complete the purchase even if her confusion is cleared up before the purchase is actually consummated. So long as the initial interest confusion lasts long enough to play a material role in a consumer's purchasing decisions, that initial interest confusion should arguably be enough to support trademark liability. The *Brookfield* court's own "driving on the highway" example implicitly recognizes the importance sunk costs and reliance expenditures play in our analysis of initial interest confusion. Having gotten off the freeway and found one video store because the consumer relied on the misleading sign, it would be a lot of trouble to turn around, get back on the freeway, and resume the search for the other video store.

Yet, as the *Brookfield* court itself recognizes, "entering a web site takes little effort—usually one click from a linked site or a search engine's list." *Brookfield Comms., Inc.*, 174 F.3d at 1057. Given the lack of sunk costs or reliance expenditures, is a momentary misdirection on the Internet likely to play a material role in a consumer's purchasing decisions? *See Bihari v. Gross*, 119 F. Supp. 2d 309, 320 n.15 (S.D.N.Y. 2000) ("Use of the highway billboard metaphor is not the best analogy to a metatag on the Internet. The harm caused by a misleading billboard on the highway is difficult to correct. In contrast, on the information superhighway, resuming one's search for the correct website is relatively simple. With one click of the mouse and a few seconds delay, a viewer can return to the search engine's results and resume searching for the original website.").

Moreover, if West Coast's use of "MovieBuff" in its metatags creates initial interest confusion, wouldn't Brookfield's use of www.moviebuff.com create initial interest confusion with West Coast's family of Movie Buff marks? Does the *Brookfield* court address this possibility? How?

4. *The Relation Between Initial Interest Confusion and the Likelihood of Confusion Factor Test.* In *Brookfield*, the court seems to treat the *Sleekcraft* factor test and initial interest confusion as independent bases for liability, applying the first to the www.moviebuff.com domain name and the second to the use of "MovieBuff" in West Coast's metatags. In a footnote, the court attempted to justify this treatment:

> The *Dr. Seuss* court discussed initial interest confusion within its purchaser care analysis. As a district court within our circuit

recognized in a recent case involving a claim of trademark infringement via metatags usage, "this case . . . is not a standard trademark case and does not lend itself to the systematic application of the eight factors." *Playboy Enters. v. Welles*, 7 F. Supp. 2d 1098 (S.D. Cal. 1998). Because we agree that the traditional eight-factor test is not well-suited for analyzing the metatags issue, we do not attempt to fit our discussion into one of the *Sleekcraft* factors.

Brookfield Comms., Inc., 174 F.3d at 1062 n.24.

How does the *Interstellar Starship Services, Ltd.* court address the possibility of initial interest confusion? Does it analyze initial interest confusion independently of the *Sleekcraft* factors? How does it incorporate initial interest confusion into the *Sleekcraft* factors or does it? Does *Interstellar Starship Services, Ltd.* overrule *Brookfield Comms., Inc.* on how courts in the Ninth Circuit should address initial interest confusion?

5.   *Initial Interest Confusion and Competition*. Consider the following case: Looking for a triathlon bike on eBay, a consumer enters the search term "Trek"—a popular brand of road and triathlon bikes. The search returns hundreds of results for bikes. Many are Trek-brand bicycles. But there are also some listings for other brands. In some case, sellers listed another brand, such as Specialized, Felt, or Cervelo, and then added to their product title phrases such as "(not Trek, Giant, Cannondale)." As a result, when a consumer searches for "Trek" or another popular bike brand, seller's less-popular, though still competing, brand of bike will come up as well. Given the detailed information given for each listed bike, you may assume that no consumer will actually follow through and purchase a Specialized bike believing that it is a Trek. However, some Trek-searching consumers will end up purchasing a non-Trek brand as a result of these diverse offerings. If Trek sued these individual sellers, alleging initial interest confusion, how should a court resolve the issue?

6.   *Cybersquatting*. In *Interstellar Starship Services, Ltd.*, Epix, in addition to alleging traditional trademark infringement, also alleged a violation of the Anticybersquatting Consumer Protection Act. Enacted in 1999, Congress intended the ACPA to address a specific practice: individuals registering domain names that corresponded to well-known brick-and-mortar trademarks and then demanding payment from the trademark's owner to release the domain name.

Although Congress did not act until 1999, the problem did not wait for Congress. "In the early 1990s, the domain name registry service, Network Solutions, Inc., or InterNIC, registered domain names on a first-come-first-served basis, requiring initially no, and then only a token, fee for registration. With businesses generally being slow to recognize the commercial potential of the net, entrepreneurs (or thieves, depending on whom you asked) rushed in to register well-known trademarks as domain names with the idea of selling them to the highest bidder. Initially, the price to a trademark owner for purchasing the corresponding domain name from the initial registrant was little more than token, an acknowledgement, as it were, of the registrant's cleverness. But by 1994, prices had started to escalate, and trademark owners turned to the courts to obtain by judicial decree what they thought they already owned and hence should not have had to purchase in the marketplace." Lunney, *Trademarks on the Internet*, 97 TRADEMARK REPORTER at 933–34.

Addressing cybersquatting through traditional trademark infringement or dilution doctrines presented several seemingly insurmountable hurdles. First, to establish liability, both trademark infringement and dilution require that a defendant "use" the allegedly infringing mark "in commerce." Typically, cybersquatters simply registered a domain name and then sat on it, waiting for an opportunity to sell. No use would seem to mean no liability. Second, trademark infringement requires that a defendant use the allegedly infringing mark "in connection with the sale, offering for sale, distribution, or advertising of any goods or services." Similarly, the federal dilution statute in force in 1995 required that a defendant use the mark commercially. Even when cybersquatters set up a website in connection with a domain name, these websites were usually simply placeholders and did not typically offer any goods or services for sale. Again, no commercial use or use in connection with the sale of goods or services would seem to mean no liability. Third, while many of the trademarks at issue were known in their specific industries, few satisfied the seemingly-stringent fame requirement of the Federal Trademark Dilution Act. Without fame, there would again seem to be no federal dilution liability.

Even before Congress enacted the ACPA, courts had little trouble, however, creatively re-writing the Trademark Act to address cybersquatting. While acknowledging that mere registration of a domain name did not constitute the requisite use, the courts held that registration of a domain name with the intent to resell to the rightful trademark owner was itself a commercial use or a use in connection with goods or services sufficient to satisfy those elements of trademark liability. *See, e.g., Panavision International, L.P. v. Toeppen*, 141 F.3d 1316, 1319 (9th Cir. 1998). As for fame, courts simply watered the requirement down, holding that trademarks such as Panavision and Intermatic were sufficiently famous to warrant dilution protection. *Id.; Intermatic Inc. v. Toeppen*, 947 F.Supp. 1227 (N.D. Ill. 1996).

These rewritings enabled courts to address cybersquatting through traditional trademark and dilution, and rendered the ACPA largely superfluous. Moreover, as we saw in Chapter 8, they also forced Congress in 2006 to revisit the Federal Trademark Dilution Act in an attempt to revitalize the fame requirement. *See* Trademark Dilution Revision Act of 2006, Pub. L. 312, 109th Cong., 2d Sess., § 2, 120 Stat. 1730 (2006), *codified at* 15 U.S.C. § 1125(c)(2)(A) (2015) ("[A] mark is famous if it is widely recognized by the general consuming public of the United States. . . .").

In any event, by 1999, the real problem trademark owners faced was not that they could not prevail on a trademark claim against a cybersquatter, but that the expense of bringing a federal lawsuit gave the cybersquatter considerable room to negotiate a substantial payment. In short, it was far cheaper to purchase the domain name than to litigate for it. For example, the $25,000 "settlement" proposed by Tchou's attorney in *Interstellar Starship* was likely much less than the legal fees and other expenses Epix incurred to pursue the domain name through federal trademark litigation. While the ACPA gave trademark owners another arrow in their litigation quiver, it did little to reduce the cost of forcing a domain name transfer through litigation.

An alternative to litigation arrived in 1999. In that year, the Internet Corporation for Assigned Names and Numbers ("ICANN"), which had been created in 1998 to take over responsibility for assigning domain names, adopted as part of its domain name service the Uniform Dispute Resolution Procedure (the "UDRP"). Agreed to by every domain name registrant as part of the registration process, the UDRP aims to provide a lower cost alternative for a trademark owner seeking to recover a domain name corresponding to its trademark.

Substantively, its standards are similar to those set forth in the ACPA. Specifically, Paragraph 4(a) of the UDRP provides a remedy where a trademark owner can prove that: (i) another has registered a domain name "identical or confusingly similar" to its trademark; (ii) that the registrant has "no rights or legitimate interests in respect of the domain name"; and (iii) the domain name was "registered and is being used in bad faith." UDRP, ¶ 4 (Aug. 26, 1999). However, rather than federal court litigation, the UDRP relies on binding arbitration, conducted largely through e-mail and electronic filings. As a result, the UDRP enables a trademark owner to recover the corresponding domain name from a cybersquatter at a much lower cost.

Although the problem the ACPA intended to address was thus already solved by the time of its enactment both by courts creatively rewriting the Trademark Act, and by the UDRP alternative, the ACPA nevertheless remains on the books as a potential trap for people like Tchou. How does the *Interstellar Starship Servs., Ltd.* court resolve the ACPA claim against Tchou? Under the ACPA, one of the central issues is whether the party registered the domain name with a bad faith intent to profit. How easy will it be to separate cybersquatters from good-faith registrants, such as Tchou? What provable facts can we reliably use to separate the two? One of the key factors set forth in the ACPA is the "registration or acquisition of multiple domain names which the person knows are identical or confusingly similar to marks of others. . . ." 15 U.S.C. § 1125(d)(1)(B)(i)(VIII). In order to earn a living as a cybersquatter, an individual would almost certainly have to register and then re-sell multiple domain names. Thus, we can separate Tchou who had registered only the one domain name, from Toeppen who had registered more than one hundred. *See Panavision International, L.P. v. Toeppen*, 141 F.3d 1316, 1319 (9th Cir. 1998). Yet, once the ACPA was on the books, it presented a potential obstacle even for good faith registrants. Watch for how the courts resolve the ACPA claims in the following section, dealing with the issue of cyber-griping.

B. CYBER-GRIPING

Alongside the cybersquatters in the early frontier days of the Internet, a second group sprung up to take advantage of the failure of established entities to claim their corresponding domain names. While some members of this second group might be willing to sell a domain name at the right price, their primary purpose was to criticize, ridicule, or otherwise complain about the trademark owner. In the first such case, Richard Bucci, the host of "Catholic Radio," a radio program in New York, and an active participant in the anti-abortion movement, registered in August 1996 the domain name www.plannedparenthood.com. On the associated website, he promoted and included links to portions of a friend's anti-abortion book, *The Cost of Abortion*. In response, Planned Parenthood sued alleging trademark infringement and dilution. *Planned Parenthood Fed'n v. Bucci*, 42 U.S.P.Q.2d (BNA) 1430 (S.D.N.Y. 1997), *aff'd w/o op.* 152 F.3d 920 (2d Cir.), *cert. denied*, 525 U.S. 834 (1998). Bucci argued that he could not be liable for trademark infringement because he did not offer any goods or services for sale on his website.

In granting a preliminary injunction against Bucci, the district court identified three ways in which he was using the domain name "in connection with the sale ... of any goods or services," as required by section 32(1)(a) for trademark infringement. First, Bucci was using the website to "plug" his friend's book. Second, he was using the website to promote his own anti-abortion views—a type of informational service. Third, Bucci's website was likely to prevent some Internet users from reaching plaintiff's own Internet web site. As the district court explained: "Prospective users of plaintiff's services who mistakenly access defendant's web site may fail to continue to search for plaintiff's own home page, due to anger, frustration, or the belief that plaintiff's home page does not exist." *See Planned Parenthood Fed'n*, 42 U.S.P.Q.2d at 1435. For these reasons, the court found that Bucci was using his site in connection with the sale of goods. Finding a likelihood of confusion, the court enjoined Bucci's use of the www.plannedparenthood.com domain name. *Id.*

Later decisions followed the *Planned Parenthood* court's lead. *See People for the Ethical Treatment of Animals v. Doughney*, 263 F.3d 359 (4th Cir. 2001) (holding that using peta.com for a website for "people eating tasty animals" was actionable infringement); *Jews For Jesus v. Brodsky*, 993 F. Supp. 282 (D.N.J. 1998) (enjoining use of "jewforjesus.org" by a third party to criticize the organization).

At about the same time, however, courts approved of domain names that used another's trademark, but also expressly indicated their critical nature. Thus, in 1998, a district court granted summary judgment on trademark infringement and dilution claims to a defendant who was using the domain name www.compupix.com/ballysucks for a website devoted to complaints about Bally Fitness's health clubs. *See Bally Total Fitness Health Holding Corp. v. Faber*, 29 F. Supp. 2d 1161, 1166–67 (C.D. Cal. 1998). In doing so, the court emphasized the valuable informational role Farber was serving:

> [T]he average Internet user may want to receive all the information available on Bally. The user may want to access the official Internet site to see how Bally sells itself. Likewise, the user may also want to be apprised of the opinions of others about Bally.

Id. at 1165.

Through these initial decisions, the courts struck a balance between the trademark owner's interests in owning its corresponding domain name and the interests of those who wanted to criticize the trademark owner on the Internet. Critics could use the trademark as part of a longer domain name, such as www.trademarksucks.com, which made plain the critical nature of the website, but they could not use a domain name consisting of www.trademark.com alone. Is that the right balance? Consider the following two cases.

BOSLEY MEDICAL INSTITUTE, INC. V. KREMER

403 F.3d 672 (9th Cir. 2005)

SILVERMAN, J.

Defendant Michael Kremer was dissatisfied with the hair restoration services provided to him by the Bosley Medical Institute, Inc. In a bald-faced effort to get even, Kremer started a website at www.BosleyMedical.com, which, to put it mildly, was uncomplimentary of the Bosley Medical Institute. The problem is that "Bosley Medical" is the registered trademark of the Bosley Medical Institute, Inc., which brought suit against Kremer for trademark infringement and like claims. Kremer argues that noncommercial use of the mark is not actionable as infringement under the Lanham Act. Bosley responds that Kremer is splitting hairs.

Like the district court, we agree with Kremer. We hold today that the noncommercial use of a trademark as the domain name of a website—the subject of which is consumer commentary about the products and services represented by the mark—does not constitute infringement under the Lanham Act.

Bosley Medical's cybersquatting claim is another matter. The issue under the Anticybersquatting Consumer Protection Act was whether

Kremer had a "bad faith intent to profit" from the use of the trademark in his domain name, such as by making an extortionate offer to sell the BosleyMedical.com site to Bosley. Because discovery regarding that claim had not been completed, and the issue itself was not within the scope of the summary judgment motions, the district court erred in granting summary judgment to Kremer as to cybersquatting.

Finally, we hold that the district court should not have granted Kremer's motion to strike Bosley Medical's state-law claims pursuant to the California anti-SLAPP statute. Bosley Medical's complaint about the unauthorized use of its trademark as Kremer's domain name was not so lacking in merit as to be susceptible to an anti-SLAPP motion to strike at an early stage of the case.

I.   Background

Bosley Medical provides surgical hair transplantation, restoration, and replacement services to the public. Bosley Medical owns the registered trademark "BOSLEY MEDICAL," has used the mark "BOSLEY MEDICAL" since 1992, and registered the mark with the United States Patent and Trademark Office in January 2001. Bosley has spent millions of dollars on advertising and promotion throughout the United States and the rest of the world.

Michael Kremer is a dissatisfied former patient of Bosley. Unhappy with the results of a hair replacement procedure performed by a Bosley physician in Seattle, Washington, he filed a medical malpractice lawsuit against Bosley Medical in 1994. That suit was eventually dismissed.

In January 2000, Kremer purchased the domain name www.Bosley Medical.com, the subject of this appeal, as well as the domain name www. BosleyMedicalViolations.com, which is not challenged by Bosley. Five days after registering the domain name, Kremer went to Bosley Medical's office in Beverly Hills, California and delivered a two-page letter to Dr. Bosley, Founder and President of Bosley Medical. The first page read:

> Let me know if you want to discuss this. Once it is spread over
> the internet it will have a snowball effect and be too late to stop.
> M. Kremer [phone number]. P.S. I always follow through on my
> promises.

The second page was entitled "Courses of action against BMG" and listed eleven items. The first item stated: "1. Net web sites disclosing true operating nature of BMG. Letter 3/14/96 from LAC D.A. Negative testimonials from former clients. Links. Provide BMG competitors with this information." The letter contains no mention of domain names or any other reference to the Internet.

Kremer began to use www.BosleyMedical.com in 2001. His site summarizes the Los Angeles County District Attorney's 1996 investigative findings about Bosley, and allows visitors to view the entire document. It also contains other information that is highly critical of Bosley. Kremer earns no revenue from the website and no goods or services are sold on the website. There are no links to any of Bosley's competitors' websites. BosleyMedical.com does link to Kremer's sister site, BosleyMedicalViolations.com, which links to a newsgroup entitled alt.baldspot, which in turn contains advertisements for companies that compete with Bosley. BosleyMedical.com also contained a link to the Public Citizen website. Public Citizen is the organization that represents Kremer in this case.

Bosley brought this suit alleging trademark infringement, dilution, unfair competition, various state law claims, and a libel claim that was eventually settled. Bosley sought to take discovery aimed at the trademark and libel claims. The magistrate judge granted limited discovery on the libel claims. Following discovery, Bosley dismissed the libel claims and amended the complaint.

Kremer moved to dismiss the First Amended Complaint and in addition moved for partial summary judgment on the issues of commercial use and likelihood of confusion. Bosley filed a cross-motion for partial summary judgment on the infringement and dilution claims. Kremer agreed that the facts were undisputed with regard to the issues of commercial use and likelihood of confusion, and that these issues were ripe for summary judgment.

Ruling that Kremer's use of "Bosley Medical" in the domain name was noncommercial and unlikely to cause confusion, the district court entered summary judgment for Kremer on the federal claims and dismissed the state law claims under California's anti-SLAPP statute. Bosley now appeals.

II. Jurisdiction and Standard of Review

We have jurisdiction under 28 U.S.C. § 1291 and review a district court's grant of summary judgment de novo, viewing the evidence in the light most favorable to the non-moving party. *Prison Legal News v. Lehman*, 397 F.3d 692, 698 (9th Cir. 2005). A district court's grant of a special motion to strike under California's anti-SLAPP statute, Cal. Civ. P. Code § 425.16, is also reviewed de novo. *Vess v. Ciba-Geigy Corp.*, 317 F.3d 1097, 1102 (9th Cir. 2003).

III. Analysis

A. Trademark Infringement and Dilution Claims

The Trademark Act of 1946 ("Lanham Act") prohibits uses of trademarks, trade names, and trade dress that are likely to cause confusion about the source of a product or service. *See* 15 U.S.C. §§ 1114,

1125(a). In 1996, Congress amended § 43 of the Lanham Act to provide a remedy for the dilution of a famous mark. *See* 15 U.S.C. § 1125(c).

Infringement claims are subject to a commercial use requirement. The infringement section of the Lanham Act, 15 U.S.C. § 1114, states that any person who "uses in commerce any reproduction, counterfeit, copy, or colorable imitation of a registered mark in connection with the sale, offering for sale, distribution, or advertising of any goods or services on or in connection with which such use is likely to cause confusion, or to cause mistake, or to deceive . . ." can be held liable for such use. 15 U.S.C. § 1114(1)(a).

In 1996, Congress expanded the scope of federal trademark law when it enacted the Federal Trademark Dilution Act ("FTDA"). The FTDA allows the "owner of a famous mark" to obtain "an injunction against another person's *commercial use in commerce* of a mark or trade name. . . ." 15 U.S.C. § 1125(c)(1) (emphasis added). While the meaning of the term "commercial use in commerce" is not entirely clear, we have interpreted the language to be roughly analogous to the "in connection with" sale of goods and services requirement of the infringement statute. *See Mattel, Inc. v. MCA Records, Inc.*, 296 F.3d 894, 903 (9th Cir. 2002) ("Although this statutory language is ungainly, its meaning seems clear: It refers to a use of a famous and distinctive mark to sell goods other than those produced or authorized by the mark's owner."); *see also Huthwaite, Inc. v. Sunrise Assisted Living, Inc.*, 261 F. Supp. 2d 502, 517 (E.D. Va. 2003) (holding that the commercial use requirement of the FTDA is "virtually synonymous with the 'in connection with the sale, offering for sale, distribution, or advertising of goods and services' requirement" of the Lanham Act).

The inclusion of these requirements in the Lanham Act serves the Act's purpose: "to secure to the owner of the mark the goodwill of his business and to protect the ability of consumers to distinguish among competing producers." *Two Pesos, Inc. v. Taco Cabana, Inc.*, 505 U.S. 763, 774 (1992) (internal quotation marks and citations omitted). In other words, the Act is designed to protect consumers who have formed particular associations with a mark from buying a competing product using the same or substantially similar mark and to allow the mark holder to distinguish his product from that of his rivals. *See Avery Dennison Corp. v. Sumpton*, 189 F.3d 868, 873 (9th Cir. 1999).

The Supreme Court has made it clear that trademark infringement law prevents only unauthorized uses of a trademark in connection with a commercial transaction in which the trademark is being used to confuse potential consumers. *See Prestonettes, Inc. v. Coty*, 264 U.S. 359, 368 (1924) ("A trademark only gives the right to prohibit the use of it so far as to protect the owner's good will against *the sale of another's product as his*." [emphasis added]); *see also Mishawaka Rubber & Woolen Mfg. Co. v.*

S.S. Kresge Co., 316 U.S. 203, 205 (1942) (explaining that the main purpose of the Lanham Act is to prevent the use of identical or similar marks in a way that confuses the public about the actual source of goods and services).

As the Second Circuit held, "the Lanham Act seeks to prevent consumer confusion that enables a seller to pass off his goods as the goods of another. . . . Trademark infringement protects only against mistaken *purchasing decisions* and not against confusion generally." *Lang v. Ret. Living Publ'g Co., Inc.*, 949 F.2d 576, 582–83 (2d Cir. 1991) (internal quotation marks and citation omitted) (emphasis added).

As a matter of First Amendment law, commercial speech may be regulated in ways that would be impermissible if the same regulation were applied to noncommercial expressions. *Florida Bar v. Went For It, Inc.*, 515 U.S. 618, 623 (1995). "The First Amendment may offer little protection for a competitor who labels its commercial good with a confusingly similar mark, but trademark rights do not entitle the owner to quash an unauthorized use of the mark by another who is communicating ideas or expressing points of view." *Mattel*, 296 F.3d at 900 (internal quotation marks and citations omitted).

The district court ruled that Kremer's use of Bosley's mark was noncommercial. To reach that conclusion, the court focused on the "use in commerce" language rather than the "use in connection with the sale of goods" clause. This approach is erroneous. "Use in commerce" is simply a jurisdictional predicate to any law passed by Congress under the Commerce Clause. *See Steele v. Bulova Watch Co.*, 344 U.S. 280, 283 (1952); *OBH, Inc. v. Spotlight Magazine, Inc.*, 86 F. Supp. 2d 176, 185 (W.D.N.Y. 2000). 15 U.S.C. § 1127 states that "unless the contrary is plainly apparent from the context . . . the word 'commerce' means all commerce which may lawfully be regulated by Congress." Therefore, the district court should have determined instead whether Kremer's use was "in connection with a sale of goods or services" rather than a "use in commerce." However, we can affirm the district court's grant of summary judgment on any ground supported by the record. *Lamps Plus, Inc. v. Seattle Lighting Fixture Co.*, 345 F.3d 1140, 1143 (9th Cir. 2003). The question before us, then, boils down to whether Kremer's use of Bosley Medical as his domain name was "in connection with a sale of goods or services." If it was not, then Kremer's use was "noncommercial" and did not violate the Lanham Act.

Bosley argues that it has met the commercial use requirement in three ways. First, it argues that a mark used in an otherwise noncommercial website or as a domain name for an otherwise noncommercial website is nonetheless used in connection with goods and services where a user can click on a link available on that website to reach a commercial site. *Nissan Motor Co. v. Nissan Computer Corp.*, 378

F.3d 1002 (9th Cir. 2004). However, Bosley's reliance on *Nissan* is unfounded.

In *Nissan*, Nissan Motor Company sued Nissan Computer Corporation for using the Internet websites www.Nissan.com and www. Nissan.net. *Id.* at 1006. In *Nissan*, however, commercial use was undisputed, as the core function of the defendant's website was to advertise his computer business. *Id.* Additionally, the defendant in *Nissan*, like the defendant in *Taubman Co. v. Webfeats*, 319 F.3d 770 (6th Cir. 2003), placed links to other commercial businesses directly on their website. 319 F.3d at 772–73. Kremer's website contains no commercial links, but rather contains links to a discussion group, which in turn contains advertising. This roundabout path to the advertising of others is too attenuated to render Kremer's site commercial. At no time did Kremer's BosleyMedical.com site offer for sale any product or service or contain paid advertisements from any other commercial entity. *See TMI, Inc. v. Maxwell*, 368 F.3d 433, 435, 438 (5th Cir. 2004) (holding that the commercial use requirement is not satisfied where defendant's site had no outside links).

Bosley also points out that Kremer's site contained a link to Public Citizen, the public interest group representing Kremer throughout this litigation. We hold that Kremer's identification of his lawyers and his provision of a link to same did not transform his noncommercial site into a commercial one.

Bosley's second argument that Kremer's website satisfies the "in connection with the sale of goods or services" requirement of the Lanham Act is that Kremer created his website to enable an extortion scheme in an attempt to profit from registering BosleyMedical.com. In *Panavision International, L.P. v. Toeppen*, 141 F.3d 1316 (9th Cir. 1998), this court held that a defendant's "commercial use was his attempt to sell the trademarks themselves." *Id.* at 1325. Similarly, in *Intermatic Inc. v. Toeppen*, 947 F. Supp. 1227 (N.D. Ill. 1996), the court found that "Toeppen's intention to arbitrage the 'intermatic.com' domain name constituted a commercial use." *Id.* at 1239; *see also Boston Prof'l Hockey Ass'n., Inc. v. Dallas Cap & Emblem Mfg., Inc.*, 510 F.2d 1004, 1010 (5th Cir. 1975) (holding that trademark law protects the trademark itself, despite the fact that only "a reproduction of the trademark itself is being sold, unattached to any other goods or services").

However, in this case, there is no evidence that Kremer was trying to sell the domain name itself. The letter delivered by Kremer to Bosley's headquarters is a threat to expose negative information about Bosley on the Internet, but it makes no reference whatsoever to ransoming Bosley's trademark or to Kremer's use of the mark as a domain name.

Bosley argues that it was denied an opportunity to pursue discovery on commercial use, and had it been allowed to proceed with discovery, it could further establish that Kremer has attempted to sell the domain name. However, in opposing Kremer's motion for summary judgment, Bosley did not make any such objections. Bosley failed to request further discovery under Federal Rule of Civil Procedure 56(f), but instead moved for summary judgment itself. Although Bosley's reply brief supporting its own motion for summary judgment complained about limited discovery in a footnote, Bosley did not move for leave to take discovery. The district court did not abuse its discretion in granting the summary judgment without permitting further discovery.

Bosley's third and final argument that it satisfied the commercial use requirement of the Lanham Act is that Kremer's use of Bosley's trademark was in connection with *Bosley's* goods and services. In other words, Kremer used the mark "in connection with goods and services" because he prevented users from obtaining the plaintiff's goods and services. *See People for the Ethical Treatment of Animals v. Doughney*, 263 F.3d 359 (4th Cir. 2001) ("PETA"). In *PETA*, defendants created a site that promoted ideas antithetical to those of the PETA group. *Id.* at 362–63. The Fourth Circuit held that the defendant's parody site, though not having a commercial purpose and not selling any goods or services, violated the Lanham Act because it "prevented users from obtaining or using PETA's goods or services." *Id.* at 365.

However, in *PETA*, the defendant's website "provided links to more than 30 commercial operations offering goods and services." *Id.* at 366. To the extent that the *PETA* court held that the Lanham Act's commercial use requirement is satisfied because the defendant's use of the plaintiff's mark as the domain name may deter customers from reaching the plaintiff's site itself, we respectfully disagree with that rationale. While it is true that www.BosleyMedical.com is not sponsored by Bosley Medical, it is just as true that it is *about* Bosley Medical. The *PETA* approach would place most critical, otherwise protected consumer commentary under the restrictions of the Lanham Act. Other courts have also rejected this theory as over-expansive. *See L.L. Bean, Inc. v. Drake Publishers, Inc.*, 811 F.2d 26, 33 (1st Cir. 1987); *see also Ford Motor Co. v. 2600 Enters.*, 177 F. Supp. 2d 661, 664 (E.D. Mich. 2001).

The *PETA* court's reading of the Lanham Act would encompass almost all uses of a registered trademark, even when the mark is merely being used to identify the object of consumer criticism. This broad view of the Lanham Act is supported by neither the text of the statute nor the history of trademark laws in this country. "Trademark laws are intended to protect" consumers from purchasing the products of an infringer "under the mistaken assumption that they are buying a product produced or sponsored by [the trademark holder]." *Beneficial Corp. v. Beneficial Capital Corp.*, 529 F. Supp. 445, 450 (S.D.N.Y. 1982). Limiting the Lanham Act to cases where a defendant is trying to profit from a plaintiff's trademark is consistent with the Supreme Court's view that "[a trademark's] function is simply to designate the goods as the product of a particular trader and to protect his good will against the sale of another's product as his." *United Drug Co. v. Theodore Rectanus Co.*, 248 U.S. 90, 97 (1918); *see also* 1 McCarthy on Trademarks and Unfair Competition § 2:7 (4th ed. 2004).

The Second Circuit held in *United We Stand America, Inc. v. United We Stand, America New York, Inc.*, 128 F.3d 86, 90 (2d Cir. 1997), that the "use in connection with the sale of goods and services" requirement of the Lanham Act does not require any actual *sale* of goods and services. Thus, the appropriate inquiry is whether Kremer offers *competing* services to the public. Kremer is not Bosley's competitor; he is their critic. His use of the Bosley mark is not in connection with a sale of goods or services—it is in connection with the expression of his opinion *about* Bosley's goods and services.

The dangers that the Lanham Act was designed to address are simply not at issue in this case. The Lanham Act, expressly enacted to be applied in commercial contexts, does not prohibit all unauthorized uses of a trademark. Kremer's use of the Bosley Medical mark simply cannot mislead consumers into buying a competing product—no customer will mistakenly purchase a hair replacement service from Kremer under the belief that the service is being offered by Bosley. Neither is Kremer capitalizing on the good will Bosley has created in its mark. Any harm to Bosley arises not from a competitor's sale of a similar product under Bosley's mark, but from Kremer's criticism of their services. Bosley cannot use the Lanham Act either as a shield from Kremer's criticism, or as a sword to shut Kremer up.

B. Anticybersquatting Consumer Protection Act

In 1999, Congress passed the Anticybersquatting Consumer Protection Act ("ACPA"), 15 U.S.C. § 1125(d), as an amendment to the Lanham Act to prohibit cybersquatting.

> Cybersquatting occurs when a person other than the trademark holder registers the domain name of a well known trademark and then attempts to profit from this by either ransoming the domain name back to the trademark holder or by using the domain name to divert business from the trademark holder to the domain name holder.

DaimlerChrysler v. The Net Inc., 388 F.3d 201, 204 (6th Cir. 2004) (internal quotation marks omitted).

The ACPA states:

> A person shall be liable in a civil action by the owner of a mark ... if, without regard to the goods or services of the parties, that

person (i) has a bad faith intent to profit from that mark . . .; and (ii) registers, traffics in, or uses a domain name [that is confusingly similar to another's mark or dilutes another's famous mark].

15 U.S.C. § 1125(d)(1)(A) (2004).

The district court dismissed Bosley's ACPA claim for the same reasons that it dismissed the infringement and dilution claims—namely, because Kremer did not make commercial use of Bosley's mark. However, the ACPA does not contain a commercial use requirement, and we therefore reverse.

Kremer argues that the "noncommercial use" proviso that appears in the dilution portion of § 1125 applies to cybersquatting claims with equal force. Admittedly, the language in § 1125 is confusing. 15 U.S.C. § 1125(c)(4) reads: "The following shall not be actionable under this section: . . . (B) Non-commercial use of a mark." 15 U.S.C. § 1125(c)(4)(B). Kremer asserts that by using the word "section," rather than the more precise term "subsection," Congress meant for the proviso to apply to all of § 1125, as opposed to subsection (c).

This argument fails for two reasons. The noncommercial use exception, which appears in a different part of the Lanham Act, is in direct conflict with the language of the ACPA. The ACPA makes it clear that "use" is only one possible way to violate the Act ("registers, traffics in, *or* uses"). Allowing a cybersquatter to register the domain name with a bad faith intent to profit but get around the law by making noncommercial use of the mark would run counter to the purpose of the Act. "The use of a domain name in connection with a site that makes a noncommercial or fair use of the mark does not necessarily mean that the domain name registrant lacked bad faith." *Coca-Cola Co. v. Purdy*, 382 F.3d 774, 778 (8th Cir. 2004) (internal quotation marks and citation omitted); *see also* H.R. Rep. No. 106–412 at 11 (1999) ("This factor is not intended to create a loophole that otherwise might swallow the bill, however, by allowing a domain name registrant to evade application of the Act by merely putting up a noninfringing site under an infringing domain name."). "It is a well-established canon of statutory construction that a court should go beyond the literal language of a statute if reliance on that language would defeat the plain purpose of the statute." *Bob Jones Univ. v. United States*, 461 U.S. 574, 586 (1983); *see also Albertson's, Inc. v. Commissioner*, 42 F.3d 537, 546 (9th Cir. 1994).

Additionally, one of the nine factors listed in the statute that courts must consider is the registrant's "bona fide non-commercial or fair use of the mark in a site accessible under the domain name." 15 U.S.C. § 1125(d)(1)(B)(i)(IV). This factor would be meaningless if the statute exempted all non-commercial uses of a trademark within a domain name. We try to avoid, where possible, an interpretation of a statute "that renders any part of it superfluous and does not give effect to all of the words used by Congress." *Nevada v. Watkins*, 939 F.2d 710, 715 (9th Cir. 1991) (internal quotation marks and citation omitted).

Finally, other courts that have construed the ACPA have not required commercial use. In *DaimlerChrysler*, the Sixth Circuit held that a

> trademark owner asserting a claim under the ACPA must establish the following: (1) it has a valid trademark entitled to protection; (2) its mark is distinctive or famous; (3) the defendant's domain name is identical or confusingly similar to, or in the case of famous marks, dilutive of, the owner's mark; and (4) the defendant used, registered, or trafficked in the domain name (5) with a bad faith intent to profit.

388 F.3d at 204. *See also Ford Motor Co. v. Catalanotte*, 342 F.3d 543, 546 (6th Cir. 2003); *E. & J. Gallo Winery v. Spider Webs Ltd.*, 129 F. Supp. 2d 1033, 1047–48 (S. D. Tex. 2001), *aff'd*, 286 F.3d 270 (5th Cir. 2002) ("As reflected by the language of the ACPA and the case law interpreting it, there is no requirement . . . that the 'use' be a commercial use to run afoul of the ACPA").

The district court erred in applying the commercial use requirement to Bosley's ACPA claim. Rather, the court should confine its inquiry to the elements of the ACPA claim listed in the statute, particularly to whether Kremer had a bad faith intent to profit from his use of Bosley's mark in his site's domain name. Bosley has met the first prong of the ACPA (that the domain name is identical to the mark) because Kremer used an unmodified version of Bosley's mark as his domain name.

Concluding that all of Bosley's claims, including the ACPA claim, were subject to a commercial use requirement, the district judge granted summary judgment in Kremer's favor. But the ACPA claim was not in front of the district court in the motions for summary judgment. The court did not provide notice to Bosley that it would rule on this claim, and did not give Bosley an opportunity to conduct discovery on the issue. *See Celotex Corp. v. Catrett*, 477 U.S. 317, 326 (1986). For this reason, the district court erred in granting summary judgment for Kremer on the ACPA claim. It remains to be seen whether Bosley can establish that Kremer registered the domain name in bad faith or can authenticate other letters that Bosley alleges were written and sent by Kremer.

. . .

IV. Conclusion

We affirm the district court's entry of summary judgment in favor of Kremer with respect to the infringement and dilution claims. We remand the ACPA claim for further proceedings. The district court's grant of the anti-SLAPP motion to strike the state law claims is reversed.

AFFIRMED in part, REVERSED in part, and REMANDED. No costs allowed.

LUCAS NURSERY & LANDSCAPING, INC. V. GROSSE
359 F.3d 806 (6th Cir. 2004)

COLE, J.

Lucas Nursery and Landscaping, Inc. ("Lucas Nursery") appeals the district court's grant of summary judgment for Defendant-Appellee Michelle Grosse in this action alleging that Grosse violated the Anticybersquatting Consumer Protection Act, 15 U.S.C. § 1125(d)(1)(A) (2000) ("the ACPA"), by registering the domain name "lucasnursery.com" and creating a web site on which she detailed her complaints against Lucas for its allegedly bad service in landscaping her front yard. The central issue on appeal is whether the district court erred in granting summary judgment in favor of Grosse based upon its conclusion that the she did not act in bad faith within the meaning of the ACPA. For the reasons that follow, we AFFIRM the judgment of the district court.

I.   BACKGROUND

This case arises from a dispute related to landscaping work that was performed by Lucas Nursery at the residence of Michelle Grosse. In March 2000, Grosse hired Lucas Nursery to correct a dip in the soil (known as a swale) that ran horizontally through the center of her front yard. Lucas Nursery's representative, Bob Lucas, Jr., stated that the swale could be corrected by using five large loads of topsoil. Lucas Nursery performed the work on May 16, 2000.

Grosse contends that the work was performed inadequately. After allegedly contacting Lucas Nursery on numerous occasions to express her displeasure with the work and to seek some repair, Grosse filed a complaint with the Better Business Bureau ("the BBB"). After the BBB ended its investigation without making a recommendation, Grosse remained dissatisfied by what she felt had been poor service by Lucas Nursery, and decided to inform others about her experience with the company.

On August 12, 2000, Grosse registered the domain name "lucasnursery.com." She then posted a web page for the sole purpose of relaying her story to the public. The web page was titled, "My Lucas Landscaping Experience." The web page included complaints regarding the poor preparation of the soil prior to Lucas Nursery's laying of the sod, the hasty nature of Lucas Nursery's work, the ineffectiveness of the BBB in addressing her complaint, and the fact that she had to pay an additional $5,400 to a second contractor to repair the work originally performed by Lucas Nursery.

On September 27, 2000, Grosse received a letter from Lucas Nursery's attorney demanding that she cease operating the web site. On October 2, 2000, Grosse removed the web site's content. However, after removing the web site's content, Grosse contacted the Michigan Bureau of Commercial Services Licensing Division and the U.S. Patent & Trademark Office to determine whether there was a registered trademark for Lucas Nursery. After learning that no trademark registration existed, Grosse concluded that Lucas Nursery could not prevent her from retaining the web site. On April 13, 2001, Grosse posted a new narrative on the web site, again describing her experience with Lucas Nursery.

Lucas Nursery filed suit against Grosse on August 17, 2001. Thereafter, each party moved for summary judgment. On April 23, 2002, the district court denied Lucas Nursery's motion for summary judgment and granted Grosse's motion for summary judgment.

II.   ANALYSIS

A.   Standard of Review

We review a district court's decision to grant summary judgment *de novo*. *Stephenson v. AllState Ins. Co.*, 328 F.3d 822, 826 (6th Cir. 2003). Summary judgment is proper if "the pleadings, depositions, answers to interrogatories, and admissions on file, together with the affidavits, if any, show that there is no genuine issue of material fact and that the moving party is entitled to a judgment as a matter of law." Fed. R. Civ. P. 56(c). When reviewing a motion for summary judgment, the evidence, all facts, and any inferences that may be drawn from the facts must be viewed in the light most favorable to the nonmoving party. *Matsushita Elec. Indus. Co. v. Zenith Radio Corp.*, 475 U.S. 574, 587 (1986). However, a "mere scintilla" of evidence is insufficient; the evidence must be such that a reasonable jury could find in favor of the plaintiff. *Anderson v. Liberty Lobby, Inc.*, 477 U.S. 242, 252 (1986).

B.   The ACPA

"The ACPA was enacted in 1999 in response to concerns over the proliferation of cybersquatting—the Internet version of a land grab." *Virtual Works, Inc. v. Volkswagen of America, Inc.*, 238 F.3d 264, 267 (4th Cir. 2001). It was enacted because then-existing law did not expressly prohibit the practice of cybersquatting, and cybersquatters had begun to insulate themselves from liability under the Federal Trademark Dilution Act, 15 U.S.C. § 1125. *Id.*

In the Senate Report accompanying the ACPA, cybersquatters are defined as those who: (1) "register well-known brand names as Internet domain names in order to extract payment from the rightful owners of the marks;" (2) "register well-known marks as domain names and warehouse those marks with the hope of selling them to the highest bidder;" (3) "register well-known marks to prey on consumer confusion by misusing the domain name to divert customers from the mark owner's site to the cybersquatter's own site;" (4) "target distinctive marks to defraud consumers, including to engage in counterfeiting activities." S. Rep. No. 106–140 at 5–6.

. . .

1. Non-Commercial Activity and the ACPA

Although there is some dispute between the parties as to whether the ACPA covers non-commercial activity, we see no reason to consider these arguments, as the statute directs a reviewing court to consider only a defendant's "bad faith intent to profit" from the use of a mark held by another party. We, therefore, turn to this consideration.

2. Bad Faith Analysis

In order for liability to attach under the ACPA a court must conclude that the defendant's actions constitute "bad faith." ACPA § 3002 (codified at 15 U.S.C. § 1125(d)(1)(A)–(B)). An analysis of whether a defendant's actions constitute bad faith within the meaning of the ACPA usually begins with consideration of several factors, nine of which are listed in the ACPA. *See Sporty's Farm v. Sportsman's Market, Inc.*, 202 F.3d 489, 498 (2d Cir. 2000). The first four factors are those that militate against a finding of bad faith by providing some reasonable basis for why a defendant might have registered the domain name of another mark holder. These factors focus on: whether the defendant has trademark or other rights in the domain name; the extent to which the domain name consists of the defendant's legal name or other common name; any prior use of the domain name for the offering of goods and services; and the bona fide noncommercial use of the site.

Each of the first three factors cuts against Grosse. She does not hold a trademark or other intellectual property rights to the domain name or names included in the registered domain name. The domain name neither consists of her legal name or any name used to refer to her. Grosse has also not used the domain name in connection with any offering of goods or services. The fourth factor cuts in Grosse's favor because the site was used for noncommercial purposes.

Factors five through eight are indicative of the presence of bad faith on the part of the defendant. These factors focus on: whether the defendant seeks to divert consumers from the mark holder's online location either in a way that could harm good will or tarnish or disparage the mark by creating a confusion regarding the sponsorship of the site; whether there has been an offer to transfer or sell the site for financial gain; whether the defendant provided misleading contact information when registering the domain name; and whether the defendant has acquired multiple domain names which may be duplicative of the marks of others.

The paradigmatic harm that the ACPA was enacted to eradicate—the practice of cybersquatters registering several hundred domain names in an effort to sell them to the legitimate owners of the mark—is simply not present in any of Grosse's actions. In its report on the ACPA, the Senate Judiciary Committee distilled the crucial elements of bad faith to mean an "intent to trade on the goodwill of another's mark." S. Rep. No. 106–140, at 9. *See also Ford Motor Co. v. Catalanotte*, 342 F.3d 543, 549 (6th Cir. 2003) ("Registering a famous trademark as a domain name and then offering it for sale to the trademark owner is exactly the wrong Congress intended to remedy when it passed the ACPA."). There is no evidence that this was Grosse's intention when she registered the Lucas Nursery domain name and created her web site. It would therefore stretch the ACPA beyond the letter of the law and Congress's intention to declare anything to the contrary.

None of these factors militates against Grosse. There is no dispute that Lucas Nursery did not have an online location, and hence Grosse's creation of a web site to complain about Lucas Nursery's services could not have been intended "to divert consumers from the mark owners's online location." Nor is there any evidence that Grosse ever sought to mislead consumers with regard to the site's sponsorship. The web site explicitly stated that the site was established by Grosse for the purposes of relaying her experience with Lucas Nursery. Moreover, Grosse never offered to sell the site to Lucas Nursery. She also did not provide misleading contact information when she registered the domain name. Finally, she has not acquired any additional domain names, which would be indicative of either an intent to sell such names to those entities whose trademarks were identical or similar, or exploit them for other uses.

Lucas Nusery contends that the Fourth Circuit's decision in *People for the Ethical Treatment of Animals (PETA) v. Doughney*, 263 F.3d 359 (4th Cir. 2001), is applicable to the instant action. Although the defendant in *Doughney* did not make commercial use of his web site, the court concluded that he had, nonetheless, acted with a bad faith intent to profit. Doughney had "made statements on his website and in the press recommending that PETA attempt to 'settle' with him and 'make him an offer'" and that he had "registered other domain names that [were] identical or similar to the marks or names of other famous people and organizations." *Id*. at 369. Here, Grosse has engaged in no such offensive conduct.

Lucas Nursery seeks to buttress its argument with *Toronto-Dominion Bank v. Karpachev*, 188 F. Supp. 2d 110 (D. Mass. 2002).

There, the district court granted Toronto-Dominion's motion for summary judgment against the defendant, concluding that there was sufficient evidence to show that the defendant had acted in bad faith under the ACPA. The defendant, a disgruntled customer, registered sixteen domain names composed of various misspellings of the name tdwaterhouse.com. *Id.* at 111. On the web sites associated with these names, the defendant attacked Toronto-Dominion for "webfacism" and involvement with white collar crime, among other things. *Id.* at 112. The court concluded that the defendant had acted in bad faith, citing four factors: (1) his intention to divert customers from the "tdwaterhouse" web site by creating confusion as to its source or sponsorship; (2) the fact that he had registered sixteen domain names; (3) the fact that he offered no goods or services on the site; and (4) the fact that he had no intellectual property rights in the site. *See id.* at 114.

Although Grosse's actions would arguably satisfy three of the four aforementioned factors, she does not fall within the factor that we consider central to a finding of bad faith. She did not register multiple web sites; she only registered one. Further, it is not clear to this Court that the presence of simply one factor that indicates a bad faith intent to profit, without more, can satisfy an imposition of liability within the meaning of the ACPA. The role of the reviewing court is not simply to add factors and place them in particular categories, without making some sense of what motivates the conduct at issue. The factors are given to courts as a guide, not as a substitute for careful thinking about whether the conduct at issue is motivated by a bad faith intent to profit. Perhaps most important to our conclusion are, Grosse's actions, which seem to have been undertaken in the spirit of informing fellow consumers about the practices of a landscaping company that she believed had performed inferior work on her yard. One of the ACPA's main objectives is the protection of consumers from slick internet peddlers who trade on the names and reputations of established brands. The practice of informing fellow consumers of one's experience with a particular service provider is surely not inconsistent with this ideal.

CONCLUSION

For the foregoing reasons, we AFFIRM the district court's grant of summary judgment in favor of Grosse.

NOTES FOR DISCUSSION

1. *Consumer Welfare: Use versus Confusion.* Neither of these cases deals with the issue directly in terms of the competing consumer interests at stake. What are those interests? On the one side is our traditional concern regarding confusion. How significant is that interest in these cases? The costs of confusion are highest when a consumer purchases a product from one company mistakenly believing that it comes from another. Is there any

likelihood that a consumer will purchase a product from one of these defendants thinking she is purchasing a product from the corresponding plaintiff? What other costs are there? The existence of Grosse's and Kremer's websites likely increase consumer search costs somewhat, making it slightly more difficult to find the authorized site, but in the absence of any mistaken purchases, that additional search cost is not likely to be very large. Against that cost we must balance the value of the information that Grosse and Kremer are attempting to convey. How valuable to a consumer is that additional information? Would it limit the value of that information significantly if Kremer had to use www.bosleymedicalviolations.com and Grosse had to use www.lucasnurserysucks.com. Could consumers interested in their perspectives still easily find their criticism sites?

Does the "use . . . in connection with the sale . . . of goods or services" language for the trademark infringement standard or the "commercial use" language of the dilution provision attempt to balance these competing consumer interests? Does the likelihood of confusion test, in conjunction with fair use, attempt to balance these issues? Why do both courts focus on the nature of the use rather than examine the likelihood of confusion question directly? Is it because the initial interest confusion doctrine forecloses any attempt to balance sensibly the competing consumer interests in these cases? If the plaintiffs could show the requisite use, how would a court most likely resolve the likelihood of confusion issue? Could either defendant have prevailed on a summary judgment motion on the likelihood of confusion issue?

2. *Distinguishing and Rejecting the Earlier Cases.* In *Bosley Medical, Inc.*, how does the Ninth Circuit deal with the earlier cases, such as *People for the Ethical Treatment of Animals* (or *"PETA"*), in granting Kremer summary judgment? First, it distinguishes *PETA* on the grounds that the defendant in *PETA* had direct links to commercial websites, where Kremer did not. *Bosley Medical Institute, Inc.*, 403 F.3d at 679. Second, it rejected the *PETA* court's view that a plaintiff could establish the requisite "use in connection with the sale of goods" by showing that "defendant's use of the plaintiff's mark as the domain name may deter customers from reaching the plaintiff's site itself." *Id.* Do you agree with the Ninth Circuit on this issue or the Fourth? If Doughney, the defendant in *PETA*, had removed the commercial links, should that have made Doughney's use permissible under trademark law? What if Bucci had not promoted his friend's book on his plannedparenthood.com site, but had limited himself to asserting his anti-abortion perspectives, should Bucci's use no longer be trademark infringement?

Or is there some other reason we should treat these cases differently? Is it that People Eating Tasting Animals and Bucci's antiabortion views are unseemly or more offensive to their likely audience, *i.e.* consumers expecting to find the official website? Is it a judicial judgment about the respective value of the defendants' perspective, in which Kremer and Grosse have legitimate concerns, but Doughney and Bucci do not? Is it that Kremer and

Grosse are conveying factual information, where Doughney and Bucci are expressing opinions or value judgments? Which websites come closer to the sorts of speech that lie at the core of the First Amendment's free speech guarantees? Which websites offer political speech? Which websites offer speech on matters of public concern? Which websites come closest to merely proposing a commercial transaction? Is seeking to persuade a consumer not to make a purchase commercial or noncommercial speech?

3. *Use: Section 1114(1)(a) versus 1125(a).* In *Bosley Medical*, the plaintiff had registered its trademark and the court therefore focused on the language of section 32(a), which sets forth the infringement standard for registered trademarks. In relevant part, that section imposes liability on "any person who shall . . . use in commerce any reproduction . . . or colorable imitation of a registered mark *in connection with the sale, offering for sale, distribution, or advertising* of any goods or services" where such use creates a likelihood of confusion. 15 U.S.C. § 1114(1)(a) (2015). In contrast, section 43(a), which sets forth the infringement standard for unregistered marks, imposes liability on "[a]ny person who, *on or in connection with any goods or services* . . . uses in commerce any word . . . which is likely to cause confusion." 15 U.S.C. § 1125(a)(1)(A) (2015). Even if one agrees with the *Bosley Medical* court that Bosley did not use the mark in connection with "the sale, offering for sale . . . of any goods," did he use the mark "in connection with any goods or services"? Did he use the mark in connection with his criticism of Bosley Medical's services? Is this enough to establish Kremer's liability under section 43(a)? Why would the infringement standard be broader for unregistered marks than for registered trademarks?

4. *The ACPA's Focus on Bad Faith Intent to Profit.* Unlike trademark infringement and dilution, the ACPA contains no use in commerce element. Congress intentionally omitted this element so that a trademark owner could reach traditional cybersquatters, who often registered domain names without using them. Is the ACPA nonetheless within the scope of Congress's Commerce Clause power? Does the act of registering a domain name constitute interstate commerce? Given the absence of a use requirement, both Kremer and Grosse are potentially liable under the ACPA. Moreover, they have both registered as a domain name another's trademark, satisfying two of the three elements of an ACPA cause of action. The only remaining question is whether they did so with a "bad faith intent to profit." How did each court rule on this issue? Will we be able to separate good faith criticizers such as Kremer and Grosse readily from bad faith cybersquatters? Which of the statutory factors are most helpful?

Even with respect to Grosse, who as the *Lucas Nursery* court recognizes is about as far from a cybersquatter as imaginable, how many of the factors weigh in favor of finding bad faith? How many more would have to weigh in favor of finding bad faith before Lucas Nursery would prevail? How many more before Grosse's good or bad faith becomes a genuine issue of fact that would preclude summary judgment? Would it be enough if Lucas Nursery had had its own official website? What if Grosse had been Internet savvy and to ensure that consumers could find her website, she had registered six additional domain names covering the likely misspellings of www.lucas nursery.com? Is that the sort of behavior Congress meant when it included registration of "multiple domain names" as a factor indicating bad faith? Or was Congress referring to someone like Toeppen who registered multiple domain names corresponding to a number of different trademarks? What if Grosse, rather than her attorney, in walking out of court one morning had responded to a press inquiry by saying "Well, if he wants the website so bad, he can make me an offer." *See People for the Ethical Treatment of Animals v. Doughney*, 263 F.3d 359, 368 (4th Cir. 2001) (finding a bad faith intent to profit where "Doughney made statements to the press and on his website recommending that PETA attempt to 'settle' with him and 'make him an offer'").

5.   *Good Faith, Bad Faith, and Mixed Motives.* What if Kremer in registering Bosley Medical's trademark as a domain name had said to himself: "This will make a great site on which to criticize them, and who knows maybe Bosley will pay me a lot of money to get their domain name back." Is that a bad faith intent to profit under the ACPA? Or does Kremer's good faith intent to use the site to criticize Bosley Medical prevail?

In *Virtual Works, Inc. v. Volkswagen of America, Inc.*, these facts arose almost exactly. 238 F.3d 264 (4th Cir. 2001). Virtual Works wanted to register a simple form of its corporate name as a domain name. When it learned that www.vw.net was available, it registered the domain name for its own business. In a deposition, one of the owners admitted that while they "decided to register the address for their own use, [they] left open the possibility of one day selling the site to Volkswagen 'for a lot of money.'" *Id.* at 269. Given this admission, the Fourth Circuit affirmed the district court's grant of summary judgment finding an ACPA violation. *Id.* at 270.

C. THE USE OF TRADEMARKS IN SEARCH ENGINES

As the Internet developed into a commercial platform, search engines began selling trademarks as keywords. When a consumer would enter a given trademark into a search engine, the search engine would return search results and sponsored links tied to the trademark. Company A could purchase Company B's trademark as a keyword from the search engine, so that when a consumer entered the trademark into the search engine, a link to Company A's website would appear either as one of the search results or as a sponsored link. Trademark owners objected to the use of their trademarks to generate business for their competitors, and litigation ensued. A number of questions arose. Were the search engines liable for selling trademarks as keywords, or for providing sponsored links keyed to the entry of certain trademarks? Were the competitors who purchased another's trademarks as keywords liable? And in either case, was the appropriate theory of liability direct liability or secondary liability?

From a consumer welfare perspective, using trademarks as keywords to trigger links to competing products entails the familiar trade-off between confusion and competition. Using a trademark as a keyword creates some risk that a consumer will buy a product from Company A by mistake, believing that she is buying a product from Company B. Yet, it also offers a consumer more information on the full range of competing products available, allowing the consumer to make a more informed and therefore better purchasing decision.

When litigation on keyword use began, courts initially focused on likelihood of confusion as the central doctrine for resolving these disputes. However, the broad reach, and factually intensive nature, of the likelihood of confusion doctrine, particularly in its initial interest confusion incarnation, made avoiding trial and potential liability difficult for search engines. It also tended to focus exclusively on one side of the consumer welfare balance and ignore the enhanced competition keyword advertising could bring.

Rather than litigate through trial the issue of likelihood of confusion for every keyword-triggered advertisement, search engines advanced a different argument to foreclose liability for keyword-triggered advertisements. They argued that the unauthorized use of a trademark to trigger an advertisement, pop-up, or sponsored link did not constitute use sufficient to trigger liability for trademark infringement in the first place. As a result, there would be no need to consider whether any given keyword-triggered advertisement was confusing.

As we have seen, the plain language of the Trademark Act requires "use" for trademark infringement under sections 1114(a) for registered marks and 1125(a)(1) for unregistered marks, and also requires "use" for dilution liability under Section 1125(c). The Trademark Act expressly defines "use in commerce" of a trademark as "plac[ing the mark] in any manner on the goods." 15 U.S.C. § 1127 (2015). Moreover, the common law has long distinguished between internal and external uses of a mark, as we saw in Chapter 2 in cases such as *Blue Bell, Inc. v. Farah Mfg. Co.* Taken together, the statutory language and the common law's internal-external use distinction provided a basis to argue that a company's purely internal use of a mark, such as in the software coding of a search engine, to cause the display of an advertisement did not constitute trademark use in the first place.

Beginning with a district court in *U-Haul International, Inc. v. WhenU.com, Inc.*, 279 F. Supp. 2d 723 (E.D. Va. 2003), a number of district courts accepted these arguments and held that the use of a trademark to trigger a banner advertisement, search result, or pop-up did not constitute trademark use at all. *See Merck & Co. v. Mediplan Health*

Consulting, 425 F. Supp. 2d 402, 415–16 (S.D.N.Y. 2006); *Wells Fargo & Co. v. WhenU.com, Inc.*, 293 F. Supp. 2d 734 (E.D. Mich. 2003). Having decided that such use was not use sufficient to establish trademark liability, there was no need to discuss whether the advertisement created a likelihood of confusion or dilution. In the absence of use, there could be no trademark liability.

In 2005, in *1-800 Contacts, Inc. v. WhenU.com, Inc.*, 414 F.3d 400 (2d Cir. 2005), the Second Circuit accepted the "it's not a use" argument. The case concerned a proprietary software program that would monitor a computer user's internet activity. When that user accessed specific websites, such as www.1800contacts.com, the program would open several pop-up windows with advertisements for competing or complementary products or services. After the district court issued a preliminary injunction, the defendant, WhenU.com, appealed. The Second Circuit reversed the injunction and dismissed the claims against WhenU.com, holding that there was no use sufficient to establish trademark liability as a matter of law.

With respect to the inclusion of www.1800contacts.com in WhenU's computer program as a trigger for pop-ups, the court held that this did not constitute "use." As the court explained:

> At the outset, we note that WhenU does not "use" 1-800's trademark in the manner ordinarily at issue in an infringement claim: it does not "place" 1-800 trademarks on any goods or services in order to pass them off as emanating from or authorized by 1-800. *See U-Haul*, 279 F. Supp. 2d at 728; cf. *L.L. Bean, Inc. v. Drake Publishers, Inc.*, 811 F.2d 26, 32–34 (1st Cir. 1987); *Societe Comptoir de L'Industrie Cotonniere Etablissements Boussac v. Alexander's Dep't Stores, Inc.*, 299 F.2d 33, 37 (2d Cir. 1962). The fact is that WhenU does not reproduce or display 1-800's trademarks at all, nor does it cause the trademarks to be displayed to a C-user. Rather, WhenU reproduces 1-800's website address, «www.1800contacts.com.», which is similar, but not identical, to 1-800's 1-800CONTACTS trademark. *See 1-800 Contacts*, 309 F. Supp. 2d at 478–79.

> The district court found that the differences between 1-800's trademarks and the website address utilized by WhenU were insignificant because they were limited to the addition of the "www." and ".com" and the omission of the hyphen and a space. *See id.* We conclude that, to the contrary, the differences between the marks are quite significant because they transform 1-800's trademark—which is entitled to protection under the Lanham Act—into a word combination that functions more or less like a public key to 1-800's website.

Moreover, it is plain that WhenU is using 1-800's website address precisely because it is a website address, rather than because it bears any resemblance to 1-800's trademark, because the only place WhenU reproduces the address is in the SaveNow directory. Although the directory resides in the C-user's computer, it is inaccessible to both the C-user and the general public. *See id.* at 476 (noting that directory is scrambled to preclude access). Thus, the appearance of 1-800's website address in the directory does not create a possibility of visual confusion with 1-800's mark. More important, a WhenU pop-up ad cannot be triggered by a C-user's input of the 1-800 trademark or the appearance of that trademark on a webpage accessed by the C-user. Rather, in order for WhenU to capitalize on the fame and recognition of 1-800's trademark—the improper motivation both 1-800 and the district court ascribe to WhenU— it would have needed to put the actual trademark on the list.

In contrast to some of its competitors, moreover, WhenU does not disclose the proprietary contents of the SaveNow directory to its advertising clients nor does it permit these clients to request or purchase specified keywords to add to the directory. *See GEICO v. Google, Inc.,* 330 F. Supp. 2d 700, 703–04 (E.D. Va. 2004) (distinguishing WhenU's conduct from defendants' practice of selling "keywords" to its advertising clients), *claim dism'd,* Order, Dec. 15, 2004 (dismissing Lanham Act claim following bench trial on finding no likelihood of confusion); *see also U-Haul,* 279 F. Supp. 2d at 728 (discussing other practices).

A company's internal utilization of a trademark in a way that does not communicate it to the public is analogous to an individual's private thoughts about a trademark. Such conduct simply does not violate the Lanham Act, which is concerned with the use of trademarks in connection with the sale of goods or services in a manner likely to lead to consumer confusion as to the source of such goods or services.

1-800 Contacts, Inc. v. WhenU.com, Inc., 414 F.3d at 408–09.

In addition, the panel also held that the triggered pop-up advertisement did not constitute use of the plaintiff's trademark. "The fatal flaw with [the district court's] holding [that the pop-up ads constitute use of the plaintiff's trademark] is that WhenU's pop-up ads *do not* display the 1-800 trademark." *Id.* at 410 (emphasis in original).

Following the *1-800-Contacts v. WhenU.com* decision, a fierce debate sprang up among academics. Professors Stacey Dogan and Mark Lemley took the lead in arguing that the *1-800-Contacts v. WhenU.com* case was correctly decided. *See* Stacey L. Dogan and Mark A. Lemley, *Grounding Trademark Law Through Use,* 92 IOWA L. REV. 1669 (2007). On the other side, Professors Graeme Dinwoodie and Mark Janis, among others, argued that the decision was fundamentally flawed. *See* Graeme B. Dinwoodie & Mark D. Janis, *Confusion over Use: Contextualism in Trademark Law*, 92 IOWA L. REV. 1597 (2007); Graeme B. Dinwoodie & Mark D. Janis, *Lessons from the Trademark Use Debate*, 92 IOWA L. REV. 1703 (2007). From the Dinwoodie & Janis perspective, the decision was flawed because the definition of use in the Act and the internal-external distinction of the common law both defined the type of use necessary to acquire trademark rights. Neither was concerned with what sort of use was sufficient to establish infringement.

Whether because of this academic debate or despite it, the Second Circuit decided to take a second look at the use issue in *Rescuecom Corp. v. Google, Inc.*, 562 F.3d 123 (2d Cir. 2009). In its opinion, the *Rescuecom Corp.* court decisively rejected the "it's not a use" argument. In doing so, the court focused on the fact that Google sells Rescuecom's trademark specifically to competitors as a keyword. As the court explained:

> First, in contrast to *1-800*, where we emphasized that the defendant made no use whatsoever of the plaintiff's trademark, here what Google is recommending and selling to its advertisers is Rescuecom's trademark. Second, in contrast with the facts of *1-800* where the defendant did not "use or display," much less sell, trademarks as search terms to its advertisers, here Google displays, offers, and sells Rescuecom's mark to Google's advertising customers when selling its advertising services. In addition, Google encourages the purchase of Rescuecom's mark through its Keyword Suggestion Tool.

Rescuecom Corp., 562 F.3d at 129.

As this passage reflects, technically, the *Rescuecom Corp.* distinguished, rather than reversed, the *1-800-Contacts v. WhenU.com* decision. As a result, the "it's not a use" argument remains available, but since *Rescuecom Corp.*, it has not been successful at the appellate level in any circuit.

As a practical matter then, *Rescuecom Corp.* returned us to where we started: Does the unauthorized use of a trademark as a keyword to trigger certain advertisements or sponsored links create a likelihood of confusion? If so, who is liable, and on what theory? It is to these issues we now turn by looking at a second *1-800-Contacts* case.

1-800 CONTACTS, INC. V. LENS.COM, INC.

722 F.3d 1229 (10th Cir. 2013)

HARTZ, J.

The Lanham Act, 15 U.S.C. §§ 1051–1127, prohibits the infringement of trademarks (used to identify products) and service marks (used to identify services). It was enacted in 1946, but because it speaks in general terms it can be applied to technologies unimagined at the time of enactment. One such technology, the Internet, has created a number of challenging issues. The case before us concerns Internet search engines, which present advertisers with new means of targeting prospective customers and therefore new possibilities for claims under the Lanham Act. The dispute arises out of advertising through AdWords, a program offered by the Internet search engine Google. An advertiser using AdWords pays Google to feature one of its ads onscreen whenever a designated term, known as a keyword, is used in a Google search. We must resolve whether the Lanham Act was violated by an advertiser's use of keywords that resembled a competitor's service mark. For the most part, we hold that there was no violation.

Plaintiff 1-800 Contacts, Inc. (1-800) dominates the retail market for replacement contact lenses. It owns the federally registered service mark 1800CONTACTS. Defendant Lens.com, Inc. is one of 1-800's competitors. To police the use of its mark, 1-800 enters different variations of the mark into Google searches and monitors what search results are displayed. When 1-800 found that several searches generated paid ads for Lens.com's websites, it concluded that Lens.com had reserved the mark as a keyword. After attempting to resolve the situation informally, 1-800 sued Lens.com for service-mark infringement. Its primary claim was that Lens.com itself had infringed the 1800CONTACTS mark by purchasing keywords resembling the mark. According to 1-800, this conduct had directed potential customers for 1-800 to Lens.com by creating what is known as "initial-interest confusion," which can be actionable under the Lanham Act. As the case progressed, 1-800 supplemented its claim of direct infringement by alleging that certain third-party marketers hired by Lens.com, known as affiliates, had also purchased keywords resembling the mark and that at least one affiliate was using the mark in the text of its online ads. 1-800 sought to hold Lens.com secondarily liable for its affiliates' conduct. The theories of secondary liability, which will be discussed more fully below, were common-law agency and contributory infringement.

The district court awarded summary judgment to Lens.com on all claims. On the direct-liability claim and most of the secondary-liability claims, the court ruled that 1-800 had raised no genuine issue of fact regarding the likelihood of initial-interest confusion. On the remaining secondary-liability claims—which concerned the use of 1-800's mark in the content of ads displayed on Google's site—the court ruled that 1-800's evidence was insufficient to hold Lens.com liable for any misconduct of its affiliates.

1-800 appeals the summary judgment. To the extent that the court based summary judgment on the ground that no likelihood of confusion existed, we affirm. Traditional analysis and actual marketplace data reveal that the keyword use by Lens.com and its affiliates was highly unlikely to divert consumers. As for the remaining secondary-liability claims, we affirm the denial of liability under agency law because the affiliates, even if agents (or more precisely, subagents) of Lens.com, lacked authority to include 1-800's mark in ads for Lens.com. But we reverse the denial of liability for contributory infringement because the evidence could support a reasonable finding that Lens.com did not take reasonable steps to halt the display of 1-800's marks in affiliate ads once it learned of such display. . . .

I.   BACKGROUND

A.   The Dispute

1-800 is the world's leading retailer of replacement contact lenses. It sells lenses via telephone, by mail order, and over the Internet. In 2003 it registered with the federal trademark register the nonstylized word mark "1800CONTACTS" as one of its service marks. The mark achieved incontestable status under 15 U.S.C. § 1065 in 2008. Lens.com is one of 1-800's competitors in the replacement-lens retail market. Unlike 1-800, which advertises through several different media and which derived approximately 40% of its gross sales from sources other than Internet orders in 2007, Lens.com advertises and does business almost exclusively online.

This dispute arose in the summer of 2005, when 1-800 discovered that paid advertisements for Lens.com appeared when one searched for the phrase "1800 CONTACTS" on Google. 1-800 concluded that Lens.com was using the 1800CONTACTS mark in its online marketing. To explain this concern properly, we must first review some mechanics of Internet advertising through search engines. Because 1-800's arguments on appeal focus solely on Lens.com's use of AdWords, a program offered by Google, we describe only AdWords and no other search engines or advertising services.

At the time of the proceedings below, a typical Google search simultaneously yielded two different kinds of results: organic results and sponsored links. Organic results were the links generated by Google's search algorithms, which sorted web pages according to their relevance to the user's search as well as their quality. An advertiser could not pay Google to have its web page displayed among the organic results. Through AdWords, however, an advertiser could pay to be displayed as a sponsored link. A sponsored link would include advertising copy and the advertiser's website address. A user who clicked on the ad would be connected to the website. Sponsored links usually appeared either above or to the right of the organic results. The notice "Sponsored Links" was displayed next to each cluster of ads. Google placed background shading behind several of the sponsored links to set them apart visually from the organic results, which appeared on a plain white background.

For its ad to appear as a sponsored link when a user initiated a Google search, an advertiser had to bid to reserve a particular word or phrase—known as a keyword—that would trigger the display of its ad. The advertiser specified whether its ad should appear as the result of (1) a broad match—that is, whenever a Google search contained a phrase that was either similar to or a relevant variation of the keyword; (2) a phrase match—whenever the search contained the exact keyword; or (3) an exact match—whenever the search contained the exact keyword and nothing more. The advertiser could also use negative matching, which instructed Google not to display the ad when a certain search term was used. Negative matching allowed the advertiser to filter out irrelevant searches. For example, if a seller of contact lenses had purchased the keyword contacts, it might have wanted to exclude searches for marketing contacts.

The display of a sponsored link in response to a user's search was known as an impression. An advertiser paid Google only if the user actually clicked on its impression; its bid for the keyword represented the amount per click that it was willing to pay. Advertisers who bid higher amounts generally received superior placement among the sponsored links. A click that led to a sale through the advertiser's web page was called a conversion, which did not incur an additional charge to the advertiser from Google.

1-800 apparently reasoned that a Google search for "1800 CONTACTS" could generate an ad for Lens.com only if Lens.com—or someone working on its behalf—had bid on that exact term or on some phrase containing that exact term. In September 2005 it sent Lens.com two letters reporting that online searches for that term were resulting in ads for Lens.com. One of the letters was accompanied by screenshots that showed Google search results for the phrases "1-800 contacts," "1-800-contacts," and "1800contacts." In each screenshot an ad for Lens.com appeared among the sponsored links, along with ads for 1-800 and other retailers. Lens.com responded that it had looked into the matter, had determined who appeared to be responsible, and would advise them not to bid on "1-800-CONTACTS" as a keyword in the future.

The parties who appeared to be responsible, Lens.com told 1-800, were affiliates. Advertisers like Lens.com might pay third-party affiliates to publish ads for them through AdWords and other search-engine programs. An Internet user who clicked on an ad published by a Lens.com affiliate would be routed directly to one of Lens.com's four websites— www.Lens.com, www.JustLenses.com, www.1-800GetLens.com, and www.ContactsAmerica.com—or instead would be taken to the affiliate's own website, where links to Lens.com's websites were displayed. When the user made a purchase at one of Lens.com's websites as a result of clicking on the affiliate's ad, the affiliate earned a commission.

Lens.com did not recruit individual affiliates directly; rather, it worked with Commission Junction (CJ), which managed a network of affiliates. Under the arrangement in this case, CJ agreed to pay the commissions to the affiliates for their conversions, and Lens.com agreed to reimburse CJ. According to Lens.com's chief executive officer, Lens.com had four different accounts with CJ in 2009, and through those accounts more than 10,000 affiliates were signed up to promote Lens.com and its brands.

Whatever action Lens.com took in response to 1-800's September 2005 notices, 1-800 continued to express concerns. In November and December 2005 it again contacted Lens.com and advised that Google searches for "1800contacts," "1800 contacts," "1-800-contacts," and "1-800 contacts" were still generating Lens.com's ads. Lens.com replied that it would try to determine who was publishing the ads in question. The next relevant communication did not occur until April 2007, when 1-800's counsel emailed Lens.com's counsel once more to complain that the problem was recurring. Attached to the email were screenshots of search results from Google and another search engine. Lens.com's counsel replied that he would confer with his client to see whether the problem could be fixed.

1-800 filed a complaint against Lens.com in August 2007 in the United States District Court for the District of Utah. The complaint stated that 1-800 had "discovered that Lens.com had purchased sponsored advertisements from Google, and other search engines, for Plaintiff's Marks to trigger advertising and/or a link to the Lens.com Websites." It further alleged that Lens.com had "use[d] the 1800 CONTACTS trademark as a triggering keyword to display and promote Lens.com's directly competitive goods and services." To support this allegation, the complaint included a screenshot of Google search results for the term "1800 CONTACTS" in which an ad for Lens.com was featured.

The complaint also alleged that Lens.com had used the 1800CONTACTS mark in its advertising copy, and it included a second screenshot that, unlike any of the screenshots that it had previously disclosed to Lens.com, showed a sponsored link featuring the term "1-800 Contacts" in the ad's text. The Internet address beneath this text was www.JustLenses.com, one of Lens.com's websites.

1-800's chief legal claims were that Lens.com had infringed on its 1800CONTACTS mark under § 32 of the Lanham Act, 15 U.S.C. § 1114(1), which provides a cause of action for the infringement of a federally registered mark, and § 43(a), 15 U.S.C. § 1125(a), which provides a cause of action for the infringement of unregistered as well as registered marks. . . .

    B.   Service-Mark Infringement Under the Lanham Act

A service mark, similar to a trademark, is defined by the Lanham Act as "any word, name, symbol, or device, or any combination thereof" that is used "to identify and distinguish the services of one person, including a unique service, from the services of others and to indicate the source of the services, even if that source is unknown." 15 U.S.C. § 1127 (2006). 1800CONTACTS is such a mark. The Lanham Act's private causes of action for trademark infringement are available to the owners of service marks. *See Vail Assocs., Inc. v. Vend-Tel-Co., Ltd.*, 516 F.3d 853, 857 & n.1 (10th Cir. 2008); *Donchez v. Coors Brewing Co.*, 392 F.3d 1211, 1215 (10th Cir. 2004). . . .

The elements of an infringement claim under § 43(a) are (1) that the plaintiff has a protectable interest in the mark; (2) that the defendant has used "an identical or similar mark" in commerce, *Donchez*, 392 F.3d at 1215 (brackets and internal quotation marks omitted); and (3) that the defendant's use is likely to confuse consumers. *See Utah Lighthouse Ministry v. Found. for Apologetic Info. & Research*, 527 F.3d 1045, 1050 (10th Cir. 2008). An infringement claim under § 32 has nearly identical elements, *see Jordache Enters., Inc. v. Hogg Wyld, Ltd.*, 828 F.2d 1482, 1484 (10th Cir. 1987), except that the registration of a mark serves as prima facie evidence of both the mark's validity and the registrant's exclusive right to use it in commerce, *see* 15 U.S.C. § 1115(a) (2002). The central question in a typical infringement action under either § 32 or § 43(a) is whether the defendant's use of the plaintiff's mark is likely to cause consumer confusion. . . .

The type of confusion alleged by 1-800 is an additional variety—namely, initial-interest confusion, a distinct theory that we recognized in *Australian Gold*. Initial-interest confusion "results when a consumer seeks a particular trademark holder's product and instead is lured to the product of a competitor by the competitor's use of the same or a similar mark." *Australian Gold*, 436 F.3d at 1238. As the name implies, the improper confusion occurs even if the consumer becomes aware of the defendant's actual identity before purchasing the product. *See id.* at 1238–39. . . .

We have identified six factors (the *King of the Mountain* factors) as relevant to whether a likelihood of confusion exists:

        (a) the degree of similarity between the marks;

        (b) the intent of the alleged infringer in adopting its mark;

        (c) evidence of actual confusion;

(d) the relation in use and the manner of marketing between the goods or services marketed by the competing parties;

(e) the degree of care likely to be exercised by purchasers; and

(f) the strength or weakness of the marks.

King of the Mountain Sports, Inc. v. Chrysler Corp., 185 F.3d 1084, 1089–90 (10th Cir. 1999). These factors are not exhaustive. *See id.* at 1090. And they should not be applied mechanically; some factors may carry far more weight than others depending on the circumstances. *See id.* ("[T]he weight afforded to some of the factors differs when applied in . . . separate contexts.").

A defendant may be held liable for service-mark infringement even though it has not directly infringed on the plaintiff's mark through its own acts. Two theories of secondary liability are pertinent here. First, we have joined the Third Circuit in recognizing that the Lanham Act incorporates common-law agency principles: a principal may be held vicariously liable for the infringing acts of an agent. *See Procter & Gamble Co. v. Haugen*, 317 F.3d 1121, 1127–28 (10th Cir. 2003); *AT & T Co. v. Winback & Conserve Program, Inc.*, 42 F.3d 1421, 1433–34 (3d Cir. 1994); 4 McCarthy § 25:21.25. Second, in *Inwood Laboratories, Inc. v. Ives Laboratories, Inc.*, 456 U.S. 844, 853–54 (1982), the Supreme Court ruled that contributory infringement can violate the Lanham Act. Akin to aiding and abetting, contributory infringement generally consists of either intentionally causing or knowingly facilitating the infringement of the plaintiff's mark by a third party. The *Inwood* Court formulated the theory as follows:

> [L]iability for trademark infringement can extend beyond those who actually mislabel goods with the mark of another. Even if a manufacturer does not directly control others in the chain of distribution, it can be held responsible for their infringing activities under certain circumstances. Thus, if a manufacturer or distributor intentionally induces another to infringe a trademark, or if it continues to supply its product to one whom it knows or has reason to know is engaging in trademark infringement, the manufacturer or distributor is contributorially responsible for any harm done as a result of the deceit.

Id. at 853–54 (footnote omitted).

C. Proceedings Before the District Court

1-800 moved for partial summary judgment on the issues of direct and secondary liability for service-mark infringement. Except for the few ads that used the mark in their text, 1-800's only clearly expressed theory of infringement was initial-interest confusion. . . .

In an effort to show actual confusion (the third *King of the Mountain* factor), 1-800 offered an example of one confused consumer and the results of a consumer survey conducted by its expert, Carl Degen. Lens.com moved to strike the survey as unreliable. It also moved for summary judgment on all claims. The district court granted Lens.com's motion to strike the survey. And it awarded summary judgment to Lens.com. See *1-800 Contacts, Inc. v. Lens.com, Inc.*, 755 F. Supp. 2d 1151, 1191 (D. Utah 2010). . . .

On appeal 1-800 argues (1) that there were disputed facts regarding likelihood of confusion and (2) that the evidence would support findings of secondary liability under theories of both vicarious liability and contributory infringement. . . . We affirm on all issues but one: contributory infringement. We disagree with the district court's ruling that there was insufficient evidence that Lens.com had the necessary actual or constructive knowledge to be held contributorially liable for the conduct of its affiliates. . . . Therefore, we reverse and remand for further proceedings on the contributory-infringement claim.

II. DISCUSSION

We first resolve the issues presented by 1-800's appeal. . . .

A. Direct Liability for Ads Placed by Lens.com

The district court awarded summary judgment to Lens.com on 1-800's claim that Lens.com was directly liable for infringing on its service mark. It ruled that 1-800 had created no genuine factual issue regarding whether Lens.com's keyword use was likely to cause confusion. It asserts that this ruling was error. It argues generally about likelihood of confusion, not distinguishing its § 32 infringement claims from its § 43(a) claims. We, too, need not differentiate between the two provisions, as the tests for likelihood of confusion under § 32 and § 43(a) do not differ materially. *See Jordache*, 828 F.2d at 1484. . . .

Again, the elements of an infringement claim under the Lanham Act are (1) that the plaintiff has a protectable interest in the mark, (2) that the defendant has used an identical or similar mark in commerce, and (3) that the defendant's use is likely to confuse consumers. That 1-800 has a protectable interest in its mark is not in dispute. And the district court ruled that purchasing the Challenged Keywords satisfied the use-in-commerce requirement, a premise that we will assume without deciding. Thus, the only contested issue is likelihood of confusion. 1-800's theory of confusion is initial-interest confusion. Its essential contention is that although Lens.com never published any ads with 1-800's mark in their text, its bidding on the nine Challenged Keywords caused its ads to appear in response to searches for the mark, thereby diverting customer interest away from 1-800's website and toward Lens.com's websites. . . .

In this case, one item of evidence particularly suggests an absence of initial-interest confusion, the variety of consumer confusion on which 1-800 relies. As we explained in *Australian Gold*, initial-interest confusion occurs when a consumer in search of the plaintiff's product "is *lured* to the product of a competitor." 436 F.3d at 1238 (emphasis added); *see Vail Assocs.*, 516 F.3d at 872 ("Initial interest confusion is a 'bait and switch' tactic that permits a competitor to *lure* consumers away from a service provider by passing off services as those of the provider, notwithstanding that the confusion is dispelled by the time of sale." (emphasis added)). Applying that description to this case, initial-interest confusion would arise as follows: a consumer enters a query for "1-800 Contacts" on Google; sees a screen with an ad for Lens.com that is generated because of Lens.com's purchase of one of the nine Challenged Keywords; becomes confused about whether Lens.com is the same source as, or is affiliated with, 1-800; and therefore clicks on the Lens.com ad to view the site. Lens.com has exploited its use of 1-800's mark to lure the confused consumer to its website. Ordinarily, the likelihood of such luring would need to be estimated by what we can call "informed judgment," which is assisted by analyzing the six *King of the Mountain* factors.

Here, however, we have AdWords data setting an upper limit on how often consumers really were lured in such fashion. A report by Lens.com's expert explained that Lens.com's use of the nine Challenged Keywords yielded 1,626 impressions for Lens.com or its associated websites over eight months. In only 25 (1.5%) of these 1,626 instances did the user click on the ad for Lens.com. (We do not know how many of the 25 made a purchase from Lens.com.) The users in those 25 instances may have been confused into thinking that Lens.com was affiliated with 1-800, or they may simply have wished to look at the offerings of those whom they knew to be 1-800's competitors. What we can say, though, is that initial-interest confusion occurred at most 1.5% of the time that a Lens.com ad was generated by a Challenged Keyword in those eight months. This number cannot support an inference that Lens.com's keyword activity was likely to "lure[ ]" consumers away from 1-800. *Australian Gold*, 436 F.3d at 1238. It is thus insufficient to justify relief. *See Universal Money Ctrs.*, 22 F.3d at 1534, 1537 (characterizing a 2.6% confusion rate as de minimis); *cf. CareFirst*, 434 F.3d at 268 (survey reporting a confusion rate of 2% was "hardly a sufficient showing of actual confusion"); *Henri's Food Prods. Co., Inc. v. Kraft, Inc.*, 717 F.2d 352, 358–59 (7th Cir. 1983) (survey reporting a confusion rate of 7.6% weighed against a finding of infringement).

Moreover, 1-800's arguments based on other *King of the Mountain* factors does not suggest a contrary conclusion. It points to the district court's determination that the likelihood of confusion is supported by factors (4) and (5): the parties offer the same services in the same channels of trade (retail sales of replacement contact lenses over the

Internet) and "it is unlikely that consumers exercise a high degree of care in selecting this service." In addition, it challenges the district court's determination on factor (6) that 1-800's mark is "only moderately strong"; and on factor (1), it argues that the relevant marks were identical or nearly identical, because the consumer was using the 1800CONTACTS mark as a search term and Lens.com had triggered the ad by using a nearly identical mark.

This analysis by 1-800 illustrates the danger of applying the factors mechanically without attention to context. The specific issue before us is the likelihood that a consumer who conducts an Internet search for 1-800 Contacts and then sees an ad for Lens.com on the results page will be confused into thinking that Lens.com has a business association with 1-800. To begin with, even if consumers in general may not much care what retailer supplies their contact lenses, the consumers relevant to this suit are looking for a particular retailer. Presumably they have narrowed their search because they have already selected 1-800 as the preferred retailer and are searching for its website or perhaps commentary on its performance. Given the purpose of the search, the shoppers will be attentive to click on those results that will connect them with sites relating to 1-800. In addition, once the consumers see the results page, the substantial dissimilarity between "1-800 Contacts" and "Lens.com" (or its other websites) can be expected to greatly reduce the chance that the consumers will think that the parties are related enterprises; the similarity of the search term and 1-800's mark is of minor relevance.

Perhaps in the abstract, one who searches for a particular business with a strong mark and sees an entry on the results page will naturally infer that the entry is for that business. But that inference is an unnatural one when the entry is clearly labeled as an advertisement and clearly identifies the source, which has a name quite different from the business being searched for. It is for this reason that the Ninth Circuit considered "the labeling and appearance of the advertisements and the surrounding context on the screen displaying the results page" to be a critical factor in finding no likelihood of confusion in a case in which the alleged infringer used a competitor's mark as a keyword. *Network Automation v. Advanced Sys. Concepts*, 638 F.3d 1137, 1154 (9th Cir. 2011). We conclude that the factors other than evidence of actual confusion (even if we assume that 1-800's mark is a strong one) firmly support the unlikelihood of confusion. This case is readily distinguishable from *Australian Gold*, in which the alleged infringer used its competitor's trademarks on its websites. *See* 436 F.3d at 1239.

We now turn to 1-800's arguments regarding actual confusion. First, it cites what it claims to be anecdotal evidence of actual confusion in the marketplace: a customer-service record disclosed by Lens.com reported that a customer called Lens.com in July 2006 to cancel her order, apparently because she had just realized that Lens.com was not 1-800. Lens.com counters that the customer-service record cannot be probative of the relevant confusion in this case because, among other reasons, it gives no indication how the customer found Lens.com to place her order initially. We agree. It would be speculation to assume that she had clicked on a Lens.com ad after specifically searching for 1-800. Moreover, a single customer-service record is entitled to little weight. *See King of the Mountain*, 185 F.3d at 1092 ("[I]solated instances of actual confusion may be de minimis." (brackets and internal quotation marks omitted)); *Universal Money Ctrs.*, 22 F.3d at 1535–36 (characterizing limited evidence of actual confusion as de minimis). . . .

Next, 1-800 argues that its consumer-confusion survey was wrongly excluded and that it, too, demonstrated actual confusion. Respondents to this survey were recruited through an online questionnaire and were limited to consumers who said that they either had bought contact lenses in the previous 12 months or were considering buying them in the next 12 months. During the survey they were told to imagine that they had just conducted a Google search for "1800contacts," and then they viewed screenshots of search results in which an ad for Lens.com appeared among the sponsored links. After studying the screenshots, they were asked whether they thought that the Lens.com ad either "originate[d] from 1-800-CONTACTS," or "ha[d] sponsorship or approval from 1-800-CONTACTS." The district court excluded the survey results under Fed. R. Evid. 702 on the ground that methodological flaws undermined the survey's reliability. It focused on two perceived flaws. First, it ruled that the population of respondents was too broad, as it was not limited to prospective Internet consumers of contact lenses. Second, it ruled that the questions were ambiguous and leading. The ambiguity arose from the first question's failure to clarify whether "1-800-CONTACTS" referred to a search term or a company. And in the court's view the questions were leading because they suggested the possibility of a connection between Lens.com and 1-800 when the respondents might not have considered such a connection on their own. The court found it unnecessary to address Lens.com's arguments concerning other alleged flaws because the survey would have been inadmissible regardless. . . .

We, too, are concerned about the reliability of the survey. We note only the ambiguity of a key question. Respondents were told that they had entered "1800contacts" into a Google search and were then asked whether they thought that the ad for Lens.com on the results screen "originates from 1-800-CONTACTS." As the district court noted, respondents may have believed that they were being asked whether the ad had resulted from use of the search term "1-800-CONTACTS." An affirmative answer based on this belief would not have been at all probative of the likelihood of confusion that 1-800 has alleged. In presenting the survey responses, 1-800's expert lumped together the affirmative responses to the ambiguous question with the affirmative responses to the question whether the respondent believed that the Lens.com ad "ha[d] sponsorship or approval from 1-800-CONTACTS." As a result, the court had no way of accurately discounting the survey data for any misunderstandings that might have arisen from the ambiguity of the first question's language.

In any event, even assuming that the survey should have been admitted, it does not warrant reversal of summary judgment because it was insufficiently probative of confusion to overcome the factors discussed above. The survey revealed that the relevant confusion was fairly low. To isolate confusion arising specifically from the use of 1-800's mark as a search term and keyword, the survey used a control group; respondents in this group were told to imagine that they had searched for the term contact lenses rather than the term 1800contacts. When these control-group respondents were asked whether they thought that the Lens.com ad either originated from 1-800 or had sponsorship or approval from 1-800, 11.9% answered in the affirmative. By comparison, 19.4% of respondents in the first noncontrol group and 19.2% of respondents in the second noncontrol group answered likewise. Subtracting the control group's 11.9% rate of confusion, one is left with net confusion rates of only 7.5% and 7.3% for the two noncontrol groups, or an average net confusion rate of only 7.4%. *See* 6 J. Thomas McCarthy, McCarthy on Trademarks and Unfair Competition § 32:187 at 32–432 (4th ed. 2013) (6 McCarthy) (noting use of such corrections to eliminate the "general background noise" of confusion in predicting the likelihood of confusion (internal quotation marks omitted)). The 7.4% figure is at (or below) the lowest confusion rate that, together with other evidence supporting confusion, could justify a conclusion that consumer confusion was likely. . . . The great weight of authority appears to be that "[w]hen the percentage results of a confusion survey dip below 10%, they can become evidence which will indicate that confusion is not likely." 6 McCarthy § 32:189 at 32–440 (emphasis added).

Thus, 1-800's survey is entitled to no more than minimal weight. And that minimal weight cannot sustain a finding of likelihood of confusion in the circumstances presented here. The other factors, including the hard data noted above, overwhelmingly indicate the unlikelihood of confusion. Even if the survey was admissible evidence, summary judgment for Lens.com was required.

B.   Secondary Liability for Ads Placed by Lens.com Affiliates

1-800 claims that Lens.com should have been denied summary judgment on the claims of secondary liability for infringement allegedly committed by affiliates who published ads on its behalf. 1-800's arguments focus exclusively on the conduct of two affiliates, Goggans and McCoy. Both Goggans and McCoy purchased keywords that were either identical or closely similar to 1-800's service mark. In addition, McCoy published at least one ad for www.JustLenses.com that featured a close variation of the mark in its text.

Again, 1-800's theories of secondary liability are vicarious liability and contributory infringement. Vicarious liability arises when common-law principles of agency impose liability on the defendant for the infringing acts of its agent. *See Procter & Gamble*, 317 F.3d at 1127–28. Contributory infringement occurs when the defendant either (1) intentionally induces a third party to infringe on the plaintiff's mark or (2) enables a third party to infringe on the mark while knowing or having reason to know that the third party is infringing, yet failing to take reasonable remedial measures. *See Inwood*, 456 U.S. at 853–54. Vicarious and contributory liability must be predicated on some direct infringement by the third party. Lens.com therefore cannot incur secondary liability unless one of the affiliates in question directly violated the Lanham Act.

As noted, the low ratio of clicks to impressions associated with Lens.com's own keyword use and the other *King of the Mountain* factors convince us that summary judgment was appropriate on 1-800's direct-infringement claim. The same factors and similar data convince us that insofar as Goggans and McCoy used keywords that resulted in ads for Lens.com entities that did not display 1-800's mark in their text, no genuine factual issue exists regarding likelihood of confusion. As for hard data, the record reveals that McCoy's use of "1800Contacts" or some variation thereof as a keyword generated more than 448,000 impressions whose text did not display the mark. Of these impressions, at most 3,163—or about .7%—resulted in clicks. Likewise, one of 1-800's own exhibits revealed that Goggans's use of "1800Contacts" as a keyword generated 242,864 impressions for www.JustLenses.com that did not display the mark in their text, and only 1,445 of the impressions—also fewer than 1%—resulted in clicks. 1-800 does not dispute these numbers, which are even more in Lens.com's favor than the 1.5% clicks-to-impressions rate for 1-800's direct-liability claim. Thus, to the extent that 1-800's secondary-liability claim derives from keyword use by Goggans and McCoy that did not generate ads containing the 1800CONTACTS mark, there is insufficient evidence of direct infringement. And absent any evidence of direct infringement, Lens.com cannot be secondarily liable. The district court properly granted summary judgment to Lens.com on this keyword use.

1-800's only remaining claim is that Lens.com is secondarily liable for McCoy's publication of ads that featured variations of the 1-800 mark in their text. We examine vicarious and contributory infringement on this claim.

1. Vicarious Liability.

The district court granted summary judgment to Lens.com on 1-800's vicarious-liability theory, ruling that the evidence would not support a reasonable inference that the affiliates were Lens.com's agents. We have some concerns with the district court's analysis and Lens.com's arguments that there was no agency relationship. . . .

We need not resolve, however, whether the evidence was sufficient to establish an agency relationship between Lens.com and its affiliates. Assuming without deciding that the affiliates were agents of Lens.com, we note that a principal is subject to liability for its agent's tortious conduct only if the conduct "is within the scope of the agent's actual authority or ratified by the principal." *Id.* § 7.04. 1-800 does not contend that Lens.com ratified McCoy's allegedly infringing ad. And although Lens.com argues broadly that its affiliates "ha[d] no authority, apparent or actual, to act on behalf of Lens.com," we can affirm summary judgment without going so far. The issue is not whether McCoy had authority to act on Lens.com's behalf at all, but merely whether he had actual authority to publish an ad displaying a variation of 1-800's mark in its text. An agent acts with actual authority if it "reasonably believes, in accordance with the principal's manifestations to the agent, that the principal wishes the agent so to act." Restatement (Third) of Agency § 2.01. As the Restatement further explains,

> Lack of actual authority is established by showing either that the agent did not believe, or could not reasonably have believed, that the principal's grant of actual authority encompassed the act in question. This standard requires that the agent's belief be reasonable, an objective standard, and that the agent actually hold the belief, a subjective standard.

Id. § 2.02 cmt. e (emphases added). The subjective component of actual authority is determinative here.

The record contains undisputed evidence that McCoy did not hold the belief that Lens.com authorized him to publish ads displaying 1-800's mark in their text. McCoy did not place any such ads himself. Rather, the ads were composed and published by one of his employees without his knowledge. Asked during a deposition whether he would agree that placing the phrase "1-800 Contacts" in the text of an ad for www.JustLenses.com "probably isn't proper," McCoy replied, "Yes, I would." Pressed further on whether he would have "stopped that practice" if he had known about it sooner, McCoy responded, "Absolutely." The unavoidable inference is that McCoy never believed, reasonably or otherwise, that Lens.com authorized him to place the ads. Thus, the subjective component of actual authority was absent. We affirm summary judgment on the vicarious-liability claim on this ground.

2.   Contributory Infringement.

a.   Sufficiency of the Evidence.

The district court granted summary judgment on contributory infringement solely on the ground that the principles of contributory liability did not allow McCoy's offending ads—the ones featuring 1-800's mark in their text—to be imputed to Lens.com. Accordingly, we focus only on those principles without deciding whether the ads themselves directly infringed 1-800's mark.

We agree with the district court that the record cannot support a reasonable inference that Lens.com intentionally induced its affiliates to place the mark in the text of their ads. As to the second *Inwood* alternative, however, we must reverse summary judgment. In our view, a rational juror could find that Lens.com knew that at least one of its affiliates was using 1-800's service mark in its ads yet did not make reasonable efforts to halt the affiliate's practice. True, the record contains no evidence that before 1-800 filed its complaint on August 13, 2007, Lens.com either knew or had reason to know that any affiliates were using 1-800's mark in their ad copy. But the complaint alleged that an ad for www.JustLenses.com had displayed the 1800CONTACTS mark in its text, and it copied a screenshot of the ad. And Lens.com did not take corrective action until three months later, on November 14, when it apparently asked CJ to contact McCoy with instructions to remove the offending ads.

Lens.com argues that during these three months it was communicating with CJ in an effort to identify the culpable affiliate and that absent such identification it did not have the actual or constructive knowledge that Inwood demands. It points out that 1-800's complaint did not reveal which of the more than 10,000 affiliates in Lens.com's network had published the ad displaying 1-800's mark. But Lens.com does not dispute 1-800's assertion that "Lens.com had an effective tool to stop its affiliates' infringement—by merely communicating to them that they may not use 1-800's mark ... in the language of sponsored links. Where Lens.com has instituted such prohibitions in the past, affiliates ceased their infringing conduct." The record reflects that Lens.com could communicate with all its affiliates at one time through an email blast from CJ or a monthly newsletter sent by CJ to every Lens.com affiliate. Thus, Lens.com may well not have needed to identify the offending affiliate to halt the placement of 1-800's mark in affiliate ad copy.

We can readily distinguish the two cases that Lens.com cites to support its contention that it had no duty to act until it knew the specific offender. In both cases knowledge of the specific offender was necessary for the defendant to take effective action. One case concerned Google's policies permitting advertisers to use trademarks as keywords and, to a limited extent, to feature them in the text of advertisements themselves.

See Rosetta Stone, 676 F.3d at 151–52. Rosetta Stone sued Google for
contributory infringement because the policies enabled sellers of
counterfeit Rosetta Stone software to mislead consumers by placing ads
that appeared when consumers conducted searches for "Rosetta Stone."
See id. at 151–52, 163. The circuit court referred to the district court's
finding that "there is little Google can do beyond expressly prohibiting
advertisements for counterfeit goods, taking down those advertisements
when it learns of their existence, and creating a team dedicated to
fighting advertisements for counterfeit goods." *Id.* at 164 (brackets and
internal quotation marks omitted). In this context, it made sense for the
court to write:

> It is not enough to have general knowledge that some
> percentage of the purchasers of a product or service is using it to
> engage in infringing activities; rather, the defendant must
> supply its product or service to identified individuals that it
> knows or has reason to know are engaging in trademark
> infringement.

Id. at 163 (emphasis added) (internal quotation marks omitted).

The second case, *Tiffany (NJ) Inc. v. eBay, Inc.*, 600 F.3d 93, 103 (2d
Cir. 2010), reviewed a suit by Tiffany against the online auction service
eBay, in which Tiffany alleged that eBay had contributorially infringed
on the Tiffany trademark by allowing third parties to list counterfeit
Tiffany goods for sale on its website. The circuit court noted the
significant efforts made by eBay to prevent sales of counterfeit Tiffany
goods, pointing out that when "complaints gave eBay reason to know that
certain sellers had been selling counterfeits, those sellers' listings were
removed and repeat offenders were suspended from the eBay site." *Id.* at
109. Nevertheless, Tiffany argued that eBay was a contributory infringer
because it "continued to supply its services to the sellers of counterfeit
Tiffany goods while knowing or having reason to know that such sellers
were infringing Tiffany's mark." *Id.* at 106. The court rejected the
argument. It wrote: "For contributory trademark infringement liability to
lie, a service provider must have more than a general knowledge or
reason to know that its service is being used to sell counterfeit goods.
Some contemporary knowledge of which particular listings are infringing
or will infringe in the future is necessary." *Id.* at 107.

As we read the opinions in *Rosetta Stone* and *Tiffany*, they support
rather than contradict 1-800's theory of liability here. Both defendants,
Google and eBay, had established means by which a third party could
engage in trademark infringement—by letting third parties advertise
counterfeit products. The discussion in both opinions implicitly assumed
that once the defendant knew of an identified third party's infringing ads,
it would be a contributory infringer if it did not halt the ads. But the
plaintiff did not describe any way for the defendant to stop an

unidentified infringer without also interfering with legitimate advertising (as by, say, halting all use of "Rosetta Stone" as a keyword or all ads for Tiffany products). A defendant has no obligation under contributory-infringement doctrine to stop a practice—such as accepting ads for Tiffany products—simply because the practice might be exploited by infringers. *Cf. Inwood*, 456 U.S. at 854 n.13 (contributory liability cannot be imposed merely for the defendant's failure to "reasonably anticipate" infringement by third parties (internal quotation marks omitted)). The obvious rationale for ordinarily requiring that the defendant know the identity of the infringer is that otherwise the defendant could not halt the infringement without also stopping perfectly proper conduct—throwing the baby out with the bath water, so to speak. But what if, as argued in the case before us, the defendant need not know the identity of the infringer to stop the allegedly infringing practice without affecting legitimate conduct? We do not infer from *Rosetta Stone* and *Tiffany* that either court would have required knowledge of the particular offender to impose contributory liability in such a situation.

In our view, if Lens.com could have stopped the use of ads using 1-800's mark by simply requiring CJ to send an email blast to its affiliates forbidding such use, then Lens.com's failure to proceed in that manner after learning of such ads could constitute contributory infringement. Lens.com does not dispute that once it learned that one of its affiliates had used 1-800's mark in the content of an ad, it had an obligation to conduct an investigation to determine which affiliate was the publisher and then order that affiliate to halt the practice. *See Coach, Inc.*, 717 F.3d at 505 (when flea market operator had been informed that vendors were selling counterfeit goods, he was "properly held liable for contributory trademark infringement because he knew or had reason to know of the infringing activities and yet continued to facilitate those activities by providing space and storage units to vendors without undertaking a reasonable investigation or taking other appropriate remedial measures"). Why then can it not be held liable for failing to take the far easier step of ordering an email blast that would necessarily reach the publisher and stop the publication, and would not interfere with any lawful conduct of other affiliates? When modern technology enables one to communicate easily and effectively with an infringer without knowing the infringer's specific identity, there is no reason for a rigid line requiring knowledge of that identity, so long as the remedy does not interfere with lawful conduct. . . .

In sum, a reasonable jury could find that during the period between the filing of 1-800's complaint and Lens.com's corrective action, Lens.com knew that at least one of its affiliates was publishing an ad bearing 1-800's mark, yet it did not take reasonable action to promptly halt the practice. We conclude that 1-800 has presented enough evidence to support a claim of contributory infringement. . . .

III. CONCLUSION

We AFFIRM summary judgment on all claims of infringement based on keyword use that did not result in ads displaying 1-800's mark in their text. With respect to the secondary-liability claims related to ads that did display the mark in their text, we AFFIRM summary judgment on vicarious infringement but REVERSE and REMAND on contributory infringement.

NOTES FOR DISCUSSION

1. *Initial Interest Confusion and the Factor Test.* As we saw in the previous section, one way to confine the potential overbreadth of the initial interest confusion doctrine is to subject it to the *Sleekcraft* (in the Ninth Circuit) or *Polaroid* (in the Second Circuit) or *King of the Mountain* (in the Tenth Circuit) factor test, rather than rely on it as a stand-alone basis for infringement. This forces a court not only to articulate a story about how initial interest confusion might arise, as the *Brookfield Comms.* court did, but to examine whether there is evidence that such confusion is, in fact, likely.

In the *1-800-Contacts v. Lens.com* case, what are the key factors that the court looks to on the direct infringement issue? The court compares click-through rates to the percentage of respondents who evince confusion in surveys to justify its conclusion that initial interest confusion is not likely, as a matter of law. Is that an appropriate comparison? What could 1-800-Contacts have done differently or additionally to bolster its claim?

In the *1-800-Contacts v. Lens.com* case, the Tenth Circuit remands for further proceedings on contributory infringement by assuming that the inclusion of the 1-800-Contacts trademark in the text of a competitor's ad creates initial interest confusion. Is that assumption sound, substantively and procedurally? Substantively, does every ad that contains a competitor's trademark create actionable confusion? Presumably not, or else a great deal of comparative advertisement would be illegal. Procedurally, who had the burden of introducing evidence sufficient to create a triable issue with respect to that issue at the summary judgment stage? If no such evidence was introduced, was it proper procedurally to assume that the use of 1-800-Contacts' trademark in the text of the ad was likely to create initial interest confusion?

2. *What is Initial Interest Confusion?* A key issue with respect to the reach of initial interest confusion is whether it reaches every instance where the unauthorized use of another's trademark diverts consumer attention or whether it requires something more than mere diversion, and if so, what that something more is. How does the Tenth Circuit resolve this issue? What is the difference between mere diversion and luring?

The Ninth Circuit has seemed to recognize a similar distinction. In *Network Automation, Inc. v. Advanced Systems Concepts, Inc.*, the Ninth Circuit held that because "the *sine qua non* of trademark infringement is consumer confusion, when we examine initial interest confusion, the owner of the mark must demonstrate likely confusion, not mere diversion." 638 F.3d 1137, 1149 (9th Cir. 2011). What is the difference between confusion and diversion?

In *Playboy Enters., Inc. v. Netscape Comms. Corp.*, Judge Berzon concurring wrote:

> There is a big difference between hijacking a customer to another website by making the customer think he or she is visiting the trademark owner's website (even if only briefly), which is what may be happening in this case when the banner advertisements are not labeled, and just distracting a potential customer with another *choice,* when it is clear that it is a choice.

Playboy Enters., Inc., 354 F.3d 1020, 1035 (9th Cir. 2004) (Berzon, J., concurring). Like the Tenth Circuit's distinction between mere diversion and luring, Judge Berzon suggests a distinction between hijacking and distracting. How do we know whether any given use is hijacking or distracting?

Judge Berzon also suggests that the key issue may be whether the advertisement or search result is labeled. But what does it mean for an advertisement or search result to be properly labeled? Should we rely on the trademark owner to identify the official website and authorized resellers, and forbid competitors only from expressly misleading consumers? Or should we require competitors to disclaim an affiliation expressly?

How would you resolve the following case: Amazon.com is the world's largest online retailer. Multi Time Machine (or MTM) is a manufacturer of high-end, military style watches. Amazon.com does not sell MTM watches, but does sell several competing brands. If a consumer searches on Amazon.com for "MTM Special Ops," a particular model of MTM watch, the search results display several competing brands—each plainly labeled by manufacturer and model. The search results do not expressly state however that Amazon.com does not carry MTM Special Ops watches. MTM has sued Amazon.com and alleged initial interest confusion. *See Multi Time Machine, Inc. v. Amazon.com, Inc.*, ___ F.3d ___, 2015 WL 6161600 (9th Cir. 2015) (affirming grant of summary judgment for Amazon.com: "Here, the products at issue are clearly labeled by Amazon to avoid any likelihood of initial interest confusion by a reasonably prudent consumer accustomed to online shopping.").

3.   *Use.* Did the Tenth Circuit resolve the question whether Lens.com's use of 1-800-Contacts as a keyword constituted "use in commerce" sufficient to sustain a trademark infringement cause of action? The Trademark Act provides:

> For purposes of this chapter, a mark shall be deemed to be in use in commerce—

(1) on goods when—

(A) it is placed in any manner on the goods or their containers or the displays associated therewith or on the tags or labels affixed thereto, or if the nature of the goods makes such placement impracticable, then on documents associated with the goods or their sale. . . .

15 U.S.C. § 1127 (2015). Did Lens.com make such a use of 1-800-Contacts's service mark?

Do you agree with the following analysis?

[A] customer walks into a bar or restaurant and orders a Coke. Without ever saying a word, the bartender or waiter serves the customer a Pepsi. That is undoubtedly a classic example of passing off and, so long as Coke is a trademark, constitutes trademark infringement. Yet, under the Second Circuit's approach in *1-800 Contacts*, so long as the bartender or waiter never spoke (or otherwise displayed) the word "Coke," there could be no trademark or unfair competition liability.

Such a conclusion makes no sense, however. The customer ordered using the word "coke" and the business responded to it. We use language not only when we speak words, but when we hear them and respond to them. Under both the statute and the common law, the [bartender's] . . . response to the customer's statement constitutes a use sufficient to establish liability. The Ninth Circuit took this view in *Playboy v. Netscape*. Although Netscape did not expressly attach the word "Playboy" or any of PEI's other trademarks to the infringing banner advertisements, it displayed those advertisements specifically in response to a user's entry of one of PEI's trademarks. Because the consumer had typed in "playboy" and received certain ads in reply, from the consumer's perspective, the banners were implicitly labeled with PEI's trademarks, just as the customer's drink was implicitly labeled "Coke."

Glynn S. Lunney, Jr., *Trademarks on the Internet: The United States Experience,* 97 TRADEMARK REPORTER 931, 967–68 (2007).

4.   *Secondary Liability.* In the *1-800-Contacts* case, the plaintiff alleges that Lens.com is liable for the actions of its affiliates under a theory of secondary liability and not as a direct infringer. What practical difference would the theory of liability make? As we saw in Chapter 7, secondary liability is relatively narrow in trademark law and arises only if a defendant knows specifically about the infringing actions of another and contributes to them. 1-800-Contacts could not establish Lens.com's liability under trademark's secondary liability doctrine by showing that Lens.com knew that some of its advertisements would create confusion; 1-800-Contacts would have to show that Lens.com knew specifically that a particular advertisement was likely to create confusion and did not take action to remove the

advertisement. The Tenth Circuit holds that Lens.com had such knowledge after 1-800-Contacts filed its lawsuit.

Does the Tenth Circuit's ruling effectively create a notice-and-takedown regime? Under a notice-and-takedown regime, when an entity receives notice of a specific infringing use, it has the requisite actual knowledge to trigger contributory liability (assuming that it has the ability to stop or remove the specific infringing use). To avoid such liability, the entity must take down the specific infringing use. Does the Tenth Circuit's ruling extend to search engines themselves that sell trademarks as keywords? If so, under what circumstances would a search engine be contributorily liable?

As we shall see in Chapter 11, often the only relief courts provide to a successful trademark plaintiff is an injunction. Monetary damages are rarely awarded. If the only relief available to 1-800-Contacts is an injunction, should Lens.com take the specific advertisement down when it receives the requisite actual notice, or should it wait for the court to find infringement? Revisit this issue again after you have studied remedies, and ask whether if 1-800-Contacts prevails, it could recover damages in this context?

5.   *Nominative Fair Use.* May a competitor defend the use of another's trademarks as a keyword on the grounds of nominative fair use? In *Playboy Enters., Inc. v. Netscape Comms. Corp.*, Netscape sought to defend its sale of the trademarks Playboy and Playmate to Playboy's competitors as keywords as a nominative fair use. 354 F.3d 101 (9th Cir. 2004). The Ninth Circuit rejected Netscape's nominative fair use defense on the grounds that Netscape did not need to use the words "playboy" or "playmate" to satisfy its consumers who were looking for photographs of nude women on the Internet. In the court's view, there were other words that Netscape and its search engine users could rely on to find such images. *Id.* at 1030. Yet, not all nude images are the same. If a consumer was looking specifically for Playboy-style images, and not the more hardcore style of images associated with Penthouse or Hustler magazines, how could the consumer search for his specific preferences without using the Playboy trademark? Is that specific style of nude image, popularized by Playboy magazine, its own genus? Is "playboy" the generic name for that style of image? Is the consumer who enters "playboy" into a search looking for photographs originally made by and published in Playboy magazine or for photographs with a similar style and subject matter?

In the end, nominative fair use failed in *Playboy* because the search engine used the marks at issue to search for pornographic images generally rather than limit the results to Playboy-brand images. How would you resolve the following case: Farzad and Lisa Tabari are auto brokers—the personal shoppers of the automotive world. They contact authorized dealers, solicit bids and arrange for customers to buy from the dealer offering the best combination of location, availability and price. Consumers like this service, as it increases competition among dealers, resulting in greater selection at lower prices. For many of the same reasons, auto manufacturers and dealers aren't so keen on it, as it undermines dealers' territorial exclusivity and lowers profit margins. The Tabaris offered this service for consumers who want to purchase a Lexus automobile at buy-a-lexus.com and buyorleaselexus.com. When customers purchase a Lexus through the Tabaris, they receive a genuine Lexus car sold by an authorized Lexus dealer. Nevertheless, Toyota sues, alleging trademark infringement and dilution. *See Toyota Motor Sales, U.S.A., Inc. v. Tabari*, 610 F.3d 1171 (9th Cir. 2010) (holding that the use constitutes non-infringing nominative fair use as a matter of law).

6. *Consumer Welfare and Trademark Owner Welfare.* Is there any real risk of material consumer confusion in keyword-triggered advertisements? Is there any chance that keyword-triggered advertisements or search results will prevent a consumer determined to find the official site from finding it? Have you ever used a search engine? Have you ever confused the sponsored search results with the organic search results? If you have searched for an official site, have you ever clicked on another site by mistake, thinking that it was the official site? Have you made that mistake more than once?

In *Toyota Motor Sales, U.S.A. v. Tabari*, Judge Kozinski wrote:

> When a domain name making nominative use of a mark does not actively suggest sponsorship or endorsement, the worst that can happen is that some consumers may arrive at the site uncertain as to what they will find. But in the age of FIOS, cable modems, DSL and T1 lines, reasonable, prudent and experienced internet consumers are accustomed to such exploration by trial and error. They skip from site to site, ready to hit the back button whenever they're not satisfied with a site's contents. They fully expect to find some sites that aren't what they imagine based on a glance at the domain name or search engine summary. Outside the special case of trademark.com, or domains that actively claim affiliation with the trademark holder, consumers don't form any firm expectations about the sponsorship of a website until they've seen the landing page—if then. This is sensible agnosticism, not consumer confusion.

Toyota Motor Sales, U.S.A., Inc., 610 F.3d at 1179. Do you agree with Judge Kozinski's assertions regarding consumer behavior?

Are consumers better or worse off as a result of competitors' and search engines' use of trademark as keywords? The competing consumer interests here should be familiar by now: increased search costs and the potential for welfare-diminishing confusion, on the one hand, against increased information about competitors and a resulting increase in competition on the other. What sort of advertisements or sponsored search results triggered in response to consumer searches on 1-800-Contacts would plausibly reduce consumer welfare? What if a banner advertisement was expressly misleading and stated that it was the official 1-800-Contacts® website when it was not?

From 1-800-Contacts's perspective, does any use of its trademark to trigger advertisements or search results for competitors make it worse off? Should a search engine's sale or a competitor's purchase of 1-800-Contacts trademarks as keywords constitute *per se* trademark infringement in that it impermissibly trades on the fame of, and 1-800-Contacts's investment in, its trademarks? Does such use illegally "free ride" on 1-800-Contacts's goodwill? Does it constitute dilution?

CHAPTER 11

REMEDIES

■ ■ ■

The Lanham Trademark Act provides a trademark or unfair competition plaintiff with several remedy options. First, the Act gives courts the "power to grant injunctions, according to the principles of equity and upon such terms as the court may deem reasonable," for either infringement of a registered trademark or to prevent a violation of section 43(a), (c), or (d). 15 U.S.C. § 1116(a) (2015). Second, for the infringement of a registered trademark, a violation of section 43(a) or (d), or a willful violation of section 43(c), the Act states that "the plaintiff shall be entitled . . . to recover (1) the defendant's profits, (2) any damages sustained by the plaintiff, and (3) the costs of the action." 15 U.S.C. § 1117(a) (2015). Third, the Act also provides for an award of reasonable attorney fees to the prevailing party "in exceptional cases." *Id.*

In addition to these fairly standard remedy options, the Act also authorizes a court to order the seizure and destruction of infringing articles and marketing materials. 15 U.S.C. § 1118 (2015). Further, in civil cases involving the use of a counterfeit mark, the Act mandates an award of exemplary damages and attorney's fees, 15 U.S.C. § 1117(b) (2015), or alternatively, authorizes a plaintiff to elect an award of statutory damages instead. 15 U.S.C. § 1117(c) (2015).

Despite the availability of this full range of remedies, in the typical case involving trademark infringement or unfair competition, however, the central, and often only, relief sought is an injunction, and so we begin our study of remedies with the legal rules courts have developed for determining when injunctive relief is appropriate in trademark cases.

A. INJUNCTIVE RELIEF: PRELIMINARY AND PERMANENT

As a general rule, courts are reluctant to grant injunctive relief when an award of damages will adequately remedy the harm a plaintiff has suffered. In part, the reasons for this reluctance are historical. In England, by the early part of the fourteenth century, relief could be obtained from the common law courts only if the injury at issue fell within the scope of a limited set of writs reflecting a correspondingly limited set of common law forms of action. When no writ applied or relief was not otherwise available from the common law courts, the injured party could petition the king for redress. In the latter part of the fourteenth century, the King's Chancellor became responsible for hearing these petitions. Early on in this process, the rule developed that relief from the King's Chancellor would not be available if the common courts at law could provide an adequate remedy. When the power of the King's Chancellor was vested in the Court of Chancery, and subsequently the Court of Equity, the procedures and remedies available were not constrained by the common law forms, but the limitation that equitable relief would be available only in the absence of an adequate remedy at law remained. Today, although the power of equitable and at law remedies are combined in a single court system, this historic limitation on the availability of equitable relief remains. There is also a more pragmatic concern. An award of damages is usually easier to enforce and requires less ongoing judicial supervision than an injunction. For that reason, injunctions will usually not issue absent a showing of irreparable harm—a harm that cannot be adequately or effectively remedied through an award of monetary damages.

In trademark law, however, courts have long presumed that once a plaintiff has established a likelihood of success on the merits, for a preliminary injunction, or infringement for a permanent injunction, money damages alone will not adequately remedy the plaintiff's harm. As Chief Judge Friendly explained in *Omega Importing Corp. v. Petri-Kine Camera Co.*, 451 F.2d 1190 (2d Cir. 1971), there are several reasons for this:

> Where there is, then, such high probability of confusion, injury irreparable in the sense that it may not be fully compensable in damages almost inevitably follows. While an injured plaintiff would be entitled to recover the profits on the infringing items, this is often difficult to determine; moreover, a defendant may have failed to earn profits because of the poor quality of its product or its own inefficiency. Indeed, confusion may cause purchasers to refrain from buying either product and to turn to those of other competitors. Yet to prove the loss of sales due to infringement is also notoriously difficult. Furthermore, if an infringer's product is of poor quality, or simply not worth the price, a more lasting but not readily measurable injury may be inflicted on the plaintiff's reputation in the market.

Id. at 1195.

For these reasons, courts have routinely granted trademark owners injunctive relief once the plaintiff has adequately shown either a likelihood of success on the merits (for a preliminary injunction) or has prevailed at trial (for a permanent injunction). Although the presumptions of irreparable harm and no adequate remedy at law were well-established in trademark law, in May 2006, the Court issued its decision in *eBay Inc. v. MercExchange, L.L.C.*, 547 U.S. 388 (2006). In *eBay*, the Court rejected a parallel set of presumptions in a patent infringement case. Rather than presuming irreparable harm and no adequate remedy at law from a successful showing of patent infringement, the Court insisted that permanent injunctive relief was appropriate only where equity's well-established four-part test for injunctive relief was satisfied. Under this test,

> [a] plaintiff must demonstrate: (1) that it has suffered an irreparable injury; (2) that remedies available at law, such as monetary damages, are inadequate to compensate for that injury; (3) that, considering the balance of hardships between the plaintiff and defendant, a remedy in equity is warranted; and (4) that the public interest would not be disserved by a permanent injunction.

eBay Inc., 547 U.S. at 391. In 2008, in *Winter v. National Resources Defense Counsel*, 555 U.S. 7 (2008), the Court extended the reasoning of *eBay* and held that in order to obtain a preliminary injunction, a plaintiff must show both: (i) that it was likely to succeed on the merits of its claim; and (ii) likely to suffer irreparable injury in the absence of an injunction. In *Winter*, the Court recognized these as separate elements and expressly rejected a sliding scale approach under which a strong showing of success on the merits would relax the required showing of irreparable injury.

Although neither *eBay* nor *Winter* was a trademark case, the Court in the course of its opinions suggested that its reasoning governed the availability of injunctions generally. The question therefore arose whether *eBay* and *Winter* should govern the availability of permanent and preliminary injunctive relief in trademark cases as well, and if so, whether a court could permissibly continue to presume irreparable harm and no adequate remedy at law, given a showing of trademark infringement or a likelihood of success on the merits in trademark cases. The Ninth Circuit has extended *eBay* and *Winter* to trademark claims in the following case.

HERB REED ENTERS., LLC V. FLORIDA ENTERTAINMENT MANAGEMENT

736 F.3d 1239 (9th Cir. 2013)

McKEOWN, CIRCUIT JUDGE

"The Platters"—the legendary name of one of the most successful vocal performing groups of the 1950s—lives on. With 40 singles on the Billboard Hot 100 List, the names of The Platters' hits ironically foreshadowed decades of litigation—"Great Pretender," "Smoke Gets In Your Eyes," "Only You," and "To Each His Own." Larry Marshak and his company Florida Entertainment Management, Inc. (collectively

"Marshak") challenge the district court's preliminary injunction in favor of Herb Reed Enterprises ("HRE"), enjoining Marshak from using the "The Platters" mark in connection with any vocal group with narrow exceptions. We consider an issue of first impression in our circuit: whether the likelihood of irreparable harm must be established—rather than presumed, as under prior Ninth Circuit precedent—by a plaintiff seeking injunctive relief in the trademark context. In light of Supreme Court precedent, the answer is yes, and we reverse the district court's order granting the preliminary injunction.

Background

The Platters vocal group was formed in 1953, with Herb Reed as one of its founders. Paul Robi, David Lynch, Zola Taylor, and Tony Williams, though not founders, have come to be recognized as the other "original" band members. The group became a "global sensation" during the latter half of the 1950s, then broke up in the 1960s as the original members left one by one. After the break up, each member continued to perform under some derivation of the name "The Platters." Marshak v. Reed, No. 96 CV 2292 (NG) (MLO), 2001 WL 92225, at *4 (E.D.N.Y. and S.D.N.Y. Feb. 1, 2001) ("Marshak I").

Litigation has been the byproduct of the band's dissolution; there have been multiple legal disputes among the original members and their current and former managers over ownership of "The Platters" mark. Much of the litigation stemmed from employment contracts executed in 1956 between the original members and Five Platters, Inc. ("FPI"), the company belonging to Buck Ram, who became the group's manager in 1954. As part of the contracts, each member assigned to FPI any rights in the name "The Platters" in exchange for shares of FPI stock. *Marshak I,* 2001 WL 92225, at *3. According to Marshak, FPI later transferred its rights to the mark to Live Gold, Inc., which in turn transferred the rights to Marshak in 2009. Litigation over the validity of the contracts and ownership of the mark left a trail of conflicting decisions in various jurisdictions, which provide the backdrop for the present controversy. What follows is a brief summary of the tangled web of multi-jurisdictional litigation that spans more than four decades.

In 1972, FPI sued Robi and Taylor for trademark infringement in California, resulting in a 1974 judgment in Robi's favor, which held that FPI "was a sham used by Mr. Ram to obtain ownership of the name 'Platters.'" Robi v. Five Platters, Inc., 838 F.2d 318, 320 (9th Cir. 1988) ("*Robi I*") (quoting the 1974 decision). By contrast, an analogous dispute between FPI and Williams in New York resulted in a 1982 decision holding that FPI had lawfully acquired exclusive ownership of the name. *Marshak I,* 2001 WL 92225, at *7 (citing the 1982 decision). Williams attempted to circumvent the New York decision by seeking declaratory judgment in the Central District of California based on the 1974 judgment in favor of Robi. He was ultimately unsuccessful; on appeal, we reasoned that Williams could not avoid the claim preclusive effect of the New York judgment by relying on issue preclusion from another case in which he was not a party. *Robi I*, 838 F.2d at 328. We upheld the judgment in favor of Robi, *id.*at 330, and later affirmed the district court's award of compensatory and punitive damages to Robi as well as its cancellation of FPI's three registered trademarks using the words "The Platters." *Robi v. Five Platters, Inc.*, 918 F.2d 1439, 1441 (9th Cir. 1990) ("*Robi II*").

In 1984, FPI sued Reed for trademark infringement in the Southern District of Florida. *Marshak I*, 2001 WL 92225, at *9. The court denied Reed's motion for summary judgment based on the preclusive effect of the 1974 California judgment against FPI. *Id.* Preferring to avoid trial, Reed signed a court-approved stipulation of settlement in 1987, under which he assigned to FPI all rights he had in FPI stock, retained the right to perform as "Herb Reed and the Platters," and agreed not to perform under the name "The Platters." However, the settlement included an "escape clause":

> In the event that a court of competent jurisdiction enters a final order with all appeals being exhausted that provides that The Five Platters, Inc. has no right in the name "The Platters," then nothing contained herein shall be construed to limit Herbert Reed's rights in the name "The Platters" and this agreement shall not inure to any party other than The Five Platters, Inc., and its successors and assigns or Herbert Reed.

A key question is whether the escape clause has now been triggered.

In 2001, Marshak, FPI, and other plaintiffs sued Reed and others for trademark infringement in the Eastern District of New York; Reed counterclaimed, also alleging trademark infringement. *Marshak I*, 2001 WL 92225, at *1. The court interpreted the 1987 settlement as "barr[ing] Reed from asserting that he has any right to the name 'The Platters' as against FPI or those claiming through FPI except as specifically allowed in that agreement, or from otherwise interfering with plaintiffs' rights to the use of 'The Platters.'"*Id.* at *15. The court determined that the settlement's escape clause had not been triggered either by *Robi I*, because the Ninth Circuit reversed the judgment in favor of Williams indicating that FPI still had some rights to "The Platters" mark, or by *Robi II*, because cancellation of FPI's federal mark registration did not resolve the question whether FPI was entitled to use the name "The Platters." *Id.* at *19–20. The district court enjoined Reed from, among other things, interfering with FPI and Marshak's use of the name "The Platters" except as permitted in the 1987 settlement ("the 2001 injunction"). *Id.* at *21. The Second Circuit affirmed. *Marshak v. Reed*, 13 Fed. Appx. 19 (2d Cir. 2001).

Reed appealed *Marshak I* a second time on the basis that an unpublished Ninth Circuit memorandum issued around the same time triggered the 1987 settlement's escape clause. The Second Circuit vacated and remanded *Marshak I,* Marshak v. Reed, 34 Fed. Appx. 8 (2d Cir. 2002), but later affirmed the district court's decision to adhere to its earlier decisions because the Ninth Circuit memorandum left "open the possibility, however remote, that FPI can establish a common law trademark right to the name 'The Platters.'" *Marshak II*, 229 F. Supp. 2d at 185, *aff'd, Marshak v. Reed*, 87 Fed. Appx. 208 (2d Cir. 2004).

HRE, which manages Reed's business affairs and holds his rights, sued FPI and other defendants for trademark infringement in the District of Nevada in 2010. To get around the restrictions in the 1987 settlement, HRE creatively alleged that it owned the "Herb Reed and the Platters" mark and that defendants used a confusingly similar mark, namely "The Platters." *Herb Reed Enters., Inc. v. Bennett*, No. 2:10–CV–1981 JCM (RJJ), 2011 WL 220221, at *1 (D. Nev. Jan. 21, 2011). FPI was not represented—according to Marshak, FPI was by this time a defunct corporation that had already transferred and no longer owned any rights to "The Platters" mark. The action resulted in a 2011 default judgment and permanent injunction declaring that (1) FPI "never used the mark 'The Platters' in a manner that [was] not false and misleading and thus never acquired common law rights to the mark," and (2) "Reed, having first used the mark 'The Platters' in commerce in 1953, and having continuously used the mark in commerce since then has superior rights to the mark to all others," including FPI and "anyone claiming rights from or through" FPI. *Herb Reed Enters., Inc. v. Monroe Powell's Platters, LLC*, 842 F. Supp. 2d 1282, 1287 (D. Nev. 2012) (quoting the 2011 judgment).

In 2012, HRE successfully obtained a preliminary injunction against Monroe Powell, FPI's former performer employee, and his company in a trademark infringement action in the District of Nevada. *Id.* at 1284. Because Powell claimed to have acquired rights to "The Platters" mark through FPI, there was a question as to whether the 1987 settlement limited Reed's ability to pursue a remedy. The district court held that, "even assuming that the 1987 stipulation applies, the escape clause has been triggered and no longer bars Reed from suing FPI or those claiming through FPI for trademark infringement." *Id.* at 1288. The court reasoned that the 2011 Nevada default judgment, which "determined that FPI 'has no right in the name "The Platters'" as required by the 1987 stipulation," was "a final order with all appeals being exhausted" because the judgment was never appealed. *Id.* at 1288–89 (quoting the 2011 judgment).

In the period between the filing of the two Nevada actions, Marshak sued Reed for civil contempt in the Eastern District of New York, alleging that Reed's first Nevada lawsuit violated the 2001 injunction. *Marshak v.*

Reed, Nos. 96–CV–2292 (NG) (RML), 11–CV–2582 (NG) (RML), 2012 WL 832269 (E.D.N.Y. Mar. 12, 2012). The court denied Marshak's motion, holding that neither Reed's use of the mark "Herb Reed and the Platters" nor Reed's suit in Nevada protecting that mark constituted a violation of the injunction. *Id.* at *3–5.

Last year brought yet another lawsuit. HRE commenced the present litigation in 2012 against Marshak in the District of Nevada, alleging trademark infringement and seeking a preliminary injunction against Marshak's continued use of "The Platters" mark. The district court held that HRE was not precluded from asserting a right in "The Platters" mark either by the 1987 settlement—the escape clause of which had been triggered by the 2011 Nevada default judgment—or by the equitable doctrine of laches. *Herb Reed Enters., LLC v. Fla. Entm't Mgmt., Inc.*, No. 2:12–CV–00560–MMD–GWF, 2012 WL 3020039, at *8 (D. Nev. Jul. 24, 2012). The district court found that HRE had established a likelihood of success on the merits, a likelihood of irreparable harm, a balance of hardships in its favor, and that a preliminary injunction would serve public interest. *Id.* at * 8–17. Accordingly, the district court granted the preliminary injunction and set the bond at $10,000. *Id.* at *19. Marshak now appeals from the preliminary injunction.

Analysis

I. Res Judicata

As an initial matter, we address whether HRE is foreclosed from bringing the underlying suit by the New York actions, *Marshak I* and *Marshak II,* which resulted in the 2001 injunction barring Reed from interfering with Marshak's use of "The Platters" mark except as permitted by the 1987 settlement. The district court correctly held that the New York actions do not have res judicata effect. . . .

II. Laches

Next, we consider whether HRE is barred from challenging Marshak's use of "The Platters" mark by laches—"an equitable time limitation on a party's right to bring suit, resting on the maxim that one who seeks the help of a court of equity must not sleep on his rights." *Jarrow Formulas, Inc. v. Nutrition Now, Inc.*, 304 F.3d 829, 835 (9th Cir. 2002) (internal quotation marks and citations omitted). The district court properly determined that laches does not foreclose this suit. . . .

III. Preliminary Injunction

To obtain a preliminary injunction, HRE "must establish that [it] is likely to succeed on the merits, that [it] is likely to suffer irreparable harm in the absence of preliminary relief, that the balance of equities tips in [its] favor, and that an injunction is in the public interest." *Winter v. Natural Res. Def. Council, Inc.*, 555 U.S. 7, 20 (2008). . . .

Marshak's key arguments are that the district court erred in concluding that HRE had established a likelihood of success on the merits because Reed abandoned "The Platters" mark and that the district court erred in finding a likelihood of irreparable harm.

A. Likelihood of Success on the Underlying Trademark Dispute

As to its trademark infringement claim, to establish a likelihood of success on the merits HRE must show that it is "(1) the owner of a valid, protectable mark, and (2) that the alleged infringer is using a confusingly similar mark." *Grocery Outlet, Inc. v. Albertson's, Inc.*, 497 F.3d 949, 951 (9th Cir. 2007) (per curiam). Tellingly, Marshak does not challenge the district court's conclusions on these two points, except by asserting the affirmative defense of abandonment on the alleged basis that Reed abandoned "The Platters" mark by signing the 1987 Florida settlement. But "[a]bandonment of a trademark, being in the nature of a forfeiture, must be strictly proved." *Prudential Ins. Co. of Am. v. Gibraltar Fin. Corp. of Cal.*, 694 F.2d 1150, 1156 (9th Cir. 1982). The district court did not err in concluding that Marshak failed to meet that burden. . . .

B. Likelihood of Irreparable Harm

We next address the likelihood of irreparable harm. As the district court acknowledged, two recent Supreme Court cases have cast doubt on the validity of this court's previous rule that the likelihood of "irreparable injury may be *presumed* from a showing of likelihood of success on the merits of a trademark infringement claim." *Brookfield Commc'ns, Inc. v. W. Coast Entm't Corp.*, 174 F.3d 1036, 1066 (9th Cir. 1999) (emphasis added). Since *Brookfield,* the landscape for benchmarking irreparable harm has changed with the Supreme Court's decisions in *eBay Inc. v. MercExchange, L.L.C.*, 547 U.S. 388, in 2006, and *Winter* in 2008.

In *eBay,* the Court held that the traditional four-factor test employed by courts of equity, including the requirement that the plaintiff must establish irreparable injury in seeking a permanent injunction, applies in the patent context. 547 U.S. at 391. Likening injunctions in patent cases to injunctions under the Copyright Act, the Court explained that it "has consistently rejected . . . a rule that an injunction automatically follows a determination that a copyright has been infringed," and emphasized that a departure from the traditional principles of equity "should not be lightly implied." *Id.* at 391–93 (citations omitted). The same principle applies to trademark infringement under the Lanham Act. Just as "[n]othing in the Patent Act indicates that Congress intended such a departure," so too nothing in the Lanham Act indicates that Congress intended a departure for trademark infringement cases. *Id.* at 391–92. Both statutes provide that injunctions may be granted in accordance with "the principles of equity." 35 U.S.C. § 283; 15 U.S.C. § 1116(a).

In *Winter,* the Court underscored the requirement that the plaintiff seeking a preliminary injunction "demonstrate that irreparable injury is *likely* in the absence of an injunction." 555 U.S. at 22 (emphasis in original) (citations omitted). The Court reversed a preliminary injunction because it was based only on a "possibility" of irreparable harm, a standard that is "too lenient." *Id. Winter's* admonition that irreparable harm must be shown to be likely in the absence of a preliminary injunction also forecloses the presumption of irreparable harm here.

Following *eBay* and *Winter,* we held that likely irreparable harm must be demonstrated to obtain a preliminary injunction in a copyright infringement case and that actual irreparable harm must be demonstrated to obtain a permanent injunction in a trademark infringement action. *Flexible Lifeline Sys. v. Precision Lift, Inc.,* 654 F.3d 989, 998 (9th Cir. 2011); *Reno Air Racing Ass'n, Inc., v. McCord,* 452 F.3d 1126, 1137–38 (9th Cir. 2006). Our imposition of the irreparable harm requirement for a permanent injunction in a trademark case applies with equal force in the preliminary injunction context. *Amoco Prod. Co. v. Village of Gambell, AK,* 480 U.S. 531, 546 n. 12 (1987) (explaining that the standard for a preliminary injunction is essentially the same as for a permanent injunction except that "likelihood of" is replaced with "actual"). We now join other circuits in holding that the *eBay* principle— that a plaintiff must establish irreparable harm—applies to a preliminary injunction in a trademark infringement case. *See* N. *Am. Med. Corp. v. Axiom Worldwide, Inc.,* 522 F.3d 1211, 1228–29 (11th Cir. 2008); *Audi AG v. D'Amato,* 469 F.3d 534, 550 (6th Cir. 2006) (applying the requirement to a permanent injunction in a trademark infringement action).

Having anticipated that the Supreme Court's decisions in *eBay* and *Winter* signaled a shift away from the presumption of irreparable harm, the district court examined irreparable harm in its own right, explaining that HRE must "establish that remedies available at law, such as monetary damages, are inadequate to compensate" for the injury arising from Marshak's continuing allegedly infringing use of the mark. HRE, 2012 WL 3020039, at *15. Although the district court identified the correct legal principle, we conclude that the record does not support a determination of the likelihood of irreparable harm.

Marshak asserts that the district court abused its discretion by relying on "unsupported and conclusory statements regarding harm [HRE] *might* suffer." We agree.

The district court's analysis of irreparable harm is cursory and conclusory, rather than being grounded in any evidence or showing offered by HRE. To begin, the court noted that it "cannot condone trademark infringement simply because it has been occurring for a long time and may continue to occur." The court went on to note that to do so "could encourage wide-scale infringement on the part of persons hoping to tread on the goodwill and fame of vintage music groups." Fair enough. Evidence of loss of control over business reputation and damage to goodwill could constitute irreparable harm. *See, e.g., Stuhlbarg Int'l Sales Co., Inc. v. John D. Brush and Co., Inc.*, 240 F.3d 832, 841 (9th Cir. 2001) (holding that evidence of loss of customer goodwill supports finding of irreparable harm). Here, however, the court's pronouncements are grounded in platitudes rather than evidence, and relate neither to whether "irreparable injury is *likely* in the absence of an injunction," *Winter*, 555 U.S. at 22, nor to whether legal remedies, such as money damages, are inadequate in this case. It may be that HRE could establish the likelihood of irreparable harm. But missing from this record is any such evidence.

In concluding its analysis, the district court simply cited to another district court case in Nevada "with a substantially similar claim" in which the court found that "the harm to Reed's reputation caused by a different unauthorized Platters group warranted a preliminary injunction." *HRE*, 2012 WL 3020039, at *15–16. As with its speculation on future harm, citation to a different case with a different record does not meet the standard of showing "likely" irreparable harm.

Even if we comb the record for support or inferences of irreparable harm, the strongest evidence, albeit evidence not cited by the district court, is an email from a potential customer complaining to Marshak's booking agent that the customer wanted Herb Reed's band rather than another tribute band. This evidence, however, simply underscores customer confusion, not irreparable harm.

The practical effect of the district court's conclusions, which included no factual findings, is to reinsert the now-rejected presumption of irreparable harm based solely on a strong case of trademark infringement. Gone are the days when "[o]nce the plaintiff in an infringement action has established a likelihood of confusion, it is ordinarily presumed that the plaintiff will suffer irreparable harm if injunctive relief does not issue." *Rodeo Collection, Ltd. v. W. Seventh*, 812 F.2d 1215, 1220 (9th Cir. 1987) (*citing Apple Computer, Inc. v. Formula International Inc.*, 725 F.2d 521, 526 (9th Cir. 1984)). This approach collapses the likelihood of success and the irreparable harm factors. Those seeking injunctive relief must proffer evidence sufficient to establish a likelihood of irreparable harm. As in *Flexible Lifeline*, 654 F.3d at 1000, the fact that the "district court made no factual findings that would support a likelihood of irreparable harm," while not necessarily establishing a lack of irreparable harm, leads us to reverse the preliminary injunction and remand to the district court.

In light of our determination that the record fails to support a finding of likely irreparable harm, we need not address the balance of equities and public interest factors.

REVERSED and REMANDED.

NOTES FOR DISCUSSION

1. *Extending eBay: Other Circuits.* As the Ninth Circuit noted in its opinion, both the Eleventh and the Sixth Circuits have extended *eBay* and *Winter* to trademark cases and expressly required a showing of irreparable harm. The Third Circuit has similarly extended *eBay* and *Winter* to false adverting cases brought under section 43(a)(1)(B) of the Trademark Act. *See Ferring Pharmaceuticals, Inc. v. Watson Pharmaceuticals, Inc.,* 765 F.3d 205 (3d Cir. 2014). The Fifth Circuit, however, has continued to presume irreparable harm in the trademark setting after *eBay. See Abraham v. Alpha Chi Omega,* 708 F.3d 614 (5th Cir. 2013). In *Abraham,* immediately after citing the *eBay* Court's enunciation of the four-part standard for obtaining a permanent injunction, the Fifth Circuit quoted language from a pre-*eBay* version of Professor McCarthy's treatise on the first two factors, irreparable injury and no adequate remedy at law:

> As to the first factor, a leading treatise states, "All that must be proven to establish liability and the need for an injunction against infringement is the likelihood of confusion—injury is presumed." 5 McCarthy on Trademarks and Unfair Competition § 30:2 (4th ed. 2001). As to the second, the same treatise states, "[T]here seems little doubt that money damages are 'inadequate' to compensate [owner] for continuing acts of [infringer]." Id.

Abraham, 708 F.3d at 627. Is this a sufficient basis for continuing to presume irreparable harm and no adequate remedy after *eBay* and *Winter*?

2. *Showing Irreparable Injury.* If a trademark plaintiff must show irreparable injury and no adequate remedy at all, how can they do so? What sorts of injury count, and when are monetary damages an inadequate remedy? In the *Herb Reed* opinion, the Ninth Circuit suggested that "Evidence of loss of control over business reputation and damage to goodwill could constitute irreparable harm." Beyond showing a likelihood of confusion, what more is needed to show such a "loss of control" or "damage to goodwill"? Would a showing of actual confusion suffice? Is such a showing now necessary to obtain injunctive relief?

In *Herb Reed,* the trademark claim at issue is a relatively plain vanilla claim that purchasers of The Platters services will be confused and get the wrong band at the time of sale. Even in that context, the Ninth Circuit required the plaintiff to show something more than a mere likelihood of confusion to obtain injunctive relief. What does that suggest for our more exotic confusion theories? What is required to show irreparable harm for initial interest or post-sale confusion claims? Or to show irreparable harm with respect to affiliation or association confusion, or with respect to endorsement or authorization confusion? What about in the dilution context? Is it necessary or sufficient to show an actual loss of distinctiveness—that is actual dilution?

3. *Injunctions and Delay.* Even before *eBay* and *Winter*, one of the most common grounds for denying a preliminary injunction is delay in either bringing the trademark infringement suit or in seeking injunctive relief. *See, e.g., Majorica, S.A. v. R.H. Macy & Co.,* 762 F.2d 7 (2d Cir. 1985) (overturning trial court's grant of preliminary injunction where plaintiff filed action in April 1984, but did not request injunction until November 1984); *Citibank, N.A. v. Citytrust,* 756 F.2d 273 (2d Cir. 1985) (overturning trial court's preliminary injunction where ten weeks passed between the time the defendant's alleged infringement began and the time the plaintiff filed its complaint and sought injunctive relief). Delay plays other roles in trademark litigation as well. If a plaintiff delays too long in bringing the lawsuit, so that the plaintiff's and defendant's respective uses have been going on for more than a few years, such coexistence may, if no confusion has arisen to date, suggest that confusion is not likely to arise in the future. *See, e.g., Cohn v. Petsmart, Inc.,* 281 F.3d 837, 842–43 (9th Cir. 2002). In addition, as we saw in Chapter 9, undue delay in bringing a lawsuit may also help establish laches, acquiescence, or estoppel, and thus limit the availability of either injunctive or monetary relief.

4. *Preliminary Injunctions and Bonds.* Under the ordinary standard, a plaintiff must show a likelihood of success on the merits in order to receive a preliminary injunction. What happens if a trial court believes, based upon the evidence presented at the preliminary injunction hearing, that the plaintiff is likely to succeed on the merits, grants a preliminary injunction barring defendant's conduct at issue, yet then rules against the plaintiff at a subsequent full trial on the merits? While the preliminary injunction in such a case would be dissolved following the trial, the court, at plaintiff's request, has prohibited the defendant from engaging in conduct, that, as it turns out, was perfectly legal.

To compensate the defendant for the losses such a mistaken preliminary injunction may cause, Rule 65(c) of the Federal Rules of Civil Procedure requires the plaintiff to post an injunction bond "in an amount that the court considers proper to pay the costs and damages sustained by any party found to have been wrongfully enjoined or restrained." Fed. R. Civ. P. 65(c). Should an injunction prove to have been wrongfully issued, the bond is the defendant's sole remedy for any damages the injunction may have caused. While courts will sometimes set a low bond, *see, e.g., Brookfield Comms. v. West Coast Enter. Corp.,* 174 F.3d 1036, 1043 (9th Cir. 1999). (setting an injunction bond at $25,000), courts will sometimes require a very high bond. *See, e.g., Nintendo of America, Inc. v. Lewis Galoob Toys, Inc.,* 16 F.3d 1032 (9th Cir.) (affirming district court's decision to award entire $15 million injunction bond to the defendant where preliminary injunction prevented the defendant from selling its Game Genie device for approximately one year), *cert. denied,* 513 U.S. 822 (1994). The amount of the bond will depend on the revenue that the enjoined conduct at issue would otherwise have generated for the defendant. The cost of posting the necessary bond can make a preliminary injunction prohibitively expensive for some litigants.

5. *Preliminary Injunctive Relief versus Summary Judgment.* As a plaintiff in trademark litigation, there are two principal procedural devices for obtaining an early resolution[1] of the dispute: moving for a preliminary injunction or moving for summary judgment. There are several important differences in the legal standards a plaintiff must satisfy for these motions, however, that an attorney should consider in deciding which to pursue. To obtain a preliminary injunction, a plaintiff must show, as one of the key issues, a likelihood of success on the merits. In determining whether a plaintiff has shown such a likelihood of success, a trial court may resolve credibility disputes between witnesses and disputed factual issues, not in a final manner binding on the eventual trier of fact, but as a preliminary matter, to predict which party is more likely to prevail should the case proceed to trial. In contrast, a plaintiff may obtain summary judgment only where there is no genuinely disputed issue of material fact. In determining whether to grant a summary judgment, the trial court may not resolve credibility disputes nor resolve disputed factual issues, at least where the factual dispute is genuine in the sense that a jury could reasonably resolve the issue either way.

In order to think about the practical implications of these rules, consider the following scenario: In New Orleans, Louisiana, there is a beer company, Dixie Brewing, that sells its Dixie beer primarily in Louisiana but also has some sales in the rest of the country. Because of New Orleans's Mardi Gras traditions, Dixie begins advertising its beer using a poster that contains the slogan "BEER OF KINGS." Anheuser-Busch learns of the poster and sends Dixie Brewing a cease and desist letter, claiming infringement of its "KING OF BEERS" trademark, and a lawsuit alleging the usual panoply of infringement, unfair competition, and dilution claims is subsequently filed. As the lawsuit progresses, Anheuser-Busch obtains survey evidence which its expert witness is prepared to testify demonstrates that 32 percent of respondents believe that Dixie "had to get" permission from Anheuser-Busch to use the poster. However, the poster has been in use in New Orleans and other cities for nearly four years and Anheuser Busch can point to no evidence of actual confusion. If Anheuser Busch wants to stop Dixie's use now, rather than wait for trial, would you as Anheuser Busch's attorney recommend that it file for a preliminary injunction or for summary judgment? Why?

In addition to the differences in the standards for granting a preliminary injunction or summary judgment, these two procedural devices are also different in terms of the availability of appellate review. As a general rule of federal appellate procedure, a party may appeal the decision of a district

---

[1] Of course, as a formal matter, a preliminary injunction does not finally resolve the case. Even if a preliminary injunction issues, the defendant may still press forward for trial and hope for a different eventual outcome. Often, however, in trademark cases, the eventual trier of fact and the person who decides whether to issue a preliminary injunction are the same person—the district court judge. Thus, the district judge's resolution of the question whether a plaintiff is likely to succeed on the merits—the relevant legal standard at the preliminary injunction stage—is usually an excellent predictor of the district judge's likely eventual decision were the case to go to trial.

court only if it represents a final judgment. *See* 28 U.S.C. § 1291 (2015) ("The courts of appeals . . . shall have jurisdiction of appeals from all final decisions of the district courts of the United States. . . ."). However, while neither the grant nor the denial of a preliminary injunction represents a final judgment, the grant or denial of a preliminary injunction is immediately appealable as an express exception to the final judgment rule. *See* 28 U.S.C. § 1292(a) (2015) (creating appellate jurisdiction to review "[i]nterlocutory orders of the district courts of the United States, . . . granting, continuing, modifying, refusing or dissolving injunctions. . . ."). In contrast, a party may appeal the grant of a summary judgment only if it finally resolves the case. A partial summary judgment is not appealable, as a matter of right. Thus, if a court grants summary judgment with respect to particular issues within a case, such as validity, ownership, functionality, or infringement, but leaves other issues for trial, or denies summary judgment entirely, a party may not appeal the summary judgment order until the remaining issues are resolved at trial. *See, e.g., Parker Bros. v. Tuxedo Monopoly, Inc.*, 757 F.2d 254, 255 (Fed. Cir. 1985) ("An order denying a motion for summary judgment is interlocutory, non-final, and non-appealable."). If a party feels that the partial summary judgment resolves its strongest claims or defenses adversely, the party can work around the final judgment rule in order to obtain an immediate appeal in two ways. First, the party can stipulate, or settle with respect, to the remaining disputed factual issues in order to convert a partial summary judgment into a final judgment, and hence, render it immediately appealable. Second and alternatively, the federal rules allow a party to appeal a nonfinal judgment if a district court's decision on an issue "involves a controlling question of law as to which there is substantial ground for difference of opinion and . . . an immediate appeal from the order may materially advance the ultimate termination of the litigation." 28 U.S.C. § 1292(b) (2015). However, to appeal under this provision, a party must obtain a written order from the district court stating that the decision involves such a controlling question of law. *Id.* Moreover, even if the district court so states, the appellate court still has discretion to decide whether to hear the appeal or wait for a final judgment. *Id.*

B. MONETARY DAMAGES AND ATTORNEYS' FEES

The Trademark Act phrases the availability of damages in seemingly mandatory language:

> (a) When a violation of any right of the registrant of a mark registered in the Patent and Trademark Office, a violation under section 1125(a) or (d), or a willful violation under section 1125(c) of this title, shall have been established in any civil action action arising under this chapter, the plaintiff shall be entitled, . . . subject to the principles of equity, to recover (1) the defendant's profits, (2) any damages sustained by the plaintiff, and (3) the costs of the action.

15 U.S.C. § 1117(a) (2015).

Yet, as a practical matter, damage awards are far from routine in the typical trademark infringement case. Two principal reasons account for this. First, because Congress included the words "subject to the principles of equity" in the statutory language, courts have sometimes restricted recovery of a defendant's profits under the first prong of the statute to cases that satisfy the general equitable requirements for unjust enrichment, and hence require proof that the defendant's infringement was willful, in bad faith, or deliberate. Second, because the causal link between a plaintiff's lost sales and the defendant's infringement is difficult to prove, courts have also circumscribed the availability of a monetary recovery under the "any damages sustained by the plaintiff" prong of the statute, by requiring proof of actual confusion.

MALTINA CORPORATION V. CAWY BOTTLING CO.
613 F.2d 582 (5th Cir. 1980)

SAM D. JOHNSON, CIRCUIT JUDGE

I.   The Facts

Cawy Bottling Company (Cawy), defendant below, appeals from the judgment of the district court in favor of the plaintiffs Maltina Corporation and Julio Blanco-Herrera in their trademark infringement action. The district court enjoined Cawy from further infringement, awarded the plaintiffs $35,000 actual damages, and ordered the defendant to account for $55,050 of gross profit earned from the sale of infringing products.

Julio Blanco-Herrera fled to this country from Cuba in late 1960 after that country nationalized the company of which he was president and, along with his family, majority stockholder. Before that year, this company was one of the largest breweries and beverage distributors in Cuba. Among its products was malta, a dark, non-alcoholic carbonated beverage brewed similar to beer. The Cuban company distributed malta under the trademarks "Malta Cristal" and "Cristal" in Cuba and in the United States. The Cuban company had registered the marks both in Cuba and the United States. When Blanco-Herrera arrived in the United States, he formed the Maltina Corporation and assigned the "Cristal" trademark to it. He attempted to produce and distribute "Cristal" in this country, but despite his efforts Maltina Corporation was never able to obtain sufficient financial backing to produce more than $356 worth of "Cristal".

Cawy Bottling, however, had an altogether different experience in producing malta. At the outset, it attempted to register the "Cristal" trademark so that it might be utilized in marketing the product. This attempt was rejected by the Patent Office because of plaintiffs' prior registration. After this attempted registration and with the knowledge of the plaintiffs' ownership of the trademark, Cawy began producing and distributing malta under the "Cristal" label in February 1968.

In 1970 the plaintiffs sued Cawy under 15 U.S.C. § 1117 for trademark infringement and unfair competition. They sought an injunction against further use of their mark, damages, and an accounting. The district court dismissed the suit on the ground that Cuba's confiscation of the assets of Blanco-Herrera's Cuban corporation made Blanco-Herrera's assignment of the "Cristal" mark to the Maltina Corporation invalid. This Court reversed, holding Cuba's confiscation decree did not extend to the "Cristal" mark registered by the United States Patent Office. On remand, the district court determined that the plaintiffs had a valid trademark. Cawy appealed, and we affirmed.

At trial on the merits, from which this appeal is taken, the district court determined that Cawy had infringed the plaintiffs' mark and assigned the case to a magistrate for determination of what recovery was appropriate under 15 U.S.C. Section 1117. Before holding a hearing the magistrate wrote a memorandum to the district court stating that he thought that the plaintiffs were entitled to an injunction but not to an accounting for defendant's profits.

After holding the hearing, however, the magistrate changed his recommendation. He noted that Cawy designed its "Cristal" label to resemble the label used by Maltina's predecessor in Cuba. He found that Cawy intended to exploit the reputation and good will of the "Cristal" mark and to deceive and mislead the Latin community into believing that the "Cristal" once sold in Cuba was now being sold in the United States. The magistrate further found that Cawy wilfully infringed the plaintiffs' mark and had been unjustly enriched to the detriment of plaintiffs' reputation and good will. He recommended that Cawy account to the plaintiffs for the profit it earned from the infringement, and he directed Cawy to report its sales of "Cristal" and associated costs to the plaintiffs for determination of its profits. The magistrate also found Cawy's infringement damaged the reputation and good will of the plaintiffs in the amount of $35,000. He recommended that Cawy compensate plaintiffs in that amount.

The district court, after a complete and independent review of the record, adopted the magistrate's recommendations as its order. As more fully discussed below, the district court eventually found Cawy liable to the plaintiffs for its gross profits from the sale of "Cristal", $55,050. The court entered judgment against Cawy for $55,050 gross profits plus $35,000 damages and enjoined Cawy from any further infringement of the plaintiffs' mark.

Cawy presents three arguments on appeal. First, it argues that an accounting was inappropriate. Second, that if an accounting was appropriate, the district court erred in awarding to the plaintiff Cawy's entire gross profits from the sales of "Cristal". Third, Cawy argues that the award of $35,000 actual damages cannot stand in the absence of any evidence to support it. We accept this final contention, but reject the first two. Cawy does not complain on appeal of the district court's enjoining it from further infringement of the plaintiffs' mark.

II. Was an Accounting Appropriate?

Section 1117, 15 U.S.C., entitles a markholder to recover, subject to the principles of equity, the profits earned by a defendant from infringement of the mark. The courts have expressed two views of the circumstances in which an accounting is proper under 15 U.S.C. § 1117. Some courts view the award of an accounting as simply a means of compensating a markholder for loss or diverted sales. Other courts view an accounting not as compensation for lost or diverted sales, but as redress for the defendant's unjust enrichment and as a deterrent to further infringement. In this case, the plaintiffs never sold any appreciable amount of "Cristal" in the United States so they cannot claim that Cawy diverted any of their sales. Accordingly, we must decide whether diversion of sales is a prerequisite to an award of an accounting. We hold that it is not.

In *Maier Brewing* the Ninth Circuit awarded an accounting to a plaintiff who was not in direct competition with a defendant and who, accordingly, had not suffered any diversion of sales from the defendant's infringement. The court noted that the defendant had wilfully and deliberately infringed. It reasoned that awarding an accounting would further Congress' purpose in enacting 15 U.S.C. Section 1117 of making infringement unprofitable. This Court is in accord with this reasoning. The Fifth Circuit has not addressed the issue whether an accounting only compensates for diverted sales or whether an accounting serves the broader functions of remedying an infringers unjust enrichment and deterring future infringement. A recent opinion by this Court, however, recognizes that a trademark is a protected property right. This recognition of a trademark as property is consistent with the view that an accounting is proper even if the defendant and plaintiff are not in direct competition, and the defendants' infringement has not diverted sales from the plaintiff. The Ninth Circuit in *Maier Brewing* noted that the infringer had used the markholder's property to make a profit and that an accounting would force the infringer to disgorge its unjust enrichment. 390 F.2d at 121. Here, the only valuable property Blanco-Herrera had when he arrived in this country was his right to the "Cristal" mark. Cawy used this property, and an accounting is necessary to partially remedy its unjust enrichment.

The district court relied, in part, on *W. E. Bassett Co. v. Revlon, Inc.,* 435 F.2d 656 (2d Cir. 1970), in ordering an accounting. That case held that an accounting should be granted "if the defendant is unjustly enriched, if the plaintiff sustained damages from the infringement, or if an accounting is necessary to deter a willful infringer from doing so again." *Id.* at 664. Revlon sold a cuticle trimmer embossed with a "Cuti-Trim" mark "in the teeth of the patent office's refusal to register" that mark. *Id.* at 662. This was willful infringement that an accounting would deter in the future. In the instant case, the district court found that Cawy's "infringement was willful and that such infringement resulted in [Cawy] being unjustly enriched. . . ." Cawy used the "Cristal" mark after the patent office refused to register it. This clearly and explicitly supports the finding of willful infringement. An injunction alone will not adequately deter future infringement. In short, we find the district court properly ordered Cawy to account to the plaintiffs for the profits it earned from its willful infringement. This accounting serves two purposes: remedying unjust enrichment and deterring future infringement.

III. Did the District Court Err in Requiring Cawy to Account for Its Entire Gross Profit from the Sale of "Cristal"?

The district court ordered Cawy to account to the plaintiffs for $55,050, the entire gross profit (total revenue less cost of goods sold) from the sale of "Cristal". The district court did not allow Cawy to deduct overhead and other expenses. These expenses would have produced a net loss from the sale of "Cristal" and, if allowed, would have enabled Cawy to escape liability to the plaintiffs for its infringement.

Under 15 U.S.C. Section 1117, the plaintiff has the burden of showing the amount of the defendant's sales of the infringing product. The defendant has the burden of showing all elements of cost and other deductions. In this case, the court ordered Cawy to report its total sales of "Cristal" and associated costs to the plaintiffs. If the plaintiffs objected to Cawy's estimate of its net profits from "Cristal", they were to file their objection with the court. The record on appeal reflects that Cawy submitted three exhibits showing its net loss on "Cristal" sales. . . . The plaintiffs filed their objections to Cawy's figures with the court. They accepted Cawy's estimate of gross revenues from the sale of "Cristal" and the cost of goods sold. Thus, they met the burden of proving the amount of sales of the infringing product. The plaintiffs, however, did not accept other deductions claimed by Cawy. Cawy claimed deductions for "EXPENSES SPECIFICALLY IDENTIFIED WITH MALTA CRISTAL". . . . Plaintiffs objected to these claimed deductions because Cawy did not show they were actually spent on "Cristal". Cawy also claimed deductions for general overhead, apportioned to "Cristal" on the basis of the ratio of "Cristal" sales to Cawy's total sales. . . . The plaintiffs objected to the overhead deductions because the infringing product constituted only a small percentage of the defendant's business.

Cawy responded to the plaintiffs' objections by asserting that it did have "specific and detailed figures and corroborating sales slips, invoices and the like to support" its claims of expenses attributable to "Cristal". Cawy failed, however, to submit any of this corroboration to the district court.

The district court, after noting that Cawy had the burden of establishing deductions from gross profits, disallowed Cawy's claims of expenses specifically attributable to "Cristal".... The court stated that it could not determine whether the advertising, sales commissions, legal fees, telephone, and other expenses claimed by Cawy related to "Cristal" sales or to the sales of other products. It then held that Cawy failed to sustain its burden of proof with respect to those claimed expenses. We cannot say that the district court erred in its holding. The record on appeal, like the record before the district court, simply affords no support for the contention that the claimed "EXPENSES SPECIFICALLY IDENTIFIED WITH MALTA CRISTAL" actually related to "Cristal" sales. Furthermore, Cawy's claims of deductions of legal fees, as the district court noted, would not be allowable in any case. While we cannot tell whether these fees related to this suit, if they did, they would not be deductible.

The district court also disallowed Cawy's deductions of a proportionate part of its overhead expenses ... Again, we must agree with the district court that Cawy failed to meet its burden of showing its expenses in the absence from the record on appeal of any evidence that Cawy's production of "Cristal" actually increased its overhead expenses. Furthermore, we note that a proportionate share of overhead is not deductible when the sales of an infringing product constitute only a small percentage of total sales. Here, on the average, infringing sales constituted just over 6% of total sales. Accordingly, we think it unlikely, especially in the absence of any evidence to the contrary, that Cawy's production of "Cristal" increased its overhead expenses.

The district court properly ordered Cawy to account for its entire gross profit from the sale of "Cristal". Cawy failed to meet its burden of showing that the overhead and other expenses that it claimed ... actually related to the production of "Cristal".

IV. Did the District Court Err in Awarding the Plaintiffs $35,000 as Actual Damages for Cawy's Infringement?

The district court awarded the plaintiffs $35,000 as actual damages from Cawy's infringement. The record, however, is wholly devoid of support for this figure. Accordingly, we must reverse as to this element.

The plaintiffs have never been able to get sufficient financial backing to produce more than a very small amount of "Cristal" in the United States. That inability makes proof of actual damages from Cawy's infringement unlikely. In any event, the plaintiffs have had an opportunity to show their damages and have failed to do so. This Court concludes that plaintiffs should not have another opportunity to show their damages just as Cawy should not have another opportunity to prove its expenses.

In the ten years since the plaintiffs filed their original petition, this case has been before us three times. All litigation must end. We remand only for entry of judgment in accordance with this opinion.

TEXAS PIG STANDS, INC. V. HARD ROCK CAFÉ INTERNATIONAL, INC.
951 F.2d 684 (5th Cir. 1992)

JOHN R. BROWN, CIRCUIT JUDGE

We traverse the barbecue heartland of the South to resolve this trademark dispute between Texas Pig Stands, Inc. (TPS), and Hard Rock Cafe International, Inc. ("Hard Rock" or "Hard Rock Cafe"). The controversy centers around the two restaurant chains' use of the term "pig sandwich" to describe a Tennessee dish of barbecued pig meat on wheat or white bun. TPS owns a registration on the term and brought suit contending that Hard Rock's use of it in its Dallas restaurant constituted an infringement on TPS' rights to the two-word title. TPS sought equitable relief and attorney's fees.

At the trial below, the jury agreed with TPS that Hard Rock was guilty of deliberate infringement on TPS' mark, which it determined was capable of registration, and concluded also that TPS could recover for Hard Rock's unjust enrichment. The trial court accepted the jury finding of infringement but reversed its finding of unjust enrichment, essentially granting a j.n.o.v. Consequently, the court refused to award TPS the profits Hard Rock gained from pushing the porcine fare under the "pig sandwich" moniker. Finally, the trial court awarded TPS attorney's fees. Both parties appealed to this Court.

We affirm the trial court's holding that the term "pig sandwich" is protectable and capable of registration. We also affirm the court's reversal of the jury finding of unjust enrichment. Finally, we conclude that the court abused its discretion in awarding TPS attorney's fees for bringing this litigation.

This Little Piggy Went to Market

The pig sandwich's long and illustrious career has its origins in the hills of western Tennessee. The porcine delicacy has endeared itself to the hearts and stomachs of the citizenry there since the turn of the century. The founder of the Hard Rock Cafe, Isaac Tigrett, grew up in this area, and Jesse Kirby, one of the founders of the predecessor company to TPS, traveled extensively in the heartland of pig sandwiches in the early 1920's. Both men were apparently inspired by the dish's popularity and eventually included the garnished barbecued pork sandwich in their menus.

TPS' predecessor, Pig Stands Company, Inc. (Pig Stands), opened its very first "Pig Stand" in Dallas on September 15, 1921, which quickly enjoyed great success. In the early years of its operation, Pig Stands was in veritable hog-heaven, with over one hundred Pig Stands opening up from California to New York. The entire time, the term "pig sandwich" was used to describe its barbecued pork sandwich. The term had also become part of its distinctive sign, menus, and promotional advertising items.

Alas, however, the nation's love affair with pig sandwiches eventually chilled, resulting in the widespread closing of most Pig Stands. The last Pig Stand in Dallas closed in September, 1985, and currently less than ten Pig Stands still operate in Texas.

Tigrett first offered a barbecued pork sandwich with the name "pig sandwich" at the Hard Rock Cafe restaurant he opened in Jackson, Tennessee, in 1982. Tigrett later introduced the pig sandwich to New York and Stockholm, Sweden, when he opened Hard Rock Cafe restaurants in those cities. Then, in November 1986, just over a year after TPS closed its last Stand in Dallas, Tigrett opened up a Hard Rock Cafe restaurant there, featuring the pig sandwich on its menu.

This Little Piggy Went to See His Lawyer

TPS notified Hard Rock in writing on October 20, 1987, of TPS' claim to rights to the term "pig sandwich" and demanded that Hard Rock cease its infringement. Hard Rock contends that at the time it did not know that TPS even existed, much less that it claimed any rights to the term "pig sandwich." Believing that it had the right to use the term "pig sandwich" as the generic name for its barbecued pork sandwich, Hard Rock refused to cease using it and instead chose to stay in its house and let TPS try to blow it down. Whether Hard Rock's legal edifice is made of brick, twigs, or straw remains to be seen.

TPS commenced this action against Hard Rock in 1989 claiming trademark and service mark infringement and unfair competition under the Lanham Act. In its complaint, TPS requested a permanent injunction against Hard Rock's use of the term "pig sandwich," as well as an award of Hard Rock's profits, reasonable attorney's fees, prejudgment interest, and costs. The case was tried to a jury on nine special issues. The jury found in favor of TPS on each issue, concluding both that Hard Rock's infringement was willful and that Hard Rock was unjustly enriched by its infringement.

The trial court conducted a post-trial hearing to consider the amount of Hard Rock's profits and the question whether TPS should be awarded attorney's fees. While the trial court found that Hard Rock profited from its sale of pig sandwiches, it refused to award any profits to TPS, stating that it was "convinced that [Hard Rock] would have sold just as many pig sandwiches by any other name." Further, the trial court asserted that "the jury's finding of unjust enrichment is not supported by the record and cannot stand." The trial court then granted the sought-for injunction and, in a subsequent damages hearing, awarded attorney's fees and costs in excess of $400,000.

Neither party was pleased with this decision, and a flurry of appeals and cross appeals ensued. TPS contests the trial court's refusal to award profits in accordance with the jury's finding of unjust enrichment. Hard Rock returns the volley, contending that . . . the trial court erred . . . in awarding attorney's fees to TPS. . . .

Unjust Enrichment—Did Hard Rock Bring Home the Bacon?

[The appeals court initially considered whether the phrase "pig sandwich" was descriptive or generic and, if descriptive, whether there was evidence of secondary meaning. After reviewing the parties's conflicting evidence, the court eventually concluded to support the jury's verdict that the phrase was descriptive, rather than generic, and that secondary meaning had been established. The appeals court also rejected several other challenges raised by Hard Rock against the mark.] With the underlying determination of the protectability of "pig sandwich" intact, we move on to the trial court's rejection of the jury's unjust enrichment finding. As TPS argues, the trial court's order vitiates the jury findings, effectively granting partial j.n.o.v. against TPS. During the post-trial damages hearing, the trial court stated: "having heard all the evidence in the case, [the court] is of the opinion that monetary relief is not warranted in this case." Later in its holding, however, the court specifically rejected the jury finding of unjust enrichment.

Had the court gone no further than its first statement, and not overturned the jury finding, we would review this issue under a much different standard. Under 15 U.S.C. § 1117(a) (Supp.1990), the trial court has wide discretion to increase or reduce the amount of profits recoverable by the plaintiff "if the court shall find that the amount of the recovery based on profits is either inadequate or excessive . . . according to the circumstances of the case." Under an abuse of discretion standard, we would have little difficulty upholding the trial court's determination that monetary relief is not warranted. *See id.* However, because the court did not merely adjust the amount of the recovery, but rather threw out the jury finding for recovery altogether, we must again apply the *Boeing* standard. *See e.g., Oxford Indus. Inc. v. Hartmarx Corp.,* 15 U.S.P.Q.2d 1648, 1655 (N.D.Ill.1990) (while the origins of unjust enrichment are both legal and equitable, a jury finding of fact in favor of unjust enrichment may be overturned "only under the standards for granting a motion for judgment notwithstanding the verdict") (citing *Hussein v. Oshkosh Motor Truck Co.,* 816 F.2d 348, 355 (7th Cir. 1987)).

The definition of unjust enrichment provided to the jury accurately frames the questions that must be answered here: (i) Would Hard Rock's retention of its profits for pig sandwich sales be unjust and inequitable? and (ii) Did Hard Rock use the reputation and good will of TPS to sell its own pig sandwiches? In assessing the evidence presented, while no single evidentiary fact carries the day, from the totality of the circumstances present we conclude that the jury did not have before it sufficient competent evidence "of such quality and weight that reasonable and fairminded men in the exercise of impartial judgment," *Boeing,* 411 F.2d at 374, might arrive at a finding of unjust enrichment.

(i) Palming Off—A Pork Purveyor Has His Pride

Returning to the origins of the pig sandwich, we first point out that the term was widely used in Tennessee in the early 1920's as providing the impetus for its being included in Hard Rock menus in Jackson, New York, and Stockholm as early as 1982. Consequently, when Hard Rock came to Dallas, it brought the term "pig sandwich" with it. The great weight of the evidence supports Hard Rock's position that its use of "pig sandwich" had nothing whatsoever to do with TPS' use of the term. At no time have TPS and Hard Rock either competed or operated restaurants in the same town simultaneously. In fact, TPS left the Dallas market over a year prior to Hard Rock's entering it, and other restaurants had been and were currently using a similar, if not identical, term in their menus. Consequently, the trial court described the situation best: "While the Court believes defendant sold pig sandwiches knowing of plaintiff's mark, it appears this was done not as an attempt to profit from the mark but rather in simple disregard of plaintiff's rights." Furthermore, as the court aptly stated: "the high degree of success [Hard Rock has] enjoyed all over the world militates against the existence of any motive to seek such an association or to use pig sandwiches to promote its overall restaurant operations."

On a review of the evidence, we conclude that there is simply no indication that Hard Rock attempted to "palm off" its pig sandwiches as those of TPS, nor did they attempt to associate their operation with TPS. TPS acknowledges that it did not lose a single sale due to Hard Rock's use of "pig sandwich." While the diversion of sales is not a prerequisite to an award of profits, *Maltina Corp. v. Cawy Bottling Co.,* 613 F.2d 582, 585, 205 U.S.P.Q. (BNA) 489 (5th Cir. 1980), it is one of the factors to be considered. The same is true of palming off—while it is not a prerequisite to finding unjust enrichment, it is an important circumstance bearing on the determination. Here, the total absence of all of these factors fatally undercuts the jury's conclusion.

(ii) Did Hard Rock Hog TPS' Good Will?

We also do not find any evidence whatsoever of Hard Rock's using TPS' good will to sell its pig sandwiches. As the trial court pointed out, while "there are people in Dallas with vivid memories of TPS, there was no proof as to the value of plaintiff's good will in Dallas today." Indeed, despite being high on the hog decades ago, the closing of practically all the Texas Pig Stands, and all outlets in Dallas well prior to Hard Rock's entry into that market, evidences the fact that TPS' good will there is between low and nill. The trial court correctly concluded, therefore, that Hard Rock "would have sold just as many pig sandwiches by any other name" and that "there is no basis for inferring that any of the profits received by [Hard Rock] from the sale of pig sandwiches are attributable to infringement."

In sum, we hold that the evidence before the jury simply was not of the quality and weight necessary to support a finding of unjust enrichment. The granted permanent injunction adequately remedies the complained-of infringement, and awarding TPS any of Hard Rock's profits would be far from equitable—it would be a windfall.

Award of Attorney Fees—Did the Trial Court Go Hog Wild?

After throwing out the jury's unjust enrichment finding at the post-trial damages hearing, the trial court also determined that this case was "exceptional" under § 1117(a), and awarded attorney's fees to TPS accordingly. Under this section of the Lanham Act, the trial court judge may, in his discretion, award attorney's fees in "exceptional" cases to the prevailing party. Hard Rock contests this determination, arguing that this case fell far short of the interpretation the courts have uniformly given to the term "exceptional."

We emphasize that here we are not dealing with the *Boeing* sanctity of the jury verdict. Imposition of attorney's fees on the unsuccessful infringer is not a matter for the jury. In the first place, the unique situation of this case and its trial reflects that no monetary awards were before the jury on the infringer's substantive liability. More than that, the imposition of attorney's fees by nature and statute, *see* 15 U.S.C. § 1117(a), is reserved to the trial judge. This means that, unlike a jury verdict or a finding of fact as such, the standard or review is whether the court abused its discretion. For the reasons set forth, we hold that it did.

In support of the award, the trial court determined that Hard Rock acted "in simple disregard of plaintiff's rights." This disregard, the trial court held, made the case "exceptional." The trial court then justified this holding by making a notable observation which reveals its true conception of "exceptional":

The large, prosperous company was unwilling to show any respect to the smaller, struggling business. . . . The larger, guilty company can more easily absorb the loss than the smaller, innocent one. If plaintiff had to pay its own fees, it would suffer for having to protect its trademark and service mark rights.

This noble sentiment, perhaps fitting for Sherwood Forest, does not meet the congressional standard of "exceptional." The legislative history of § 1117 suggests that an "exceptional case" is one in which the defendant's trademark infringement "can be characterized as 'malicious,' 'fraudulent,' 'deliberate,' or 'willful.'" S. Rep. No. 93–1400, 93rd Cong., 2d Sess., *reprinted in* 1974 U.S. Code Cong. & Admin. News 7132, 7133. The statutory provision has been interpreted by courts to require a showing of a high degree of culpability on the part of the infringer, for example, bad faith or fraud. On the other hand, the parties' relative economic positions should not enter into the determination, even when an award of punitive damages would serve as an example to deter other infringers. As one court has stated:

> [Plaintiff] gives a persuasive argument as to the sound reason for allowing attorney's fees, that is to seek to prevent by example others from pirating trademarks belonging to those who have them registered and who will properly and legally be using them and that argument has great merit and perhaps should be the law, but as I read the statute it is not the law.

Plough, Inc. v. Sun Fun Prods., Inc., 200 U.S.P.Q. 236, 237 (M.D.Fla.1977).

The trial court pointed to the jury determination that Hard Rock's infringement was willful in an attempt to bring its determination in line with this established precedent, but this attempt is unavailing. A jury finding of willfulness does not bind the trial court in determining whether this case is "exceptional"; it may, however, serve as a guide. Here, the guide is a poor one due to the definition of "willful" provided in the special interrogatories: "An act is done 'willfully' if it is done voluntarily and intentionally and not because of accident or other innocent reason." This standard falls far short of the kind of culpability required to render a case "exceptional." While we do not condone Hard Rock's infringement, its actions do not approach "deliberate pirating" or "egregious conduct."

The trial court's own conclusions built Hard Rock's house, brick by brick, that neither the court nor TPS could blow down—one wall, the absence of palming off; the second wall, the lack of any intent to deceive or confuse; the third wall, the lack of any attempt to profit from such infringement; and to complete the structure, the finding of a total lack of any damage or hardship to TPS' business and good will. Hard Rock's financial success and size do not undermine this construction; these facts do not even enter into it. This being an "unexceptional" case, we hold that the trial court abused its discretion in awarding attorney's fees to TPS under § 1117(a).

D-D-Dt D-D-Dt That's All, Folks!

TPS now leaves this legal barnyard with its mark intact, but we cannot allow it to attain a windfall on account of Hard Rock's infringement. While the jury had sufficient evidence to find "pig sandwich" to be a descriptive mark that had acquired secondary meaning, Hard Rock's infringement merits only the grant of a permanent injunction, and not an award of profits. Furthermore, though not entirely kosher, Hard Rock's actions were not sufficiently swinish to bring this case to the "exceptional" level required for an award of attorney's fees. Thus, the trial court order granting a permanent injunction for trademark infringement and denying the award of profits is AFFIRMED, and the order awarding attorney's fees is REVERSED.

JOHNSON, CIRCUIT JUDGE, dissenting.

Regrettably, I cannot agree with the majority's view of this case, and therefore must respectfully dissent.

To understand the essence of this dissent it is necessary to recite a number of critically important jury findings. The jury found that Hard Rock used an imitation of Texas Pig Stands' registered trademark. The jury found that the imitation trademark used by Hard Rock was similar enough to Texas Pig Stands' mark that it was likely to confuse consumers as to whether the product was sponsored or endorsed by Texas Pig Stands. The jury found that Hard Rock used the imitation of Texas Pig Stands' mark willfully and in bad faith, maliciously, or fraudulently. All of these jury findings are amply supported by the evidence. None of these findings has been set aside or overturned.

Despite the majority's attempt to diminish the jury's finding of a knowing, deliberate infringement, the majority quotes with seeming approval the district court's assessment of the evidence that the "defendant sold pig sandwiches knowing of plaintiff's mark . . . in simple disregard of plaintiff's rights." There can be no question that Hard Rock deliberately infringed on Texas Pig Stands' trademark. It knew of that mark and openly refused to honor it. In such a case, trademark law demands that the infringer be penalized, lest such infringement be encouraged and the valuable protections of the trademark laws vitiated. Mistakenly, in this writer's opinion, the majority today goes to great lengths to avoid imposing any penalty whatsoever on an admittedly willful and deliberate infringer.

Upon a finding of a knowing trademark violation, the victim of the violation is entitled to both injunctive and monetary relief. 15 U.S.C. §§ 1114, 1117. There is no question here that it was appropriate to enjoin Hard Rock from further use of Texas Pig Stands' mark in the future. The question here is whether Texas Pig Stands should have been afforded any monetary recovery for previous violations. The prior cases of this Court and the purposes of the trademark laws demand that Hard Rock be required to pay a monetary penalty, in order to render its deliberate infringement unprofitable. . . .

In this case there were two potential penalties which might, in equity, have been imposed on Hard Rock for its deliberate violation of federal law. Either would have rendered Hard Rock's infringement unprofitable and provided an appropriate deterrent. Based on the facts found by the jury, the district court in this case could have either 1) forced Hard Rock to disgorge the profits it made selling food under Texas Pig Stands' trademark, or 2) compelled Hard Rock to pay Texas Pig Stands' attorneys' fees. The district court, exercising its discretion to fashion an equitable result, chose the second of these options. The majority of this panel, substituting its judgment for that of the district court, now refuses to allow the imposition of *any* penalty and allows Hard Rock to keep whatever profits accrued from Hard Rock's willful and deliberate infringement. . . .

The majority's oft-expressed concern about a "windfall" for the plaintiffs has led it to an unjust and unwarranted result. For one thing, there would be no windfall here. Awarding attorneys' fees to Texas Pig Stands would not in any way constitute a windfall—such fees would do no more than provide appropriate compensation to Texas Pig Stands for its efforts to vindicate its protected economic rights. Moreover, even if there were a windfall, certainly it is far better to allow a windfall to the innocent victim than to place the entire burden of the litigation on that victim and allow the culpable party to profit from its infringement.

The message conveyed by the majority's determination here is that despite what this Court has heretofore written, it may now be permissible and profitable to infringe on the trademark of another. While the Fifth Circuit might eventually put a stop to that illegal infringement, that infringement nonetheless still could be profitable. The trademark laws generally, and section 1117 in particular, do not countenance such a result. The message this Court should send is that infringement—and particularly the knowing, deliberate, and willful infringement—will have two consequences. It will be enjoined and it will be made unprofitable.

As the majority does not send that message, I must respectfully dissent.

NOTES FOR DISCUSSION

1. *The Final Chapter.* Following the panel decision, Texas Pig Stands petitioned for a rehearing en banc and attacked the panel's decision as "inconsistent with and in conflict with" the Fifth Circuit's earlier decision in

Maltina Corp. The panel took the petition for rehearing en banc as a petition for rehearing and responded to the plaintiff's contention as follows:

> Nothing in the Court's opinion affords any basis for this attack. In the first place, the opinion does not slight the case since *Maltina* was cited twice. This Court recognizes *Maltina* to be the law of the Fifth Circuit in its holding that (i) absence of competitors or (ii) failure of proof showing diversion of the mark owner's sales is no defense to the claim for Defendant's profits under 15 U.S.C. § 1117.

> The reason why Hard Rock Cafe's profits were not awarded was not based on (i) absence of competitors or (ii) no evidence of diversion; it was, rather, based solely on the lack of evidence showing that any of Defendant's profits were the result of its infringement of the mark.

> The trial court in granting j.n.o.v. on unjust enrichment expressly found:

>> Hard Rock 'would have sold just as many pig sandwiches by any other name' and that 'there is no basis for inferring that any of the profits received by [Hard Rock] from the sale of pig sandwiches are attributable to infringement.'

> The overriding principle comes from the Supreme Court that as to recovery of infringer's profits:

>> The plaintiff, of course, is not entitled to profits demonstrably not attributable to the unlawful use of his mark.

> *Mishawaka Rubber & Woolen Mfg. Co. v. S.S. Kresge Co.*, 316 U.S. 203, 206 (1941).

> ... Treating the suggestion for rehearing en banc as a petition for panel rehearing, it is ordered that the petition for panel rehearing is denied.

Are you persuaded? What about the discussion in *Maltina* about the need to deter willful infringement? What are the factual differences between the two cases that might justify the different outcomes?

The Fifth Circuit recognized the tension between *Maltina* and *Texas Pig Stands,* and in a later case, attempted to reconcile them. *See Pebble Beach Co. v. Tour 18 I*, 155 F.3d 526, 555 (5th Cir. 1998). "Whether an award of [defendant's] profits is appropriate," the court wrote, will depend upon a consideration of six factors drawn from the two cases: "(1) whether the defendant had the intent to confuse or deceive, (2) whether sales have been diverted, (3) the adequacy of other remedies, (4) any unreasonable delay by the plaintiff in asserting his rights, (5) the public interest in making the misconduct unprofitable, and (6) whether it is a case of palming off." *Id.* Is this approach consistent with the two cases? Does it reconcile them or simply jumble them together?

2. *Monetary Damages, Deterrence, and Penalties.* In the section authorizing an award of profits and damages, Congress included the following language:

> In assessing damages the court may enter judgment, according to the circumstances of the case, for any sum above the amount found as actual damages, not exceeding three times such amount. If the court shall find that the amount of the recovery based on profits is either inadequate or excessive the court may in its discretion enter judgment for such sum as the court shall find to be just, according to the circumstances of the case. Such sum in either of the above circumstances shall constitute compensation and not a penalty.

15 U.S.C. § 1117(a) (2015).

Is an award of damages in order to deter willful infringement necessarily a penalty and not compensation? If so, is such an award permissible under the statute?

3. *eBay Redux.* Are the plaintiffs in *Texas Pig Stands* and *Maltina Co.,* for all practical purposes, nonpracticing trademark owners, at least in the defendant's geographic markets? Both cases were decided well before the Court's decision in *eBay,* and both, following the usual practice in trademark cases, grant permanent injunctions once the plaintiffs established trademark infringement. If the courts had applied the *eBay* analysis, should the injunctions have been denied and the plaintiffs relegated to their monetary remedies?

4. *Monetary Relief: Plantiff's Losses.* As a general rule, while a plaintiff need not prove actual confusion to obtain injunctive relief, courts require proof of actual confusion for a plaintiff to recovery monetary damages. *See, e.g., Brunswick Corp. v. Spirit Reel Co.,* 832 F.2d 513, 525 (10th Cir. 1987) ("Likelihood of confusion is insufficient; to recover damages plaintiff must prove it has been damaged by actual consumer confusion or deception resulting from the violation."); *see also Schutt Mfg. Co. v. Riddell, Inc.,* 673 F.2d 202 (7th Cir. 1982) ("A higher standard of proof is required for the grant of money damages, however. A party seeking such relief is required to show not only the likelihood of such confusion, but must demonstrate that it has been damaged by actual consumer reliance on the misleading statements."). Proof of actual confusion establishes the necessary causal link between the plaintiff's lost sales and the defendant's infringement.

In the Second Circuit, Judge Learned Hand once tied the availability of monetary remedies to proof of actual confusion: "It is of course true that to recover damages or profits, whether for infringement of a trade-mark or for unfair competition, it is necessary to show that buyers, who wished to buy the plaintiff's goods, have been actually misled into buying the defendant's." *G.H. Mumm Champagne v. Eastern Wine Corp.,* 142 F.2d 499, 501 (2d Cir. 1944). Today, the Second Circuit requires proof of either actual confusion, or of a defendant's bad faith sufficient to infer actual confusion, in order for a plaintiff to recover for its own lost sales. *See, e.g., Boosey & Hawkes Music Pubs., Ltd. v. Walt Disney Co.,* 145 F.3d 481, 493 (2d Cir. 1998).

   5.   *Monetary Relief: Defendant's Profits.* Both *Maltina* and *Texas Pig Stands* are from the Fifth Circuit and address the rule for recovering the defendant's profits in that circuit. Other circuits have their own rules with respect to the recovery of the defendant's profits. As a general rule, however, all of the circuits require something more than simple proof of infringement before they will award a defendant's profits as a monetary remedy. The circuits phrase the something more differently, however. The Third and Fourth Circuit follow the multifactor approach the Fifth Circuit adopted in *Pebble Beach Co. See Synergistic Int'l, LLC v. Korman,* 470 F.3d 162, 175 (4th Cir. 2006); *Banjo Buddies, Inc. v. Renosky,* 399 F.3d 168, 175 (3d Cir. 2005).

   Some circuits, including the District of Columbia, the Second, and the Eleventh, permit a plaintiff to recover the defendant's profits if the plaintiff demonstrates that the defendant acted willfully, deliberately, or in bad faith. *See, e.g., International Star Class Racing Assoc. v. Tommy Hilfiger, U.S.A., Inc.,* 80 F.3d 749, 753 (2d Cir. 1996) ("In order to recover an accounting of an infringer's profits, a plaintiff must prove that the infringer acted in bad faith."); *Babbit Elecs. v. Dynascan Corp.,* 38 F.3d 1161, 1183 (11th Cir. 1994) ("Where the defendant's infringement is deliberate and willful, as in this case, an accounting for profits is proper under a theory of unjust enrichment."); *Foxtrap, Inc. v. Foxtrap, Inc.,* 671 F.2d 636, 641 (D.C. Cir. 1982). Mere knowledge of the plaintiff's mark, or "willfulness" in the sense of "done voluntarily and intentionally," is usually insufficient to justify an award of the defendant's products. Rather, "courts have insisted on a relatively egregious display of bad faith, e.g., an 'aura of indifference to plaintiff's rights and a smug willingness that the good will plaintiff sought to foster could safely be treated as a nullity.'" *Foxtrap, Inc.,* 671 F.2d at 641 (*quoting W. E. Bassett Co. v. Revlon, Inc.,* 435 F.2d 656, 662 (2d Cir. 1970)).

   The First Circuit has articulated three justifications for awarding a plaintiff the defendant's profits in a trademark case: "(1) as a rough measure of the harm to plaintiff; (2) to avoid unjust enrichment of the defendant; or (3) if necessary to protect the plaintiff by deterring a willful infringer from further infringement." *Tamko Roofing Prods., Inc. v. Ideal Roofing Co., Ltd.,* 282 F.3d 23, 36 (1st Cir. 2002). While the First Circuit has recognized that proof that the defendant acted in bad faith may be necessary to justify an award of the defendant's profits under the unjust enrichment and deterrence rationales, it is not necessary to recover the defendant's profits attributable to the infringement under the first rationale. *Id.* So long as the parties compete, a finding of likelihood of confusion may suffice to award the plaintiff the defendant's profits on the theory "that defendant's profits would have gone to plaintiff if there was no violation." *Aktiebolaget Electrolux v. Armatron Int'l, Inc.,* 999 F.2d 1, 5 (1st Cir. 1993).

   6.   *Monetary Damages and Jury Trials.* Because of the difficulty of satisfying the standards to obtain monetary damages in trademark infringement, plaintiffs in many cases ask only for injunctive relief. This has

an important consequence, however, in that a request for monetary relief, including statutory damages, implicates the Seventh Amendment's right to a jury trial. *See Feltner v. Columbia Picts. Television, Inc.*, 523 U.S. 340, 352–53 (1998) (holding that plaintiff's claim of statutory damages under Copyright Act implicates Seventh Amendment right to a jury trial). Under the Court's jurisprudence, a plaintiff cannot avoid the Seventh Amendment by casting its claim for damages in equitable terms, as an "accounting," or characterizing the damages as incidental to the equitable relief sought. *See Dairy Queen, Inc. v. Wood*, 369 U.S. 469, 477–79 (1962); *Beacon Theatres, Inc. v. Westover*, 359 U.S. 500, 508–11 (1959). However, if *only* equitable relief is sought, the Seventh Amendment right to a jury trial does not attach and so a judge, not a jury, will resolve any disputed factual issues should the case go to trial. If a party anticipates trademark litigation, and has a preference for whether a judge or a jury will try the case, what can a party do to obtain their preference? Which party, the plaintiff or the defendant, will typically control whether factual issues will eventually be tried to a judge or a jury in a trademark case?

In thinking about these rules, recall the Anheuser-Busch v. Dixie Brewing hypothetical, *supra*. As Anheuser-Busch's attorney, would you prefer that the issues be resolved by a New Orleans judge or a New Orleans jury? Assuming that you prefer the judge as your trier of fact, how should you draft your complaint to eliminate the possibility of a jury trial?

7. *Attorneys' Fees.* The Trademark Act authorizes an award of a reasonable attorney fees to the prevailing party "in exceptional cases." 15 U.S.C. § 1117(a) (2015). As the *Texas Pig Stands* court notes, the Senate Report accompanying the attorneys' fees provision stated that a case is exceptional when the defendant's infringement "can be characterized as 'malicious,' 'fraudulent,' 'deliberate,' or 'willful.'" S.Rep. No. 93–1400, 93rd Cong., 2d Sess., *reprinted in* 1974 U.S. Code Cong. & Admin. News 7132, 7133. While the statute provides the same "exceptional case" standard whether the prevailing party is the plaintiff or the defendant, courts have applied different standards in awarding fees. For a prevailing defendant to receive an award of attorneys' fees, courts typically require the defendant to show that the suit was "groundless, unreasonable, vexatious, or pursued in bad faith." *See, e.g., Gracie v. Gracie*, 217 F.3d 1060, 1071 (9th Cir. 2000). In contrast, courts allow a prevailing plaintiff to recover attorneys' fees either on that basis or, following the Senate Report, by showing that the defendant's infringement was "malicious, fraudulent, deliberate, or willful." *See, e.g., Earthquake Sound Corp. v. Bumper Industries*, 352 F.3d 1210, 1216 (9th Cir. 2003).

In 2014, the Supreme Court decided *Octane Fitness, LLC v. Icon Health & Fitness, LLC,* 134 S.Ct. 1749 (2014). Although the case involved a claim of patent, rather than trademark, infringement, the Patent Act provides for an award of attorneys' fees to the prevailing party using the same "exceptional" case language as the Trademark Act. 35 U.S.C. § 285. Before the Court stepped in, the Federal Circuit had defined an "exceptional case" under the Patent Act as one which either involves "material inappropriate conduct" or is both "objectively baseless" and "brought in subjective bad faith." Brooks Furniture Mfg., Inc. v. Dutailier Int'l, Inc., 393 F.3d 1378, 1381 (Fed. Cir. 2005). In *Octane Fitness, LLC*, the Court rejected this standard as too restrictive and inflexible. 134 S.Ct. at 1756–57. Giving the term "exceptional" its ordinary meaning at the time it was added to the Patent Act in 1952, the Court defined an "exceptional" case as "simply one that stands out from others with respect to the substantive strength of a party's litigating position (considering both the governing law and the facts of the case) or the unreasonable manner in which the case was litigated." *Id.* at 1756. Whether this interpretation of the Patent Act will spill over into trademark law remains to be seen, but given that both Acts use the same "exceptional" case standard, an attorney could reasonably argue that *Octane Fitness* should govern for trademark cases as well.

8. *Counterfeiting.* Why didn't the plaintiffs in *Texas Pig Stands* and *Maltina Co.* claim that the defendants were counterfeiters? In addition to the criminal penalties available against counterfeiters that we shall study later in this Chapter, the Trademark Act also provides for heightened penalties in civil actions arising out of counterfeit marks. For such civil actions, section 1117(b) modifies the ordinary damages and attorneys' fees rules set forth in section 1117(a) as follows:

> In assessing damages under subsection (a), the court shall, unless the court finds extenuating circumstances, enter judgment for three times such profits or damages, whichever is greater, together with a reasonable attorney's fee, in the case of any violation of section 1114(1)(a) of this title . . . that consists of intentionally using a mark or designation, knowing such mark or designation is a counterfeit mark (as defined in section 1116(d) of this title), in connection with the sale, offering for sale, or distribution of goods or services.

17 U.S.C. § 1117(b) (2015). In terms of the remedies available, how does this provision differ from subsection (a)?

In addition, in a civil action arising out of the use of a counterfeit mark, section 1117(c) states that "the plaintiff may elect, at any time before final judgment is rendered, to recover, instead of actual damages and profits under subsection (a), an award of statutory damages, as an alternative to recovering actual damages, . . . in the amount of—(1) not less than $500 or more than $100,000 per counterfeit mark . . . ; or (2) if the court finds that the use of the counterfeit mark was willful, not more than $1,000,000 per counterfeit mark. . . ." 17 U.S.C. § 1117(c) (2015). Section 1117(c) does not expressly address, one way or the other, whether an award of attorneys' fees is available with an award of statutory damages. Based upon the statutory language, if a plaintiff elects to recover statutory damages under section 1117(c), may the plaintiff also recover a reasonable attorneys' fee award under section 1117(a) or (b)? *See K & N Eng'g, Inc. v. Bulat*, 510 F.3d 1079 (9th Cir. 2007) (no).

Importantly, these counterfeiting remedies are not restricted to stereotypical black market goods. To the contrary, section 1116(d)(1)(B) states that a " 'counterfeit mark' means—(i) a counterfeit of a mark that is registered on the principal register . . . for such goods or services sold, offered for sale, or distributed and that is in use, whether or not the person against whom relief is sought knew such mark was so registered. . . ." 17 U.S.C. § 1116(d)(1)(B) (2015).

Does the definition in section 1116(d) apply to the defendants in either *Maltina Corp.* or *Texas Pig Stands?* Is either using a mark that is registered on the principal register? Is either using it for the goods or services for which it is registered? Are the plaintiffs in each case still using the mark for those goods or services? Are those three requirements all that is required under section 1116(d) for a defendant's marks to constitute a counterfeit mark?

If so, was an award of the defendant's profits and a reasonable attorneys' fees mandatory under section 1117(b)? What does the language "intentionally using a mark . . . , knowing such mark . . . is a counterfeit mark" in section 1117(b) mean? Does it require a specific intent to infringe or proof that the infringement is otherwise willful? *See Lindy Pen Co. v. Bic Pen Corp.*, 982 F.2d 1400, 1409–10 (9th Cir. 1993) (requiring intentional infringement to invoke section 1117(b), and holding that it is not enough that defendant used an identical mark on identical goods and on the goods for which the plaintiff's mark was federally registered); *Chanel, Inc. v. Italian Activewear of Florida, Inc.*, 931 F.2d 1472, 1476–77 (11th Cir. 1991) (same). Can we reconcile requiring a specific intent to infringe to establish counterfeiting, with the statutory damages provision in section 1117(c) which reserves heightened statutory damages for "willful" use of a counterfeit mark? Could either defendant claim "extenuating circumstances"? *See Lindy Pen Co.*, 982 F.2d at 1409 (suggesting that "extenuating circumstances may be inferred" where *inter alia* the defendant was " 'unaware of [the plaintiff's] registered trademark' ").

9. *State Law Alternatives.* If a plaintiff cannot satisfy the federal Trademark Act's exacting standards for obtaining damages, enhanced damages, or attorneys' fees, state law may sometimes provide a viable alternative. While state law varies, some states provide a relaxed standard for awarding enhanced damages, punitive damages, or attorneys' fees in trademark and unfair competition cases. New Hampshire law, for example, provides for enhanced damages and an award of attorneys' fees "automatically upon a showing that the violation was willful or knowing." *See Attrezzi, LLC v. Maytag Corp.*, 436 F.3d 32, 40–41 (1st Cir. 2006). In addition, many states authorize, as a general principle, punitive damages for willful torts. The laws of the states of, among others, Illinois, and as we shall see later in this Chapter, Colorado extend this principle and authorize an award of punitive damages to cases involving willful trademark infringement. *See JCW Invs., Inc. v. Novelty, Inc.*, 482 F.3d 910, 917 (7th Cir. 2007). Are such state law remedies preempted by the stricter standards the Lanham

Trademark Act provides? *See JCW Invs., Inc.*, 482 F.2d at 917–18 (no); *Attrezzi, LCC*, 436 F.2d at 41 (no).

C. THE SPECIAL CASE OF REVERSE CONFUSION

As the *Texas Pig Stands* case reflects, and despite the seemingly mandatory language of the statute, obtaining an award of monetary damages in trademark litigation can prove difficult. There is one notable exception to this rule, however. In the relatively small number of cases involving reverse confusion, courts have routinely made very significant monetary awards to prevailing trademark plaintiffs, as the following cases illustrate.

BIG O TIRE DEALERS, INC. v. GOODYEAR TIRE & RUBBER CO.

561 F.2d 1365 (10th Cir. 1977)

LEWIS, C.J.

This civil action was brought by Big O Tire Dealers, Inc., ("Big O") asserting claims of unfair competition against the Goodyear Tire & Rubber Co. ("Goodyear") based upon false designation of origin under 15 U.S.C. § 1125(a) and common law trademark infringement. After a ten-day trial and three days of deliberation, the jury returned the following verdict:

> We the jury in the above entitled cause, upon our oath do say that we find the following as our verdict herein:
>
> Upon the claim of liability for trademark infringement we find for Big O Inc.
>
> Upon the claim of liability for false designation of origin we find for Goodyear.
>
> Upon the claim for trademark disparagement we find for Big O Inc.
>
> We find that plaintiff has proven special compensatory damages in the amount of $None.
>
> We find that plaintiff has proven general compensatory damages in the amount of $2,800,000.
>
> We assess punitive or exemplary damages in the amount of $16,800,000.
>
> Dated September 4, 1975.

Filing a comprehensive post-trial opinion the United States District Court for the District of Colorado entered judgment on the jury's verdict, permanently enjoined Goodyear from infringing on Big O's trademark, and dismissed Goodyear's counterclaim for equitable relief. 408 F. Supp. 1219. Goodyear appeals that judgment.

Big O is a tire-buying organization which provides merchandising techniques, advertising concepts, operating systems, and other aids to approximately 200 independent retail tire dealers in 14 states who identify themselves to the public as Big O dealers. These dealers sell replacement tires using the Big O label on "private brand" tires. They also sell other companies' brands such as B.F. Goodrich and Michelin Tires. At the time of trial Big O's total net worth was approximately $200,000.

Goodyear is the world's largest tire manufacturer. In 1974 Goodyear's net sales totaled more than $5.25 billion and its net income after taxes surpassed $157 million. In the replacement market Goodyear sells through a nationwide network of company-owned stores, franchise dealers, and independent retailers.

In the fall of 1973 Big O decided to identify two of its lines of private brand tires as "Big O Big Foot 60" and "Big O Big Foot 70." These names were placed on the sidewall of the respective tires in raised white letters. The first interstate shipment of these tires occurred in February 1974. Big O dealers began selling these tires to the public in April 1974. Big O did not succeed in registering "Big Foot" as a trademark with the United States Patent and Trademark Office.

In the last three months of 1973 Goodyear began making snowmobile replacement tracks using the trademark "Bigfoot." From October 1973 to August 1975 Goodyear made only 671 "Bigfoot" snowmobile tracks and sold only 411 tracks. In December 1973 Goodyear filed an application to register "Bigfoot" as a trademark for snowmobile tracks with the United States Patent and Trademark Office; the registration was granted on October 15, 1974.

In July 1974 Goodyear decided to use the term "Bigfoot" in a nationwide advertising campaign to promote the sale of its new "Custom Polysteel Radial" tire. The name "Custom Polysteel Radial" was molded into the tire's sidewall. Goodyear employed a trademark search firm to conduct a search for "Bigfoot" in connection with tires and related products. This search did not uncover any conflicting trademarks. After this suit was filed Goodyear filed an application to register "Bigfoot" as a trademark for tires but withdrew it in 1975. Goodyear planned to launch its massive, nationwide "Bigfoot" advertising campaign on September 16, 1974.

On August 24, 1974, Goodyear first learned of Big O's "Big Foot" tires. Goodyear informed Big O's president, Norman Affleck, on August 26 of Goodyear's impending "Bigfoot" advertising campaign. Affleck was asked to give Goodyear a letter indicating Big O had no objection to this use of "Bigfoot." When Affleck replied he could not make this decision alone, it was suggested Affleck talk with John Kelley, Goodyear's vice-president for advertising.

Affleck called Kelley and requested more information on Goodyear's impending advertising campaign. A Goodyear employee visited Affleck on August 30 and showed him rough versions of the planned Goodyear "Bigfoot" commercials and other promotional materials. On September 10, Affleck and two Big O directors met in New Orleans, with Kelley and Goodyear's manager of consumer market planning to discuss the problem further. At this time the Big O representatives objected to Goodyear using "Bigfoot" in connection with tires because they believed any such use would severely damage Big O. They made it clear they were not interested in money in exchange for granting Goodyear the right to use the "Bigfoot" trademark, and asked Goodyear to wind down the campaign as soon as possible. Goodyear's response to this request was indefinite and uncertain.

During the trial several Goodyear employees conceded it was technically possible for Goodyear to have deleted the term "Bigfoot" from its television advertising as late as early September. However, on September 16, 1974, Goodyear launched its nationwide "Bigfoot" promotion on ABC's Monday Night Football telecast. By August 31, 1975, Goodyear had spent $9,690,029 on its massive, saturation campaign.

On September 17 Affleck wrote Kelley a letter setting forth his understanding of the New Orleans meeting that Goodyear would wind up its "Bigfoot" campaign as soon as possible. Kelley replied on September 20, denying any commitment to discontinue use of "Bigfoot" and declaring Goodyear intended to use "Bigfoot" as long as it continued to be a helpful advertising device.

On October 9 Kelley told Affleck he did not have the authority to make the final decision for Goodyear and suggested that Affleck call Charles Eaves, Goodyear's executive vice-president. On October 10 Affleck called Eaves and Eaves indicated the possibility of paying Big O for the use of the term "Bigfoot." When Affleck stated no interest in the possibility Eaves told him Goodyear wished to avoid litigation but that if Big O did sue, the case would be in litigation long enough that Goodyear might obtain all the benefits it desired from the term "Bigfoot."

This was the final communication between the parties until Big O filed suit on November 27, 1974. The district court denied Big O's request for a temporary restraining order and a preliminary injunction. After judgment was entered on the jury's verdict for Big O, Goodyear appealed to this court. Goodyear's allegations of error are discussed below.

I.

The district court instructed the jury it must decide whether "the term BIG FOOT [is] merely descriptive of a quality or characteristic of the Big O BIG FOOT 60 and Big O BIG FOOT 70 tires." The court further charged the jury that if it decided "Big Foot is merely descriptive as applied to these Big O tires, then [it must] consider whether the evidence shows that before September 16, 1974, the plaintiff had so used Big Foot as to develop a secondary meaning such as to associate that term with Big O Tire Dealers, Inc. in the minds of a significant number of the consuming public."

Goodyear argues that Big Foot is descriptive in nature as a matter of law or fact and that the evidence is not sufficient to support the issue of secondary meaning and therefore Goodyear is entitled to judgment notwithstanding the verdict. Goodyear bases its descriptiveness argument on the premise that "Big Foot" is a combination of two common English words which together are descriptive of the big footprint characteristic of tires. At trial, Goodyear presented evidence showing it had used the term "BIG FOOT TRACTION" in brochures produced in 1964 and 1969. Goodyear also presented evidence of the use of the term "footprint" in connection with tires.

Big O presented evidence that it adopted the mark "Big Foot" after the Abominable Snowman, or the Sasquatch Monster Bigfoot. Thus, Big O asserts the term "Big Foot" is totally arbitrary in relation to automobile tires, having no descriptive significance.

Words which are merely descriptive of the qualities, ingredients, or composition of an article cannot be appropriated as a trademark and are not entitled to protection unless they have acquired a secondary meaning. In testing the validity of common law trademarks the critical question is what the designation meant to the purchasing public; not what the designation meant to those in the industry. Mindful of these principles, we hold the trial court did not err in refusing to rule as a matter of law that "Big Foot" is merely descriptive of the big footprint characteristic of tires. . . .

IV.

The district court charged the jury:

A trademark is infringed when a second person (later user) uses it in a manner which is likely to cause confusion among ordinarily prudent purchasers or prospective purchasers as to the source of the products. The test is not one of actual confusion; it is the likelihood of confusion.

The effect of this instruction was to permit the jury to base liability on a likelihood of any kind of confusion. Big O does not claim nor was any evidence presented showing Goodyear intended to trade on the goodwill of Big O or to palm off Goodyear products as being those of Big O. Instead, Big O contends Goodyear's use of Big O's trademark created a likelihood of confusion concerning the source of Big O's "Big Foot" tires.

The facts of this case are different from the usual trademark infringement case. As the trial judge stated, the usual trademark infringement case involves a claim by a plaintiff with a substantial investment in a well established trademark. The plaintiff would seek recovery for the loss of income resulting from a second user attempting to trade on the goodwill associated with that established mark by suggesting to the consuming public that his product comes from the same origin as the plaintiff's product. The instant case, however, involves reverse confusion wherein the infringer's use of plaintiff's mark results in confusion as to the origin of plaintiff's product. Only one reported decision involves the issue of reverse confusion. In *Westward Coach Mfg. Co. v. Ford Motor Co.*, 7 Cir., 388 F.2d 627, *cert. denied*, 392 U.S. 927, the court held reverse confusion is not actionable as a trademark infringement under Indiana law.

Consequently, Goodyear argues the second use of a trademark is not actionable if it merely creates a likelihood of confusion concerning the source of the first user's product. Since both parties agree Colorado law is controlling in this case, we must decide whether this so-called reverse confusion is actionable under Colorado law. To our knowledge, the Colorado courts have never considered whether a second use creating the likelihood of confusion about the source of the first user's products is actionable. However, the Colorado Court of Appeals in deciding a trade name infringement case involving an issue of first impression, cogently pointed out that the Colorado Supreme Court

> has consistently recognized and followed a policy of protecting established trade names and preventing public confusion and the tendency has been to widen the scope of that protection.

Wood v. Wood's Homes Inc., 33 Colo. App. 285.

Using that language as a guiding light in divining what Colorado law is on this issue of first impression, we hold that the Colorado courts, if given the opportunity, would extend its common law trademark infringement actions to include reverse confusion situations. Such a rule would further Colorado's "policy of protecting trade names and preventing public confusion" as well as having "the tendency [of widening] the scope of that protection."

The district court very persuasively answered Goodyear's argument that liability for trademark infringement cannot be imposed without a showing that Goodyear intended to trade on the goodwill of Big O or to palm off Goodyear products as being those of Big O's when it said

> The logical consequence of accepting Goodyear's position would be the immunization from unfair competition liability of a company with a well established trade name and with the

economic power to advertise extensively for a product name taken from a competitor. If the law is to limit recovery to passing off, anyone with adequate size and resources can adopt any trademark and develop a new meaning for that trademark as identification of the second user's products. The activities of Goodyear in this case are unquestionably unfair competition through an improper use of a trademark and that must be actionable.

408 F. Supp. at 1236.

Goodyear further argues there was no credible evidence from which the jury could have found a likelihood of reverse confusion. A review of the record demonstrates the lack of merit in this argument. Big O presented more than a dozen witnesses who testified to actual confusion as to the source of Big O's "Big Foot" tires after watching a Goodyear "Bigfoot" commercial. The jury could have reasonably inferred a likelihood of confusion from these witnesses' testimony of actual confusion. Moreover, two of Goodyear's executive officers, Kelley and Eaves, testified confusion was likely or even inevitable.

. . .

VII.

Finally, Goodyear challenges the jury's verdict awarding Big O $2.8 million in compensatory damages and $16.8 million in punitive damages. Goodyear contends Big O failed to prove either the fact or the amount of damages. Big O asserts the evidence supporting the fact of damages falls into two categories: (1) Goodyear's enormous effort to adopt, use, and absorb Big O's trademark virtually destroyed Big O's ability to make any effective use of its "Big Foot" trademark and (2) Goodyear's false statements that "Bigfoot" was available only from Goodyear created the appearance of dishonesty and wrongful conduct by Big O thereby harming its reputation within the trade and with the public. We agree with the district court that there is sufficient evidence to support the jury's finding of the fact of damages.

Big O also asserts the evidence provided the jury with a reasonable basis for determining the amount of damages. Big O claims the only way it can be restored to the position it was in before Goodyear infringed its trademark is to conduct a corrective advertising campaign. Big O insists it should be compensated for the advertising expenses necessary to dispel the public confusion caused by Goodyear's infringement. Goodyear spent approximately $10 million on its "Bigfoot" advertising campaign. Thus, Big O advances two rationales in support of the $2.8 million award: (1) there were Big O Tire Dealers in 28 percent of the states (14 of 50) and 28 percent of $10 million equals the amount of the award; and (2) the Federal Trade Commission generally orders businesses who engage in misleading advertising to spend approximately 25 percent of their advertising budget on corrective advertising and this award is roughly 25 percent of the amount Goodyear spent infringing on Big O's trademark. The district court used the first rationale in denying Goodyear's motion to set the verdict aside. The second rationale was presented by Big O at oral argument.

The purpose of general compensatory damages is to make the plaintiff whole. Big O concedes it was unable to prove with precision the amount necessary to make itself whole. However, the district court concluded "the damages awarded by the jury would enable Big O to do an equivalent volume of advertising in the states in which there are Big O dealers to inform their customers, potential customers, and the public as a whole about the true facts in this dispute or anything else necessary to eliminate the confusion." 408 F. Supp. at 1232. Moreover, the Supreme Court has pointed out that a plaintiff's inability to prove with precision that amount necessary to make itself whole does not preclude recovery since

> the most elementary conceptions of justice and public policy require that the wrongdoer shall bear the risk of the uncertainty which his own wrong has created.

Bigelow v. RKO Radio Pictures, Inc., 327 U.S. 251, 265.

There is precedent for the recovery of corrective advertising expenses incurred by a plaintiff to counteract the public confusion resulting from a defendant's wrongful conduct. *E.g., Petersime & Son v. Robbins*, 10 Cir., 81 F.2d 295, *cert. denied*, 299 U.S. 553; *Maytag Co. v. Meadows Mfg. Co.*, 7 Cir., 45 F.2d 299, *cert. denied*, 283 U.S. 843; *Truzzolino Food Products Co. v. F. W. Woolworth Co.*, 108 Mont. 408; *Den Norske Ameriekalinje Actiesselskabet v. Sun Printing and Pub. Ass'n*, 226 N.Y. 1. Unlike the wronged parties in those cases Big O did not spend any money prior to trial in advertising to counteract the confusion from the Goodyear advertising. It is clear from the record Big O did not have the economic resources to conduct an advertising campaign sufficient to counteract Goodyear's $9,690,029 saturation advertising campaign. We are thus confronted with the question whether the law should apply differently to those who have the economic power to help themselves concurrently with the wrong than to those who must seek redress through the courts. Under the facts of this case we are convinced the answer must be no. Goodyear contends the recovery of advertising expenses should be limited to those actually incurred prior to trial. In this case the effect of such a rule would be to recognize that Big O has a right to the exclusive use of its trademark but has no remedy to be put in the position it was in prior to September 16, 1974, before Goodyear effectively usurped Big O's trademark. The impact of Goodyear's "Bigfoot" campaign was devastating. The infringing mark was seen repeatedly by millions of consumers. It is clear from the record that Goodyear deeply penetrated the public consciousness. Thus, Big O is entitled to recover a reasonable amount equivalent to that of a concurrent corrective advertising campaign.

As the district court pointed out, the jury's verdict of $2.8 million corresponds to 28 percent of the approximately $10 million Goodyear spent infringing Big O's mark. Big O has dealers in 14 states which equals 28 percent of the 50 states. Big O also points out the jury's award is close to 25 percent of the amount Goodyear spent infringing on Big O's mark. Big O emphasizes that the Federal Trade Commission often requires businesses who engage in misleading advertising to spend 25 percent of their advertising budget on corrective advertising.

Taking cognizance of these two alternative rationales for the jury's award for compensatory damages we are convinced the award is not capable of support as to any amount in excess of $678,302. As the district court implied in attempting to explain the jury's verdict, Big O is not entitled to the total amount Goodyear spent on its nationwide campaign since Big O only has dealers in 14 states, thus making it unnecessary for Big O to run a nationwide advertising campaign. Furthermore, implicit in the FTC's 25 percent rule in corrective advertising cases is the fact that dispelling confusion and deception in the consuming public's mind does not require a dollar-for-dollar expenditure. In keeping with " 'the constant tendency of the courts . . . to find some way in which damages can be awarded where a wrong has been done,' " we hold that the maximum amount which a jury could reasonably find necessary to place Big O in the position it was in before September 16, 1974, vis-a-vis its "Big Foot" trademark, is $678,302. We arrive at this amount by taking 28 percent of the $9,690,029 it was stipulated Goodyear spent on its "Bigfoot" campaign, and then reducing that figure by 75 percent in accordance with the FTC rule, since we agree with that agency's determination that a dollar-for-dollar expenditure for corrective advertising is unnecessary to dispel the effects of confusing and misleading advertising.

Under Colorado law exemplary damages must bear some relation to the compensatory award. *Barnes v. Lehman*, 118 Colo. 161, 163, 193 P.2d 273. The district court in its post-trial opinion upheld the jury's punitive damage award of $16.8 million as not being disproportionate under Colorado law. We find the district court's determination of the reasonableness of a six-to-one exemplary to compensatory ratio to be persuasive, and thus we defer to the district court's interpretation of Colorado law. Therefore, in light of the reduction in compensatory damages proved, the punitive damage award is similarly reduced to $4,069,812, thus maintaining the jury's and district court's six-to-one exemplary to compensatory ratio.

We have considered the numerous other contentions presented by Goodyear as constituting error but are convinced that the hard core of the issues was presented to the jury without error or accumulation of error requiring reversal. As modified the judgment is affirmed.

The case is remanded to the trial court with directions to vacate its judgment and enter judgment in compliance with this opinion.

SANDS, TAYLOR & WOOD CO. V. QUAKER OATS CO.
978 F.2d 947 (7th Cir. 1992)

CUDAHY, CIRCUIT JUDGE

Sands, Taylor & Wood Company (STW) brought this action against The Quaker Oats Company (Quaker) for federal trademark infringement and related state-law claims, alleging that Quaker's use of the words "Thirst Aid" in its advertising slogan "Gatorade is Thirst Aid" infringed STW's registered trademark for THIRST-AID. The district court agreed, and entered judgment for STW in the amount of $42,629,399.09, including prejudgment interest and attorney's fees. The court also permanently enjoined Quaker from using the words "Thirst Aid." Not surprisingly, Quaker appeals.

I.

Plaintiff STW is a small, Vermont-based company that for the past 180 years has sold bagged flour at retail under the brand name "King Arthur Flour." In 1973, STW acquired Joseph Middleby, Jr., Inc. (Middleby), a manufacturer of soft drinks, soda fountain syrups and ice cream toppings. STW thereby became the owner of three trademarks registered to Middleby: (1) THIRST-AID "First Aid for Your Thirst," issued October 10, 1950, for use on "nonalcoholic maltless beverages, sold as soft drinks, and syrups therefor"; (2) THIRST-AID, issued August 26, 1952, for use on various ice cream toppings as well as "fruits and sauces used in the making of ice cream"; and (3) THIRST-AID, issued March 24, 1953, for use on "soda fountain syrups used in the preparation of maltless soft drinks."

From 1921 to 1973, Middleby used the THIRST-AID mark on a wide variety of beverage products and syrups that it sold to soda fountains, ice cream parlors and food service outlets. Middleby also supplied its THIRST-AID customers with various items displaying the name THIRST-AID, including streamers, banners, glasses and pitchers, for in-store advertising and promotion. STW continued these activities after it acquired Middleby, which it operated as a wholly-owned subsidiary.

In the late 1970s sales of THIRST-AID soft drinks declined as consumers turned increasingly to bottles and cans rather than soda fountains and ice cream parlors for their soft drinks. In addition, between

1979 and 1983 STW underwent a period of severe economic hardship during which its annual gross revenues dropped from $40 million to approximately $3.1 million. In the spring of 1980, Pet, Inc. (Pet), negotiated with STW a nationwide license to use the name THIRST-AID on a new isotonic beverage intended to compete with the very popular Gatorade brand isotonic beverage manufactured by Stokely Van Camp Company (Stokely). Pet began test-marketing the product in twenty stores in Columbia, South Carolina in June of 1980. Pet's THIRST-AID was advertised through the same media as Gatorade, and was sold through the same channels of trade (grocery stores) to the same customers. During the five-month period of the test, Pet's THIRST-AID captured approximately 25% of the isotonic beverage market in the test area. Nevertheless, for reasons that are not important here, Pet decided not to enter the market with the new product and in June of 1981 its license to use the name THIRST-AID expired.

In December of 1981, STW sold the assets of Middleby (now renamed Johnson-Middleby) to L. Karp & Sons (Karp), a distributor of bakery products. As part of the sale, STW assigned to Karp all of the registered THIRST-AID trademarks. STW obtained a simultaneous exclusive license back for retail use of the trademark on certain "Products" defined as "jams, jellies, pie fillings" and various other bakery supplies.

In August of 1983, Stokely, the manufacturer of Gatorade, was acquired by Quaker. Shortly thereafter, Quaker solicited proposals for a new advertising campaign intended to educate consumers about Gatorade's ability to quench thirst and replace fluids and minerals lost by the human body through strenuous exercise. One of the candidates was the slogan "Gatorade is Thirst Aid for That Deep Down Body Thirst."

Pursuant to Quaker's regular practice, the proposed "Thirst Aid" campaign was submitted to the legal department for approval in February or March of 1984. Quaker's in-house counsel, Charles Lannin, concluded that the words "Thirst Aid" did not raise any trademark problems because they were used to describe an attribute of the product rather than as a designation of source or affiliation. Lannin therefore did not conduct a trademark search for the term "Thirst Aid" at this time.

Shortly thereafter, an employee of Quaker's research and development division telephoned Lannin and informed him that Pet had previously test-marketed an isotonic beverage called THIRST-AID. Lannin contacted Pet and was told that Pet had discontinued its isotonic beverage a few years before. Some weeks later, another Quaker employee informed Lannin that he thought a "Thirst Aid" beverage was being marketed in Florida. At this point, on May 2, 1984, Lannin obtained a trademark search of the phrase "Thirst Aid." The search revealed the three THIRST-AID registrations by Middleby as well as the sale of the marks to Karp. Lannin directed a trademark paralegal employed by

Quaker to contact Karp in order to determine what products it was selling under the THIRST-AID name; the Karp employee to whom the paralegal spoke stated that "they [sic] didn't think they marketed anything under that name."

On May 12, 1984, the first "Gatorade is Thirst Aid" commercials ran on television. On May 31, 1984, Karp's lawyer, Russell Hattis, called Quaker regarding Quaker's use of "Thirst Aid." Hattis claimed that Quaker was infringing Karp's trademarks, to which Lannin responded that there was no infringement because Quaker was using the words "Thirst Aid" descriptively. In a subsequent meeting between the two, Lannin learned from Hattis that the THIRST-AID mark had not been used on soft drinks or beverages since the Pet test-market. On June 2, Quaker sought an opinion from outside trademark counsel, Robert Newbury, who essentially agreed with Lannin that there was no infringement because Quaker was using the words "Thirst Aid" descriptively rather than as a trademark.

On June 4, Lannin was contacted by Frank Sands, the president of STW, who stated that STW owned the rights to use the THIRST-AID mark at retail under a license-back agreement with Karp. Sands claimed that Quaker was infringing those rights, although he acknowledged that STW did not sell any THIRST-AID products at that time.

Quaker did not hear from either Karp or STW again until the commencement of this litigation. In the interim, STW entered into a written agreement with Karp under which STW paid Karp $1 for an assignment of Karp's trademark registrations. Sands filed suit one week later, alleging that the slogan "Gatorade is Thirst Aid for That Deep Down Body Thirst" infringed its registrations and constituted unfair competition under the Lanham Act, 15 U.S.C. §§ 1051 *et seq.,* state common law and various state statutes. After granting summary judgment in favor of STW on Quaker's fair use defense, the district court held a bench trial on the remaining issues. On December 18, 1990, the court issued its opinion holding that Quaker had infringed STW's trademark and awarding STW 10% of Quaker's pre-tax profits on Gatorade for the period during which Quaker used "Thirst Aid" in its advertising. *Sands, Taylor & Wood v. The Quaker Oats Co.,* 18 U.S.P.Q.2D (BNA) 1457 (N.D. Ill. 1990). The court also awarded STW attorney's fees and costs as well as prejudgment interest. Gatorade appeals.

II.

As we have noted, the district court granted summary judgment in favor of STW on Quaker's defense that it had made a "fair use" of the phrase "Thirst Aid." The fair use doctrine is based on the principle that no one should be able to appropriate descriptive language through trademark registration. *William R. Warner & Co. v. Eli Lilly & Co.,* 265

U.S. 526, 528 (1924). To prevail on the fair use defense, the defendant must establish that its use of a registered "term or device" is "otherwise than as a trade or service mark," that the term or device is "descriptive of" the defendant's goods or services and that the defendant is using the term or device "fairly and in good faith only to describe to users" those goods and services. 15 U.S.C. § 1115(b)(4). The district court found that the term "Thirst Aid" was not descriptive of Gatorade but rather was "suggestive." The court also found that even if "Thirst Aid" were descriptive, Quaker could not prevail on the fair use defense because it had used the term as a trademark in its ads. Quaker challenges both of these conclusions.

[The Court found "thirst aid" descriptive, but affirmed the district court's rejection of Quaker's fair use defense as follows:]

The evidence of Quaker's advertisements supports the district court's conclusion that Quaker used "Thirst Aid" as a trademark. Quaker's ads do not simply use the words "Thirst Aid" in a sentence describing Gatorade, but as an "attention-getting symbol." In many of the ads, the words "Thirst Aid" appear more prominently and in larger type than does the word "Gatorade." Further, given the rhyming quality of "Gatorade" and "Thirst Aid," the association between the two terms created by Quaker's ads is likely to be very strong, so that "Thirst Aid" appears as part of a memorable slogan that is uniquely associated with Quaker's product. Quaker presented no evidence that its "Thirst Aid" ads do not have this effect on consumers. "The plain language of Rule 56(c) mandates the entry of summary judgment . . . against a party who fails to make a showing sufficient to establish the existence of an element essential to that party's case, and on which that party will bear the burden of proof at trial." The district court did not err in concluding that Quaker used "Thirst Aid" as a trademark.

III.

Because trademark rights derive from the use of a mark in commerce and not from mere registration of the mark, the owner of a mark will lose his exclusive rights if he fails actually to use it. 15 U.S.C. § 1127. A mark is deemed to be thus "abandoned" when "its use has been discontinued with intent not to resume such use." *Id.* Two years of nonuse create a prima facie case of abandonment, which may be rebutted by "evidence explaining the nonuse or demonstrating the lack of an intent not to resume use." *Roulo v. Russ Berrie & Co.*, 886 F.2d 931, 938 (7th Cir. 1989). Quaker argues that the district court erred in finding that STW or its predecessors had not abandoned through nonuse the THIRST-AID mark for a beverage sold at retail.

. . . The district court found that STW's efforts to license THIRST-AID for use on a soft drink during this period were sufficient evidence of intent to resume use to rebut a prima facie case of abandonment.

Although the district court erred in focusing on the intent of STW rather than of Karp during the three years that Karp owned the marks, the court at least implicitly found that Karp's efforts to license THIRST-AID to Shasta and Tropicana were sufficient to establish Karp's intent to resume use. Karp did not abandon the right to use THIRST-AID for a beverage.

. . .

A.   Reverse Confusion

The "keystone" of trademark infringement is "likelihood of confusion" as to source, affiliation, connection or sponsorship of goods or services among the relevant class of customers and potential customers. 2 McCarthy, *supra* § 23:1, at 42–43, 46–47. Usually, the confusion alleged is "forward confusion," which occurs "when customers mistakenly think that the junior user's goods or services are from the same source as or are connected with the senior user's goods or services." *Id.* at 48. In such a case, the junior user attempts to capitalize on the senior user's good will and established reputation by suggesting that his product comes from the same source as does the senior user's product. *Big O Tire Dealers v. Goodyear Tire & Rubber Co.*, 561 F.2d 1365 (10th Cir. 1977).

In this case, however, STW relies not on classic forward confusion but on the doctrine of "reverse confusion." Reverse confusion occurs when a large junior user saturates the market with a trademark similar or identical to that of a smaller, senior user. In such a case, the junior user does not seek to profit from the good will associated with the senior user's mark. Nonetheless, the senior user is injured because

> . . . the public comes to assume that the senior user's products are really the junior user's or that the former has become somehow connected to the latter. The result is that the senior user loses the value of the trademark—its product identity, corporate identity, control over its goodwill and reputation, and ability to move into new markets.

Ameritech, Inc. v. American Information Technologies Corp., 811 F.2d 960, 964 (6th Cir. 1987); *see also Banff, Ltd.*, 841 F.2d at 490–91; *Big O Tire Dealers*, 561 F.2d at 1372. Although this court has not previously recognized reverse confusion as the basis for a claim under the Lanham Act, several other circuits have endorsed the concept. We agree with those courts that "the objectives of the Lanham Act—to protect an owner's interest in its trademark by keeping the public free from confusion as to the source of goods and ensuring fair competition—are as important in a case of reverse confusion as in typical trademark infringement." *Banff, Ltd.*, 841 F.2d at 490. We therefore hold that reverse confusion is a redressable injury under the Lanham Act.

Quaker does not really dispute the validity of the reverse confusion theory. Rather, Quaker argues that there is no likelihood of confusion of any sort here because STW has no "product in commerce" about which customers could be confused. We now turn to that issue.

B.   Likelihood of Confusion

Modern trademark law prohibits use of a senior user's mark not only on products that are in direct competition with those of the senior user but also on products that are considered to be "closely related" to the senior user's. *International Kennel Club*, 846 F.2d at 1089. A "closely related" product is one "which would reasonably be thought by the buying public to come from the same source, or thought to be affiliated with, connected with, or sponsored by, the trademark owner." 2 McCarthy, *supra* § 24:3, at 166; *see also International Kennel Club*, 846 F.2d at 1089. Thus, the use of the mark VERA on cosmetics and perfume has been found to infringe the mark VERA on designer apparel and household linens. *Scarves by* Vera, Inc. v. Todo Imports, Ltd., 544 F.2d 1167 (2d Cir. 1976).

One of the reasons courts have given for protecting trademark owners against the use of confusingly similar marks on closely related products is to protect the owner's ability to enter product markets in which it does not now trade but into which it might reasonably be expected to expand in the future. Protecting the trademark owner's interest in capitalizing on the good will associated with its mark by moving into new markets is especially compelling in the context of a reverse confusion case, where the junior user so overwhelms the senior user's mark that the senior user may come to be seen as the infringer. Such a scenario is particularly likely if the senior user were to attempt to expand into the precise field where the junior user has created a strong association between its product and the senior user's mark. "When it appears extremely likely . . . that the trademark owner will soon enter the defendant's field, this . . . factor weighs heavily in favor of injunctive relief." *Interpace*, 721 F.2d at 464.

In this case, STW has manifested a serious intent to market (or license someone else to market) an isotonic beverage in direct competition with Gatorade under the THIRST-AID name. Karp continued those efforts during the period that it owned the THIRST-AID marks. Those efforts might well have been successful but for Quaker's "Thirst Aid" campaign. The Pet test product is a fair representation of what an isotonic beverage marketed by STW or its licensee would look like. As Quaker notes, the district court's finding of likelihood of confusion was based largely on the Pet test product. The district court did not err in taking this approach, despite the fact that the Pet product is not currently on the market. *Cf. Roulo,* 886 F.2d at 937–38 (finding likelihood of confusion between defendant's product and plaintiff's product, although the latter had not been on market for more than two years).

Nor do we find any merit in Quaker's challenge to the district court's determination that there would likely be confusion between Gatorade and an isotonic beverage marketed by STW under the name THIRST-AID. This court has identified seven factors to be used in analyzing likelihood of confusion:

> The degree of similarity between the marks in appearance and suggestion; the similarity of the products for which the name is used; the areas and manner of concurrent use; the degree of care likely to be exercised by consumers; the strength of the complainant's mark; actual confusion; and an intent on the part of the alleged infringer to palm off his products as those of another.

Forum Corp., 903 F.2d at 439. Quaker argues that the district court misapplied (or failed to apply) all but one of these factors. The trial court's ultimate conclusion as to likelihood of confusion is a finding of fact, which we review under the clearly erroneous standard. *Id.* at 438. We do, however, "review the district court's statement of the law de novo for legal error and its conclusions for signs that the court's application of the law was infected with legal error." *Id.*

Quaker argues, first, that the district court erred in finding a likelihood of confusion because it failed even to consider the strength of STW's mark. According to Quaker, the "extensive" use of the words "thirst aid" on other products "establishes the weakness of plaintiff's marks and weighs heavily against a finding of likelihood of confusion." Br. at 22–23. Although Quaker is correct that the district court failed to factor in the strength of STW's mark, we disagree with Quaker as to the significance of that factor in this case. "Whether a mark is weak or not is of little importance where the conflicting mark is identical and the goods are closely related." 1 McCarthy, *supra* § 11:24, at 505–06. Here, both the marks and the goods Quaker's Gatorade and the isotonic beverage that STW would market but for Quaker's actions—are virtually identical.

Further, "the term 'strength' as applied to trademarks refers to the distinctiveness of the mark, or more precisely, its tendency to identify the goods sold under the mark as emanating from a particular . . . source." *McGregor-Doniger, Inc. v. Drizzle, Inc.*, 599 F.2d 1126, 1131 (2d Cir. 1979). In a reverse confusion case, then, it may make more sense to consider the strength of the mark in terms of its association with the junior user's goods. Here, there was abundant evidence that consumers strongly associate the words "thirst aid" with Gatorade, even when those words appear on a product label along with a different brand name. Thus, to the extent that the district court erred in failing to consider the strength of the THIRST-AID mark, that error did not tend to favor STW.

Quaker also argues that the district court erred in finding that the marks are similar because the court (1) "incorrectly relied on the Pet product and on plaintiff's registrations" and (2) failed to consider that Quaker's "Thirst Aid" ads always included the well-known brand name "Gatorade." The first of these arguments is clearly foreclosed by our conclusion, above, that the district court correctly relied on the Pet product in determining likelihood of confusion; both the Pet label and STW's registrations are appropriate evidence of how the THIRST-AID mark would appear on an isotonic beverage marketed by STW, particularly since STW, as the senior user, has no obligation to label its product in such a way as to avoid confusion with Quaker's product. As for the second argument, it is precisely the strong association between Gatorade and "Thirst Aid" created by Quaker's ads that is likely to create confusion in this case. Under the circumstances, the linking of the plaintiffs' mark with the defendant's brand name is an aggravation, not a justification.

Quaker also argues that the district court erred in finding similarity of products and distribution chains because it relied on the Pet product. Again, this claim is foreclosed by our conclusion that the district court's reliance was appropriate.

Quaker next contends that the district court's finding that there was "no evidence of actual confusion by any customers" precludes any likelihood of confusion. As we have stated many times, however, the plaintiff need not show actual confusion in order to establish likelihood of confusion. The Weilbacher slogan study, which showed a strong association between Gatorade and "Thirst Aid" on the part of consumers, tends to show that consumers faced with an isotonic beverage marketed under the name "Thirst Aid" would be likely to think it was produced either by the manufacturer of Gatorade or by another manufacturer who was trading off Gatorade's good will.

Further, we think that the district court erred in rejecting STW's evidence of another study performed by Weilbacher in which 24 percent of customers who were shown the label from the Pet test product stated that they thought the product was produced by Gatorade. This is precisely the sort of study that this court has held to be the correct methodology for assessing consumer confusion. *James Burrough*, 540 F.2d at 278–79. The district court, however, refused to rely on the study because it did not expose the consumer to a product which he or she would find in the current marketplace. Given the court's use of the Pet product in assessing other factors and our view that the Pet product fairly represents the isotonic beverage STW would like to market but for Quaker's "Thirst Aid" campaign, we think that the district court erred in finding this evidence not probative of confusion. The Weilbacher label study clearly demonstrates that consumers would be likely to confuse an isotonic beverage marketed under the name "Thirst Aid" with Gatorade unless the producer of the new beverage made some special effort to distinguish its product. As we have noted, however, the senior user of the mark has no duty to take such measures.

Finally, Quaker contends that the district court erred in considering Quaker's intent in analyzing likelihood of confusion. We agree. Even in a traditional case of forward confusion the defendant's intent is relevant to the issue of likelihood of confusion only if he intended "to palm off his products as those of another," thereby profiting from confusion. In a reverse confusion case, of course, the defendant by definition is not palming off or otherwise attempting to create confusion as to the source of his product. Thus, the "intent" factor of the likelihood of confusion analysis is essentially relevant in a reverse confusion case. As the district court noted, however, "[a] finding of fraudulent intent or bad faith is not essential to prove infringement where likelihood of confusion already exists." *Sands, Taylor & Wood*, 18 U.S.P.Q.2D (BNA) at 1471. The district court's analysis of the other factors is sufficient to support its finding that there was a likelihood of confusion and, therefore, infringement.

V.

The district court awarded STW ten percent of Quaker's profits on sales of Gatorade for the period during which the "Thirst Aid" campaign ran—$24,730,000—based on its finding that Quaker had acted in bad faith. The court also ordered Quaker to pay STW's attorney's fees, again based on the finding of bad faith, as well as prejudgment interest on the award of profits beginning from May 12, 1984. Quaker challenges all three of these rulings.

A.   Profits

Quaker argues that an award of its profits was inappropriate here because there was no evidence that Quaker intended to trade on STW's good will or reputation; indeed, such an intent is necessarily absent in a reverse confusion case. According to Quaker, an award of the defendant's profits is justified only where the defendant has been unjustly enriched by appropriating the plaintiff's good will. There is some support for this position in the case law. "To obtain an accounting of profits, the courts usually require that defendant's infringement infer some connotation of 'intent,' or a knowing act denoting an intent, to infringe or reap the harvest of another's mark and advertising." 2 McCarthy, *supra* § 30:25, at 498. The law of this circuit is not, however, so limited. As we stated in *Roulo*:

> The Lanham Act specifically provides for the awarding of profits in the discretion of the judge subject only to principles of equity. As stated by this Court, "The trial court's primary function is to make violations of the Lanham Act unprofitable to

the infringing party." Other than general equitable considerations, there is no express requirement that the parties be in direct competition or that the infringer willfully infringe the trade dress to justify an award of profits. Profits are awarded under different rationales including unjust enrichment, deterrence, and compensation.

886 F.2d at 941. This broader view seems to be more consistent with the language of the Lanham Act than is the narrower (though perhaps more logical) rule espoused by Quaker. We decline to adopt Quaker's restrictive interpretation in light of Seventh Circuit precedent.

Nevertheless, we are mindful of the fact that awards of profits are to be limited by "equitable considerations." The district court justified the award of profits based on its finding that Quaker acted in bad faith. The evidence of bad faith in this case, however, is pretty slim. The court based its finding on (1) Quaker's "failure to conduct a basic trademark search until days before the airing of the Thirst Aid commercial," and its "anonymous, cursory investigations" of Karp's use of the mark once it obtained such a search; (2) Quaker's decision to continue with the "Thirst Aid" campaign after it discovered Karp's registrations; (3) the fact that Quaker did not seek a formal legal opinion regarding potential trademark issues until after the first "Thirst Aid" commercials were aired; and (4) Quaker's failure to take "reasonable precautions" to avoid the likelihood of confusion. *Sands, Taylor & Wood*, 18 U.S.P.Q.2D (BNA) at 1472–73.

None of these facts is particularly good evidence of bad faith. For example, Quaker's in-house counsel, Lannin, testified at trial that his review of the "Thirst Aid" campaign in February or March of 1984 did not include a trademark search because he concluded that the proposed advertisements used the words "Thirst Aid" descriptively, and not as a trademark, and therefore did not raise any trademark issues. The district court apparently accepted this testimony, but nonetheless found Quaker's failure to investigate indicative of bad faith. Further, the court stated that it is a "close question" whether "Thirst Aid" is a descriptive term. Indeed, this court has found that the district court erred in concluding that "Thirst Aid" was not descriptive as a matter of law. A party who acts in reasonable reliance on the advice of counsel regarding a close question of trademark law generally does not act in bad faith.

Nor does Quaker's decision to proceed with the "Thirst Aid" campaign once it learned of Karp's registrations necessarily show bad faith. Based both on his earlier conclusion that "Thirst Aid" was descriptive and on his investigation into Karp's use of the term, which revealed that Karp was not currently using the THIRST-AID mark on any products sold at retail, Lannin concluded that Quaker's ads did not infringe Karp's rights in its marks. That conclusion was confirmed by the opinion Quaker obtained a few weeks later from its outside counsel, which concluded that Quaker was making a fair use of "Thirst Aid" because " 'THIRST-AID' [sic] is not used as a trademark on the product but rather clearly as a positioning statement or claim in advertising. It is used descriptively to inform the purchaser that the product will aid your thirst, and as a play on the words 'First Aid.' " Mem. *re Use of Term "THIRST-AID" as Advertising Claim for Gatorade* at 7–8 (undated). "The fact that one believes he has a right to adopt a mark already in use because in his view no conflict exists since the products are separate and distinct cannot, by itself, stamp his conduct as in bad faith." *Nalpac, Ltd. v. Corning Glass Works*, 784 F.2d 752, 755 (6th Cir. 1986). Even the defendant's refusal to cease using the mark upon demand is not necessarily indicative of bad faith. Absent more, courts should "not make an inference of bad faith from evidence of conduct that is compatible with a good faith business judgment." *Munters Corp. v. Matsui America, Inc.*, 730 F. Supp. 790, 799–800 (N.D. Ill. 1989), *aff'd*, 909 F.2d 250 (7th Cir. 1990).

Quaker's failure to obtain a formal legal opinion from outside counsel until after the "Thirst Aid" campaign began is similarly weak evidence of bad faith. Given Lannin's sincere, reasonable conclusion that Quaker's ads used "Thirst Aid" descriptively, so that no trademark issue was raised, Quaker had no reason to seek the opinion of outside trademark counsel. Similarly, Quaker had no reason to take any precautions to avoid likelihood of confusion; Quaker's research had revealed that there was no product about which people were likely to be confused.

A determination of bad faith is a finding of fact subject to the clearly erroneous standard of review. We cannot say on this record that the district court's conclusion was clearly erroneous. We do think, however, that the evidence of bad faith here is marginal at best. Further, this is not a case where the senior user's trademark is so well-known that the junior user's choice of a confusingly similar mark, out of the infinite number of marks in the world, itself supports an inference that the junior user acted in bad faith. 2 McCarthy, *supra* § 23:33, at 147. There is no question that Quaker developed the "Thirst Aid" campaign entirely independently, with no knowledge of STW's marks. In such a case, an award of $24 million in profits is not "equitable"; rather, it is a windfall to the plaintiff. Quaker may have been unjustly enriched by using STW's mark without paying for it, but the award of profits bears no relationship to that enrichment. A reasonable royalty, perhaps related in some way to the fee STW was paid by Pet, would more accurately reflect both the extent of Quaker's unjust enrichment and the interest of STW that has been infringed. We therefore reverse the district court's award of profits and remand for a redetermination of damages. A generous approximation of the royalties Quaker would have had to pay STW for the use of the THIRST-AID mark had it recognized the validity of STW's claims seems to us an appropriate measure of damages, although perhaps not the only one. In any event, we can conceive of no rational measure of damages that would yield $24 million.

B.   Attorney's Fees

The Lanham Act provides for recovery of attorney's fees by the prevailing party in "exceptional cases." 15 U.S.C. § 1117(a). The district court concluded that this was such an exceptional case based on its finding that Quaker acted in bad faith. Because we affirm that finding, we also affirm the award of attorney's fees. The "equitable considerations" which lead us to reverse the award of profits do not apply to this issue. . . .

VI.

For the foregoing reasons, the decision of the district court is AFFIRMED in part, REVERSED in part and REMANDED for further proceedings.

RIPPLE, CIRCUIT JUDGE, concurring. I join the judgment of the court and all but part V of Judge Cudahy's comprehensive and thoughtful opinion. In my view, Quaker's corporate conduct in this matter deserves a somewhat less charitable appraisal than that presented in part V. Therefore, in assessing damages, I believe the district court, in the exercise of its discretion, might well place substantial emphasis on deterrence. Therefore, I doubt very much that damages measured by a "reasonable royalty" (opinion 29)—a speculative approximation itself— necessarily would suffice in this case. Nevertheless, I agree with Judge Cudahy that the district court's use of a "percentage of profits" benchmark for the award of damages is difficult to sustain. I therefore concur in his conclusion that a more precise determination is appropriate.

FAIRCHILD, SENIOR CIRCUIT JUDGE, dissenting in part. Twenty-four million dollars ($24 million) is, indeed, a big number. It is, however, only 10% of the profit realized by Quaker out of the product it marketed by using STW's mark. We are affirming the finding that Quaker used the mark in bad faith. The real question, it seems to me, is one of causation. What portion of Quaker's profit resulted from its use of THIRST AID, and therefore constituted unjust enrichment? I am unable to say that the district court's estimate of 10% was unreasonable or clearly erroneous. Quaker made no showing that it should have been a different number. The 90% ($216 million) of profit which Quaker retains is no paltry reward for everything it contributed to the success of the venture.

Therefore, I respectfully dissent from the decision to reverse the award.

NOTES FOR DISCUSSION

1. *Remand.* On remand, the district court "reduced" the award to Sands, Taylor, and Woods from the original, twenty-four million dollars, to $26,088,235. This sum consisted of $10,328,411 that the district court found to be a reasonable royalty for Quaker Oats' use of Sands, Taylor, and Woods' mark, which the district court doubled in order "to deter conduct such as defendants," together with $5,431,413 in prejudgment interest. Quaker Oats again appealed the award. On the second appeal, Judge Ripple, writing for the majority, affirmed the reasonable royalty and the award of prejudgment interest, but questioned whether the doubling of the royalty in order to deter the infringement constituted an impermissible penalty. The Seventh Circuit therefore vacated that portion of the award and remanded to the district court "to permit the district court to state with more clarity the reasons for the enhancement." *Sands, Taylor & Wood v. Quaker Oats*, 34 F.3d 1340, 1352–53 (7th Cir. 1994). Judge Fairchild joined Judge Ripple's opinion, but also wrote separately stating that he would have affirmed the award in its entirety. *Id.* at 1353–54.

The author of the original panel opinion, Judge Cudahy, dissented. As he explained:

> My viewpoint on damages is certainly somewhat colored by my role as author of the opinion on liability in this case. This is a thin case, as I think my opinion for the panel makes clear. In fact, a finding of bad faith was made here only with considerable reluctance. The THIRST-AID mark was essentially a shelf item, attached to no good will of an ongoing business. It was a mark looking for a product and a business which might find it of some value.

Id. at 1354.

He would therefore have affirmed the award of the $10 million as a reasonable royalty. Indeed, he characterized the award as "a most generous calculation, and . . . beyond the wildest dreams of STW. . . ." *Id.* However, he believed that there was no basis in the record for doubling the award and would therefore have preferred to reverse the district court on that issue rather than vacate and remand. *Id.*

On the second remand, the district court reinstated its enhancement. In response to Judge Ripple's request for further clarification of the reasons for the enhancement, the district court wrote *inter alia*: "The enhancement is not a penalty. It reflects the inadequacy of the base royalty award in light of the 'circumstances of the case,' the extraordinary profits defendant realized as a consequence of its deliberate infringement." Quaker Oats did not appeal again.

Even from a property-based perspective on trademarks, what justification is there for awarding Sands, Taylor & Woods over twenty million dollars for the infringement of a mark that "was essentially a shelf item"?

2. *The Consumer Interest.* Think again about how consumers are harmed by reverse confusion. Under the reverse confusion scenario, the risk is that a consumer will buy the product of the senior, but less well-known user, believing that he or she is buying the product of the junior, but more well-known user, and be disappointed. In other words, a consumer purchases a tire from Big O, or a drink from Sands, Taylor & Woods, and expecting a product from Goodyear or Quaker Oats, is disappointed with the quality of the plaintiff's products. How exactly does awarding Big O or Sands, Taylor & Woods millions of dollars remedy this harm? Aren't the plaintiffs profiting from the confusion directly?

You can argue that the award may deter similarly situated potential defendants in the future and thereby eliminate the risk of confusion before it ever begins. Yet, compare the willingness of courts to award very large sums in reverse confusion cases to their general reluctance to award damages in more traditional, forward confusion cases. Wouldn't a very large award in a forward confusion case similarly deter infringements and thereby minimize the risk of consumer confusion? Moreover, in forward confusion cases, who profits from the consumer confusion: the plaintiff, as in reverse confusion cases, or the defendant? Shouldn't we therefore be more willing to award very large damages in forward confusion cases if deterrence is our goal?

Why isn't an injunction sufficient deterrence in these cases? Won't the threatened loss of its entire advertising investment be sufficient to encourage Goodyear and Quaker Oats to be more careful? How would you measure the monetary loss to Goodyear or Quaker Oats from the injunctions in these cases? How much additional loss do the damage awards impose? Which provides the more substantial deterrence?

3. *Capping a Reverse Confusion Plaintiff's Recovery.* If your car is damaged in an accident, and the cost of repairing it exceeds its pre-accident market value, will your insurance company pay you the cost of repair or the market value? As a general rule, insurance companies in such a situation "total" the car and pay its pre-accident market value. Should we adopt a similar rule in the reverse confusion cases and cap a plaintiff's recovery at the pre-infringement market value of its trademark? Or would such a cap amount to an inappropriate forced sale of the trademark?

Just two months after the *Sands, Taylor & Woods* decision, the Seventh Circuit suggested such a rule in *Zazu Hair Designs*, which we considered in Chapter 2:

> Any compensatory award depends on loss, and in treating the need for advertising as a "loss" the court overlooked the principle that a trademark cannot be worth less than zero. "Corrective advertising" is a method of repair. Defendant diminishes the value of plaintiff's trademark, and advertising restores that mark to its original value. . . . Expenses for repair cannot be justified when they exceed the value of the asset. If a car worth $4,000 is crushed in a

collision and repair would cost $10,000, the court awards damages of $4,000, not $10,000. . . .

To justify damages to pay for corrective advertising a plaintiff must show that the confusion caused by the defendant's mark injured the plaintiff and that "repair" of the old trademark, rather than adoption of a new one, is the least expensive way to proceed.

Zazu Designs v. L'Oreal, S.A., 979 F.2d 499, 506 (7th Cir. 1992) (Easterbrook, J.).

Alternatively, could we cap the monetary award only in cases where the defendant had a good faith and reasonable belief that it was not infringing? Did Goodyear or Quaker Oats have such a belief?

D. COUNTERFEIT GOODS

In addition to the civil remedies available, Congress in 1984 enacted the Trademark Counterfeiting Act and made trademark counterfeiting a federal crime. Under the Act, a person who "intentionally traffics . . . in goods or services and knowingly uses a counterfeit mark on or in connection with such goods or services . . . , the use of which is likely to cause confusion . . . shall be fined not more than $2,000,000 or imprisoned not more than 10 years. . . ." 18 U.S.C. § 2320 (2015). The following case examines the reach of the Act's criminal liability.

UNITED STATES V. TORKINGTON
812 F.2d 1347 (11th Cir. 1987)

KRAVITCH, CIRCUIT JUDGE

The definition of the term "counterfeit mark" under section 2320(d)(1)(A) of the Trademark Counterfeiting Act of 1984 (the Act), 15 U.S.C. §§ 1116–1118, 18 U.S.C. § 2320, is at issue in this case of first impression. The district court held that a mark is not "counterfeit" under section 2320(d)(1)(A) unless the use of the mark in connection with the goods in question would be likely to cause direct purchasers to be confused, mistaken or deceived. The court found that, given the enormous price differential between the allegedly counterfeit goods and the authentic goods, it was unlikely, as a matter of law, that direct purchasers would be confused, mistaken or deceived. The court therefore dismissed the indictment.

We find that the district court's ruling that section 2320(d)(1)(A) requires a showing that direct purchasers would be likely to be confused, mistaken or deceived is not supported by either the language or the legislative history of the section. Accordingly, we hold that section 2320(d)(1)(A) does not require a showing that direct purchasers would be confused, mistaken or deceived; rather, the section is satisfied where it is shown that members of the purchasing public would be likely to be confused, mistaken or deceived. Moreover, we find that this likely confusion test includes the likelihood of confusion in a post-sale context.

I. BACKGROUND

On June 2, 1985, Edward Little, a private investigator with Rolex Watch U.S.A., Inc., visited a booth operated by appellee John Torkington at the Thunderbird Swap Shop Indoor Flea Market in Fort Lauderdale, Florida. Little noticed a salesman at the booth showing customers two watches bearing both the name "Rolex" and the Rolex crown trademark emblem. The watches were virtually indistinguishable from authentic Rolex watches. These allegedly counterfeit Rolex watches had been kept under the counter; there were no such watches on display.

Little asked to see those watches as well as other models of replica Rolex watches. The salesman showed him several. The salesman said that the watches were $27 each. Little asked the salesman whether the watches were guaranteed. The salesman responded that they were not guaranteed but said that Little could return any watch that broke to the booth and the salesman would fix it. Little purchased a watch. The salesman handed it to him in a pouch bearing the Rolex crown mark. It is undisputed that Little knew that he had purchased a replica Rolex watch and not an authentic one.

On June 23, 1985, a deputy marshal executed a search and seizure order on Torkington's booth at the Thunderbird Flea Market. He seized 742 replica Rolex watches bearing both the Rolex name and crown trademarks.

On October 3, 1985, a federal grand jury in the Southern District of Florida charged Torkington with two counts of trafficking and attempting to traffic in counterfeit Rolex watches, in violation of 18 U.S.C. § 2320(a). Count I of the indictment is based on the June 2, 1985 sale of the watch to Little. Count II is based on the 742 replica Rolex watches that were seized from Torkington's booth on June 23, 1985.

Torkington filed two motions to dismiss the indictment pursuant to Fed.R.Crim.P. 12(b). Following hearings on the matter, the court issued an order on February 10, 1986 dismissing both counts of the indictment on the ground that the replica Rolex watches were not "counterfeit" under section 2320(d)(1)(A). The United States appealed.

II. DEFINITION OF "COUNTERFEIT MARK"

The district court concluded that the replica Rolex watches in question were not "counterfeit" under section 2320(d)(1)(A)(iii) because it determined that the section is not satisfied unless the use of the mark would be likely to cause direct purchasers of the allegedly counterfeit goods to be confused, mistaken or deceived. The court concluded that the government could not prove a section 2320 violation in the instant case because "it [is] unlikely ... that the purchaser of a replica or fake Rolex watch that sold for $27.00 would be confused, mistaken or deceived into thinking that he was purchasing a genuine Rolex watch, which may sell for approximately $1,000 to $8,000." The court also ruled that the likely confusion of members of the public who encounter the allegedly counterfeit watches in a post-sale context is irrelevant to the section 2320(d)(1)(A)(iii) inquiry. We disagree with both of these conclusions.

Section 2320 of the Trademark Counterfeiting Act was enacted in order to increase the sanctions for the counterfeiting of certain registered trademarks above the purely civil remedies available under the Trademark Act of 1946, 15 U.S.C. § 1051 *et seq.* [hereinafter the Lanham Act]. *Report of the Committee on the Judiciary*, H.R.Rep. No. 997, 98th Cong., 2d Sess. 1, 4 (1984) [hereinafter H.R.Rep. No. 997]; *Report of the Senate Committee on the Judiciary*, S.Rep. No. 526, 98th Cong., 2d Sess. 1, *reprinted in*, 1984 U.S. Code Cong. & Admin.News 3182, 3627 [hereinafter S.Rep. No. 526].

Section 2320 is narrower in scope than is the Lanham Act, however. In particular, its sanctions are available only where the defendant "knowingly uses a counterfeit mark on or in connection with" the goods or services in question. 18 U.S.C. § 2320(a).

The section defines "counterfeit mark" as:

(A) a spurious mark—

(i) that is used in connection with trafficking in goods or services;

(ii) that is identical with, or substantially indistinguishable from, a mark registered for those goods or services on the principal register in the United States Patent and Trademark Office and in use, whether or not the defendant knew such mark was so registered; and

(iii) the use of which is likely to cause confusion, to cause mistake, or to deceive;

18 U.S.C. § 2320(d)(1)(A) (emphasis added).

A. *Confusion of the Purchasing Public*

The "likely to cause confusion, to cause mistake, or to deceive" test of section 2320(d)(1)(A)(iii) is broadly worded. Nothing in the plain meaning of the section restricts its scope to the use of marks that would be likely to cause direct purchasers of the goods to be confused, mistaken or deceived.

The legislative history indicates that Congress intentionally omitted such limiting language. Congress easily could have inserted language restricting the scope of section 2320(d)(1)(A)(iii) to cases where it is likely that direct purchasers would be confused, mistaken or deceived. Congress in fact had used such limiting language in a similar context in the original version of section 1114(1) of the Lanham Act. *Syntex Laboratories, Inc. v. Norwich Pharmacal Co.*, 437 F.2d 566, 568 (2d Cir. 1971); *Rolls-Royce Motors Ltd. v. A & A Fiberglass, Inc.*, 428 F. Supp. 689, 694 n. 10 (N.D.Ga.1977). Congress therefore had before it language it could have used to restrict section 2320(d)(1)(A)(iii) to situations where direct purchasers would be likely to be confused, mistaken, or deceived. Congress chose not to use either this or similar limiting language and we will not construe section 2320(d)(1)(A)(iii) in a way that adds a restriction that Congress chose not to include.

Moreover, not only did Congress omit the limiting language of the original version of section 1114(1) from section 2320(d)(1)(A)(iii), but it explicitly employed the language of the current version of section 1114(1) of the Lanham Act. H.R.Rep. No. 997, at 12; *Joint Statement on Trademark Counterfeiting Legislation*, Cong. Rec. H12,078 (daily ed. Oct. 10, 1984) [hereinafter *Joint Statement*]. In our view, Congress thereby manifested its intent that section 2320(d)(1)(A)(iii) be given the same interpretation as is given the identical language in section 1114(1) of the Lanham Act. *See* H.R.Rep. No. 997, at 8, 12; *Joint Statement*, Cong.Rec. at H12,078; *see also United States v. Gonzalez*, 630 F. Supp. 894, 896 (S.D.Fla.1986).

It is clear from the legislative history that Congress intentionally employed the language of § 1114(1) when it drafted § 2320(d)(1)(A)(iii). *Report of the Committee on the Judiciary*, H.R.Rep. No. 997, 98th Cong., 2d Sess. 12 (1984) [hereinafter H.R.Rep. No. 997]; *Joint Statement on Trademark Counterfeiting Legislation*, Cong.Rec. at H12,078 (daily ed. Oct. 10, 1984) [hereinafter *Joint Statement*]. Congress employed the identical language in order "to ensure that no conduct will be criminalized by this act that does not constitute trademark infringement under the Lanham Act." *Joint Statement*, Cong.Rec. at H12,078. In particular, Congress used this language to limit the scope of the criminal act to marks in commercial use, H.R.Rep. No. 997, at 12, a limitation that is explicit in the Lanham Act, 15 U.S.C. §§ 1114(1), 1125(a), but is not explicit in § 2320(d)(1)(A).

The legislative history does not suggest that Congress intended for § 2320(d)(1)(A)(iii) to serve a purpose other than that of linking the test for a criminal trademark violation to the test used in the civil context. There certainly is no indication that Congress intended for the § 2320(d)(1)(A)(iii) test to be more restrictive than is the test under the Lanham Act. As Congress observed in the *Joint Statement, supra*:

> Proposed subsection 18 U.S.C. § 2320(d)(1)(A)(iii) states that 'counterfeit mark' must be one the use of which is likely 'to cause confusion, to cause mistake, or to deceive.' This is the key phrase

in the remedial section of the Lanham Act, 15 U.S.C. § 1114, and
its inclusion here is intended to ensure that no conduct will be
criminalized by this act that does not constitute trademark
infringement under the Lanham Act. *As a practical matter,
however, this element should be easily satisfied if the other
elements of a 'counterfeit mark' have been proven—since a
counterfeit mark is the most egregious example of a mark that 'is
likely to cause confusion'.*

Cong.Rec. at H12,078 (emphasis added).

The current version of section 1114(1) of the Lanham Act differs from
the original version in that it does not contain the likely to confuse direct
purchasers requirement of the original section. Courts interpreting the
current version of section 1114(1) have held that the section does not
require a showing that direct purchasers would be likely to be confused,
mistaken or deceived. Instead, they construe section 1114(1) to require
simply the likely confusion of the purchasing public—a term that includes
individuals who are potential purchasers of the trademark holders goods
as well as those who are potential direct purchasers of the allegedly
counterfeit goods. *Levi Strauss v. Blue Bell, Inc.*, 632 F.2d 817, 822 (9th
Cir. 1980); *AMP Inc. v. Foy*, 540 F.2d 1181, 1183 (4th Cir. 1976); *Rolex
Watch U.S.A. v. Canner*, 645 F. Supp. 484, 492 (S.D.Fla.1986); *Rolls-
Royce Motors*, 428 F. Supp. at 695–96 & n.10; *see Boston Professional
Hockey Ass'n v. Dallas Cap & Emblem Mfg., Inc.*, 510 F.2d 1004, 1012
(5th Cir.), *cert. denied*, 423 U.S. 868 (1975); *Syntex Laboratories*, 437 F.2d
at 568; *see also John H. Harland Co. v. Clarke Checks, Inc.*, 711 F.2d 966,
972 (11th Cir. 1983) (the test is whether there is a likelihood of confusion
between the registered mark and the allegedly infringing mark).

Given our conclusion that section 2320(d)(1)(A)(iii) should be
interpreted similarly to the identical language in section 1114(1), we hold
that section 2320(d)(1)(A)(iii) also is satisfied when the use of the mark in
connection with the goods or services in question would be likely to
confuse the purchasing public. *See United States v. Infurnari*, 647 F.
Supp. 57, 59–60 (W.D.N.Y.1986); *Gonzalez*, 630 F. Supp. at 896.

B. *Post-Sale Context*

In its order the district court also concluded that the likelihood of
post-sale confusion is irrelevant to the section 2320(d)(1)(A)(iii) inquiry.
We disagree.

Under section 1114(1) of the Lanham Act, the likely to confuse test is
satisfied when potential purchasers of the trademark holder's products
would be likely to be confused should they encounter the allegedly
counterfeit goods in a post-sale context—for example, in a direct
purchaser's possession. *Lois Sportswear, U.S.A., Inc. v. Levi Strauss &
Co.*, 799 F.2d 867, 871, 872–73 (2d Cir. 1986); *Blue Bell*, 632 F.2d at 822;

Rolex Watch, 645 F. Supp. at 488, 493–95; *Rolls-Royce Motors*, 428 F. Supp. at 694; *see Syntex Laboratories*, 437 F.2d at 568 (likelihood of confusion need not be that of purchasers, any kind of likelihood of confusion is sufficient); *see also Boston Professional Hockey Ass'n*, 510 F.2d at 1012 (the likely to confuse standard is met where defendant duplicated and sold protected trademarks to the public knowing the public would identify them as those of the trademark holder). Consequently we conclude that the likely to confuse test of section 2320(d)(1)(A)(iii) also is satisfied by a showing that it is likely that members of the public would be confused, mistaken or deceived should they encounter the allegedly counterfeit goods in a post-sale context. *See Infurnari*, 647 F. Supp. at 59–60; *Gonzalez*, 630 F. Supp. at 896.

This conclusion is supported by the policy goals of the Trademark Counterfeiting Act. Like the Lanham Act, the Trademark Counterfeiting Act is not simply an anti-consumer fraud statute. *See Infurnari*, 647 F. Supp. at 59–60; *Gonzalez*, 630 F. Supp. 894. Rather, a central policy goal of the Act is to protect trademark holders' ability to use their marks to identify themselves to their customers and to link that identity to their reputations for quality goods and services. S.Rep. No. 526, at 1–2, 4–5, 1984 U.S. Code Cong. & Admin.News, at 3627–28, 3630–31; H.R.Rep. No. 997, at 5–6; *See Infurnari*, 647 F. Supp. at 59–60; *Gonzalez*, 630 F. Supp. at 896; *See also Lois Sportswear*, 799 F.2d at 872 (same conclusion with respect to the Lanham Act), *E. Remy Martin & Co. v. Shaw-Ross International Imports, Inc.*, 756 F.2d 1525, 1530 (11th Cir. 1985) (same); *Rolex Watch*, 645 F. Supp. at 488 (same).

It is essential to the Act's ability to serve this goal that the likely to confuse standard be interpreted to include post-sale confusion. A trademark holder's ability to use its mark to symbolize its reputation is harmed when potential purchasers of its goods see unauthentic goods and identify these goods with the trademark holder. H.R.Rep. No. 997, at 5–6; *See Lois Sportswear*, 799 F.2d at 872–73; *Remy Martin*, 756 F.2d at 1530; *Grotrian, Helfferich, Schulz, Th. Steinweg Nachf. v. Steinway & Sons*, 523 F.2d 1331, 1342 (2d Cir. 1975). This harm to trademark holders is no less serious when potential purchasers encounter these counterfeit goods in a post-sale context. *See Lois Sportswear*, 799 F.2d at 872–73; *Steinway*, 523 F.2d at 1342; *Blue Bell*, 632 F.2d at 822; *Rolex Watch*, 645 F. Supp. at 494–95; *Gonzalez*, 630 F. Supp. at 896. Moreover, verbal disclaimers by sellers of counterfeit goods do not prevent this harm.

III. WHETHER DISMISSAL IS APPROPRIATE

Based on the discussion above, we conclude that the district court employed the wrong legal standard when it dismissed the indictment on the ground that the government could not show that it is likely that direct purchasers would be confused, mistaken or deceived. This error does not in and of itself necessitate reversal of the district court, however. Reversal is required in this case because we find that, under the proper legal standard, dismissal of the indictment is improper.

Under Fed.R.Crim.P. 12(b) an indictment may be dismissed where there is an infirmity of law in the prosecution; a court may not dismiss an indictment, however, on a determination of facts that should have been developed at trial. *United States v. Korn*, 557 F.2d 1089, 1090–91 (5th Cir. 1977); *see United States v. Cadillac Overall Supply Co.*, 568 F.2d 1078, 1082 (5th Cir.) (on a motion to dismiss the indictment the district court must not pierce the pleadings or make a premature resolution of the merits of the allegations), *cert. denied*, 437 U.S. 903, 98 S.Ct. 3088, 57 L.Ed.2d 1133 (1978).

On review, this court must reverse a dismissal if it concludes that the factual allegations in the indictment, when viewed in the light most favorable to the government, were sufficient to charge the offense as a matter of law. *See United States v. Mann*, 517 F.2d 259, 266 (5th Cir. 1975), *cert. denied*, 423 U.S. 1087 (1976); *see also Cadillac Overall Supply*, 568 F.2d at 1082 (on a motion to dismiss an indictment the district court must take the allegations to be true).

This circuit has defined seven factors that should be considered when analyzing whether there is a likelihood of confusion between two marks under section 1114(1) of the Lanham Act, *John H. Harland*, 711 F.2d at 972; we now employ these factors here. These factors are: (1) the type of trademark, (2) the similarity of design, (3) the similarity of product, (4) the identity of retail outlets and purchasers, (5) the similarity of advertising media used, (6) defendant's intent and (7) actual confusion. *Id.* at 972; *see Univ. of Georgia Athletic Ass'n v. Laite*, 756 F.2d 1535, 1542 (11th Cir. 1985) (employing the same seven factors in determining likelihood of confusion under section 43(a) of the Lanham Act).

None of these factors, however, is essential to a finding of likely confusion. *See Marathon Mfg. Co. v. Enerlite Prods. Corp.*, 767 F.2d 214, 218 (5th Cir. 1985); *John H. Harland Co.*, 711 F.2d at 973, rather, the likely to confuse determination involves a weighing of the seven factors. This determination therefore is generally a question of fact. *See Marathon Mfg.*, 767 F.2d at 217; *Conagra v. Singleton*, 743 F.2d 1508, 1514 (11th Cir. 1984); *John H. Harland Co.*, 711 F.2d at 973; *Boston Professional Hockey Ass'n*, 510 F.2d at 1012.

Given our conclusions that a likelihood of post-sale confusion satisfies section 2320(d)(1)(A)(iii) and that the determination of whether there is a likelihood of confusion should be based on the above seven factor test, we hold that the district court was incorrect in granting the motion to dismiss the indictment in the instant case. In addition to an indictment that alleges all the elements of the crime, the district court had before it evidence that the allegedly counterfeit watches are externally identical to authentic Rolex watches and bear both the name "Rolex" and the Rolex crown trademark emblem. This evidence that the allegedly counterfeit watches bear Rolex's trademark, are of identical design, and are the same type of product is sufficient to support the allegation that the marks used in connection with the replica Rolex watches are likely to cause the purchasing public to be confused, mistaken or deceived. *See Infurnari*, 647 F. Supp. at 59–60; *Gonzalez*, 630 F. Supp. at 895–96; *see also Rolls-Royce*, 428 F. Supp. at 695 (granting summary judgment in part for plaintiff on similar facts). This evidence therefore is at least sufficient to enable the government to overcome the motion to dismiss the indictment. *See Infurnari*, 647 F. Supp. at 60 (declining to dismiss an indictment based on similar facts); *Gonzalez*, 630 F. Supp. at 896 (same).

We therefore hold that the district court erred in dismissing the indictment because it was incorrect in concluding that the marks are not counterfeit as a matter of law. Accordingly, we REVERSE the dismissal of the indictment and REMAND.

REVERSED and REMANDED.

NOTES FOR DISCUSSION

1. *Counterfeiting and Consumer Welfare.* In a footnote, the court explained that its decision benefitted not only Rolex, but also consumers:

> It also is important to recognize that the enforcement of trademark laws benefits consumers even in cases where there is no possibility that consumers will be defrauded. For, to the extent that trademarks provide a means for the public to distinguish between manufacturers, they also provide incentives for manufacturers to provide quality goods. *See U.S. International Trade Commission's Final Report on Investigation No. 332–158 Under Section 332(b) of the Tariff Act of 1930, The Effects of Foreign Product Counterfeiting on United States Industry*, U.S. Int'l Trade Comm'n Pub. 1479, *reprinted in part in* 82 Pat. & Trademark Rev. 471, 483 (1984). Traffickers of these counterfeit goods, however, attract some customers who would otherwise purchase the authentic goods. Trademark holders' returns to their investments in quality are thereby reduced. This reduction in profits may cause trademark holders to decrease their investments in quality below what they would spend were there no counterfeit goods. This in turn harms those consumers who wish to purchase higher quality goods.

United States v. Torkington, 812 F.2d at 1353 n.6.

Are you persuaded?

2. *Criminal Penalties: A Comparison of Patent, Copyright, and Trademark.* Congress has added criminal penalties for intentional violations of both the Copyright Act and the Trademark Act, but not the Patent Act. Why the difference?

CHAPTER 12

FALSE AND MISLEADING ADVERTISING

■ ■ ■

In addition to prohibiting the use of "any word, term, name, symbol, or device . . . which is likely to cause confusion," 15 U.S.C. § 1125(a)(1)(A) (2015), section 43(a) of the Trademark Act also prohibits:

> [A]ny false or misleading description of fact . . . or false or misleading representation of fact, which . . . in commercial advertising or promotion, misrepresents the nature, characteristics, qualities, or geographic origin of his or her or another person's goods, services, or commercial activities.

15 U.S.C. § 1125(a)(1)(B) (2015).

In this Chapter, we study the scope of this prohibition.

A. "FALSE OR MISLEADING"

AMERICAN HOME PRODUCTS CORP. V. JOHNSON & JOHNSON
577 F.2d 160 (2d Cir. 1978)

OAKS, CIRCUIT JUDGE

Comparative advertising in which the competing product is explicitly named is a relatively new weapon in the Madison Avenue arsenal. These cross-appeals by two of the leading manufacturers of analgesics—pain relief tablets—raise questions regarding the permissible boundaries of this novel approach to consumer persuasion. The parties appeal from an order of the United States District Court for the Southern District of New York, Charles E. Stewart, *Judge*, enjoining the use in television and printed advertising of certain product superiority claims of "Anacin" over "Tylenol." *American Home Products Corp. v. Johnson & Johnson*, 436 F. Supp. 785 (S.D.N.Y. 1977). The order was issued in an action for a declaratory judgment initiated by appellant American Home Products Corp. (AHP), the manufacturer of Anacin, against McNeil Laboratories, Inc., the manufacturer of Tylenol, and its parent corporation, Johnson & Johnson (collectively McNeil), seeking a ruling that the advertising is not false. McNeil counterclaimed, alleging, *inter alia*, that the advertisements were false and misleading under Section 43(a) of the Lanham Act, 15 U.S.C. § 1125(a). The district court found that the advertising violated Section 43(a), and accordingly the judgment enjoined AHP from representing that Anacin provides superior analgesia to Tylenol "in the context of a representation as to any anti-inflammatory property of Anacin. . . ."

AHP argues on appeal that (1) even on the basis of the district court's findings, there is no ground for relief under Section 43(a); (2) the findings are clearly erroneous in concluding that (a) the Anacin advertising claims greater pain relief (Claims One and Two); (b) the disputed claim of superiority in reducing pain from inflammatory conditions (Claim Two) is false; and (c) the anti-inflammatory claim for the conditions listed in the advertising (Claim Three) is unsubstantiated; and (3) the terms of the injunction are too indefinite to comply with Fed. R. Civ. P. 65(d). McNeil appeals from the district court's refusal to enjoin those portions of the Anacin advertising which, McNeil asserts, present misleading claims of Anacin's faster onset of analgesia and harmlessness to the stomach. Since we are of the view that Judge Stewart's order is based upon sound legal principles, that his findings are not clearly erroneous, and that the injunction as framed is proper in scope and specificity, we affirm.

I.   THE FACTS

AHP's product, Anacin, is a compound of aspirin (ASA), its analgesic component, and caffeine. McNeil's product, Tylenol, affords analgesia through the ingredient acetaminophen (APAP). Anacin advertises more heavily than the other leading aspirin brands. It took over the Number One pain reliever spot from another aspirin-based product, Bayer Aspirin, a few years ago. Since the summer of 1976, however, Tylenol has replaced Anacin as the largest selling over-the-counter (OTC) internal analgesic product. Anacin remains the largest selling aspirin-based analgesic.

The lawsuit arose out of two Anacin advertisements initiated shortly after Tylenol became market leader. The first is a thirty-second television commercial initially aired by CBS in late November, 1976, and by NBC in early December, 1976. It commences with the phrase: "Your body knows the difference between these pain relievers . . . and Adult Strength Anacin," and asserts its superiority to Datril, Tylenol and Extra-Strength Tylenol.[3] The second advertisement was introduced in national magazines in late January, 1977. It carries a similar theme, stating that

---

[3]   The "story board" of the television commercial is printed in Judge Stewart's opinion below, 436 F. Supp. 785, 788 (S.D.N.Y. 1977). The script for the commercial reads as follows:

SPOKESMAN: Your body knows the difference between these pain relievers [showing other products] and Adult Strength Anacin. For pain other than headache Anacin reduces the inflammation that often comes with pain. These do not. (SFX: MUTED KETTLE DRUM.) Specifically, inflammation of tooth extraction[,] muscle strain (SFX BUILDS)[,] backache (SFX BUILDS), or if your doctor diagnoses tendonitis[,] neuritis. (SFX FADES.) Anacin reduces that inflammation (SFX OUT) as Anacin relieves pain fast. These do not. Take Adult Strength Anacin.

"Anacin can reduce inflammation that comes with most pain," "Tylenol cannot."[4]

The controversy began when McNeil protested the television commercial to the networks and the magazine advertisement to the print media on the ground that they were deceptive and misleading. McNeil also complained to the National Advertising Division of the Better Business Bureau. These protests were, for the most part, unsuccessful. CBS, NBC and the print media, continued to carry the two advertisements without alteration. As a result of the protests, AHP filed a declaratory judgment action under 28 U.S.C. § 2201 and sought to enjoin McNeil from interfering with the dissemination of the commercial and the printed advertisement. McNeil counterclaimed under Section 43(a) of the Lanham Act, 15 U.S.C. § 1125(a), urging that the following claims contained in AHP's advertisements were false: (A) that Anacin is a superior analgesic to Tylenol, (B) that Anacin is an efficacious anti-inflammatory drug for the conditions listed in the advertisements, (C) that Anacin provides faster relief than Tylenol, and (D) that Anacin does not harm the stomach. It sought declaratory relief and an injunction prohibiting AHP from continuing to make false claims which disparaged Tylenol.

Section 43(a) provides in pertinent part:

> Any person who shall . . . use in connection with any goods . . . any false description or representation, including words or other symbols tending falsely to describe or represent the same, and shall cause such goods . . . to enter into commerce, . . . shall be liable to a civil action . . . by any person who believes that he is or is likely to be damaged by the use of any such false description or representation.

15 U.S.C. § 1125(a).

After denying McNeil's motion for a preliminary injunction, Judge Stewart held an expedited trial on the merits. Principally on the basis of consumer reaction surveys, he concluded that the advertisements made the following representations: (1) the television commercial represented

---

[4]   The print advertisement is reproduced in Judge Stewart's opinion, 436 F. Supp. at 789. It reads in substantial part as follows:

> Anacin can reduce inflammation that comes with most pain. Tylenol cannot.

> With any of these pains, your body knows the difference between the pain reliever in Adult-Strength Anacin and other pain relievers like Tylenol. Anacin can reduce the inflammation that often comes with these pains.

> Tylenol cannot. Even Extra-Strength Tylenol cannot. And Anacin relieves pain fast as it reduces inflammation.

> Get fast relief. Take Adult-Strength Anacin. Millions take Anacin with no stomach upset. Anacin.

"These pains" referred to in the text are depicted as located on the human body by spots and include sinusitis, tooth extraction, neuritis, tendonitis, muscular backache, muscle strain, and sprains.

that "Anacin is a superior analgesic generally, and not only with reference to particular conditions such as those enumerated in the ad [*see* note 3 *supra*] or to Anacin's alleged ability to reduce inflammation," *id.* at 796 (Claim One); (2) the print advertisement claimed that "Anacin is a superior analgesic for certain kinds of pain because Anacin can reduce inflammation," *id.* (Claim Two) and (3) both advertisements represented that Anacin reduces inflammation associated with the conditions specified in the advertisements. *Id.* (Claim Three). The district court then concluded that the preponderance of the evidence indicated that Claims One and Two—that Anacin is a superior analgesic in general to Tylenol and a superior analgesic for conditions which have an inflammatory component—were false. *Id.* at 801–03. The court further held that it could not be determined on the basis of the evidence presented whether OTC dosages of Anacin reduce inflammation to a clinically significant extent in the conditions specified by the advertisements. Thus, Judge Stewart could not reach a definitive conclusion on the truth or falsity of the third claim. *Id.* at 801, 803. Nevertheless, he determined that because the three claims are "integral and inseparable," *id.* at 803, "the advertisements as a whole make false representations for Anacin and falsely disparages [sic] Tylenol in violation of the Lanham Act." *Id.* at 803. Accordingly, he held that McNeil was entitled to an injunction against AHP, given the "substantial evidence that consumers have been and will continue to be deceived as to the relative efficacy of the two products and that this deception is injuring, and will continue to injure, Tylenol's reputation among consumers." *Id.* The injunction prohibits AHP from publishing or inducing television, radio or print media to publish

> any advertisement or promotional material which contains, in the context of a representation as to any anti-inflammatory property of ANACIN or aspirin sold by AHP, any representation that at over-the-counter levels ANACIN or aspirin provides superior analgesia to acetaminophen including TYLENOL either (1) generally, or (2) for conditions which are associated with inflammation or have inflammatory components, or (3) because ANACIN or aspirin reduces inflammation. . . .

II. THE PRINCIPAL APPEAL

A. *Whether Relief May be Afforded under Section 43(a) on the Basis of the District Court's Findings.*

AHP's first contention is based on the following premises. The advertisements contain no express claim for greater analgesia; they merely assert Anacin's superiority to Tylenol in reducing inflammation, a claim which the district court found not to be false. AHP further assumes that the anti-inflammatory claim was held to be true and is in fact unambiguous. The argument is that a truthful and unambiguous product claim cannot be barred under Section 43(a) even though consumers mistakenly perceive a different and incorrect meaning. Thus, appellants urge, the court erred in finding a violation of Section 43(a) by not relying on express claims of superior pain relief, but by interpreting consumer reaction tests—one of which, incidentally, was introduced by AHP and the other of which was not objected to by AHP—as indicating that consumers derive a message of greater pain relief from the explicit "truthful" claim.

Whatever abstract validity AHP's argument may have, an issue we need not decide, it is clear that in this case the language of the advertisements is not unambiguous. The "truthfulness" of the claims, therefore, cannot be established until the ambiguity is resolved. Moreover, Judge Stewart expressly refused to characterize the anti-inflammatory claims as truthful.[10] But even assuming the literal truthfulness of the anti-inflammatory claims, appellant's position is no stronger because of the ambiguity of the total message which, as the district court found, conveys additional claims (Claims One and Two).[11]

That Section 43(a) of the Lanham Act encompasses more than literal falsehoods cannot be questioned. *American Brands, Inc. v. R. J. Reynolds Tobacco Co.*, 413 F. Supp. 1352, 1357 (S.D.N.Y. 1976); 1 R. Callmann, *The Law of Unfair Competition, Trademarks and Monopolies* §§ 19.1(a), at 631; 19.1(e), at 644; 19.2(a)(1), at 656; 19.2(b)(1), at 665–67 (3d ed. 1967); *cf. FTC v. Sterling Drug, Inc.*, 317 F.2d 669, 674–75 (2d Cir. 1963) (Federal Trade Commission suit). Were it otherwise, clever use of innuendo, indirect intimations, and ambiguous suggestions could shield the advertisement from scrutiny precisely when protection against such sophisticated deception is most needed. It is equally well established that the truth or falsity of the advertisement usually should be tested by the

---

[10] The flaw in appellant's logic is its conclusion of truthfulness from the district court's candid recognition that it could not determine whether the anti-inflammatory claim was true or false. Judge Stewart did not find this claim truthful:

> Accordingly, we find that there is no reliable evidence showing that ASA reduces inflammation to a clinically significant extent in the conditions listed in the advertisements at OTC dosages. On the other hand, we think that McNeil has not proved by a preponderance of the evidence that this claim is, or tends to be, false.

436 F. Supp. at 801.

[11] Appellants apparently solely refer to the claims of superior anti-inflammatory effect as the "truthful and unambiguous product claim." We have already pointed out, note 10 *supra*, the fallacy of interpreting the district court's finding of unsubstantiation as a finding of truthfulness. Additionally, appellants err in their failure to recognize that the advertisement must be viewed in its entirety. As stated by Judge Kaufman in *FTC v. Sterling Drug, Inc.*, 317 F.2d 669, 674 (2d Cir. 1963):

> It is therefore necessary ... to consider the advertisement in its entirety and not to engage in disputatious dissection. The entire mosaic should be viewed rather than each tile separately. "The buying public does not ordinarily carefully study or weigh each word in an advertisement. The ultimate impression upon the mind of the reader arises from the sum total of not only what is said but also of all that is reasonably implied." *Aronberg v. Federal Trade Commission*, 132 F.2d 165, 167 (7th Cir. 1942).

By paraphrasing the language of the advertisements simply to state that Anacin reduces inflammation while Tylenol cannot, they overlook the obvious ambiguous nature of the advertisements.

reactions of the public. 1 R. Callmann, *The Law of Unfair Competition, Trademarks and Monopolies, supra,* §§ 18.2(b), at 623; 19.2(a), at 655; 19.2(a)(1), at 656; 19.2(b)(1), at 665–69. Judge Lasker astutely articulated these legal principles in *American Brands, Inc. v. R. J. Reynolds Co., supra,* 413 F. Supp. at 1356–57 (emphasis added), a false advertising case involving ambiguous claims:

> Deceptive advertising or merchandising statements may be judged in various ways. If a statement is actually false, relief can be granted on the court's own findings without reference to the reaction of the buyer or consumer of the product. . . .

> The subject matter here is different. We are dealing not with statements which are literally or grammatically untrue. . . . Rather, we are asked to determine whether a statement acknowledged to be *literally true and grammatically correct nevertheless has a tendency to mislead, confuse or deceive.* As to such a proposition "the public's reaction to [the] advertisement will be the starting point in any discussion of the likelihood of deception. . . . If an advertisement is designed to impress . . . customers, . . . the reaction of [that] groups [*sic*] will be determinative." 1 Callmann: Unfair Competition, Trademarks & Monopolies at 19.2(a)(1) (3rd ed. 1967). A court may, of course, construe and parse the language of the advertisement. It may have personal reactions as to the defensibility or indefensibility of the deliberately manipulated words. It may conclude that the language is far from candid and would never pass muster under tests otherwise applied—for example, the Securities Acts' injunction that "thou shalt disclose"; but the court's reaction is at best not determinative and at worst irrelevant. *The question in such cases is—what does the person to whom the advertisement is addressed find to be the message?*

Applying these principles to the facts of this case, we are convinced that the district court's use of consumer response data was proper. We believe that the claims of both the television commercial and the print advertisement are ambiguous. This obscurity is produced by several references to "pain" and body sensation accompanying the assertions that Anacin reduces inflammation. A reader of or listener to these advertisements could reasonably infer that Anacin is superior to Tylenol in reducing pain generally (Claim One) and in reducing certain kinds of pain (Claim Two). Given this rather obvious ambiguity, Judge Stewart was warranted in examining, and may have been compelled to examine, consumer data to determine first the messages conveyed in order to determine ultimately the truth or falsity of the messages.

It was also proper to construe Section 43(a) to prohibit the representations, assuming for the moment the correctness of Judge

Stewart's findings on consumer reaction, *see* Part II, B, 1, *infra*, and on falsity. *See* Part II, B, 2, *infra*. Contrary to appellant's contentions, Judge Stewart did not use Section 43(a) to prohibit truthful representations mistakenly construed by consumers. *See* notes 10–11 *supra*. We have here deliberate ambiguity and unsubstantiated anti-inflammatory claims determined by the district court to be understood by the public as proclaiming superior analgesic results. Given the audience reaction to the advertisements, as found by the district court, the statute's proscription of "words or other symbols tending falsely to describe or represent [the goods]" was violated.

B.   *Whether the Findings Are Supported by the Evidence.*

1.   *The findings that the advertising makes claims of greater pain relief generally and for specific conditions.*

AHP argues that even if Judge Stewart was correct in evaluating consumer perceptions, he arrived at the conclusion that the advertisements claim greater pain relief (Claims One and Two) by misinterpreting the consumer reaction data and erroneously affording no weight to the testimony of market research experts concerning the messages conveyed by the advertising. Initially, we note that the district court did take into account the expert testimony offered by both sides on the meaning of the advertisements. Recognizing that in some circumstances such testimony should be given substantial weight, Judge Stewart refrained from doing so here largely because it was neither reliable nor helpful to an understanding of the test data which it purported to interpret. The testimony, however, was used to corroborate the surveys.

The test data itself has some inherent weaknesses. However, it was in the district court's province as trier of fact to weigh the evidence, and in particular the opinion research. *See Grotrian, Helfferich, Schulz, Th. Steinweg Nachf. v. Steinway & Sons*, 523 F.2d 1331, 1341 (2d Cir. 1975) (trademark infringement case). Additionally, the district court's findings, based not only on its analysis of the surveys but also on the corroborating testimony of the market research experts, are entitled to the usual clearly erroneous standard of review under Fed. R. Civ. P. 52(a). *See, e.g., Grotrian, Helfferich, Schulz, Th. Steinweg Nachf. v. Steinway & Sons, supra*, 523 F.2d at 1339 n.16. And our review of the record reveals that the findings on consumer interpretation of the advertising are not erroneous.

The analysis of its test data by ASI Market Research, Inc. (ASI) which was made for and at the request of AHP and was heavily relied on by Judge Stewart, completely supports his finding that the television commercial made a superiority claim which was not limited to pain associated with inflammation. It states that the commercial produced a reasonable level of "competitive superiority" type of recall. It is fairly clear from the qualitative group discussions that the side by side comparison to other named brands was being translated into a general "better than" rather than a specific "better for inflammation."

It also reveals: "Heavy symptom-relief response was occurring, predominantly in the area of relief of 'pain.' Relief of headaches was secondary, somewhat more visible for 'Muscle' [another commercial] than for [this commercial]." Translated from survey jargon, the ASI survey concludes that the "Your Body Knows" television commercial produced a recollection in the selected audience of 250 members that Anacin is a superior pain reliever generally, even though the advertisement may have been phrased in terms of comparing inflammation relief.

AHP's advertising executives may, indeed, have intended to communicate that Anacin is better for relieving pain. They noted that 74% of the specifically selected audience thought of the commercial in terms of pain relief, while none thought of inflammation as such unless attention was directed specifically to inflammation. Nevertheless, they pointed out that because the references to inflammation triggered pain association, it was not necessary that inflammation relief be recalled.

What the ASI test shows, then, is the powerful "subliminal" influence of modern advertisements. *See generally* M. McLuhan & Q. Fiore, *The Medium Is the Massage* (1967). The survey reveals that the word "inflammation" triggers pain association, and pain association is what both advertisements are all about. The district court properly relied on these conclusions in finding that the commercial claimed general analgesic superiority. . . .

We conclude, therefore, that the judge correctly held, principally on the basis of consumer reaction tests, that both advertisements claim greater pain relief. On the assumption that this claim is false, *see* Part II, B, 2, *infra*, as the district court held, it was perfectly proper for the trial court to enjoin future advertisements containing superior analgesic claims.

2.   *The findings of falsity and inconclusiveness.*

Appellant apparently does not attack the district court's finding that Claim One (Anacin is a superior pain reliever in general to Tylenol, *see ante* slip op. at 2880–81) is false. It does dispute the findings on Claims Two and Three. *See id.* It first argues: "Even assuming that AHP's advertising claims greater pain relief for inflammatory conditions [Claim Two, we believe], the advertising is truthful. . . ." Brief for Appellant at 17; *see id.* at 46. Second, appellant asserts: "The District Court found that . . . the anti-inflammatory claim for the conditions listed in AHP's advertising [Claim Three] is not false. However, the District Court erred in failing to find expressly that Anacin does reduce inflammation for the listed conditions." *Id*. at 45.

We conclude that Judge Stewart's determination that ASA and APAP are equipotent as pain relievers for inflammatory conditions is not clearly erroneous. It was based on his careful consideration of medical studies, medical literature and expert testimony. The studies, which we have also examined, reveal that with one exception—in the case of rheumatoid arthritis—there is little to indicate that in OTC dosages ASA is more effective in reducing pain from inflammatory conditions than APAP.

Judge Stewart found the second study, nearly 20 years old, to be methodologically unsound in comparison to the numerous other scientific reports introduced. Additionally, the study does not seem very helpful in resolving the issues below because it measured pain relief by noting differences in grip strength and joint stiffness. We have difficulty, therefore, understanding whether and when its conclusions are directed to pain relief (relevant to Claim Two) or to inflammation relief (relevant to Claim Three).

The district court recognized that the medical experts' testimony as well as the scientifically unsupported opinions of certain members of the medical community were more conflicting. Judge Stewart was unwilling to give much weight to AHP's experts, who hypothesized that Anacin reduces pain associated with inflammation better than Tylenol, because much of this evidence admittedly consisted of mere speculation. In sum, Judge Stewart found most of the studies on the comparative analgesic effectiveness of ASA and APAP more reliable and convincing. Given the conflicting testimony of each party's experts and the sound scientific basis underlying the studies, we cannot say that Judge Stewart erred in his evaluation and weighing of the evidence.

We also conclude that on the basis of the evidence introduced at trial, the judge was justified in holding that he could not determine whether Anacin, at OTC dosages, reduces inflammation in the conditions listed in the advertisements. We think it unnecessary to detail the conflicting evidence presented on each of the conditions. For determining the validity of the district court's holding of lack of substantiation, it is sufficient to note that for each condition mentioned in the advertisements there was credible evidence suggesting that Anacin does not reduce inflammation.

There was testimony that aspirin is not used to control *inflammation* following tooth extraction because of its well-documented propensity to increase post-operative hemorrhaging. With respect to neuritis, perhaps an out-moded term, there was evidence that all but two neuropathies are noninflammatory in nature, and that the only two which are inherently inflammatory—leprosy and shingles—are not treated by aspirin. The evidence regarding sinusitis revealed that while aspirin can make the patient more comfortable by reducing fever and relieving headache and muscle ache, it has no effect whatsoever on the underlying sinus infection. There was evidence that aspirin is not used for reduction of inflammation from sprains and strains; indeed it can be counterproductive by prolonging and increasing hemorrhaging at the site of the injury. There was basic disagreement on whether tendonitis, to be distinguished from tenosynovitis, is a degenerative or an inherently inflammatory disease. Thus, it could not be determined whether aspirin at OTC dosages provides any therapeutic effect on tendonitis other than pain relief. Backaches have so many different causes, so many of which are not inherently inflammatory in origin, that the advertising simply cannot be accepted as true.

Moreover, Judge Stewart painstakingly considered the evidence most favorable to appellant's position—studies on aspirin's effectiveness in reducing inflammation from rheumatoid arthritis. However, he concluded that these studies did not sufficiently resolve the question whether at OTC levels Anacin reduces inflammation in the specified conditions, particularly in light of the conflicting medical literature and expert testimony on the subject.

Our discussion of the evidence relied on by the district court is an overall review of the thousands of pages of transcripts and documentary evidence. Nevertheless, we are confident that Judge Stewart's findings, based on his thorough review of the evidence, are not "clearly erroneous."

C.   *Whether the Injunction is Sufficiently Specific.*

AHP argues that the injunctive order, *see ante* slip op. at 2880–81, does not comply with Fed. R. Civ. P. 65(d) which requires specificity in terms and description in reasonable detail of the acts sought to be restrained. In particular, appellant asserts that the injunction as framed effectively bars AHP from discussing Anacin's anti-inflammatory benefits in a comparative advertisement because such claims may also contain an implicit representation of superior analgesia. Apparently, AHP objects to the fact that the injunction is not limited to express claims for superior analgesia.

We think the district court did a commendable job of drafting an order which specifies, as clearly as possible under the circumstances, the acts to be enjoined. Representations as to any anti-inflammatory properties of Anacin are enjoined only to the extent that they contain or imply three clearly described claims of analgesic superiority at OTC levels. In our view, Rule 65(d) is satisfied. More explicit language, if this is possible, will not diminish AHP's asserted difficulty in determining whether proposed advertising conveys a message of superior pain relief. We note, moreover, that the district court has retained jurisdiction to enable the parties "to apply to this court at any time for such other orders and directions as may be necessary or appropriate for the modification, construction or carrying out of [the] judgment." *American Home Products*

Corp. v. Johnson & Johnson, supra, 436 F. Supp. 785. If AHP encounters difficulties under the decree, it can apply to the court for guidance at such time.

III. THE CROSS-APPEAL

The district court rejected McNeil's contentions that the printed advertisement contains claims of Anacin's faster onset of analgesia and harmlessness to the stomach. We have some difficulty with this conclusion because the advertisement suggests to us that Anacin produces analgesia faster than Tylenol and that Anacin is gentle to the stomach. But we agree with Judge Lasker's statement in *American Brands, Inc. v. R. J. Reynolds Tobacco Co., supra,* 413 F. Supp. at 1357, that "the court's reaction [to language of an advertisement] is at best not determinative and at worst irrelevant." A court should turn to consumers' reactions to determine whether the advertising in question makes false representations, *see id.*; 1 R. Callmann, *The Law of Unfair Competition, Trademarks and Monopolies, supra,* §§ 18.2(b), at 623; 19.2(a), at 655; 19.2(a)(1), at 656; 19.2(b)(1), at 665–69, as Judge Stewart did. While the evidence could have supported a contrary result, we cannot hold that his findings of insufficient evidence to sustain either of McNeil's claims are clearly erroneous. The consumer surveys did not sufficiently buttress the contention that the literally true statement of the print advertisement, "millions take Anacin with no stomach upset," produces the message that Anacin causes no harm to the stomach. Only three out of the forty-three women questioned in the G & R survey reported such a claim. This surely was a proper basis for the district court's finding that this number is too small to support, by a preponderance of the evidence, the existence of the representation.

The surveys were contradictory on whether the commercials convey a claim of faster relief. The G & R print advertisement test showed 49% reporting "fast acting." Judge Stewart's review of the verbatims revealed that most of the 49%, about one-third of the test audience, reported a "faster" claim. The ASI data, however, indicated that only 1% of the television viewers reported this message. Judge Stewart rejected the G & R results because he considered the ASI data more reliable, it "so strongly undercut" the G & R data, and the expert testimony supporting the McNeil position simply did not take the ASI study sufficiently into account. 436 F. Supp. at 794–95. We are persuaded by the district court's clearly articulated reasoning that its weighing of the evidence was reasonable.

The judgment is affirmed.

UNITED INDUSTRIES CORP. v. THE CLOROX CO.

140 F.3d 1175 (8th Cir. 1998)

WOLLMAN, CIRCUIT JUDGE

The Clorox Company appeals from the district court's denial of its motion for preliminary injunctive relief brought within the context of its counterclaim against United Industries Corporation for false advertising under section 43(a) of the Lanham Act, 15 U.S.C. § 1125(a). We affirm.

I.

Clorox and United Industries are competing producers of roach bait insecticide products. Clorox manufactures and sells Combat, the top-selling brand of roach bait, while United Industries manufactures and sells the Maxattrax brand of roach bait, a small and relatively new participant in this market. United Industries initiated this action against Clorox, seeking a declaratory judgment that the packaging of its Maxattrax product, which predominantly asserts that it "Kills Roaches in 24 Hours," did not constitute false advertising or unfair competition under the Lanham Act. In response, Clorox moved to dismiss the complaint, contending that no actual case or controversy existed between the two parties regarding the packaging claims. Shortly thereafter, however, Clorox withdrew its motion to dismiss and filed an answer and counterclaim, which subsequently was amended. Clorox's amended counterclaim alleged, primarily, that a Maxattrax television commercial that United Industries had recently released for broadcast constituted false, deceptive, and misleading advertising in violation of section 43(a) of the Lanham Act, 15 U.S.C. § 1125(a)(1)(B).

The commercial at issue, entitled "Side by Side" by the advertising firm that produced it, depicts a split-screen view of two roach bait products on two kitchen countertops. The lighting is dark. On the left, one sees the Maxattrax box; on the right, a generic "Roach Bait" box that is vaguely similar to the packaging of the Combat brand sold by Clorox. An announcer asks the question: "Can you guess which bait kills roaches in 24 hours?" The lights then come up as the camera pans beyond the boxes to reveal a clean, calm, pristine kitchen, uninhabited by roaches, on the Maxattrax side. On the other side, the kitchen is in a chaotic state: cupboards and drawers are opening, items on the counter are turning over, paper towels are spinning off the dispenser, a spice rack is convulsing and losing its spices, all the apparent result of a major roach infestation. At the same time, the message "Based on lab tests" appears in small print at the bottom of the screen. The two roach bait boxes then reappear on the split-screen, and several computer-animated roaches on the "Roach Bait" side appear to kick over the generic box and dance gleefully upon it. The final visual is of the Maxattrax box only, over which the announcer concludes, "To kill roaches in 24 hours, it's hot-shot

Maxattrax. Maxattrax, it's the no-wait roach bait." The final phrase is also displayed in print on the screen. The entire commercial runs fifteen seconds.

Clorox filed a motion for a preliminary injunction against this commercial. After expedited discovery and a two-day hearing, the district court denied the motion.

II.

In deciding a motion for a preliminary injunction, district courts are instructed to consider what have come to be known as the *Dataphase* factors:

(1) The probability of success on the merits;

(2) The threat of irreparable harm to the movant;

(3) The balance between this harm and the injury that granting injunction will inflict on other interested parties; and

(4) Whether the issuance of an injunction is in the public interest.

Sanborn Mfg. Co., Inc. v. Campbell Hausfeld/Scott Fetzer Co., 997 F.2d 484, 485–86 (8th Cir. 1993) (citing *Dataphase Sys., Inc. v. C L Sys., Inc.*, 640 F.2d 109, 114 (8th Cir. 1981) (en banc)); *see also Minnesota Mining and Mfg. Co. v. Rauh Rubber, Inc.*, 130 F.3d 1305, 1307 (8th Cir. 1997).

No single factor in itself is dispositive; rather, each factor must be considered to determine whether the balance of equities weighs toward granting the injunction. *See Sanborn*, 997 F.2d at 486; *Calvin Klein Cosmetics Corp. v. Lenox Labs., Inc.*, 815 F.2d 500, 503 (8th Cir. 1987).

We have noted that by enacting the Lanham Act, Congress apparently intended to encourage competitors to seek injunctions as a method of combating false advertising, and, in such cases that ultimately prove to have merit, injunctive relief is not to be issued reluctantly. *See Black Hills Jewelry Mfg. Co. v. Gold Rush, Inc.*, 633 F.2d 746, 753 n.7 (8th Cir. 1980). With regard to a preliminary injunction, however, the burden on the movant is heavy, in particular where, as here, "granting the preliminary injunction will give [the movant] substantially the relief it would obtain after a trial on the merits." *Sanborn*, 997 F.2d at 486 (quoting *Dakota Indus., Inc. v. Ever Best Ltd.*, 944 F.2d 438, 440 (8th Cir. 1991)). Caution must therefore be exercised in a court's deliberation, and "the essential inquiry in weighing the propriety of issuing a preliminary injunction is whether the balance of other factors tips decidedly toward the movant and the movant has also raised questions so serious and difficult as to call for more deliberate investigation." *General Mills, Inc. v. Kellogg Co.*, 824 F.2d 622, 624–25 (8th Cir. 1987).

A district court has broad discretion when ruling on requests for preliminary injunctions, and we will reverse only for clearly erroneous factual determinations, an error of law, or an abuse of that discretion. *See Sanborn*, 997 F.2d at 486 (citing *Calvin Klein*, 815 F.2d 500 at 503). A district court's finding is "clearly erroneous" when, although evidence may exist to support it, upon review of the entire record we are left with the definite and firm conviction that error has occurred. *See Prufrock Ltd., Inc. v. Lasater*, 781 F.2d 129, 133 (8th Cir. 1986); *Anderson v. City of Bessemer City*, 470 U.S. 564, 573–74 (1985). This deferential standard of review "rests upon the unique opportunity afforded the trial court judge to evaluate the credibility of witnesses and to weigh the evidence." *Inwood Lab., Inc. v. Ives Lab., Inc.*, 456 U.S. 844, 855 (1982).

A.

In our analysis of the *Dataphase* factors, we begin by assessing the probability of Clorox's ultimate success on the merits. At the early stage of a preliminary injunction motion, the speculative nature of this particular inquiry militates against any wooden or mathematical application of the test. *See Calvin Klein*, 815 F.2d at 503. Instead, "a court should flexibly weigh the case's particular circumstances to determine whether the balance of equities so favors the movant that justice requires the court to intervene to preserve the status quo until the merits are determined." *Id.* (quoting *Dataphase*, 640 F.2d at 113). Clorox asserts Lanham Act violations and seeks, primarily, permanent injunctive relief against the alleged false claims contained in the Maxattrax "Side by Side" commercial.

Section 43(a) of the Lanham Act

The Lanham Act was intended, in part, to protect persons engaged in commerce against false advertising and unfair competition. *See Two Pesos, Inc. v. Taco Cabana, Inc.*, 505 U.S. 763, 767–68 (1992) (quoting 15 U.S.C. § 1127); 3 J. Thomas McCarthy, *McCarthy on Trademarks and Unfair Competition* § 27:25 at 27–40 (West Group 1997). In particular, the Act prohibits commercial advertising or promotion that misrepresents the nature, characteristics, qualities, or geographic origin of the advertiser's or another person's goods, services, or commercial activities. *See Rhone-Poulenc Rorer Pharm., Inc. v. Marion Merrell Dow, Inc.*, 93 F.3d 511, 514 (8th Cir. 1996) (citing 15 U.S.C. § 1125(a)(1)(B)); *Sanborn*, 997 F.2d at 486.

To establish a claim under the false or deceptive advertising prong of the Lanham Act, a plaintiff must prove: (1) a false statement of fact by the defendant in a commercial advertisement about its own or another's product; (2) the statement actually deceived or has the tendency to deceive a substantial segment of its audience; (3) the deception is material, in that it is likely to influence the purchasing decision; (4) the defendant caused its false statement to enter interstate commerce; and

(5) the plaintiff has been or is likely to be injured as a result of the false statement, either by direct diversion of sales from itself to defendant or by a loss of goodwill associated with its products. *See Southland Sod Farms v. Stover Seed Co.*, 108 F.3d 1134, 1139 (9th Cir. 1997); *Johnson & Johnson-Merck Consumer Pharm. Co. v. Rhone-Poulenc Rorer Pharm., Inc.*, 19 F.3d 125, 129 (3d Cir. 1994). In addition, to recover money damages under the Act, a "plaintiff must prove both actual damages and a causal link between defendant's violation and those damages." *Rhone-Poulenc*, 93 F.3d at 515.

The false statement necessary to establish a Lanham Act violation generally falls into one of two categories: (1) commercial claims that are literally false as a factual matter; and (2) claims that may be literally true or ambiguous but which implicitly convey a false impression, are misleading in context, or likely to deceive consumers. *See Southland*, 108 F.3d at 1139; *National Basketball Ass'n v. Motorola, Inc.*, 105 F.3d 841, 855 (2d Cir. 1997); *Abbott Lab. v. Mead Johnson & Co.*, 971 F.2d 6, 13 (7th Cir. 1992). Many claims will actually fall into a third category, generally known as "puffery" or "puffing." Puffery is "exaggerated advertising, blustering, and boasting upon which no reasonable buyer would rely and is not actionable under § 43(a)." *Southland*, 108 F.3d at 1145; *see also Castrol Inc. v. Pennzoil Co.*, 987 F.2d 939, 945 (3d Cir. 1993). Nonactionable puffery includes representations of product superiority that are vague or highly subjective. *See Southland*, 108 F.3d at 1145; *Cook, Perkiss & Liehe, Inc. v. Northern California Collection Serv., Inc.*, 911 F.2d 242, 246 (9th Cir. 1990) (advertising that merely states in general terms that one product is superior is not actionable). However, false descriptions of specific or absolute characteristics of a product and specific, measurable claims of product superiority based on product testing are not puffery and are actionable. *See Southland*, 108 F.3d at 1145; *Castrol*, 987 F.2d at 945.

1. Literally false claims

If a plaintiff proves that a challenged claim is literally false, a court may grant relief without considering whether the buying public was actually misled; actual consumer confusion need not be proved. *See Rhone-Poulenc*, 93 F.3d at 516; *Johnson & Johnson-Merck*, 19 F.3d at 129; *McNeil-P.C.C., Inc. v. Bristol-Myers Squibb Co.*, 938 F.2d 1544, 1549 (2d Cir. 1991) (where advertisement is shown to be literally false, court may enjoin it without reference to its impact on consumers). In assessing whether an advertisement is literally false, a court must analyze the message conveyed within its full context. *See Rhone-Poulenc*, 93 F.3d at 516; *Southland*, 108 F.3d at 1139. In some circumstances, even a visual image, or a visual image combined with an audio component, may be literally false:

We find, therefore, that the squeezing-pouring sequence in the Jenner commercial is false on its face. The visual component of the ad makes an explicit representation that Premium Pack is produced by squeezing oranges and pouring the freshly-squeezed juice directly into the carton. This is not a true representation of how the product is prepared. Premium Pack juice is heated and sometimes frozen prior to packaging.

Coca-Cola Co. v. Tropicana Products, Inc., 690 F.2d 312, 318 (2d Cir. 1982); *see also Rhone-Poulenc*, 93 F.3d at 516 (drug manufacturer's advertisements featuring images such as two similar gasoline pumps or airline tickets with dramatically different prices, accompanied by slogan, "Which one would you choose?" was literally false message that competing drugs could be indiscriminately substituted). The greater the degree to which a message relies upon the viewer or consumer to integrate its components and draw the apparent conclusion, however, the less likely it is that a finding of literal falsity will be supported. Commercial claims that are implicit, attenuated, or merely suggestive usually cannot fairly be characterized as literally false.

The district court determined that the Maxattrax commercial conveyed an explicit message that the product killed roaches in 24 hours and found that this message was literally true. The court concluded that scientific testing performed both by United Industries and Clorox sufficiently demonstrated that Maxattrax, which contains the fast-acting nerve toxin known as chlorpyrifos or Dursban, will actually kill a roach within 24 hours of its coming into contact with the product. In response, Clorox argues that the district court erroneously "ignored the explicit visual statements in United's advertising that, as a matter of law, combine with its express audio statements to determine its literal meaning." Brief for Appellant at 16. Clorox contends that the Maxattrax commercial conveyed three additional explicit messages that are literally false: (1) that Maxattrax controls roach infestations in consumers' homes within 24 hours; (2) that Combat and other roach baits are entirely ineffective in consumers' homes within 24 hours; and (3) that Maxattrax provides superior performance in consumers' homes in comparison to Combat and other roach baits.

Our review of the record satisfies us that the district court's determination that the commercial was literally true is not clearly erroneous. The court was clearly correct in its assessment that the audio and print components of the advertisement are literally true. The scientific evidence and expert testimony contained in the record satisfactorily established that Maxattrax roach bait "kills roaches in 24 hours." Clorox protests that this statement is literally true only in circumstances where a particular roach actually comes into contact with the product. This complaint rings hollow. The requirement that roaches must come into contact with the poison for it to be effective is the central premise of the roach bait line of products. We will not presume the average consumer to be incapable of comprehending the essential nature of a roach trap.

Similarly, we conclude that the district court did not err in determining that the Maxattrax commercial did not convey explicit visual messages that were literally false. The depiction of a Maxattrax box in a pristine, roach-free kitchen, coupled with the depiction of a kitchen in disarray in which animated roaches happily dance about on a generic roach trap, is not sufficient, in our view, to constitute literal falsity in the manner in which it was presented. When the context is considered as a whole, moreover, the audio component of the advertisement, emphasizing only the 24-hour time frame and quick roach kill with no mention of complete infestation control, fosters ambiguity regarding the intended message and renders the commercial much more susceptible to differing, plausible interpretations. Thus, in our view, the district court's finding that the commercial did not explicitly convey a literally false message that Maxattrax will completely control a home roach infestation within 24 hours is not clearly erroneous.

Clorox also contends that the commercial conveys an explicit message of comparative superiority that is literally false. We have recently distinguished between two types of comparative advertising claims brought under the Lanham Act: (1) "my product is better than yours" and (2) "*tests prove* that my product is better than yours." *Rhone-Poulenc*, 93 F.3d at 514 (emphasis in original). When challenging a claim of superiority that does not make express reference to testing, a plaintiff must prove that the defendant's claim of superiority is actually false, not simply unproven or unsubstantiated. *See id.* Under a "tests prove" claim, in which a defendant has buttressed a claim of superiority by attributing it to the results of scientific testing, a plaintiff must prove only "that the tests [relied upon] were not sufficiently reliable to permit one to conclude with reasonable certainty that they established the proposition for which they were cited." *Id.* at 514–15 (quoting *Castrol, Inc. v. Quaker State Corp.*, 977 F.2d 57, 62–63 (2d Cir. 1992)). However, "to ensure vigorous competition and to protect legitimate commercial speech, courts applying this standard should give advertisers a fair amount of leeway, at least in the absence of a clear intent to deceive or substantial consumer confusion." *Rhone-Poulenc*, 93 F.3d at 515.

The Maxattrax commercial indicates in small print at the bottom of the screen that its implied answer to the posed question, "Can you guess which bait kills roaches in 24 hours?" is, "Based on lab tests." In order for this claim to be considered literally false, then, Clorox must establish that the tests to which the commercial referred were not sufficiently reliable to support its claims with reasonable certainty. *See id.* at 514–15. The district court determined that the scientific research provided by United Industries was reliable and supported the commercial's claims. We agree with this conclusion. Laboratory testing indicates that the toxin contained in Maxattrax kills within 24 hours those roaches that come into contact with it. Some other roach bait products will not kill a roach within that interval and, in fact, are not even intended to do so.

Any additional messages in the Maxattrax commercial perceived by Clorox, visual or otherwise, are not sufficiently explicit or unambiguous so as to constitute specific false claims of a literal nature. Thus, we cannot say that the court committed clear error in its determinations regarding the scope of the commercial's explicit claims of superiority (that it kills roaches within 24 of hours and that a generic competitor does not), or in finding that claim to be literally true. *See L & F Products, a Div. of Sterling Winthrop, Inc. v. Procter & Gamble Co.*, 45 F.3d 709, 712 (2d Cir. 1995) (district court's determination with respect to facial falsity was not clearly erroneous).

2.   Implicitly false or misleading claims

Statements that are literally true or ambiguous but which nevertheless have a tendency to mislead or deceive the consumer are actionable under the Lanham Act. *See Southland*, 108 F.3d 1134 at 1140; *Sandoz Pharm. Corp. v. Richardson-Vicks, Inc.*, 902 F.2d 222, 228–29 (3d Cir. 1990); *American Home Products Corp. v. Johnson & Johnson*, 577 F.2d 160, 165 (2d Cir. 1978). Where a commercial claim is not literally false but is misleading in context, proof that the advertising actually conveyed the implied message and thereby deceived a significant portion of the recipients becomes critical. *See William H. Morris Co. v. Group W, Inc.*, 66 F.3d 255, 258 (9th Cir. 1995) (per curiam); *Johnson & Johnson * Merck Consumer Pharm. Co. v. Smithkline Beecham Corp.*, 960 F.2d 294, 297–98 (2d Cir. 1992).

> If a plaintiff does not prove the claim to be literally false, he must prove that it is deceptive or misleading, which depends on the message that is conveyed to consumers. Public reaction is the measure of a commercial's impact. As the district court noted, the success of the claim usually turns on the persuasiveness of a consumer survey.

Johnson & Johnson-Merck, 19 F.3d at 129–30 (internal citations omitted).

. . . Therefore, unless a commercial claim is literally false, or a trier of fact has determined that a competitor acted willfully with intent to deceive or in bad faith, a party seeking relief under this section of the Lanham Act bears the ultimate burden of proving actual deception by using reliable consumer or market research. *See Smithkline Beecham*, 960 F.2d at 297 ("It is not for the judge to determine, based solely upon his or her intuitive reaction, whether the advertisement is deceptive.");

AT & T, 42 F.3d 1421 at 1443 (quoting *Sandoz*, 902 F.2d 222 at 228–29) ("It cannot obtain relief by arguing how consumers *could* react; it must show how consumers *actually* do react.").

At the preliminary injunction stage, however, full-blown consumer surveys or market research are not an absolute prerequisite, and expert testimony or other evidence may at times be sufficient to obtain preliminary injunctive relief in cases involving implicitly false or misleading claims. *See Abbott*, 971 F.2d at 15; 3 McCarthy § 27:55 at 27–81 ("However, on a motion for a preliminary injunction, a survey is not always necessary and it is sufficient if plaintiff introduces expert testimony or any other evidence showing that a significant number of consumers received the claimed message from the advertisement.").

Clorox contends that when one assesses the comparative visuals and implicit messages in the commercial, a consumer might be misled to construe them as a claim that Maxattrax will completely control an infestation by killing all of the roaches in one's home within 24 hours, while its competitors will fail to do the same. In fact, Maxattrax will kill only those roaches which come into contact with the product; actual control of a roach problem may take several weeks. Whether one accepts the district court's more literal interpretation of the commercial's message or Clorox's proposed construction, however, is highly dependent upon context and inference, and Clorox's view is unsupported at this point by expert testimony, surveys, or consumer reaction evidence of any kind. It is, in other words, a classic question of fact, the resolution of which we will not disturb absent a showing of clear error by the district court. Clorox has not made such a showing.

In sum, then, the district court did not err in concluding that Clorox had not shown a likelihood of success on the merits of the claim.

B.

The remaining *Dataphase* factors do not tip the balance of equities decidedly in favor of Clorox. We have stated that the failure to demonstrate the threat of irreparable harm is, by itself, a sufficient ground upon which to deny a preliminary injunction. *See Adam-Mellang v. Apartment Search, Inc.*, 96 F.3d 297, 299 (8th Cir. 1996). When injunctive relief is sought under the Lanham Act, the finding of a tendency to deceive satisfies the requisite showing of irreparable harm. *See Black Hills Jewelry*, 633 F.2d at 753 ("To obtain an injunction under section 43(a) appellees need only show that the falsities complained of had a tendency to deceive."); *McNeilab, Inc. v. American Home Products Corp.*, 848 F.2d 34, 38 (2d Cir. 1988) (where challenged advertisement directly, but falsely, proclaims superiority of defendant's product over plaintiff's, irreparable harm may be presumed). Absent such a showing, however, irreparable harm cannot be presumed where, as here, plaintiff has not established any prospect of success upon the merits. *See Sanborn*,

997 F.2d at 489; *Johnson & Johnson v. Carter-Wallace, Inc.*, 631 F.2d 186, 192 (2d Cir. 1980) ("While proof of actual diversion of sales is not required for a § 43(a) injunction to issue, proof that the advertising complained of is in fact false is essential."). Clorox has not otherwise sufficiently demonstrated the threat of irreparable injury so as to tip this factor in its favor.

The district court did not make an explicit finding concerning the balance of harm to Clorox stemming from the commercial and the injury to United Industries that would result from an injunction. In light of the district court's conclusion that Clorox had failed to demonstrate a probability of ultimate success, the possibility that it will suffer any harm from the continuing airing of the commercial is highly speculative and therefore does not serve to tip the balance of equities in Clorox's favor. *See generally Sanborn*, 997 F.2d at 489–90.

Finally, "although the public interest favors enjoining false statements," *id.* at 490, absent a more substantial showing that Clorox has a viable claim, this factor likewise does not tilt the equities toward granting preliminary injunctive relief. *See id.* Therefore, because we believe that it committed no clear error in its factual findings or legal conclusions, we conclude that the district court did not abuse its broad discretion in denying Clorox's motion for preliminary injunction. . . .

The order denying preliminary injunctive relief is affirmed.

NOTES FOR DISCUSSION

1. *Why Regulate Advertisements?* Are consumers better or worse off as a result of the Trademark Act's attempt to prohibit false or misleading advertisements? Although this may seem self-evident, we do not generally regulate political advertisements, except to require that the funding source for the advertisement be accurately identified. Attempting to regulate the accuracy of advertisements may lead consumers to rely more heavily on statements that seem like factual representations in advertisements. With regulation and greater reliance, businesses may spend more resources trying to present advertisements that appear accurate, but are in fact misleading, knowing that consumers will rely on them. In the absence of regulation, consumers would distrust factual statements in advertisements even more than they already do.

How would companies respond in a market without regulation? What has happened in the market for political advertisements? Would a refusal to regulate advertising accuracy undermine the utility of advertising? Has it done so in the political sphere? Or would advertising continue to convey useful information?

At the very least, the fact that a company has paid money to prepare and place its advertisements would remain. Can a consumer rely on that expenditure as a signal of product quality? Consider two companies, one of which manufactures a high quality product, the other a low quality product. Which will advertise more heavily? If a consumer cannot determine product quality *ex ante*, advertising by the low-quality company will generate a one-time bump in purchases. New customers will try the product in response to the advertisement, but then having experienced the product and discovering its low quality, will not purchase it again. In contrast, advertising by the high-quality company will generate a stream of repeat purchases. New customers will try the product, and being satisfied, will return to purchase it again. As a result, if the profit from each sale of the high- and low-quality products is similar, the stream of sales generated for the high-quality product will likely yield a higher return on any given advertising expenditure than the one-time bump for the low-quality product. While advertising expenditures will not always accurately separate high-and low-quality products, it can serve as an accurate signal in many cases. Should we therefore leave advertising unregulated?

2.   *Alternative Dispute Resolution.* As an alternative to litigation under section 43(a), the Better Business Bureau provides an alternative dispute resolution mechanism through its National Advertising Division (or NAD). The NAD mechanism offers a number of advantages compared to litigation, including: (i) generally less expensive and quicker; (ii) reviews national advertisements for truth and accuracy and has a special set of rules governing advertisements directed at children; and (iii) relies on decision-makers with special expertise in advertising, rather than lay juries or judges, to evaluate claims.

3.   *Standing.* Section 43(a) allows "any person who believes that he is or is likely to be damaged by such act" to bring a cause of action for false advertising. 15 U.S.C. § 1125(a)(1) (2015). Despite the broad language, courts have universally held that consumers do not have standing to bring false advertising claims under section 43(a). *See Phoenix of Broward, Inc. v. McDonald's Corp.*, 489 F.3d 1156, 1170 (11th Cir. 2007) ("'[T]he several circuits that have dealt with the question are uniform in their categorical denial of Lanham Act standing to consumers.'" (*quoting Made in the USA Found. v. Phillips Foods, Inc.*, 365 F.3d 278, 281 (4th Cir. 2004))). Consumers may have standing to sue under parallel state laws, however. *See Kwikset Corp. v. Superior Court*, 51 Cal.4th 310, 120 Cal.Rptr.3d 741, 246 P.3d 877 (2011) (holding that the purchasers of goods falsely labeled "made in U.S.A." had standing under the California Unfair Competition Law and Fair Advertising Law when the purchasers alleged that the false labeling induced them to purchase the goods and they would not have purchased them otherwise).

As our first two cases illustrate, direct competitors have standing under the Trademark Act. But aside from consumers and direct competitors, what about others, who, while not direct competitors, play some role in the supply chain? The question arose in *Lexmark Int'l, Inc. v. Static Control Components, Inc.* 134 S.Ct. 1377 (2014). Lexmark manufactures and sells, *inter alia,* laser printers. To implement a form of price discrimination, known as metering, Lexmark tries to control the sale of printer cartridges that are compatible with its printers. This permits Lexmark to charge a lower price for its printers and a higher price for its printer cartridges, and thus charge those who use its printers more intensively a higher price. Because the printer cartridges carry a monopoly surcharge, there is an opportunity for others to offer compatible cartridges at a lower price. However, Lexmark installs a "lock-out" chip on its cartridges so that only its cartridges will work on its printers. Static Control developed its own microchip that duplicated the functionality of Lexmark's lock-out chip. This allowed third parties to refurbish used Lexmark cartridges, install Static Control's replacement chip, and offer the refurbished cartridges in competition with Lexmark's cartridges. Static Control did not sell refurbished cartridges directly, rather it sold the replacement microchip to third-party remanufacturers.

In response, Lexmark sued Static Control for copyright infringement and violation of the Digital Millennium Copyright Act, asserting that its lock-out chip contained a copyrighted computer program and served as technical protection measure. Static Control counterclaimed, asserting that Lexmark had engaged in false or misleading advertising. In its counterclaim, Static Control alleged that Lexmark had made two types of false or misleading statements. First, Static Control alleged that "Lexmark 'purposefully misleads end-users' to believe that they are legally bound . . . to return the cartridge to Lexmark after a single use. Second, it alleged that . . . Lexmark 'sent letters to most of the companies in the toner cartridge remanufacturing business' falsely advising those companies that it was illegal to sell refurbished . . . cartridges and, in particular, that it was illegal to use Static Control's products to refurbish those cartridges." *Lexmark Int'l, Inc.*, 134 S.Ct. at 1384.

The district court dismissed on prudential standing grounds finding that, while Static Control fell within the literal reach of section 43(a)'s broad standing language, Static Control was not itself a direct competitor of Lexmark. In response, Static Control appealed. In its opinion, the Sixth Circuit identified three different approaches to the standing issue. The Third, Fifth, Eighth, and Eleventh applied a multi-factor prudential standing doctrine similar to the one applied by the district court. The Seventh, Ninth, and Tenth applied a categorical standing rule, limiting standing to direct competitors. The Second Circuit applied a broad standing doctrine consistent with the Act's broad language, asking if the claimant has a reasonable interest to be protected against the false advertising and a reasonable basis to believe that that interest is likely to be damaged. The Sixth Circuit adopted the Second Circuit's approach and reversed.

Lexmark petitioned the Supreme Court for *certiorari*. The Court granted *certiorari* and affirmed the Sixth Circuit. Although the Court cautioned against reading the statute as broadly as its literal language might suggest, the Court identified two elements that a claimant must satisfy to have standing. First, the claimant's injury must fall within the zone of interests Congress intended to protect. For false advertising claims under the

Trademark Act, this zone of interest includes "an injury to a commercial interest in reputation or sales," but not the loss experienced by a "hoodwinked" consumer. *Lexmark Int'l, Inc.*, 134 S.Ct. at 1390. Second, the false or misleading advertising must also be the proximate cause of the alleged injury. As the Court explained, "the harm alleged [must have] a sufficiently close connection to the conduct the statute prohibits." *Id.* The harm must not be "too remote" from the false advertising at issue and must not be "purely derivative of 'misfortunes visited upon a third person by the defendant's acts.' " *Id.* at 1391.

Applying this two-part standard, the Court held that Static Control had standing to assert its false advertising claims against Lexmark. With respect to the first part, "Static Control's alleged injuries—lost sales and damage to its business reputation—are injuries to precisely the sorts of commercial interests the Act protects." *Id.* at 1393. With respect to the second, the Court acknowledged that Static Control's alleged injuries were somewhat indirect. The false advertising at issue tended to interfere most directly with the sale of refurbished printer cartridges. However, in this case, Static Control was the sole source of the replacement microchips necessary to sell refurbished printer cartridges. As a result, "if the remanufacturers sold 10,000 fewer refurbished cartridges because of Lexmark's false advertising, then it would follow more or less automatically that Static Control sold 10,000 fewer microchips for the same reason, without the need for any 'speculative . . . proceedings' or 'intricate, uncertain inquiries.' " *Id.* at 1394. The Court therefore held that Static Control satisfied the proximate cause element for standing as well.

4. *Literally False.* What are the express statements made in each of the advertisements at issue in *American Home Prods.* and *United Indus. Corp.*? Are any of these statements literally (or facially) false? If a statement in an advertisement, such as "kills roaches within twenty-four hours," has two possible meanings, one of which is false ("kills all roaches in your house within twenty-four hours"), the other of which is true ("kills all roaches that contact the poison within twenty-four hours"), is that a case of literal falsity?

What are the legal differences between literal falsity and implied falsity? First, a judge determines literal falsity by examining the literal statements in the advertisement. Surveys of consumer perception to determine the advertisement's meanings are unnecessary. Second, if a statement is literally false, courts will presume that the statement is also deceptive.

5. *Impliedly False or Misleading.* An advertisement is impliedly false or misleading if a substantial or significant number of consumers perceive the advertisement as making an implicit representation and that implicit representation is not true. Because it relies on consumers' interpretation of the advertisements, rather than statements plain on the advertisement's face, a plaintiff advancing a theory of impliedly false or misleading representations must usually introduce consumer survey evidence to establish how consumers interpret the advertisement at issue.

In *American Home Prods. Corp.*, what are the literal statements that the advertisement makes? What are the implied representations that McNeil contended the advertisements conveyed? How did McNeil attempt to establish each of these implied representations? Which implied representations did the district court find a substantial or significant number of consumers would interpret the advertisement as making? Which did the district court reject? Did the appeals court agree with the district court on each of these? What was the standard of review and what role did it play in the appeals court's analysis of this issue?

6. *Surveying Consumer Perception.* To establish that a survey is impliedly false or misleading, a plaintiff must usually rely on survey evidence. Survey formats vary in the false advertising context, but usually begin with an open-ended question, where a respondent is shown the commercial and then asked: "What ideas did the advertiser try to get across about [the product] in the commercial?" Often a commercial will present several ideas, and so surveys will typically follow the initial open-ended question with "probes," such as "What other ideas did they try to get across?" or simply "What else?" Sometimes, a survey will also pursue more specific inquiries focusing on particular statements in the advertisement. For example, a survey might ask: "In the advertisement, they say [quote a portion of the advertisement]. What does that statement mean to you?" As in the likelihood of confusion context, that some consumers perceive the alleged representation is not sufficient. In this context, courts typically require twenty percent or more of the survey respondents to perceive the alleged representation. *See, e.g., Johnson & Johnson-Merck Consumer Pharm. Co. v. Rhone-Poulenc Rorer Pharms., Inc.*, 19 F.3d 125, 134 n.14 (3d Cir. 1994).

In *Johnson & Johnson-Merck Consumer Pharm. Co. v. Rhone-Poulenc Rorer Pharms., Inc.*, for example, Rorer ran ads touting its Extra Strength Maalox Plus as "the strongest antacid there is." 19 F.3d at 126. Johnson & Johnson, the maker of Mylanta, sued, alleging a violation of section 43(a)(1)(B). *Id.* As it turns out, laboratory tests showed that Maalox had a slightly higher acid-neutralizing capacity than Mylanta. *Id.* at 127. The statement was not therefore literally false. *Id.* at 132. Nevertheless, Johnson & Johnson argued that consumers would interpret the advertisements as a representation that Maalox provided superior relief. Because tests conducted by both parties showed the two antacids were equally effective at relieving the symptoms of acid ingestion, *id.* at 127, an implicit representation of superior relief would be false.

To support its argument Johnson & Johnson introduced a consumer survey, which contained an open-ended "What ideas" question, followed by repeated probes, as well as a specific "The advertisement states that Maalox is the strongest. What does that mean to you?" question. Rorer's expert testified that only the responses to the open-ended question, unprobed, were reliable and found that only 7.5 percent of respondents interpreted the "strongest" claim as an implicit representation of superior relief. *Id.* at 133–34. In contrast, Johnson & Johnson's expert considered the responses to all of the questions and found that over half of the respondents understood "strongest" to mean "superior relief." *Id.* at 134. In resolving the plaintiff's motion for a preliminary injunction, the district court accepted the testimony of Rorer's expert and rejected the testimony of Johnson & Johnson's expert. In the district court's view, the repeated probes and the more specific "The advertisements says . . . What does that mean?" question were leading and therefore not reliable evidence of how consumers would interpret the advertisement on their own. As a result, Johnson & Johnson had failed to show that a substantial or significant number of consumers were misled. *Id.* at 134 n.14. The court therefore denied Johnson & Johnson's request for a preliminary injunction. On appeal, the Third Circuit affirmed. *Id.*

7. *Impliedly False and Deceptive Intent.* While courts usually require a consumer survey to establish the presence of impliedly false representations, courts will presume the existence of such representations when a plaintiff shows that the defendant had an actual intent to deceive consumers. The *United Industries Corp.* court acknowledged this alternative method of proof, but did not apply it: "Therefore, unless a commercial claim is literally false, or a trier of fact has determined that a competitor acted willfully with intent to deceive or in bad faith, a party seeking relief under this section of the Lanham Act bears the ultimate burden of proving actual deception by using reliable consumer or market research." 140 F.3d at 1183. However, courts have emphasized that a plaintiff must show "deliberate conduct" of an "egregious nature" to establish the requisite intent. *Johnson & Johnson-Merck Consumer Pharm. Co.*, 19 F.3d at 132.

8. *Taking Advantage of Public Misconceptions.* What if an advertisement makes a statement that is literally true, but when linked into a popular misconception, creates a false or misleading impression? If an advertiser tailors its advertisements specifically to take advantage of such a misconception, is that actionable under section 43(a)(1)(B)?

In an earlier antacid case, Johnson & Johnson sued, alleging that Smithkline Beecham, the maker of TUMS, was doing precisely that. *Johnson & Johnson * Merck Consumer Pharms. Co v. Smithkline Beecham Corp.*, 960 F.2d 294 (2d Cir. 1992). Specifically, while TUMS uses calcium carbonate to neutralize excess stomach acid, Mylanta uses aluminum hydroxide and magnesium hydroxide. Moreover, there is a popular misperception that the ingestion of aluminum causes Alzheimer's disease. In its initial advertisement, Smithkline stated that Mylanta contains aluminum and magnesium, and that TUMS contains calcium. The advertisement's tagline was "Calcium-rich, aluminum-free TUMS." When Johnson & Johnson complained, Smithkline modified its ad, by deleting the reference to TUMS as "aluminum-free" and emphasizing that TUMS contained calcium and that calcium was good for you. Not satisfied with these changes, Johnson & Johnson sued.

As the court phrased it:

> J&J*Merck contends that, even though the content of the challenged commercials is literally true, Ingredients-Revised preys upon a publicly held misperception that the ingestion of aluminum causes Alzheimer's disease. According to J&J*Merck, the commercials accomplish this by repeatedly juxtaposing the absence of aluminum in TUMS with its presence in MYLANTA. In turn, this repetition supposedly links MYLANTA with an allegedly popularly held, yet unsubstantiated concern that aluminum is associated with Alzheimer's. Since the aluminum/Alzheimer's connection has not been scientifically established, J&J*Merck argues that Ingredients-Revised purposefully taps into a preexisting body of public misinformation in order to communicate the false and misleading message that aluminum-based antacids are harmful.

> The gravamen of J&J*Merck's claim is that advertisers may be held liable for the knowing exploitation of public misperception.

Id. at 297. According to the court, Johnson & Johnson's "argument presents a novel theory of Lanham Act liability". Should the court accept the theory? If Smithkline's advertisement had stated "Mylanta causes Alzheimer's disease," that would be actionable, without a doubt. If Smithkline's advertisement had stated "Mylanta contains aluminum and ingesting aluminum causes Alzheimer's disease," that too would be actionable, absent evidence to establish the connection. But what if Smithkline only says "Mylanta contains aluminum" and leaves it to a misinformed public to make the Alzheimer's connection?

In the end, the court did not resolve whether taking advantage of a common misperception would constitute actionable misrepresentation. Instead, the court found as a factual matter that Johnson & Johnson's survey evidence, although it showed that some consumers made the Alzheimer's connection, had failed to establish that a significant or substantial number of consumers interpreted the advertisements as an implicit representation of a causal link between Mylanta, aluminum, and Alzheimer's. *Id.* at 299.

9.   *Visual Claims: Literally False or Misleading?* Can a visual claim be false or misleading? The *United Industries Corp.* court states that a visual component of an advertisement can make express and implied representations. The voice-over in the Maxattrax advertisements states that Maxattrax kills roaches in twenty-four hours. The accompanying visual image shows a kitchen initially at night and when the light comes on (the next day?), a roach-free kitchen. Taken together, do the words and the image establish the express representation for which Clorox contends: "Maxattrax will completely control a roach infestation within twenty-four hours." In what way is the message ambiguous? Do you agree with the district court's finding that the commercial is not literally false? What role does the standard of review play in insulating the district court's finding on this issue from appellate review? How does the district court's finding of an ambiguity

compare to the orange juice commercial in which the Second Circuit had found literal falsity?

In that earlier case, Tropicana Products, Inc. had run a television commercial for its Premium Pack orange juice showing the renowned American Olympic athlete Bruce Jenner squeezing an orange while saying "It's pure, pasteurized juice as it comes from the orange." Jenner then pours the fresh-squeezed juice into a Tropicana carton while the audio states "It's the only leading brand not made with concentrate and water." In fact, the juice is pasteurized (heated to about 200 degrees Fahrenheit) and sometimes frozen prior to packaging. In that case, the court found the advertisement literally false. *See Coca-Cola Co. v. Tropicana Products, Inc.*, 690 F.2d 312, 318 (2d Cir. 1982). Are there any ambiguities in the audio and visual presentation of Tropicana's commercial?

What about the following case? In August 1999, Clorox introduced a 15-second and a 30-second television commercial, each depicting an S.C. Johnson Ziploc Slide-Loc resealable storage bag side-by-side with a Clorox Glad-Lock bag. The bags are identified in the commercials by brand name. Both commercials show an animated, talking goldfish in water inside each of the bags. In the commercials, the bags are turned upside-down, and the Slide-Loc bag leaks rapidly while the Glad-Lock bag does not leak at all. In both the 15-and 30-second commercials, the Slide-Loc goldfish says, in clear distress, "My Ziploc Slider is dripping. Wait a minute!," while the Slide-Loc bag is shown leaking at a rate of approximately one drop per one to two seconds. At the end of both commercials, the Slide-Loc goldfish exclaims, "Can I borrow a cup of water!!!"

S.C. Johnson sued alleging that the advertisement was false or misleading. It retained Dr. Phillip DeLassus, an outside expert, who conducted "torture testing," in which Slide-Loc bags were filled with water, rotated for 10 seconds, and held upside-down for an additional 20 seconds. He testified about the results of the tests he performed, emphasizing that 37 percent of all Slide-Loc bags tested did not leak at all. Of the remaining 63 percent that did leak, only a small percentage leaked at the rate depicted in the television commercials. The vast majority leaked at a rate between two and twenty times slower than that depicted in the commercials. *See S.C. Johnson & Son, Inc. v. Clorox Co.*, 241 F.3d 232, 240 (2d Cir. 2001) (literally false).

Keep in mind that Clorox will have another bite at the apple in *United Industries, Inc.* This court's decision is just the first, preliminary injunction round. For trial, Clorox can and almost certainly will have a consumer survey prepared. Do you think twenty percent of more of the survey respondents will interpret the Maxattrax commercials as a representation that Maxattrax will solve your roach problem in twenty-four hours?

10. *Deception.* As the *United Indus. Corp.* court notes, to establish a cause of action under section 43(a)(1)(B), a plaintiff must also show that the false or misleading representation of fact "actually deceived or has the

tendency to deceive a substantial segment of its audience." 140 F.3d at 1180. However, if the representation is literally false, courts will presume deception. *See, e.g., Cashmere & Camel Hair Mfrs. Inst. v. Saks Fifth Ave.,* 284 F.3d 302, 314–15 (1st Cir.), *cert. denied,* 537 U.S. 1001 (2002). Courts will also presume deception where the defendant intended to deceive consumers. *See, e.g., id.* at 316.

As a practical matter, these presumptions mean that a plaintiff must prove deception only for impliedly false or misleading claims. For such claims, a plaintiff must already introduce survey evidence showing that consumers interpret an advertisement as making an implicit representation that is false. Does the plaintiff need a second survey to establish that the implied falsehood is also deceptive? The usual answer here is no. The same survey that establishes that consumers interpret an advertisement as making an implicit representation will also usually suffice to show deceptiveness. This is the approach the *American Home Prods. Corp.* court followed. One survey established both that the consumers interpreted the advertisements as a representation that aspirin provided superior pain relief and that consumers were thereby deceived. *See also United Indus. Corp.,* 140 F.3d at 1182 ("Where a commercial claim is not literally false but is misleading in context, proof that the advertising actually conveyed the implied message and thereby deceived a significant portion of the recipients becomes critical.").

11. *Causation and Harm.* To establish the final element for establishing a claim for relief under section 43(a)(1)(B), a plaintiff must show that it "has been or is likely to be injured as a result of the statement at issue." *United Indus. Corp.,* 140 F.3d at 1180. As an initial matter, courts distinguish between the showing a plaintiff must make under this element to obtain injunctive relief and the showing a plaintiff must make to obtain monetary damages. To obtain injunctive relief, a plaintiff need show only "a reasonable basis for the belief that the plaintiff is likely to be damaged as a result of the false advertising." *Johnson & Johnson v. Carter-Wallace, Inc.,* 631 F.2d 186, 190 (2d Cir. 1980). The standard for injunctive relief was not historically high. All that was required is "some indication of actual injury and causation to satisfy Lanham Act standing requirements and to ensure a plaintiff's injury was not speculative." *McNeilab, Inc. v. American Home Products Corp.,* 848 F.2d 34, 38 (2d Cir. 1988). As discussed in Chapter 11, however, the Supreme Court's decisions in *eBay* and *Winter* may require proof of irreparable harm and no adequate remedy at law in this context as well. The Third Circuit has already held that *eBay* and *Winter* require such a showing. *See Ferring Pharmaceuticals, Inc. v. Watson Pharmaceuticals, Inc.,* 765 F.3d 205 (3d Cir. 2014).

In contrast, to recover monetary damages, a plaintiff, as a general rule, must show "both actual damages and a causal link between defendant's violation and those damages." *Rhone-Poulenc Rorer Pharm., Inc. v. Marion Merrell Dow, Inc.,* 93 F.3d 511, 515 (8th Cir. 1996). Proving such a causal link does not require direct evidence, however; circumstantial evidence can be sufficient. *See EFCO Corp. v. Symons Corp.*, 219 F.3d 734, 740 (8th Cir. 2000) (finding sufficient evidence of causal link where plaintiff's revenues were decreasing at the same rate as the defendant's revenues were increasing, together with "evidence that its sales force was losing clients to" the defendant).

As with other elements of a false advertising claim, courts have established presumptions to assist a plaintiff on this element as well. First, where the false or misleading advertisement issue mentions a competitor by name, courts will presume causation and harm sufficient to justify an award of injunctive relief. *See McNeilab, Inc.*, 848 F.2d at 38 ("A misleading comparison to a specific competing product necessarily diminishes that product's value in the minds of the consumer."). Second, in cases involving comparative advertising and a finding of intentional deception, courts will presume causation and injury in fact sufficient to justify an award of monetary damages. *See Porous Media Corp. v. Pall Corp.*, 110 F.3d 1329, 1336 (8th Cir. 1997). Although the plaintiff in such a case still bears the "burden of proving an evidentiary basis to justify any monetary recovery," *id.*, uncertainties with respect to the proper amount of an award, rather than with respect to the fact of causation and injury, will not foreclose an award of damages. *Id.; see also PPX Enters. v. Audiofidelity Enters.*, 818 F.2d 266, 271 (2d Cir. 1987) (noting that "courts may engage in 'some degree of speculation in computing the amount of damages, particularly when the inability to compute them is attributable to the defendant's wrongdoing'") (*quoting Burndy Corp. v. Teledyne Indus.*, 748 F.2d 767, 771 (2d Cir. 1984)).

For example, in *PPX Enters.*, the defendant, Audiofidelity, sold eight albums "purporting to contain feature performances by Jimi Hendrix, but which either did not contain Hendrix performances at all or contained performances in which Hendrix was merely a background performer or undifferentiated session player." *Id.* at 268. Although its advertisements for the albums were false, the defendant argued that a jury could not properly award damages because the plaintiff failed to offer consumer surveys or other evidence of consumer reaction. *Id.* at 272. The Second Circuit rejected the argument:

> The jury's conclusion that consumers actually were deceived by Audiofidelity's misrepresentations is supported by the false advertising contained on the record albums and the fact that Audiofidelity successfully sold the albums on the market. Given the egregious nature of Audiofidelity's actions, we see no need to require appellant to provide consumer surveys or reaction tests in order to prove entitlement to damages. The only possible conclusion to be derived from Audiofidelity's conduct was that consumers actually were deceived by the misrepresentations. . . .

> Audiofidelity's products were patently fraudulent, and the advertising accompanying those products was the vehicle employed to perpetrate the fraud.

Id. at 272–73.

B. MATERIALITY AND PUFFERY

PIZZA HUT, INC. v. PAPA JOHN'S INTERNATIONAL, INC.
227 F.3d 489 (5th Cir. 2000), *cert. denied*, 532 U.S. 920 (2001)

E. GRADY JOLLY, CIRCUIT JUDGE

This appeal presents a false advertising claim under section 43(a) of the Lanham Act, resulting in a jury verdict for the plaintiff, Pizza Hut. At the center of this appeal is Papa John's four word slogan "Better Ingredients. Better Pizza."

The appellant, Papa John's International Inc. ("Papa John's"), argues that the slogan "cannot and does not violate the Lanham Act" because it is "not a misrepresentation of fact." The appellee, Pizza Hut, Inc., argues that the slogan, when viewed in the context of Papa John's overall advertising campaign, conveys a false statement of fact actionable under section 43(a) of the Lanham Act. The district court, after evaluating the jury's responses to a series of special interrogatories and denying Papa John's motion for judgment as a matter of law, entered judgment for Pizza Hut stating:

> When the 'Better Ingredients. Better Pizza.' slogan is considered in light of the entirety of Papa John's post-May 1997 advertising which violated provisions of the Lanham Act and in the context in which it was juxtaposed with the false and misleading statements contained in Papa John's print and broadcast media advertising, the slogan itself became tainted to the extent that its continued use should be enjoined.

We conclude that (1) the slogan, standing alone, is not an objectifiable statement of fact upon which consumers would be justified in relying, and thus not actionable under section 43(a); and (2) while the slogan, when utilized in connection with some of the post-May 1997 comparative advertising—specifically, the sauce and dough campaigns—conveyed objectifiable and misleading facts, Pizza Hut has failed to adduce any evidence demonstrating that the facts conveyed by the slogan were material to the purchasing decisions of the consumers to which the slogan was directed. Thus, the district court erred in denying Papa John's motion for judgment as a matter of law. We therefore reverse the judgment of the district court denying Papa John's motion for judgment as a matter of law, vacate its final judgment, and remand the case to the district court for entry of judgment for Papa John's.

I

A

Pizza Hut is a wholly owned subsidiary of Tricon Global Restaurants. With over 7000 restaurants (both company and franchisee-owned), Pizza Hut is the largest pizza chain in the United States. In 1984, John Schnatter founded Papa John's Pizza in the back of his father's tavern. Papa John's has grown to over 2050 locations, making it the third largest pizza chain in the United States.

In May 1995, Papa John's adopted a new slogan: "Better Ingredients. Better Pizza." In 1996, Papa John's filed for a federal trademark registration for this slogan with the United States Patent & Trademark Office ("PTO"). Its application for registration was ultimately granted by the PTO. Since 1995, Papa John's has invested over $300 million building customer goodwill in its trademark "Better Ingredients. Better Pizza." The slogan has appeared on millions of signs, shirts, menus, pizza boxes, napkins and other items, and has regularly appeared as the "tag line" at the end of Papa John's radio and television ads, or with the company logo in printed advertising.

On May 1, 1997, Pizza Hut launched its "Totally New Pizza" campaign. This campaign was the culmination of "Operation Lightning Bolt," a nine-month, $50 million project in which Pizza Hut declared "war" on poor quality pizza. From the deck of a World War II aircraft carrier, Pizza Hut's president, David Novak, declared "war" on "skimpy, low quality pizza." National ads aired during this campaign touted the "better taste" of Pizza Hut's pizza, and "dared" anyone to find a "better pizza."

In early May 1997, Papa John's launched its first national ad campaign. The campaign was directed towards Pizza Hut, and its "Totally New Pizza" campaign. In a pair of TV ads featuring Pizza Hut's co-founder Frank Carney, Carney touted the superiority of Papa John's pizza over Pizza Hut's pizza. Although Carney had left the pizza business in the 1980's, he returned as a franchisee of Papa John's because he liked the taste of Papa John's pizza better than any other pizza on the market. The ad campaign was remarkably successful. During May 1997, Papa John's sales increased 11.7 percent over May 1996 sales, while Pizza Hut's sales were down 8 percent.

On the heels of the success of the Carney ads, in February 1998, Papa John's launched a second series of ads touting the results of a taste test in which consumers were asked to compare Papa John's and Pizza Hut's pizzas. In the ads, Papa John's boasted that it "won big time" in taste tests. The ads were a response to Pizza Hut's "dare" to find a "better pizza." The taste test showed that consumers preferred Papa John's traditional crust pizzas over Pizza Hut's comparable pizzas by a 16-point margin (58% to 42%). Additionally, consumers preferred Papa John's thin crust pizzas by a fourteen-point margin (57% to 43%).

Following the taste test ads, Papa John's ran a series of ads comparing specific ingredients used in its pizzas with those used by its "competitors." During the course of these ads, Papa John's touted the superiority of its sauce and its dough. During the sauce campaign, Papa John's asserted that its sauce was made from "fresh, vine-ripened tomatoes," which were canned through a process called "fresh pack," while its competitors—including Pizza Hut—make their sauce from remanufactured tomato paste. During the dough campaign, Papa John's stated that it used "clear filtered water" to make its pizza dough, while the "biggest chain" uses "whatever comes out of the tap." Additionally, Papa John's asserted that it gives its yeast "several days to work its magic," while "some folks" use "frozen dough or dough made the same day." At or near the close of each of these ads, Papa John's punctuated its ingredient comparisons with the slogan "Better Ingredients. Better Pizza."

Pizza Hut does not appear to contest the truthfulness of the underlying factual assertions made by Papa John's in the course of these ads. Pizza Hut argues, however, that its own independent taste tests and other "scientific evidence" establishes that filtered water makes no difference in pizza dough, that there is no "taste" difference between Papa John's "fresh-pack" sauce and Pizza Hut's "remanufactured" sauce, and that fresh dough is not superior to frozen dough. In response to Pizza Hut's "scientific evidence," Papa John's asserts that "each of these 'claims' involves a matter of common sense choice (fresh versus frozen, canned vegetables and fruit versus remanufactured paste, and filtered versus unfiltered water) about which individual consumers can and do form preferences every day without 'scientific' or 'expert' assistance."

In November 1997, Pizza Hut filed a complaint regarding Papa John's "Better Ingredients. Better Pizza." advertising campaign with the National Advertising Division of the Better Business Bureau, an industry self-regulatory body. This complaint, however, did not produce satisfactory results for Pizza Hut.

B

On August 12, 1998, Pizza Hut filed a civil action in the United States District Court for the Northern District of Texas charging Papa John's with false advertising in violation of Section 43(a)(1)(B) of the Lanham Act. The suit sought relief based on the above-described TV ad campaigns, as well as on some 249 print ads. On March 10, 1999, Pizza Hut filed an amended complaint. Papa John's answered the complaints by denying that its advertising and slogan violated the Lanham Act. Additionally, Papa John's asserted a counterclaim, charging Pizza Hut with engaging in false advertising. The parties consented to a jury trial before a United States magistrate judge. The parties further agreed that the liability issues were to be decided by the jury, while the equitable injunction claim and damages award were within the province of the court.

The trial began on October 26, 1999, and continued for over three weeks. At the close of Pizza Hut's case, and at the close of all evidence, Papa John's moved for a judgment as a matter of law. The motions were denied each time. The district court, without objection, submitted the liability issue to the jury through special interrogatories. The special issues submitted to the jury related to (1) the slogan and (2) over Papa John's objection, certain classes of groups of advertisements referred to as "sauce claims," "dough claims," "taste test claims," and "ingredients claims."

On November 17, 1999, the jury returned its responses to the special issues finding that Papa John's slogan, and its "sauce claims" and "dough claims" were false or misleading and deceptive or likely to deceive consumers. The jury also determined that Papa John's "taste test" ads were not deceptive or likely to deceive consumers, and that Papa John's "ingredients claims" were not false or misleading. As to Papa John's counterclaims against Pizza Hut, the jury found that two of the three Pizza Hut television ads at issue were false or misleading and deceptive or likely to deceive consumers.

On January 3, 2000, the trial court, based upon the jury's verdict and the evidence presented by the parties in support of injunctive relief and on the issue of damages, entered a Final Judgment and issued a Memorandum Opinion and Order. The court concluded that the "Better Ingredients. Better Pizza." slogan was "consistent with the legal definition of non-actionable puffery" from its introduction in 1995 until May 1997. However, the slogan "became tainted . . . in light of the entirety of Papa John's post-May 1997 advertising." Based on this conclusion, the magistrate judge permanently enjoined Papa John's from "using any slogan in the future that constitutes a recognizable variation of the phrase 'Better Ingredients. Better Pizza.'" or which uses the adjective "Better" to modify the terms "ingredients" and/or "pizza." Additionally, the court enjoined Papa John's from identifying Frank Carney as a co-founder of Pizza Hut, "unless such advertising includes a voice-over, printed statement or a superimposed message which states that Frank Carney has not been affiliated with Pizza Hut since 1980," and enjoined the dissemination of any advertising that was produced or disseminated prior to the date of this judgment and that explicitly or implicitly states or suggests that "Papa John's component is superior to the same component of Pizza Hut's pizzas." Finally, the court enjoined Papa John's from "explicitly or implicitly claiming that a component of Papa John's pizza is superior to the same component of Pizza Hut's unless the superiority claim is supported by either (1) scientifically demonstrated attributes of superiority or (2) taste test surveys." Additionally, the injunction required that if the claim is supported by taste test surveys, the advertising shall include a printed statement, voice-over or "super," whichever is appropriate, stating the localities where the tests were conducted, the inclusive dates on which the surveys were performed, and the specific pizza products that were tested. The court also awarded Pizza Hut $467,619.75 in damages for having to run corrective ads.

On January 20, 2000, Papa John's filed a notice of appeal with our court. On January 26, we granted Papa John's motion to stay the district court's injunction pending appeal.

II

We review the district court's denial of a motion for judgment as a matter of law de novo applying the same standards as the district court. *See Ensley v. Cody Resources, Inc.*, 171 F.3d 315, 319 (5th Cir. 1999) (citing *Hidden Oaks Ltd. v. City of Austin*, 138 F.3d 1036, 1042 (5th Cir. 1998)); *Nero v. Industrial Molding Corp.*, 167 F.3d 921, 925 (5th Cir. 1999). In ruling on a motion for judgment as a matter of law, we will consider all of the evidence—not just the evidence that supports the non-movant's case—but in the light most favorable to the non-movant. *Id.* The granting of a judgment as a matter of law will be appropriate "if, after a party has been fully heard by the jury on an issue, 'there is no legally sufficient evidentiary basis for a reasonable jury to [find] for that party with respect to that issue.'" *Rutherford v. Harris County, Texas*, 197 F.3d 173, 179 (5th Cir. 1999) (quoting *Aetna Cas. & Sur. Co., v. Pendleton Detectives of Miss., Inc.*, 182 F.3d 376, 377–78 (5th Cir. 1999)).

Thus, for purposes of this appeal, we will review the evidence, in the most favorable light to Pizza Hut, to determine if, as a matter of law, it is sufficient to support a claim of false advertising under section 43(a) of the Lanham Act.

III

A

Section 43(a) of the Lanham Act, codified at 15 U.S.C. § 1125, provides in relevant part:

> Any person who . . . in commercial advertising or promotion, misrepresents the nature, characteristics, quality, or geographic origin of his or another person's goods, services, or commercial activities, shall be liable in a civil action by any person who believes that he or she is likely to be damaged by such act.

15 U.S.C. § 1125 (a)(1)(B) (West 1999).

We have interpreted this section of the Lanham Act as providing "protection against a 'myriad of deceptive commercial practices,' including false advertising or promotion." *Seven-Up Co. v. Coca-Cola Co.*, 86 F.3d 1379, 1387 (5th Cir. 1996) (quoting *Resource Developers v. Statue of Liberty-Ellis Island Found.*, 926 F.2d 134, 139 (2d Cir. 1991)).

A prima facie case of false advertising under section 43(a) requires the plaintiff to establish:

(1) A false or misleading statement of fact about a product;

(2) Such statement either deceived, or had the capacity to deceive a substantial segment of potential consumers;

(3) The deception is material, in that it is likely to influence the consumer's purchasing decision;

(4) The product is in interstate commerce; and

(5) The plaintiff has been or is likely to be injured as a result of the statement at issue.

See Taquino v. Teledyne Monarch Rubber, 893 F.2d 1488, 1500 (5th Cir. 1990); *Cook, Perkiss and Liehe, Inc. v. Northern Cal. Collection Serv. Inc.*, 911 F.2d 242, 246 (9th Cir. 1990); 4 J. Thomas McCarthy, *McCarthy on Trademarks and Unfair Competition*, § 27:24 (4th ed. 1996).

The failure to prove the existence of any element of the prima facie case is fatal to the plaintiff's claim. *Id.*

B

The law governing false advertising claims under section 43(a) of the Lanham Act is well settled. In order to obtain monetary damages or equitable relief in the form of an injunction, "a plaintiff must demonstrate that the commercial advertisement or promotion is either literally false, or that [if the advertisement is not literally false,] it is likely to mislead and confuse consumers." *Seven-Up*, 86 F.3d at 1390 (citing *McNeil-P.C.C., Inc. v. Bristol-Myers Squibb Co.*, 938 F.2d 1544, 1548–49 (2d Cir. 1991)); *see also Johnson & Johnson v. Smithkline Beecham Corp.*, 960 F.2d 294, 298 (2d Cir. 1992). If the statement is shown to be misleading, the plaintiff must also introduce evidence of the statement's impact on consumers, referred to as materiality. *American Council of Certified Podiatric Physicians and Surgeons v. American Bd. of Podiatric Surgery, Inc.*, 185 F.3d 606, 614 (6th Cir. 1999).

(1)

(a)

Essential to any claim under section 43(a) of the Lanham Act is a determination of whether the challenged statement is one of fact— actionable under section 43(a)—or one of general opinion—not actionable under section 43(a). Bald assertions of superiority or general statements of opinion cannot form the basis of Lanham Act liability. *See Presidio Enters., Inc. v. Warner Bros. Distrib. Corp.*, 784 F.2d 674, 685 (5th Cir. 1986); *Groden v. Random House, Inc.*, 61 F.3d 1045, 1051 (2d Cir. 1995) (citing Restatement (Third) of Unfair Competition § 3 (1993)). Rather the statements at issue must be a "specific and measurable claim, capable of being proved false or of being reasonably interpreted as a statement of objective fact." *Coastal Abstract Serv., Inc. v. First Am. Title Ins. Co.*, 173 F.3d 725, 731 (9th Cir. 1999); *see also American Council*, 185 F.3d at 614 (stating that "a Lanham Act claim must be based upon a statement of fact, not of opinion"). As noted by our court in *Presidio*: "[A] statement of fact is one that (1) admits of being adjudged true or false in a way that (2) admits of empirical verification." *Presidio*, 784 F.2d at 679; *see also Southland Sod Farms v. Stover Seed Co.*, 108 F.3d 1134, 1145 (9th Cir. 1997) (stating that in order to constitute a statement of fact, a statement must make "a specific and measurable advertisement claim of product superiority").

(b)

One form of non-actionable statements of general opinion under section 43(a) of the Lanham Act has been referred to as "puffery." Puffery has been discussed at some length by other circuits. The Third Circuit has described "puffing" as "advertising that is not deceptive for no one would rely on its exaggerated claims." *U.S. Healthcare, Inc. v. Blue Cross of Greater Philadelphia*, 898 F.2d 914 (3d Cir. 1990). Similarly, the Ninth Circuit has defined "puffing" as "exaggerated advertising, blustering and boasting upon which no reasonable buyer would rely and is not actionable under 43(a)." *Southland Sod Farms v. Stover Seed Co.*, 108 F.3d 1134, 1145 (9th Cir. 1997) (quoting 3 J. Thomas McCarthy, *McCarthy on Trademarks and Unfair Competition* § 27.04[4][d] (3d ed. 1994)); *see also Cook*, 911 F.2d at 246 (stating that "puffing has been described by most courts as involving outrageous generalized statements, not making specific claims, that are so exaggerated as to preclude reliance by consumers").

These definitions of puffery are consistent with the definitions provided by the leading commentaries in trademark law. A leading authority on unfair competition has defined "puffery" as an "exaggerated advertising, blustering, and boasting upon which no reasonable buyer would rely," or "a general claim of superiority over a comparative product that is so vague, it would be understood as a mere expression of opinion." 4 J. Thomas McCarthy, *McCarthy on Trademark and Unfair Competition* § 27.38 (4th ed. 1996). Similarly, *Prosser and Keeton on Torts* defines "puffing" as "a seller's privilege to lie his head off, so long as he says nothing specific, on the theory that no reasonable man would believe him, or that no reasonable man would be influenced by such talk." W. Page

Keeton, et al., *Prosser and Keeton on the Law of Torts* § 109, at 757 (5th ed. 1984).

Drawing guidance from the writings of our sister circuits and the leading commentators, we think that non-actionable "puffery" comes in at least two possible forms: (1) an exaggerated, blustering, and boasting statement upon which no reasonable buyer would be justified in relying; or (2) a general claim of superiority over comparable products that is so vague that it can be understood as nothing more than a mere expression of opinion.

(2)

(a)

With respect to materiality, when the statements of fact at issue are shown to be literally false, the plaintiff need not introduce evidence on the issue of the impact the statements had on consumers. *See Castrol, Inc. v. Quaker State Corp.*, 977 F.2d 57, 62 (2d Cir. 1992); *Avila v. Rubin*, 84 F.3d 222, 227 (7th Cir. 1996). In such a circumstance, the court will assume that the statements actually misled consumers. *See American Council*, 185 F.3d at 614; *Johnson & Johnson, Inc. v. GAC Int'l, Inc.*, 862 F.2d 975, 977 (2d Cir. 1988); *U-Haul International, Inc. v. Jartran, Inc.*, 793 F.2d 1034, 1040 (9th Cir. 1986). On the other hand, if the statements at issue are either ambiguous or true but misleading, the plaintiff must present evidence of actual deception. *See American Council*, 185 F.3d at 616; *Smithkline*, 960 F.2d at 297 (stating that when a "plaintiff's theory of recovery is premised upon a claim of implied falsehood, a plaintiff must demonstrate, by extrinsic evidence, that the challenged commercials tend to mislead or confuse"); *Avila*, 84 F.3d at 227. The plaintiff may not rely on the judge or the jury to determine, "based solely upon his or her own intuitive reaction, whether the advertisement is deceptive." *Smithkline*, 960 F.2d at 297. Instead, proof of actual deception requires proof that "consumers were actually deceived by the defendant's ambiguous or true-but-misleading statements." *American Council*, 185 F.3d at 616; *see also Avis Rent A Car Sys., Inc. v. Hertz Corp.*, 782 F.2d 381, 386 (2d Cir. 1986) (stating that the plaintiff's claim fails due to its failure to introduce evidence establishing that the public was actually deceived by the statements at issue).

(b)

The type of evidence needed to prove materiality also varies depending on what type of recovery the plaintiff seeks. Plaintiffs looking to recover monetary damages for false or misleading advertising that is not literally false must prove actual deception. *See Balance Dynamics Corp. v. Schmitt Ind.*, 204 F.3d 683, 690 (6th Cir. 2000); *Resource Developers*, 926 F.2d at 139. Plaintiffs attempting to prove actual deception have to produce evidence of actual consumer reaction to the challenged advertising or surveys showing that a substantial number of consumers were actually misled by the advertisements. *See, e.g., PPX Enters., Inc. v. Autofidelity Enters., Inc.*, 818 F.2d 266, 271 (2d Cir. 1987) ("Actual consumer confusion often is demonstrated through the use of direct evidence, e.g., testimony from members of the buying public, as well as through circumstantial evidence, e.g., consumer surveys or consumer reaction tests.").

Plaintiffs seeking injunctive relief must prove that defendant's representations "have a tendency to deceive consumers." *Balance Dynamics*, 204 F.3d 683 at 690. *See also Resource Developers*, 926 F.2d at 139; *Blue Dane Simmental Corp. v. American Simmental Assoc.*, 178 F.3d 1035, 1042–43 (8th Cir. 1999); *Black Hills Jewelry Mfg. Co. v. Gold Rush, Inc.*, 633 F.2d 746, 753 (8th Cir. 1980); 4 *McCarty on Trademark and Unfair Competition* § 27:36 (4th ed.). Although this standard requires less proof than actual deception, plaintiffs must still produce evidence that the advertisement tends to deceive consumers. *See Coca-Cola Co. v. Tropicana Prod., Inc.*, 690 F.2d 312, 317 (2d Cir. 1982) (noting that when seeking a preliminary injunction barring an advertisement that is implicitly false, "its tendency to violate the Lanham Act by misleading, confusing or deceiving should be tested by public reaction"). To prove a tendency to deceive, plaintiffs need to show that at least some consumers were confused by the advertisements. *See, e.g., American Council*, 185 F.3d at 618 ("Although plaintiff need not present consumer surveys or testimony demonstrating actual deception, it must present evidence of some sort demonstrating that consumers were misled.")

IV

We turn now to consider the case before us. Reduced to its essence, the question is whether the evidence, viewed in the most favorable light to Pizza Hut, established that Papa John's slogan "Better Ingredients. Better Pizza." is misleading and violative of section 43(a) of the Lanham Act. In making this determination, we will first consider the slogan "Better Ingredients. Better Pizza." standing alone to determine if it is a statement of fact capable of deceiving a substantial segment of the consuming public to which it was directed. Second, we will determine whether the evidence supports the district court's conclusion that after May 1997, the slogan was tainted, and therefore actionable, as a result of its use in a series of ads comparing specific ingredients used by Papa John's with the ingredients used by its "competitors."

A

The jury concluded that the slogan itself was a "false or misleading" statement of fact, and the district court enjoined its further use. Papa John's argues, however, that this statement "quite simply is not a statement of fact, [but] rather, a statement of belief or opinion, and an argumentative one at that." Papa John's asserts that because "a statement of fact is either true or false, it is susceptible to being proved or disproved. A statement of opinion or belief, on the other hand, conveys the speaker's state of mind, and even though it may be used to attempt to persuade the listener, it is a subjective communication that may be accepted or rejected, but not proven true or false." Papa John's contends that its slogan "Better Ingredients. Better Pizza." falls into the latter category, and because the phrases "better ingredients" and "better pizza" are not subject to quantifiable measures, the slogan is non-actionable puffery.

We will therefore consider whether the slogan standing alone constitutes a statement of fact under the Lanham Act. Bisecting the slogan "Better Ingredients. Better Pizza.," it is clear that the assertion by Papa John's that it makes a "Better Pizza." is a general statement of opinion regarding the superiority of its product over all others. This simple statement, "Better Pizza.," epitomizes the exaggerated advertising, blustering, and boasting by a manufacturer upon which no consumer would reasonably rely. *See, e.g., In re Boston Beer Co.*, 198 F.3d 1370, 1372 (Fed. Cir. 1999) (stating that the phrase "The Best Beer in America" was "trade puffery" and that such a general claim of superiority "should be freely available to all competitors in any given field to refer to their products or services"); *Atari Corp. v. 3DO Co.*, 1994 WL 723601, *2 (N.D. Cal. 1994) (stating that a manufacturer's slogan that its product was "the most advanced home gaming system in the universe" was non-actionable puffery); *Nikkal Indus., Ltd. v. Salton, Inc.*, 735 F. Supp. 1227, 1234 (S.D.N.Y. 1990) (stating that a manufacturer's claim that its ice cream maker was "better" than competition ice cream makers is non-actionable puffery). Consequently, it appears indisputable that Papa John's assertion "Better Pizza." is non-actionable puffery.

Moving next to consider separately the phrase "Better Ingredients.," the same conclusion holds true. Like "Better Pizza.," it is typical puffery. The word "better," when used in this context is unquantifiable. What makes one food ingredient "better" than another comparable ingredient, without further description, is wholly a matter of individual taste or preference not subject to scientific quantification. Indeed, it is difficult to think of any product, or any component of any product, to which the term "better," without more, is quantifiable. As our court stated in *Presidio*:

> The law recognizes that a vendor is allowed some latitude in claiming merits of his wares by way of an opinion rather than an absolute guarantee, so long as he hews to the line of rectitude in matters of fact. Opinions are not only the lifestyle of democracy, they are the brag in advertising that has made for the wide dissemination of products that otherwise would never have reached the households of our citizens. If we were to accept the thesis set forth by the appellees, [that all statements by

advertisers were statements of fact actionable under the Lanham Act,] the advertising industry would have to be liquidated in short order.

Presidio, 784 F.2d at 685.

Thus, it is equally clear that Papa John's assertion that it uses "Better Ingredients." is one of opinion not actionable under the Lanham Act.

Finally, turning to the combination of the two non-actionable phrases as the slogan "Better Ingredients. Better Pizza.," we fail to see how the mere joining of these two statements of opinion could create an actionable statement of fact. Each half of the slogan amounts to little more than an exaggerated opinion of superiority that no consumer would be justified in relying upon. It has not been explained convincingly to us how the combination of the two phrases, without more, changes the essential nature of each phrase so as to make it actionable. We assume that "Better Ingredients." modifies "Better Pizza." and consequently gives some expanded meaning to the phrase "Better Pizza," i.e., our pizza is better because our ingredients are better. Nevertheless, the phrase fails to give "Better Pizza." any more quantifiable meaning. Stated differently, the adjective that continues to describe "pizza" is "better," a term that remains unquantifiable, especially when applied to the sense of taste. Consequently, the slogan as a whole is a statement of non-actionable opinion. Thus, there is no legally sufficient basis to support the jury's finding that the slogan standing alone is a "false or misleading" statement of fact.

B

We next will consider whether the use of the slogan "Better Ingredients. Better Pizza." in connection with a series of comparative ads found by the jury to be misleading—specifically, ads comparing Papa John's sauce and dough with the sauce and dough of its competitors— "tainted" the statement of opinion and made it misleading under section 43(a) of the Lanham Act. Before reaching the ultimate question of whether the slogan is actionable under the Lanham Act, we will first examine the sufficiency of the evidence supporting the jury's conclusion that the comparison ads were misleading.

(1)

After the jury returned its verdict, Papa John's filed a post-verdict motion under Federal Rule of Civil Procedure 50 for a judgment as a matter of law. In denying Papa John's motion, the district court, while apparently recognizing that the slogan "Better Ingredients. Better Pizza." standing alone is non-actionable puffery under the Lanham Act, concluded that after May 1997, the slogan was transformed as a result of its use in connection with a series of ads that the jury found misleading.

These ads had compared specific ingredients used by Papa John's with the ingredients used by its competitors. In essence, the district court held that the comparison ads in which the slogan appeared as the tag line gave objective, quantifiable, and fact-specific meaning to the slogan. Consequently, the court concluded that the slogan was misleading and actionable under section 43(a) of the Lanham Act and enjoined its further use.

(2)

We are obligated to accept the findings of the jury unless the facts point so overwhelmingly in favor of one party that no reasonable person could arrive at a different conclusion. *See Scottish Heritable Trust v. Peat Marwick Main & Co.*, 81 F.3d 606, 610 (5th Cir. 1996). In examining the record evidence, we must view it the way that is most favorable to upholding the verdict. *See Hiltgen v. Sumrall*, 47 F.3d 695, 700 (5th Cir. 1995). Viewed in this light, it is clear that there is sufficient evidence to support the jury's conclusion that the sauce and dough ads were misleading statements of fact actionable under the Lanham Act.

Turning first to the sauce ads, the evidence establishes that despite the differences in the methods used to produce their competing sauces: (1) the primary ingredient in both Pizza Hut and Papa John's sauce is vine-ripened tomatoes; (2) at the point that the competing sauces are placed on the pizza, just prior to putting the pies into the oven for cooking, the consistency and water content of the sauces are essentially identical; and (3) as noted by the district court, at no time "prior to the close of the liability phase of trial was any credible evidence presented [by Papa John's] to demonstrate the existence of demonstrable differences" in the competing sauces. Consequently, the district court was correct in concluding that: "Without any scientific support or properly conducted taste preference test, by the written and/or oral negative connotations conveyed that pizza made from tomato paste concentrate is inferior to the 'fresh pack' method used by Papa John's, its sauce advertisements conveyed an impression which is misleading. . . ." Turning our focus to the dough ads, while the evidence clearly established that Papa John's and Pizza Hut employ different methods in making their pizza dough, again, the evidence established that there is no quantifiable difference between pizza dough produced through the "cold or slow-fermentation method" (used by Papa John's), or the "frozen dough method" (used by Pizza Hut). Further, although there is some evidence indicating that the texture of the dough used by Papa John's and Pizza Hut is slightly different, this difference is not related to the manufacturing process used to produce the dough. Instead, it is due to a difference in the wheat used to make the dough. Finally, with respect to the differences in the pizza dough resulting from the use of filtered water as opposed to tap water, the evidence was sufficient for the jury to conclude that there is no quantifiable difference between dough produced with tap water, as opposed to dough produced with filtered water.

We should note again that Pizza Hut does not contest the truthfulness of the underlying factual assertions made by Papa John's in the course of the sauce and dough ads. Pizza Hut concedes that it uses "remanufactured" tomato sauce to make its pizza sauce, while Papa John's uses "fresh-pack." Further, in regard to the dough, Pizza Hut concedes the truth of the assertion that it uses tap water in making its pizza dough, which is often frozen, while Papa John's uses filtered water to make its dough, which is fresh—never frozen. Consequently, because Pizza Hut does not contest the factual basis of Papa John's factual assertions, such assertions cannot be found to be factually false, but only impliedly false or misleading.

Thus, we conclude by saying that although the ads were true about the ingredients Papa John's used, it is clear that there was sufficient evidence in the record to support the jury's conclusion that Papa John's sauce and dough ads were misleading—but not false—in their suggestion that Papa John's ingredients were superior.

(3)

Thus, having concluded that the record supports a finding that the sauce and dough ads are misleading statements of fact, we must now determine whether the district court was correct in concluding that the use of the slogan "Better Ingredients. Better Pizza." in conjunction with these misleading ads gave quantifiable meaning to the slogan making a general statement of opinion misleading within the meaning of the Lanham Act.

In support of the district court's conclusion that the slogan was transformed, Pizza Hut argues that "in construing any advertising statement, the statement must be considered in the overall context in which it appears." Building on the foundation of this basic legal principle, see Avis, 782 F.2d at 385, Pizza Hut argues that "the context in which Papa John's slogan must be viewed is the 2 1/2 year campaign during which its advertising served as 'chapters' to demonstrate the truth of the 'Better Ingredients. Better Pizza.' book." Pizza Hut argues, that because Papa John's gave consumers specific facts supporting its assertion that its sauce and dough are "better"—specific facts that the evidence, when viewed in the light most favorable to the verdict, are irrelevant in making a better pizza—Papa John's statement of opinion that it made a "Better Pizza" became misleading. In essence, Pizza Hut argues, that by using the slogan "Better Ingredients. Better Pizza." in combination with the ads comparing Papa John's sauce and dough with the sauce and dough of its competitions, Papa John's gave quantifiable meaning to the word "Better" rendering it actionable under section 43(a) of the Lanham Act.

We agree that the message communicated by the slogan "Better Ingredients. Better Pizza." is expanded and given additional meaning when it is used as the tag line in the misleading sauce and dough ads. The slogan, when used in combination with the comparison ads, gives consumers two fact-specific reasons why Papa John's ingredients are "better." Consequently, a reasonable consumer would understand the slogan, when considered in the context of the comparison ads, as conveying the following message: Papa John's uses "better ingredients," which produces a "better pizza" because Papa John's uses "fresh-pack" tomatoes, fresh dough, and filtered water. In short, Papa John's has given definition to the word "better." Thus, when the slogan is used in this context, it is no longer mere opinion, but rather takes on the characteristics of a statement of fact. When used in the context of the sauce and dough ads, the slogan is misleading for the same reasons we have earlier discussed in connection with the sauce and dough ads.

(4)

Concluding that when the slogan was used as the tag line in the sauce and dough ads it became misleading, we must now determine whether reasonable consumers would have a tendency to rely on this misleading statement of fact in making their purchasing decisions. We conclude that Pizza Hut has failed to adduce evidence establishing that the misleading statement of fact conveyed by the ads and the slogan was material to the consumers to which the slogan was directed. Consequently, because such evidence of materiality is necessary to establish liability under the Lanham Act, the district court erred in denying Papa John's motion for judgment as a matter of law.

As previously discussed, none of the underlying facts supporting Papa John's claims of ingredient superiority made in connection with the slogan were literally false. Consequently, in order to satisfy its prima facie case, Pizza Hut was required to submit evidence establishing that the impliedly false or misleading statements were material to, that is, they had a tendency to influence the purchasing decisions of, the consumers to which they were directed. *See American Council*, 185 F.3d at 614 (stating that "a plaintiff relying upon statements that are literally true yet misleading cannot obtain relief by arguing how consumers could react; it must show how consumers actually do react"); *Smithkline*, 960 F.2d at 298; *Sandoz Pharm. Corp. v. Richardson-Vicks, Inc.*, 902 F.2d 222, 228–29 (3d Cir. 1990); *Avis*, 782 F.2d at 386; see also 4 J. Thomas McCarthy, *McCarthy on Trademarks and Unfair Competition*, § 27:35 (4th ed. 1997) (stating that the "plaintiff must make some showing that the defendant's misrepresentation was 'material' in the sense that it would have some effect on consumers' purchasing decision"). We conclude that the evidence proffered by Pizza Hut fails to make an adequate showing.

In its appellate brief and during the course of oral argument, Pizza Hut directs our attention to three items of evidence in the record that it asserts establishes materiality to consumers. First, Pizza Hut points to the results of a survey conducted by an "independent expert" (Dr. Dupont) regarding the use of the slogan "Better Ingredients. Better Pizza." as written on Papa John's pizza box (the box survey). The results of the box survey, however, were excluded by the district court. Consequently, these survey results provide no basis for the jury's finding.

Second, Pizza Hut points to two additional surveys conducted by Dr. Dupont that attempted to measure consumer perception of Papa John's "taste test" ads. This survey evidence, however, fails to address Pizza Hut's claim of materiality with respect to the slogan. Moreover, the jury rejected Pizza Hut's claims of deception with regard to Papa John's "taste test" ads—the very ads at issue in these surveys.

Finally, Pizza Hut attempts to rely on Papa John's own tracking studies and on the alleged subjective intent of Papa John's executives "to create a perception that Papa John's in fact uses better ingredients" to demonstrate materiality. Although Papa John's 1998 Awareness, Usage & Attitude Tracking Study showed that 48% of the respondents believe that "Papa John's has better ingredients than other national pizza chains," the study failed to indicate whether the conclusions resulted from the advertisements at issue, or from personal eating experiences, or from a combination of both. Consequently, the results of this study are not reliable or probative to test whether the slogan was material. Further, Pizza Hut provides no precedent, and we are aware of none, that stands for the proposition that the subjective intent of the defendant's corporate executives to convey a particular message is evidence of the fact that consumers in fact relied on the message to make their purchases. Thus, this evidence does not address the ultimate issue of materiality.

In short, Pizza Hut has failed to offer probative evidence on whether the misleading facts conveyed by Papa John's through its slogan were material to consumers: that is to say, there is no evidence demonstrating that the slogan had the tendency to deceive consumers so as to affect their purchasing decisions. *See American Council*, 185 F.3d at 614; *Blue Dane*, 178 F.3d at 1042–43; *Sandoz Pharm. Corp. v. Richardson-Vicks, Inc.*, 902 F.2d 222, 228–29 (3d Cir. 1990). Thus, the district court erred in denying Papa John's motion for judgment as a matter of law.

V

In sum, we hold that the slogan "Better Ingredients. Better Pizza." standing alone is not an objectifiable statement of fact upon which consumers would be justified in relying. Thus, it does not constitute a false or misleading statement of fact actionable under section 43(a) of the Lanham Act.

Additionally, while the slogan, when appearing in the context of some of the post-May 1997 comparative advertising—specifically, the sauce and dough campaigns—was given objectifiable meaning and thus became misleading and actionable, Pizza Hut has failed to adduce sufficient evidence establishing that the misleading facts conveyed by the slogan were material to the consumers to which it was directed. Thus, Pizza Hut failed to produce evidence of a Lanham Act violation, and the district court erred in denying Papa John's motion for judgment as a matter of law.

Therefore, the judgment of the district court denying Papa John's motion for judgment as a matter of law is REVERSED; the final judgment of the district court is VACATED; and the case is REMANDED for entry of judgment for Papa John's.

NOTES FOR DISCUSSION

1.   *Puffery.* Section 43(a) prohibits only "false or misleading description . . . or representation of fact." The *Papa John's* court distinguishes statements of opinion or puffery from statements of fact. As a policy matter, why is puffery not actionable? Would a reasonable consumer rely on the statement "Better Ingredients. Better Pizza"? Is there some criteria by which we can determine whether Papa John's uses "Better Ingredients" or makes a "Better Pizza"? What tests does the court offer to separate opinion from fact?

Are you persuaded by the court's holding that the statement "Better Ingredients" and the statement "Better Pizza", each taken on its own, is not a representation of fact, but an expression of opinion? Are you persuaded by the court's reasoning that if each alone is opinion, then the combined statement "Better Ingredients. Better Pizza" must also be non-actionable opinion? Can we perform a consumer taste test to resolve whether Papa John's pizza is in fact better? Is "better pizza" a representation of better taste, or of something else, perhaps better nutritional value? Is the line between opinion and fact a question for the court to resolve based upon its own impression of the advertisements, or is it a question of consumer perception that requires survey or other evidence that demonstrates how consumers perceived the advertisement?

Assuming that the slogan, "Better Ingredients. Better Pizza," is a statement of opinion on its own, how does it become factual when combined with the "dough" and "sauce" advertisements? Does the court rely on consumer surveys or other consumer perception evidence to support its conclusion that the slogan, "Better Ingredients. Better Pizza," became factual as a result of the "dough" and "sauce" advertisements? What measurable attributes are associated with the slogan when it is used in conjunction with the "dough" and "sauce" advertisements? In the "dough" and "sauce" advertisements, Papa John's defines what it means by "better ingredients"— "fresh-pack" tomatoes, fresh dough, and filtered water. Certainly, we now have express representations—that Papa John's uses "fresh-pack tomatoes, fresh dough, and filtered water"—that, if false, would form a basis for liability. How do this listing of specific ingredients make the slogan "Better Ingredients. Better Pizza" factual? Can we now test whether these ingredients are, in fact, "better" in a way that we could not before? Do "dough" and "sauce" advertisements make clear that the "better" claim is related to taste, as opposed to nutrition?

Accepting the court's conclusion that the slogan, "Better Ingredients. Better Pizza," became factual when used in the "dough" and "sauce" advertisements, did the slogan become literally false or only implicitly false or misleading? Can a plaintiff establish that an advertisement is implicitly false or misleading without evidence of how consumers perceive the advertisement? Did Pizza Hut present such evidence?

Are the following statements puffery?

a) The tag line "Whiter is not possible" used in conjunction with a clothes detergent with a whitening agent. *See Clorox Co. v. Proctor & Gamble Commer. Co.*, 228 F.3d 24, 39 (1st Cir. 2000) ("[I]t is a specific, measurable claim, and hence not puffing.").

b) A mobile telephone service made the following statement in its advertisements: "We ask you: Would you prefer to do business with the phone company with the best technology, lower rates, and better customer service?" *See Metro Mobile CTS, Inc. v. Newvector Communications, Inc.*, 643 F.Supp. 1289 (D. Ariz.) (granting preliminary injunction), *rev'd without opinion*, 803 F.2d 724 (9th Cir. 1986) (puffing).

c) Pennzoil claimed that its motor oil provides "longer engine life and better engine protection." *See Castrol, Inc. v. Pennzoil Co.*, 987 F.2d 939, 946 (3d Cir. 1993) (not puffing: "Pennzoil's claim of engine protection by contrast involves more than a mere generality. Here, the claim is both specific and measurable by comparative research.").

d) A debt collection service, NCC, runs the following advertisement:

DO YOU PAY FOR AN ATTORNEY TO DO YOUR COLLECTION WORK? And pay. And pay. And pay! Were you quoted a really low "collection fee" only to find that "costs" are eating you alive? Do you find that you are doing all the "leg work" for your lawyer? Then call us—we're the low cost commercial collection experts.

In addition to any express representation(s) in the advertisement, the court finds that the ad also implicitly asserts that "NCC offers the same collection services as lawyers at a lower or more competitive price." *Cook, Perkiss & Liehe, Inc. v. Northern California Collection Serv. Inc.*, 911 F.2d 242, 246 (9th Cir. 1990) (puffery: "the alleged misrepresentations in NCC's advertisement . . . are general assertions of superiority rather than factual misrepresentations").

2.   *Materiality.* According to the Fifth Circuit, does a plaintiff have to prove materiality with respect to literally false statements? Why or why not?

Does a plaintiff have to prove materiality with respect to implicitly false or misleading statements? Why or why not?

Other circuits disagree with the Fifth Circuit's dicta suggesting that materiality is presumed if a statement is literally false. *See Johnson & Johnson Vision Care, Inc. v. 1-800-Contacts, Inc.*, 299 F.3d 1242, 1250 (11th Cir. 2002) ("The plaintiff must establish materiality even when a court finds that the defendant's advertisement is literally false."); *Cashmere & Camel Hair Mfrs. Inst. v. Saks Fifth Ave.*, 284 F.3d 302, 312 n.10 (1st Cir.) (same), *cert. denied*, 537 U.S. 1001 (2002); *S.C. Johnson & Son, Inc. v. Clorox Co.*, 241 F.3d 232, 238 (2d Cir. 2001) (same).

In any event, how does a plaintiff go about proving materiality? What if Pizza Hut could show that Papa John's market share jumped from 22.2 percent to 32.1 percent of the market shortly after Papa John's began airing the "Better Ingredients. Better Pizza" advertisements? Would that demonstrate materiality? If not, could Pizza Hut perform a survey to test for materiality? What would such a survey ask?

How else can a plaintiff demonstrate materiality? What if a defendant is selling coats as "Cashmere and Wool" and the label states that the coats "contain 70 percent wool, 20 percent nylon, and 10 percent cashmere," yet tests demonstrate that the coats contain no cashmere at all? Is it enough that the false statement relates to "an inherent quality or characteristic" of the product? In *Cashmere & Camel Hair Mfrs. Inst. v. Saks Fifth Ave.*, the First Circuit held that it was.

> [I]t seems obvious that cashmere is a basic ingredient of a cashmere-blend garment; without it, the product could not be deemed a cashmere-blend garment or compete in the cashmere-blend market. Thus, it seems reasonable to conclude that defendants' misrepresentation of the blazers' cashmere content is material because it relates to a characteristic that defines the product at issue, as well as the market in which it is sold.

284 F.3d at 312.

Isn't it equally obvious that a misleading claim with respect to whether Papa John's pizza is "better" will prove material? Why is Papa John's using the slogan if it is not "likely to influence the purchasing decision"?

Is the following misrepresentation material? In the late 1990s, Motorola offered the SportsTrax a pager service that provided continuously updated scores from various sporting games. Motorola advertised that the "SportsTrax provides 'updated game information direct from each arena' which 'originates from the press table in each arena' and on a statement appearing on the spine of the retail box and on the retail display stand that SportsTrax provides 'game updates from the arena.'" In fact, Motorola collects the information it transmits on the SportsTrax service from radio and television broadcasts of the games. *See National Basketball Ass'n v. Motorola, Inc.*, 105 F.3d 841, 855 (2d Cir. 1997) (not material).

CHAPTER 13

THE RIGHT OF PUBLICITY

∎ ∎ ∎

A. ORIGINS AND JUSTIFICATIONS

At the turn of the twentieth century, there was no legal or equitable right to control the use of an individual's image or likeness for advertising or otherwise, beyond that available through libel. In the United States, the Georgia Supreme Court in *Pavesich v. New England Life Ins. Co.* was the first to recognize and grant relief for the unauthorized use of an individual's photograph in connection with an advertisement for a life insurance company's products. 122 Ga. 190, 50 S.E. 68 (1905). The court held that such an unauthorized commercial use trespassed upon the plaintiff's right of privacy. Not all courts agreed, however. Just three years earlier, the New York Court of Appeals had refused to recognize such a right to privacy in a case in which a woman's photograph was used without her permission under the heading "Flour of the Family" in advertisements for Franklin Mills flour. *Roberson v. Rochester Folding Box Co.*, 171 N.Y. 538, 64 N.E. 442 (1902).

Even where courts recognized a cause of action against unauthorized commercial use under the right of privacy, dealing with such uses as a privacy issue created two different problems. First, to the extent the right to control such advertising (or commercial) uses arose from the right of privacy—the right to be let alone—courts consistently held that individuals who had become famous or otherwise publicly well known had waived their right to control such advertising uses. Courts therefore almost universally permitted the unauthorized use of an individual's name or likeness for advertising purposes so long as the individual was famous or otherwise publicly known. *See, e.g., Atkinson v. John E. Doherty & Co.*, 121 Mich. 372, 80 N.W. 285 (1899). Second, the right of privacy is inherently personal. For that reason, tying the right to control advertising uses of an individual's name or likeness to the right of privacy suggests that such a right is also personal. Making the right a personal, rather than a property, right, raised questions as to whether the right was transferable and whether it survived a person's death.

It was not until 1953 that a court suggested that a person had a property right to control the commercial use of his or her name, image, or likeness, and the right of publicity was born.

HAELAN LABORATORIES, INC. v. TOPPS CHEWING GUM, INC.

202 F.2d 866 (2d Cir.), *cert. denied*, 346 U.S. 816 (1953)

FRANK, CIRCUIT JUDGE

After a trial without a jury, the trial judge dismissed the complaint on the merits. The plaintiff maintains that defendant invaded plaintiff's exclusive right to use the photographs of leading baseball-players. Probably because the trial judge ruled against plaintiff's legal contentions, some of the facts were not too clearly found.

1.   So far as we can now tell, there were instances of the following kind:

(a). The plaintiff, engaged in selling chewing-gum, made a contract with a ball-player providing that plaintiff for a stated term should have the exclusive right to use the ball-player's photograph in connection with the sales of plaintiff's gum; the ball-player agreed not to grant any other gum manufacturer a similar right during such term; the contract gave plaintiff an option to extend the term for a designated period.

(b). Defendant, a rival chewing-gum manufacturer, knowing of plaintiff's contract, deliberately induced the ball-player to authorize defendant, by a contract with defendant, to use the player's photograph in connection with the sales of defendant's gum either during the original or extended term of plaintiff's contract, and defendant did so use the photograph.

Defendant argues that, even if such facts are proved, they show no actionable wrong, for this reason: The contract with plaintiff was no more than a release by the ball-player to plaintiff of the liability which, absent the release, plaintiff would have incurred in using the ball-player's photograph, because such a use, without his consent, would be an invasion of his right of privacy under Section 50 and Section 51 of the New York Civil Rights Law; this statutory right of privacy is personal, not assignable; therefore, plaintiff's contract vested in plaintiff no "property" right or other legal interest which defendant's conduct invaded.

Both parties agree, and so do we, that, on the facts here, New York "law" governs. And we shall assume, for the moment, that, under the New York decisions, defendant correctly asserts that any such contract between plaintiff and a ball-player, in so far as it merely authorized plaintiff to use the player's photograph, created nothing but a release of liability. On that basis, were there no more to the contract, plaintiff would have no actionable claim against defendant. But defendant's argument neglects the fact that, in the contract, the ball-player also promised not to give similar releases to others. If defendant, knowing of the contract, deliberately induced the ball-player to break that promise, defendant behaved tortiously. . . .

2.   The foregoing covers the situations where defendant, by itself or through its agent, induced breaches. But in those instances where Russell induced the breach, we have a different problem; and that problem also confronts us in instances—alleged in one paragraph of the complaint and to which the trial judge in his opinion also (although not altogether clearly) refers—where defendant, "with knowledge of plaintiff's exclusive rights, used a photograph of a ball-player without his consent during the term of his contract with plaintiff."

With regard to such situations, we must consider defendant's contention that none of plaintiff's contracts created more than a release of liability, because a man has no legal interest in the publication of his picture other than his right of privacy, i.e., a personal and non-assignable right not to have his feelings hurt by such a publication.

A majority of this court rejects this contention. We think that, in addition to and independent of that right of privacy (which in New York derives from statute), a man has a right in the publicity value of his photograph, i.e., the right to grant the exclusive privilege of publishing his picture, and that such a grant may validly be made "in gross," i.e., without an accompanying transfer of a business or of anything else. Whether it be labeled a "property" right is immaterial; for here, as often elsewhere, the tag "property" simply symbolizes the fact that courts enforce a claim which has pecuniary worth.

This right might be called a "right of publicity." For it is common knowledge that many prominent persons (especially actors and ball-players), far from having their feelings bruised through public exposure of their likenesses, would feel sorely deprived if they no longer received money for authorizing advertisements, popularizing their countenances, displayed in newspapers, magazines, busses, trains and subways. This right of publicity would usually yield them no money unless it could be made the subject of an exclusive grant which barred any other advertiser from using their pictures. . . .

3.   We must remand to the trial court for a determination (on the basis of the present record and of further evidence introduced by either party) of these facts: (1) the date and contents of each of plaintiff's contracts, and whether plaintiff exercised its option to renew; (2) defendant's or Players' conduct with respect to each such contract.

Of course, if defendant made a contract with a ball-player which was not executed—or which did not authorize defendant to use the player's photograph—until the expiration of the original or extended term of plaintiff's contract with that player, or which did not induce a breach of the agreement to renew, then defendant did no legal wrong to plaintiff.

The same is true of instances where neither defendant nor Players induced a breach of plaintiff's contract, and defendant did not use the player's photograph until after the expiration of such original or extended or option term.

If, upon further exploration of the facts, the trial court, in the light of our opinion, concludes that defendant is liable, it will, of course, ascertain damages and decide what equitable relief is justified.

Reversed and remanded.

SWAN, CHIEF JUDGE (concurring in part).

I agree that the cause should be reversed and remanded, and I concur in so much of the opinion as deals with the defendant's liability for intentionally inducing a ball-player to breach a contract which gave plaintiff the exclusive privilege of using his picture.

CARDTOONS, L.C. v. MAJOR LEAGUE BASEBALL PLAYERS ASS'N
95 F.3d 959 (10th Cir. 1996)

TACHA, CIRCUIT JUDGE

Cardtoons, L.C., ("Cardtoons") brought this action to obtain a declaratory judgment that its parody trading cards featuring active major league baseball players do not infringe on the publicity rights of members of the Major League Baseball Players Association ("MLBPA"). The district court held that the trading cards constitute expression protected by the First Amendment and therefore read a parody exception into Oklahoma's statutory right of publicity. MLBPA appeals, arguing that . . . Cardtoons does not have a First Amendment right to market its trading cards. . . . Because Cardtoons' First Amendment right to free expression outweighs MLBPA's proprietary right of publicity, we affirm.

I.   Background

Cardtoons formed in late 1992 to produce parody trading cards featuring caricatures of major league baseball players. Cardtoons contracted with a political cartoonist, a sports artist, and a sports author and journalist, who designed a set of 130 cards. The majority of the cards, 71, have caricatures of active major league baseball players on the front and humorous commentary about their careers on the back. The balance of the set is comprised of 20 "Big Bang Bucks" cards (cartoon drawings of currency with caricatures of the most highly paid players on the front, yearly salary statistics on the back), 10 "Spectra" cards (caricatures of active players on the front, nothing on the back), 10 retired player cards (caricatures of retired players on the front, humorous commentary about their careers on the back), 11 "Politics in Baseball" cards (cartoons featuring caricatures of political and sports figures on the front, humorous text on the back), 7 standing cards (caricatures of team logos on the front, humorous text on the back), and 1 checklist card. Except for the Spectra cards, the back of each card bears the Cardtoons logo and the following statement: "Cardtoons baseball is a parody and is NOT licensed by Major League Baseball Properties or Major League Baseball Players Association."

A person reasonably familiar with baseball can readily identify the players lampooned on the parody trading cards. The cards use similar names, recognizable caricatures, distinctive team colors, and commentary about individual players. For example, the card parodying San Francisco Giants' outfielder Barry Bonds calls him "Treasury Bonds," and features a recognizable caricature of Bonds, complete with earring, tipping a bat boy for a 24 carat gold "Fort Knoxville Slugger." The back of the card has a team logo (the "Gents"), and the following text:

> Redemption qualities and why Treasury Bonds is the league's most valuable player:
>
>   1.   Having Bonds on your team is like having money in the bank.
>
>   2.   He plays so hard he gives 110 percent, compounded daily.
>
>   3.   He turned down the chance to play other sports because he has a high interest rate in baseball.
>
>   4.   He deposits the ball in the bleachers.
>
>   5.   He is into male bonding.
>
>   6.   He is a money player.
>
>   7.   He has a 24-karat Gold Glove.
>
>   8.   He always cashes in on the payoff pitch.
>
> NOTICE: Bonds is not tax-free in all states but is double exempt.

At the end of the 1992 season, Barry Bonds was a two-time winner of the National League's Most Valuable Player award, a three-time winner of a Gold Glove award, and had just signed a six-year contract for $43.75 million, making him the highest-paid player in baseball. Richard Hoffer, *The Importance of Being Barry: The Giants' Barry Bonds is the Best Player in the Game Today—Just Ask Him*, Sports Illustrated, May 24, 1993, at 13. No one the least bit familiar with the game of baseball would mistake Cardtoons' "Treasury Bonds" for anyone other than the Giants' Barry Bonds. Other caricatures, such as "Ken Spiffy, Jr." of the "Mari-Nerds" (Ken Griffey, Jr., of the Seattle Mariners), are equally identifiable.

The trading cards ridicule the players using a variety of themes. A number of the cards, including the "Treasury Bonds" card and all of the Big Bang Bucks cards, humorously criticize players for their substantial salaries. (The irony of MLBPA's counterclaim for profits from the cards is not lost on this panel.) Other trading cards mock the players' narcissism, as exemplified by the card featuring "Egotisticky Henderson" of the "Pathetics," parodying Ricky Henderson, then of the Oakland Athletics. The card features a caricature of Henderson raising his finger in a "number one" sign while patting himself on the back, with the following text:

> Egotisticky Henderson, accepting the "Me-Me Award" from himself at the annual "Egotisticky Henderson Fan Club" banquet, sponsored by Egotisticky Henderson:
>
>> I would just like to thank myself for all I have done. (Pause for cheers.) I am the greatest of all time. (Raise arms triumphantly.) I love myself. (Pause for more cheers.) I am honored to know me. (Pause for louder cheers.) I wish there were two of me so I could spend more time with myself. (Wipe tears from eyes.) I couldn't have done it without me. (Remove cap and hold it aloft.) It's friends like me that keep me going. (Wave to crowd and acknowledge standing ovation.)

The remainder of the cards poke fun at things such as the players' names ("Chili Dog Davis" who "plays the game with relish," a parody of designated hitter Chili Davis), physical characteristics ("Cloud Johnson," a parody of six-foot-ten-inch pitcher Randy Johnson), and onfield behavior (a backflipping "Ozzie Myth," a parody of shortstop Ozzie Smith).

The format of the parody trading cards is similar to that of traditional baseball cards. The cards, printed on cardboard stock measuring 2 1/2 by 3 1/2 inches, have images of players on the front and player information on the back. Like traditional cards, the parody cards use a variety of special effects, including foil embossing, stamping, spectra etching, and U-V coating. Cardtoons also takes advantage of a number of trading card industry techniques to enhance the value of its cards, such as limiting production, serially numbering cases of the cards, and randomly inserting subsets and "chase cards" (special trading cards) into the sets.

After designing its trading cards, Cardtoons contracted with a printer (Champs Marketing, Inc.) and distributor (TCM Associates) and implemented a marketing plan. As part of that plan, Cardtoons placed an advertisement in the May 14, 1993, issue of Sports Collectors Digest. That advertisement tipped off MLBPA, the defendant in this action, and prompted its attorney to write cease and desist letters to both Cardtoons and Champs.

MLBPA is the exclusive collective bargaining agent for all active major league baseball players, and operates a group licensing program in which it acts as the assignee of the individual publicity rights of all active players. Since 1966, MLBPA has entered into group licensing arrangements for a variety of products, such as candy bars, cookies, cereals, and, most importantly, baseball trading cards, which generate over seventy percent of its licensing revenue. MLBPA receives royalties from these sales and distributes the money to individual players.

After receiving the cease and desist letter from MLBPA, Champs advised Cardtoons that it would not print the parody cards until a court of competent jurisdiction had determined that the cards did not violate MLBPA' rights. Cardtoons then filed this suit seeking a declaratory judgment that its cards do not violate the publicity or other property rights of MLBPA or its members. Cardtoons also sought damages for tortious interference with its contractual relationship with Champs, as well as an injunction to prevent MLBPA from threatening legal action against Champs or other third parties with whom Cardtoons had contracted concerning the cards. MLBPA moved to dismiss for lack of subject matter jurisdiction, and counterclaimed for a declaratory judgment, injunction, and damages for violation of its members' rights of publicity under Oklahoma law.

The district court referred the case to a magistrate, who issued his Report and Recommendation in favor of MLBPA. The magistrate stated that the parody cards infringed on MLBPA's right of publicity and that, under either a trademark balancing test or a copyright fair use test, Cardtoons did not have a First Amendment right to market its cards without a license from MLBPA. The district court initially adopted the magistrate's Report and Recommendation, *Cardtoons, L.C. v. Major League Baseball Players Association*, 838 F. Supp. 1501 (N.D. Okla. 1993), but subsequently vacated that decision and issued *Cardtoons, L.C. v. Major League Baseball Players Association*, 868 F. Supp. 1266 (N.D. Okla. 1994). In its second opinion, the court wholly rejected application of a trademark balancing test to the right of publicity, and instead applied a copyright fair use analysis. Unlike the magistrate, however, the court held that a fair use analysis requires recognition of a parody exception to the Oklahoma publicity rights statute, and issued a declaratory judgment in favor of Cardtoons. This appeal followed. . . .

III. The Merits

Cardtoons asks for a declaration that it can distribute its parody trading cards without the consent of MLBPA. There are three steps to our analysis of this issue. First, we determine whether the cards infringe upon MLBPA's property rights as established by either the Lanham Act or Oklahoma's right of publicity statute. If so, we then ascertain whether the cards are protected by the First Amendment. Finally, if both parties have cognizable rights at stake, we proceed to a final determination of the relative importance of those rights in the context of this case.

A. MLBPA's Property Rights

1. The Lanham Act

We begin by determining whether the cards violate MLBPA's property rights under the Lanham Act. Section 43(a)(1) of the Lanham Act, 15 U.S.C. § 1125(a)(1), creates a federal remedy for false representations or false designations of origin used in connection with the sale of a product. . . .

The hallmark of a Lanham Act suit is proof of the likelihood of confusion, which occurs "when consumers make an incorrect mental association between the involved commercial products or their producers." *San Francisco Arts & Athletics, Inc. v. United States Olympic Comm.*, 483 U.S. 522, 564 (1987) (Brennan, J., dissenting), *quoted with approval in Jordache Enters., Inc. v. Hogg Wyld, Ltd.*, 828 F.2d 1482, 1484 (10th Cir. 1987).

Likelihood of confusion is a question of fact that we review for clear error. *Jordache*, 828 F.2d at 1484. The district court found that Cardtoons' parody cards created no likelihood of confusion. We agree that no one would mistake MLBPA and its members as anything other than the targets of the parody cards. Most of the cards have a Cardtoons logo and a statement that they are not licensed by MLBPA. In addition, as with all successful parodies, the effect of the cards is to amuse rather than confuse. "A parody relies upon a *difference* from the original mark, presumably a humorous difference, in order to produce its desired effect." *Id.* at 1486 (emphasis added). Cardtoons' success depends upon the humorous association of its parody cards with traditional, licensed baseball cards, not upon public confusion as to the source of the cards. The district court's decision that the parody cards do not create a likelihood of confusion is not clearly erroneous, and thus the cards do not infringe upon MLBPA's property rights under the Lanham Act.

2. The Right of Publicity

The right of publicity is the right of a person to control the commercial use of his or her identity. 1 J. Thomas McCarthy, *The Rights of Publicity and Privacy* § 1.1[A][1] (1996); *see Restatement (Third) of Unfair Competition* § 46 (1995). While the right was originally intertwined with the right of privacy, courts soon came to recognize a distinction between the personal right to be left alone and the business right to control use of one's identity in commerce. *McCarthy, supra,* §§ 1.1–1.6; Michael Madow, *Private Ownership of Public Image: Popular Culture and Publicity Rights*, 81 Cal. L. Rev. 127, 167–78 (1993). The latter was first acknowledged as a distinct privilege and termed the "right of publicity" in *Haelan Laboratories, Inc. v. Topps Chewing Gum, Inc.*,

202 F.2d 866 (2d Cir.), *cert. denied*, 346 U.S. 816, 98 L.Ed. 343, 74 S.Ct. 26 (1953). . . . The development of this new intellectual property right was further cultivated by Melville Nimmer in his seminal article *The Right of Publicity*, 19 Law & Contemp. Probs. 203 (1954). Nimmer, who was counsel for Paramount Pictures at the time, Madow, *supra*, at 174 n.238, referred to "the needs of Broadway and Hollywood" in describing the foundations and parameters of the right, Nimmer, *supra*, at 203. The right of publicity is now recognized by common law or statute in twenty-five states. McCarthy, *supra*, § 6.1[B].

Like trademark and copyright, the right of publicity involves a cognizable property interest. *Zacchini v. Scripps-Howard Broadcasting Co.*, 433 U.S. 562, 573, 53 L.Ed.2d 965, 97 S.Ct. 2849 (1977); *Restatement (Third) of Unfair Competition* § 46 cmt. g. Most formulations of the right protect against the unauthorized use of certain features of a person's identity—such as name, likeness, or voice—for commercial purposes. *See* McCarthy, *supra*, §§ 4.9–4.15. Although publicity rights are related to laws preventing false endorsement, they offer substantially broader protection. Suppose, for example, that a company, Mitchell Fruit, wanted to use pop singer Madonna in an advertising campaign to sell bananas, but Madonna never ate its fruit and would not agree to endorse its products. If Mitchell Fruit posted a billboard featuring a picture of Madonna and the phrase, "Madonna may have ten platinum albums, but she's never had a Mitchell banana," Madonna would not have a claim for false endorsement. She would, however, have a publicity rights claim, because Mitchell Fruit misappropriated her name and likeness for commercial purposes. Publicity rights, then, are a form of property protection that allows people to profit from the full commercial value of their identities.

Oklahoma first recognized the right of publicity as early as 1965, but expanded the right in a 1985 statute that is virtually identical to California's right of publicity statute, Cal. Civ. Code §§ 990 and 3344. The heart of the Oklahoma statute provides that:

> Any person who knowingly uses another's name, voice, signature, photograph, or likeness, in any manner, on or in products, merchandise, or goods, or for purposes of advertising or selling, or soliciting purchases of, products, merchandise, goods, or services, without such persons prior consent, . . . shall be liable for any damages sustained by the person or persons injured as a result thereof, and any profits from the unauthorized use that are attributable to the use shall be taken into account in computing the actual damages.

Okla. Stat. tit. 12, § 1449(A). Thus, a civil suit for infringement of MLBPA's publicity right under § 1449(A) requires proof of three elements: (1) knowing use of player names or likenesses (2) on products, merchandise, or goods (3) without MLBPA's prior consent. If MLBPA proves these three elements, then the burden shifts to Cardtoons to raise a valid defense.

There is little question that Cardtoons knowingly uses the names and likenesses of major league baseball players. This is evident from an examination of the cards and the testimony of the president of Cardtoons, who conceded that the cards borrow the likenesses of active players. Indeed, the caricatures are only humorous because they, along with the parodied name, team, and commentary, are accurate enough to allow identification of the players being parodied. The second and third elements of the statute are also satisfied. The cards are clearly a product, designed to be widely marketed and sold for profit. In addition, the parties have stipulated that MLBPA has not consented to Cardtoons' use of player likenesses. Cardtoons' parody cards, then, do infringe upon MLBPA's publicity right as defined in § 1449(A).

The Oklahoma publicity statute contains two exceptions designed to accommodate the First Amendment. The first, a "news" exception, exempts use of a person's identity in connection with any news, public affairs, or sports broadcast or account, or any political campaign, from the dictates of the statute. Okla. stat. tit. 12, § 1449(D). The second exception, roughly analogous to the First Amendment concept of "incidental use," exempts use in a commercial medium that is not directly connected with commercial sponsorship or paid advertising. Okla. stat. tit. 12, § 1449(F). The news and incidental use exceptions, however, provide no haven for Cardtoons. Cardtoons' commercial venture is not in connection with any news account. Moreover, the company's use of player likenesses is directly connected with a proposed commercial endeavor; indeed, the players were specifically selected for their wide market appeal. Thus, notwithstanding any First Amendment defense, Cardtoons' use of player likenesses on its cards violates the Oklahoma statute and infringes upon the property rights of MLBPA.

B. Cardtoons' First Amendment Right

Because the parody trading cards infringe upon MLBPA's property rights, we must consider whether Cardtoons has a countervailing First Amendment right to publish the cards. The First Amendment only protects speech from regulation by the government. Although this is a civil action between private parties, it involves application of a state statute that Cardtoons claims imposes restrictions on its right of free expression. Application of that statute thus satisfies the state action requirement of Cardtoons' First Amendment claim. *See New York Times Co. v. Sullivan*, 376 U.S. 254, 265 (1964).

Cardtoons' parody trading cards receive full protection under the First Amendment. The cards provide social commentary on public figures, major league baseball players, who are involved in a significant commercial enterprise, major league baseball. While not core political speech (the cards do not, for example, adopt a position on the Ken Griffey, Jr., for President campaign), this type of commentary on an important social institution constitutes protected expression.

The cards are no less protected because they provide humorous rather than serious commentary. Speech that entertains, like speech that informs, is protected by the First Amendment because "the line between the informing and the entertaining is too elusive for the protection of that basic right." *Winters v. New York*, 333 U.S. 507, 510 (1948); *see Zacchini*, 433 U.S. at 562, 578. Moreover, Cardtoons makes use of artistic and literary devices with distinguished traditions. Parody, for example, is a humorous form of social commentary that dates to Greek antiquity, and has since made regular appearances in English literature. *See L.L. Bean, Inc. v. Drake Publishers, Inc.*, 811 F.2d 26, 28 (1st Cir.), *appeal dismissed and cert. denied*, 483 U.S. 1013 (1987). In addition, cartoons and caricatures, such as those in the trading cards, have played a prominent role in public and political debate throughout our nation's history. *See Hustler Magazine v. Falwell*, 485 U.S. 46, 53–55 (1988). Thus, the trading cards' commentary on these public figures and the major commercial enterprise in which they work receives no less protection because the cards are amusing.

MLBPA contends that Cardtoons' speech receives less protection because it fails to use a traditional medium of expression. The protections afforded by the First Amendment, however, have never been limited to newspapers and books. The Supreme Court has relied on the First Amendment to strike down ordinances that ban the distribution of pamphlets, *Lovell v. Griffin*, 303 U.S. 444, 451–52 (1938), the circulation of handbills, *Jamison v. Texas*, 318 U.S. 413, 416 (1943), and the display of yard signs, *City of Ladue v. Gilleo*, 512 U.S. 43 (1994). Moreover, many untraditional forms of expression are also protected by the First Amendment. *See, e.g., Texas v. Johnson*, 491 U.S. 397 (1989) (flag burning); *Schad v. Mount Ephraim*, 452 U.S. 61 (1981) (nude dancing); *Cohen v. California*, 403 U.S. 15 (1971) (wearing a jacket bearing the words "Fuck the Draft"). Thus, even if the trading cards are not a traditional medium of expression, they nonetheless contain protected speech.

Moreover, even if less common mediums of expression were to receive less First Amendment protection (perhaps out of concern for whether they contain any expression at all), trading cards do not fall into that category. Baseball cards have been an important means of informing the public about baseball players for over a century. "Trading, collecting and learning about players are the most common reasons for children to purchase baseball cards. . . . They are, in other words, an education in baseball." *Fleer Corp. v. Topps Chewing Gum, Inc.*, 501 F. Supp. 485,

495–96 (E.D. Pa. 1980), *rev'd on other grounds*, 658 F.2d 139 (3d Cir. 1981), *cert. denied*, 455 U.S. 1019 (1982). . . .

MLBPA also maintains that the parody trading cards are commercial merchandise rather than protected speech. However, we see no principled distinction between speech and merchandise that informs our First Amendment analysis. The fact that expressive materials are sold neither renders the speech unprotected, *Virginia State Bd. of Pharmacy v. Virginia Citizens Consumer Council, Inc.*, 425 U.S. 748, 761, 48 L.Ed.2d 346, 96 S.Ct. 1817 (1976), nor alters the level of protection under the First Amendment, *Lakewood v. Plain Dealer Publishing Co.*, 486 U.S. 750, 756 n.5, 100 L.Ed.2d 771, 108 S.Ct. 2138 (1988). Cardtoons need not give away its trading cards in order to bring them within the ambit of the First Amendment. *See Lakewood*, 486 U.S. at 756 n.5.

MLBPA further argues that the parody cards are commercial speech and should therefore receive less protection under the First Amendment. The Supreme Court has defined commercial speech as "expression related solely to the economic interests of the speaker and its audience." *Central Hudson Gas & Elec. Corp. v. Public Serv. Comm'n*, 447 U.S. 557, 561, 65 L.Ed.2d 341, 100 S.Ct. 2343 (1980). Speech that does no more than propose a commercial transaction, for example, is commercial speech. *See Virginia State Bd. of Pharmacy*, 425 U.S. at 762. Thus, commercial speech is best understood as speech that merely advertises a product or service for business purposes, *see 44 Liquormart, Inc. v. Rhode Island*, 134 L.Ed.2d 711, 116 S.Ct. 1495, 1504 (1996) (plurality opinion) (outlining a brief history of commercial speech that is, essentially, a history of advertising). As such, commercial speech may receive something less than the strict review afforded other types of speech. *Id.* at 1507.

Cardtoons' trading cards, however, are not commercial speech—they do not merely advertise another unrelated product. Although the cards are sold in the marketplace, they are not transformed into commercial speech merely because they are sold for profit. *Virginia State Bd. of Pharmacy*, 425 U.S. at 761. Contrary to MLBPA's argument, therefore, the cards are unlike the parody in the only other circuit court decision addressing the constitutional tensions inherent in a celebrity parody, *White v. Samsung Electronics America, Inc.*, 971 F.2d 1395 (9th Cir.), *cert. denied*, 508 U.S. 951, 124 L.Ed.2d 660, 113 S.Ct. 2443 (1993). In that case, defendant Samsung published an advertisement featuring a costumed robot that parodied Vanna White, the letter-turner on television's Wheel of Fortune, and White sued for violation of her right of publicity. The court noted that in cases of noncommercial parodies, "the first amendment hurdle will bar most right of publicity actions against those activities." *Id.* at 1401 n.3. However, without engaging in a methodical commercial speech analysis of Samsung's First Amendment defense, the court ruled that White's claim was sufficient to withstand Samsung's motion for summary judgment. We disagree with the result in that case for reasons discussed in the two dissents that it engendered. *Id.* at 1407–08 (Alarcon, J., concurring in part and dissenting in part); *White v. Samsung Elecs. Am., Inc.*, 989 F.2d 1512, 1512–23 (9th Cir. 1993) (denial of rehearing en banc) (Kozinski, J., dissenting). Moreover, our case is distinguished by the fact that the speech involved is not commercial, but rather speech subject to full First Amendment protection. *White*, therefore, is inapposite, and we must directly confront the central problem in this case: whether Cardtoons' First Amendment right trumps MLBPA's property right.

C. Balancing Free Speech Rights with Property Rights

In resolving the tension between the First Amendment and publicity rights in this case, we find little guidance in cases involving parodies of other forms of intellectual property. Trademark and copyright, for example, have built-in mechanisms that serve to avoid First Amendment concerns of this kind. As discussed above, proof of trademark infringement under the Lanham Act requires proof of a likelihood of confusion, but, in the case of a good trademark parody, there is little likelihood of confusion, since the humor lies in the difference between the original and the parody. The Copyright Act of 1976 contains a similar mechanism, the fair use exception, which permits the use of copyrighted materials for purposes such as criticism and comment. 17 U.S.C. § 107; *see Campbell v. Acuff-Rose Music, Inc.*, 510 U.S. 569, 114 S.Ct. 1164, 127 L.Ed.2d 500 (1994) (applying the fair use exception to parody). Oklahoma's right of publicity statute, however, does not provide a similar accommodation for parody, and we must therefore confront the First Amendment issue directly.

MLBPA urges us to adopt the framework established in *Lloyd Corp. v. Tanner*, 407 U.S. 551, 33 L.Ed.2d 131, 92 S.Ct. 2219 (1972), in order to reconcile the free speech and property rights at stake in this case. The issue in *Lloyd* was whether a private shopping center could prevent the distribution of handbills on its premises. The Court focused on the availability of "adequate alternative avenues of communication":

> It would be an unwarranted infringement of property rights to require [the shopping center] to yield to the exercise of First Amendment rights under circumstances where adequate alternative avenues of communication exist. Such an accommodation would diminish property rights without significantly enhancing the asserted right of free speech.

Id. at 567. The Court held that the First Amendment did not require the shopping center to allow distribution of the handbills because the public sidewalks and streets surrounding the center provided an adequate alternative avenue of communication. *Id.* at 567–68. This type of analysis, usually applied to time, place, and manner restrictions, has also been applied in several cases where intellectual property rights have conflicted with the right to free expression. *E.g., Mutual of Omaha Ins. Co. v. Novak*, 836 F.2d 397, 402–03 (8th Cir. 1987) (holding that "Mutant of Omaha," a parody of Mutual of Omaha's logo, constitutes trademark infringement), *cert. denied*, 488 U.S. 933, 102 L.Ed.2d 344, 109 S.Ct. 326 (1988); *Dallas Cowboys Cheerleaders, Inc. v. Pussycat Cinema, Ltd.*, 604 F.2d 200, 206 (2d Cir. 1979) (holding that the use of Dallas Cowboys Cheerleader uniforms in the film *Debbie Does Dallas* constitutes trademark infringement).

MLBPA argues that application of the *Lloyd* analysis requires protection of its proprietary right of publicity. First, MLBPA maintains that there are many ways that Cardtoons could parody the institution of baseball that would not require use of player names and likenesses. Cardtoons could, for example, use generic images of baseball players to poke fun at the game. Second, MLBPA contends that Cardtoons could use recognizable players in a format other than trading cards, such as a newspaper or magazine, without infringing on its right of publicity. MLBPA argues that these alternative means of communication are adequate and, therefore, that we may uphold its property rights without seriously infringing upon Cardtoons' right to free expression.

We find, however, that in the context of intellectual property, *Lloyd's* "no adequate alternative avenues" test does not sufficiently accommodate the public's interest in free expression. *See Rogers v. Grimaldi*, 875 F.2d 994, 999 (2d Cir. 1989); *Mutual of Omaha Ins. Co.*, 836 F.2d at 405–06 (Heaney, J., dissenting). Intellectual property, unlike real estate, includes the words, images, and sounds that we use to communicate, and "we cannot indulge in the facile assumption that one can forbid particular words without also running a substantial risk of suppressing ideas in the process," *Cohen*, 403 U.S. at 26; *see San Francisco Arts & Athletics*, 483 U.S. at 569–570 (Brennan, J., dissenting). Restrictions on the words or images that may be used by a speaker, therefore, are quite different than restrictions on the time, place, or manner of speech. *Rogers*, 875 F.2d at 999; *see* Robert Denicola, *Trademarks as Speech: Constitutional Implications of the Emerging Rationales for the Protection of Trade Symbols*, 1982 Wisc. L. Rev. 158, 206.

In this case, Cardtoons' expression requires use of player identities because, in addition to parodying the institution of baseball, the cards also lampoon individual players. Further, Cardtoons' use of the trading card format is an essential component of the parody because baseball cards have traditionally been used to celebrate baseball players and their accomplishments. Cardtoons expresses ideas through the use of major league baseball player identities, and MLBPA's attempts to enjoin the parody thus goes to the content of the speech, not merely to its time, place, or manner. For that reason, the *Lloyd* test is inapplicable in this case.

This case instead requires us to directly balance the magnitude of the speech restriction against the asserted governmental interest in protecting the intellectual property right. We thus begin our analysis by examining the importance of Cardtoons' right to free expression and the consequences of limiting that right. We then weigh those consequences against the effect of infringing on MLBPA's right of publicity.

1. The Effect of Infringing upon Cardtoons' Right to Free Speech

Cardtoons' interest in publishing its parody trading cards implicates some of the core concerns of the First Amendment. "Parodies and caricatures," noted Aldous Huxley, "are the most penetrating of criticisms." *Point Counter Point*, ch. 13 (1928); *see Hustler Magazine*, 485 U.S. at 53–55. A parodist can, with deft and wit, readily expose the foolish and absurd in society. Parody is also a valuable form of self-expression that allows artists to shed light on earlier works and, at the same time, create new ones. Thus, parody, both as social criticism and a means of self-expression, is a vital commodity in the marketplace of ideas.

Parodies of celebrities are an especially valuable means of expression because of the role celebrities play in modern society. As one commentator explained, celebrities are "common points of reference for millions of individuals who may never interact with one another, but who share, by virtue of their participation in a mediated culture, a common experience and a collective memory." John B. Thompson, *Ideology and Modern Culture: Critical Social Theory in the Era of Mass Communication* 163 (1990). Through their pervasive presence in the media, sports and entertainment celebrities come to symbolize certain ideas and values. Commentator Michael Madow gives the following example:

> In December 1990, . . . shortly before the outbreak of the Gulf War, a story circulated in Washington that President Bush had boasted to a congressional delegation that Saddam Hussein was "going to get his ass kicked." When reporters pressed Bush to confirm the statement, he did not answer directly. Instead, he hitched up his pants in the manner of John Wayne. Everyone got the point.

Madow, *supra*, at 128 (footnotes omitted). Celebrities, then, are an important element of the shared communicative resources of our cultural domain.

Because celebrities are an important part of our public vocabulary, a parody of a celebrity does not merely lampoon the celebrity, but exposes the weakness of the idea or value that the celebrity symbolizes in society. Cardtoons' trading cards, for example, comment on the state of major league baseball by turning images of our sports heroes into modern-day personifications of avarice. In order to effectively criticize society, parodists need access to images that mean something to people, and thus celebrity parodies are a valuable communicative resource. Restricting the use of celebrity identities restricts the communication of ideas.

Without First Amendment protection, Cardtoons' trading cards and their irreverent commentary on the national pastime cannot be freely distributed to the public. Instead, as required by Oklahoma law, the production and distribution of the cards would be subject to MLBPA's consent. The problem with this scheme, as the Supreme Court noted in the context of copyright parody, is that "the unlikelihood that creators of imaginative works will license critical reviews or lampoons of their own productions removes such uses from the very notion of a potential licensing market." *Campbell*, 114 S.Ct. at 1178. The potential for suppression is even greater in the context of publicity rights because the product involved is the celebrity's own persona. Indeed, the director of licensing for MLBPA testified that MLBPA would never license a parody which poked fun at the players. Thus, elevating the right of publicity above the right to free expression would likely prevent distribution of the parody trading cards. This would not only allow MLBPA to censor criticism of its members, but would also have a chilling effect upon future celebrity parodies. Such a result is clearly undesirable, for "the last thing we need, the last thing the First Amendment will tolerate, is a law that lets public figures keep people from mocking them." *White*, 989 F.2d at 1519 (Kozinski, J., dissenting).

2. The Effect of Infringing upon MLBPA's Right of Publicity

We now turn to an evaluation of society's interest in protecting MLBPA's publicity right. The justifications offered for the right of publicity fall into two categories, economic and noneconomic. The right is thought to further economic goals such as stimulating athletic and artistic achievement, promoting the efficient allocation of resources, and protecting consumers. In addition, the right of publicity is said to protect various noneconomic interests, such as safeguarding natural rights, securing the fruits of celebrity labors, preventing unjust enrichment, and averting emotional harm. We examine the applicability of each of these justifications to the facts of this case.

The principal economic argument made in support of the right of publicity is that it provides an incentive for creativity and achievement. *See, e.g., Zacchini*, 433 U.S. at 576–77; *Carson v. Here's Johnny Portable Toilets, Inc.*, 698 F.2d 831, 837 (6th Cir. 1983). Under this view, publicity rights induce people to expend the time, effort, and resources to develop the talents prerequisite to public recognition. While those talents provide immediate benefit to those with commercially valuable identities, the products of their enterprise—such as movies, songs, and sporting events—ultimately benefit society as a whole. Thus, it is argued, society has an interest in a right of publicity that is closely analogous to its interest in other intellectual property protections such as copyright and patent law. *Zacchini*, 433 U.S. at 576.

This incentives argument is certainly a compelling justification for other forms of intellectual property. Copyright law, for example, protects the primary, if not only, source of a writer's income, and thus provides a significant incentive for creativity and achievement. The incentive effect of publicity rights, however, has been overstated. Most sports and entertainment celebrities with commercially valuable identities engage in activities that themselves generate a significant amount of income; the commercial value of their identities is merely a by-product of their performance values. *See Restatement (Third) of Unfair Competition* § 46 cmt. c. Although no one pays to watch Cormac McCarthy write a novel, many people pay a lot of money to watch Demi Moore "act" and Michael Jordan play basketball. Thus, the analogy to the incentive effect of other intellectual property protections is strained because "abolition of the right of publicity would leave entirely unimpaired a celebrity's ability to earn a living from the activities that have generated his commercially marketable fame." Madow, *supra*, at 209.

This distinction between the value of a person's identity and the value of his performance explains why *Zacchini v. Scripps-Howard Broadcasting Co.*, 433 U.S. 562, 53 L.Ed.2d 965, 97 S.Ct. 2849 (1977), the Supreme Court's sole case involving a right of publicity claim, is a red herring. Hugo Zacchini, a performer in a human cannonball act, brought an action against a television station to recover damages he suffered when the station videotaped and broadcast his entire performance. The Supreme Court held that the First Amendment did not give the station the right to broadcast Zacchini's entire act in contravention of his state protected right of publicity. *Id.* at 574–75. Zacchini, however, complained of the appropriation of the economic value of his *performance*, not the economic value of his *identity*. The Court's incentive rationale is obviously more compelling in a right of performance case than in a more typical right of publicity case involving the appropriation of a celebrity's identity. *See Restatement (Third) of Unfair Competition* § 46 reporters' note cmt. c.

Moreover, the additional inducement for achievement produced by publicity rights are often inconsequential because most celebrities with valuable commercial identities are already handsomely compensated. Actor Jim Carrey, for example, received twenty million dollars for starring in the movie *The Cable Guy*, *see* Bernard Weinraub, *How a Sure Summer Hit Missed*, N.Y. Times, June 27, 1996, at C11, and major league baseball players' salaries currently average over one million dollars per year, *see* Bill Brashler, *Booooooooooooooooo! Let's Hear It for Pampered, Preening, Overpaid Whiners: The Jocks*, Chi. Trib., July 28, 1996,

(Magazine), at 12. Such figures suggest that "even without the right of publicity the rate of return to stardom in the entertainment and sports fields is probably high enough to bring forth a more than 'adequate' supply of creative effort and achievement." Madow, *supra*, at 210. In addition, even in the absence of publicity rights, celebrities would still be able to reap financial reward from authorized appearances and endorsements. The extra income generated by licensing one's identity does not provide a necessary inducement to enter and achieve in the realm of sports and entertainment. Thus, while publicity rights may provide some incentive for creativity and achievement, the magnitude and importance of that incentive has been exaggerated.

The argument that publicity rights provide valuable incentives is even less compelling in the context of celebrity parodies. Since celebrities will seldom give permission for their identities to be parodied, granting them control over the parodic use of their identities would not directly provide them with any additional income. It would, instead, only allow them to shield themselves from ridicule and criticism. . . .

We recognize that publicity rights do provide some incentive to achieve in the fields of sports and entertainment. However, the inducements generated by publicity rights are not nearly as important as those created by copyright and patent law, and the small incentive effect of publicity rights is reduced or eliminated in the context of celebrity parodies. In sum, it is unlikely that little leaguers will stop dreaming of the big leagues or major leaguers will start "dogging it" to first base if MLBPA is denied the right to control the use of its members' identities in parody.

The second economic justification for the right of publicity is that it promotes the efficient allocation of resources, a version of the familiar tragedy of the commons argument used to prove the superiority of private property over common property. *See, e.g., Matthews v. Wozencraft*, 15 F.3d 432, 437–38 (5th Cir. 1994). Without the artificial scarcity created by publicity rights, identities would be commercially exploited until the marginal value of each use is zero. *Id.* "Creating artificial scarcity preserves the value to [the celebrity], to advertisers who contract for the use of his likeness, and in the end, to consumers, who receive information from the knowledge that he is being paid to endorse the product." *Id.* at 438. Giving people control of the commercial use of their identities, according to this analysis, maximizes the economic and informational value of those identities.

This efficiency argument is most persuasive in the context of advertising, where repeated use of a celebrity's likeness to sell products may eventually diminish its commercial value. The argument is not as persuasive, however, when applied to nonadvertising uses. It is not clear, for example, that the frequent appearance of a celebrity's likeness on t-shirts and coffee mugs will reduce its value; indeed, the value of the likeness may increase precisely because "everybody's got one." Madow, *supra*, at 222. Further, celebrities with control over the parodic use of their identities would not use the power to "ration the use of their names in order to maximize their value over time," *Matthews*, 15 F.3d at 438 n.2. They would instead use that power to suppress criticism, and thus permanently remove a valuable source of information about their identity from the marketplace.

The final economic argument offered for rights of publicity is that they protect against consumer deception. *See, e.g., Restatement (Third) of Unfair Competition* § 46 cmt. c; McCarthy, *supra*, § 2.4; Peter L. Felcher & Edward L. Rubin, *Privacy, Publicity, and the Portrayal of Real People by the Media*, 88 Yale L.J. 1577, 1600 (1979). The Lanham Act, however, already provides nationwide protection against false or misleading representations in connection with the sale of products. Moreover, as discussed above, the use of celebrity names or likenesses in parodies in general, and in Cardtoons' trading cards in particular, are not likely to confuse or deceive consumers. Thus, this final economic justification has little merit.

There are also several noneconomic reasons advanced for the right of publicity. First, some believe that publicity rights stem from some notion of natural rights. McCarthy, for example, argues that a natural rights rationale, resting more upon "visceral impulses of 'fairness'" than upon reasoned argument, "seems quite sufficient to provide a firm support for the existence of a Right of Publicity." McCarthy, *supra*, § 2.1[A]. McCarthy, however, offers little reason for this assertion, and blind appeals to first principles carry no weight in our balancing analysis.

The second noneconomic justification is that publicity rights allow celebrities to enjoy the fruits of their labors. *See, e.g., Zacchini*, 433 U.S. at 573; *Uhlaender v. Henricksen*, 316 F. Supp. 1277, 1282 (D. Minn. 1970). According to this argument, "[a] celebrity must be considered to have invested his years of practice and competition in a public personality which eventually may reach marketable status." *Uhlaender*, 316 F. Supp. at 1282. People deserve the right to control and profit from the commercial value of their identities because, quite simply, they've earned it. Thus, in this view, the right of publicity is similar to the right of a commercial enterprise to profit from the goodwill it has built up in its name. *Ali v. Playgirl, Inc.*, 447 F. Supp. 723, 728–29 (S.D.N.Y. 1978).

Celebrities, however, are often not fully responsible for their fame. Indeed, in the entertainment industry, a celebrity's fame may largely be the creation of the media or the audience. *See* Madow, *supra* at 184–96 (discussing the role of factors beyond a celebrity's control in developing a commercially marketable persona). As one actor put it, "Only that audience out there makes a star. It's up to them. You can't do anything about it. . . . Stars would all be Louis B. Mayer's cousins if you could make 'em up." Jack Nicholson, *quoted in* Jib Fowles, *Starstruck: Celebrity Performers and the American Public* 84 (1992). Professional athletes may be more responsible for their celebrity status, however, because athletic success is fairly straightforwardly the result of an athlete's natural talent and dedication. Thus, baseball players may deserve to profit from the commercial value of their identities more than movie stars. Once again, however, the force of this justification is diminished in the case of parody, because there is little right to enjoy the fruits of socially undesirable behavior.

The third, related justification for publicity rights is the prevention of unjust enrichment. *See, e.g., Zacchini*, 433 U.S. at 576; *Ali*, 447 F. Supp. at 728–29. In this view, whether the commercial value of an identity is the result of a celebrity's hard work, media creation, or just pure dumb luck, no social purpose is served by allowing others to freely appropriate it. Cardtoons, however, is not merely hitching its wagon to a star. As in all celebrity parodies, Cardtoons added a significant creative component of its own to the celebrity identity and created an entirely new product. Indeed, allowing MLBPA to control or profit from the parody trading cards would actually sanction the theft of Cardtoons' creative enterprise.

A final justification offered for the right of publicity is that it prevents emotional injuries. For example, commercial misappropriation may greatly distress a celebrity who finds all commercial exploitation to be offensive. *Lugosi v. Universal Pictures*, 25 Cal. 3d 813, 603 P.2d 425, 439 n.11, 160 Cal. Rptr. 323 (Cal. 1979) (Bird, C.J., dissenting). Even celebrities who crave public attention might find particular uses of their identities to be distressing. *See, e.g., O'Brien v. Pabst Sales Co.*, 124 F.2d 167, 170 (5th Cir. 1942) (professional football player, active in an organization devoted to discouraging alcohol use among young people, sued to stop the use of his image in a Pabst Blue Ribbon beer advertising calendar). The right of publicity allows celebrities to avoid the emotional distress caused by unwanted commercial use of their identities. Publicity rights, however, are meant to protect against the loss of financial gain, not mental anguish. *Zacchini*, 433 U.S. at 573; *Lugosi*, 603 P.2d at 438–39 (Bird, C.J., dissenting). Laws preventing unfair competition, such as the Lanham Act, and laws prohibiting the intentional infliction of emotional distress adequately cover that ground. Moreover, fame is a double-edged sword—the law cannot allow those who enjoy the public limelight to so easily avoid the ridicule and criticism that sometimes accompany public prominence.

Thus, the noneconomic justifications for the right of publicity are no more compelling than the economic arguments. Those justifications further break down in the context of parody, where the right to profit from one's persona is reduced to the power to suppress criticism. In sum, the effect of limiting MLBPA's right of publicity in this case is negligible.

IV. Conclusion

One of the primary goals of intellectual property law is to maximize creative expression. The law attempts to achieve this goal by striking a proper balance between the right of a creator to the fruits of his labor and the right of future creators to free expression. Underprotection of intellectual property reduces the incentive to create; overprotection creates a monopoly over the raw material of creative expression. The application of the Oklahoma publicity rights statute to Cardtoons' trading cards presents a classic case of overprotection. Little is to be gained, and much lost, by protecting MLBPA's right to control the use of its members' identities in parody trading cards. The justifications for the right of publicity are not nearly as compelling as those offered for other forms of intellectual property, and are particularly unpersuasive in the case of celebrity parodies. The cards, on the other hand, are an important form of entertainment and social commentary that deserve First Amendment protection. Accordingly, we AFFIRM.

NOTES FOR DISCUSSION

1.   *Justification at Inception.* What justification does the *Haelan Labs.* court offer for creating a legal right to control the commercial use of one's name, image, or likeness? Or does the court treat the desirability of recognizing such a legal right as self-evident?

2.   *Economic Justifications.* The *Cardtoons, L.C.* court offers three economic justifications for recognizing the right of publicity. The first is incentives. We should recognize a legal right to control the value that arises from commercial uses of one's name or likeness because that will encourage people to invest in developing such value. As we saw in Chapter 1, this is the classic justification for patent and copyright. Does it provide much support for a right of publicity? Does the *Cardtoons, L.C.* court find it persuasive? How much do celebrities get paid for their endorsements? The court emphasizes the high salaries celebrities and star athletes receive. Are their endorsement deals simply icing on the cake or are they the cake? It depends. In 1997, Forbes reported that Michael Jordan earned $31.3 million in salary and $47 million in endorsements; boxing champion Evander Holyfield earned $53 million in salary and $1.3 million in endorsements; and Tiger Woods earned $2.1 million in salary and $24 million in endorsements. If providing incentives is the justification for the right, what does it suggest about the right's limits?

The second is that in the absence of legal control, a person's image or likeness will be overused and its value thereby diminished. Both courts and academics have advanced this argument, using analogies to overuse of common pools and to the economic principle of congestion externalities to justify a right of publicity. *See, e.g., Matthews v. Wozencraft,* 15 F.3d 432,

437–38 & n.2 (5th Cir. 1994); RICHARD A. POSNER, THE ECONOMICS OF JUSTICE 248 (1981); William M. Landes & Richard A. Posner, *Indefinitely Renewable Copyright*, 70 U. CHI. L. REV. 471, 487 (2003) (arguing that "unlimited reproduction of the name or the likeness could prematurely exhaust the celebrity's commercial value, just as unlimited drilling from a common pool of oil or gas would deplete the pool prematurely"); Mark F. Grady, *A Positive Economic Theory of the Right of Publicity*, 1 UCLA ENT. L. REV. 97 (1994). How does the *Cardtoons, L.C.* court address this justification? Is there anything to this overuse argument? Does a three word answer—"Ho, Ho, Ho"—completely rebut the claim? In other words, if the overuse argument is right, shouldn't Santa Claus and all of his buddies in the public domain, ranging from the Easter Bunny to Dr. Frankenstein and his monster, have no value as advertising icons? Yet, every year, when the holiday season rolls out, here comes the Jolly Old Elf as pitchman for an array of products. Why? Are these theories simply wrong?

How does the price drop that occurs as a result of the widespread unauthorized use of a celebrity's name, image, or likeness differ from the price drop that accompanies competitive entry more generally? When a new competitor enters a market that was, prior to the entry, a monopoly, prices in the market fall. The reduction in price affects both the new entrant, that caused it, and the existing market participant(s). At one time, economists used the phrase "pecuniary externality" to refer to the effects of such a price drop on the other market participants. Is the response of prices to competitive entry an externality? If so, is it an externality that leads to inefficiency? Is the price drop that might result from widespread unauthorized commercial use of a celebrity's image the same thing we see with competitive entry generally? Is the price drop not a congestion externality, but a pecuniary externality? Is the fall in price brought about by such unauthorized use an externality at all?

The third economic concern is the risk of consumer deception. How does the *Cardtoons, L.C.* court treat that concern? Is this justification merely circular? That is, in the absence of a right of publicity, would consumers perceive an endorsement if a celebrity's image were used to promote a particular product? Do you agree with the court that the availability of Lanham Trademark Act relief for false endorsement eliminates the need for a separate right of publicity? Do you agree with the court's Madonna-Mitchell Fruit billboard example? Or would consumers perceive an endorsement from the use of Madonna's image despite the billboard's text?

3. *Noneconomic Justifications.* The *Cardtoons, L.C.* court also offers four noneconomic justifications for the right of publicity: (i) unauthorized use of another's name or image to promote a product is viscerally unfair; (ii) a right to control use is justified by labor-dessert theory or natural rights; (iii) a right to control such use prevents unjust enrichment; and (iv) a right to control such use prevents emotional injuries. Does the *Cardtoons, L.C.* court find any of these justifications persuasive? When would they be persuasive? For example, should a college football player, whose religion forbids the

consumption of alcohol, be able to prevent the use of his name or image in connection with a beer advertisement? Why or why not? In the absence of a right of publicity, he could not. *See O'Brien v. Pabst Sales Co.*, 124 F.2d 167, 170 (5th Cir. 1942). Does that offend you?

4.   *The Value of Celebrity Endorsement.* Celebrity endorsements are valuable. Consumers rely on them. Why? If you are deciding between the products of two companies, and one company has a paid celebrity endorser, while the other does not, from which should you purchase? Assume further that, although you cannot tell from an ex ante examination of the products, one of the products is high quality, while the other is low quality. You will not know which is which until after you make the purchase and live with the product for a few years. What means are available to a consumer to determine which company's products is higher quality? A consumer could talk to a friend, or read a review by a neutral evaluator, such as Consumer Reports. Can the consumer rely on a celebrity's endorsement?

In this situation, which company will pay more for the celebrity endorsement? For the low quality company, a celebrity endorsement offers a one-time opportunity to recoup the celebrity's fee. In response to the endorsement, some consumers will purchase the company's product and the company will make a corresponding profit. However, having been sucked in by the endorsement, consumers will discover the product's low quality, and will not make that mistake again. In contrast, for the high quality company, a celebrity endorsement generates both: (i) an initial response; *and* (ii) repeat sales to the new, and newly satisfied, customers. Often, although the high quality company's profit per-sale will be lower because it spends more on ensuring the quality of its product, the high quality company will earn more from the stream of business a celebrity endorsement creates than the low quality company earns from its one-time sales bump. As a result, in many cases, a company's willingness to spend money on a celebrity endorsement accurately signals the higher quality of its products. Can we justify a right of publicity in order to enable companies to signal product quality by paying high prices for celebrity endorsements?

5.   *Celebrities and Non-Celebrities.* Should the right of publicity extend to non-celebrities? Should a company be able to use your name, image, or likeness to advertise its products without your permission? Which of the possible justifications for the right of publicity would support extending the right to celebrities and non-celebrities alike?

6.   *Duration.* How long should the right of publicity last? Should it end with a person's death? Or should it last as long as a person's name, image, or likeness retains a commercial value? What does each of the proffered justifications for the right suggest in this regard? When the issue arose through common law development, courts divided on the issue. *Compare Factors Etc., Inc. v. Pro Arts, Inc.*, 579 F.2d 215, 221 (2d Cir. 1978) (holding that where right to exploit Elvis's likeness was assigned before Elvis died the right survived his death), *cert. denied,* 440 U.S. 908 (1979), *with Memphis Dev. Foundation v. Factors Etc., Inc.*, 616 F.2d 956, 960 (6th Cir.) (holding

that right of publicity ended with celebrity's death even if celebrity had assigned right before his death), *cert. denied*, 449 U.S. 953 (1980). As an issue of state law, the Tennessee legislature has the power to define the right of publicity's term for Elvis. What term do you think the Tennessee legislature set on the right? *See* Tenn. Code Ann. § 47–25–1104(a), (b) (2010) (providing that the right of publicity endures for ten years after an individual's death, and further providing that if commercial exploitation of the right begins within that period, the exclusive right to such exploitation will endure until abandoned through two years of nonuse).

B. EXPANSION

MIDLER V. FORD MOTOR CO.

849 F.2d 460 (9th Cir. 1988)

JOHN T. NOONAN, CIRCUIT JUDGE

This case centers on the protectibility of the voice of a celebrated chanteuse from commercial exploitation without her consent. Ford Motor Company and its advertising agency, Young & Rubicam, Inc., in 1985 advertised the Ford Lincoln Mercury with a series of nineteen 30 or 60 second television commercials in what the agency called "The Yuppie Campaign." The aim was to make an emotional connection with Yuppies, bringing back memories of when they were in college. Different popular songs of the seventies were sung on each commercial. The agency tried to get "the original people," that is, the singers who had popularized the songs, to sing them. Failing in that endeavor in ten cases the agency had the songs sung by "sound alikes." Bette Midler, the plaintiff and appellant here, was done by a sound alike.

Midler is a nationally known actress and singer. She won a Grammy as early as 1973 as the Best New Artist of that year. Records made by her since then have gone Platinum and Gold. She was nominated in 1979 for an Academy award for Best Female Actress in *The Rose*, in which she portrayed a pop singer. *Newsweek* in its June 30, 1986 issue described her as an "outrageously original singer/comedian." *Time* hailed her in its March 2, 1987 issue as "a legend" and "the most dynamic and poignant singer-actress of her time."

When Young & Rubicam was preparing the Yuppie Campaign it presented the commercial to its client by playing an edited version of Midler singing "Do You Want To Dance," taken from the 1973 Midler album, "The Divine Miss M." After the client accepted the idea and form of the commercial, the agency contacted Midler's manager, Jerry Edelstein. The conversation went as follows: "Hello, I am Craig Hazen from Young and Rubicam. I am calling you to find out if Bette Midler would be interested in doing" . . . ? Edelstein: "Is it a commercial?" "Yes." "We are not interested."

Undeterred, Young & Rubicam sought out Ula Hedwig whom it knew to have been one of "the Harlettes" a backup singer for Midler for ten years. Hedwig was told by Young & Rubicam that "they wanted someone who could sound like Bette Midler's recording of [Do You Want To Dance]." She was asked to make a "demo" tape of the song if she was interested. She made an a capella demo and got the job.

At the direction of Young & Rubicam, Hedwig then made a record for the commercial. The Midler record of "Do You Want To Dance" was first played to her. She was told to "sound as much as possible like the Bette Midler record," leaving out only a few "aahs" unsuitable for the commercial. Hedwig imitated Midler to the best of her ability.

After the commercial was aired Midler was told by "a number of people" that it "sounded exactly" like her record of "Do You Want To Dance." Hedwig was told by "many personal friends" that they thought it was Midler singing the commercial. Ken Fritz, a personal manager in the entertainment business not associated with Midler, declares by affidavit that he heard the commercial on more than one occasion and thought Midler was doing the singing.

Neither the name nor the picture of Midler was used in the commercial; Young & Rubicam had a license from the copyright holder to use the song. At issue in this case is only the protection of Midler's voice. The district court described the defendants' conduct as that "of the average thief." They decided, "If we can't buy it, we'll take it." The court nonetheless believed there was no legal principle preventing imitation of Midler's voice and so gave summary judgment for the defendants. Midler appeals.

The First Amendment protects much of what the media do in the reproduction of likenesses or sounds. A primary value is freedom of speech and press. *Time, Inc. v. Hill*, 385 U.S. 374, 388 (1967). The purpose of the media's use of a person's identity is central. If the purpose is "informative or cultural" the use is immune; "if it serves no such function but merely exploits the individual portrayed, immunity will not be granted." Felcher and Rubin, *Privacy, Publicity and the Portrayal of Real People by the Media*, 88 Yale L.J. 1577, 1596 (1979). Moreover, federal copyright law preempts much of the area. "Mere imitation of a recorded performance would not constitute a copyright infringement even where one performer deliberately sets out to simulate another's performance as exactly as possible." Notes of Committee on the Judiciary, 17 U.S.C. § 114(b). It is in the context of these First Amendment and federal copyright distinctions that we address the present appeal.

Nancy Sinatra once sued Goodyear Tire and Rubber Company on the basis of an advertising campaign by Young & Rubicam featuring "These Boots Are Made For Walkin'," a song closely identified with her; the female singers of the commercial were alleged to have imitated her voice and style and to have dressed and looked like her. The basis of Nancy Sinatra's complaint was unfair competition; she claimed that the song and the arrangement had acquired "a secondary meaning" which, under California law, was protectible. This court noted that the defendants "had paid a very substantial sum to the copyright proprietor to obtain the license for the use of the song and all of its arrangements." To give Sinatra damages for their use of the song would clash with federal copyright law. Summary judgment for the defendants was affirmed. *Sinatra v. Goodyear Tire & Rubber Co.*, 435 F.2d 711, 717–718 (9th Cir. 1970), *cert. denied*, 402 U.S. 906 (1971). If Midler were claiming a secondary meaning to "Do You Want To Dance" or seeking to prevent the defendants from using that song, she would fail like Sinatra. But that is not this case. Midler does not seek damages for Ford's use of "Do You Want To Dance," and thus her claim is not preempted by federal copyright law. Copyright protects "original works of authorship fixed in any tangible medium of expression." 17 U.S.C. § 102(a). A voice is not copyrightable. The sounds are not "fixed." What is put forward as protectible here is more personal than any work of authorship.

Bert Lahr once sued Adell Chemical Co. for selling Lestoil by means of a commercial in which an imitation of Lahr's voice accompanied a cartoon of a duck. Lahr alleged that his style of vocal delivery was distinctive in pitch, accent, inflection, and sounds. The First Circuit held that Lahr had stated a cause of action for unfair competition, that it could be found "that defendant's conduct saturated plaintiff's audience, curtailing his market." *Lahr v. Adell Chemical Co.*, 300 F.2d 256, 259 (1st Cir. 1962). That case is more like this one. But we do not find unfair competition here. One-minute commercials of the sort the defendants put on would not have saturated Midler's audience and curtailed her market. Midler did not do television commercials. The defendants were not in competition with her. *See Halicki v. United Artists Communications, Inc.*, 812 F.2d 1213 (9th Cir. 1987).

California Civil Code section 3344 is also of no aid to Midler. The statute affords damages to a person injured by another who uses the person's "name, voice, signature, photograph or likeness, in any manner." The defendants did not use Midler's name or anything else whose use is prohibited by the statute. The voice they used was Hedwig's, not hers. The term "likeness" refers to a visual image not a vocal imitation. The statute, however, does not preclude Midler from pursuing any cause of action she may have at common law; the statute itself implies that such common law causes of action do exist because it says its remedies are merely "cumulative." *Id.* § 3344(g).

The companion statute protecting the use of a deceased person's name, voice, signature, photograph or likeness states that the rights it recognizes are "property rights." *Id.* § 990(b). By analogy the common law rights are also property rights. Appropriation of such common law rights is a tort in California. *Motschenbacher v. R.J. Reynolds Tobacco Co.*, 498 F.2d 821 (9th Cir. 1974). In that case what the defendants used in their television commercial for Winston cigarettes was a photograph of a famous professional racing driver's racing car. The number of the car was changed and a wing-like device known as a "spoiler" was attached to the car; the car's features of white pinpointing, an oval medallion, and solid red coloring were retained. The driver, Lothar Motschenbacher, was in the car but his features were not visible. Some persons, viewing the commercial, correctly inferred that the car was his and that he was in the car and was therefore endorsing the product. The defendants were held to have invaded a "proprietary interest" of Motschenbacher in his own identity. *Id.* at 825.

Midler's case is different from Motschenbacher's. He and his car were physically used by the tobacco company's ad; he made part of his living out of giving commercial endorsements. But, as Judge Koelsch expressed it in *Motschenbacher*, California will recognize an injury from "an appropriation of the attributes of one's identity." *Id.* at 824. It was irrelevant that Motschenbacher could not be identified in the ad. The ad suggested that it was he. The ad did so by emphasizing signs or symbols associated with him. In the same way the defendants here used an imitation to convey the impression that Midler was singing for them.

Why did the defendants ask Midler to sing if her voice was not of value to them? Why did they studiously acquire the services of a sound-alike and instruct her to imitate Midler if Midler's voice was not of value to them? What they sought was an attribute of Midler's identity. Its value was what the market would have paid for Midler to have sung the commercial in person.

A voice is more distinctive and more personal than the automobile accouterments protected in *Motschenbacher*. A voice is as distinctive and personal as a face. The human voice is one of the most palpable ways identity is manifested. We are all aware that a friend is at once known by a few words on the phone. At a philosophical level it has been observed that with the sound of a voice, "the other stands before me." D. Ihde, *Listening and Voice* 77 (1976). A fortiori, these observations hold true of singing, especially singing by a singer of renown. The singer manifests herself in the song. To impersonate her voice is to pirate her identity. *See* W. Keeton, D. Dobbs, R. Keeton, D. Owen, *Prosser & Keeton on Torts* 852 (5th ed. 1984).

We need not and do not go so far as to hold that every imitation of a voice to advertise merchandise is actionable. We hold only that when a distinctive voice of a professional singer is widely known and is deliberately imitated in order to sell a product, the sellers have appropriated what is not theirs and have committed a tort in California.

Midler has made a showing, sufficient to defeat summary judgment, that the defendants here for their own profit in selling their product did appropriate part of her identity.

REVERSED AND REMANDED FOR TRIAL.

WHITE V. SAMSUNG ELECTRONICS AMERICA, INC.
971 F.2d 1395 (9th Cir. 1992)

GOODWIN, CIRCUIT JUDGE

This case involves a promotional "fame and fortune" dispute. In running a particular advertisement without Vanna White's permission, defendants Samsung Electronics America, Inc. (Samsung) and David Deutsch Associates, Inc. (Deutsch) attempted to capitalize on White's fame to enhance their fortune. White sued, alleging infringement of various intellectual property rights, but the district court granted summary judgment in favor of the defendants. We affirm in part, reverse in part, and remand.

Plaintiff Vanna White is the hostess of "Wheel of Fortune," one of the most popular game shows in television history. An estimated forty million people watch the program daily. Capitalizing on the fame which her participation in the show has bestowed on her, White markets her identity to various advertisers.

The dispute in this case arose out of a series of advertisements prepared for Samsung by Deutsch. The series ran in at least half a dozen publications with widespread, and in some cases national, circulation. Each of the advertisements in the series followed the same theme. Each depicted a current item from popular culture and a Samsung electronic product. Each was set in the twenty-first century and conveyed the message that the Samsung product would still be in use by that time. By hypothesizing outrageous future outcomes for the cultural items, the ads created humorous effects. For example, one lampooned current popular notions of an unhealthy diet by depicting a raw steak with the caption: "Revealed to be health food. 2010 A.D." Another depicted irreverent "news"-show host Morton Downey Jr. in front of an American flag with the caption: "Presidential candidate. 2008 A.D."

The advertisement which prompted the current dispute was for Samsung video-cassette recorders (VCRs). The ad depicted a robot, dressed in a wig, gown, and jewelry which Deutsch consciously selected to resemble White's hair and dress. The robot was posed next to a game board which is instantly recognizable as the Wheel of Fortune game show set, in a stance for which White is famous. The caption of the ad read: "Longest-running game show. 2012 A.D." Defendants referred to the ad as the "Vanna White" ad. Unlike the other celebrities used in the campaign, White neither consented to the ads nor was she paid.

Following the circulation of the robot ad, White sued Samsung and Deutsch in federal district court under: (1) California Civil Code § 3344; (2) the California common law right of publicity; and (3) § 43(a) of the Lanham Act, 15 U.S.C. § 1125(a). The district court granted summary judgment against White on each of her claims. White now appeals.

I. *Section 3344*

White first argues that the district court erred in rejecting her claim under section 3344. Section 3344(a) provides, in pertinent part, that "any person who knowingly uses another's name, voice, signature, photograph, or likeness, in any manner, . . . for purposes of advertising or selling, . . . without such person's prior consent . . . shall be liable for any damages sustained by the person or persons injured as a result thereof."

. . . In this case, Samsung and Deutsch used a robot with mechanical features, and not, for example, a manikin molded to White's precise features. Without deciding for all purposes when a caricature or impressionistic resemblance might become a "likeness," we agree with the district court that the robot at issue here was not White's "likeness" within the meaning of section 3344. Accordingly, we affirm the court's dismissal of White's section 3344 claim.

II. *Right of Publicity*

White next argues that the district court erred in granting summary judgment to defendants on White's common law right of publicity claim. In *Eastwood v. Superior Court,* 149 Cal.App.3d 409 (1983), the California court of appeal stated that the common law right of publicity cause of action "may be pleaded by alleging (1) the defendant's use of the plaintiff's identity; (2) the appropriation of plaintiff's name or likeness to defendant's advantage, commercially or otherwise; (3) lack of consent; and (4) resulting injury." *Id.* at 417 (citing Prosser, Law of Torts (4th ed. 1971) § 117, pp. 804–807). The district court dismissed White's claim for failure to satisfy *Eastwood's* second prong, reasoning that defendants had not appropriated White's "name or likeness" with their robot ad. We agree that the robot ad did not make use of White's name or likeness. However, the common law right of publicity is not so confined.

The *Eastwood* court did not hold that the right of publicity cause of action could be pleaded only by alleging an appropriation of name or likeness. *Eastwood* involved an unauthorized use of photographs of Clint Eastwood and of his name. Accordingly, the *Eastwood* court had no occasion to consider the extent beyond the use of name or likeness to which the right of publicity reaches. That court held only that the right of publicity cause of action "may be" pleaded by alleging, *inter alia,* appropriation of name or likeness, not that the action may be pleaded *only* in those terms.

The "name or likeness" formulation referred to in *Eastwood* originated not as an element of the right of publicity cause of action, but as a description of the types of cases in which the cause of action had been recognized. The source of this formulation is Prosser, *Privacy,* 48 Cal.L.Rev. 383, 401–07 (1960), one of the earliest and most enduring articulations of the common law right of publicity cause of action. In looking at the case law to that point, Prosser recognized that right of publicity cases involved one of two basic factual scenarios: name appropriation, and picture or other likeness appropriation. *Id.* at 401–02, nn.156–57.

Even though Prosser focused on appropriations of name or likeness in discussing the right of publicity, he noted that "it is not impossible that there might be appropriation of the plaintiff's identity, as by impersonation, without the use of either his name or his likeness, and that this would be an invasion of his right of privacy." *Id.* at 401, n.155. At the time Prosser wrote, he noted however, that "no such case appears to have arisen." *Id.*

Since Prosser's early formulation, the case law has borne out his insight that the right of publicity is not limited to the appropriation of name or likeness. In *Motschenbacher v. R.J. Reynolds Tobacco Co.,* 498 F.2d 821 (9th Cir. 1974), the defendant had used a photograph of the plaintiff's race car in a television commercial. Although the plaintiff appeared driving the car in the photograph, his features were not visible. Even though the defendant had not appropriated the plaintiff's name or likeness, this court held that plaintiff's California right of publicity claim should reach the jury.

In *Midler,* this court held that, even though the defendants had not used Midler's name or likeness, Midler had stated a claim for violation of her California common law right of publicity because "the defendants . . . for their own profit in selling their product did appropriate part of her identity" by using a Midler sound-alike. *Id.* at 463–64.

In *Carson v. Here's Johnny Portable Toilets, Inc.,* 698 F.2d 831 (6th Cir. 1983), the defendant had marketed portable toilets under the brand name "Here's Johnny"—Johnny Carson's signature "Tonight Show" introduction—without Carson's permission. The district court had dismissed Carson's Michigan common law right of publicity claim because the defendants had not used Carson's "name or likeness." *Id.* at 835. In reversing the district court, the sixth circuit found "the district court's conception of the right of publicity . . . too narrow" and held that the right was implicated because the defendant had appropriated Carson's identity by using, *inter alia,* the phrase "Here's Johnny." *Id.* at 835–37.

These cases teach not only that the common law right of publicity reaches means of appropriation other than name or likeness, but that the specific means of appropriation are relevant only for determining whether the defendant has in fact appropriated the plaintiff's identity. The right of publicity does not require that appropriations of identity be accomplished through particular means to be actionable. It is noteworthy that the *Midler* and *Carson* defendants not only avoided using the plaintiff's name or likeness, but they also avoided appropriating the celebrity's voice, signature, and photograph. The photograph in *Motschenbacher* did include the plaintiff, but because the plaintiff was not visible the driver could have been an actor or dummy and the analysis in the case would have been the same.

Although the defendants in these cases avoided the most obvious means of appropriating the plaintiffs' identities, each of their actions directly implicated the commercial interests which the right of publicity is designed to protect. As the *Carson* court explained:

> the right of publicity has developed to protect the commercial interest of celebrities in their identities. The theory of the right is that a celebrity's identity can be valuable in the promotion of products, and the celebrity has an interest that may be protected from the unauthorized commercial exploitation of that identity. . . . If the celebrity's identity is commercially exploited, there has been an invasion of his right whether or not his "name or likeness" is used.

Carson, 698 F.2d at 835. It is not important *how* the defendant has appropriated the plaintiff's identity, but *whether* the defendant has done so. *Motschenbacher, Midler,* and *Carson* teach the impossibility of treating the right of publicity as guarding only against a laundry list of specific means of appropriating identity. A rule which says that the right of publicity can be infringed only through the use of nine different methods of appropriating identity merely challenges the clever advertising strategist to come up with the tenth.

Indeed, if we treated the means of appropriation as dispositive in our analysis of the right of publicity, we would not only weaken the right but effectively eviscerate it. The right would fail to protect those plaintiffs most in need of its protection. Advertisers use celebrities to promote their products. The more popular the celebrity, the greater the number of people who recognize her, and the greater the visibility for the product. The identities of the most popular celebrities are not only the most attractive for advertisers, but also the easiest to evoke without resorting to obvious means such as name, likeness, or voice.

. . . Viewed separately, the individual aspects of the advertisement in the present case say little. Viewed together, they leave little doubt about the celebrity the ad is meant to depict. The female-shaped robot is wearing a long gown, blond wig, and large jewelry. Vanna White dresses exactly like this at times, but so do many other women. The robot is in the process of turning a block letter on a game-board. Vanna White dresses like this while turning letters on a game-board but perhaps similarly attired Scrabble-playing women do this as well. The robot is standing on what looks to be the Wheel of Fortune game show set. Vanna White dresses like this, turns letters, and does this on the Wheel of Fortune game show. She is the only one. Indeed, defendants themselves referred to their ad as the "Vanna White" ad. We are not surprised.

Television and other media create marketable celebrity identity value. Considerable energy and ingenuity are expended by those who have achieved celebrity value to exploit it for profit. The law protects the celebrity's sole right to exploit this value whether the celebrity has achieved her fame out of rare ability, dumb luck, or a combination thereof. We decline Samsung and Deutch's invitation to permit the evisceration of the common law right of publicity through means as facile as those in this case. Because White has alleged facts showing that Samsung and Deutsch had appropriated her identity, the district court erred by rejecting, on summary judgment, White's common law right of publicity claim.

III. *The Lanham Act*

White's final argument is that the district court erred in denying her claim under § 43(a) of the Lanham Act, 15 U.S.C. § 1125(a). The version of section 43(a) applicable to this case provides, in pertinent part, that "any person who shall . . . use, in connection with any goods or services . . . any false description or representation . . . shall be liable to a civil action . . . by any person who believes that he is or is likely to be damaged by the use of any such false description or designation." 15 U.S.C. § 1125(a).

To prevail on her Lanham Act claim, White is required to show that in running the robot ad, Samsung and Deutsch created a likelihood of confusion over whether White was endorsing Samsung's VCRs.

This circuit recognizes several different multi-factor tests for determining whether a likelihood of confusion exists. None of these tests is correct to the exclusion of the others. *Eclipse Associates Ltd. v. Data General Corp.,* 894 F.2d 1114, 1118 (9th Cir. 1990). Normally, in reviewing the district court's decision, this court will look to the particular test that the district court used. *Academy,* 944 F.2d at 1454, n.3; *Eclipse,* 894 F.2d at 1117–1118. However, because the district court in this case apparently did not use any of the multi-factor tests in making its likelihood of confusion determination, and because this case involves an appeal from summary judgment and we review de novo the district court's determination, we will look for guidance to the 8-factor test enunciated in *AMF Inc. v. Sleekcraft Boats,* 599 F.2d 341 (9th Cir. 1979). . . . We turn now to consider White's claim in light of each factor.

In cases involving confusion over endorsement by a celebrity plaintiff, "mark" means the celebrity's persona. *See Allen*, 610 F.Supp. at 627. The "strength" of the mark refers to the level of recognition the celebrity enjoys among members of society. *See Academy*, 944 F.2d at 1455. If Vanna White is unknown to the segment of the public at whom Samsung's robot ad was directed, then that segment could not be confused as to whether she was endorsing Samsung VCRs. Conversely, if White is well-known, this would allow the possibility of a likelihood of confusion. For the purposes of the *Sleekcraft* test, White's "mark," or celebrity identity, is strong.

In cases concerning confusion over celebrity endorsement, the plaintiff's "goods" concern the reasons for or source of the plaintiff's fame. Because White's fame is based on her televised performances, her "goods" are closely related to Samsung's VCRs. Indeed, the ad itself reinforced the relationship by informing its readers that they would be taping the "longest-running game show" on Samsung's VCRs well into the future.

The third factor, "similarity of the marks," both supports and contradicts a finding of likelihood of confusion. On the one hand, all of the aspects of the robot ad identify White; on the other, the figure is quite clearly a robot, not a human. This ambiguity means that we must look to the other factors for resolution.

The fourth factor does not favor White's claim because she has presented no evidence of actual confusion.

Fifth, however, White has appeared in the same stance as the robot from the ad in numerous magazines, including the covers of some. Magazines were used as the marketing channels for the robot ad. This factor cuts toward a likelihood of confusion.

Sixth, consumers are not likely to be particularly careful in determining who endorses VCRs, making confusion as to their endorsement more likely.

Concerning the seventh factor, "defendant's intent," the district court found that, in running the robot ad, the defendants had intended a spoof of the "Wheel of Fortune." The relevant question is whether the defendants "intended to profit by confusing consumers" concerning the endorsement of Samsung VCRs. *Toho*, 645 F.2d 788 (9th Cir. 1981). We do not disagree that defendants intended to spoof Vanna White and "Wheel of Fortune." That does not preclude, however, the possibility that defendants also intended to confuse consumers regarding endorsement. The robot ad was one of a series of ads run by defendants which followed the same theme. Another ad in the series depicted Morton Downey Jr. as a presidential candidate in the year 2008. Doubtless, defendants intended to spoof presidential elections and Mr. Downey through this ad. Consumers, however, would likely believe, and would be correct in so believing, that Mr. Downey was paid for his permission and was endorsing Samsung products. Looking at the series of advertisements as a whole, a jury could reasonably conclude that beneath the surface humor of the series lay an intent to persuade consumers that celebrity Vanna White, like celebrity Downey, was endorsing Samsung products.

Finally, the eighth factor, "likelihood of expansion of the product lines," does not appear apposite to a celebrity endorsement case such as this.

Application of the *Sleekcraft* factors to this case indicates that the district court erred in rejecting White's Lanham Act claim at the summary judgment stage. In so concluding, we emphasize two facts, however. First, construing the motion papers in White's favor, as we must, we hold only that White has raised a genuine issue of material fact concerning a likelihood of confusion as to her endorsement. *Cohen v. Paramount Pictures Corp.,* 845 F.2d 851, 852–53 (9th Cir. 1988). Whether White's Lanham Act claim should succeed is a matter for the jury. Second, we stress that we reach this conclusion in light of the peculiar facts of this case. In particular, we note that the robot ad identifies White and was part of a series of ads in which other celebrities participated and were paid for their endorsement of Samsung's products.

IV. *The Parody Defense*

In defense, defendants cite a number of cases for the proposition that their robot ad constituted protected speech. The only cases they cite which are even remotely relevant to this case are *Hustler Magazine v. Falwell,* 485 U.S. 46 (1988) and *L.L. Bean, Inc. v. Drake Publishers, Inc.,* 811 F.2d 26 (1st Cir. 1987). Those cases involved parodies of advertisements run for the purpose of poking fun at Jerry Falwell and L.L. Bean, respectively. This case involves a true advertisement run for the purpose of selling Samsung VCRs. The ad's spoof of Vanna White and Wheel of Fortune is subservient and only tangentially related to the ad's primary message: "buy Samsung VCRs." Defendants' parody arguments are better addressed to non-commercial parodies. The difference between a "parody" and a "knock-off" is the difference between fun and profit.

V. *Conclusion*

In remanding this case, we hold only that White has pleaded claims which can go to the jury for its decision.

AFFIRMED IN PART, REVERSED IN PART, and REMANDED.

ALARCON, CIRCUIT JUDGE, concurring in part, dissenting in part:

Vanna White seeks recovery from Samsung based on three theories: the right to privacy, the right to publicity, and the Lanham Act. I concur in the majority's conclusions on the right to privacy. I respectfully dissent from its holdings on the right to publicity and the Lanham Act claims.

I.

. . .

The protection of intellectual property presents the courts with the necessity of balancing competing interests. On the one hand, we wish to protect and reward the work and investment of those who create intellectual property. In so doing, however, we must prevent the creation of a monopoly that would inhibit the creative expressions of others. We have traditionally balanced those interests by allowing the copying of an idea, but protecting a unique expression of it. Samsung clearly used the idea of a glamorous female game show hostess. Just as clearly, it avoided appropriating Vanna White's expression of that role. Samsung did not use a likeness of her. The performer depicted in the commercial advertisement is unmistakably a lifeless robot. Vanna White has presented no evidence that any consumer confused the robot with her identity. Indeed, no reasonable consumer could confuse the robot with Vanna White or believe that, because the robot appeared in the advertisement, Vanna White endorsed Samsung's product.

I would affirm the district court's judgment in all respects.

Aftermath

Following the panel's decision, Samsung filed a motion asking the panel for a rehearing and suggested that the Ninth Circuit as a whole review the case *en banc*. Such motions are commonly filed, but rarely granted. *White v. Samsung Electronics* is in that regard no exception. The panel rejected the motion for rehearing, and the suggestion for a rehearing *en banc* failed to receive support from a majority of the active judges on the Ninth Circuit, and as result, failed. Judge Kozinski, however, joined by two of his colleagues, wrote a spirited dissent from this denial. While his dissent, like any dissent, is not binding law, it articulates some of the policy concerns an expanding right of publicity implicate.

WHITE V. SAMSUNG ELECTRONICS AMERICA, INC.
989 F.2d 1512 (9th Cir. 1993)

KOZINSKI, CIRCUIT JUDGE, with whom CIRCUIT JUDGES O'SCANNLAIN and KLEINFELD join, dissenting from the order rejecting the suggestion for rehearing en banc.

I

Saddam Hussein wants to keep advertisers from using his picture in unflattering contexts. Clint Eastwood doesn't want tabloids to write about him. Rudolf Valentino's heirs want to control his film biography. The Girl Scouts don't want their image soiled by association with certain activities. George Lucas wants to keep Strategic Defense Initiative fans from calling it "Star Wars." Pepsico doesn't want singers to use the word "Pepsi" in their songs. Guy Lombardo wants an exclusive property right to ads that show big bands playing on New Year's Eve. Uri Geller thinks he should be paid for ads showing psychics bending metal through telekinesis. Paul Prudhomme, that household name, thinks the same about ads featuring corpulent bearded chefs. And scads of copyright holders see purple when their creations are made fun of.

Something very dangerous is going on here. Private property, including intellectual property, is essential to our way of life. It provides an incentive for investment and innovation; it stimulates the flourishing of our culture; it protects the moral entitlements of people to the fruits of their labors. But reducing too much to private property can be bad medicine. Private land, for instance, is far more useful if separated from other private land by public streets, roads and highways. Public parks, utility rights-of-way and sewers reduce the amount of land in private hands, but vastly enhance the value of the property that remains.

So too it is with intellectual property. Overprotecting intellectual property is as harmful as underprotecting it. Creativity is impossible without a rich public domain. Nothing today, likely nothing since we tamed fire, is genuinely new: Culture, like science and technology, grows by accretion, each new creator building on the works of those who came before. Overprotection stifles the very creative forces it's supposed to nurture.

The panel's opinion is a classic case of overprotection. Concerned about what it sees as a wrong done to Vanna White, the panel majority erects a property right of remarkable and dangerous breadth: Under the majority's opinion, it's now a tort for advertisers to *remind* the public of a celebrity. Not to use a celebrity's name, voice, signature or likeness; not to imply the celebrity endorses a product; but simply to evoke the celebrity's image in the public's mind. This Orwellian notion withdraws far more from the public domain than prudence and common sense allow. It conflicts with the Copyright Act and the Copyright Clause. It raises serious First Amendment problems. It's bad law, and it deserves a long, hard second look. . . .

Intellectual property rights aren't free: They're imposed at the expense of future creators and of the public at large. Where would we be if Charles Lindbergh had an exclusive right in the concept of a heroic solo aviator? If Arthur Conan Doyle had gotten a copyright in the idea of the detective story, or Albert Einstein had patented the theory of relativity? If every author and celebrity had been given the right to keep people from mocking them or their work? Surely this would have made the world poorer, not richer, culturally as well as economically.

This is why intellectual property law is full of careful balances between what's set aside for the owner and what's left in the public domain for the rest of us: The relatively short life of patents; the longer, but finite, life of copyrights; copyright's idea-expression dichotomy; the fair use doctrine; the prohibition on copyrighting facts; the compulsory license of television broadcasts and musical compositions; federal preemption of overbroad state intellectual property laws; the nominative use doctrine in trademark law; the right to make soundalike recordings. All of these diminish an intellectual property owner's rights. All let the public use something created by someone else. But all are necessary to maintain a free environment in which creative genius can flourish.

The intellectual property right created by the panel here has none of these essential limitations: No fair use exception; no right to parody; no idea-expression dichotomy. It impoverishes the public domain, to the detriment of future creators and the public at large. Instead of well-defined, limited characteristics such as name, likeness or voice, advertisers will now have to cope with vague claims of "appropriation of identity," claims often made by people with a wholly exaggerated sense of their own fame and significance. *See* pp. 1–3 & notes 1–10 *supra.* Future Vanna Whites might not get the chance to create their personae, because their employers may fear some celebrity will claim the persona is too similar to her own. The public will be robbed of parodies of celebrities, and our culture will be deprived of the valuable safety valve that parody and mockery create.

Moreover, consider the moral dimension, about which the panel majority seems to have gotten so exercised. Saying Samsung "appropriated" something of White's begs the question: *Should* White have the exclusive right to something as broad and amorphous as her "identity"? Samsung's ad didn't simply copy White's schtick—like all parody, it created something new. True, Samsung did it to make money, but White does whatever she does to make money, too; the majority talks of "the difference between fun and profit," 971 F.2d at 1401, but in the entertainment industry fun *is* profit. Why is Vanna White's right to exclusive for-profit use of her persona—a persona that might not even be her own creation, but that of a writer, director or producer—superior to Samsung's right to profit by creating its own inventions? Why should she have such absolute rights to control the conduct of others, unlimited by the idea-expression dichotomy or by the fair use doctrine?

To paraphrase only slightly *Feist Publications, Inc.* v. *Rural Telephone Service Co.,* 113 L.Ed.2d 358, 111 S.Ct. 1282, 1289–90 (1991), it may seem unfair that much of the fruit of a creator's labor may be used by others without compensation. But this is not some unforeseen byproduct of our intellectual property system; it is the system's very essence. Intellectual property law assures authors the right to their original expression, but encourages others to build freely on the ideas that underlie it. This result is neither unfair nor unfortunate: It is the means by which intellectual property law advances the progress of science and art. We give authors certain exclusive rights, but in exchange we get a richer public domain. The majority ignores this wise teaching, and all of us are the poorer for it. . . .

Finally, I can't see how giving White the power to keep others from evoking her image in the public's mind can be squared with the First Amendment. Where does White get this right to control our thoughts? The majority's creation goes way beyond the protection given a trademark or a copyrighted work, or a person's name or likeness. All those things control one particular way of expressing an idea, one way of referring to an object or a person. But not allowing any means of reminding people of someone? That's a speech restriction unparalleled in First Amendment law.

What's more, I doubt even a name-and-likeness-only right of publicity can stand without a parody exception. The First Amendment isn't just about religion or politics—it's also about protecting the free development of our national culture. Parody, humor, irreverence are all vital components of the marketplace of ideas. The last thing we need, the last thing the First Amendment will tolerate, is a law that lets public figures keep people from mocking them, or from "evoking" their images in the mind of the public. 971 F.2d at 1399.

The majority dismisses the First Amendment issue out of hand because Samsung's ad was commercial speech. *Id.* at 1401 & n.3. So what? Commercial speech may be less protected by the First Amendment than noncommercial speech, but less protected means protected nonetheless. *Central Hudson Gas & Elec. Corp.* v. *Public Serv. Comm'n,* 447 U.S. 557 (1980). And there are very good reasons for this. Commercial speech has a profound effect on our culture and our attitudes. Neutral-seeming ads influence people's social and political attitudes, and themselves arouse political controversy. "Where's the Beef?" turned from an advertising catchphrase into the only really memorable thing about the 1984 presidential campaign. Four years later, Michael Dukakis called George Bush "the Joe Isuzu of American politics."

In our pop culture, where salesmanship must be entertaining and entertainment must sell, the line between the commercial and noncommercial has not merely blurred; it has disappeared. Is the Samsung parody any different from a parody on Saturday Night Live or in Spy Magazine? Both are equally profit-motivated. Both use a celebrity's identity to sell things—one to sell VCRs, the other to sell advertising. Both mock their subjects. Both try to make people laugh. Both add something, perhaps something worthwhile and memorable, perhaps not, to our culture. Both are things that the people being portrayed might dearly want to suppress. . . .

For better or worse, we are the Court of Appeals for the Hollywood Circuit. Millions of people toil in the shadow of the law we make, and much of their livelihood is made possible by the existence of intellectual property rights. But much of their livelihood—and much of the vibrancy of our culture—also depends on the existence of other intangible rights: The right to draw ideas from a rich and varied public domain, and the right to mock, for profit as well as fun, the cultural icons of our time.

In the name of avoiding the "evisceration" of a celebrity's rights in her image, the majority diminishes the rights of copyright holders and the public at large. In the name of fostering creativity, the majority suppresses it. Vanna White and those like her have been given something they never had before, and they've been given it at our expense. I cannot agree.

NOTES FOR DISCUSSION

1.   *False Signals and Imitations.* If Ford had used Midler's actual voice without permission, then there is no question but that Ford would have been liable. As a policy matter, why would such an unauthorized use be actionable? Does that same policy justify extending liability for an imitation? Why does the *Midler* court find Ford's imitation of Bette Midler's voice in its commercial to be actionable? Recall our discussion after *Cardtoons, L.C.* suggesting that spending a lot of money to obtain a celebrity's endorsement can serve as an accurate signal of the associated product's quality. By using an imitator, can Ford send a "false" signal? That is consumers will perceive the commercial as a Midler endorsement, and believing that Ford had spent a lot of money to obtain Midler's endorsement, both perceive and rely on the informal guarantee of high quality such an expenditure signals. By using an imitator, Ford will get the benefit of Midler's endorsement without paying its cost, and consumers will be misled. Which part is more troubling? That Ford gets Midler's apparent endorsement without paying for it or that consumers are misled? Of the cost of the advertising campaign, including shooting the commercial, paying the singer, and paying for the airtime, what fraction of that total cost would a Midler endorsement represent? Is simply paying for the airtime itself an accurate signal?

Does this false signaling rationale justify the outcome in the *White* case? Will the use of the robot send the same false signal?

2.   *Imitations and False Endorsement: Unjust Enrichment.* Alternatively, is the problem in the *Midler* case that Ford is unjustly enriched? Is it receiving the benefit of Midler's endorsement without paying for it? Is this justification ultimately circular? If the court permitted Ford to use an imitator, then presumably others could as well. If everyone did use imitators, would consumers rely on the fact that Ford aired an advertisement with a voice that sounded like Midler's as a signal of high product quality? If imitations were permitted and became common, what would that do to the value of, and market for, celebrity endorsements? If Ford had actually hired

Midler, how could it make that plain to consumers? Would unauthorized uses crowd out authorized uses?

Was Samsung unjustly enriched? Whatever the legal rules, are consumers likely to perceive the use of the robot as an implicit statement that White has endorsed Samsung? Or will consumers see it as simply a clever advertisement?

3.   *Perceived Endorsement.* Which of the justifications for the right of publicity implicitly or expressly rely on an underlying factual belief that consumers will perceive a given advertisement as an expression of the celebrity's endorsement? Consider first the three economic rationales: (i) providing incentives; (ii) preventing overuse; and (iii) preventing consumer confusion. What about the four noneconomic rationales: (i) unfairness; (ii) labor-dessert; (iii) unjust enrichment; and (iv) emotional injury?

4.   *Similarities, Differences.* What are the similarities in the *Midler* and *White* cases that lead the courts to reach the same outcome? What are the differences?

5.   *Parody, Permission.* Is the ad in the *White* case a parody of White? Is it making fun of her in some way? Is it as much a parody as the baseball trading cards we saw in *Cardtoons, L.C.*? Given the court's ruling, Samsung will have to get White's permission to air the advertisement. Is there any chance that White will give it?

6.   *Big Deal, No Deal.* Judge Kozinski is clearly worked up about the *White* decision. Does the outcome merit his outrage? How much does it change our society? Will Samsung still be able to sell and advertise its products? Will people still be able to make fun of White? What difference does the *White* decision make? We lose a clever advertisement, and probably foreclose that style of advertisement in the future. How broadly will companies read the *White* decision? Will it have the chilling effects that Judge Kozinski suggests? Will companies avoid any references to celebrities in their advertisements in order to avoid the risks of having a court declare an advertisement impermissible and losing their investment it? Why did Samsung prepare the White robot advertisement? Surely, it knew there was some risk that a court would rule in White's favor. Is it possible that Samsung prepared the advertisement specifically to get sued, hoping for the free publicity such a lawsuit would inevitably generate?

On the other hand, how would our society be different if White had lost? Which society would you prefer to live in, one in which the advertisement was permissible or one in which it was not? Why?

C. LIMITS

ETW CORP. v. JIREH PUBLISHING, INC.
332 F.3d 915 (6th Cir. 2003)

GRAHAM, DISTRICT JUDGE

Plaintiff-Appellant ETW Corporation ("ETW") is the licensing agent of Eldrick "Tiger" Woods ("Woods"), one of the world's most famous professional golfers. Woods, chairman of the board of ETW, has assigned to it the exclusive right to exploit his name, image, likeness, and signature, and all other publicity rights. ETW owns a United States trademark registration for the mark "TIGER WOODS" (Registration No. 2,194,381) for use in connection with "art prints, calendars, mounted photographs, notebooks, pencils, pens, posters, trading cards, and unmounted photographs."

Defendant-Appellee Jireh Publishing, Inc. ("Jireh") of Tuscaloosa, Alabama, is the publisher of artwork created by Rick Rush ("Rush"). Rush, who refers to himself as "America's sports artist," has created paintings of famous figures in sports and famous sports events. A few examples include Michael Jordan, Mark McGuire, Coach Paul "Bear" Bryant, the Pebble Beach Golf Tournament, and the America's Cup Yacht Race. Jireh has produced and successfully marketed limited edition art prints made from Rush's paintings.

In 1998, Rush created a painting entitled *The Masters of Augusta*, which commemorates Woods's victory at the Masters Tournament in Augusta, Georgia, in 1997. At that event, Woods became the youngest player ever to win the Masters Tournament, while setting a 72-hole record for the tournament and a record 12-stroke margin of victory. In the foreground of Rush's painting are three views of Woods in different poses. In the center, he is completing the swing of a golf club, and on each side he is crouching, lining up and/or observing the progress of a putt. To the left of Woods is his caddy, Mike "Fluff" Cowan, and to his right is his final round partner's caddy. Behind these figures is the Augusta National Clubhouse. In a blue background behind the clubhouse are likenesses of famous golfers of the past looking down on Woods. These include Arnold Palmer, Sam Snead, Ben Hogan, Walter Hagen, Bobby Jones, and Jack Nicklaus. Behind them is the Masters leader board.

The limited edition prints distributed by Jireh consist of an image of Rush's painting which includes Rush's signature at the bottom right hand corner. Beneath the image of the painting, in block letters, is its title, "The Masters Of Augusta." Beneath the title, in block letters of equal height, is the artist's name, "Rick Rush," and beneath the artist's name, in smaller upper and lower case letters, is the legend "Painting America Through Sports." . . .

ETW filed suit against Jireh on June 26, 1998, in the United States District Court for the Northern District of Ohio, alleging trademark infringement in violation of the Lanham Act, 15 U.S.C. § 1114; dilution of the mark under the Lanham Act, 15 U.S.C. § 1125(c); unfair competition and false advertising under the Lanham Act, 15 U.S.C. § 1125(a); unfair competition and deceptive trade practices under Ohio Revised Code § 4165.01; unfair competition and trademark infringement under Ohio common law; and violation of Woods's right of publicity under Ohio common law. Jireh counterclaimed, seeking a declaratory judgment that Rush's art prints are protected by the First Amendment and do not violate the Lanham Act. Both parties moved for summary judgment. The district court granted Jireh's motion for summary judgment and dismissed the case. *See ETW Corp. v. Jireh Pub., Inc.*, 99 F. Supp. 2d 829 (N.D. Ohio 2000). ETW timely perfected an appeal to this court.

I.   *Standard of Review*

We review the district court's grant of summary judgment de novo. *Sperle v. Michigan Dep't of Corr.*, 297 F.3d 483, 490 (6th Cir. 2002). Summary judgment is proper where there exists no issue of material fact and the moving party is entitled to judgment as a matter of law. Fed.R.Civ.P. 56(c). In considering such a motion, the court construes all reasonable factual inferences in favor of the nonmoving party. *Matsushita Elec. Indus. Co. v. Zenith Radio Corp.*, 475 U.S. 574, 587 (1986). The central issue is "whether the evidence presents a sufficient disagreement to require submission to a jury or whether it is so one-sided that one party must prevail as a matter of law." *Anderson v. Liberty Lobby, Inc.*, 477 U.S. 242, 251–52 (1986).

II.   *Trademark Claims Based on the Unauthorized Use of the Registered Trademark "Tiger Woods"*

ETW claims that the prints of Rush's work constitute the unauthorized use of a registered trademark in violation of the Lanham Act, 15 U.S.C. § 1114, and Ohio law. Because trademark claims under Ohio law follow the same analysis as those under the Lanham Act, our discussion of the federal trademark claims will therefore encompass the state trademark claims as well. *Rock & Roll Hall of Fame & Museum, Inc. v. Gentile Prods.*, 134 F.3d 749, 754 (6th Cir. 1998) (citing *Daddy's Junky Music Stores, Inc. v. Big Daddy's Family Music Ctr.*, 109 F.3d 275, 288 (6th Cir. 1997)).

ETW claims that Jireh infringed the registered mark "Tiger Woods" by including these words in marketing materials which accompanied the prints of Rush's painting. The words "Tiger Woods" do not appear on the face of the prints, nor are they included in the title of the painting. The words "Tiger Woods" do appear under the flap of the envelopes which contain the prints, and Woods is mentioned twice in the narrative which accompanies the prints.

The Lanham Act provides a defense to an infringement claim where the use of the mark "is a use, otherwise than as a mark, . . . which is descriptive of and used fairly and in good faith only to describe the goods . . . of such party[.]" 15 U.S.C. § 1115(b)(4); *see San Francisco Arts and Athletics, Inc. v. United States Olympic Comm.*, 483 U.S. 522, 565 (1987); *Herman Miller, Inc. v. Palazzetti Imports and Exports, Inc.*, 270 F.3d 298, 319 (6th Cir. 2001)("Under the doctrine of 'fair use,' the holder of a trademark *cannot* prevent others from using the word that forms the trademark in its *primary* or *descriptive* sense.")(emphasis in the original); *Car-Freshner Corp. v. S.C. Johnson & Son, Inc.*, 70 F.3d 267, 270 (2d Cir. 1995)("Fair use permits others to use a protected mark to describe aspects of their own goods[.]"). In evaluating a defendant's fair use defense, a court must consider whether defendant has used the mark: (1) in its descriptive sense; and (2) in good faith. *Victoria's Secret Stores v. Artco Equip. Co.,*, 194 F. Supp. 2d 704, 724 (S.D. Ohio 2002); *see also Cairns v. Franklin Mint Co.*, 292 F.3d 1139, 1151 (9th Cir. 2002).

A celebrity's name may be used in the title of an artistic work so long as there is some artistic relevance. *See Rogers v. Grimaldi*, 875 F.2d 994, 997 (2d Cir. 1989); *New York Racing Ass'n v. Perlmutter Publ'g, Inc.*, No. 95–CV–994, 1996 WL 465298 at *4 (N.D.N.Y. July 19, 1996) (finding the use of a registered mark on the title of a painting protected by the First Amendment). The use of Woods's name on the back of the envelope containing the print and in the narrative description of the print are purely descriptive and there is nothing to indicate that they were used other than in good faith. The prints, the envelopes which contain them, and the narrative materials which accompany them clearly identify Rush as the source of the print. Woods is mentioned only to describe the content of the print.

The district court properly granted summary judgment on ETW's claim for violation of its registered mark, "Tiger Woods," on the grounds that the claim was barred by the fair use defense as a matter of law.

III. *Trademark Claims Under 15 U.S.C. § 1125(a) Based on the Unauthorized Use of the Likeness of Tiger Woods*

. . . ETW claims protection under the Lanham Act for any and all images of Tiger Woods. This is an untenable claim. ETW asks us, in effect, to constitute Woods himself as a walking, talking trademark. Images and likenesses of Woods are not protectable as a trademark because they do not perform the trademark function of designation. They do not distinguish and identify the source of goods. They cannot function as a trademark because there are undoubtedly thousands of images and likenesses of Woods taken by countless photographers, and drawn, sketched, or painted by numerous artists, which have been published in many forms of media, and sold and distributed throughout the world. No reasonable person could believe that merely because these photographs or paintings contain Woods's likeness or image, they all originated with Woods.

We hold that, as a general rule, a person's image or likeness cannot function as a trademark. Our conclusion is supported by the decisions of other courts which have addressed this issue. In *Pirone v. MacMillan, Inc.*, 894 F.2d 579 (2d Cir. 1990), the Second Circuit rejected a trademark claim asserted by the daughters of baseball legend Babe Ruth. The plaintiffs objected to the use of Ruth's likeness in three photographs which appeared in a calendar published by the defendant. The court rejected their claim, holding that "a photograph of a human being, unlike a portrait of a fanciful cartoon character, is not inherently 'distinctive' in the trademark sense of tending to indicate origin." *Id.* at 583. The court noted that Ruth "was one of the most photographed men of his generation, a larger than life hero to millions and an historical figure[.]" *Id.* The Second Circuit Court concluded that a consumer could not reasonably believe that Ruth sponsored the calendar:

> An ordinarily prudent purchaser would have no difficulty discerning that these photos are merely the subject matter of the calendar and do not in any way indicate sponsorship. No reasonable jury could find a likelihood of confusion.

Id. at 585. The court observed that "under some circumstances, a photograph of a person may be a valid trademark—if, for example, a particular photograph was consistently used on specific goods." *Id.* at 583. The court rejected plaintiffs' assertion of trademark rights in every photograph of Ruth. . . .

Here, ETW does not claim that a particular photograph of Woods has been consistently used on specific goods. Instead, ETW's claim is identical to that of the plaintiffs in *Pirone*, a sweeping claim to trademark rights in every photograph and image of Woods. Woods, like Ruth, is one of the most photographed sports figures of his generation, but this alone does not suffice to create a trademark claim.

The district court properly granted summary judgment on ETW's claim of trademark rights in all images and likenesses of Tiger Woods.

IV. *Lanham Act Unfair Competition and False Endorsement Claims, Ohio Right to Privacy Claims, and the First Amendment Defense*

A. *Introduction*

ETW's claims under § 43(a) of the Lanham Act, 15 U.S.C. § 1125(a), include claims of unfair competition and false advertising in the nature of false endorsement. ETW has also asserted a claim for infringement of the right of publicity under Ohio law. The elements of a Lanham Act false endorsement claim are similar to the elements of a right of publicity claim under Ohio law. In fact, one legal scholar has said that a Lanham Act false endorsement claim is the federal equivalent of the right of publicity. *See* Bruce P. Keller, *The Right of Publicity: Past, Present, and Future,* 1207 PLI Corp. Law and Prac. Handbook, 159, 170 (October 2000). Therefore, cases which address both these types of claims should be instructive in determining whether Jireh is entitled to summary judgment on those claims.

In addition, Jireh has raised the First Amendment as a defense to all of ETW's claims, arguing that Rush's use of Woods's image in his painting is protected expression. Cases involving Lanham Act false endorsement claims and state law claims of the right of publicity have considered the impact of the First Amendment on those types of claims. We will begin with a discussion of the scope of First Amendment rights in the context of works of art, and will then proceed to examine how First Amendment rights have been balanced against intellectual property rights in cases involving the Lanham Act and state law rights of publicity. Finally, we will apply the relevant legal principles to the facts of this case.

B. *First Amendment Defense*

The protection of the First Amendment is not limited to written or spoken words, but includes other mediums of expression, including music, pictures, films, photographs, paintings, drawings, engravings, prints, and sculptures. *See Hurley v. Irish-American Gay, Lesbian and Bisexual Group of Boston*, 515 U.S. 557, 569 (1995)("The Constitution looks beyond written or spoken words as mediums of expression."); *Ward v. Rock Against Racism*, 491 U.S. 781, 790 (1989) ("Music, as a form of expression and communication, is protected under the First Amendment."); *Zacchini v. Scripps-Howard Broadcasting Co.*, 433 U.S. 562, 578 (1977)("There is no doubt that entertainment, as well as news, enjoys First Amendment protection."); *Kaplan v. California*, 413 U.S. 115, 119–120 (1973) ("Pictures, films, paintings, drawings, and engravings ... have First Amendment protection[.]"); *Bery v. City of New York*, 97 F.3d 689, 695 (2d Cir. 1996) ("Visual art is as wide ranging in its depiction of ideas, concepts and emotions as any book, treatise, pamphlet or other writing, and is similarly entitled to full First Amendment protection.").

Speech is protected even though it is carried in a form that is sold for profit. The fact that expressive materials are sold does not diminish the degree of protection to which they are entitled under the First Amendment.

Publishers disseminating the work of others who create expressive materials also come wholly within the protective shield of the First Amendment.

Even pure commercial speech is entitled to significant First Amendment protection. Commercial speech is "speech which does 'no more than propose a commercial transaction[.]'" *Virginia State Bd. of*

Pharmacy, 425 U.S. at 762 (quoting *Pittsburgh Press Co. v. Pittsburgh Comm'n on Human Relations*, 413 U.S. 376, 385 (1973)); *see also Central Hudson Gas and Electric Corp.*, 447 U.S. at 566 (articulating a four part test to bring commercial speech within the protection of the First Amendment).

Rush's prints are not commercial speech. They do not propose a commercial transaction. Accordingly, they are entitled to the full protection of the First Amendment. Thus, we are called upon to decide whether Woods's intellectual property rights must yield to Rush's First Amendment rights.

C. *Lanham Act False Endorsement Claim*

The district court did not specifically discuss ETW's false endorsement claim in granting summary judgment to Jireh. The gist of the false endorsement claim is that the presence of Woods's image in Jireh's print implies that he has endorsed Jireh's product. *See* McCarthy, The Rights of Publicity and Privacy, § 5:30 (2d ed. 2000) (hereinafter "McCarthy on Publicity and Privacy"). Courts have recognized false endorsement claims under § 43(a) of the Lanham Act where a celebrity's image or persona is used in association with a product so as to imply that the celebrity endorses the product.

False endorsement occurs when a celebrity's identity is connected with a product or service in such a way that consumers are likely to be misled about the celebrity's sponsorship or approval of the product or service. *See, e.g., Wendt v. Host Int'l, Inc.*, 125 F.3d 806 (9th Cir. 1997) (animatronic robotic figures resembling actors in *Cheers* television program used to advertise chain of airport bars modeled on Cheers set); *Abdul-Jabbar v. General Motors Corp.*, 85 F.3d 407 (9th Cir. 1996) (athlete's name and accomplishments used in television advertisement for Oldsmobile automobiles); *Waits v. Frito-Lay, Inc.*, 978 F.2d 1093 (9th Cir. 1992) (imitation of singer's unique voice used in radio commercial advertising Dorito Chips); *White v. Samsung Electronics America, Inc.*, 971 F.2d 1395 (9th Cir. 1992) (female robot bearing resemblance to television celebrity, Vanna White, turning letters in what appeared to be the "Wheel of Fortune" game show set in television commercial advertising electronics products); *Allen v. National Video, Inc.*, 610 F. Supp. 612 (S.D.N.Y. 1985) (photograph of Woody Allen look-alike in national advertising campaign for video club).

. . .

In the ordinary false endorsement claim, the controlling issue is likelihood of confusion. This court has formulated an eight-factor test to determine the likelihood of confusion. *See Landham*, 227 F.3d at 626; *Wynn Oil Co. v. Thomas*, 839 F.2d 1183, 1186 (6th Cir. 1988). However, for the reasons discussed below, we conclude that where the defendant has articulated a colorable claim that the use of a celebrity's identity is protected by the First Amendment, the likelihood of confusion test is not appropriate because it fails to adequately consider the interests protected by the First Amendment.

In *Rogers v. Grimaldi*, 875 F.2d 994 (2d Cir. 1989), Ginger Rogers, the surviving member of one of the most famous duos in show business history, brought suit against the producers and distributors of a movie entitled *Ginger and Fred*. The film was not about Ginger Rogers and Fred Astaire, but about two fictional Italian cabaret performers who imitated Rogers and Astaire and became known in Italy as "Ginger and Fred." Rogers asserted claims under § 43(a) of the Lanham Act. The Second Circuit began its analysis by noting that "movies, plays, books, and songs are all indisputably works of artistic expression and deserve protection." *Id.* at 997. The court concluded that "because overextension of Lanham Act restrictions in the area of titles might intrude on First Amendment values, we must construe the Act narrowly to avoid such a conflict." *Id.* at 998.

The Second Circuit court rejected Rogers' argument that First Amendment concerns are implicated only where the author has no alternative means of expression. Her argument was based on *Lloyd Corp. v. Tanner*, 407 U.S. 551, 566–67 (1972), where the Supreme Court held that respondents had no First Amendment right to distribute handbills in the interior mall area of petitioner's privately-owned shopping center, noting that respondents had adequate alternative means of communication. Noting that this test had been applied by several courts in the trademark context, the *Rogers* court rejected the "no alternative means" test because it "does not sufficiently accommodate the public's interest in free expression[.]" 875 F.2d at 999. The court concluded:

> We believe that in general the Act should be construed to apply to artistic works only where the public interest in avoiding consumer confusion outweighs the public interest in free expression. In the context of allegedly misleading titles using a celebrity's name, that balance will normally not support application of the Act unless the title has no artistic relevance to the underlying work whatsoever, or, if it has some artistic relevance, unless the title explicitly misleads as to the source or the content of the work.

Id.

... Like Rogers, ETW argues that the district court should have considered whether alternative means existed for Jireh to express itself without violating Woods's intellectual property rights. We agree with the Second Circuit's conclusion that the "no alternative means" test does not sufficiently accommodate the public's interest in free expression. ... We thus apply the *Rogers* test to the facts before us.

D. *Right of Publicity Claim*

ETW claims that Jireh's publication and marketing of prints of Rush's painting violates Woods's right of publicity. The right of publicity is an intellectual property right of recent origin which has been defined as the inherent right of every human being to control the commercial use of his or her identity. *See* McCarthy on Publicity and Privacy, § 1:3. The right of publicity is a creature of state law and its violation gives rise to a cause of action for the commercial tort of unfair competition. *Id.*

. . .

There is an inherent tension between the right of publicity and the right of freedom of expression under the First Amendment. This tension becomes particularly acute when the person seeking to enforce the right is a famous actor, athlete, politician, or otherwise famous person whose exploits, activities, accomplishments, and personal life are subject to constant scrutiny and comment in the public media. . . .

In *Comedy III Productions, Inc. v. Gary Saderup, Inc.*, 25 Cal. 4th 387, 106 Cal. Rptr. 2d 126, 21 P.3d 797 (2001), the California Supreme Court adopted a transformative use test in determining whether the artistic use of a celebrity's image is protected by the First Amendment. Saderup, an artist with over twenty-five years experience in making charcoal drawings of celebrities, created a drawing of the famous comedy team, The Three Stooges. The drawings were used to create lithographic and silk screen masters, which were then used to produce lithographic prints and silk screen images on T-shirts. Comedy III, the owner of all rights to the former comedy act, brought suit against Saderup under a California statute, which grants the right of publicity to successors in interest of deceased celebrities.

The California Supreme Court found that Saderup's portraits were entitled to First Amendment protection because they were "expressive works and not an advertisement or endorsement of a product." *Id.* at 396, 21 P.3d at 802. In discussing the tension between the right of publicity and the First Amendment, the court observed:

> Because celebrities take on personal meanings to many individuals in the society, the creative appropriation of celebrity images can be an important avenue of individual expression. As one commentator has stated: "Entertainment and sports celebrities are the leading players in our Public Drama. We tell tales, both tall and cautionary, about them. We monitor their comings and goings, their missteps and heartbreaks. We copy their mannerisms, their styles, their modes of conversation and of consumption. Whether or not celebrities are 'the chief agents of moral change in the United States,' they certainly are widely used—far more than are our institutionally anchored elites—to

symbolize individual aspirations, group identities and cultural values. Their images are thus important expressive and communicative resources: the peculiar, yet familiar idiom in which we conduct a fair portion of our cultural business and everyday conversation." (Madow, *Private Ownership of Public Image: Popular Culture and Publicity Rights* (1993) 81 Cal. L. Rev. 125 at 128) (Madow, italics and fns. omitted).

Id. at 397, 21 P.3d at 803.

The court rejected the proposition that Saderup's lithographs and T-shirts lost their First Amendment protection because they were not original single works of art, but were instead part of a commercial enterprise designed to generate profit solely from the sale of multiple reproductions of likenesses of The Three Stooges:

This position has no basis in logic or authority. No one would claim that a published book, because it is one of many copies, receives less First Amendment protection than the original manuscript. . . . [A] reproduction of a celebrity image that, as explained above, contains significant creative elements is entitled to as much First Amendment protection as an original work of art.

Id. at 408, 21 P.3d at 810.

Borrowing part of the fair use defense from copyright law, the California court proposed the following test for distinguishing between protected and unprotected expression when the right of publicity conflicts with the First Amendment:

When artistic expression takes the form of a literal depiction or imitation of a celebrity for commercial gain, directly trespassing on the right of publicity without adding significant expression beyond that trespass, the state law interest in protecting the fruits of artistic labor outweighs the expressive interests of the imitative artist.

On the other hand, when a work contains significant transformative elements, it is not only especially worthy of First Amendment protection, but it is also less likely to interfere with the economic interest protected by the right of publicity. . . .

Accordingly, First Amendment protection of such works outweighs whatever interest the state may have in enforcing the right of publicity.

Id. at 405, 21 P.3d at 808 (footnote and citations omitted). . . .

We conclude that in deciding whether the sale of Rush's prints violate Woods's right of publicity, we will look to the Ohio case law and the Restatement (Third) of Unfair Competition. In deciding where the line should be drawn between Woods's intellectual property rights and the First Amendment, we find ourselves in agreement with the dissenting judges in *White*, . . . and we will follow them in determining whether Rush's work is protected by the First Amendment. Finally, we believe that the transformative elements test adopted by the Supreme Court of California in *Comedy III Productions*, will assist us in determining where the proper balance lies between the First Amendment and Woods's intellectual property rights. We turn now to a further examination of Rush's work and its subject.

E. *Application of the Law to the Evidence in this Case*

The evidence in the record reveals that Rush's work consists of much more than a mere literal likeness of Woods. It is a panorama of Woods's victory at the 1997 Masters Tournament, with all of the trappings of that tournament in full view, including the Augusta clubhouse, the leader board, images of Woods's caddy, and his final round partner's caddy. These elements in themselves are sufficient to bring Rush's work within the protection of the First Amendment. The Masters Tournament is probably the world's most famous golf tournament and Woods's victory in the 1997 tournament was a historic event in the world of sports. A piece of art that portrays a historic sporting event communicates and celebrates the value our culture attaches to such events. It would be ironic indeed if the presence of the image of the victorious athlete would deny the work First Amendment protection. Furthermore, Rush's work includes not only images of Woods and the two caddies, but also carefully crafted likenesses of six past winners of the Masters Tournament: Arnold Palmer, Sam Snead, Ben Hogan, Walter Hagen, Bobby Jones, and Jack Nicklaus, a veritable pantheon of golf's greats. Rush's work conveys the message that Woods himself will someday join that revered group.

Turning first to ETW's Lanham Act false endorsement claim, we agree with the courts that hold that the Lanham Act should be applied to artistic works only where the public interest in avoiding confusion outweighs the public interest in free expression. The *Rogers* test is helpful in striking that balance in the instant case. We find that the presence of Woods's image in Rush's painting *The Masters of Augusta* does have artistic relevance to the underlying work and that it does not explicitly mislead as to the source of the work. . . .

We find, like the court in *Rogers*, that plaintiff's survey evidence, even if its validity is assumed, indicates at most that some members of the public would draw the incorrect inference that Woods had some connection with Rush's print. The risk of misunderstanding, not engendered by any explicit indication on the face of the print, is so outweighed by the interest in artistic expression as to preclude application of the Act. We disagree with the dissent's suggestion that a jury must decide where the balance should be struck and where the boundaries should be drawn between the rights conferred by the Lanham Act and the protections of the First Amendment.

In regard to the Ohio law right of publicity claim, we conclude that Ohio would construe its right of publicity as suggested in the Restatement (Third) of Unfair Competition, Chapter 4, Section 47, Comment d., which articulates a rule analogous to the rule of fair use in copyright law. Under this rule, the substantiality and market effect of the use of the celebrity's image is analyzed in light of the informational and creative content of the defendant's use. Applying this rule, we conclude that Rush's work has substantial informational and creative content which outweighs any adverse effect on ETW's market and that Rush's work does not violate Woods's right of publicity.

We further find that Rush's work is expression which is entitled to the full protection of the First Amendment and not the more limited protection afforded to commercial speech. When we balance the magnitude of the speech restriction against the interest in protecting Woods's intellectual property right, we encounter precisely the same considerations weighed by the Tenth Circuit in *Cardtoons*. These include consideration of the fact that through their pervasive presence in the media, sports and entertainment celebrities have come to symbolize certain ideas and values in our society and have become a valuable means of expression in our culture. As the Tenth Circuit observed "celebrities . . . are an important element of the shared communicative resources of our cultural domain." *Cardtoons*, 95 F.3d at 972.

In balancing these interests against Woods's right of publicity, we note that Woods, like most sports and entertainment celebrities with commercially valuable identities, engages in an activity, professional golf, that in itself generates a significant amount of income which is unrelated to his right of publicity. Even in the absence of his right of publicity, he would still be able to reap substantial financial rewards from authorized appearances and endorsements. It is not at all clear that the appearance of Woods's likeness in artwork prints which display one of his major achievements will reduce the commercial value of his likeness.

While the right of publicity allows celebrities like Woods to enjoy the fruits of their labors, here Rush has added a significant creative component of his own to Woods's identity. Permitting Woods's right of publicity to trump Rush's right of freedom of expression would extinguish Rush's right to profit from his creative enterprise.

After balancing the societal and personal interests embodied in the First Amendment against Woods's property rights, we conclude that the effect of limiting Woods's right of publicity in this case is negligible and significantly outweighed by society's interest in freedom of artistic expression.

Finally, applying the transformative effects test adopted by the Supreme Court of California in *Comedy III*, we find that Rush's work does contain significant transformative elements which make it especially worthy of First Amendment protection and also less likely to interfere with the economic interest protected by Woods' right of publicity. Unlike the unadorned, nearly photographic reproduction of the faces of The Three Stooges in *Comedy III*, Rush's work does not capitalize solely on a literal depiction of Woods. Rather, Rush's work consists of a collage of images in addition to Woods's image which are combined to describe, in artistic form, a historic event in sports history and to convey a message about the significance of Woods's achievement in that event. Because Rush's work has substantial transformative elements, it is entitled to the full protection of the First Amendment. In this case, we find that Woods's right of publicity must yield to the First Amendment.

V. *Conclusion*

In accordance with the foregoing, the judgment of the District Court granting summary judgment to Jireh Publishing is affirmed.

C.B.C. DISTRIBUTION AND MKTG., INC. v. MAJOR LEAGUE BASEBALL ADVANCED MEDIA, L.P.

505 F.3d 818 (8th Cir. 2007), *cert. denied*, 128 S.Ct. 2872 (2008)

ARNOLD, CIRCUIT JUDGE.

C.B.C. Distribution and Marketing, Inc., brought this action for a declaratory judgment against Major League Baseball Advanced Media, L.P., to establish its right to use, without license, the names of and information about major league baseball players in connection with its fantasy baseball products. Advanced Media counter-claimed, maintaining that CBC's fantasy baseball products violated rights of publicity belonging to major league baseball players and that the players, through their association, had licensed those rights to Advanced Media, the interactive media and Internet company of major league baseball. The Major League Baseball Players Association intervened in the suit, joining in Advanced Media's claims and further asserting a breach of contract claim against CBC. The district court granted summary judgment to CBC, *see C.B.C. Distrib. and Mktg., Inc. v. Major League Baseball Advanced Media, L.P.*, 443 F. Supp. 2d 1077 (E.D. Mo. 2006), and Advanced Media and the Players Association appealed. We affirm.

I.

CBC sells fantasy sports products via its Internet website, e-mail, mail, and the telephone. Its fantasy baseball products incorporate the names along with performance and biographical data of actual major league baseball players. Before the commencement of the major league baseball season each spring, participants form their fantasy baseball teams by "drafting" players from various major league baseball teams. Participants compete against other fantasy baseball "owners" who have also drafted their own teams. A participant's success, and his or her team's success, depends on the actual performance of the fantasy team's players on their respective actual teams during the course of the major league baseball season. Participants in CBC's fantasy baseball games pay fees to play and additional fees to trade players during the course of the season.

From 1995 through the end of 2004, CBC licensed its use of the names of and information about major league players from the Players Association pursuant to license agreements that it entered into with the association in 1995 and 2002. The 2002 agreement, which superseded in its entirety the 1995 agreement, licensed to CBC "the names, nicknames, likenesses, signatures, pictures, playing records, and/or biographical data of each player" (the "Rights") to be used in association with CBC's fantasy baseball products.

In 2005, after the 2002 agreement expired, the Players Association licensed to Advanced Media, with some exceptions, the exclusive right to use baseball players' names and performance information "for exploitation via all interactive media." Advanced Media began providing fantasy baseball games on its website, MLB.com, the official website of major league baseball. It offered CBC, in exchange for a commission, a license to promote the MLB.com fantasy baseball games on CBC's website but did not offer CBC a license to continue to offer its own fantasy baseball products. This conduct by Advanced Media prompted CBC to file the present suit, alleging that it had "a reasonable apprehension that it will be sued by Advanced Media if it continues to operate its fantasy baseball games."

The district court granted summary judgment to CBC. It held that CBC was not infringing any state-law rights of publicity that belonged to major league baseball players. *C.B.C.*, 443 F. Supp. 2d at 1106–07. The court reasoned that CBCs fantasy baseball products did not use the names of major league baseball players as symbols of their identities and with an intent to obtain a commercial advantage, as required to establish an infringement of a publicity right under Missouri law (which all parties concede applies here). *Id.* at 1085–89. The district court further held that even if CBC were infringing the players' rights of publicity, the first amendment preempted those rights. *Id.* at 1091–1100. The court rejected, however, CBC's argument that federal copyright law preempted the rights of publicity claim. *Id.* at 1100–03. . . .

Because this appeal is from the district court's grant of summary judgment, our review is *de novo*, and we apply "the same standards as the district court and view[ ] the evidence in the light most favorable to the nonmoving party." *Travelers Prop. Cas. Co. of Am. v. General Cas. Ins.*

Co., 465 F.3d 900, 903 (8th Cir. 2006). Summary judgment is appropriate only if "there is no genuine issue as to any material fact and . . . the moving party is entitled to judgment as a matter of law." Fed. R. Civ. P. 56(c); *Celotex Corp. v. Catrett*, 477 U.S. 317, 322 (1986). We also review *de novo* the district court's interpretation of state law, including its interpretation of Missouri law regarding the right of publicity. *See Hammer v. City of Osage Beach*, 318 F.3d 832, 841 (8th Cir. 2003). When state law is ambiguous, we must "predict how the highest court of that state would resolve the issue." *Clark v. Kellogg Co.*, 205 F.3d 1079, 1082 (8th Cir. 2000).

II.

A.

An action based on the right of publicity is a state-law claim. *See Zacchini v. Scripps-Howard Broad. Co.*, 433 U.S. 562, 566 (1977). In Missouri, "the elements of a right of publicity action include: (1) That defendant used plaintiff's name as a symbol of his identity (2) without consent (3) and with the intent to obtain a commercial advantage." *Doe v. TCI Cablevision*, 110 S.W.3d 363, 369 (Mo. 2003), *cert. denied*, 540 U.S. 1106 (2004). The parties all agree that CBC's continued use of the players' names and playing information after the expiration of the 2002 agreement was without consent. The district court concluded, however, that the evidence was insufficient to make out the other two elements of the claim, and we address each of these in turn.

With respect to the symbol-of-identity element, the Missouri Supreme Court has observed that " 'the name used by the defendant must be understood by the audience as referring to the plaintiff.' " The state court had further held that "[i]n resolving this issue, the fact-finder may consider evidence including 'the nature and extent of the identifying characteristics used by the defendant, the defendant's intent, the fame of the plaintiff, evidence of actual identification made by third persons, and surveys or other evidence indicating the perceptions of the audience.' " *Doe*, 110 S.W.3d at 370 (quoting Restatement (Third) of Unfair Competition § 46 cmt. d).

Here, we entertain no doubt that the players' names that CBC used are understood by it and its fantasy baseball subscribers as referring to actual major league baseball players. CBC itself admits that: In responding to the appellants' argument that "this element is met by the mere confirmation that the name used, in fact, refers to the famous person asserting the violation," CBC stated in its brief that "if this is all the element requires, CBC agrees that it is met." We think that by reasoning that "identity," rather than "mere use of a name," "is a critical element of the right of publicity," the district court did not understand that when a name alone is sufficient to establish identity, the defendant's use of that name satisfies the plaintiff's burden to show that a name was used as a symbol of identity.

It is true that with respect to the "commercial advantage" element of a cause of action for violating publicity rights, CBC's use does not fit neatly into the more traditional categories of commercial advantage, namely, using individuals' names for advertising and merchandising purposes in a way that states or intimates that the individuals are endorsing a product. *Cf.* Restatement (Third) of Unfair Competition § 47 cmt. a, b. But the Restatement, which the Missouri Supreme Court has recognized as authority in this kind of case, *see Doe*, 110 S.W.3d at 368, also says that a name is used for commercial advantage when it is used "in connection with services rendered by the user" and that the plaintiff need not show that "prospective purchasers are likely to believe" that he or she endorsed the product or service. Restatement (Third) of Unfair Competition § 47 & cmt. a. We note, moreover, that in Missouri, "the commercial advantage element of the right of publicity focuses on the defendant's intent or purpose to obtain a commercial benefit from use of the plaintiff's identity." *Doe*, 110 S.W.3d at 370–71. Because we think that it is clear that CBC uses baseball players' identities in its fantasy baseball products for purposes of profit, we believe that their identities are being used for commercial advantage and that the players therefore offered sufficient evidence to make out a cause of action for violation of their rights of publicity under Missouri law.

B.

CBC argues that the first amendment nonetheless trumps the right-of-publicity action that Missouri law provides. Though this dispute is between private parties, the state action necessary for first amendment protections exists because the right-of-publicity claim exists only insofar as the courts enforce state-created obligations that were "never explicitly assumed" by CBC. *See Cohen v. Cowles Media Co.*, 501 U.S. 663, 668 (1991).

The Supreme Court has directed that state law rights of publicity must be balanced against first amendment considerations, *see Zacchini v. Scripps-Howard Broad.*, 433 U.S. 562 (1977), and here we conclude that the former must give way to the latter. First, the information used in CBC's fantasy baseball games is all readily available in the public domain, and it would be strange law that a person would not have a first amendment right to use information that is available to everyone. It is true that CBC's use of the information is meant to provide entertainment, but "[s]peech that entertains, like speech that informs, is protected by the First Amendment because '[t]he line between the informing and the entertaining is too elusive for the protection of that basic right.'" *Cardtoons, L.C. v. Major League Baseball Players Ass'n*, 95 F.3d 959, 969 (10th Cir. 1996) (quoting *Winters v. New York*, 333 U.S. 507, 510 (1948));

see also Zacchini, 433 U.S. at 578. We also find no merit in the argument that CBC's use of players' names and information in its fantasy baseball games is not speech at all. We have held that "the pictures, graphic design, concept art, sounds, music, stories, and narrative present in video games" is speech entitled to first amendment protection. *See Interactive Digital Software Ass'n v. St. Louis County, Mo.*, 329 F.3d 954, 957 (8th Cir. 2003). Similarly, here CBC uses the "names, nicknames, likenesses, signatures, pictures, playing records, and/or biographical data of each player" in an interactive form in connection with its fantasy baseball products. This use is no less expressive than the use that was at issue in *Interactive Digital*.

Courts have also recognized the public value of information about the game of baseball and its players, referring to baseball as "the national pastime." *Cardtoons*, 95 F.3d at 972. A California court, in a case where Major League Baseball was itself defending its use of players' names, likenesses, and information against the players' asserted rights of publicity, observed, "Major league baseball is followed by millions of people across this country on a daily basis . . . The public has an enduring fascination in the records set by former players and in memorable moments from previous games . . . The records and statistics remain of interest to the public because they provide context that allows fans to better appreciate (or deprecate) today's performances." *Gionfriddo v. Major League Baseball*, 94 Cal. App. 4th 400, 411, 114 Cal. Rptr. 2d 307 (2001). The Court in *Gionfriddo* concluded that the "recitation and discussion of factual data concerning the athletic performance of [players on Major League Baseball's website] command a substantial public interest, and, therefore, is a form of expression due substantial constitutional protection." *Id*. We find these views persuasive.

In addition, the facts in this case barely, if at all, implicate the interests that states typically intend to vindicate by providing rights of publicity to individuals. Economic interests that states seek to promote include the right of an individual to reap the rewards of his or her endeavors and an individual's right to earn a living. Other motives for creating a publicity right are the desire to provide incentives to encourage a person's productive activities and to protect consumers from misleading advertising. *See Zacchini*, 433 U.S. at 573, 576; *Cardtoons*, 95 F.3d at 973. But major league baseball players are rewarded, and handsomely, too, for their participation in games and can earn additional large sums from endorsements and sponsorship arrangements. Nor is there any danger here that consumers will be misled, because the fantasy baseball games depend on the inclusion of all players and thus cannot create a false impression that some particular player with "star power" is endorsing CBC's products.

Then there are so-called non-monetary interests that publicity rights are sometimes thought to advance. These include protecting natural rights, rewarding celebrity labors, and avoiding emotional harm. *See Cardtoons*, 95 F.3d at 973. We do not see that any of these interests are especially relevant here, where baseball players are rewarded separately for their labors, and where any emotional harm would most likely be caused by a player's actual performance, in which case media coverage would cause the same harm. We also note that some courts have indicated that the right of publicity is intended to promote only economic interests and that non-economic interests are more directly served by so-called rights of privacy. *See, e.g., id.* at 967; *Gionfriddo*, 94 Cal. App. 4th at 409 (2001); *see also Haelan Laboratories v. Topps Chewing Gum*, 202 F.2d 866, 868 (2d Cir. 1953). For instance, although the court in *Cardtoons*, 95 F.3d at 975–76, conducted a separate discussion of non-economic interests when weighing the countervailing rights, it ultimately concluded that the non-economic justifications for the right of publicity were unpersuasive as compared with the interest in freedom of expression. "Publicity rights . . . are meant to protect against the loss of financial gain, not mental anguish." *Id.* at 976. We see merit in this approach.

Because we hold that CBC's first amendment rights in offering its fantasy baseball products supersede the players' rights of publicity, we need not reach CBC's alternative argument that federal copyright law preempts the players' state law rights of publicity.

III.

. . .

IV.

For the foregoing reasons, the district court's grant of summary judgment to CBC is affirmed.

NOTES FOR DISCUSSION

1. *The First Amendment Interest.* Why does each court focus on the First Amendment's protection of free speech as the appropriate limit on the plaintiff's rights of publicity? How would things be different if the courts came out the other way? In *ETW*, if Tiger Woods could control such paintings, then only licensed paintings would exist. Similarly, in *CBC*, if major league players could control the use of their stats in fantasy baseball leagues, then only licensed leagues would exist. How is the choice between allowing only authorized paintings or fantasy baseball leagues, and allowing unauthorized paintings and leagues a First Amendment free speech issue? Are the courts simply pretending that there is a First Amendment interest so that they can more closely examine whether there is any justification for extending the right of publicity to the uses before them? Why can't they just examine that

issue directly? Are the courts really just asking whether society would be better or worse off in a world where Woods could control paintings of himself or in a world where ball players could control the use of their stats for fantasy leagues? Would you prefer to live in a world where Woods and the players could control these uses or one where they may not? Why?

2. *The First Amendment, the Right of Publicity, and News Reporting.* From its inception, courts have worried that a broad right to control the use of one's name, image, or likeness could potentially interfere with the free speech interest in news reporting. Way back in 1905, when the Georgia Supreme Court, first recognized the right to control the unauthorized commercial use of one's name, image, or likeness, the court acknowledged the potential conflict:

> The stumbling block which many have encountered in the way of a recognition of the existence of a right of privacy has been that the recognition of such right would inevitably tend to curtail the liberty of speech and of the press.

Pavesich v. New England Life Ins. Co., 122 Ga. 190, 202, 50 S.E. 68, 73 (1905). And the court expressly recognized that "[t]he right of privacy is unquestionably limited by the right to speak and print." *Id.* at 204.

Yet, since the formal recognition of the right of publicity in 1953, courts have struggled to balance the competing interests at stake. In *Zacchini v. Scripps-Howard Broad. Co.*, 433 U.S. 562 (1977), the question of how to strike that balance came before the United States Supreme Court. In *Zacchini,* a television station filmed and then, as a segment on its nightly news program, broadcast Zacchini's entire fifteen-second, human cannonball act, over Zacchini's objection. *Id.* at 563–64. The Court held that in doing so, the station had violated Zacchini's right of publicity. *Id.* at 578. Although the Court acknowledged that there is a First Amendment interest in "entertainment, as well as news," *id.,* this was outweighed by the threat the broadcast posed to the incentives for Zacchini to invest his talent and energy in creating his act. *Id.* at 575–76. In the Court's view:

> [I]f the public can see the act free on television, it will be less willing to pay to see it at the fair. The effect of a public broadcast of the performance is similar to preventing petitioner from charging an admission fee.

Id.

The Court cites no evidence in support of these assertions. Do you believe that they are right? Or will more people go to the circus as a result of the news broadcast?

The Court went on:

> But it is important to note that neither the public nor respondent will be deprived of the benefit of petitioner's performance as long as his commercial stake in his act is

appropriately recognized. Petitioner does not seek to enjoin the broadcast of his performance; he simply wants to be paid for it.

Id. at 578.

If the Court had refused to recognize Zacchini's rights, would Zacchini stop performing his human cannonball act? Would such a decision lead potential future circus performers to forego the circus and devote their energy and effort to some other activity? Would society be worse off as a result?

Alternatively, can we protect the First Amendment interests in these cases by recognizing the plaintiff's rights, but limiting the plaintiff to a damages remedy? If Zacchini had asked for an injunction, would that have changed the outcome in *Zacchini*? Would Zacchini be entitled to an injunction under the four-part standard the Court articulated in *eBay Inc. v. MercExchange, L.L.C.*, 547 U.S. 388 (2006), that we studied in Chapter 11? Do damages provide a fully adequate remedy in these cases? Should we limit the remedy available to Bette Midler and Vanna White to damages? Similarly, in the *ETW* and *CBC* cases, would recognizing the plaintiff's rights of publicity while limiting their relief to damages be a better resolution? Is money the real issue or is control?

How would you resolve the following cases?

a) A comedian, Pat Paulsen, announces his presidential candidacy, tongue-in-cheek, and a poster marketer sells, without his authorization, a poster with his image and, at the bottom, the words "For President." Paulsen sues, asking for a preliminary injunction based upon, *inter alia,* his right of publicity. *See Paulsen v. Personality Posters, Inc.*, 59 Misc.2d 444, 299 N.Y.S.2d 501, 507 (N.Y. Sup. Ct. 1968) ("When a well-known entertainer enters the presidential ring, tongue in cheek or otherwise, it is clearly newsworthy and of public interest. A poster which portrays plaintiff in that role, and reflects the spirit in which he approaches said role, is a form of public interest presentation to which [First Amendment] protection must be extended.").

b) In the 1950s, Mickey Dora was a surfing legend in Malibu, California. In 1987, Frontline Video puts together a documentary entitled, "The Legends of Malibu." The documentary focuses on surfing at Malibu. The documentary includes, without Dora's authorization, photos, an interview, and contemporary footage of Dora. Dora sues, alleging, among other causes of action, a violation of his right of publicity. *See Dora v. Frontline Video, Inc.*, 15 Cal.App.4th 536, 18 Cal.Rptr.2d 790 (2nd Dist., Ct. App. 1993) (finding that surfing is a matter of public interest and that the defendant's First Amendment interests therefore outweigh the plaintiff's right of publicity interests).

c) In the winter of 1957–1958, Shirley Booth, a prominent actress at the time, was vacationing at the "Round Hill" resort in Jamaica. *Holiday* magazine was there to do a story on the resort and its prominent guests. Ms. Booth's photograph was taken and included in the February 1959 issue of *Holiday* magazine in connection with the story. Subsequently, *Holiday* used

Ms. Booth's photograph in prominent full-page advertisements for *Holiday* magazine in two other periodicals, the *New Yorker* and *Advertising Age*. Ms. Booth sued, alleging a violation of her right of publicity. *See* Booth v. Curtis Pub. Co., 15 A.D.2d 343, 223 N.Y.S.2d 737, 744 (Sup. Ct. N.Y. Appellate Div. 1962) (holding that no violation occurred "so long as the reproduction was used to illustrate the quality and content of the periodical in which it originally appeared").

3. *The First Amendment and Criticism, Parody, or Comment.* As we saw in *Cardtoons, L.C.*, courts have also recognized a First Amendment interest in uses that criticize, parody, or comment. In *ETW*, the court balances the defendant's First Amendment interest against the plaintiff's right of publicity interests by asking to what extent the defendant "transforms" Woods' image. Is "transformation" a First Amendment value? The focus on transformation as a tool to separate infringing from non-infringing uses originated in copyright's fair use doctrine. *See Campbell v. Acuff-Rose Music, Inc.*, 510 U.S. 569 (1994). In that context, courts use the extent to which a defendant's work transforms the plaintiff's original work as a key factor in assessing whether the defendant's work is fair or infringing. *Id.* at 579–80. In attempting to increase the production of original and creative works, focusing on this issue makes perfect sense. It identifies both: (i) whether the defendant's use is likely to cut into sales of, and reduce thereby, the incentives for the plaintiff's original work; and (ii) the extent to which the defendant's work represents a valuable creative contribution in its own right.

How well does a focus on "transformation" work in balancing the plaintiff's right of publicity interests and the defendant's First Amendment interests? While the *ETW* court draws the transformation test from *Comedy III Prods., Inc.*, the *ETW* court reaches a different outcome than *Comedy III Prods.* Why? In what sense is Rush's painting in *ETW* more transformative than Saderup's charcoal sketch in *Comedy III Prods.*? Irrespective of that answer, in what way is the painting in *ETW* more deserving of First Amendment protection than the charcoal sketch in *Comedy III Prods.*? Does the First Amendment provide more protection for less realistic schools of art, such as impressionism, while it provides less protection for realistic sketches? What language in the Constitution suggests such a value choice?

Is the court using the test, not in truth as a balancing of First Amendment interests, but as an attempt to isolate factually the source of the "real" value of the defendant's use? In *Comedy III Prods.*, the defendant's products sell primarily because of the Three Stooges, while in *ETW*, the defendant's paintings sell primarily because of the defendant's talent, rather than his subject. Is that factually accurate? Even if it is, in what sense does that indicate a stronger First Amendment interest in permitting Rush's use? Putting to one side the First Amendment window dressing, is that a sensible approach to deciding whether a use violates the right of publicity? Are some of the purposes of the right of publicity in line with the purposes of copyright? Which ones? Does the copyright balance make sense then as a way of limiting the scope of the right of publicity in cases where the right of publicity serves the same incentive-based purpose as copyright? Should we apply the copyright balance embedded in "transformation" to other cases, such as *White*?

4.   *Consumer Welfare.* Would consumers be better or worse off if Tiger Woods could control the use in *ETW* and if baseball players could control the use in *CBC*? As we have seen elsewhere, such control would tend to limit competition, lead to higher prices, lower quality, and less variety. Without control, fantasy leagues would have to strive continually to improve and distinguish themselves from each other in order to attract a larger share of the available customers. Similarly, without control, anyone can paint scenes of Tiger winning the Masters, and Rush will have to compete against other painters to offer better and more creative paintings at a lower price. Is there any doubt that consumers would be better off with competition in these markets?

As we saw back in Chapter 1, we generally recognize two arguments for limiting competition. The first, traditionally associated with patents and copyrights, is the incentive argument. Protection will create incentives to invest and lead to greater output of the protected activity. The second, more traditionally associated with trademarks, is the consumer deception argument. Protection will reduce consumer search costs and reduce the likelihood that a consumer will purchase one company's product by mistake. Does either of these arguments support the exclusive rights that Tiger Woods and baseball players seek in *ETW* and *CBC*, respectively? Construct the best argument you can from either an incentives or a consumer deception perspective to support the plaintiff's position in each case. Is either argument particularly persuasive? Which argument is more persuasive?

Balance the incentives and deception concerns against the benefits competition, if allowed, would bring. Is there any reasonable argument that consumers would be better off if the courts had reached the opposite conclusions in *ETW* or *CBC*? Why do both courts dress their analyses up in First Amendment terms, rather than address the welfare implications of their decisions directly?

5.   *Consumer Confusion.* In analyzing whether Rush's paintings creates the potential for consumer deception, would a survey matter? As it happens, the plaintiff's attorneys introduced a survey into evidence. According to the court:

> Respondents in the survey were handed a copy of Rush's print and were asked the question: "Do you believe that Tiger Woods has an affiliation or connection with this print or that he has given his approval or has sponsored it?" Sixty-two percent answered "Yes"; eleven percent said "No"; and twenty-seven percent said "Don't Know."

ETW Corp., 332 F.3d at 937 n.19.

Should this change the outcome in the case? Judge Clay, in dissent, insisted that it established a genuine issue of material fact with respect to likelihood of confusion. *Id.* at 942–43. He would therefore have remanded the case for trial on the likelihood of confusion issue. The majority disagreed and criticized the survey:

> The terms "affiliated with" and "connected with" were not defined. Some respondents may have thought that Woods's mere presence in the print was itself an affiliation or connection. No control questions were asked to clarify this. Furthermore, the respondents were not given the packaging in which Jireh distributed the prints which prominently features Rush and contains no suggestion that Woods sponsored or approved the print.

Id. at 937 n.19.

Would a properly conducted survey have made a difference? How should the plaintiff have changed its survey to address the court's concerns? If the survey had asked respondents if they believed that Tiger Woods "had approved" the painting, would that have established a triable issue with respect to likelihood of confusion? How material is such confusion likely to be with respect to the consumer's purchasing decision? If a consumer believes that all paintings of Woods and all fantasy leagues are authorized, will that affect his or her decision as to whether, and if so, which of them to purchase or patronize?

In any event, is this a case where whatever harm may result from confusion is plainly outweighed by the benefits of competition? In analyzing this, an important question is whether whatever confusion exists will persist over time. If anyone can paint Tiger Woods and if anyone can run a fantasy baseball website, will an "appreciable number of ordinarily prudent consumers" continue to believe that all such uses are authorized or will they adjust their expectations to the realities of the marketplace?

6.   *Of Tribute Bands and Elvis Impersonators.* Tribute bands imitate well-known or popular performers or bands, such as Elvis Presley or the Beatles. As a class, tribute bands range from those who simply sing the original performer's or band's songs to those that seek to imitate the original as precisely as possible, in looks, styling, musical phrasing, and in every other respect. Some bands, such as KISS, Aerosmith, Metallica, and the Dave Matthews band, have embraced their imitators. Others, such as the Beatles and Elvis's estate, have sued them.

While copyright law leaves room for tribute bands, should the right of publicity bar such bands? States have reached differing conclusions. At one end of the spectrum, the state of Nevada expressly exempts tribute bands in its right of publicity statute, Nev. Rev. Stat. Ann. § 597.790(2)(d) (2010), protecting Las Vegas's ubiquitous Elvis impersonators. In contrast, trial courts in California, New Jersey, and Tennessee have held that tribute bands violate the original performer's or band's right of publicity, at least when they go beyond merely playing the music of the original artist and begin to imitate recognizable aspects of the original artist's or band's looks or performance style. *See Apple Corps. Ltd. v. A.D.P.R., Inc.*, 843 F.Supp. 342 (M.D. Tenn. 1993); *Estate of Elvis Presley v. Russen*, 513 F.Supp. 1339 (D.N.J. 1981); *Apple Corps Ltd. v. Leber*, 229 U.S.P.Q. (BNA) 1015 (Cal. Super. Ct. 1986). Should such bands violate the right of publicity? Why or why not?

INDEX

References are to Pages